P9-CQE-401

Eighth Edition

Rules *for* WRITERS

Diana Hacker

Nancy Sommers
Harvard University

Contributing ESL Specialist

Kimberli Huster
Robert Morris University

Bedford/St. Martin's
A Macmillan Education Imprint
Boston • New York

For Bedford/St. Martin's

Vice President, Editorial, Macmillan Higher Education Humanities: Edwin Hill
Editorial Director, English and Music: Karen S. Henry
Publisher for Composition: Leasa Burton
Executive Editors: Michelle M. Clark and Brendan Baruth
Senior Editor: Mara Weible
Senior Media Editor: Barbara G. Flanagan
Assistant Editor: Stephanie Thomas
Senior Production Editor: Gregory Erb
Senior Production Supervisor: Jennifer Wetzel
Marketing Manager: Emily Rowin
Copy Editor: Hilly van Loon
Indexer: Ellen Kuhl Repetto
Director of Rights and Permissions: Hilary Newman
Permissions Manager: Kalina Ingham
Photo Editor: Martha Friedman
Senior Art Director: Anna Palchik
Text Design: Claire Seng-Niemoeller
Cover Design: William Boardman
Composition: Cenveo Publisher Services
Printing and Binding: RR Donnelley and Sons

0 9 8 7 6 5
f e d c b a

For information, write: Bedford/St. Martin's, 75 Arlington Street, Boston, MA 02116 (617-399-4000)

ISBN 978-1-4576-8304-6 (Student Edition) Manufactured in China
ISBN 978-1-319-01134-5 (Instructor's Edition) Manufactured in U.S.
ISBN 978-1-319-01131-4 (Student Edition with Writing about Literature) Manufactured in China

Acknowledgments

Acknowledgments and copyrights appear on the same page as the text and art selections they cover; these acknowledgments and copyrights constitute an extension of the copyright page. It is a violation of the law to reproduce these selections by any means whatsoever without the written permission of the copyright holder.

Photo by Mara Weible

A letter from the author

Dear Students:

Welcome to *Rules for Writers*—your college writing handbook. One of the pleasures of college writing is exploring ideas and discovering what you think about a subject. You may find that the writing process leads you in unexpected directions—the more you read about a topic, the more questions arise for you to consider; new questions may lead you to challenge your initial assumptions. It is in the *process* of writing—of thinking in depth about ideas—that you learn what's interesting in a subject and why you care about it. And it is through this process that you figure out not just what you think, but why you think it. *Rules for Writers* will be your companion throughout the writing process, helping you to develop your authority as a thoughtful and effective writer.

College offers many opportunities to write and to learn from the process of writing and revising. In a criminal justice course, for example, you may be asked to write a policy memo or a legal brief; in a nursing course, you may be asked to write a case study or a nursing practice paper. To write in these courses is to learn how to think like a criminologist or a nurse and to contribute your ideas to the discipline's important conversations and debates. As you write college papers, you'll have questions about how to engage with other writers who have written about your topic, how to support your ideas with well-documented evidence, and how to communicate your points effectively. *Rules for Writers* provides the guidance you'll need to write successful college papers in all your courses.

As you flip through *Rules for Writers*, you'll see that it's easy to use and convenient to keep with you as you draft and revise. You'll find answers to all your writing questions — forming a thesis, developing an argument, evaluating and citing sources, and managing information to avoid plagiarism. You'll find documentation models and formatting advice in MLA and APA. You'll also find answers to your questions about grammar, punctuation, and mechanics — how to tighten wordy sentences, for example, or how to use commas or quotation marks correctly.

The more you rely on *Rules for Writers* and learn from its advice, the more successful you'll be as a college writer. For each assignment, flag sections that contain information you need to write a successful paper. And when you get feedback on a draft, flag sections to help you address your writing challenges.

Rules for Writers supports your writing in every college course. Use it. Being a successful college writer starts here.

With all good wishes,

Nancy Sommers

Making the most of your handbook

Want to be successful with writing assignments in all your college courses? Using *Rules for Writers* is a key first step. Make the most of your handbook by turning to it whenever you're writing, revising, conducting research, or documenting sources. You'll find advice you can use for nearly every college writing assignment, starting with answers to common questions like these:

- How can I improve my thesis? *1c*
- How should I format a research essay in MLA style? *57a, 57b*
- What is critical reading? Why does it matter? *4a–4e, 5a–5e*
- How do I write a speech? *7a–7d*
- What are multimodal texts, and how do I write about them? *5a–5e*
- I've gotten feedback on a draft. What do I do next? *2a–2i*
- How can I make my writing flow better? *3d*
- What is the right way to use an apostrophe? *36a–36e*
- How do I know whether a source is reliable and worth my time? *52a–52e*
- How should I introduce a source in my paper? *55c (MLA) and 60c (APA)*
- Are there easy ways to avoid plagiarism? *54 (MLA) and 59 (APA)*
- How do I cite online videos and social media posts? *56 (MLA) and 61 (APA)*

Quick tips for finding more help

Whatever writing and research questions you have, finding help in *Rules for Writers* is easy. The following reference aids offer convenient, reliable help for writing assignments in any course.

- **The brief and detailed contents** inside the front and back covers allow you to quickly spot the help you need.
- **The index** includes user-friendly terms such as "flow" to point to help with coherence.
- **Color-coded MLA and APA sections** give discipline-specific advice for working with sources. Directories at the beginning of each section list documentation models.
- **The glossaries** in the Appendixes offer useful definitions and help with commonly confused or misused words such as *affect* and *effect*.

If your instructor has assigned this book with LaunchPadSolo for *Rules for Writers*, use the activation code to access the exercises, sample student papers, and LearningCurve game-like quizzing. Visit macmillanhighered.com/rules8e to log in.

- **260 writing, grammar, and research exercises** help you improve your writing and integrate sources.
- **39 sample student papers** provide guidance in writing and formatting your work in any course.
- **30 LearningCurve adaptive quizzes** offer game-like sentence-level practice and let you track your progress.

References to additional online support appear throughout *Rules for Writers*.

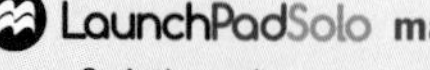

macmillanhighered.com/rules8e

8 Active verbs

> Exercises: 8–2 to 8–6

> LearningCurve: Active and passive voice

Preface for instructors

Dear Colleagues:

As college teachers, we have an important mission. We prepare students to write for different purposes and for different audiences. We show students how to read critically and write effectively, preparing them to join ongoing research conversations as contributors (not just consumers) of ideas. In college, students learn to write, and they learn through writing. Effective writing is fundamental to academic success — across the disciplines.

When you adopt *Rules for Writers* for your students, you send an important message: Writing is worth studying and learning. And you give students the resource to answer their questions and to learn from the answers. College writing is high stakes: Students learn to become nurses and teachers, biologists and criminal justice professionals through writing. They might focus on psychology or economics, but they'll most likely write in each college class they take. *Rules for Writers* is the *one* text that students will need for all their college work.

When students have a trusted handbook to answer their writing questions, they become more confident writers. Confident college writers are more flexible learners; they're more willing to try new approaches, and they feel comfortable thinking critically. I recently surveyed 700 first-year writers about the relationship between handbook use and writer confidence. When students were asked about this relationship, 79% of survey participants, many of whom use *Rules for Writers*, reported that using a handbook made them more confident academic writers. Students reported that using *Rules for Writers* helped them become more efficient and effective writers than if they had simply searched the Internet for answers to their questions about comma usage, for example, or about citing and documenting sources. A Google search might call up 46 million results to their question about comma usage, but these results are often more confusing than illuminating, and never as straightforward and authoritative as the confidence-building instruction they receive from relying on *Rules for Writers.*

Each new feature in the eighth edition is designed to answer students' writing questions and address specific problems students face as college writers. And each new feature of *Rules for Writers* is designed to support your teaching with the handbook. One such feature is an emphasis on the relationship between reading critically and writing effectively. The eighth edition shows students how to read carefully to understand an author's ideas, how to read with skepticism to question those ideas, and how to present their own ideas in response. The entire academic writing section is focused on the important reading and writing relationship, because the more students learn to take from their reading, the more they have to give as writers.

My goal in revising *Rules for Writers* was to create an even more useful classroom resource to save you time and increase students' learning. The eighth edition is informed by teachers and students who use it and who helped me look squarely at the writing problems students face and the practical solutions they need to become confident academic writers. You'll find new instruction on effective peer review, successful paraphrasing, accurate citation of online sources, and meaningful research — turning topics into questions; finding entry points in debates; and evaluating, integrating, and citing sources. And you'll find step-by-step writing guides to help students write common assignments, such as an annotated bibliography.

Teaching with *Rules for Writers* has become easier than ever. The eighth edition is now available with LaunchPad Solo for *Rules for Writers* — an online product with assignable exercises, sample student writing, and other resources. I've included "Writing Practice" prompts to help students apply handbook advice to their own drafts and to offer practice with core academic skills — thesis statements, research questions, peer review, and more. You and your students will also find videos; practice exercises for grammar, style, and citation; and LearningCurve, game-like adaptive quizzing.

As the author of *Rules for Writers*, I bring to this handbook the belief that writing *is* worth studying and learning — that all students who use this book will learn to read deeply and write clearly, that they will find in their reading ideas they care about, and that they will write about these ideas with care and depth.

I am eager to share this handbook with you, knowing that in the eighth edition you'll find everything you and your students trust and value about *Rules for Writers.*

Nancy Sommers

Acknowledgments

I am grateful for the expertise, enthusiasm, and classroom experience that so many individuals brought to the eighth edition.

Reviewers

I thank those instructors who offered detailed feedback on various parts of the handbook and its supplements: Kirk Adams, Tarrant County College; Kathryn Allen, University of North Carolina–Pembroke; David Arnold, University of Wisconsin–Stevens Point; Kevin Burke, University of Delaware; Sherry Clark, Hopkinsville Community College; Kristen di Gennaro, Pace University; Marylynne Diggs, Clark College; Kimberly Dozier, College of the Desert; Candice Floyd, Prince George's Community College; Ann Guess, Alvin Community College; Derek Handley, Community College of Allegheny County; Peter Harvan, Beachwood High School; Anne Helms, Alamance Community College; Elizabeth Joseph, Tarrant County College; Chippy McLain, Walters State Community College; L. Adam Mekler, Morgan State University; Matt Miller, Oxford High School; Candice Rowe, University of Massachusetts–Boston; Tony Russell, Central Oregon Community College; Jim Schrantz, Tarrant County College; Art Schuhart, Northern Virginia Community College; Cynthia Scurria, Alcorn State University; Alex Tavares, Hillsborough Community College; Janel Mays Thompson, Durham Technical Community College; Brandon Wallace, Montgomery College; Sander Zulauf, County College of Morris.

Contributors

I am grateful to the following individuals, fellow teachers of writing, for their smart revisions of important content: Kimberli Huster, ESL Specialist at Robert Morris University, updated the advice for multilingual writers, and Sara McCurry, Instructor of English at Shasta College, coauthored the second edition of *Teaching with Hacker Handbooks* with Jonathan Cullick, Professor of English and Chair of the Department of English at Northern Kentucky University.

Students

I would like to thank the following students who have let us adapt their papers as models: Ned Bishop, Sophie Harba, Sam

Jacobs, Luisa Mirano, Michelle Nguyen, Emilia Sanchez, and Ren Yoshida. Thanks also to Alyson D'Amato and Marisa Williamson for permission to use their multimodal projects as models.

Bedford/St. Martin's

A comprehensive handbook is a collaborative writing project, and it is my pleasure to acknowledge and thank the enormously talented Bedford/St. Martin's editorial team, whose deep commitment to students informs each new feature of *Rules for Writers*. Edwin Hill, vice president for the humanities, Leasa Burton, publisher for composition, and Karen Henry, editorial director for English, have helped shape the handbook's identity and have guided us with their insights about how the college handbook market is changing and how we can continue to meet the needs of today's college writer.

Michelle Clark, executive editor, is a treasured friend and colleague and an endless source of creativity and clarity. Michelle combines wisdom with patience and imagination with practicality. Mara Weible, senior editor, brings to the eighth edition her superb editorial judgment and her teacher's sensibility. It is a deep personal and professional pleasure to work with an editor as thoughtful and talented as Mara. Her creativity has shaped the eighth edition and made it an even more practical and innovative handbook. Barbara Flanagan, senior media editor, has worked on the Hacker handbooks for more than 25 years and brings attention to detail, keen insights, and unrivaled expertise in documentation and media. Thanks to Stephanie Thomas, assistant editor, for help with art and permissions, for managing the review process, and for developing several ancillaries. Many thanks to Gregory Erb, senior production editor, for keeping us on schedule and for producing the book with skill and care. And I am grateful to the media team—especially media producer Allison Hart—for creating engaging media for the writing course. Practical advice from Bedford colleagues Emily Rowin, Brendan Baruth, Jimmy Fleming, and Nick Carbone, who, like me, spend many, many hours on the road and in faculty offices, is always treasured. Thanks to Hilly van Loon, copy editor, for her thoroughness and attention to detail; to Claire Seng-Niemoeller, text designer, who crafted another open and beautifully designed edition of the book; and to William Boardman, art director, who has given the book a strikingly beautiful cover.

Last, but never least, I offer thanks to my own students who, over many years, have shaped my teaching and helped me understand their challenges in becoming college writers. Thanks to my friends and colleagues Suzanne Lane, Maxine Rodburg, Laura Saltz, and Kerry Walk for sustaining conversations about the teaching of writing. And thanks to my family: to Joshua Alper, an attentive reader of life and literature, for his steadfastness across the drafts; to my parents, Walter and Louise Sommers, and my aunt Elsie Adler, who encouraged me to write and set me forth on a career of writing and teaching; to my extended family, Ron, Charles Mary, Alexander, Demian, Devin, Liz, Kate, and Sam for their good humor and good cheer; and to Rachel and Curran, to Alexandra and Brian, witty and wise beyond measure, always generous with their instruction and inspiration in all things that matter. And to Lailah Dragonfly, my granddaughter, thanks for the joy and sweetness you bring to life.

Nancy Sommers

Welcome to the eighth edition

Rules for Writers speaks to everything student writers need. Many students want to turn to popular search engines for quick answers, but the real shortcut is right in their hands. *Rules for Writers* provides authoritative, trustworthy advice that's easy to understand and apply. No guesswork involved. And while writing-related resources on the Web offer *information* (sometimes accurate, sometimes not), they don't offer the *instruction* students will find in their handbook. With the eighth edition, students have access to reference content that has been class-tested by millions of students, along with the following new content to meet their evolving needs.

An emphasis on critical reading The second section of *Rules for Writers* — Academic Reading, Writing, and Speaking — has been substantially revised to emphasize the importance of reading to college research and writing. The handbook offers students a reading process, teaching them to analyze various types of texts, sources they discover through research, their own writing, and the work of their peers.

Help with analyzing multimodal texts A new chapter, "Reading and writing about multimodal texts" (pp. 80–91), introduces new genres and practical strategies for analysis.

More help for composing in a variety of genres Writing guides throughout *Rules for Writers* (see pp. 76–77 for an example) help students work through college assignments in a variety of genres. New annotated sample papers provide helpful models.

Practical advice for public speaking A new chapter, "Speaking confidently" (pp. 119–23), helps students develop effective oral communication strategies, whether they're writing a speech from scratch or turning a paper into a presentation.

More help with peer review and revising with comments A new chapter, "Revising, editing, and reflecting" (pp. 30–49), advises students on giving and receiving comments on assignments and applying feedback to revisions of their own work.

Research and documentation help for every course Substantially revised sections teach students to find an entry point in a debate and develop authority as a researcher. Students will find new practical advice for writing a research proposal. *Rules for Writers* now includes more than 200 documentation models for sources in MLA and APA styles. And because some sources are especially hard to cite, new how-to boxes address tricky issues such as authorship of reposted online content.

LaunchPadSolo for *Rules for Writers*—handbook-specific online assignments and exercises

LaunchPad Solo for *Rules for Writers*, available free when packaged with the print text, includes 36 interactive writing prompts related to specific handbook content; 260 writing, grammar, and research exercises; 39 additional sample student papers in MLA and APA styles; and 30 adaptive LearningCurve quizzes. Targeted cross-references throughout the handbook connect you and your students to related resources in LaunchPad Solo for *Rules for Writers*. ISBN 978-1-319-05719-0

LaunchPadSolo macmillanhighered.com/rules8e

8 Active verbs
> Exercises: 8-2 to 8-6
> LearningCurve: Active and passive voice

***Writer's Help 2.0 for Hacker Handbooks*—a complete online handbook, and more**

For searchable, assignable Hacker handbook content online, you can package *Rules for Writers* with *Writer's Help 2.0 for Hacker Handbooks*. Instead of turning to Google for hit-or-miss advice, students can search *Writer's Help 2.0* for the same straightforward, reliable content they find in their handbook as well as exercises, videos, and additional coverage of topics such as writing in the disciplines and analyzing and composing multimodal texts. With *Writer's Help 2.0*, you can assign online pages and activities and track students' use and progress. User-friendly help for college writers also means useful data for instructors and administrators—two benefits of *Writer's Help 2.0 for Hacker Handbooks*. ISBN 978-1-319-05725-1

***LaunchPad Solo for Readers and Writers*—prebuilt teaching and learning units**

Rules for Writers can be packaged with *LaunchPad Solo for Readers and Writers*, which provides multimedia content and assessments—including LearningCurve adaptive quizzing—organized into prebuilt, curated units for easy assigning and assessment of student progress. ISBN 978-1-319-05722-0

Supplements and media

Visit the catalog page for *Rules for Writers* to see a complete list of instructor supplements, including *Teaching with Hacker Handbooks*, student supplements, e-books (various formats), and other media: macmillanhighered.com/rules/catalog.

Custom solutions

Many schools opt for a custom edition of *Rules for Writers*. Some programs choose to add a section about course outcomes and policies; others choose to customize by adding sample writing by their own students. Custom covers with the school's name and school colors or a photo help emphasize that the handbook provides advice students can count on in all their courses, across the disciplines and throughout their college careers.

Contents

The Writing Process

The Writing Process 1

The Writing Process

College offers many opportunities to write and learn from the process of writing and revising.

As you write, you will read and respond to what others have written, use evidence to support your ideas, and develop your ability to think carefully and creatively. In a sociology class, you might be asked to write a field report; in a nursing class, a case study; and in a literature class, a critical analysis. By writing in these classes, you contribute your ideas and join thinkers and writers who share interests, ideas, and ways of communicating with one another. Developing the following habits of mind — curiosity, engagement, responsibility, and reflection — will help you write successfully in all of your college courses.

Be curious. Good college writing starts with curiosity. What issues intrigue you? What questions need to be explored? Writing is more interesting and rewarding when you explore questions you don't have answers to, questions that matter to you and to those in the discipline in which you are writing.

Be engaged. Writing is a social activity that brings you into conversations with scholars, instructors, classmates, librarians, and writing center tutors. Reading actively allows you to consider and respond to the ideas of other writers. Participating in classroom or online discussions deepens your thinking and gives you opportunities to engage with your peers. Effective college writers reach out to readers who can help shape their work in progress.

Be responsible. Engaging with the ideas of other writers and thinkers requires responsibility — to represent their ideas accurately and honestly and to acknowledge their contributions to your work. By giving credit to your sources and differentiating your own ideas from those of your sources, you encourage your readers to trust you and take you seriously.

Be reflective. Being reflective in a writing class often means stopping to think about your own writing habits or approaches to writing assignments. By examining your decisions, successes, and challenges, you'll be able to figure out what's working and what needs more work and to transfer skills from one writing assignment to the next.

1 Exploring, planning, and drafting

Writing is a process of figuring out what you think, not a matter of recording already developed thoughts. Since it's not possible to think about everything all at once, you'll find the process more manageable if you handle a piece of writing in stages. You will generally move from planning to drafting to revising, but as your ideas develop, you will find yourself circling back and returning to earlier stages.

Before composing a first draft, spend some time generating ideas. Mull over your subject while listening to music, taking a walk, or driving to work; or jot down inspirations or explore your questions with a willing listener. Consider these questions: What do you find puzzling, striking, or interesting about your subject? What would you like to know more about? Be curious and open to new ideas and different points of view. Explore questions you don't have answers to.

1a Assess the writing situation.

Begin by taking a look at your writing situation. The key elements of a writing situation include the following:

- subject
- purpose
- audience
- genre
- sources of information
- constraints (length, document design, reviewers, deadlines)

It is likely that you will make final decisions about all of these matters later in the writing process—after a first draft, for example—but you will become a more effective writer if you think about as many of them as possible in advance. For a quick checklist, see the chart on pages 4–5.

Checklist for assessing the writing situation

Subject

- Has the subject (or a range of possible subjects) been assigned to you, or are you free to choose your own?
- What interests you about your subject? What questions would you like to explore?
- Why is your subject worth writing about? How might readers benefit?
- Do you need to narrow your subject (because of length restrictions, for instance)?

Purpose and audience

- Why are you writing: To inform readers? To persuade them? To call them to action? To offer an interpretation of a text? Do you have more than one purpose for writing?
- Who are your readers? How well informed are they about the subject? What do you want them to learn?
- How interested and attentive are your readers likely to be? Will they resist any of your ideas? What possible objections will you need to anticipate and counter?
- What is your relationship to your readers: Student to instructor? Citizen to citizen? Expert to novice? Employee to supervisor?

Genre

- What genre (type of writing) does your assignment require: A report? A proposal? An analysis of data? An essay?
- If the genre is not assigned, what genre is appropriate for your subject, purpose, and audience?
- What are the expectations and conventions of your assigned genre? For instance, what type of evidence is typically used in the genre?
- Does the genre require a specific design format or method of organization?
- Does the genre require or benefit from visuals, such as photos, drawings, or graphs?

Sources of information

- Where will your information come from: Reading? Research? Direct observation? Interviews? Questionnaires?

- What type of evidence suits your subject, purpose, audience, and genre?
- What documentation style is required: MLA? APA?

Length and format

- Do you have any length specifications? If not, what length seems appropriate, given your subject, purpose, audience, and genre?
- Is a particular format required? If so, do you have guidelines to follow or examples to consult?

Deadlines

- What are your deadlines? How much time will you need to allow for the various stages of writing, including proofreading and printing or posting the final draft?

Academic English What counts as good writing varies from culture to culture and even among groups within cultures. In some situations, you will need to become familiar with the writing styles — such as direct or indirect, personal or impersonal, plain or embellished — that are valued by the culture or discipline for which you are writing.

Subject

Frequently your subject will be given to you. In a psychology class, for example, you might be asked to discuss Bruno Bettelheim's Freudian analysis of fairy tales. In a composition course, assignments often ask you to analyze texts and evaluate arguments. In the business world, you may be assigned to draft a marketing plan. When you are free to choose your own subject, let your own curiosity focus your choice. Make connections between yourself and what you are learning. If you are studying television, radio, and the Internet in a communications course, for example, you might ask yourself which of these subjects interests you most. Perhaps you want to learn more about the role streaming video can play in activism and social change. Look through your readings and class notes to see if you can identify questions you'd like to explore further in an essay.

Make sure that you can reasonably investigate your subject in the space you have. If you are limited to a few pages, for example, you could not do justice to a broad subject such as "videos as agents of social change." You could, however, focus on one aspect of the subject — perhaps contradictory claims about the effectiveness of creating video content for small, specific audiences.

If your interest in a subject stems from your personal experience, you will want to ask what it is about your experience that would interest your audience and why. For example, if you have volunteered at a homeless shelter, you might have spent some time talking to homeless children and learning about their needs. Perhaps you can use your experience to broaden your readers' understanding of the issues, to persuade an organization to fund an after-school program for homeless children, or to propose changes in legislation.

Whether or not you choose your own subject, it's important to be aware of the expectations of each writing situation. The following chart suggests ways to interpret assignments.

Understanding an assignment

Determining the purpose of an assignment

The wording of an assignment may suggest its purpose. You might be expected to do one or more of the following in a college writing assignment:

- summarize information from course materials or research (See 4c.)
- analyze ideas and concepts (See 4d.)
- take a position on a topic and defend it with evidence (See 6h.)
- synthesize (combine ideas from) several sources and create an original argument (See 55d and 60d.)

Understanding how to answer an assignment's question

Many assignments will ask you to answer a *how* or *why* question. You cannot answer such questions using only facts; instead, you will need to take a position. For example, the question "*What* are the survival rates for leukemia patients?" can be answered with facts. The question "*Why* are the survival rates for leukemia patients in one state lower than those in a neighboring state?" must be answered with both a claim and facts.

If a list of questions appears in the assignment, be careful — instructors rarely expect you to answer all the questions in order. Look instead for topics or themes that will help you ask your own questions.

Recognizing implied questions

When you are asked to *discuss, analyze, agree or disagree with*, or *consider* a topic, your instructor will often expect you to answer a *how* or *why* question.

Discuss the effects of the No Child Left Behind Act on special education programs.	=	*How* has the No Child Left Behind Act affected special education programs?
Consider the recent rise of attention deficit hyperactivity disorder diagnoses.	=	*Why* are diagnoses of attention deficit hyperactivity disorder rising?

Purpose

Your purpose, or reason for writing, will often be dictated by your writing situation. Perhaps you have been asked to draft a proposal requesting funding for a student organization, to report the results of a psychology experiment, or to write about the controversy surrounding genetically modified foods for the school newspaper. Even though your overall purpose may be fairly obvious in such situations, a closer look at the assignment can help you make some necessary decisions. How detailed should the proposal be? How technical does your psychology professor expect your report to be? Do you want to inform students about the controversy surrounding genetically modified foods or to change their attitudes toward it?

In many writing situations, part of your challenge will be discovering a purpose. Asking yourself why readers should care about what you are saying can help you decide what your purpose might be. Perhaps your subject is magnet schools — schools that draw students from different neighborhoods because of features such as advanced science classes or a concentration on the arts. If you have discussed magnet schools in class, a description of how these schools work probably will not interest you or your readers. But maybe you have discovered that your county's magnet schools are not promoting diversity as had been planned, and you want to call your readers to action.

Although no precise guidelines will lead you to a purpose, you can begin by asking, "Why am I writing?" and "What is my goal?" Identify which one or more of the following aims you hope to accomplish.

PURPOSES FOR WRITING

to inform	to evaluate
to persuade	to recommend
to entertain	to request
to call readers to action	to propose
to change attitudes	to provoke thought
to analyze	to express feelings
to argue	to summarize
to reflect	to synthesize

Writers often misjudge their own purposes, summarizing when they should be analyzing, or expressing feelings about problems instead of proposing solutions. Before beginning any writing task, pause to ask, "Why am I communicating with my readers?" This question will lead you to another important question: "Just who are my readers?"

Audience

Take time to ask questions about your readers and their expectations. Consider questions such as these: Who will be reading your draft? What is your relationship to your readers? What information will your audience need to understand your ideas? The choices you make as you write will tell readers who you think they are (novices or experts, for example) and will show respect for your readers' perspectives.

Academic audiences In college writing, considerations of audience can be more complex than they seem at first. Your instructors will read your essay, of course, but most instructors play multiple roles while reading. Their first and most obvious roles are as coach and evaluator; but they are also intelligent and objective readers, the kind of people who might be informed or called to action by what you have to say and who want to learn from your insights and ideas.

Business audiences Writers in the business world often find themselves writing for multiple audiences. A letter to a client, for instance, might be distributed to sales representatives as well. Readers of a report might include people with and without technical expertise, or readers who want details and those who prefer a quick overview.

Public audiences Writers in communities often write to a specific audience — a legislative representative, readers of a local newspaper, fellow members of a social group. With public writing, it is more likely that you are familiar with the views your readers hold and the assumptions they make, so you may be better able to judge how to engage those readers.

For help with audience when composing e-mail messages, see the following chart.

Considering audience when writing e-mail messages

In academic, business, and public contexts, you will want to show readers that you value their time. Here are some strategies for writing effective e-mails:

- Use a concise, meaningful subject line to help readers sort messages and set priorities.
- State your main point at the beginning so that your reader sees it without scrolling.
- Write concisely; keep paragraphs short.
- Avoid writing in all capital letters or all lowercase letters.
- Proofread for typos and obvious errors that are likely to slow down readers.

You will also want to follow conventions of etiquette and academic integrity. Here are some strategies for writing responsible e-mails:

- E-mail messages can easily be forwarded to others and reproduced. Do not write anything that you would not want attributed to you.
- Do not forward another person's message without asking his or her permission.
- If you write an e-mail message that includes someone else's words — opinions, statistics, song lyrics, and so forth — let your reader know the source for that material and where any borrowed material begins and ends.
- Choose your words carefully because e-mail messages can easily be misread. Without hearing your voice or seeing your facial gestures or body language, readers can misunderstand your message.

Genre

When writing for a college course, pay close attention to the genre, or type of writing, assigned. Each genre is a category of writing meant for a specific purpose and audience, with its own set of agreed-upon expectations and conventions for style, structure, and document design. Sometimes an assignment specifies the genre — an essay in a writing class, a policy memo in a criminal justice class, or an executive summary in a business class. Sometimes the genre is yours to choose, and you need to decide if a particular genre — a poster presentation, an audio essay, a Web page, or a podcast, for example — will help you communicate your purpose and reach readers.

If the genre has been assigned, the following questions will help you figure out how to present your ideas:

- Do you have access to sample projects in the genre that has been assigned?
- Who is the audience? What specialized vocabulary do readers expect in the genre?
- What type of evidence is usually required in the genre?
- What format, organization, and citation style are expected?

If you are free to choose the genre, consider the following questions when deciding which genre to use:

- What is your purpose: To argue a position? To instruct? To present a process? To inspire? To propose? Do you have more than one purpose?
- Who is your audience? What do you know about your readers or viewers?
- What method of presenting information would appeal to your audience: Reasoned paragraphs? Diagrams? Video? Slides?

Sources of information

Where will your evidence — facts, details, and examples — come from? What kind of reading, observation, or research is necessary to meet the expectations of your assignment?

Reading Reading is an important way to deepen your understanding of a topic and expand your perspective. It will be your primary source of information for many college assignments.

Read with an open mind to learn from the insights and research of others. Take notes on your thoughts, impressions, and questions. Your notes can be a way to enter a conversation with the authors of the texts you read. (See 51c.) And always keep careful records of any sources you read and consult. (See 51c.)

Observation Observation is an excellent means of collecting information about a wide range of subjects, such as gender relationships on a popular television program, the clichéd language of sports announcers, or a current exhibit at the local art museum. For such subjects, do not rely on your memory alone; your information will be fresher and more detailed if you actively collect it, with a notebook, laptop, or voice recorder.

Interviews and questionnaires Interviews and questionnaires can supply detailed and interesting information on many subjects. A nursing student interested in the care of terminally ill patients might interview hospice nurses, for example.

It is a good idea to record interviews to preserve any vivid quotations that you might want to weave into your essay. Circulating questionnaires by e-mail or on a Web site will facilitate responses. Keep questions simple, and specify a deadline to ensure that you get a reasonable number of replies.

Length and format

Writers seldom have complete control over length requirements. Journalists usually write within strict word limits set by their editors, businesspeople routinely aim for conciseness, and most college assignments specify an approximate length.

Your writing situation may also require a certain format. In the academic world, you may need to learn precise disciplinary and genre conventions for formatting lab reports, critiques, research papers, and so on. For most undergraduate essays, a standard academic format is acceptable. (See pp. 597–607.)

EXERCISE 1–1 Narrow three of the following subjects into topics that would be manageable for an essay of two to five pages.

1. Treatments for mental illness
2. An experience with racism or sexism
3. Cyberbullying
4. Images of women in video games
5. Public health care

EXERCISE 1–2 Suggest a purpose and an audience for three of the following subjects.

More practice: LaunchPadSolo

1. Genetic modification of cash crops
2. Government housing for military veterans
3. The future of print magazines
4. Working with special needs children
5. Hybrid cars

1b Explore your subject.

Experiment with one or more techniques for exploring your subject and discovering your purpose: talking and listening; reading and annotating texts; asking questions; brainstorming and freewriting; keeping a journal; blogging.

Whatever technique you turn to, the goal is the same: to generate ideas that will lead you to a question, a problem, or a topic that you want to explore further.

Talking and listening

Conversation can help you develop your ideas before you begin to write them down. By talking and listening to others, you can also discover what they find interesting, what they are curious about, and where they disagree with you. If you are planning to develop an argument, you can try it out on listeners with other points of view.

LaunchPadSolo **macmillanhighered.com/rules8e**

1 Exploring, planning, and drafting
> Writing practice: Exploring a subject
> Exercise: 1–3

Reading and annotating texts

Reading is an important way to deepen your understanding of a topic, learn from the insights and research of others, and expand your perspective. Annotating a text, written or visual, encourages you to read actively — to highlight key concepts, to note contradictions in an argument, or to raise questions for further research and investigation.

Asking questions

Whenever you are writing about ideas, events, or people, whether current or historical, asking questions is one way to get started. You might try the questions journalists routinely ask themselves: *Who? What? When? Where? Why?* and *How?* If you were writing about a negative reaction to a film, for instance, you might want to ask — *Who* objected to the film and *why? What* were the objections and *when* were they voiced? Such questions will help you investigate your subject to discover important facts.

In academic writing, scholars often generate ideas by posing questions related to a specific discipline. If you are writing in a particular discipline, try to find out which questions its scholars typically explore. Look for clues in assigned readings, assignments, and class discussions to understand how a discipline's questions help you understand its concerns.

Brainstorming and freewriting

Brainstorming and freewriting are good ways to figure out what you know and what questions you have. Write whatever comes to mind without pausing to think about word choice, spelling, or even meaning. The goal is to write quickly and freely to discover what questions are on your mind and what directions you might pursue.

Keeping a journal

A journal is a collection of informal, exploratory, sometimes experimental writing. In a journal, often meant for your eyes only, you can take risks. You might freewrite, pose questions, comment on an interesting idea from one of your classes, or keep a list of questions that occur to you while reading. You might imagine a conversation between yourself and your readers or stage a debate to understand opposing positions.

Blogging

Although a blog is a type of journal, it is a public writing space rather than a private one. You can explore an idea for a paper by blogging about it in different ways or from different angles. Since most blogs have a commenting feature, you can create a conversation by inviting readers to give you feedback—ask questions, make counterarguments, or suggest other sources on a topic.

1c Draft and revise a working thesis statement.

For many types of writing, you will be able to state your central idea in a sentence or two. Such a statement, which ordinarily appears in the opening paragraph of your finished essay, is called a *thesis*.

Understanding what makes an effective thesis statement

An effective thesis statement is a central idea that conveys your purpose—your reason for writing—and requires support.

Keep the following guidelines in mind to help you develop an effective thesis statement:

- A thesis should take a position that needs to be explained and supported.
- A thesis should be your answer to a question, your solution to a problem, or your position on a topic or debate.
- A thesis should be appropriate for the length requirements of the assignment. It should not be too broad or too narrow.
- A thesis should be sharply focused. Use concrete language and make sure your thesis lets readers know what you plan to discuss.
- A thesis should stand up to the "So what?" question. (See p. 16.)

Drafting a working thesis

As you explore your topic, you will begin to see possible ways to focus your material. At this point, try to settle on a *tentative* central idea, or working thesis statement. The more complex your topic, the more your focus may change. Think of your working thesis as preliminary, open for consideration and revision, as you clarify your purpose and consider the expectations of your audience. As your ideas develop, you'll need to revisit your working thesis to see if it presents the position you want to take and if it can be supported by the sources of evidence you have accumulated.

You'll find that the process of answering a question you have posed, resolving a problem you have identified, or taking a position on a debatable topic will focus your thinking and lead you to develop a working thesis. Here, for example, are one student's efforts to pose a question and draft a working thesis for an essay in his ethics course.

> QUESTION
>
> Should athletes who enhance their performance through biotechnology be banned from athletic competition?
>
> WORKING THESIS
>
> Athletes who boost their performance through biotechnology should be banned from athletic competition.

The working thesis offers a useful place to start writing — a way to limit the topic and focus a first draft — but it doesn't take into consideration the expectations of readers who will ask "Why?" and "So what?" The student has taken a position — athletes who boost their performance through biotechnology should be banned from athletic competition — but he hasn't answered *why* athletes should be banned. To fully answer his own question and to claim something specific in his thesis, he might push his own thinking with the word *because*.

> STRONGER WORKING THESIS
>
> Athletes who boost their performance through biotechnology should be banned from athletic competition *because* biotechnology gives athletes an unfair advantage and disrupts the sense of fair play.

Revising a working thesis

As you move to a clearer and more specific position you want to take, you'll start to see ways to revise your working thesis. You may find that the evidence you have collected supports a different thesis; or you may find that your position has changed as you learned more about your topic. Revision is ongoing; as your ideas evolve, your working thesis will evolve, too. One effective way to revise a working thesis is to put it to the "So what?" test (see the box below). A test like this can help you keep audience and purpose — and the expectations of your assignment — in mind as you revise.

Putting your working thesis to the "So what?" test

Use the following questions to help you revise your working thesis.

- Why would readers want to read an essay with this thesis? How would you respond to a reader who hears your thesis and asks "So what?" or "Why does it matter?"
- Will any readers disagree with this thesis? If so, how might your thesis respond to a counter perspective?
- Is the thesis too obvious? If you cannot come up with interpretations that oppose your own, consider revising your thesis.
- Can you support your thesis with the evidence available?

Using a problem/strategy approach as you revise

Revising a working thesis is easier if you have a method or an approach. The following problem/strategy approach is an effective way to evaluate and revise a working thesis, especially if you tend to start out with thesis statements that are too factual, too broad, too narrow, or too vague.

A thesis should require proof or further development through facts and details; it cannot itself be a fact or a description.

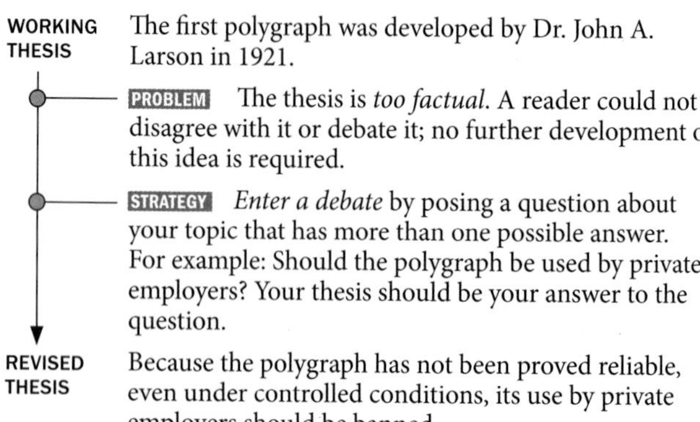

WORKING THESIS
The first polygraph was developed by Dr. John A. Larson in 1921.
PROBLEM
The thesis is *too factual.* A reader could not disagree with it or debate it; no further development of this idea is required.
STRATEGY
Enter a debate by posing a question about your topic that has more than one possible answer. For example: Should the polygraph be used by private employers? Your thesis should be your answer to the question.
REVISED THESIS
Because the polygraph has not been proved reliable, even under controlled conditions, its use by private employers should be banned.

A thesis should be an answer to a question, not a question itself.

WORKING THESIS Would John F. Kennedy have continued to escalate the war in Vietnam if he had lived?

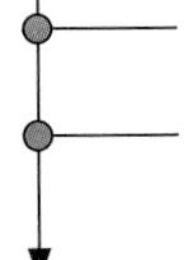

PROBLEM The thesis is *a question*, not an answer to a question.

STRATEGY *Take a position* on your topic by answering the question you have posed. Your thesis should be your answer to the question.

REVISED THESIS Although John F. Kennedy sent the first American troops to Vietnam before he died, an analysis of his foreign policy suggests that he would not have escalated the war had he lived.

A thesis should be of sufficient scope for your assignment; it should not be too broad.

WORKING THESIS Mapping the human genome has many implications for health and science.

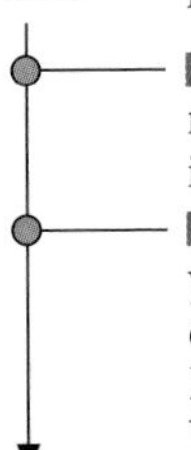

PROBLEM The thesis is *too broad*. Even in a very long research paper, you would not be able to discuss all the implications of mapping the human genome.

STRATEGY *Focus on a subtopic of your original topic*. Once you have chosen a subtopic, take a position in an ongoing debate and pose a question that has more than one answer. For example: Should people be tested for genetic diseases? Your thesis should be your answer to the question.

REVISED THESIS Although scientists can now detect genetic predisposition for specific diseases, policymakers should establish clear guidelines about whom to test and under what circumstances.

A thesis also should not be too narrow.

WORKING THESIS A person who carries a genetic mutation linked to a particular disease might or might not develop that disease.

PROBLEM The thesis is *too narrow*. It does not suggest any argument or debate about the topic.

STRATEGY *Identify challenging questions* that readers might ask about your topic. Then pose a question that has more than one answer. For example: Do the risks of genetic testing outweigh its usefulness? Your thesis should be your answer to this question.

REVISED THESIS Though positive results in a genetic test do not guarantee that the disease will develop, such results can cause psychological trauma; genetic testing should therefore be avoided if possible.

A thesis should be sharply focused, not too vague. Avoid fuzzy, hard-to-define words such as *interesting*, *good*, or *disgusting*.

WORKING THESIS The Vietnam Veterans Memorial is an interesting structure.

PROBLEM This thesis is *too fuzzy and unfocused*. It's difficult to define *interesting*, and the sentence doesn't give readers any cues about where the essay is going.

STRATEGY *Focus your thesis with concrete language and a clear plan.* Pose a question about the topic that has more than one answer. For example: How does the physical structure of the Vietnam Veterans Memorial shape the experience of visitors? Your thesis — your answer to the question — should use specific language.

REVISED THESIS By inviting visitors to see their own reflections in the wall, the Vietnam Veterans Memorial creates a link between the present and the past.

EXERCISE 1–4 In each of the following pairs, which sentence might work well as a thesis for a short paper? What is the problem with the other one? Is it too factual? Too broad? Too vague? Use the problem/strategy approach from pages 16–18 to evaluate each thesis.

More practice: LaunchPadSolo

1. a. By networking with friends, a single parent can manage to strike a balance among work, school, a social life, and family.
   b. Single parents face many challenges as they try to juggle all of their responsibilities.
2. a. At the Special Olympics, athletes with disabilities show that, with hard work and support from others, they can accomplish anything — that they can indeed be winners.
   b. Working with the Special Olympics program is rewarding.
3. a. History 201, taught by Professor Brown, is offered at 10:00 a.m. on Tuesdays and Thursdays.
   b. Whoever said that history is nothing but polishing tombstones must have missed History 201, because in Professor Brown's class history is vibrantly alive.
4. a. So far, research suggests that zero-emissions vehicles are not a sensible solution to the problem of steadily increasing air pollution.

LaunchPadSolo **macmillanhighered.com/rules8e**
1 Exploring, planning, and drafting
> Writing practice: Revising a thesis
> Exercises: 1–5 and 1–6

b. Because air pollution is of serious concern to many people today, several US government agencies have implemented plans to begin solving the problem.

5. a. Anorexia nervosa is a dangerous and sometimes deadly eating disorder occurring mainly in young, upper-middle-class teens.

b. The eating disorder anorexia nervosa is rarely cured by one treatment alone; only by combining drug therapy with psychotherapy and family therapy can the client begin the long journey to wellness.

1d Draft a plan.

Once you have drafted a working thesis, listing and organizing your supporting ideas can help you flesh out the thesis. Creating outlines, whether informal or formal, can help you make sure your writing is focused and logical and can help you identify any gaps in your support.

When to use an informal outline

You might want to sketch an informal outline to see how you will support your thesis and to figure out a tentative structure for your ideas. Informal outlines can take many forms. Perhaps the most common is simply the thesis followed by a list of major ideas.

Working thesis: In the *Hunger Games*, the games help transform Katniss Everdeen's love for her sister into the spark of revolution.

- Pitting the districts against each other in the games helps the Capitol maintain control by discouraging widespread revolt.
- Before the games, Katniss and Gale think about leaving the district in search of a better life for their families. They don't imagine ways of improving life within their district or across districts.
- Katniss volunteers for the games to save her sister, Prim, with whom Katniss shares a close bond.
- In the arena, Katniss acts like a big sister to Rue, who reminds her of Prim.
- By protecting Rue and mourning her death, Katniss begins to use the Capitol's instrument of control — the games — to undermine the Capitol's hold on the districts.
- More than a temporary alliance, the sister-like bond between Katniss and Rue gives Katniss, and the rest of Panem, an opportunity to imagine a world in which members of one district might fight for the well-being of those in another.

If you began by jotting down a list of ideas, you can turn the list into a rough outline by crossing out some ideas, adding others, and putting the ideas in a logical order.

When to use a formal outline

Early in the writing process, rough outlines have certain advantages: They can be produced quickly, they are obviously tentative, and they can be revised easily. However, a formal outline may be useful later in the writing process, after you have written a rough draft, especially if your topic is complex. It can help you see whether the parts of your essay work together and whether your essay's structure is logical.

The following formal outline brought order to the research paper that appears in 57b, on regulating healthy eating. The student's thesis is an important part of the outline. Everything else in the outline supports it, directly or indirectly.

FORMAL OUTLINE

Thesis: In the name of public health and safety, state governments have the responsibility to shape public health policies and to regulate healthy eating choices, especially since doing so offers a potentially large social benefit for a relatively small cost.

I. Debates surrounding food regulation have a long history in the United States.
   A. The 1906 Pure Food and Drug Act guarantees inspection of meat and dairy products.
   B. Such regulations are considered reasonable because consumers are protected from harm with little cost.
   C. Consumers consider reasonable regulations to be an important government function to stop harmful items from entering the marketplace.

II. Even though food meets safety standards, there is a need for further regulation.
   A. The typical American diet—processed sugars, fats, and refined flours—is damaging over time.
   B. Related health risks are diabetes, cancer, and heart problems.
   C. Passing chronic-disease-related legislation is our single most important public health challenge.

III. Food legislation is not a popular solution for most Americans.
    A. A proposed New York City regulation banning sale of soft drinks greater than twelve ounces failed in 2012, and in California, a proposed soda tax failed in 2011.
    B. Many consumers find such laws to be unreasonable restrictions on freedom of choice.
    C. Opposition to food and beverage regulation is similar to the opposition to early tobacco legislation; the public views the issue as one of personal responsibility.
    D. Counterpoint: Freedom of "choice" is a myth; our choices are heavily influenced by marketing.

IV. The United States has a history of regulations to discourage unhealthy behaviors.
    A. Tobacco-related restrictions faced opposition.
    B. Seat belt laws are a useful analogy.
    C. The public seems to support laws that have a good cost-benefit ratio; the cost of food/beverage regulations is low, and most people agree that the benefits would be high.

V. Americans believe that personal choice is lost when regulations such as taxes and bans are instituted.
    A. Regulations open up the door to excessive control and interfere with cultural and religious traditions.
    B. Counterpoint: Burdens on individual liberty are a reasonable price to pay for large social health benefits.

VI. Public opposition continues to stand in the way of food regulation to promote healthier eating. We must consider whether to allow the costly trend of rising chronic disease to continue in the name of personal choice, or whether we are willing to support the legal changes and public health policies that will reverse that trend.

Planning with headings

When drafting a research paper or a business document, consider using headings to guide your planning and to help your readers follow the organization of your final draft. While drafting, you can insert your working thesis, experiment with possible headings, and type chunks of text beneath each heading. You may need to try grouping your ideas in a few different ways to suit your purpose and audience.

NOTE: Headings help writers plan and readers understand a document. See page 41 for help using headings and page 585 for a sample paper organized with headings.

1e Draft an introduction.

The introduction to a piece of writing announces the main point; the body develops it; and the conclusion drives it home. You can begin drafting, however, at any point. If you find it difficult to introduce a paper that you have not yet written, try drafting the body first and saving the introduction for later.

Your introduction will usually be a paragraph of 50 to 150 words (in a longer paper, it may be more than one paragraph). Perhaps the most common strategy is to open with a few sentences that engage, or hook, the reader and that establish your purpose for writing and your central idea, or thesis. In the following introduction, the thesis is highlighted.

> As the United States industrialized in the nineteenth century, using immigrant labor, social concerns took a backseat to the task of building a prosperous nation. The government did not regulate industries and did not provide an effective safety net for the poor or for those who became sick or injured on the job. Immigrants and the poor did have a few advocates, however. Settlement houses such as Hull-House in Chicago provided information, services, and a place for reform-minded individuals to gather and work to improve the conditions of the urban poor. Alice Hamilton was one of these reformers. Her work at Hull-House spanned twenty-two years and later expanded throughout the nation. Hamilton's efforts helped to improve the lives of immigrants and drew attention and respect to the problems and people that until then had been ignored.
>
> —Laurie McDonough, student

Each sentence leading to your thesis should engage readers by drawing them into the world of the essay and showing them why your essay is worth reading.

Whether you are writing for a scholarly audience, a professional audience, a public audience, or a general audience, you cannot assume your readers' interest in the topic. The hook should spark readers' curiosity and offer them a reason to continue.

The chart that follows provides strategies for drafting an introduction.

NOTE: Different writing situations call for different introductions. For more examples of effective introductions, see pages 88 (Yoshida), 112 (Jacobs), and 517 (Harba).

Strategies for drafting an introduction

The following strategies can provide a hook for your reader, whether you are composing a traditional essay or a multimodal work such as a slide show presentation or a video (see p. 80).

- Offer a startling statistic or an unusual fact
- Ask a question
- Introduce a quotation or a bit of dialogue
- Provide historical background
- Define a term or concept
- Propose a problem, contradiction, or dilemma
- Use a vivid example or image
- Develop an analogy
- Relate an anecdote

As you draft your introduction, think about your writing situation, especially your genre. For some types of writing, it may be difficult or impossible to express the central idea in a thesis statement; or it may be unwise or unnecessary to put a thesis statement in the essay itself. A literacy narrative, for example, may have a focus too subtle to be distilled in a single sentence. Strictly informative writing, like that found in many business memos or nursing reports, may be difficult to summarize in a thesis. In such instances, do not try to force the central idea into a thesis statement. Instead, think in terms of an overriding purpose and of the genre's conventions and expectations. (See 1a and 1c.)

LaunchPadSolo **macmillanhighered.com/rules8e**

1 Exploring, planning, and drafting
> Writing practice: Revising an introduction
> Exercise: 1–7

Academic English If you come from a culture that prefers an indirect approach in writing, you may feel that asserting a thesis early in an essay sounds unrefined and even rude. In the United States, however, readers appreciate a direct approach; when you state your point as directly as possible, you show that you understand your topic and value your readers' time.

1f Draft the body.

The body of your essay develops support for your thesis, so it's important to have at least a working thesis before you start writing. What does your thesis promise readers? What question are you trying to answer? What problem are you trying to solve? What is your position on the topic? Keep these questions in mind as you draft the body of your essay.

Asking questions as you draft

You may already have written an introduction that includes your working thesis. If not, as long as you have a draft thesis, you can begin developing the body and return later to the introduction. If your thesis suggests a plan or if you have sketched a preliminary outline, try to organize your paragraphs accordingly.

Draft the body of your essay by writing at least one paragraph about each supporting point you listed in the planning stage. If you do not have a plan, pause for a few moments and sketch one. As you draft the body, keep asking questions; keep anticipating what your readers may need to know.

Keep in mind that often you might not know what you want to say until you have written a draft. It is possible to begin without a plan—assuming you are prepared to treat your first attempt as a "discovery draft" that may be radically rewritten once you discover what you really want to say. Whether or not you have a plan when you begin drafting, you can often figure out a workable order for your ideas by stopping each time you start a new paragraph to think about what your readers will need to know to follow your train of thought.

For more detailed help with drafting and developing paragraphs, see 3.

USING SOURCES RESPONSIBLY: As you draft, keep careful notes and records of any sources you read and consult (see 51). If you quote, paraphrase, or summarize a source, include a citation, even in your draft. You will save time and avoid plagiarism if you follow the rules of citation while drafting.

Adding visuals as you draft

As you draft, you may decide that some of the support for your thesis could come from one or more visuals. Visuals can convey information concisely and powerfully. Graphs and tables, for example, can simplify complex numerical information. Images — including photographs and diagrams — often express an idea more vividly than words can. Keep in mind that if you download a visual — or use published information to create your own visual — you must credit your source.

Always consider how a visual conveys your purpose and how your audience might respond to it. Choose visuals to support your writing, not to substitute for it. For an example of an effective use of a visual, see page 46. In writing about the shift from print to online news, student writer Sam Jacobs used a screen shot of a link embedded in a news article to illustrate his argument (see 6k).

The chart on pages 26–27 describes eight types of visuals and their purposes.

1g Draft a conclusion.

A conclusion should remind readers of the essay's main idea without repeating it. Often the concluding paragraph can be relatively short. By the end of the essay, readers should already understand your main point; your conclusion drives it home and, perhaps, gives readers something more to consider.

Strategies for drafting a conclusion

In addition to echoing your main idea, a conclusion might do any of the following:

- Briefly summarize your essay's key points
- Propose a course of action
- Offer a recommendation
- Discuss the topic's wider significance or implications
- Redefine a key term or concept
- Pose a question for future study

Choosing visuals to suit your purpose

Pie chart

Pie charts compare a part or parts to the whole. Segments of the pie represent percentages of the whole (and always total 100 percent).

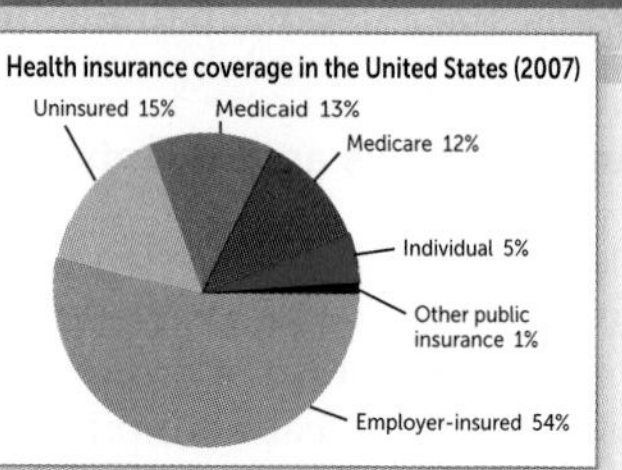

Bar graph (or line graph)

Bar graphs highlight trends over a period of time or compare numerical data. Line graphs display the same data as bar graphs; the data are graphed as points, and the points are connected with lines.

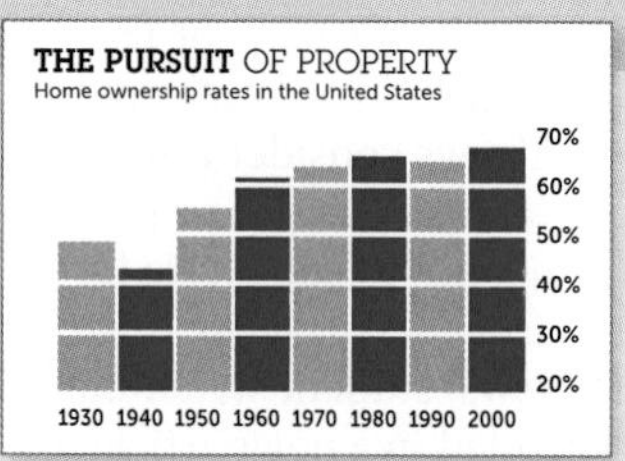

Infographic

An infographic presents data in a visually engaging form. The data are usually numerical, as in bar graphs or line graphs, but they are represented by a graphic element instead of by bars or lines.

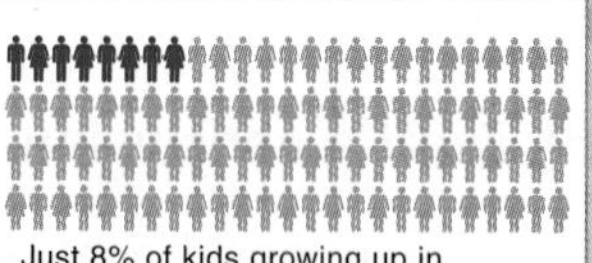

Just 8% of kids growing up in low-income communities graduate from college by age 24.

Table

Tables display numbers and words in columns and rows. They can be used to organize complicated numerical information into an easily understood format.

Prices of daily doses of AIDS drugs ($US)

Drug	*Brazil*	*Uganda*	*Côte d'Ivoire*	*US*
3TC (Lamuvidine)	1.66	3.28	2.95	8.70
ddC (Zalcitabine)	0.24	4.17	3.75	8.80
Didanosine	2.04	5.26	3.48	7.25
Efavirenz	6.96	n/a	6.41	13.13
Indinavir	10.32	12.79	9.07	14.93
Nelfinavir	4.14	4.45	4.39	6.47
Nevirapine	5.04	n/a	n/a	8.48
Saquinavir	6.24	7.37	5.52	6.50
Stavudine	0.56	6.19	4.10	9.07
ZDV/3TC	1.44	7.34	n/a	18.78
Zidovudine	1.06	4.34	2.43	10.12

Source: UNAIDS, 2000

Photograph

Photographs vividly depict people, scenes, or objects discussed in a text.

Behrouz Mehri/AFP/Getty Images

Diagram

Diagrams, useful in scientific and technical writing, concisely illustrate processes, structures, or interactions.

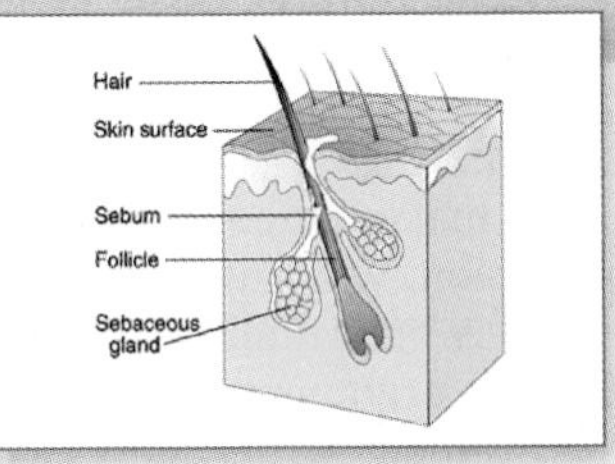

NIAMS

Flowchart

Flowcharts show structures (the hierarchy of employees at a company, for example) or steps in a process and their relation to one another. (See also p. 145 for another example.)

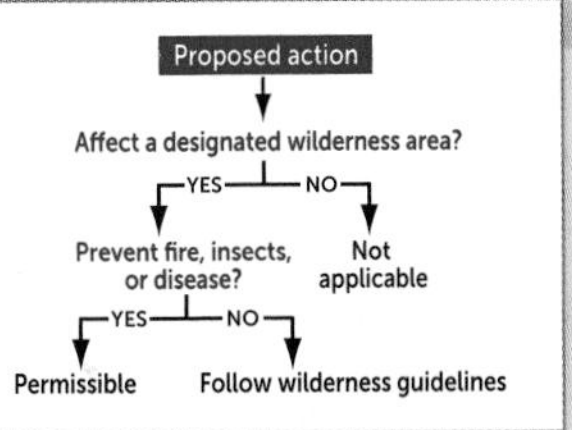

Map

Maps illustrate distances, historical information, or demographics and often use symbols for geographic features and points of interest.

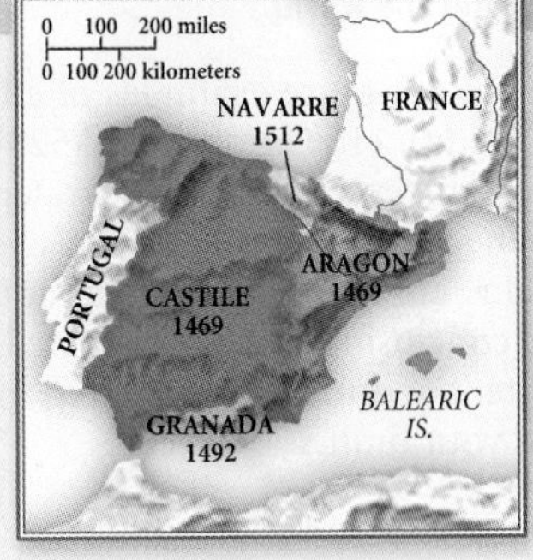

To conclude an essay analyzing the shifting roles of women in the military services, one student discusses her topic's implications for society as a whole.

> As the military continues to train women in jobs formerly reserved for men, our understanding of women's roles in society will no doubt continue to change. And as news reports of women training for and taking part in combat operations become commonplace, reports of women becoming CEOs, police chiefs, and even president of the United States will cease to surprise us. Or perhaps we have already reached this point.
>
> — Rosa Broderick, student

To make the conclusion memorable and to give a sense of completion, you might bring readers full circle by returning to the thesis or including a detail from the introduction. To conclude his argument essay about the shift from print to online news, student writer Sam Jacobs returns to the phrase "fit to print" from his introduction, and echoes his thesis to show the wider significance of his argument. (See pp. 112–117.)

> The Internet has enabled consumers to participate in a new way in reading, questioning, interpreting, and reporting the news. Decisions about appropriate content and coverage are no longer exclusively in the hands of news editors. Ordinary citizens now have a meaningful voice in the conversation — a hand in deciding what's "fit to print." Some skeptics worry about the apparent free-for-all and loss of tradition. But the expanding definition of news provides opportunities for consumers to be more engaged with events in their communities, their nations, and the world.

To see more examples of effective conclusions, see pages 91 (Yoshida), 116 (Jacobs), and 523 (Harba).

Whatever concluding strategy you choose, keep in mind that an effective conclusion is decisive and unapologetic. Avoid introducing completely new ideas at the end of an essay. And because the conclusion is so closely tied to the rest of the essay in both content and tone, be prepared to revise it or rewrite it as you revise your draft.

LaunchPadSolo **macmillanhighered.com/rules8e**
1 Exploring, planning, and drafting
> Writing practice: Revising a conclusion

1h Manage your files.

Keeping track of all your notes, outlines, rough drafts, and final drafts can be challenging. Be sure to give your files distinct names that reflect the appropriate stage of your writing process, and store them in a logical place.

Writing online or in a word processing program can make drafting and revising easier. You can undo changes or return to an earlier draft if a revision misfires. Applying the following steps can help you explore drafting and revising possibilities with little risk.

- Create folders and subfolders for each assignment. Save notes, outlines, and drafts together.
- Label revised drafts with different file names and dates.
- Print hard copies, make backup copies, and press the Save button often (every five to ten minutes).
- Always record complete bibliographic information about any sources you might use, including visuals.
- Use a comment function to make notes to yourself or to respond to the drafts of peers.

MANAGING FILES

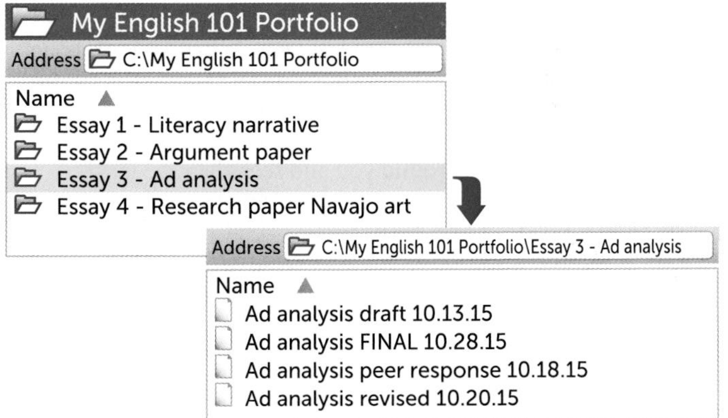

macmillanhighered.com/rules8e

1 Exploring, planning, and drafting
 > Writing practice: Managing your files

2 Revising, editing, and reflecting

Revising is rarely a one-step process. Global matters — thesis, purpose, organization, content, and overall strategy — generally receive attention first because global revisions involve bigger changes, including rewrites of paragraphs or whole sections of a paper. Improvements in sentence structure and word choice usually come later; it's a good idea to make sure global revisions are complete before you spend time fine-tuning sentences. Revising at the sentence level gives you a chance to reconsider whether a particular point could be stronger or clearer or if a certain word or phrase sends the message you intended.

Editing is a step that is best left for the end of the writing process. It involves identifying errors or patterns of errors, such as using commas and quotation marks correctly, making subjects and verbs agree, or using the right form of a pronoun. See 2b for advice on keeping an editing log.

Writing multiple drafts allows you to write in stages, seek feedback, and strengthen your paper through both revising and editing.

2a See revision as a social process.

To revise is to *re-see*, and the comments you receive from reviewers — instructors, peers, and writing center tutors — will help you re-see your draft from your readers' point of view. When you ask readers for their comments, revision becomes a social experience, connecting you with the suggestions and insights of readers who help you shape your work in progress. As you write for college courses, form a community of readers around you and seek their feedback.

Feedback gives you perspective on what's working and not working in your draft and keeps the expectations of your readers in mind. Simple questions such as "What would you say is my main idea?" and "Is my draft focused and organized?" will help you see your draft through readers' eyes. The checklist for global revision on page 42 may help you and your reviewers get started.

2b Use peer review: Revise with comments.

Peer review gives you an opportunity to see your draft through the eyes of readers. When peers — classmates and fellow students — read your work, they offer feedback, pointing out where they are intrigued or confused. They offer their insights and suggestions, answer your questions, and help you strengthen your draft. Think of peer review as an opportunity to talk about your writing with a coach, an advocate, who will help you achieve your purpose for writing.

The following guidelines will help you learn from your reviewers' comments and revise successfully.

Be active. Help reviewers understand your purpose for writing and provide background about why you chose your topic, why it matters to you, and what you hope to accomplish in your draft. Let your reviewers know your specific questions and concerns so they can provide focused feedback.

Listen with an open mind. After you've worked hard on a draft, you might be surprised to hear reviewers tell you it still needs more development. Don't take criticism personally. Your readers are responding to your essay, not you. If comments show that a reviewer doesn't understand what you're trying to do, don't be defensive. Instead, consider why your reader is confused, and figure out how to clarify your point. Responding to readers' objections—instead of dismissing them—may strengthen your ideas and make your essay more persuasive. Taking feedback seriously will make you a stronger writer.

Weigh feedback carefully. As you begin revising, you may find yourself sorting through suggestions from many people, including instructors, writing tutors, and peer reviewers. Sometimes these readers will agree, but often their advice will differ. Your reviewers will probably make more suggestions than you can use, so be strategic. It's important to sort through all the comments you receive with your original goals in mind and to focus on global concerns first (see p. 42)—otherwise, you'll be facing the impossible task of trying to incorporate everyone's advice.

Keep a revision and editing log. Make a clear and simple list of the global and sentence-level concerns that keep coming up in most of your reviewers' comments. That list can serve as a starting point each time you revise a paper to help you learn about your strengths and weaknesses as a writer. When you take charge of your own writing in this way, comments will become a valuable resource.

NOTE: Some instructors suggest that writers acknowledge their reviewers in a brief note at the end of their finished paper.

LaunchPadSolo **macmillanhighered.com/rules8e**

2 Revising, editing, and reflecting
> Writing practice: Using reviewers' comments
> Exercises: 2–1 and 2–2

Strategies for revising with comments

Often the comments you'll receive are written as shorthand commands—"Be specific!"—and sometimes as questions—"What is your main point?" Such comments don't immediately show you *how* to revise, but they do identify where revision might improve your draft. Don't hesitate to ask your reviewers to explain their comments if you don't understand them. The following sample comments and revision strategies will help you think about how to apply reviewer feedback to your own writing—and where you might look in *Rules for Writers* for help.

THE COMMENT: *Unfocused introduction*

Understanding the comment When readers point out that your introduction needs to be "focused," the comment often signals that the beginning sentences of your essay are vague, unconnected to the rest of your essay, and don't establish your purpose for writing.

Strategies for revising

- ***Reread your introduction and ask questions.*** Are the sentences leading to your thesis specific enough to engage readers and communicate your purpose? Do these sentences lead logically to your thesis? Do they spark your readers' curiosity and offer them a reason to continue reading? (***See 1e.***)
- ***Try engaging readers with a "hook"*** in your introduction—a question, a quotation, a vivid example, or a startling statistic. (***See the chart on p. 23.***)

THE COMMENT: *Consider opposing viewpoints*

Understanding the comment When readers suggest that you "consider opposing viewpoints," the comment often signals that you need to recognize and respond to possible objections to your argument.

Strategies for revising

- ***Read more*** to learn about the debates surrounding the topic. Understand the various sides of your issue so you can anticipate and counter objections to your argument. (***See 50a and 50b.***)
- ***Be open-minded.*** Although it might seem illogical to introduce opposing arguments, you'll show your knowledge of the topic by recognizing that not everyone draws the same conclusions or holds the same point of view. (***See 6i and p. 438.***)
- ***Introduce and counter objections*** with phrases like these: "Some readers might point out that . . ." or "Critics of this view argue that. . . ." (***See p. 110.***)

2c Use peer review: Give constructive comments.

Peer review gives you an opportunity to read the work of your classmates and to learn from each other. As you offer advice about how to strengthen a peer's thesis or how to use a visual to convey concise information, you are thinking about the purpose of a thesis and the role of visuals. When you propose a strategy for focusing an introduction or for anticipating a counterargument, you not only help your classmate, but you also benefit from the process of thinking strategically about revision.

As a peer reviewer, your work is to engage with a writer as a reader. It isn't your job to rewrite, correct, or proofread the work of your peers. It is your job, though, to offer thoughtful, positive, encouraging comments to show peers what they're doing well and how they might build upon their strengths as writers.

The following guidelines will help you offer constructive comments to your peers.

Be specific. Your comments will be more constructive if you point to specific places in a draft and show your classmate how, why, and where a draft is effective or confusing. Instead of saying "I like your draft," be specific about what you like: "You do a great job of using a startling statistic in your introduction to hook me as a reader." Or instead of offering a generality such as "Your draft doesn't have much support," give a specific suggestion: "A bar graph in the third paragraph might support your thesis and be convincing visual evidence."

View yourself as a coach, not a judge. Think of yourself as asking questions and proposing possibilities, not dictating solutions. It is the writer, after all, who will have to grapple with revising. Help the writer identify the strengths of a draft and conceive possible solutions to address the draft's problems. Try phrasing comments this way: "Have you thought about . . ." "What if you tried . . ." or "How can you help a reader understand this important point. . . ."

Pay attention to global issues first. Focus on the big picture—purpose, thesis, organization, and content—before sentence structure, word choice, and grammar. As a reader, do you understand the writer's main idea? Can you follow the train of thought? Restate the writer's thesis and main ideas to check your understanding. Use the checklist for global revision (p. 42) to guide your comments.

The following excerpt from an online peer review session shows a peer reviewer offering constructive comments:

EXCERPT FROM AN ONLINE PEER REVIEW SESSION

Juan (Peer Reviewer): *Rachel, your essay makes a great point that credit card companies often hook students on a cycle of spending. But it sounds as if you're blaming students for their spending habits and credit card companies for their deceptive actions. Is this what you want to say?*

Peer reviewer restates writer's main point and asks a question to help her clarify her ideas.

Rachel (Writer): ***No, I want to keep the focus on the credit card companies. I didn't realize I was blaming students. What could I change?***

Writer takes comment seriously and asks reviewer for specific suggestion.

Juan (Reviewer): *In paragraphs three and four, you group all students together as if all students have the same bad spending habits. If students are your audience, you'll be insulting them. What reader is motivated to read something that's alienating? What is your purpose for writing this draft?*

Peer reviewer points to specific places in the draft and asks questions to help writer focus on audience and purpose.

Rachel (Writer): ***Well . . . It's true that students don't always have good spending habits, but I don't want to blame students. My purpose is to call students to action about the dangers of credit card debt. Any suggestions for narrowing the focus?***

Writer is actively engaged with peer reviewer's comments and doesn't take criticism personally.

Juan (Reviewer): *Most students know about the dangers of credit card debt, but they might not know about specific deceptive practices companies use to lure them. Maybe ask yourself what would surprise your audience about these practices?*

Peer reviewer responds as a reader and acts as a coach to suggest possible solutions.

Rachel (Writer): ***Juan, that's a good idea. I'll try it.***

Writer thanks reviewer for his help and leaves session with a specific revision strategy.

POST COMMENT

2d Highlights of one student's peer review process.

Student writer Michelle Nguyen wrote a draft in response to the following assignment:

> How have your experiences with writing, positive or negative, shaped you as a writer? Write a literacy narrative (500–1,000 words) to explore this question. Select one or more key experiences that you think best illustrate how you became the writer you are today. In addition to telling a story, your narrative should make a larger point about learning to write that will be of interest to your readers.

Below is the draft Nguyen submitted to her three peer reviewers. Here are questions she gave her peer reviewers to focus their feedback.

QUESTIONS FROM NGUYEN TO PEER REVIEWERS

Alex, Brian, and Sameera: Thanks for reading my draft. Here are three questions I have about my draft: Is my focus clear? Is there anything that confuses you? What specifically should I cut or add to strengthen my draft?

ROUGH DRAFT WITH PEER COMMENTS

Rough Draft

My family used to live in the heart of Hanoi, Vietnam. The neighborhood was small but swamped with crime. Drug addicts scoured the alleys and stole the most mundane things—old clothes, worn slippers, even license plates of motorbikes. Like anyone else in Vietnam in the '90s, we struggled with poverty. There was no entertainment device in our house aside from an 11" black-and-white television. Even then, electricity went off for hours on a weekly basis.

I was particularly close to a Vietnam War veteran. My parents were away a lot, so the old man became like a grandfather to me. He taught me how to ride a bicycle, how to read, how to take care of

Alex F: You might want to add a title to focus readers.

Sameera K: I really like your introduction. It's so vivid. Think about adding a photo of your neighborhood so readers can relate. What does Hanoi look like?

Brian S: You have great details here to set the scene in Hanoi, but why does it matter that you didn't have an "entertainment device"? Maybe choose the most interesting among all these details.

small pets. He worked sporadically from home, fixing bicycle tires and broken pedals. He was a wrinkly old man who didn't talk much. His vocal cords were damaged during the war, and it caused him pain to speak. In a neighborhood full of screaming babies and angry shop owners and slimy criminals, his home was my quiet haven. I could read and write and think and bond with someone whose worldliness came from his wordlessness.

Brian S: Worldliness came from wordlessness—great phrase! Is this part of your main idea? What is your main idea?

The tiny house he lived in stood at the far end of our neighborhood. It always smelled of old clothes and forgotten memories. He was a slight man, but his piercing black eyes retained their intensity even after all these years. He must have made one fierce soldier.

Sameera K: You do a good job of showing us why this Vietnam veteran was important to you, but it seems like this draft is more a story about the man and not about you. What do you want readers to understand about you?

"I almost died once," he said, dusting a picture frame. It was one of those rare instances he ever mentioned his life during the war. As he talked, I perched myself on the side of an armchair, rested my head on my tiny hands, and listened intently. I didn't understand much. I just liked hearing his low, humming voice. The concept of war for me was strictly confined to the classroom, and even then, the details of combat were always murky. The teachers just needed us to know that the communist troops enjoyed a glorious victory.

"I was the only survivor of my unit. 20 guys. All dead within a year. Then they let me go," he said. His voice cracked a little and his eyes misted over as he stared at pictures from his combatant past. "We didn't even live long enough to understand what we were fighting for."

He finished the sentence with a drawn-out sigh, a small set of wrinkles gathering at the end of his eyes.

Years later, as I thought about his stories, I started to wonder why he referred to his deceased comrades by the collective pronoun "we." It was as if a little bit of him died on the battlefield with them too.

Three years after my family left the neighborhood, I learned that the old man became stricken with cancer. When I came home the next summer, I visited his house and sat by his sickbed. His shoulder-length mop of salt and pepper hair now dwarfed his rail-thin figure. We barely exchanged a word. He just held my hands tightly until my mother called for me to leave, his skeletal fingers leaving a mark on my pale palms. Perhaps he was trying to transmit to me some of his worldliness and his wisdom. Perhaps he was telling me to go out into the world and live the free life he never had.

Some people say that writers are selfish and vain. The truth is, I learned to write because it gave me peace in the much too noisy world of my Vietnamese childhood. In the quiet of the old man's house, I gazed out the window, listened to my thoughts, and wrote them down. It all started with a story about a wrinkly Vietnam War veteran who didn't talk much.

Sameera K: I'm curious to hear more about you and why this man was so important to you. What did he teach you about writing? What did he see in you?

Alex F: This sentence is confusing. Your draft doesn't seem to be about the selfishness or vanity of writers.

Brian S: What does "it" refer to? I think you're trying to say something important about silence and noise and literacy, but I'm not sure what it is.

After reading her draft and considering the feedback from her classmates, Nguyen realized that she had chosen a good direction but that she hadn't focused her draft to meet the expectations of the assignment. Her classmates offered her valuable suggestions about adding a photograph of her Hanoi neighborhood and clarifying her main idea. With her classmates' specific questions and suggestions in mind, and their encouragement to see the undeveloped possibilities in her draft, Nguyen developed some goals for revising.

MICHELLE NGUYEN'S REVISION GOALS

- Add a title.
- Revise introduction to set the scene more dramatically. Use Sameera's idea to include a photo of my neighborhood.
- Make the story my story, not the man's story. Answer Sameera's question: What did the man see in me and I in him? Delete extra material about the old man.
- Answer Brian's question: What is my main idea?
- Follow Brian's suggestion about the connection between wordlessness and worldliness. Make the contrasts sharper between the neighborhood and the man's house.
- Figure out what main idea I'm trying to communicate. See if there is a possible idea in the various contrasts. The surprise was finding writing in silence, not in the noisy exchange of voices in my neighborhood.

See page 45 for Nguyen's revised draft.

2e Approach global revision in cycles.

Revision is more effective when you approach it in cycles, rather than attempting to change everything all at once. Four common cycles of global revision are discussed in this section:

- Engaging the audience
- Sharpening the focus
- Improving the organization
- Strengthening the content

Engaging the audience

Sometimes a rough draft needs an overhaul because it is directed at no particular audience. A good question to ask yourself and your reviewers is the toughest question a reader might ask: "So what?" or "Why does it matter?" If your draft can't pass the "So what?" test, you may need to rethink your approach.

Once you have made sure that your draft is directed at an audience—readers who have a stake in the topic—you may still need to refine your tone. The tone of a piece of writing expresses the writer's feelings toward the audience and the topic, so it is important to get it right. When you seek responses to your draft, ask your readers about your tone. If they respond that your tone seems self-centered, flippant, bossy, patronizing, or hostile, for example, you'll want to modify it to show respect for your readers.

The following paragraph was drafted by a student who hoped to persuade his audience to buy organic produce.

A PARAGRAPH THAT ALIENATES READERS

> If you choose to buy organic produce, you are supporting local farmers as well as demonstrating your opposition to chemical pesticides. As more and more supermarkets carry organic fruits and vegetables, consumers have fewer reasons not to buy organic. Some consumers do not buy organic produce because they are not willing to spend the extra money. But if you care at all about the environment or the small farmer, you should be willing to support organic farms in your area.

When the student asked a classmate to review his draft, his classmate commented that the tone was harsh and alienating. His peer reviewer questioned why he assumed his readers didn't care about the environment.

A PARAGRAPH THAT RESPECTS READERS

> By choosing to buy organic produce, you have the opportunity to support local farmers, to oppose the use of chemical pesticides, and to taste some of the freshest produce available. Because more supermarkets carry organic produce than ever, you won't even have to miss out on any of your favorite fruits or vegetables. Although organic produce can be more expensive than conventional produce, the costs are not prohibitive. For example, a pound of organic bananas at my local grocery store is eighty-nine cents, while the conventional bananas are sixty-nine cents a pound. If you can afford this small price difference, you will have the opportunity to make a difference for the environment and for the small farmer.
>
> —Leon Nage, student

Sharpening the focus

A clearly focused draft fixes readers' attention on one central idea and does not stray from that idea. You can sharpen the focus of a draft by clarifying the introduction (especially the thesis) and by deleting any text that is off point.

Clarifying the introduction Reread your introduction to see if it clearly states the essay's main idea. To help you revise, ask your reviewers questions such as the following:

- Does the introduction let readers know what to expect as they read on?
- Does it make the significance of the subject clear so that readers will want to keep reading?
- Can readers tell where the introduction stops and the body of the essay begins? Have you included material in the introduction that should appear in the body instead? Is your introduction too broad or unfocused?
- Does the thesis accurately state the main idea of the essay?

Deleting text that is off the point Compare the introduction, especially the thesis statement, with the body of the essay. Does the body fulfill the promise of the introduction? If not, you will need to adjust one or the other. Either rebuild the introduction to fit the body or keep the introduction and delete body sentences or paragraphs that stray from its point.

Improving the organization

A draft is well organized when its major divisions are logical and easy to follow. To improve the organization of your draft, you may need to take one or more of the following actions: adding or sharpening topic sentences, moving blocks of text, and inserting headings.

Adding or sharpening topic sentences Topic sentences state the main ideas of the paragraphs in the body of an essay. (See 3a.) You can review the organization of a draft by reading only the topic sentences. Do the topic sentences clearly support the essay's main idea? Can you turn them into a reasonable sentence outline of the paper? (See 1d.) If your draft lacks topic sentences, add them unless you have a good reason for omitting them.

Moving blocks of text Improving the organization of a draft can be as simple as moving a few sentences from one paragraph to another or reordering paragraphs. You may also find that you can clarify the organization of a draft by combining choppy paragraphs or by dividing those that are too long for easy reading. (See 3e.) Often, however, the process is more complex. As you move blocks of text, you may need to supply transitions to make the text fit smoothly in the new positions; you may also need to rework topic sentences to make your new organization clear.

Before moving text, consider sketching a revised outline. Divisions in the outline might become topic sentences in the restructured essay. (See 3e.)

Inserting headings In long documents, such as complex research papers or business reports, headings can help readers follow your organization. Typically, headings are presented as phrases, declarative or imperative sentences, or questions. To draw attention to headings, you can center them, put them in boldface, underline them, use all capital letters, or do some combination of these techniques. (See also 58b for use of headings in APA papers.)

Strengthening the content

In reviewing the content of a draft, first consider whether your argument is sound. Second, consider whether you should add or delete any text (sentences or paragraphs). If your purpose is to argue a point, consider how persuasively you have supported your point. If your purpose is to inform, be sure that you have presented your ideas clearly and with enough detail to meet your readers' expectations.

Rethinking your argument A first draft presents you with an opportunity to rethink your argument. You can often develop your ideas about a subject by asking yourself some questions:

- Is your claim more sweeping than the evidence supports?
- Have you left out an important step in the argument?
- Have you dealt fairly with opposing arguments?
- Is your draft free of faulty reasoning? (See 6a.)

Adding text If any paragraphs or sections of the essay are too skimpy to be clear and convincing (a common problem in rough drafts), add specific facts, details, and examples. You may need to go back to the beginning of the writing process: listing specifics, brainstorming ideas with friends or classmates, perhaps doing more research. As you revise paragraphs, it's helpful to ask questions such as Why? and How?

Deleting text Look for sentences and paragraphs that can be cut without serious loss of meaning. Ask your reviewers if they can show you sentences where you have repeated yourself or strayed from your point. Maybe you have given too much emphasis to minor ideas. Cuts may also be necessitated by word limits, such as those imposed by a college assignment or by the realities of the business world, where readers are often pressed for time.

Checklist for global revision

Purpose and audience

- Does the draft address a question, a problem, or an issue that readers care about?
- Is the draft appropriate for its audience? Does it account for the audience's knowledge of and possible attitudes toward the subject?
- Is the tone respectful?

Focus

- Is the thesis clear? Is it prominently placed?
- Does the thesis answer a reader's "So what?" question? (See p. 16.)
- If the draft has no thesis, is there a good reason for omitting one?

Organization and paragraphing

- Is each paragraph unified around a main point?
- Does each paragraph support and develop the thesis?
- Have you provided organizational cues for readers such as topic sentences and headings?
- Have you presented ideas in a logical order?
- Are any paragraphs too long or too short for easy reading?

Content

- Is the supporting material relevant and persuasive?
- Which ideas need further development? Have you left your readers with any unanswered questions?
- Are the parts proportioned sensibly? Do major ideas receive enough attention?
- Should you delete any material? Look for redundant or irrelevant information.

Point of view

- Is the dominant point of view — first person (*I* or *we*), second person (*you*), or third person (*he*, *she*, *it*, *one*, or *they*) — appropriate for your purpose and audience? (See 1a.)

2f Revise and edit sentences.

When you *revise* sentences, you focus on clarity and effectiveness; when you *edit*, you check for correctness. Sentences that are wordy, vague, or rambling may distract readers and make it hard for readers to focus on your purpose or grasp your ideas. Read each sentence slowly to determine if it is as specific and clear as possible. You might find it helpful to read your work aloud and trust your ears to detect awkwardness, wordiness, or a jarring repetition. Your goal, as you revise your sentences, is to make each word count to keep the attention and interest of your readers.

Here, for example, is a rough-draft paragraph as one student made changes to solve a variety of sentence-level problems.

> Although some cities have found creative ways to improve access to public transportation for passengers with physical disabilities, ~~and to fund other programs, there have been problems in~~ our city has struggled with ~~due to the need to address~~ budget constraints and competing ~~needs~~ priorities. ~~This~~ The budget crunch has led citizens to question how funds are distributed.~~?~~ For example, last year ~~when~~ city officials voted to use available funds to support ~~had to choose between allocating funds for accessible transportation or allocating funds to~~ after-school programs rather than transportation upgrades.~~, they voted for the after-school programs.~~ It is not clear to some citizens why ~~these~~ after-school programs are more important.

The original paragraph was too wordy, a problem that can be addressed through any number of revisions to clarify the meaning of each sentence. The following revision would also be acceptable.

> Some cities have funded improved access to public transportation for passengers with physical disabilities. Because of budget constraints, our city chose to fund after-school programs rather than transportation programs. As a result, citizens have begun to question how funds are distributed and why certain programs are more important than others.

Some of the improvements in the first revision do not involve choice and must be edited to avoid confusion and misunderstanding. For example, the hyphen in *after-school programs* is necessary; a noun must be substituted for the pronoun *these* in the last sentence; and the question mark in the second sentence must be changed to a period.

NOTE: You can use an editing log to keep a personal list of your common errors and learn the rules to correct the errors. To begin your log, review all the grammar, punctuation, and spelling errors identified in your last piece of writing. For each error, list the handbook section that provides advice or examples for you to review as you edit.

2g Proofread the final manuscript.

Proofreading is a special kind of reading: a slow and methodical search for misspellings, typographical mistakes, and omitted words or word endings. Such errors can be difficult to spot in your own work because you may read what you intended to write, not what is actually on the page.

Although proofreading may be slow, it is crucial. Errors in an essay can be distracting and annoying. If the writer doesn't care about this piece of writing, the reader might wonder, why should I? A carefully proofread essay, however, sends a positive message: It shows that you value your writing and respect your readers.

As you proofread, pay attention to formatting your final draft and follow your instructor's directions for formatting documents. (See the document design gallery [pp. 597–607] for formatting guidelines for MLA and APA.)

Proofreading tips

- Remove distractions and allow yourself ten to fifteen minutes of pure concentration; turn off the TV and your cell phone and find a quiet place, away from people who are talking.
- Proofread out loud, articulating each word as it is actually written.
- Proofread your sentences in reverse order.
- Proofread hard copy pages; mistakes can be difficult to catch on-screen.
- Don't rely too heavily on spell checkers and grammar checkers. Before automatically accepting their changes, consider their accuracy and appropriateness.
- Ask a volunteer (a friend, roommate, or co-worker) to proofread after you. A second reader may catch something you didn't.

2h Sample student revision

On pages 35–37, you'll find Michelle Nguyen's first draft, along with the highlights of her peer review process. Comments from her peer reviewers helped Nguyen see her draft through her readers' eyes and to develop a revision plan (see p. 38). One reviewer asked: "What is your main idea?" Another reviewer asked: "What do you want readers to understand about you?" As she revised, Nguyen made both global revisions and sentence-level revisions to clarify her main idea and to delete extra material that might distract readers from her story. Here is Nguyen's final draft, "A Place to Begin."

Nguyen 1

Michelle Nguyen
Professor Wilson
English 101
22 September 2014

Nguyen formats her final draft using MLA guidelines.

A Place to Begin

I grew up in the heart of Hanoi, Vietnam—Nhà Dầu—a small but busy neighborhood swamped with crime. Houses, wedged in among cafés and other local businesses (see fig. 1), measured uniformly about 200 square feet, and the walls were so thin that we could hear every heated debate and impassioned disagreement. Drug addicts scoured the vicinity and stole the most mundane things—old clothes, worn slippers, even license plates of motorbikes. It was a neighborhood where dogs howled and kids ran amok and where the earth was always moist and marked with stains. It was the 1990s Vietnam in miniature, with all the turmoil and growing pains of a newly reborn nation.

Nguyen revises her introduction to engage readers with vivid details.

In a city perpetually inundated with screaming children and slimy criminals, I found my place in the home

Sentences revised for clarity and specificity.

Marginal annotations indicate MLA-style formatting and **effective writing**.

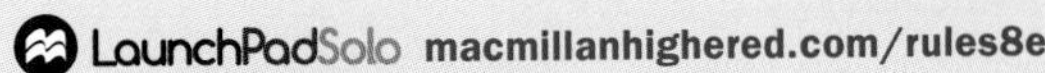
LaunchPadSolo **macmillanhighered.com/rules8e**
2 Revising, editing, and reflecting
> Sample student writing: Nguyen, "A Place to Begin" (literacy narrative)

Nguyen 2

Fig. 1 Nhà Dầu neighborhood in Hanoi (personal photograph by author)

As her peer reviewers suggested, Nguyen adds a photograph to help readers visualize Hanoi.

Nguyen focuses on one key story in response to reviewers' questions.

Nguyen's revisions clarify her main idea.

of a Vietnam War veteran. My parents were away a lot, so the old man became like a grandfather to me. He was a slight man who didn't talk much. His vocal cords had been damaged during the war, and it caused him pain to speak. In his quiet home, I could read and write in the presence of someone whose worldliness grew from his wordlessness.

His tiny house stood at the far end of our neighborhood and always smelled of old clothes and forgotten memories. His wall was plastered with pictures from his combatant past, pictures that told his life story when his own voice couldn't. "I almost died once," he said, dusting a picture frame. It was one of those rare instances he ever mentioned his life during the war.

I perched myself on the side of the armchair, rested my head on my tiny hands, and listened intently. I didn't understand much. I just liked hearing his low, raspy voice.

Nguyen develops her narrative with dialogue.

"I was the only survivor of my unit. Twenty guys. All dead within a year. Then they let me go."

Nguyen 3

He finished the sentence with a drawn-out sigh, a small set of wrinkles gathering at the corner of his eye.

I wanted to hear the details of that story yet was too afraid to ask. But the bits and pieces I did hear, I wrote down in a notebook. I wanted to make sure that there were not only photos but also written words to bear witness to the old veteran's existence.

Once, I caught him looking at the jumbled mess of sentences I'd written. I ran to the table and snatched my notebook, my cheeks warmed with a bright tinge of pink. I was embarrassed. But mostly, I was terrified that he'd hate me for stealing his life story and turning it into a collection of words and characters and ambivalent feelings.

Nguyen revises to keep the focus on her story and not the old man's, as her peer reviewers suggested.

"I'm sorry," I muttered, my gaze drilling a hole into the tiled floor.

Quietly, he peeled the notebook from my fingers and placed it back on the table.

In his muted way, with his mouth barely twisted in a smile, he seemed to be granting me permission and encouraging me to keep writing. Maybe he saw a storyteller and a writer in me, a little girl with a pencil and too much free time.

The last time I visited Nhà Dầu was for the veteran's funeral two years ago. It was a cold November afternoon, but the weather didn't dampen the usual tumultuous spirit of the neighborhood. I could hear the jumble of shouting voices and howling dogs, yet it didn't bother me. For a minute I closed my eyes, remembering myself as a little girl with a big pencil, gazing out a window and scribbling words in my first notebook.

Nguyen revises her final two paragraphs, circling back to the scene from the introduction, giving the narrative coherence.

Many people think that words emerge from words and from the exchange of voices. Perhaps this is true. But the surprising paradox of writing for me is that I started to

Nguyen revises final paragraph to show readers the significance of her narrative.

Nguyen 4

write in the presence of silence. It was only in the utter stillness of a Vietnam War veteran's house that I could hear my thoughts for the first time, appreciate language, and find the confidence to put words on a page. With one notebook and a pencil, and with the encouragement of a wordless man to tell his story, I began to write. Sometimes that's all a writer needs, a quiet place to begin.

Following a peer reviewer's advice, Nguyen chooses words from her final sentence for her title.

2i Prepare a portfolio; reflect on your writing.

At the end of the semester, your instructor may ask you to submit a portfolio, or collection, of your writing. A writing portfolio often consists of drafts, revisions, and reflections that demonstrate a writer's thinking and learning processes or that showcase the writer's best work. Your instructor may give you the choice of submitting your portfolio on paper or electronically.

As early in the course as possible, be sure you know the answers to the following questions:

- Should the portfolio be a paper collection or an electronic one? Is it your choice?
- Will the portfolio be checked or assessed before the end of the term? If so, when or how often? By whom?
- Are you free to choose any or all of the pieces to include?
- Are you free to include a variety of items (not just rough and final drafts of papers), such as outlines and notes, journal entries, photographs or other visuals, comments from reviewers, sound files, or video clips?
- Will your instructor be the primary or only audience for the portfolio? Or will the portfolio be shared with peers or with other instructors?

TIP: Save your notes, drafts, and reviewers' comments for possible use in your portfolio. The more you have assembled, the more you have to choose from to represent your best work. Keep your documents organized in a paper or electronic file system for easy access. (See 1h.)

Reflection — the process of stepping back periodically to examine your decisions, preferences, strengths, and challenges as a writer — helps you recognize your growth as a writer and is the backbone of portfolio keeping.

When you submit your portfolio for a final evaluation or reading, you may be asked to include a reflective opening statement — a cover letter, an introduction, a preface, a memo, or an essay.

Reflective writing allows you to do the following:

- show that you can identify the strengths and weaknesses of your writing
- comment on the progress you've made in the course
- understand your own writing process
- demonstrate that you've made good writing decisions
- comment on how you might use skills developed in or experiences from your writing course in other courses where writing is assigned

Check with your instructor about the guidelines for your reflective opening statement.

3 Building effective paragraphs

A paragraph is a group of sentences that focuses on one main point or example. Except for special-purpose paragraphs, such as introductions and conclusions (see 1e and 1g), body paragraphs function to develop and support an essay's main point or thesis. Aim for paragraphs that are well developed, organized, coherent, and neither too long nor too short for easy reading. Note that there is no ideal length for a paragraph, but your instructor may have specific guidelines.

3a Focus on a main point.

A paragraph should be unified around a main point. The point should be clear to readers, and all sentences in the paragraph should relate to it.

Stating the main point in a topic sentence

As readers move into a paragraph, they need to know where they are — in relation to the whole essay — and what to expect in the sentences to come. A good topic sentence, a one-sentence summary of the paragraph's main point, acts as a signpost pointing in two directions: backward toward the thesis of the essay and forward toward the body of the paragraph.

Like a thesis statement (see 1c), a topic sentence is more general than the material supporting it. Usually the topic sentence (highlighted in the following example) comes first in the paragraph.

> All living creatures manage some form of communication. The dance patterns of bees in their hive help to point the way to distant flower fields or announce successful foraging. Male stickleback fish regularly swim upside-down to indicate outrage in a courtship contest. Male deer and lemurs mark territorial ownership by rubbing their own body secretions on boundary stones or trees. Everyone has seen a frightened dog put his tail between his legs and run in panic. We, too, use gestures, expressions, postures, and movement to give our words point.
>
> — Olivia Vlahos, *Human Beginnings*

In college writing, topic sentences are often necessary for advancing or clarifying lines of an argument and introducing evidence from a source. In the following paragraph on the effects of the 2010 oil spill in the Gulf of Mexico, the writer uses a topic sentence (highlighted) to state that the extent of the threat is unknown before quoting three sources that illustrate her point.

> To date, the full ramifications [of the oil spill] remain a question mark. An August report from the National Oceanic and Atmospheric Administration estimated that 75 percent of the oil had "either evaporated or been burned, skimmed, recovered from the wellhead, or dispersed." However, Woods Hole Oceanographic Institution researchers reported that a 1.2-mile-wide, 650-foot-high plume caused by the spill "had and will persist for some time." And University of Georgia scientists concluded that almost 80 percent of the released oil hadn't been recovered and "remains a threat to the ecosystem."
>
> — Michele Berger, "Volunteer Army"

LaunchPadSolo macmillanhighered.com/rules8e
3 Building effective paragraphs
> Writing practice: Creating unity
> LearningCurve: Topics and main ideas
> LearningCurve: Topic sentences and supporting details

Occasionally the topic sentence may be withheld until the end of the paragraph — but only if the earlier sentences hang together so well that readers perceive their direction, if not their exact point.

Sticking to the point

Sentences that do not support the topic sentence destroy the unity of a paragraph. If the paragraph is otherwise focused, such sentences can simply be deleted or perhaps moved elsewhere. In the following paragraph describing the inadequate facilities in a high school, the information about the chemistry instructor (highlighted) is clearly off the point.

> As the result of tax cuts, the educational facilities of Lincoln High School have reached an all-time low. Some of the books date back to 1990 and have long since shed their covers. The few computers in working order must share one printer. The lack of lab equipment makes it necessary for four or five students to work at one table, with most watching rather than performing experiments. Also, the chemistry instructor left to have a baby at the beginning of the semester, and most of the students don't like the substitute. As for the furniture, many of the upright chairs have become recliners, and the desk legs are so unbalanced that they play seesaw on the floor.

EXERCISE 3–1 Underline the topic sentence in the following paragraph and cross out any material that does not clarify or develop the central idea. *More practice:* LaunchPadSolo

> Quilt making has served as an important means of social, political, and artistic expression for women. In the nineteenth century, quilting circles provided one of the few opportunities for women to forge social bonds outside of their families. Once a week or more, they came together to sew as well as trade small talk, advice, and news. They used dyed cotton fabrics much like the fabrics quilters use today; surprisingly, quilters' basic materials haven't changed that much over the years. Sometimes the women joined their efforts in support of a political cause, making quilts that would be raffled to raise money for temperance societies, hospitals for sick and wounded soldiers, and the fight against slavery. Quilt making also afforded women a means of artistic expression at a time when they had few other creative outlets. Within their socially acceptable roles as homemakers, many quilters subtly pushed back at the restrictions placed on them by experimenting with color, design, and technique.

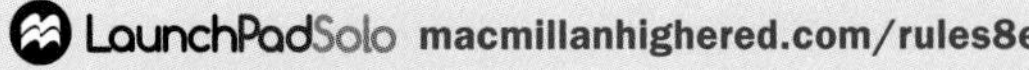
LaunchPadSolo macmillanhighered.com/rules8e
3 Building effective paragraphs
> Exercise: 3–2

3b Develop the main point.

Though an occasional short paragraph is fine, particularly if it functions as a transition or emphasizes a point, a series of brief paragraphs suggests inadequate development. How much development is enough? That varies, depending on the writer's purpose and audience.

For example, when health columnist Jane Brody wrote a paragraph attempting to convince readers that it is impossible to lose fat quickly, she knew that she would have to present a great deal of evidence because many dieters want to believe the opposite. She did *not* write only the following:

> When you think about it, it's impossible to lose — as many diets suggest — 10 pounds of *fat* in ten days, even on a total fast. Even a moderately active person cannot lose so much weight so fast. A less active person hasn't a prayer.

This three-sentence paragraph is too skimpy to be convincing. But the paragraph that Brody did write contains enough evidence to convince even skeptical readers.

> When you think about it, it's impossible to lose — as many . . . diets suggest — 10 pounds of *fat* in ten days, even on a total fast. A pound of body fat represents 3,500 calories. To lose 1 pound of fat, you must expend 3,500 more calories than you consume. Let's say you weigh 170 pounds and, as a moderately active person, you burn 2,500 calories a day. If your diet contains only 1,500 calories, you'd have an energy deficit of 1,000 calories a day. In a week's time that would add up to a 7,000-calorie deficit, or 2 pounds of real fat. In ten days, the accumulated deficit would represent nearly 3 pounds of lost body fat. Even if you ate nothing at all for ten days and maintained your usual level of activity, your caloric deficit would add up to 25,000 calories. . . . At 3,500 calories per pound of fat, that's still only 7 pounds of lost fat.
>
> — Jane Brody, *Jane Brody's Nutrition Book*

3c Choose a suitable pattern of organization.

Although paragraphs (and indeed whole essays) may be patterned in any number of ways, certain patterns of organization occur frequently, either alone or in combination: examples and illustrations,

LaunchPadSolo **macmillanhighered.com/rules8e**
3 Building effective paragraphs
> LearningCurve: Patterns of organization

narration, description, process, comparison and contrast, analogy, cause and effect, classification and division, and definition. These patterns (sometimes called *methods of development*) have different uses, depending on the writer's subject and purpose.

Examples and illustrations

Examples, perhaps the most common pattern of development, are appropriate whenever the reader might be tempted to ask, "For example?" Though examples are just selected instances, not a complete catalog, they are enough to suggest the truth of many topic sentences, as in the following paragraph.

> Normally my parents abided scrupulously by "The Budget," but several times a year Dad would dip into his battered black strongbox and splurge on some irrational, totally satisfying luxury. Once he bought over a hundred comic books at a flea market, doled out to us thereafter at the tantalizing rate of two a week. He always got a whole flat of pansies, Mom's favorite flower, for us to give her on Mother's Day. One day a boy stopped at our house selling fifty-cent raffle tickets on a sailboat, and Dad bought every ticket the boy had left — three books' worth.
>
> — Connie Hailey, student

Illustrations are extended examples, frequently presented in story form. Because they require several sentences apiece, they are used more sparingly than examples. When well selected, however, they can be a vivid and effective means of developing a point. The writer of the following paragraph uses illustrations to demonstrate that Harriet Tubman, the underground railroad's most famous conductor, was a genius at eluding her pursuers.

> Part of [Harriet Tubman's] strategy of conducting was, as in all battle-field operations, the knowledge of how and when to retreat. Numerous allusions have been made to her moves when she suspected that she was in danger. When she feared the party was closely pursued, she would take it for a time on a train southward bound. No one seeing Negroes going in this direction would for an instant suppose them to be fugitives. Once on her return she was at a railroad station. She saw some men reading a poster and she heard one of them reading it aloud. It was a description of her, offering a reward for her capture. She took a southbound train to avert suspicion. At another time when Harriet heard men talking about her, she pretended to read a book which she carried. One man remarked, "This can't be the woman. The one we want can't read or write." Harriet devoutly hoped the book was right side up.
>
> — Earl Conrad, *Harriet Tubman*

Narration

A paragraph of narration tells a story or part of a story. Narrative paragraphs are usually arranged in chronological order, but they may also contain flashbacks, interruptions that take the story back to an earlier time. The following paragraph recounts one of the author's experiences in the African wild.

> One evening when I was wading in the shallows of the lake to pass a rocky outcrop, I suddenly stopped dead as I saw the sinuous black body of a snake in the water. It was all of six feet long, and from the slight hood and the dark stripes at the back of the neck I knew it to be a Storm's water cobra — a deadly reptile for the bite of which there was, at that time, no serum. As I stared at it an incoming wave gently deposited part of its body on one of my feet. I remained motionless, not even breathing, until the wave rolled back into the lake, drawing the snake with it. Then I leaped out of the water as fast as I could, my heart hammering.
>
> — Jane Goodall, *In the Shadow of Man*

Description

A descriptive paragraph sketches a portrait of a person, place, or thing by using concrete and specific details that appeal to one or more of our senses — sight, sound, smell, taste, and touch. Consider, for example, the following description of the grasshopper invasions that devastated the midwestern landscape in the United States in the late 1860s.

> They came like dive bombers out of the west. They came by the millions with the rustle of their wings roaring overhead. They came in waves, like the rolls of the sea, descending with a terrifying speed, breaking now and again like a mighty surf. They came with the force of a williwaw and they formed a huge, ominous, dark brown cloud that eclipsed the sun. They dipped and touched earth, hitting objects and people like hailstones. But they were not hail. These were *live* demons. They popped, snapped, crackled, and roared. They were dark brown, an inch or longer in length, plump in the middle and tapered at the ends. They had transparent wings, slender legs, and two black eyes that flashed with a fierce intelligence.
>
> — Eugene Boe, "Pioneers to Eternity"

Process

A process paragraph is structured in chronological order. A writer may choose this pattern either to describe how something is made or done or to explain to readers, step-by-step, how to do something. Here is a paragraph explaining how to perform a "roll cast," a popular fly-fishing technique.

> Begin by taking up a suitable stance, with one foot slightly in front of the other and the rod pointing down the line. Then begin a smooth, steady draw, raising your rod hand to just above shoulder height and lifting the rod to the 10:30 or 11:00 position. This steady draw allows a loop of line to form between the rod top and the water. While the line is still moving, raise the rod slightly, then punch it rapidly forward and down. The rod is now flexed and under maximum compression, and the line follows its path, bellying out slightly behind you and coming off the water close to your feet. As you power the rod down through the 3:00 position, the belly of line will roll forward. Follow through smoothly so that the line unfolds and straightens above the water.
>
> — *The Dorling Kindersley Encyclopedia of Fishing*

Comparison and contrast

To compare two subjects is to draw attention to their similarities, although the word *compare* also has a broader meaning that includes a consideration of differences. To contrast is to focus only on differences.

Whether a paragraph stresses similarities or differences, it may be patterned in one of two ways. The two subjects may be presented one at a time, as in the following paragraph of contrast.

> So Grant and Lee were in complete contrast, representing two diametrically opposed elements in American life. Grant was the modern man emerging; beyond him, ready to come on the stage, was the great age of steel and machinery, of crowded cities and a restless, burgeoning vitality. Lee might have ridden down from the old age of chivalry, lance in hand, silken banner fluttering over his head. Each man was the perfect champion of his cause, drawing both his strengths and his weaknesses from the people he led.
>
> — Bruce Catton, "Grant and Lee: A Study in Contrasts"

Or a paragraph may proceed point by point, treating the two subjects together, one aspect at a time. The following paragraph uses the point-by-point method to contrast speeches given by Abraham Lincoln in 1860 and Barack Obama in 2008.

> Two men, two speeches. The men, both lawyers, both from Illinois, were seeking the presidency, despite what seemed their crippling connection with extremists. Each was young by modern

standards for a president. Abraham Lincoln had turned fifty-one just five days before delivering his speech. Barack Obama was forty-six when he gave his. Their political experience was mainly provincial, in the Illinois legislature for both of them, and they had received little exposure at the national level — two years in the House of Representatives for Lincoln, four years in the Senate for Obama. Yet each was seeking his party's nomination against a New York senator of longer standing and greater prior reputation — Lincoln against Senator William Seward, Obama against Senator Hillary Clinton.

— Garry Wills, "Two Speeches on Race"

Analogy

Analogies draw comparisons between items that appear to have little in common. Writers turn to analogies for a variety of reasons: to make the unfamiliar seem familiar, to provide a concrete understanding of an abstract topic, to argue a point, or to provoke fresh thoughts or changed feelings about a subject. In the following paragraph, physician Lewis Thomas draws an analogy between the behavior of ants and that of humans.

> Ants are so much like human beings as to be an embarrassment. They farm fungi, raise aphids as livestock, launch armies into wars, use chemical sprays to alarm and confuse enemies, capture slaves. The families of weaver ants engage in child labor, holding their larvae like shuttles to spin out the thread that sews the leaves together for their fungus gardens. They exchange information ceaselessly. They do everything but watch television.
>
> — Lewis Thomas, "On Societies as Organisms"

Although analogies can be a powerful tool for illuminating a subject, they should be used with caution in arguments. Just because two things may be alike in one respect, we cannot conclude that they are alike in all respects. (See "false analogy," p. 94.)

Cause and effect

When causes and effects are a matter of argument, they are too complex to be reduced to a simple pattern (see p. 95). However, if a writer wishes merely to describe a cause-and-effect relationship that is generally accepted, then the effect may be stated in the topic sentence, with the causes listed in the body of the paragraph.

> The fantastic water clarity of the Mount Gambier sinkholes results from several factors. The holes are fed from aquifers holding rainwater that fell decades — even centuries — ago, and that has been filtered through miles of limestone. The high level of calcium that limestone adds causes the silty detritus from dead plants and animals to cling together and settle quickly to the bottom. Abundant bottom vegetation in the shallow sinkholes also helps bind the silt. And the rapid turnover of water prohibits stagnation.
>
> — Hillary Hauser, "Exploring a Sunken Realm in Australia"

Or the paragraph may move from cause to effects, as in this paragraph from a student paper on the effects of the industrial revolution on American farms.

> The rise of rail transport in the nineteenth century forever changed American farming — for better and for worse. Farmers who once raised crops and livestock to sustain just their own families could now make a profit by selling their goods in towns and cities miles away. These new markets improved the living standard of struggling farm families and encouraged them to seek out innovations that would increase their profits. On the downside, the competition fostered by the new markets sometimes created hostility among neighboring farm families where there had once been a spirit of cooperation. Those farmers who couldn't compete with their neighbors left farming forever, facing poverty worse than they had ever known.
>
> — Chris Mileski, student

Classification and division

Classification is the grouping of items into categories according to some consistent principle. For example, an elementary school teacher might classify children's books according to their level of difficulty, but a librarian might group them by subject matter. The principle of classification that a writer chooses ultimately depends on the purpose of the classification. The following paragraph classifies species of electric fish.

> Scientists sort electric fishes into three categories. The first comprises the strongly electric species like the marine electric rays or the freshwater African electric catfish and South American electric eel. Known since the dawn of history, these deliver a punch strong enough to stun a human. In recent years, biologists have focused on a second category: weakly electric fish in the

South American and African rivers that use tiny voltages for communication and navigation. The third group contains sharks, nonelectric rays, and catfish, which do not emit a field but possess sensors that enable them to detect the minute amounts of electricity that leak out of other organisms.

—Anne and Jack Rudloe, "Electric Warfare: The Fish That Kill with Thunderbolts"

Division takes one item and divides it into parts. As with classification, division should be made according to some consistent principle. The following passage describes the components that make up a baseball.

Like the game itself, a baseball is composed of many layers. One of the delicious joys of childhood is to take apart a baseball and examine the wonders within. You begin by removing the red cotton thread and peeling off the leather cover—which comes from the hide of a Holstein cow and has been tanned, cut, printed, and punched with holes. Beneath the cover is a thin layer of cotton string, followed by several hundred yards of woolen yarn, which makes up the bulk of the ball. Finally, in the middle is a rubber ball, or "pill," which is a little smaller than a golf ball. Slice into the rubber and you'll find the ball's heart—a cork core. The cork is from Portugal, the rubber from southeast Asia, the covers are American, and the balls are assembled in Costa Rica.

—Dan Gutman, *The Way Baseball Works*

Definition

A definition puts a word or concept into a general class and then provides enough details to distinguish it from others in the same class. In the following paragraph, the writer defines *envy* as a special kind of desire.

Envy is so integral and so painful a part of what animates behavior in market societies that many people have forgotten the full meaning of the word, simplifying it into one of the synonyms of desire. It is that, which may be why it flourishes in market societies: democracies of desire, they might be called, with money for ballots, stuffing permitted. But envy is more or less than desire. It begins with an almost frantic sense of emptiness inside oneself, as if the pump of one's heart were sucking on air. One has to be blind to perceive the emptiness, of course, but that's just what envy is, a selective blindness. *Invidia*, Latin for envy, translates as "non-sight," and Dante has the envious plodding along under

> cloaks of lead, their eyes sewn shut with leaden wire. What they are blind to is what they have, God-given and humanly nurtured, in themselves.
>
> —Nelson W. Aldrich Jr., *Old Money*

3d Make paragraphs coherent.

When sentences and paragraphs flow from one to another without discernible bumps, gaps, or shifts, they are said to be coherent. Coherence can be improved by strengthening the ties between old information and new. A number of techniques for strengthening those ties are detailed in this section.

Linking ideas clearly

Readers expect to learn a paragraph's main point in a topic sentence early in the paragraph. Then, as they move into the body of the paragraph, they expect to encounter specific details, facts, or examples that support the topic sentence—either directly or indirectly.

If a sentence does not support the topic sentence directly, readers expect it to support another sentence in the paragraph and therefore to support the topic sentence indirectly. The following paragraph begins with a topic sentence. The highlighted sentences are direct supports, and the rest of the sentences are indirect supports.

> Though the open-space classroom works for many children, it is not practical for my son, David. First, David is hyperactive. When he was placed in an open-space classroom, he became distracted and confused. He was tempted to watch the movement going on around him instead of concentrating on his own work. Second, David has a tendency to transpose letters and numbers, a tendency that can be overcome only by individual attention from the instructor. In the open classroom he was moved from teacher to teacher, with each one responsible for a different subject. No single teacher worked with David long enough to diagnose the problem, let alone help him with it. Finally, David is not a highly motivated learner. In the open classroom, he was graded "at his own level," not by criteria for a certain grade. He could receive a B in reading and still be a grade level behind, because he was doing satisfactory work "at his own level."
>
> —Margaret Smith, student

Repeating key words

Repetition of key words is an important technique for gaining coherence. To prevent repetitions from becoming dull, you can use variations of a key word (*hike, hiker, hiking*), pronouns referring to the word (*gamblers . . . they*), and synonyms (*run, spring, race, dash*). In the following paragraph describing plots among indentured servants in the seventeenth century, historian Richard Hofstadter binds sentences together by repeating the key word *plots* and echoing it with a variety of synonyms (which are highlighted).

> Plots hatched by several servants to run away together occurred mostly in the plantation colonies, and the few recorded servant uprisings were entirely limited to those colonies. Virginia had been forced from its very earliest years to take stringent steps against mutinous plots, and severe punishments for such behavior were recorded. Most servant plots occurred in the seventeenth century: a contemplated uprising was nipped in the bud in York County in 1661; apparently led by some left-wing offshoots of the Great Rebellion, servants plotted an insurrection in Gloucester County in 1663, and four leaders were condemned and executed; some discontented servants apparently joined Bacon's Rebellion in the 1670's. In the 1680's the planters became newly apprehensive of discontent among the servants "owing to their great necessities and want of clothes," and it was feared they would rise up and plunder the storehouses and ships; in 1682 there were plant-cutting riots in which servants and laborers, as well as some planters, took part.
>
> — Richard Hofstadter, *America at 1750*

Using parallel structures

Parallel structures are frequently used within sentences to underscore the similarity of ideas (see 9). They may also be used to bind together a series of sentences expressing similar information. In the following passage describing folk beliefs, anthropologist Margaret Mead presents similar information in parallel grammatical form.

> Actually, almost every day, even in the most sophisticated home, something is likely to happen that evokes the memory of some old folk belief. The salt spills. A knife falls to the floor. Your nose tickles. Then perhaps, with a slightly embarrassed smile, the person who spilled the salt tosses a pinch over his left shoulder. Or someone recites the old rhyme, "Knife falls, gentleman calls." Or as you rub your nose you think, That means a letter. I wonder who's writing?
>
> — Margaret Mead, "New Superstitions for Old"

Maintaining consistency

Coherence suffers whenever a draft shifts confusingly from one point of view to another or from one verb tense to another. (See 13.) In addition, coherence can suffer when new information is introduced with the subject of each sentence. As a rule, a sentence's subject should echo a subject or an object in the previous sentence.

Providing transitions

Transitions help readers move from sentence to sentence; they also alert readers to more global connections of ideas — those between paragraphs or even larger blocks of text.

Sentence-level transitions Certain words and phrases signal connections between (or within) sentences. Frequently used transitions are included in the chart on page 63.

Skilled writers use transitional expressions with care, making sure, for example, not to use *consequently* when *also* would be more precise. They are also careful to select transitions with an appropriate tone, perhaps preferring *so* to *thus* in an informal piece, *in summary* to *in short* for a scholarly essay.

In the following paragraph, taken from an argument that dinosaurs had the "'right-sized' brains for reptiles of their body size," biologist Stephen Jay Gould uses transitions (highlighted) with skill.

> I don't wish to deny that the flattened, minuscule head of large bodied Stegosaurus houses little brain from our subjective, top-heavy perspective, but I do wish to assert that we should not expect more of the beast. First of all, large animals have relatively smaller brains than related, small animals. The correlation of brain size with body size among kindred animals (all reptiles, all mammals, for example) is remarkably regular. As we move from small to large animals, from mice to elephants or small lizards to Komodo dragons, brain size increases, but not so fast as body size. In other words, bodies grow faster than brains, and large animals have low ratios of brain weight to body weight. In fact, brains grow only about two-thirds as fast as bodies. Since we have no reason to believe that large animals are consistently stupider than their smaller relatives, we must conclude that large animals require relatively less brain to do as well as smaller animals. If we do not recognize this relationship, we are likely to underestimate the mental power of very large animals, dinosaurs in particular.
>
> — Stephen Jay Gould, "Were Dinosaurs Dumb?"

Academic English Choose transitions carefully and vary them appropriately. Each transition has a different meaning (see the chart below). If you do not use a transition with an appropriate meaning, you might confuse your readers.

► **Although taking eight o'clock classes may seem unappealing, coming to school early has its advantages. ~~Moreover,~~ For example, students who arrive early typically avoid the worst traffic and find the best parking spaces.**

Paragraph-level transitions Paragraph-level transitions usually link the *first* sentence of a new paragraph with the *first* sentence of the previous paragraph. In other words, the topic sentences signal global connections.

Look for opportunities to allude to the subject of a previous paragraph (as summed up in its topic sentence) in the topic sentence of the next one. In his essay "Little Green Lies," Jonathan H. Adler uses this strategy in the following topic sentences, which appear in a passage describing the benefits of plastic packaging.

> Consider aseptic packaging, the synthetic packaging for the "juice boxes" so many children bring to school with their lunch. One criticism of aseptic packaging is that it is nearly impossible to recycle, yet on almost every other count, aseptic packaging is environmentally preferable to the packaging alternatives. Not only do aseptic containers not require refrigeration to keep their contents from spoiling, but their manufacture requires less than one-10th the energy of making glass bottles.
>
> What is true for juice boxes is also true for other forms of synthetic packaging. The use of polystyrene, which is commonly (and mistakenly) referred to as "Styrofoam," can reduce food waste dramatically due to its insulating properties. (Thanks to these properties, polystyrene cups are much preferred over paper for that morning cup of coffee.) Polystyrene also requires significantly fewer resources to produce than its paper counterpart.

LaunchPadSolo **macmillanhighered.com/rules8e**
3 Building effective paragraphs
> Writing practice: Using transitions
> Exercise: 3–3

Common transitions

TO SHOW ADDITION and, also, besides, further, furthermore, in addition, moreover, next, too, first, second

TO GIVE EXAMPLES for example, for instance, to illustrate, in fact, specifically

TO COMPARE also, in the same manner, similarly, likewise

TO CONTRAST but, however, on the other hand, in contrast, nevertheless, still, even though, on the contrary, yet, although

TO SUMMARIZE OR CONCLUDE in short, in summary, in conclusion, to sum up, therefore

TO SHOW TIME after, as, before, next, during, later, finally, meanwhile, then, when, while, immediately

TO SHOW PLACE OR DIRECTION above, below, beyond, nearby, opposite, close, to the left

TO INDICATE LOGICAL RELATIONSHIP if, so, therefore, consequently, thus, as a result, for this reason, because, since

Transitions between blocks of text In long essays, you will need to alert readers to connections between blocks of text that are more than one paragraph long. You can do this by inserting transitional sentences or short paragraphs at key points in the essay. Here, for example, is a transitional paragraph from a student research paper. It announces that the first part of the paper (about how apes demonstrate language skills) has come to a close and the second part (about whether they understand grammar) is about to begin.

> Although the great apes have demonstrated significant language skills, one central question remains: Can they be taught to use that uniquely human language tool we call grammar, to learn the difference, for instance, between "ape bite human" and "human bite ape"? In other words, can an ape create a sentence?

Another strategy to help readers move from one block of text to another is to insert headings in your essay. Headings, which usually sit above blocks of text, allow you to announce a new topic boldly, without the need for subtle transitions.

3e If necessary, adjust paragraph length.

Most readers feel comfortable reading paragraphs that range between one hundred and two hundred words. Shorter paragraphs require too much starting and stopping, and longer ones strain readers' attention span. There are exceptions to this guideline, however. Paragraphs longer than two hundred words frequently appear in scholarly writing, where scholars explore complex ideas. Paragraphs shorter than one hundred words occur in newspapers because of narrow columns; in informal essays to quicken the pace; and in business writing and Web sites, where readers routinely skim for main ideas.

In an essay, the first and last paragraphs will ordinarily be the introduction and the conclusion. These special-purpose paragraphs are likely to be shorter than the paragraphs in the body of the essay. Typically, the body paragraphs will follow the essay's outline: one paragraph per point in short essays, several paragraphs per point in longer ones. Some ideas require more development than others, however, so it is best to be flexible. If an idea stretches to a length unreasonable for a paragraph, you should divide the paragraph, even if you have presented comparable points in the essay in single paragraphs.

Paragraph breaks are not always made for strictly logical reasons. Writers use them for the following reasons as well.

REASONS FOR BEGINNING A NEW PARAGRAPH

- to mark off the introduction and the conclusion
- to signal a shift to a new idea
- to indicate an important shift in time or place
- to emphasize a point (by placing it at the beginning or the end, not in the middle, of a paragraph)
- to highlight a contrast
- to signal a change of speakers (in dialogue)
- to provide readers with a needed pause
- to break up text that looks too dense

Beware of using too many short, choppy paragraphs, however. Readers want to see how your ideas connect, and they become irritated when you break their momentum by forcing them to pause every few sentences. Here are some reasons you might have for combining some of the paragraphs in a rough draft.

REASONS FOR COMBINING PARAGRAPHS

- to clarify the essay's organization
- to connect closely related ideas
- to bind together text that looks too choppy

Academic Reading, Writing, and Speaking

Academic Reading, Writing, and Speaking 65

Academic Reading, Writing, and Speaking

4 Reading and writing critically

College writing requires you to become a critical reader — questioning and conversing with the texts you read. When you read critically, you read with an open, curious mind to understand both what is said and why. And when you write critically, you respond to a text, with thoughtful questions and insights, offering your judgment of *how* the parts of a text contribute to its overall effect. The texts you'll be asked to read and analyze may be written — many books, articles, and case studies, for example, convey meaning solely through written words. Or they may be multimodal, combining one or more modes — words, images, and sounds — such as videos, podcasts, advertisements. Whether you're reading and writing about a written text or a multimodal text, many of the same strategies apply. This chapter covers strategies that will help you analyze any text. Chapter 5 offers specific advice for analyzing multimodal texts.

4a Read actively.

Reading, like writing, is an active process that happens in steps. Most texts, such as the ones assigned in college, don't yield their meaning with one quick reading. Rather, they require you to read and reread to grasp the main points and to comprehend a text's layers of meaning.

When you read actively, you pay attention to details you would miss if you just skimmed a text. First, you read to understand the main ideas. Then you pay attention to your own reactions by making note of what interests, surprises, or puzzles you. Active readers preview a text, annotate it, and then converse with it.

Previewing a text

Previewing — looking quickly through a text before you read — helps you understand its basic features and structure. A text's title, for example, may reveal an author's purpose; a text's format or design may reveal what kind of text it is — a book, a report, a policy memo, a video, and so on. As you preview, you can browse for images, scan headings, and gain a sense of the text's subsections

LaunchPadSolo macmillanhighered.com/rules8e
4 Reading and writing critically
> Writing practice: Reading actively
> LearningCurve: Critical reading

and intended audience. The more you know about a text before you read it, the easier it will be to dig deeper into it.

Annotating a text

Annotating helps you capture and record your responses to a text. As you annotate, you take notes — jot down questions and reactions in the margins of the text or on electronic or paper sticky notes. You might circle or underline the author's main points. Or you might develop your own system of annotating by placing question marks, asterisks, or stars by the text's thesis, message, or major pieces of evidence.

As you annotate and think about a text, you are starting to write about it. Responding with notes helps you frame what *you* want to say about the author's ideas or questions you want to address in response to the text. On a second or third reading, you may notice contradictions — statements the author makes that, put side-by-side, just don't seem to make sense — or surprising insights that may lead to further investigation. Each rereading will raise new questions and lead to a better understanding of the text.

The following example shows how one student, Emilia Sanchez, annotated an article from *CQ Researcher*, a newsletter about social and political issues.

ANNOTATED ARTICLE

Big Box Stores Are Bad for Main Street

BETSY TAYLOR

Opening strategy — the problem is not x, it's y.

There is plenty of reason to be concerned about the proliferation of Wal-Marts and other so-called "big box" stores. The question, however, is not whether or not these types of stores create jobs (although several studies claim they produce a net job loss in local communities) or whether they ultimately save consumers money. The real concern about having a 25-acre slab of concrete with a 100,000 square foot box of stuff land on a town is whether it's good for a community's soul.

Sentimental — what is a community's soul? I would think job security and a strong economy are better for a community's "soul" than small stores that have to lay people off or close.

Lumps all big boxes together.

The worst thing about "big boxes" is that they have a tendency to produce Ross Perot's famous "big sucking sound" — sucking the life out of cities and small towns across the country. On the other hand, small businesses are great for a community. They offer more personal service; they won't threaten to pack up and leave town if they don't get tax breaks, free roads and other blandishments; and small-business owners are much

(*Continued*)

Big Box Stores Are Bad for Main Street (Continued)

more responsive to a customer's needs. (Ever try to complain about bad service or poor quality products to the president of Home Depot?)

Logic problem? Why couldn't customer complain to store manager?

Assumes all small businesses are attentive.

Yet, if big boxes are so bad, why are they so successful? One glaring reason is that we've become a nation of hyper-consumers, and the big-box boys know this. Downtown shopping districts comprised of small businesses take some of the efficiency out of overconsumption. There's all that hassle of having to travel from store to store, and having to pull out your credit card so many times. Occasionally, we even find ourselves chatting with the shopkeeper, wandering into a coffee shop to visit with a friend or otherwise wasting precious time that could be spent on acquiring more stuff.

True?

Taylor wishes for a time that is long gone or never was.

But let's face it — bustling, thriving city centers are fun. They breathe life into a community. They allow cities and towns to stand out from each other. They provide an atmosphere for people to interact with each other that just cannot be found at Target, or Wal-Mart or Home Depot.

Author's either/or thinking isn't working. Stores like Home Depot try to encourage a community feel.

Community vs. economy. What about prices?

Is it anti-American to be against having a retail giant set up shop in one's community? Some people would say so. On the other hand, if you board up Main Street, what's left of America?

Emotional appeal seems too simplistic.

Conversing with a text

Conversing with a text — responding to a text and its author — helps you move beyond your initial notes to draw conclusions about what you've read. Perhaps you ask additional questions, point out something that doesn't make sense, or explain how the author's points suggest wider implications. As you respond to a text, you look more closely at how the author works through a topic, and you evaluate the author's evidence and conclusions.

Conversing takes your understanding of a text to the next level. For example, student writer Emilia Sanchez noticed on a first reading that her assigned text closed with an emotional appeal to the reader. On a second reading, she started to question whether the emotional appeal was too simplistic.

Many writers use a double-entry notebook to converse with a text and its author and to generate ideas and insights. To create one, draw a line down the center of a notebook page or create a two-column table in your word processing program. On the left side, record what the author says; include quotations, sentences, and key terms from the text. On the right side, record your observations and questions. With each rereading of a text, you can return to your notebook to add new insights or questions.

A double-entry notebook allows you to begin to see the difference between what a text says and what it means and to visualize the conversation between you and the author as it develops.

Here is an excerpt from student writer Emilia Sanchez's double-entry notebook.

IDEAS FROM THE TEXT	MY RESPONSES
"The question, however, is not whether or not these types of stores create jobs (although several studies claim they produce a net job loss in local communities) or whether they ultimately save consumers money" (1011).	*Why are big-box stores bad if they create jobs or save people money? Taylor dismisses these possibilities without acknowledging their importance. My family needs to save money and needs jobs more than "chatting with the shopkeeper" (1011).*
"The real concern . . . is whether [big-box stores are] good for a community's soul" (1011). "[S]mall businesses are great for a community" (1011).	*Taylor is missing something here. Are all big-box stores bad? Are all small businesses great? Would getting rid of big-box stores save the "soul" of America? Is Main Street the "soul" of America? Taylor sounds overly sentimental. She assumes that people spend more money because they shop at big-box stores. And she assumes that small businesses are always better for consumers.*

USING SOURCES RESPONSIBLY: Put quotation marks around words you have copied from the source and keep an accurate record of page numbers for quotations and ideas.

Asking the "So what?" question

As you read and annotate a text, make sure you understand its thesis, or central idea. Ask yourself: "What is the author's thesis?" Then put the author's thesis to the "So what?" test: "Why does this thesis matter? Why does it need to be argued?" Perhaps you'll conclude that the thesis is too obvious and doesn't matter at all — or that it matters so much that you feel the author stopped short and overlooked key details. Or perhaps you'll think that a reasonable person might draw different conclusions about the issue. You'll be in a stronger position to analyze a text after putting its thesis to the "So what?" test.

Guidelines for active reading

Preview a written text.

- Who is the author? What are the author's credentials?
- What is the author's purpose: To inform? To persuade? To call to action?
- Who is the expected audience?
- When was the text written? Where was it published?
- What kind of text is it: A book? A report? A scholarly article? A policy memo?

Annotate a written text.

- What surprises, puzzles, or intrigues you about the text?
- What question does the text attempt to answer? Or what problem does it attempt to solve?
- What is the author's thesis, or central claim?
- What type of evidence does the author provide to support the thesis? How persuasive is this evidence?

Converse with a written text.

- What are the strengths and limitations of the text?
- Has the author drawn conclusions that you want to question? Do you have a different interpretation of the evidence?
- Does the text raise questions that it does not answer?
- Does the author consider opposing points of view and treat them fairly?

Ask the "So what?" question.

- Why does the author's thesis need to be argued, explained, or explored? What's at stake?
- What has the author overlooked in presenting this thesis? What's missing?
- Could a reasonable person draw different conclusions about the issue?
- To put an author's thesis to the "So what?" test, use phrases like the following: *The author overlooks this important point: . . .* and *The author's argument is convincing because. . . .*

4b Outline a text to identify main ideas.

You are probably familiar with using an outline as a planning tool to help you organize your ideas. An outline is a useful tool for reading, too. Outlining a text — identifying its main idea and major parts — can be an important step in your reading process.

As you outline, look closely for a text's thesis statement (main idea) and topic sentences because they serve as important signposts for readers. A thesis statement often appears in the introduction, usually in the first or second paragraph. Topic sentences often can be found at the beginning of body paragraphs, where they announce a shift to a new idea. (See 1e and 3a.)

Put the author's thesis and key points in your own words. Here, for example, are the points Emilia Sanchez identified as she prepared to write her summary and analysis of the text printed on page 67. Notice that Sanchez does not simply trace the author's ideas paragraph by paragraph; instead, she sums up the article's central points.

OUTLINE OF "BIG BOX STORES ARE BAD FOR MAIN STREET"

Thesis: Whether or not they take jobs away from a community or offer low prices to consumers, we should be worried about "big-box" stores like Wal-Mart, Target, and Home Depot because they harm communities by taking the life out of downtown shopping districts.

I. Small businesses are better for cities and towns than big-box stores are.
   A. Small businesses offer personal service; big-box stores do not.
   B. Small businesses don't make demands on community resources as big-box stores do.
   C. Small businesses respond to customer concerns; big-box stores do not.

II. Big-box stores are successful because they cater to consumption at the expense of benefits to the community.
   A. Buying everything in one place is convenient.
   B. Shopping at small businesses may be inefficient, but it provides opportunities for socializing.
   C. Downtown shopping districts give each city or town a special identity.

Conclusion: Although some people say that it's anti-American to oppose big-box stores, actually these stores threaten the communities that make up America by encouraging buying at the expense of the traditional interactions of Main Street.

Reading online

For many college assignments, you will be asked to read online sources. It is tempting to skim and browse online texts rather than read them carefully. When you skim a text, you are less likely to remember what you have read and less inclined to reread to grasp layers of meaning.

The following strategies will help you read critically online.

Read slowly. Instead of sweeping your eyes across the page, consciously slow down the pace of your reading to focus on each sentence.

Avoid multitasking. Close other applications, especially messaging and social media. If you follow a link for background or the definition of a term, return to the text immediately.

Annotate electronically. Use software tools, such as sticky notes, highlighting, and commenting features, to record your thoughts as you read online texts.

Print the text. If you prefer to read and annotate printed texts, make a copy for close reading and note taking. Be sure to record information about the online source so that you can find it again, if needed, and cite it properly.

4c Summarize to deepen your understanding.

Your goal in summarizing a text is to state the work's main ideas and key points simply, objectively, and accurately in your own words. Writing a summary does not require you to judge the author's ideas; it requires you to *understand* the author's ideas. In summarizing, you condense information, put an author's ideas in your own words, and test your understanding of what a text says. If you have sketched a brief outline of the text (see 4b), refer to it as you draft your summary.

Following is Emilia Sanchez's summary of the article that is printed on page 67.

In her essay "Big Box Stores Are Bad for Main Street," Betsy Taylor argues that chain stores harm communities by taking the life out of downtown shopping districts. Explaining that a community's "soul" is more important than low prices or consumer convenience, she argues that small businesses are better than stores like Home Depot and Target because they emphasize personal interactions and don't place demands on a community's resources. Taylor asserts that big-box stores are successful because "we've become a nation of hyper-consumers" (1011), although the convenience of shopping in these stores comes at the expense of benefits to the community. She concludes by suggesting that it's not "anti-American" to oppose big-box stores because the damage they inflict on downtown shopping districts extends to America itself.

—Emilia Sanchez, student

Guidelines for writing a summary

- In the first sentence, mention the title of the text, the name of the author, and the author's thesis.
- Maintain a neutral tone; be objective.
- As you present the author's ideas, use the third-person point of view and the present tense: *Taylor argues. . . .* (If you are writing in APA style, see 60c.)
- Keep your focus on the text. Don't state the author's ideas as if they were your own.
- Put all or most of your summary in your own words; if you borrow a phrase or a sentence from the text, put it in quotation marks and provide the page number in parentheses.
- Limit yourself to presenting the text's key points.
- Be concise; make every word count.

4d Analyze to demonstrate your critical reading.

Whereas a summary most often answers the question of *what* a text says, an analysis looks at *how* a text conveys its main idea. As you read and reread a text—previewing, annotating, and conversing—you are asking questions and generating ideas to form a judgment of it. When you analyze a text, you say to readers: "Here's my reading of this text. This is what the text means and why it matters." Assignments calling for an analysis of a text vary widely, but they usually ask you to look at how the text's parts contribute to its central argument or purpose, often with the aim of evaluating its evidence or overall effect.

NOTE: Writing about a text often requires you to quote directly from the text. See 55 for guidelines for integrating quotations.

Balancing summary with analysis

If you have written a summary of a text, you may find it useful to refer to the main points of the summary as you write your analysis. Your readers may or may not be familiar with the text you are analyzing, so you need to summarize the text briefly to help readers understand the basis of your analysis. The following strategies will help you balance summary with analysis.

- Remember that readers are interested in your ideas about a text.
- Pose questions that lead to an interpretation or a judgment of a text rather than to a summary. The questions on page 70 can help steer you away from summary and toward analysis.
- Focus your analysis on the text's thesis and main ideas or some prominent feature of the reading.
- Pay attention to your topic sentences to make sure they signal analysis.
- Ask peer reviewers to give you feedback: Do you summarize too much and need to analyze more?

Here is an example of how student writer Emilia Sanchez balances summary with analysis in her essay about Betsy Taylor's article (see p. 67). Before stating her thesis, Sanchez summarizes the article's purpose and central idea.

Summary

[In her essay "Big Box Stores Are Bad for Main Street," Betsy Taylor focuses not on the economic effects of large chain stores but on the effects these stores have on the "soul" of America. She argues that stores like Home Depot, Target, and Wal-Mart are bad for America because they draw people out of downtown shopping districts and cause them to focus on consumption. In contrast, she believes that small businesses are good for America because they provide personal attention, encourage community interaction, and make each city and town unique.] [But Taylor's argument is unconvincing because it is based on sentimentality—on idealized images of a quaint Main Street—rather than on the roles that businesses play in consumers' lives and communities.]

Analysis

Drafting an analytical thesis statement

An effective thesis statement for analytical writing responds to a question about a text or tries to resolve a problem in the text. Remember that your thesis isn't the same as the text's thesis or main idea. Your thesis presents your judgment of the text's argument.

If student writer Emilia Sanchez had started her analysis of "Big Box Stores Are Bad for Main Street" (p. 67) with the following thesis statement, she merely would have repeated the main idea of the article.

INEFFECTIVE THESIS STATEMENT

> Big-box stores such as Wal-Mart and Home Depot promote consumerism by offering endless goods at low prices, but they do nothing to promote community.

Instead, Sanchez wrote the following thesis statement, which offers her judgment of Taylor's argument.

EFFECTIVE THESIS STATEMENT

> By ignoring the complex economic relationship between large chain stores and their communities, Taylor incorrectly assumes that simply getting rid of big-box stores would have a positive effect on America's communities.

As you draft your thesis, try asking *what*, *why*, and *how* questions to form a judgment about a text you are reading.

- What has the text's author overlooked or failed to consider? Why does this matter?
- Why might a reasonable person draw a different set of conclusions about the subject matter?
- How does the text clarify or complicate your understanding of the subject?

NOTE: When you analyze a text, you integrate words and ideas from the source into your own writing. For advice on quoting, paraphrasing, and using signal phrases, see 55 (MLA) or 60 (APA).

LaunchPadSolo **macmillanhighered.com/rules8e**

4 Reading and writing critically

> Writing practice: Drafting and revising an analytical thesis

> Writing practice: Analyzing a text

> Writing practice: Developing an analysis

Writing guide | Analytical essay

An **analysis** of a text allows you to examine the parts of a text to understand *what* it means and *how* it makes its meaning. Your goal is to offer your judgment of the text and to persuade readers to see it through your analytical perspective. A sample analytical essay begins on page 78.

Key features

- **A careful and critical reading** of a text reveals what the text says, how it works, and what it means. In an analytical essay, you pay attention to the details of the text, especially its thesis and evidence.
- **A thesis that offers a clear judgment** of a text anchors your analysis. Your thesis might be the answer to a question you have posed about a text or the resolution of a problem you have identified in the text.
- **Support for the thesis** comes from evidence in the text. You summarize, paraphrase, and quote passages that support the claims you make about the text.
- **A balance of summary and analysis** helps readers who may not be familiar with the text you are analyzing. Summary answers the question of *what* a text says; an analysis looks at *how* a text makes its point.

Writing your analytical essay

EXPLORE

Explore ideas by asking questions about the text. Let your questions help you understand what the text says, how it works, and what it means. Look for patterns among your questions to discover what interests you about the text's thesis, evidence, and key passages. Explore ideas for your analysis by asking questions such as the following:

- What is the text about?
- What do you find most interesting, surprising, or puzzling about this text?
- What is the author's thesis or central idea? Put the author's thesis to the "So what?" test. (See p. 69.)
- What do your annotations of the text reveal about your response to it?

DRAFT

- Draft a working thesis to focus your analysis. Remember that your thesis is not the same as the author's thesis. Your thesis presents *your* judgment and interpretation of the text.
- Draft a plan to organize your paragraphs. Your introductory paragraph will briefly summarize the text and offer your thesis. Your body paragraphs will support your thesis with evidence from the text. Your conclusion will pull together the major points and show the significance of your analysis. (See 1d.)
- Identify specific words, phrases, and sentences as evidence to support your thesis.

REVISE

Ask your reviewers to give you specific comments. You can use the following questions to guide their feedback.

- Is the introduction effective and engaging?
- Is summary balanced with analysis?
- Does the thesis offer a clear judgment of the text?
- What objections might other writers pose to your analysis?
- Is the analysis well organized? Are there clear topic sentences and transitions?
- Is there sufficient evidence? Is the evidence analyzed?
- Have you cited words, phrases, or sentences that are summarized or quoted?

4e Sample student writing: Analysis of an article

Following is Emilia Sanchez's analysis of the article by Betsy Taylor (see p. 67). Sanchez used MLA (Modern Language Association) style to format her paper and cite the source.

LaunchPadSolo macmillanhighered.com/rules8e
4 Reading and writing critically
> Sample student writing: Sanchez, "Rethinking Big-Box Stores" (analysis of an article)

Sanchez 1

Emilia Sanchez

Professor Goodwin

English 10

23 October 2014

Rethinking Big-Box Stores

Opening briefly summarizes the article's purpose and thesis.

In her essay "Big Box Stores Are Bad for Main Street," Betsy Taylor focuses not on the economic effects of large chain stores but on the effects these stores have on the "soul" of America. She argues that stores like Home Depot, Target, and Wal-Mart are bad for America because they draw people out of downtown shopping districts and cause them to focus on consumption. In contrast, she believes that small businesses are good for America because they provide personal attention, encourage community interaction, and make each city and town unique. But Taylor's argument is unconvincing because it is based on sentimentality—on idealized images of a quaint Main Street—rather than on the roles that businesses play in consumers' lives and communities. By ignoring the complex economic relationship between large chain stores and their communities, Taylor incorrectly assumes that simply getting rid of big-box stores would have a positive effect on America's communities.

Sanchez begins to analyze Taylor's argument.

Thesis expresses Sanchez's judgment of Taylor's article.

Taylor's use of colorful language reveals that she has a sentimental view of American society and does not understand economic realities. In her first paragraph, Taylor refers to a big-box store as a "25-acre slab of concrete with a 100,000 square foot box of stuff" that "land[s] on a town," evoking images of a powerful monster crushing the American way of life (1011). But she oversimplifies a complex issue. Taylor does not consider that many

Signal phrase introduces quotations from the source; Sanchez uses an MLA in-text citation.

Marginal annotations indicate MLA-style formatting and **effective writing**.

Sanchez 2

downtown business districts failed long before chain stores moved in, when factories and mills closed and workers lost their jobs. In cities with struggling economies, big-box stores can actually provide much-needed jobs. Similarly, while Taylor blames big-box stores for harming local economies by asking for tax breaks, free roads, and other perks, she doesn't acknowledge that these stores also enter into economic partnerships with the surrounding communities by offering financial benefits to schools and hospitals.

Sanchez identifies and challenges Taylor's assumptions.

Taylor's assumption that shopping in small businesses is always better for the customer also seems driven by nostalgia for an old-fashioned Main Street rather than by the facts. While she may be right that many small businesses offer personal service and are responsive to customer complaints, she does not consider that many customers appreciate the service at big-box stores. Just as customer service is better at some small businesses than at others, it is impossible to generalize about service at all big-box stores. For example, customers depend on the lenient return policies and the wide variety of products at stores like Target and Home Depot.

Clear topic sentence announces a shift to a new topic.

Sanchez refutes Taylor's claim.

Taylor blames big-box stores for encouraging American "hyper-consumerism," but she oversimplifies by equating big-box stores with bad values and small businesses with good values. Like her other points, this claim ignores the economic and social realities of American society today. Big-box stores do not force Americans to buy more. By offering lower prices in a convenient setting, however, they allow consumers to save time and purchase goods they might not be able to afford from small businesses. The existence of more small businesses would not change what

Sanchez 3

most Americans can afford, nor would it reduce their desire to buy affordable merchandise.

Sanchez treats the author fairly.

Taylor may be right that some big-box stores have a negative impact on communities and that small businesses offer certain advantages. But she ignores the economic conditions that support big-box stores as well as the fact that Main Street was in decline before the big-box store arrived. Getting rid of big-box stores will not bring back a simpler America populated by thriving, unique Main Streets; in reality, Main Street will not survive if consumers cannot afford to shop there.

Conclusion returns to the thesis and shows the wider significance of Sanchez's analysis.

Sanchez 4

Work Cited

Work cited page is in MLA style.

Taylor, Betsy. "Big Box Stores Are Bad for Main Street." *CQ Researcher* 9.44 (1999): 1011. Print.

5 Reading and writing about multimodal texts

In many of your college classes, you'll have the opportunity to read and write about multimodal texts, such as advertisements, maps, videos, and Web sites. These texts are called multimodal because they use written words and images or moving images and sound or some other combination of modes to convey meaning. You might be asked to analyze an advertisement for a composition course, a map for a geology course, or a YouTube video for a sociology course. All texts can be approached in a critical way. You can engage with them by studying how they work to communicate their message and by discovering within them something that is surprising, interesting, and worthy of interpretation. The strategies and advice offered in Chapter 4 for critically reading and writing about texts apply to multimodal texts. In this chapter, you'll find additional advice specific to analyzing multimodal texts.

5a Read actively.

Any multimodal text can be read — that is, examined to understand *what* it says and *how* it communicates its purpose and reaches its audience. As you read, think about the words, images, and sounds separately, and then analyze how they work together.

When you read a multimodal text, you'll find it helpful to preview, annotate, and converse with the text.

Previewing a multimodal text

Previewing starts when you look at the basic details of a multimodal text and pay attention to first impressions. You ask questions about the text's subject matter and design, its context and composer or creator, and its purpose and intended audience. The more you can gather from a first look, the easier it will be to dig deeper into the meaning of a text. The following questions will help you preview a multimodal text:

- What kind of text is it: Advertisement? Video? Slide show?
- What is your first reaction to the text? Does it elicit an emotional response?
- What strikes you right away about the various modes — words, images (moving or static), or sound? Does one mode seem to stand out more than the others?
- What does the subject matter and design suggest about the intended audience?

Annotating a multimodal text

Annotating a text — jotting down observations, reactions, and questions — helps you read actively to answer the basic question "What is this text about?" In annotating, you generate ideas by

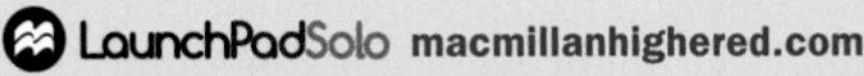

5 Reading and writing about multimodal texts
> Writing practice: Reading visual texts actively

paying close attention to each mode. You notice what surprises and intrigues you about the text, and you observe what is present and absent. For example, you might question the choice of classical music in an audio essay and wonder what this choice implies about the intended audience. Or in viewing a public service video, you might notice the presence of black-and-white photographs and the absence of words, spoken or written, and question how these design choices serve the video's message.

The following guidelines will help you annotate a multimodal text:

- **Identify the different modes used and examine them separately.** Thinking about each mode on its own is a helpful first step to evaluating the text as a whole. What modes are present — written words, static images, moving images, or sound?
- **Identify the role of each mode within the text.** For example, do written words convey information? Does audio evoke an emotional response?
- **Identify the features of each mode.** How do various features help convey the text's meaning and serve its purpose? For example, if written words are the mode being used, are they boldface or italic, large or small, black or in color? What differences do these features make?
- **Keep track of details.** For example, if you are making notes about an audio or a video file, include a time stamp with each observation so that you can easily find that moment again to check your notes or to include a clip in your analysis: *04:21 The music stops abruptly, and a single word, "Care," appears on-screen.*

The example on page 83 shows how one student, Ren Yoshida, annotated an advertisement.

Conversing with a multimodal text

Conversing with a text — or responding to a text and its author — helps you move beyond your early notes to form judgments about the text you're examining. You might choose to examine the choice of mode — why the message is conveyed in moving images rather than printed words, for example — or the features of a mode — why the background music becomes much louder at one point. You might point out something that

ANNOTATED ADVERTISEMENT

What is being exchanged?

Why is "fairly traded" so difficult to read?

"Empowering" — why in an elegant font? Who is empowering farmers?

"Farmers" in all capital letters — shows strength?

Straightforward design and not much text.

Outstretched hands. Is she giving a gift? Inviting a partnership?

Hands: heart-shaped, foregrounded.

Raw coffee is earthy, natural.

When you choose Equal Exchange fairly traded coffee, tea or chocolate, you join a network that empowers farmers in Latin America, Africa, and Asia to:

- **Stay on their land**
- **Care for the environment**
- **Farm organically**
- **Support their family**
- **Plan for the future**

www.equalexchange.coop

Photo: Jesus Choqueheranca de Quevero, Coffee farmer & CEPICAFE Cooperative member, Peru

Positive verbs: consumers choose, join, empower; farmers stay, care, farm, support, plan.

What does it mean to join a network?

How do consumers know their money helps farmers stay on their land?

is puzzling, contradictory, or provocative about the interplay between modes or their features. In his annotations to the Equal Exchange ad, Ren Yoshida asks why two words, *empowering* and *farmers*, are in different fonts (see p. 83) and why the farmer's hands are outstretched. As Yoshida moves beyond his annotations to form judgments about the text, he focuses his attention on the contradictions between the ad's emotional and logical appeals. He notices that the ad appeals to consumers' emotions, and yet such appeals raise logical questions about what is being exchanged and who is becoming empowered.

Many writers use a double-entry notebook to converse with a text and generate ideas for writing (see pp. 68–69 for guidelines on creating a double-entry notebook and sample entries). As you record details and features of a multimodal text on the left side of the notebook page and your own responses on the right side, you can visualize the conversation as it develops.

5b Outline to identify main ideas.

When you outline a text, you identify its main idea or purpose and its major parts. One approach for outlining a multimodal text is to define its main idea or purpose and sketch a list of its key elements. Because ads, Web sites, and videos may not include an explicit statement of purpose, such as a thesis statement, you may have to puzzle it out from the details in the work.

Here is the informal outline Ren Yoshida developed as he prepared to write an analysis of the advertisement on page 83. Notice that Yoshida makes an attempt to state the ad's purpose and sum up its message.

INFORMAL OUTLINE OF EQUAL EXCHANGE ADVERTISEMENT

Purpose: To persuade consumers that they can improve the lives of organic farmers and their families by purchasing Equal Exchange coffee.

Key features:

- The farmer's heart-shaped hands are outstretched, offering the viewer partnership and the product of her hard work.
- The raw coffee is surprisingly fruitlike and fresh—natural and healthy looking.
- A variety of fonts are used for emphasis, such as the elegant font for "empowering."

- Consumer support leads to a higher quality of life for the farmers and for all people, since these farmers care for the environment and plan for the future.
- The simplicity of the design reflects the simplicity of the exchange. The consumer only has to buy a cup of coffee to make a difference.

Conclusion: Equal Exchange is selling more than a product—coffee. It is selling the message that together farmers and consumers hold the future of land, environment, farms, and families in their hands.

5c Summarize to deepen your understanding.

Your goal in summarizing a multimodal text is to state the work's central idea and key points simply, objectively, and accurately, in your own words, and usually in paragraph form. As you present the central idea, use the third-person point of view and the present tense. If you have sketched a brief outline of the text (see 5b), refer to it as you draft your summary.

To summarize a multimodal text, begin with essential information, such as who composed the text and why, who the intended audience is, and when and where the work appeared. Briefly explain the text's main idea and identify its key features. Divide the summary into a few major and minor ideas. Since a summary must be fairly short, you must make judgments about what is most important.

Here is the summary Ren Yoshida developed as he prepared to write an analysis of the advertisement on page 83. Notice how Yoshida composes the summary in his own words, uses the third-person point of view ("The Equal Exchange advertisement is . . ."), and uses present tense ("The ad suggests . . .").

> The Equal Exchange advertisement is selling the message that together farmers and consumers hold the future of the planet in their hands. At the center of the ad is a farmer whose outstretched hands, full of raw coffee, offer the fruit of her labor and a partnership with consumers. The ad suggests that in a global world producers and consumers are bound together. A cup of coffee is more than just a morning ritual; a cup of coffee is part of an equal exchange that empowers farmers to stay on their land and empowers consumers to do the right thing.
>
> —Ren Yoshida, student

5d Analyze to demonstrate your critical reading.

A summary most often answers the question of *what* a text says, whereas an analysis looks at *how* a text conveys its main idea or message. As you read a multimodal text — previewing, annotating, and conversing — you are forming a judgment of it. Your analysis says to readers: "Here's my reading of this text. This is what the text means and why it matters." When you are assigned to analyze a multimodal text, you will usually be expected to look at how the different modes (sound, words, moving or static images) and their features (loud or quiet, bold or italic, fast or slow) contribute to its central purpose, often with the aim of judging how effective the text is in achieving its purpose.

Balancing summary with analysis

If you have written a summary of a text, you may find it useful to refer to the main points of the summary as you write your analysis. Your readers may or may not be familiar with the multimodal text you are analyzing and will need at least some summary to ground your analysis. For example, student writer Ren Yoshida summarizes the Equal Exchange advertisement on page 83 by describing part of the text first, allowing readers to get their bearings, and then moving to an analytical statement about that particular part of the text.

Summary: [A farmer, her hardworking hands full of raw coffee, reaches out from an Equal Exchange advertisement. The hands, in the shape of a heart, offer to consumers the fruit of the farmer's labor. The ad's message is straightforward: in choosing Equal Exchange, consumers become global citizens, partnering with farmers to help save the planet.]

Analysis: [Suddenly, a cup of coffee is more than just a morning ritual; a cup of coffee is a moral choice that empowers both consumers and farmers.]

These strategies will help you balance summary with analysis.

- Remember that readers are interested in your ideas about a text.
- Pose questions that lead to an interpretation or a judgment of a text rather than to a summary. Go beyond describing what you see or hear to ask "why" and "how" questions.
- Focus on a few significant features rather than listing every detail. For example, evaluate the size and arrangement of written words or the pitch (high or low) or pace (fast or slow) of the audio.
- Pay attention to the role of each mode within the text. For example, how do images convey information or emotion?
- Ask peer reviewers to give you feedback: Do you summarize too much and need to analyze more?

Drafting an analytical thesis statement

An effective thesis statement for analytical writing about a multimodal text responds to a question about the text or tries to resolve a problem in the text. Remember that your thesis isn't the same as the text's main idea. Your thesis presents your judgment of the text's argument. If your draft thesis restates the text's message, return to the questions you asked earlier in the process as you revise.

INEFFECTIVE THESIS STATEMENT

> Consumers who purchase coffee from farmers in the Equal Exchange network are helping farmers stay on their land.

The thesis is ineffective because it summarizes the ad; it doesn't present an analysis. Ren Yoshida focused the thesis by questioning a single detail in the work.

QUESTIONS

> The ad promises an equal exchange, but is the exchange equal between consumers and farmers? Do the words *equal exchange* and *empowering farmers* appeal to consumers' emotions?

EFFECTIVE THESIS STATEMENT

> Although the ad works successfully on an emotional level, it is less successful on a logical level because of its promise for an equal exchange between consumers and farmers.

LaunchPadSolo macmillanhighered.com/rules8e
5 Reading and writing about multimodal texts
> Writing practice: Drafting and revising an analytical thesis (multimodal)
> Writing practice: Learning from other writers

5e Sample student writing: Analysis of an advertisement

On the following pages is Ren Yoshida's analysis of the Equal Exchange advertisement that appears on page 83.

Yoshida 1

Ren Yoshida

Professor Marcotte

English 101

4 November 2014

Sometimes a Cup of Coffee Is Just a Cup of Coffee

A farmer, her hardworking hands full of coffee beans, reaches out from an Equal Exchange advertisement (Equal Exchange). The hands, in the shape of a heart, offer to consumers the fruit of the farmer's labor. The ad's message is straightforward: in choosing Equal Exchange, consumers become global citizens, partnering with farmers to help save the planet. Suddenly, a cup of coffee is more than just a morning ritual; a cup of coffee is a moral choice that empowers both consumers and farmers. This simple exchange appeals to a consumer's desire to be a good person—to protect the environment and do the right thing. Yet the ad is more complicated than it first seems, and its design raises some logical questions about such an exchange. Although the ad works successfully on an emotional level, it is less successful on a logical level because of its promise for an equal exchange between consumers and farmers.

The source is cited in the text. No page number is available for the online source.

Yoshida summarizes the content of the ad.

Thesis expresses Yoshida's analysis of the ad.

Marginal annotations indicate MLA-style formatting and **effective writing.**

LaunchPadSolo **macmillanhighered.com/rules8e**

5 Reading and writing about multimodal texts

> Sample student writing: Yoshida, "Sometimes a Cup of Coffee Is Just a Cup of Coffee" (analysis of an advertisement)

> Sample student writing: D'Amato, "Loose Leaf Teas" (Web site); Williamson, "To the Children of America" (video essay)

Yoshida 2

The focus of the ad is a farmer, Jesus Choqueheranca de Quevero, and, more specifically, her outstretched, cupped hands. Her hands are full of red, raw coffee, her life's work. The ad successfully appeals to consumers' emotions, assuming they will find the farmer's welcoming face and hands, caked with dirt, more appealing than startling statistics about the state of the environment or the number of farmers who lose their land each year. It seems almost rude not to accept the farmer's generous offering since we know her name and, as the ad implies, have the choice to "empower" her. In fact, how can a consumer resist helping the farmer "[c]are for the environment" and "[p]lan for the future," when it is a simple matter of choosing the right coffee? The ad sends the message that our future is a global future in which producers and consumers are bound together.

Details show how the ad appeals to consumers' emotions.

Yoshida interprets details such as the farmer's hands.

First impressions play a major role in the success of an advertisement. Consumers are pulled toward a product, or pushed away, by an ad's initial visual and emotional appeal. Here, the intended audience is busy people, so the ad tries to catch viewers' attention and make a strong impression immediately. Yet with a second or third viewing, consumers might start to ask some logical questions about Equal Exchange before buying their morning coffee. Although the farmer extends her heart-shaped hands to consumers, they are not actually buying a cup of coffee or the raw coffee directly from her. In reality, consumers are buying from Equal Exchange, even if the ad substitutes the more positive word *choose* for *buy*. Furthermore, consumers aren't actually empowering the farmer; they are joining "a network that empowers farmers." The idea of a network makes a simple transaction more complicated. How do consumers know their

Yoshida begins to challenge the logic of the ad.

Yoshida 3

Words from the ad serve as evidence.

Clear topic sentence announces a shift.

Summary of the ad's key features serves Yoshida's analysis.

money helps farmers "[s]tay on their land" and "[p]lan for the future" as the ad promises? They don't.

The ad's design elements raise questions about the use of the key terms *equal exchange* and *empowering farmers*. The Equal Exchange logo suggests symmetry and equality, with two red arrows facing each other, but the words of the logo appear almost like an eye exam poster, with each line decreasing in font size and clarity. The words *fairly traded* are tiny. Below the logo, the words *empowering farmers* are presented in contradictory fonts. *Empowering* is written in a flowing, cursive font, almost the opposite of what might be considered empowering, whereas *farmers* is written in a plain, sturdy font. The ad's varying fonts communicate differently and make it hard to know exactly what is being exchanged and who is becoming empowered.

What is being exchanged? The logic of the ad suggests that consumers will improve the future by choosing Equal Exchange. The first exchange is economic: consumers give one thing—dollars—and receive something in return—a cup of coffee—and the farmer stays on her land. The second exchange is more complicated because it involves a moral exchange. The ad suggests that if consumers don't choose "fairly traded" products, farmers will be forced off their land and the environment destroyed. This exchange, when put into motion by consumers choosing to purchase products not "fairly traded," has negative consequences for both consumers and farmers. The message of the ad is that the actual exchange taking place is not economic but moral; after all, nothing is being bought, only chosen. Yet the logic of this exchange quickly falls apart. Consumers aren't empowered to become global citizens simply by choosing Equal Exchange, and farmers aren't empowered to plan for the future by

Yoshida 4

consumers' choices. And even if all this empowerment magically happened, there is nothing equal about such an exchange.

Advertisements are themselves about empowerment—encouraging viewers to believe they can become someone or do something by identifying, emotionally or logically, with a product. In the Equal Exchange ad, consumers are emotionally persuaded to identify with a farmer whose face is not easily forgotten and whose heart-shaped hands hold a collective future. On a logical level, though, the ad raises questions because empowerment, although a good concept to choose, is not easily or equally exchanged. Sometimes a cup of coffee is just a cup of coffee.

Yoshida shows why his thesis matters.

Conclusion includes a detail from the introduction.

Conclusion returns to Yoshida's thesis.

Yoshida 5

Work Cited

Equal Exchange. Advertisement. *Equal Exchange*. Equal Exchange, n.d. Web. 14 Oct. 2014.

6 Reading and writing arguments

Many of your college assignments will ask you to read and write arguments about debatable issues. The questions being debated might be matters of public policy (*Should corporations be allowed to advertise on public school property?* or *What is the least dangerous way to dispose of hazardous waste?*), or they might be scholarly issues (*What role do genes play in determining behavior?* or *What were the causes of the Vietnam War?*). On such questions, reasonable people may disagree.

As you read arguments across the disciplines and enter into academic or public policy debates, pay attention to the questions being asked, the evidence being presented, and the various positions being argued. It's helpful to approach all arguments with an open, curious mind. Reasonable people disagree on topics worth debating, so dive into the center of these disagreements to understand what's at stake in the arguments being debated. You'll find the critical reading strategies introduced in chapter 4—previewing, annotating, and conversing with texts—to be useful as you ask questions about an argument's logic, evidence, and use of appeals. Many arguments can stand up to critical scrutiny. Sometimes, however, a line of argument that at first seems reasonable turns out to be illogical, unfair, or both.

As you write for various college courses, you'll be asked to take positions in academic debates, propose solutions to problems, and persuade readers to accept your arguments. Just as you evaluate arguments with openness, you'll want to construct arguments with the same openness—acknowledging disagreements and opposing views and presenting your arguments fully and fairly to your readers.

See sections 6a–6c for advice about reading arguments. Sections 6d–6k address writing arguments.

6a Distinguish between reasonable and fallacious argumentative tactics.

When you evaluate an argument, look closely at the reasoning and evidence behind it. A number of unreasonable argumentative tactics are known as *logical fallacies*. Most of the fallacies—such as hasty generalizations and false analogies—are misguided or dishonest uses of legitimate strategies. The examples in this section suggest when such strategies are reasonable and when they are not.

Generalizing (inductive reasoning)

Writers and thinkers generalize all the time. We look at a sample of data and conclude that data we have not observed will most likely conform to what we have seen. From a spoonful of soup, we conclude just how salty the whole bowl will be. After numerous unpleasant experiences with an airline, we decide to book future flights with a competitor.

When we draw a conclusion from an array of facts, we are engaged in inductive reasoning. Such reasoning deals in probability, not certainty. For a conclusion to be highly probable, it must be based on evidence that is sufficient, representative, and relevant. (See the chart on p. 94.)

> **Academic English** Many hasty generalizations contain words such as *all*, *ever*, *always*, and *never*, when qualifiers such as *most*, *many*, *usually*, and *seldom* would be more accurate.

The fallacy known as *hasty generalization* is a conclusion based on insufficient or unrepresentative evidence.

HASTY GENERALIZATION

In a single year, scores on standardized tests in California's public schools rose by ten points. Therefore, more children than ever are succeeding in America's public school systems.

Data from one state do not justify a conclusion about the whole United States.

A *stereotype* is a hasty generalization about a group. Here are a few examples.

STEREOTYPES

Women are bad bosses.

Politicians are corrupt.

Children are always curious.

Stereotyping is common because of our tendency to perceive selectively. We tend to see what we want to see; we notice evidence confirming our already formed opinions and fail to notice evidence to the contrary. For example, if you have concluded that politicians are corrupt, your stereotype will be confirmed by news reports of legislators being indicted — even though every day the media describe conscientious officials serving the public honestly and well.

Drawing analogies

An analogy points out a similarity between two things that are otherwise different. Analogies can be an effective means of arguing a point. It is not always easy to draw the line between a reasonable and an unreasonable analogy. At times, however, an analogy is clearly off base, in which case it is called a *false analogy.*

FALSE ANALOGY

If we can send a spacecraft to Pluto, we should be able to find a cure for the common cold.

The writer has falsely assumed that because two things are alike in one respect, they must be alike in others. Exploring the outer reaches of the solar system and finding a cure for the common cold are both scientific challenges, but the problems confronting medical researchers are quite different from those solved by space scientists.

Testing inductive reasoning

Though inductive reasoning leads to probable and not absolute truth, you can assess a conclusion's likely probability by asking three questions. This chart shows how to apply those questions to a sample conclusion based on a survey.

CONCLUSION The majority of students on our campus would volunteer at least five hours a week in a community organization if the school provided a placement service for volunteers.

EVIDENCE In a recent survey, 723 of 1,215 students questioned said they would volunteer at least five hours a week in a community organization if the school provided a placement service for volunteers.

1. ***Is the evidence sufficient?*** That depends. On a small campus (say, 3,000 students), the pool of students surveyed would be sufficient for market research, but on a large campus (say, 30,000), 1,215 students are only 4 percent of the population. If that 4 percent were known to be truly representative of the other 96 percent, however, even such a small sample would be sufficient (see question 2).
2. ***Is the evidence representative?*** The evidence is representative if those responding to the survey reflect the characteristics of the entire student population: age, sex, race, field of study, number of extracurricular commitments, and so on. If most of those surveyed are majors in a field like social work, the researchers should question the survey's conclusion.
3. ***Is the evidence relevant?*** Yes. The survey results are directly linked to the conclusion. Evidence based on a survey about the number of hours students work for pay would not be relevant because it would not be about *choosing to volunteer.*

Tracing causes and effects

Demonstrating a connection between causes and effects is rarely simple. For example, to explain why a chemistry course has a high failure rate, you would begin by listing possible causes: inadequate preparation of students, poor teaching, lack of qualified tutors, and so on. Next you would investigate each possible cause. Only after investigating the possible causes would you be able to weigh the relative impact of each cause and suggest appropriate remedies.

Because cause-and-effect reasoning is so complex, it is not surprising that writers frequently oversimplify it. In particular, writers sometimes assume that because one event follows another, the first is the cause of the second. This common fallacy is known as *post hoc*, from the Latin *post hoc, ergo propter hoc*, meaning "after this, therefore because of this."

POST HOC FALLACY

> Since Governor Cho took office, unemployment among minorities in the state has decreased by 7 percent. Governor Cho should be applauded for reducing unemployment among minorities.

Is the governor solely responsible for the decrease? Are there other reasons? The writer must show that Governor Cho's policies are responsible for the decrease in unemployment; it is not enough to show that the decrease followed the governor's taking office.

Weighing options

Especially when reasoning about problems and solutions, writers must weigh options. To be fair, a writer should mention the full range of options, showing why one is superior to the others or might work well in combination with others.

It is unfair to suggest that only two alternatives exist when in fact there are more. Writers who set up a false choice between their preferred option and one that is clearly unsatisfactory are guilty of the *either . . . or* fallacy.

EITHER . . . OR FALLACY

> Our current war against drugs has not worked. Either we should legalize drugs or we should turn the drug war over to our armed forces and let them fight it.

Are these the only solutions — legalizing drugs and calling out the army? Other options, such as funding for drug abuse prevention programs, are possible.

Making assumptions

An assumption is a claim that is taken to be true — without the need of proof. Most arguments are based to some extent on assumptions, since writers rarely have the time and space to prove all the conceivable claims on which their argument is based. For example, someone arguing about the best means of limiting population growth in developing countries might assume that the goal of limiting population growth is worthwhile. For most audiences, there would be no need to articulate this assumption or to defend it.

There is a danger, however, in failing to spell out and prove a claim that is clearly controversial. Consider the following short argument, in which a key claim is missing.

ARGUMENT WITH MISSING CLAIM

> Violent crime is increasing. Therefore, we should vigorously enforce the death penalty.

The writer seems to be assuming that the death penalty deters violent criminals and that it is a fair punishment — and that most audiences will agree. These are not reasonable assumptions; the writer will need to state and support both claims.

When a missing claim is an assertion that few would agree with, we say that a writer is guilty of a *non sequitur* (Latin for "does not follow").

NON SEQUITUR

> Christopher gets plenty of sleep; therefore, he will be a successful student in the university's pre-med program.

Does it take more than sleep to be a successful student? Few people would agree with the missing claim — that people with good sleep habits always make successful students.

Deducing conclusions (deductive reasoning)

When we deduce a conclusion, we put things together, like any good detective. We establish that a general principle is true, that a specific case is an example of that principle, and that therefore a particular conclusion about that case is a certainty.

Deductive reasoning can often be structured in a three-step argument called a *syllogism*. The three steps are the major premise, the minor premise, and the conclusion.

1. Anything that increases radiation in the environment is dangerous to public health. (Major premise)
2. Nuclear reactors increase radiation in the environment. (Minor premise)
3. Therefore, nuclear reactors are dangerous to public health. (Conclusion)

The major premise is a generalization. The minor premise is a specific case. The conclusion follows from applying the generalization to the specific case.

Deductive arguments break down if one of the premises is not true or if the conclusion does not follow logically from the premises. In the following argument, the major premise is very likely untrue.

UNTRUE PREMISE

The police do not give speeding tickets to people driving less than five miles per hour over the limit. Dominic is driving fifty-nine miles per hour in a fifty-five-mile-per-hour zone. Therefore, the police will not give Dominic a speeding ticket.

The conclusion is true only if the premises are true. If the police sometimes give tickets for driving less than five miles per hour over the limit, Dominic cannot safely conclude that he will avoid a ticket.

In the following argument, both premises might be true, but the conclusion does not follow logically from them.

CONCLUSION DOES NOT FOLLOW

All members of our club ran in this year's Boston Marathon. Jay ran in this year's Boston Marathon. Therefore, Jay is a member of our club.

The fact that Jay ran the race is no guarantee that he is a member of the club. Presumably, many runners are nonmembers.

Assuming that both premises are true, the following argument holds up.

CONCLUSION FOLLOWS

All members of our club ran in this year's Boston Marathon. Jay is a member of our club. Therefore, Jay ran in this year's Boston Marathon.

6b Distinguish between legitimate and unfair emotional appeals.

There is nothing wrong with appealing to readers' emotions. After all, many issues worth arguing about have an emotional as well as a logical dimension. Even the Greek logician Aristotle lists *pathos* (emotion) as a legitimate argumentative tactic. For example, in an essay criticizing big-box stores (see p. 67), writer Betsy Taylor has a good reason for tugging at readers' emotions: Her subject is the decline of city and town life. In her conclusion, Taylor appeals to readers' emotions by invoking their national pride.

LEGITIMATE EMOTIONAL APPEAL

> Is it anti-American to be against having a retail giant set up shop in one's community? Some people would say so. On the other hand, if you board up Main Street, what's left of America?

Emotional appeals, however, are frequently misused. Many of the arguments we see in the media, for instance, strive to win our sympathy rather than our intelligent agreement. A TV commercial suggesting that you will be thin and attractive if you drink a certain diet beverage is making a pitch to emotions. So is a political speech that recommends electing a candidate because he is a devoted husband and father who serves as a volunteer firefighter.

The following passage illustrates several types of unfair emotional appeals.

UNFAIR EMOTIONAL APPEALS

> This progressive proposal to build a ski resort in the state park has been carefully researched by Western Trust, the largest bank in the state; furthermore, it is favored by a majority of the local merchants. The only opposition comes from tree huggers who care more about trees than they do about people. One of their leaders was actually arrested for disturbing the peace several years ago.

Words with strong positive or negative connotations, such as *progressive* and *tree hugger*, are examples of *biased language*. Attacking the people who hold a belief (environmentalists) rather than refuting their argument is called *ad hominem*,

LaunchPadSolo macmillanhighered.com/rules8e
6 Reading and writing arguments
> Writing practice: Identifying appeals

Evaluating ethical, logical, and emotional appeals as a reader

Ancient Greek rhetoricians distinguished among three kinds of appeals used to influence readers — ethical, logical, emotional. As you evaluate arguments, identify these appeals and question their effectiveness. Are they appropriate for the audience and the argument? Are they balanced and legitimate or lopsided and misleading?

Ethical appeals (*ethos*)

Ethical arguments call upon a writer's character, knowledge, and authority. Ask questions such as the following when you evaluate the ethical appeal of an argument.

- Is the writer informed and trustworthy? How does the writer establish authority and credibility?
- Is the writer fair-minded and unbiased? How does the writer establish reasonableness?
- Does the writer use sources knowledgeably and responsibly?
- How does the writer describe the views of others and deal with opposing views?

Logical appeals (*logos*)

Reasonable arguments appeal to readers' sense of logic, rely on evidence, and use inductive and deductive reasoning. Ask questions such as the following to evaluate the logical appeal of an argument.

- Is the evidence sufficient, representative, and relevant?
- Is the reasoning sound?
- Does the argument contain any logical fallacies or unwarranted assumptions?
- Are there any missing or mistaken premises?

Emotional appeals (*pathos*)

Emotional arguments appeal to readers' beliefs and values. Ask questions such as the following to evaluate the emotional appeal of an argument.

- What values or beliefs does the writer address, either directly or indirectly?
- Are the emotional appeals legitimate and fair?
- Does the writer oversimplify or dramatize an issue?
- Do the emotional arguments highlight or shift attention away from the evidence?

a Latin term meaning "to the man." Associating a prestigious name (Western Trust) with the writer's side is called *transfer*. Claiming that an idea should be accepted because a large number of people (the majority of merchants) are in favor is called the *bandwagon appeal*. Bringing in irrelevant issues (the arrest) is a *red herring*, named after a trick used in fox hunts to mislead the dogs by dragging a smelly fish across the trail.

Advertising makes use of ethical, logical, and emotional appeals to persuade consumers to buy a product or embrace a brand. This Patagonia ad makes an ethical appeal with its copy that invites customers to rethink their purchasing practices.

6c Judge how fairly a writer handles opposing views.

The way in which a writer deals with opposing views is revealing. Some writers address the arguments of the opposition fairly, conceding points when necessary and countering others, all in a civil spirit. Other writers will do almost anything to win an argument: either ignoring opposing views altogether or misrepresenting such views and attacking their proponents.

Writers build credibility—*ethos*—by addressing opposing arguments fairly. As you read arguments, assess the credibility of your sources by looking at how they deal with views not in agreement with their own.

Describing the views of others

Some writers and speakers deliberately misrepresent the views of others. One way they do this is by setting up a "straw man," a character so weak that he is easily knocked down. The *straw man* fallacy consists of an oversimplification or outright distortion of opposing views. For example, in a California debate over attempts to control the mountain lion population, pro-lion groups characterized their opponents as trophy hunters bent on shooting harmless animals. In truth, hunters were only one faction of those who saw a need to control the lion population.

During the District of Columbia's struggle for voting representation, some politicians set up a straw man, as shown in the following example.

STRAW MAN FALLACY

> Washington, DC, residents are lobbying for statehood. Giving a city such as the District of Columbia the status of a state would be unfair.

The straw man wanted statehood. In fact, most DC citizens lobbied for voting representation in any form, not necessarily through statehood.

Quoting opposing views

Writers often quote the words of writers who hold opposing views. In general, this is a good idea, for it assures some level of fairness and accuracy. At times, though, both the fairness and the accuracy are an illusion.

A source may be misrepresented when it is quoted out of context. All quotations are to some extent taken out of context, but a fair writer will explain the context to readers. To select a provocative sentence from a source and to ignore the more moderate sentences surrounding it is both unfair and misleading. Sometimes a writer deliberately distorts a source through the device of ellipsis dots. Ellipsis dots tell readers that words have been omitted from the original source. When those words are crucial to an author's meaning, omitting them is obviously unfair. (See also 39d.)

ORIGINAL SOURCE

> Johnson's *History of the American West* is riddled with inaccuracies and astonishing in its blatantly racist description of the Indian wars.
>
> — B. R., reviewer

MISLEADING QUOTATION

Johnson's *History of the American West* is "astonishing in its . . . description of the Indian wars."

Checklist for reading and evaluating arguments

- What is the writer's thesis, or central claim?
- Are there any gaps in reasoning? Does the argument contain any logical fallacies (see 6a)?
- What assumptions does the argument rest on? Are there any unstated assumptions?
- What appeals — ethical, logical, or emotional — does the writer make? Are these appeals effective?
- What evidence does the writer use? Could there be alternative interpretations of the evidence?
- How does the writer handle opposing views?
- If you are not persuaded by the writer's argument, what counter-arguments could you make to the writer?

EXERCISE 6–1 Explain what is illogical in the following brief arguments. It may be helpful to identify the logical fallacy or fallacies by name. Answers appear in the back of the book.

More practice: LaunchPadSolo

a. My roommate, who is an engineering major, is taking a course called Structures of Tall Buildings. All engineers have to know how to design tall buildings.
b. If you're old enough to vote, you're old enough to drink. Therefore, the drinking age should be lowered to eighteen.
c. If you're not part of the solution, you're part of the problem.
d. American students could be outperforming students in schools around the globe if it weren't for the outmoded, behind-the-times thinking of many statewide education departments.
e. Charging a fee for curbside trash pickup will encourage everyone to recycle more because no one in my town likes to spend extra money.

LaunchPadSolo **macmillanhighered.com/rules8e**

6 Reading and writing arguments
> Writing practice: Evaluating an argument
> Exercise: 6–2

6d When writing arguments, consider purpose and context.

Evaluating the arguments of other writers prepares you to construct your own. When you ask questions about the logic and evidence of the arguments you read, you become more aware of such needs in your own writing. And when you pose objections to arguments, you more readily anticipate and counter objections to your own arguments.

In constructing an argument, you take a stand on a debatable issue. Your purpose is to explain your understanding of the truth about a subject or to propose the best solution to a problem, reasonably and logically, without being combative. Your aim is to persuade your readers to reconsider their positions by offering new reasons to question existing viewpoints.

It's best to start by informing yourself about the debate or conversation around a subject—sometimes called its *context*. If you are planning to write about the subject of offshore drilling, you might want to read sources that shed light on the social context (the concerns of consumers, the ideas of lawmakers, the proposals of environmentalists) and sources that may inform you about the intellectual context (scientific or theoretical responses by geologists, oceanographers, or economists) in which the debate is played out. Because your readers may be aware of the social and intellectual contexts in which your issue is grounded, you will be at a disadvantage if you are not informed. Conduct some research before preparing your argument. Consulting even a few sources can help to deepen your understanding of the conversation around the issue.

6e View your audience as a panel of jurors.

Do not assume that your audience already agrees with you. Instead, envision skeptical readers who, like a panel of jurors, will make up their minds after listening to all sides of the argument. If you are arguing a public policy issue, aim your paper at readers who represent a variety of positions. In the case of a debate over offshore drilling, for example, imagine a jury that represents those who have a stake in the matter: consumers, policymakers, and environmentalists.

At times, you can deliberately narrow your audience. If you are working within a word limit, for example, you might not have the space in which to address the concerns of all interested

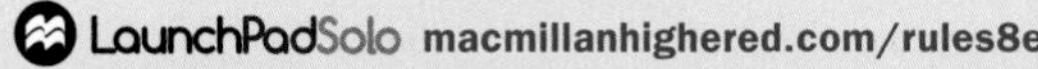

6 Reading and writing arguments
> Writing practice: Joining a conversation

parties. Or you might be primarily interested in reaching just a segment of a larger audience, such as consumers. Once you identify a specific audience, it's helpful to think about what kinds of arguments and evidence will appeal to that audience.

NOTE: Your assignment may require a specific audience, or you may be free to identify a broader group of readers. Check with your instructor before you make your case.

Using ethical, logical, and emotional appeals as a writer

To construct a convincing argument, you must establish your credibility (*ethos*) and appeal to your readers' sense of logic and reason (*logos*) as well as to their values and beliefs (*pathos*). When using these appeals, make sure they are appropriate for your audience and your argument.

Ethical appeals (*ethos*)

To accept your argument, a reader must perceive you as trustworthy, fair, and reasonable. When you acknowledge alternative positions, you build common ground with readers and gain their trust by showing that you are knowledgeable. And when you use sources responsibly (summarizing, paraphrasing, or quoting the views of others respectfully), you inspire readers' confidence in your judgment.

Logical appeals (*logos*)

To persuade readers, you need to appeal to their sense of logic and sound reasoning. When you provide sufficient evidence, you offer readers logical support for your argument. And when you clarify the assumptions that underlie your arguments and avoid logical fallacies, you appeal to readers' desire for reason.

Emotional appeals (*pathos*)

To establish common ground with readers, you need to appeal to their beliefs and values as well as to their minds. When you offer readers vivid examples and illustrations, startling statistics, or compelling visuals, you engage readers and deepen their interest in your argument. And when you balance emotional appeals with logical appeals, you highlight the human dimension of an issue to show readers why they should care about your argument.

LaunchPadSolo **macmillanhighered.com/rules8e**
6 Reading and writing arguments
> Writing practice: Appealing to your readers

Academic English Some cultures value writers who argue with force; other cultures value writers who argue subtly or indirectly. Academic audiences in the United States will expect your writing to be assertive and confident — neither aggressive nor passive. You can create an assertive tone by acknowledging different positions and supporting your ideas with specific evidence.

TOO AGGRESSIVE	Of course only registered organ donors should be eligible for organ transplants. It's selfish and shortsighted to think otherwise.
TOO PASSIVE	I might be wrong, but I think that maybe people should have to register as organ donors if they want to be considered for a transplant.
ASSERTIVE TONE	If only registered organ donors are eligible for transplants, more people will register as donors.

If you are uncertain about the tone of your work, ask for help at your school's writing center.

6f In your introduction, establish credibility and state your position.

When you are constructing an argument, make sure your introduction includes a thesis statement that establishes your position on the issue you have chosen to debate. In the sentences leading up to the thesis, establish your credibility (*ethos*) with readers by showing that you are knowledgeable and fair-minded. If possible, build common ground (*pathos*) with readers who may not at first agree with your views, and show them why they should consider your thesis. For advice about writing effective thesis statements, see 1c.

In the following introduction, student writer Kevin Smith presents himself as someone worth listening to. Because Smith introduces both sides of the debate, readers are likely to approach his essay with an open mind.

Smith shows that he is familiar with the legal issues surrounding school prayer.

Although the Supreme Court has ruled against prayer in public schools on First Amendment grounds, many people still feel that prayer should be allowed. Such people value prayer as a practice central to their faith and believe that prayer is a way for schools to reinforce moral principles. They also compellingly point out a paradox in the First Amendment itself: at what point does the separation of church and state restrict the freedom of those who wish to practice their religion? What proponents of school prayer fail to realize, however, is that the Supreme Court's decision, although it was made on legal grounds, makes sense on religious grounds as well. Prayer is too important to be trusted to our public schools.

Smith is fair-minded, presenting the views of both sides.

Thesis builds common ground.

— Kevin Smith, student

TIP: A good way to test a thesis while drafting and revising is to imagine a counterargument to your argument (see 6i). If you can't think of an opposing point of view, rethink your thesis and ask a classmate or writing center tutor to respond to your argument.

6g Back up your thesis with persuasive lines of argument.

Arguments of any complexity contain lines of argument that, when taken together, might reasonably persuade readers that the thesis has merit. The following, for example, are the main lines of argument that student writer Sam Jacobs used in his paper about the shift from print to online news (see pp. 112–17).

CENTRAL CLAIM

Thesis: The shift from print to online news provides unprecedented opportunities for readers to become more engaged with the news, to hold journalists accountable, and to participate as producers, not simply as consumers.

SUPPORTING CLAIMS

- Print news has traditionally had a one-sided relationship with its readers, delivering information for passive consumption.
- Online news invites readers to participate in a collaborative process—to question and even contribute to the content.

- Links within news stories provide transparency, allowing readers to move easily from the main story to original sources, related articles, or background materials.
- Technology has made it possible for readers to become news producers—posting text, audio, images, and video of news events.
- Citizen journalists can provide valuable information, sometimes more quickly than traditional journalists can.

If you sum up your main lines of argument, as Jacobs did, you will have a rough outline of your essay. In your paper, you will provide evidence for each of these claims.

6h Support your claims with specific evidence.

You will need to support your central claim and any subordinate claims with evidence: facts, statistics, examples and illustrations, visuals (such as graphs or photos), expert opinion, and so on. Debatable topics require that you consult some written sources to establish your *ethos* and to persuade your audience. As you read through or view the sources, you will learn more about the arguments and counterarguments at the center of your debate.

USING SOURCES RESPONSIBLY: Whether your sources provide facts or statistics, examples or illustrations, visuals, or expert opinion, remember that you must cite them. Documenting sources gives credit to authors and shows readers how to locate a source in case they want to assess its credibility or explore the issue further. For help citing sources, see 56a and 56b (MLA) and 61a and 61b (APA).

Using facts and statistics

A fact is something that is known with certainty because it has been objectively verified: The capital of Wyoming is Cheyenne. Carbon has an atomic weight of 12. John F. Kennedy was assassinated on November 22, 1963. Statistics are collections of numerical facts: Alcohol abuse is a factor in nearly 40 percent of traffic fatalities. More than four in ten businesses in the United States are owned by women.

LaunchPadSolo macmillanhighered.com/rules8e
6 Reading and writing arguments
> Writing practice: Drafting your central claim and supporting claims

Most arguments are supported, at least to some extent, by facts and statistics. For example, in the following passage the writer uses statistics to show that college students carry unreasonably high credit card debt.

> A 2009 study by Sallie Mae revealed that undergraduates are carrying record-high credit card balances and are relying on credit cards more than ever, especially in the economic downturn. The average credit card debt per college undergraduate is more than three thousand dollars, and three-quarters of undergraduates carry balances and incur finance charges each month (Hunter).

Writers often use statistics in selective ways to bolster their own positions. If you suspect that a writer's handling of statistics is not quite fair, track down the original sources for those statistics or read authors with opposing views, who may give you a fuller understanding of the numbers.

Using examples and illustrations

Examples and illustrations (extended examples, often in story form) rarely prove a point by themselves, but when used in combination with other forms of evidence, they flesh out an argument with details and bring it to life. Because examples are often concrete and sometimes vivid, they can reach readers in ways that statistics and abstract ideas cannot.

In a paper arguing that online news provides opportunities for readers that print does not, Sam Jacobs describes how regular citizens using only cell phones and laptops helped save lives during Hurricane Katrina by sending important updates to the rest of the world.

> Citizen reporting made a difference in the wake of Hurricane Katrina in 2005. Armed with cell phones and laptops, regular citizens relayed critical news updates in a rapidly developing crisis, often before traditional journalists were even on the scene.

Using visuals

Visuals — charts, graphs, diagrams, photographs — can support your argument by providing vivid and detailed evidence and by capturing your readers' attention. Bar or line graphs, for instance, describe and organize complex statistical data; photographs can immediately and evocatively convey abstract ideas. (See pp. 26–27.)

As you consider using visual evidence, ask yourself the following questions:

- Is the visual accurate, credible, and relevant?
- How will the visual appeal to readers: Logically? Ethically? Emotionally?
- How will the visual evidence function? Will it provide background information? Present complex numerical information or convey an abstract idea? Lend authority? Refute counterarguments?

Citing expert opinion

Although they are no substitute for careful reasoning of your own, the views of an expert can contribute to the force of your argument. For example, to help make the case that print journalism has a one-sided relationship with its readers, student writer Sam Jacobs integrates an expert's key description.

> With the rise of the Internet, however, this model has been criticized by journalists such as Dan Gillmor, founder of the Center for Citizen Media, who argues that traditional print journalism treats "news as a lecture," whereas online news is "more of a conversation" (xxiv).

When you rely on expert opinion, make sure that your source is an expert in the field you are writing about. In some cases, you may need to provide credentials showing why your source is worth listening to, such as listing the person's position or title alongside his or her name. When including expert testimony in your paper, you can summarize or paraphrase the expert's opinion or you can quote the expert's exact words. You will, of course, need to document the source, as Jacobs did.

6i Anticipate objections; counter opposing arguments.

Readers who already agree with you need no convincing, but skeptical readers may resist your arguments. To be willing to give up a position that seems reasonable, readers need to see that

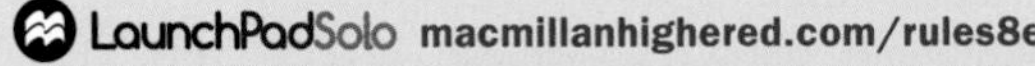

6 Reading and writing arguments
> Writing practice: Practicing counterargument

another position is even more reasonable. In addition to presenting your own case, therefore, you should consider the opposing arguments and attempt to counter them.

Anticipating and countering objections

To anticipate a possible objection to your argument, consider the following questions.

- Could a reasonable person draw a different conclusion from your facts or examples?
- Might a reader question any of your assumptions or offer an alternative explanation?
- Is there any evidence that might weaken your position?

The following questions may help you respond to a reader's potential objection.

- Can you concede the point to the opposition but challenge the point's importance or usefulness?
- Can you explain why readers should consider a new perspective or question a piece of evidence?
- Should you explain how your position responds to contradictory evidence?
- Can you suggest a different interpretation of the evidence?

When you write, use phrasing to signal to readers that you're about to present an objection. Often the signal phrase can go in the lead sentence of a paragraph.

Critics of this view argue that . . .
Some readers might point out that . . .
Researchers challenge these claims by . . .

It might seem at first that drawing attention to an opposing point of view or contradictory evidence would weaken your argument. But by anticipating and countering objections, you show yourself as a reasonable and well-informed writer who has a thorough understanding of the significance of the issue.

There is no best place in an essay to deal with opposing views. Often it is useful to summarize the opposing position early in your essay. After stating your thesis, but before developing your own arguments, you might have a paragraph that addresses the most important counterargument. Or you can anticipate objections paragraph by paragraph as you develop your case.

Wherever you decide to address opposing arguments, you will enhance your credibility if you explain the arguments of others accurately and fairly.

6j Build common ground.

As you counter opposing arguments, try to seek out one or two assumptions you might share with readers who do not initially agree with your views. If you can show that you share their concerns, your readers will be more likely to accept that your argument is valid. For example, to persuade people opposed to controlling the deer population with a regulated hunting season, a state wildlife commission would have to show that it too cares about preserving deer and does not want them to die needlessly. Having established these values in common, the commission might be able to persuade critics that reducing the total number of deer prevents starvation caused by overpopulation.

People believe that intelligence and decency support their side of an argument. To be persuaded, they must see these qualities in your argument. Otherwise, they will persist in their opposition.

6k Sample student writing: Argument

In the paper that begins on the next page, student writer Sam Jacobs argues that the shift from print to online news benefits readers by providing them with opportunities to produce news and to think more critically as consumers of news. Notice how he appeals to his readers by presenting opposing views fairly before providing his own arguments.

In writing the paper, Jacobs consulted both print and online sources. When he quotes, summarizes, or paraphrases information from a source, he cites the source with an MLA (Modern Language Association) in-text citation. Citations in the paper refer readers to the list of works cited at the end of the paper. (For more details about citing sources, see 54.)

A guide to writing an argument essay appears on pages 118–19.

LaunchPadSolo macmillanhighered.com/rules8e

6 Reading and writing arguments

> Sample student writing: Jacobs, "From Lecture to Conversation: Redefining What's 'Fit to Print'" (argument)

Jacobs 1

Sam Jacobs

Professor Alperini

English 101

5 November 2013

From Lecture to Conversation:

Redefining What's "Fit to Print"

In his opening sentences, Jacobs provides background for his thesis.

"All the news that's fit to print," the motto of the *New York Times* since 1896, plays with the word *fit*, asserting that a news story must be newsworthy and must not exceed the limits of the printed page. The increase in online news consumption, however, challenges both meanings of the word *fit*, allowing producers and consumers alike to rethink who decides which topics are worth covering and how extensive that coverage should be. Any cultural shift usually means that something is lost, but in this case there are clear gains. The shift from print to online news provides unprecedented opportunities for readers to become more engaged with the news, to hold journalists accountable, and to participate as producers, not simply as consumers.

Thesis states the main point.

Jacobs does not need a citation for common knowledge.

Guided by journalism's code of ethics—accuracy, objectivity, and fairness—print news reporters have gathered and delivered stories according to what editors decide is fit for their readers. Except for op-ed pages and letters to the editor, print news has traditionally had a one-sided relationship with its readers. The print news media's reputation for objective reporting has been held up as "a stop sign" for readers, sending a clear message that no further inquiry is necessary (Weinberger). With the rise of the Internet, however, this model has been criticized by journalists such as Dan Gillmor, founder of the Center for

Source is cited in MLA style.

Marginal annotations indicate MLA-style formatting and **effective writing**.

Jacobs 2

Citizen Media, who argues that traditional print journalism treats "news as a lecture," whereas online news is "more of a conversation" (xxiv). Print news arrives on the doorstep every morning as a fully formed lecture, a product created without participation from its readership. By contrast, online news invites readers to participate in a collaborative process—to question and even help produce the content.

One of the most important advantages online news offers over print news is the presence of built-in hyperlinks, which carry readers from one electronic document to another. If readers are curious about the definition of a term, the roots of a story, or other perspectives on a topic, links provide a path. Links help readers become more critical consumers of information by engaging them in a totally new way. For instance, the link embedded in the story "Credit-Shy: Younger Generation Is More Likely to Stick to a Cash-Only Policy" (Sapin) allows readers to find out more about the financial trends of young adults and provides statistics that confirm the article's accuracy (see fig. 1). Other links in the article widen the conversation. These kinds of links give readers the opportunity to conduct their own evaluation of the evidence and verify the journalist's claims.

Transition moves from Jacobs's main argument to specific examples.

Links provide a kind of transparency impossible in print because they allow readers to see through online news to the "sources, disagreements, and the personal assumptions and values" that may have influenced a news story (Weinberger). The International Center for Media and the Public Agenda underscores the importance of news organizations letting "customers in on the often tightly held little secrets of journalism." To do so, they suggest, will lead to "accountability and accountability leads to

Jacobs clarifies key terms (*transparency* and *accountability*).

Jacobs 3

credibility" ("Openness"). These tools alone don't guarantee that news producers will be responsible and trustworthy, but they encourage an open and transparent environment that benefits news consumers.

Jacobs develops the thesis.

Not only has technology allowed readers to become more critical news consumers, but it also has helped some to become news producers. The Web gives ordinary people the power to report on the day's events. Anyone with an Internet connection can publish on blogs and Web sites, engage in online discussion forums, and contribute video and audio recordings. Citizen journalists with laptops, cell phones, and digital camcorders have become news producers alongside large news organizations.

Opposing views are presented fairly.

Not everyone embraces the spread of unregulated news reporting online. Critics point out that citizen journalists are not necessarily trained to be fair or ethical, for example, nor are they subject to editorial oversight. Acknowledging that citizen reporting is more immediate and experimental, critics also question its accuracy and accountability: "While it has its place . . . it really isn't journalism at all, and it opens up information flow to the strong probability of fraud and abuse. . . . Information without journalistic standards is called gossip," writes David Hazinski in the *Atlanta Journal-Constitution* (23A). In his book *Losing the News*, media specialist Alex S. Jones argues that what passes for news today is in fact "pseudo news" and is "far less reliable" than traditional print news (27). Even a supporter like Gillmor is willing to agree that citizen journalists are "nonexperts," but he argues that they are "using technology to make a profound contribution, and a real difference" (140).

Jacobs counters opposing arguments.

Jacobs 4

Citizen reporting made a difference in the wake of Hurricane Katrina in 2005. Armed with cell phones and laptops, regular citizens relayed critical news updates in a rapidly developing crisis, often before traditional journalists were even on the scene. In 2006, the enormous

A vivid example helps Jacobs make his point.

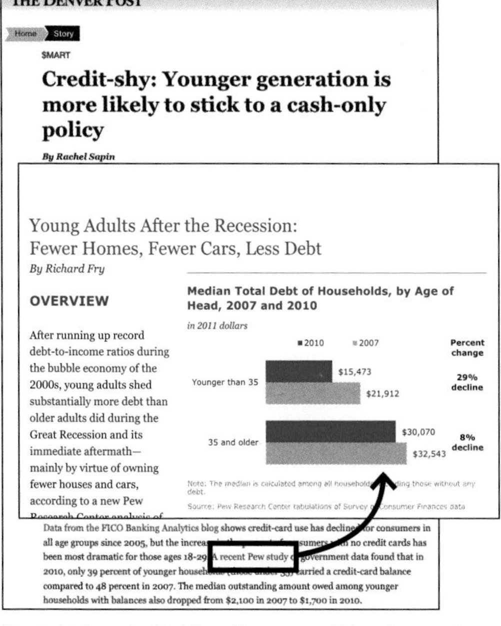

THE DENVER POST

Home › Story

$MART

Credit-shy: Younger generation is more likely to stick to a cash-only policy

By Rachel Sapin

Young Adults After the Recession: Fewer Homes, Fewer Cars, Less Debt

By Richard Fry

OVERVIEW

After running up record debt-to-income ratios during the bubble economy of the 2000s, young adults shed substantially more debt than older adults did during the Great Recession and its immediate aftermath—mainly by virtue of owning fewer houses and cars, according to a new Pew Research Center analysis of

Median Total Debt of Households, by Age of Head, 2007 and 2010

in 2011 dollars

	2010	2007	Percent change
Younger than 35	$15,473	$21,912	29% decline
35 and older	$30,070	$32,543	8% decline

Note: The median is calculated among all households [illegible]ding those without any debt.

Source: Pew Research Center tabulations of Survey [illegible] Consumer Finances data

Data from the FICO Banking Analytics blog shows credit-card use has decline[illegible] for consumers in all age groups since 2005, but the increa[illegible]sumers [illegible] no credit cards has been most dramatic for those ages 18-29. A recent Pew study [illegible] government data found that in 2010, only 39 percent of younger househ[illegible] carried a credit-card balance compared to 48 percent in 2007. The median outstanding amount owed among younger households with balances also dropped from $2,100 in 2007 to $1,700 in 2010.

Fig. 1. Links embedded in online news articles allow readers to move from the main story to original sources, related articles, or background materials. The link in this online article (Sapin) points to a statistical report by the Pew Research Center, the original source of the author's data on young adults' spending practices.

Jacobs 5

contributions of citizen journalists were recognized when the New Orleans *Times-Picayune* received the Pulitzer Prize in public service for its online coverage—largely citizen-generated—of Hurricane Katrina. In recognizing the paper's "meritorious public service," the Pulitzer Prize board credited the newspaper's blog for "heroic, multi-faceted coverage of [the storm] and its aftermath" ("2006 Pulitzer"). Writing for the *Online Journalism Review,* Mark Glaser emphasizes the role that blog updates played in saving storm victims' lives. Further, he calls the *Times-Picayune*'s partnership with citizen journalists a "watershed for online journalism."

Jacobs uses specific evidence for support.

The Internet has enabled consumers to participate in a new way in reading, questioning, interpreting, and reporting the news. Decisions about appropriate content and coverage are no longer exclusively in the hands of news editors. Ordinary citizens now have a meaningful voice in the conversation—a hand in deciding what's "fit to print." Some skeptics worry about the apparent free-for-all and loss of tradition. But the expanding definition of news provides opportunities for consumers to be more engaged with events in their communities, their nations, and the world.

Conclusion echoes the thesis without repeating it.

Jacobs 6

Works Cited

Works cited page uses MLA style.

Gillmor, Dan. *We the Media: Grassroots Journalism by the People, for the People*. Sebastopol: O'Reilly, 2006. Print.

Glaser, Mark. "NOLA.com Blogs and Forums Help Save Lives after Katrina." *OJR: The Online Journalism Review*. Knight Digital Media Center, 13 Sept. 2005. Web. 23 Oct. 2013.

Hazinski, David. "Unfettered 'Citizen Journalism' Too Risky." *Atlanta Journal-Constitution* 13 Dec. 2007: 23A. *General OneFile*. Web. 21 Oct. 2013.

Jones, Alex S. *Losing the News*: *The Future of the News That Feeds Democracy*. New York: Oxford UP, 2009. Print.

"Openness and Accountability: A Study of Transparency in Global Media Outlets." *ICMPA: International Center for Media and the Public Agenda*. Intl. Center for Media and the Public Agenda, 2006. Web. 21 Oct. 2013.

Sapin, Rachel. "Credit-Shy: Younger Generation Is More Likely to Stick to a Cash-Only Policy." *Denverpost.com*. Denver Post, 26 Aug. 2013. Web. 23 Oct. 2013.

"The 2006 Pulitzer Prize Winners: Public Service." *The Pulitzer Prizes*. Columbia U, n.d. Web. 21 Oct. 2013.

Weinberger, David. "Transparency Is the New Objectivity." *Joho the Blog*. David Weinberger, 19 July 2009. Web. 22 Oct. 2013.

List is alphabetized by authors' last names (or by title when a work has no author).

Abbreviation "n.d." indicates that the online source has no update date.

Writing guide | Argument essay

Composing an **argument** gives you the opportunity to take a position on a debatable issue. You say to your readers: "Here is my position, here is the evidence that supports the position, and here is my response to other positions on the issue." A sample argument essay begins on page 112.

Key features

- **A thesis, stated as a clear position on a debatable issue,** frames an argument essay. The issue is debatable because reasonable people disagree about it.
- **An examination of the issue's context** indicates why the issue is important, why readers should care about it, or how your position fits into the debates surrounding the topic.
- **Sufficient, representative, and relevant evidence** supports the argument's claims. Evidence needs to be specific and persuasive; quoted, summarized, or paraphrased fairly and accurately; and cited correctly.
- **Opposing positions are summarized and countered.** By anticipating and countering objections to your position, you establish common ground with readers and show yourself as a reasonable and well-informed writer.

Writing your argument

EXPLORE

Generate ideas by brainstorming responses to questions such as the following.

- What is the debate around your issue? What sources will help you learn more about your issue?
- What position will you take? Why does your position need to be argued?
- What evidence supports your position? What evidence makes you question your position?
- What types of appeals — *ethos*, *logos*, *pathos* — might you use to persuade readers? How will you build common ground with your readers?
- Might a reader question any of your assumptions or offer an alternative perspective? If so, how might you anticipate and counter objections to your position?

DRAFT

Try to figure out the best way to structure your argument. A typical outline might include the following steps: Capture readers' attention; state your position; give background information; outline your major claims with specific evidence; recognize and respond to opposing points of view; and end by reinforcing your point and why it matters.

As you draft, think about the best order for your claims. You could organize by strength, building to your strongest argument (instead of starting with your strongest), or by concerns your audience might have.

REVISE

Ask your reviewers for specific feedback. Here are some questions to guide their comments.

- Is the thesis clear? Is the issue debatable?
- Is the evidence persuasive? Is more needed?
- Is your argument organized logically?
- Are there any flaws in your reasoning or assumptions that weaken the argument?
- Have you presented yourself as a knowledgeable, trustworthy writer?
- Does the conclusion pull together your entire argument? How might the conclusion be more effective?

7 Speaking confidently

Speaking and writing draw on many of the same skills. Effective speakers, like effective writers, identify their purpose, audience, and context. They project themselves as informed and reasonable, establish common ground with listeners, and use specific, memorable language and techniques to capture their audience's attention.

In many college classes, you'll be assigned to give oral presentations. The more comfortable you become speaking in different settings, the easier it will be when you give a formal presentation.

You can develop informal speaking skills by contributing to class discussions, responding to the comments of fellow students, and playing an active role in team-based learning.

7a Identify your purpose, audience, and context.

In planning your presentation, strategize a bit: Identify your purpose (reason) for speaking; your audience (listeners); and the context (situation) in which you will speak.

PURPOSE	Begin by asking: Why am I speaking? What is my goal? Possible goals might include the following: to inform, persuade, evaluate, recommend, and call to action.
AUDIENCE	Effective speakers identify the expectations of their audience and shape their material to these expectations. Assess what your audience may already know and believe, what objections you might need to anticipate, and how you might interact with your listeners.
CONTEXT	Ask: What is the situation for my speech? An assignment for a course? The presentation of a group project? A community meeting? And how much time do I have to speak? The answers to these questions will help you shape the presentation for your particular speaking situation.

7b Prepare a presentation.

Knowing your subject

You need to know your subject well in order to talk about it confidently. Although you can't pack too much material into a short speech, you need to speak knowledgeably to engage your audience. In preparing your speech, do some research to collect evidence — facts, statistics, visuals, expert testimony — that will support your points.

Developing a clear structure

A good presentation is easily followed because it has a clear beginning, middle, and end. In your introduction, forecast the purpose and structure of your presentation and the question or problem you are addressing so your audience can anticipate where you are going. Organize the body of an informative speech to help your audience remember key points of information, and conclude your presentation by giving listeners a sense of completion. Restate the key points, and borrow an image or phrasing from your opening to make the speech come full circle.

Using signposts and repetition

As you speak, use signpost language to remind the audience of your purpose and key points. Signposts guide listeners—"The shift to online news has three important benefits for consumers"—and help them to understand the transition from one point to the next—"The second benefit is. . . ." By repeating phrases, you emphasize the importance of key points and help listeners remember them.

Writing for the ear, not the eye

Use an engaging, lively style so that the audience will enjoy listening to you. Be sure to use straightforward spoken language that's easy on the ear, not too complicated or too abstract. Keep your sentences short and direct so that listeners can easily follow your presentation.

Integrating sources with signal language

If you are using sources, do so responsibly. As you speak, be sure to acknowledge your sources with signal phrases ("According to *New York Times* columnist David Brooks . . ."). If you have slides, signal phrases or citations can be included on the slides.

Using multimedia purposefully

Well-chosen visuals or audio can enhance your presentation and add variety. A photograph might highlight an environmental problem, a line graph can quickly show a trend over time, and a brief video clip can offer visual evidence to capture listeners' attention. Multimedia elements can convey information powerfully, but always consider how they support your purpose and how your audience will respond.

LaunchPadSolo **macmillanhighered.com/rules8e**
7 Speaking confidently
> Writing practice: Preparing a presentation

7c Focus on delivery.

Establishing a relationship

If you give an audience your full attention, they will return it. Before delivering your speech, make steady eye contact with your listeners, introduce yourself, and help your audience connect with you.

Starting strong and ending strong

Beginnings and endings of speeches are critical to gain and hold an audience's attention. Plan your opening strategy: Will you pose a question and ask for a show of hands? Will you tell a brief personal story? End strong by looking directly at your audience as you review your key points. Finish by thanking your audience and inviting questions.

Boosting your confidence

Effective speaking starts with a good script and a clear message. However, pay attention to additional details that will boost your confidence and strengthen your presentation:

- Dress for the occasion.
- Make eye contact; use body language and hand gestures to emphasize points.
- Practice, practice, practice. Speak out loud in front of a mirror or a friend, and practice using visual aids.
- Time your rehearsal.
- Know the setting in which you'll deliver your talk.

NOTE: Speakers have the main role in presentations, but audience members have important roles, too. Speakers need encouragement, so look at the speaker, make eye contact, and be ready with a question about an interesting or surprising point.

LaunchPadSolo **macmillanhighered.com/rules8e**

7 Speaking confidently
> Writing practice: Focusing on your delivery
> Writing practice: Learning from another speaker (persuasive speech)
> Writing practice: Learning from another speaker (informative speech)

7d Remix an essay for a presentation.

You may be assigned to adapt an essay that you have already written for delivery to a listening audience. Student writer Sam Jacobs revised his essay as he prepared a speaking script. Compare the first paragraph of Jacob's essay (p. 112) with the opening lines for his presentation below.

Good afternoon, everyone. I'm Sam Jacobs.

Friendly opening establishes a relationship with the audience.

Jacobs starts with his key question and engages the audience immediately.

Today I want to explore this question: How do consumers benefit from reading news online? But first let me have a quick show of hands: How many of you read news online? If you answered yes, you are part of the 71% of young Americans, ages 18 to 29, who read their news online, according to the Pew Center. We've grown up in a digital generation, consuming news on every possible mobile device, especially our cell phones. Most of us don't miss the newspaper arriving on the doorstep every morning. And because we expect to read news online, we take it for granted. But if we take it for granted, we might miss the benefits of participating as producers of news, not simply as consumers. The three benefits I want to explore are . . .

Jacobs uses a source responsibly and integrates it well.

Establishes common ground with the audience.

Jacobs repeats words and phrases for emphasis and uses signposts to make it easier for his listeners to follow his ideas.

LaunchPadSolo macmillanhighered.com/rules8e

7 Speaking confidently

> Writing practice: Remixing an essay for an oral presentation

Clarity

Grammar

Multilingual Writers and ESL Challenges

Clarity 125

Grammar 187

Multilingual Writers and ESL Challenges 255

Clarity

8 Prefer active verbs.

As a rule, choose an active verb and pair it with a subject that names the person or thing doing the action. Active verbs express meaning more emphatically and vigorously than their weaker counterparts — verbs in the passive voice or forms of the verb *be*.

PASSIVE	The pumps *were destroyed* by a surge of power.
BE VERB	A surge of power *was* responsible for the destruction of the pumps.
ACTIVE	A surge of power *destroyed* the pumps.

Verbs in the passive voice lack strength because their subjects receive the action instead of doing it. Forms of the verb *be* (*be, am, is, are, was, were, being, been*) lack vigor because they convey no action.

Although passive verbs and the forms of *be* have legitimate uses, choose an active verb whenever possible. Even among active verbs, some are more vigorous and colorful than others. Carefully selected verbs can energize a piece of writing.

▶ **The goalie crouched low, ~~reached~~ swept out his stick, and ~~sent~~ hooked the rebound away from the mouth of the net.**

> **Academic English** Although you may be tempted to avoid the passive voice completely, keep in mind that some writing situations call for it, especially scientific writing. For appropriate uses of the passive voice, see page 127; for advice about forming the passive voice, see 28b and 47c.

8a Use the active voice unless you have a good reason for choosing the passive.

In the active voice, the subject does the action; in the passive voice, the subject receives the action (see also 47c). Although both voices are grammatically correct, the active voice is usually more effective because it is clearer and more direct.

ACTIVE	Hernando *caught* the fly ball.
PASSIVE	The fly ball *was caught* by Hernando.

Passive sentences often identify the actor in a *by* phrase, as in the preceding example. Sometimes, however, that phrase is omitted, and who or what is responsible for the action becomes unclear: *The fly ball was caught.*

Most of the time, you will want to emphasize the actor, so you should use the active voice. To replace a passive verb with an active one, make the actor the subject of the sentence.

The settlers stripped the land of timber before realizing
► ~~The land was stripped of timber before the settlers realized~~ **the** ^ **consequences of their actions.**

The revision emphasizes the actors (*settlers*) by naming them in the subject.

Appropriate uses of the passive

The passive voice is appropriate if you want to emphasize the receiver of the action or to minimize the importance of the actor.

APPROPRIATE PASSIVE	Many Hawaiians *were forced* to leave their homes after the earthquake.
APPROPRIATE PASSIVE	Near harvest time, the tobacco plants *are sprayed* with a chemical to slow the growth of suckers.

The writer of the first sentence wished to emphasize the receiver of the action, *Hawaiians*. The writer of the second sentence wished to focus on the tobacco plants, not on the people spraying them.

In much scientific writing, the passive voice properly emphasizes the experiment or process being described, not the researcher. Check with your instructor for the preference in your discipline.

8b Replace *be* verbs that result in dull or wordy sentences.

Not every *be* verb needs replacing. The forms of *be* (*be, am, is, are, was, were, being, been*) work well when you want to link a subject to a noun that clearly renames it or to an adjective that describes it: *Orchard House was the home of Louisa May Alcott. The harvest will be bountiful after the summer rains.*

Be verbs also are essential as helping verbs before present participles (*is flying, are disappearing*) to express ongoing action: *Derrick was fighting the fire when his wife went into labor.* (See 27f.)

If using a *be* verb makes a sentence needlessly dull and wordy, however, consider replacing it. Often a phrase following the verb contains a noun or an adjective (such as *violation, resistant*) that suggests a more vigorous, active verb (*violate, resist*).

► **Burying nuclear waste in Antarctica would ~~be in violation of~~ violate an international treaty.**

Violate is less wordy and more vigorous than *be in violation of.*

► **When Rosa Parks ~~was resistant to~~ resisted giving up her seat on the bus, she became a civil rights hero.**

Resisted is stronger than *was resistant to.*

8c As a rule, choose a subject that names the person or thing doing the action.

In weak, unemphatic prose, both the actor and the action may be buried in sentence elements other than the subject and the verb. In the following weak sentence, for example, both the actor and the action appear in prepositional phrases, word groups that do not receive much attention from readers.

WEAK	The institution of the New Deal had the effect of reversing some of the economic inequalities of the Great Depression.
EMPHATIC	The New Deal reversed some of the economic inequalities of the Great Depression.

Consider the subjects and verbs of the two versions — *institution had* versus *New Deal reversed.* The second version expresses the writer's point more emphatically.

► **~~The use of~~ Pure oxygen can ~~cause~~ heal~~ing in~~ wounds that are otherwise untreatable.**

In the original sentence, the subject and verb — *use can cause* — express the point blandly. *Pure oxygen can heal* makes the point more emphatically and directly.

EXERCISE 8–1 Revise unemphatic sentences by replacing passive verbs or *be* verbs with active alternatives. You may need to name in the subject the person or thing doing the action. If a sentence is emphatic, do not change it. Possible revisions appear in the back of the book. *More practice:* LaunchPadSolo

> The ranger doused the campfire before giving us
> ~~The campfire was doused by the ranger before we were given~~ a ticket for unauthorized use of a campsite.

a. The Prussians were victorious over the Saxons in 1745.
b. The entire operation is managed by Ahmed, the producer.
c. The sea kayaks were expertly paddled by the tour guides.
d. At the crack of rocket and mortar blasts, I jumped from the top bunk and landed on my buddy below, who was crawling on the floor looking for his boots.
e. There were shouting protesters on the courthouse steps.

9 Balance parallel ideas.

If two or more ideas are parallel, they are easier to grasp when expressed in parallel grammatical form. Single words should be balanced with single words, phrases with phrases, clauses with clauses.

> A kiss can be a comma, a question mark, or an exclamation point. —Mistinguett

> This novel is not to be tossed lightly aside, but to be hurled with great force. —Dorothy Parker

> In matters of principle, stand like a rock; in matters of taste, swim with the current. —Thomas Jefferson

Writers often use parallelism to create emphasis. (See 14f.)

LaunchPadSolo **macmillanhighered.com/rules8e**

8 Active verbs
> Exercises: 8-2 to 8-6
> LearningCurve: Active and passive voice

9a Balance parallel ideas in a series.

Readers expect items in a series to appear in parallel grammatical form. When one or more of the items violate readers' expectations, a sentence will be needlessly awkward.

▶ **Children who study music also learn confidence, discipline, and ~~they are creative.~~** creativity.

The revision presents all the items in the series as nouns: *confidence*, *discipline*, and *creativity*.

▶ **Impressionist painters believed in focusing on ordinary subjects, capturing the effects of light on those subjects, and ~~to use~~** using **short brushstrokes.**

The revision uses *-ing* forms for all the items in the series: *focusing*, *capturing*, and *using*.

▶ **Racing to get to work on time, Sam drove down the middle of the road, ran one red light, and** ignored **two stop signs.**

The revision adds a verb to make the three items parallel: *drove*, *ran*, and *ignored*.

In headings and lists, aim for as much parallelism as the content allows.

9b Balance parallel ideas presented as pairs.

When pairing ideas, underscore their connection by expressing them in similar grammatical form. Paired ideas are usually connected in one of these ways:

- with a coordinating conjunction such as *and*, *but*, or *or*
- with a pair of correlative conjunctions such as *either . . . or* or *not only . . . but also*
- with a word introducing a comparison, usually *than* or *as*

Parallel ideas linked with coordinating conjunctions

Coordinating conjunctions (*and*, *but*, *or*, *nor*, *for*, *so*, and *yet*) link ideas of equal importance. When those ideas are closely parallel in content, they should be expressed in parallel grammatical form.

▶ **Emily Dickinson's poetry features the use of dashes and ~~capitalizing~~ the capitalization of common words.**

The revision balances the nouns *use* and *capitalization*.

▶ **Many states are reducing property taxes for home owners and ~~extend~~ extending tax credits to renters.**

The revision balances the verb *reducing* with the verb *extending*.

Parallel ideas linked with correlative conjunctions

Correlative conjunctions come in pairs: *either . . . or*, *neither . . . nor*, *not only . . . but also*, *both . . . and*, *whether . . . or*. Make sure that the grammatical structure following the second half of the pair is the same as that following the first half.

▶ **Thomas Edison was not only a prolific inventor but also ~~was~~ a successful entrepreneur.**

The words *a prolific inventor* follow *not only*, so *a successful entrepreneur* should follow *but also*. Repeating *was* creates an unbalanced effect.

▶ **The clerk told me either to change my flight or to take the train.**

To change my flight, which follows *either*, should be balanced with *to take the train*, which follows *or*.

Comparisons linked with *than* or *as*

In comparisons linked with *than* or *as*, the elements being compared should be expressed in parallel grammatical structure.

▶ **It is easier to speak in abstractions than ~~grounding~~ to ground one's thoughts in reality.**

To speak is balanced with *to ground*.

Comparisons should also be logical and complete. (See 10c.)

▶ **In Pueblo culture, according to Silko, ~~to write~~ writing down the stories of a tribe is not the same as "keeping track of all the stories" (290).**

When you are quoting from a source, parallel grammatical structure—such as *writing . . . keeping*—helps create continuity between your sentence and the words from the source. (See 56a on citing sources in MLA style.)

9c Repeat function words to clarify parallels.

Function words such as prepositions (*by*, *to*) and subordinating conjunctions (*that*, *because*) signal the grammatical nature of the word groups to follow. Although you can sometimes omit them, be sure to include them whenever they signal parallel structures that readers might otherwise miss.

▶ **Our study revealed that left-handed students were more likely to have trouble with classroom desks and** that **rearranging desks for exam periods was useful.**

A second subordinating conjunction helps readers sort out the two parallel ideas: *that* left-handed students have trouble with classroom desks and *that* rearranging desks was useful.

EXERCISE 9–1 Edit the following sentences to correct faulty parallelism. Possible revisions appear in the back of the book.

More practice: LaunchPadSolo

Rowena began her workday by pouring a cup of coffee and ~~checked~~ checking **her e-mail.**

a. Police dogs are used for finding lost children, tracking criminals, and the detection of bombs and illegal drugs.

LaunchPadSolo **macmillanhighered.com/rules8e**

9 Parallel ideas

> Exercises: 9–2 to 9–6

> LearningCurve: Parallelism

b. Hannah told her rock-climbing partner that she bought a new harness and of her desire to climb Otter Cliffs.
c. It is more difficult to sustain an exercise program than starting one.
d. During basic training, I was not only told what to do but also what to think.
e. Jan wanted to drive to the wine country or at least Sausalito.

10 Add needed words.

Sometimes writers leave out words intentionally, and the meaning of the sentence is not affected. But leaving out words can occasionally cause confusion for readers or make the sentence ungrammatical. Readers need to see at a glance how the parts of a sentence are connected.

Multilingual

Languages sometimes differ in the need for certain words. In particular, be alert for missing articles, verbs, subjects, or expletives. See 29, 30a, and 30b.

10a Add words needed to complete compound structures.

In compound structures, words are often left out for economy: *Tom is a man who means what he says and* [*who*] *says what he means.* Such omissions are acceptable as long as the omitted words are common to both parts of the compound structure.

If a sentence defies grammar or idiom because an omitted word is not common to both parts of the compound structure, the simplest solution is to put the word back in.

▶ **Advertisers target customers whom they identify through demographic research or** ^who **have purchased their product in the past.**

The word *who* must be included because *whom . . . have purchased* is not grammatically correct.

accepted
▶ **Mayor Davis never has and never will accept a bribe.**
^

Has . . . accept is not grammatically correct.

in
▶ **Many South Pacific islanders still believe and live by ancient laws.**
^

Believe . . . by is not idiomatic in English. (For a list of common idioms, see 18d.)

NOTE: Even when the omitted word is common to both parts of the compound structure, occasionally it must be inserted to avoid ambiguity.

My favorite *professor* and *mentor* influenced my choice of a career. [Professor and mentor are the same person.]

My favorite *professor* and *my mentor* influenced my choice of a career. [Professor and mentor are two different people; *my* must be repeated.]

10b Add the word *that* if there is any danger of misreading without it.

If there is no danger of misreading, the word *that* may be omitted when it introduces a subordinate clause. *The value of a principle is the number of things* [*that*] *it will explain.* When a sentence might be misread without *that*, however, include the word.

▶ **In his famous obedience experiments, psychologist Stanley**
that
Milgram discovered ordinary people were willing to inflict
^
physical pain on strangers.

Milgram didn't discover ordinary people; he discovered that ordinary people were willing to inflict pain on strangers. The word *that* tells readers to expect a clause, not just *ordinary people*, as the direct object of *discovered*.

10c Add words needed to make comparisons logical and complete.

Comparisons should be made between items that are alike. To compare unlike items is illogical and distracting.

▸ **The forests of North America are much more extensive than** those of **Europe.** ^

Forests must be compared with forests, not with all of Europe.

▸ **Some say that Ella Fitzgerald's renditions of Cole Porter's songs are better than any other** ~~**singer.**~~ singer's. ^

Ella Fitzgerald's renditions cannot logically be compared with a singer. The revision uses the possessive form *singer's*, with the word *renditions* being implied.

Sometimes the word *other* must be inserted to make a comparison logical.

▸ **Jupiter is larger than any** other ^ **planet in our solar system.**

Jupiter is a planet, and it cannot be larger than itself.

Sometimes the word *as* must be inserted to make a comparison grammatically complete.

▸ **The city of Lowell is as old,** as ^ **if not older than, the neighboring city of Lawrence.**

The construction *as old* is not complete without a second *as*: *as old as . . . the neighboring city of Lawrence.*

Comparisons should be complete enough to ensure clarity. The reader should understand what is being compared.

INCOMPLETE Brand X is less salty.

COMPLETE Brand X is less salty than Brand Y.

Finally, comparisons should leave no ambiguity for readers. If more than one interpretation is possible, revise the sentence to state clearly which interpretation you intend. In the following ambiguous sentence, two interpretations are possible.

AMBIGUOUS Ken helped me more than my roommate.

CLEAR Ken helped me more than *he helped* my roommate.

CLEAR Ken helped me more than my roommate *did*.

10d Add the articles *a*, *an*, and *the* where necessary for grammatical completeness.

It is not always necessary to repeat articles with paired items: *We bought a computer and printer.* However, if one of the items requires *a* and the other requires *an*, both articles must be included.

an
► **We bought a computer and antivirus program.**
^

Articles are sometimes omitted in recipes and other instructions that are meant to be followed while they are being read. In nearly all other forms of writing, whether formal or informal, such omissions are inappropriate.

Multilingual

Choosing and using articles can be challenging for multilingual writers. See 29.

EXERCISE 10–1 Add any words needed for grammatical or logical completeness in the following sentences. Possible revisions appear in the back of the book. *More practice:* LaunchPadSolo

that
The officer feared the prisoner would escape.
^

a. A grapefruit or orange is a good source of vitamin C.
b. The women entering the military academy can expect haircuts as short as the male cadets.
c. Looking out the family room window, Sarah saw her favorite tree, which she had climbed as a child, was gone.
d. The graphic designers are interested and knowledgeable about producing posters for the balloon race.
e. The Great Barrier Reef is larger than any coral reef in the world.

LaunchPadSolo macmillanhighered.com/rules8e
10 Needed words
> Exercises: 10-2 to 10-5

11 Untangle mixed constructions.

A mixed construction contains sentence parts that do not sensibly fit together. The mismatch may be a matter of grammar or of logic.

11a Untangle the grammatical structure.

Once you begin a sentence, your choices are limited by the range of grammatical patterns in English. (See 47 and 48.) You cannot begin with one grammatical plan and switch without warning to another. Often you must rethink the purpose of the sentence and revise.

MIXED — For most drivers who have a blood alcohol content of .05 percent double their risk of causing an accident.

The writer begins the sentence with a long prepositional phrase and makes it the subject of the verb *double.* But a prepositional phrase can serve only as a modifier; it cannot be the subject of a sentence.

REVISED — For most drivers who have a blood alcohol content of .05 percent, the risk of causing an accident is doubled.

REVISED — Most drivers who have a blood alcohol content of .05 percent double their risk of causing an accident.

In the first revision, the writer begins with the prepositional phrase and finishes the sentence with a proper subject and verb (*risk . . . is doubled*). In the second revision, the writer stays with the original verb (*double*) and heads into the sentence another way, making *drivers* the subject of *double.*

Electing
▶ **~~When the country elects~~ a president is the most important** ^ **responsibility in a democracy.**

The adverb clause *When the country elects a president* cannot serve as the subject of the verb *is.* The revision replaces the adverb clause with a gerund phrase, a word group that can function as a subject. (See 48b and 48e.)

▸ **Although the United States is a wealthy nation, ~~but~~ more than 20 percent of our children live in poverty.**

The coordinating conjunction *but* cannot link a subordinate clause (*Although the United States . . .*) with an independent clause (*more than 20 percent of our children live in poverty*).

Occasionally a mixed construction is so tangled that it defies grammatical analysis. When this happens, back away from the sentence, rethink what you want to say, and then rewrite the sentence.

MIXED In the whole-word method, children learn to recognize entire words rather than by the phonics method in which they learn to sound out letters and groups of letters.

REVISED The whole-word method teaches children to recognize entire words; the phonics method teaches them to sound out letters and groups of letters.

Multilingual

English does not allow double subjects, nor does it allow an object or an adverb to be repeated in an adjective clause. Unlike some other languages, English does not allow a noun and a pronoun to be repeated in a sentence if they have the same grammatical function. See 30c and 30d.

▸ **My father ~~he~~ moved to Peru before he met my mother.**

▸ **~~The final exam~~ I should really study for ~~it~~ to pass the course.** [inserted: the final exam]

11b Straighten out the logical connections.

The subject and the predicate (the verb and its modifiers) should make sense together; when they don't, the error is known as *faulty predication.*

▸ **The court decided that ~~Tiffany's welfare~~ [inserted: Tiffany] would not be safe living with her abusive parents.**

Tiffany, not her welfare, may not be safe.

double personal exemption for the
▶ **Under the revised plan, the elderly, ~~who now receive a double personal exemption,~~ will be abolished.**

The exemption, not the elderly, will be abolished.

An appositive is a noun that renames a nearby noun. When an appositive and the noun it renames are not logically equivalent, the error is known as *faulty apposition.* (See 48c.)

Tax accounting,
▶ **~~The tax accountant,~~ a very lucrative profession, requires intelligence, patience, and attention to mathematical detail.**

The tax accountant is a person, not a profession.

11c Avoid *is when, is where,* and *reason . . . is because* constructions.

In formal English, many readers object to *is when, is where,* and *reason . . . is because* constructions on either grammatical or logical grounds.

Grammatically, the verb *is* (as well as *are, was,* and *were*) should be followed by a noun that renames the subject or by an adjective that describes the subject, not by an adverb clause beginning with *when, where,* or *because.* (See 48b and 48e.) Logically, the words *when, where,* or *because* suggest relations of time, place, and cause—relations that do not always make sense with *is, are, was,* or *were.*

▶ **The ~~reason the~~ experiment failed ~~is~~ because conditions in the lab were not sterile.**

The writer might have changed *because* to *that* (*The reason the experiment failed is that conditions in the lab were not sterile*), but the preceding revision is more concise.

a disorder suffered by people who
▶ **Anorexia nervosa is ~~where people~~ think they are too fat and diet to the point of starvation.**

Where refers to places. Anorexia nervosa is a disorder, not a place.

EXERCISE 11–1 Edit the following sentences to untangle mixed constructions. Possible revisions appear in the back of the book.

More practice: LaunchPadSolo

Taking
~~By taking~~ **the oath of allegiance made Ling a US citizen.**
^

a. Using surgical gloves is a precaution now worn by dentists to prevent contact with patients' blood and saliva.
b. A physician, the career my brother is pursuing, requires at least ten years of challenging work.
c. The reason the pharaohs had bad teeth was because tiny particles of sand found their way into Egyptian bread.
d. Recurring bouts of flu among team members set a record for number of games forfeited.
e. In this box contains the key to your future.

12 Repair misplaced and dangling modifiers.

Modifiers, whether they are single words, phrases, or clauses, should point clearly to the words they modify. As a rule, related words should be kept together.

12a Put limiting modifiers in front of the words they modify.

Limiting modifiers such as *only*, *even*, *almost*, *nearly*, and *just* should appear in front of a verb only if they modify the verb: *At first, I couldn't even touch my toes, much less grasp them.* If they limit the meaning of some other word in the sentence, they should be placed in front of that word.

► **The literature reveals that students ~~only~~ learn new vocabulary**
only
words when they are encouraged to read.
^

Only limits the meaning of the *when* clause.

LaunchPadSolo **macmillanhighered.com/rules8e**
11 Mixed constructions
> Exercises: 11-2 to 11-5

just
▶ **If you ~~just~~ interview ^ chemistry majors, your picture of the student body's response to the new grading policies will be incomplete.**

The adverb *just* limits the meaning of *chemistry majors*, not *interview*.

When the limiting modifier *not* is misplaced, the sentence usually suggests a meaning the writer did not intend.

not
▶ **In the United States in 1860, ^ all black southerners were ~~not~~ slaves.**

The original sentence says that no black southerners were slaves. The revision makes the writer's real meaning clear: Some (but not all) black southerners were slaves.

12b Place phrases and clauses so that readers can see at a glance what they modify.

Although phrases and clauses can appear at some distance from the words they modify, make sure your meaning is clear. When phrases or clauses are oddly placed, absurd misreadings can result.

MISPLACED	The soccer player returned to the clinic where he had undergone emergency surgery in 2004 in a limousine sent by Adidas.
REVISED	Traveling in a limousine sent by Adidas, the soccer player returned to the clinic where he had undergone emergency surgery in 2004.

The revision corrects the false impression that the soccer player underwent emergency surgery in a limousine.

On the walls
▶ ^ **~~There~~ are many pictures of comedians who have performed at Gavin's. ^ ~~on the walls.~~**

The comedians weren't performing on the walls; the pictures were on the walls.

170-pound,
▶ **The robber was described as a ^ six-foot-tall man with a heavy mustache. ^ ~~weighing 170 pounds.~~**

The robber, not the mustache, weighed 170 pounds.

Occasionally the placement of a modifier leads to an ambiguity — a squinting modifier. In such a case, two revisions will be possible, depending on the writer's intended meaning.

AMBIGUOUS	The exchange students we met for coffee occasionally questioned us about our latest slang.
CLEAR	The exchange students we occasionally met for coffee questioned us about our latest slang.
CLEAR	The exchange students we met for coffee questioned us occasionally about our latest slang.

In the original version, it was not clear whether the meeting or the questioning happened occasionally. Both revisions eliminate the ambiguity.

12c Move awkwardly placed modifiers.

As a rule, a sentence should flow from subject to verb to object, without lengthy detours along the way. When a long adverbial word group separates a subject from its verb, a verb from its object, or a helping verb from its main verb, the result is often awkward.

▶ **~~Hong Kong,~~ A ~~a~~fter more than 150 years of British rule, Hong Kong was transferred back to Chinese control in 1997.**

There is no reason to separate the subject, *Hong Kong*, from the verb, *was transferred*, with a long phrase.

Multilingual

English does not allow an adverb to appear between a verb and its object. See 30f.

▶ **Yolanda lifted easily ~~easily~~ the fifty-pound weight.**

12d Avoid split infinitives when they are awkward.

An infinitive consists of *to* plus the base form of a verb: *to think, to breathe, to dance.* When a modifier appears between *to* and the verb, an infinitive is said to be "split": *to carefully balance, to completely understand.*

When a long word or a phrase appears between the parts of the infinitive, the result is usually awkward.

If possible, the
► **~~The~~ patient should try to ~~if possible~~ avoid going up and down stairs.**

Attempts to avoid split infinitives can result in equally awkward sentences. When alternative phrasing sounds unnatural, most experts allow—and even encourage—splitting the infinitive.

AWKWARD We decided actually to enforce the law.

BETTER We decided to actually enforce the law.

At times, neither the split infinitive nor its alternative sounds particularly awkward. In such situations, it is usually better not to split the infinitive, especially in formal writing.

► **Nursing students learn to ~~accurately~~ record a patient's vital signs/** accurately.

EXERCISE 12–1 Edit the following sentences to correct misplaced or awkwardly placed modifiers. Possible revisions appear in the back of the book. *More practice:* LaunchPadSolo

in a telephone survey
Answering questions can be annoying. ~~in a telephone survey.~~

a. More research is needed to effectively evaluate the risks posed by volcanoes in the Pacific Northwest.
b. Many students graduate with debt from college totaling more than fifty thousand dollars.
c. It is a myth that humans only use 10 percent of their brains.
d. A coolhunter is a person who can find in the unnoticed corners of modern society the next wave of fashion.
e. All geese do not fly beyond Narragansett for the winter.

LaunchPadSolo **macmillanhighered.com/rules8e**
12 Modifiers
> Exercises: 12–2 to 12–5
> LearningCurve: Modifiers

12e Repair dangling modifiers.

A dangling modifier fails to refer logically to any word in the sentence. Dangling modifiers are easy to repair, but they can be hard to recognize, especially in your own writing.

Recognizing dangling modifiers

Dangling modifiers are usually word groups (such as verbal phrases) that suggest but do not name an actor. When a sentence opens with such a modifier, readers expect the subject of the next clause to name the actor. If it doesn't, the modifier dangles.

- **Understanding the need to create checks and balances on power,** ^the framers of^ **the Constitution divided the government into three branches.**

  The framers of the Constitution (not the document itself) understood the need for checks and balances.

- **After completing seminary training,** ~~**women's**~~ ^women were often denied^ **access to the priesthood.** ~~**has often been denied.**~~

  Women (not their access to the priesthood) complete the training.

The following sentences illustrate four common kinds of dangling modifiers.

DANGLING *Deciding to join the navy*, the recruiter enthusiastically pumped Joe's hand. [Participial phrase]

DANGLING *Upon entering the doctor's office*, a skeleton caught my attention. [Preposition followed by a gerund phrase]

DANGLING *To satisfy her mother*, the piano had to be practiced every day. [Infinitive phrase]

DANGLING *Though not eligible for the clinical trial*, the doctor prescribed the drug for Ethan on compassionate grounds. [Elliptical clause with an understood subject and verb]

These dangling modifiers falsely suggest that the recruiter decided to join the navy, that the skeleton entered the doctor's office, that the piano intended to satisfy the mother, and that the doctor was not eligible for the clinical trial.

Although most readers will understand the writer's intended meaning in such sentences, the inadvertent humor can be distracting.

Repairing dangling modifiers

To repair a dangling modifier, you can revise the sentence in one of two ways:

- Name the actor in the subject of the sentence.
- Name the actor in the modifier.

Depending on your sentence, one of these revision strategies may be more appropriate than the other.

ACTOR NAMED IN SUBJECT

► **Upon entering the doctor's office, ^I noticed a skeleton. ~~caught my attention.~~**

► **To satisfy her mother, ^Jing-mei had to practice the piano ~~had to be practiced~~ every day.**

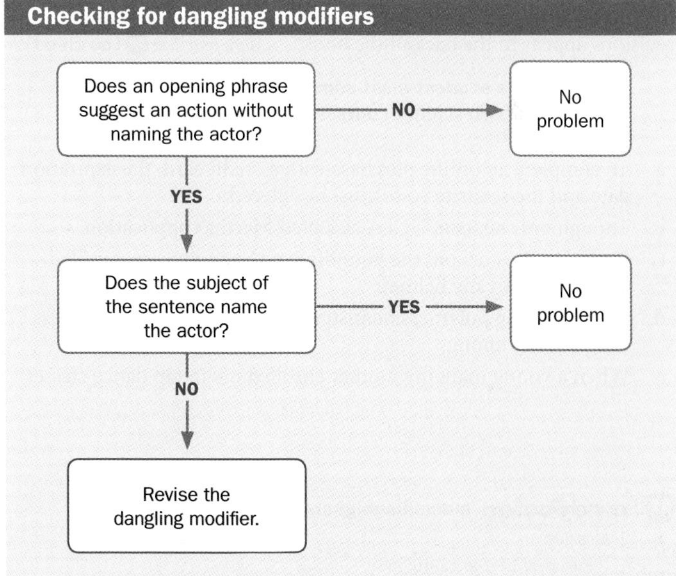
Checking for dangling modifiers
Does an opening phrase suggest an action without naming the actor?
NO
No problem
YES
Does the subject of the sentence name the actor?
YES
No problem
NO
Revise the dangling modifier.

ACTOR NAMED IN MODIFIER

When Joe decided
▸ ~~Deciding~~ to join the navy, the recruiter enthusiastically
his
pumped ~~Joe's~~ hand.

Ethan was
▸ Though not eligible for the clinical trial, the doctor prescribed
him
the drug for ~~Ethan~~ on compassionate grounds.

NOTE: You cannot repair a dangling modifier just by moving it. Consider, for example, the sentence about the skeleton. If you put the modifier at the end of the sentence (*A skeleton caught my attention upon entering the doctor's office*), you are still suggesting — absurdly, of course — that the skeleton entered the office. The only way to avoid the problem is to put the word *I* in the sentence, either as the subject or in the modifier.

I noticed
▸ Upon entering the doctor's office, a skeleton. ~~caught my attention.~~

As I entered
▸ ~~Upon entering~~ the doctor's office, a skeleton caught my attention.

EXERCISE 12–6 Edit the following sentences to correct dangling modifiers. Most sentences can be revised in more than one way. Possible revisions appear in the back of the book. *More practice:* LaunchPadSolo

a student must complete
To graduate, two science courses. ~~must be completed.~~

a. To complete an online purchase with a credit card, the expiration date and the security code must be entered.
b. Though only sixteen, UCLA accepted Martha's application.
c. Settled in the cockpit, the pounding of the engine was muffled only slightly by my helmet.
d. After studying polymer chemistry, computer games seemed less complex to Phuong.
e. When a young man, my mother enrolled me in tap dance classes.

LaunchPadSolo **macmillanhighered.com/rules8e**
12 Modifiers
> Exercises: 12–7 to 12–10
> LearningCurve: Modifiers

13 Eliminate distracting shifts.

The following sections can help you avoid unnecessary shifts that might distract or confuse your readers: shifts in point of view, in verb tense, in mood or voice, or from indirect to direct questions or quotations.

13a Make the point of view consistent in person and number.

The point of view of a piece of writing is the perspective from which it is written: first person (*I* or *we*), second person (*you*), or third person (*he*, *she*, *it*, *one*, *they*, or any noun).

The *I* (or *we*) point of view, which emphasizes the writer, is a good choice for informal letters and writing based primarily on personal experience. The *you* point of view, which emphasizes the reader, works well for giving advice or explaining how to do something. The third-person point of view, which emphasizes the subject, is appropriate in formal academic and professional writing.

Writers who have trouble settling on an appropriate point of view sometimes shift confusingly from one to another. The solution is to choose a suitable perspective and stay with it.

► **Our class practiced rescuing a victim trapped in a wrecked car. We learned to dismantle the car with the essential tools. ~~You~~ ^We were graded on ~~your~~ ^our speed and ~~your~~ ^our skill in freeing the victim.**

The writer should have stayed with the *we* point of view. *You* is inappropriate because the writer is not addressing readers directly. *You* should not be used in a vague sense meaning "anyone." (See 23d.)

► **~~One needs~~ ^You need a password and a credit card number to access the database. You will be billed at an hourly rate.**

You is an appropriate choice because the writer is giving advice directly to readers.

EXERCISE 13–1 Edit the following paragraph to eliminate distracting shifts in point of view (person and number).

More practice: LaunchPadSolo

When online dating first became available, many people thought that it would simplify romance. We believed that you could type in a list of criteria — sense of humor, college education, green eyes, good job — and a database would select the perfect mate. Thousands of people signed up for services and filled out their profiles, confident that true love was only a few mouse clicks away. As it turns out, however, virtual dating is no easier than traditional dating. I still have to contact the people I find, exchange e-mails and phone calls, and meet him in the real world. Although a database might produce a list of possibilities and screen out obviously undesirable people, you can't predict chemistry. More often than not, people who seem perfect online just don't click in person. Electronic services do help a single person expand their pool of potential dates, but it's no substitute for the hard work of romance.

13b Maintain consistent verb tenses.

Consistent verb tenses clearly establish the time of the actions being described. When a passage begins in one tense and then shifts without warning and for no reason to another, readers are distracted and confused.

► **There was no way I could fight the current and win. Just as I was losing hope, a stranger ~~jumps~~** jumped **off a passing boat and ~~swims~~** swam **toward me.**

The writer thought that the present tense (*jumps*, *swims*) would convey immediacy and drama. But having begun in the past tense (*could fight*, *was losing*), the writer should follow through in the past tense.

Writers often encounter difficulty with verb tenses when writing about literature. Because fictional events occur outside the time frames of real life, the past tense and the present tense may seem equally appropriate. The literary convention is to describe fictional events consistently in the present tense. (See pp. 249–50.)

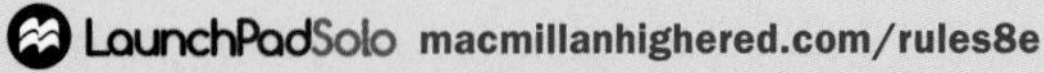

13 Shifts

> Exercises: 13–2, 13–9 to 13–11

> LearningCurve: Shifts

▶ **The scarlet letter is a punishment sternly placed on Hester's breast by the community, and yet it ~~was~~ is a fanciful and imaginative product of Hester's own needlework.**

EXERCISE 13–3 Edit the following paragraphs to eliminate distracting shifts in tense. *More practice:* LaunchPadSolo

The English colonists who settled in Massachusetts received assistance at first from the local Indian tribes, but by 1675 there had been friction between the English and the Indians for many years. On June 20 of that year, Metacomet, whom the colonists called Philip, leads the Wampanoag tribe in the first of a series of attacks on the colonial settlements. The war, known today as King Philip's War, rages on for more than a year and leaves three thousand Indians and six hundred colonists dead. Metacomet's attempt to retain power in his native land failed. Finally he too is killed, and the victorious colonists sell his wife and children into slavery.

The Indians did not leave records of their encounters with the English settlers, but the settlers recorded some of their experiences at the hands of the Indians. One of the few accounts to survive was written by a captured colonist, Mrs. Mary Rowlandson. She is a minister's wife who is kidnapped by an Indian war party and held captive for eleven weeks in 1676. Her history, *A Narrative of the Captivity and Restoration of Mrs. Mary Rowlandson*, tells the story of her experiences with the Wampanoags. Although it did not paint a completely balanced picture of the Indians, Rowlandson's narrative, which is considered a classic early American text, showed its author to be a keen observer of life in an Indian camp.

13c Make verbs consistent in mood and voice.

Unnecessary shifts in the mood of a verb can be distracting and confusing to readers. There are three moods in English: the *indicative*, used for facts, opinions, and questions; the *imperative*, used for orders or advice; and the *subjunctive*, used in certain contexts to express wishes or conditions contrary to fact (see 27g).

The following passage shifts confusingly from the indicative to the imperative mood.

LaunchPadSolo macmillanhighered.com/rules8e
13 Shifts
> Exercises: 13–4, 13–9 to 13–11
> LearningCurve: Shifts

▶ The counselor advised us to spread out our core requirements over two three semesters. ~~Also,~~ ^She also suggested that we^ pay attention to prerequisites for elective courses.

The writer began by reporting the counselor's advice in the indicative mood (*counselor advised*) and switched to the imperative mood (*pay attention*); the revision puts both sentences in the indicative.

A verb may be in either the active voice (with the subject doing the action) or the passive voice (with the subject receiving the action). (See 8a.) If a writer shifts without warning from one to the other, readers may be left wondering why.

▶ Each student completes a self-assessment~~.~~, ^gives it^ ~~The self-assessment is then given~~ to the teacher, and a copy ^exchanges^ ~~is exchanged~~ with a classmate.

Because the passage began in the active voice (*student completes*) and then switched to the passive (*self-assessment is given, copy is exchanged*), readers are left wondering who gives the self-assessment to the teacher and the classmate. The active voice, which is clearer and more direct, leaves no ambiguity.

13d Avoid sudden shifts from indirect to direct questions or quotations.

An indirect question reports a question without asking it: *We asked whether we could visit Miriam.* A direct question asks directly: *Can we visit Miriam?* Sudden shifts from indirect to direct questions are awkward. In addition, sentences containing such shifts are impossible to punctuate because indirect questions must end with a period and direct questions must end with a question mark. (See 38b.)

▶ I wonder whether Karla knew of the theft and, if so, ~~did she report~~ ^whether she reported^ it to the police~~?~~.

The revision poses both questions indirectly. The writer could also ask both questions directly: *Did Karla know of the theft, and, if so, did she report it to the police?*

An indirect quotation reports someone's words without quoting word for word: *Annabelle said that she is a Virgo.* A direct quotation presents the exact words of a speaker or writer, set off with quotation marks: *Annabelle said, "I am a Virgo."* Unannounced shifts from indirect to direct quotations are distracting and confusing, especially when the writer fails to insert the necessary quotation marks, as in the following example.

▶ **The patient said she had been experiencing heart palpitations**
asked me to
and ~~please~~ run as many tests as possible to identify the problem.
^

The revision reports the patient's words indirectly. The writer also could quote the words directly: *The patient said, "I have been experiencing heart palpitations. Please run as many tests as possible to identify the problem."*

EXERCISE 13–5 Edit the following sentences to make the verbs consistent in mood and voice and to eliminate distracting shifts from indirect to direct questions or quotations. Possible revisions appear in the back of the book. *More practice:* LaunchPadSolo

As a public relations intern, I wrote press releases, managed the
fielded all phone calls.
Web site, and ~~all phone calls were fielded by me.~~
^

a. An incredibly talented musician, Ray Charles mastered R&B, soul, and gospel styles. Even country music was performed well by him.
b. Environmentalists point out that shrimp farming in Southeast Asia is polluting water and making farmlands useless. They warn that action must be taken by governments before it is too late.
c. The samples were observed for five days before we detected any growth.
d. In his famous soliloquy, Hamlet contemplates whether death would be preferable to his difficult life and, if so, is he capable of committing suicide?
e. The lawyer told the judge that Miranda Hale was innocent and allow her to prove the allegations false.

LaunchPadSolo **macmillanhighered.com/rules8e**
13 Shifts
> Exercises: 13-7, 13-9 to 13-11
> LearningCurve: Shifts

EXERCISE 13–6 Edit the following sentences to eliminate distracting shifts. Possible revisions appear in the back of the book.

More practice: LaunchPadSolo

For many first-year engineering students, adjusting to a rigorous course load can be so challenging that ~~you~~ they sometimes feel overwhelmed.

a. A courtroom lawyer has more than a touch of theater in their blood.
b. The interviewer asked if we had brought our proof of citizenship and did we bring our passports?
c. The experienced reconnaissance scout knows how to make fast decisions and use sophisticated equipment to keep their team from being detected.
d. After the animators finish their scenes, the production designer arranges the clips according to the storyboard. Synchronization notes must also be made for the sound editor and the composer.
e. Madame Defarge is a sinister figure in Dickens's *A Tale of Two Cities.* On a symbolic level, she represents fate; like the Greek Fates, she knitted the fabric of individual destiny.

14 Emphasize key ideas.

Within each sentence, emphasize your point by expressing it in the subject and verb of an independent clause, the words that receive the most attention from readers (see 14a–14e).

Within longer stretches of prose, you can draw attention to ideas deserving special emphasis by using a variety of techniques, often involving an unusual twist or some element of surprise (see 14f).

14a Coordinate equal ideas; subordinate minor ideas.

When combining two or more ideas in one sentence, you have two choices: coordination or subordination. Choose coordination to indicate that the ideas are equal or nearly equal in

importance. Choose subordination to indicate that one idea is less important than another.

Coordination

Coordination draws attention equally to two or more ideas. To coordinate single words or phrases, join them with a coordinating conjunction or with a pair of correlative conjunctions: *bananas and strawberries*; *not only a lackluster plot but also inferior acting* (see 46g).

To coordinate independent clauses — word groups that express a complete thought and that can stand alone as a sentence — join them with a comma and a coordinating conjunction or with a semicolon:

, and	, but	, or	, nor
, for	, so	, yet	;

The semicolon is often accompanied by a conjunctive adverb such as *moreover*, *furthermore*, *therefore*, or *however* or by a transitional phrase such as *for example*, *in other words*, or *as a matter of fact*. (For a longer list, see p. 154.)

Assume, for example, that your intention is to draw equal attention to the following two ideas.

> Social networking Web sites offer ways for people to connect in the virtual world. They do not replace face-to-face forms of social interaction.

To coordinate these ideas, you can join them with a comma and the coordinating conjunction *but* or with a semicolon and the conjunctive adverb *however*.

> Social networking Web sites offer ways for people to connect in the virtual world, but they do not replace face-to-face forms of social interaction.

> Social networking Web sites offer ways for people to connect in the virtual world; however, they do not replace face-to-face forms of social interaction.

It is important to choose a coordinating conjunction or conjunctive adverb appropriate to your meaning. In the preceding example, the two ideas contrast with each other, calling for *but* or *however*. (For specific coordination strategies, see the chart on p. 154.)

Using coordination to combine sentences of equal importance

1. Consider using a comma and a coordinating conjunction. (See 32a.)

, and	, but	, or	, nor
, for	, so	, yet	

► **In Orthodox Jewish funeral ceremonies, the shroud is a simple linen**
and the
vestment/, ~~The~~ coffin is plain wood.

2. Consider using a semicolon with a conjunctive adverb or transitional phrase. (See 34b.)

also	however	next
as a result	in addition	now
besides	in fact	of course
consequently	in other words	otherwise
finally	in the first place	still
for example	meanwhile	then
for instance	moreover	therefore
furthermore	nevertheless	thus

in addition, she
► **Alicia scored well on the SAT/; ~~She also~~ had excellent grades and a record of community service.**

3. Consider using a semicolon alone. (See 34a.)

in
► **In youth we learn/; ~~In~~ age we understand.**

Subordination

To give unequal emphasis to two or more ideas, express the major idea in an independent clause and place any minor ideas in subordinate clauses or phrases. (For specific subordination strategies, see the chart on p. 156.)

Let your intended meaning determine which idea you emphasize. Consider the two ideas about social networking Web sites.

> Social networking Web sites offer ways for people to connect in the virtual world. They do not replace face-to-face forms of social interaction.

If your purpose is to stress the ways that people can connect in the virtual world rather than the limitations of these connections, subordinate the idea about the limitations.

> Although they do not replace face-to-face forms of social interaction, social networking Web sites offer ways for people to connect in the virtual world.

To focus on the limitations of the virtual world, subordinate the idea about the ways people connect on these Web sites.

> Although social networking Web sites offer ways for people to connect in the virtual world, they do not replace face-to-face forms of social interaction.

EXERCISE 14–1 Use the coordination or subordination technique in brackets to combine each pair of independent clauses. Possible revisions appear in the back of the book. *More practice:* LaunchPadSolo

> **Ted Williams was one of the best hitters in the history of** baseball, but he **~~baseball. He~~ never won a World Series ring.** [*Use a comma and a coordinating conjunction.*]

a. Williams played for the Boston Red Sox from 1939 to 1960. He managed the Washington Senators and the Texas Rangers for several years after retiring as a player. [*Use a comma and a coordinating conjunction.*]

b. In 1941, Williams finished the season with a batting average of .406. No player has hit over .400 for a season since then. [*Use a semicolon.*]

c. Williams acknowledged that Joe DiMaggio was a better all-around player. Williams felt that he was a better hitter than DiMaggio. [*Use the subordinating conjunction* although.]

d. Williams was a stubborn man. He always refused to tip his cap to the crowd after a home run because he claimed that fans were fickle. [*Use a semicolon and the transitional phrase* for example.]

e. Williams's relationship with the media was unfriendly at best. He sarcastically called baseball writers the "knights of the keyboard" in his memoir. [*Use a semicolon.*]

LaunchPadSolo **macmillanhighered.com/rules8e**

14 Emphasis

> Exercises: 14–3 to 14–7

> LearningCurve: Coordination and subordination

Using subordination to combine sentences of unequal importance

1. Consider putting the less important idea in a subordinate clause beginning with one of the following words. (See 48e.)

after	before	that	which
although	even though	unless	while
as	if	until	who
as if	since	when	whom
because	so that	where	whose

When
► **Elizabeth Cady Stanton proposed a convention to discuss the status of women in America/, Lucretia Mott agreed.**

that she
► **My sister owes much of her recovery to a yoga program/~~She~~ began ~~the program~~ three years ago.**

2. Consider putting the less important idea in an appositive phrase. (See 48c.)

► **Karate, ~~is~~ a discipline based on the philosophy of nonviolence/, ~~It~~ teaches the art of self-defense.**

3. Consider putting the less important idea in a participial phrase. (See 48b.)

E
► **~~American essayist Cheryl Peck was~~ encouraged by friends to write about her life/~~She~~ began combining humor and irony in her essays about being overweight.**
, American essayist Cheryl Peck

14b Combine choppy sentences.

Short sentences demand attention, so you should use them primarily for emphasis. Too many short sentences, one after the other, make for a choppy style.

If an idea is not important enough to deserve its own sentence, try combining it with a sentence close by. Put any minor ideas in subordinate structures such as phrases or subordinate clauses. (See 48.)

► **The Parks Department keeps the use of insecticides to a minimum/ because the ~~The~~ city is concerned about the environment.**

The writer wanted to emphasize that the Parks Department minimizes its use of chemicals, so she put the reason in a subordinate clause beginning with *because.*

► **The Chesapeake and Ohio Canal, ~~is~~ a 184-mile waterway constructed in the 1800s/, ~~It~~ was a major source of transportation for goods during the Civil War.**

A minor idea is now expressed in an appositive phrase (*a 184-mile waterway constructed in the 1800s*).

Although subordination is ordinarily the most effective technique for combining short, choppy sentences, coordination is appropriate when the ideas are equal in importance.

► **At 3:30 p.m., Forrest displayed a flag of truce/ and ~~Forrest~~ sent in a demand for unconditional surrender.**

Combining two short sentences by joining their predicates (*displayed . . . sent*) is an effective coordination technique.

Multilingual

Unlike some other languages, English does not repeat objects or adverbs in adjective clauses. The relative pronoun (*that, which, whom*) or relative adverb (*where*) in the adjective clause represents the object or adverb. See 30d.

► **The apartment that we rented ~~it~~ needed repairs.**

The pronoun *it* cannot repeat the relative pronoun *that.*

EXERCISE 14–2 Combine the following sentences by subordinating minor ideas or by coordinating ideas of equal importance. You must decide which ideas are minor because the sentences are given out of context. Possible revisions appear in the back of the book.

More practice: LaunchPadSolo

Agnes, ~~was~~ another girl I worked with/, ~~She~~ was a hyperactive child.

a. The X-Men comic books and Japanese woodcuts of kabuki dancers were part of Marlena's research project on popular culture. They covered the tabletop and the chairs.
b. Our waitress was costumed in a kimono. She had painted her face white. She had arranged her hair in a lacquered beehive.
c. Students can apply for a spot in the leadership program. The program teaches thinking and communication skills.
d. Shore houses were flooded up to the first floor. Beaches were washed away. Brant's Lighthouse was swallowed by the sea.
e. Laura Thackray is an engineer at Volvo Car Corporation. She addressed women's safety needs. She designed a pregnant crash-test dummy.

14c Avoid ineffective or excessive coordination.

Coordinate structures are appropriate only when you intend to draw readers' attention equally to two or more ideas: *Professor Sakellarios praises loudly, and she criticizes softly.* If one idea is more important than another — or if a coordinating conjunction does not clearly signal the relationship between the ideas — you should subordinate the less important idea.

INEFFECTIVE COORDINATION	Closets were taxed as rooms, and most colonists stored their clothes in chests or clothespresses.
IMPROVED WITH SUBORDINATION	Because closets were taxed as rooms, most colonists stored their clothes in chests or clothespresses.

The revision subordinates the less important idea (*closets were taxed as rooms*) by putting it in a subordinate clause. Notice that

LaunchPadSolo **macmillanhighered.com/rules8e**
14 Emphasis
> Exercises: 14–3 to 14–7
> LearningCurve: Coordination and subordination

the subordinating conjunction *Because* signals the relation between the ideas more clearly than the coordinating conjunction *and.*

Because it is so easy to string ideas together with *and*, writers often rely too heavily on coordination in their rough drafts. The cure for excessive coordination is simple: Look for opportunities to tuck minor ideas into subordinate clauses or phrases.

When shareholders
▶ ~~**Shareholders**~~ **exchanged investment tips at the company's annual meeting,** ~~**and**~~ **they learned that different approaches can yield similar results.**

The minor idea has become a subordinate clause beginning with *When.*

After four hours,
▶ ~~**Four hours went by, and**~~ **a rescue truck finally arrived, but by that time we had been evacuated in a helicopter.**

Three independent clauses were excessive. The least important idea has become a prepositional phrase.

EXERCISE 14–8 The following sentences show coordinated ideas (ideas joined with a coordinating conjunction or a semicolon). Restructure the sentences by subordinating minor ideas. You must decide which ideas are minor because the sentences are given out of context. Possible revisions appear in the back of the book. *More practice:* LaunchPadSolo

where they
The rowers returned to shore, ~~**and**~~ **had a party on the beach**
to celebrate
~~**and celebrated**~~ **the start of the season.**

a. These particles are known as "stealth liposomes," and they can hide in the body for a long time without detection.

b. Irena is a competitive gymnast and majors in biology; her goal is to apply her athletic experience and her science degree to a career in sports medicine.

c. Students, textile workers, and labor unions have loudly protested sweatshop abuses, so apparel makers have been forced to examine their labor practices.

LaunchPadSolo **macmillanhighered.com/rules8e**

14 Emphasis
> Exercises: 14-9
> LearningCurve: Coordination and subordination

d. IRC (Internet relay chat) was developed in a European university; it was created as a way for a group of graduate students to talk about projects from their dorm rooms.

e. The cafeteria's new menu has an international flavor, and it includes everything from enchiladas and pizza to pad thai and sauerbraten.

14d Do not subordinate major ideas.

If a sentence buries its major idea in a subordinate construction, readers may not give the idea enough attention. Make sure to express your major idea in an independent clause and to subordinate any minor ideas.

defeated Thomas E. Dewey,

▸ **Harry S. Truman, who was the unexpected winner of the 1948 presidential election, ~~defeated Thomas E. Dewey.~~**

The writer wanted to focus on Truman's unexpected victory, but the original sentence buried this information in an adjective clause. The revision puts the more important idea in an independent clause and tucks the less important idea into an adjective clause (*who defeated Thomas E. Dewey*).

As

▸ **I was driving home from my new job, heading down Ranchitos Road, ~~when~~ my car suddenly overheated.**

The writer wanted to emphasize that the car overheated, not the fact of driving home. The revision expresses the major idea in an independent clause and places the less important idea in an adverb clause (*As I was driving home from my new job*).

14e Do not subordinate excessively.

In attempting to avoid short, choppy sentences, writers sometimes go to the opposite extreme, putting more subordinate ideas into a sentence than its structure can bear. If a sentence collapses under its own weight, occasionally it can be restructured. More often, however, such sentences must be divided.

► **In *Animal Liberation*, Peter Singer argues that animals possess nervous systems and can feel pain. ~~and that~~ He believes that "the ethical principle on which human equality rests requires us to extend equal consideration to animals" (1).**

Excessive subordination makes it difficult for the reader to focus on the quoted passage. By splitting the original sentence into two separate sentences, the writer draws attention to Peter Singer's main claim, that humans should give "equal consideration to animals." (See 56a on citing sources in MLA style.)

EXERCISE 14–10 In each of the following sentences, the idea that the writer wished to emphasize is buried in a subordinate construction. Restructure each sentence so that the independent clause expresses the major idea, as indicated in brackets, and lesser ideas are subordinated. Possible revisions appear in the back of the book.

More practice: LaunchPadSolo

Although Catherine has weathered many hardships, ~~although~~ she has rarely become discouraged. [*Emphasize that Catherine has rarely become discouraged.*]

a. Gina helped the relief effort, distributing food and medical supplies. [*Emphasize distributing food and medical supplies.*]

b. Janbir spent every Saturday learning tabla drumming, noticing with each hour of practice that his memory for complex patterns was growing stronger. [*Emphasize Janbir's memory.*]

c. The rotor hit, gouging a hole about an eighth of an inch deep in my helmet. [*Emphasize that the rotor gouged a hole in the helmet.*]

d. My grandfather, who raised his daughters the old-fashioned way, was born eighty years ago in Puerto Rico. [*Emphasize how the grandfather raised his daughters.*]

e. The Narcan reversed the depressive effect of the drug, saving the patient's life. [*Emphasize that the patient's life was saved.*]

LaunchPadSolo **macmillanhighered.com/rules8e**

14 Emphasis

> Exercises: 14–11 and 14–12

> LearningCurve: Coordination and subordination

14f Experiment with techniques for gaining special emphasis.

By experimenting with certain techniques, usually involving some element of surprise, you can draw attention to ideas that deserve special emphasis. Use such techniques sparingly, however, or they will lose their punch. The writer who tries to emphasize everything ends up emphasizing nothing.

Using sentence endings for emphasis

You can highlight an idea simply by withholding it until the end of a sentence. The technique works something like a punch line. In the following example, the sentence's meaning is not revealed until its very last word.

> The only completely consistent people are the dead.
> — Aldous Huxley

Using parallel structure for emphasis

Parallel grammatical structure draws special attention to paired ideas or to items in a series. (See 9.) When parallel ideas are paired, the emphasis falls on words that underscore comparisons or contrasts, especially when they occur at the end of a phrase or clause.

> We must *stop talking* about the *American dream* and *start listening* to the *dreams of Americans*. — Reubin Askew

In a parallel series, the emphasis falls at the end, so it is generally best to end with the most dramatic or climactic item in the series.

> Sister Charity enjoyed passing out writing punishments: translate the Ten Commandments into Latin, type a thousand-word essay on good manners, copy the New Testament with a quill pen. — Marie Visosky, student

15 Provide some variety.

When a rough draft is filled with too many sentences that begin the same way or have the same structure, try injecting some variety—as long as you can do so without sacrificing clarity or ease of reading.

15a Vary your sentence openings.

Most sentences in English begin with the subject, move to the verb, and continue to the object, with modifiers tucked in along the way or put at the end. For the most part, such sentences are fine. Put too many of them in a row, however, and they become monotonous.

Adverbial modifiers are easily movable when they modify verbs; they can often be inserted ahead of the subject. Such modifiers might be single words, phrases, or clauses.

Eventually a
► **~~A~~ few drops of sap ~~eventually~~ began to trickle into the bucket.**

Like most adverbs, *eventually* does not need to appear close to the verb it modifies (*began*).

Just as the sun was coming up, a
► **~~A~~ pair of black ducks flew over the pond. ~~just as the sun was coming up.~~**

The adverb clause, which modifies the verb *flew*, is as clear at the beginning of the sentence as it is at the end.

Adjectives and participial phrases can frequently be moved to the beginning of a sentence without loss of clarity.

Dejected and withdrawn,
► **Edward ~~, dejected and withdrawn,~~ nearly gave up his search for a job.**

A / John and I
► **~~John and I,~~ ~~a~~nticipating a peaceful evening, sat down at the campfire to brew a cup of coffee.**

TIP: When beginning a sentence with an adjective or a participial phrase, make sure that the subject of the sentence names the person or thing described in the introductory phrase. If it doesn't, the phrase will dangle. (See 12e.)

15b Use a variety of sentence structures.

A writer should not rely too heavily on simple sentences and compound sentences, for the effect tends to be both monotonous and choppy. (See 14b and 14c.) Too many complex or compound-complex sentences, however, can be equally monotonous. If your style tends to one or the other extreme, try to achieve a better mix of sentence types.

The major sentence types are illustrated in the following sentences, all taken from Flannery O'Connor's "The King of the Birds," an essay describing the author's pet peafowl.

SIMPLE	Frequently the cock combines the lifting of his tail with the raising of his voice.
COMPOUND	Any chicken's dusting hole is out of place in a flower bed, but the peafowl's hole, being the size of a small crater, is more so.
COMPLEX	The peacock does most of his serious strutting in the spring and summer when he has a full tail to do it with.
COMPOUND-COMPLEX	The cock's plumage requires two years to attain its pattern, and for the rest of his life, this chicken will act as though he designed it himself.

For a fuller discussion of sentence types, see 49a.

15c Try inverting sentences occasionally.

A sentence is inverted if it does not follow the normal subject-verb-object pattern (see 47c). Many inversions sound artificial and should be avoided, except in the most formal contexts. But if an inversion sounds natural, it can provide a welcome touch of variety.

Set at the top two corners of the stage were huge
► ~~**Huge**~~ **lavender hearts outlined in bright white lights.** ~~**were set at the top two corners of the stage.**~~

In the revision, the subject, *hearts*, appears after the verb, *were set*. Notice that the two parts of the verb are also inverted — and separated from each other (*Set . . . were*) — without any awkwardness or loss of meaning.

Inverted sentences are used for emphasis as well as for variety (see 14f).

EXERCISE 15–1 Improve sentence variety in each of the following sentences by using the technique suggested in brackets. Possible revisions appear in the back of the book. *More practice:* LaunchPadSolo

> To protect endangered marine turtles, fishing
> **~~Fishing~~ crews place turtle excluder devices in fishing nets.** ^ ^
>
> **~~to protect endangered marine turtles.~~** [***Begin the sentence with the adverbial infinitive phrase.***]

a. The exhibits for insects and spiders are across the hall from the fossils exhibit. [*Invert the sentence.*]

b. Sayuri becomes a successful geisha after growing up desperately poor. [*Move the adverb clause to the beginning of the sentence.*]

c. Researchers have been studying Mount St. Helens for years. They believe that earthquakes may have caused the 1980 eruption. [*Combine the two sentences into a complex sentence.*]

d. Ice cream typically contains 10 percent milk fat. Premium ice cream may contain up to 16 percent milk fat and has less air in it. [*Combine the two sentences as a compound sentence.*]

e. The economy may recover quickly if home values climb. [*Move the adverb clause to the beginning of the sentence.*]

EXERCISE 15–2 Edit the following paragraph to increase sentence variety.

Making architectural models is a skill that requires patience and precision. It is an art that illuminates a design. Architects come up with a grand and intricate vision. Draftspersons convert that vision into blueprints. The model maker follows the blueprints. The model maker builds a miniature version of the structure. Modelers can work in traditional materials like wood and clay and paint. Modelers can work in newer materials like Styrofoam and liquid polymers. Some modelers still use cardboard, paper, and glue. Other modelers prefer glue guns, deformable plastic, and thin aluminum and brass wire. The modeler may seem to be making a small mess in the early stages of model building. In the end the modeler has completed a small-scale structure. Architect Rem Koolhaas has insisted that plans reveal the logic of a design. He has argued that models expose the architect's vision. The model maker's art makes this vision real.

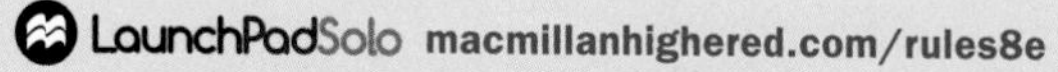

15 Variety
> Exercise: 15–3

16 Tighten wordy sentences.

Long sentences are not necessarily wordy, nor are short sentences always concise. A sentence is wordy if it can be tightened without loss of meaning.

16a Eliminate redundancies.

Writers often repeat themselves unnecessarily, thinking that expressions such as *cooperate together*, *yellow in color*, or *basic essentials* add emphasis to their writing. Such redundancies, though, do just the opposite. There is no need to say the same thing twice.

► **Daniel ~~is now employed~~ works at a private rehabilitation center ~~working~~ as a registered physical therapist.**

Though modifiers ordinarily add meaning to the words they modify, occasionally they are redundant.

► **Sylvia ~~very hurriedly~~ scribbled her name, address, and phone number on a greasy napkin.**

The word *scribbled* already suggests that Sylvia wrote *very hurriedly.*

► **Gabriele Muccino's film *The Pursuit of Happyness* tells the story of a single father determined ~~in his mind~~ to pull himself and his son out of homelessness.**

The word *determined* contains the idea that his resolution formed in his mind.

16b Avoid unnecessary repetition of words.

Though words may be repeated deliberately for effect, repetitions will seem awkward if they are clearly unnecessary. When a more concise version is possible, choose it.

▸ Our fifth patient, in room six, is ~~a~~ mentally ill. ~~patient.~~

▸ The best teachers help each student ~~become a better student~~ grow both academically and emotionally.

16c Cut empty or inflated phrases.

An empty phrase can be cut with little or no loss of meaning. Common examples are introductory word groups that weaken the writer's authority by apologizing or hedging: *in my opinion*, *I think that*, *it seems that*, *one must admit that*, and so on.

▸ ~~In my opinion, o~~ Our current immigration policy is misguided.

Readers understand without being told that they are hearing the writer's opinion.

Inflated phrases can be reduced to a word or two without loss of meaning.

INFLATED	CONCISE
along the lines of	like
as a matter of fact	in fact
at all times	always
at the present time	now, currently
at this point in time	now, currently
because of the fact that	because
by means of	by
by virtue of the fact that	because
due to the fact that	because
for the purpose of	for
for the reason that	because
have the ability to	be able to, can
in light of the fact that	because
in order to	to
in spite of the fact that	although, though
in the event that	if

INFLATED	CONCISE
in the final analysis	finally
in the nature of	like
in the neighborhood of	about
until such time as	until

16d Simplify the structure.

If the structure of a sentence is needlessly indirect, try simplifying it. Look for opportunities to strengthen the verb.

▶ **The financial analyst claimed that because of volatile market conditions she could not ~~make an~~ estimate ~~of~~ the company's future profits.**

The verb *estimate* is more vigorous and concise than *make an estimate of.*

The colorless verbs *is*, *are*, *was*, and *were* frequently generate excess words.

studied

▶ **Investigators ~~were involved in studying~~ the effect of classical music on unborn babies.**

The revision is more direct and concise. The action (*studying*), originally appearing in a subordinate structure, has become a strong verb, *studied.*

The expletive constructions *there is* and *there are* (or *there was* and *there were*) can also lead to wordy sentences. The same is true of expletive constructions beginning with *it.* (See 47c.)

A

▶ **~~There is~~ ~~a~~nother module ~~that~~ tells the story of Charles Darwin and introduces the theory of evolution.**

Finally, verbs in the passive voice may be needlessly indirect. When the active voice expresses your meaning as effectively, use it. (See 8a.)

our coaches have recruited

▶ **All too often, athletes with marginal academic skills. ~~have been recruited by our coaches.~~**

16e Reduce clauses to phrases, phrases to single words.

Word groups functioning as modifiers can often be made more compact. Look for any opportunities to reduce clauses to phrases or phrases to single words.

► **We took a side trip to Monticello, ~~which was~~ the home of Thomas Jefferson.**

this
► **In ~~the~~ essay, ~~that follows,~~ I argue against Immanuel Kant's**
problematic
claim that we should not lie under any circumstances, .
~~which is a problematic claim.~~

EXERCISE 16–1 Edit the following sentences to reduce wordiness. Possible revisions appear in the back of the book.

More practice: LaunchPadSolo

even though
The Wilsons moved into the house ~~in spite of the fact that~~ the back door was only ten yards from the train tracks.

a. Martin Luther King Jr. was a man who set a high standard for future leaders to meet.
b. Alice has been deeply in love with cooking since she was little and could first peek over the edge of a big kitchen tabletop.
c. In my opinion, Bloom's race for the governorship is a futile exercise.
d. It is pretty important in being a successful graphic designer to have technical knowledge and at the same time an eye for color and balance.
e. Your task will be the delivery of correspondence to all employees in the company.

LaunchPadSolo **macmillanhighered.com/rules8e**
16 Wordy sentences
> Exercises: 16–3 to 16–7

EXERCISE 16–2 Edit the following business memo to reduce wordiness.

To: District managers
From: Margaret Davenport, Vice President
Subject: Customer database

It has recently been brought to my attention that a percentage of our sales representatives have been failing to log reports of their client calls in our customer database each and every day. I have also learned that some representatives are not checking the database on a routine basis.

Our clients sometimes receive a multiple number of sales calls from us when a sales representative is not cognizant of the fact that the client has been contacted at a previous time. Repeated telephone calls from our representatives annoy our customers. These repeated telephone calls also portray our company as one that is lacking in organization.

Effective as of immediately, direct your representatives to do the following:

- Record each and every customer contact in the customer database at the end of each day, without fail.
- Check the database at the very beginning of each day to ensure that telephone communications will not be initiated with clients who have already been called.

Let me extend my appreciation to you for cooperating in this important matter.

17 Choose appropriate language.

Language is appropriate when it suits your subject, engages your audience, and blends naturally with your own voice.

To some extent, your choice of language will be governed by the conventions of the genre in which you are writing. When in doubt about the conventions of a particular genre — lab reports, informal essays, business memos, and so on — consult your instructor or look at models written by experts in the field.

17a Stay away from jargon.

Jargon is specialized language used among members of a trade, profession, or group. Use jargon only when readers will be familiar with it and only when plain English will not do as well.

JARGON We outsourced the work to an outfit in Ohio because we didn't have the bandwidth to tackle it in-house.

REVISED We hired a company in Ohio because we had too few employees to do the work.

Broadly defined, jargon includes puffed-up language designed more to impress readers than to inform them. The following are common examples from business, government, higher education, and the military, with plain English alternatives in parentheses.

ameliorate (improve)	indicator (sign)
commence (begin)	optimal (best, most favorable)
components (parts)	parameters (boundaries, limits)
endeavor (try)	peruse (read, look over)
exit (leave)	prior to (before)
facilitate (help)	utilize (use)
impact (v.) (affect)	viable (workable)

Sentences filled with jargon are hard to read, and they are often wordy as well.

► **The CEO should ~~dialogue~~ [talk] with investors about ~~partnering~~ [working] with clients to ~~purchase~~ [buy] land in ~~economically deprived zones.~~ [poor neighborhoods.]**

17b Avoid pretentious language, most euphemisms, and "doublespeak."

Hoping to sound profound or poetic, some writers embroider their thoughts with large words and flowery phrases. Such pretentious language is so ornate and wordy that it obscures the writer's meaning.

▶ Taylor's ~~employment of multihued means of expression draws back the curtains and lets slip the~~ use of colorful language reveals that she has a nostalgic ~~vantage point from which she observes~~ view of American society ~~as well as her lack of comprehension of~~ and does not understand economic realities.

Euphemisms — nice-sounding words or phrases substituted for words thought to sound harsh or ugly — are sometimes appropriate. Many cultures, for example, accept euphemisms when speaking or writing about excretion (*I have to go to the bathroom*), sexual intercourse (*They did not sleep together*), and the like. Most euphemisms, however, are needlessly evasive or even deceitful. Like pretentious language, they obscure the intended meaning.

EUPHEMISM	PLAIN ENGLISH
adult entertainment	pornography
preowned automobile	used car
economically deprived	poor
negative savings	debts
strategic withdrawal	retreat or defeat
revenue enhancers	taxes
chemical dependency	drug addiction
downsize	lay off, fire
correctional facility	prison

The term *doublespeak* applies to any deliberately evasive or deceptive language, including euphemisms. Doublespeak is especially common in politics and business. A military retreat is described as *tactical redeployment*; *enhanced interrogation* is a euphemism for "torture"; and *downsizing* really means "firing employees."

LaunchPadSolo macmillanhighered.com/rules8e
17 Appropriate language
> Exercises: 17-3 and 17-4
> LearningCurve: Word choice and appropriate language

EXERCISE 17–1 Edit the following sentences to eliminate jargon, pretentious or flowery language, euphemisms, and doublespeak. You may need to make substantial changes in some sentences. Possible revisions appear in the back of the book. *More practice:* LaunchPadSolo

After two weeks in the legal department, Sue has ~~worked into~~ mastered the office routine, ~~of the office,~~ and her performance has ~~functional and self-management skills have~~ exceeded all expectations.

a. In my youth, my family was under the constraints of difficult financial circumstances.
b. In order that I may increase my expertise in the area of delivery of services to clients, I feel that participation in this conference will be beneficial.
c. The prophetic meteorologist cautioned the general populace regarding the possible deleterious effects of the impending tempest.
d. Government-sanctioned investigations into the continued value of after-school programs indicate a perceived need in the public realm at large.
e. Passengers should endeavor to finalize the customs declaration form prior to exiting the aircraft.

EXERCISE 17–2 Edit the following e-mail message to eliminate jargon.

Dear Ms. Jackson:

We members of the Nakamura Reyes team value our external partnering arrangements with Creative Software, and I look forward to seeing you next week at the trade show in Fresno. Per Mr. Reyes, please let me know when you'll have some downtime there so that he and I can conduct a strategizing session with you concerning our production schedule. It's crucial that we all be on the same page re our 2015–2016 product release dates.

Before we have some face time, however, I have some findings to share. Our customer-centric approach to the new products will necessitate that user testing periods trend upward. The enclosed data should help you effectuate any adjustments to your timeline; let me know ASAP if you require any additional information to facilitate the above.

Before we convene in Fresno, Mr. Reyes and I will agendize any further talking points. Thanks for your help.

Sincerely,

Sylvia Nakamura

17c In most contexts, avoid slang, regional expressions, and nonstandard English.

Slang is an informal and sometimes private vocabulary that expresses the solidarity of a group such as teenagers, rock musicians, or sports fans; it is subject to more rapid change than Standard English. For example, the slang teenagers use to express approval changes every few years; *cool*, *groovy*, *neat*, *awesome*, *sick*, and *crunk* have replaced one another within the last several decades. Sometimes slang becomes so widespread that it is accepted as standard vocabulary. *Jazz*, for example, started out as slang but is now a standard term for a style of music.

Although slang has a certain vitality, it is a code that not everyone understands, and it is very informal. Therefore, it is inappropriate in most written work.

we lost
▶ **When the server crashed unexpectedly, three hours of unsaved**
data. ~~went down the tubes.~~

disgust you.
▶ **The government's "filth" guidelines for food will ~~gross you out.~~**

Regional expressions are common to a group in a geographic area. *Let's talk with the bark off* (for *Let's speak frankly*) is an expression in the southern United States, for example. Regional expressions have the same limitations as slang and are therefore inappropriate in most writing.

▶ **John was four blocks from the house before he remembered to**
turn off
~~cut~~ the headlights. ~~off.~~

▶ **Seamus wasn't ~~for~~ sure, but he thought the whales might be migrating during his visit to Oregon.**

Standard English is the language used in all academic, business, and professional fields. Nonstandard English is spoken by people with a common regional or social heritage. Although nonstandard English may be appropriate when spoken within a close group, it is out of place in most formal and informal writing.

▶ **The governor said he ~~don't~~ doesn't know if he will approve the budget without the clean air provision.**

If you speak a nonstandard dialect, try to identify the ways in which your dialect differs from Standard English. Look especially for the following features of nonstandard English, which commonly cause problems in writing.

Misusing verb forms such as *began* and *begun* (See 27a.)

Leaving *-s* endings off verbs (See 27c.)

Leaving *-ed* endings off verbs (See 27d.)

Leaving out necessary verbs (See 27e.)

Using double negatives (See 26e.)

17d Choose an appropriate level of formality.

In deciding on a level of formality, consider both your subject and your audience. Does the subject demand a dignified treatment, or is a relaxed tone more suitable? Will readers be put off if you assume too close a relationship with them, or might you alienate them by seeming too distant?

For most college and professional writing, some degree of formality is appropriate. In a job application letter, for example, it is a mistake to sound too breezy and informal.

TOO INFORMAL	I'd like to get that sales job you've got in the paper.
MORE FORMAL	I would like to apply for the position of sales associate advertised in the *Peoria Journal Star*.

Informal writing is appropriate for private letters, personal e-mail and text messages, and business correspondence between close associates. Like spoken conversation, informal writing allows contractions (*don't*, *I'll*) and colloquial words (*kids*, *kinda*). Vocabulary and sentence structure are rarely complex.

In choosing a level of formality, above all be consistent. When a writer's voice shifts from one level of formality to another, readers receive mixed messages.

► **Once a pitcher for the Blue Jays, Jorge shared with me the secrets of his trade. His lesson ~~commenced~~ *began* with his famous curveball, ~~implemented~~ *thrown* by tucking the little finger behind the ball. Next he ~~elucidated~~ *revealed* the mysteries of the sucker pitch, a slow ball coming behind a fast windup.**

Words such as *commenced* and *elucidated* are inappropriate for the subject matter, and they clash with informal terms such as *sucker pitch* and *fast windup.*

EXERCISE 17–5 Revise the following passage so that the level of formality is appropriate for a letter to the editor of a major newspaper.

> In pop culture, college grads who return home to live with the folks are seen as good-for-nothing losers who mooch off their families. And many older adults seem to feel that the trend of moving back home after school, which was rare in their day, is becoming too commonplace today. But society must realize that times have changed. Most young adults want to live on their own ASAP, but they graduate with heaps of debt and need some time to get back on their feet. College tuition and the cost of housing have increased way more than salary increases in the past fifty years. Also, the job market is tighter and more jobs require advanced degrees than in the past. So before people go off on college graduates who move back into their parents' house for a spell, they'd better consider all the facts.

17e Avoid sexist language.

Sexist language is language that stereotypes or demeans women or men. Using nonsexist language is a matter of courtesy — of respect for and sensitivity to the feelings of others.

Recognizing sexist language

Some sexist language is easy to recognize because it reflects genuine disdain for women: referring to a woman as a "chick," for example, or calling a lawyer a "lady lawyer."

Other forms of sexist language are less blatant. The following practices, while they may not result from conscious sexism, reflect stereotypical thinking: referring to members of one profession as exclusively male or exclusively female (teachers as women or computer engineers as men, for instance), using different conventions when naming or identifying women and men, or assuming an exclusively male or female audience.

STEREOTYPICAL LANGUAGE

After a nursing student graduates, *she* must face a difficult state board examination. [Not all nursing students are women.]

Running for city council are Boris Stotsky, an attorney, and *Mrs.* Cynthia Jones, a professor of English and *mother of three.* [The title *Mrs.* and the phrase *mother of three* are irrelevant.]

Still other forms of sexist language result from outdated traditions. The pronouns *he*, *him*, and *his*, for instance, were traditionally used to refer generically to persons of either sex. Nowadays, to avoid that sexist usage, some writers use *she*, *her*, and *hers* generically or substitute the female pronouns alternately with the male pronouns.

GENERIC PRONOUNS

A journalist is motivated by *his* deadline.

A good interior designer treats *her* clients' ideas respectfully.

But both forms are sexist — for excluding one sex entirely and for making assumptions about the members of particular professions.

Similarly, the nouns *man* and *men* were once used to refer generically to persons of either sex. Current usage demands gender-neutral terms for references to both men and women.

INAPPROPRIATE	APPROPRIATE
chairman	chairperson, moderator, chair, head
congressman	member of Congress, representative, legislator
fireman	firefighter
foreman	supervisor
mailman	mail carrier, postal worker, letter carrier
to man	to operate, to staff
mankind	people, humans
manpower	personnel, staff
policeman	police officer
weatherman	forecaster, meteorologist

Revising sexist language

When revising sexist language, you may be tempted to substitute *he or she* and *his or her*. These terms are inclusive but wordy; fine in small doses, they can become awkward when repeated throughout an essay. A better revision strategy is to write in the plural; yet another strategy is to recast the sentence so that the problem does not arise.

SEXIST

A journalist is motivated by *his* deadline.

A good interior designer treats *her* clients' ideas respectfully.

ACCEPTABLE BUT WORDY

A journalist is motivated by *his or her* deadline.

A good interior designer treats *his or her* clients' ideas respectfully.

BETTER: USING THE PLURAL

Journalists are motivated by *their* deadlines.

Good interior designers treat *their* clients' ideas respectfully.

BETTER: RECASTING THE SENTENCE

A journalist is motivated by *a* deadline.

A good interior designer treats clients' ideas respectfully.

For more examples of these revision strategies, see 22.

EXERCISE 17–6 Edit the following sentences to eliminate sexist language or sexist assumptions. Possible revisions appear in the back of the book. *More practice:* LaunchPadSolo

Scholarship athletes ... their

~~A scholarship athlete~~ must be as concerned about ~~his~~

they are ... their

academic performance as ~~he is~~ about ~~his~~ athletic performance.

a. Mrs. Geralyn Farmer, who is the mayor's wife, is the chief surgeon at University Hospital. Dr. Paul Green is her assistant.
b. Every applicant wants to know how much he will earn.
c. An elementary school teacher should understand the concept of nurturing if she intends to be effective.

LaunchPadSolo **macmillanhighered.com/rules8e**

17 Appropriate language

> Exercises: 17-8 to 17-10

> LearningCurve: Word choice and appropriate language

d. An obstetrician needs to be available to his patients at all hours.

e. If man does not stop polluting his environment, mankind will perish.

EXERCISE 17–7 Eliminate sexist language or sexist assumptions in the following job posting for an elementary school teacher.

> We are looking for qualified women for the position of elementary school teacher. The ideal candidate should have a bachelor's degree, a state teaching certificate, and one year of student teaching. She should be knowledgeable in all elementary subject areas, including science and math. While we want our new teacher to have a commanding presence in the classroom, we are also looking for motherly characteristics such as patience and trustworthiness. She must be able to both motivate an entire classroom and work with each student one-on-one to assess his individual needs. She must also be comfortable communicating with the parents of her students. For salary and benefits information, including maternity leave policy, please contact the Martin County School Board. Any qualified applicant should submit her résumé by March 15.

17f Revise language that may offend groups of people.

Your writing should be respectful and free of stereotypical, biased, or other offensive language. Be especially careful when describing or labeling people. Labels can become dated, and it is important to recognize when their continued use is not acceptable. When naming groups of people, choose labels that the groups currently use themselves. For example, instead of *Eskimos*, use *Inuit*.

▶ **North Dakota takes its name from the ~~Indian~~ ^Lakota word meaning "friend" or "ally."**

▶ **Many ~~Oriental~~ ^Asian immigrants have recently settled in our town.**

Negative stereotypes (such as "drives like a teenager" or "sour as a spinster") are of course offensive. But you should avoid stereotyping a person or a group even if you believe your generalization to be positive.

▶ **It was no surprise that Greer, ~~a Chinese American,~~ ^an excellent math and science student, was selected for the honors chemistry program.**

18 Find the exact words.

Two reference works (or their online equivalents) will help you find words to express your meaning exactly: a good dictionary, such as *The American Heritage Dictionary* or *Merriam-Webster* online, and a collection of synonyms and antonyms, such as *Roget's International Thesaurus.*

TIP: Do not turn to a thesaurus in search of flowery or impressive words. Look instead for words that exactly express your meaning.

18a Select words with appropriate connotations.

In addition to their strict dictionary meanings (or *denotations*), words have *connotations*, emotional colorings that affect how readers respond to them. The word *steel* denotes "commercial iron that contains carbon," but it also calls up a cluster of images associated with steel. These associations give the word its connotations—cold, hard, smooth, unbending.

If the connotation of a word does not seem appropriate for your purpose, your audience, or your subject matter, you should change the word. When a more appropriate synonym does not come quickly to mind, consult a dictionary or a thesaurus.

► **As I covered the boats with marsh grass, the ~~perspiration~~ sweat I had worked up evaporated in the wind, and the cold morning air seemed even colder.**

The word *perspiration* is too dainty for the context, which suggests vigorous exercise.

EXERCISE 18–1 Use a dictionary and a thesaurus to find at least four synonyms for each of the following words. Be prepared to explain any slight differences in meaning.

1. decay (verb)
2. difficult (adjective)
3. hurry (verb)
4. pleasure (noun)
5. secret (adjective)
6. talent (noun)

18b Prefer specific, concrete nouns.

Unlike general nouns, which refer to broad classes of things, specific nouns point to particular items. *Film*, for example, names a general class, *fantasy film* names a narrower class, and *The Golden Compass* is more specific still. Other examples: *team*, *football team*, *Denver Broncos*; *music*, *symphony*, *Beethoven's Ninth*.

Unlike abstract nouns, which refer to qualities and ideas (*justice*, *beauty*, *realism*, *dignity*), concrete nouns point to immediate, often sensory experience and to physical objects (*steeple*, *asphalt*, *lilac*, *stone*, *garlic*).

Specific, concrete nouns express meaning more vividly than general or abstract ones. Although general and abstract language is sometimes necessary to convey your meaning, use specific, concrete words whenever possible.

▶ **The senator spoke about the challenges of the future:**
pollution, dwindling resources, and terrorism.
~~the environment and world peace.~~
^

Nouns such as *thing*, *area*, *aspect*, *factor*, and *individual* are especially dull and imprecise.

motherhood, and memory.
▶ **Toni Morrison's *Beloved* is about slavery, ~~among other things.~~**
^

18c Do not misuse words.

If a word is not in your active vocabulary, you may find yourself misusing it, sometimes with embarrassing consequences. When in doubt, check the dictionary.

climbing
▶ **The fans were ~~migrating~~ up the bleachers in search of seats.**
^

permeated
▶ **The Internet has so ~~diffused~~ our culture that it touches all**
^
segments of society.

Be especially alert for misused word forms — using a noun such as *absence* or *significance*, for example, when your meaning requires the adjective *absent* or *significant*.

► Most dieters are not ~~persistence~~ persistent enough to make a permanent change in their eating habits.

EXERCISE 18–2 Edit the following sentences to correct misused words. Possible revisions appear in the back of the book.

More practice: LaunchPadSolo

These days the training required for a ballet dancer is ~~all-absorbent.~~ all-absorbing.

a. We regret this delay; thank you for your patients.
b. Ada's plan is to require education and experience to prepare herself for a position as property manager.
c. Serena Williams, the penultimate competitor, has earned millions of dollars just in endorsements.
d. Many people take for granite that public libraries have up-to-date computer systems.
e. The affect of Gao Xinjian's novels on Chinese exiles is hard to gauge.

18d Use standard idioms.

Idioms are speech forms that follow no easily specified rules. The English say "Bernice went *to hospital*," an idiom strange to American ears, which are accustomed to hearing *the* in front of *hospital.* Native speakers of a language seldom have problems with idioms, but prepositions (such as *with*, *to*, *at*, and *of*) sometimes cause trouble, especially when they follow certain verbs and adjectives. When in doubt, consult a dictionary.

UNIDIOMATIC	IDIOMATIC
abide with (a decision)	abide by (a decision)
according with	according to
agree to (an idea)	agree with (an idea)
angry at (a person)	angry with (a person)
capable to	capable of

LaunchPadSolo **macmillanhighered.com/rules8e**
18 Exact words
> Exercises: 18–3 and 18–4
> LearningCurve: Word choice and appropriate language

comply to	comply with
desirous to	desirous of
different than (a person or thing)	different from (a person or thing)
intend on doing	intend to do
off of	off
plan on doing	plan to do
preferable than	preferable to
prior than	prior to
similar than	similar to
superior than	superior to
sure and	sure to
think on	think of, about
try and	try to
type of a	type of

Multilingual

Because idioms follow no particular rules, you must learn them individually. You may find it helpful to keep a list of idioms that you frequently encounter in conversation and in reading.

EXERCISE 18–5 Edit the following sentences to eliminate errors in the use of idiomatic expressions. If a sentence is correct, write "correct" after it. Revisions appear in the back of the book. *More practice:* LaunchPadSolo

We agreed to abide ~~with~~ by the decision of the judge.

a. Queen Anne was so angry at Sarah Churchill that she refused to see her again.

b. Jean-Pierre's ambitious travel plans made it impossible for him to comply with the residency requirement for in-state tuition.

LaunchPadSolo macmillanhighered.com/rules8e
18 Exact words
> Exercises: 18–6 and 18–7
> LearningCurve: Word choice and appropriate language

c. The parade moved off of the street and onto the beach.
d. The frightened refugees intend on making the dangerous trek across the mountains.
e. What type of a wedding are you planning?

18e Do not rely heavily on clichés.

The pioneer who first announced that he had "slept like a log" no doubt amused his companions with a fresh and unlikely comparison. Today, however, that comparison is a cliché, a saying that can no longer add emphasis or surprise.

To see just how predictable clichés are, put your hand over the right-hand column in the following list and then finish the phrases on the left.

cool as a	cucumber
beat around	the bush
blind as a	bat
busy as a	bee, beaver
crystal	clear
dead as a	doornail
out of the frying pan and	into the fire
light as a	feather
like a bull	in a china shop
playing with	fire
nutty as a	fruitcake
selling like	hotcakes
starting out at the bottom	of the ladder
water under the	bridge
white as a	sheet, ghost
avoid clichés like the	plague

The solution for clichés is simple: Just delete them or rewrite them.

► **When I received a full scholarship from my second-choice school, I ~~found myself between a rock and a hard place.~~** felt pressured to settle for second best.

Sometimes you can write around a cliché by adding an element of surprise. One student, for example, who had written that she had butterflies in her stomach, revised her cliché like this:

> If all of the action in my stomach is caused by butterflies, there must be a horde of them, with horseshoes on.

The image of butterflies wearing horseshoes is fresh and unlikely, not predictable like the original cliché.

18f Use figures of speech with care.

A figure of speech is an expression that uses words imaginatively (rather than literally) to make abstract ideas concrete. Most often, figures of speech compare two seemingly unlike things to reveal surprising similarities.

In a *simile*, the writer makes the comparison explicitly, usually by introducing it with *like* or *as*: *By the time cotton had to be picked, Grandfather's neck was as red as the clay he plowed.* In a *metaphor*, the *like* or *as* is omitted, and the comparison is implied. For example, in the Old Testament Song of Solomon, a young woman compares the man she loves to a fruit tree: *With great delight I sat in his shadow, and his fruit was sweet to my taste.*

Although figures of speech are useful devices, writers sometimes use them without thinking through the images they evoke. The result is sometimes a *mixed metaphor*, the combination of two or more images that don't make sense together.

► **Our manager decided to put all controversial issues ~~in a holding pattern~~ on a back burner until after the annual meeting.**

Here the writer is mixing airplanes and stoves. Simply deleting one of the images corrects the problem.

► **Crossing Utah's salt flats in a new convertible, my cousin flew ~~under a full head of steam~~.** [inserted: at jet speed.]

Flew suggests an airplane, whereas under a full head of steam suggests a steamboat or train. To clarify the image, the writer should stick with one comparison or the other.

EXERCISE 18–8 Edit the following sentences to replace worn-out expressions and clarify mixed figures of speech. Possible revisions appear in the back of the book. *More practice:* LaunchPadSolo

the color drained from his face.
When he heard about the accident, ~~he turned white as a sheet.~~ ^

a. John stormed into the room like a bull in a china shop.
b. Some people insist that they'll always be there for you, even when they haven't been before.
c. The Cubs easily beat the Mets, who were in the soup early in the game today at Wrigley Field.
d. We ironed out the sticky spots in our relationship.
e. My mother accused me of beating around the bush when in fact I was just talking off the top of my head.

LaunchPadSolo **macmillanhighered.com/rules8e**
18 Exact words
> Exercises: 18–9 and 18–10
> LearningCurve: Word choice and appropriate language

Grammar

19 Repair sentence fragments.

A sentence fragment is a word group that pretends to be a sentence. Sentence fragments are easy to recognize when they appear out of context, like these:

> When the cat leaped onto the table.
>
> Running for the bus.

When fragments appear next to related sentences, however, they are harder to spot.

> We had just sat down to dinner. When the cat leaped onto the table.
>
> I tripped and twisted my ankle. Running for the bus.

Recognizing sentence fragments

To be a sentence, a word group must consist of at least one independent clause. An independent clause includes a subject and a verb, and it either stands alone or could stand alone.

To test whether a word group is a complete sentence or a fragment, use the flowchart on page 189. By using the flowchart, you can see exactly why *When the cat leaped onto the table* is a fragment: It has a subject (*cat*) and a verb (*leaped*), but it begins with a subordinating word (*When*), which makes the word group a dependent clause. *Running for the bus* is a fragment because it lacks a subject and a verb (*Running* is a verbal, not a verb). (See also 48b and 48e.)

Repairing sentence fragments

You can repair most fragments in one of two ways:

- Pull the fragment into a nearby sentence.
- Rewrite the fragment as a complete sentence.

► **We had just sat down to dinner/ ~~When~~ [when] the cat leaped onto the table.**

► **[Running for the bus,] I tripped and twisted my ankle. ~~Running for the bus.~~**

Test for fragments

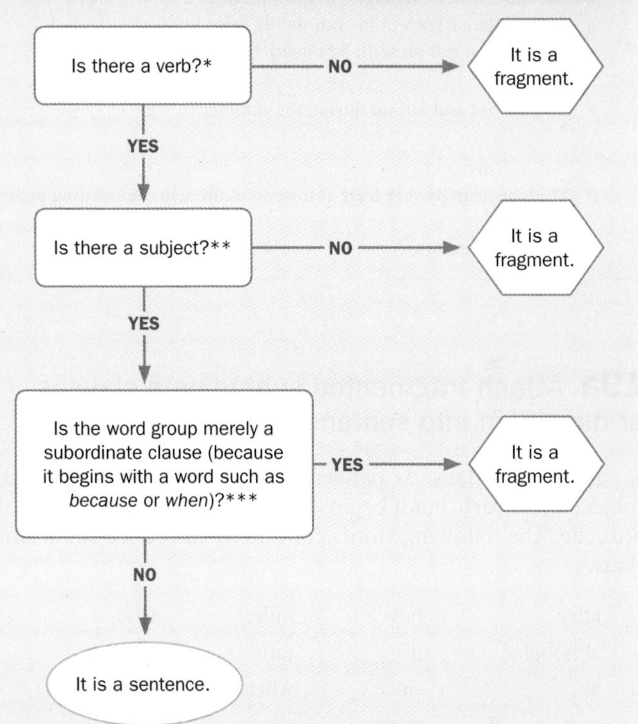
Is there a verb?*
NO
It is a fragment.
YES
Is there a subject?**
NO
It is a fragment.
YES
Is the word group merely a subordinate clause (because it begins with a word such as *because* or *when*)?***
YES
It is a fragment.
NO
It is a sentence.

*Do not mistake verbals for verbs. A verbal is a verb form (such as *walking, to act*) that does not function as a verb of a clause. (See 48b.)

**The subject of a sentence may be *you*, understood but not present in the sentence. (See 47a.)

***A sentence may open with a subordinate clause, but the sentence must also include an independent clause. (See 19a and 49a.)

If you find any fragments, try one of these methods of revision (see 19a–19c):

1. Attach the fragment to a nearby sentence.
2. Rewrite the fragment as a complete sentence.

Multilingual

Unlike some other languages, English requires a subject and a verb in every sentence (except in commands, where the subject *you* is understood but not present: *Sit down*). See 30a and 30b.

► ~~Is~~ It is often hot and humid during the summer.

► Students are usually very busy at the end of the semester writing papers and taking exams.

19a Attach fragmented subordinate clauses or turn them into sentences.

A subordinate clause is patterned like a sentence, with both a subject and a verb, but it begins with a word that marks it as subordinate. The following words commonly introduce subordinate clauses.

after	how	unless	who
although	if	until	whom
as	since	when	whose
as if	so that	where	why
because	than	whether	
before	that	which	
even though	though	while	

Subordinate clauses function within sentences as adjectives, as adverbs, or as nouns. They cannot stand alone. (See 48e.)

Most fragmented clauses beg to be pulled into a sentence nearby.

► Americans have come to fear the West Nile virus/ ~~Because~~ because it is transmitted by the common mosquito.

Because introduces a subordinate clause, so it cannot stand alone. (For punctuation of subordinate clauses appearing at the end of a sentence, see 33f.)

► **Although psychiatrist Peter Kramer expresses concerns about Prozac~~.~~, ~~Many~~ many other doctors believe that the benefits of antidepressants outweigh the risks.**

Although introduces a subordinate clause, which cannot stand alone. (For punctuation of subordinate clauses at the beginning of a sentence, see 32b.)

If a fragmented clause cannot be attached to a nearby sentence or if you feel that attaching it would be awkward, try turning the clause into a sentence. The simplest way to do this is to delete the opening word or words that mark the clause as subordinate.

► **Population increases and uncontrolled development are taking a deadly toll on the environment. ~~So that across~~ Across the globe, fragile ecosystems are collapsing.**

19b Attach fragmented phrases or turn them into sentences.

Like subordinate clauses, phrases function within sentences as adjectives, as adverbs, or as nouns. They cannot stand alone. Fragmented phrases are often prepositional or verbal phrases; sometimes they are appositives, words or word groups that rename nouns or pronouns. (See 48a, 48b, and 48c.)

Often a fragmented phrase may simply be pulled into a nearby sentence.

► **The archaeologists worked slowly~~.~~, ~~Examining~~ examining and labeling every pottery shard they uncovered.**

The word group beginning with *Examining* is a verbal phrase, so it cannot stand alone.

► **The patient displayed symptoms of ALS~~.~~, ~~A~~ a neurodegenerative disease.**

A neurodegenerative disease is an appositive renaming the noun *ALS*. (For punctuation of appositives, see 32e.)

If a fragmented phrase cannot be pulled into a nearby sentence effectively, turn the phrase into a sentence. You may need to add a subject, a verb, or both.

▶ **In the training session, Jamie explained how to access our new database. ~~Also~~ [She also taught us] how to submit expense reports and request vendor payments.**

The revision turns the fragmented phrase into a sentence by adding a subject and a verb.

19c Attach other fragmented word groups or turn them into sentences.

Other word groups that are commonly fragmented include parts of compound predicates, lists, and examples introduced by *for example*, *in addition*, or similar expressions.

Parts of compound predicates

A predicate consists of a verb and its objects, complements, and modifiers (see 47b). A compound predicate includes two or more predicates joined with a coordinating conjunction such as *and*, *but*, or *or*. Because the parts of a compound predicate have the same subject, they should appear in the same sentence.

▶ **The woodpecker finch of the Galápagos Islands carefully selects a twig of a certain size and shape/ ~~And~~ [and] then uses this tool to pry out grubs from trees.**

The subject is *finch*, and the compound predicate is *selects . . . and . . . uses*. (For punctuation of compound predicates, see 33a.)

Lists

To correct a fragmented list, often you can attach it to a nearby sentence with a colon or a dash. (See 35a and 39a.)

▶ **It has been said that there are only three indigenous American art forms/: ~~Musical~~ [musical] comedy, jazz, and soap opera.**

Sometimes terms like *especially*, *namely*, *like*, and *such as* introduce fragmented lists. Such fragments can usually be attached to the preceding sentence.

▶ **In the twentieth century, the South produced some great American writers~~.~~, ~~Such~~ such as Flannery O'Connor, William Faulkner, Alice Walker, and Tennessee Williams.**

Examples introduced by *for example*, *in addition*, or similar expressions

Other expressions that introduce examples or explanations can lead to unintentional fragments. Although you may begin a sentence with some of the following words or phrases, make sure that what follows has a subject and a verb.

also	for example	mainly
and	for instance	or
but	in addition	that is

Often the easiest solution is to turn the fragment into a sentence.

▶ **In his memoir, Primo Levi describes the horrors of living in a concentration camp. For example, ~~working~~ he worked without food and ~~suffering~~ suffered emotional abuse.**

The writer corrected this fragment by adding a subject — *he* — and substituting verbs for the verbals *working* and *suffering*.

▶ **Deborah Tannen's research reveals that men and women have different ideas about communication. For example, Tannen explains that a woman "expects her husband to be a new and improved version of her best friend" (441).**

A quotation must be part of a complete sentence. *That a woman "expects her husband to be a new and improved version of her best friend"* is a fragment — a subordinate clause. In this case, adding a signal phrase that includes a subject and a verb (*Tannen explains*) corrects the fragment and clarifies that the quotation is from Tannen.

19d Exception: A fragment may be used for effect.

Writers occasionally use sentence fragments for special purposes.

FOR EMPHASIS	Following the dramatic Americanization of their children, even my parents grew more publicly confident. *Especially my mother.* — Richard Rodriguez
TO ANSWER A QUESTION	Are these new drug tests 100 percent reliable? *Not in the opinion of most experts.*
TRANSITIONS	*And now the opposing arguments.*
EXCLAMATIONS	*Not again!*
IN ADVERTISING	*Fewer carbs. Improved taste.*

Although fragments are sometimes appropriate, writers and readers do not always agree on when they are appropriate. That's why you will find it safer to write in complete sentences.

EXERCISE 19–1 Repair any fragment by attaching it to a nearby sentence or by rewriting it as a complete sentence. If a word group is correct, write "correct" after it. Possible revisions appear in the back of the book. *More practice:* LaunchPadSolo

One Greek island that should not be missed is Mykonos~~.~~, ~~A~~ a vacation spot for Europeans and a playground for the rich and famous.

a. Listening to the CD her sister had sent, Mia was overcome with a mix of emotions. Happiness, homesickness, and nostalgia.

b. Cortés and his soldiers were astonished when they looked down from the mountains and saw Tenochtitlán. The magnificent capital of the Aztecs.

c. Although my spoken Spanish is not very good. I can read the language with ease.

d. There are several reasons for not eating meat. One reason being that dangerous chemicals are used throughout the various stages of meat production.

e. To learn how to sculpt beauty from everyday life. This is my intention in studying art and archaeology.

LaunchPadSolo **macmillanhighered.com/rules8e**

19 Sentence fragments
> Exercises: 19–3 to 19–7
> LearningCurve: Sentence fragments

EXERCISE 19–2 Repair each fragment in the following passage by attaching it to a sentence nearby or by rewriting it as a complete sentence.

> Digital technology has revolutionized information delivery. Forever blurring the lines between information and entertainment. Yesterday's readers of books and newspapers are today's readers of e-books and news blogs. Countless readers have moved on from print information entirely. Choosing instead to scroll their way through a text on their Amazon Kindle or in an online forum. Once a nation of people spoon-fed television commercials and the six o'clock evening news. We are now seemingly addicted to YouTube. Remember the family trip when Dad or Mom wrestled with a road map? On the way to St. Louis or Seattle? No wrestling is required with a GPS navigator by the driver's side. Unless it's Mom and Dad wrestling over who gets to program the address. Accessing information now seems to be America's favorite pastime. John Horrigan, associate director for research at the Pew Internet and American Life Project, reports that 31 percent of American adults are "elite" users of technology. Who are "highly engaged" with digital content. As a country, we embrace information and communication technologies. Which include iPads, smartphones, and other handheld devices. Children rely on such devices and the Internet from an early age. For activities like reading, socializing, gaming, and information gathering.

20 Revise run-on sentences.

Run-on sentences are independent clauses that have not been joined correctly. An independent clause is a word group that can stand alone as a sentence. (See 49a.) When two independent clauses appear in one sentence, they must be joined in one of these ways:

- with a comma and a coordinating conjunction (*and*, *but*, *or*, *nor*, *for*, *so*, *yet*)
- with a semicolon (or occasionally with a colon or a dash)

Recognizing run-on sentences

There are two types of run-on sentences. When a writer puts no mark of punctuation and no coordinating conjunction between independent clauses, the result is called a *fused sentence.*

FUSED Air pollution poses risks to all humans it can be deadly for asthma sufferers.
(INDEPENDENT CLAUSE / INDEPENDENT CLAUSE)

A far more common type of run-on sentence is the *comma splice*—two or more independent clauses joined with a comma but without a coordinating conjunction. In some comma splices, the comma appears alone.

COMMA SPLICE Air pollution poses risks to all humans, it can be deadly for asthma sufferers.

In other comma splices, the comma is accompanied by a joining word that is *not* a coordinating conjunction. There are only seven coordinating conjunctions in English: *and, but, or, nor, for, so,* and *yet.*

COMMA SPLICE Air pollution poses risks to all humans, however, it can be deadly for asthma sufferers.

However is a transitional expression and cannot be used with only a comma to join two independent clauses (see 20b).

Recognizing run-on sentences

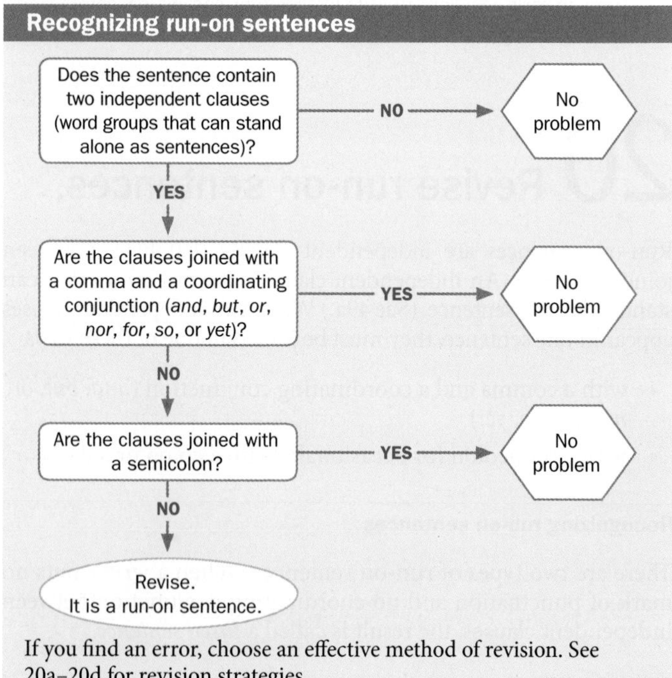
Does the sentence contain two independent clauses (word groups that can stand alone as sentences)?
NO
No problem
YES
Are the clauses joined with a comma and a coordinating conjunction (and, but, or, nor, for, so, or yet)?
YES
No problem
NO
Are the clauses joined with a semicolon?
YES
No problem
NO
Revise. It is a run-on sentence.

If you find an error, choose an effective method of revision. See 20a–20d for revision strategies.

Revising run-on sentences

To revise a run-on sentence, you have four choices.

1. Use a comma and a coordinating conjunction (*and*, *but*, *or*, *nor*, *for*, *so*, *yet*).

► **Air pollution poses risks to all humans, ^but it can be deadly for people with asthma.**

2. Use a semicolon (or, if appropriate, a colon or a dash). A semicolon may be used alone or with a transitional expression.

► **Air pollution poses risks to all humans~~,~~; it can be deadly for people with asthma.**

► **Air pollution poses risks to all humans~~,~~; ^however, it can be deadly for people with asthma.**

3. Make the clauses into separate sentences.

► **Air pollution poses risks to all humans~~,~~. ~~it~~ ^It can be deadly for people with asthma.**

4. Restructure the sentence, perhaps by subordinating one of the clauses.

► ^Although air ~~**Air**~~ **pollution poses risks to all humans, it can be deadly for people with asthma.**

One of these revision techniques usually works better than the others for a particular sentence. The fourth technique, the one requiring the most extensive revision, is often the most effective.

20a Consider separating the clauses with a comma and a coordinating conjunction.

There are seven coordinating conjunctions in English: *and*, *but*, *or*, *nor*, *for*, *so*, and *yet*. When a coordinating conjunction joins independent clauses, it is usually preceded by a comma. (See 32a.)

▶ Some lesson plans include exercises, ^but completing them should not be the focus of all class periods.

▶ Many government officials privately admit that the polygraph is unreliable, ~~however,~~ ^yet they continue to use it as a security measure.

However is a transitional expression, not a coordinating conjunction, so it cannot be used with only a comma to join independent clauses. (See also 20b.)

20b Consider separating the clauses with a semicolon (or, if appropriate, with a colon or a dash).

When the independent clauses are closely related and their relation is clear without a coordinating conjunction, a semicolon is an acceptable method of revision. (See 34a.)

▶ Tragedy depicts the individual confronted with the fact of death/^; comedy depicts the adaptability of human society.

A semicolon is required between independent clauses that have been linked with a transitional expression (such as *however, therefore, moreover, in fact,* or *for example*). For a longer list, see 34b.

▶ In his film adaptation of the short story "Killings," director Todd Field changed key details of the plot/^; in fact, he added whole scenes that do not appear in the story.

A colon or a dash may be more appropriate if the first independent clause introduces the second or if the second clause summarizes or explains the first. (See 35a and 39a.) In formal writing, the colon is usually preferred to the dash.

▶ Nuclear waste is hazardous: ~~this~~ ^This is an indisputable fact.

▶ The female black widow spider is often a widow of her own making/^— she has been known to eat her partner after mating.

A colon is an appropriate method of revision if the first independent clause introduces a quoted sentence.

► **Nobel Peace Prize winner Al Gore had this to say about climate change/: "The truth is that our circumstances are not only new; they are completely different than they have ever been in all of human history."**

20c Consider making the clauses into separate sentences.

► **Why should we spend money on expensive space exploration/? ~~we~~ We have enough underfunded programs here on Earth.**

A question and a statement should be separate sentences.

► **Some studies have suggested that the sexual relationships of bonobos set them apart from common chimpanzees/. ~~according~~ According to Stanford (1998), these differences have been exaggerated.**

Using a comma to join two independent clauses creates a comma splice. In this example, an effective revision is to separate the first independent clause (*Some studies . . .*) from the second independent clause (*these differences . . .*) and to keep the signal phrase with the second clause. (See also 61a on citing sources in APA style.)

NOTE: When two quoted independent clauses are divided by explanatory words, make each clause its own sentence.

► **"It's always smart to learn from your mistakes," quipped my supervisor/. ~~"it's~~ "It's even smarter to learn from the mistakes of others."**

20d Consider restructuring the sentence, perhaps by subordinating one of the clauses.

If one of the independent clauses is less important than the other, turn the less important clause into a subordinate clause or phrase. (For more about subordination, see 14, especially the chart on p. 156.)

▶ **One of the most famous advertising slogans is Wheaties cereal's "Breakfast of Champions," ~~it~~ which was penned in 1933.**

▶ **Mary McLeod Bethune, ~~was~~ the seventeenth child of former slaves, ~~she~~ founded the National Council of Negro Women in 1935.**

Minor ideas in these sentences are now expressed in subordinate clauses or phrases.

EXERCISE 20–1 Revise the following run-on sentences using the method of revision suggested in brackets. Possible revisions appear in the back of the book. *More practice:* LaunchPadSolo

Because Daniel had been obsessed with his weight as a teenager, he rarely ate anything sweet. [*Restructure the sentence.*]

a. The city had one public swimming pool, it stayed packed with children all summer long. [*Restructure the sentence.*]
b. The building is being renovated, therefore at times we have no heat, water, or electricity. [*Use a comma and a coordinating conjunction.*]
c. The view was not what the travel agent had described, where were the rolling hills and the shimmering rivers? [*Make two sentences.*]
d. Walker's coming-of-age novel is set against a gloomy scientific backdrop, the earth's rotation has begun to slow down. [*Use a semicolon.*]
e. City officials had good reason to fear a major earthquake, most of the business district was built on landfill. [*Use a colon.*]

LaunchPadSolo macmillanhighered.com/rules8e
20 Run-on sentences
> Exercises: 20–4 to 20–9
> LearningCurve: Run-on sentences

EXERCISE 20–2 Revise any run-on sentences using a technique that you find effective. If a sentence is correct, write "correct" after it. Possible revisions appear in the back of the book.

> **Crossing so many time zones on an eight-hour flight, I knew I would be tired when I arrived, ~~however,~~ but I was too excited to sleep on the plane.**

a. Wind power for the home is a supplementary source of energy, it can be combined with electricity, gas, or solar energy.
b. Aidan viewed Sofia Coppola's *Lost in Translation* three times and then wrote a paper describing the film as the work of a mysterious modern painter.
c. In the Middle Ages, the streets of London were dangerous places, it was safer to travel by boat along the Thames.
d. "He's not drunk," I said, "he's in a state of diabetic shock."
e. Are you able to endure extreme angle turns, high speeds, frequent jumps, and occasional crashes, then supermoto racing may be a sport for you.

EXERCISE 20–3 In the following rough draft, revise any run-on sentences.

Some parents and educators argue that requiring uniforms in public schools would improve student behavior and performance. They think that uniforms give students a more professional attitude toward school, moreover, they believe that uniforms help create a sense of community among students from diverse backgrounds. But parents and educators should consider the drawbacks to requiring uniforms in public schools.

Uniforms do create a sense of community, they do this, however, by stamping out individuality. Youth is a time to express originality, it is a time to develop a sense of self. One important way young people express their identities is through the clothes they wear. The self-patrolled dress code of high school students may be stricter than any school-imposed code, nevertheless, trying to control dress habits from above will only lead to resentment or to mindless conformity.

If children are going to act like adults, they need to be treated like adults, they need to be allowed to make their own choices. Telling young people what to wear to school merely prolongs their childhood. Requiring uniforms undermines the educational purpose of public schools, which is not just to teach facts and figures but to help young people grow into adults who are responsible for making their own choices.

21 Make subjects and verbs agree.

In the present tense, verbs agree with their subjects in number (singular or plural) and in person (first, second, third): *I sing, you sing, he sings, she sings, we sing, they sing.* Even if your ear recognizes the standard subject-verb combinations presented in 21a, you will no doubt encounter tricky situations such as those described in 21b–21k.

21a Learn to recognize the standard subject-verb combinations.

This section describes the basic guidelines for making present-tense verbs agree with their subjects. The present-tense ending *-s* (or *-es*) is used on a verb if its subject is third-person singular (*he, she, it*, and singular nouns); otherwise, the verb takes no ending. Consider, for example, the present-tense forms of the verbs *love* and *try*, given at the beginning of the chart on page 204.

The verb *be* varies from this pattern; it has special forms in *both* the present and the past tense. These forms appear at the end of the chart.

If you aren't sure of the standard forms, use the charts on pages 204 and 205 as you proofread your work for subject-verb agreement. You may also want to look at 27c on *-s* endings of regular and irregular verbs.

21b Make the verb agree with its subject, not with a word that comes between.

Word groups often come between the subject and the verb. Such word groups, usually modifying the subject, may contain a noun that at first appears to be the subject. By mentally stripping away such modifiers, you can isolate the noun that is in fact the subject.

The *samples* on the tray in the lab *need* testing.

- ▶ **High levels of air pollution cause~~s~~ damage to the respiratory tract.**

  The subject is *levels*, not *pollution*. Strip away the phrase *of air pollution* to hear the correct verb: *levels cause.*

- ▶ **The slaughter of pandas for their pelts ~~have~~ has caused the panda population to decline drastically.**

  The subject is *slaughter*, not *pandas* or *pelts*.

NOTE: Phrases beginning with the prepositions *as well as*, *in addition to*, *accompanied by*, *together with*, and *along with* do not make a singular subject plural.

- ▶ **The governor as well as his press secretary ~~were~~ was on the plane.**

  To emphasize that two people were on the plane, the writer could use *and* instead: *The governor and his press secretary were on the plane.*

21c Treat most subjects joined with *and* as plural.

A subject with two or more parts is said to be compound. If the parts are connected with *and*, the subject is almost always plural.

Leon and Jan often *jog* together.

- ▶ **The Supreme Court's willingness to hear the case and its affirmation of the original decision ~~has~~ have set a new precedent.**

EXCEPTION 1: When the parts of the subject form a single unit or when they refer to the same person or thing, treat the subject as singular.

Fish and chips was a last-minute addition to the menu.

Sue's friend and adviser was surprised by her decision.

Subject-verb agreement at a glance

Present-tense forms of *love* and *try* (typical verbs)

	SINGULAR		PLURAL	
FIRST PERSON	I	love	we	love
SECOND PERSON	you	love	you	love
THIRD PERSON	he/she/it*	loves	they**	love

	SINGULAR		PLURAL	
FIRST PERSON	I	try	we	try
SECOND PERSON	you	try	you	try
THIRD PERSON	he/she/it*	tries	they**	try

Present-tense forms of *have*

	SINGULAR		PLURAL	
FIRST PERSON	I	have	we	have
SECOND PERSON	you	have	you	have
THIRD PERSON	he/she/it*	has	they**	have

Present-tense forms of *do* (including negative forms)

	SINGULAR		PLURAL	
FIRST PERSON	I	do/don't	we	do/don't
SECOND PERSON	you	do/don't	you	do/don't
THIRD PERSON	he/she/it*	does/doesn't	they**	do/don't

Present-tense and past-tense forms of *be*

	SINGULAR		PLURAL	
FIRST PERSON	I	am/was	we	are/were
SECOND PERSON	you	are/were	you	are/were
THIRD PERSON	he/she/it*	is/was	they**	are/were

*And singular nouns (*child, Roger*)
**And plural nouns (*children, the Mannings*)

When to use the -s (or -es) form of a present-tense verb

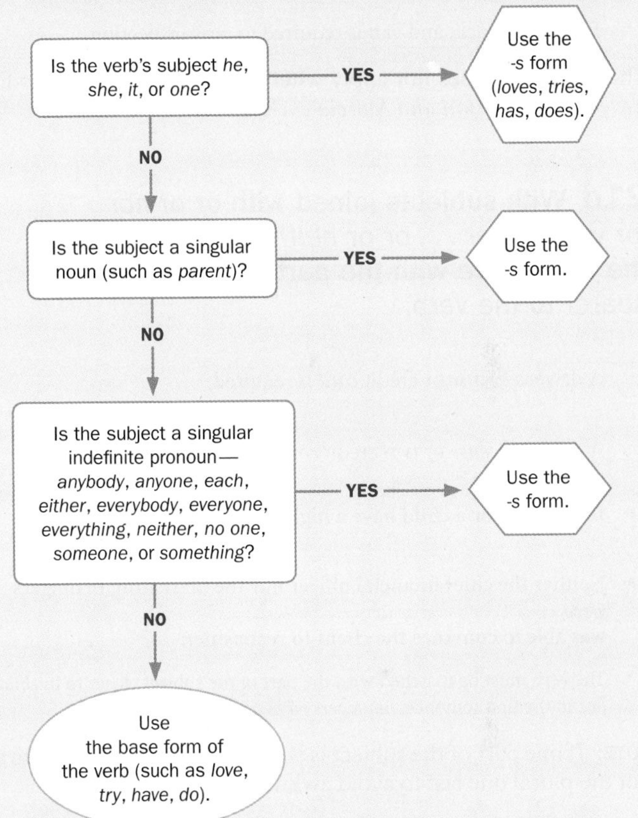
Is the verb's subject *he*, *she*, *it*, or *one*?
YES
Use the -s form (*loves*, *tries*, *has*, *does*).
NO
Is the subject a singular noun (such as *parent*)?
YES
Use the -s form.
NO
Is the subject a singular indefinite pronoun— *anybody*, *anyone*, *each*, *either*, *everybody*, *everyone*, *everything*, *neither*, *no one*, *someone*, or *something*?
YES
Use the -s form.
NO
Use the base form of the verb (such as *love*, *try*, *have*, *do*).

EXCEPTION: Choosing the correct present-tense form of *be* (*am*, *is*, or *are*) is not quite so simple. See the chart on the previous page for both present- and past-tense forms of *be*.

TIP: Do not use the *-s* form of a verb if it follows a modal verb such as *can*, *must*, or *should* or another helping verb. (See 28c.)

EXCEPTION 2: When a compound subject is preceded by *each* or *every*, treat it as singular.

Every car, truck, and van is required to pass inspection.

This exception does not apply when a compound subject is followed by *each*: *Alan and Marcia each have different ideas.*

21d With subjects joined with *or* or *nor* (or with *either . . . or* or *neither . . . nor*), make the verb agree with the part of the subject nearer to the verb.

A driver's *license* or credit *card is* required.

A driver's *license* or two credit *cards are* required.

▸ **If an infant or a child ~~have~~ has a high fever, call a doctor.**

▸ **Neither the chief financial officer nor the marketing managers ~~was~~ were able to convince the client to reconsider.**

The verb must be matched with the part of the subject closer to it: *child has* in the first sentence, *managers were* in the second.

NOTE: If one part of the subject is singular and the other is plural, put the plural one last to avoid awkwardness.

21e Treat most indefinite pronouns as singular.

Indefinite pronouns are pronouns that do not refer to specific persons or things. The following commonly used indefinite pronouns are singular.

anybody	each	everyone	nobody	somebody
anyone	either	everything	no one	someone
anything	everybody	neither	nothing	something

Many of these words appear to have plural meanings, and they are often treated as such in casual speech. In formal written English, however, they are nearly always treated as singular.

Everyone on the team *supports* the coach.

► **Each of the essays ~~have~~ been graded.** [has]

► **Nobody who participated in the clinical trials ~~were~~ given a placebo.** [was]

The subjects of these sentences are *Each* and *Nobody.* These indefinite pronouns are third-person singular, so the verbs must be *has* and *was.*

A few indefinite pronouns (*all, any, none, some*) may be singular or plural depending on the noun or pronoun they refer to.

SINGULAR *Some* of our *luggage was* lost.

None of his *advice makes* sense.

PLURAL *Some* of the *rocks are* slippery.

None of the *eggs were* broken.

NOTE: When the meaning of *none* is emphatically "not one," *none* may be treated as singular: *None* [meaning "Not one"] *of the eggs was broken.* Using *not one* instead is sometimes clearer: *Not one of the eggs was broken.*

21f Treat collective nouns as singular unless the meaning is clearly plural.

Collective nouns such as *jury, committee, audience, crowd, troop, family,* and *couple* name a class or a group. In American English, collective nouns are nearly always treated as singular: They emphasize the group as a unit. Occasionally, when there is some reason to draw attention to the individual members of the group, a collective noun may be treated as plural. (See also 22b.)

SINGULAR The *class respects* the teacher.

PLURAL The *class are* debating among themselves.

To underscore the notion of individuality in the second sentence, many writers would add a clearly plural noun.

PLURAL The class *members are* debating among themselves.

▶ **The board of trustees ~~meet~~ meets in Denver twice a year.**

The board as a whole meets; there is no reason to draw attention to its individual members.

▶ **A young couple ~~was~~ were arguing about politics while holding hands.**

The meaning is clearly plural. Only separate individuals can argue and hold hands.

NOTE: The phrase *the number* is treated as singular, *a number* as plural.

SINGULAR *The number* of school-age children *is* declining.

PLURAL *A number* of children *are* attending the wedding.

NOTE: In general, when fractions or units of measurement are used with a singular noun, treat them as singular; when they are used with a plural noun, treat them as plural.

SINGULAR *Three-fourths* of the salad *has* been eaten.

Twenty *inches* of wallboard *was* covered with mud.

PLURAL *One-fourth* of the drivers *were* texting.

Two *pounds* of blueberries *were* used to make the pie.

21g Make the verb agree with its subject even when the subject follows the verb.

Verbs ordinarily follow subjects. When this normal order is reversed, it is easy to become confused. Sentences beginning with *there is* or *there are* (or *there was* or *there were*) are inverted; the subject follows the verb.

There *are* surprisingly few *honeybees* left in southern China.

▶ **There ~~was~~ ^were a social worker and a journalist at the meeting.**

The subject, *worker and journalist*, is plural, so the verb must be *were*.

Occasionally, you may decide to invert a sentence for variety or effect. When you do so, check to make sure that your subject and verb agree.

▶ **Of particular concern ~~is~~ ^are penicillin and tetracycline, antibiotics used to make animals more resistant to disease.**

The subject, *penicillin and tetracycline*, is plural, so the verb must be *are*.

21h Make the verb agree with its subject, not with a subject complement.

One basic sentence pattern in English consists of a subject, a linking verb, and a subject complement: *Jack is a lawyer.* Because the subject complement (*lawyer*) names or describes the subject (*Jack*), it is sometimes mistaken for the subject. (See 47b on subject complements.)

These *exercises are* a way to test your ability to perform under pressure.

▶ **A tent and a sleeping bag ~~is~~ ^are the required equipment.**

Tent and bag is the subject, not *equipment*.

▶ **A major force in today's economy ~~are~~ is children — as consumers, decision makers, and trend spotters.**

Force is the subject, not *children*. If the corrected version seems too awkward, make *children* the subject: *Children are a major force in today's economy — as consumers, decision makers, and trend spotters.*

21i *Who*, *which*, and *that* take verbs that agree with their antecedents.

Like most pronouns, the relative pronouns *who*, *which*, and *that* have antecedents, nouns or pronouns to which they refer. Relative pronouns used as subjects of subordinate clauses take verbs that agree with their antecedents.

Take a *course that prepares* you for classroom management.

One of the

Constructions such as *one of the students who* [or *one of the things that*] cause problems for writers. Do not assume that the antecedent must be *one*. Instead, consider the logic of the sentence.

▶ **Our ability to use language is one of the things that ~~sets~~ set us apart from animals.**

The antecedent of *that* is *things*, not *one*. Several things set us apart from animals.

Only one of the

When the phrase *the only* comes before *one*, you are safe in assuming that *one* is the antecedent of the relative pronoun.

▶ **Veronica was the only one of the first-year Spanish students who ~~were~~ was fluent enough to apply for the exchange program.**

The antecedent of *who* is *one*, not *students*. Only one student was fluent enough.

21j Words such as *athletics*, *economics*, *mathematics*, *physics*, *politics*, *statistics*, *measles*, and *news* are usually singular, despite their plural form.

is
▸ **Politics ~~are~~ among my mother's favorite pastimes.**

EXCEPTION: Occasionally some of these words, especially *economics*, *mathematics*, *politics*, and *statistics*, have plural meanings: *Office politics often sway decisions about hiring and promotion. The economics of the building plan are prohibitive.*

21k Titles of works, company names, words mentioned as words, and gerund phrases are singular.

describes
▸ ***Lost Cities* ~~describe~~ the discoveries of fifty ancient civilizations.**

specializes
▸ **Delmonico Brothers ~~specialize~~ in organic produce.**

is
▸ ***Controlled substances* ~~are~~ a euphemism for illegal drugs.**

A gerund phrase consists of an *-ing* verb form followed by any objects, complements, or modifiers (see 48b). Treat gerund phrases as singular.

makes
▸ **Encountering long hold times ~~make~~ customers impatient with telephone tech support.**

EXERCISE 21–1 Edit the following sentences to eliminate problems with subject-verb agreement. If a sentence is correct, write "correct" after it. Answers appear in the back of the book.

More practice: LaunchPadSolo

were
Jack's first days in the infantry ~~was~~ grueling.

a. One of the main reasons for elephant poaching are the profits received from selling the ivory tusks.

b. Not until my interview with Dr. Hwang were other possibilities opened to me.
c. A number of students in the seminar was aware of the importance of joining the discussion.
d. Batik cloth from Bali, blue and white ceramics from Delft, and a bocce ball from Turin has made Angelie's room the talk of the dorm.
e. The board of directors, ignoring the wishes of the neighborhood, has voted to allow further development.

EXERCISE 21–2 For each sentence in the following passage, underline the subject (or compound subject) and then select the verb that agrees with it. (If you have trouble identifying the subject, consult 47a.)

More practice: LaunchPadSolo

Loggerhead sea turtles (migrate / migrates) thousands of miles before returning to their nesting location every two to three years. The nesting season for loggerhead turtles (span / spans) the hottest months of the summer. Although the habitat of Atlantic loggerheads (range / ranges) from Newfoundland to Argentina, nesting for these turtles (take / takes) place primarily along the southeastern coast of the United States. Female turtles that have reached sexual maturity (crawl / crawls) ashore at night to lay their eggs. The cavity that serves as a nest for the eggs (is / are) dug out with the female's strong flippers. Deposited into each nest (is / are) anywhere from fifty to two hundred spherical eggs, also known as a *clutch*. After a two-month incubation period, all eggs in the clutch (begin / begins) to hatch, and within a few days the young turtles attempt to make their way into the ocean. A major cause of the loggerhead's decreasing numbers (is / are) natural predators such as raccoons, birds, and crabs. Beach erosion and coastal development also (threaten / threatens) the turtles' survival. For example, a crowd of curious humans or lights from beachfront residences (is / are) enough to make the female abandon her nesting plans and return to the ocean. Since only one in one thousand loggerheads survives to adulthood, special care should be taken to protect this threatened species.

LaunchPadSolo **macmillanhighered.com/rules8e**

21 Subject-verb agreement
> Exercises: 21–3 to 21–6
> LearningCurve: Subject-verb agreement

22 Make pronouns and antecedents agree.

A pronoun is a word that substitutes for a noun. (See 46b.) Many pronouns have antecedents, nouns or pronouns to which they refer. A pronoun and its antecedent agree when they are both singular or both plural.

SINGULAR *Dr. Ava Berto* finished *her* rounds.

PLURAL The hospital *interns* finished *their* rounds.

> The pronouns *he*, *his*, *she*, *her*, *it*, and *its* must agree in gender (masculine, feminine, or neuter) with their antecedents, not with the words they modify.
>
> *Steve* visited *his* [not *her*] sister in Seattle.
>
> Multilingual

22a Do not use plural pronouns to refer to singular antecedents.

Writers are frequently tempted to use plural pronouns to refer to two kinds of singular antecedents: indefinite pronouns and generic nouns.

Indefinite pronouns

Indefinite pronouns refer to nonspecific persons or things. Even though some of the following indefinite pronouns may seem to have plural meanings, treat them as singular in formal English.

anybody	each	everyone	nobody	somebody
anyone	either	everything	no one	someone
anything	everybody	neither	nothing	something

Everyone performs at *his or her* [not *their*] own fitness level.

When a plural pronoun refers mistakenly to a singular indefinite pronoun, you can usually choose one of three options for revision:

1. Replace the plural pronoun with *he or she* (or *his or her*).
2. Make the antecedent plural.
3. Rewrite the sentence so that no problem of agreement exists.

► **When someone travels outside the United States for the first time, ~~they need~~** *he or she needs* **to apply for a passport.**

► **When ~~someone travels~~** *people travel* **outside the United States for the first time, they need to apply for a passport.**

► **~~When someone~~** *Anyone who* **travels outside the United States for the first time, ~~they need~~** *needs* **to apply for a passport.**

Because the *he or she* construction is wordy, often the second or third revision strategy is more effective. Using *he* (or *his*) to refer to persons of either sex, while less wordy, is considered sexist, as is using *she* (or *her*) for all persons. Some writers alternate male and female pronouns throughout a text, but the result is often awkward. See 17e and the chart on page 216 for strategies that avoid sexist language.

NOTE: If you change a pronoun from singular to plural (or vice versa), check to be sure that the verb agrees with the new pronoun (see 21e).

Generic nouns

A generic noun represents a typical member of a group, such as a typical student, or any member of a group, such as any lawyer. Although generic nouns may seem to have plural meanings, they are singular.

Every *runner* must train rigorously if *he or she wants* [not *they want*] to excel.

When a plural pronoun refers mistakenly to a generic noun, you will usually have the same three revision options as mentioned at the top of this page for indefinite pronouns.

he or she wants
▶ A medical student must study hard if ~~they want~~ to succeed.

Medical students
▶ ~~A medical student~~ must study hard if they want to succeed.

▶ A medical student must study hard ~~if they want~~ to succeed.

22b Treat collective nouns as singular unless the meaning is clearly plural.

Collective nouns such as *jury*, *committee*, *audience*, *crowd*, *class*, *troop*, *family*, *team*, and *couple* name a group. Ordinarily the group functions as a unit, so the noun should be treated as singular; if the members of the group function as individuals, however, the noun should be treated as plural. (See also 21f.)

AS A UNIT — The *committee* granted *its* permission to build.

AS INDIVIDUALS — The *committee* put *their* signatures on the document.

When treating a collective noun as plural, many writers prefer to add a clearly plural antecedent such as *members* to the sentence: *The members of the committee put their signatures on the document.*

▶ **Defense attorney Clarence Darrow surprisingly urged the jury to find his client, John Scopes, guilty so that he could appeal the case to a higher court. The jury complied, returning ~~their~~ its verdict in only nine minutes.**

There is no reason to draw attention to the individual members of the jury, so *jury* should be treated as singular.

22c Treat most compound antecedents joined with *and* as plural.

In 1987, *Reagan and Gorbachev* held a summit where *they* signed the Intermediate-Range Nuclear Forces Treaty.

Choosing a revision strategy that avoids sexist language

Because many readers object to sexist language, avoid using *he*, *him*, and *his* (or *she*, *her*, and *hers*) to refer to both men and women. Also try to avoid the wordy expressions *he or she* and *his or her*. More graceful alternatives are usually possible.

Use an occasional *he or she* (or *his or her*).

► In our office, everyone works at ~~their~~ [his or her] own pace.

Make the antecedent plural.

► ~~An employee~~ [Employees] on extended disability leave may continue their life insurance.

Recast the sentence.

► The amount of vacation time a federal worker may accrue depends on ~~their~~ length of service.

► ~~If a~~ [A] child ~~is~~ born to parents who are both tall/ ~~they have~~ [has] a high chance of being tall.

► In his autobiography, Benjamin Franklin suggests that anyone can achieve success ~~as long as they live~~ [by living] a virtuous life and ~~work~~ [working] hard.

22d With compound antecedents joined with *or* or *nor* (or with *either . . . or* or *neither . . . nor*), make the pronoun agree with the nearer antecedent.

Either *Bruce* or *Tom* should receive first prize for *his* poem.

Neither the *mouse* nor the *rats* could find *their* way through the maze.

NOTE: If one of the antecedents is singular and the other plural, as in the second example, put the plural one last to avoid awkwardness.

EXCEPTION: If one antecedent is male and the other female, do not follow the traditional rule. The sentence *Either Bruce or Elizabeth should receive first prize for her short story* makes no sense. The best solution is to recast the sentence: *The prize for best short story should go to either Bruce or Elizabeth.*

EXERCISE 22–1 Edit the following sentences to eliminate problems with pronoun-antecedent agreement. Most of the sentences can be revised in more than one way, so experiment before choosing a solution. If a sentence is correct, write "correct" after it. Possible revisions appear in the back of the book. *More practice:* LaunchPadSolo

Recruiters
~~The recruiter~~ **may tell the truth, but there is much that they choose not to tell.**

a. Every presidential candidate must appeal to a wide variety of ethnic and social groups if they want to win the election.
b. David lent his motorcycle to someone who allowed their friend to use it.
c. The aerobics teacher motioned for everyone to move their arms in wide, slow circles.
d. The parade committee was unanimous in its decision to allow all groups and organizations to join the festivities.
e. The applicant should be bilingual if they want to qualify for this position.

EXERCISE 22–2 Edit the following paragraph to eliminate problems with pronoun-antecedent agreement or sexist language.

A common practice in businesses is to put each employee in their own cubicle. A typical cubicle resembles an office, but their walls don't reach the ceiling. Many office managers feel that a cubicle floor plan has its advantages. Cubicles make a large area feel spacious. In addition, they can be moved around so that each new employee can be accommodated in his own work area. Of course, the cubicle model also has problems. The typical employee is not as happy with a cubicle

LaunchPadSolo **macmillanhighered.com/rules8e**
22 Pronoun-antecedent agreement
> Exercises: 22–3 to 22–6
> LearningCurve: Pronoun agreement and pronoun reference

as they would be with a traditional office. Also, productivity can suffer. Neither a manager nor a frontline worker can ordinarily do their best work in a cubicle because of noise and lack of privacy. Each worker can hear his neighbors tapping on computer keyboards, making telephone calls, and muttering under their breath.

23 Make pronoun references clear.

Pronouns substitute for nouns; they are a kind of shorthand. In a sentence like *After Andrew intercepted the ball, he kicked it as hard as he could*, the pronouns *he* and *it* substitute for the nouns *Andrew* and *ball.* The word a pronoun refers to is called its *antecedent.*

23a Avoid ambiguous or remote pronoun reference.

Ambiguous pronoun reference occurs when a pronoun could refer to two possible antecedents.

The pitcher broke when Gloria set it

▶ **~~When Gloria set the pitcher~~ on the glass-topped table/. ~~it broke.~~**

"You have

▶ **Tom told James, ~~that he had~~ won the lottery."**

What broke — the pitcher or the table? Who won the lottery — Tom or James? The revisions eliminate the ambiguity.

Remote pronoun reference occurs when a pronoun is too far away from its antecedent for easy reading.

▶ **After the court ordered my ex-husband to pay child support, he refused. Eight months later, the judge ordered him to make payments directly to the court, which would in turn pay me.**

my ex-husband
After six months, payments stopped. Again ~~he~~ was summoned to appear in court; he did not respond.

The pronoun *he* was too distant from its antecedent, *ex-husband*, which appeared several sentences earlier.

23b Generally, avoid broad reference of *this*, *that*, *which*, and *it*.

For clarity, the pronouns *this*, *that*, *which*, and *it* should ordinarily refer to specific antecedents rather than to whole ideas or sentences. When a pronoun's reference is needlessly broad, either replace the pronoun with a noun or supply an antecedent to which the pronoun clearly refers.

► **By advertising on television, pharmaceutical companies gain exposure for their prescription drugs. Patients respond to ~~this~~ by requesting drugs they might not need.** the ads

For clarity, the writer substituted the noun *ads* for the pronoun *this*, which referred broadly to the idea expressed in the preceding sentence.

► **Romeo and Juliet were both too young to have acquired much wisdom, ~~and~~ that accounts for their rash actions.** a fact

The writer added an antecedent (*fact*) that the pronoun *that* clearly refers to.

23c Do not use a pronoun to refer to an implied antecedent.

A pronoun should refer to a specific antecedent, not to a word that is implied but not present in the sentence.

► **After braiding Ann's hair, Sue decorated ~~them~~ with ribbons.** the braids

The pronoun *them* referred to Ann's braids (implied by the term *braiding*), but the word *braids* did not appear in the sentence.

Modifiers, such as possessives, cannot serve as antecedents. A modifier may strongly imply the noun that a pronoun might logically refer to, but it is not itself that noun.

► **In ~~Jamaica Kincaid's~~ "Girl," ~~she~~** Jamaica Kincaid **describes the advice a mother gives her daughter, including the mysterious warning not to be "the kind of woman who the baker won't let near the bread" (454).**

Using the possessive form of an author's name to introduce a source leads to a problem later in this sentence: The pronoun *she* cannot refer logically to a possessive modifier (*Jamaica Kincaid's*). The revision substitutes the noun *Jamaica Kincaid* for the pronoun *she*, thereby eliminating the problem. (For more on writing with sources in MLA style, see 55.)

23d Avoid the indefinite use of *they*, *it*, and *you*.

Do not use the pronoun *they* to refer indefinitely to persons who have not been specifically mentioned. *They* should always refer to a specific antecedent.

► **In June, ~~they~~** the board **voted to charge a fee for students to participate in sports and music programs.**

The word *it* should not be used indefinitely in constructions such as *It is said on television* . . . or *In the article, it says that*. . . .

► The **~~In the~~ encyclopedia ~~it~~ states that male moths can smell female moths from several miles away.**

The pronoun *you* is appropriate only when the writer is addressing the reader directly: *Once you have kneaded the dough, let it rise in a warm place.* Except in informal contexts, however, *you* should not be used to mean "anyone in general." Use a noun instead.

► **Ms. Pickersgill's *Guide to Etiquette* stipulates that ~~you~~** a guest **should not arrive at a party too early or leave too late.**

23e To refer to persons, use *who, whom,* or *whose,* not *which* or *that.*

In most contexts, use *who, whom,* or *whose* to refer to persons, *which* or *that* to refer to animals or things. *Which* is reserved only for animals or things; it is impolite to use it to refer to persons.

▶ **All thirty-two women in the study, half of ~~which~~ whom were unemployed for more than six months, reported higher self-esteem after job training.**

Although *that* is sometimes used to refer to persons, many readers will find such references dehumanizing. It is more polite to use a form of *who* — a word reserved only for people.

▶ **During the two-day festival El Día de los Muertos (Day of the Dead), Mexican families celebrate loved ones ~~that~~ who have died.**

EXERCISE 23–1 Edit the following sentences to correct errors in pronoun reference. In some cases, you will need to decide on an antecedent that the pronoun might logically refer to. Possible revisions appear in the back of the book. *More practice:* LaunchPadSolo

Although Apple makes the most widely recognized smartphone, other companies have gained a share of the market. ~~This~~ The competition has kept prices from skyrocketing.

a. They say that engineering students should have hands-on experience with dismantling and reassembling machines.

b. She had decorated her living room with posters from chamber music festivals. This led her date to believe that she was interested in classical music. Actually, she preferred rock.

c. In my high school, you didn't need to get all A's to be considered a success; you just needed to work to your ability.

LaunchPadSolo **macmillanhighered.com/rules8e**

23 Pronoun reference

> Exercises: 23–3 to 23–6

> LearningCurve: Pronoun agreement and pronoun reference

d. Marianne told Jenny that she was worried about her mother's illness.
e. Though Lewis cried for several minutes after scraping his knee, eventually it subsided.

EXERCISE 23–2 Edit the following passage to correct errors in pronoun reference. In some cases, you will need to decide on an antecedent that the pronoun might logically refer to.

> Since its launch in the 1980s, the Internet has grown to be one of the largest communications forums in the world. The Internet was created by a team of academics who were building on a platform that government scientists had started developing in the 1950s. They initially viewed it as a noncommercial enterprise that would serve only the needs of the academic and technical communities. But with the introduction of user-friendly browser technology in the 1990s, it expanded tremendously. By the late 1990s, many businesses were connecting to the Internet with high-speed broadband and fiber-optic connections, which is also true of many home users today. Accessing information, shopping, and communicating are easier than ever before. This, however, can lead to some possible drawbacks. You forfeit privacy when you search, shop, and communicate. They say that avoiding disclosure of personal information and routinely adjusting your privacy settings on social media sites are the best ways to protect yourself on the Internet.

24 Distinguish between pronouns such as *I* and *me*.

The personal pronouns in the following chart change what is known as *case form* according to their grammatical function in a sentence. Pronouns functioning as subjects or subject complements appear in the *subjective* case; those functioning as objects appear in the *objective* case; and those showing ownership appear in the *possessive* case.

	SUBJECTIVE CASE	OBJECTIVE CASE	POSSESSIVE CASE
SINGULAR	I	me	my
	you	you	your
	he/she/it	him/her/it	his/her/its

	SUBJECTIVE CASE	OBJECTIVE CASE	POSSESSIVE CASE
PLURAL	we	us	our
	you	you	your
	they	them	their

Pronouns in the subjective and objective cases are frequently confused. Most of the rules in this section specify when to use one or the other of these cases. Section 24g explains a special use of pronouns and nouns in the possessive case.

24a Use the subjective case (*I, you, he, she, it, we, they*) for subjects and subject complements.

When personal pronouns are used as subjects, ordinarily your ear will tell you the correct pronoun. Problems sometimes arise, however, with compound word groups containing a pronoun, so it is not always safe to trust your ear.

▶ **Joel ran away because his stepfather and ~~him~~ [he] had quarreled.**

His stepfather and he is the subject of the verb *had quarreled.* If we strip away the words *his stepfather and*, the correct pronoun becomes clear: *he had quarreled* (not *him had quarreled*).

When a pronoun is used as a subject complement (a word following a linking verb), your ear may mislead you, since the incorrect form is frequently heard in casual speech. (See "subject complements," 47b.)

▶ **During the Lindbergh trial, Bruno Hauptmann repeatedly denied that the kidnapper was ~~him.~~ [he.]**

If *kidnapper was he* seems too stilted, rewrite the sentence: . . . *Bruno Hauptmann repeatedly denied that he was the kidnapper.*

24b Use the objective case (*me, you, him, her, it, us, them*) for all objects.

When a personal pronoun is used as a direct object, an indirect object, or the object of a preposition, ordinarily your ear will lead you to the correct pronoun. When an object is compound, however, you may occasionally become confused.

- ▶ **Janice was indignant when she realized that the salesclerk was insulting her mother and ~~she.~~** her.

  Her mother and her is the direct object of the verb *was insulting.* Strip away the words *her mother and* to hear the correct pronoun: *was insulting her* (not *was insulting she*).

- ▶ **The most traumatic experience for her father and ~~I~~** me **occurred long after her operation.**

  Her father and me is the object of the preposition *for.* Strip away the words *her father and* to test for the correct pronoun: *for me* (not *for I*).

When in doubt about the correct pronoun, some writers try to avoid making the choice by using a reflexive pronoun such as *myself.* Using a reflexive pronoun in such situations is nonstandard.

- ▶ **Nidra gave my cousin and ~~myself~~** me **some good tips on traveling in New Delhi.**

  My cousin and me is the indirect object of the verb *gave.* For correct uses of *myself,* see the glossary of usage in the appendixes.

24c Put an appositive and the word to which it refers in the same case.

Appositives are noun phrases that rename nouns or pronouns. A pronoun used as an appositive has the same function (usually subject or object) as the word(s) it renames.

- ▶ **The managers, Dr. Bell and ~~me,~~** I, **could not agree on a plan.**

  The appositive *Dr. Bell and I* renames the subject, *managers.* Test: *I could not agree* (not *me could not agree*).

- ▶ **The reporter interviewed only two witnesses, the bicyclist and ~~I.~~** me.

  The appositive *the bicyclist and me* renames the direct object, *witnesses.* Test: *interviewed me* (not *interviewed I*).

24d Following *than* or *as*, choose the pronoun that expresses your meaning.

When a comparison begins with *than* or *as*, your choice of a pronoun will depend on your intended meaning. To test for the correct pronoun, mentally complete the sentence: *My roommate likes football more than I* [*do*].

- ▶ **In our report on nationalized health care in the United States, we argued that Canadians are much better off than ~~us.~~** ^we.

  We is the subject of the verb *are*, which is understood: *Canadians are much better off than we* [*are*]. If the correct English seems too formal, you can always add the verb.

- ▶ **We respected no other candidate for the city council as much as ~~she.~~** ^her.

  This sentence means that we respected no other candidate as much as *we respected her. Her* is the direct object of the understood verb *respected.*

24e For *we* or *us* before a noun, choose the pronoun that would be appropriate if the noun were omitted.

- ▶ ^We **~~Us~~ tenants would rather fight than move.**

- ▶ **Management is shortchanging** ^us **~~we~~ tenants.**

  No one would say *Us would rather fight than move* or *Management is shortchanging we.*

24f Use the objective case for subjects and objects of infinitives.

An infinitive is the word *to* followed by the base form of a verb. (See 48b.) Subjects of infinitives are an exception to the rule that subjects must be in the subjective case. Whenever an infinitive has a subject, it must be in the objective case. Objects of infinitives also are in the objective case.

► **Sue asked John and ~~I~~ [me] to drive the senator and ~~she~~ [her] to the airport.**

John and me is the subject of the infinitive *to drive*; *senator and her* is the direct object of the infinitive.

24g Use the possessive case to modify a gerund.

A pronoun that modifies a gerund or a gerund phrase should be in the possessive case (*my*, *our*, *your*, *his*, *her*, *its*, *their*). A gerund is a verb form ending in *-ing* that functions as a noun. Gerunds frequently appear in phrases; when they do, the whole gerund phrase functions as a noun. (See 48b.)

► **The chances of ~~you~~ [your] being hit by lightning are about two million to one.**

Your modifies the gerund phrase *being hit by lightning.*

Nouns as well as pronouns may modify gerunds. To form the possessive case of a noun, use an apostrophe and an *-s* (*victim's*) or just an apostrophe (*victims'*). (See 36a.)

► **The old order in France paid a high price for the ~~aristocracy~~ [aristocracy's] exploiting the lower classes.**

The possessive noun *aristocracy's* modifies the gerund phrase *exploiting the lower classes.*

EXERCISE 24–1 Edit the following sentences to eliminate errors in pronoun case. If a sentence is correct, write "correct" after it. Answers appear in the back of the book. *More practice:* LaunchPadSolo

Papa chops wood for neighbors much younger than ~~him.~~ [he.]

LaunchPadSolo **macmillanhighered.com/rules8e**

24 Pronoun case

> Exercises: 24–3 to 24–5

> Exercises: 24/25–6 and 24/25–7 (pronoun review)

a. Rick applied for the job even though he heard that other candidates were more experienced than he.
b. The volleyball team could not believe that the coach was she.
c. She appreciated him telling the truth in such a difficult situation.
d. The director has asked you and I to draft a proposal for a new recycling plan.
e. Five close friends and myself rented a station wagon, packed it with food, and drove two hundred miles to Mardi Gras.

EXERCISE 24–2 In the following paragraph, choose the correct pronoun in each set of parentheses.

> We may blame television for the number of products based on characters in children's TV shows — from Big Bird to SpongeBob — but in fact merchandising that capitalizes on a character's popularity started long before television. Raggedy Ann began as a child's rag doll, and a few years later books about (she / her) and her brother, Raggedy Andy, were published. A cartoonist named Johnny Gruelle painted a cloth face on a family doll and applied for a patent in 1915. Later Gruelle began writing and illustrating stories about Raggedy Ann, and in 1918 (he / him) and a publisher teamed up to publish the books and sell the dolls. He was not the only one to try to sell products linked to children's stories. Beatrix Potter published the first of many Peter Rabbit picture books in 1902, and no one was better than (she / her) at making a living from spin-offs. After Peter Rabbit and Benjamin Bunny became popular, Potter began putting pictures of (they / them) and their little animal friends on merchandise. Potter had fans all over the world, and she understood (them / their) wanting to see Peter Rabbit not only in books but also on teapots and plates and lamps and other furnishings for the nursery. Potter and Gruelle, like countless others before and since, knew that entertaining children could be a profitable business.

25 Distinguish between *who* and *whom*.

The choice between *who* and *whom* (or *whoever* and *whomever*) occurs primarily in subordinate clauses and in questions. *Who* and *whoever*, subjective-case pronouns, are used for subjects and subject complements. *Whom* and *whomever*, objective-case pronouns, are used for objects. (See 25a and 25b.)

An exception to this general rule occurs when the pronoun functions as the subject of an infinitive (see 25c). See also 24f.

25a Use *who* and *whom* correctly in subordinate clauses.

When *who* and *whom* (or *whoever* and *whomever*) introduce subordinate clauses, their case is determined by their function *within the clause they introduce.*

In the following two examples, the pronouns *who* and *whoever* function as the subjects of the clauses they introduce.

▶ **First prize goes to the runner ~~whom~~** who **earns the most points.**

The subordinate clause is *who earns the most points.* The verb of the clause is *earns*, and its subject is *who.*

▶ **Maya Angelou's *I Know Why the Caged Bird Sings* should be read by ~~whomever~~** whoever **is interested in the effects of racial prejudice on children.**

The writer selected the pronoun *whomever*, thinking that it was the object of the preposition *by.* However, the object of the preposition is the entire subordinate clause *whoever is interested in the effects of racial prejudice on children.* The verb of the clause is *is*, and the subject of the verb is *whoever.*

When functioning as an object in a subordinate clause, *whom* (or *whomever*) also appears out of order, before the subject and verb. To choose the correct pronoun, you can mentally restructure the clause.

▶ **You will work with our senior traders, ~~who~~** whom **you will meet later.**

The subordinate clause is *whom you will meet later.* The subject of the clause is *you*, and the verb is *will meet. Whom* is the direct object of the verb. The correct choice becomes clear if you mentally restructure the clause: *you will meet whom.*

When functioning as the object of a preposition in a subordinate clause, *whom* is often separated from its preposition.

▶ **The tutor ~~who~~** whom **I was assigned to was very supportive.**

Whom is the object of the preposition *to.* In this sentence, the writer might choose to drop *whom*: *The tutor I was assigned to was very supportive.*

NOTE: Inserted expressions such as *they know*, *I think*, and *she says* should be ignored in determining whether to use *who* or *whom*.

▶ **The speech pathologist reported a particularly difficult session with a stroke patient ~~whom~~ [who] she knew was suffering from aphasia.**

Who is the subject of *was suffering*, not the object of *knew*.

25b Use *who* and *whom* correctly in questions.

When *who* and *whom* (or *whoever* and *whomever*) are used to open questions, their case is determined by their function within the question. In the following example, *who* functions as the subject of the question.

▶ **~~Whom~~ [Who] was responsible for creating that computer virus?**

Who is the subject of the verb *was*.

When *whom* functions as the object of a verb or the object of a preposition in a question, it appears out of normal order. To choose the correct pronoun, you can mentally restructure the question.

▶ **~~Who~~ [Whom] did the Democratic Party nominate in 2008?**

Whom is the direct object of the verb *did nominate*. This becomes clear if you restructure the question: *The Democratic Party did nominate whom in 2008?*

25c Use *whom* for subjects or objects of infinitives.

An infinitive is the word *to* followed by the base form of a verb. (See 48b.) Subjects of infinitives are an exception to the rule that subjects must be in the subjective case. The subject of an infinitive must be in the objective case. Objects of infinitives also are in the objective case.

▶ **When it comes to money, I know ~~who~~ [whom] to believe.**

The infinitive phrase *whom to believe* is the direct object of the verb *know*, and *whom* is the subject of the infinitive *to believe*.

NOTE: In spoken English, *who* is frequently used when the correct *whom* sounds too stuffy. Although some readers will accept constructions like *Who* [not *Whom*] *did Senator Boxer replace?* in informal written English, it is safer to use *whom* in formal writing.

EXERCISE 25–1 Edit the following sentences to eliminate errors in the use of *who* and *whom* (or *whoever* and *whomever*). If a sentence is correct, write "correct" after it. Answers appear in the back of the book.

More practice: LaunchPadSolo

What is the address of the artist ~~who~~ whom Antonio hired?

a. Arriving late for rehearsal, we had no idea who was supposed to dance with whom.

b. The environmental policy conference featured scholars who I had never heard of.

c. Whom did you support in last month's election for student government president?

d. Daniel always gives a holiday donation to whomever needs it.

e. So many singers came to the audition that Natalia had trouble deciding who to select for the choir.

26 Choose adjectives and adverbs with care.

Adjectives modify nouns or pronouns. They usually come before the word they modify; occasionally they function as complements following the word they modify. Adverbs modify verbs, adjectives, or other adverbs. (See 46d and 46e.)

Many adverbs are formed by adding *-ly* to adjectives (*normal*, *normally*; *smooth*, *smoothly*). But don't assume that all words ending in *-ly* are adverbs or that all adverbs end in *-ly*. Some adjectives end in *-ly* (*lovely*, *friendly*), and some adverbs don't (*always*, *here*, *there*). When in doubt, consult a dictionary.

LaunchPadSolo **macmillanhighered.com/rules8e**

25 *Who and whom*

> Exercises: 25–2 and 25–3

> Exercises: 24/25–6 and 24/25–7 (pronoun review)

Multilingual

Placement of adjectives and adverbs can be a tricky matter for multilingual writers. See 30f and 30h.

26a Use adjectives to modify nouns.

Adjectives ordinarily precede the nouns they modify. But they can also function as subject complements or object complements, following the nouns they modify.

Multilingual

In English, adjectives are not pluralized to agree with the words they modify:

► The ~~reds~~ red roses were a surprise.

Subject complements

A subject complement follows a linking verb and completes the meaning of the subject. (See 47b.) When an adjective functions as a subject complement, it describes the subject.

Justice is *blind.*

Problems can arise with verbs such as *smell*, *taste*, *look*, and *feel*, which sometimes, but not always, function as linking verbs. If the word following one of these verbs describes the subject, use an adjective; if the word following the verb modifies the verb, use an adverb.

ADJECTIVE The detective looked *cautious.*

ADVERB The detective looked *cautiously* for fingerprints.

The adjective *cautious* describes the detective; the adverb *cautiously* modifies the verb *looked.*

Linking verbs suggest states of being, not actions. Notice, for example, the different meanings of *looked* in the preceding examples. To look cautious suggests the state of being cautious; to look cautiously is to perform an action in a cautious way.

▶ **The lilacs in our backyard smell especially ~~sweetly~~ sweet this year.**

The verb *smell* suggests a state of being, not an action. Therefore, it should be followed by an adjective, not an adverb.

▶ **The drawings looked ~~well~~ good after the architect made a few changes.**

The verb *looked* is a linking verb suggesting a state of being, not an action. The adjective *good* is appropriate following the linking verb to describe *drawings*. (See also 26c.)

Object complements

An object complement follows a direct object and completes its meaning. (See 47b.) When an adjective functions as an object complement, it describes the direct object.

Sorrow makes *us wise*.

Object complements occur with verbs such as *call*, *consider*, *create*, *find*, *keep*, and *make*. When a modifier follows the direct object of one of these verbs, use an adjective to describe the direct object; use an adverb to modify the verb.

ADJECTIVE The referee called the plays *perfect*.

ADVERB The referee called the plays *perfectly*.

The first sentence means that the referee considered the plays to be perfect; the second means that the referee did an excellent job of calling the plays.

26b Use adverbs to modify verbs, adjectives, and other adverbs.

When adverbs modify verbs (or verbals), they nearly always answer the question When? Where? How? Why? Under what conditions? How often? or To what degree? When adverbs modify adjectives or other adverbs, they usually qualify or intensify the meaning of the word they modify. (See 46e.)

Adjectives are often used incorrectly in place of adverbs in casual or nonstandard speech.

► **The travel arrangement worked out ~~perfect~~ perfectly for everyone.**

► **The manager must see that the office runs ~~smooth~~ smoothly and ~~efficient.~~ efficiently.**

The adverb *perfectly* modifies the verb *worked out*; the adverbs *smoothly* and *efficiently* modify the verb *runs.*

► **The chance of recovering any lost property looks ~~real~~ really slim.**

Only adverbs can modify adjectives or other adverbs. *Really* intensifies the meaning of the adjective *slim.*

26c Distinguish between *good* and *well*, *bad* and *badly*.

Good is an adjective (*good performance*). *Well* is an adverb when it modifies a verb (*speak well*). The use of the adjective *good* in place of the adverb *well* to modify a verb is nonstandard and especially common in casual speech.

► **We were glad that Sanya had done ~~good~~ well on the CPA exam.**

The adverb *well* modifies the verb *had done.*

Confusion can arise because *well* is an adjective when it modifies a noun or pronoun and means "healthy" or "satisfactory" (*The babies were well and warm*).

► **Adrienne did not feel ~~good,~~ well, but she performed anyway.**

As an adjective following the linking verb *did feel*, *well* describes Adrienne's health.

Bad is always an adjective and should be used to describe a noun; *badly* is always an adverb and should be used to modify a verb. The adverb *badly* is often used inappropriately to describe a noun, especially following a linking verb.

▶ **The sisters felt ~~badly~~ [bad] when they realized they had left their brother out of the planning.**

The adjective *bad* is used after the linking verb *felt* to describe the noun *sisters.*

26d Use comparatives and superlatives with care.

Most adjectives and adverbs have three forms: the positive, the comparative, and the superlative.

POSITIVE	COMPARATIVE	SUPERLATIVE
soft	softer	softest
fast	faster	fastest
careful	more careful	most careful
bad	worse	worst
good	better	best

Comparative versus superlative

Use the comparative to compare two things, the superlative to compare three or more.

▶ **Which of these two low-carb drinks is ~~best?~~ [better?]**

▶ **Though Shaw and Jackson are impressive, Zhao is the ~~more~~ [most] qualified of the three candidates running for mayor.**

Forming comparatives and superlatives

To form comparatives and superlatives of most one- and two-syllable adjectives, use the endings *-er* and *-est*: *smooth, smoother, smoothest*; *easy, easier, easiest.* With longer adjectives, use *more* and *most* (or *less* and *least* for downward comparisons): *exciting, more exciting, most exciting*; *helpful, less helpful, least helpful.*

Some one-syllable adverbs take the endings *-er* and *-est* (*fast, faster, fastest*), but longer adverbs and all of those ending in *-ly* form the comparative and superlative with *more* and *most* (or *less* and *least*).

The comparative and superlative forms of some adjectives and adverbs are irregular: *good, better, best*; *well, better, best*; *bad, worse, worst*; *badly, worse, worst.*

▶ **The Kirov is the ~~talentedest~~ most talented ballet company we have seen.**

▶ **According to our projections, sales at local businesses will be ~~worser~~ worse than those at the chain stores this winter.**

Double comparatives or superlatives

Do not use double comparatives or superlatives. When you have added *-er* or *-est* to an adjective or adverb, do not also use *more* or *most* (or *less* or *least*).

▶ **Of all her family, Julia is the ~~most~~ happiest about the move.**

▶ **All the polls indicated that Gore was more ~~likelier~~ likely to win than Bush.**

Absolute concepts

Avoid expressions such as *more straight*, *less perfect*, *very round*, and *most unique*. Either something is unique or it isn't. It is illogical to suggest that absolute concepts come in degrees.

▶ **That is the most ~~unique~~ unusual wedding gown I have ever seen.**

▶ **The painting is even more ~~priceless~~ valuable because it is signed.**

26e Avoid double negatives.

Standard English allows two negatives only if a positive meaning is intended: *The orchestra was not unhappy with its performance* (meaning that the orchestra was happy). Using a double negative to emphasize a negative meaning is nonstandard.

Negative modifiers such as *never*, *no*, and *not* should not be paired with other negative modifiers or with negative words such as *neither*, *none*, *no one*, *nobody*, and *nothing*.

▶ **The county is not doing ~~nothing~~ *anything* to see that the trash is picked up.**

The double negative *not . . . nothing* is nonstandard.

The modifiers *hardly, barely,* and *scarcely* are considered negatives in standard English, so they should not be used with negatives such as *not, no one,* or *never.*

▶ **Maxine is so weak that she ~~can't~~ *can* hardly climb stairs.**

EXERCISE 26–1 Edit the following sentences to eliminate errors in the use of adjectives and adverbs. If a sentence is correct, write "correct" after it. Answers appear in the back of the book.

More practice: LaunchPadSolo

We weren't surprised by how ~~good~~ *well* the sidecar racing team flowed through the tricky course.

a. Do you expect to perform good on the exam next week?
b. With the budget deadline approaching, our office hasn't hardly had time to handle routine correspondence.
c. Some flowers smell surprisingly bad.
d. The customer complained that he hadn't been treated nice by the agent on the phone.
e. Of all the smart people in my family, Aunt Ida is the most cleverest.

EXERCISE 26–2 Edit the following passage to eliminate errors in the use of adjectives and adverbs.

Doctors recommend that to give skin the most fullest protection from ultraviolet rays, people should use plenty of sunscreen, limit sun exposure, and wear protective clothing. The commonest sunscreens today are known as "broad spectrum" because they block out both UVA and UVB rays. These lotions don't feel any differently on the skin from the old UVA-only types, but they work best at preventing premature aging and skin cancer. Many sunscreens claim to be waterproof, but they won't hardly provide adequate coverage after extended periods of swimming or perspiring. To protect good, even waterproof sunscreens should be reapplied liberal and often. All areas of exposed skin, including ears, backs of hands, and tops of feet, need to be coated good to avoid burning or damage. Some people's skin reacts bad to PABA, or para-aminobenzoic acid, so PABA-free (hypoallergenic) sunscreens are widely available. In addition to recommending sunscreen, doctors almost unanimously agree that people should stay out of the sun when rays are the most strongest — between 10:00 a.m. and 3:00 p.m. — and should limit time in the sun. They also suggest that people wear long-sleeved shirts, broad-brimmed hats, and long pants whenever possible.

27 Choose appropriate verb forms, tenses, and moods in Standard English.

In speech, some people use verb forms and tenses that match a home dialect or variety of English. In writing, use Standard English verb forms unless you are quoting nonstandard speech or using alternative forms for literary effect. (See 17c.)

Except for the verb *be*, all verbs in English have five forms. The following list shows the five forms and provides a sample sentence in which each might appear.

BASE FORM	Usually I (*walk*, *ride*).
PAST TENSE	Yesterday I (*walked*, *rode*).
PAST PARTICIPLE	I have (*walked*, *ridden*) many times before.
PRESENT PARTICIPLE	I am (*walking*, *riding*) right now.
-S FORM	He/she/it (*walks*, *rides*) regularly.

The verb *be* has eight forms instead of the usual five: *be*, *am*, *is*, *are*, *was*, *were*, *being*, *been*.

27a Choose Standard English forms of irregular verbs.

For all regular verbs, the past-tense and past-participle forms are the same (ending in *-ed* or *-d*), so there is no danger of confusion. This is not true, however, for irregular verbs, such as the following.

BASE FORM	PAST TENSE	PAST PARTICIPLE
go	went	gone
break	broke	broken
fly	flew	flown
sing	sang	sung

The past-tense form always occurs alone, without a helping verb. It expresses action that occurred entirely in the past: *I rode to work yesterday. I walked to work last Tuesday.* The past participle is used with a helping verb. It forms the perfect tenses with *has, have*, or *had*; it forms the passive voice with *be, am, is, are, was, were, being*, or *been*. (See 46c for a complete list of helping verbs and 27f for a survey of tenses.)

PAST TENSE	Last July, we *went* to Paris.
HELPING VERB + PAST PARTICIPLE	We *have gone* to Paris twice.

The list of common irregular verbs beginning below will help you distinguish between the past tense and the past participle. Choose the past-participle form if the verb in your sentence requires a helping verb; choose the past-tense form if the verb does not require a helping verb. (See verb tenses in 27f.)

► **Yesterday we ~~seen~~ saw a documentary about Isabel Allende.**

The past-tense *saw* is required because there is no helping verb.

► **The truck was apparently ~~stole~~ stolen while the driver ate lunch.**

► **By Friday, the stock market had ~~fell~~ fallen two hundred points.**

Because of the helping verbs *was* and *had*, the past-participle forms are required: *was stolen, had fallen.*

Common irregular verbs

BASE FORM	PAST TENSE	PAST PARTICIPLE
arise	arose	arisen
awake	awoke, awaked	awaked, awoke, awoken
be	was, were	been

BASE FORM	PAST TENSE	PAST PARTICIPLE
beat	beat	beaten, beat
become	became	become
begin	began	begun
bend	bent	bent
bite	bit	bitten, bit
blow	blew	blown
break	broke	broken
bring	brought	brought
build	built	built
burst	burst	burst
buy	bought	bought
catch	caught	caught
choose	chose	chosen
cling	clung	clung
come	came	come
cost	cost	cost
deal	dealt	dealt
dig	dug	dug
dive	dived, dove	dived
do	did	done
drag	dragged	dragged
draw	drew	drawn
dream	dreamed, dreamt	dreamed, dreamt
drink	drank	drunk
drive	drove	driven
eat	ate	eaten
fall	fell	fallen
fight	fought	fought
find	found	found
fly	flew	flown
forget	forgot	forgotten, forgot
freeze	froze	frozen
get	got	gotten, got

(*continued*)

BASE FORM	PAST TENSE	PAST PARTICIPLE
give	gave	given
go	went	gone
grow	grew	grown
hang (execute)	hanged	hanged
hang (suspend)	hung	hung
have	had	had
hear	heard	heard
hide	hid	hidden
hurt	hurt	hurt
keep	kept	kept
know	knew	known
lay (put)	laid	laid
lead	led	led
lend	lent	lent
let (allow)	let	let
lie (recline)	lay	lain
lose	lost	lost
make	made	made
prove	proved	proved, proven
read	read	read
ride	rode	ridden
ring	rang	rung
rise (get up)	rose	risen
run	ran	run
say	said	said
see	saw	seen
send	sent	sent
set (place)	set	set
shake	shook	shaken
shoot	shot	shot
shrink	shrank	shrunk
sing	sang	sung
sink	sank	sunk

BASE FORM	PAST TENSE	PAST PARTICIPLE
sit (be seated)	sat	sat
slay	slew	slain
sleep	slept	slept
speak	spoke	spoken
spin	spun	spun
spring	sprang	sprung
stand	stood	stood
steal	stole	stolen
sting	stung	stung
strike	struck	struck, stricken
swear	swore	sworn
swim	swam	swum
swing	swung	swung
take	took	taken
teach	taught	taught
throw	threw	thrown
wake	woke, waked	waked, woken
wear	wore	worn
wring	wrung	wrung
write	wrote	written

27b Distinguish among the forms of *lie* and *lay*.

Writers and speakers frequently confuse the various forms of *lie* (meaning "to recline or rest on a surface") and *lay* (meaning "to put or place something"). *Lie* is an intransitive verb; it does not take a direct object: *The forms lie on the table.* The verb *lay* is transitive; it takes a direct object: *Please lay the forms on the table.* (See 47b.)

In addition to confusing the meaning of *lie* and *lay*, writers and speakers are often unfamiliar with the Standard English forms of these verbs.

BASE FORM	PAST TENSE	PAST PARTICIPLE	PRESENT PARTICIPLE
lie (recline)	lay	lain	lying
lay (put)	laid	laid	laying

▶ **Sue was so exhausted that she ~~laid~~ lay down for a nap.**

The past-tense form of *lie* ("to recline") is *lay.*

▶ **The patient had ~~laid~~ lain in an uncomfortable position all night.**

The past-participle form of *lie* ("to recline") is *lain.* If the correct English seems too stilted, recast the sentence: *The patient had been lying in an uncomfortable position all night.*

▶ **The prosecutor ~~lay~~ laid the pistol on a table close to the jurors.**

The past-tense form of *lay* ("to place") is *laid.*

▶ **Letters dating from 1915 were ~~laying~~ lying in a corner of the chest.**

The present participle of *lie* ("to rest on a surface") is *lying.*

EXERCISE 27–1 Edit the following sentences to eliminate problems with irregular verbs. If a sentence is correct, write "correct" after it. Answers appear in the back of the book. *More practice:* LaunchPadSolo

The ranger ~~seen~~ saw the forest fire ten miles away.

a. When I get the urge to exercise, I lay down until it passes.

b. Grandmother had drove our new hybrid to the sunrise church service, so we were left with the station wagon.

c. A pile of dirty rags was laying at the bottom of the stairs.

d. How did the game know that the player had went from the room with the blue ogre to the hall where the gold was heaped?

e. Abraham Lincoln took good care of his legal clients; the contracts he drew for the Illinois Central Railroad could never be broke.

27c Use *-s* (or *-es*) endings on present-tense verbs that have third-person singular subjects.

All singular nouns (*child, tree*) and the pronouns *he, she,* and *it* are third-person singular; indefinite pronouns such as *everyone*

LaunchPadSolo **macmillanhighered.com/rules8e**

27 Verb forms, tenses, and moods
> Exercises: 27–2 to 27–4
> LearningCurve: Verbs

and *neither* are also third-person singular. When the subject of a sentence is third-person singular, its verb takes an *-s* or *-es* ending in the present tense. (See also 21.)

	SINGULAR		PLURAL	
FIRST PERSON	I	know	we	know
SECOND PERSON	you	know	you	know
THIRD PERSON	he/she/it	knows	they	know
	child	knows	parents	know
	everyone	knows		

▸ **My neighbor ~~drive~~ [drives] to Marco Island every weekend.**

▸ **Sulfur dioxide ~~turn~~ [turns] leaves yellow, ~~dissolve~~ [dissolves] marble, and ~~eat~~ [eats] away iron and steel.**

The subjects *neighbor* and *sulfur dioxide* are third-person singular, so the verbs must end in *-s*.

TIP: Do not add the *-s* ending to the verb if the subject is not third-person singular. The writers of the following sentences, knowing they sometimes dropped *-s* endings from verbs, overcorrected by adding the endings where they don't belong.

▸ **I prepares program specifications and logic diagrams for every installation.**

The writer mistakenly concluded that the *-s* ending belongs on present-tense verbs used with *all* singular subjects, not just *third-person* singular subjects. The pronoun *I* is first-person singular, so its verb does not require the *-s*.

▸ **The dirt floors requires continual sweeping.**

The writer mistakenly thought that the verb needed an *-s* ending because of the plural subject. But the *-s* ending is used only on present-tense verbs with third-person *singular* subjects.

Has versus *have*

In the present tense, use *has* with third-person singular subjects; all other subjects require *have*.

	SINGULAR		PLURAL	
FIRST PERSON	I	have	we	have
SECOND PERSON	you	have	you	have
THIRD PERSON	he/she/it	has	they	have

▸ **This respected musician almost always ~~have~~ has a message to convey in his work.**

The subject *musician* is third-person singular, so the verb should be *has*.

▸ **My law classes ~~has~~ have helped me understand contracts.**

The subject of this sentence — *classes* — is third-person plural, so Standard English requires *have. Has* is used only with third-person singular subjects.

Does versus *do* and *doesn't* versus *don't*

In the present tense, use *does* and *doesn't* with third-person singular subjects; all other subjects require *do* and *don't*.

	SINGULAR		PLURAL	
FIRST PERSON	I	do/don't	we	do/don't
SECOND PERSON	you	do/don't	you	do/don't
THIRD PERSON	he/she/it	does/doesn't	they	do/don't

▸ **Grandfather really ~~don't~~ doesn't have a place to call home.**

Grandfather is third-person singular, so the verb should be *doesn't*.

Am, is, and *are*; *was* and *were*

The verb *be* has three forms in the present tense (*am, is, are*) and two in the past tense (*was, were*).

	SINGULAR		PLURAL	
FIRST PERSON	I	am/was	we	are/were
SECOND PERSON	you	are/were	you	are/were
THIRD PERSON	he/she/it	is/was	they	are/were

▸ **Did you think you ~~was~~ were going to drown?**

The subject *you* is second-person singular, so the verb should be *were*.

27d Do not omit -*ed* endings on verbs.

Speakers who do not fully pronounce -*ed* endings sometimes omit them unintentionally in writing. Failure to pronounce -*ed* endings is common in many dialects and in informal speech, even in Standard English. In the following frequently used words and phrases, for example, the -*ed* ending is not always fully pronounced.

advised	developed	prejudiced	supposed to
asked	fixed	pronounced	used to
concerned	frightened	stereotyped	

When a verb is regular, both the past tense and the past participle are formed by adding -*ed* (or -*d*) to the base form of the verb.

Past tense

Use the ending -*ed* or -*d* to express the past tense of regular verbs. The past tense is used when the action occurred entirely in the past.

fixed
▶ **Over the weekend, Ed ~~fix~~ ^ his brother's skateboard and tuned up his mother's 1991 Fiat.**

advised
▶ **Last summer, my counselor ~~advise~~ ^ me to ask my chemistry instructor for help.**

Past participles

Past participles are used in three ways: (1) following *have, has,* or *had* to form one of the perfect tenses; (2) following *be, am, is, are, was, were, being,* or *been* to form the passive voice; and (3) as adjectives modifying nouns or pronouns. The perfect tenses are listed on page 248, and the passive voice is discussed in 8a. For a discussion of participles as adjectives, see 48b.

asked
▶ **Robin has ~~ask~~ ^ for more housing staff for next year.**

Has asked is present perfect tense (*have* or *has* followed by a past participle).

▸ **Though it is not a new phenomenon, domestic violence is now** publicized ~~publicize~~ **more than ever.**

Is publicized is a verb in the passive voice (a form of *be* followed by a past participle).

▸ **All kickboxing classes end in a cool-down period to stretch** tightened ~~tighten~~ **muscles.**

The past participle *tightened* functions as an adjective modifying the noun *muscles*.

27e Do not omit needed verbs.

Although Standard English allows some linking verbs and helping verbs to be contracted in informal contexts, it does not allow them to be omitted.

Linking verbs, used to link subjects to subject complements, are frequently a form of *be*: *be, am, is, are, was, were, being, been*. (See 47b.) Some of these forms may be contracted (*I'm, she's, we're, you're, they're*), but they should not be omitted altogether.

▸ **When we** ^are **quiet in the evening, we can hear the crickets.**

Helping verbs, used with main verbs, include forms of *be*, *do*, and *have* and the modal verbs *can, will, shall, could, would, should, may, might*, and *must*. (See 46c.) Some helping verbs may be contracted (*he's leaving, we'll celebrate, they've been told*), but they should not be omitted altogether.

▸ **We** ^have **been in Chicago since last Thursday.**

▸ **Do you know someone who** ^would **be good for the job?**

Multilingual

Some languages do not require a linking verb between a subject and its complement. English, however, requires a verb in every sentence. See 30a.

▸ **Every night, I read a short book to my daughter. When I** ^am **too busy, my husband reads to her.**

EXERCISE 27–5 Edit the following sentences to eliminate problems with *-s* and *-ed* verb forms and with omitted verbs. If a sentence is correct, write "correct" after it. Answers appear in the back of the book.

More practice: LaunchPadSolo

The Pell Grant sometimes ~~cover~~ covers the student's full tuition.

a. The glass sculptures of the Swan Boats was prominent in the brightly lit lobby.

b. Visitors to the glass museum were not suppose to touch the exhibits.

c. Our church has all the latest technology, even a closed-circuit television.

d. Christos didn't know about Marlo's promotion because he never listens. He always talking.

e. Most psychologists agree that no one performs well under stress.

27f Choose the appropriate verb tense.

Tenses indicate the time of an action in relation to the time of the speaking or writing about that action.

The most common problem with tenses — shifting confusingly from one tense to another — is discussed in section 13. Other problems with tenses are detailed in this section, after the following survey of tenses.

Survey of tenses

Tenses are classified as present, past, and future, with simple, perfect, and progressive forms for each.

Simple tenses The simple tenses indicate relatively simple time relations. The *simple present* tense is used primarily for actions occurring at the same time they are being discussed or for actions occurring regularly. The *simple past* tense is used for actions completed in the past. The *simple future* tense is used for actions that will occur in the future. In the following table, the simple tenses

LaunchPadSolo **macmillanhighered.com/rules8e**
27 Verb forms, tenses, and moods
> Exercises: 27-6 to 27-8
> LearningCurve: Verbs

are given for the regular verb *walk*, the irregular verb *ride*, and the highly irregular verb *be*.

SIMPLE PRESENT

SINGULAR		PLURAL	
I	walk, ride, am	we	walk, ride, are
you	walk, ride, are	you	walk, ride, are
he/she/it	walks, rides, is	they	walk, ride, are

SIMPLE PAST

SINGULAR		PLURAL	
I	walked, rode, was	we	walked, rode, were
you	walked, rode, were	you	walked, rode, were
he/she/it	walked, rode, was	they	walked, rode, were

SIMPLE FUTURE

I, you, he/she/it, we, they	will walk, ride, be

Perfect tenses More complex time relations are indicated by the perfect tenses. A verb in one of the perfect tenses (a form of *have* plus the past participle) expresses an action that was or will be completed at the time of another action.

PRESENT PERFECT

I, you, we, they	have walked, ridden, been
he/she/it	has walked, ridden, been

PAST PERFECT

I, you, he/she/it, we, they	had walked, ridden, been

FUTURE PERFECT

I, you, he/she/it, we, they	will have walked, ridden, been

Progressive forms The simple and perfect tenses have progressive forms that describe actions in progress. A progressive verb consists of a form of *be* followed by a present participle. The progressive forms are not normally used with certain verbs, such as *believe*, *know*, *hear*, *seem*, and *think*.

PRESENT PROGRESSIVE

I	am walking, riding, being
he/she/it	is walking, riding, being
you, we, they	are walking, riding, being

PAST PROGRESSIVE

I, he/she/it	was walking, riding, being
you, we, they	were walking, riding, being

FUTURE PROGRESSIVE

I, you, he/she/it, we, they	will be walking, riding, being

PRESENT PERFECT PROGRESSIVE

I, you, we, they	have been walking, riding, being
he/she/it	has been walking, riding, being

PAST PERFECT PROGRESSIVE

I, you, he/she/it, we, they	had been walking, riding, being

FUTURE PERFECT PROGRESSIVE

I, you, he/she/it, we, they	will have been walking, riding, being

Multilingual

See 28a for more specific examples of verb tenses that can be challenging for multilingual writers.

Special uses of the present tense

Use the present tense when expressing general truths, when writing about literature, and when quoting, summarizing, or paraphrasing an author's views.

General truths or scientific principles should appear in the present tense unless such principles have been disproved.

► **Galileo taught that the earth ~~revolved~~ revolves around the sun.**

Because Galileo's teaching has not been discredited, the verb should be in the present tense. The following sentence, however, is acceptable: *Ptolemy taught that the sun revolved around the earth.*

When writing about a work of literature, you may be tempted to use the past tense. The convention, however, is to describe fictional events in the present tense.

▶ **In Masuji Ibuse's *Black Rain*, a child ~~reached~~ reaches for a pomegranate in his mother's garden, and a moment later he ~~was~~ is dead, killed by the blast of the atomic bomb.**

When you are quoting, summarizing, or paraphrasing the author of a nonliterary work, use present-tense verbs such as *writes*, *reports*, *asserts*, and so on to introduce the source. This convention is usually followed even when the author is dead (unless a date or the context specifies the time of writing).

▶ **Dr. Jerome Groopman ~~argued~~ argues that doctors are "susceptible to the subtle and not so subtle efforts of the pharmaceutical industry to sculpt our thinking" (9).**

In MLA style, signal phrases are written in the present tense, not the past tense. (See also 55c.)

APA NOTE: When you are documenting a paper with the APA (American Psychological Association) style of in-text citations, use past tense verbs such as *reported* or *demonstrated* or present perfect verbs such as *has reported* or *has demonstrated* to introduce the source. (See also 60c.)

E. Wilson (1994) reported that positive reinforcement alone was a less effective teaching technique than a mixture of positive reinforcement and constructive criticism.

The past perfect tense

The past perfect tense consists of a past participle preceded by *had* (*had worked, had gone*). This tense is used for an action already completed by the time of another past action or for an action already completed at some specific past time.

Everyone *had spoken* by the time I arrived.

I pleaded my case, but Paula *had made up* her mind.

Writers sometimes use the simple past tense when they should use the past perfect.

▶ **We built our cabin high on a pine knoll, forty feet above an abandoned quarry that ~~was~~ had been flooded in 1920 to create a lake.**

The building of the cabin and the flooding of the quarry both occurred in the past, but the flooding was completed before the time of building.

▶ **By the time dinner was served, the guest of honor had left.**

The past perfect tense is needed because the action of leaving was already completed at a specific past time (when dinner was served).

Some writers tend to overuse the past perfect tense. Do not use the past perfect if two past actions occurred at the same time.

▶ **When Ernest Hemingway lived in Cuba, he ~~had written~~ wrote *For Whom the Bell Tolls*.**

Sequence of tenses with infinitives and participles

An infinitive is the base form of a verb preceded by *to*. (See 48b.) Use the present infinitive to show action at the same time as or later than the action of the verb in the sentence.

▶ **Sonia had hoped to ~~have paid~~ pay the bill by May 1.**

The action expressed in the infinitive (*to pay*) occurred later than the action of the sentence's verb (*had hoped*).

Use the perfect form of an infinitive (*to have* followed by the past participle) for an action occurring earlier than that of the verb in the sentence.

▶ **Dan would like to ~~join~~ have joined the navy, but he went to college first.**

The liking occurs in the present; the joining would have occurred in the past.

Like the tense of an infinitive, the tense of a participle is governed by the tense of the sentence's verb. Use the present participle (ending in *-ing*) for an action occurring at the same time as that of the sentence's verb.

Hiking the Appalachian Trail, we spotted many wildflowers.

Use the past participle (such as *given* or *helped*) or the present perfect participle (*having* plus the past participle) for an action occurring before that of the verb.

> *Discovered* off the coast of Florida, the Spanish galleon yielded many treasures.
>
> *Having worked* her way through college, Lee graduated debt-free.

27g Use the subjunctive mood in the few contexts that require it.

There are three moods in English: the *indicative*, used for facts, opinions, and questions; the *imperative*, used for orders or advice; and the *subjunctive*, used in certain contexts to express wishes, requests, or conditions contrary to fact. For many writers, the subjunctive causes the most problems.

Forms of the subjunctive

In the subjunctive mood, present-tense verbs do not change form to indicate the number and person of the subject (see 21). Instead, the subjunctive uses the base form of the verb (*be*, *drive*, *employ*) with all subjects.

> It is important that you *be* [not *are*] prepared for the interview.
>
> We asked that she *drive* [not *drives*] more slowly.

Also, in the subjunctive mood, there is only one past-tense form of *be*: *were* (never *was*).

> If I *were* [not *was*] you, I'd try a new strategy.

Uses of the subjunctive

The subjunctive mood appears only in a few contexts: in contrary-to-fact clauses beginning with *if* or expressing a wish; in *that* clauses following verbs such as *ask*, *insist*, *recommend*, *request*, and *suggest*; and in certain set expressions.

In contrary-to-fact clauses beginning with *if* When a subordinate clause beginning with *if* expresses a condition contrary to fact, use the subjunctive *were* in place of *was*.

▶ If I ~~was~~ were a member of the management team, I would organize more social events for employees.

▶ The astronomers would be able to see the moons of Jupiter tonight if the weather ~~was~~ were clearer.

The verbs in these sentences express conditions that do not exist: The writer is not a member of Congress, and the weather is not clear.

Do not use the subjunctive mood in *if* clauses expressing conditions that exist or may exist.

If Dana *wins* the contest, she will leave for Barcelona in June.

In contrary-to-fact clauses expressing a wish In formal English, use the subjunctive *were* in clauses expressing a wish or desire.

INFORMAL	I wish that Dr. Vaughn *was* my professor.
FORMAL	I wish that Dr. Vaughn *were* my professor.

In *that* clauses following verbs such as *ask*, *insist*, *request*, and *suggest* Because requests have not yet become reality, they are expressed in the subjunctive mood.

▶ Professor Moore insists that her students ~~are~~ be on time for every class.

▶ We recommend that Mrs. Lambert ~~files~~ file form 1050 as soon as possible.

In certain set expressions The subjunctive mood, once more widely used, remains in certain set expressions: *Be that as it may*, *as it were*, *far be it from me*, and so on.

EXERCISE 27–9 Edit the following sentences to eliminate errors in verb tense or mood. If a sentence is correct, write "correct" after it. Answers appear in the back of the book. *More practice:* LaunchPadSolo

After the path ~~was~~ had been plowed, we were able to walk in the park.

a. The palace of Knossos in Crete is believed to have been destroyed by fire around 1375 BCE.
b. Watson and Crick discovered the mechanism that controlled inheritance in all life: the workings of the DNA molecule.
c. When city planners proposed rezoning the waterfront, did they know that the mayor promised to curb development in that neighborhood?
d. Tonight's concert begins at 9:30. If it was earlier, I'd consider going.
e. The math position was filled by the woman who had been running the tutoring center.

LaunchPadSolo **macmillanhighered.com/rules8e**

27 Verb forms, tenses, and moods
 > Exercises: 27–10 to 27–12
 > LearningCurve: Verbs

Multilingual Writers and ESL Challenges

This section of *Rules for Writers* is primarily for multilingual writers. You may find this section helpful if you learned English as a second language (ESL) or if you speak a language other than English with your friends and family.

28 Verbs

Both native and nonnative speakers of English encounter challenges with verbs. Section 28 focuses on specific challenges that multilingual writers sometimes face. You can find more help with verbs in other sections in the book:

making subjects and verbs agree (21)
using irregular verb forms (27a, 27b)
leaving off verb endings (27c, 27d)
choosing the correct verb tense (27f)
avoiding inappropriate uses of the passive voice (8a)

28a Use the appropriate verb form and tense.

This section offers a brief review of English verb forms and tenses. For additional help, see 27 and 46c.

Basic verb forms

Every main verb in English has five forms, which are used to create all of the verb tenses in standard English. The chart at the top of page 257 shows these forms for the regular verb *help* and the irregular verbs *give* and *be*. See 27a for the forms of other common irregular verbs.

Verb tenses

Section 27f describes all the verb tenses in English, showing the forms of a regular verb, an irregular verb, and the verb *be* in each tense. The chart on pages 257–59 provides more details about the tenses commonly used in the active voice in writing; the chart on page 260 gives details about tenses commonly used in the passive voice.

Basic verb forms

	REGULAR VERB *HELP*	IRREGULAR VERB *GIVE*	IRREGULAR VERB *BE**
BASE FORM	help	give	be
PAST TENSE	helped	gave	was, were
PAST PARTICIPLE	helped	given	been
PRESENT PARTICIPLE	helping	giving	being
-S FORM	helps	gives	is

**Be* also has the forms *am* and *are*, which are used in the present tense.

Verb tenses commonly used in the active voice

For descriptions and examples of all verb tenses, see 27f. For verb tenses commonly used in the passive voice, see the chart on page 260.

Simple tenses

For general facts, states of being, habitual actions

Simple present	**Base form or *-s* form**
• general facts	College students often *study* late at night.
• states of being	Water *becomes* steam at 100 degrees centigrade.
• habitual, repetitive actions	We *donate* to a different charity each year.
• scheduled future events	The train *arrives* tomorrow at 6:30 p.m.

NOTE: For uses of the present tense in writing about literature, see page 249.

Simple past	**Base form + *-ed* or *-d* or irregular form**
• completed actions at a specific time in the past	The storm *destroyed* their property. She *drove* to Montana three years ago.
• facts or states of being in the past	When I *was* young, I usually *walked* to school with my sister.

Simple future	***will* + base form**
• future actions, promises, or predictions	I *will exercise* tomorrow. The snowfall *will begin* around midnight.

→

Verb tenses commonly used in the active voice, continued

Simple progressive forms
For continuing actions

Present progressive	***am, is, are* + present participle**
• actions in progress at the present time, not continuing indefinitely	The students *are taking* an exam in Room 105. The valet *is parking* the car.
• future actions (with *leave, go, come, move,* etc.)	I *am leaving* tomorrow morning.
Past progressive	***was, were* + present participle**
• actions in progress at a specific time in the past	They *were swimming* when the storm struck.
• *was going to, were going to* for past plans that did not happen	We *were going to* drive to Florida for spring break, but the car broke down.

NOTE: Some verbs are not normally used in the progressive: *appear, believe, belong, contain, have, hear, know, like, need, see, seem, taste, understand,* and *want.*

► I ~~am wanting~~ want to see August Wilson's *Radio Golf.*

Perfect tenses
For actions that happened or will happen before another time

Present perfect	***has, have* + past participle**
• repetitive or constant actions that began in the past and continue to the present	I *have loved* cats since I was a child. Alicia *has worked* in Kenya for ten years.
• actions that happened at an unknown or unspecific past time	Stephen *has visited* Wales three times.
Past perfect	***had* + past participle**
• actions that began or occurred before another time in the past	She *had* just *crossed* the street when the runaway car crashed into the building.

NOTE: For more discussion of uses of the past perfect, see 27f. For uses of the past perfect in conditional sentences, see 28e.

→

Verb tenses commonly used in the active voice, continued	
Perfect progressive forms *For continuous past actions before another time*	
Present perfect progressive	***has, have* + *been* + present participle**
• continuous actions that began in the past and continue to the present	Yolanda *has been trying* to get a job in Boston for five years.
Past perfect progressive	***had* + *been* + present participle**
• actions that began and continued in the past until another past action	By the time I moved to Georgia, I *had been supporting* myself for five years.

28b To write a verb in the passive voice, use a form of *be* with the past participle.

When a sentence is written in the passive voice, the subject receives the action instead of doing it. (See "Passive transformations" in 47c.)

The solution *was measured* by the lab assistant.

To form the passive voice, use a form of *be* — *am, is, are, was, were, being, be,* or *been* — followed by the past participle of the main verb: *was chosen, are remembered.* (Sometimes a form of *be* follows another helping verb: *will be considered, could have been broken.*)

▶ ***Dreaming in Cuban* was ~~writing~~ written by Cristina García.**

In the passive voice, the past participle *written*, not the present participle *writing*, must follow *was* (the past tense of *be*).

▶ **The child is being ~~test.~~ tested.**

The past participle *tested*, not the base form *test*, must be used with *is being* to form the passive voice.

For details on forming the passive in various tenses, consult the chart on page 260. (For appropriate uses of the passive voice, see 8a.)

Verb tenses commonly used in the passive voice

For details about verb tenses in the active voice, see pages 257–59.

Simple tenses (passive voice)

Simple present	***am, is, are* + past participle**
• general facts	Breakfast *is served* daily.
• habitual, repetitive actions	The receipts *are counted* every night.
Simple past	***was, were* + past participle**
• completed past actions	He *was rewarded* for being on time.
Simple future	***will be* + past participle**
• future actions, promises, or predictions	The decision *will be made* by the committee next week.

Simple progressive forms (passive voice)

Present progressive	***am, is, are* + *being* + past participle**
• actions in progress at the present time	The new stadium *is being built* with private money.
• future actions (with *leave, go, come, move,* etc.)	Jo *is being promoted* to a new job next month.
Past progressive	***was, were* + *being* + past participle**
• actions in progress at a specific time in the past	We thought we *were being followed.*

Perfect tenses (passive voice)

Present perfect	***has, have* + *been* + past participle**
• actions that began in the past and continue to the present	The flight *has been delayed* because of storms in the Midwest.
• actions that happened at an unknown or unspecific time in the past	Wars *have been fought* throughout history.
Past perfect	***had* + *been* + past participle**
• actions that began or occurred before another time in the past	He *had been given* all the hints he needed to complete the puzzle.

NOTE: Future progressive, future perfect, and perfect progressive forms are not used in the passive voice.

NOTE: Only transitive verbs, those that take direct objects, may be used in the passive voice. Intransitive verbs such as *occur, happen, sleep, die, become,* and *fall* are not used in the passive. (See 47b.)

► **The accident ~~was~~ happened suddenly.**

EXERCISE 28–1 Revise the following sentences to correct errors in verb forms and tenses in the active and the passive voice. You may need to look at 27a for the correct form of some irregular verbs and at 27f for help with tenses. Answers appear in the back of the book.

More practice: LaunchPadSolo

The meeting ~~begin~~ begins tonight at 7:30.

a. In the past, tobacco companies deny any connection between smoking and health problems.
b. The volunteer's compassion has touch many lives.
c. I am wanting to register for a summer tutoring session.
d. By the end of the year, the state will have test 139 birds for avian flu.
e. The golfers were prepare for all weather conditions.

28c Use the base form of the verb after a modal.

The modal verbs are *can, could, may, might, must, shall, should, will,* and *would.* (*Ought to* is also considered a modal verb.) The modals are used with the base form of a verb to show ability, certainty, necessity, permission, obligation, or possibility.

Modals and the verbs that follow them do not change form to indicate tense. For a summary of modals and their meanings, see the chart on pages 262–63. (See also 27e.)

► **The art museum will ~~launches~~ launch its fundraising campaign next month.**

The modal *will* must be followed by the base form *launch,* not the present tense *launches.*

LaunchPadSolo **macmillanhighered.com/rules8e**
28 Verbs
> Exercises: 28–2, 28–3, and 28–13 (verb review)
> LearningCurve: Verbs for multilingual writers

Modals and their meanings	
can	
• general ability (present)	Ants *can survive* anywhere, even in space. Jorge *can run* a marathon faster than his brother.
• informal requests or permission	*Can* you *tell* me where the light is? Sandy *can borrow* my calculator.
could	
• general ability (past)	Lea *could read* when she was only three years old.
• polite, informal requests or permission	*Could* you *give* me that pen?
may	
• formal requests or permission	*May* I *see* the report? Students *may park* only in the yellow zone.
• possibility	I *may try* to finish my homework tonight, or I *may wake up* early and *finish* it tomorrow.
might	
• possibility	Funding for the language lab *might double* by 2019.
NOTE: *Might* usually expresses a stronger possibility than *may*.	
must	
• necessity (present or future)	To be effective, welfare-to-work programs *must provide* access to job training.
• strong probability	Amy *must be* nervous. [She is probably nervous.]
• near certainty (present or past)	I *must have left* my wallet at home. [I almost certainly left my wallet at home.]
should	
• suggestions or advice	Diabetics *should drink* plenty of water every day.
• obligations or duties	The government *should protect* citizens' rights.
• expectations	The books *should arrive* soon. [We expect the books to arrive soon.]

will	
• certainty	If you don't leave now, you *will be* late for your rehearsal.
• requests	*Will* you *help* me study for my psychology exam?
• promises and offers	Jonah *will arrange* the carpool.
would	
• polite requests	*Would* you *help* me carry these books? I *would like* some coffee. [*Would like* is more polite than *want*.]
• habitual or repeated actions (past)	Whenever Elena needed help with sewing, she *would call* her aunt.

► **The translator could ~~spoke~~ speak many languages, so the ambassador hired her for the European tour.**

The modal *could* must be followed by the base form *speak*, not the past tense *spoke*.

TIP: Do not use *to* in front of a main verb that follows a modal.

► **Gina can ~~to~~ drive us home if we miss the last train.**

For the use of modals in conditional sentences, see 28e.

EXERCISE 28–4 Edit the following sentences to correct errors in the use of verb forms with modals. You may find it helpful to consult the chart on pages 262–63. If a sentence is correct, write "correct" after it. Answers appear in the back of the book. *More practice:* LaunchPadSolo

We should ~~to~~ order pizza for dinner.

a. A major league pitcher can to throw a baseball more than ninety-five miles per hour.

LaunchPadSolo **macmillanhighered.com/rules8e**
28 Verbs
> Exercises: 28–5 and 28–6
> LearningCurve: Verbs for multilingual writers

b. The writing center tutor will helps you revise your essay.
c. A reptile must adjusted its body temperature to its environment.
d. In some states, individuals may renew a driver's license online.
e. My uncle, a cartoonist, could sketched a face in less than two minutes.

28d To make negative verb forms, add *not* in the appropriate place.

If the verb is the simple present or past tense of *be* (*am*, *is*, *are*, *was*, *were*), add *not* after the verb.

Gianna *is not* a member of the club.

For simple present-tense verbs other than *be*, use *do* or *does* plus *not* before the base form of the verb. (For the correct forms of *do* and *does*, see the chart on p. 204.)

▶ **Mariko ~~no~~ [does not] want more dessert.**

▶ **Mariko does not want~~s~~ more dessert.**

For simple past-tense verbs other than *be*, use *did* plus *not* before the base form of the verb.

▶ **They did not ~~planted~~ [plant] corn this year.**

In a verb phrase consisting of one or more helping verbs and a present or past participle (*is watching*, *were living*, *has played*, *could have been driven*), use the word *not* after the first helping verb.

▶ **Inna should [not] have ~~not~~ gone dancing last night.**

▶ **Bonnie is ~~no~~ [not] singing this weekend.**

NOTE: English allows only one negative in an independent clause to express a negative idea; using more than one is an error known as a *double negative* (see 26e).

▶ **We could not find ~~no~~ [any] books about the history of our school.**

28e In a conditional sentence, choose verb tenses according to the type of condition expressed in the sentence.

Conditional sentences contain two clauses: a subordinate clause (usually starting with *if*, *when*, or *unless*) and an independent clause. The subordinate clause (sometimes called the *if* or *unless* clause) states the condition or cause; the independent clause states the result or effect. In each example in this section, the subordinate clause (*if* clause) is marked SUB, and the independent clause is marked IND. (See 48e on subordinate clauses.)

Factual

Factual conditional sentences express relationships based on facts. If the relationship is a scientific truth, use the present tense in both clauses.

SUB [If water *cools* to 32 degrees Fahrenheit,] IND [it *freezes*.]

If the sentence describes a condition that is (or was) habitually true, use the same tense in both clauses.

SUB [When Sue *jogs* along the canal,] IND [her dog *runs* ahead of her.]

SUB [Whenever the coach *asked* for help,] IND [I *volunteered*.]

Predictive

Predictive conditional sentences are used to predict the future or to express future plans or possibilities. To form a predictive sentence, use a present-tense verb in the subordinate clause; in the independent clause, use the modal *will*, *can*, *may*, *should*, or *might* plus the base form of the verb.

SUB [If you *practice* regularly,] IND [your tennis game *should improve*.]

IND [We *will lose* our remaining wetlands] SUB [unless we *act* now.]

TIP: In all types of conditional sentences (factual, predictive, and speculative), *if* or *unless* clauses do not use the modal verb *will*.

▶ **If Jenna ~~will pass~~ ^passes^ her history test, she will graduate this year.**

Speculative

Speculative conditional sentences express unlikely, contrary-to-fact, or impossible conditions. English uses the past or past perfect tense in the *if* clause, even for conditions in the present or the future.

Unlikely possibilities If the condition is possible but unlikely in the present or the future, use the past tense in the subordinate clause; in the independent clause, use *would*, *could*, or *might* plus the base form of the verb.

SUB — IND

If I *won* the lottery, I *would travel* to Egypt.

The writer does not expect to win the lottery. Because this is a possible but unlikely present or future situation, the past tense is used in the subordinate clause.

Conditions contrary to fact In conditions that are currently unreal or contrary to fact, use the past-tense verb *were* (not *was*) in the *if* clause for all subjects. (See also 27g on the subjunctive mood.)

▶ **If I ~~was~~ were president, I would make children's issues a priority.**

The writer is not president, so *were* is correct in the *if* clause.

Events that did not happen In a conditional sentence that speculates about an event that did not happen or was impossible in the past, use the past perfect tense in the *if* clause; in the independent clause, use *would have*, *could have*, or *might have* with the past participle. (See also past perfect tense, p. 258.)

SUB — IND

If I *had saved* more money, I *would have visited* Laos last year.

The writer did not save more money and did not travel to Laos. This sentence shows a possibility that did not happen.

SUB — IND

If Aunt Grace *had been* alive for your graduation, she *would have been* very proud.

Aunt Grace was not alive at the time of the graduation. This sentence shows an impossible situation in the past.

EXERCISE 28–7 Edit the following sentences to correct problems with verbs. In some cases, more than one revision is possible. Possible revisions appear in the back of the book. *More practice:* LaunchPadSolo

> had
> **If I ~~have~~ time, I would study both French and Russian next semester.**

a. The electrician might have discovered the broken circuit if she went through the modules one at a time.
b. If Verena wins a scholarship, she would go to graduate school.
c. Whenever a rainbow appears after a storm, everybody came out to see it.
d. Sarah did not understood the terms of her internship.
e. If I live in Budapest with my cousin Szusza, she would teach me Hungarian cooking.

28f Become familiar with verbs that may be followed by gerunds or infinitives.

A gerund is a verb form that ends in *-ing* and is used as a noun: *sleeping, dreaming*. (See 48b on verbal phrases.) An infinitive is the word *to* plus the base form of the verb: *to sleep, to dream*. The word *to* is an infinitive marker, not a preposition, in this use. (See 48b on infinitive phrases.)

A few verbs may be followed by either a gerund or an infinitive; others may be followed by a gerund but not by an infinitive; still others may be followed by an infinitive but not by a gerund.

Verb + gerund or infinitive (no change in meaning)

The following commonly used verbs may be followed by a gerund or an infinitive, with little or no difference in meaning:

begin	hate	love
continue	like	start

I love *skiing*. I love *to ski*.

LaunchPadSolo **macmillanhighered.com/rules8e**
28 Verbs
> Exercises: 28–8, 28–9, and 28–13 (verb review)
> LearningCurve: Verbs for multilingual writers

Verb + gerund or infinitive (change in meaning)

With a few verbs, the choice of a gerund or an infinitive changes the meaning dramatically:

forget	remember	stop	try

She stopped *speaking* to Lucia. [She no longer spoke to Lucia.]

She stopped *to speak* to Lucia. [She paused so that she could speak to Lucia.]

Verb + gerund

These verbs may be followed by a gerund but not by an infinitive:

admit	discuss	imagine	put off	risk
appreciate	enjoy	miss	quit	suggest
avoid	escape	postpone	recall	tolerate
deny	finish	practice	resist	

Bill enjoys *playing* [not *to play*] the piano.

Jamie quit *smoking*.

Verb + infinitive

These verbs may be followed by an infinitive but not by a gerund:

agree	decide	manage	plan	wait
ask	expect	mean	pretend	want
beg	help	need	promise	wish
claim	hope	offer	refuse	would like

Jill has offered *to water* [not *watering*] the plants while we are away.

Joe finally managed *to find* a parking space.

A few of these verbs may be followed either by an infinitive directly or by a noun or pronoun plus an infinitive:

ask	help	promise	would like
expect	need	want	

We asked *to speak* to the congregation.

We asked *Rabbi Abrams to speak* to our congregation.

Verb + noun or pronoun + infinitive

With certain verbs in the active voice, a noun or pronoun must come between the verb and the infinitive that follows it. The noun or pronoun usually names a person who is affected by the action of the verb.

advise	convince	order	tell
allow	encourage	persuade	urge
cause	have (own)	remind	warn
command	instruct	require	

V N INF

The class encouraged Luis to tell the story of his escape.

The counselor *advised Haley to take* four courses instead of five.

Verb + noun or pronoun + unmarked infinitive

An unmarked infinitive is an infinitive without *to*. A few verbs (often called *causative verbs*) may be followed by a noun or pronoun and an unmarked infinitive.

have (cause)	let (allow)
help	make (force)

Jorge *had the valet park* his car.

► **Rose had the attendant ~~to~~ wash the windshield.**

► **Frank made me ~~to~~ carry his book for him.**

NOTE: *Help* can be followed by a noun or pronoun and either an unmarked or a marked infinitive.

Emma *helped Brian wash* the dishes.
Emma *helped Brian to wash* the dishes.

NOTE: The infinitive is used in some typical constructions with *too* and *enough*.

TOO + ADJECTIVE + INFINITIVE	The gift is *too large to wrap*.
ENOUGH + NOUN + INIFINITIVE	Our emergency pack has *enough bottled water to last* a week.
ADJECTIVE + *ENOUGH* + INFINITIVE	Some of the hikers felt *strong enough to climb* another thousand feet.

EXERCISE 28–10 Form sentences by adding gerund or infinitive constructions to the following sentence openings. In some cases, more than one kind of construction is possible. Possible answers appear in the back of the book. *More practice:* LaunchPadSolo

Please remind your sister to call me.

a. I enjoy
b. The tutor told Samantha
c. The team hopes
d. Ricardo and his brothers miss
e. Jon remembered

29 Articles

Articles (*a*, *an*, *the*) are part of a category of words known as *noun markers* or *determiners*.

29a Be familiar with articles and other noun markers.

Standard English uses noun markers to help identify the nouns that follow. In addition to articles (*a*, *an*, and *the*), noun markers include the following:

- possessive nouns, such as *Elena's* (See 36a.)
- possessive pronoun/adjectives: *my*, *your*, *his*, *her*, *its*, *our*, *their* (See 46b.)
- demonstrative pronoun/adjectives: *this*, *that*, *these*, *those* (See 46b.)
- quantifiers: *all*, *any*, *each*, *either*, *every*, *few*, *many*, *more*, *most*, *much*, *neither*, *several*, *some*, and so on (See 29d.)
- numbers: *one*, *twenty-three*, and so on

Using articles and other noun markers

Articles and other noun markers always appear before nouns; sometimes other modifiers, such as adjectives, come between a noun marker and a noun.

ART N
Felix is reading a book about mythology.

ART ADJ N
We took an exciting trip to Alaska last summer.

NOUN MARKER ADV ADJ N
That very delicious meal was expensive.

In most cases, do not use an article with another noun marker.

► **~~The~~ Natalie's older brother lives in Wisconsin.**

Expressions like *a few*, *the most*, and *all the* are exceptions: *a few potatoes*, *all the rain*. See also 29d.

Types of articles and types of nouns

To choose an appropriate article for a noun, you must first determine whether the noun is *common* or *proper*, *count* or *noncount*, *singular* or *plural*, and *specific* or *general*. The chart on pages 273–74 describes the types of nouns.

Articles are classified as *indefinite* and *definite*. The indefinite articles, *a* and *an*, are used with general nouns. The definite article, *the*, is used with specific nouns. (The last section of the chart on pp. 273–74 explains general and specific nouns.)

A and *an* both mean "one" or "one among many." Use *a* before a consonant sound: *a banana*, *a vacation*, *a picture*, *a happy child*, *a united family*. Use *an* before a vowel sound: *an eggplant*, *an occasion*, *an uncle*, *an honorable person*. (See also *a*, *an* in the glossary of usage.)

The shows that a noun is specific; use *the* with one or more than one specific thing: *the newspaper*, *the soldiers*.

29b Use *the* with most specific common nouns.

The definite article, *the*, is used with most nouns—both count and noncount—that the reader can identify specifically. Usually the identity will be clear to the reader for one of the six reasons on pages 272–74. (See also the chart on p. 275.)

1. The noun has been previously mentioned.

► **A truck cut in front of our van. When** ^the **truck skidded a few seconds later, we almost crashed into it.**

The article *A* is used before *truck* when the noun is first mentioned. When the noun is mentioned again, it needs the article *the* because readers can now identify which truck skidded — the one that cut in front of the van.

2. A phrase or clause following the noun restricts its identity.

► **Bryce warned me that** ^the **GPS in his car was not working.**

The phrase *in his car* identifies the specific GPS.

NOTE: Descriptive adjectives do not necessarily make a noun specific. A specific noun is one that readers can identify within a group of nouns of the same type.

► **If I win the lottery, I will buy** ~~the~~ ^a **brand-new bright red sports car.**

The reader cannot identify which specific brand-new bright red sports car the writer will buy. Even though *car* has many adjectives in front of it, it is a general noun in this sentence.

3. A superlative adjective such as *best* or *most intelligent* makes the noun's identity specific. (See also 26d on comparatives and superlatives.)

► **Our petite daughter dated** ^the **tallest boy in her class.**

The superlative *tallest* makes the noun *boy* specific. Although there might be several tall boys, only one boy can be the tallest.

4. The noun describes a unique person, place, or thing.

► **During an eclipse, one should not look directly at** ^the **sun.**

There is only one sun in our solar system, so its identity is clear.

5. The context or situation makes the noun's identity clear.

► **Please don't slam** ^the **door when you leave.**

Both the speaker and the listener know which door is meant.

Types of nouns

Common or proper

Common nouns	**Examples**	
• name general persons, places, things, or ideas • begin with lowercase	religion knowledge rain	beauty student country

Proper nouns	**Examples**	
• name specific persons, places, things, or ideas • begin with capital letter	Hinduism Philip Vietnam	President Adams Blue Mosque Renaissance

Count or noncount (common nouns only)

Count nouns	**Examples**
• name persons, places, things, or ideas that can be counted • have plural forms	girl, girls city, cities goose, geese philosophy, philosophies

Noncount nouns	**Examples**	
• name things or abstract ideas that cannot be counted • cannot be made plural	water silver furniture	patience knowledge air

NOTE: See the chart on page 276 for commonly used noncount nouns.

Singular or plural (both common and proper)

Singular nouns (count and noncount)	**Examples**	
• represent one person, place, thing, or idea	backpack country woman achievement	rain beauty Nile River Block Island

Plural nouns (count only)	**Examples**	
• represent more than one person, place, thing, or idea • must be count nouns	backpacks countries women	Ural Mountains Falkland Islands achievements

→

Types of nouns, continued

Specific (definite) or general (indefinite) (count and noncount)

Specific nouns	Examples
• name persons, places, things, or ideas that can be identified within a group of the same type	*The students* in Professor Martin's *class* should study. *The airplane* carrying *the senator* was late. *The furniture* in *the truck* was damaged.
General nouns	**Examples**
• name categories of persons, places, things, or ideas (often plural)	*Students* should study. *Books* bridge *gaps* between *cultures.* *The airplane* has made commuting between *cities* easy.

6. The noun is singular and refers to a scientific class or category of items (most often animals, musical instruments, and inventions).

▶ **~~Tin~~ [The tin] whistle is common in traditional Irish music.**

The writer is referring to the tin whistle as a class of musical instruments.

29c Use *a* (or *an*) with common singular count nouns that refer to "one" or "any."

If a count noun refers to one unspecific item (not a whole category), use the indefinite article, *a* or *an*. *A* and *an* usually mean "one among many" but can also mean "any one." (See the chart on p. 275.)

▶ **My English professor asked me to bring [a] dictionary to class.**

The noun *dictionary* refers to "one unspecific dictionary" or "any dictionary."

▶ We want to rent ^an apartment close to the lake.

The noun *apartment* refers to "any apartment close to the lake," not a specific apartment.

Choosing articles for common nouns

Use *the*

- if the reader has enough information to identify the noun specifically

COUNT: Please turn on *the lights*. We're going to *the lake* tomorrow.

NONCOUNT: *The food* throughout Italy is excellent.

Use *a* or *an*

- if the noun refers to one item

and

- if the item is singular but not specific

COUNT: Bring *a pencil* to class. Charles wrote *an essay* about his first job.

NOTE: Do not use *a* or *an* with plural or noncount nouns.

Use a quantifier (*enough*, *many*, *some*, etc.)

- if the noun represents an unspecified amount of something
- if the amount is more than one but not all items in a category

COUNT (plural): Amir showed us *some photos* of India. *Many turtles* return to the same nesting site each year.

NONCOUNT: We didn't get *enough rain* this summer.

NOTE: Sometimes no article conveys an unspecified amount: *Amir showed us photos of India.*

Use no article

- if the noun represents all items in a category

COUNT (plural): *Students* can attend the show for free.

- if the noun represents a category in general

NONCOUNT: *Coal* is a natural resource.

NOTE: *The* is occasionally used when a singular count noun refers to all items in a class or a specific category: *The bald eagle is no longer endangered in the United States.*

Commonly used noncount nouns

Food and drink

beef, bread, butter, candy, cereal, cheese, cream, meat, milk, pasta, rice, salt, sugar, water, wine

Nonfood substances

air, cement, coal, dirt, gasoline, gold, paper, petroleum, plastic, rain, silver, snow, soap, steel, wood, wool

Abstract nouns

advice, anger, beauty, confidence, courage, employment, fun, happiness, health, honesty, information, intelligence, knowledge, love, poverty, satisfaction, wealth

Use no article

biology (and other areas of study), clothing, equipment, furniture, homework, jewelry, luggage, machinery, mail, money, news, poetry, pollution, research, scenery, traffic, transportation, violence, weather, work

NOTE: A few noncount nouns (such as *love*) can also be used as count nouns: *He had two loves: music and archery.*

29d Use a quantifier such as *some* or *more*, not *a* or *an*, with a noncount noun to express an approximate amount.

Do not use *a* or *an* with noncount nouns. Also do not use numbers or words such as *several* or *many*; they must be used with plural nouns, and noncount nouns do not have plural forms. (See the chart above for a list of commonly used noncount nouns.)

▸ **Dr. Snyder gave us ~~an~~ information about the Peace Corps.**

▸ **Do you have ~~many~~ money with you?**

You can use quantifiers such as *enough*, *less*, and *some* to suggest approximate amounts or nonspecific quantities of noncount nouns: *a little salt*, *any homework*, *enough wood*, *less information*, *much pollution*.

- ▶ **Vincent's mother told him that she had ~~a~~ [some] news that would surprise him.**

29e Do not use articles with nouns that refer to all of something or something in general.

When a noncount noun refers to all of its type or to a concept in general, it is not marked with an article.

- ▶ **~~The kindness~~ [Kindness] is a virtue.**

  The noun represents kindness in general; it does not represent a specific type of kindness, such as *the kindness he showed me after my mother's death*.

- ▶ **In some parts of the world, ~~the~~ rice is preferred to all other grains.**

  The noun *rice* represents rice in general. To refer to a specific type or serving of rice, the definite article is appropriate: *The rice my husband served last night is the best I've ever tasted.*

In most cases, when you use a count noun to represent a general category, make the noun plural. Do not use unmarked singular count nouns to represent whole categories.

- ▶ **~~Fountain is~~ [Fountains are] an expensive element of landscape design.**

  Fountains is a count noun that represents fountains in general.

EXCEPTION: In some cases, *the* can be used with singular count nouns to represent a class or specific category: *The Chinese alligator is smaller than the American alligator*. See also number 6 in 29b.

29f Do not use articles with most singular proper nouns. Use *the* with most plural proper nouns.

Since singular proper nouns are already specific, they typically do not need an article: *Prime Minister Cameron*, *Jamaica*, *Lake Huron*, *Mount Etna*.

There are, however, many exceptions. In most cases, if the proper noun consists of a common noun with modifiers (adjectives or an *of* phrase), use *the* with the proper noun.

► **We visited** the **Great Wall of China last year.**

► **Rob wants to be a translator for** the **Central Intelligence Agency.**

The is used with most plural proper nouns: *the McGregors, the Bahamas, the Finger Lakes, the United States.*

Geographic names create problems because there are so many exceptions to the rules. When in doubt, consult the chart on page 279, check a dictionary, or ask a native speaker.

EXERCISE 29–1 Edit the following sentences for proper use of articles and nouns. If a sentence is correct, write "correct" after it. Answers appear in the back of the book. *More practice:* LaunchPadSolo

~~The~~ Josefina's dance routine was flawless.

a. Doing volunteer work often brings a satisfaction.
b. As I looked out the window of the plane, I could see the Cape Cod.
c. Melina likes to drink her coffees with lots of cream.
d. Recovering from abdominal surgery requires patience.
e. I completed the my homework assignment quickly.

EXERCISE 29–2 Articles have been omitted from the following description of winter weather. Insert the articles *a*, *an*, and *the* where English requires them and be prepared to explain the reasons for your choices.

> Many people confuse terms *hail*, *sleet*, and *freezing rain*. Hail normally occurs in thunderstorm and is caused by strong updrafts that lift growing chunks of ice into clouds. When chunks of ice, called hailstones, become too heavy to be carried by updrafts, they fall to ground. Hailstones can cause damage to crops, windshields, and people. Sleet occurs during winter storms and is caused by snowflakes falling from layer of cold air into warm layer, where they become raindrops, and then into another cold layer. As they

29 Articles
> Exercises: 29–3 to 29–6
> LearningCurve: Articles and nouns for multilingual writers

fall through last layer of cold air, raindrops freeze and become small ice pellets, forming sleet. When it hits car windshield or windows of house, sleet can make annoying racket. Driving and walking can be hazardous when sleet accumulates on roads and sidewalks. Freezing rain is basically rain that falls onto ground and then freezes after it hits ground. It causes icy glaze on trees and any surface that is below freezing.

Using *the* with geographic nouns

When to omit *the*	
streets, squares, parks	Ivy Street, Union Square, Denali National Park
cities, states, counties	Miami, New Mexico, Bee County
most countries, continents	Italy, Nigeria, China, South America, Africa
bays, single lakes	Tampa Bay, Lake Geneva
single mountains, islands	Mount Everest, Crete

When to use *the*	
country names with *of* phrase	the United States (of America), the People's Republic of China
large regions, deserts	the East Coast, the Sahara
peninsulas	the Baja Peninsula, the Sinai Peninsula
oceans, seas, gulfs	the Pacific Ocean, the Dead Sea, the Persian Gulf
canals and rivers	the Panama Canal, the Amazon
mountain ranges	the Rocky Mountains, the Alps
groups of islands	the Solomon Islands

30 Sentence structure

Although their structure can vary widely, sentences in English generally flow from subject to verb to object or complement: *Bears eat fish.* This section focuses on the major challenges that multilingual students face when writing sentences in English. For more details on the parts of speech and the elements of sentences, consult sections 46–49.

30a Use a linking verb between a subject and its complement.

Some languages, such as Russian and Turkish, do not use linking verbs (*is*, *are*, *was*, *were*) between subjects and complements (nouns or adjectives that rename or describe the subject). Every English sentence, however, must include a verb. For more on linking verbs, see 27e.

► **Jim ^is intelligent.**

► **Many streets in San Francisco ^are very steep.**

30b Include a subject in every sentence.

Some languages, such as Spanish and Japanese, do not require a subject in every sentence. Every English sentence, however, needs a subject. Commands are an exception: The subject *you* is understood but not present in the sentence ([*You*] *Give me the book*).

► **Your aunt is very energetic. ~~Seems~~ ^She seems young for her age.**

The word *it* is used as the subject of a sentence describing the weather or temperature, stating the time, indicating distance, or suggesting an environmental fact.

► **~~Is~~ ^It is raining in the valley and snowing in the mountains.**

► **~~Is~~ ^It is 9:15 a.m.**

In most English sentences, the subject appears before the verb. Some sentences, however, are inverted: The subject comes after the verb. In these sentences, a placeholder called an *expletive* (*there* or *it*) often comes before the verb.

There [EXP] are [V] many people [S] here today. (Many people [S] are [V] here today.)

There is
▸ ~~Is~~ an apple pie in the refrigerator.

there are
▸ As you know, many religious sects in India.

Notice that the verb agrees with the subject that follows it: *apple pie is*, *sects are*. (See 21g.)

Sometimes an inverted sentence has an infinitive (*to work*) or a noun clause (*that she is intelligent*) as the subject. In such sentences, the placeholder *it* is needed before the verb. (See also 48b and 48e.)

EXP V — S — — S — V
It is important to study daily. (To study daily is important.)

it
▸ **Because the road is flooded, is necessary to change our route.**

TIP: The words *here* and *there* are not used as subjects. When they mean "in this place" (*here*) or "in that place" (*there*), they are adverbs, not nouns.

It
▸ **I just returned from a vacation in Japan. ~~There~~ is very**
there.
beautiful/

This school that school
▸ **~~Here~~ offers a master's degree in physical therapy; ~~there~~ has only a bachelor's program.**

30c Do not use both a noun and a pronoun to perform the same grammatical function in a sentence.

English does not allow a subject to be repeated in its own clause.

▸ **The doctor ~~she~~ advised me to cut down on salt.**

The pronoun *she* cannot repeat the subject, *doctor*.

Do not add a pronoun even when a word group comes between the subject and the verb.

▸ **The watch that I lost on vacation ~~it~~ was in my backpack.**

The pronoun *it* cannot repeat the subject, *watch*.

Some languages allow "topic fronting," placing a word or phrase (a "topic") at the beginning of a sentence and following it with an independent clause that explains something about the topic. This form is not allowed in English because the sentence seems to start with one subject but then introduces a new subject in an independent clause.

TOPIC — IND CLAUSE

INCORRECT The seeds I planted them last fall.

The sentence can be corrected by bringing the topic (*seeds*) into the independent clause.

the seeds

▶ **~~The seeds~~ I planted ~~them~~ last fall.**

30d Do not repeat a subject, an object, or an adverb in an adjective clause.

Adjective clauses begin with relative pronouns (*who, whom, whose, which, that*) or relative adverbs (*when, where*). Relative pronouns usually serve as subjects or objects in the clauses they introduce; another word in the clause cannot serve the same function. Relative adverbs should not be repeated by other adverbs later in the clause.

ADJ CLAUSE

The cat ran under the car that was parked on the street.

▶ **The cat ran under the car that ~~it~~ was parked on the street.**

The relative pronoun *that* is the subject of the adjective clause, so the pronoun *it* cannot be added as a subject.

▶ **Myrna enjoyed the investment seminars that she attended ~~them~~ last week.**

The relative pronoun *that* is the object of the verb *attended*. The pronoun *them* cannot also serve as an object.

Sometimes the relative pronoun is understood but not present in the sentence. In such cases, do not add another word with the same function as the omitted pronoun.

► **Myrna enjoyed the seminars she attended ~~them~~ last week.**

The relative pronoun *that* is understood after *seminars* even though it is not present in the sentence.

If the clause begins with a relative adverb, do not use another adverb with the same meaning later in the clause.

► **The office where I work ~~there~~ is one hour from the city.**

The adverb *there* cannot repeat the relative adverb *where.*

EXERCISE 30–1 In the following sentences, add needed subjects or expletives and delete any repeated subjects, objects, or adverbs. Answers appear in the back of the book. *More practice:* LaunchPadSolo

The new geology professor is the one whom we saw ~~him~~ on TV this morning.

a. Are some cartons of ice cream in the freezer.
b. I don't use the subway because am afraid.
c. The prime minister she is the most popular leader in my country.
d. We tried to get in touch with the same manager whom we spoke to him earlier.
e. Recently have been a number of earthquakes in Turkey.

30e Avoid mixed constructions beginning with *although* or *because*.

A word group that begins with *although* cannot be linked to a word group that begins with *but* or *however*. The result is an error called a *mixed construction* (see also 11a). Similarly, a word group that begins with *because* cannot be linked to a word group that begins with *so* or *therefore*.

If you want to keep *although* or *because*, drop the other linking word (see the examples on p. 284).

LaunchPadSolo **macmillanhighered.com/rules8e**
30 Sentence structure
> Exercises: 30–2 and 30–3
> LearningCurve: Sentence structure for multilingual writers

► **Although Nikki Giovanni is best known for her poetry for adults, ~~but~~ she has written several books for children.**

► **Because German and Dutch are related languages, ~~therefore~~ tourists from Berlin can usually read a few signs in Amsterdam.**

If you want to keep the other linking word, omit *although* or *because.*

► **~~Although~~ Nikki Giovanni is best known for her poetry for adults, but she has written several books for children.**

► **~~Because~~ German and Dutch are related languages~~,~~; therefore, tourists from Berlin can usually read a few signs in Amsterdam.**

For advice about using commas and semicolons with linking words, see 32a and 34b.

30f Do not place an adverb between a verb and its direct object.

Adverbs modifying verbs can appear in various positions: at the beginning or end of a sentence, before or after a verb, or between a helping verb and its main verb.

Slowly, we drove along the rain-slick road.

Mia handled the teapot very *carefully*.

Martin *always* wins our tennis matches.

Christina is *rarely* late for our lunch dates.

My daughter has *often* spoken of you.

The election results were being *closely* followed by analysts.

However, an adverb cannot appear between a verb and its direct object.

► **Mother** carefully **wrapped ~~carefully~~ the gift.**

The adverb *carefully* cannot appear between the verb, *wrapped*, and its direct object, *the gift*.

EXERCISE 30–4 Edit the following sentences for proper sentence structure. If a sentence is correct, write "correct" after it. Answers appear in the back of the book. *More practice:* LaunchPadSolo

She peeled ~~slowly~~ the banana. [slowly. inserted]

a. Although freshwater freezes at 32 degrees Fahrenheit, however ocean water freezes at 28 degrees Fahrenheit.

b. Because we switched cable packages, so our channel lineup has changed.

c. The competitor mounted confidently his skateboard.

d. My sister performs well the *legong*, a Balinese dance.

e. Because product development is behind schedule, we will have to launch the product next spring.

30g Distinguish between present participles and past participles used as adjectives.

Both present and past participles may be used as adjectives. The present participle always ends in *-ing*. Past participles usually end in *-ed*, *-d*, *-en*, *-n*, or *-t*. (See 27a.)

PRESENT PARTICIPLES	confusing, speaking, boring
PAST PARTICIPLES	confused, spoken, bored

Like all other adjectives, participles can come before nouns; they also can follow linking verbs, in which case they describe the subject of the sentence. (See 47b.)

Use a present participle to describe a person or thing *causing or stimulating an experience.*

The *boring lecture* put us to sleep. [The lecture caused boredom.]

Use a past participle to describe a person or thing *undergoing an experience.*

The *audience* was *bored* by the lecture. [The audience experienced boredom.]

LaunchPadSolo **macmillanhighered.com/rules8e**

30 Sentence structure

> Exercises: 30–5 and 30–6

> LearningCurve: Sentence structure for multilingual writers

Participles that describe emotions or mental states often cause the most confusion.

annoying/annoyed	exhausting/exhausted
boring/bored	fascinating/fascinated
confusing/confused	frightening/frightened
depressing/depressed	satisfying/satisfied
exciting/excited	surprising/surprised

► **Our afternoon hike to Thundering Brook Falls was ~~exhausted.~~** exhausting.

Exhausting suggests that the hike caused exhaustion.

► **The ~~exhausting~~** exhausted **hikers reached the campground just before midnight.**

Exhausted describes how the hikers felt.

EXERCISE 30–7 Edit the following sentences for proper use of present and past participles. If a sentence is correct, write "correct" after it. Answers appear in the back of the book.

More practice: LaunchPadSolo

Danielle and Monica were very ~~exciting~~ excited **to be going to a Broadway show for the first time.**

a. Listening to everyone's complaints all day was irritated.

b. The long flight to Singapore was exhausted.

c. His skill at chess is amazing.

d. After a great deal of research, the scientist made a fascinated discovery.

e. Surviving that tornado was one of the most frightened experiences I've ever had.

LaunchPadSolo **macmillanhighered.com/rules8e**

30 Sentence structure

> Exercises: 30–8 and 30–9

> LearningCurve: Sentence structure for multilingual writers

30h Place cumulative adjectives in an appropriate order.

Adjectives usually come before the nouns they modify and may also come after linking verbs. (See 46d and 47b.)

> ADJ N V ADJ
> Janine wore a new necklace. Janine's necklace was new.

Cumulative adjectives, which cannot be joined by the word *and* or separated by commas, must come in a particular order. If you use cumulative adjectives before a noun, see the chart on this page. The chart is only a guide; don't be surprised if you encounter exceptions. (See also 33d.)

> stained red plastic
> ▶ **My dorm room has only a desk and a ~~plastic red stained~~ chair.**

Order of cumulative adjectives

FIRST

ARTICLE OR OTHER NOUN MARKER a, an, the, her, Joe's, two, many, some

EVALUATIVE WORD attractive, dedicated, delicious, ugly, disgusting

SIZE large, enormous, small, little

LENGTH OR SHAPE long, short, round, square

AGE new, old, young, antique

COLOR yellow, blue, crimson

NATIONALITY French, Peruvian, Vietnamese

RELIGION Catholic, Protestant, Jewish, Muslim

MATERIAL silver, walnut, wool, marble

LAST **NOUN/ADJECTIVE** tree (as in *tree* house), kitchen (as in *kitchen* table)

THE NOUN MODIFIED house, coat, bicycle, bread, woman, coin

My large blue wool coat is in the attic.

Joe's collection includes *two small antique silver* coins.

EXERCISE 30–10 Using the chart on page 287 as necessary, arrange the following modifiers and nouns in their proper order. Answers appear in the back of the book. *More practice:* LaunchPadSolo

two new French racing bicycles
new, French, two, bicycles, racing

a. sculptor, young, an, Vietnamese, intelligent
b. dedicated, a, priest, Catholic
c. old, her, sweater, blue, wool
d. delicious, Joe's, Scandinavian, bread
e. many, boxes, jewelry, antique, beautiful

31 Prepositions and idiomatic expressions

31a Become familiar with prepositions that show time and place.

The most frequently used prepositions in English are *at*, *by*, *for*, *from*, *in*, *of*, *on*, *to*, and *with*. Prepositions can be difficult to master because the differences among them are subtle and idiomatic. The chart on page 289 is limited to three troublesome prepositions that show time and place: *at*, *on*, and *in*.

Not every possible use is listed in the chart, so don't be surprised when you encounter exceptions and idiomatic uses that you must learn one at a time. For example, in English a person rides *in* a car but *on* a bus, plane, train, or subway.

▶ **My first class starts ~~on~~ at 8:00 a.m.**

▶ **The farmers go to market ~~in~~ on Wednesday.**

LaunchPadSolo **macmillanhighered.com/rules8e**
30 Sentence structure
> Exercises: 30–11 and 30–12
> LearningCurve: Sentence structure for multilingual writers

At, *on*, and *in* to show time and place

Showing time

AT	*at* a specific time: *at* 7:20, *at* dawn, *at* dinner
ON	*on* a specific day or date: *on* Tuesday, *on* June 4
IN	*in* a part of a 24-hour period: *in* the afternoon, *in* the daytime [but *at* night]
	in a year or month: *in* 2008, *in* July
	in a period of time: finished *in* three hours

Showing place

AT	*at* a meeting place or location: *at* home, *at* the club
	at the edge of something: sitting *at* the desk
	at the corner of something: turning *at* the intersection
	at a target: throwing the snowball *at* Lucy
ON	*on* a surface: placed *on* the table, hanging *on* the wall
	on a street: the house *on* Spring Street
	on an electronic medium: *on* television, *on* the Internet
IN	*in* an enclosed space: *in* the garage, *in* an envelope
	in a geographic location: *in* San Diego, *in* Texas
	in a print medium: *in* a book, *in* a magazine

EXERCISE 31–1 In the following sentences, replace prepositions that are not used correctly. You may need to refer to the chart on this page. If a sentence is correct, write "correct" after it. Answers appear in the back of the book. *More practice:* LaunchPadSolo

at
The play begins ~~on~~ 7:20 p.m.

a. Whenever we eat at the Centerville Café, we sit at a small table on the corner of the room.

b. In the 1990s, entrepreneurs created new online businesses in record numbers.

c. In Thursday, Nancy will attend her first home repair class at the community center.

LaunchPadSolo **macmillanhighered.com/rules8e**

31 Prepositions and idiomatic expressions

> Exercises: 31–2 and 31–3

> LearningCurve: Prepositions for multilingual writers

d. Alex began looking for her lost mitten in another location.

e. We decided to go to a restaurant because there was no fresh food on the refrigerator.

31b Use nouns (including -ing forms) after prepositions.

In a prepositional phrase, use a noun (not a verb) after the preposition. Sometimes the noun will be a gerund, the *-ing* verb form that functions as a noun (see 48b).

► **Our student government is good at ~~save~~** saving **money.**

Distinguish between the preposition *to* and the infinitive marker *to*. If *to* is a preposition, it should be followed by a noun or a gerund.

► **We are dedicated to ~~help~~** helping **the poor.**

If *to* is an infinitive marker, it should be followed by the base form of the verb.

► **We want to ~~helping~~** help **the poor.**

To test whether *to* is a preposition or an infinitive marker, insert a word that you know is a noun after the word *to*. If the noun makes sense in that position, *to* is a preposition. If the noun does not make sense after *to*, then *to* is an infinitive marker.

Zoe is addicted *to* ____________________.

They are planning *to* ____________________.

In the first sentence, a noun (such as *magazines*) makes sense after *to*, so *to* is a preposition and should be followed by a noun or a gerund: Zoe is addicted *to magazines*. Zoe is addicted *to running*.

In the second sentence, a noun (such as *magazines*) does not make sense after *to*, so *to* is an infinitive marker and must be followed by the base form of the verb: They are planning *to build* a new school.

31c Become familiar with common adjective + preposition combinations.

Some adjectives appear only with certain prepositions. These expressions are idiomatic and may be different from the combinations used in your native language.

▸ **Paula is married ~~with~~ *to* Jon.**

Check an ESL dictionary for combinations that are not listed in the chart at the bottom of this page.

31d Become familiar with common verb + preposition combinations.

Many verbs and prepositions appear together in idiomatic phrases. Pay special attention to the combinations that are different from the combinations used in your native language.

▸ **Your success depends ~~of~~ *on* your effort.**

Check an ESL dictionary for combinations that are not listed in the chart on page 292.

Adjective + preposition combinations

accustomed to	connected to	guilty of	preferable to
addicted to	covered with	interested in	proud of
afraid of	dedicated to	involved in	responsible for
angry with	devoted to	involved with	satisfied with
ashamed of	different from	known as	scared of
aware of	engaged in	known for	similar to
committed to	engaged to	made of (*or* made from)	tired of
concerned about	excited about	married to	worried about
concerned with	familiar with	opposed to	
	full of		

Verb + preposition combinations

agree with	compare with	forget about	speak to (or speak with)
apply to	concentrate on	happen to	stare at
approve of	consist of	hope for	succeed at
arrive at	count on	insist on	succeed in
arrive in	decide on	listen to	take advantage of
ask for	depend on	participate in	take care of
believe in	differ from	rely on	think about
belong to	disagree with	reply to	think of
care about	dream about	respond to	wait for
care for	dream of	result in	wait on
compare to	feel like	search for	

Punctuation

Mechanics

Grammar Basics

Punctuation 293

Mechanics 337

Grammar Basics 361

Punctuation

32 The comma

The comma was invented to help readers. Without it, sentence parts can collide into one another unexpectedly, causing misreadings.

CONFUSING If you cook Elmer will do the dishes.

CONFUSING While we were eating a rattlesnake approached our campsite.

Add commas in the logical places (after *cook* and *eating*), and suddenly all is clear. No longer is Elmer being cooked, the rattlesnake being eaten.

Various rules have evolved to prevent such misreadings and to speed readers along through complex grammatical structures. Those rules are detailed in this section. (Section 33 explains when not to use commas.)

32a Use a comma before a coordinating conjunction joining independent clauses.

When a coordinating conjunction connects two or more independent clauses — word groups that could stand alone as separate sentences — a comma must precede it. There are seven coordinating conjunctions in English: *and*, *but*, *or*, *nor*, *for*, *so*, and *yet*.

A comma tells readers that one independent clause has come to a close and that another is about to begin.

▶ **The department sponsored a seminar on college survival skills, and it also hosted a barbecue for new students.**

EXCEPTION: If the two independent clauses are short and there is no danger of misreading, the comma may be omitted.

The plane took off and we were on our way.

TIP: As a rule, do *not* use a comma with a coordinating conjunction that joins only two words, phrases, or subordinate clauses. (See 33a.)

▶ **A good money manager controls expenses, and invests surplus dollars to meet future needs.**

The word group following *and* is not an independent clause; it is the second half of a compound predicate (*controls . . . and invests*).

32b Use a comma after an introductory clause or phrase.

The most common introductory word groups are clauses and phrases functioning as adverbs. Such word groups usually tell when, where, how, why, or under what conditions the main action of the sentence occurred. (See 48a, 48b, and 48e.)

A comma tells readers that the introductory clause or phrase has come to a close and that the main part of the sentence is about to begin.

▶ **When Irwin was ready to iron, his cat tripped on the cord.**

Without the comma, readers may have Irwin ironing his cat. The comma signals that *his cat* is the subject of a new clause, not part of the introductory one.

▶ **Near a small stream at the bottom of the canyon, the park rangers discovered an abandoned mine.**

The comma tells readers that the introductory prepositional phrase has come to a close.

EXCEPTION: The comma may be omitted after a short adverb clause or phrase if there is no danger of misreading: *In no time we were at 2,800 feet.*

Sentences also frequently begin with participial phrases that function as adjectives, describing the noun or pronoun immediately following them. The comma tells readers that they are about to learn the identity of the person or thing described; therefore, the comma is usually required even when the phrase is short. (See 48b.)

▶ **Buried under layers of younger rocks, the earth's oldest rocks contain no fossils.**

NOTE: Other introductory word groups include transitional expressions and absolute phrases (see 32f).

EXERCISE 32–1 Add or delete commas where necessary in the following sentences. If a sentence is correct, write "correct" after it. Answers appear in the back of the book. *More practice:* LaunchPadSolo

Because we had been saving molding for a few weeks, we had enough wood to frame all thirty paintings.

a. Alisa brought the injured bird home, and fashioned a splint out of Popsicle sticks for its wing.
b. Considered a classic of early animation *The Adventures of Prince Achmed* used hand-cut silhouettes against colored backgrounds.
c. If you complete the evaluation form and return it within two weeks you will receive a free breakfast during your next stay.
d. After retiring from the New York City Ballet in 1965, legendary dancer Maria Tallchief went on to found the Chicago City Ballet.
e. Roger had always wanted a handmade violin but he couldn't afford one.

EXERCISE 32–2 Add or delete commas where necessary in the following sentences. If a sentence is correct, write "correct" after it. Answers appear in the back of the book.

The car had been sitting idle for a month, so the battery was completely dead.

a. J. R. R. Tolkien finished writing his draft of *The Lord of the Rings* trilogy in 1949 but the first book in the series wasn't published until 1954.
b. In the first two minutes of its ascent the space shuttle had broken the sound barrier and reached a height of over twenty-five miles.
c. German shepherds can be gentle guide dogs or they can be fierce attack dogs.
d. Some former professional cyclists claim that the use of performance-enhancing drugs is widespread in cycling and they argue that no rider can be competitive without doping.
e. As an intern, I learned most aspects of the broadcasting industry but I never learned about fundraising.

LaunchPadSolo **macmillanhighered.com/rules8e**

32 The comma

> Exercises: 32–3 and 32–4

> LearningCurve: Commas

32c Use a comma between all items in a series.

When three or more items are presented in a series, those items should be separated from one another with commas. Items in a series may be single words, phrases, or clauses.

- **Langston Hughes's poetry is concerned with racial pride, social justice, and the diversity of the African American experience.**

- **Bubbles of air, leaves, ferns, bits of wood, and insects are often found trapped in amber.**

Although some writers view the last comma in a series as optional, most experts advise using the comma because its omission can result in ambiguity or misreading.

- **My uncle willed me all of his property, houses, and boats.**

  Did the uncle will his property *and* houses *and* boats — or simply his property, consisting of houses and boats? If the former meaning is intended, a comma is necessary to prevent ambiguity.

- **The activities include touring the White House, visiting the Air and Space Museum, attending a lecture about the Founding Fathers, and kayaking on the Potomac River.**

  Without the comma, the activities might seem to include a lecture about kayaking, not participating in kayaking. The comma makes it clear that *kayaking on the Potomac River* is a separate item in the series.

32d Use a comma between coordinate adjectives not joined with *and*. Do not use a comma between cumulative adjectives.

When two or more adjectives each modify a noun separately, they are coordinate.

Roberto is a *warm, gentle, affectionate* father.

If the adjectives can be joined with *and*, the adjectives are coordinate, so you should use commas: *warm* and *gentle* and *affectionate* (*warm*, *gentle*, *affectionate*).

Adjectives that do not modify the noun separately are cumulative.

Three large gray shapes moved slowly toward us.

Beginning with the adjective closest to the noun *shapes*, these modifiers lean on one another, piggyback style, with each modifying a larger word group. *Gray* modifies *shapes*, *large* modifies *gray shapes*, and *three* modifies *large gray shapes*. Cumulative adjectives cannot be joined with *and* (not *three* and *large* and *gray shapes*).

COORDINATE ADJECTIVES

► **Should patients with severe, irreversible brain damage be put on life support systems?**

Adjectives that can be connected with *and* are coordinate: *severe and irreversible.*

CUMULATIVE ADJECTIVES

► **Ira ordered a rich/chocolate/layer cake.**

Ira didn't order a cake that was rich and chocolate and layer: He ordered a *layer cake* that was *chocolate*, a *chocolate layer cake* that was *rich.*

EXERCISE 32–5 Add or delete commas where necessary in the following sentences. If a sentence is correct, write "correct" after it. Answers appear in the back of the book. *More practice:* LaunchPadSolo

We gathered our essentials, took off for the great outdoors, and ignored the fact that it was Friday the 13th.

a. The cold impersonal atmosphere of the university was unbearable.
b. An ambulance threaded its way through police cars, fire trucks and irate citizens.
c. The *1812 Overture* is a stirring, magnificent piece of music.

LaunchPadSolo **macmillanhighered.com/rules8e**

32 The comma

> Exercises: 32–7 and 32–8

> LearningCurve: Commas

d. After two broken arms, three cracked ribs and one concussion, Ken quit the varsity football team.
e. My cat's pupils had constricted to small black shining slits.

EXERCISE 32–6 Add or delete commas where necessary in the following sentences. If a sentence is correct, write "correct" after it. Answers appear in the back of the book.

> **Good social workers excel in patience, diplomacy, and positive thinking.**

a. NASA's rovers on Mars are equipped with special cameras that can take close-up high-resolution pictures of the terrain.
b. A baseball player achieves the triple crown by having the highest batting average, the most home runs, and the most runs batted in during the regular season.
c. If it does not get enough sunlight, a healthy green lawn can turn into a shriveled brown mess within a matter of days.
d. Love, vengeance, greed and betrayal are common themes in Western literature.
e. Many experts believe that shark attacks on surfers are a result of the sharks' mistaking surfboards for small, injured seals.

32e Use commas to set off nonrestrictive (nonessential) elements. Do not use commas to set off restrictive (essential) elements.

Certain word groups that modify nouns or pronouns can be restrictive or nonrestrictive — that is, essential or not essential to the meaning of a sentence. These word groups are usually adjective clauses, adjective phrases, or appositives.

Restrictive elements

A restrictive element defines or limits the meaning of the word it modifies; it is therefore essential to the meaning of the sentence and is not set off with commas. If you remove a restrictive modifier from a sentence, the meaning changes significantly, becoming more general than you intended.

RESTRICTIVE (NO COMMAS)

The campers need clothes *that are durable.*

Scientists *who study the earth's structure* are called geologists.

The first sentence does not mean that the campers need clothes in general. The intended meaning is more limited: The campers need durable clothes. The second sentence does not mean that scientists in general are called geologists; only those scientists who specifically study the earth's structure are called geologists. The italicized word groups are essential and are therefore not set off with commas.

Nonrestrictive elements

A nonrestrictive modifier describes a noun or pronoun whose meaning has already been clearly defined or limited. Because the modifier contains nonessential or parenthetical information, it is set off with commas. If you remove a nonrestrictive element from a sentence, the meaning does not change dramatically. Some meaning may be lost, but the defining characteristics of the person or thing described remain the same.

NONRESTRICTIVE (WITH COMMAS)

The campers need sturdy shoes, *which are expensive.*

The scientists, *who represented eight different universities,* met to review applications for the Advancements in Science Award.

In the first sentence, the campers need sturdy shoes, and the shoes happen to be expensive. In the second sentence, the scientists met to review applications for the award; that they represented eight different universities is informative but not critical to the meaning of the sentence. The nonessential information in both sentences is set off with commas.

NOTE: Often it is difficult to tell whether a word group is restrictive or nonrestrictive without seeing it in context and considering the writer's meaning. Both of the following sentences are grammatically correct, but their meaning is slightly different.

The dessert made with fresh raspberries was delicious.

The dessert, made with fresh raspberries, was delicious.

In the first example, the phrase *made with fresh raspberries* tells readers which of two or more desserts the writer is referring to. In the example with commas, the phrase merely adds information about the dessert.

Adjective clauses

Adjective clauses are patterned like sentences, containing subjects and verbs, but they function within sentences as modifiers of nouns or pronouns. They always follow the word they modify, usually immediately. Adjective clauses begin with a relative pronoun (*who*, *whom*, *whose*, *which*, *that*) or with a relative adverb (*where*, *when*). (See also 48e.)

Nonrestrictive adjective clauses are set off with commas; restrictive adjective clauses are not.

NONRESTRICTIVE CLAUSE (WITH COMMAS)

▶ **Ed's house, which is located on thirteen acres, was completely furnished with bats in the rafters and mice in the kitchen.**

The adjective clause *which is located on thirteen acres* does not restrict the meaning of *Ed's house*; the information is nonessential and is therefore set off with commas.

RESTRICTIVE CLAUSE (NO COMMAS)

▶ **The giant panda/that was born at the San Diego Zoo in 2003/ was sent to China in 2007.**

Because the adjective clause *that was born at the San Diego Zoo in 2003* identifies one particular panda out of many, the information is essential and is therefore not set off with commas.

NOTE: Use *that* only with restrictive (essential) clauses. Many writers prefer to use *which* only with nonrestrictive (nonessential) clauses, but usage varies.

Adjective phrases

Prepositional or verbal phrases functioning as adjectives may be restrictive or nonrestrictive. Nonrestrictive phrases are set off with commas; restrictive phrases are not.

NONRESTRICTIVE PHRASE (WITH COMMAS)

▶ **The helicopter, with its million-candlepower spotlight illuminating the area, circled above.**

The *with* phrase is nonessential because its purpose is not to specify which of two or more helicopters is being discussed. The phrase is not required for readers to understand the meaning of the sentence.

RESTRICTIVE PHRASE (NO COMMAS)

► **One corner of the attic was filled with newspapers/ dating from the early 1900s.**

Dating from the early 1900s restricts the meaning of *newspapers*, so the comma should be omitted.

► **The bill/ proposed by the Illinois representative/ would lower taxes for middle-income families.**

Proposed by the Illinois representative identifies exactly which bill is meant.

Appositives

An appositive is a noun or noun phrase that renames a nearby noun. Nonrestrictive appositives are set off with commas; restrictive appositives are not.

NONRESTRICTIVE APPOSITIVE (WITH COMMAS)

► **Darwin's most important book, *On the Origin of Species,* was the result of many years of research.**

Most important restricts the meaning to one book, so the appositive *On the Origin of Species* is nonrestrictive and should be set off with commas.

RESTRICTIVE APPOSITIVE (NO COMMAS)

► **The song/ "Viva la Vida/" was blasted out of huge amplifiers.**

Once they've read *song*, readers still don't know precisely which song the writer means. The appositive following *song* restricts its meaning, so the appositive should not be set off with commas.

EXERCISE 32–9 Add or delete commas where necessary in the following sentences. If a sentence is correct, write "correct" after it. Answers appear in the back of the book. *More practice:* LaunchPadSolo

My sister, who plays center on the Sparks, now lives at The Sands, a beach house near Los Angeles.

a. Choreographer Alvin Ailey's best-known work *Revelations* is more than just a crowd-pleaser.
b. Twyla Tharp's contemporary ballet *Push Comes to Shove* was made famous by the Russian dancer Baryshnikov. [*Tharp has written more than one contemporary ballet.*]
c. The glass sculptor sifting through hot red sand explained her technique to the other glassmakers. [*There is more than one glass sculptor.*]
d. A member of an organization, that provides job training for teens, was also appointed to the education commission.
e. Brian Eno who began his career as a rock musician turned to meditative compositions in the late 1970s.

32f Use commas to set off transitional and parenthetical expressions, absolute phrases, and word groups expressing contrast.

Transitional expressions

Transitional expressions serve as bridges between sentences or parts of sentences. They include conjunctive adverbs such as *however*, *therefore*, and *moreover* and transitional phrases such as *for example*, *as a matter of fact*, and *in other words*. (For complete lists of these expressions, see 34b.)

When a transitional expression appears between independent clauses in a compound sentence, it is preceded by a semicolon and is usually followed by a comma. (See 34b.)

► **Minh did not understand our language; moreover, he was unfamiliar with our customs.**

When a transitional expression appears at the beginning of a sentence or in the middle of an independent clause, it is usually set off with commas.

► **As a matter of fact, American football was established in the mid-nineteenth century by fans who wanted to play a more organized game of rugby.**

LaunchPadSolo **macmillanhighered.com/rules8e**
32 The comma
> Exercise: 32-10
> LearningCurve: Commas

► **Natural foods are not always salt free; celery, for example, contains more sodium than most people would imagine.**

EXCEPTION: If a transitional expression blends smoothly with the rest of the sentence, calling for little or no pause in reading, it does not need to be set off with a comma. Expressions such as *also*, *at least*, *certainly*, *consequently*, *indeed*, *of course*, *moreover*, *no doubt*, *perhaps*, *then*, and *therefore* do not always call for a pause.

Alice's bicycle is broken; *therefore* you will need to borrow Sue's.

Parenthetical expressions

Expressions that are distinctly parenthetical, providing only supplemental information, should be set off with commas. They interrupt the flow of a sentence or appear at the end as afterthoughts.

► **Evolution, as far as we know, doesn't work this way.**

Absolute phrases

An absolute phrase, which modifies the whole sentence, usually consists of a noun followed by a participle or participial phrase. (See 48d.) Absolute phrases may appear at the beginning or at the end of a sentence and should be set off with commas.

ABSOLUTE PHRASE
N PARTICIPLE
The sun appearing for the first time in a week, we were at last able to begin the archaeological dig.

► **Elvis Presley made music industry history in the 1950s, his records having sold more than ten million copies.**

NOTE: Do not insert a comma between the noun and the participle in an absolute construction.

► **The next contestant/ being five years old, the host adjusted the height of the microphone.**

Word groups expressing contrast

Sharp contrasts beginning with words such as *not*, *never*, and *unlike* are set off with commas.

► **The Epicurean philosophers sought mental, not bodily, pleasures.**

► **Unlike Robert, Rae Marie enjoyed managing the household budget.**

32g Use commas to set off nouns of direct address, the words *yes* and *no*, interrogative tags, and mild interjections.

► **Forgive me, Angela, for forgetting your birthday.**

► **Yes, the loan will probably be approved.**

► **The film was faithful to the book, wasn't it?**

► **Well, cases like these are difficult to decide.**

32h Use commas with expressions such as *he said* to set off direct quotations.

► **In his "Letter from Birmingham Jail," Martin Luther King Jr. wrote, "We know through painful experience that freedom is never voluntarily given by the oppressor; it must be demanded by the oppressed" (225).**

See 37 on the use of quotation marks and pages 467–68 on citing literary sources in MLA style.

32i Use commas with dates, addresses, titles, and numbers.

Dates

In dates, set off the year from the rest of the sentence with a pair of commas.

► **On December 12, 1890, orders were sent out for the arrest of Sitting Bull.**

EXCEPTIONS: Commas are not needed if the date is inverted or if only the month and year are given.

The security alert system went into effect on 15 April 2009.

February 2015 was an extremely snowy month.

Addresses

The elements of an address or a place name are separated with commas. A zip code, however, is not preceded by a comma.

► **John Lennon was born in Liverpool, England, in 1940.**

► **Please send the package to Greg Tarvin at 708 Spring Street, Washington, IL 61571.**

Titles

If a title follows a name, set off the title from the rest of the sentence with a pair of commas.

► **Ann Hall, MD, has been appointed to the board of trustees.**

Numbers

In numbers more than four digits long, use commas to separate the numbers into groups of three, starting from the right. In numbers four digits long, a comma is optional.

3,500 [*or* 3500]

100,000

5,000,000

EXCEPTIONS: Do not use commas in street numbers, zip codes, telephone numbers, or years with four or fewer digits.

32j Use a comma to prevent confusion.

In certain situations, a comma is necessary to prevent confusion. If the writer has intentionally left out a word or phrase, for example, a comma may be needed to signal the omission.

► **To err is human; to forgive, divine.**

If two words in a row echo each other, a comma may be needed for ease of reading.

► **The catastrophe that we had feared might happen, happened.**

Sometimes a comma is needed to prevent readers from grouping words in ways that do not match the writer's intention.

► **Patients who can, walk up and down the halls every day.**

EXERCISE 32–11 This exercise covers the major uses of the comma described in 32a–32e. Add or delete commas where necessary. If a sentence is correct, write "correct" after it. Answers appear in the back of the book. *More practice:* LaunchPadSolo

Even though our brains actually can't focus on two tasks at a time, many people believe they can multitask.

a. Cricket which originated in England is also popular in Australia, South Africa and India.
b. At the sound of the starting pistol the horses surged forward toward the first obstacle, a sharp incline three feet high.
c. After seeing an exhibition of Western art Gerhard Richter escaped from East Berlin, and smuggled out many of his notebooks.
d. Corrie's new wet suit has an intricate, blue pattern.
e. We replaced the rickety, old, spiral staircase with a sturdy, new ladder.

LaunchPadSolo **macmillanhighered.com/rules8e**

32 The comma

> Exercises: 32–13 to 32–17

> LearningCurve: Commas

EXERCISE 32–12 This exercise covers all uses of the comma. Add or delete commas where necessary in the following sentences. If a sentence is correct, write "correct" after it. Answers appear in the back of the book.

> **"Yes, neighbors, we must work together to save the community center," urged Mr. Owusu.**

a. On January 15, 2008 our office moved to 29 Commonwealth Avenue, Mechanicsville VA 23111.
b. The coach having bawled us out thoroughly, we left the locker room with his harsh words ringing in our ears.
c. Ms. Carlson you are a valued customer whose satisfaction is very important to us.
d. Mr. Mundy was born on July 22, 1939 in Arkansas, where his family had lived for four generations.
e. Her board poised at the edge of the half-pipe, Nina waited her turn to drop in.

33 Unnecessary commas

Many common misuses of the comma result from a misunderstanding of the major comma rules presented in 32.

33a Do not use a comma with a coordinating conjunction that joins only two words, phrases, or subordinate clauses.

Though a comma should be used before a coordinating conjunction joining independent clauses (see 32a) or with a series of three or more elements (see 32c), these rules should not be extended to other compound word groups.

▶ **Ron discovered a leak, and came back to fix it.**

The coordinating conjunction *and* links two verbs in a compound predicate: *discovered* and *came*.

► We knew that she had won, but that the election was close.

The coordinating conjunction *but* links two subordinate clauses, each beginning with *that*.

33b Do not use a comma to separate a verb from its subject or object.

A sentence should flow from subject to verb to object without unnecessary pauses. Commas may appear between these major sentence elements only when a specific rule calls for them.

► Zoos large enough to give the animals freedom to roam, are becoming more popular.

The comma should not separate the subject, *Zoos*, from the verb, *are becoming*.

33c Do not use a comma before the first or after the last item in a series.

Though commas are required between items in a series (32c), do not place them either before or after the whole series.

► Other causes of asthmatic attacks are, stress, change in temperature, and cold air.

► Ironically, even novels that focus on horror, evil, and alienation, often have themes of spiritual renewal and redemption as well.

33d Do not use a comma between cumulative adjectives, between an adjective and a noun, or between an adverb and an adjective.

Commas are required between coordinate adjectives (those that can be joined with *and*), but they do not belong between cumulative adjectives (those that cannot be joined with *and*). (For a full discussion, see 32d.)

► **In the corner of the closet, we found an old/maroon hatbox.**

A comma should never be used between an adjective and the noun that follows it.

► **It was a senseless, dangerous/mission.**

Nor should a comma be used between an adverb and an adjective that follows it.

► **The Hillside is a good home for severely/disturbed youths.**

33e Do not use commas to set off restrictive elements.

Restrictive elements are modifiers or appositives that restrict the meaning of the nouns they follow. Because they are essential to the meaning of the sentence, they are not set off with commas. (For a full discussion of restrictive and nonrestrictive elements, see 32e.)

► **Drivers/who think they own the road/make cycling a dangerous sport.**

The modifier *who think they own the road* restricts the meaning of *Drivers* and is essential to the meaning of the sentence. Putting commas around the *who* clause falsely suggests that all drivers think they own the road.

► **Margaret Mead's book/*Coming of Age in Samoa*/stirred up considerable controversy when it was published in 1928.**

Since Mead wrote more than one book, the appositive contains information essential to the meaning of the sentence.

33f Do not use a comma to set off a concluding adverb clause that is essential for meaning.

When adverb clauses introduce a sentence, they are nearly always followed by a comma (see 32b). When they conclude a sentence, however, they are not set off by commas if their content is essential to the meaning of the earlier part of the sentence. Adverb clauses beginning with *after, as soon as, because, before, if, since, unless, until,* and *when* are usually essential.

▸ **Don't visit Paris at the height of the tourist season/unless you have booked hotel reservations.**

Without the *unless* clause, the meaning of the sentence might at first seem broader than the writer intended.

When a concluding adverb clause is nonessential, it should be preceded by a comma. Clauses beginning with *although, even though, though,* and *whereas* are usually nonessential.

▸ **The lecture seemed to last only a short time, although the clock said it had gone on for more than an hour.**

33g Do not use a comma after a phrase that begins an inverted sentence.

Though a comma belongs after most introductory phrases (see 32b), it does not belong after phrases that begin an inverted sentence. In an inverted sentence, the subject follows the verb, and a phrase that ordinarily would follow the verb is moved to the beginning (see 47c).

▸ **At the bottom of the hill/sat the stubborn mule.**

33h Avoid other common misuses of the comma.

Do not use a comma in the following situations.

AFTER A COORDINATING CONJUNCTION (*AND, BUT, OR, NOR, FOR, SO, YET*)

▸ **Occasionally TV talk shows are performed live, but/more often they are taped.**

AFTER *SUCH AS* OR *LIKE*

► **Shade-loving plants such as/ begonias, impatiens, and coleus can add color to a shady garden.**

AFTER *ALTHOUGH*

► **Although/ the air was balmy, the water was too cold for swimming.**

BEFORE A PARENTHESIS

► **Though Sylvia's ACT score was low/ (only 15), her admissions essay was superior.**

TO SET OFF AN INDIRECT (REPORTED) QUOTATION

► **Samuel Goldwyn once said/ that a verbal contract isn't worth the paper it's written on.**

WITH A QUESTION MARK OR AN EXCLAMATION POINT

► **"Why don't you try it?/" she coaxed. "You can't do any worse than the rest of us."**

EXERCISE 33–1 Delete any unnecessary commas in the following sentences. If a sentence is correct, write "correct" after it. Answers appear in the back of the book. *More practice:* LaunchPadSolo

In his Silk Road Project, Yo-Yo Ma incorporates work by musicians such as/ Kayhan Kalhor and Richard Danielpour.

a. After the morning rains cease, the swimmers emerge from their cottages.

b. Tricia's first artwork was a bright, blue, clay dolphin.

LaunchPadSolo **macmillanhighered.com/rules8e**

33 Unnecessary commas

> Exercises: 33–3 to 33–5

> LearningCurve: Commas

c. Some modern musicians, (trumpeter John Hassell is an example) blend several cultural traditions into a unique sound.
d. Myra liked hot, spicy foods such as, chili, kung pao chicken, and buffalo wings.
e. On the display screen, was a soothing pattern of light and shadow.

EXERCISE 33–2 Delete unnecessary commas in the following passage.

Each spring since 1970, New Orleans has hosted the Jazz and Heritage Festival, an event that celebrates the music, food, and culture, of the region. Although, it is often referred to as "Jazz Fest," the festival typically includes a wide variety of musical styles such as, gospel, Cajun, blues, zydeco, and, rock and roll. Famous musicians who have appeared regularly at Jazz Fest, include Dr. John, B. B. King, and Aretha Franklin. Large stages are set up throughout the fairgrounds in a way, that allows up to ten bands to play simultaneously without any sound overlap. Food tents are located throughout the festival, and offer popular, local dishes like crawfish Monica, jambalaya, and fried, green tomatoes. Following Hurricane Katrina in 2005, Jazz Fest revived quickly, and attendance has steadily increased each year. Fans, who cannot attend the festival, still enjoy the music by downloading songs, and watching performances online.

34 The semicolon

The semicolon is used to connect major sentence elements of equal grammatical rank.

34a Use a semicolon between closely related independent clauses not joined with a coordinating conjunction.

When two independent clauses appear in one sentence, they are usually linked with a comma and a coordinating conjunction (*and*, *but*, *or*, *nor*, *for*, *so*, *yet*). The coordinating conjunction signals the relation between the clauses. If the clauses are closely related and the relation is clear without a conjunction, they may be linked with a semicolon instead.

> In film, a low-angle shot makes the subject look powerful; a high-angle shot does just the opposite.

A semicolon must be used whenever a coordinating conjunction has been omitted between independent clauses. To use merely a comma creates a type of run-on sentence known as a *comma splice.* (See 20.)

▶ **In 1800, a traveler needed six weeks to get from New York City to Chicago~~,~~; in 1860, the trip by railroad took only two days.**

34b Use a semicolon between independent clauses linked with a transitional expression.

Transitional expressions include conjunctive adverbs and transitional phrases.

CONJUNCTIVE ADVERBS

accordingly	furthermore	moreover	still
also	hence	nevertheless	subsequently
anyway	however	next	then
besides	incidentally	nonetheless	therefore
certainly	indeed	now	thus
consequently	instead	otherwise	
conversely	likewise	similarly	
finally	meanwhile	specifically	

TRANSITIONAL PHRASES

after all	even so	in fact
as a matter of fact	for example	in other words
as a result	for instance	in the first place
at any rate	in addition	on the contrary
at the same time	in conclusion	on the other hand

When a transitional expression appears between independent clauses, it is preceded by a semicolon and usually followed by a comma.

► Many corals grow very gradually/; in fact, the creation of a coral reef can take centuries.

When a transitional expression appears in the middle or at the end of the second independent clause, the semicolon goes *between the clauses.*

► Biologists have observed laughter in primates other than humans/; chimpanzees, however, sound more like they are panting than laughing.

Transitional expressions should not be confused with the coordinating conjunctions *and, but, or, nor, for, so,* and *yet,* which are preceded by a comma when they link independent clauses. (See 32a.)

34c Use a semicolon between items in a series containing internal punctuation.

► Classic science fiction sagas are *Star Trek,* with Mr. Spock/; *Battlestar Galactica,* with its Cylons/; and *Star Wars,* with Han Solo, Luke Skywalker, and Darth Vader.

Without the semicolons, the reader would have to sort out the major groupings, distinguishing between important and less important pauses according to the logic of the sentence. By inserting semicolons at the major breaks, the writer does this work for the reader.

34d Avoid common misuses of the semicolon.

Do not use a semicolon in the following situations.

BETWEEN A SUBORDINATE CLAUSE AND THE REST OF THE SENTENCE

► Although children's literature was added to the National Book Awards in 1969;/, it has had its own award, the Newbery Medal, since 1922.

BETWEEN AN APPOSITIVE AND THE WORD IT REFERS TO

► **The scientists were fascinated by the species *Argyroneta aquatica*;/, a spider that lives underwater.**

TO INTRODUCE A LIST

► **Some of my favorite celebrities have been animal rights advocates;/: Betty White, Casey Affleck, and Dave Navarro.**

BETWEEN INDEPENDENT CLAUSES JOINED BY *AND, BUT, OR, NOR, FOR, SO,* OR *YET*

► **Five of the applicants had worked with spreadsheets;/, but only one was familiar with database management.**

EXCEPTIONS: If one or both of the independent clauses contain a comma, you may use a semicolon with a coordinating conjunction between the clauses.

EXERCISE 34–1 Add commas or semicolons where needed in the following well-known quotations. If a sentence is correct, write "correct" after it. Answers appear in the back of the book. *More practice:* LaunchPadSolo

If an animal does something, we call it instinct; if we do the same thing, we call it intelligence. — Will Cuppy

a. Do not ask me to be kind just ask me to act as though I were. — Jules Renard

b. When men talk about defense they always claim to be protecting women and children but they never ask the women and children what they think. — Pat Schroeder

c. When I get a little money I buy books if any is left I buy food and clothes. — Desiderius Erasmus

d. America is a country that doesn't know where it is going but is determined to set a speed record getting there. — Laurence J. Peter

e. Wit has truth in it wisecracking is simply calisthenics with words. — Dorothy Parker

LaunchPadSolo **macmillanhighered.com/rules8e**

34 The semicolon

> Exercises: 34–3 to 34–6

> LearningCurve: Semicolons and colons

EXERCISE 34–2 Edit the following sentences to correct errors in the use of the comma and the semicolon. If a sentence is correct, write "correct" after it. Answers appear in the back of the book.

> **Love is blind; envy has its eyes wide open.**

a. Strong black coffee will not sober you up, the truth is that time is the only way to get alcohol out of your system.
b. Margaret was not surprised to see hail and vivid lightning, conditions had been right for violent weather all day.
c. There is often a fine line between right and wrong; good and bad; truth and deception.
d. My mother always says that you can't learn common sense; either you're born with it or you're not.
e. Severe, unremitting pain is a ravaging force; especially when the patient tries to hide it from others.

35 The colon

The colon is used primarily to call attention to the words that follow it. In addition, the colon has some conventional uses.

35a Use a colon after an independent clause to direct attention to a list, an appositive, a quotation, or a summary or an explanation.

A LIST

The daily routine should include at least the following: twenty knee bends, fifty sit-ups, and five minutes of running in place.

AN APPOSITIVE

My roommate is guilty of two of the seven deadly sins: gluttony and sloth.

A QUOTATION

Consider the words of Benjamin Franklin: "There never was a good war or a bad peace."

A SUMMARY OR AN EXPLANATION

Faith is like love: It cannot be forced.

The novel is clearly autobiographical: The author even gives his own name to the main character.

NOTE: For other ways of introducing quotations, see "Introducing quoted material" on pages 327–28. When an independent clause follows a colon, begin with a capital letter. Some disciplines use a lowercase letter instead. See 45f for variations.

35b Use a colon according to convention.

SALUTATION IN A LETTER Dear Sir or Madam:

HOURS AND MINUTES 5:30 p.m.

PROPORTIONS The ratio of women to men was 2:1.

TITLE AND SUBTITLE *The Glory of Hera: Greek Mythology and the Greek Family*

BIBLIOGRAPHIC ENTRIES Boston: Bedford, 2014

CHAPTER AND VERSE IN SACRED TEXT Luke 2:14, Qur'an 67:3

35c Avoid common misuses of the colon.

A colon must be preceded by a full independent clause. Therefore, avoid using it in the following situations.

BETWEEN A VERB AND ITS OBJECT OR COMPLEMENT

► **Some important vitamins found in vegetables are:/vitamin A, thiamine, niacin, and vitamin C.**

BETWEEN A PREPOSITION AND ITS OBJECT

► **The heart's two pumps each consist of:/an upper chamber, or atrium, and a lower chamber, or ventricle.**

AFTER *SUCH AS*, *INCLUDING*, OR *FOR EXAMPLE*

► **The NCAA regulates college athletic teams, including:/ basketball, baseball, softball, and football.**

EXERCISE 35–1 Edit the following sentences to correct errors in the use of the comma, the semicolon, or the colon. If a sentence is correct, write "correct" after it. Answers appear in the back of the book.

More practice: LaunchPadSolo

Lifting the cover gently, Luca found the source of the odd sound;: a marble in the gears.

a. We always looked forward to Thanksgiving in Vermont: It was our only chance to see our Grady cousins.
b. If we have come to fight, we are far too few, if we have come to die, we are far too many.
c. The travel package includes: a round-trip ticket to Athens, a cruise through the Cyclades, and all hotel accommodations.
d. The news article portrays the land use proposal as reckless; although 62 percent of the town's residents support it.
e. Psychologists Kindlon and Thompson (2000) offer parents a simple starting point for raising male children, "Teach boys that there are many ways to be a man" (p. 256).

36 The apostrophe

36a Use an apostrophe to indicate that a noun is possessive.

Possessive nouns usually indicate ownership, as in *Tim's hat, the lawyer's desk.* Frequently, however, ownership is only loosely implied: *the tree's roots, a day's work.* If you are not sure whether a noun is possessive, try turning it into an *of* phrase: *the roots of the tree, the work of a day.* (Pronouns also have possessive forms. See 36b and 36e.)

When to add -'s

1. If the noun does not end in -*s*, add -*'s*.

   Luck often propels a rock musician's career.

LaunchPadSolo **macmillanhighered.com/rules8e**

35 The colon

> Exercises: 35-2 and 35-3

> LearningCurve: Semicolons and colons

The Children's Defense Fund is a nonprofit organization that supports programs for poor and minority children.

2. If the noun is singular and ends in *-s* or an *s* sound, add *-'s* to indicate possession.

   Lois's sister spent last year in India.

   Her article presents an overview of Marx's teachings.

NOTE: To avoid potentially awkward pronunciation, some writers use only the apostrophe with a singular noun ending in *-s*: *Sophocles'*.

When to add only an apostrophe

If the noun is plural and ends in *-s*, add only an apostrophe.

Both diplomats' briefcases were searched by guards.

Joint possession

To show joint possession, use *-'s* or (*-s'*) with the last noun only; to show individual possession, make all nouns possessive.

Have you seen Joyce and Greg's new camper?

John's and Marie's expectations of marriage couldn't have been more different.

Joyce and Greg jointly own one camper. John and Marie individually have different expectations.

Compound nouns

If a noun is compound, use *-'s* (or *-s'*) with the last element.

My father-in-law's memoir about his childhood in Sri Lanka was published in October.

36b Use an apostrophe and *-s* to indicate that an indefinite pronoun is possessive.

Indefinite pronouns refer to no specific person or thing: *everyone, someone, no one, something.* (See 46b.)

Someone's raincoat has been left behind.

36c Use an apostrophe to mark omissions in contractions and numbers.

In a contraction, the apostrophe takes the place of one or more missing letters. *It's* stands for *it is*, *can't* for *cannot*.

It's a shame that Frank can't go on the tour.

The apostrophe is also used to mark the omission of the first two digits of a year (*the class of '08*) or years (*the '60s generation*).

36d Do not use an apostrophe in certain situations.

An apostrophe typically is not used to pluralize numbers, letters, abbreviations, and words mentioned as words. Note the few exceptions and be consistent throughout your paper.

Plural of numbers

Do not use an apostrophe in the plural of any numbers.

Oksana skated nearly perfect figure 8s.

The 1920s are known as the Jazz Age.

Plural of letters

Italicize the letter and use roman (regular) font style for the *-s* ending. Do not italicize academic grades.

Two large *P*s were painted on the door.

He received two Ds for the first time in his life.

EXCEPTIONS: To avoid misreading, use an apostrophe to form the plural of lowercase letters and the capital letters *A* and *I*.

Beginning readers often confuse *b*'s and *d*'s.

Students with straight A's earn high honors.

MLA NOTE: MLA recommends using an apostrophe for the plural of single capital and lowercase letters: *H*'s, *p*'s.

Plural of abbreviations

Do not use an apostrophe to pluralize an abbreviation.

Harriet has thirty DVDs on her desk.

Marco earned two PhDs before his thirtieth birthday.

Plural of words mentioned as words

Generally, omit the apostrophe to form the plural of words mentioned as words. If the word is italicized, the *-s* ending appears in roman (regular) type.

We've heard enough *maybe*s.

Words mentioned as words may also appear in quotation marks. When you choose this option, use the apostrophe.

We've heard enough "maybe's."

36e Avoid common misuses of the apostrophe.

Do not use an apostrophe with nouns that are not possessive or with the possessive pronouns *its*, *whose*, *his*, *hers*, *ours*, *yours*, and *theirs*.

► **Some ~~outpatient's~~ outpatients have special parking permits.**

► **Each area has ~~it's~~ its own conference room.**

It's means "it is." The possessive pronoun *its* contains no apostrophe despite the fact that it is possessive.

► **We attended a reading by Junot Díaz, ~~who's~~ whose work focuses on the Dominican immigration experience.**

Who's means "who is." The possessive pronoun is *whose*.

EXERCISE 36–1 Edit the following sentences to correct errors in the use of the apostrophe. If a sentence is correct, write "correct" after it. Answers appear in the back of the book. *More practice:* LaunchPadSolo

Our favorite barbecue restaurant is Poor ~~Richards~~ Richard's Ribs.

a. This diet will improve almost anyone's health.

b. The innovative shoe fastener was inspired by the designers young son.
c. Each days menu features a different European country’s dish.
d. Sue worked overtime to increase her families earnings.
e. Ms. Jacobs is unwilling to listen to students complaints about computer failures.

EXERCISE 36–2 Edit the following passage to correct errors in the use of the apostrophe.

> Its never too soon to start holiday shopping. In fact, some people choose to start shopping as early as January, when last seasons leftover’s are priced at their lowest. Many stores try to lure customers in with promise’s of savings up to 90 percent. Their main objective, of course, is to make way for next years inventory. The big problem with postholiday shopping, though, is that there isn’t much left to choose from. Store’s shelves have been picked over by last-minute shoppers desperately searching for gifts. The other problem is that its hard to know what to buy so far in advance. Next year’s hot items are anyones guess. But proper timing, mixed with lot’s of luck and determination, can lead to good purchases at great price’s.

37 Quotation marks

Writers use quotation marks primarily to enclose direct quotations of another person’s spoken or written words. You will also find these other uses and exceptions:

- for quotations within quotations (single quotation marks: 37b)
- for titles of short works (37c)
- for words used as words (37d)
- with other marks of punctuation (37e)
- with brackets and ellipsis marks (39c, 39d)
- no quotation marks for indirect quotations, paraphrases, and summaries (p. 324)
- no quotation marks for long quotations (p. 324)

LaunchPadSolo **macmillanhighered.com/rules8e**
36 The apostrophe
> Exercises: 36–3 to 36–5
> LearningCurve: Apostrophes

37a Use quotation marks to enclose direct quotations.

Direct quotations of a person's words, whether spoken or written, must be in quotation marks.

> “Twitter,” according to social media researcher Jameson Brown, “is the best social network for brand to customer engagement.”

In dialogue, begin a new paragraph to mark a change in speaker.

> “Mom, his name is Willie, not William. A thousand times I've told you, it's *Willie.*”
>
> “Willie is a derivative of William, Lester. Surely his birth certificate doesn't have Willie on it, and I like calling people by their proper names.”
>
> “Yes, it does, ma'am. My mother named me Willie K. Mason.”
>
> — Gloria Naylor

If a single speaker utters more than one paragraph, introduce each paragraph with a quotation mark, but do not use a closing quotation mark until the end of the speech.

Exception: Indirect quotations

Do not use quotation marks around indirect quotations. An indirect quotation reports someone's ideas without using that person's exact words. In academic writing, indirect quotation is called *paraphrase* or *summary*. (See pp. 412–14.)

> Social media researcher Jameson Brown claims that Twitter is the best social media tool for companies that want to reach their consumers.

Exception: Long quotations

Long quotations of prose or poetry are generally set off from the text by indenting. Quotation marks are not used because the indented format tells readers that the quotation is taken word-for-word from the source.

> After making an exhaustive study of the historical record, James Horan evaluates Billy the Kid like this:
>
> > The portrait that emerges of [the Kid] from the thousands of pages of affidavits, reports, trial transcripts, his letters,

> and his testimony is neither the mythical Robin Hood nor the stereotyped adenoidal moron and pathological killer. Rather Billy appears as a disturbed, lonely young man, honest, loyal to his friends, dedicated to his beliefs, and betrayed by our institutions and the corrupt, ambitious, and compromising politicians in his time. (158)

The long quotation and the page number in parentheses are handled according to MLA style. (See 56a.)

MLA and APA have specific guidelines for what constitutes a long quotation and how it should be indented (see pp. 449 and 541, respectively).

37b Use single quotation marks to enclose a quotation within a quotation.

> Megan Marshall notes that Elizabeth Peabody's school focused on "not merely 'teaching' but 'educating children morally and spiritually as well as intellectually from the first' " (107).

37c Use quotation marks around the titles of short works.

Short works include newspaper and magazine articles, poems, short stories, songs, episodes of television and radio programs, and chapters or subdivisions of books.

> James Baldwin's story "Sonny's Blues" tells the story of two brothers who come to understand each other's suffering.

NOTE: Titles of long works such as books, plays, television and radio programs, films, magazines, and newspapers are put in italics. (See 42a.)

37d Quotation marks may be used to set off words used as words.

Although words used as words are ordinarily italicized (see 42d), quotation marks are also acceptable. Be consistent throughout your paper.

The words “accept” and “except” are frequently confused.

The words *accept* and *except* are frequently confused.

37e Use punctuation with quotation marks according to convention.

This section describes the conventions American publishers use in placing various marks of punctuation inside or outside quotation marks. It also explains how to punctuate when introducing quoted material. (For the use of quotation marks in MLA and APA styles, see 56a and 61a, respectively. The examples in this section show MLA style.)

Periods and commas

Place periods and commas inside quotation marks.

> “I'm here as part of my service-learning project,” I told the classroom teacher. “I'm hoping to become a reading specialist.”

This rule applies to single quotation marks as well as double quotation marks. (See 37b.) It also applies to all uses of quotation marks: for quoted material, for titles of works, and for words used as words.

EXCEPTION: In MLA and APA styles of parenthetical in-text citations, the period follows the citation in parentheses.

> James M. McPherson comments, approvingly, that the Whigs “were not averse to extending the blessings of American liberty, even to Mexicans and Indians” (48).

Colons and semicolons

Put colons and semicolons outside quotation marks.

> Harold wrote, “I regret that I am unable to attend the fundraiser for AIDS research”; his letter, however, came with a donation.

Question marks and exclamation points

Put question marks and exclamation points inside quotation marks unless they apply to the whole sentence.

> Dr. Abram's first question was “What are your goals?”
>
> Have you heard the old proverb “Do not climb the hill until you reach it”?

In the first sentence, the question mark applies only to the quoted question. In the second sentence, the question mark applies to the whole sentence.

NOTE: In MLA and APA styles for a quotation that ends with a question mark or an exclamation point, the parenthetical citation and a period should follow the entire quotation.

> Rosie Thomas asks, “Is nothing in life ever straight and clear, the way children see it?” (77).

Introducing quoted material

After a word group introducing a quotation, choose a colon, a comma, or no punctuation at all, whichever is appropriate in context.

Formal introduction If a quotation is formally introduced, a colon is appropriate. A formal introduction is a full independent clause, not just an expression such as *he said* or *she remarked.*

> Thomas Friedman provides a challenging yet optimistic view of the future: “We need to get back to work on our country and on our planet. The hour is late, the stakes couldn’t be higher, the project couldn’t be harder, the payoff couldn’t be greater” (25).

Expression such as *he writes* If a quotation is introduced with an expression such as *he writes* or *she remarked* — or if it is followed by such an expression — a comma is needed.

> “With regard to air travel,” Stephen Ambrose notes, “Jefferson was a full century ahead of the curve” (53).
>
> “Unless another war is prevented it is likely to bring destruction on a scale never before held possible and even now hardly conceived,” Albert Einstein wrote in the aftermath of the atomic bomb (29).

Blended quotation When a quotation is blended into the writer’s own sentence, either a comma or no punctuation is appropriate, depending on the way in which the quotation fits into the sentence structure.

> The future champion could, as he put it, “float like a butterfly and sting like a bee.”
>
> Virginia Woolf wrote in 1928 that “a woman must have money and a room of her own if she is to write fiction” (4).

Beginning of sentence If a quotation appears at the beginning of a sentence, use a comma after it unless the quotation ends with a question mark or an exclamation point.

> "I've always thought of myself as a reporter," American poet Gwendolyn Brooks once stated (162).
>
> "What is it?" she asked, bracing herself.

Interrupted quotation If a quoted sentence is interrupted by explanatory words, use commas to set off the explanatory words. If two successive quoted sentences from the same source are interrupted by explanatory words, use a comma before the explanatory words and a period after them.

> "Everyone agrees journalists must tell the truth," Bill Kovach and Tom Rosenstiel write. "Yet people are befuddled about what 'the truth' means" (37).

37f Avoid common misuses of quotation marks.

Do not use quotation marks to draw attention to familiar slang, to disown trite expressions, or to justify an attempt at humor.

► **The economist estimated that single-family home prices would decline another 5 percent by the end of the year, emphasizing that this was only a "ballpark figure."**

Do not use quotation marks around the title of your own essay.

EXERCISE 37–1 Add or delete quotation marks as needed and make any other necessary changes in punctuation in the following sentences. If a sentence is correct, write "correct" after it. Answers appear in the back of the book. *More practice:* LaunchPadSolo

> **Gandhi once said, "An eye for an eye only ends up making the whole world blind."**

LaunchPadSolo **macmillanhighered.com/rules8e**
37 Quotation marks
> Exercises: 37–3 to 37–5

a. As for the advertisement "Sailors have more fun", if you consider chipping paint and swabbing decks fun, then you will have plenty of it.
b. Even after forty minutes of discussion, our class could not agree on an interpretation of Robert Frost's poem "The Road Not Taken."
c. After winning the lottery, Juanita said that "she would give half the money to charity."
d. After the movie, Vicki said, "The reviewer called this flick "trash of the first order." I guess you can't believe everything you read."
e. "Cleaning your house while your kids are still growing," said Phyllis Diller, "is like shoveling the walk before it stops snowing."

EXERCISE 37–2 Add or delete quotation marks as needed and make any other necessary changes in punctuation in the following passage. Citations should conform to MLA style (see 54b).

In his article The Moment of Truth, former vice president Al Gore argues that global warming is a genuine threat to life on Earth and that we must act now to avoid catastrophe. Gore calls our situation a "true *planetary emergency*" and cites scientific evidence of the greenhouse effect and its consequences (170–71). "What is at stake, Gore insists, is the survival of our civilization and the habitability of the Earth (197)." With such a grim predicament at hand, Gore questions why so many political and economic leaders are reluctant to act. "Is it simply more convenient to ignore the warnings," he asks (171)?

The crisis, of course, will not go away if we just pretend it isn't there. Gore points out that in Chinese two symbols form the character for the word crisis. The first of those symbols means "danger", and the second means "opportunity." The danger we face, he claims, is accompanied by "unprecedented opportunity." (172) Gore contends that throughout history we have won battles against seemingly unbeatable evils such as slavery and fascism and that we did so by facing the truth and choosing the moral high ground. Gore's final appeal is to our humanity:

> "Ultimately, [the fight to end global warming] is not about any scientific discussion or political dialogue; it is about who we are as human beings. It is about our capacity to transcend our limitations, to rise to this new occasion. To see with our hearts, as well as our heads, the response that is now called for." (244)

Gore feels that the fate of our world rests in our own hands, and his hope is that we will make the choice to save the planet.

Source of quotations: Al Gore; "The Moment of Truth"; *Vanity Fair* May 2006: 170+; print.

38 End punctuation

38a The period

Use a period to end all sentences except direct questions or genuine exclamations. Also use periods in abbreviations according to convention.

To end sentences

Most sentences should end with a period. A sentence that reports a question instead of asking it directly, (an indirect question) should end with a period, not a question mark.

► **The professor asked whether talk therapy was more beneficial than antidepressants?.**

If a sentence is not a genuine exclamation, it should end with a period, not an exclamation point. (See also 38c.)

► **After years of working her way through school, Geeta finally graduated with high honors!.**

In abbreviations

A period is conventionally used in abbreviations of titles and Latin words or phrases, including the time designations for morning and afternoon.

Mr.	i.e.	a.m. (or AM)
Ms.	e.g.	p.m. (or PM)
Dr.	etc.	

NOTE: If a sentence ends with a period marking an abbreviation, do not add a second period.

Do not use a period with US Postal Service abbreviations for states: MD, TX, CA.

Current usage is to omit the period in abbreviations of organization names, academic degrees, and designations for eras.

NATO	UNESCO	UCLA	BS	BC
IRS	AFL-CIO	NIH	PhD	BCE

38b The question mark

A direct question should be followed by a question mark.

What is the horsepower of a 777 engine?

TIP: Do not use a question mark after an indirect question, one that is reported rather than asked directly. Use a period instead.

► **He asked me who was teaching the math course this year~~?~~.**

38c The exclamation point

Use an exclamation point after a word group or sentence to express exceptional feeling or to provide special emphasis. The exclamation point is rarely appropriate in academic writing.

When Gloria entered the room, I switched on the lights, and we all yelled, "Surprise!"

TIP: Do not overuse the exclamation point.

► **In the fisherman's memory, the fish lives on, increasing in length and weight with each passing year, until at last it is big enough to shade a fishing boat~~!~~.**

This sentence doesn't need to be pumped up with an exclamation point. It is emphatic enough without it.

EXERCISE 38–1 Add appropriate end punctuation in the following paragraph.

> Although I am generally rational, I am superstitious I never walk under ladders or put shoes on the table If I spill the salt, I go into frenzied calisthenics picking up the grains and tossing them over my left shoulder As a result of these curious activities, I've always wondered whether knowing the roots of superstitions would quell my irrational responses Superstition has it, for example, that one should never place a hat on the bed This superstition arises from a time when head lice were common and placing a guest's hat on the bed stood a good chance of spreading lice through the host's bed Doesn't this make good sense And doesn't it stand to reason that, if I know that my guests don't have lice, I shouldn't care where their hats go Of course it does It is fair to ask, then, whether I have changed my ways and place hats on beds Are you kidding I wouldn't put a hat on a bed if my life depended on it

39 Other punctuation marks

39a The dash

When typing, use two hyphens to form a dash (--). Do not put spaces before or after the dash. If your word processing program has what is known as an "em-dash" (—), you may use it instead, with no space before or after it.

Use a dash to set off parenthetical material that deserves emphasis.

> Everything that went wrong — from the peeping Tom at her window last night to my head-on collision today — we blamed on our move.

Use a dash to set off appositives that contain commas. An appositive is a noun or noun phrase that renames a nearby noun. Ordinarily, most appositives are set off with commas (32e), but when the appositive itself contains commas, a pair of dashes helps readers see the relative importance of all the pauses.

> In my hometown, people's basic needs — food, clothing, and shelter — are less costly than in a big city like Los Angeles.

A dash can also introduce a list, a restatement, an amplification, or a dramatic shift in tone or thought.

> Along the wall are the bulk liquids — sesame seed oil, honey, safflower oil, and that half-liquid "peanuts only" peanut butter.
>
> In his last semester, Peter tried to pay more attention to his priorities — applying to graduate school and getting financial aid.
>
> Everywhere we looked there were little kids — a bag of Skittles in one hand and their mommy or daddy's sleeve in the other.
>
> Kiere took a few steps back, came running full speed, kicked a mighty kick — and missed the ball.

In the first two examples, the writer could also use a colon. (See 35a.) The colon is more formal than the dash and not quite as dramatic.

TIP: Unless there is a specific reason for using the dash, avoid it. Unnecessary dashes create a choppy effect.

39b Parentheses

Use parentheses to enclose supplemental material, minor digressions, and afterthoughts.

> Nurses record patients' vital signs (temperature, pulse, and blood pressure) several times a day.

Use parentheses to enclose letters or numbers labeling items in a series.

> Regulations stipulated that only the following equipment could be used on the survival mission: (1) a knife, (2) thirty feet of parachute line, (3) a book of matches, (4) two ponchos, (5) an E tool, and (6) a signal flare.

TIP: Rough drafts are likely to contain unnecessary parentheses. As writers head into a sentence, they often think of additional details, using parentheses to work them in as best they can. Such sentences usually can be revised to include the details without parentheses.

▶ **Researchers have said that** *from* **seventeen million** ~~**(estimates run as high as**~~ *to* **twenty-three million)** **Americans have diabetes.**

39c Brackets

Use brackets to enclose any words or phrases that you have inserted into an otherwise word-for-word quotation.

> *Audubon* reports that "if there are not enough young to balance deaths, the end of the species [California condor] is inevitable" (4).

The sentence quoted from the *Audubon* article did not contain the words *California condor* (since the context of the full article made clear what species was meant), so the writer needed to add the name in brackets.

The Latin word "sic" in brackets indicates that an error in a quoted sentence appears in the original source.

> According to the review, Nelly Furtado's performance was brilliant, "exceding [sic] the expectations of even her most loyal fans."

Do not overuse "sic," however, since calling attention to others' mistakes can appear snobbish. The preceding quotation, for example, might have been paraphrased instead: *According to the review, even Nelly Furtado's most loyal fans were surprised by the brilliance of her performance.*

39d The ellipsis mark

The ellipsis mark consists of three spaced periods. Use an ellipsis mark to indicate that you have deleted words from an otherwise word-for-word quotation.

> Shute (2010) acknowledges that treatment for autism can be expensive: "Sensory integration therapy . . . can cost up to $200 an hour" (82).

If you delete a full sentence or more in the middle of a quoted passage, use a period before the three ellipsis dots.

> "If we don't properly train, teach, or treat our growing prison population," says longtime reform advocate Luis Rodríguez, "somebody else will. . . . This may well be the safety issue of the new century" (16).

TIP: Ordinarily, do not use the ellipsis mark at the beginning or at the end of a quotation. Readers will understand that the quoted material is taken from a longer passage. If you have cut some words from the end of the final quoted sentence, however, MLA requires an ellipsis mark.

In quoted poetry, use a full line of ellipsis dots to indicate that you have dropped a line or more from the poem, as in this example from "To His Coy Mistress" by Andrew Marvell:

> Had we but world enough, and time,
> This coyness, lady, were no crime.
> . . . .
> But at my back I always hear
> Time's wingèd chariot hurrying near; (1–2, 21–22)

39e The slash

Use the slash to separate two or three lines of poetry that have been run into your text. Add a space both before and after the slash.

> In the opening lines of "Jordan," George Herbert pokes gentle fun at popular poems of his time: "Who says that fictions only and false hair / Become a verse? Is there in truth no beauty?" (1–2).

Four or more lines of poetry should be handled as an indented quotation. (See pp. 324–25.)

The slash may occasionally be used to separate paired terms such as *pass/fail* and *producer/director*. Do not use a space before or after the slash. Be sparing in this use of the slash. In particular, avoid the use of *and/or*, *he/she*, and *his/her*. Instead of using *he/she* and *his/her* to solve sexist language problems, you can usually find more graceful alternatives. (See 17e and 22a.)

EXERCISE 39–1 Edit the following sentences to correct errors in punctuation, focusing especially on appropriate use of the dash, parentheses, brackets, the ellipsis mark, and the slash. If a sentence is correct, write "correct" after it. Answers appear in the back of the book.

More practice: LaunchPadSolo

> **Social insects/—bees, for example/—are able to communicate complicated messages to one another.**

LaunchPadSolo **macmillanhighered.com/rules8e**
39 Other punctuation marks
> Exercises: 39-2 and 39-3

a. A client left his/her cell phone in our conference room after the meeting.
b. The films we made of Kilauea — on our trip to Hawaii Volcanoes National Park — illustrate a typical spatter cone eruption.
c. Although he was confident in his course selections, Greg chose the pass/fail option for Chemistry 101.
d. Of three engineering fields, chemical, mechanical, and materials, Keegan chose materials engineering for its application to toy manufacturing.
e. The writer Chitra Divakaruni explained her work with other Indian American immigrants: "Many women who came to Maitri [a women's support group in San Francisco] needed to know simple things like opening a bank account or getting citizenship. . . . Many women in Maitri spoke English, but their English was functional rather than emotional. They needed someone who understands their problems and speaks their language."

Mechanics

40 Abbreviations

Use abbreviations only when they are clearly appropriate and universally understood (such as *Dr.*, *a.m.*, *PhD*, and so on). This section provides details about common abbreviations and about how to handle abbreviations that might not be familiar to your audience.

40a Use standard abbreviations for titles immediately before and after proper names.

TITLES BEFORE PROPER NAMES	TITLES AFTER PROPER NAMES
Mr. Rafael Zabala	William Albert Sr.
Ms. Nancy Linehan	Thomas Hines Jr.
Dr. Margaret Simmons	Robert Simkowski, MD
Rev. John Stone	Margaret Chin, LLD

Do not abbreviate a title if it is not used with a proper name.

- ▶ **My history ~~prof.~~ *professor* is an expert on race relations in South Africa.**

Avoid redundant titles such as *Dr. Amy Day, MD.* Choose one title or the other: *Dr. Amy Day* or *Amy Day, MD.*

40b Use abbreviations only when you are sure your readers will understand them.

Familiar abbreviations for the names of organizations, companies, countries, academic degrees, and common terms, written without periods, are generally acceptable.

CIA	FBI	MD	NAACP
NBA	CEO	PhD	DVD
YMCA	CBS	USA	ESL

Talk show host Conan O'Brien is a Harvard graduate with a BA in history.

The YMCA has opened a new gym close to my office.

When using an unfamiliar abbreviation (such as NASW for National Association of Social Workers) or a potentially ambiguous abbreviation (such as *AMA*, which might refer to the American Medical Association or the American Management Association), write the full name followed by the abbreviation in parentheses at the first mention of the name. Then use just the abbreviation throughout the rest of the paper.

NOTE: An abbreviation that can be pronounced as a word is called an *acronym*: *NATO, MADD, OPEC.*

40c Use *BC, AD, a.m., p.m., No.*, and $ only with specific dates, times, numbers, and amounts.

The abbreviation *BC* ("before Christ") follows a date, and *AD* ("*anno Domini*") precedes a date. Acceptable alternatives are *BCE* ("before the common era") and *CE* ("common era"), both of which follow a date.

40 BC (or 40 BCE)	4:00 a.m. (or AM)	No. 12 (or no. 12)
AD 44 (or 44 CE)	6:00 p.m. (or PM)	$150

Avoid using *a.m., p.m., No.*, or *$* when not accompanied by a specific numeral: *in the morning* (not *in the a.m.*).

40d Units of measurement

The following are typical abbreviations for units of measurement. Most social sciences and related fields use metric units (*km, mg*), but in other fields and in everyday use, US standard units (*mi, lb*) are typical. As a general rule, use the abbreviations for units when they appear with numerals; spell out the units when they are used alone or when they are used with spelled-out numbers (see also 41a).

METRIC UNITS	US STANDARD UNITS
m, cm, mm	yd, ft, in.
km, kph	mi, mph
kg, g, mg	lb, oz

Results were measured in pounds.
Runners in the 5-km race had to contend with a stiff headwind.

Use no periods after abbreviations for units of measurement, except for the abbreviation for "inch" (*in.*), to distinguish it from the preposition *in*.

40e Be sparing in your use of Latin abbreviations.

Latin abbreviations are acceptable in footnotes and bibliographies.

cf. (Latin *confer*, "compare")
e.g. (Latin *exempli gratia*, "for example")
et al. (Latin *et alia*, "and others")
etc. (Latin *et cetera*, "and so forth")
i.e. (Latin *id est*, "that is")
N.B. (Latin *nota bene*, "note well")

In most academic writing, use the appropriate English phrases.

► **Many obsolete laws remain on the books. A law in Vermont, ~~e.g.,~~** for example, **forbids an unmarried man and woman to sit closer than six inches apart on a park bench.**

40f Plural of abbreviations

To form the plural of most abbreviations, add *-s*, without an apostrophe: *PhDs*, *DVDs*. Do not add *-s* to indicate the plural of units of measurement: *mm* (not *mms*), *lb* (*lbs*), *in.* (not *ins.*).

40g Avoid inappropriate abbreviations.

In academic writing, abbreviations for the following are not commonly accepted.

PERSONAL NAMES Charles (not Chas.)
DAYS OF THE WEEK Monday (not Mon.)
HOLIDAYS Christmas (not Xmas)
MONTHS January, February, March (not Jan., Feb., Mar.)
COURSES OF STUDY political science (not poli. sci.)

DIVISIONS OF WRITTEN WORKS chapter, page (not ch., p.)

STATES AND COUNTRIES Massachusetts (not MA or Mass.)

PARTS OF A BUSINESS NAME Adams Lighting Company (not Adams Lighting Co.); Kim and Brothers (not Kim and Bros.)

NOTE: Use abbreviations for units of measurement when they are preceded by numerals (*13 cm*). Do not abbreviate them when they are used alone. (See 40d.)

EXCEPTION: Abbreviate states and provinces in complete addresses, and always abbreviate *DC* when used with *Washington.*

EXERCISE 40–1 Edit the following sentences to correct errors in abbreviations. If a sentence is correct, write "correct" after it. Answers appear in the back of the book. *More practice:* LaunchPadSolo

This year ~~Xmas~~ [Christmas] will fall on a ~~Tues.~~ [Tuesday.]

a. Since its inception, the BBC has maintained a consistently high standard of radio and television broadcasting.

b. Some combat soldiers are trained by govt. diplomats to be sensitive to issues of culture, history, and religion.

c. Mahatma Gandhi has inspired many modern leaders, including Martin Luther King Jr.

d. How many lb. have you lost since you began running four miles a day?

e. Denzil spent all night studying for his psych. exam.

41 Numbers

41a Follow the conventions in your discipline for spelling out or using numerals to express numbers.

In the humanities, which generally follow Modern Language Association (MLA) style, use numerals only for specific numbers above one hundred: *353, 1,020.* Spell out numbers one hundred and below and large round numbers: *eleven, thirty-five, sixty, fifteen million.*

LaunchPadSolo **macmillanhighered.com/rules8e**

40 Abbreviations

> Exercises: 40–2 and 40–3

The social sciences and other disciplines that follow American Psychological Association (APA) style use numerals for all but the numbers one through nine. Spell out numbers from one to nine even when they are used with related numerals in a passage: *The survey found that nine of the 157 respondents had not taken a course on alcohol use.* (An exception is the abstract of a paper, where numerals are used for all numbers. See 62a on APA manuscript format.)

If a sentence begins with a number, spell out the number or rewrite the sentence.

One hundred fifty
▶ ~~150~~ **children in our program need expensive dental treatment.**
^

Rewriting the sentence may be less awkward if the number is long: *In our program, 150 children need expensive dental treatment.*

41b Use numerals according to convention in dates, addresses, and so on.

DATES July 4, 1776; 56 BC; AD 30

ADDRESSES 77 Latches Lane, 519 West 42nd Street

PERCENTAGES 55 percent (or 55%)

FRACTIONS, DECIMALS ⅞, 0.047

SCORES 7 to 3, 21–18

STATISTICS average age 37, average weight 180

SURVEYS 4 out of 5

EXACT AMOUNTS OF MONEY $105.37, $106,000

DIVISIONS OF BOOKS volume 3, chapter 4, page 189

DIVISIONS OF PLAYS act 3, scene 3 (or act III, scene iii)

TIME OF DAY 4:00 p.m., 1:30 a.m.

NOTE: When not using *a.m.* or *p.m.*, write out the time in words (*two o'clock in the afternoon, twelve noon, seven in the morning*).

EXERCISE 41–1 Edit the following sentences to correct errors in the use of numbers. If a sentence is correct, write "correct" after it. Answers appear in the back of the book. *More practice:* LaunchPadSolo

$3.06
By the end of the evening, Ashanti had only ~~three dollars~~
^
~~and six cents~~ left.

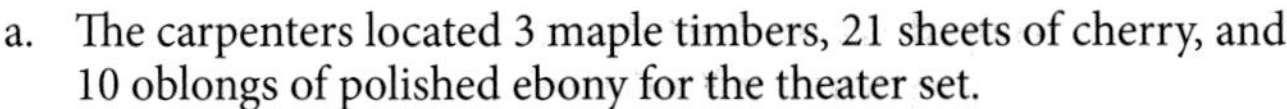

a. The carpenters located 3 maple timbers, 21 sheets of cherry, and 10 oblongs of polished ebony for the theater set.
b. The program's cost is well over one billion dollars.
c. The score was tied at 5–5 when the momentum shifted and carried the Standards to a decisive 12–5 win.
d. 8 students in the class had been labeled "learning disabled."
e. The Vietnam Veterans Memorial in Washington, DC, had fifty-eight thousand one hundred thirty-two names inscribed on it when it was dedicated in 1982.

42 Italics

This section describes conventional uses for italics. (If your instructor requires underlining, simply substitute underlining for italics in the examples in this section.)

Some software applications do not allow for italics. To indicate words that should be italicized, you can use underscore marks or asterisks before and after the words.

> I will write my senior thesis on _And the Mountains Echoed_.

NOTE: Excessive use of italics to emphasize words or ideas, especially in academic writing, is distracting and should be avoided.

42a Italicize the titles of works according to convention.

Titles of the following types of works should be italicized.

TITLES OF BOOKS *The Color Purple*, *The Round House*

MAGAZINES *Time*, *Scientific American*, *Slate*

NEWSPAPERS the *Baltimore Sun*, the *Orlando Sentinel Online*

PAMPHLETS *Common Sense*, *Facts about Marijuana*

LONG POEMS *The Waste Land*, *Paradise Lost*

PLAYS *'Night Mother*, *Wicked*

FILMS *Casablanca*, *Argo*

TELEVISION PROGRAMS *The Voice*, *Frontline*

RADIO PROGRAMS *All Things Considered*

MUSICAL COMPOSITIONS *Porgy and Bess*

CHOREOGRAPHIC WORKS *Brief Fling*

WORKS OF VISUAL ART *American Gothic*

DATABASES [MLA] *ProQuest*

WEB SITES *Salon*, *Google*

COMPUTER SOFTWARE OR APPS [MLA] *Photoshop*, *Instagram*

The titles of other works—including short stories, essays, episodes of radio and television programs, songs, and short poems—are enclosed in quotation marks. (See 37c.)

NOTE: Do not use italics when referring to the Bible, titles of books in the Bible (Genesis, not *Genesis*), or titles of legal documents (the Constitution, not the *Constitution*).

42b Italicize the names of specific ships, spacecraft, and aircraft.

Queen Mary 2, *Endeavour*, *Wright Flyer*

The success of the Soviets' *Sputnik* energized the US space program.

42c Italicize foreign words used in an English sentence.

Shakespeare's Falstaff is a comic character known for both his excessive drinking and his general *joie de vivre*.

EXCEPTION: Do not italicize foreign words that have become a standard part of the English language—"laissez-faire," "fait accompli," "modus operandi," and "per diem," for example.

42d Italicize words mentioned as words, letters mentioned as letters, and numbers mentioned as numbers.

Tomás assured us that the chemicals could probably be safely mixed, but his *probably* stuck in our minds.

Some toddlers have trouble pronouncing the letters *f* and *s*.

A big *3* was painted on the stage door.

NOTE: Quotation marks may be used instead of italics to set off words mentioned as words. (See 37d.)

EXERCISE 42–1 Edit the following sentences to correct errors in the use of italics. If a sentence is correct, write "correct" after it. Answers appear in the back of the book. *More practice:* LaunchPadSolo

The lecture was about Gini Alhadeff's memoir *The Sun at Midday*. Correct

a. Howard Hughes commissioned the Spruce Goose, a beautifully built but thoroughly impractical wooden aircraft.
b. The old man *screamed* his anger, *shouting* to all of us, "I will not leave my money to you worthless layabouts!"
c. I learned the Latin term ad infinitum from an old nursery rhyme about fleas: "Great fleas have little fleas upon their back to bite 'em, / Little fleas have lesser fleas and so on ad infinitum."
d. Cinema audiences once gasped at hearing the word *damn* in *Gone with the Wind.*
e. Neve Campbell's lifelong interest in ballet inspired her involvement in the film "The Company," which portrays a season with the Joffrey Ballet.

43 Spelling

You learned to spell from repeated experience with words in both reading and writing. As you proofread, you can probably tell if a word doesn't look quite right. In such cases, the solution is simple: Look up the word in the dictionary. (See 43b.)

43a Become familiar with the major spelling rules.

i before *e* except after *c*

In general, use *i* before *e* except after *c* and except when sounded like *ay*, as in *neighbor* and *weigh*.

LaunchPadSolo macmillanhighered.com/rules8e
42 Italics
> Exercises: 42–2 and 42–3

I BEFORE *E*	relieve, believe, sieve, niece, fierce, frieze
E BEFORE *I*	receive, deceive, sleigh, freight, eight
EXCEPTIONS	seize, either, weird, height, foreign, leisure

Suffixes

Final silent *-e* Generally, drop a final silent *-e* when adding a suffix that begins with a vowel. Keep the final *-e* if the suffix begins with a consonant.

combine, combination	achieve, achievement
desire, desiring	care, careful
prude, prudish	entire, entirety
remove, removable	gentle, gentleness

Words such as *changeable*, *judgment*, *argument*, and *truly* are exceptions.

Final *-y* When adding *-s* or *-d* to words ending in *-y*, ordinarily change *-y* to *-ie* when the *-y* is preceded by a consonant but not when it is preceded by a vowel.

comedy, comedies	monkey, monkeys
dry, dried	play, played

With proper names ending in *-y*, however, do not change the *-y* to *-ie* even if it is preceded by a consonant: *the Doughertys* (*the Dougherty family*).

Final consonants If a final consonant is preceded by a single vowel *and* the consonant ends a one-syllable word or a stressed syllable, double the consonant when adding a suffix beginning with a vowel.

bet, betting	occur, occurrence
commit, committed	

Plurals

-s* or *-es Add *-s* to form the plural of most nouns; add *-es* to singular nouns ending in *-s*, *-sh*, *-ch*, and *-x*.

table, tables	church, churches
paper, papers	dish, dishes

Ordinarily add *-s* to nouns ending in *-o* when the *-o* is preceded by a vowel. Add *-es* when it is preceded by a consonant.

radio, radios	hero, heroes
video, videos	tomato, tomatoes

Other plurals To form the plural of a hyphenated compound word, add *-s* to the chief word even if it does not appear at the end.

mother-in-law, mothers-in-law

English words derived from other languages such as Latin, Greek, or French sometimes form the plural as they would in their original language.

medium, media	chateau, chateaux
criterion, criteria	

Multilingual

Spelling varieties among English-speaking countries can cause confusion. Following is a list of some common words with different American and British spellings. Consult a dictionary for others.

AMERICAN	BRITISH
canceled, traveled	cancelled, travelled
color, humor	colour, humour
judgment	judgement
check	cheque
realize, apologize	realise, apologise
defense	defence
anemia, anesthetic	anaemia, anaesthetic
theater, center	theatre, centre
fetus	foetus
mold, smolder	mould, smoulder
civilization	civilisation
connection, inflection	connexion, inflexion
licorice	liquorice

43b Become familiar with your dictionary.

A good dictionary, whether print or online — such as *The Random House College Dictionary* or *Merriam-Webster* online — is an indispensable writer's aid.

A sample print dictionary entry, taken from *The American Heritage Dictionary*, appears at the bottom of this page.

A sample online dictionary entry, taken from *Merriam-Webster* online, appears on page 349.

Spelling, word division, pronunciation

The main entry (*re·gard* in the sample entries) shows the correct spelling of the word. When there are two correct spellings of a word (as in *collectible, collectable*, for example), both are given, with the preferred spelling usually appearing first.

PRINT DICTIONARY ENTRY

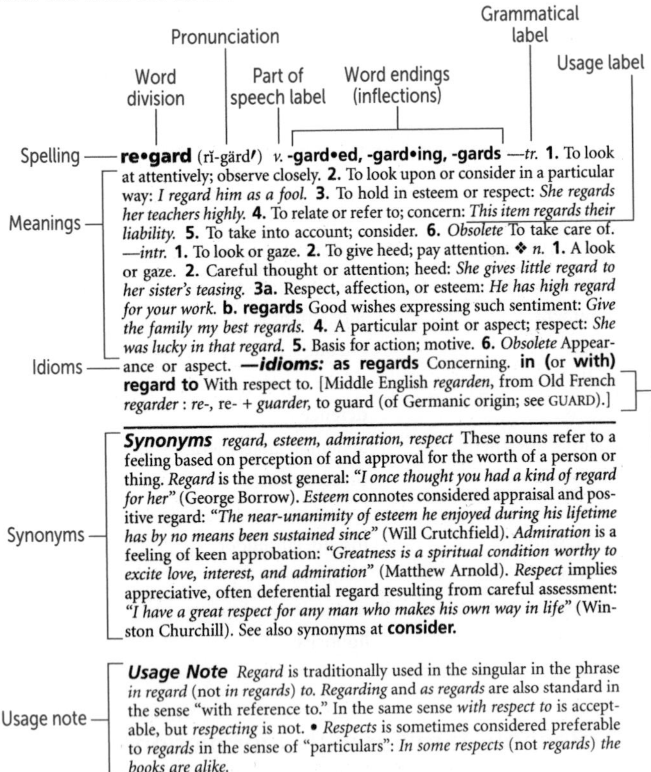

re•gard (rĭ-gärd′) *v.* **-gard•ed, -gard•ing, -gards** —*tr.* **1.** To look at attentively; observe closely. **2.** To look upon or consider in a particular way: *I regard him as a fool.* **3.** To hold in esteem or respect: *She regards her teachers highly.* **4.** To relate or refer to; concern: *This item regards their liability.* **5.** To take into account; consider. **6.** *Obsolete* To take care of. —*intr.* **1.** To look or gaze. **2.** To give heed; pay attention. ❖ *n.* **1.** A look or gaze. **2.** Careful thought or attention; heed: *She gives little regard to her sister's teasing.* **3a.** Respect, affection, or esteem: *He has high regard for your work.* **b. regards** Good wishes expressing such sentiment: *Give the family my best regards.* **4.** A particular point or aspect; respect: *She was lucky in that regard.* **5.** Basis for action; motive. **6.** *Obsolete* Appearance or aspect. ***—idioms:*** **as regards** Concerning. **in** (or **with**) **regard to** With respect to. [Middle English *regarden*, from Old French *regarder* : *re-*, re- + *guarder*, to guard (of Germanic origin; see GUARD).]

Synonyms *regard, esteem, admiration, respect* These nouns refer to a feeling based on perception of and approval for the worth of a person or thing. *Regard* is the most general: "*I once thought you had a kind of regard for her*" (George Borrow). *Esteem* connotes considered appraisal and positive regard: "*The near-unanimity of esteem he enjoyed during his lifetime has by no means been sustained since*" (Will Crutchfield). *Admiration* is a feeling of keen approbation: "*Greatness is a spiritual condition worthy to excite love, interest, and admiration*" (Matthew Arnold). *Respect* implies appreciative, often deferential regard resulting from careful assessment: "*I have a great respect for any man who makes his own way in life*" (Winston Churchill). See also synonyms at **consider.**

Usage Note *Regard* is traditionally used in the singular in the phrase *in regard* (not *in regards*) *to. Regarding* and *as regards* are also standard in the sense "with reference to." In the same sense *with respect to* is acceptable, but *respecting* is not. • *Respects* is sometimes considered preferable to *regards* in the sense of "particulars": *In some respects* (not *regards*) *the books are alike.*

ONLINE DICTIONARY ENTRY

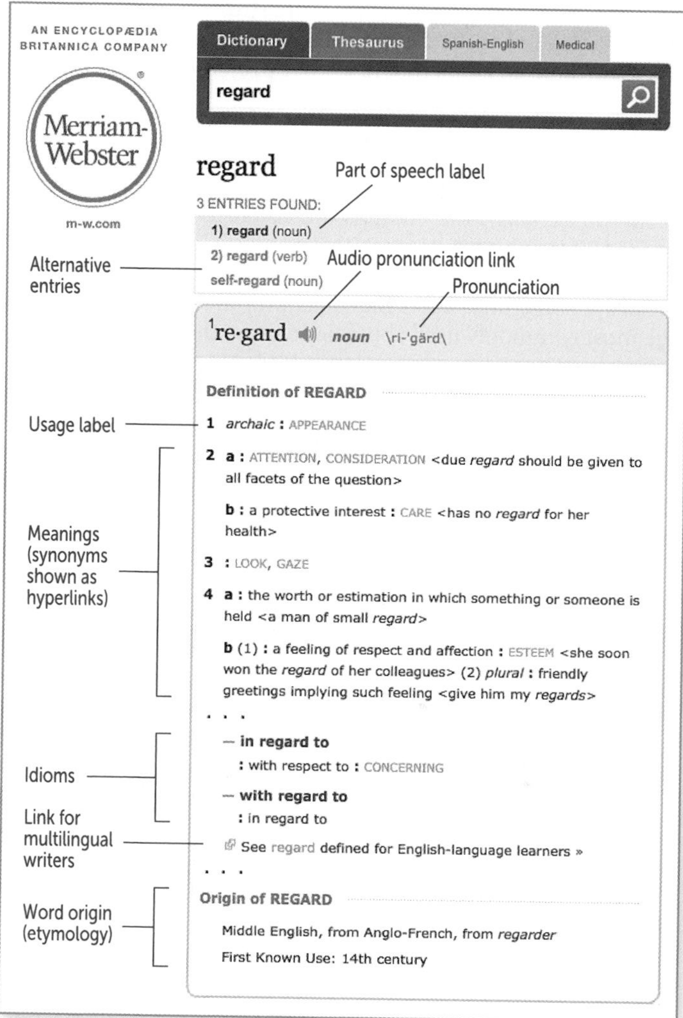

The dot between *re* and *gard* separates the two syllables and indicates where the word should be divided if it can't fit at the end of a line of type (see 44f). When a word is compound, the main entry shows how to write it: as one word (*crossroad*), as a hyphenated word (*cross-stitch*), or as two words (*cross section*).

The word's pronunciation is given just after the main entry. The accents indicate which syllables are stressed; the other marks are explained in the dictionary's pronunciation key. Many online entries include an audio link to a voice pronouncing the word.

Word endings and grammatical labels

When a word takes endings to indicate grammatical functions (called *inflections*), the endings are listed in boldface, as with *-garded*, *-garding*, and *-gards* in the sample print entry (p. 348).

Labels for the parts of speech and for other grammatical terms are sometimes abbreviated, as they are in the print entry. The most commonly used abbreviations are these:

n.	noun	adj.	adjective
pl.	plural	adv.	adverb
sing.	singular	pron.	pronoun
v.	verb	prep.	preposition
tr.	transitive verb	conj.	conjunction
intr.	intransitive verb	interj.	interjection

Meanings, word origin, synonyms, and antonyms

Sometimes a word can be used as more than one part of speech (*regard*, for instance, can be used as either a verb or a noun). In such a case, all the meanings for one part of speech are given before all the meanings for another, as in the sample entries.

The origin of the word, called its *etymology*, appears in brackets after all the meanings in the print and online versions.

Synonyms, words similar in meaning to the main entry, are frequently listed. In the sample print entry, the dictionary draws distinctions in meaning among the various synonyms. In the online entry, synonyms appear as hyperlinks. Antonyms, which do not appear in the sample entries, are words having a meaning opposite from that of the main entry.

Usage

Usage labels indicate when, where, or under what conditions a particular meaning for a word is appropriately used. Common labels are *informal* (or *colloquial*), *slang*, *archaic*, *poetic*, *non-standard*, *dialect*, *obsolete*, and *British*. In the sample print entry

(p. 348), two meanings of *regard* are labeled *obsolete* because they are no longer in use. The sample online entry (p. 349) has one meaning labeled *archaic*.

Dictionaries sometimes include usage notes as well. Advice in the notes is based on the opinions of many experts and on actual usage in current publications.

43c Discriminate between words that sound alike but have different meanings.

Words that sound alike or nearly alike but have different meanings and spellings are called *homophones*. The following sets of words are commonly confused. (See also the glossary of usage in the appendixes.)

affect (verb: to exert an influence)
effect (verb: to accomplish; noun: result)

its (possessive pronoun: of or belonging to it)
it's (contraction of *it is* or *it has*)

loose (adjective: free, not securely attached)
lose (verb: to fail to keep, to be deprived of)

principal (adjective: most important; noun: head of a school)
principle (noun: a fundamental guideline or truth)

their (possessive pronoun: belonging to them)
they're (contraction of *they are*)
there (adverb: that place or position)

who's (contraction of *who is* or *who has*)
whose (possessive form of *who*)

your (possessive pronoun: belonging to you)
you're (contraction of *you are*)

43d Be alert to commonly misspelled words.

absence
academic
accidentally
accommodate
achievement
acknowledge
acquaintance
acquire
address
all right
amateur
analyze
answer
apparently
appearance
arctic
argument
arithmetic
arrangement
ascend
athlete
athletics
attendance
basically

beautiful
beginning
believe
benefited
bureau
business
calendar
candidate
cemetery
changeable
column
commitment
committed
committee
competitive
completely
conceivable
conscience
conscientious
conscious
criticism
criticize
decision
definitely
descendant
desperate
dictionary
different
disastrous
eighth
eligible
embarrass
emphasize
entirely
environment
especially
exaggerated
exercise
exhaust
existence
extraordinary
extremely
familiar
fascinate
February
foreign
forty
fourth
friend
government
grammar
guard
harass
height
humorous
incidentally
incredible
independence
indispensable
inevitable
intelligence
irrelevant
irresistible
knowledge
library
license
lightning
loneliness
maintenance
maneuver
marriage
mathematics
mischievous
necessary
noticeable
occasion
occurred
occurrence
pamphlet
parallel
particularly
pastime
permanent
permissible
perseverance
phenomenon
physically
playwright
practically
precede
preference
preferred
prejudice
presence
prevalent
privilege
proceed
professor
pronunciation
publicly
quiet
quite
quizzes
receive
recognize
referred
restaurant
rhythm
roommate
sandwich
schedule
seize
separate
sergeant
siege
similar
sincerely
sophomore
strictly
subtly
succeed
surprise
thorough
tomorrow
tragedy
transferred
tries
truly
unnecessarily
usually
vacuum
vengeance
villain
weird
whether
writing

EXERCISE 43–1 The following memo has been run through a spell checker. Proofread it carefully, editing the spelling and typographical errors that remain. *More practice:* 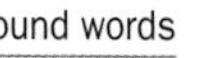

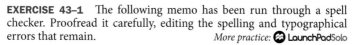

November 3, 2014

To: Patricia Wise
From: Constance Mayhew
Subject: Express Tours annual report

Thank you for agreeing to draft the annual report for Express Tours. Before you begin you're work, let me outline the initial steps.

First, its essential for you to include brief profiles of top management. Early next week, I'll provide profiles for all manages accept Samuel Heath, who's biographical information is being revised. You should edit these profiles carefully and than format them according to the enclosed instructions. We may ask you to include other employee's profiles at some point.

Second, you should arrange to get complete financial information for fiscal year 2014 from our comptroller, Richard Chang. (Helen Boyes, to, can provide the necessary figures.) When you get this information, precede according tot he plans we discuss in yesterday's meeting. By the way, you will notice from the figures that the sale of our Charterhouse division did not significantly effect net profits.

Third, you should e-mail a first draft of the report by December 15. Of coarse, you should proofread you writing.

I am quiet pleased that you can take on this project. If I can answers questions, don't hesitate to call.

44 The hyphen

In addition to the guidelines in this section, a dictionary will help you make decisions about hyphenation.

44a Consult the dictionary to determine how to treat a compound word.

The dictionary shows whether to treat a compound word as a hyphenated compound (*water-repellent*), one word (*waterproof*),

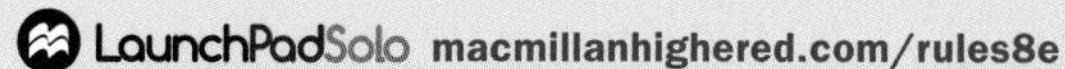
43 Spelling
> Exercise: 43-2

or two words (*water table*). If the compound word is not in the dictionary, treat it as two words.

► **The prosecutor chose not to cross-examine any witnesses.**

► **All students are expected to record their data in a small note book.**

► **Alice walked through the looking/glass into a backward world.**

44b Hyphenate two or more words used together as an adjective before a noun.

► **Many teachers use Web-delivered content in the classroom.**

► **Richa Gupta is not yet a well-known candidate.**

Web-delivered in the first example and *well-known* in the second example are adjectives used before the nouns *content* and *candidate.*

Generally, do not use a hyphen when such compounds follow the noun.

► **After our television campaign, Richa Gupta will be well/known.**

Do not use a hyphen to connect *-ly* adverbs to the words they modify.

► **A slowly/moving truck tied up traffic.**

NOTE: When two or more hyphenated adjectives in a row modify the same noun, you can suspend the hyphens. *Do you prefer first-, second-, or third-class tickets?*

44c Hyphenate fractions and certain numbers when they are spelled out.

For numbers written as words, use a hyphen in all fractions (*two-thirds*) and in all forms of compound numbers from twenty-one to ninety-nine (*thirty-five, sixty-seventh*).

► **One-fourth of my income goes to pay my child care expenses.**

44d Use a hyphen with the prefixes *all-*, *ex-* (meaning "former"), and *self-* and with the suffix *-elect*.

► **The private foundation is funneling more money into self-help projects.**

► **The Student Senate bylaws require the president-elect to attend all senate meetings between the election and the official transfer of office.**

44e Use a hyphen to clarify certain words.

Without the hyphen, there would be no way to distinguish between words such as *re-creation* and *recreation.*

> Bicycling in the city is my favorite form of recreation.
>
> The film was praised for its astonishing re-creation of nineteenth-century London.

Hyphens are sometimes used to separate awkward double or triple letters in compound words (*anti-intellectual, cross-stitch*).

44f Check for correct word breaks when words must be divided at the end of a line.

Some word processing programs and other computer applications automatically generate word breaks at the ends of lines. For academic writing, it's best to disable automatic hyphenation. This setting will ensure that only words already containing a hyphen (such as *long-distance*, *pre-Roman*) will be hyphenated at the ends of lines.

E-mail addresses and URLs need special attention when they occur at the end of a line of text or in bibliographic citations. You can't rely on your word processor to divide these terms correctly, so you must make a decision in each case. Do not insert a hyphen to divide electronic addresses. Instead, break an e-mail address after the @ symbol or before a period. It is common practice to break a URL before most punctuation marks. (For variations in MLA and APA styles, see 57a and 62a, respectively.)

> I repeatedly e-mailed Janine at janine.r.rose@dunbaracademy .org before I gave up and called her cell phone.
>
> To avoid standing in line, I now order stamps online at http://www .usps.com.

EXERCISE 44–1 Edit the following sentences to correct errors in hyphenation. If a sentence is correct, write "correct" after it. Answers appear in the back of the book. *More practice:* LaunchPadSolo

> **Émile Zola's first readers were scandalized by his slice-of-life novels.**

a. Gold is the seventy-ninth element in the periodic table.

b. The swiftly-moving tugboat pulled alongside the barge and directed it away from the oil spill in the harbor.

c. The Moche were a pre-Columbian people who established a sophisticated culture in ancient Peru.

d. Your dog is well-known in our neighborhood.

e. Road-blocks were set up along all the major highways leading out of the city.

45 Capitalization

In addition to the rules in this section, a good dictionary can tell you when to use capital letters.

45a Capitalize proper nouns and words derived from them; do not capitalize common nouns.

Proper nouns are the names of specific persons, places, and things. All other nouns are common nouns. The following types of words are usually capitalized: names of deities, religions,

LaunchPadSolo **macmillanhighered.com/rules8e**

44 The hyphen

> Exercises: 44–2 and 44–3

religious followers, sacred books; words of family relationship used as names; particular places; nationalities and their languages, races, tribes; educational institutions, departments, degrees, particular courses; government departments, organizations, political parties; historical movements, periods, events, documents; and trade names.

PROPER NOUNS	COMMON NOUNS
God (used as a name)	a god
Book of Common Prayer	a sacred book
Uncle Pedro	my uncle
Father (used as a name)	my father
Lake Superior	a picturesque lake
the Capital Center	a center for advanced studies
the South	a southern state
Wrigley Field	a baseball stadium
University of Wisconsin	a state university
Geology 101	geology
Environmental Protection Agency	a federal agency
the Democratic Party	a political party
the Enlightenment	the eighteenth century
the Treaty of Versailles	a treaty
Advil	a painkiller

Months, holidays, and days of the week are treated as proper nouns; the seasons and numbers of the days of the month are not.

> Our academic year begins on a Tuesday in early September, right after Labor Day.
>
> Graduation is in late spring, on the second of June.

EXCEPTION: Capitalize Fourth of July (or July Fourth) when referring to the holiday.

Names of school subjects are capitalized only if they are names of languages. Names of particular courses are capitalized.

> This semester Lee is taking math, geography, geology, French, and English.
>
> Professor Obembe offers Modern American Fiction 501 to undergraduate students.

The terms *Web* and *Internet* are typically capitalized, but related common nouns are not: *home page, operating system*. Usage varies widely, however, so check with your instructor about whether you should follow the guidelines for MLA or APA style (57a or 62a, respectively).

CAUTION: Do not capitalize common nouns to make them seem important.

45b Capitalize titles of persons when used as part of a proper name but usually not when used alone.

Professor Margaret Barnes; Dr. Sinyee Sein; John Scott Williams Jr.

District Attorney Marshall was reprimanded for badgering the witness.

The district attorney was elected for a two-year term.

Usage varies when the title of an important public figure is used alone: *The president* [or *President*] *vetoed the bill.*

45c Capitalize the first, last, and all major words in titles and subtitles of works such as books, articles, songs, and online documents.

In both titles and subtitles of works mentioned in the text of a paper, major words such as nouns, pronouns, verbs, adjectives, and adverbs should be capitalized. Minor words such as articles, prepositions, and coordinating conjunctions are not capitalized unless they are the first or last word of a title or subtitle.

Capitalize the second part of a hyphenated term in a title if it is a major word but not if it is a minor word. Capitalize chapter titles and the titles of other major divisions of a work following the same guidelines used for titles of complete works.

Seizing the Enigma: The Race to Break the German U-Boat Codes
A River Runs through It
"I Want to Hold Your Hand"
The Canadian Green Page

To see why some of the titles in the list are italicized and some are put in quotation marks, see 42a and 37c.

Titles of works are handled differently in the APA reference list. See "Preparing the list of references" in 62a.

45d Capitalize the first word of a sentence.

The first word of a sentence should be capitalized. When a sentence appears within parentheses, capitalize its first word unless the parentheses appear within another sentence.

> Early detection of breast cancer significantly increases survival rates. (See table 2.)
>
> Early detection of breast cancer significantly increases survival rates (see table 2).

45e Capitalize the first word of a quoted sentence but not a quoted word or phrase.

> Loveless writes, "If failing schools are ever to be turned around, much more must be learned about how schools age as institutions" (25).
>
> Russell Baker has written that in this country, sports are "the opiate of the masses" (46).

If a quoted sentence is interrupted by explanatory words, do not capitalize the first word after the interruption. (See 37e.)

> "If you want to go out," he said, "tell me now."

When quoting poetry, copy the poet's capitalization exactly. Many poets capitalize the first word of every line of poetry; a few contemporary poets dismiss capitalization altogether.

> it was the week   that
> i felt the city's narrow breezes rush about
> me   —Don L. Lee

45f Capitalize the first word after a colon if it begins an independent clause.

If a group of words following a colon could stand on its own as a complete sentence, capitalize the first word (see p. 360).

Clinical trials called into question the safety profile of the drug: A high percentage of participants reported hypertension and kidney problems.

Preferences vary among academic disciplines. See 57a and 62a.

Always use lowercase for a list or an appositive that follows a colon (see 35a).

Students were divided into two groups: residents and commuters.

EXERCISE 45–1 Edit the following sentences to correct errors in capitalization. If a sentence is correct, write "correct" after it. Answers appear in the back of the book. *More practice:* LaunchPadSolo

On our trip to the West, we visited the ~~g~~rand ~~c~~anyon and the ~~g~~reat ~~s~~alt ~~d~~esert. [handwritten corrections: G, C, G, S, D]

a. Assistant dean Shirin Ahmadi recommended offering more world language courses.

b. We went to the Mark Taper Forum to see a production of *Angels in America*.

c. Kalindi has an ambitious semester, studying differential calculus, classical hebrew, brochure design, and greek literature.

d. Lydia's Aunt and Uncle make modular houses as beautiful as modernist works of art.

e. We amused ourselves on the long flight by discussing how Spring in Kyoto stacks up against Summer in London.

LaunchPadSolo **macmillanhighered.com/rules8e**

45 Capitalization

> Exercises: 45–2 and 45–3

> LearningCurve: Capitalization

Grammar Basics

46 Parts of speech

Traditional grammar recognizes eight parts of speech: noun, pronoun, verb, adjective, adverb, preposition, conjunction, and interjection. Many words can function as more than one part of speech. For example, depending on its use in a sentence, the word *paint* can be a noun (*The paint is wet*) or a verb (*Please paint the ceiling next*).

46a Nouns

A noun is the name of a person, place, thing, or concept.

> N N N
> The *lion* in the *cage* growled at the *zookeeper*.

Nouns sometimes function as adjectives modifying other nouns. Because of their dual roles, nouns used in this manner may be called *noun/adjectives*.

> N/ADJ N/ADJ
> The *leather* notebook was tucked in the *student's* backpack.

Nouns are classified in a variety of ways. *Proper* nouns are capitalized, but *common* nouns are not (see 45a). For clarity, writers choose between *concrete* and *abstract* nouns (see 18b). The distinction between *count* nouns and *noncount* nouns can be especially helpful to multilingual writers (see 29a). Most nouns have singular and plural forms; *collective* nouns may be either singular or plural, depending on how they are used (see 21f and 22b). *Possessive* nouns require an apostrophe (see 36a).

EXERCISE 46–1 Underline the nouns (and noun/adjectives) in the following sentences. Answers appear in the back of the book.

More practice: LaunchPadSolo

The best part of dinner was the chef's newest dessert.

LaunchPadSolo **macmillanhighered.com/rules8e**

46 Parts of speech

> Exercises: 46–2 to 46–4, 46–19, 46–20

> LearningCurve: Nouns and pronouns

a. The stage was set for a confrontation of biblical proportions.
b. The courage of the mountain climber was an inspiration to the rescuers.
c. The need to arrive before the guest of honor motivated us to navigate the thick fog.
d. The defense attorney made a final appeal to the jury.
e. A national museum dedicated to women artists opened in 1987.

46b Pronouns

A pronoun is a word used in place of a noun. Usually the pronoun substitutes for a specific noun, known as its *antecedent*.

ANT PN
When the *battery* wears down, we recharge *it*.

Although most pronouns function as substitutes for nouns, some can function as adjectives modifying nouns. Such pronouns may be called *pronoun/adjectives*.

PN/ADJ
That bird was at the same window yesterday morning.

Pronouns are classified as personal, possessive, intensive and reflexive, relative, interrogative, demonstrative, indefinite, and reciprocal.

Personal pronouns Personal pronouns refer to specific persons or things. They always function as subsitutes for nouns.

Singular: I, me, you, she, her, he, him, it

Plural: we, us, you, they, them

Possessive pronouns Possessive pronouns indicate ownership.

Singular: my, mine, your, yours, her, hers, his, its

Plural: our, ours, your, yours, their, theirs

Some of these possessive pronouns function as adjectives modifying nouns: *my, your, his, her, its, our, their.*

Intensive and reflexive pronouns Intensive pronouns emphasize a noun or another pronoun (The senator *herself* met us at the door). Reflexive pronouns name a receiver of an action identical with the doer of the action (Paula cut *herself*).

Singular: myself, yourself, himself, herself, itself

Plural: ourselves, yourselves, themselves

Relative pronouns Relative pronouns introduce subordinate clauses functioning as adjectives (The writer *who won the award* refused to accept it). The relative pronoun, in this case *who*, also points back to a noun or pronoun that the clause modifies (*writer*). (See 48e.)

who, whom, whose, which, that

The pronouns *whichever*, *whoever*, *whomever*, *what*, and *whatever* are sometimes considered relative pronouns. These words introduce noun clauses, however; they do not point back to a noun or pronoun. (See "Noun clauses" in 48e.)

Interrogative pronouns Interrogative pronouns introduce questions (*Who* is expected to win the election?).

who, whom, whose, which, what

Demonstrative pronouns Demonstrative pronouns identify or point to nouns. Frequently they function as adjectives (*This* chair is my favorite), but they may also function as substitutes for nouns (*This* is my favorite chair).

this, that, these, those

Indefinite pronouns Indefinite pronouns refer to nonspecific persons or things. Most are always singular (*everyone*, *each*); some are always plural (*both*, *many*); a few may be singular or plural (see 21e). Most indefinite pronouns function as substitutes for nouns (*Something* is burning), but some can also function as adjectives (*All* campers must check in at the lodge).

all	anything	everyone	nobody	several
another	both	everything	none	some
any	each	few	no one	somebody
anybody	either	many	nothing	someone
anyone	everybody	neither	one	something

Reciprocal pronouns Reciprocal pronouns refer to individual parts of a plural antecedent (By turns, the penguins fed *one another*).

each other, one another

NOTE: See also pronoun-antecedent agreement (22), pronoun reference (23), distinguishing between pronouns such as *I* and *me* (24), and distinguishing between *who* and *whom* (25).

EXERCISE 46–5 Underline the pronouns (and pronoun/adjectives) in the following sentences. Answers appear in the back of the book.

More practice: LaunchPadSolo

We were intrigued by the video that the fifth graders produced as their final project.

a. The governor's loyalty was his most appealing trait.
b. In the fall, the geese that fly south for the winter pass through our town in huge numbers.
c. As Carl Sandburg once said, even he himself did not understand some of his poetry.
d. I appealed my parking ticket, but you did not get one.
e. Angela did not mind gossip as long as no one gossiped about her.

46c Verbs

The verb of a sentence usually expresses action (*jump*, *think*) or being (*is*, *become*). It is composed of a main verb possibly preceded by one or more helping verbs.

The horses *exercise* [MV] every day.

The task force report *was* [HV] not *completed* [MV] on schedule.

No one *has* [HV] *been* [HV] *defended* [MV] with more passion than our mayor.

LaunchPadSolo **macmillanhighered.com/rules8e**

46 Parts of speech

> Exercises: 46–6 to 46–8, 46–19, 46–20

> LearningCurve: Nouns and pronouns

Notice that words, usually adverbs, can intervene between the helping verb and the main verb (was *not* completed). (See 46e.)

Helping verbs

There are twenty-three helping verbs in English: forms of *have*, *do*, and *be*, which may also function as main verbs; and nine modals, which function only as helping verbs. *Have*, *do*, and *be* change form to indicate tense; the nine modals do not.

FORMS OF *HAVE*, *DO*, AND *BE*

have, has, had

do, does, did

be, am, is, are, was, were, being, been

MODALS

can, could, may, might, must, shall, should, will, would

The verb phrase *ought to* is often classified as a modal as well.

Main verbs

The main verb of a sentence is always the kind of word that would change form if put into these test sentences:

BASE FORM	Usually I (*walk*, *ride*).
PAST TENSE	Yesterday I (*walked*, *rode*).
PAST PARTICIPLE	I have (*walked*, *ridden*) many times before.
PRESENT PARTICIPLE	I am (*walking*, *riding*) right now.
-S FORM	Usually he/she/it (*walks*, *rides*).

If a word doesn't change form when slipped into the test sentences, you can be certain that it is not a main verb. For example, the noun *revolution*, though it may seem to suggest an action, can never function as a main verb. Just try to make it behave like one (*Today I revolution . . . Yesterday I revolutioned . . .*) and you'll see why.

When both the past-tense and the past-participle forms of a verb end in *-ed*, the verb is regular (*walked*, *walked*). Otherwise, the verb is irregular (*rode*, *ridden*). (See 27a.)

The verb *be* is highly irregular, having eight forms instead of the usual five: the base form *be*; the present-tense forms *am*, *is*, and *are*; the past-tense forms *was* and *were*; the present participle *being*; and the past participle *been*. Helping verbs combine with main verbs to create tenses. For a survey of tenses, see 28a.

NOTE: Some verbs are followed by *particles*, words that look like prepositions but that are actually part of the verbs. Common verb-particle combinations include *bring up*, *call off*, *drop off*, *give in*, *look up*, *run into*, and *take off*.

Sharon *packed up* her broken laptop and *sent* it *off* to the repair shop.

TIP: For more information about using verbs, see these sections: active verbs (8), subject-verb agreement (21), Standard English verb forms (27), verb tense and mood (27f and 27g), and multilingual/ESL challenges with verbs (28).

EXERCISE 46–9 Underline the verbs in the following sentences, including helping verbs and particles. If a verb is part of a contraction (such as *is* in *isn't* or *would* in *I'd*), underline only the letters that represent the verb. Answers appear in the back of the book.

More practice: LaunchPadSolo

The ground under the pine trees wasn't wet from the rain.

a. My grandmother always told me a soothing story before bed.
b. There were fifty apples on the tree before the frost killed them.
c. Morton brought down the box of letters from the attic.
d. Stay on the main road and you'll arrive at the base camp before us.
e. The fish struggled vigorously but was trapped in the net.

46d Adjectives

An adjective is a word used to modify, or describe, a noun or pronoun. An adjective usually answers one of these questions: Which one? What kind of? How many?

ADJ
the *frisky* horse [Which horse?]

ADJ ADJ
cracked old plates [What kind of plates?]

LaunchPadSolo macmillanhighered.com/rules8e
46 Parts of speech
> Exercises: 46-10 to 46-12, 46-19, 46-20
> LearningCurve: Verbs, adjectives, and adverbs

ADJ
nine months [How many months?]

ADJ
qualified applicants [What kind of applicants?]

Adjectives usually precede the words they modify. They may also follow linking verbs, in which case they describe the subject. (See 47b.)

ADJ
The decision was *unpopular.*

The definite article *the* and the indefinite articles *a* and *an* are also classified as adjectives.

ART ART ART
A defendant should be judged on *the* evidence provided to *the* jury, not on hearsay.

Some possessive, demonstrative, and indefinite pronouns can function as adjectives: *their*, *its*, *this*, *all* (see 46b). And nouns can function as adjectives when they modify other nouns: *apple pie* (the noun *apple* modifies the noun *pie*; see 46a).

TIP: You can find more details about using adjectives in 26. If you are a multilingual writer, you may find help with articles and specific uses of adjectives in 29, 30g, and 30h.

46e Adverbs

An adverb is a word used to modify, or qualify, a verb (or verbal), an adjective, or another adverb. It usually answers one of these questions: When? Where? How? Why? Under what conditions? To what degree?

Pull *firmly* on the emergency handle. [Pull how?]

Read the text *first* and *then* complete the exercises. [Read when? Complete when?]

Adverbs modifying adjectives or other adverbs usually intensify or limit the intensity of the word they modify.

ADV
Be *extremely* kind, and you will have many friends.

ADV
We proceeded *very* cautiously in the dark house.

The words *not* and *never* are classified as adverbs.

A word such as *cannot* contains the helping verb *can* and the adverb *not*. The word *can't* contains the helping verb *can* and a contracted form of *not* (see 36c).

TIP: You can find more details about using adverbs in 26b–26d. Multilingual writers can find more about the placement of adverbs in 30f.

EXERCISE 46–13 Underline the adjectives and circle the adverbs in the following sentences. If a word is a noun or pronoun functioning as an adjective, underline it and mark it as a noun/adjective or pronoun/adjective. Also treat the articles *a*, *an*, and *the* as adjectives. Answers appear in the back of the book. *More practice:* LaunchPadSolo

Finding an available room during the convention was (not) easy.

a. Generalizations lead to weak, unfocused essays.
b. The Spanish language is wonderfully flexible.
c. The wildflowers smelled especially fragrant after the steady rain.
d. I'd rather be slightly hot than bitterly cold.
e. The cat slept soundly in its wicker basket.

46f Prepositions

A preposition is a word placed before a noun or pronoun to form a phrase that modifies another word in the sentence. The prepositional phrase nearly always functions as an adjective or as an adverb.

> The road *to* (P) the summit travels *past* (P) craters *from* (P) an extinct volcano.

To the summit functions as an adjective modifying the noun *road*; *past craters* functions as an adverb modifying the verb *travels*;

from an extinct volcano functions as an adjective modifying the noun *craters*. (For more on prepositional phrases, see 48a.)

English has a limited number of prepositions. The most common are included in the following list.

about	beside	from	outside	toward
above	besides	in	over	under
across	between	inside	past	underneath
after	beyond	into	plus	unlike
against	but	like	regarding	until
along	by	near	respecting	unto
among	concerning	next	round	up
around	considering	of	since	upon
as	despite	off	than	with
at	down	on	through	within
before	during	onto	throughout	without
behind	except	opposite	till	
below	for	out	to	

Some prepositions are more than one word long. *Along with, as well as, in addition to, next to,* and *rather than* are common examples.

TIP: Prepositions are used in idioms such as *capable of* and *dig up* (see 18d). For specific issues for multilingual writers, see 31.

46g Conjunctions

Conjunctions join words, phrases, or clauses, and they indicate the relation between the elements joined.

Coordinating conjunctions A coordinating conjunction is used to connect grammatically equal elements. (See 9b and 14a.) The coordinating conjunctions are *and, but, or, nor, for, so,* and *yet.*

> The sociologist interviewed children *but* not their parents.
>
> Write clearly, *and* your readers will appreciate your efforts.

In the first sentence, *but* connects two noun phrases; in the second, *and* connects two independent clauses.

Correlative conjunctions Correlative conjunctions come in pairs; they connect grammatically equal elements.

either . . . or whether . . . or
neither . . . nor both . . . and
not only . . . but also

Either the painting was brilliant *or* it was a forgery.

Subordinating conjunctions A subordinating conjunction introduces a subordinate clause and indicates the relation of the clause to the rest of the sentence. (See 48e.) The most common subordinating conjunctions are *after*, *although*, *as*, *as if*, *because*, *before*, *if*, *in order that*, *once*, *since*, *so that*, *than*, *that*, *though*, *unless*, *until*, *when*, *where*, *whether*, and *while*. (For a complete list, see p. 390.)

When the fundraiser ends, we will have raised a million dollars.

Conjunctive adverbs Conjunctive adverbs connect independent clauses and indicate the relation between the clauses. They can be used with a semicolon to join two independent clauses in one sentence, or they can be used alone with an independent clause. The most common conjunctive adverbs are *finally*, *furthermore*, *however*, *moreover*, *nevertheless*, *similarly*, *then*, *therefore*, and *thus*. (For a complete list, see p. 374.)

The photographer failed to take a light reading; *therefore*, all the pictures were underexposed.

During the day, the kitten sleeps peacefully. *However*, when night falls, the kitten is wide awake and ready to play.

Conjunctive adverbs can appear at the beginning or in the middle of a clause.

When night falls, *however*, the kitten is wide awake and ready to play.

TIP: Recognizing conjunctive adverbs and coordinating conjunctions will help you avoid run-on sentences and make punctuation decisions (see 20, 32a, and 32f). Recognizing subordinating conjunctions will help you avoid sentence fragments (see 19).

46h Interjections

An interjection is a word used to express surprise or emotion (*Oh! Hey! Wow!*).

LaunchPadSolo **macmillanhighered.com/rules8e**

46 Parts of speech

> Exercises: 46–19 and 46–20 (all parts of speech)

> LearningCurve: Prepositions and conjunctions

Parts of speech

- A **noun** names a person, place, thing, or concept.

  N N N
  Repetition does not transform a *lie* into *truth.*

- A **pronoun** substitutes for a noun.

  PN PN PN PN
  Before the attendant let *us* board the small plane, *he* weighed *us* and *our* baggage.

  PERSONAL PRONOUNS: I, me, you, he, him, she, her, it, we, us, they, them

  POSSESSIVE PRONOUNS: my, mine, your, yours, her, hers, his, its, our, ours, their, theirs

  INTENSIVE AND REFLEXIVE PRONOUNS: myself, yourself, himself, herself, itself, ourselves, yourselves, themselves

  RELATIVE PRONOUNS: that, which, who, whom, whose

  INTERROGATIVE PRONOUNS: who, whom, whose, which, what

  DEMONSTRATIVE PRONOUNS: this, that, these, those

  INDEFINITE PRONOUNS

all	each	many	one
another	either	neither	several
any	everybody	nobody	some
anybody	everyone	none	somebody
anyone	everything	no one	someone
anything	few	nothing	something
both			

  RECIPROCAL PRONOUNS: each other, one another

- A **helping verb** comes before a main verb.

  MODALS: can, could, may, might, must, shall, should, will, would (*also* ought to)

  FORMS OF *BE*: be, am, is, are, was, were, being, been

  FORMS OF *HAVE*: have, has, had

  FORMS OF *DO*: do, does, did

(The forms of *be, have,* and *do* may also function as main verbs.)

- A **main verb** shows action or a state of being.

MV
The novel *opens* with a tense description of a grim murder, but

HV MV
the author *does* not *maintain* the initial level of suspense.

A main verb will always change form when put into these positions in sentences:

Usually I ________.	(*walk, ride*)
Yesterday I ________.	(*walked, rode*)
I have ________ many times before.	(*walked, ridden*)
I am ________ right now.	(*walking, riding*)
Usually he ________.	(*walks, rides*)

The highly irregular verb *be* has eight forms: *be, am, is, are, was, were, being, been.*

- An **adjective** modifies a noun or pronoun, usually answering one of these questions: Which one? What kind of? How many? The articles *a, an,* and *the* are also adjectives.

PN/ADJ N/ADJ ADJ ADJ PN/ADJ
Our family's strong ties gave us *welcome* comfort in *our* grief.

- An **adverb** modifies a verb, an adjective, or an adverb, usually answering one of these questions: When? Where? Why? How? Under what conditions? To what degree?

ADV ADV
Young people *often* approach history *skeptically.*

- A **preposition** indicates the relationship between the noun or pronoun that follows it and another word in the sentence.

P P
A journey *of* a thousand miles begins *with* a single step.

Parts of speech, continued

COMMON PREPOSITIONS

about	besides	like	since
above	between	near	than
across	beyond	next	through
after	but	next to	throughout
against	by	of	till
along	concerning	off	to
along with	considering	on	toward
among	despite	onto	under
around	down	opposite	underneath
as	during	out	unlike
as well as	except	outside	until
at	for	over	unto
because of	from	past	up
before	in	plus	upon
behind	in addition to	rather than	with
below	inside	regarding	within
beside	into	respecting	without

- A **conjunction** connects words or word groups.

  COORDINATING CONJUNCTIONS: and, but, or, nor, for, so, yet

  SUBORDINATING CONJUNCTIONS: after, although, as, as if, because, before, even though, if, in order that, once, since, so that, than, that, though, unless, until, when, where, whether, while

  CORRELATIVE CONJUNCTIONS: either . . . or; neither . . . nor; not only . . . but also; both . . . and; whether . . . or

  CONJUNCTIVE ADVERBS: accordingly, also, anyway, besides, certainly, consequently, conversely, finally, furthermore, hence, however, incidentally, indeed, instead, likewise, meanwhile, moreover, nevertheless, next, nonetheless, now, otherwise, similarly, specifically, still, subsequently, then, therefore, thus

- An **interjection** expresses surprise or emotion (*Oh! Wow! Hooray!*).

47 Sentence patterns

The vast majority of sentences in English conform to one of these five patterns:

subject/verb/subject complement
subject/verb/direct object
subject/verb/indirect object/direct object
subject/verb/direct object/object complement
subject/verb

Adverbial modifiers (single words, phrases, or clauses) may be added to any of these patterns, and they may appear nearly anywhere — at the beginning, in the middle, or at the end.

Predicate is the grammatical term given to the verb plus its objects, complements, and adverbial modifiers.

For a quick-reference chart of sentence patterns, see page 380.

47a Subjects

The subject of a sentence names whom or what the sentence is about. The simple subject is always a noun or pronoun; the complete subject consists of the simple subject and any words or word groups modifying the simple subject.

The complete subject

To find the complete subject, ask Who? or What?, insert the verb, and finish the question. The answer is the complete subject.

COMPLETE SUBJECT
The devastating effects of famine can last for many years.

Who or what can last for many years? *The devastating effects of famine.*

COMPLETE SUBJECT
Adventure novels that contain multiple subplots are often made into successful movies.

Who or what are often made into movies? *Adventure novels that contain multiple subplots.*

COMPLETE SUBJECT

In our program, student teachers work full-time for ten months.

Who or what works full-time for ten months? *Student teachers.* Notice that *In our program, student teachers* is not a sensible answer to the question. (It is not safe to assume that the subject must always appear first in a sentence.)

The simple subject

To find the simple subject, strip away all modifiers in the complete subject. This includes single-word modifiers such as *the* and *devastating,* phrases such as *of famine,* and subordinate clauses such as *that contain multiple subplots.*

SS

The devastating effects of famine can last for many years.

SS

Adventure novels that contain multiple subplots are often made into successful movies.

A sentence may have a compound subject containing two or more simple subjects joined with a coordinating conjunction such as *and, but,* or *or.*

SS SS

Great commitment and a little luck make a successful actor.

Understood subjects

In imperative sentences, which give advice or issue commands, the subject is understood but not actually present in the sentence. The subject of an imperative sentence is understood to be *you.*

[*You*] Put your hands on the steering wheel.

Subject after the verb

Although the subject ordinarily comes before the verb (*The planes took off*), occasionally it does not. When a sentence begins with *There is* or *There are* (or *There was* or *There were*), the subject follows the verb. In such inverted constructions, the word *There* is an expletive, an empty word serving merely to get the sentence started.

SS
There are *eight planes waiting to take off.*

Occasionally a writer will invert a sentence for effect.

SS
Joyful is *the child whose school closes for snow.*

Joyful is an adjective, so it cannot be the subject. Turn this sentence around and its structure becomes obvious.

The *child* whose school closes for snow is joyful.

In questions, the subject frequently appears between the helping verb and the main verb.

HV SS MV
Do *Kenyan marathoners* train year-round?

TIP: The ability to recognize the subject of a sentence will help you edit for fragments (19), subject-verb agreement (21), pronouns such as *I* and *me* (24), missing subjects (30b), and repeated subjects (30c).

EXERCISE 47–1 In the following sentences, underline the complete subject and write *SS* above the simple subject(s). If the subject is an understood *you*, insert *you* in parentheses. Answers appear in the back of the book. *More practice:* LaunchPadSolo

SS SS
Parents and their children often look alike.

a. The hills and mountains seemed endless, and the snow atop them glistened.
b. In foil fencing, points are scored by hitting an electronic target.
c. Do not stand in the aisles or sit on the stairs.
d. There were hundreds of fireflies in the open field.
e. The evidence against the defendant was staggering.

LaunchPadSolo **macmillanhighered.com/rules8e**
47 Sentence patterns
> Exercises: 47–2 to 47–4

47b Verbs, objects, and complements

Section 46c explains how to find the verb of a sentence. A sentence's verb is classified as linking, transitive, or intransitive, depending on the kinds of objects or complements the verb can (or cannot) take.

Linking verbs and subject complements

Linking verbs connect the subject to a subject complement, a word or word group that completes the meaning of the subject by renaming or describing it.

If the subject complement renames the subject, it is a noun or noun equivalent (sometimes called a *predicate noun*).

S V SC
An e-mail requesting personal information may be a scam.

If the subject complement describes the subject, it is an adjective or adjective equivalent (sometimes called a *predicate adjective*).

S V SC
Last month's temperatures were mild.

Whenever they appear as main verbs (rather than helping verbs), the forms of *be* — *be, am, is, are, was, were, being, been* — usually function as linking verbs. In the preceding examples, for instance, the main verbs are *be* and *were*.

Verbs such as *appear, become, feel, grow, look, make, seem, smell, sound,* and *taste* are linking when they are followed by a word or word group that renames or describes the subject.

S V SC
As it thickens, the sauce will look unappealing.

Transitive verbs and direct objects

A transitive verb takes a direct object, a word or word group that names a receiver of the action.

S V DO
The hungry cat clawed the bag of dry food.

The simple direct object is always a noun or pronoun, in this case *bag*. To find it, simply strip away all modifiers.

Transitive verbs usually appear in the active voice, with the subject doing the action and a direct object receiving the action. Active-voice sentences can be transformed into the passive voice, with the subject receiving the action instead. (See 47c.)

Transitive verbs, indirect objects, and direct objects

The direct object of a transitive verb is sometimes preceded by an indirect object, a noun or pronoun telling to whom or for whom the action of the sentence is done.

S V IO ┌─ DO ─┐ S ┌─ V ─┐ IO ┌─ DO ─┐
You give her some yarn, and she will knit you a scarf.

The simple indirect object is always a noun or pronoun. To test for an indirect object, insert the word *to* or *for* before the word or word group in question. If the sentence makes sense, the word or word group is an indirect object.

You give [to] *her* some yarn, and she will knit [for] *you* a scarf.

An indirect object may be turned into a prepositional phrase using *to* or *for*: *You give some yarn to her, and she will knit a scarf for you.*

Only certain transitive verbs take indirect objects. Some examples are *ask, bring, find, get, give, hand, lend, make, offer, pay, promise, read, send, show, teach, tell, throw,* and *write.*

Transitive verbs, direct objects, and object complements

The direct object of a transitive verb is sometimes followed by an object complement, a word or word group that renames or describes the object.

S V DO ┌─ OC ─┐
People often consider chivalry a thing of the past.

┌─ S ─┐ V DO ┌─ OC ─┐
The kiln makes clay firm and strong.

When the object complement renames the direct object, it is a noun or pronoun (such as *thing*). When it describes the direct object, it is an adjective (such as *firm* and *strong*).

Intransitive verbs

Intransitive verbs take no objects or complements.

S V
The audience laughed.

S V
The driver accelerated in the straightaway.

Nothing receives the actions of laughing and accelerating in these sentences, so the verbs are intransitive. Notice that such verbs may or may not be followed by adverbial modifiers. In the second sentence, *in the straightaway* is an adverbial prepositional phrase modifying *accelerated.*

Sentence patterns

Subject / linking verb / subject complement

S V SC
Acting is art. [*Art* renames *Acting.*]

S V SC
Good researchers are curious. [*Curious* describes *researchers.*]

Subject / transitive verb / direct object

S V DO
An antihistamine may prevent an allergic reaction.

Subject / transitive verb / indirect object / direct object

S V IO DO
The elevator's rapid ascent gave Irina an attack of vertigo.

Subject / transitive verb / direct object / object complement

S V DO OC
The reviewer called the film a masterpiece. [*Masterpiece* renames *film.*]

S V DO OC
The new double-glazed windows made the house warmer. [*Warmer* describes *house.*]

Subject / intransitive verb

S V
The kettle whistles.

NOTE: The dictionary will tell you whether a verb is transitive or intransitive. Some verbs have both transitive and intransitive functions.

TRANSITIVE	Sandra *flew* her small plane over the canyon.
INTRANSITIVE	A flock of migrating geese *flew* overhead.

In the first example, *flew* has a direct object that receives the action: *her small plane*. In the second example, the verb is followed by an adverb (*overhead*), not by a direct object.

EXERCISE 47–5 Label the subject complements and direct objects in the following sentences, using the labels *SC* and *DO*. If a subject complement or direct object consists of more than one word, bracket and label all of it. Answers appear in the back of the book.

DO (most drivers)
The sharp right turn confused most drivers.

a. Textbooks are expensive.
b. Samurai warriors never fear death.
c. Successful coaches always praise their players' efforts.
d. St. Petersburg was the capital of the Russian Empire for two centuries.
e. The medicine tasted bitter.

EXERCISE 47–6 Each of the following sentences has either an indirect object followed by a direct object or a direct object followed by an object complement. Label the objects and complements, using the labels *IO*, *DO*, and *OC*. If an object or a complement consists of more than one word, bracket and label all of it. Answers appear in the back of the book.

More practice: LaunchPadSolo

DO (their own experience) *OC* (normal)
Most people consider their own experience normal.

a. Stress can make adults and children weary.
b. The dining hall offered students healthy meal choices.
c. Consider the work finished.
d. We showed the agent our tickets, and she gave us boarding passes.
e. Zita has made community service her priority this year.

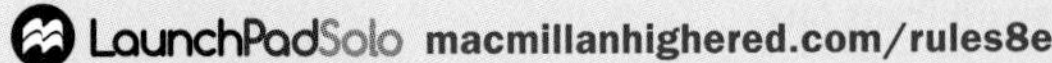

47 Sentence patterns
> Exercises: 47-7 to 47-12

47c Pattern variations

Although most sentences follow one of the five patterns in the chart on page 380, variations of these patterns commonly occur in questions, commands, sentences with delayed subjects, and passive transformations.

Questions and commands

Questions are sometimes patterned in normal word order, with the subject preceding the verb.

S ┌— V —┐
Who will have the most hits this season?

Sometimes the pattern of a question is inverted, with the subject appearing between the helping verb and the main verb or after the verb.

HV S MV
Will he have the most hits this season?

V ┌—— S ——┐
Why is the number of hits an important statistic?

In commands, the subject of the sentence is an understood *you*.

S V
[You] Pay attention to the road.

Sentences with delayed subjects

Writers sometimes choose to delay the subject of a sentence to achieve a special effect such as suspense or humor.

V ┌— S —┐
Behind the phony tinsel of Hollywood lies the real tinsel.

The subject of the sentence is also delayed in sentences opening with the expletive *There* or *It*. When used as expletives, the words *There* and *It* have no strict grammatical function; they serve merely to get the sentence started.

V ┌—— S ——┐
There are thirty thousand spectators in the stadium.

V ┌—— S ——┐
It is best to avoid trans fats.

The subject in the second example is an infinitive phrase. (See 48b.)

Passive transformations

Transitive verbs, those that can take direct objects, usually appear in the active voice. In the active voice, the subject does the action, and a direct object receives the action.

S V DO

ACTIVE The fireworks display dazzled the viewers on the Esplanade.

Sentences in the active voice may be transformed into the passive voice, with the subject receiving the action instead.

S HV MV

PASSIVE The viewers on the Esplanade were dazzled by the fireworks display.

What was once the direct object (*the viewers on the Esplanade*) has become the subject in the passive-voice transformation, and the original subject appears in a prepositional phrase beginning with *by*. The *by* phrase is frequently omitted in passive-voice constructions.

PASSIVE The viewers on the Esplanade were dazzled.

Verbs in the passive voice can be identified by their form alone. The main verb is always a past participle, such as *dazzled* (see 46c), preceded by a form of *be* (*be*, *am*, *is*, *are*, *was*, *were*, *being*, *been*): *were dazzled*. Sometimes adverbs intervene (*were usually dazzled*).

TIP: Avoid using the passive voice when the active voice would be more appropriate (see 8a).

48 Subordinate word groups

Subordinate word groups include phrases and clauses. Phrases are subordinate because they lack a subject and a verb; they are classified as prepositional, verbal, appositive, and absolute (see 48a–48d). Subordinate clauses have a subject and a verb, but they begin with a word (such as *although*, *that*, or *when*) that marks them as subordinate (see 48e).

48a Prepositional phrases

A prepositional phrase begins with a preposition such as *at, by, for, from, in, of, on, to,* or *with* (see 46f) and usually ends with a noun or noun equivalent: *on the table, for him, by sleeping late.* The noun or noun equivalent is known as the *object of the preposition.*

Prepositional phrases function either as adjectives or as adverbs. When functioning as an adjective, a prepositional phrase nearly always appears immediately following the noun or pronoun it modifies.

The hut had *walls of mud.*

Adjective phrases usually answer one or both of the questions Which one? and What kind of? If we ask Which walls? or What kind of walls? we get a sensible answer: *walls of mud.*

Adverbial prepositional phrases usually modify the verb, but they can also modify adjectives or other adverbs. When a prepositional phrase modifies the verb, it can appear nearly anywhere in a sentence.

James *walked* his dog *on a leash.*

Sabrina *in time adjusted* to life in Ecuador.

During a mudslide, the terrain *can change* drastically.

If a prepositional phrase is movable, you can be certain that it is adverbial.

In the cave, the explorers found well-preserved prehistoric drawings.

The explorers found well-preserved prehistoric drawings *in the cave.*

Adverbial word groups usually answer one of these questions: When? Where? How? Why? Under what conditions? To what degree?

James walked his dog *how*? *On a leash.*

Sabrina adjusted to life in Ecuador *when*? *In time.*

The terrain can change drastically *under what conditions*? *During a mudslide.*

In questions and subordinate clauses, a preposition may appear after its object.

> *What* are you afraid *of*?
> We avoided the bike trail *that* John had warned us *about*.

EXERCISE 48–1 Underline the prepositional phrases in the following sentences. Tell whether each one is an adjective phrase or an adverb phrase and what it modifies in the sentence. Answers appear in the back of the book. *More practice:* LaunchPadSolo

> **Flecks of mica glittered in the new granite floor.** (Adjective phrase modifying "Flecks"; adverb phrase modifying "glittered")

a. In northern Italy, we met many people who speak German as their first language.
b. William completed the three-mile hike through the thick forest with ease.
c. To my boss's dismay, I was late for work again.
d. The traveling exhibit of Mayan artifacts gave viewers new insight into pre-Columbian culture.
e. In 2002, the euro became the official currency in twelve European countries.

48b Verbal phrases

A verbal is a verb form that does not function as the verb of a clause. Verbals include infinitives (the word *to* plus the base form of the verb), present participles (the *-ing* form of the verb), and past participles (the verb form usually ending in *-d*, *-ed*, *-n*, *-en*, or *-t*). (See 27a and 46c.)

INFINITIVE	PRESENT PARTICIPLE	PAST PARTICIPLE
to dream	dreaming	dreamed
to choose	choosing	chosen
to build	building	built
to grow	growing	grown

LaunchPadSolo **macmillanhighered.com/rules8e**
48 Subordinate word groups
> Exercises: 48-2 to 48-5
> LearningCurve: Coordination and subordination

Instead of functioning as the verb of a clause, a verbal functions as an adjective, a noun, or an adverb.

ADJECTIVE	*Broken* promises cannot be fixed.
NOUN	Constant *complaining* becomes wearisome.
ADVERB	Can you wait *to celebrate*?

Verbals with objects, complements, or modifiers form verbal phrases.

In my family, *singing loudly* is more appreciated than *singing well.*

Governments exist *to protect the rights of minorities.*

Like verbals, verbal phrases function as adjectives, nouns, or adverbs. Verbal phrases are ordinarily classified as participial, gerund, and infinitive.

Participial phrases

Participial phrases always function as adjectives. Their verbals are either present participles (such as *dreaming, asking*) or past participles (such as *stolen, reached*).

Participial phrases frequently appear immediately following the noun or pronoun they modify.

Congress shall make no *law abridging the freedom of speech or of the press.*

Participial phrases are often movable. They can precede the word they modify.

Being a weight-bearing joint, the *knee* is among the most frequently injured.

They may also appear at some distance from the word they modify.

Last night we saw a *play* that affected us deeply, *written with profound insight into the lives of immigrants.*

Gerund phrases

Gerund phrases are built around present participles (verb forms that end in *-ing*), and they always function as nouns: usually as subjects, subject complements, direct objects, or objects of a preposition.

S
Rationalizing a fear can eliminate it.

SC
The key to a good sauce is browning the mushrooms.

DO
Lizards usually enjoy sunning themselves.

The American Heart Association has documented the benefits of
OBJ OF PREP
diet and exercise in reducing the risk of heart attack.

Infinitive phrases

Infinitive phrases, usually constructed around *to* plus the base form of the verb (*to call*, *to drink*), can function as nouns, as adjectives, or as adverbs. When functioning as a noun, an infinitive phrase may appear in almost any noun slot in a sentence, usually as a subject, subject complement, or direct object.

S
To live without health insurance is risky.

Infinitive phrases functioning as adjectives usually appear immediately following the noun or pronoun they modify.

The Nineteenth Amendment gave women the *right to vote.*

The infinitive phrase modifies the noun *right*. Which right? *The right to vote.*

Adverbial infinitive phrases usually qualify the meaning of the verb, telling when, where, how, why, under what conditions, or to what degree an action occurred.

Volunteers *rolled up* their pants *to wade through the floodwaters.*

Why did they roll up their pants? *To wade through the floodwaters.*

NOTE: In some constructions, the infinitive is unmarked; that is, the *to* does not appear. (See 28f.)

Graphs and charts can help researchers [*to*] *present complex data.*

EXERCISE 48–6 Underline the verbal phrases in the following sentences. Tell whether each phrase is participial, gerund, or infinitive and how each is used in the sentence. Answers appear in the back of the book. *More practice:* LaunchPadSolo

Do you want to watch that documentary? (Infinitive phrase used as direct object of "Do want")

a. Updating your software will fix the computer glitch.
b. The challenge in decreasing the town budget is identifying nonessential services.
c. Cathleen tried to help her mother by raking the lawn.
d. Understanding little, I had no hope of passing my biology final.
e. Working with animals gave Steve a sense of satisfaction.

48c Appositive phrases

Appositive phrases describe nouns or pronouns. Instead of modifying nouns or pronouns, however, appositive phrases rename them. In form they are nouns or noun equivalents.

> Bloggers, *conversationalists at heart*, are the online equivalent of radio talk show hosts.

Appositives are said to be "in apposition to" the nouns or pronouns they rename. *Conversationalists at heart* is in apposition to the noun *Bloggers*.

48d Absolute phrases

An absolute phrase modifies a whole clause or sentence, not just one word. It consists of a noun or noun equivalent usually followed by a participial phrase.

> *Her words reverberating in the hushed arena*, the senator urged the crowd to support her former opponent.

LaunchPadSolo macmillanhighered.com/rules8e

48 Subordinate word groups
> Exercises: 48–7 to 48–9
> LearningCurve: Coordination and subordination

48e Subordinate clauses

Subordinate clauses are patterned like sentences, having subjects and verbs and sometimes objects or complements. But they function within sentences as adjectives, adverbs, or nouns. They cannot stand alone as complete sentences.

A subordinate clause usually begins with a subordinating conjunction or a relative pronoun. The chart on page 390 classifies these words according to the kinds of clauses (adjective, adverb, or noun) they introduce.

Adjective clauses

Adjective clauses modify nouns or pronouns, usually answering the question Which one? or What kind of? Most adjective clauses begin with a relative pronoun (*who*, *whom*, *whose*, *which*, or *that*). In addition to introducing the clause, the relative pronoun points back to the noun that the clause modifies.

The coach chose *players who would benefit from intense drills.*

A *book that goes unread* is a writer's worst nightmare.

Relative pronouns are sometimes "understood."

The things [*that*] *we cherish most* are the things [*that*] *we might lose.*

Occasionally an adjective clause is introduced by a relative adverb, usually *when*, *where*, or *why*.

The aging actor returned to the *stage where he had made his debut as Hamlet half a century earlier.*

The parts of an adjective clause are often arranged as in sentences (subject/verb/object or complement).

Sometimes it is our closest friends who (S) disappoint (V) us (DO).

Frequently, however, the object or complement appears first, out of the normal order of subject/verb/object.

They can be the very friends whom (DO) we (S) disappoint (V).

TIP: For punctuation of adjective clauses, see 32e and 33e. For advice about avoiding repeated words in adjective clauses, see 30d.

Words that introduce subordinate clauses

Words introducing adjective clauses

RELATIVE PRONOUNS: that, which, who, whom, whose

RELATIVE ADVERBS: when, where, why

Words introducing adverb clauses

SUBORDINATING CONJUNCTIONS: after, although, as, as if, because, before, even though, if, in order that, since, so that, than, that, though, unless, until, when, where, whether, while

Words introducing noun clauses

RELATIVE PRONOUNS: that, which, who, whom, whose

OTHER PRONOUNS: what, whatever, whichever, whoever, whomever

OTHER SUBORDINATING WORDS: how, if, when, whenever, where, wherever, whether, why

Adverb clauses

Adverb clauses modify verbs, adjectives, or other adverbs, usually answering one of these questions: When? Where? Why? How? Under what conditions? To what degree? They always begin with a subordinating conjunction (such as *after*, *although*, *because*, *that*, *though*, *unless*, or *when*). (For a complete list, see the chart on this page.)

When the sun went down, the hikers *prepared* their camp.

Kate *would have made* the team *if she hadn't broken her ankle.*

Adverb clauses are usually movable when they modify a verb. In the preceding examples, for instance, the adverb clauses can be moved without affecting the meaning of the sentences.

The hikers prepared their camp *when the sun went down.*

If she hadn't broken her ankle, Kate would have made the team.

When an adverb clause modifies an adjective or an adverb, it is not movable; it must appear next to the word it modifies. In the following examples, the *when* clause modifies the adjective *Uncertain*, and the *than* clause modifies the adverb *better*.

Uncertain *when the baby would be born*, Ray and Leah stayed close to home.

Jackie can dance better *than I can walk.*

Adverb clauses are sometimes elliptical, with some of their words being understood but not appearing in the sentence.

When [*it is*] *renovated*, the dorm will hold six hundred students.

Noun clauses

A noun clause functions just like a single-word noun, usually as a subject, a subject complement, a direct object, or an object of a preposition. It usually begins with one of the following words: *how*, *if*, *that*, *what*, *whatever*, *when*, *where*, *whether*, *which*, *who*, *whoever*, *whom*, *whomever*, *whose*, *why*. (For a complete list, see the box on p. 390.)

S

Whoever leaves the house last must double-lock the door.

DO

Copernicus argued that the sun is the center of the universe.

The subordinating word introducing the clause may or may not play a significant role in the clause. In the preceding example sentences, *Whoever* is the subject of its clause, but *that* does not perform a function in its clause.

As with adjective clauses, the parts of a noun clause may appear in normal order (subject/verb/object or complement) or out of their normal order.

S V DO OC

Loyalty is what keeps a friendship strong.

DO S V

New Mexico is where we live.

EXERCISE 48–10 Underline the subordinate clauses in the following sentences. Tell whether each clause is an adjective, adverb, or noun clause and how it is used in the sentence. Answers appear in the back of the book. *More practice:* LaunchPadSolo

Show the committee the latest draft before you print the final report. (Adverb clause modifying "Show")

a. The city's electoral commission adjusted the voting process so that every vote would count.
b. A marketing campaign that targets baby boomers may not appeal to young professionals.
c. After the Tambora volcano erupted in the southern Pacific in 1815, no one realized that it would contribute to the "year without a summer" in Europe and North America.
d. The concept of peak oil implies that at a certain point there will be no more oil to extract from the earth.
e. Details are easily overlooked when you are rushing.

49 Sentence types

Sentences are classified in two ways: according to their structure (simple, compound, complex, and compound-complex) and according to their purpose (declarative, imperative, interrogative, and exclamatory).

49a Sentence structures

Depending on the number and the types of clauses they contain, sentences are classified as simple, compound, complex, or compound-complex.

Clauses come in two varieties: independent and subordinate. An independent clause contains a subject and a predicate, and it either stands alone or could stand alone as a sentence. A subordinate clause also contains a subject and a predicate, but it functions within a sentence as an adjective, an adverb, or a noun; it cannot stand alone. (See 48e.)

Simple sentences

A simple sentence is one independent clause with no subordinate clauses.

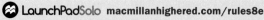

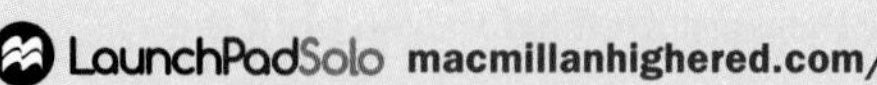

48 Subordinate word groups
> Exercises: 48–11 to 48–15
> LearningCurve: Coordination and subordination

INDEPENDENT CLAUSE
Without a passport, Eva could not visit her grandparents in Hungary.

A simple sentence may contain compound elements—a compound subject, verb, or object, for example—but it does not contain more than one full sentence pattern. The following sentence is simple because its two verbs (*comes in* and *goes out*) share a subject (*Spring*).

INDEPENDENT CLAUSE
Spring comes in like a lion and goes out like a lamb.

Compound sentences

A compound sentence is composed of two or more independent clauses with no subordinate clauses. The independent clauses are usually joined with a comma and a coordinating conjunction (*and*, *but*, *or*, *nor*, *for*, *so*, *yet*) or with a semicolon. (See 14a.)

INDEPENDENT CLAUSE / INDEPENDENT CLAUSE
The car broke down, but a rescue van arrived within minutes.

INDEPENDENT CLAUSE / INDEPENDENT CLAUSE
A shark was spotted near shore; people left immediately.

Complex sentences

A complex sentence is composed of one independent clause with one or more subordinate clauses. (See 48e.)

SUBORDINATE CLAUSE
ADJECTIVE The pitcher who won the game is a rookie.

SUBORDINATE CLAUSE
ADVERB If you leave late, take a cab home.

SUBORDINATE CLAUSE
NOUN What matters most to us is a quick commute.

Compound-complex sentences

A compound-complex sentence contains at least two independent clauses and at least one subordinate clause. The following sentence contains two independent clauses, each of which contains a subordinate clause.

INDEPENDENT CLAUSE [SUB CL] / INDEPENDENT CLAUSE [SUB CL]

Tell the doctor how you feel, and she will decide whether you can go home.

49b Sentence purposes

Writers use declarative sentences to make statements, imperative sentences to issue requests or commands, interrogative sentences to ask questions, and exclamatory sentences to make exclamations.

DECLARATIVE	The echo sounded in our ears.
IMPERATIVE	Love your neighbor.
INTERROGATIVE	Did the better team win tonight?
EXCLAMATORY	We're here to save you!

EXERCISE 49–1 Identify the following sentences as simple, compound, complex, or compound-complex. Identify the subordinate clauses and classify them according to their function: adjective, adverb, or noun. (See 48e.) Answers appear in the back of the book. *More practice:* LaunchPadSolo

The deli in Courthouse Square was crowded with lawyers at lunchtime. (Simple)

a. Fires that are ignited in dry areas spread especially quickly.
b. The early Incas were advanced; they used a calendar and developed a decimal system.
c. Elaine's jacket was too thin to block the wintry air.
d. Before we leave for the station, we always check the Amtrak Web site.
e. Decide when you want to leave, and I will be there to pick you up.

LaunchPadSolo **macmillanhighered.com/rules8e**
49 Sentence types
> Exercises: 49–2 and 49–3

Research

Research 395

Research

50 Thinking like a researcher; gathering sources

A college research assignment asks you to pose questions worth exploring, to read widely in search of possible answers, to interpret what you read, to draw reasoned conclusions, and to support those conclusions with evidence. In short, it asks you to enter a research conversation by engaging with the ideas of other writers and thinkers who have explored and studied your topic. As you listen to and learn from the voices already in the conversation, you'll find entry points where you can add your own insights and ideas.

Becoming a confident researcher means figuring out how to respond to and engage with ideas, find your own voice, and present your ideas alongside other people's thoughts. It also requires embracing the idea that writing with sources is a process that takes time. As your ideas evolve, you may find that the process leads you in unexpected directions — perhaps new questions in the conversation require you to create a new search strategy, find additional sources, and challenge your initial assumptions. Keep an open mind throughout the process, be curious, and enjoy the work of finding answers to questions that matter to you.

50a Manage the project.

When you begin a research project, you need to understand the assignment, choose a direction, and quickly grasp the big picture for the topic you choose. The following tips will help you manage the beginning phase of research.

Managing time

When you receive your assignment, set a realistic schedule of deadlines. Think about how much time you might need for each step of your project. One student created a calendar to map out her tasks for a research paper assigned on October 3 and due October 31, keeping in mind that some tasks might overlap or need to be repeated.

Keeping a research log

Research is a process. As your topic evolves, you may find yourself asking new questions that require you to create a new search

SAMPLE CALENDAR FOR A RESEARCH ASSIGNMENT

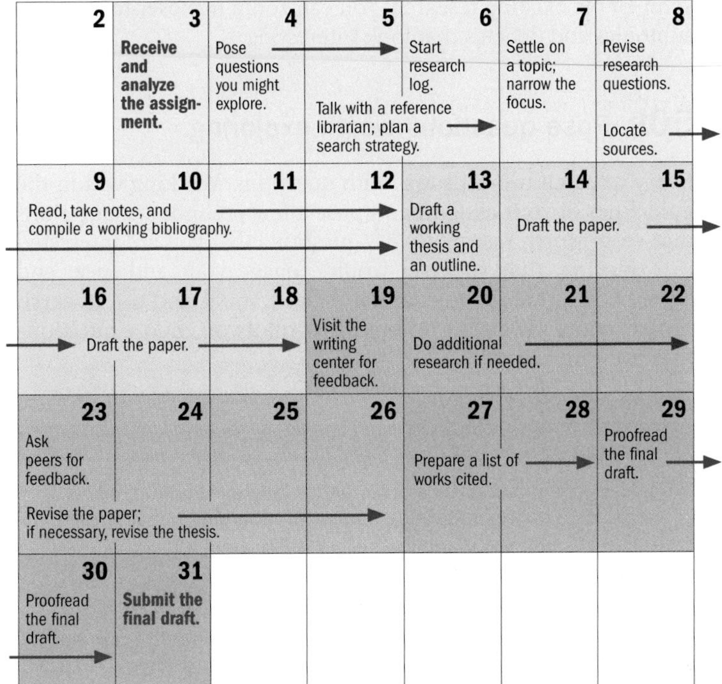

strategy, find additional sources, and revise your initial assumptions. A research log helps you bring order to this process by keeping accurate records of the sources you read and your ideas about them. You might want to use a separate hardcopy notebook for your log or create a digital set of files. Keeping an accurate source trail and working bibliography, and separating your own insights and ideas from those of your sources, will help you become a more efficient researcher.

2
3
Receive and analyze the assignment.
4
Pose questions you might explore.
5
6
Start research log.
Talk with a reference librarian; plan a search strategy.
7
Settle on a topic; narrow the focus.
8
Revise research questions.
Locate sources.
9
10
11
12
Read, take notes, and compile a working bibliography.
13
Draft a working thesis and an outline.
14
15
Draft the paper.
16
17
18
Draft the paper.
19
Visit the writing center for feedback.
20
21
22
Do additional research if needed.
23
Ask peers for feedback.
24
25
26
Revise the paper; if necessary, revise the thesis.
27
28
Prepare a list of works cited.
29
Proofread the final draft.
30
Proofread the final draft.
31
Submit the final draft.

Getting the big picture

As you consider a possible research topic, set aside some time to learn what people are saying about it by reading sources on the Web or in library databases. Ask yourself questions such as these:

- What aspects of the topic are generating the most debate?
- Why and on what points are people disagreeing?
- Which arguments and approaches seem worth exploring?

Once you have an aerial view of the topic and are familiar with some of the existing research, you can zoom in closer to examine subtopics and debates that look interesting.

50b Pose questions worth exploring.

Every research project starts with questions. Working within the guidelines of your assignment, pose a few preliminary questions that seem worth researching — questions that you are interested in exploring, that you feel would engage your audience, and about which there is substantial debate. You'll find the research process more rewarding and meaningful if you choose questions that you care about.

Thinking like a researcher

To develop your authority as a researcher, you need to think like a researcher — asking interesting questions, becoming well informed through reading and evaluating sources, and citing sources to acknowledge other researchers.

Be curious. What makes you angry, concerned, or perplexed? What topics and debates do you care about? What problems do you want to help solve? Explore your topic from multiple perspectives, and let your curiosity drive your project.

Be engaged. Talk with a librarian and learn how to use your library's research tools and resources. Once you find promising sources, let one source lead you to another; follow clues (in the source's list of works cited, if one exists) to learn who else has written about your topic. Listen to the key voices in the research conversation you've joined — and then respond.

Be responsible. Use sources to develop and support your ideas rather than patching them together to let them speak for you. From the start of your research project, keep careful track of sources you read or view (see 51), place quotation marks around words copied from sources, and maintain accurate records for all bibliographic information.

Be reflective. Keep a research log, and use your log to explore various points you are developing and to pose counterarguments to your research argument. Research is never a straightforward path, so use your log to reflect on the evolution of your project as well as your evolution as a researcher.

Here are some preliminary questions jotted down by students enrolled in a variety of college courses.

- Why are boys diagnosed with attention deficit disorder more often than girls are?
- Do nutritional food labels inform consumers or confuse them?
- Should states require public schools to adopt antibullying policies?
- Why was amateur archaeologist Heinrich Schliemann such a controversial figure in his own time?

As you think about possible questions, choose those that are focused (not too broad), challenging (not just factual), and grounded (not too speculative) as possible entry points in a conversation.

Choosing a focused question

If your initial question is too broad, given the length of the paper you plan to write, look for ways to restrict your focus. Here, for example, is how two students narrowed their initial questions.

TOO BROAD	FOCUSED
What are the benefits of stricter auto emissions standards?	How will stricter auto emissions standards create new auto industry jobs and make US carmakers more competitive in the world market?
What causes depression?	How has the widespread use of antidepressant drugs affected teenage suicide rates?

Choosing a challenging question

Your research paper will be more interesting to both you and your audience if you base it on an intellectually challenging line of inquiry. Avoid factual questions that fail to provoke thought or engage readers in a debate; such questions lead to reports or lists of facts, not to researched arguments.

TOO FACTUAL	CHALLENGING
Is autism on the rise?	Why is autism so difficult to treat?
Where is wind energy being used?	What makes wind farms economically viable?

You will need to address a factual question in the course of answering a more challenging one. For example, if you were writing about promising treatments for autism, you would no doubt answer the question "What is autism?" at some point in your paper and even analyze competing definitions of autism to help support your arguments about the challenges of treating the condition. It would be unproductive, however, to use the factual question as the focus for the entire paper.

Choosing a grounded question

Make sure that your research question is grounded, not too speculative. Although speculative questions — such as those that address morality or beliefs — are worth asking in a research paper, they are unsuitable central questions. For most college courses, the central argument of a research paper should be grounded in evidence and should not be based entirely on beliefs.

TOO SPECULATIVE	GROUNDED
Is it wrong to share pornographic personal photos by cell phone?	What role should the US government play in regulating mobile content?
Do medical scientists have the right to experiment on animals?	How have technical breakthroughs made medical experiments on animals increasingly unnecessary?

Finding an entry point in a research conversation

As you pose preliminary research questions, you may wonder where and how to step into a research conversation. To find entry points, you may need to ask:

- Who are the major writers or thinkers in the debate? What positions have they taken?
- How and why do the major writers or thinkers disagree?
- What hasn't been said in the conversation and needs to be pointed out?

LaunchPadSolo **macmillanhighered.com/rules8e**

50 Thinking like a researcher; gathering sources

> Exercise: 50–1

> Writing practice: Entering a research conversation (with video)

As you orient yourself, try using the following statements to help you find points of entry in a research conversation.

> On one side of the debate is position X, on the other side is Y, but there is a middle position, Z.
>
> The conventional view about the problem or issue needs to be challenged because . . .
>
> Key details in this debate that have been overlooked are . . .
>
> Researchers have drawn conclusion X from the evidence, but one could also draw conclusion Y.

Testing a research question

- Does the question allow you to enter into a research conversation that you care about?
- Is the question flexible enough to allow for many possible answers?
- Is the question clear, focused, interesting?
- Is the question narrow enough, given the length of the assignment?
- Put the question to the "So what?" test. Can you show readers why the question needs to be asked and why the answer matters? (See p. 16.)

50c Map out a search strategy.

A search strategy is a systematic plan for tracking down sources. To create a search strategy appropriate for your research question, it may help to consult a librarian and take a look at your library's Web site, which will give you an overview of available resources.

No single search strategy works for every topic. For some topics, it may be useful to search for information in popular newspapers, magazines, and Web sites. For others, the best sources might be found in scholarly journals, books, and specialized reference works. Still other topics might be enhanced by field research — interviews, surveys, or observation.

With the help of a librarian, each of the students whose research essays can be found in this handbook constructed a search strategy appropriate for the research question.

Sophie Harba (See her full paper in 57b.) Sophie Harba's topic, the role of government in legislating food choices, is debated in scholarly articles and in publications aimed at the general public. To find information on her topic, Harba decided to

- search the Web to locate current news, government publications, and information from organizations that focus on the issues surrounding government regulation of food
- check a library database for current peer-reviewed research articles
- use the library catalog to search for a recently published book that was cited in a blog post on her topic and on several well-respected Web sites

Luisa Mirano (See her full paper in 62b.) Luisa Mirano's topic, the limitations of medication for childhood obesity, is the subject of psychological studies as well as articles in newspapers and magazines aimed at the general public. Thinking that both scholarly and popular sources would be appropriate, Mirano decided to

- search the Web to see what issues about childhood obesity might be interesting
- focus her search on medications reported in newspaper and magazine articles, advocacy Web sites, and government sites
- search specialized databases related to psychology and medicine for recent scholarly and scientific articles
- track down an article that several of her sources cited as an influential study

USING SOURCES RESPONSIBLY: Use your research log (see p. 396) to record information for each source you read or view, especially page numbers and URLs. If you gather complete publication information from the start of your project, you'll easily find it when you need to document your sources.

50d Search efficiently; master a few shortcuts to finding good sources.

Most students use a combination of library databases and the Web in their research. You can save yourself a lot of time by becoming an efficient searcher.

LaunchPadSolo macmillanhighered.com/rules8e
50 Thinking like a researcher; gathering sources
> Writing practice: Mapping out a search strategy

Using the library

The Web site hosted by your college library is full of useful information. In addition to dozens of databases and links to other references, many libraries offer online subject guides as well as one-on-one help from reference librarians through e-mail or chat. You can save yourself time if you get advice from your instructor, a librarian, or your library's Web site about the best place to start your search for sources.

Visiting your library can also be helpful. You can consult personally with reference librarians, who can show you what resources are available, help you refine your keywords for catalog or database searches, or suggest ways to narrow your search.

Savvy searchers cut down on the clutter of a broad search by adding additional search terms, limiting a search to recent publications, or selecting a database option to look at only one type of source, such as peer-reviewed articles, if that's what is needed. When looking for books, you can broaden a catalog search by asking "What kind of book might contain the information I need?" After you've identified a promising book on the library shelves, looking through the books on nearby shelves can also be valuable.

Using the Web

When using a search engine, it's a good idea to use terms that are as specific as possible and to enclose search phrases in quotation marks. You can refine your search by date or domain; for example, *autism site:.gov* will search for information about autism on government (.gov) Web sites. Use clues in what you find (such as organizations or government agencies that seem particularly informative) to refine your search.

As you examine sites, look for "about" links to learn about the site's author or sponsoring agency. Examine URLs for clues. Those that contain .k12 may be intended for young audiences; URLs ending in .gov lead to official information from US government entities. URLs may also offer clues about the country of origin: .au for Australia, .uk for United Kingdom, .in for India, and so on. If you aren't sure where a page originated, erase everything in the URL after the first slash in your address bar; the result should be the root page of the site, which may offer useful information about the site's purpose and audience (see p. 404). Avoid sites that provide information but no explanation of who the authors are or why the site was created. They may simply be advertising platforms attracting visitors with commonly sought information that is not original or substantial. For more on evaluating Web sites, see 52e.

CHECK URLS FOR CLUES ABOUT SPONSORSHIP

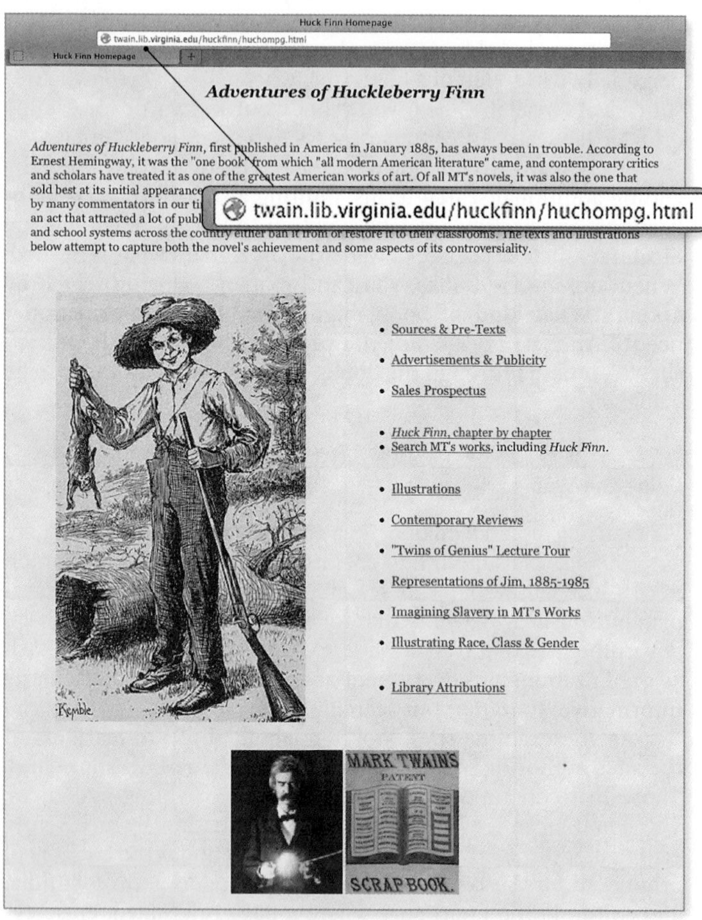

This source, from an internal page of a Web site, provides no indication of an author or a sponsor. Shortening the URL to http://twain.lib.virginia.edu/ leads to a main page that lists a university literature professor as the author and the University of Virginia Library as the sponsor.

Using bibliographies and citations as shortcuts

Scholarly books and articles list the works the author has cited, usually at the end. These lists are useful shortcuts to additional reliable sources on your topic. For example, most of the scholarly articles that student writer Luisa Mirano consulted contained citations to related research studies, selected by experts in the field. Through these citations, she quickly located other sources related to her topic, treatments for childhood obesity. Even popular sources such as news articles, videos, and interviews may refer to additional relevant sources that may be worth tracking down.

Using a variety of online tools and databases

You will probably find that your instructor, your librarian, or your library's Web site can be helpful in pointing you in the right direction once you have a topic and a research question. If you are still seeking some guidance about which Web sites, directories, databases, and other sources might yield useful searches, the URL at the bottom of the page will lead you to lists of sources that might provide the jump start you are looking for.

Tips for smart searching

For currency. If you need current information, news outlets such as the *New York Times* and the BBC, think tanks, government agencies, and advocacy groups may provide appropriate sources for your research. When using Google, you can limit a search to the most recent year, month, week, or day.

For authority. As you search, keep an eye out for any experts being cited in sources you examine. Following the citation trail may lead you to sources by those experts — or the organizations they represent — that may be even more helpful. You can limit a Google search by type of Web site and type of source. Add *site:.gov* to focus on government sources or *filetype:pdf* to zero in on reports and research papers as PDF files.

For scholarship. When you need scholarly or peer-reviewed articles, use a library database to look for reports of original research written by the people who conducted it. Scholarly articles provide information about where the authors work (such as universities or research centers), use a formal writing style, and include footnotes or a bibliography.

→

LaunchPadSolo **macmillanhighered.com/rules8e**
50 Thinking like a researcher; gathering sources
> Finding research help: Locating sources using online tools and databases

Tips for smart searching, continued

For context. Books are important sources in many fields such as history, philosophy, and sociology, and they often do a better job than scholarly articles of putting ideas in context. You may find a single chapter or even a few pages that are just what you need to gain a deeper perspective. Consider publication dates with your topic in mind.

For firsthand authenticity. In some fields, primary sources may be required. In historical research, for example, a primary source is one that originated in the historical period under discussion or is a firsthand account from a witness. In the sciences, a primary source (sometimes called a *primary article*) is a published report of research written by the scientist who conducted it. For more information, see page 423.

50e Conduct field research, if appropriate.

Your own field research can enhance or be the focus of a writing project. For a composition class, for example, you might want to interview a local politician about a current issue, such as the initiation of a city bike-share program. For a sociology class, you might decide to conduct a survey about campus trends in community service.

RESEARCH NOTE: Colleges and universities often require researchers to submit projects to an institutional review board (IRB) if the research involves human subjects outside a classroom setting. Before administering a survey or conducting other fieldwork, check with your instructor to see if IRB approval is required.

Interviewing

Interviews can often shed new light on a topic. Look for an expert who has firsthand knowledge of the subject, or seek out a key participant whose personal experience provides a valuable perspective.

When asking for an interview, be clear about who you are, what the purpose of the interview is, and how you would prefer to conduct it: by e-mail, over the phone, or in person. Ask questions that lead to facts, anecdotes, and opinions that will add a meaningful dimension to your paper.

INEFFECTIVE INTERVIEW QUESTIONS

How many years have you spent studying childhood obesity?

Is your work interesting?

EFFECTIVE INTERVIEW QUESTIONS

What are some current interpretations of the causes of childhood obesity?

What treatments have you found to be most effective? Why do you think they work?

USING SOURCES RESPONSIBLY: When quoting your source (the interviewee) in your paper, be accurate and fair. Do not change the meaning of your interviewee's words or take them out of context. To ensure accuracy, you might want to ask permission to record the interview or conduct it by e-mail.

Surveying opinion

For some topics, you may find it useful to survey opinions through written questionnaires, telephone or e-mail polls, or questions posted on a social media site. Many people are reluctant to fill out long questionnaires, so for a good response rate, limit your questions with your purpose in mind.

Surveys with yes/no questions or multiple-choice options can be completed quickly, and the results are easy to tally. You may also want to ask a few open-ended questions to elicit more individual responses, some of which may be worth quoting in your paper.

SAMPLE YES/NO QUESTION

Do you favor the use of Internet surveillance in the workplace?

SAMPLE OPEN-ENDED QUESTION

What, if any, experiences have you had with Internet surveillance in the workplace?

Other field methods

Your firsthand visits to and observations of significant places, people, or events can enhance a paper in a variety of disciplines. If you aren't able to visit an organization, a company, or a historic site, you may find useful information on an official Web site or a phone number or e-mail address to use to contact a representative.

50f Write a research proposal.

One effective way to manage your research project and focus your thinking is to write a research proposal. A proposal gives you an opportunity to look back — to remind you why you decided to enter a specific research conversation — and to look forward — to predict any difficulties or obstacles that might arise during your project. Your objective is to make a case for the question you plan to explore, the sources you plan to use, and the feasibility of the project, given the time and resources available. As you take stock of your project, you also have the valuable opportunity to receive comments from your instructor and classmates about your proposed research question and search strategy.

The following points will help you organize your proposal.

- **Research question.** What question will you be exploring? Why does this question need to be asked? What do you hope to learn from the project?
- **Research conversation.** What have you learned so far about the debate or specific research conversation you will enter? What entry point have you found to offer your own insights and ideas?
- **Search strategy.** Explain your search strategy: What kinds of sources will you use to explore your question? What sources have you found most useful, and why? How will you locate a variety of sources (print and visual, primary and secondary, for example)?
- **Research challenges.** What challenges, if any, do you anticipate (locating sufficient sources, managing the project, finding a position to take)? What resources are available to help you meet these challenges?

51 Managing information; taking notes responsibly

An effective researcher is a good record keeper. Whether you decide to keep records in your research log or in a file on your computer, you will need methods for managing information: maintaining a working bibliography (see 51a), keeping track of source materials (see 51b), and taking notes without plagiarizing your sources (see 51c). (For more on avoiding plagiarism, see 54 for MLA style and 59 for APA style.)

51a Maintain a working bibliography.

Keep a record of each source you read or view. This record, called a *working bibliography*, will help you compile the list of sources that will appear at the end of your paper. The format of this list depends on the documentation style you are using (for MLA style, see 56b; for APA style, see 61b). Using the proper style in your working bibliography will ensure that you have all the information you need to correctly cite any sources you use. (See 52f for advice on using your working bibliography as the basis for an annotated bibliography.)

Most researchers save bibliographic information from the library's catalog and databases and from the Web. The information you need is given in the chart on page 411. If you download a visual, you must gather the same information as for a print source.

For Web sources, some bibliographic information may not be available, but spend time looking for it before assuming that it doesn't exist. When information isn't available on the home page, you may have to follow links to interior pages. (See also pp. 405 and 425 for more details about finding bibliographic information in online sources.)

USING SOURCES RESPONSIBLY: Use care when printing or saving articles from a database or Web site. The files themselves may not include some of the elements you need to cite the source properly, especially page numbers. You may need to record additional information from the database or Web site where you accessed the file.

RESEARCH TIP: Your school may provide citation software, which automatically formats citations in any style using bibliographic information submitted by researchers. You must carefully proofread the results from these programs, however, because the citations often include errors.

51b Keep track of source materials.

The best way to keep track of source materials is to save a copy of each potential source as you conduct your research. Many database services will allow you to e-mail, save, or print citations or full texts of articles, and you can easily download, copy, or take screen shots of information from the Web.

Working with photocopies, printouts, and electronic files — as opposed to relying on memory or hastily written notes — has several benefits. You can highlight key passages, perhaps even color-coding them to reflect topics in your outline. You can get a head start on note taking. Finally, you reduce the chances of unintentional plagiarism since you will be able to compare your use of a source in your paper with the actual source, not just with your notes.

51c Take notes carefully to avoid unintentional plagiarism.

When you take notes from sources and jot down ideas, use your own words. Avoid copying passages — or cutting and pasting texts from electronic sources — without using quotation marks to indicate which words are yours and which ones you've taken from a source. Even if you half-copy the author's sentences — either by mixing the author's phrases with your own without using quotation marks or by plugging your synonyms into the author's sentence structure — you are committing plagiarism, a serious academic offense. (For examples of this kind of plagiarism, sometimes referred to as *patchwriting*, see 54b and 59b.)

To take notes responsibly, make sure you understand the ideas in the source. What are the major arguments? What is the evidence? Then, resist the temptation to look at the source as you take notes — except when you are quoting. Keep the source close by so that you can check for accuracy, but don't try to put ideas in your own words with the source's sentences in front of you. When you include a quotation in your notes, make sure you copy the words exactly and put quotation marks around them.

For strategies for avoiding plagiarism when using sources from the Web, see page 415.

Information to collect for a working bibliography

For an entire book

- All authors; any editors or translators
- Title and subtitle
- Edition (if not the first)
- Publication information: city, publisher, and date
- Medium: print, Web, and so on
- Date you retrieved the source (for an online source)

For an article

- All authors of the article
- Title and subtitle of the article
- Title of the journal, magazine, or newspaper
- Date; volume, issue, and page numbers
- Medium: print, Web, DVD, and so on
- Date you retrieved the source (for an online source)

For an article retrieved from a database (in addition to preceding information)

- Name of the database
- Accession number or other number assigned by the database
- Digital object identifier (DOI), if there is one
- URL of the journal's home page, if there is no DOI
- Date you retrieved the source

For a Web source (including visual, audio, and multimedia sources)

- All authors, editors, or composers of the source
- Editor or compiler of the Web source, if there is one
- Title and subtitle of the source
- Title of the longer work, if the source is contained in a longer work
- Title of the Web site
- Print publication information for the source, if available
- Online page or paragraph numbers, if any
- Date of online publication (or latest update)
- Sponsor of the site
- Date you accessed the source
- The site's URL

NOTE: For the exact bibliographic format to use in your working bibliography and in the final paper, see 56b (MLA) and 61b (APA).

USING SOURCES RESPONSIBLY: Be especially careful when using copy-and-paste functions in electronic files. Some researchers plagiarize their sources because they lose track of which words came from sources and which are their own. To prevent unintentional plagiarism, put quotation marks around any source text that you copy during your research.

There are three kinds of note taking: summarizing, paraphrasing, and quoting. Be sure to keep track of exact page references for all three types of notes; you will need the page numbers later if you use the information in your paper. And it is good practice to indicate in your notes if you have summarized, paraphrased, or quoted an author's words to avoid unintentionally plagiarizing a source.

Summarizing without plagiarizing

A summary condenses information and captures main ideas, perhaps reducing a chapter to a short paragraph or a paragraph to a single sentence. A summary should be written in your own words; if you use phrases from the source, put them in quotation marks.

> **Academic English** Even in the early stages of note taking, it is important to keep in mind that in the United States written texts are considered an author's property. (This "property" isn't a physical object, so it is often referred to as *intellectual property*.) The author (or the publisher) owns the language as well as any original ideas contained in the writing, whether the source is published in print or digital form. When you use another author's property in your own writing, you are required to follow certain conventions for citing the material, or you risk committing *plagiarism*.

Here is a passage about marine pollution from a National Oceanic and Atmospheric Administration (NOAA) Web site. Following the passage are the student's annotations on the source—notes and questions that help him figure out the meaning—and then his summary of the passage. (The bibliographic information is recorded in MLA style.)

ORIGINAL SOURCE

A question that is often posed to the NOAA Marine Debris Program (MDP) is "How much debris is actually out there?"

The MDP has recognized the need for this answer as well as the growing interest and value of citizen science. To that end, the MDP is developing and testing two types of monitoring and assessment protocols: 1) rigorous scientific survey and 2) volunteer at-sea visual survey. These types of monitoring programs are necessary in order to compare marine debris, composition, abundance, distribution, movement, and impact data on national and global scales.

— NOAA Marine Debris Program. "Efforts and Activities Related to the 'Garbage Patches.'" *Marine Debris*. NOAA Marine Debris Program, 2012. Web. 28 Nov. 2012.

ORIGINAL SOURCE WITH STUDENT ANNOTATIONS

by whom? ocean trash

A question that is often posed to the NOAA Marine Debris Program (MDP) is "How much debris is actually out there?" The MDP has recognized the need for this answer as well as the growing interest and value of citizen science. To that end, the MDP

ways of gathering information

is developing and testing two types of monitoring and assessment protocols: 1) rigorous scientific survey and 2) volunteer at-sea visual survey. These types of monitoring programs are necessary in order

kinds of materials how much?

to compare marine debris, composition, abundance, distribution,

why it matters

movement, and impact data on national and global scales.

SUMMARY

Source: NOAA Marine Debris Program. "Efforts and Activities Related to the 'Garbage Patches.'" *Marine Debris*. NOAA Marine Debris Program, 2012. Web. 28 Nov. 2012.

Having to field citizens' questions about the size of debris fields in Earth's oceans, the Marine Debris Program, an arm of the US National Oceanic and Atmospheric Administration, is currently implementing methods to monitor and draw conclusions about our oceans' patches of pollution (NOAA Marine Debris Program).

Paraphrasing without plagiarizing

Like a summary, a paraphrase is written in your own words; but whereas a summary reports significant information in fewer words than the source, a paraphrase restates the information in roughly the same number of words. A successful paraphrase also uses sentence structure that's different from the original. If you retain occasional choice phrases from the source, use quotation marks so that later you will know which phrases are not your own. If you paraphrase a source, you must still cite the source.

As you read the following paraphrase of the original source (see pp. 412–13), notice that the language is significantly different from that in the original.

PARAPHRASE

Source: NOAA Marine Debris Program. "Efforts and Activities Related to the 'Garbage Patches.'" *Marine Debris*. NOAA Marine Debris Program, 2012. Web. 28 Nov. 2012.

Citizens concerned and curious about the amount, makeup, and locations of debris patches in our oceans have been pressing NOAA's Marine Debris Program for answers. In response, the organization is preparing to implement plans and standards for expert study and nonexpert observation, both of which will yield results that will be helpful in determining the significance of the pollution problem (NOAA Marine Debris Program).

Using quotation marks to avoid plagiarizing

A quotation consists of the exact words from a source. In your notes, put all quoted material in quotation marks; do not assume that you will remember later which words, phrases, and passages you have quoted and which are your own. When you quote, be sure to copy the words of your source exactly, including punctuation and capitalization.

QUOTATION

Source: NOAA Marine Debris Program. "Efforts and Activities Related to the 'Garbage Patches.'" *Marine Debris*. NOAA Marine Debris Program, 2012. Web. 28 Nov. 2012.

> The NOAA Marine Debris Program has noted that, as our oceans become increasingly polluted, surveillance is "necessary in order to compare marine debris, composition, abundance, distribution, movement, and impact data on national and global scales."

Note that because the source is from a Web site without page numbers, the in-text citation includes only the author name and not a page number.

Avoiding plagiarism from the Web

Understand what plagiarism is. When you use another author's intellectual property — language, visuals, or ideas — in your own writing without giving proper credit, you commit a kind of academic theft called *plagiarism*.

Treat Web sources the same way you treat print sources. Any language that you find on the Web must be cited, even if the material is in the public domain (which generally includes older works no longer protected by copyright law) or is publicly accessible on free sites. When you use material from Web sites sponsored by federal, state, or municipal governments (.gov sites) or by nonprofit organizations (.org sites), you must acknowledge that material, too, as intellectual property owned by those agencies.

Keep track of which words come from sources and which are your own. To prevent unintentional plagiarism when you copy and paste passages from Web sources to an electronic file, put quotation marks around any text that you have inserted into your own work. During note taking and drafting, you might use a different color font or highlighting to draw attention to text taken from sources so that material from articles, Web sites, and other sources stands out unmistakably as someone else's words.

Avoid Web sites that bill themselves as "research services" and sell essays. When you use Web search engines to research a topic, you will often see links to sites that appear to offer legitimate writing support but that actually sell college essays. Of course, submitting a paper that you have purchased is cheating, but even using material from such a paper is considered plagiarism.

For details on avoiding plagiarism while working with sources, see 54b (MLA) and 59b (APA).

52 Evaluating sources

You can often locate dozens or even hundreds of potential sources for your topic — far more than you will have time to read. Your challenge will be to determine what kinds of sources you need to answer your research questions and to zero in on a reasonable number of trustworthy sources. This kind of decision making is referred to as *evaluating sources*. When you evaluate a source, you make a judgment about how useful the source is to your project.

Evaluating sources isn't something you do in one sitting. Being an effective researcher doesn't mean following a formula (*find some sources* > *evaluate those sources* > *write the paper*). Rather, it means seeing the process as more dynamic. After you do some planning, searching, and reading, for example, you may reflect on the information you have collected and conclude that you need to rethink your research question — and so you return to assessing the kinds of sources you need. You may be midway through drafting your paper when you begin to question a particular source's credibility, at which point you return to searching and reading.

52a Think about how sources might contribute to your writing.

How you plan to use sources in your paper will affect how you evaluate them. Not every source must directly support your thesis; sources can have a range of functions in a paper. They can do any of the following:

- provide background information or context for your topic
- explain terms or concepts that your readers might not understand
- provide evidence for your argument
- lend authority to your argument
- identify a gap or contradiction in the conversation
- offer counterarguments and alternative interpretations to your argument

Viewing evaluation as a process

When you use sources in your writing, make a habit of evaluating, or judging the value of, those sources at each stage of your project. The following questions may help.

Evaluate as you PLAN

What kinds of sources do I need?

What do I need these sources to help me do: Define? Persuade? Inform?

Evaluate as you SEARCH

How can I find reliable sources that help me answer my research question?

Which sources will help me build my credibility as a researcher?

Evaluate as you READ

What positions do these sources take in the debate on my topic? What are their biases?

How do these sources inform my understanding of the topic and the position I will take?

Evaluate as you WRITE

How do the sources I've chosen help me make my point?

How do my own ideas fit into the conversation on my research topic?

As you plan, you will need to think through the kinds of sources that will help you fulfill your purpose. The following are notes that one student took as she planned a paper.

Purpose: to persuade

My argument: that public funding for the arts should be granted on artistic merit alone and not on so-called decency standards

Sources I could use for background/context:	1998 Supreme Court decision (*National Endowment for the Arts v. Finley*) First Amendment
Sources that support my argument:	interviews of controversial artists Karen Finley and Tim Miller
Source that represents an alternative viewpoint:	passages from a profile of conservative North Carolina senator Jesse Helms

With her overall purpose in mind, the student judged each source according to the specific role it would play in her argument. For more examples of how student writers use sources for a variety of purposes, see 53c and 58c.

52b Select sources worth your time and attention.

As you search for sources in databases, the library catalog, and search engines, you're likely to get many more results than you can read or use. This section explains how to scan through the results for the most promising sources, and how to preview them to see whether they will help you answer your research question.

Scanning search results

As you scan through a list of search results, look for clues indicating whether a source might be useful for your purposes or not worth pursuing. You will need to use somewhat different strategies when scanning search results from a database, a library catalog, and a Web search engine.

Databases Most databases list at least the following information, which can help you decide if a source is relevant, current, and scholarly (see the chart on p. 421).

Title and brief description (How relevant?)

Date (How current?)

Name of periodical or other publication (How scholarly?)

Length (How extensive in coverage?)

Many databases allow you to sort your list of results by relevance or date; sorting may help you scan the information more efficiently.

Library catalogs The library's catalog usually lists basic information about books, periodicals, DVDs, and other material—enough to give you a first impression. As in database search results, the title and date of publication of books and other sources listed in the catalog will often be your first clues as to whether the source is worth consulting. If a title looks interesting, you can click on it for information about the subject matter and length. For books, reports, or other long sources, a table of contents may also be available.

Web search engines Reliable and unreliable sources live side-by-side online. As you scan through search results, look for the following clues about the probable relevance, currency, and reliability of a Web site.

The title, keywords, headings, and lead-in text (How relevant?)

A date (How current?)

An indication of the site's sponsor or purpose (How reliable?)

The URL, especially the URL ending: for example, .com, .edu, .gov, or .org (How relevant? How reliable?)

At the bottom of this page are a few of the results that student writer Luisa Mirano retrieved after typing the keywords *childhood obesity* into a search engine; she limited her search to works with those words in the title.

Mirano found the first site, sponsored by a research-based organization, promising enough to explore for her paper. The second and fourth sites held less promise because they seemed to offer popular rather than scholarly information. In addition, the second site was full of distracting advertisements. Mirano rejected the third source not because she doubted its reliability — in fact, research from the National Institutes of Health was what she hoped to find — but because a review of its contents revealed that the information was too general for her purposes.

EVALUATING SEARCH RESULTS: INTERNET SEARCH ENGINE

Content from a research-based organization. Promising.	American **Obesity** Association - **Childhood Obesity** **Childhood Obesity**. **Obesity** in **children** ... Note: The term "**childhood obesity**" may refer to both **children** and adolescents. In general, we ... www.**obesity**.org/subs/**childhood**/ - 17k - Jan 8, 2005 - Cached - Similar pages
Popular rather than scholarly source. Not relevant.	**Childhood Obesity** KS Logo, **Childhood Obesity**. advertisement. Source. ERIC Clearinghouse on Teaching and Teacher Education. Contents. ... Back to the Top Causes of **Childhood Obesity**. ... www.kidsource.com/kidsource/content2/**obesity**.html - 18k - Cached - Similar pages
Content too general. Not relevant.	**Childhood Obesity**, June 2002 Word on Health - National Institutes ... **Childhood Obesity** on the Rise, an article in the June 2002 edition of The NIH Word on Health - Consumer Information Based on Research from the National ... www.nih.gov/news/WordonHealth/ jun2002/**childhoodobesity**.htm - 22k - Cached - Similar pages
Popular and too general. Not relevant.	MayoClinic.com - **Childhood obesity**: Parenting advice ... **Childhood obesity**: Parenting advice By Mayo Clinic staff. ... Here are some other tips to help your **obese child** — and yourself: Be a positive role model. ... www.mayoclinic.com/invoke.cfm?id=FL00058 - 42k - Jan 8, 2005 - Cached - Similar pages

Previewing sources

Once you have decided that a source looks promising, preview it quickly to see whether it lives up to its promise. If you can evaluate as you search, rejecting irrelevant or unreliable sources before actually reading them, you will save yourself time.

PREVIEWING AN ARTICLE

- Consider the publication in which the article is printed. Is it a scholarly journal (see the chart on p. 421)? A popular magazine? A newspaper with a national reputation?
- For a magazine or journal article, look for an abstract or a statement of purpose at the beginning; also look for a summary at the end.
- For a newspaper article, focus on the headline and the opening paragraphs for relevance.
- Scan any headings and look at any visuals — charts, graphs, diagrams, or illustrations — that might indicate the article's focus and scope.

PREVIEWING A BOOK

- Glance through the table of contents, keeping your research question in mind. Even if the entire book is not relevant, parts of it may prove useful.
- Scan the preface in search of a statement of the author's purposes.
- Use the index to look up a few words related to your topic.
- If a chapter looks useful, read its opening and closing paragraphs and skim any headings.

PREVIEWING A WEB SITE

- Check to see if the sponsor is a reputable organization, a government agency, or a university. Is the group likely to look at only one side of a debatable issue?
- If you have landed on an internal page of a site and no author or sponsor is evident, try navigating to the home page, either through a link or by truncating the URL (see the tip on p. 404).
- Try to determine the purpose of the Web site. Is the site trying to sell a product? Promote an idea? Inform the public? Is the purpose consistent with your research?

- If the Web site includes statistical data (tables, graphs, charts), can you tell how and by whom the statistics were compiled? Is research cited?
- Find out when the site was created or last updated. Is it current enough for your purposes?

52c Select appropriate versions of online sources.

An online source may appear as an abstract, an excerpt, or a full-text article or book. It is important to distinguish among these versions of sources and to use a complete version of a source, preferably one with page numbers, for your research.

Abstracts and excerpts are shortened versions of complete works. An abstract — a summary of a work's contents — might appear in a database record for a source and can give you clues

Determining if a source is scholarly

For many college assignments, you will be asked to use scholarly sources. These are written by experts for a knowledgeable audience and usually go into more depth than books and articles written for a general audience. (Scholarly sources are sometimes called *refereed* or *peer-reviewed* because the work is evaluated by experts in the field before publication.) To determine if a source is scholarly, you should look for the following:

- Formal language and presentation
- Authors who are academics or scientists
- Footnotes or a bibliography documenting the works cited by the author in the source
- Original research and interpretation (rather than a summary of other people's work)
- Quotations from and analysis of primary sources (in humanities disciplines such as literature, history, and philosophy)
- A description of research methods or a review of related research (in the sciences and social sciences)

NOTE: In some databases, searches can be limited to refereed or peer-reviewed journals.

about the usefulness of the source for your research. An excerpt is the first few sentences or paragraphs of a newspaper or magazine article and sometimes appears in a list of results from an online search. Abstracts and excerpts often provide enough information for you to determine whether the complete article would be useful for your paper. Both are brief (usually fewer than five hundred words) and generally do not contain enough information to function alone as sources in a research paper. Reading the complete article is the best way to understand the author's argument before referring to it in your own writing. If an article is available in multiple file formats, work with the file that includes page numbers. Numbering will help you with accurate note taking and citation.

52d Read with an open mind and a critical eye.

As you begin reading the sources you have chosen, keep an open mind. Do not let your personal beliefs prevent you from listening to new ideas and opposing viewpoints. Be curious about the wide range of positions in the research conversation you are entering. Your research question should guide you as you engage your sources.

When you read critically, you are examining an author's assumptions, assessing evidence, and weighing conclusions.

Reading critically means

- reading carefully (*What does the source say?*)
- reading skeptically (*Are any of the author's points or conclusions problematic?*)
- reading evaluatively (*How does this source help me make my argument?*)

For one student's careful reading of a source text, see 5a.

USING SOURCES RESPONSIBLY: Take time to read the entire source and try to understand an author's arguments, assumptions, and conclusions. Try to avoid taking quotations from the first few pages of a source before you understand if the words and ideas are representative of the work as a whole.

Distinguishing between primary and secondary sources

As you begin assessing evidence in a source, determine whether you are reading a primary or a secondary source. Primary sources include original documents such as letters, diaries, legislative bills, laboratory studies, field research reports, and eyewitness accounts. Secondary sources are commentaries on primary sources — another writer's opinions about or interpretation of a primary source.

Although a primary source is not necessarily more reliable than a secondary source, it has the advantage of being a firsthand account. You can better evaluate what a secondary source says if you have first read any primary sources it discusses.

Being alert for signs of bias

Bias is a way of thinking, a tendency to be partial, that prevents people and publications from viewing a topic objectively. Both in print and online, some sources are more objective than others. If you are exploring the rights of organizations like WikiLeaks to distribute sensitive government documents over the Internet, for example, you may not find objective, unbiased information in a US State Department report. If you are researching timber harvesting practices, you are likely to encounter bias in publications sponsored by environmental groups. As a researcher, you will need to consider any suspected bias as you assess the source. If you are uncertain about a source's special interests, seek the help of a reference librarian.

Like publishers, some authors are more objective than others. If you have reason to believe that a writer is particularly biased, you will want to assess his or her arguments with special care. For a list of questions worth asking, see the chart on page 424.

Assessing the author's argument

In nearly all subjects worth writing about, there is some element of argument, so expect to encounter debates and disagreements among authors. In fact, areas of disagreement give you entry points in a research conversation. The questions in the chart on page 424 can help you weigh the strengths and weaknesses of each author's arguments.

Evaluating all sources

Checking for signs of bias

- Does the author or publisher endorse political or religious views that could affect objectivity?
- Is the author or publisher associated with a special-interest group, such as PETA or the National Rifle Association, that might present only one side of an issue?
- Are alternative views presented and addressed? How fairly does the author treat opposing views? (See 6c.)
- Does the author's language show signs of bias?

Assessing an argument

- What is the author's central claim or thesis?
- How does the author support this claim — with relevant and sufficient evidence or with just a few anecdotes or emotional examples?
- Are statistics consistent with those you encounter in other sources? Have they been used fairly? Does the author explain where the statistics come from?
- Are any of the author's assumptions questionable?
- Does the author consider opposing arguments and refute them persuasively? (See 6c.)
- Does the author fall prey to any logical fallacies? (See 6a.)

52e Assess Web sources with care.

Sources found on the Web can provide valuable information, but verifying their credibility may take time. Before using a Web source in your paper, make sure you know who created the material and for what purpose. Sites with reliable information can stand up to careful scrutiny. For a checklist on evaluating Web sources, see the chart on page 425. (See also an evaluation of two sample Web sites on pp. 426–27.)

LaunchPadSolo **macmillanhighered.com/rules8e**
52 Evaluating sources
> Writing practice: Evaluating sources you find on the Web

Evaluating sources you find on the Web

Authorship

- Does the Web site or document have an author? You may need to do some clicking and scrolling to find the author's name. If you have landed directly on an internal page of a site, for example, you may need to navigate to the home page or find an "about this site" link to learn the name of the author.
- If there is an author, can you tell whether he or she is knowledgeable and credible? When the author's qualifications aren't listed on the site itself, look for links to the author's home page, which may provide evidence of his or her interests and expertise.

Sponsorship

- Who, if anyone, sponsors the site? The sponsor of a site is often named and described on the home page.
- What does the URL tell you? The domain name extension often indicates the type of group hosting the site: commercial (.com), educational (.edu), nonprofit (.org), governmental (.gov), military (.mil), or network (.net). URLs may also indicate a country of origin: .uk (United Kingdom) or .jp (Japan), for instance.

Purpose and audience

- Why was the site created: To argue a position? To sell a product? To inform readers?
- Who is the site's intended audience?

Currency

- How current is the site? Check for the date of publication or the latest update, often located at the bottom of the home page or at the beginning or end of an internal page.
- How current are the site's links? If many of the links no longer work, the site may be too dated for your purposes.

EVALUATING A WEB SITE: CHECKING RELIABILITY

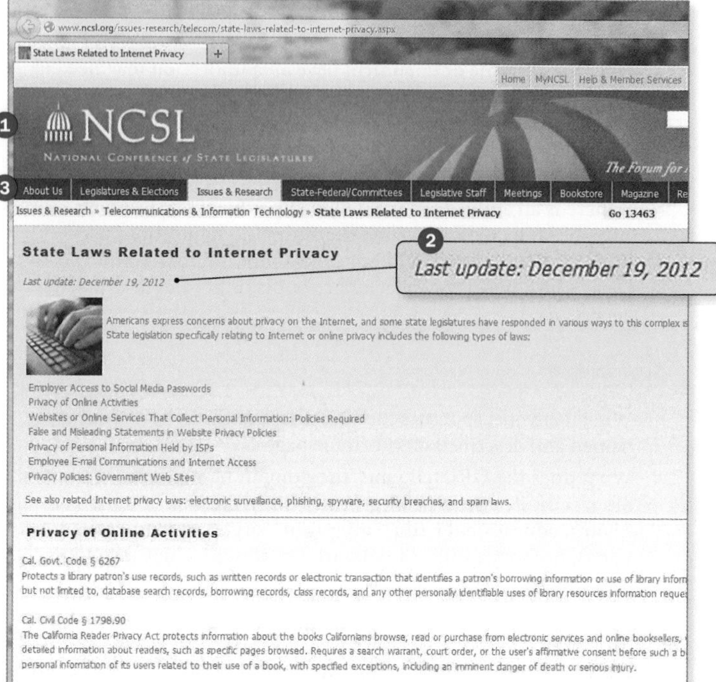

1 This page on Internet monitoring and workplace privacy appears on a Web site sponsored by the National Conference of State Legislatures. The NCSL is a bipartisan group that functions as a clearinghouse of ideas and research of interest to state lawmakers. It is also a lobby for state issues before the US government.

2 A clear date of publication shows currency.

3 An "About Us" page provides an opportunity to verify the organization's credentials. When you know something about the creator of the site, you will be in a good position to evaluate the worth and reliability of its information.

EVALUATING A WEB SITE: CHECKING PURPOSE

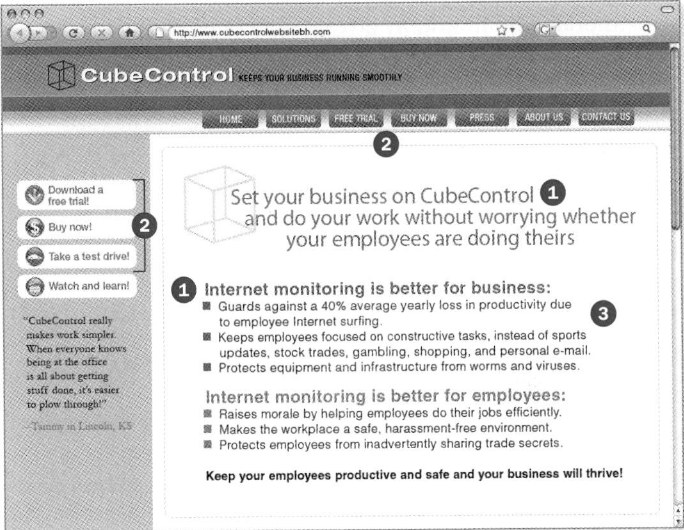

1 The site is sponsored by a company that specializes in employee-monitoring software.

2 Repeated links for trial downloads and purchase suggest the site's intended audience: consumers seeking to purchase software (probably not researchers seeking detailed information about employees' use of the Internet in the workplace).

3 The site appears to provide information and even shows statistics from studies, but ultimately the purpose of the site is to sell a product.

52f Construct an annotated bibliography.

Section 51a describes how to write a working bibliography, a document that helps you keep track of publication information for all of the sources you may be considering for your project. At some point during your research process, or as a separate assignment, your instructor may ask you to write an annotated

LaunchPadSolo macmillanhighered.com/rules8e

52 Evaluating sources

> Writing practice: Developing an annotated bibliography

> Sample student writing: Orlov, "Online Monitoring: A Threat to Employee Privacy in the Wired Workplace: An Annotated Bibliography" (annotated bibliography; MLA)

> Sample student writing: Niemeyer, "Keynesian Policy: Implications for the Current U.S. Economic Crisis" (annotated bibliography; APA)

Writing guide | Annotated bibliography

An **annotated bibliography** gives you an opportunity to summarize, evaluate, and record publication information for your sources before drafting your research paper. You summarize each source to understand its main ideas; you evaluate each source for accuracy, quality, and relevance. Finally, you reflect, asking yourself how the source will contribute to your research project. A sample annotated bibliography entry appears on page 430.

Key features

- **A list of sources arranged in alphabetical order by author** includes complete bibliographic information for each source.
- **A brief entry for each source** is typically one hundred to two hundred words.
- **A summary** of each source states the work's main ideas and key points briefly and accurately. The summary is written in the third person and the present tense. Summarizing helps you test your understanding of a source and convey its meaning responsibly.
- **An evaluation** of the source's role and usefulness in your project includes an assessment of the source's strengths and limitations, the author's qualifications and expertise, and the function of the source in your project. Evaluating a source helps you analyze how the source fits into your project and separate the source's ideas from your own.

Writing your annotated bibliography

EXPLORE

For each source, begin by brainstorming responses to questions such as the following.

- What is the purpose of the source? Who is the author's intended audience?
- What is the author's thesis? What evidence supports the thesis?
- What qualifications and expertise does the author bring? Does the author have any biases or make any questionable assumptions?
- Why do you think this source is useful for your project?
- How does this source relate to the other sources in your bibliography?

○ DRAFT

- Arrange the sources in alphabetical order by author (or by title for works with no author).
- Provide consistent bibliographic information for each source. For the exact bibliographic format, see 56b (MLA) or 61b (APA).
- Start your summary by identifying the thesis and purpose of the source as well as the credentials of the source's author.
- Keep your research question in mind. How does this source contribute to your project? How does it help you take your place in the conversation?

● REVISE

Ask reviewers for specific feedback. Here are some questions to guide their comments.

- Is each source summarized clearly? Have you identified the author's main idea?
- For each source, have you made a clear judgment about how and why the source is useful for your project?
- Have you used quotation marks around exact words from a source?

bibliography entry for one or more of the sources you've gathered. When annotating a bibliography entry, you provide citation information for the source and, in your own words, a summary of its contents. Summarizing key points of a source will help you identify how the source relates to your argument and will help you judge whether the source is relevant and appropriate for your project. Evaluating your sources' ideas will help you separate them from your own ideas, and it will also help you move toward a draft in which you synthesize sources and present your own thesis. (See 55d and 60d for more on synthesis.) For a sample annotated bibliography, see page 430. For more help with writing an annotated bibliography, see the Writing Guide that begins on page 428.

SAMPLE ANNOTATED BIBLIOGRAPHY ENTRY (MLA STYLE)

Resnik, David. "Trans Fat Bans and Human Freedom." *American Journal of Bioethics* 10.3 (2010): 27-32. *Academic Search Premier*. Web. 17 Apr. 2013.

Summarize the source using present tense.

Annotations should be three to seven sentences long.

In this scholarly article, bioethicist David Resnik argues that bans on unhealthy foods threaten our personal freedom. He claims that researchers don't have enough evidence to know whether banning trans fats will save lives or money; all we know is that such bans restrict dietary choices. Resnik explains why most Americans oppose food restrictions, noting our multiethnic and regional food traditions as well as our resistance to government limitations on personal freedoms. He acknowledges that few people would miss eating trans fats, but he fears that bans on such substances could lead to widespread restrictions on red meat, sugary sodas, and other foods known to have harmful effects. Resnik offers a well-reasoned argument, but he goes too far by insisting that all proposed food restrictions will do more harm than good. This article contributes important perspectives on American resistance to government intervention in food choice and counters arguments in other sources that support the idea of food legislation to advance public health.

Evaluate the source for bias and relevance.

Evaluate the source for its contribution to the research project.

Writing Papers in MLA Style

Writing Papers in MLA Style 431

Writing Papers in MLA Style

Directory to MLA in-text citation models

Directory to MLA works cited models

Directory to MLA works cited models, continued

Books and other long works

Web sites and parts of Web sites

Directory to MLA works cited models, continued

Most English instructors and some humanities instructors will ask you to document your sources with the Modern Language Association (MLA) system of citations described in chapter 56.

When writing an MLA paper that is based on sources, you face three main challenges: (1) supporting a thesis, (2) citing your sources accurately and avoiding plagiarism, and (3) integrating source material effectively.

Examples in chapters 53–55 are drawn from a student's research about the role of government in legislating food choices. Sophie Harba's research paper, in which she argues that state governments have the responsibility to advance health policies and to regulate healthy eating choices, appears on pages 517–25.

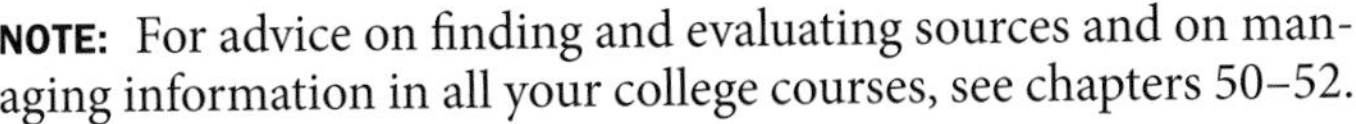

NOTE: For advice on finding and evaluating sources and on managing information in all your college courses, see chapters 50–52.

53 Supporting a thesis

Most research assignments ask you to form a thesis, or main idea, and to support that thesis with well-organized evidence. (See also 1c.)

53a Form a working thesis.

Once you have read a variety of sources, considered your issue from different perspectives, and chosen an entry point in the research conversation (see 50b), you are ready to form a working thesis to focus your project: a one-sentence (or occasionally a two-sentence) statement of your central idea. (See also 1c and 53d.) The working thesis expresses more than your opinion; it expresses your informed, reasoned answer to your research question—a question about which people might disagree. As you learn more about your subject, your ideas may change, and your working thesis will evolve, too. You can revise your thesis as you draft.

In a research paper, your thesis will answer the central research question that you pose (see 50b). Here, for example, are student writer Sophie Harba's research question and working thesis.

RESEARCH QUESTION

Should the government enact laws to regulate healthy eating choices?

WORKING THESIS

Government has the responsibility to regulate healthy eating choices because of the rise of chronic diseases.

LaunchPadSolo **macmillanhighered.com/rules8e**

53 Supporting a thesis
> Writing practice: Writing a working thesis for a research paper
> Exercises: 53–1 and 53–2

After you have written a rough draft and perhaps done more reading, you may decide to revise your thesis, as Harba did, to give it a sharper and more specific focus.

REVISED THESIS

In the name of public health and safety, state governments have the responsibility to advance health policies and to regulate healthy eating choices, especially since doing so offers a potentially large social benefit for a relatively small cost.

The thesis usually appears at the end of the introductory paragraph. To read Sophie Harba's thesis in her introduction, see page 517.

Testing your thesis

When drafting and revising a thesis statement, make sure it answers your central research question and that you can effectively develop it with the sources available to you. Keeping the following guidelines in mind will help you develop an effective thesis statement.

- A thesis should take a position that needs to be argued and supported. It should not be a fact or description.
- A thesis should match the scope of the research project. If your thesis is too broad, explore a subtopic of your original topic. If your thesis is too narrow, pose a research question that has more than one answer.
- A thesis should be sharply focused. Avoid vague words such as *interesting* or *good.* Use concrete language and make sure your thesis lets readers know your position.
- A thesis should stand up to the "So what?" question. Ask yourself why readers should care about your thesis. If your thesis matters to you, your readers are more likely to find your ideas engaging.

53b Organize your ideas.

The body of your paper will consist of evidence in support of your thesis. It will be useful to sketch an informal plan that helps you begin to organize your ideas. Sophie Harba, for example, used this simple plan to outline the structure of her argument:

- Debates about the government's role in regulating food have a long history in the United States.

- Some experts argue that we should focus on the dangers of unhealthy eating habits and on preventing chronic diseases linked to diet.
- But food regulations are not a popular solution because many Americans object to government restrictions on personal choice.
- Food regulations designed to prevent chronic disease don't ask Americans to give up their freedom; they ask Americans to see health as a matter of public good.

After you have written a rough draft, a formal outline can help you organize your argument (see 1d).

53c Use sources to inform and support your argument.

Used thoughtfully, the source materials you have gathered will make your argument more developed and convincing for readers. Sources can play several different roles to support your thesis and develop your points.

Providing background information or context

You can use facts and statistics to support generalizations or to establish the importance of your topic, as student writer Sophie Harba does to demonstrate the large social benefits of laws designed to prevent chronic disease.

> To give just one example, Marion Nestle, New York University professor of nutrition and public health, notes that "a 1% reduction in intake of saturated fat across the population would prevent more than 30,000 cases of coronary heart disease annually and save more than a billion dollars in health care costs" (7).

Explaining terms or concepts

If readers are unfamiliar with a term or a concept, you will want to define or explain it; or if your argument depends on a term with multiple meanings, you will want to explain your use of the term. Quoting or paraphrasing a source can help you define terms and concepts in accessible language. Harba defines the term *refined grains* as part of her claim that the typical American diet is getting less healthy over time.

> A diet that is low in nutritional value and high in sugars, fats, and refined grains—grains that have been processed to increase shelf life but that sacrifice fiber, iron, and B vitamins—can be damaging over time (United States, Dept. of Agriculture and Dept. of Health and Human Services 36).

Supporting your claims

As you develop your argument, back up your assertions with facts, examples, and other evidence from your research. (See also 6h.) Harba, for example, uses factual evidence to make the point that the typical American diet is damaging.

> Michael Pollan, who has written extensively about Americans' unhealthy eating habits, cites the Centers for Disease Control in arguing that "fully three quarters of US health care spending goes to treat chronic diseases, most of which are preventable and linked to diet: heart disease, stroke, type 2 diabetes, and at least a third of all cancers."

Lending authority

Expert opinion can add weight and credibility to your argument. (See also 6h.) But don't rely on experts to make your points for you. State your ideas in your own words and, when appropriate, cite the judgment of an authority in the field to support your position.

> Debates surrounding the government's role in regulating food have a long history in the United States. According to Lorine Goodwin, a food historian, nineteenth-century reformers who sought to purify the food supply were called "fanatics" and "radicals" by critics who argued that consumers should be free to buy and eat what they want (77).

Anticipating and countering objections

Do not ignore sources that seem contrary to your position. Instead, use them to give voice to opposing points of view and to state potential objections to your argument before you counter them (see 6i). By anticipating her readers' argument that many Americans oppose laws to limit what they eat, Sophie Harba creates an opportunity to counter that objection and build common ground with her readers.

> Why is the public largely resistant to laws that would limit unhealthy choices or penalize those choices with so-called fat taxes? Many consumers and civil rights advocates find such laws to be an unreasonable restriction on individual freedom of choice. As health policy experts Mello, Studdert, and Brennan point out, opposition to food and beverage regulation is similar to the opposition to early tobacco legislation: the public views the issue as one of personal responsibility rather than one requiring government intervention (2602). In other words, if a person eats unhealthy food and becomes ill as a result, that is his or her choice. But those who favor legislation claim that freedom of choice is a myth because of the strong influence of food and beverage industry marketing on consumers' dietary habits.

53d Draft an introduction for your thesis.

In a research paper, readers are accustomed to seeing the thesis statement — the paper's main point — at the end of the first or second paragraph. The advantage of putting it in the first paragraph is that readers can easily recognize your position. The advantage of delaying the thesis until the second paragraph is that you can provide a fuller context for your main idea.

As you draft your introduction, you may revise your working thesis, either because you have refined your thinking or because new wording fits more smoothly into the context you have created for it.

In addition to stating your thesis, an introduction should hook readers (see 1e). For example, in your first sentence or two you might introduce readers to the research conversation by connecting your topic to a recent news item or by pointing to emerging trends in an academic discipline. Other strategies are to pose a puzzling problem or to cite a startling statistic. Sophie Harba begins her paper by engaging readers with her research question: "Should the government enact laws to regulate healthy eating choices?" She then highlights the research conversation around the question before offering her perspective in her thesis (see p. 517).

53e Draft the paper in an appropriate voice.

A chatty, breezy voice is usually not appropriate in a research paper, but neither is a vague, timid one.

TOO CHATTY

> What's up with these people who think food isn't important and don't want the government in their kitchen? People who are against food regulation seem so irrational and unreasonable.

MORE FORMAL

> Why is the public largely resistant to laws that would limit unhealthy choices or penalize those choices with so-called fat taxes? Many consumers and civil rights advocates find such laws to be an unreasonable restriction on individual freedom of choice.

TOO VAGUE

> It has been concluded that a majority of Americans don't want the government to restrict their food access.

MORE SPECIFIC

> According to a nationwide poll, 75 percent of Americans are opposed to laws that restrict or put limitations on access to unhealthy foods (Neergaard and Agiesta).

TOO TIMID

> I may not be an expert on food policy, but it seems to me that eating unhealthy foods contributes to chronic disease and lots of other problems.

MORE AUTHORITATIVE

> Mounting scientific evidence points to unhealthy foods as a significant contributing factor to chronic disease, which we know is straining our health care system, decreasing our quality of life, and leading to unnecessary premature deaths.

54 Citing sources; avoiding plagiarism

In a research paper, you will draw on the work of other writers, and you must document their contributions by citing your sources. Sources are cited for two reasons:

1. to tell readers where your information comes from — so that they can assess its reliability and, if interested, find and read the original source
2. to give credit to the writers from whom you have borrowed words and ideas

Borrowing another writer's language, sentence structures, or ideas without proper acknowledgment is a form of dishonesty known as *plagiarism.*

You must include a citation when you quote from a source, when you summarize or paraphrase, and when you borrow facts that are not common knowledge (see also 54b).

54a Understand how the MLA system works.

Most English professors and some humanities professors require the MLA (Modern Language Association) system of in-text citations. Here, briefly, is how the MLA citation system usually works. (See 56 for more details and model citations. See 57b for a sample research paper with in-text citations and a works cited list in MLA style.)

1. The source is introduced by a signal phrase that names its author.
2. The material being cited is followed by a page number in parentheses (unless the source is an unpaginated Web source).
3. At the end of the paper, a list of works cited (arranged alphabetically by authors' last names) gives complete publication information for the source.

IN-TEXT CITATION

Bioethicist David Resnik emphasizes that such policies "open the door to excessive government control over food, which could restrict dietary choices, interfere with cultural, ethnic, and religious traditions, and exacerbate socioeconomic inequalities" (31).

ENTRY IN THE LIST OF WORKS CITED

Resnik, David. "Trans Fat Bans and Human Freedom." *American Journal of Bioethics* 10.3 (2010): 27-32. *Academic Search Premier*. Web. 17 Apr. 2013.

NOTE: When you use an MLA in-text citation, a period appears after the parenthetical citation. This basic MLA format varies for different types of sources. For a detailed discussion and other models, see 56.

54b Avoid plagiarism when quoting, summarizing, and paraphrasing sources.

In a research paper, you draw on the work of other writers, and you must document their contributions by citing your sources. When you acknowledge your sources, you avoid plagiarism, a serious academic offense. (See also 51c.)

In general, these three acts are considered plagiarism: (1) failing to cite quotations and borrowed ideas, (2) failing to enclose borrowed language in quotation marks, and (3) failing to put summaries and paraphrases in your own words. Definitions of plagiarism may vary; it's a good idea to find out how your school defines academic dishonesty.

Citing quotations and borrowed ideas

You must cite all direct quotations. You must also cite any ideas borrowed from a source: summaries and paraphrases; statistics and other specific facts; and visuals such as cartoons, graphs, and diagrams.

The only exception is common knowledge—information that your readers could easily find in any number of general sources. For example, a quick search could tell you that Joel Coen directed *Fargo* in 1996 and that Emily Dickinson published only a handful of her many poems during her lifetime.

As a rule, when you have seen information repeatedly in your reading, you don't need to cite it. However, when information has appeared in only one or two sources, when it is highly specific (as with statistics), or when it is controversial, you should cite the source. If a topic is new to you and you are not sure what is considered common knowledge or what is controversial, ask your instructor, a reference librarian, or someone else with expertise. When in doubt, cite the source. (See 56 for details.)

Enclosing borrowed language in quotation marks

To indicate that you are using a source's exact phrases or sentences, you must enclose them in quotation marks unless they have been set off from the text by indenting (see 55b). To omit the quotation marks is to claim—falsely—that the language is your own, as in the example below. Such an omission is plagiarism even if you have cited the source.

ORIGINAL SOURCE

> Although these policies may have a positive impact on human health, they open the door to excessive government control over food, which could restrict dietary choices, interfere with cultural, ethnic, and religious traditions, and exacerbate socioeconomic inequalities.
>
> —David Resnik, "Trans Fat Bans and Human Freedom," p. 31

PLAGIARISM

> Bioethicist David Resnik points out that policies to ban trans fats may protect human health, but they open the door to excessive government control over food, which could restrict dietary choices and interfere with cultural, ethnic, and religious traditions (31).

BORROWED LANGUAGE IN QUOTATION MARKS

> Bioethicist David Resnik points out that policies to ban trans fats may protect human health, but they "open the door to excessive government control over food, which could restrict dietary choices, interfere with cultural, ethnic, and religious traditions, and exacerbate socioeconomic inequalities" (31).

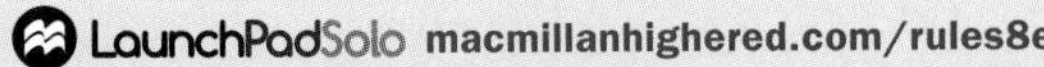
LaunchPadSolo macmillanhighered.com/rules8e

54 Citing sources; avoiding plagiarism

> Exercises: 54–1 to 54–6

Putting summaries and paraphrases in your own words

Summaries and paraphrases are written in your own words. A summary condenses information from a source; a paraphrase uses roughly the same number of words as the original source to convey the information. When you summarize or paraphrase, it is not enough to name the source; you must restate the source's meaning using your own language. (See also 51c and 55a.) Half-copying the author's sentences by using the author's phrases in your own sentences without quotation marks or by plugging synonyms into the author's sentence structure (sometimes called patchwriting) is a form of plagiarism.

The first paraphrase of the following source is plagiarized. Even though the source is cited, too much of its language is borrowed from the original. The highlighted strings of words have been copied exactly (without quotation marks). In addition, the writer has closely echoed the sentence structure of the source, merely substituting some synonyms (*interfere with lifestyle choices* for *paternalistic intervention into lifestyle choices* and *decrease the feeling of personal responsibility* for *enfeeble the notion of personal responsibility*).

ORIGINAL SOURCE

> [A]ntiobesity laws encounter strong opposition from some quarters on the grounds that they constitute paternalistic intervention into lifestyle choices and enfeeble the notion of personal responsibility. Such arguments echo those made in the early days of tobacco regulation.
>
> —Michelle M. Mello, David M. Studdert, and Troyen A. Brennan, "Obesity—The New Frontier of Public Health Law," p. 2602

PLAGIARISM: UNACCEPTABLE BORROWING

> Health policy experts Mello, Studdert, and Brennan argue that antiobesity laws encounter strong opposition from some quarters because they interfere with lifestyle choices and decrease the feeling of personal responsibility. These arguments mirror those made in the early days of tobacco regulation (2602).

To avoid plagiarizing an author's language, resist the temptation to look at the source while you are summarizing or paraphrasing. After you have read the passage you want to paraphrase, set the source aside. Ask yourself, "What is the author's meaning?" In your own words, state your understanding of the author's ideas.

Return to the source and check that you haven't used the author's language or sentence structure or misrepresented the author's ideas. Following these steps will help you avoid plagiarizing the source. When you fully understand another writer's meaning, you can more easily and accurately represent those ideas in your own words.

ACCEPTABLE PARAPHRASE

As health policy experts Mello, Studdert, and Brennan point out, opposition to food and beverage regulation is similar to the opposition to early tobacco legislation: the public views the issue as one of personal responsibility rather than one requiring government intervention (2602).

55 Integrating sources

Your research paper draws on and borrows from the work of others — your sources — to help you develop and support your ideas. As you conduct research, you gather language and ideas from your sources that you might want to use in your paper. Section 54 shows you how to acknowledge those sources to avoid plagiarism. This section will help you integrate those sources seamlessly and effectively into your paper, so that readers understand how your use of quotation, summary, and paraphrase contributes to your argument.

As you integrate sources, you need to find a balance between the words of your sources and your own voice. Readers should always know who is speaking in your paper — you or your source. You can use several strategies to integrate research sources into your paper while maintaining your own voice.

- Use sources as concisely as possible so that your own thinking and voice aren't lost (55a and 55b).
- Use signal phrases and avoid dropping quotations into your paper without indicating the boundary between your words and the source's words (55c).

- Discuss and analyze your sources to show readers how each source supports your argument and how the sources relate to one another (55d).

55a Summarize and paraphrase effectively.

In your academic writing, keep the emphasis on your ideas and your language; use your own words to summarize and to paraphrase your sources and to explain your points. Whether you choose to summarize or paraphrase a source depends on your purpose.

Summarizing

When you summarize a source, you express another writer's ideas in your own words, condensing the author's key points and using fewer words than the author. The following guidelines will help you decide when summary is the most effective method for integrating your source.

WHEN TO USE A SUMMARY

- When a passage is lengthy and you want to condense a chapter to a short paragraph or a paragraph to a single sentence
- When you want to state the source's main ideas simply and briefly in your own words
- When you want to compare arguments or ideas from various sources
- When you want to provide readers with an understanding of the source's argument before you respond to it or launch your own

Paraphrasing

When you paraphrase, you express an author's ideas in your own words, using approximately the same number of words and details as in the source. The following guidelines will help you decide when paraphrase is the most effective method for integrating your source.

WHEN TO USE A PARAPHRASE

- When the ideas and information are important but the author's exact words are not needed for accuracy or emphasis
- When you want to restate the source's ideas in your own words
- When you need to simplify and explain a technical or complicated source
- When you need to reorder a source's ideas

Even though you use your own words to summarize and paraphrase, the original idea remains the intellectual property of the author, so you must include a citation. (See 54b.)

55b Use quotations effectively.

When you quote a source, you borrow some of the author's exact words and enclose them in quotation marks. Quotation marks show your readers that both the idea and the words belong to the author.

WHEN TO USE QUOTATIONS

- When language is especially vivid or expressive
- When exact wording is needed for technical accuracy
- When it is important to let the debaters of an issue explain their positions in their own words
- When the words of an authority lend weight to an argument
- When the language of a source is the topic of your discussion (as in an analysis or interpretation)

Limiting your use of quotations

Although it is tempting to insert many quotations in your paper and to use your own words only for connecting passages, do not quote excessively.

It is not always necessary to quote full sentences from a source. To reduce your reliance on the words of others, you can often

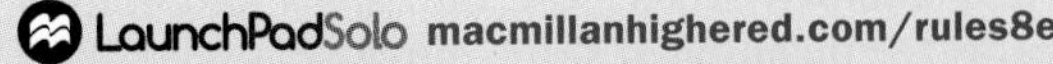

55 Integrating sources

> Exercises: 55-1 to 55-5

integrate language from a source into your own sentence structure. (For the use of signal phrases in integrating quotations, see 55c.)

> Resnik acknowledges that his argument relies on the "slippery slope" fallacy, but he insists that "social and political pressures" regarding food regulations make his concerns valid (31).

Using the ellipsis mark and brackets

Two useful marks of punctuation, the ellipsis mark and brackets, allow you to keep quoted material to a minimum and to integrate it smoothly into your text.

The ellipsis mark To condense a quoted passage, you can use the ellipsis mark (three periods, with spaces between) to indicate that you have left words out. What remains must be grammatically complete.

> In Mississippi, legislators passed "a ban on bans—a law that forbids . . . local restrictions on food or drink" (Conly A23).

The writer has omitted from the source the words *municipalities to place* before *local restrictions* to condense the quoted material.

On the rare occasions when you want to leave out one or more full sentences, use a period before the three ellipsis dots.

> Legal scholars Gostin and Gostin argue that "individuals have limited willpower to defer immediate gratification for longer-term health benefits. . . . A person understands that high-fat foods or a sedentary lifestyle will cause adverse health effects, or that excessive spending or gambling will cause financial hardship, but it is not always easy to refrain" (217).

Ordinarily, do not use an ellipsis mark at the beginning or at the end of a quotation. Your readers will understand that the quoted material is taken from a longer passage, so such marks are not necessary. The only exception occurs when you have dropped words at the end of the final quoted sentence. In such cases, put three ellipsis dots before the closing quotation mark and parenthetical reference.

USING SOURCES RESPONSIBLY: Make sure omissions and ellipsis marks do not distort the meaning of your source.

Brackets Brackets allow you to insert your own words into quoted material. You can insert words in brackets to clarify a confusing reference or to keep a sentence grammatical in your context. You also use brackets to indicate that you are changing a letter from capital to lowercase (or vice versa) to fit into your sentence.

> Neergaard and Agiesta argue that "a new poll finds people are split on how much the government should do to help [find solutions to the national health crisis]—and most draw the line at attempts to force healthier eating."

In this example, the writer inserted words in brackets to clarify the meaning of *help*.

To indicate an error such as a misspelling in a quotation, insert [sic], including the brackets, right after the error.

> "While Americans of every race, gender and ethnicity are affected by this disease, diabetes disproportionately effects [sic] minority populations."

Do not overuse [sic] to call attention to errors in a source. Sometimes paraphrasing is a better option. (See 39c.)

Setting off long quotations

When you quote more than four typed lines of prose or more than three lines of poetry, set off the quotation by indenting it one inch from the left margin.

Long quotations should be introduced by an informative sentence, often followed by a colon. Quotation marks are unnecessary because the indented format tells readers that the passage is taken word-for-word from the source.

> In response to critics who claim that laws aimed at stopping us from eating whatever we want are an assault on our freedom of choice, Conly offers a persuasive counterargument:
>
> > [L]aws aren't designed for each one of us individually. Some of us can drive safely at 90 miles per hour, but we're bound by the same laws as the people who can't, because individual speeding laws aren't practical. Giving up a little liberty is something we agree to when we agree to live in a democratic society that is governed by laws. (A23)

Notice that at the end of an indented quotation the parenthetical citation goes outside the final mark of punctuation. (When a quotation is run into your text, the opposite is true. See the sample citations on p. 448.)

55c Use signal phrases to integrate sources.

Whenever you include a paraphrase, summary, or direct quotation of another writer's work in your paper, prepare your readers for it with introductory words called a *signal phrase.* A signal phrase usually names the author of the source and often provides some context for the source material.

Using signal phrases in MLA papers

To avoid monotony, try to vary both the language and the placement of your signal phrases.

Model signal phrases

Michael Pollan, who has written extensively about Americans' unhealthy eating habits, argues that ". . ."

As health policy experts Mello, Studdert, and Brennan point out, ". . ."

Marion Nestle, New York University professor of nutrition and public health, notes, ". . ."

Conly offers a persuasive counterargument: ". . ."

Verbs in signal phrases

acknowledges	comments	endorses	reasons
adds	compares	grants	refutes
admits	confirms	illustrates	rejects
agrees	contends	implies	reports
argues	declares	insists	responds
asserts	denies	notes	suggests
believes	disputes	observes	thinks
claims	emphasizes	points out	writes

When you write a signal phrase, choose a verb that is appropriate for the way you are using the source. Are you providing background, explaining a concept, supporting a claim, lending authority, or refuting a belief (see 53c)? Refer to the chart on page 450 for a list of verbs commonly used in signal phrases.

NOTE: MLA style calls for verbs in the present or present perfect tense (*argues, has argued*) to introduce source material unless you include a date that specifies the time of the original author's writing.

Marking boundaries

Readers need to move from your words to the words of a source without feeling a jolt. Avoid dropping quotations into the text without warning. Instead, provide clear signal phrases, including at least the author's name, to indicate the boundary between your words and the source's words. (The signal phrase is highlighted in the second example.)

DROPPED QUOTATION

> Laws designed to prevent chronic disease by promoting healthier food and beverage consumption also have potential economic benefits. "[A] 1% reduction in the intake of saturated fat across the population would prevent more than 30,000 cases of coronary heart disease annually and would save more than a billion dollars in health care costs" (Nestle 7).

QUOTATION WITH SIGNAL PHRASE

> Laws designed to prevent chronic disease by promoting healthier food and beverage consumption also have potential economic benefits. Marion Nestle, New York University professor of nutrition and public health, notes that "a 1% reduction in the intake of saturated fat across the population would prevent more than 30,000 cases of coronary heart disease annually and would save more than a billion dollars in health care costs" (7).

Establishing authority

The first time you mention a source, include in the signal phrase the author's title, credentials, or experience to help your readers recognize the source's authority and your own credibility as a responsible researcher who has located reliable sources. (Signal phrases are highlighted in the next two examples.)

SOURCE WITH NO CREDENTIALS

Michael Pollan notes that "the Centers for Disease Control estimates that fully three quarters of US health care spending goes to treat chronic diseases, most of which are preventable and linked to diet: heart disease, stroke, type 2 diabetes, and at least a third of all cancers."

SOURCE WITH CREDENTIALS

Journalist Michael Pollan, who has written extensively about Americans' unhealthy eating habits, notes that "the Centers for Disease Control estimates that fully three quarters of US health care spending goes to treat chronic diseases, most of which are preventable and linked to diet: heart disease, stroke, type 2 diabetes, and at least a third of all cancers."

Introducing summaries and paraphrases

Introduce most summaries and paraphrases with a signal phrase that names the author and places the material in the context of your argument. (See also 55c.) Readers will then understand that everything between the signal phrase and the parenthetical citation summarizes or paraphrases the cited source.

Without the signal phrase (highlighted) in the following example, readers might think that only the quotation at the end is being cited, when in fact the whole paragraph is based on the source.

To improve public health, advocates such as Bowdoin College philosophy professor Sarah Conly contend that it is the government's duty to prevent people from making harmful choices whenever feasible and whenever public benefits outweigh the costs. In response to critics who claim that laws aimed at stopping us from eating whatever we want are an assault on our freedom of choice, Conly asserts that "laws aren't designed for each one of us individually" (A23).

There are times when a summary or a paraphrase does not require a signal phrase naming the author. When the context makes clear where the cited material begins, you may omit the signal phrase and include the author's last name in parentheses.

Using signal phrases with statistics and other facts

When you cite a statistic or another specific fact, a signal phrase is often not necessary. Readers usually will understand that the citation refers to the statistic or fact (not the whole paragraph).

> Seventy-five percent of Americans are opposed to laws that restrict or put limitations on access to unhealthy foods (Neergaard and Agiesta).

There is nothing wrong, however, with using signal phrases to introduce statistics or other facts.

Putting source material in context

Readers should not have to guess why source material appears in your paper. A signal phrase can help you make the connection between your own ideas and those of another writer by clarifying how the source will contribute to your paper (see 52a).

If you use another writer's words, you must explain how they relate to your argument. Quotations don't speak for themselves; you must support them by creating a context for readers. Embed each quotation between sentences of your own: Introduce the quotation with a signal phrase, and follow it with interpretive comments that link the quotation to your paper's argument (see also 55d).

QUOTATION WITH EFFECTIVE CONTEXT

> In response to critics who claim that laws aimed at stopping us from eating whatever we want are an assault on our freedom of choice, Conly offers a persuasive counterargument:
>
> > [L]aws aren't designed for each one of us individually. Some of us can drive safely at 90 miles per hour, but we're bound by the same laws as the people who can't, because individual speeding laws aren't practical. Giving up a little

> liberty is something we agree to when we agree to live in a democratic society that is governed by laws. (A23)

As Conly suggests, we need to change our either/or thinking (either we have complete freedom of choice *or* we have government regulations and lose our freedom) and instead need to see health as a matter of public good, not individual liberty.

55d Synthesize sources.

When you synthesize multiple sources in a research paper, you create a conversation about your research topic. Your argument includes your active analysis and integration of ideas, not just a series of quotations and paraphrases. Your synthesis will show how your sources relate to one another; one source may support, extend, or counter the ideas of another. Not every source has to "speak" to another in a research paper, but readers should be able to see how each one functions in your argument (see 52a).

Considering how sources relate to your argument

Before you integrate sources and show readers how they relate to one another, consider how each one might contribute to your own argument. As student writer Sophie Harba became more informed about her research topic, she asked herself these questions: *What have I learned from my sources? Which sources might support my ideas or illustrate the points I want to make? What counterarguments do I need to address to strengthen my position?* She annotated a passage from one of her sources—a nonprofit group's assertion that our choices about food are skewed by marketing messages.

STUDENT NOTES ON THE ORIGINAL SOURCE

useful factual information

The food and beverage industry spends approximately $2 billion per year marketing to children. — "Facts on Junk Food"

could use this to counter the point about personal choice in Mello et al.

Placing sources in conversation

You can show readers how the ideas of one source relate to those of another by connecting and analyzing the ideas in your own voice. After all, you've done the research and thought through the issues, so you should control the conversation. When you effectively synthesize sources, the emphasis is still on your own writing; the thread of your argument should be easy to identify and to understand, with or without your sources.

SAMPLE SYNTHESIS

Student writer Sophie Harba sets up her synthesis with a question.

A signal phrase indicates how the source contributes to Harba's argument and shows that the idea that follows is not her own.

Harba interprets a paraphrased source.

Harba uses a source to support her counter-argument.

Why is the public largely resistant to laws that would limit unhealthy choices or penalize those choices with so-called fat taxes? Many consumers and civil rights advocates find such laws to be an unreasonable restriction on individual freedom of choice. [Student writer] As health policy experts Mello, Studdert, and Brennan point out, opposition to food and beverage regulation is similar to the opposition to early tobacco legislation: the public views the issue as one of personal responsibility rather than one requiring government intervention (2602). [Source 1] In other words, if a person eats unhealthy food and becomes ill as a result, that is his or her choice. But those who favor legislation claim that freedom of choice is a myth because of the strong influence of food and beverage industry marketing on consumers' dietary habits. [Student writer] According to one nonprofit health advocacy group, food and beverage companies spend roughly two billion dollars per year marketing directly to children. As a result, kids see about four thousand ads per year encouraging them to consume unhealthy food and drinks ("Facts on Junk Food"). [Source 2] As was the case with antismoking laws passed in recent decades, taxes and legal restrictions on junk food sales could help to counter the strong marketing messages that promote unhealthy products. [Student writer]

The United States has a history of state and local public health laws that have successfully promoted a particular behavior by punishing an undesirable behavior. The decline in tobacco use as a result of antismoking taxes and laws is perhaps the most obvious example. Another example is legislation requiring the use of seat belts, which have significantly reduced fatalities in car crashes. One government agency reports that seat belt use saved an average of more than fourteen thousand lives per year in the United States between 2000 and 2010 (United States, Dept. of Transportation, Natl. Highway Traffic Safety Administration 231). Perhaps seat belt laws have public support because the cost of wearing a seat belt is small, especially when compared with the benefit of saving fourteen thousand lives per year.

Harba uses a statistic to extend the argument and follows the source with a closing thought of her own.

Source 3

Student writer

In this synthesis, Harba uses her own analysis to shape the conversation among her sources. She does not simply string quotations together or allow them to overwhelm her writing. She guides her readers through a conversation about a variety of laws that could promote and have promoted public health. She finds points of intersection among her sources, acknowledges the contributions of others in the research conversation, and shows readers, in her own voice, how the various sources support her argument.

When synthesizing sources, ask yourself the following questions:

- How do your sources speak to your research question?
- How do your sources speak to each other?
- Have you varied the function of sources — to provide background, to explain concepts, to lend authority, and to anticipate counterarguments?
- Do you connect and analyze sources in your own voice?
- Is your own argument easy to identify and to understand, with or without your sources?

Reviewing an MLA paper: Use of sources

Use of quotations

- Have you used quotation marks around quoted material (unless it has been set off from the text)? (See 54b.)
- Have you checked that quoted language is word-for-word accurate? If not, do ellipsis marks or brackets indicate the omissions or changes? (See pp. 448–49.)
- Does a clear signal phrase (usually naming the author) prepare readers for each quotation and for the purpose the quotation serves? (See 55c.)
- Does a parenthetical citation follow each quotation? (See 56a.)
- Have you embedded each quotation between sentences of your own to put the source in context? (See 55c.)

Use of summaries and paraphrases

- Are summaries and paraphrases free of plagiarized wording — not copied or half-copied from the source? (See 54b.)
- Are summaries and paraphrases documented with parenthetical citations? (See 54b and 56a.)
- Do readers know where the cited material begins? In other words, does a signal phrase mark the boundary between your words and the summary or paraphrase? Or does the context alone make clear exactly what you are citing? (See 55c.)
- Does a signal phrase prepare readers for the purpose the summary or paraphrase has in your argument?

Use of statistics and other facts

- Are statistics and facts (other than common knowledge) documented with parenthetical citations? (See 54b and 56a.)
- If there is no signal phrase, will readers understand exactly which facts are being cited? (See 55c.)

56 Documenting sources in MLA style

In English and other humanities classes, you may be asked to use the MLA (Modern Language Association) system for documenting sources, which is set forth in the *MLA Handbook for Writers of Research Papers*, 7th ed. (New York: MLA, 2009).

MLA recommends in-text citations that refer readers to a list of works cited. A typical in-text citation names the author of the source, often in a signal phrase, and gives a page number in parentheses. At the end of the paper, the list of works cited provides publication information about the source; the list is alphabetized by authors' last names (or by titles for works without authors). There is a direct connection between the in-text citation and the alphabetical listing. In the following example, that connection is highlighted.

IN-TEXT CITATION

Bioethicist David Resnik emphasizes that such policies, despite their potential to make our society healthier, "open the door to excessive government control over food, which could restrict dietary choices, interfere with cultural, ethnic, and religious traditions, and exacerbate socioeconomic inequalities" (31).

ENTRY IN THE LIST OF WORKS CITED

Resnik, David. "Trans Fat Bans and Human Freedom." *American Journal of Bioethics* 10.3 (2010): 27-32. *Academic Search Premier*. Web. 17 Apr. 2013.

For a list of works cited that includes this entry, see page 524.

56a MLA in-text citations

MLA in-text citations are made with a combination of signal phrases and parenthetical references. A signal phrase introduces information taken from a source (a quotation, summary, paraphrase, or fact); usually the signal phrase includes the author's name. The parenthetical reference comes after the cited material, often at the end of the sentence. It includes at least a page number (except for unpaginated sources, such as those found on the Web). In the models in 56a, the elements of the in-text citation are highlighted.

IN-TEXT CITATION

> Resnik acknowledges that his argument relies on "slippery slope" thinking, but he insists that "social and political pressures" regarding food regulation make his concerns valid (31).

Readers can look up the author's last name in the alphabetized list of works cited, where they will learn the work's title and other publication information. If readers decide to consult the source, the page number will take them straight to the cited passage.

General guidelines for signal phrases and page numbers

Items 1–5 explain how the MLA system usually works for all sources — in print, on the Web, in other media, and with or without authors and page numbers. Items 6–27 give variations on the basic guidelines.

■ **1. Author named in a signal phrase** Ordinarily, introduce the material being cited with a signal phrase that includes the author's name. In addition to preparing readers for the source, the signal phrase allows you to keep the parenthetical citation brief.

> According to Lorine Goodwin, a food historian, nineteenth-century reformers who sought to purify the food supply were called "fanatics" and "radicals" by critics who argued that consumers should be free to buy and eat what they want (77).

The signal phrase — *According to Lorine Goodwin* — names the author; the parenthetical citation gives the page number of the book in which the quoted words may be found.

Notice that the period follows the parenthetical citation. When a quotation ends with a question mark or an exclamation point, leave the end punctuation inside the quotation mark and add a period at the end of your sentence. (See the example at the top of page 460.)

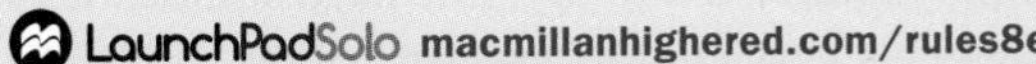

LaunchPadSolo **macmillanhighered.com/rules8e**

56 Documenting sources in MLA style

> Exercises: 56-1 to 56-3

Burgess asks a critical question: "How can we think differently about food labeling?" (51).

■ **2. Author named in parentheses** If you do not give the author's name in a signal phrase, put the last name in parentheses along with the page number (if the source has one). Use no punctuation between the name and the page number: (Moran 351).

According to a nationwide poll, 75% of Americans are opposed to laws that restrict or put limitations on access to unhealthy foods (Neergaard and Agiesta).

■ **3. Author unknown** If a source has no author, the works cited entry will begin with the title. In your in-text citation, either use the complete title in a signal phrase or use a short form of the title in parentheses. Titles of books and other long works are italicized; titles of articles and other short works are put in quotation marks (see also p. 514).

As a result, kids see nearly four thousand ads per year encouraging them to eat unhealthy food and drinks ("Facts on Junk Food").

NOTE: If the author is a corporation or a government agency, see items 8 and 17 on pages 462 and 465, respectively.

■ **4. Page number unknown** Do not include the page number if a work lacks page numbers, as is the case with many Web sources. Do not use page numbers from a printout from a Web site. (When the pages of a Web source are stable, as in PDF files, supply a page number in your in-text citation.)

Michael Pollan points out that "cheap food" actually has "significant costs—to the environment, to public health, to the public purse, even to the culture."

If a source has numbered paragraphs or sections, use "par." (or "pars.") or "sec." (or "secs.") in the parentheses: (Smith, par. 4). Notice that a comma follows the author's name.

■ **5. One-page source** If the source is one page long, MLA allows (but does not require) you to omit the page number. It's a good idea to include the page number because without it readers may not know where your citation ends or, worse, may not realize that you have provided a citation at all.

NO PAGE NUMBER IN CITATION

Sarah Conly uses John Stuart Mill's "harm principle" to argue that citizens need their government to intervene to prevent them from taking harmful actions—such as driving too fast or buying unhealthy foods—out of ignorance of the harm they can do. But government intervention may overstep in the case of food choices.

PAGE NUMBER IN CITATION

Sarah Conly uses John Stuart Mill's "harm principle" to argue that citizens need their government to intervene to prevent them from taking harmful actions—such as driving too fast or buying unhealthy foods—out of ignorance of the harm they can do (A23). But government intervention may overstep in the case of food choices.

Variations on the general guidelines

This section describes the MLA guidelines for handling a variety of situations not covered in items 1–5.

■ **6. Two or three authors** Name the authors in a signal phrase, as in the following example, or include their last names in the parenthetical reference: (Gostin and Gostin 214).

As legal scholars Gostin and Gostin explain, "[I]nterventions that do not pose a truly significant burden on individual liberty" are justified if they "go a long way towards safeguarding the health and well-being of the populace" (214).

When you name three authors in the parentheses, separate the names with commas: (Alton, Davies, and Rice 56).

■ **7. Four or more authors** Name all authors or include only the first author's name followed by "et al." (Latin for "and others"). The format you use should match the format in your works cited entry (see item 3 on p. 472).

The study was extended for two years, and only after results were reviewed by an independent panel did the researchers publish their findings (Blaine et al. 35).

■ **8. Organization as author** When the author is a corporation or an organization, name that author either in the signal phrase or in the parentheses. (For a government agency as author, see item 17 on p. 465.)

The American Diabetes Association estimates that the cost of diagnosed diabetes in the United States in 2012 was $245 billion.

In the list of works cited, the American Diabetes Association is treated as the author and alphabetized under *A*. When you give the organization name in parentheses, abbreviate common words in the name: "Assn.," "Dept.," "Natl.," "Soc.," and so on.

The cost of diagnosed diabetes in the United States in 2012 was estimated at $245 billion (Amer. Diabetes Assn.).

■ **9. Authors with the same last name** If your list of works cited includes works by two or more authors with the same last name, include the author's first name in the signal phrase or first initial in the parentheses.

One approach to the problem is to introduce nutrition literacy at the K-5 level in public schools (E. Chen 15).

■ **10. Two or more works by the same author** Mention the title of the work in the signal phrase or include a short version of the title in the parentheses.

The American Diabetes Association tracks trends in diabetes across age groups. In 2012, more than 200,000 children and adolescents had diabetes ("Fast Facts"). Because of an expected dramatic increase in diabetes in young people over the next forty years, the association encourages "strategies for implementing childhood obesity prevention programs and primary prevention programs for youth at risk of developing type 2 diabetes" ("Number of Youth").

Titles of articles and other short works are placed in quotation marks; titles of books and other long works are italicized. (See also p. 514.)

In the rare case when both the author's name and a short title must be given in parentheses, separate them with a comma.

> Researchers have estimated that "the number of youth with type 2 [diabetes] could quadruple and the number with type 1 could triple" by 2050, "with an increasing proportion of youth with diabetes from minority populations" (Amer. Diabetes Assn., "Number of Youth").

■ **11. Two or more works in one citation** To cite more than one source in the parentheses, list the authors (or titles) in alphabetical order and separate them with a semicolon.

> The prevalence of early-onset Type 2 diabetes has been well documented (Finn 68; Sharma 2037; Whitaker 118).

It may be less distracting to use an information note for multiple citations (see 56c).

■ **12. Repeated citations from the same source** When you are writing about a single work, you do not need to include the author's name each time you quote from or paraphrase the work. After you mention the author's name at the beginning of your paper, you may include just the page number in your parenthetical citations.

> In Susan Glaspell's short story "A Jury of Her Peers," two women accompany their husbands and a county attorney to an isolated house where a farmer named John Wright has been choked to death in his bed with a rope. The chief suspect is Wright's wife, Minnie, who is in jail awaiting trial. The sheriff's wife, Mrs. Peters, has come along to gather some personal items for Minnie, and Mrs. Hale has joined her. Early in the story, Mrs. Hale sympathizes with Minnie and objects to the way the male investigators are "snoopin' round and criticizin'" her kitchen (249). In contrast, Mrs. Peters shows respect for the law, saying that the men are doing "no more than their duty" (249).

In a paper with multiple sources, if you are citing a source more than once in a paragraph, you may omit the author's name after the first mention in the paragraph as long as it is clear that you are still referring to the same source.

■ **13. Encyclopedia or dictionary entry** When an encyclopedia or a dictionary entry does not have an author, it will be alphabetized in the list of works cited under the word or entry that you consulted (see item 28 on p. 486). Either in your text or in your parenthetical citation, mention the word or entry. No page number is required because readers can easily look up the word or entry.

> The word *crocodile* has a complex etymology ("Crocodile").

■ **14. Multivolume work** If your paper cites more than one volume of a multivolume work, indicate in the parentheses the volume you are referring to, followed by a colon and the page number.

> In his studies of gifted children, Terman describes a pattern of accelerated language acquisition (2: 279).

If you cite only one volume of a multivolume work, you will include the volume number in the list of works cited and will not need to include it in the parentheses. (See the second example in item 38 on p. 493.)

■ **15. Entire work** Use the author's name in a signal phrase or a parenthetical citation. There is no need to use a page number.

> Pollan explores the issues surrounding food production and consumption from a political angle.

■ **16. Selection in an anthology** Put the name of the author of the selection (not the editor of the anthology) in the signal phrase or the parentheses.

> In "Love Is a Fallacy," the narrator's logical teachings disintegrate when Polly declares that she should date Petey because "[h]e's got a raccoon coat" (Shulman 391).

In the list of works cited, the work is alphabetized under *Shulman*, the author of the story, not under the name of the editor of the anthology. (See item 35 on p. 491.)

Shulman, Max. "Love Is a Fallacy." *Current Issues and Enduring Questions*. Ed. Sylvan Barnet and Hugo Bedau. 9th ed. Boston: Bedford, 2011. 383-91. Print.

■ **17. Government document** When a government agency is the author, you will alphabetize it in the list of works cited under the name of the government, such as United States or Great Britain (see item 72 on p. 510). For this reason, you must name the government as well as the agency in your in-text citation.

> One government agency reports that seat belt use saved an average of more than fourteen thousand lives per year in the United States between 2000 and 2010 (United States, Dept. of Transportation, Natl. Highway Traffic Safety Administration 231).

■ **18. Historical document** For a historical document, such as the United States Constitution or the Canadian Charter of Rights and Freedoms, provide the document title, neither italicized nor in quotation marks, along with relevant article and section numbers. In parenthetical citations, use common abbreviations such as "art." and "sec." and abbreviations of well-known titles: (US Const., art. 1, sec. 2).

> While the United States Constitution provides for the formation of new states (art. 4, sec. 3), it does not explicitly allow or prohibit the secession of states.

Cite other historical documents as you would any other work, by the first element in the works cited entry (see item 74 on p. 510).

■ **19. Legal source** For a legislative act (law) or court case, name the act or case either in a signal phrase or in parentheses. Italicize the names of cases but not the names of acts. (See also items 75 and 76 on p. 511.)

> The Jones Act of 1917 granted US citizenship to Puerto Ricans.

> In 1857, Chief Justice Roger B. Taney declared in *Dred Scott v. Sandford* that blacks, whether enslaved or free, could not be citizens of the United States.

■ **20. Visual such as a table, a chart, or another graphic** To cite a visual that has a figure number in the source, use the abbreviation "fig." and the number in place of a page number in your parenthetical citation: (Manning, fig. 4). If you refer to the figure in your text, spell out the word "figure" in the text.

To cite a visual that does not have a figure number in a print source, use the visual's title or a description in your text and cite the author and page number as for any other source.

For a visual not in a print source, identify the visual in your text and then in parentheses use the first element in the works cited entry: the artist's or photographer's name or the title of the work. (See items 65–70 on pp. 505–8.)

> Photographs such as *Woman Aircraft Worker* (Bransby) and *Women Welders* (Parks) demonstrate the US government's attempt to document the contributions of women during World War II.

■ **21. Personal communication and social media** Cite personal letters, personal interviews, e-mail messages, and social media posts by the name listed in the works cited entry, as you would for any other source. Identify the type of source in your text if you feel it is necessary for clarity. (See items 27d, 29c, and 77–81 in section 56b.)

■ **22. Web source** Your in-text citation for a source from the Web should follow the same guidelines as for other sources. If the source lacks page numbers but has numbered paragraphs, sections, or divisions, use those numbers with the appropriate abbreviation in your in-text citation: "par.," "sec.," "ch.," "pt.," and so on. Do not add such numbers if the source itself does not use them; simply give the author or title in your in-text citation.

> Julian Hawthorne points out profound differences between his father and Ralph Waldo Emerson but concludes that, in their lives and their writing, "together they met the needs of nearly all that is worthy in human nature" (ch. 4).

■ **23. Indirect source (source quoted in another source)** When a writer's or a speaker's quoted words appear in a source written by someone else, begin the parenthetical citation with the abbreviation "qtd. in." (See also item 12 on p. 476.) In the following example, Gostin and Gostin are the authors of the source given in the works cited list; the source contains a quotation by Beauchamp.

Public health researcher Dan Beauchamp has said that "public health practices are 'communal in nature, and concerned with the well-being of the community as a whole and not just the well-being of any particular person'" (qtd. in Gostin and Gostin 217).

Literary works and sacred texts

Literary works and sacred texts are usually available in a variety of editions. Your list of works cited will specify which edition you are using, and your in-text citation will usually consist of a page number from the edition you consulted (see item 24). When possible, give enough information — such as book parts, play divisions, or line numbers — so that readers can locate the cited passage in any edition of the work (see items 25–27).

■ **24. Literary work without parts or line numbers** Many literary works, such as most short stories and many novels and plays, do not have parts or line numbers. In such cases, simply cite the page number.

> At the end of Kate Chopin's "The Story of an Hour," Mrs. Mallard drops dead upon learning that her husband is alive. In the final irony of the story, doctors report that she has died of a "joy that kills" (25).

■ **25. Verse play or poem** For verse plays, give act, scene, and line numbers that can be located in any edition of the work. Use arabic numerals and separate the numbers with periods.

> In Shakespeare's *King Lear*, Gloucester, blinded for suspected treason, learns a profound lesson from his tragic experience: "A man may see how this world goes / with no eyes" (4.2.148-49).

For a poem, cite the part, stanza, and line numbers, if it has them, separated by periods.

> The Green Knight claims to approach King Arthur's court "because the praise of you, prince, is puffed so high, / And your manor and your men are considered so magnificent" (1.12.258-59).

For poems that are not divided into numbered parts or stanzas, use line numbers. For a first reference, use the word "lines": (lines 5–8). Thereafter use just the numbers: (12–13).

■ **26. Novel with numbered divisions** When a novel has numbered divisions, put the page number first, followed by a semicolon, and then the book, part, or chapter in which the passage may be found. Use abbreviations such as "bk.," "pt.," and "ch."

> One of Kingsolver's narrators, teenager Rachel, pushes her vocabulary beyond its limits. For example, Rachel complains that being forced to live in the Congo with her missionary family is "a sheer tapestry of justice" because her chances of finding a boyfriend are "dull and void" (117; bk. 2, ch. 10).

■ **27. Sacred text** When citing a sacred text such as the Bible or the Qur'an, name the edition you are using in your works cited entry (see item 39 on p. 493). In your parenthetical citation, give the book, chapter, and verse (or their equivalent), separated with periods. Common abbreviations for books of the Bible are acceptable.

> Consider the words of Solomon: "If your enemy is hungry, give him bread to eat; and if he is thirsty, give him water to drink" (*Oxford Annotated Bible*, Prov. 25.21).

The title of a sacred work is italicized when it refers to a specific edition of the work, as in the preceding example. If you refer to the book in a general sense in your text, neither italicize it nor put it in quotation marks (see also the note on p. 344 in section 42a).

> The Bible and the Qur'an provide allegories that help readers understand how to lead a moral life.

56b MLA list of works cited

The elements you will need for the works cited list will differ slightly for some sources, but the main principles apply to all sources, whether in print or from the Web: You should identify an author, a creator, or a producer whenever possible; give a title; provide the date on which the source was produced; and indicate the medium of delivery. Some sources will require page numbers;

some will require a sponsoring person or organization; and some will require other identifying information.

Section 56b provides details for how to cite many of the sources you are likely to encounter. It also provides hints for what you can do when a source does not match one of the models exactly. When you cite sources, your goals are to show that your sources are reliable and relevant, to provide readers with enough information to find sources easily, and to provide that information consistently according to MLA conventions.

▸ Directory to MLA works cited models, page 432
▸ General guidelines for the works cited list, page 470

General guidelines for listing authors

The formatting of authors' names in items 1–12 applies to all sources — books, articles, Web sites — in print, on the Web, or in other media. For more models of specific source types, see items 13–81.

1. Single author

author: last name first | title (book) | city of publication | publisher | date | medium

Bowker, Gordon. *James Joyce: A New Biography*. New York: Farrar, 2012. Print.

2. Two or three authors

first author: last name first | second author: in normal order | title (book) | city of publication | publisher | date | medium

Gourevitch, Philip, and Errol Morris. *Standard Operating Procedure*. New York: Penguin, 2008. Print.

first author: last name first | other authors: in normal order | title (newspaper article) | newspaper title | date of publication | page | medium

Farmer, John, John Azzarello, and Miles Kara. "Real Heroes, Fake Stories." *New York Times* 14 Sept. 2008: WK10. Print.

General guidelines for the works cited list

In the list of works cited, include only sources that you have quoted, summarized, or paraphrased in your paper.

Authors and titles

- Arrange the list alphabetically by authors' last names or by titles for works with no authors.
- For the first author, place the last name first, a comma, and the first name. For subsequent authors, put their names in normal order (first name followed by last name).
- In titles of works, capitalize all words except articles (*a*, *an*, *the*), prepositions (*at*, *between*, *from*, *under*, and so on), coordinating conjunctions (*and*, *but*, *or*, *nor*, *for*, *so*, *yet*), and the *to* in infinitives—unless the word is first or last in the title or subtitle.
- Use quotation marks for titles of articles and other short works.
- Italicize titles of books and other long works.

Place of publication and publisher

- For sources that require a place of publication, give the city of publication without a state or country name.
- Shorten publishers' names, usually to the first principal word ("Wiley" for "John Wiley and Sons," for instance). For university publishers, use "U" and "P" for "University" and "Press": UP of Florida.
- If a work has two publishers, give the city and name for both (in the order listed on the title page), separated with a semicolon.
- List a sponsor or a publisher for most sources from the Web.
- If a source has no sponsor or publisher, use "N.p." (for "No publisher").
- For a work found in a database, give the title of the database but not a sponsor.

Dates

- For a print source, give the most recent date on the title page or the copyright page.
- For a Web source, use the copyright date or the most recent update.
- For books and for most journals, use the year of publication.
- For monthly magazines, use the month and the year. Abbreviate all months except May, June, and July.

- For weekly magazines and newspapers, give the day, month, and year, with no commas (18 Feb. 2013). Abbreviate all months except May, June, and July.
- If there is no date of publication or update, use "n.d." (for "no date").
- For sources found on the Web or in a database, give your date of access.

Page numbers

- For most articles and other short works, give page numbers when they are available.
- If page numbers are not available (as is often the case with sources on the Web), use "n. pag." (for "no pagination") in place of page numbers.
- Do not use the page numbers from a printout of a source.
- If an article does not appear on consecutive pages, give the number of the first page followed by a plus sign: 35+.

Medium

- Include the medium in which a work was published, produced, or delivered.
- Capitalize the medium, but do not italicize it or put it in quotation marks.
- Typical designations for the medium are "Print," "Web," "Radio," "Television," "CD," "Film," "DVD," "Photograph," "Performance," "Lecture," "MP3 file," and "PDF file."

URLs

- MLA guidelines assume that readers can locate most Web sources by entering the author, title, or other identifying information in a search engine or a database. Consequently, MLA does not require a URL in citations for Web sources.
- If your instructor requires a URL, see the note at the end of item 47.

3. Four or more authors Either name all the authors or name the first author followed by "et al." (Latin for "and others"). In an in-text citation, use the same form for the authors' names as you use in the works cited entry. See item 7 on page 461.

first author: last name first | other authors: in normal order

Leech, Geoffrey, Marianne Hundt, Christian Mair, and Nicholas Smith.

title (book) | city of publication

Change in Contemporary English: A Grammatical Study. Cambridge:

publisher | year | medium

Cambridge UP, 2009. Print.

4. Organization or company as author

author: organization name, not abbreviated | title (book)

National Geographic. *National Geographic Visual Atlas of the World*.

city of publication | publisher, with common abbreviations | date | medium

Washington: Natl. Geographic Soc., 2008. Print.

Your in-text citation also should treat the organization as the author (see item 8 on p. 462).

5. No author listed

a. Article or other short work

article title | label | newspaper title (city in brackets)

"Policing Ohio's Online Courses." Editorial. *Plain Dealer* [Cleveland]

date | page(s) | medium

9 Oct. 2012: A5. Print.

article title | title of long work | title of Web site

"Chapter 2: What Can Be Patented?" *Inventor's Handbook*. *Lemelson-MIT*.

sponsor | no date | medium | date of access

Massachusetts Inst. of Technology, n.d. Web. 31 Oct. 2013.

b. Television program

(episode title) "Fast Times at West Philly High." (title of TV show) *Frontline*. (producer) Prod. Debbie Morton. (network) PBS.
(local station, city) KTWU, Topeka, (date of broadcast) 4 Dec. 2012. (medium) Television.

c. Book, entire Web site, or other long work

(title (Web site)) *Women of Protest: Photographs from the Records of the National Woman's Party*.
(sponsor) Lib. of Cong., (no date) n.d. (medium) Web. (date of access) 29 Sept. 2013.

TIP: Often the author's name is available but is not easy to find. It may appear at the end of the page, in tiny print, or on another page of the site, such as the home page. Also, an organization or a government may be the author (see items 4 and 72).

■ **6. Two or more works by the same author** First alphabetize the works by title (ignoring the article *A*, *An*, or *The* at the beginning of a title). Use the author's name for the first entry; for subsequent entries, use three hyphens and a period. The three hyphens must stand for exactly the same name as in the first entry.

García, Cristina. *Dreams of Significant Girls*. New York: Simon, 2011. Print.

---. *The Lady Matador's Hotel*. New York: Scribner, 2010. Print.

■ **7. Two or more works by the same group of authors** To list multiple works by the same group of two or more authors, alphabetize the works by title (ignoring the article *A*, *An*, or *The* at the beginning of a title). Use all authors' names for the first entry; begin subsequent entries with three hyphens and a period. The three hyphens must stand for all the authors' names.

Agha, Hussein, and Robert Malley. "The Arab Counterrevolution." *New York Review of Books*. NYREV, 29 Sept. 2011. Web. 12 Dec. 2013.

---. "This Is Not a Revolution." *New York Review of Books*. NYREV, 8 Nov. 2012. Web. 12 Dec. 2013.

■ **8. Editor or translator** Begin with the editor's or translator's name. For one editor, use "ed." after the name; for more than one, use "eds." Use "trans." for one or more translators. (See p. 474.)

first editor: last name first — other editor(s): in normal order — title (book) — city of publication — publisher — year — medium

Jones, Russell M., and John H. Swanson, eds. *Dear Helen: Wartime Letters from a Londoner to Her American Pen Pal*. Columbia: U of Missouri P, 2009. Print.

■ **9. Author with editor or translator** Begin with the name of the author. Place the editor's or translator's name after the title. "Ed." or "Trans." means "Edited by" or "Translated by," so it is the same for one or more editors or translators.

author: last name first — title (book) — translator: in normal order — city of publication — publisher — year — medium

Scirocco, Alfonso. *Garibaldi: Citizen of the World*. Trans. Allan Cameron. Princeton: Princeton UP, 2007. Print.

How to answer the basic question "Who is the author?"

PROBLEM: Sometimes when you need to cite a source, it's not clear who the author is. This is especially true for sources on the Web or other nonprint sources, which may have been created by one person and uploaded by a different person or an organization. Whom do you cite as the author in such a case? How do you determine who *is* the author?

EXAMPLE: The video "Surfing the Web on the Job" (see below) was uploaded to YouTube by CBSNewsOnline. Is the person or organization who uploads the video the author of the video? Not necessarily.

Surfing the Web on The Job

Uploaded on Nov 12, 2009
As the Internet continues to emerge as a critical facet of everyday life, CBS News' Daniel Sieberg reports that companies are cracking down on employees' personal Web use.

10. Graphic narrative or other illustrated work If a work has both an author and an illustrator, the order in your citation will depend on which of those persons you emphasize in your paper. (See also p. 476.)

a. Author first If you emphasize the author's work, begin with the author's name. After the title, use the abbreviation "Illus." (meaning "Illustrated by") followed by the illustrator's name.

Moore, Alan. *V for Vendetta*. Illus. David Lloyd. New York: Vertigo-DC Comics, 2008. Print.

b. Illustrator first If you emphasize the illustrator, begin your citation with the illustrator's name, followed by the abbreviation "illus." (meaning "illustrator"). After the title of the work, put the author's name, preceded by "By."

Weaver, Dustin, illus. *The Tenth Circle*. By Jodi Picoult. New York: Washington Square, 2006. Print.

STRATEGY: After you view or listen to the source a few times, ask yourself whether you can tell who is chiefly responsible for creating the content in the source. It could be an organization. It could be an identifiable individual. This video consists entirely of reporting by Daniel Sieberg, so in this case the author is Sieberg.

CITATION: To cite the source, you would use the basic MLA guidelines for a video found on the Web (item 56).

author: last name first | title of video | Web site title | sponsor

Sieberg, Daniel. "Surfing the Web on the Job." *YouTube*. YouTube, 12 Nov. 2009. Web. 26 Nov. 2012.

update date | medium | date of access

If you want to include the person or organization who uploaded the video, you can add it as supplementary information at the end.

author: last name first | title of video | Web site title | sponsor

Sieberg, Daniel. "Surfing the Web on the Job." *YouTube*. YouTube, 12 Nov. 2009. Web. 26 Nov. 2012. Uploaded by CBSNewsOnline.

update date | medium | date of access | supplementary information

■ **10. Graphic narrative or other illustrated work (*cont.*)**

c. Author and illustrator the same person If the illustrator and the author are the same person, cite the work as you would any other work with one author (not using the label "illus." or "by").

Smith, Lane. *Abe Lincoln's Dream*. New York: Roaring Brook, 2012. Print.

■ **11. Author using a pseudonym (pen name) or screen name** Give the author's name as it appears in the source (the pseudonym), followed by the author's real name, if available, in brackets. (For screen names in social media, see items 80 and 81 on p. 512.)

Grammar Girl [Mignon Fogarty]. "When Are Double Words OK?" *Grammar Girl: Quick and Dirty Tips for Better Writing*. Macmillan, 28 Sept. 2012. Web. 10 Nov. 2013.

Pauline. Comment. "Is This the End?" By James Atlas. *New York Times*. New York Times, 25 Nov. 2012. Web. 29 Nov. 2013.

■ **12. Author quoted by another author (indirect source)** If one of your sources uses a quotation from another source and you'd like to use the quotation, provide a works cited entry for the source in which you found the quotation. In your in-text citation, indicate that the quoted words appear in the source (see item 23 on p. 466). In the following examples, Belmaker is the source in the works cited list; Townson is quoted in Belmaker.

SOURCE (BELMAKER) QUOTING ANOTHER SOURCE (TOWNSON)

> Peter Townson, a journalist working with the DOHA Center for Press Freedom in Qatar, says there is one obvious reason that some countries in the Middle East have embraced social media so heartily. "It's kind of the preferred way for people to get news, because they know there's no self-censorship involved," Townson said in a phone interview.

WORKS CITED ENTRY

Belmaker, Genevieve. "Five Ways Journalists Can Use Social Media for On-the-Ground Reporting in the Middle East." *Poynter*. Poynter Inst., 20 Nov. 2012. Web. 24 Nov. 2013.

IN-TEXT CITATION

Peter Townson points out that social media in the Middle East are "kind of the preferred way for people to get news, because they know there's no self-censorship involved" (qtd. in Belmaker).

Articles and other short works

▸ Citation at a glance: Article in a journal, page 478
▸ Citation at a glance: Article from a database, page 480

13. Basic format for an article or other short work

a. Print

author: last name first | article title

Ferris, William R. "Southern Literature: A Blending of Oral, Visual, and Musical Voices." *Daedalus* 141.1 (2012): 139-53. Print.

journal title | volume, issue | year | page(s) | medium

b. Web

author: last name first | title of short work

Sonderman, Jeff. "Survey: Public Prefers News from Professional Journalists." *Poynter*. Poynter Inst., 29 Aug. 2012. Web. 31 Oct. 2013.

title of Web site | sponsor | update date | medium | date of access

c. Database

author: last name first | article title | journal title

Emanuel, Lynn Collins. "The Noirs: Collecting the Evidence." *American Poetry Review* 41.6 (2012): 6. *General OneFile*. Web. 14 Dec. 2013.

volume, issue | year | page(s) | database title | medium | date of access

14. Article in a journal

a. Print

author: last name first | article title

Fuqua, Amy. "'The Furrow of His Brow': Providence and Pragmatism in Toni Morrison's *Paradise*." *Midwest Quarterly* 54.1 (2012): 38-52. Print.

journal title | volume, issue | year | page(s) | medium

Citation at a glance
Article in a journal (MLA)

To cite an article in a print journal in MLA style, include the following elements:

1 Author(s) of article
2 Title and subtitle of article
3 Title of journal
4 Volume and issue numbers (if any)
5 Year of publication
6 Page number(s) of article
7 Medium

JOURNAL TABLE OF CONTENTS

FIRST PAGE OF ARTICLE

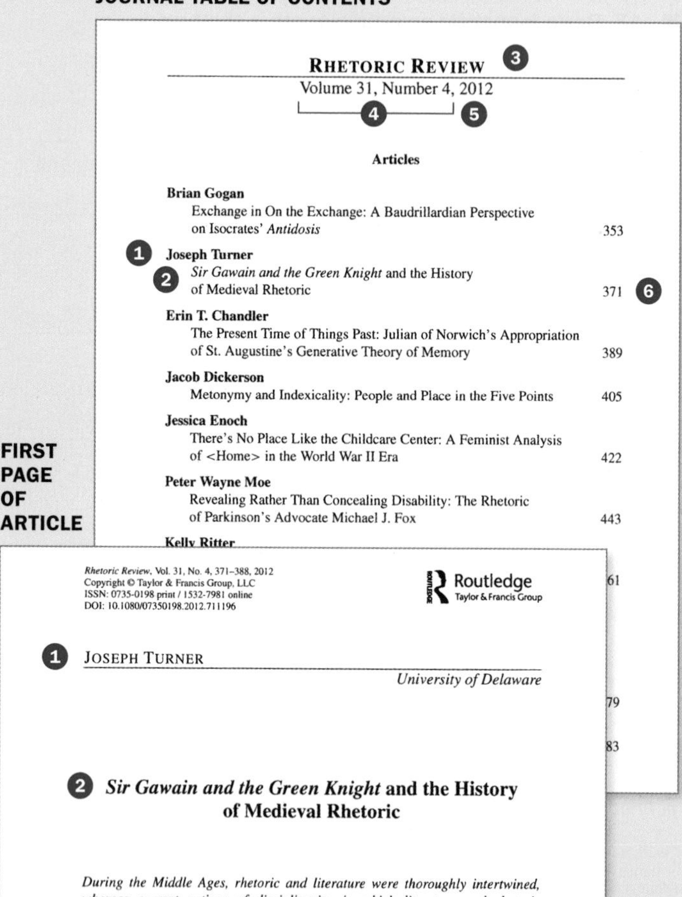

RHETORIC REVIEW 3
Volume 31, Number 4, 2012
4 5
Articles
Brian Gogan
Exchange in On the Exchange: A Baudrillardian Perspective on Isocrates' *Antidosis* 353
1 Joseph Turner
2 *Sir Gawain and the Green Knight* and the History of Medieval Rhetoric 371 6
Erin T. Chandler
The Present Time of Things Past: Julian of Norwich's Appropriation of St. Augustine's Generative Theory of Memory 389
Jacob Dickerson
Metonymy and Indexicality: People and Place in the Five Points 405
Jessica Enoch
There's No Place Like the Childcare Center: A Feminist Analysis of <Home> in the World War II Era 422
Peter Wayne Moe
Revealing Rather Than Concealing Disability: The Rhetoric of Parkinson's Advocate Michael J. Fox 443
Kelly Ritter
Rhetoric Review, Vol. 31, No. 4, 371–388, 2012
Copyright © Taylor & Francis Group, LLC
ISSN: 0735-0198 print / 1532-7981 online
DOI: 10.1080/07350198.2012.711196
Routledge
Taylor & Francis Group
1 JOSEPH TURNER
University of Delaware
2 *Sir Gawain and the Green Knight* and the History of Medieval Rhetoric
During the Middle Ages, rhetoric and literature were thoroughly intertwined, whereas current notions of disciplinarity, in which literature and rhetoric are constructed as separate traditions, muddy our understanding of medieval

WORKS CITED ENTRY FOR AN ARTICLE IN A PRINT JOURNAL

1 | 2
Turner, Joseph. "*Sir Gawain and the Green Knight* and the History of

3 | 4 | 5 | 6 | 7
Medieval Rhetoric." *Rhetoric Review* 31.4 (2012): 371-88. Print.

For more on citing articles in MLA style, see items 13–16.

■ 14. Article in a journal (*cont.*)

b. Online journal

author: last name first | article title
Cáceres, Sigfrido Burgos. "Towards Concert in Africa: Seeking Progress and

journal title | volume, issue
Power through Cohesion and Unity." *African Studies Quarterly* 12.4

year | page(s) | medium | date of access
(2011): 59-73. Web. 31 Oct. 2013.

c. Database

author: last name first | article title
Maier, Jessica. "A 'True Likeness': The Renaissance City Portrait."

journal title | volume, issue | year | page(s) | database title | medium | date of access
Renaissance Quarterly 65.3 (2012): 711-52. *JSTOR*. Web. 30 Aug. 2013.

■ 15. Article in a magazine

a. Print (monthly)

author: last name first | article title | magazine title | date | page(s)
Bryan, Christy. "Ivory Worship." *National Geographic* Oct. 2012: 28-61.

medium
Print.

b. Print (weekly)

author: last name first | article title | magazine title | date | page(s) | medium
Vick, Karl. "The Stateless Statesman." *Time* 15 Oct. 2012: 32-37. Print.

Citation at a glance
Article from a database (MLA)

To cite an article from a database in MLA style, include the following elements:

1. Author(s) of article
2. Title and subtitle of article
3. Title of journal, magazine, or newspaper
4. Volume and issue numbers (for journal)
5. Date or year of publication
6. Page number(s) of article ("n. pag." if none)
7. Name of database
8. Medium
9. Date of access

DATABASE RECORD

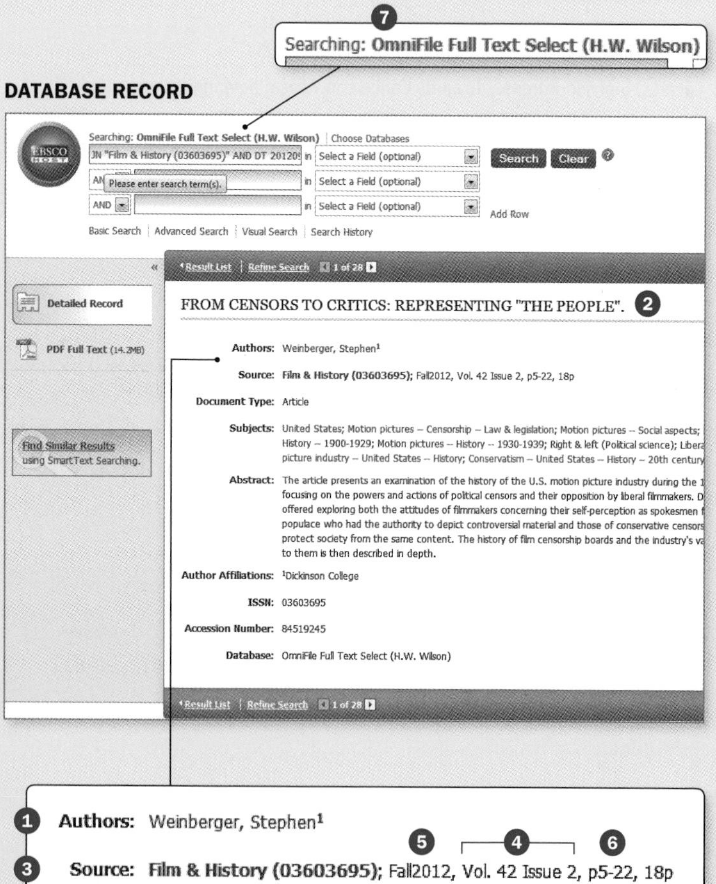

WORKS CITED ENTRY FOR AN ARTICLE FROM A DATABASE

1 | 2
Weinberger, Stephen. "From Censors to Critics: Representing 'the People.'"

3 | 4 | 5 | 6 | 7 | 8
Film & History 42.2 (2012): 5-22. *OmniFile Full Text Select*. Web.

9
12 Jan. 2014.

For more on citing articles from a database in MLA style, see items 13–16.

■ 15. Article in a magazine (*cont.*)

c. Web

d. Database

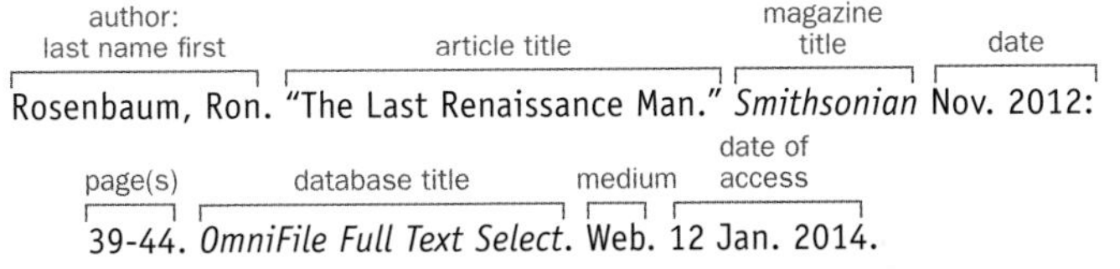

■ 16. Article in a newspaper

If the city of publication is not obvious from the title of the newspaper, include the city in brackets after the newspaper title (see item 5a).

a. Print If sections are numbered, include the section number between the date and the page number: 14 Sept. 2013, sec. 2: 21.

author: last name first | article title
Sherry, Allison. "Volunteers' Personal Touch Turns High-Tech Data into Votes."

newspaper title | date | page(s) | medium
Denver Post 30 Oct. 2012: 1A+. Print.

b. Web

author: last name first | article title

Amos, Adria. "STEM Teacher Uses 'Flip' Method to Put Classroom Focus on

Web site title | sponsor

Students, Not Educator." *Knoxnews.com*. Knoxville News Sentinel,

date | medium | date of access

1 Oct. 2012. Web. 29 Oct. 2013.

c. E-reader

article title | newspaper title | date | page(s) | medium

"Church Votes No on Female Bishops." *Boston Globe* 21 Nov. 2012: A3. E-reader.

d. Database

article title | label | newspaper title | date | page(s)

"The Road toward Peace." Editorial. *New York Times* 15 Feb. 1945: 18.

database title | medium

ProQuest Historical Newspapers: The New York Times. Web.

date of access

18 June 2013.

■ **17. Abstract or executive summary** Include the label "Abstract" or "Executive summary," neither italicized nor in quotation marks, after the title of the work.

a. Abstract of an article

Bottomore, Stephen. "The Romance of the Cinematograph." Abstract. *Film History* 24.3 (2012): 341-44. *General OneFile*. Web. 25 Oct. 2013.

b. Abstract of a paper

Dixon, Rosemary, Dmitri Iourinski, and Kyle B. Roberts. "The Opportunities and Challenges of Virtual Library Systems: A Case Study." Abstract. Paper presented at the 2011 Chicago Colloquium on Digital Humanities and Computer Science. U of Chicago. 20 Nov. 2011. Web. 28 Nov. 2013.

c. Abstract of a dissertation

Chen, Shu-Ling. "Mothers and Daughters in Morrison, Tan, Marshall, and Kincaid." Diss. U of Washington, 2000. *DAI* 61.6 (2000): AAT9975963. *ProQuest Dissertations and Theses*. Web. 22 Feb. 2013.

d. Executive summary

Pintak, Lawrence. *The Murrow Rural Information Initiative: Final Report*. Executive summary. Pullman: Murrow Coll. of Communication, Washington State U, 25 May 2012. PDF file.

■ **18. Article with a title in its title** Use single quotation marks around a title of a short work or a quoted term that appears in an article title. Italicize a title or term normally italicized.

Silber, Nina. "From 'Great Emancipator' to 'Vampire Hunter': The Many Stovepipe Hats of Cinematic Lincoln." *Cognoscenti*. WBUR, 22 Nov. 2012. Web. 13 Dec. 2013.

■ **19. Editorial** Cite as a source with no author (see item 5) and use the label "Editorial" following the article title.

"New State for the US?" Editorial. *Columbus Dispatch*. Dispatch Printing, 24 Nov. 2012. Web. 27 Nov. 2013.

■ **20. Unsigned article** Cite as a source with no author (see item 5).

"Public Health Response to a Changing Climate." *Centers for Disease Control and Prevention*. Centers for Disease Control and Prevention, 1 Oct. 2012. Web. 31 Oct. 2013.

"Harper's Index." *Harper's Magazine* Feb. 2012: 11. Print.

■ **21. Letter to the editor** Use the label "Letter" after the title. If the letter has no title, place the label after the author's name.

Fahey, John A. "Recalling the Cuban Missile Crisis." Letter. *Washington Post* 28 Oct. 2012: A16. *LexisNexis Library Express*. Web. 15 Dec. 2013.

22. Comment on an online article If the writer of the comment uses a screen name, see item 11. After the name, include the label "Comment" followed by the title of the article and the author of the article (preceded by "By"). Continue with publication information for the article.

author: screen name | label | article title

pablosharkman. Comment. "'We Are All Implicated': Wendell Berry Laments a Disconnection from Community and the Land." By Scott Carlson. *Chronicle of Higher Education*. Chronicle of Higher Educ., 23 Apr. 2012. Web. 30 Oct. 2013.

author of article | Web site title | sponsor | update date | medium | date of access

23. Paper or presentation at a conference If the paper or presentation is included in the proceedings of a conference, cite it as a selection in an anthology (see item 35; see also item 45 for proceedings of a conference). If you viewed the presentation live, cite it as a lecture or public address (see item 62).

first author: last name first | other contributors: in normal order

Zuckerman, Ethan, with Tim Berners-Lee, Esther Dyson, Jaron Lanier, and Kaitlin Thaney. "Big Data, Big Challenges, and Big Opportunities." Presentation at Wired for Change: The Power and the Pitfalls of Big Data. Ford Foundation, New York. 15 Oct. 2012. Web. 30 Oct. 2013.

presentation title | label | conference title | conference sponsor | location | date | medium | date of access

24. Book review Name the reviewer and the title of the review, if any, followed by "Rev. of" and the title and author of the work reviewed. Add the publication information for the publication in which the review appears. If the review has no author and no title, begin with "Rev. of" and alphabetize the entry by the first principal word in the title of the work reviewed.

a. Print

Flannery, Tim. "A Heroine in Defense of Nature." Rev. of *On a Farther Shore: The Life and Legacy of Rachel Carson*, by William Souder. *New York Review of Books* 22 Nov. 2012: 21-23. Print.

b. Web

Telander, Alex C. "In an MMO Far Far Away." Rev. of *Omnitopia Dawn*, by Diane Duane. *San Francisco Book Review*. 1776 Productions, 17 Jan. 2012. Web. 8 Aug. 2013.

c. Database

Petley, Christer. Rev. of *The Atlantic World and Virginia, 1550-1624*, by Peter C. Mancall. *Caribbean Studies* 38.1 (2008): 175-77. *JSTOR*. Web. 14 Oct. 2013.

■ **25. Film review or other review** Name the reviewer and the title of the review, if any, followed by "Rev. of" and the title and writer or director of the work reviewed. Add the publication information for the publication in which the review appears. If the review has no author and no title, begin with "Rev. of" and alphabetize the entry by the first principal word in the title of the work reviewed.

a. Print

Lane, Anthony. "Film within a Film." Rev. of *Argo*, dir. Ben Affleck, and *Sinister*, dir. Scott Derrickson. *New Yorker* 15 Oct. 2012: 98-99. Print.

b. Web

Cobbett, Richard. "World of Warcraft: *Mists of Pandaria* Review." Rev. of *Mists of Pandaria*, by Blizzard Entertainment. *PC Gamer*. Future Publishing, 4 Oct. 2012. Web. 13 Oct. 2013.

■ **26. Performance review** Name the reviewer and the title of the review, if any, followed by "Rev. of" and the title and author of the work reviewed. Add the publication information for the publication in which the review appears. If the review has no author and no title, begin with "Rev. of" and alphabetize the entry by the first principal word in the title of the work reviewed.

Matson, Andrew. Rev. of *Until the Quiet Comes*, by Flying Lotus. *Seattle Times*. Seattle Times, 31 Oct. 2012. Web. 10 Nov. 2013.

■ **27. Interview** Begin with the person interviewed, followed by the title of the interview (if there is one). If the interview does not have a title, include the word "Interview" after the interviewee's name. If you wish to include the name of the interviewer, put it after the title of the interview (or after the name of the interviewee if there is no title). (See also item 60 for citing transcripts of interviews.)

a. Print

Weddington, Sarah. "Sarah Weddington: Still Arguing for *Roe*." Interview by Michele Kort. *Ms*. Winter 2013: 32-35. Print.

b. Web

Kapoor, Anil. "Anil Kapoor on Q." Interview by Jian Ghomeshi. *Q*. CBC Radio, n.d. Web. 29 Oct. 2013.

c. Television or radio

Buffett, Warren, and Carol Loomis. Interview by Charlie Rose. *Charlie Rose*. PBS. WGBH, Boston, 26 Nov. 2012. Television.

d. Personal To cite an interview that you conducted, begin with the name of the person interviewed. Then write "Personal interview" or "Telephone interview," followed by the date of the interview.

Akufo, Dautey. Personal interview. 11 Apr. 2013.

■ **28. Article in a reference work (encyclopedia, dictionary, wiki)** List the author of the entry (if there is one), the title of the entry, the title of the reference work, the edition number (if any), the date of the edition, and the medium. Page numbers are not necessary, even for print sources, because the entries in the source are arranged alphabetically and are therefore easy to locate.

a. Print

Posner, Rebecca. "Romance Languages." *The Encyclopaedia Britannica: Macropaedia*. 15th ed. 1987. Print.

"Sonata." *The American Heritage Dictionary of the English Language*. 5th ed. 2011. Print.

b. Web

"Hip Hop Music." *Wikipedia*. Wikimedia Foundation, 19 Nov. 2012. Web. 18 Dec. 2013.

Durante, Amy M. "Finn Mac Cumhail." *Encyclopedia Mythica*. Encyclopedia Mythica, 17 Apr. 2011. Web. 20 Nov. 2013.

29. Letter

a. Print Begin with the writer of the letter, the words "Letter to" and the recipient, and the date of the letter (use "N.d." if it is undated). Add the title of the collection, the editor, and publication information. Add the page range before the medium.

Wharton, Edith. Letter to Henry James. 28 Feb. 1915. *Henry James and Edith Wharton: Letters, 1900-1915*. Ed. Lyall H. Powers. New York: Scribner's, 1990. 323-26. Print.

b. Web After information about the letter writer, recipient, and date (if known), give the name of the Web site or archive, italicized; the date of posting; the medium ("Web"); and your date of access.

Oblinger, Maggie. Letter to Charlie Thomas. 31 Mar. 1895. *Prairie Settlement: Nebraska Photographs and Family Letters, 1862-1912*. Lib. of Cong., 15 Sept. 2000. Web. 3 Sept. 2013.

c. Personal To cite a letter that you received, begin with the writer's name and add the phrase "Letter to the author," followed by the date. Add the medium ("MS" for "manuscript," or a handwritten letter; "TS" for "typescript," or a typed letter).

Primak, Shoshana. Letter to the author. 6 May 2013. TS.

Books and other long works

▶ Citation at a glance: Book, page 489

30. Basic format for a book

a. Print

author: last name first | book title | city | publisher | date | medium

Wolfe, Tom. *Back to Blood*. New York: Little, 2012. Print.

b. E-book

author: last name first | book title | translators: in normal order

Tolstoy, Leo. *War and Peace*. Trans. Richard Pevear and Larissa Volokhonsky.

city | publisher | date | medium

New York: Knopf, 2007. Nook file.

c. Web Give whatever print publication information is available for the work, followed by the title of the Web site, the medium, and your date of access.

author: last name first | book title | contributor(s): in normal order

Thoreau, Henry David. *Thoreau's Walden*. Ed. and introd. Raymond MacDonald Alden.

city | publisher | original date | series | Web site title

New York: Longmans, 1910. Longmans' English Classics. *Google Books*.

medium | date of access

Web. 31 Oct. 2013.

Saalman, Lora, ed. and trans. *The China-India Nuclear Crossroads*. Washington: Carnegie Endowment for Intl. Peace, 2012. *Scribd*. Web. 27 Nov. 2013.

d. Database

author: last name first | book title

Cullender, Rose. *A Tryal of Witches at the Assizes Held at Bury St. Edmonds for the Count of Suffolk on the Tenth Day of March, 1664*. London, 1682.

city and date of original

database title | medium | date of access

Early English Books Online. Web. 29 Apr. 2013.

Citation at a glance
Book (MLA)

To cite a print book in MLA style, include the following elements:

1 Author(s)
2 Title and subtitle
3 City of publication
4 Publisher
5 Date of publication (latest date)
6 Medium

TITLE PAGE

FROM COPYRIGHT PAGE

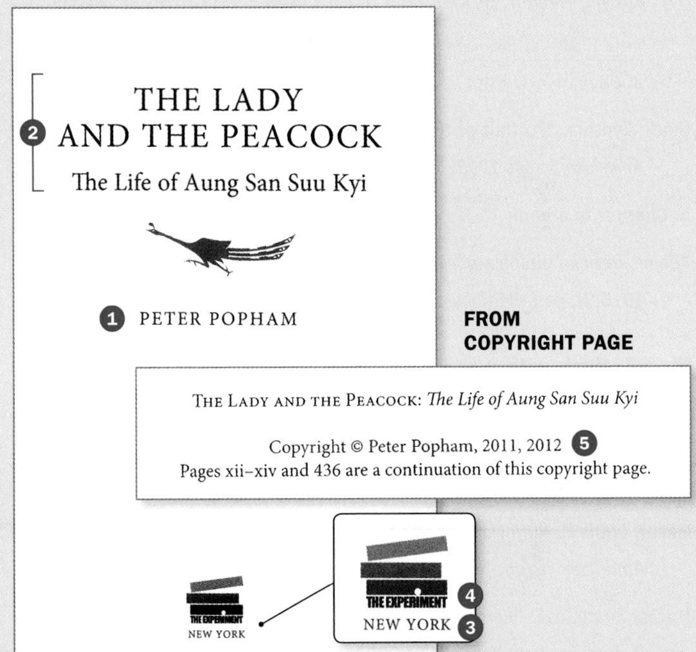

THE LADY AND THE PEACOCK
2
The Life of Aung San Suu Kyi
1 PETER POPHAM
THE EXPERIMENT
NEW YORK
THE LADY AND THE PEACOCK: The Life of Aung San Suu Kyi
Copyright © Peter Popham, 2011, 2012 5
Pages xii–xiv and 436 are a continuation of this copyright page.
THE EXPERIMENT 4
NEW YORK 3

WORKS CITED ENTRY FOR A PRINT BOOK

1 — Popham, Peter. 2 — *The Lady and the Peacock: The Life of Aung San Suu Kyi*. 3 — New York: 4 — Experiment, 5 — 2012. 6 — Print.

For more on citing books in MLA style, see items 30–42.

31. Parts of a book

a. *Foreword, introduction, preface, or afterword*

author of foreword: last name first | book part | book title | author of book: in normal order | city | imprint-publisher | date | page(s) | medium

Bennett, Hal Zina. Foreword. *Shimmering Images: A Handy Little Guide to Writing Memoir*. By Lisa Dale Norton. New York: Griffin-St. Martin's, 2008. xiii-xvi. Print.

Ozick, Cynthia. "Portrait of the Essay as a Warm Body." Introduction. *The Best American Essays 1998*. Ed. Ozick. Boston: Houghton, 1998. xv-xxi. Print.

b. *Chapter in a book*

Adams, Henry. "Diplomacy." *The Education of Henry Adams*. Boston: Houghton, 1918. N. pag. *Bartleby.com: Great Books Online*. Web. 8 Dec. 2013.

32. Book with a title in its title If the book title contains a title normally italicized, neither italicize the internal title nor place it in quotation marks. If the title within the title is normally put in quotation marks, retain the quotation marks and italicize the entire book title.

Masur, Louis P. *Runaway Dream:* Born to Run *and Bruce Springsteen's American Vision*. New York: Bloomsbury, 2009. Print.

Millás, Juan José. *"Personality Disorders" and Other Stories*. Trans. Gregory B. Kaplan. New York: MLA, 2007. Print.

33. Book in a language other than English Capitalize the title according to the conventions of the book's language. If your readers are not familiar with the language, include a translation of the title in brackets.

Vargas Llosa, Mario. *El sueño del celta* [*The Dream of the Celt*]. Madrid: Alfaguara, 2010. Print.

34. Entire anthology or collection An anthology is a collection of works, often with various authors and an editor for the entire volume. (The abbreviation "eds." is for multiple editors. If the book has only one editor, use the singular "ed.")

first editor: last name first | other editor(s): in normal order | title of anthology

Belasco, Susan, and Linck Johnson, eds. *The Bedford Anthology of American Literature*. Vol. 2. Boston: Bedford, 2008. Print.

volume | city | publisher | date | medium

35. One selection from an anthology or a collection

▸ Citation at a glance: Selection from an anthology or a collection, page 492

author of selection | title of selection | title of anthology

Lorde, Audre. "Black Mother Woman." *The Bedford Anthology of American Literature*. Ed. Susan Belasco and Linck Johnson. Vol. 2. Boston: Bedford, 2008. 1419. Print.

editor(s) of anthology | volume | city | publisher | date | page(s) | medium

36. Two or more selections from an anthology or a collection

For two or more works from the same anthology, provide an entry for the entire anthology (see item 34) and a shortened entry for each selection. Use the medium only for the complete anthology. Alphabetize the entries by authors' or editors' last names.

first editor: last name first | other editor(s): in normal order | title of anthology

Belasco, Susan, and Linck Johnson, eds. *The Bedford Anthology of American Literature*. Vol. 2. Boston: Bedford, 2008. Print.

volume | city | publisher | date | medium

author of selection | title of selection | editor(s) of anthology | page(s)

Lorde, Audre. "Black Mother Woman." Belasco and Johnson 1419.

author of selection | title of selection | editor(s) of anthology | page(s)

Silko, Leslie Marmon. "Yellow Woman." Belasco and Johnson 1475-81.

37. Edition other than the first Include the number of the edition (2nd, 3rd, and so on). If the book has a translator or an editor in addition to the author, give the name of the translator or editor before the edition number, using the abbreviation "Trans." for "Translated by" or "Ed." for "Edited by" (see item 9).

Eagleton, Terry. *Literary Theory: An Introduction*. 3rd ed. Minneapolis: U of Minnesota P, 2008. Print.

Citation at a glance

Selection from an anthology or a collection (MLA)

To cite a selection from an anthology in MLA style, include the following elements:

1. Author(s) of selection
2. Title and subtitle of selection
3. Title and subtitle of anthology
4. Editor(s) of anthology
5. City of publication
6. Publisher
7. Date of publication
8. Page numbers of selection
9. Medium

FIRST PAGE OF SELECTION

CHAPTER 3

Technology's Quiet Revolution for Women (2)

Isobel Coleman (1)

ary 2011 revolution, I happened to be in th Gamila Ismail, a longtime Egyptian pent decades opposing the Mubarak morrow?" I asked her, referring to the d for the next day in Tahrir Square. "It monitoring Twitter and Facebook feeds a young assistant had spent weeks help-ation through social media. "We think ople could join the protest. This could change." Indeed.

role of social media in the Arab upris-s given voice to youth and women in al media is just the latest in a long line driving profound changes in civil soci-irst notions of community developed

ncil on Foreign Relations, is the Director of the Coun-acy Initiative and CFR's Women and Foreign Policy Beneath Her Feet: How Women Are Transforming *and a contributing author to* Restoring the Balance: *esident (Brookings Institution Press, 2008). She has and Women Action Area at the Clinton Global Ini-one of "150 Women Who Shake the World."*

41 — 41 (8)

TITLE PAGE OF ANTHOLOGY

(3) THE UNFINISHED **REVOLUTION**

VOICES FROM THE GLOBAL FIGHT FOR WOMEN'S RIGHTS

EDITED BY MINKY WORDEN (4)

(6) Seven Stories Press
(5) NEW YORK

7
Seven Stories Press
NEW YORK

FROM COPYRIGHT PAGE

(7)
Copyright © 2012 by Minky Worden
Individual chapters © 2012 by each author

WORKS CITED ENTRY FOR A SELECTION FROM AN ANTHOLOGY

1 — Coleman, Isobel. 2 — "Technology's Quiet Revolution for Women." 3 — *The Unfinished Revolution: Voices from the Global Fight for Women's Rights.* 4 — Ed. Minky Worden. 5 — New York: 6 — Seven Stories, 7 — 2012. 8 — 41-49. 9 — Print.

Coleman, Isobel. "Technology's Quiet Revolution for Women." *The Unfinished Revolution: Voices from the Global Fight for Women's Rights.* Ed. Minky Worden. New York: Seven Stories, 2012. 41-49. Print.

For more on citing selections from anthologies in MLA style, see items 34–36.

■ **38. Multivolume work** Include the total number of volumes before the city and publisher, using the abbreviation "vols." If the volumes were published over several years, give the inclusive dates of publication. (The abbreviation "Ed." means "Edited by," so it is the same for one or more editors.)

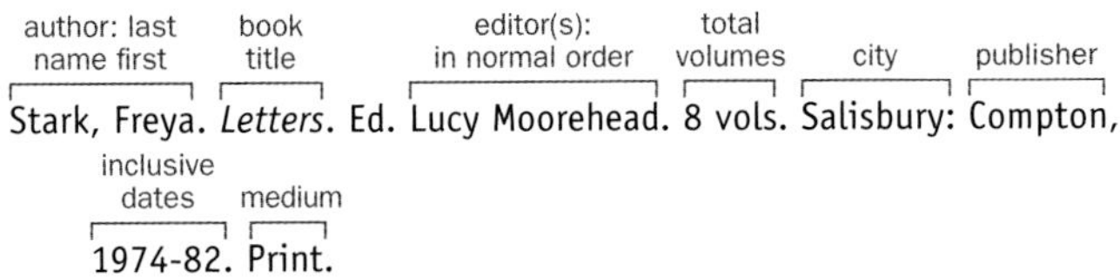

If you cite only one of the volumes in your paper, include the volume number before the city and publisher and give the date of publication for that volume. After the date, give the medium of publication followed by the total number of volumes.

author: last name first | book title | editor(s): in normal order | volume cited | city | publisher | date of volume | medium | total volumes

Stark, Freya. *Letters*. Ed. Lucy Moorehead. Vol. 5. Salisbury: Compton, 1978. Print. 8 vols.

■ **39. Sacred text** Give the title of the edition (taken from the title page), italicized; the editor's or translator's name (if any); publication information; and the medium. Add the name of the version, if there is one, after the medium.

The Oxford Annotated Bible with the Apocrypha. Ed. Herbert G. May and Bruce M. Metzger. New York: Oxford UP, 1965. Print. Rev. Standard Vers.

The Qur'an: Translation. Trans. Abdullah Yusuf Ali. Elmhurst: Tahrike, 2000. Print.

■ **40. Book in a series** After the publication information, give the medium and then the series name as it appears on the title page, followed by the series number, if any.

Denham, A. E., ed. *Plato on Art and Beauty*. New York: Palgrave, 2012. Print. Philosophers in Depth.

■ **41. Republished book** After the title of the book, give the original year of publication, followed by the current publication information. If the republished book contains new material, such as an introduction or an afterword, include information about the new material after the original date.

Trilling, Lionel. *The Liberal Imagination*. 1950. Introd. Louis Menand. New York: New York Rev. of Books, 2008. Print.

■ **42. Publisher's imprint** Give the name of the imprint (a division of a publishing company), a hyphen, and the name of the publisher.

Mantel, Hilary. *Bring Up the Bodies*. New York: Macrae-Holt, 2012. Print.

■ **43. Pamphlet, brochure, or newsletter** Cite as you would a book.

The Legendary Sleepy Hollow Cemetery. Concord: Friends of Sleepy Hollow Cemetery, 2008. Print.

■ **44. Dissertation**

a. Published For dissertations that have been published in book form, italicize the title. After the title and before the book's publication information, give the abbreviation "Diss.," the name of the institution, and the year the dissertation was accepted. Add the medium of publication at the end.

Damberg, Cheryl L. *Healthcare Reform: Distributional Consequences of an Employer Mandate for Workers in Small Firms*. Diss. Rand Graduate School, 1995. Santa Monica: Rand, 1996. Print.

b. Unpublished Begin with the author's name, followed by the dissertation title in quotation marks; the abbreviation "Diss."; the name of the institution; the year the dissertation was accepted; and the medium of the dissertation.

Jackson, Shelley. "Writing Whiteness: Contemporary Southern Literature in Black and White." Diss. U of Maryland, 2000. Print.

■ **45. Proceedings of a conference** Cite as you would a book, adding the name, date, and location of the conference after the title.

Sowards, Stacey K., Kyle Alvarado, Diana Arrieta, and Jacob Barde, eds. *Across Borders and Environments: Communication and Environmental Justice in International Contexts*. Proc. of Eleventh Biennial Conf. on Communication and the Environment, 25-28 June 2011, U of Texas at El Paso. Cincinnati: Intl. Environmental Communication Assn., 2012. PDF file.

■ **46. Manuscript** Give the author, a title or a description of the manuscript, and the date of composition. Use the abbreviation "MS" for "manuscript" (handwritten) or "TS" for "typescript." Add the name and location of the institution housing the material. For a manuscript found on the Web, give the preceding information but omit "MS" or "TS." List the title of the Web site, the medium ("Web"), and your date of access.

Arendt, Hannah. *Between Past and Future*. N.d. 1st draft. Hannah Arendt Papers. MS Div., Lib. of Cong. *Manuscript Division, Library of Congress*. Web. 24 Aug. 2013.

Web sites and parts of Web sites

■ 47. An entire Web site

a. Web site with author or editor

author or editor: last name first | title of Web site | sponsor

Railton, Stephen. *Mark Twain in His Times*. Stephen Railton and U of Virginia Lib., 2012. Web. 27 Nov. 2013.

update date | medium | date of access

Halsall, Paul, ed. *Internet Modern History Sourcebook*. Fordham U, 4 Nov. 2011. Web. 19 Sept. 2013.

47. An entire Web site (*cont.*)

b. Web site with organization as author

government | department | title of Web site | sponsor

United States. Dept. of Agriculture. *USDA*. US Dept. of Agriculture,

update date | medium | date of access

12 Feb. 2014. Web. 3 Mar. 2014.

c. Web site with no author Begin with the title of the site. If the site has no title, begin with a label such as "Home page."

Jacob Leisler Papers Project. Dept. of History, New York U, n.d. Web. 24 Aug. 2013.

d. Web site with no title Use the label "Home page" or another appropriate description in place of a title.

Gray, Bethany. Home page. Iowa State U, 2013. Web. 22 Sept. 2013.

NOTE: If your instructor requires a URL for Web sources, include the URL, enclosed in angle brackets, at the end of the entry.

Railton, Stephen. *Mark Twain in His Times*. Stephen Railton and U of Virginia Lib., 2012. Web. 27 Nov. 2013. <http://twain.lib.virginia.edu/>.

48. Short work from a Web site

▸ Citation at a glance: Short work from a Web site, page 497

a. Short work with author

author: last name first | title of short work | title of Web site

Gallagher, Sean. "The Last Nomads of the Tibetan Plateau." *Pulitzer Center*

sponsor | update date | medium | date of access

on Crisis Reporting. Pulitzer Center, 25 Oct. 2012. Web. 30 Oct. 2013.

b. Short work with no author

title of article | title of Web site

"Social and Historical Context: Vitality." *Arapesh Grammar and Digital Language*

sponsor | no date

Archive Project. Inst. for Advanced Technology in the Humanities, n.d.

medium | date of access

Web. 18 Feb. 2014.

Citation at a glance

Short work from a Web site (MLA)

To cite a short work from a Web site in MLA style, include the following elements:

1 Author(s) of short work (if any)
2 Title and subtitle of short work
3 Title and subtitle of Web site
4 Sponsor of Web site ("N.p." if none)
5 Latest update date ("n.d." if none)
6 Medium
7 Date of access

INTERNAL PAGE OF WEB SITE

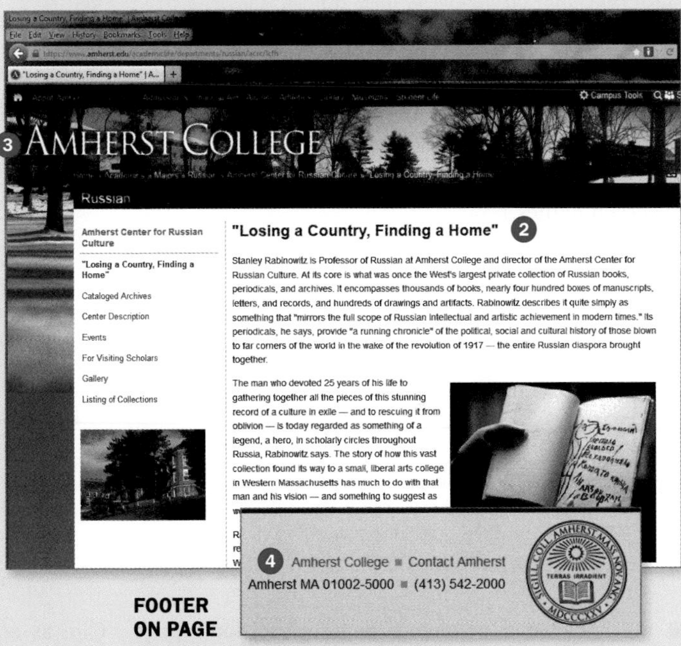

Courtesy of the Trustees of Amherst College. Reproduced by permission.

WORKS CITED ENTRY FOR A SHORT WORK FROM A WEB SITE

(2) "Losing a Country, Finding a Home." (3) *Amherst College.* (4) Amherst Coll., (5) n.d.
(6) Web. (7) 12 Jan. 2013.

For more on citing sources from Web sites in MLA style, see items 48 and 49.

49. Long work from a Web site

author: last name first — title of long work — title of Web site — sponsor

Milton, John. *Paradise Lost: Book I*. *Poetry Foundation*. Poetry Foundation,

update date — medium — date of access

2014. Web. 10 Mar. 2014.

50. Entire blog

Cite a blog as you would an entire Web site (see item 47).

Kiuchi, Tatsuro. *Tatsuro Kiuchi: News & Blog*. N.p., n.d. Web. 29 Oct. 2013.

51. Blog post or comment

Cite a blog post or comment (a response to a post) as you would a short work from a Web site (see item 48). If the post or comment has no title, use the label "Blog post" or "Blog comment." Follow with the remaining information as for an entire blog (see item 50). (See item 11 for the use of screen names.)

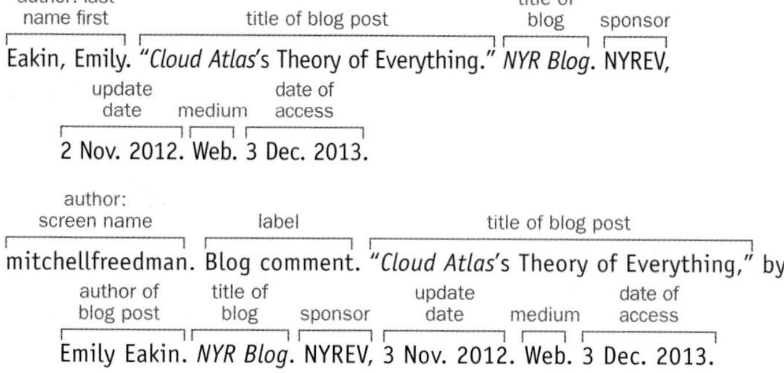

52. Academic course or department home page

Cite as a short work from a Web site (see item 48). For a course home page, begin with the name of the instructor and the title of the course or title of the page (use "Course home page" if there is no other title). For a department home page, begin with the name of the department and the label "Dept. home page."

Masiello, Regina. "355:101: Expository Writing." *Rutgers School of Arts and Sciences*. Writing Program, Rutgers U, 2013. Web. 19 Aug. 2013.

Comparative Media Studies. Dept. home page. *Massachusetts Institute of Technology*. MIT, n.d. Web. 6 Oct. 2013.

Audio, visual, and multimedia sources

■ **53. Podcast** If you view or listen to a podcast on the Web, cite it as you would a short work from a Web site (see item 48). If you download the podcast and view or listen to it on a computer or portable player, give the file type (such as "MP3 file" or "MOV file") as the medium.

a. Web

author: last name first | podcast title | Web site title | sponsor

Tanner, Laura. "Virtual Reality in 9/11 Fiction." *Literature Lab*. Dept. of English, Brandeis U, n.d. Web. 30 Oct. 2013.

no date | medium | date of access

b. Downloaded

author: last name first | podcast title | Web site title | sponsor

Tanner, Laura. "Virtual Reality in 9/11 Fiction." *Literature Lab*. Dept. of English, Brandeis U, n.d. MP3 file.

no date | medium

■ **54. Film (DVD, BD, or other format)** Generally, begin the entry with the title, followed by the director and lead performers, as in the first example. If your paper emphasizes one or more people involved with the film, you may begin with those names, as in the second example.

Typical designations for medium are "Film" (if viewed in a theater or streamed through a service such as Netflix); "DVD"; "BD" (for Blu-ray Disc); and "Web" (if viewed on a Web site). If you aren't sure of the medium, use "Film."

film title | director | major performers

Argo. Dir. Ben Affleck. Perf. Affleck, Bryan Cranston, and Alan Arkin. Warner. Bros., 2012. Film.

distributor | release date | medium

54. Film (DVD, BD, or other format) (*cont.*)

director: last name first — film title — major performers

Forster, Marc, dir. *Finding Neverland*. Perf. Johnny Depp, Kate Winslet,

distributor — release date

Julie Christie, Radha Mitchell, and Dustin Hoffman. Miramax, 2004.

medium

DVD.

55. Supplementary material accompanying a film Begin with the title of the supplementary material, in quotation marks, and the names of any important contributors, as for a film. End with information about the film, as in item 54.

"Sweeney's London." Prod. Eric Young. *Sweeney Todd: The Demon Barber of Fleet Street*. Dir. Tim Burton. DreamWorks, 2007. DVD. Disc 2.

56. Video or audio from the Web Cite video or audio that you accessed on the Web as you would a short work from a Web site (see item 48), giving information about the author before other information about the video or audio.

author: last name first — title of video — Web site title — sponsor — update date — medium

Lewis, Paul. "Citizen Journalism." *YouTube*. YouTube, 14 May 2011. Web.

date of access

24 Sept. 2013.

author: last name first — title of video — narrator (or host or speaker)

Fletcher, Antoine. "The Ancient Art of the Atlatl." Narr. Brenton Bellomy.

Web site title — sponsor — update date

Russell Cave National Monument. Natl. Park Service, 12 Feb. 2014.

medium — date of access

Web. 24 Feb. 2014.

author: last name first — title of video — Web site title

Burstein, Julie. "Four Lessons in Creativity." *TED: Ideas Worth Spreading*.

sponsor — update date — medium — date of access

TED Conf., Mar. 2012. Web. 18 Aug. 2013.

57. Video game List the developer or author of the game (if any); the title, italicized; the version ("Vers."), if there is one; the distributor and date of publication; and the platform or medium. If the game can be played on the Web, add information as for a work from a Web site (see item 48).

Firaxis Games. *Sid Meier's Civilization Revolution*. Take-Two Interactive, 2008. Xbox 360. *Edgeworld*. Atom Entertainment, 1 May 2012. Web. 15 June 2013.

58. Computer software or app Cite as a video game (see item 57), giving whatever information is available about the version, distributor, date, and platform.

Words with Friends. Vers. 5.84. Zynga, 2013. iOS 4.3.

59. Television or radio episode or program If you are citing an episode or a segment of a program, begin with the title of the episode or segment, in quotation marks. Then give the title of the program, italicized; relevant information about the program, such as the writer ("By"), director ("Dir."), performers ("Perf."), or narrator or host ("Narr."); the network; the local station and location (if any, as in item 27c; not necessary for cable networks); the date of broadcast; and the medium ("Television," "Radio").

For a program you accessed on the Web, after the information about the program give the network, the original broadcast date, the title of the Web site, the medium ("Web"), and your date of access. If you are citing an entire program (not an episode or a segment), begin your entry with the title of the program, italicized.

a. Broadcast

title of episode | program title | narrator (or host or speaker)

"Federal Role in Support of Autism." *Washington Journal*. Narr. Robb Harleston.

network | broadcast date | medium

C-SPAN. 1 Dec. 2012. Television.

The Daily Show with Jon Stewart. Comedy Central. 29 Nov. 2012. Television.

■ 59. Television or radio episode or program (*cont.*)

b. Web

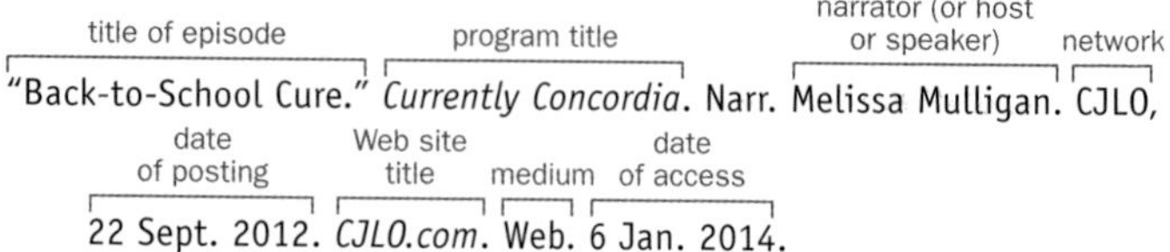

c. Podcast

How to cite a source reposted from another source

PROBLEM: Some sources that you find online, particularly on video-sharing sites, did not originate with the person who uploaded or published the source online. How do you give proper credit for such sources?

EXAMPLE: Say you need to cite President John F. Kennedy's inaugural address. You have found a video on YouTube that provides footage of the address (see image). The video was uploaded by PaddyIrishMan2 on October 29, 2006. But clearly, PaddyIrishMan2 is not the author of the video or of the address.

JFK Inaugural Address 1 of 2

Uploaded on Oct 29, 2006
President John F. Kennedy's inaugural address, January 20th 1961.

Vice President Johnson, Mr. Speaker, Mr. Chief Justice, President Eisenhower, Vice President Nixon, President Truman, reverend clergy, fellow citizens, we observe today not a victory of party, but a celebration of freedom — symbolising an end, as well as a beginning — signifying renewal, as well as change. For I have sworn before you and Almighty God the same solemn oath our forebears prescribed nearly a century and three quarters ago.

■ **60. Transcript** You might find a transcript related to an interview or a program on a radio or television Web site or in a transcript database, such as in the first example. Cite the source as you would an interview (see item 27) or a radio or television program (see item 59). Add the label "Transcript" at the end of the entry.

Cullen, Heidi. "Weather Warnings for a 'Climate Changed Planet.'" Interview by Terry Gross. *Fresh Air.* Natl. Public Radio, 25 July 2011. *LexisNexis Library Express*. Web. 5 Apr. 2013. Transcript.

"Missing Athletes Join a Long List of Olympic Defectors." Narr. Melissa Block. *All Things Considered*. Natl. Public Radio, 9 Aug. 2012. Web. 28 Aug. 2013. Transcript.

STRATEGY: Start with what you know. The source is a video that you viewed on the Web. For this particular video, John F. Kennedy is the speaker and the author of the inaugural address. PaddyIrishMan2 is identified as the person who uploaded the source to YouTube.

CITATION: To cite the source, you can combine the basic MLA guidelines for a lecture or public address (see item 62) and for a video found on the Web (see item 56).

author/speaker: last name first — title of address — Web site title — sponsor

Kennedy, John F. "JFK Inaugural Address: 1 of 2." *YouTube*. YouTube,

update date — medium — date of access

29 Oct. 2006. Web. 24 Nov. 2013.

Because Kennedy's inauguration is a well-known historical event, you can be fairly certain that this is not the only version of the inauguration video. It is a good idea, therefore, to include information about which version you viewed as supplementary information at the end of your citation.

author/speaker: last name first — title of address — Web site title — sponsor

Kennedy, John F. "JFK Inaugural Address: 1 of 2." *YouTube*. YouTube,

update date — medium — date of access — supplementary information

29 Oct. 2006. Web. 24 Nov. 2013. Uploaded by PaddyIrishMan2.

NOTE: If your work calls for a primary source, you should try to find the original source of the video; a reference librarian can help.

61. Performance For a live performance of a concert, a play, a ballet, or an opera, begin with the title of the work performed, italicized (unless it is named by form, number, and key). Then give the author or composer of the work ("By"); relevant information such as the director ("Dir."), the choreographer ("Chor."), the conductor ("Cond."), or the major performers ("Perf."); the theater, ballet, or opera company, if any; the theater and location; the date of the performance; and the label "Performance."

Wetu in the City: An Urban Black Indian Tale. By Mwalim [Morgan James Peters]. Dir. Naheem Garcia. Hibernian Hall, Boston. 16 Nov. 2012. Performance.

Symphony no. 4 in G. By Gustav Mahler. Cond. Mark Wigglesworth. Perf. Juliane Banse and Boston Symphony Orch. Symphony Hall, Boston. 17 Apr. 2009. Performance.

62. Lecture or public address Begin with the speaker's name, followed by the title of the lecture (if any), in quotation marks; the organization sponsoring the lecture; the location; the date; and a label such as "Lecture" or "Address." If you viewed the lecture on the Web, cite as you would a short work from a Web site (see item 48).

a. Live

Berry, Wendell E. "It All Turns on Affection." Natl. Endowment for the Humanities. John F. Kennedy Center for the Performing Arts, Washington. 23 Apr. 2012. Lecture.

b. Web

Clinton, Hillary Rodham. "Remarks on 'Creating an AIDS-Free Generation.'" *US Department of State: Diplomacy in Action*. US Dept. of State, 8 Nov. 2011. Web. 29 Oct. 2013.

63. Musical score For both print and online versions, begin with the composer's name; the title of the work, italicized (unless it is named by form, number, and key); and the date of composition. For a print source, give the place of publication; the name of the publisher and date of publication; and the medium. For an online source, give the title of the Web site; the publisher or sponsor of the site; the date of Web publication; the medium; and your date of access.

Beethoven, Ludwig van. Symphony no. 5 in C Minor, op. 67. 1807. *Center for Computer Assisted Research in the Humanities*. CCARH, Stanford U, 2000. Web. 23 Aug. 2013.

■ **64. Sound recording** Begin with the name of the person you want to emphasize: the composer, conductor ("Cond."), or performer ("Perf."). For a long work, give the title, italicized (unless it is named by form, number, and key); the names of pertinent artists (such as performers, readers, or musicians); and the orchestra and conductor, if relevant. End with the manufacturer, the date, and the medium ("CD," "Audiocassette"). For a song, put the title in quotation marks. If you include the name of the album or CD, italicize it.

a. CD

Bizet, Georges. *Carmen*. Perf. Jennifer Larmore, Thomas Moser, Angela Gheorghiu, and Samuel Ramey. Bavarian State Orch. and Chorus. Cond. Giuseppe Sinopoli. Warner, 1996. CD.

Blige, Mary J. "Don't Mind." *Life II: The Journey Continues (Act 1)*. Geffen, 2011. CD.

b. Downloaded

Blige, Mary J. "Don't Mind." *Life II: The Journey Continues (Act 1)*. Geffen, 2011. MP3 file.

■ **65. Work of art** (a) For an original work of art, cite the artist's name; the title of the artwork, italicized; the date of composition; the medium of composition (for instance, "Oil on canvas," "Charcoal on paper"); and the institution and city in which the artwork is located. (b) For artworks found on the Web, omit the medium of composition and include the title of the Web site, the medium ("Web"), and your date of access.

(c) If you downloaded a digital file from an archive or other online source, cite as in (a) but include the type of file as the medium ("JPEG file," "TIFF file"). (d) If you viewed the artwork as a reproduction in a print source, omit the medium of composition and add publication information about the print source, including the page number or figure number for the artwork; give the medium of reproduction at the end.

a. Original

Constable, John. *Dedham Vale*. 1802. Oil on canvas. Victoria and Albert Museum, London.

b. Web

Hessing, Valjean. *Caddo Myth*. 1976. Joslyn Art Museum, Omaha. *Joslyn Art Museum*. Web. 19 Apr. 2014.

c. Digital file

Diebenkorn, Richard. *Ocean Park No. 38*. 1971. Phillips Collection, Washington. JPEG file.

d. Reproduction (print)

O'Keeffe, Georgia. *Black and Purple Petunias*. 1925. Private collection. *Two Lives: A Conversation in Paintings and Photographs*. Ed. Alexandra Arrowsmith and Thomas West. New York: Harper, 1992. 67. Print.

■ **66. Photograph** (a) For an original photograph, cite the photographer's name; the title of the photograph, italicized; the date of composition; the medium ("Photograph"); and the institution and city in which the photograph is located. (b) For photographs found on the Web, omit the medium "Photograph" and include the title of the Web site, the medium "Web," and your date of access. (c) If you downloaded a digital file from an archive or other online source, cite as in (a) but include the type of file as the medium ("JPEG file," "TIFF file"). (d) If you viewed the photograph as a reproduction in a print source, omit the medium of composition and add publication information about the print source, including the page number or figure number for the artwork; give the medium of reproduction at the end.

a. Original

Feinstein, Harold. *Hangin' Out, Sharing a Public Bench, NYC.* 1948. Photograph. Panopticon Gallery, Boston.

b. Web

McCurry, Steve. *A World of Prayer*. 29 Oct. 2012. *Magnum Photos*. Web. 30 Apr. 2013.

c. Digital file

Lucy Branham in Occoquan Prison Dress. 1919. Lib. of Cong. JPEG file.

d. Reproduction (print)

Kertész, André. *Meudon*. 1928. *Street Photography: From Atget to Cartier-Bresson*. By Clive Scott. London: Tauris, 2011. 61. Print.

■ **67. Cartoon** Give the cartoonist's name; the title of the cartoon, if it has one, in quotation marks; the label "Cartoon" or "Comic strip"; publication information; and the medium. To cite an online cartoon, give the title of the Web site, the sponsor or publisher, the medium, and your date of access.

Zyglis, Adam. "Delta and Denial." Cartoon. *Buffalo News*. Buffalo News, 11 Jan. 2013. Web. 21 Jan. 2013.

■ **68. Advertisement** Name the product or company being advertised, followed by the word "Advertisement." Give publication information for the source in which the advertisement appears.

UnitedHealthcare. Advertisement. *Smithsonian* Dec. 2012: 27. Print.

Corolla. Advertisement. *Root*. Slate Group, 28 Nov. 2012. Web. 3 Dec. 2013.

■ **69. Visual such as a table, a chart, or another graphic** Cite a visual as you would a short work within a longer work. Use the label "Table," "Chart," or "Graphic" following the title. Add the medium and, for an online source, the sponsor or publisher and the date of access. If the visual has a number in the source, give that number immediately before the medium.

"Canada's Energy Flow 2007." Chart. *Economist*. Economist Newspaper, 26 Oct. 2012. Web. 30 Oct. 2013.

"CDC Climate Ready States and Cities Initiative." Graphic. *Centers for Disease Control and Prevention*. Centers for Disease Control and Prevention, 1 Oct. 2012. Web. 31 Oct. 2013.

■ **70. Map** Cite a map as you would a short work within a longer work. Or, if the map is published on its own, cite it as a book or another long work. Use the label "Map" following the title. Add the medium and, for an online source, the sponsor or publisher and the date of access.

"Population Origin Groups in Rural Texas." Map. *Perry-Castañeda Library Map Collection*. U of Texas at Austin, 1976. Web. 17 Mar. 2013.

How to cite course materials

PROBLEM: Sometimes you will be assigned to work with materials that an instructor has uploaded to a course Web site or has handed out in class. Complete publication information may not always be given for such sources. A PDF file or a hard copy article, for instance, may have a title and an author's name but give no other information. Or a video may not include information about the creator or the date the video was created. When you write a paper using such sources, how should you cite them in your own work?

EXAMPLE: Perhaps your instructor has included a PDF file of an article in a collection of readings on the course Web site (see image at right). You are writing a paper in which you use a passage from the work.

THE IMAGE OF THE RAILROAD IN *ANNA KARENINA*

Gary R. Jahn, University of Minnesota

The motif of the railroad recurs so frequently in Lev Tolstoj's *Anna Karenina* that the conclusion that it is somehow integral to a full understanding of the novel is inescapable. According to a recent study the railroad is mentioned at least thirty-two times in the book,[1] and every reader will remember that Anna and Vronskij first meet at a railway station, that Levin intensely dislikes the railroad, and that Anna commits suicide by leaping under a train.[2]

M. S. Al'tman once asked why Anna, having decided to do away with herself, should have selected such a gruesome method. The question is flippant only in its formulation, and a great deal of scholarly effort has been devoted to answering it. A searching of the extensive biographical data on Tolstoj has amply attested his personal aversion for the railroad. He wrote Turgenev in 1857 that "the railroad is to travel as a whore is to love,"[3] and it is known that he was discomfited to the point of nausea by the swaying of railway carriages. These facts provide a credible physiological basis for the standard, although not unanimous,[4] Soviet view that Levin's dyspeptic attitude toward the railroad is the correlative of Tolstoj's, that the highly autobiographical Levin was expressing Tolstoj's belief that the railroad served only to pander to and further inflame the already monstrous appetite of the idle and privileged for foreign luxuries, and that this belief overlies their mutual resentment of the forces tending to displace the landholding nobility from its position of inherited privilege: forces which the railroad is said to symbolize. The railroad is present in the novel so that it can be attacked, and this is precisely what Levin does in the book which he writes about contemporary Russian life.[5] There is an indubitable measure of truth in this understanding of the railway motif. It does account for Levin's view of the railroad and it is also true that for him the railroad symbolizes forces harmful to the traditional style of life of

■ **71. Digital file** A digital file is any document or image that exists in digital form, independent of a Web site. Begin with information required for the source (such as a photograph, a report, a sound recording, or a radio program), following the guidelines throughout section 56b. Then for the medium, indicate the type of file: "JPEG file," "PDF file," "MP3 file," and so on.

photographer | photograph title | date of composition | location of photograph | medium

Hine, Lewis W. *Girl in Cherryville Mill*. 1908. Prints and Photographs Div., Lib. of Cong. JPEG file.

"Back to School." *This American Life*. Narr. Ira Glass. Episode 474. Chicago Public Media, 14 Sept. 2012. MP3 file.

STRATEGY: Look through section 56b for a model that matches the type of source you're working with. Is it an article? A chapter from a book? A photograph? A video? The model or models you find will give you an idea of the information you need to gather about the source. The usual required information is (1) the author or creator, (2) the title, (3) the date the work was published or created, (4) the date you accessed the source (usually only for sources on the Web), and (5) the medium in which the source was presented (see p. 471).

CITATION: For your citation, you can give only as much of the required information as you can find in the source. In this example, you know the source is an article with an author and a title, and you accessed it as a PDF file. So you can combine items 13a (basic format for an article) and 71 (digital file) to create the works cited entry for the source. Since you can't tell when the article was published, you should use "N.d." for "No date." At the end of your citation, it is a good idea to include the description "Course materials" and supplementary information about the course (such as its title or number and the term).

author: last name first | article title | no date | medium | supplementary information

Jahn, Gary R. "The Image of the Railroad in *Anna Karenina*." N.d. PDF file. Course materials, EN101, Fall 2013.

NOTE: When in doubt about how much information to include or where to find it, consult your instructor.

71. Digital file (*cont.*)

National Institute of Mental Health. *What Rescue Workers Can Do*. Washington: US Dept. of Health and Human Services, 2006. PDF file.

Government and legal documents

72. Government document Treat the government agency as the author, giving the name of the government followed by the name of the department and the agency, if any. For print sources, add the medium at the end of the entry. For sources found on the Web, follow the model for an entire Web site (see item 47) or for short or long works from a Web site (see items 48 and 49).

government | department | agency (or agencies)

United States. Dept. of Agriculture. Food and Nutrition Service. Child Nutrition Programs. *Eligibility Manual for School Meals: Determining and Verifying Eligibility*. *National School Lunch Program*. US Dept. of Agriculture, Aug. 2012. Web. 30 Oct. 2013.

title (long work) | Web site title | sponsor | update date | medium | date of access

Canada. Minister of Indian Affairs and Northern Dev. *Gathering Strength: Canada's Aboriginal Action Plan*. Ottawa: Minister of Public Works and Govt. Services Can., 2000. Print.

73. Testimony before a legislative body

Carson, Johnnie. "Assessing US Policy on Peacekeeping Operations in Africa." Testimony before the US House Foreign Affairs Committee, Subcommittee on Africa, Global Health, and Human Rights. *US Department of State: Diplomacy in Action*. US Dept. of State, 13 Sept. 2012. Web. 29 Sept. 2013.

74. Historical document The titles of most historical documents, such as the US Constitution and the Canadian Charter of Rights and Freedoms, are neither italicized nor put in quotation marks. For a print version, cite as for a selection in an anthology (see item 35) or for a book (with the title not italicized). For an online version, cite as a short work from a Web site (see item 48).

Jefferson, Thomas. First Inaugural Address. 1801. *The American Reader*. Ed. Diane Ravitch. New York: Harper, 1990. 42-44. Print.

Constitution of the United States. 1787. *The Charters of Freedom*. US Natl. Archives and Records Administration, n.d. Web. 19 Jan. 2013.

■ **75. Legislative act (law)** Begin with the name of the act, neither italicized nor in quotation marks. Then provide the act's Public Law number; its Statutes at Large volume and page numbers; its date of enactment; and the medium.

Electronic Freedom of Information Act Amendments of 1996. Pub. L. 104-231. 110 Stat. 3048. 2 Oct. 1996. Print.

■ **76. Court case** Name the first plaintiff and the first defendant. Then give the volume, name, and page number of the law report; the court name; the year of the decision; and publication information. Do not italicize the name of the case. (In the text of the paper, the name of the case is italicized; see item 19 on p. 465.)

Utah v. Evans. 536 US 452. Supreme Court of the US. 2002. *Supreme Court Collection*. Legal Information Inst., Cornell U Law School, n.d. Web. 30 Apr. 2013.

Personal communication and social media

■ **77. E-mail message** Begin with the writer's name and the subject line. Then write "Message to" followed by the name of the recipient. End with the date of the message and the medium ("E-mail").

Lowe, Walter. "Review Questions." Message to the author. 15 Mar. 2013. E-mail.

■ **78. Text message** Cite like an e-mail message, giving the medium as "Text message."

Wiley, Joanna. Message to the author. 4 Apr. 2014. Text message.

■ **79. Posting to an online discussion list** When possible, cite archived versions of postings. If you cannot locate an archived version, keep a copy of the posting for your records. Begin with the author's name, followed by the title or subject line, in quotation marks (use the label "Online posting" if the posting has no title). Then proceed as for a short work from a Web site (see item 48).

Baker, Frank. "A New Twist on a Classic." *Developing Digital Literacies.* NCTE, 30 Nov. 2012. Web. 10 Jan. 2013.

■ **80. Facebook post or comment** Cite as a short work from a Web site (see item 48), beginning with the writer's real name followed by the screen name in parentheses, if both are given. Otherwise use whatever name is given in the source. Follow with the title of the post, if any, in quotation marks. If there is no title, use the label "Post."

Bedford/St. Martin's. "Liz Losh Discusses Teaching about Interactive Media with Comics: http://ow.ly/imucP." *Facebook*. Facebook, 5 Mar. 2013. Web. 26 Mar. 2013.

Erin Houlihan. Post. *Facebook*. Facebook, 23 Nov. 2013. Web. 26 Nov. 2013.

■ **81. Twitter post (tweet)** Begin with the writer's real name followed by the screen name in parentheses, if both are given. Otherwise use whatever name is given in the source. Give the text of the entire tweet in quotation marks, using the writer's capitalization and punctuation. Follow the text with the date and time noted on the tweet. Use "Tweet" as the medium.

Curiosity Rover. "The journey of 352,000,000 miles begins with a single launch. One year ago today, I left Earth for Mars http://twitpic.com/bgq1vn." 26 Nov. 2012, 10:10 a.m. Tweet.

56c MLA information notes (optional)

Researchers who use the MLA system of parenthetical documentation may also use information notes for one of two purposes:

1. to provide additional material that is important but might interrupt the flow of the paper

2. to refer to several sources that support a single point or to provide comments on sources

Information notes may be either footnotes or endnotes. Footnotes appear at the foot of the page; endnotes appear on a separate page at the end of the paper, just before the list of works cited. For either style, the notes are numbered consecutively throughout the paper. The text of the paper contains a raised arabic numeral that corresponds to the number of the note.

TEXT

In the past several years, employees have filed a number of lawsuits against employers because of online monitoring practices.[1]

NOTE

1. For a discussion of federal law applicable to electronic surveillance in the workplace, see Kesan 293.

57 MLA manuscript format; sample research paper

The following guidelines are consistent with advice given in the *MLA Handbook for Writers of Research Papers*, 7th ed. (New York: MLA, 2009), and with typical requirements for student papers. For a sample MLA research paper, see pages 517–25.

57a MLA manuscript format

Formatting the paper

Papers written in MLA style should be formatted as follows.

Font If your instructor does not require a specific font, choose one that is standard and easy to read (such as Times New Roman).

Title and identification MLA does not require a title page. On the first page of your paper, place your name, your instructor's name, the course title, and the date on separate lines against the left margin. Then center your title. (See p. 517 for a sample first page.)

If your instructor requires a title page, ask for formatting guidelines.

Page numbers (running head) Put the page number preceded by your last name in the upper right corner of each page, one-half inch below the top edge. Use arabic numerals (1, 2, 3, and so on).

Margins, line spacing, and paragraph indents Leave margins of one inch on all sides of the page. Left-align the text.

Double-space throughout the paper. Do not add extra space above or below the title of the paper or between paragraphs.

Indent the first line of each paragraph one-half inch from the left margin.

Capitalization, italics, and quotation marks In titles of works, capitalize all words except articles (*a*, *an*, *the*), prepositions (*to*, *from*, *between*, and so on), coordinating conjunctions (*and*, *but*, *or*, *nor*, *for*, *so*, *yet*), and the *to* in infinitives — unless the word is first or last in the title or subtitle. Follow these guidelines in your paper even if the title appears in all capital or all lowercase letters in the source.

In the text of an MLA paper, when a complete sentence follows a colon, lowercase the first word following the colon unless the sentence is a quotation or a well-known expression or principle.

Italicize the titles of books, journals, magazines, and other long works, such as Web sites. Use quotation marks around the titles of articles, short stories, poems, and other short works.

Long quotations When a quotation is longer than four typed lines of prose or three lines of poetry, set it off from the text by indenting the entire quotation one inch from the left margin. Double-space the indented quotation and do not add extra space above or below it.

Do not use quotation marks when a quotation has been set off from the text by indenting. See page 522 for an example.

URLs When you need to break a URL at the end of a line in the text of your paper, break it only after a slash or a double slash and do not insert a hyphen. For MLA rules on dividing URLs in your list of works cited, see page 516.

Headings MLA neither encourages nor discourages the use of headings and provides no guidelines for their use. If you would like to insert headings in a long essay or research paper, check first with your instructor.

Visuals MLA classifies visuals as tables and figures (figures include graphs, charts, maps, photographs, and drawings). Label each table with an arabic numeral ("Table 1," "Table 2," and so on) and provide a clear caption that identifies the subject. Capitalize the caption as you would a title (see 45c); do not italicize the label and caption or place them in quotation marks. Place the label and caption on separate lines above the table, flush with the left margin.

For a table that you have borrowed or adapted, give the source below the table in a note like the following:

Source: Boris Groysberg and Michael Slind; "Leadership Is a Conversation"; *Harvard Business Review* June 2012: 83; print.

For each figure, place the figure number (using the abbreviation "Fig.") and a caption below the figure, flush left. Capitalize the caption as you would a sentence; include source information following the caption. (When referring to the figure in your paper, use the abbreviation "fig." in parenthetical citations; otherwise spell out the word.) See page 519 for an example of a figure in a paper.

Place visuals in the text, as close as possible to the sentences that relate to them, unless your instructor prefers that visuals appear in an appendix.

Preparing the list of works cited

Begin the list of works cited on a new page at the end of the paper. Center the title "Works Cited" about one inch from the top of the page. Double-space throughout. See pages 117 and 524–25 for sample lists of works cited.

Alphabetizing the list Alphabetize the list by the last names of the authors (or editors); if a work has no author or editor, alphabetize by the first word of the title other than *A*, *An*, or *The*.

If your list includes two or more works by the same author, use the author's name for the first entry only. For subsequent entries, use three hyphens followed by a period. List the titles in alphabetical order. (See items 6 and 7 on p. 473.)

Indenting Do not indent the first line of each works cited entry, but indent any additional lines one-half inch. This technique highlights the names of the authors, making it easy for readers to scan the alphabetized list. See page 524.

URLs (Web addresses) If you need to include a URL in a works cited entry and it must be divided across lines, break the URL only after a slash or a double slash. Do not insert a hyphen at the end of the line. Insert angle brackets around the URL. (See the note following item 47 on p. 496.) If your word processing program automatically turns URLs into links (by underlining them and changing the color), turn off this feature.

57b Sample MLA research paper

On the following pages is a research paper on the topic of the role of government in legislating food choices, written by Sophie Harba, a student in a composition class. Harba's paper is documented with in-text citations and a list of works cited in MLA style. Annotations in the margins of the paper draw your attention to Harba's use of MLA style and her effective writing.

Harba 1

Sophie Harba

Professor Baros-Moon

Engl 1101

30 April 2013

What's for Dinner? Personal Choices vs. Public Health

Title is centered.

Should the government enact laws to regulate healthy eating choices? Many Americans would answer an emphatic "No," arguing that what and how much we eat should be left to individual choice rather than unreasonable laws. Others might argue that it would be unreasonable for the government not to enact legislation, given the rise of chronic diseases that result from harmful diets. In this debate, both the definition of reasonable regulations and the role of government to legislate food choices are at stake. In the name of public health and safety, state governments have the responsibility to shape health policies and to regulate healthy eating choices, especially since doing so offers a potentially large social benefit for a relatively small cost.

Opening research question engages readers.

Writer highlights the research conversation.

Thesis answers the research question and presents Harba's main point.

Debates surrounding the government's role in regulating food have a long history in the United States. According to Lorine Goodwin, a food historian, nineteenth-century reformers who sought to purify the food supply were called "fanatics" and "radicals" by critics who argued that consumers should be free to buy and eat what they want (77). Thanks to regulations, though, such as the 1906 federal Pure Food and Drug Act, food, beverages, and medicine are largely free from toxins. In addition, to prevent contamination and the spread of disease, meat and dairy products are now inspected by government agents to ensure that they meet health requirements. Such regulations

Signal phrase names the author. The parenthetical citation includes a page number.

Historical background provides context for debate.

Marginal annotations indicate MLA-style formatting and **effective writing**.

Harba explains her use of a key term, *reasonable.*

Harba establishes common ground with the reader.

Transition helps readers move from one paragraph to the next.

No page number is available for this Web source.

can be considered reasonable because they protect us from harm with little, if any, noticeable consumer cost. It is not considered an unreasonable infringement on personal choice that contaminated meat or arsenic-laced cough drops are *un*available at our local supermarket. Rather, it is an important government function to stop such harmful items from entering the marketplace.

Even though our food meets current safety standards, there is a need for further regulation. Not all food dangers, for example, arise from obvious toxins like arsenic and *E. coli*. A diet that is low in nutritional value and high in sugars, fats, and refined grains—grains that have been processed to increase shelf life but that contain little fiber, iron, and B vitamins—can be damaging over time (United States, Dept. of Agriculture and Dept. of Health and Human Services 36). A graph from the government's *Dietary Guidelines for Americans, 2010* provides a visual representation of the American diet and how far off it is from the recommended nutritional standards (see fig. 1).

Michael Pollan, who has written extensively about Americans' unhealthy eating habits, notes that "[t]he Centers for Disease Control estimates that fully three quarters of US health care spending goes to treat chronic diseases, most of which are preventable and linked to diet: heart disease, stroke, type 2 diabetes, and at least a third of all cancers." In fact, the amount of money the United States spends to treat chronic illnesses is increasing so rapidly that the Centers for Disease Control has labeled chronic disease "the public health challenge of the 21st century" (United States, Dept. of Health and Human Services 1). In fighting this epidemic, the primary challenge

Harba 3

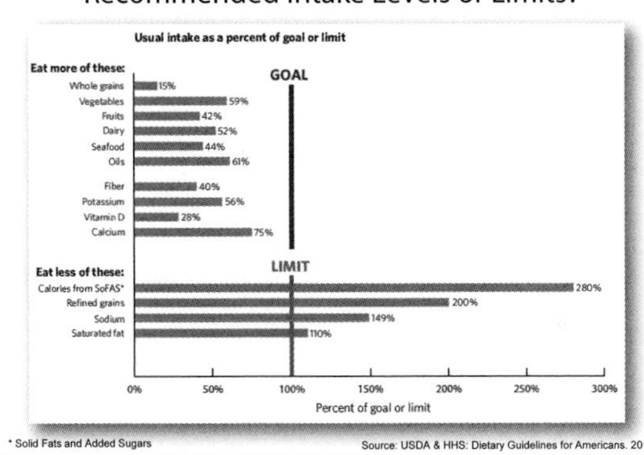

Harba uses a graph to illustrate Americans' poor nutritional choices.

Fig. 1. This graph shows that Americans consume about three times more fats and sugars and twice as many refined grains as is recommended but only half of the recommended foods (United States, Dept. of Agriculture and Dept. of Health and Human Services, fig. 5-1).

The visual includes a figure number, descriptive caption, and source information.

is not the need to find a cure; the challenge is to prevent chronic diseases from striking in the first place.

Harba sets forth the urgency of her argument.

Legislation, however, is not a popular solution when it comes to most Americans and the food they eat. According to a nationwide poll, 75% of Americans are opposed to laws that restrict or put limitations on access to unhealthy foods (Neergaard and Agiesta). When New York mayor Michael Bloomberg proposed a regulation in 2012 banning the sale of soft drinks in servings greater than twelve ounces in restaurants and movie theaters, he was ridiculed as "Nanny Bloomberg." In California in 2011, legislators failed to pass a law that would impose a penny-per-ounce tax on soda,

Harba treats both sides fairly.

Harba 4

which would have funded obesity prevention programs. And in Mississippi, legislators passed "a ban on bans—a law that forbids . . . local restrictions on food or drink" (Conly A23).

Why is the public largely resistant to laws that would limit unhealthy choices or penalize those choices with so-called fat taxes? Many consumers and civil rights advocates find such laws to be an unreasonable restriction on individual freedom of choice. As health policy experts Mello, Studdert, and Brennan point out, opposition to food and beverage regulation is similar to the opposition to early tobacco legislation: the public views the issue as one of personal responsibility rather than one requiring government intervention (2602). In other words, if a person eats unhealthy food and becomes ill as a result, that is his or her choice. But those who favor legislation claim that freedom of choice is a myth because of the strong influence of food and beverage industry marketing on consumers' dietary habits. According to one nonprofit health advocacy group, food and beverage companies spend roughly two billion dollars per year marketing directly to children. As a result, kids see nearly four thousand ads per year encouraging them to consume unhealthy food and drinks ("Facts on Junk Food"). As was the case with antismoking laws passed in recent decades, taxes and legal restrictions on junk food sales could help to counter the strong marketing messages that promote unhealthy products.

Harba anticipates objections to her idea. She counters opposing views and provides support for her argument.

The United States has a history of state and local public health laws that have successfully promoted a particular behavior by punishing an undesirable behavior. The decline in tobacco use as a result of antismoking taxes and laws is perhaps the most obvious example. Another example is legislation requiring the use of seat belts, which have significantly reduced fatalities in car

An analogy extends Harba's argument.

Harba 5

crashes. One government agency reports that seat belt use saved an average of more than fourteen thousand lives per year in the United States between 2000 and 2010 (United States, Dept. of Transportation, Natl. Highway Traffic Safety Administration 231). Perhaps seat belt laws have public support because the cost of wearing a seat belt is small, especially when compared with the benefit of saving fourteen thousand lives per year.

Laws designed to prevent chronic disease by promoting healthier food and beverage consumption also have potentially enormous benefits. To give just one example, Marion Nestle, New York University professor of nutrition and public health, notes that "a 1% reduction in intake of saturated fat across the population would prevent more than 30,000 cases of coronary heart disease annually and save more than a billion dollars in health care costs" (7). Few would argue that saving lives and dollars is not an enormous benefit. But three-quarters of Americans say they would object to the costs needed to achieve this benefit—the regulations needed to reduce saturated fat intake.

Harba introduces a direct quotation with a signal phrase and follows with a comment that shows readers why she chose to use the source.

Why do so many Americans believe there is a degree of personal choice lost when regulations such as taxes, bans, or portion limits on unhealthy foods are proposed? Some critics of anti-junk-food laws believe that even if state and local laws were successful in curbing chronic diseases, they would still be unacceptable. Bioethicist David Resnik emphasizes that such policies, despite their potential to make our society healthier, "open the door to excessive government control over food, which could restrict dietary choices, interfere with cultural, ethnic, and religious traditions, and exacerbate socioeconomic inequalities" (31). Resnik acknowledges that his argument relies on "slippery slope" thinking, but he insists that "social

Harba acknowledges critics and counterarguments.

Harba 6

and political pressures" regarding food regulation make his concerns valid (31). Yet the social and political pressures that Resnik cites are really just the desire to improve public health, and limiting access to unhealthy, artificial ingredients seems a small price to pay. As legal scholars L. O. Gostin and K. G. Gostin explain, "[I]nterventions that do not pose a truly significant burden on individual liberty" are justified if they "go a long way towards safeguarding the health and well-being of the populace" (214).

Including the source's credentials makes Harba more credible.

To improve public health, advocates such as Bowdoin College philosophy professor Sarah Conly contend that it is the government's duty to prevent people from making harmful choices whenever feasible and whenever public benefits outweigh the costs. In response to critics who claim that laws aimed at stopping us from eating whatever we want are an assault on our freedom of choice, Conly offers a persuasive counterargument:

Long quotation is introduced with a signal phrase naming the author.

> [L]aws aren't designed for each one of us individually. Some of us can drive safely at 90 miles per hour, but we're bound by the same laws as the people who can't, because individual speeding laws aren't practical. Giving up a little liberty is something we agree to when we agree to live in a democratic society that is governed by laws. (A23)

Long quotation is set off from the text. Quotation marks are omitted.

As Conly suggests, we need to change our either/or thinking (either we have complete freedom of choice *or* we have government regulations and lose our freedom) and instead need to see health as a matter of public good, not individual liberty. Proposals such as Mayor Bloomberg's that seek to limit portions of unhealthy beverages aren't about giving up liberty; they are about asking individuals to choose substantial public health benefits at a very small cost.

Long quotation is followed with comments that connect the source to Harba's argument.

Harba 7

Despite arguments in favor of regulating unhealthy food as a means to improve public health, public opposition has stood in the way of legislation. Americans freely eat as much unhealthy food as they want, and manufacturers and sellers of these foods have nearly unlimited freedom to promote such products and drive increased consumption, without any requirements to warn the public of potential hazards. Yet mounting scientific evidence points to unhealthy food as a significant contributing factor to chronic disease, which we know is straining our health care system, decreasing Americans' quality of life, and leading to unnecessary premature deaths. Americans must consider whether to allow the costly trend of rising chronic disease to continue in the name of personal choice or whether to support the regulatory changes and public health policies that will reverse that trend.

Conclusion sums up Harba's argument and provides closure.

Harba 8

Heading is centered.

Works Cited

Conly, Sarah. "Three Cheers for the Nanny State." *New York Times* 25 Mar. 2013: A23.

"The Facts on Junk Food Marketing and Kids." *Prevention Institute*. Prevention Inst., n.d. Web. 21 Apr. 2013.

Goodwin, Lorine Swainston. *The Pure Food, Drink, and Drug Crusaders, 1879-1914*. Jefferson: McFarland, 2006. Print.

Gostin, L. O., and K. G. Gostin. "A Broader Liberty: J. S. Mill, Paternalism, and the Public's Health." *Public Health* 123.3 (2009): 214-21. *Academic Search Premier*. Web. 17 Apr. 2013.

Mello, Michelle M., David M. Studdert, and Troyen A. Brennan. "Obesity—The New Frontier of Public Health Law." *New England Journal of Medicine* 354.24 (2006): 2601-10. *Expanded Academic ASAP*. Web. 22 Apr. 2013.

Neergaard, Lauran, and Jennifer Agiesta. "Obesity's a Crisis but We Want Our Junk Food, Poll Shows." *Huffington Post*. TheHuffingtonPost.com, 4 Jan. 2013. Web. 20 Apr. 2013.

Nestle, Marion. *Food Politics: How the Food Industry Influences Nutrition and Health*. Berkeley: U of California P, 2013. Print.

Pollan, Michael. "The Food Movement, Rising." *New York Review of Books*. NYREV, 10 June 2010. Web. 19 Apr. 2013.

Resnik, David. "Trans Fat Bans and Human Freedom." *American Journal of Bioethics* 10.3 (2010): 27-32. *Academic Search Premier*. Web. 17 Apr. 2013.

United States. Dept. of Agriculture and Dept. of Health and Human Services. *Dietary Guidelines for Americans, 2010*. Dept. of Agriculture and Dept. of Health and Human Services, 2010. Web. 17 Apr. 2013.

Abbreviation "n.d." indicates that the online source has no update date.

First line of each entry is at the left margin; extra lines are indented ½".

Double-spacing is used throughout.

List is alphabetized by authors' last names (or by title when a work has no author).

The government agency is used as the author of a government document.

Harba 9

United States. Dept. of Health and Human Services. Centers for Disease Control and Prevention. *The Power of Prevention*. Natl. Center for Chronic Disease Prevention and Health Promotion, 2009. Web. 19 Apr. 2013.

United States. Dept. of Transportation. Natl. Highway Traffic Safety Administration. *Traffic Safety Facts 2010: A Compilation of Motor Vehicle Crash Data from the Fatality Analysis Reporting System and the General Estimates System*. US Dept. of Transportation, 2010. Web. 12 Apr. 2013.

Writing Papers in APA Style

Writing Papers in APA Style 527

Writing Papers in APA Style

Directory to APA in-text citation models

Directory to APA reference list models

General guidelines for listing authors

Articles and other short works

Directory to APA reference list models, continued

Books and other long works

Web sites and parts of Web sites

Audio, visual, and multimedia sources

Personal communication and social media

Most instructors in the social sciences and some instructors in other disciplines will ask you to document your sources with the American Psychological Association (APA) system of in-text citations and references described in section 61.

When writing an APA-style paper that draws on sources, you face three main challenges: (1) supporting a thesis, (2) citing your sources accurately and avoiding plagiarism, and (3) integrating source material effectively.

Examples in this section are drawn from one student's research for a review of the literature on treatments for childhood obesity. Luisa Mirano's paper appears on pages 585–96.

NOTE: For advice on finding and evaluating sources and on managing information in all your college courses, see sections 50–52.

58 Supporting a thesis

Most research assignments ask you to form a thesis, or main idea, and to support that thesis with well-organized evidence. In a paper reviewing the literature on a topic, the thesis analyzes the often competing conclusions drawn by a variety of researchers.

58a Form a working thesis.

Once you have read a range of sources, considered your issue from different perspectives, and chosen an entry point in the research conversation (see 50b), you are ready to form a working thesis to focus your project: a one-sentence (or occasionally a two-sentence) statement of your central idea. (See also 1c.) The working thesis expresses more than your opinion; it expresses your informed, reasoned answer to your research question — a question about which people might disagree. As you learn more about your subject, your ideas may change, and your working thesis will evolve, too. You can revise your thesis as you draft. Here, for example, is a research question posed by Luisa Mirano, a student in a psychology class, followed by her thesis in answer to that question.

RESEARCH QUESTION

Is medication the right treatment for the escalating problem of childhood obesity?

WORKING THESIS

Treating cases of childhood obesity with medication alone is too narrow an approach for this growing problem.

The thesis usually appears at the end of the introductory paragraph. To read Luisa Mirano's thesis in the context of her introduction, see page 587.

Testing your thesis

When drafting and revising a thesis statement, make sure it answers your central research question and that you can effectively develop it with the sources available to you.

Keeping the following guidelines in mind will help you develop an effective thesis statement.

- A thesis should take a position that needs to be argued and supported. It should not be a fact or description.
- A thesis should match the scope of the research project. If your thesis is too broad, explore a subtopic of your original topic. If your thesis is too narrow, pose a research question that has more than one answer.
- A thesis should be sharply focused. Avoid vague words such as *interesting* or *good*. Use concrete language and make sure your thesis lets readers know your position.
- A thesis should stand up to the "So what?" question. Ask yourself why readers should care about your thesis. If your thesis matters to you, your readers are more likely to find your ideas engaging.

58b Organize your ideas.

The American Psychological Association (APA) encourages the use of headings to help readers follow the organization of a paper. For an original research report, the major headings often follow a standard model: Method, Results, Discussion. The introduction does not have a heading; it consists of the material between the title of the paper and the first heading.

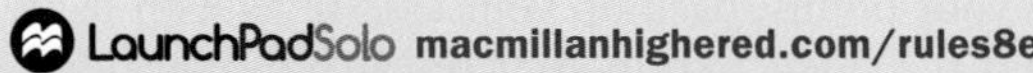

58 Supporting a thesis

> Exercises: 58–1 and 58–2

For a literature review, headings will vary. Luisa Mirano used four questions to focus her research into treatments for childhood obesity; the questions then became headings in her paper (see 62b).

58c Use sources to inform and support your argument.

Sources can play several different roles to support your thesis and develop your points.

Providing background information or context

You can use facts and statistics to support generalizations or to establish the importance of your topic, as student writer Luisa Mirano does in her introduction.

> In March 2004, U.S. Surgeon General Richard Carmona called attention to a health problem in the United States that, until recently, has been overlooked: childhood obesity. Carmona said that the "astounding" 15% child obesity rate constitutes an "epidemic." Since the early 1980s, that rate has "doubled in children and tripled in adolescents." Now more than nine million children are classified as obese.

Explaining terms or concepts

If readers are unfamiliar with a term or a concept important to your topic, you will want to define or explain it; or if your argument depends on a term with multiple meanings, you will want to explain your use of the term. Quoting or paraphrasing a source can help you define terms and concepts in accessible language. Luisa Mirano uses a scholarly source to explain how one of the major obesity drugs functions.

> Sibutramine suppresses appetite by blocking the reuptake of the neurotransmitters serotonin and norepinephrine in the brain (Yanovski & Yanovski, 2002, p. 594).

Supporting your claims

As you develop your points, back up your assertions with facts, examples, and other evidence from your research (see also 6h).

Luisa Mirano, for example, uses one source's findings to support her central idea that the medical treatment of childhood obesity has limitations.

> As journalist Greg Critser (2003) noted in his book *Fat Land*, use of weight-loss drugs is unlikely to have an effect without the proper "support system"—one that includes doctors, facilities, time, and money (p. 3).

Lending authority to your argument

Expert opinion can add weight and credibility to your argument (see also 6h). But don't rely on experts to make your points for you. State your ideas in your own words and, when appropriate, cite the judgment of an authority in the field to support your position.

> Both medical experts and policymakers recognize that solutions might come not only from a laboratory but also from policy, education, and advocacy. A handbook designed to educate doctors on obesity called for "major changes in some aspects of western culture" (Hoppin & Taveras, 2004, Conclusion section, para. 1).

Anticipating and countering alternative interpretations

Do not ignore sources that seem contrary to your position. Instead, use them to give voice to opposing points of view and alternative interpretations before you counter them (see 6i). Readers often have objections in mind already, whether or not they agree with you. Mirano uses a source to acknowledge value in her opponents' position that medication alone can successfully treat childhood obesity.

> As researchers Yanovski and Yanovski (2002) have explained, obesity was once considered "either a moral failing or evidence of underlying psychopathology" (p. 592). But this view has shifted: Many medical professionals now consider obesity a biomedical rather than a moral condition, influenced by both genetic and environmental factors. Yanovski and Yanovski have further noted that the development of weight-loss medications in the early 1990s showed that "obesity should be treated in the same manner as any other chronic disease . . . through the long-term use of medication" (p. 592).

59 Citing sources; avoiding plagiarism

In a research paper, you will draw on the work of other researchers and writers, and you must document their contributions by citing your sources. Sources are cited for two reasons:

1. to tell readers where your information comes from — so that they can assess its reliability and, if interested, find and read the original source
2. to give credit to the writers from whom you have borrowed words and ideas

You must cite anything you borrow from a source, including direct quotations; statistics and other specific facts; visuals such as tables, graphs, and diagrams; and any ideas you present in a summary or paraphrase. Borrowing without proper acknowledgment is a form of dishonesty known as *plagiarism*.

The only exception is common knowledge — information that your readers may know or could easily locate in any number of reference sources.

59a Understand how the APA system works.

The American Psychological Association recommends an author-date system of citations. The following is a brief description of how the author-date system usually works.

1. The source is introduced by a signal phrase that includes the last name of the author followed by the date of publication in parentheses.
2. The material being cited is followed by a page number in parentheses (unless the source is an unpaginated Web source).
3. At the end of the paper, an alphabetized list of references gives complete publication information for the source.

IN-TEXT CITATION

As researchers Yanovski and Yanovski (2002) have explained, obesity was once considered "either a moral failing or evidence of underlying psychopathology" (p. 592).

ENTRY IN THE LIST OF REFERENCES

Yanovski, S. Z., & Yanovski, J. A. (2002). Drug therapy: Obesity. *The New England Journal of Medicine, 346,* 591-602.

This basic APA format varies for different types of sources. For a detailed discussion and other models, see 61.

59b Avoid plagiarism when quoting, summarizing, and paraphrasing sources.

In a research paper, you draw on the work of other writers and you must document their contributions by citing your sources. When you acknowledge your sources, you avoid plagiarism, a serious academic offense.

In general, these three acts are considered plagiarism: (1) failing to cite quotations and borrowed ideas, (2) failing to enclose borrowed language in quotation marks, and (3) failing to put summaries and paraphrases in your own words. Definitions of plagiarism may vary; it's a good idea to find out how your school defines and addresses academic dishonesty.

Citing quotations and borrowed ideas

To indicate that you are using a source's exact phrases or sentences, you must enclose them in quotation marks unless they have been set off from the text by indenting (see 60b). To omit the quotation marks is to claim—falsely—that the language is your own, as in the example below. Such an omission is plagiarism even if you have cited the source.

ORIGINAL SOURCE

In an effort to seek the causes of this disturbing trend, experts have pointed to a range of important potential contributors to the rise in childhood obesity that are unrelated to media: a reduction in physical education classes and after-school athletic programs, an increase in the availability of sodas and snacks in public schools, the growth in the number of fast-food outlets across the country, the trend toward "super-sizing" food portions in restaurants, and the increasing number of highly processed high-calorie and high-fat grocery products.

—Henry J. Kaiser Family Foundation, "The Role of Media in Childhood Obesity" (2004), p. 1

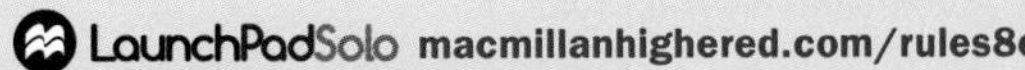

59 Citing sources; avoiding plagiarism
> Exercises: 59–1 to 59–7

PLAGIARISM

According to the Henry J. Kaiser Family Foundation (2004), experts have pointed to a range of important potential contributors to the rise in childhood obesity that are unrelated to media (p. 1).

BORROWED LANGUAGE IN QUOTATION MARKS

According to the Henry J. Kaiser Family Foundation (2004), "experts have pointed to a range of important potential contributors to the rise in childhood obesity that are unrelated to media" (p. 1).

NOTE: Quotation marks are not used when quoted sentences are set off from the text by indenting (see 60b).

Putting summaries and paraphrases in your own words

Summaries and paraphrases are written in your own words. A summary condenses information from a source; a paraphrase uses roughly the same number of words as the original source to convey information. When you summarize or paraphrase, it is not enough to name the source; you must restate the source's meaning using your own language. (See also 51c and 60a.)

Half-copying the author's sentences by using the author's phrases in your own sentences without quotation marks or by plugging synonyms into the author's sentence structure (sometimes called patchwriting) is a form of plagiarism.

The following paraphrases are plagiarized — even though the source is cited — because their language and sentence structure are too close to those of the source.

ORIGINAL SOURCE

In an effort to seek the causes of this disturbing trend, experts have pointed to a range of important potential contributors to the rise in childhood obesity that are unrelated to media.

— Henry J. Kaiser Family Foundation,
"The Role of Media in Childhood Obesity" (2004), p. 1

UNACCEPTABLE BORROWING OF PHRASES

According to the Henry J. Kaiser Family Foundation (2004), experts have indicated a range of significant potential contributors to the rise in childhood obesity that are not linked to media (p. 1).

UNACCEPTABLE BORROWING OF STRUCTURE

According to the Henry J. Kaiser Family Foundation (2004), experts have identified a variety of key factors causing a rise in childhood obesity, factors that are not tied to media (p. 1).

To avoid plagiarizing an author's language, resist the temptation to look at the source while you are summarizing or paraphrasing. After you have read the passage you want to paraphrase, set the source aside. Ask yourself, "What is the author's meaning?" In your own words, state your understanding of the author's ideas.

Return to the source and check that you haven't used the author's language or sentence structure or misrepresented the author's ideas. When you fully understand another writer's meaning, you can more easily and accurately present those ideas in your own words.

ACCEPTABLE PARAPHRASE

A report by the Henry J. Kaiser Family Foundation (2004) described causes other than media for the childhood obesity crisis.

60 Integrating sources

Your research paper draws on and borrows from the work of others — your sources — to help you develop and support your ideas. As you conduct research, you gather language and ideas from your sources that you might want to use in your paper. Section 59 shows you how to acknowledge those sources to avoid plagiarism. This section will help you integrate those sources seamlessly and effectively into your paper, so that readers understand how your use of quotation, summary, and paraphrase contributes to your argument. As you integrate sources, you need to find a balance between the words of your sources and your own voice. Readers should always know who is speaking in your paper — you or your source. You can use several strategies to integrate research sources into your paper while maintaining your own voice.

- Use sources as concisely as possible so that your own thinking and voice aren't lost (60a and 60b).
- Use signal phrases and avoid dropped quotations. Clearly indicate the boundary between your words and the source's words (60c).
- Discuss and analyze your sources to show readers how each source supports your points and how the sources relate to one another (60d).

60a Summarize and paraphrase effectively.

In your academic writing, keep the emphasis on your ideas and your language; use your own words to summarize and to paraphrase your sources and to explain your points. Whether you choose to summarize or paraphrase a source depends on your purpose.

Summarizing

When you summarize a source, you express another writer's ideas in your own words, condensing the author's key points and using fewer words than the author. Even though a summary is in your own words, the original idea remains the intellectual property of the author, so you must include a citation.

WHEN TO USE A SUMMARY

- When a passage is lengthy and you want to condense a chapter to a short paragraph or a paragraph to a single sentence
- When you want to state the source's main ideas simply and briefly in your own words
- When you want to compare or contrast arguments or ideas from various sources
- When you want to provide readers with an understanding of the source's argument before you respond to it or launch your own

Paraphrasing

When you paraphrase, you express an author's ideas in your own words, using approximately the same number of words and details as in the source. Even though the words are your own, the original idea is the author's intellectual property, so you must give a citation.

WHEN TO USE A PARAPHRASE

- When the ideas and information are important but the author's exact words are not needed for accuracy or emphasis
- When you want to restate the source's ideas in your own words
- When you need to simplify and explain a technical or complicated source
- When you need to reorder a source's ideas

Even though you use your own words to summarize and paraphrase, the original idea remains the intellectual property of the author, so you must include a citation. (See 59b.)

60b Use quotations effectively.

When you quote a source, you borrow some of the author's exact words and enclose them in quotation marks. Quotation marks show your readers that both the idea and the words belong to the author.

WHEN TO USE QUOTATIONS

- When language is especially vivid or expressive
- When exact wording is needed for technical accuracy
- When it is important to let the debaters of an issue explain their positions in their own words
- When the words of an authority lend weight to an argument
- When you want to discuss the language of a source

Limiting your use of quotations

Although it is tempting to insert many quotations in your paper and to use your own words only for connecting passages, do not quote excessively.

It is not always necessary to quote full sentences from a source. To reduce your reliance on the words of others, you can integrate language from a source into your own sentence structure. (For the use of signal phrases in integrating quotations, see 60c.)

> Carmona (2004) advised the subcommittee that the situation constitutes an "epidemic" and that the skyrocketing statistics are "astounding."

> As researchers continue to face a number of unknowns about obesity, it may be helpful to envision treating the disorder, as Yanovski and Yanovski (2002) suggested, "in the same manner as any other chronic disease" (p. 592).

Using the ellipsis mark

To condense a quoted passage, you can use the ellipsis mark (three periods, with spaces between) to indicate that you have omitted words. What remains must be grammatically complete.

> Roman (2003) reported that "social factors are nearly as significant as individual metabolism in the formation of . . . dietary habits of adolescents" (p. 345).

The writer has omitted the words *both healthy and unhealthy* from the source.

When you want to leave out one or more full sentences, use a period before the three ellipsis dots.

> According to Sothern and Gordon (2003), "Environmental factors may contribute as much as 80% to the causes of childhood obesity. . . . Research suggests that obese children demonstrate decreased levels of physical activity and increased psychosocial problems" (p. 104).

Ordinarily, do not use an ellipsis mark at the beginning or at the end of a quotation. Readers will understand that you have taken the quoted material from a longer passage. The only exception occurs when you feel it is necessary, for clarity, to indicate that your quotation begins or ends in the middle of a sentence.

USING SOURCES RESPONSIBLY: Make sure that omissions and ellipsis marks do not distort the meaning of your source.

Using brackets

Brackets allow you to insert your own words into quoted material. You can insert words in brackets to clarify a confusing reference or to keep a sentence grammatical in your context.

> The cost of treating obesity currently totals $117 billion per year—a price, according to the surgeon general, "second only to the cost of [treating] tobacco use" (Carmona, 2004).

To indicate an error such as a misspelling in a quotation, insert [*sic*], italicized and in brackets, right after the error.

Setting off long quotations

When you quote forty or more words from a source, set off the quotation by indenting it one-half inch from the left margin. Use the normal right margin and do not single-space the quotation.

Long quotations should be introduced by an informative sentence, often followed by a colon. Quotation marks are unnecessary because the indented format tells readers that the passage is taken word-for-word from the source.

> Yanovski and Yanovski (2002) have described earlier treatments of obesity that focused on behavior modification:
>
> > With the advent of behavioral treatments for obesity in the 1960s, hope arose that modification of maladaptive eating and exercise habits would lead to sustained weight loss, and that time-limited programs would produce permanent changes in weight. Medications for the treatment of obesity were proposed as short-term adjuncts for patients, who would presumably then acquire the skills necessary to continue to lose weight, reach "ideal body weight," and maintain a reduced weight indefinitely. (p. 592)

Notice that at the end of an indented quotation the parenthetical citation goes outside the final mark of punctuation. (When a quotation is run into your text, the opposite is true. See the sample citations on p. 540.)

60c Use signal phrases to integrate sources.

Whenever you include a paraphrase, summary, or direct quotation of another writer's work in your paper, prepare your readers for it with introductory words called a *signal phrase*. A signal phrase usually names the author of the source, gives the publication year in parentheses, and often provides some context. It is generally acceptable in APA style to call authors by their last name only, even on a first mention. If your paper refers to two authors with the same last name, use initials as well.

When you write a signal phrase, choose a verb that is appropriate for the way you are using the source. Are you providing background, explaining a concept, supporting a claim, lending authority, or refuting an argument (see 58c)? See the chart on page 543 for a list of verbs commonly used in signal phrases. Note that APA requires using verbs in the past tense or present perfect tense (*explained* or *has explained*) to introduce source material. Use the present tense only for discussing the applications or effects of your own results (*the data suggest*) or knowledge that has been clearly established (*researchers agree*).

Marking boundaries

Readers need to move from your words to the words of a source without feeling a jolt. Avoid dropping direct quotations into your text without warning. Instead, provide clear signal phrases, including at least the author's name and the year of publication. Signal phrases mark the boundaries between source material and your own words; they can also tell readers why a source is worth quoting. (The signal phrase is highlighted in the second example.)

DROPPED QUOTATION

Obesity was once considered in a very different light. "For many years, obesity was approached as if it were either a moral failing or evidence of underlying psychopathology" (Yanovski & Yanovski, 2002, p. 592).

QUOTATION WITH SIGNAL PHRASE

Obesity was once considered in a very different light. As researchers Yanovski and Yanovski (2002) have explained, obesity was widely thought of as "either a moral failing or evidence of underlying psychopathology" (p. 592).

Using signal phrases with summaries and paraphrases

As with quotations, you should introduce most summaries and paraphrases with a signal phrase that mentions the author and the year and places the material in the context of your own writing. Readers will then understand where the summary or paraphrase begins.

Without the signal phrase (highlighted) in the following example, readers might think that only the last sentence is being cited, when in fact the whole paragraph is based on the source.

> Carmona (2004) advised a Senate subcommittee that the problem of childhood obesity is dire and that the skyrocketing statistics—which put the child obesity rate at 15%—are cause for alarm. More than nine million children, double the number in the early 1980s, are classified as obese. Carmona warned that obesity can cause myriad physical problems that only worsen as children grow older.

There are times, however, when a summary or a paraphrase does not require a signal phrase naming the author. When the context makes clear where the cited material begins, you may omit the signal phrase and include the author's name and the year in parentheses.

Using signal phrases in APA papers

To avoid monotony, try to vary both the language and the placement of your signal phrases.

Model signal phrases

In the words of Carmona (2004), ". . ."

As Yanovski and Yanovski (2002) have noted, ". . ."

Hoppin and Taveras (2004), medical researchers, pointed out that ". . ."

". . . ," claimed Critser (2003).

". . . ," wrote Duenwald (2004), ". . ."

Researchers McDuffie et al. (2003) have offered a compelling argument for this view: ". . ."

Hilts (2002) answered objections with the following analysis: ". . ."

Verbs in signal phrases

admitted
agreed
argued
asserted
believed
claimed
compared
confirmed
contended
declared
denied
emphasized
insisted
noted
observed
pointed out
reasoned
refuted
rejected
reported
responded
suggested
thought
wrote

Integrating statistics and other facts

When you are citing a statistic or another specific fact, a signal phrase is often not necessary. In most cases, readers will understand that the citation refers to the statistic or fact (not the whole paragraph).

> In purely financial terms, the drugs cost more than $3 a day on average (Duenwald, 2004).

There is nothing wrong, however, with using a signal phrase to introduce a statistic or another fact.

Putting source material in context

Readers should not have to guess why source material appears in your paper. A signal phrase can help you make the connection between your own ideas and those of another writer by clarifying how the source will contribute to your paper.

If you use another writer's words, you must explain how they relate to your writing. Quotations don't speak for themselves; you must support them by creating a context for readers. Embed each quotation between sentences of your own: Introduce the quotation with a signal phrase, and follow it with interpretive comments that link the quotation to your own ideas. (See also 60c.)

QUOTATION WITH EFFECTIVE CONTEXT

> A report by the Henry J. Kaiser Family Foundation (2004) outlined trends that may have contributed to the childhood obesity crisis, including food advertising for children as well as
>
> > a reduction in physical education classes . . . , an increase in the availability of sodas and snacks in public schools, the growth in the number of fast-food outlets . . . , and the increasing number of highly processed high-calorie and high-fat grocery products. (p. 1)
>
> Addressing each of these areas requires more than a doctor armed with a prescription pad; it requires a broad mobilization not just of doctors and concerned parents but of educators, food industry executives, advertisers, and media representatives.

60d Synthesize sources.

When you synthesize multiple sources in a research paper, you create a conversation about your research topic. Your paper includes your active analysis and integration of ideas, not just a series of quotations and paraphrases. Your synthesis will show how your sources relate to one another; one source may support, extend, or counter the ideas of another. Not every source has to "speak" to another in a research paper, but readers should be able to see how each one functions in your argument.

SAMPLE SYNTHESIS (DRAFT)

Student writer Luisa Mirano begins with a claim that needs support.

Mirano interprets and connects sources. Each paragraph ends with her own thoughts.

Signal phrases indicate how sources contribute to Mirano's paper and show that the ideas that follow are not her own.

Medical treatments have clear costs for individual patients, including unpleasant side effects, little information about long-term use, and uncertainty that they will yield significant weight loss. The financial burden is heavy as well; [Student writer] the drugs cost more than $3 a day on average (Duenwald, 2004). [Source 1] In each of the clinical trials, use of medication was accompanied by expensive behavioral therapies, including counseling, nutrition education, fitness advising, and monitoring. [Student writer] As Critser (2003) noted in his book *Fat Land*, use of weight-loss drugs is unlikely to have an effect without the proper "support system"—one that includes doctors, facilities, time, and money (p. 3). [Source 2] For many families, this level of care is prohibitively expensive. [Student writer]

Both medical experts and policymakers recognize that solutions might come not only from a laboratory but also from policy, education, and advocacy. A handbook designed to educate doctors on obesity called for "major changes in some aspects of western culture" (Hoppin & Taveras, 2004, Conclusion section, para. 1). [Source 3] Solving the childhood obesity problem will require broad mobilization of doctors and concerned parents and also of educators, food industry executives, advertisers, and media representatives.

Student writer

In this synthesis, Mirano uses her own analyses to shape the conversation among her sources. She does not simply string quotations and statistics together or allow her sources to overwhelm her writing. The final sentence, written in her own voice, gives her an opportunity to explain to readers how her sources support and extend her argument.

When synthesizing sources, ask yourself these questions:

- How do your sources speak to your research question?
- How do your sources speak to each other?
- Have you varied the functions of sources — to provide background, explain concepts, lend authority, and anticipate counterarguments?
- Do you explain how your sources support your argument?
- Do you connect and analyze sources in your own voice?
- Is your own argument easy to identify and to understand, with or without your sources?

61 Documenting sources in APA style

In most social science classes and some humanities classes, you will be asked to use the APA system for documenting sources, which is set forth in the *Publication Manual of the American Psychological Association*, 6th ed. (Washington, DC: APA, 2010).

APA recommends in-text citations that refer readers to a list of references. An in-text citation gives the author of the source (often in a signal phrase), the year of publication, and often a page number in parentheses. At the end of the paper, a list of references provides publication information about the source; the list is alphabetized by authors' last names (or by titles for works with no authors). The direct link between the in-text citation and the entry in the reference list is highlighted in the following example.

IN-TEXT CITATION

Yanovski and Yanovski (2002) reported that "the current state of the treatment for obesity is similar to the state of the treatment of hypertension several decades ago" (p. 600).

ENTRY IN THE LIST OF REFERENCES

Yanovski, S. Z., & Yanovski, J. A. (2002). Drug therapy: Obesity. *The New England Journal of Medicine, 346*, 591-602.

For a reference list that includes this entry, see pages 595–96.

61a APA in-text citations

APA's in-text citations provide the author's last name and the year of publication, usually before the cited material, and a page number in parentheses directly after the cited material. In the following models, the elements of the in-text citation are highlighted.

NOTE: APA style requires the use of the past tense or the present perfect tense in signal phrases introducing cited material: *Smith (2012) reported, Smith (2012) has argued.* (See also p. 543.)

■ **1. Basic format for a quotation** Ordinarily, introduce the quotation with a signal phrase that includes the author's last name followed by the year of publication in parentheses. Put the page number (preceded by "p.") in parentheses after the quotation. For sources from the Web without page numbers, see item 12a on page 551.

Critser (2003) noted that despite growing numbers of overweight Americans, many health care providers still "remain either in ignorance or outright denial about the health danger to the poor and the young" (p. 5).

If the author is not named in the signal phrase, place the author's name, the year, and the page number in parentheses after the quotation: (Critser, 2003, p. 5). (See items 6 and 12 for citing sources that lack authors; item 12 also explains how to handle sources without dates or page numbers.)

NOTE: Do not include a month in an in-text citation, even if the entry in the reference list includes the month.

■ **2. Basic format for a summary or a paraphrase** As with a quotation (see item 1), include the author's last name and the year either in a signal phrase introducing the material or in parentheses following it. Use a page number, if one is available, following the cited material. For sources from the Web without page numbers, see item 12a on page 551.

> Yanovski and Yanovski (2002) explained that sibutramine suppresses appetite by blocking the reuptake of the neurotransmitters serotonin and norepinephrine in the brain (p. 594).

> Sibutramine suppresses appetite by blocking the reuptake of the neurotransmitters serotonin and norepinephrine in the brain (Yanovski & Yanovski, 2002, p. 594).

■ **3. Work with two authors** Name both authors in the signal phrase or in parentheses each time you cite the work. In the parentheses, use "&" between the authors' names; in the signal phrase, use "and."

> According to Sothern and Gordon (2003), "Environmental factors may contribute as much as 80% to the causes of childhood obesity" (p. 104).

> Obese children often engage in limited physical activity (Sothern & Gordon, 2003, p. 104).

■ **4. Work with three to five authors** Identify all authors in the signal phrase or in parentheses the first time you cite the source.

> In 2003, Berkowitz, Wadden, Tershakovec, and Cronquist concluded, "Sibutramine . . . must be carefully monitored in adolescents, as in adults, to control increases in [blood pressure] and pulse rate" (p. 1811).

In subsequent citations, use the first author's name followed by "et al." in either the signal phrase or the parentheses.

As Berkowitz et al. (2003) advised, "Until more extensive safety and efficacy data are available, . . . weight-loss medications should be used only on an experimental basis for adolescents" (p. 1811).

■ **5. Work with six or more authors** Use the first author's name followed by "et al." in the signal phrase or in parentheses.

McDuffie et al. (2002) tested 20 adolescents, aged 12-16, over a three-month period and found that orlistat, combined with behavioral therapy, produced an average weight loss of 4.4 kg, or 9.7 pounds (p. 646).

■ **6. Work with unknown author** If the author is unknown, mention the work's title in the signal phrase or give the first word or two of the title in the parentheses. Titles of short works such as articles are put in quotation marks; titles of long works such as books and reports are italicized.

Children struggling to control their weight must also struggle with the pressures of television advertising that, on the one hand, encourages the consumption of junk food and, on the other, celebrates thin celebrities ("Television," 2002).

NOTE: In the rare case when "Anonymous" is specified as the author, treat it as if it were a real name: (Anonymous, 2001). In the list of references, also use the name Anonymous as author.

■ **7. Organization as author** If the author is an organization or a government agency, name the organization in the signal phrase or in the parentheses the first time you cite the source.

Obesity puts children at risk for a number of medical complications, including Type 2 diabetes, hypertension, sleep apnea, and orthopedic problems (Henry J. Kaiser Family Foundation, 2004, p. 1).

If the organization has a familiar abbreviation, you may include it in brackets the first time you cite the source and use the abbreviation alone in later citations.

FIRST CITATION	(Centers for Disease Control and Prevention [CDC], 2012)
LATER CITATIONS	(CDC, 2012)

8. Authors with the same last name To avoid confusion if your reference list includes two or more authors with the same last name, use initials with the last names in your in-text citations.

> Research by E. Smith (1989) revealed that. . . .
>
> One 2012 study contradicted . . . (R. Smith, p. 234).

9. Two or more works by the same author in the same year When your list of references includes more than one work by the same author in the same year, you will use lowercase letters ("a," "b," and so on) with the year to order the entries in the reference list. (See item 8 on p. 557.) Use those same letters with the year in the in-text citation.

> Research by Durgin (2003b) has yielded new findings about the role of counseling in treating childhood obesity.

10. Two or more works in the same parentheses Put the works in the same order that they appear in the reference list, separated with semicolons.

> Researchers have indicated that studies of pharmacological treatments for childhood obesity are inconclusive (Berkowitz et al., 2003; McDuffie et al., 2002).

11. Multiple citations to the same work in one paragraph If you give the author's name in the text of your paper (not in parentheses) and you mention that source again in the text of the same paragraph, give only the author's name, not the date, in the later citation. If any subsequent reference in the same paragraph is in parentheses, include both the author and the date in the parentheses.

> Principal Jean Patrice said, "You have to be able to reach students where they are instead of making them come to you. If you don't, you'll lose them" (personal communication, April 10, 2006). Patrice expressed her desire to see all students get something out of their educational experience. This feeling is common among members of Waverly's faculty. With such a positive view of student potential, it is no wonder that 97% of Waverly High School graduates go on to a four-year university (Patrice, 2006).

12. Web source Cite sources from the Web as you would cite any other source, giving the author and the year when they are available.

> Atkinson (2001) found that children who spent at least four hours a day watching TV were less likely to engage in adequate physical activity during the week.

Usually a page number is not available; occasionally a Web source will lack an author or a date (see items 12a, 12b, and 12c).

a. No page numbers When a Web source lacks stable numbered pages, you may include paragraph numbers or headings to help readers locate the passage being cited.

If the source has numbered paragraphs, use the paragraph number preceded by the abbreviation "para.": (Hall, 2012, para. 5). If the source has no numbered paragraphs but contains headings, cite the appropriate heading in parentheses; you may also indicate which paragraph under the heading you are referring to, even if the paragraphs are not numbered.

> Hoppin and Taveras (2004) pointed out that several other medications were classified by the Drug Enforcement Administration as having the "potential for abuse" (Weight-Loss Drugs section, para. 6).

NOTE: For PDF documents that have stable page numbers, give the page number in the parenthetical citation.

b. Unknown author If no author is named in the source, mention the title of the source in a signal phrase or give the first word or two of the title in parentheses (see also item 6). (If an organization serves as the author, see item 7.)

> The body's basal metabolic rate, or BMR, is a measure of its at-rest energy requirement ("Exercise," 2003).

c. Unknown date When the source does not give a date, use the abbreviation "n.d." (for "no date").

> Attempts to establish a definitive link between television programming and children's eating habits have been problematic (Magnus, n.d.).

13. An entire Web site If you are citing an entire Web site, not an internal page or a section, give the URL in the text of your paper but do not include it in the reference list.

> The U.S. Center for Nutrition Policy and Promotion website (http://www.cnpp.usda.gov/) provides useful information about diet and nutrition for children and adults.

14. Multivolume work If you have used more than one volume from a multivolume work, add the volume number in parentheses with the page number.

> Banford (2009) has demonstrated stable weight loss over time from a combination of psychological counseling, exercise, and nutritional planning (Volume 2, p. 135).

15. Personal communication Interviews that you conduct, memos, letters, e-mail messages, social media posts, and similar communications that would be difficult for your readers to retrieve should be cited in the text only, not in the reference list. (Use the first initial with the last name in parentheses.)

> One of Atkinson's colleagues, who has studied the effect of the media on children's eating habits, has contended that advertisers for snack foods will need to design ads responsibly for their younger viewers (F. Johnson, personal communication, October 20, 2013).

16. Course materials Cite lecture notes from your instructor or your own class notes as personal communication (see item 15). If your instructor distributes or posts materials that contain publication information, cite as you would the appropriate source (for instance, an article, a section in a Web document, or a video). See also item 65 on page 579.

17. Part of a source (chapter, figure) To cite a specific part of a source, such as a whole chapter or a figure or table, identify the element in parentheses. Don't abbreviate terms such as "Figure," "Chapter," and "Section"; "page" is always abbreviated "p." (or "pp." for more than one page).

> The data support the finding that weight loss stabilizes with consistent therapy and ongoing monitoring (Hanniman, 2010, Figure 8-3, p. 345).

18. Indirect source (source quoted in another source) When a writer's or a speaker's quoted words appear in a source written by someone else, begin the parenthetical citation with the words "as cited in." In the following example, Critser is the author of the source given in the reference list; that source contains a quotation by Satcher.

> Former surgeon general Dr. David Satcher described "a nation of young people seriously at risk of starting out obese and dooming themselves to the difficult task of overcoming a tough illness" (as cited in Critser, 2003, p. 4).

■ **19. Sacred or classical text** Identify the text, the version or edition you used, and the relevant part (chapter, verse, line). It is not necessary to include the source in the reference list.

> Peace activists have long cited the biblical prophet's vision of a world without war: "And they shall beat their swords into plowshares, and their spears into pruning hooks; nation shall not lift up sword against nation, neither shall they learn war any more" (Isaiah 2:4, Revised Standard Version).

61b APA list of references

As you gather sources for an assignment, you will likely find sources in print, on the Web, and in other places. The information you will need for the reference list at the end of your paper will differ slightly for some sources, but the main principles apply to all sources: You should identify an author, a creator, or a producer whenever possible; give a title; and provide the date on which the source was produced. Some sources will require page numbers; some will require a publisher; and some will require retrieval information.

► General guidelines for the reference list, **page 554**

Section 61b provides specific requirements for and examples of many of the sources you are likely to encounter. When you cite sources, your goals are to show that the sources you've used are reliable and relevant to your work, to provide your readers with enough information so that they can find your sources easily, and to provide that information in a consistent way according to APA conventions.

In the list of references, include only sources that you have quoted, summarized, or paraphrased in your paper.

LaunchPadSolo **macmillanhighered.com/rules8e**

61 Documenting sources in APA style

> Exercises: 61-4 to 61-8, 61-12

General guidelines for listing authors

The formatting of authors' names in items 1–12 applies to all sources in print and on the Web — books, articles, Web sites, and so on. For more models of specific source types, see items 13–69.

General guidelines for the reference list

In APA style, the alphabetical list of works cited, which appears at the end of the paper, is titled "References."

Authors and dates

- Alphabetize entries in the list of references by authors' last names; if a work has no author, alphabetize it by its title.
- For all authors' names, put the last name first, followed by a comma; use initials for the first and middle names.
- With two or more authors, use an ampersand (&) before the last author's name. Separate the names with commas. Include names for the first seven authors; if there are eight or more authors, give the first six authors, three ellipsis dots, and the last author.
- If the author is a company or an organization, give the name in normal order.
- Put the date of publication immediately after the first element of the citation. Enclose the date in parentheses, followed by a period (outside the parentheses).
- For books, give the year of publication. For magazines, newspapers, and newsletters, give the exact date as in the publication (the year plus the month or the year plus the month and the day). For sources on the Web, give the date of posting, if it is available. Use the season if the publication gives only a season and not a month.

Titles

- Italicize the titles and subtitles of books, journals, and other long works.
- Use no italics or quotation marks for the titles of articles.
- For books and articles, capitalize only the first word of the title and subtitle and all proper nouns.
- For the titles of journals, magazines, and newspapers, capitalize all words of four letters or more (and all nouns, pronouns, verbs, adjectives, and adverbs of any length).

Place of publication and publisher

- Take the information about a book from its title page and copyright page. If more than one place of publication is listed, use only the first.
- Give the city and state for all US cities. Use postal abbreviations for all states.
- Give the city and country for all non-US cities; include the province for Canadian cities. Do not abbreviate the country and province.
- Do not give a state if the publisher's name includes it (Ann Arbor: University of Michigan Press, for example).
- In publishers' names, omit terms such as "Company" (or "Co.") and "Inc." but keep "Books" and "Press." Omit first names or initials (Norton, not W. W. Norton, for example).
- If the publisher is the same as the author, use the word "Author" in the publisher position.

Volume, issue, and page numbers

- For a journal or a magazine, give only the volume number if the publication is paginated continuously through each volume; give the volume and issue numbers if each issue begins on page 1.
- Italicize the volume number and put the issue number, not italicized, in parentheses.
- For monthly magazines, give the year and the month; for weekly magazines, add the day.
- For daily and weekly newspapers, give the month, day, and year; use "p." or "pp." before page numbers (if any). For journals and magazines, do not add "p." or "pp."
- When an article appears on consecutive pages, provide the range of pages. When an article does not appear on consecutive pages, give all page numbers: A1, A17.

URLs, DOIs, and other retrieval information

- For articles and books from the Web, use the DOI (digital object identifier) if the source has one, and do not give a URL. If a source does not have a DOI, give the URL.
- Use a retrieval date for a Web source only if the content is likely to change. Most of the examples in 61b do not show a retrieval date because the content of the sources is stable. If you are unsure about whether to use a retrieval date, include the date or consult your instructor.

1. Single author

author: last name + initial(s) | year (book) | title (book) | place of publication | publisher

Brown, S. (2014). *Mean streak*. New York, NY: Grand Central.

2. Two to seven authors List up to seven authors by last names followed by initials. Use an ampersand (&) before the name of the last author. (See items 3–5 on pp. 548–49 for citing works with multiple authors in the text of your paper.)

all authors: last name + initial(s) | year (book) | title (book) | place of publication | publisher

Stanford, D. J., & Bradley, B. A. (2012). *Across the Atlantic ice: The origins of America's Clovis culture*. Berkeley: University of California Press.

all authors: last name + initial(s) | year (journal) | title (article) | journal title | volume | page(s) | DOI

Ludwig, J., Duncan, G. J., Gennetian, L. A., Katz, L. F., Kessler, R. C., Kling, J. R., & Sanbonmatsu, L. (2012). Neighborhood effects on the long-term well-being of low-income adults. *Science*, *337*, 1505-1510. doi:10.1126/science.1224648

3. Eight or more authors List the first six authors followed by three ellipsis dots and the last author's name.

Tøttrup, A. P., Klaassen, R. H. G., Kristensen, M. W., Strandberg, R., Vardanis, Y., Lindström, Å., . . . Thorup, K. (2012). Drought in Africa caused delayed arrival of European songbirds. *Science, 338,* 1307. doi:10.1126/science.1227548

4. Organization as author

author: organization name | year | title (book) | edition | place of publication | organization as author and publisher

American Psychiatric Association. (2013). *Diagnostic and statistical manual of mental disorders* (5th ed.). Washington, DC: Author.

5. Unknown author Begin the entry with the work's title.

title (article) | year + month + day (weekly publication) | journal title | volume, issue | page(s)

The rise of the sharing economy. (2013, March 9). *The Economist, 406*(8826), 14.

title (book) | year | place of publication | publisher

New concise world atlas. (2010). New York, NY: Oxford University Press.

6. Author using a pseudonym (pen name) or screen name Use the author's real name, if known, and give the pseudonym or screen name in brackets exactly as it appears in the source. If only the screen name is known, begin with that name and do not use brackets. (See also items 47 and 68 on citing screen names in social media.)

screen name | year + month + day (daily publication) | title of original article | label | title of publication | URL for Web publication

littlebigman. (2012, December 13). Re: Who's watching? Privacy concerns persist as smart meters roll out [Comment]. *National Geographic Daily News*. Retrieved from http://news.nationalgeographic.com/

7. Two or more works by the same author Use the author's name for all entries. List the entries by year, the earliest first.

Heinrich, B. (2009). *Summer world: A season of bounty*. New York, NY: Ecco.

Heinrich, B. (2012). *Life everlasting: The animal way of death*. New York, NY: Houghton Mifflin Harcourt.

8. Two or more works by the same author in the same year List the works alphabetically by title. In the parentheses, following the year add "a," "b," and so on. Use these same letters when giving the year in the in-text citation. (See also p. 584 and item 9 on p. 550.)

Bower, B. (2012a, December 15). Families in flux. *Science News, 182*(12), 16.

Bower, B. (2012b, November 3). Human-Neandertal mating gets a new date. *Science News, 182*(9), 8.

■ **9. Editor** Begin with the name of the editor or editors; place the abbreviation "Ed." (or "Eds." for more than one editor) in parentheses following the name. (See item 10 for a work with both an author and an editor.)

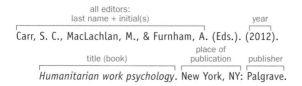

all editors: last name + initial(s) | year

Carr, S. C., MacLachlan, M., & Furnham, A. (Eds.). (2012).

title (book) | place of publication | publisher

Humanitarian work psychology. New York, NY: Palgrave.

■ **10. Author and editor** Begin with the name of the author, followed by the name of the editor and the abbreviation "Ed." For an author with two or more editors, use the abbreviation "Ed." after each editor's name: Gray, W., & Jones, P. (Ed.), & Smith, A. (Ed.).

author | editor | year | title (book)

James, W., & Pelikan, J. (Ed.). (2009). *The varieties of religious experience*.

place of publication | publisher | original publication information

New York, NY: Library of America. (Original work published 1902)

■ **11. Translator** Begin with the name of the author. After the title, in parentheses place the name of the translator (in normal order) and the abbreviation "Trans." (for "Translator"). Add the original date of publication at the end of the entry.

author | year | title (book) | translator | place of publication

Scheffer, P. (2011). *Immigrant nations* (L. Waters, Trans.). Cambridge,

publisher | original publication information

England: Polity Press. (Original work published 2007)

■ **12. Editor and translator** If the editor and translator are the same person, the same name appears in both the editor position and the translator position.

Girard, R., & Williams, J. G. (Ed.). (2012). *Resurrection from the underground* (J. G. Williams, Trans.). East Lansing: Michigan State University Press. (Original work published 1996)

Articles and other short works

▸Citation at a glance: Article in a journal or magazine, **page 560**
▸Citation at a glance: Article from a database, **page 562**

13. Article in a journal If an article from the Web or a database has no DOI, include the URL for the journal's home page.

a. Print

all authors: last name + initial(s) | year | article title

Bippus, A. M., Dunbar, N. E., & Liu, S.-J. (2012). Humorous responses to interpersonal complaints: Effects of humor style and nonverbal expression. *The Journal of Psychology, 146*, 437-453.

journal title | volume | page(s)

b. Web

all authors: last name + initial(s) | year | article title

Vargas, N., & Schafer, M. H. (2013). Diversity in action: Interpersonal networks and the distribution of advice. *Social Science Research, 42*(1), 46-58. doi:10.1016/j.ssresearch.2012.08.013

journal title | volume, issue | page(s) | DOI

author | year | article title

Brenton, S. (2011). When the personal becomes political: Mitigating damage following scandals. *Current Research in Social Psychology*. Retrieved from http://www.uiowa.edu/~grpproc/crisp/crisp.html

journal title (no volume available) | URL for journal home page

c. Database

author | year (journal) | article title

Sohn, K. (2012). The social class origins of U.S. teachers, 1860-1920. *Journal of Social History, 45*(4), 908-935. doi:10.1093/jsh/shr121

journal title | volume, issue | page(s) | DOI

Citation at a glance

Article in a journal or magazine (APA)

To cite an article in a print journal or magazine in APA style, include the following elements:

1. Author(s)
2. Year of publication for journal; complete date for magazine
3. Title and subtitle of article
4. Name of journal or magazine
5. Volume number; issue number, if required (see p. 555)
6. Page number(s) of article

JOURNAL TABLE OF CONTENTS

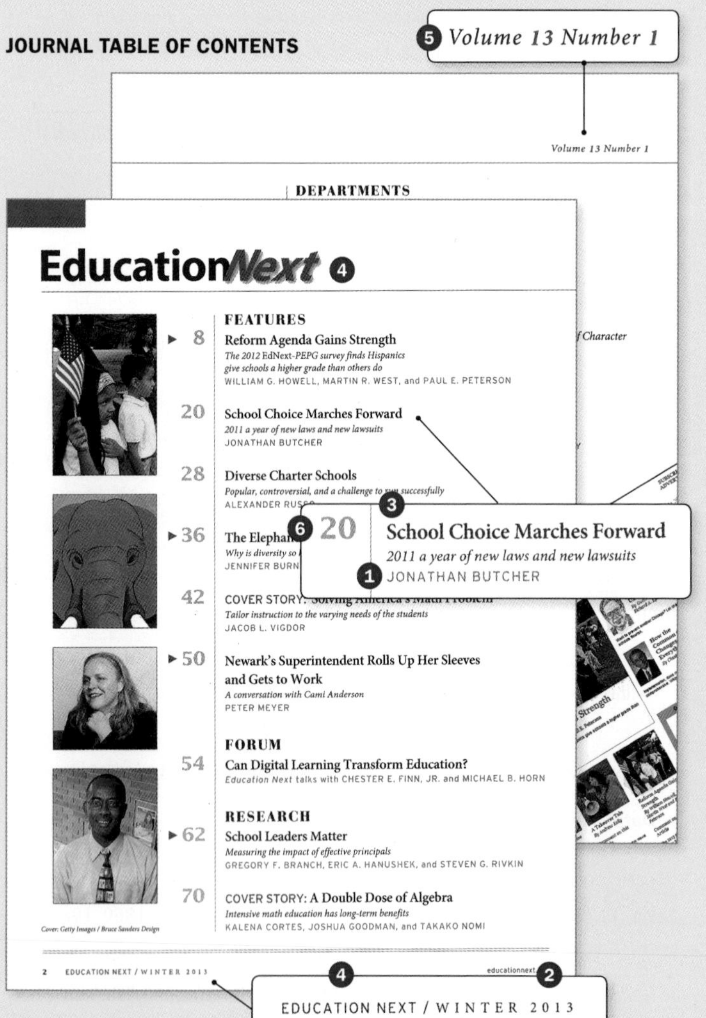

5 Volume 13 Number 1
Volume 13 Number 1
DEPARTMENTS
EducationNext 4
FEATURES
8 Reform Agenda Gains Strength
The 2012 EdNext-PEPG survey finds Hispanics give schools a higher grade than others do
WILLIAM G. HOWELL, MARTIN R. WEST, and PAUL E. PETERSON
20 School Choice Marches Forward
2011 a year of new laws and new lawsuits
JONATHAN BUTCHER
28 Diverse Charter Schools
Popular, controversial, and a challenge to run successfully
ALEXANDER RUS
36 The Elephan
Why is diversity so
JENNIFER BURN
42 COVER STORY:
Tailor instruction to the varying needs of the students
JACOB L. VIGDOR
50 Newark's Superintendent Rolls Up Her Sleeves and Gets to Work
A conversation with Cami Anderson
PETER MEYER
FORUM
54 Can Digital Learning Transform Education?
Education Next talks with CHESTER E. FINN, JR. and MICHAEL B. HORN
RESEARCH
62 School Leaders Matter
Measuring the impact of effective principals
GREGORY F. BRANCH, ERIC A. HANUSHEK, and STEVEN G. RIVKIN
70 COVER STORY: A Double Dose of Algebra
Intensive math education has long-term benefits
KALENA CORTES, JOSHUA GOODMAN, and TAKAKO NOMI
Cover: Getty Images / Bruce Sanders Design
2 EDUCATION NEXT / WINTER 2013
educationnext
6 20
3 School Choice Marches Forward
2011 a year of new laws and new lawsuits
1 JONATHAN BUTCHER
4 2
EDUCATION NEXT / WINTER 2013

FIRST PAGE OF ARTICLE

feature

School Choice Marches Forward

3

One year ago, the *Wall Street Journal* dubbed 2011 "the year of school choice," opining that "this year is shaping up as the best for reformers in a very long time." Such quotes were bound to circulate among education reformers and give traditional opponents of school choice, such as teachers unions, heartburn. Thirteen states enacted new programs that allow K–12 students to choose a public or private school instead of attending their assigned school, and similar bills were under consideration in more than two dozen states.

2011 a year of new laws and new lawsuits

By JONATHAN BUTCHER 1

With so much activity, school choice moved from the margins of education reform debates and became the headline. In January 2012, *Washington Post* education reporter Michael Alison Chandler said school choice has become "a mantra of 21st-century education reform," citing policies across the country that have traditional public schools competing for students alongside charter schools and private schools.

"It took us 20 years to pass the first 20 private school-choice programs in America and in the 21st year we passed 7 new programs," says Scott Jensen with the American Federation for Children (AFC), a school-choice advocacy group based in Washington, D.C. "So we went from passing, on average, one each year, to seven in one fell swoop."

Programs enacted in 2011 include

- a tax-credit scholarship program in North Carolina
- Arizona's education savings account system for K–12 students
- Maine's new charter school law, which brings the total number of states, along with the District of Columbia, with charter schools to 42
- a voucher program in Indiana with broad eligibility rules.

School-choice laws also passed in Wisconsin, Washington, D.C., Oklahoma,

educationnext.org WINTER 2013 / EDUCATION NEXT 21

2 4

WINTER 2013 / EDUCATION NEXT 21

REFERENCE LIST ENTRY FOR AN ARTICLE IN A PRINT JOURNAL OR MAGAZINE

1 2 3 4 5 6

Butcher, J. (2013). School choice marches forward. *Education Next, 13*(1), 20-27.

For more on citing articles in APA style, see items 13–15.

Citation at a glance
Article from a database (APA)

To cite an article from a database in APA style, include the following:

1. Author(s)
2. Year of publication for journal; complete date for magazine or newspaper
3. Title and subtitle of article
4. Name of periodical
5. Volume number; issue number, if required (see p. 555)
6. Page number(s)
7. DOI (digital object identifier)
8. URL for periodical's home page (if there is no DOI)

DATABASE RECORD

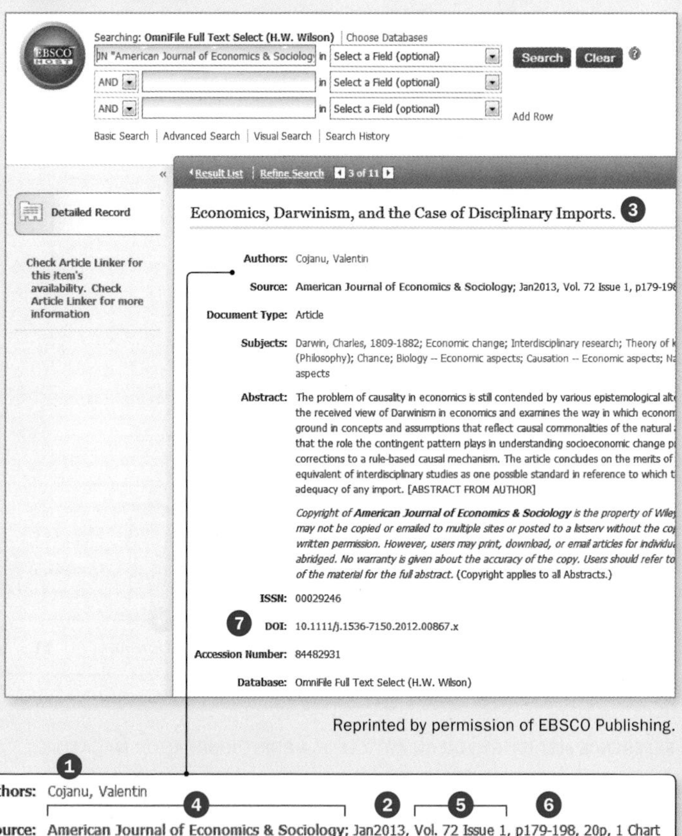

EBSCO HOST

Searching: **OmniFile Full Text Select (H.W. Wilson)** | Choose Databases

JN "American Journal of Economics & Sociolog in Select a Field (optional) Search Clear

AND in Select a Field (optional)

AND in Select a Field (optional) Add Row

Basic Search | Advanced Search | Visual Search | Search History

‹Result List | Refine Search 3 of 11

Detailed Record

Check Article Linker for this item's availability. Check Article Linker for more information

Economics, Darwinism, and the Case of Disciplinary Imports. 3

Authors: Cojanu, Valentin

Source: American Journal of Economics & Sociology; Jan2013, Vol. 72 Issue 1, p179-198

Document Type: Article

Subjects: Darwin, Charles, 1809-1882; Economic change; Interdisciplinary research; Theory of k (Philosophy); Chance; Biology -- Economic aspects; Causation -- Economic aspects; Na aspects

Abstract: The problem of causality in economics is still contended by various epistemological alt the received view of Darwinism in economics and examines the way in which econom ground in concepts and assumptions that reflect causal commonalities of the natural that the role the contingent pattern plays in understanding socioeconomic change p corrections to a rule-based causal mechanism. The article concludes on the merits of equivalent of interdisciplinary studies as one possible standard in reference to which t adequacy of any import. [ABSTRACT FROM AUTHOR]

*Copyright of **American Journal of Economics & Sociology** is the property of Wiley may not be copied or emailed to multiple sites or posted to a listserv without the co written permission. However, users may print, download, or email articles for individu abridged. No warranty is given about the accuracy of the copy. Users should refer to of the material for the full abstract.* (Copyright applies to all Abstracts.)

ISSN: 00029246

7 **DOI:** 10.1111/j.1536-7150.2012.00867.x

Accession Number: 84482931

Database: OmniFile Full Text Select (H.W. Wilson)

Reprinted by permission of EBSCO Publishing.

1 **Authors:** Cojanu, Valentin

Source: American Journal of Economics & Sociology (4); Jan2013 (2), Vol. 72 Issue 1 (5), p179-198 (6), 20p, 1 Chart

For more on citing articles from a database in APA style, see items 13–15.

REFERENCE LIST ENTRY FOR AN ARTICLE FROM A DATABASE

1 — 2 — 3

Cojanu, V. (2013). Economics, Darwinism, and the case of disciplinary

4 — 5 — 6

imports. *American Journal of Economics & Sociology, 72*, 179-198.

7

doi:10.1111/j.1536-7150.2012.00867.x

14. Article in a magazine If an article from the Web or a database has no DOI, include the URL for the magazine's home page.

a. Print

author — year + month (monthly magazine) — article title — magazine title

Comstock, J. (2012, December). The underrated sense. *Psychology Today, 45*(6), 46-47.

volume, issue — page(s)

b. Web

author — date of posting (when available) — article title — magazine title

Burns, J. (2012, December 3). The measure of all things. *The American Prospect*. Retrieved from http://prospect.org/

URL for home page

c. Database

author — year + month (monthly magazine) — article title — magazine title — volume, issue — page(s)

Tucker, A. (2012, November). Primal instinct. *Smithsonian, 43*(7), 54-63. Retrieved from http://www.smithsonianmag.com/

URL for magazine home page

15. Article in a newspaper

a. Print

author — year + month + day — article title

Swarns, R. L. (2012, December 9). A family, for a few days a year. *The New York Times*, pp. 1, 20.

newspaper title — page(s)

15. Article in a newspaper (*cont.*)

b. Web

author: last name + initial(s) | year + month + day | article title | newspaper title | URL for home page

Villanueva-Whitman, E. (2012, November 27). Working to stimulate memory function. *Des Moines Register*. Retrieved from http://www.desmoinesregister.com/

16. Abstract

Add the label "Abstract," in brackets, after the title.

a. Abstract of a journal article

Morales, J., Calvo, A., & Bialystok, E. (2013). Working memory development in monolingual and bilingual children [Abstract]. *Journal of Experimental Child Psychology, 114*, 187-202. Retrieved from http://www.sciencedirect.com/

b. Abstract of a paper

Denham, B. (2012). Diffusing deviant behavior: A communication perspective on the construction of moral panics [Abstract]. Paper presented at the AEJMC 2012 Conference, Chicago, IL. Retrieved from http://www.aejmc.org/home/2012/04/ctm-2012-abstracts/

17. Supplemental material

If an article on the Web contains supplemental material that is not part of the main article, cite the material as you would an article and add the label "Supplemental material" in brackets following the title.

Reis, S., Grennfelt, P., Klimont, Z., Amann, M., ApSimon, H., Hettelingh, J.-P., . . . Williams, M. (2012). From acid rain to climate change [Supplemental material]. *Science 338*(6111), 1153-1154. doi:10.1126/science.1226514

18. Article with a title in its title

If an article title contains another article title or a term usually placed in quotation marks, use quotation marks around the internal title or the term.

Easterling, D., & Millesen, J. L. (2012, Summer). Diversifying civic leadership: What it takes to move from "new faces" to adaptive problem solving. *National Civic Review*, 20-27. doi:10.1002/ncr.21073

19. Letter to the editor Insert the words "Letter to the editor" in brackets after the title of the letter. If the letter has no title, use the bracketed words as the title (as in the following example).

Lim, C. (2012, November-December). [Letter to the editor]. *Sierra*. Retrieved from http://www.sierraclub.org/sierra/

20. Editorial or other unsigned article

The business case for transit dollars [Editorial]. (2012, December 9). *Star Tribune*. Retrieved from http://www.startribune.com/

21. Newsletter article Cite as you would an article in a magazine, giving whatever publication information is available (volume, issue, page numbers, and so on).

Scrivener, L. (n.d.). Why is the minimum wage issue important for food justice advocates? *Food Workers—Food Justice, 15*. Retrieved from http://www.thedatabank.com/dpg/199/pm.asp?nav=1&ID=41429

22. Review Give the author and title of the review (if any) and, in brackets, the type of work, the title, and the author for a book or the year for a film. If the review has no author or title, use the material in brackets as the title.

author of review | year (journal) | book title

Aviram, R. B. (2012). [Review of the book *What do I say? The therapist's*

book author(s)

guide to answering client questions, by L. N. Edelstein & C. A. Waehler].

journal title | volume, issue | page(s) | DOI

Psychotherapy, 49(4), 570-571. doi:10.1037/a0029815

author(s) | year (journal) | review title

Bradley, A., & Olufs, E. (2012). Family dynamics and school violence

film title | year (film)

[Review of the motion picture *We need to talk about Kevin*, 2011].

journal title | volume, issue | DOI

PsycCRITIQUES, 57(49). doi:10.1037/a0030982

23. Published interview Begin with the person interviewed, and put the interviewer in brackets following the title (if any).

Githongo, J. (2012, November 20). A conversation with John Githongo [Interview by Baobab]. *The Economist*. Retrieved from http://www .economist.com/

24. Article in a reference work (encyclopedia, dictionary, wiki)

a. Print See also item 32 on citing a volume in a multivolume work.

Konijn, E. A. (2008). Affects and media exposure. In W. Donsbach (Ed.), *The international encyclopedia of communication* (Vol. 1, pp. 123-129). Malden, MA: Blackwell.

b. Web

Ethnomethodology. (2006). In *STS wiki*. Retrieved December 15, 2012, from http://www.stswiki.org/index.php?title=Ethnomethodology

25. Comment on an online article Begin with the writer's real name or screen name. If both are given, put the real name first, followed by the screen name in brackets. Before the title, use "Re" and a colon. Add "Comment" in brackets following the title.

Danboy125. (2012, November 9). Re: No flowers on the psych ward [Comment]. *The Atlantic*. Retrieved from http://www.theatlantic .com/

26. Testimony before a legislative body

Carmona, R. H. (2004, March 2). *The growing epidemic of childhood obesity*. Testimony before the Subcommittee on Competition, Foreign Commerce, and Infrastructure of the U.S. Senate Committee on Commerce, Science, and Transportation. Retrieved from http://www .hhs.gov/asl/testify/t040302.html

27. Paper presented at a meeting or symposium (unpublished)

Karimi, S., Key, G., & Tat, D. (2011, April 22). *Complex predicates in focus*. Paper presented at the West Coast Conference on Formal Linguistics, Tucson, AZ.

28. Poster session at a conference

Lacara, N. (2011, April 24). *Predicate which appositives*. Poster session presented at the West Coast Conference on Formal Linguistics, Tucson, AZ.

Books and other long works

▸Citation at a glance: Book, **page 568**

29. Basic format for a book

a. Print

author(s): last name + initial(s) | year | book title | place of publication | publisher

Child, B. J. (2012). *Holding our world together: Ojibwe women and the survival of community*. New York, NY: Viking.

b. Web (or online library) Give the URL for the home page of the Web site or the online library.

author(s) | year | book title | URL

Amponsah, N. A., & Falola, T. (2012). *Women's roles in sub-Saharan Africa*. Retrieved from http://books.google.com/

c. E-book Give the version in brackets after the title ("Kindle version," "Nook version," and so on). Include the DOI or, if a DOI is not available, the URL for the home page of the site from which you downloaded the book.

Wolf, D. A., & Folbre, N. (Eds.). (2012). *Universal coverage of long-term care in the United States* [Adobe Digital Editions version]. Retrieved from https://www.russellsage.org/

d. Database Give the URL for the database.

Beasley, M. H. (2012). *Women of the Washington press: Politics, prejudice, and persistence*. Retrieved from http://muse.jhu.edu/

Citation at a glance
Book (APA)

To cite a print book in APA style, include the following elements:

1 Author(s)
2 Year of publication
3 Title and subtitle
4 Place of publication
5 Publisher

TITLE PAGE

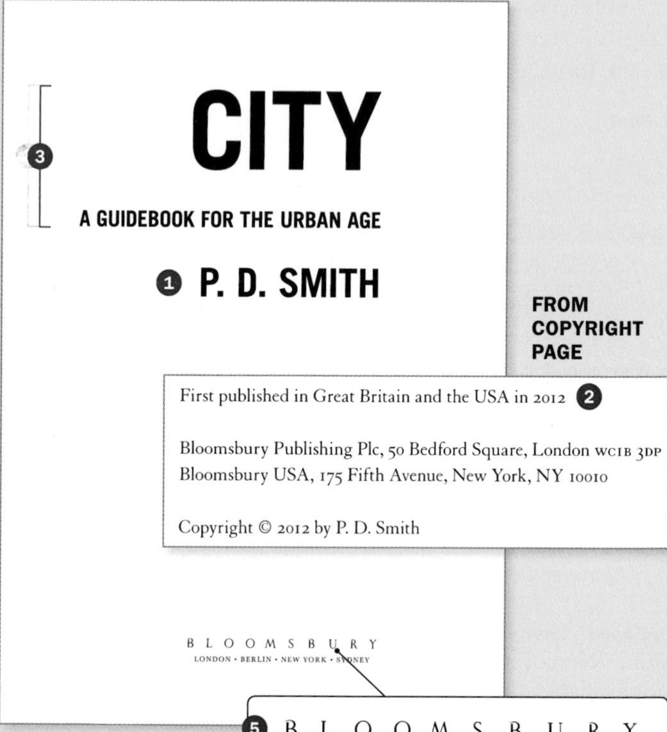

3
CITY
A GUIDEBOOK FOR THE URBAN AGE
1 P. D. SMITH
FROM COPYRIGHT PAGE
First published in Great Britain and the USA in 2012 2
Bloomsbury Publishing Plc, 50 Bedford Square, London WC1B 3DP
Bloomsbury USA, 175 Fifth Avenue, New York, NY 10010
Copyright © 2012 by P. D. Smith
BLOOMSBURY
LONDON • BERLIN • NEW YORK • SYDNEY
5 BLOOMSBURY
4 LONDON • BERLIN • NEW YORK • SYDNEY

REFERENCE LIST ENTRY FOR A PRINT BOOK

Smith, P. D. (2012). *City: A guidebook for the urban age*. London, England: Bloomsbury.

For more on citing books in APA style, see items 29–37.

30. Edition other than the first Include the edition number (abbreviated) in parentheses after the title.

Harvey, P. (2013). *An introduction to Buddhism: Teachings, history, and practices* (2nd ed.). Cambridge, England: Cambridge University Press.

31. Selection in an anthology or a collection An anthology is a collection of works on a common theme, often with different authors for the selections and usually with an editor for the entire volume.

a. Entire anthology

editor(s) · year · title of anthology · place of publication · publisher

Warren, A. E. A., Lerner, R. M., & Phelps, E. (Eds.). (2011). *Thriving and spirituality among youth: Research perspectives and future possibilities*. Hoboken, NJ: Wiley.

b. Selection in an anthology

author of selection · year · title of selection · editors of anthology · title of anthology · page numbers of selection · place of publication · publisher

Lazar, S. W. (2012). Neural correlates of positive youth development. In A. E. A. Warren, R. M. Lerner, & E. Phelps (Eds.), *Thriving and spirituality among youth: Research perspectives and future possibilities* (pp. 77-90). Hoboken, NJ: Wiley.

32. Multivolume work If the volumes have been published over several years, give the span of years in parentheses. If you have used only one volume of a multivolume work, indicate the volume number after the title of the complete work; if the volume has its own title, add that title after the volume number.

a. All volumes

Khalakdina, M. (2008-2011). *Human development in the Indian context: A socio-cultural focus* (Vols. 1-2). New Delhi, India: Sage.

b. One volume, with title

Jensen, R. E. (Ed.). (2012). *Voices of the American West: Vol. 1. The Indian interviews of Eli S. Ricker, 1903-1919*. Lincoln: University of Nebraska Press.

33. Introduction, preface, foreword, or afterword

Zachary, L. J. (2012). Foreword. In L. A. Daloz, *Mentor: Guiding the journey of adult learners* (pp. v-vii). San Francisco, CA: Jossey-Bass.

34. Dictionary or other reference work

Leong, F. T. L. (Ed.). (2008). *Encyclopedia of counseling* (Vols. 1-4). Thousand Oaks, CA: Sage.

Nichols, J. D., & Nyholm, E. (2012). *A concise dictionary of Minnesota Ojibwe*. Minneapolis: University of Minnesota Press.

35. Republished book

Mailer, N. (2008). *Miami and the siege of Chicago: An informal history of the Republican and Democratic conventions of 1968*. New York, NY: New York Review Books. (Original work published 1968)

36. Book with a title in its title If the book title contains another book title or an article title, do not italicize the internal title and do not put quotation marks around it.

Marcus, L. (Ed.). (1999). *Sigmund Freud's* The interpretation of dreams*: New interdisciplinary essays*. Manchester, England: Manchester University Press.

37. Book in a language other than English Place the English translation, not italicized, in brackets.

Carminati, G. G., & Méndez, A. (2012). *Étapes de vie, étapes de soins* [Stages of life, stages of care]. Chêne-Bourg, Switzerland: Médecine & Hygiène.

38. Dissertation

a. Published

Hymel, K. M. (2009). *Essays in urban economics* (Doctoral dissertation). Available from ProQuest Dissertations and Theses database. (AAT 3355930)

b. Unpublished

Mitchell, R. D. (2007). *The Wesleyan Quadrilateral: Relocating the conversation* (Unpublished doctoral dissertation). Claremont School of Theology, Claremont, CA.

39. Conference proceedings

Yu, F.-Y., Hirashima, T., Supnithi, T., & Biswas, G. (2011). *Proceedings of the 19th International Conference on Computers in Education: ICCE 2011*. Retrieved from http://www.apsce.net:8080/icce2011/program/proceedings/

40. Government document If the document has a number, place the number in parentheses after the title.

U.S. Transportation Department, Pipeline and Hazardous Materials Safety Administration. (2012). *Emergency response guidebook 2012*. Washington, DC: Author.

U.S. Census Bureau, Bureau of Economic Analysis. (2012, December). *U.S. international trade in goods and services, October 2012* (Report No. CB12-232, BEA12-55, FT-900 [12-10]). Retrieved from http://www.census.gov/foreign-trade/Press-Release/2012pr/10/

41. Report from a private organization If the publisher and the author are the same, begin with the publisher. For a print source, use "Author" as the publisher at the end of the entry (see item 4 on p. 556); for an online source, give the URL. If the report has a number, put it in parentheses following the title.

Ford Foundation. (2012, November). *Eastern Africa*. Retrieved from http://www.fordfoundation.org/pdfs/library/Eastern-Africa-brochure-2012.pdf

Atwood, B., Beam, M., Hindman, D. B., Hindman, E. B., Pintak, L., & Shors, B. (2012, May 25). *The Murrow Rural Information Initiative: Final report*. Pullman: Murrow College of Communication, Washington State University.

42. Legal source The title of a court case is italicized in an in-text citation, but it is not italicized in the reference list.

Sweatt v. Painter, 339 U.S. 629 (1950). Retrieved from Cornell University Law School, Legal Information Institute website: http://www.law.cornell.edu/supct/html/historics/USSC_CR_0339_0629_ZS.html

43. Sacred or classical text It is not necessary to list sacred works such as the Bible or the Qur'an or classical Greek and Roman works (such as the *Odyssey*) in your reference list. See item 19 on page 553 for how to cite these sources in the text of your paper.

Web sites and parts of Web sites

▸ Citation at a glance: Section in a Web document, **page 576**

NOTE: In an APA paper or an APA reference list entry, the word "website" is spelled all lowercase, as one word.

44. Entire Web site Do not include an entire Web site in the reference list. Give the URL in parentheses when you mention it in the text of your paper. (See item 13 on p. 552.)

45. Document from a Web site List as many of the following elements as are available: author's name, publication date (or "n.d." if there is no date), title (in italics), publisher (if any), and URL. If the publisher is known and is not named as the author, include the publisher in your retrieval statement.

Wagner, D. A., Murphy, K. M., & De Korne, H. (2012, December). *Learning first: A research agenda for improving learning in low-income countries*. Retrieved from Brookings Institution website: http://www.brookings.edu/research/papers/2012/12/learning-first-wagner-murphy-de-korne

Gerber, A. S., & Green, D. P. (2012). *Field experiments: Design, analysis, and interpretation*. Retrieved from Yale Institution for Social and Policy Studies website: http://isps.yale.edu/research/data/d081#.UUy2HFdPL5w

Centers for Disease Control and Prevention. (2012, December 10). *Concussion in winter sports*. Retrieved from http://www.cdc.gov/Features/HockeyConcussions/index.html

46. Section in a Web document Cite as you would a chapter in a book or a selection in an anthology (see item 31b on p. 569).

Pew Research Center. (2012, December 12). About the 2012 Pew global attitudes survey. In *Social networking popular across globe*. Retrieved from http://www.pewglobal.org/2012/12/12/social-networking-popular-across-globe

Chang, W.-Y., & Milan, L. M. (2012, October). Relationship between degree field and emigration. In *International mobility and employment characteristics among recent recipients of U.S. doctorates*. Retrieved from National Science Foundation website: http://www.nsf.gov/statistics/infbrief/nsf13300

■ **47. Blog post** Begin with the writer's real name or screen name. If both are given, put the real name first, followed by the screen name in brackets. Add the date of the post (or "n.d." if the post is undated). Place the label "Blog post" in brackets following the title of the post. If there is no title, use the bracketed material as the title. End with the URL for the post.

Kerssen, T. (2012, October 5). Hunger is political: Food Sovereignty Prize honors social movements [Blog post]. Retrieved from http://www.foodfirst.org/en/node/4020

■ **48. Blog comment** Cite as a blog post, but add "Re" and a colon before the title of the original post and the label "Blog comment" in brackets following the title.

Studebakerhawk_14611. (2012, December 5). Re: A people's history of MOOCs [Blog comment]. Retrieved from http://www.insidehighered.com/blogs/library-babel-fish/people's-history-moocs

Audio, visual, and multimedia sources

■ **49. Podcast**

Schulz, K. (2011, March). *Kathryn Schulz: On being wrong* [Video podcast]. Retrieved from TED on http://itunes.apple.com/

Taylor, A., & Parfitt, G. (2011, January 13). *Physical activity and mental health: What's the evidence?* [Audio podcast]. Retrieved from Open University on http://itunes.apple.com/

■ **50. Video or audio on the Web**

Kurzen, B. (2012, April 5). *Going beyond Muslim-Christian conflict in Nigeria* [Video file]. Retrieved from http://www.youtube.com/watch?v=JD8MIJOA050

50. Video or audio on the Web (*cont.*)

Malone, T. W. *Collective intelligence* [Video file]. Retrieved from http://edge.org/conversation/collective-intelligence

Bever, T., Piattelli-Palmarini, M., Hammond, M., Barss, A., & Bergesen, A. (2012, February 2). *A basic introduction to Chomsky's linguistics* [Audio file]. Retrieved from University of Arizona, College of Social & Behavioral Sciences, Department of Linguistics website: http://linguistics.arizona.edu/node/711

51. Transcript of an audio or a video file

Malone, T. W. *Collective intelligence* [Transcript of video file]. Retrieved from http://edge.org/conversation/collective-intelligence

Glass, I. (2012, September 14). *Back to school* [Transcript of audio file No. 474]. In *This American life*. Retrieved from http://www.thisamericanlife.org/

52. Film (DVD, BD, or other format) Give the director, producer, and other relevant contributors, followed by the year of the film's release and the title. In brackets, add a description of the medium. Use "Motion picture" if you viewed the film in a theater; "Video file" if you downloaded the film from the Web or through a streaming service such as Netflix; "DVD" or "BD" if you viewed the film on DVD or Blu-ray Disc. For a motion picture or a DVD or BD, add the location where the film was made and the studio. If you retrieved the film from the Web or used a streaming service, give the URL for the home page.

Affleck, B. (Director). (2012). *Argo* [Motion picture]. Burbank, CA: Warner Bros.

Ross, G. (Director and Writer), & Collins, S. (Writer). (2012). *The hunger games* [Video file]. Retrieved from http://netflix.com/

53. Television or radio program

a. Series

Hager, M. (Executive producer), & Schieffer, B. (Moderator). (2012). *Face the nation* [Television series]. Washington, DC: CBS News.

b. Episode on the air

Harleston, R. (Host). (2012, December 1). Federal role in support of autism [Television series episode]. In *Washington journal*. Washington, DC: C-SPAN.

c. Episode on the Web

Morton, D. (Producer). (2012). Fast times at West Philly High [Television series episode]. In M. Hager (Executive producer), *Frontline*. Retrieved from http://www.wgbh.org/

Glass, I. (Host). (2012, November 23). Little war on the prairie (No. 479) [Radio series episode]. In *This American life*. Retrieved from http://www.thisamericanlife.org/

■ 54. Music recording

Chibalonza, A. Jubilee. (2012). On *African voices* [CD]. Merenberg, Germany: ZYX Music.

African voices [CD]. (2012). Merenberg, Germany: ZYX Music.

■ 55. Lecture, speech, or address

Verghese, A. (2012, December 6). *Colonialism and patterns of ethnic conflict in contemporary India*. Address at the Freeman Spogli Institute, Stanford University, Stanford, CA.

Donovan, S. (2012, June 12). *Assisted housing mobility in challenging times* [Video file]. Address at the 5th National Conference on Assisted Housing Mobility, Urban Institute, Washington, DC. Retrieved from http://www.urban.org/events/HUD-Secretary-Shaun-Donovan-Speaks-on-Housing-Mobility.cfm

■ 56. Data set or graphic representation of data (graph, chart, table) Give information about the type of source in brackets following the title. If there is no title, give a brief description of the content of the source in brackets in place of the title. If the item is numbered in the source, indicate the number in parentheses after the title. If the graphic appears within a larger document, do not italicize the title of the graphic.

U.S. Department of Agriculture, Economic Research Service. (2011). *Daily intake of nutrients by food source: 2005-08* [Data set]. Retrieved from http://www.ers.usda.gov/data-products/food-consumption-and-nutrient-intakes.aspx

Citation at a glance

Section in a Web document (APA)

To cite a section in a Web document in APA style, include the following elements:

1. Author(s)
2. Date of publication or most recent update ("n.d." if there is no date)
3. Title of section
4. Title of document
5. URL of section

WEB DOCUMENT CONTENTS PAGE

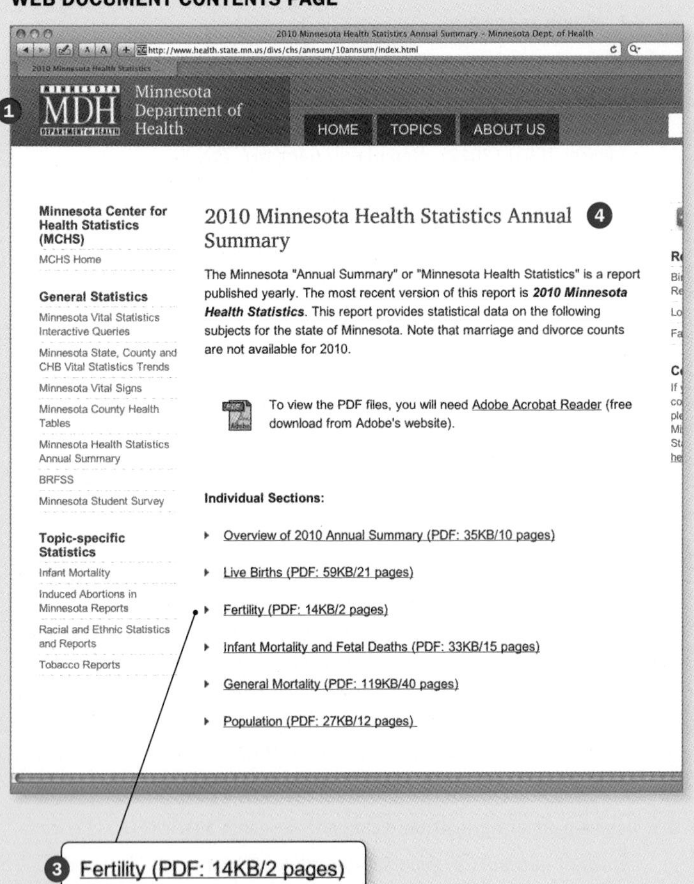

5 http://www.health.state.mn.us/divs/chs/annsum/10annsum/Fertility2010.pdf

ON-SCREEN VIEW OF DOCUMENT

http://www.health.state.mn.us/divs/chs/annsum/10annsum/Fertility2010.pdf

Fertility Table 1
Total Reported Pregnancies by Outcome and Rate
Minnesota Residents, 1981 - 2010

Year	Total Reported Pregnancies*	Live Births	Induced Abortions	Fetal Deaths	Female Population Ages 15-44	Pregnancy Rate**
1981	84,934	68,652	15,821	461	967,087	87.8
1982	84,500	68,512	15,559	429	977,905	86.4
1983	80,530	65,559	14,514	457	981,287	82.1
1984	82,736	66,715	15,556	465	985,608	83.9
1985	83,853	67,412	16,002	439	994,249	84.3
1986	81,882	65,766	15,716	400	997,501	82.1
1987	81,318	65,168	15,746	404	1,004,801	80.9
1988	83,335	66,745	16,124	466	1,020,209	81.7
1989	83,426	67,490	15,506	430	1,024,576	81.4
1990	83,714	67,985	15,280	449	1,025,919	81.6
1991	81,904	67,037	14,441	426	1,036,146	79.0
1992	79,844	65,591	13,846	407	1,049,175	76.1
1993	77,939	64,646	12,955	338	1,060,396	73.5
1994	78,344	64,277	13,702	365	1,073,649	73.0
1995	76,338	63,259	12,715	364	1,053,136	72.5
1996	76,909	63,681	12,876	352	1,066,220	72.1
1997	77,850	64,491	12,997	362	1,050,544	74.1
1998	78,646	65,207	13,050	389	1,054,458	74.6
1999	79,374	65,953	13,037	384	1,054,543	75.3
2000	81,039	67,451	13,200	388	1,082,642	74.9

Courtesy of the Minnesota Department of Health.

REFERENCE LIST ENTRY FOR A SECTION IN A WEB DOCUMENT

1 2 3 4

Minnesota Department of Health. (n.d.). Fertility. In *2010 Minnesota health statistics annual summary*. Retrieved from http://www.health .state.mn.us/divs/chs/annsum/10annsum/Fertility2010.pdf

5

For more on citing documents from Web sites in APA style, see items 45 and 46.

■ **56. Data set or graphic representation of data (*cont.*)**

Gallup. (2012, December 5). *In U.S., more cite obesity as most urgent health problem* [Graphs]. Retrieved from http://www.gallup.com /poll/159083/cite-obesity-urgent-health-problem.aspx

■ **57. Mobile application software (app)** Begin with the developer of the app, if known (as in the second example).

MindNode Touch 2.3 [Mobile application software]. (2012). Retrieved from http://itunes.apple.com/

Source Tree Solutions. (2012). mojoPortal [Mobile application software]. Retrieved from http://www.microsoft.com/web/gallery/

■ **58. Video game** Begin with the creator of the video game, if known. Add the label "Video game" in brackets after the title of the program. If the game can be played on the Web or was downloaded from the Web, give the URL instead of publication information.

Firaxis Games. (2010). Sid Meier's Civilization V [Video game]. New York, NY: Take-Two Interactive. Xbox 360.

Atom Entertainment. (2012). Edgeworld [Video game]. Retrieved from http://www.addictinggames.com/

■ **59. Map**

Ukraine [Map]. (2008). Retrieved from the University of Texas at Austin Perry-Castañeda Library Map Collection website: http://www.lib .utexas.edu/maps/cia08/ukraine_sm_2008.gif

Syrian uprising map [Map]. (2012, October). Retrieved from http://www .polgeonow.com/2012/10/syria-uprising-map-october-2012-7.html

■ **60. Advertisement**

VMware [Advertisement]. (2012, September). *Harvard Business Review, 90*(9), 27.

■ **61. Work of art or photograph**

Olson, A. (2011). *Short story* [Painting]. Museum of Contemporary Art, Chicago, IL.

Crowner, S. (2012). *Kurtyna fragments* [Painting]. Retrieved from http:// www.walkerart.org/

Weber, J. (1992). *Toward freedom* [Outdoor mural]. Sherman Oaks, CA.

62. Brochure or fact sheet

National Council of State Boards of Nursing. (2011). *A nurse's guide to professional boundaries* [Brochure]. Retrieved from https://www.ncsbn.org/

World Health Organization. (2012, September). *Road traffic injuries* (No. 358) [Fact sheet]. Retrieved from http://www.who.int/mediacentre/factsheets/fs358/en/index.html

63. Press release Generally, list the organization responsible for the press release. Give the exact date.

Urban Institute. (2012, October 11). Two studies address health policy on campaign trail [Press release]. Retrieved from http://www.urban.org/publications/901537.html

64. Presentation slides

Boeninger, C. F. (2008, August). *Web 2.0 tools for reference and instructional services* [Presentation slides]. Retrieved from http://libraryvoice.com/archives/2008/08/04/opal-20-conference-presentation-slides

65. Lecture notes or other course materials Cite materials that your instructor has posted on the Web as you would a Web document or a section in a Web document (see item 45 or 46). If the materials are handouts or printouts, cite whatever information is available in the source. Cite the instructor's personal notes or material that is not posted (such as slides) as personal communication in the text of your paper (see items 15 and 16 on p. 552).

Blum, R. (2011). Neurodevelopment in the first decade of life [Lecture notes and audio file]. In R. Blum & L. M. Blum, *Child health and development*. Retrieved from http://ocw.jhsph.edu/index.cfm/go/viewCourse/course/childhealth/coursePage/lectureNotes/

Personal communication and social media

66. E-mail E-mail messages, letters, and other personal communication are not included in the list of references. (See item 15 on p. 552 for citing these sources in the text of your paper.)

67. Online posting If an online posting is not archived, cite it as a personal communication in the text of your paper and do not include it in the list of references. If the posting is archived, give the URL and the name of the discussion list if it is not part of the URL.

McKinney, J. (2006, December 19). Adult education-healthcare partnerships [Electronic mailing list message]. Retrieved from http://www.nifl.gov/pipermail/healthliteracy/2006/000524.html

68. Twitter post (tweet) Use the author's real name, if it is given, and put the screen name in brackets exactly as it appears in the source (including capitalization and punctuation). If only the screen name is known, begin with that name and do not enclose it in brackets. Include the entire text of the tweet as the title, followed by the label "Tweet" in brackets; end with the URL.

CQ Researcher. (2012, December 5). Up to 80 percent of the 600,000 processed foods sold in America have sugar added to their recipes. See http://bit.ly/UmfA4L [Tweet]. Retrieved from https://twitter .com/cqresearcher/status/276449095521038336

69. Facebook post Use the author's name exactly as it appears in the post. In place of a title, give a few words of the post followed by the label "Facebook post" in brackets. Include the date you retrieved the source and the URL for the poster's Facebook page. If you are citing a personal Facebook page that will not be accessible to your readers, cite it as personal communication in your text, not in the reference list (see item 15 on p. 552).

U.S. Department of Education. (2012, October 9). They are resilient [Facebook post]. Retrieved October 15, 2012, from http://www .facebook.com/ED.gov

62 APA manuscript format; sample research paper

The guidelines in this section are consistent with advice given in the *Publication Manual of the American Psychological Association*, 6th ed. (Washington, DC: APA, 2010), and with typical requirements for undergraduate papers.

62a APA manuscript format

Formatting the paper

The guidelines on pages 581–83 describe APA's recommendations for formatting the text of your paper. For guidelines on preparing the reference list, see pages 583–84.

Font If your instructor does not require a specific font, choose one that is standard and easy to read (such as Times New Roman).

Title page Begin at the top left, with the words "Running head," followed by a colon and the title of your paper (shortened to no more than fifty characters) in all capital letters. Put the page number 1 flush with the right margin.

About halfway down the page, on separate lines, center the full title of your paper, your name, and your school's name. At the bottom of the page, you may add the heading "Author Note," centered, followed by a brief paragraph that lists specific information about the course or department or provides acknowledgments or contact information. See page 585 for a sample title page.

Page numbers and running head Number all pages with arabic numerals (1, 2, 3, and so on) in the upper right corner one-half inch from the top of the page. Flush with the left margin on the same line as the page number, type a running head consisting of the title of the paper (shortened to no more than fifty characters) in all capital letters. On the title page only, include the words "Running head" followed by a colon before the title. See pages 585–96.

Margins, line spacing, and paragraph indents Use margins of one inch on all sides of the page. Left-align the text.

Double-space throughout the paper. Indent the first line of each paragraph one-half inch.

Capitalization, italics, and quotation marks In headings and in titles of works that appear in the text of the paper, capitalize all words of four letters or more (and all nouns, pronouns, verbs, adjectives, and adverbs of any length). Capitalize the first word following a colon if the word begins a complete sentence.

In the body of your paper, italicize the titles of books, journals, magazines, and other long works, such as Web sites. Use quotation marks around the titles of articles, short stories, and other short works.

NOTE: APA has different requirements for titles in the reference list. See page 584.

Long quotations When a quotation is forty or more words, set it off from the text by indenting it one-half inch from the left margin. Double-space the quotation. Do not use quotation marks around it. (See p. 594 for an example. See also p. 541 for more information about integrating long quotations.)

Footnotes If you insert a footnote number in the text of your paper, place the number, raised above the line, immediately following any mark of punctuation except a dash. At the bottom of the page, begin the note with a one-half-inch indent and the superscript number corresponding to the number in the text. Insert an extra double-spaced line between the last line of text on the page and the footnote. Double-space the footnote. (See p. 587 for an example.)

Abstract and keywords An abstract is a 150-to-250-word paragraph that provides readers with a quick overview of your essay. It should express your main idea and your key points; it might also briefly suggest any implications or applications of the research you discuss in the paper.

If your instructor requires one, include an abstract on a new page after the title page. Center the word "Abstract" (in regular font, not boldface) one inch from the top of the page. Double-space the abstract and do not indent the first line.

A list of keywords follows the abstract; the keywords help readers search for a published paper on the Web or in a database. Leave one line of space after the abstract and begin the next line with the word "Keywords," italicized and indented one-half inch, followed by a colon. Then list important words related to your paper. Check with your instructor for requirements in your course. (See p. 586 for an example of an abstract.)

Headings Although headings are not always necessary, their use is encouraged in the social sciences. For most undergraduate papers, one level of heading is usually sufficient. (See pp. 588–92.)

First-level headings are centered and boldface. In research papers and laboratory reports, the major headings are "Method," "Results," and "Discussion." In other types of papers, the major headings should be informative and concise, conveying the structure of the paper.

Second-level headings are flush left and boldface. Third-level headings are indented and boldface, followed by a period and the text on the same line.

In first- and second-level headings, capitalize the first and last words and all words of four or more letters (and nouns, pronouns, verbs, adjectives, and adverbs of any length). In third-level headings, capitalize only the first word, any proper nouns, and the first word after a colon.

First-Level Heading Centered

Second-Level Heading Flush Left

Third-level heading indented. Text immediately follows.

Visuals (tables and figures) APA classifies visuals as tables and figures (figures include graphs, charts, drawings, and photographs).

Label each table with an arabic numeral (Table 1, Table 2, and so on) and provide a clear title. Place the label and title on separate lines above the table, flush left and double-spaced. Type the table number in regular font; italicize the table title.

If you have used data from an outside source or have taken or adapted the table from a source, give the source information in a note below the table. Begin with the word "Note," italicized and followed by a period. If any data in the table require an explanatory footnote, use a superscript lowercase letter in the table and in a footnote following the source note. Double-space source notes and footnotes; do not indent the first line of each note. (For an example of a note in a table, see p. 591.)

For each figure, place the figure number and a caption below the figure, flush left and double-spaced. Begin with the word "Figure" and an arabic numeral, both italicized, followed by a period. Place the caption, not italicized, on the same line. If you have taken or adapted the figure from an outside source, give the source information immediately following the caption. Use the term "From" or "Adapted from" before the source information.

In the text of your paper, discuss the most significant features of each visual. Place the visual as close as possible to the sentences that relate to it unless your instructor prefers that visuals appear in an appendix.

Preparing the list of references

Begin your list of references on a new page at the end of the paper. Center the title "References" one inch from the top of the page. Double-space throughout. For a sample reference list, see page 595.

Indenting entries Type the first line of each entry flush left and indent any additional lines one-half inch.

Alphabetizing the list Alphabetize the reference list by the last names of the authors (or editors) or by the first word of an organization name (if the author is an organization). When a work has no author or editor, alphabetize by the first word of the title other than *A*, *An*, or *The*.

If your list includes two or more works by the same author, arrange the entries by year, the earliest first. If your list includes two or more works by the same author in the same year, arrange the works alphabetically by title. Add the letters "a," "b," and so on within the parentheses after the year. For journal articles, use only the year and the letter: (2012a). For articles in magazines and newspapers, use the full date and the letter in the reference list: (2012a, July 7); use only the year and the letter in the in-text citation.

Authors' names Invert all authors' names and use initials instead of first names. Separate the names with commas. For two to seven authors, use an ampersand (&) before the last author's name. For eight or more authors, give the first six authors, three ellipsis dots, and the last author (see item 3 on p. 556).

Titles of books and articles In the reference list, italicize the titles and subtitles of books. Do not italicize or use quotation marks around the titles of articles. For both books and articles, capitalize only the first word of the title and subtitle (and all proper nouns). Capitalize names of journals, magazines, and newspapers as you would capitalize them normally (see 45c).

Abbreviations for page numbers Abbreviations for "page" and "pages" ("p." and "pp.") are used before page numbers of newspaper articles and selections in anthologies (see item 15 on p. 563 and item 31 on p. 569). Do not use "p." or "pp." before page numbers of articles in journals and magazines (see items 13 and 14 on pp. 559 and 563).

Breaking a URL or DOI When a URL or a DOI (digital object identifier) must be divided, break it after a double slash or before any other mark of punctuation. Do not insert a hyphen; do not add a period at the end.

62b Sample APA research paper

On the following pages is a research paper on the effectiveness of treatments for childhood obesity, written by Luisa Mirano, a student in a psychology class. Mirano's assignment was to write a literature review paper documented with APA-style citations and references.

LaunchPadSolo **macmillanhighered.com/rules8e**
62 APA manuscript format; sample paper
> Sample student writing: Mirano, "Can Medication Cure Obesity in Children? A Review of the Literature" (literature review)

Running head: CAN MEDICATION CURE OBESITY IN CHILDREN? 1

A running head consists of a title (shortened to no more than fifty characters) in all capital letters. On the title page, it is preceded by the label "Running head." Page numbers appear in the upper right corner.

Can Medication Cure Obesity in Children?

A Review of the Literature

Luisa Mirano

Northwest-Shoals Community College

Full title, writer's name, and school name are centered halfway down the page.

Author Note

This paper was prepared for Psychology 108, Section B, taught by Professor Kang.

An author's note lists specific information about the course or department and can provide acknowledgments and contact information.

Marginal annotations indicate APA-style formatting and **effective writing**.

Abstract appears on a separate page. Heading is centered and not boldface.

Abstract

In recent years, policymakers and medical experts have expressed alarm about the growing problem of childhood obesity in the United States. While most agree that the issue deserves attention, consensus dissolves around how to respond to the problem. This literature review examines one approach to treating childhood obesity: medication. The paper compares the effectiveness for adolescents of the only two drugs approved by the Food and Drug Administration (FDA) for long-term treatment of obesity, sibutramine and orlistat. This examination of pharmacological treatments for obesity points out the limitations of medication and suggests the need for a comprehensive solution that combines medical, social, behavioral, and political approaches to this complex problem.

Keywords help readers search for a paper on the Web or in a database.

Keywords: obesity, childhood, adolescence, medication, public policy

Can Medication Cure Obesity in Children?
A Review of the Literature

Full title, centered and not boldface.

In March 2004, U.S. Surgeon General Richard Carmona called attention to a health problem in the United States that, until recently, has been overlooked: childhood obesity. Carmona said that the "astounding" 15% child obesity rate constitutes an "epidemic." Since the early 1980s, that rate has "doubled in children and tripled in adolescents." Now more than nine million children are classified as obese.[1] While the traditional response to a medical epidemic is to hunt for a vaccine or a cure-all pill, childhood obesity is more elusive. The lack of success of recent initiatives suggests that medication might not be the answer for the escalating problem. This literature review considers whether the use of medication is a promising approach for solving the childhood obesity problem by responding to the following questions.

1. What are the implications of childhood obesity?
2. Is medication effective at treating childhood obesity?
3. Is medication safe for children?
4. Is medication the best solution?

Mirano sets up her organization by posing four questions.

Understanding the limitations of medical treatments for children highlights the complexity of the childhood obesity problem in the United States and underscores the need for physicians, advocacy groups, and policymakers to search for other solutions.

Mirano states her thesis.

[1]Obesity is measured in terms of body-mass index (BMI): weight in kilograms divided by square of height in meters. A child or an adolescent with a BMI in the 95th percentile for his or her age and gender is considered obese.

Mirano uses a footnote to define an essential term that would be cumbersome to define within the text.

Headings, centered and boldface, help readers follow the organization.

What Are the Implications of Childhood Obesity?

Obesity can be a devastating problem from both an individual and a societal perspective. Obesity puts children at risk for a number of medical complications, including Type 2 diabetes, hypertension, sleep apnea, and orthopedic problems (Henry J. Kaiser Family Foundation, 2004, p. 1). Researchers Hoppin and Taveras (2004) have noted that obesity is often associated with psychological issues such as anxiety, depression, and binge eating (Complications section, Table 4).

In a signal phrase, the word "and" links the names of two authors; the date is given in parentheses.

Obesity also poses serious problems for a society struggling to cope with rising health care costs. The cost of treating obesity currently totals $117 billion per year—a price, according to the surgeon general, "second only to the cost of [treating] tobacco use" (Carmona, 2004). And as the number of children who suffer from obesity grows, long-term costs will only increase.

Because the author (Carmona) is not named in the signal phrase, his name and the date appear in parentheses.

Is Medication Effective at Treating Childhood Obesity?

The widening scope of the obesity problem has prompted medical professionals to rethink old conceptions of the disorder and its causes. As researchers Yanovski and Yanovski (2002) have explained, obesity was once considered "either a moral failing or evidence of underlying psychopathology" (p. 592). But this view has shifted: Many medical professionals now consider obesity a biomedical rather than a moral condition, influenced by both genetic and environmental factors. Yanovski and Yanovski have further noted that the development of weight-loss medications in the early 1990s showed that "obesity should be treated in the same manner as any other chronic disease . . . through the long-term use of medication" (p. 592).

Ellipsis mark indicates omitted words.

CAN MEDICATION CURE OBESITY IN CHILDREN? 5

The search for the right long-term medication has been complicated. Many of the drugs authorized by the Food and Drug Administration (FDA) in the early 1990s proved to be a disappointment. Two of the medications—fenfluramine and dexfenfluramine—were withdrawn from the market because of severe side effects (Yanovski & Yanovski, 2002, p. 592), and several others were classified by the Drug Enforcement Administration as having the "potential for abuse" (Hoppin & Taveras, 2004, Weight-Loss Drugs section, para. 6). Currently only two medications have been approved by the FDA for long-term treatment of obesity: sibutramine (marketed as Meridia) and orlistat (marketed as Xenical). This section compares studies on the effectiveness of each.

In a parenthetical citation, an ampersand links the names of two authors.

Sibutramine suppresses appetite by blocking the reuptake of the neurotransmitters serotonin and norepinephrine in the brain (Yanovski & Yanovski, 2002, p. 594). Though the drug won FDA approval in 1998, experiments to test its effectiveness for younger patients came considerably later. In 2003, University of Pennsylvania researchers Berkowitz, Wadden, Tershakovec, and Cronquist released the first double-blind placebo study testing the effect of sibutramine on adolescents, aged 13-17, over a 12-month period. Their findings are summarized in Table 1. After 6 months, the group receiving medication had lost 4.6 kg (about 10 pounds) more than the control group. But during the second half of the study, when both groups received sibutramine, the results were more ambiguous. In months 6-12, the group that continued to take sibutramine gained an average of 0.8 kg, or roughly 2 pounds; the control group, which switched from placebo to sibutramine, lost 1.3 kg, or roughly 3 pounds (Berkowitz et al., 2003,

Mirano draws attention to an important article.

p. 1808). Both groups received behavioral therapy covering diet, exercise, and mental health.

These results paint a murky picture of the effectiveness of the medication: While initial data seemed promising, the results after one year raised questions about whether medication-induced weight loss could be sustained over time. As Berkowitz et al. (2003) advised, "Until more extensive safety and efficacy data are available, . . . weight-loss medications should be used only on an experimental basis for adolescents" (p. 1811).

When this article was first cited, all four authors were named. In subsequent citations of a work with three to five authors, "et al." is used after the first author's name.

A study testing the effectiveness of orlistat in adolescents showed similarly ambiguous results. The FDA approved orlistat in 1999 but did not authorize it for adolescents until December 2003. Roche Laboratories (2003), maker of orlistat, released results of a one-year study testing the drug on 539 obese adolescents, aged 12-16. The drug, which promotes weight loss by blocking fat absorption in the large intestine, showed some effectiveness in adolescents: an average loss of 1.3 kg, or roughly 3 pounds, for subjects taking orlistat for one year, as opposed to an average gain of 0.67 kg, or 1.5 pounds, for the control group (pp. 8-9). See Table 1.

Short-term studies of orlistat have shown slightly more dramatic results. Researchers at the National Institute of Child Health and Human Development tested 20 adolescents, aged 12-16, over a three-month period and found that orlistat, combined with behavioral therapy, produced an average weight loss of 4.4 kg, or 9.7 pounds (McDuffie et al., 2002, p. 646). The study was not controlled against a placebo group; therefore, the relative effectiveness of orlistat in this case remains unclear.

For a source with six or more authors, the first author's surname followed by "et al." is used for the first and subsequent references.

CAN MEDICATION CURE OBESITY IN CHILDREN? 7

Table 1

Effectiveness of Sibutramine and Orlistat in Adolescents

Medication	Subjects	Treatment[a]	Side effects	Average weight loss/gain
Sibutramine	Control	0-6 mos.: placebo 6-12 mos.: sibutramine	Mos. 6-12: increased blood pressure; increased pulse rate	After 6 mos.: loss of 3.2 kg (7 lb) After 12 mos.: loss of 4.5 kg (9.9 lb)
	Medicated	0-12 mos.: sibutramine	Increased blood pressure; increased pulse rate	After 6 mos.: loss of 7.8 kg (17.2 lb) After 12 mos.: loss of 7.0 kg (15.4 lb)
Orlistat	Control	0-12 mos.: placebo	None	Gain of 0.67 kg (1.5 lb)
	Medicated	0-12 mos.: orlistat	Oily spotting; flatulence; abdominal discomfort	Loss of 1.3 kg (2.9 lb)

Note. The data on sibutramine are adapted from "Behavior Therapy and Sibutramine for the Treatment of Adolescent Obesity," by R. I. Berkowitz, T. A. Wadden, A. M. Tershakovec, & J. L. Cronquist, 2003, *Journal of the American Medical Association, 289*, pp. 1807–1809. The data on orlistat are adapted from *Xenical (Orlistat) Capsules: Complete Product Information*, by Roche Laboratories, December 2003, retrieved from http://www.rocheusa.com /products/xenical/pi.pdf

[a]The medication and/or placebo were combined with behavioral therapy in all groups over all time periods.

Mirano uses a table to summarize the findings presented in two sources.

A note gives the source of the data.

A content note explains data common to all subjects.

CAN MEDICATION CURE OBESITY IN CHILDREN? 8

Is Medication Safe for Children?

While modest weight loss has been documented for both medications, each carries risks of certain side effects. Sibutramine has been observed to increase blood pressure and pulse rate. In 2002, a consumer group claimed that the medication was related to the deaths of 19 people and filed a petition with the Department of Health and Human Services to ban the medication (Hilts, 2002). The sibutramine study by Berkowitz et al. (2003) noted elevated blood pressure as a side effect, and dosages had to be reduced or the medication discontinued in 19 of the 43 subjects in the first six months (p. 1809).

The main side effects associated with orlistat were abdominal discomfort, oily spotting, fecal incontinence, and nausea (Roche Laboratories, 2003, p. 13). More serious for long-term health is the concern that orlistat, being a fat-blocker, would affect absorption of fat-soluble vitamins, such as vitamin D. However, the study found that this side effect can be minimized or eliminated if patients take vitamin supplements two hours before or after administration of orlistat (p. 10). With close monitoring of patients taking the medication, many of the risks can be reduced.

Is Medication the Best Solution?

The data on the safety and efficacy of pharmacological treatments of childhood obesity raise the question of whether medication is the best solution for the problem. The treatments have clear costs for individual patients, including unpleasant side effects, little information about long-term use, and uncertainty that they will yield significant weight loss.

CAN MEDICATION CURE OBESITY IN CHILDREN? 8

In purely financial terms, the drugs cost more than $3 a day on average (Duenwald, 2004). In each of the clinical trials, use of medication was accompanied by an expensive regime of behavioral therapies, including counseling, nutritional education, fitness advising, and monitoring. As journalist Greg Critser (2003) noted in his book *Fat Land*, use of weight-loss drugs is unlikely to have an effect without the proper "support system"—one that includes doctors, facilities, time, and money (p. 3). For some, this level of care is prohibitively expensive.

A third complication is that the studies focused on adolescents aged 12-16, but obesity can begin at a much younger age. Little data exist to establish the safety or efficacy of medication for treating very young children.

While the scientific data on the concrete effects of these medications in children remain somewhat unclear, medication is not the only avenue for addressing the crisis. Both medical experts and policymakers recognize that solutions might come not only from a laboratory but also from policy, education, and advocacy. A handbook designed to educate doctors on obesity called for "major changes in some aspects of western culture" (Hoppin & Taveras, 2004, Conclusion section, para. 1). Cultural change may not be the typical realm of medical professionals, but the handbook urged doctors to be proactive and "focus [their] energy on public policies and interventions" (Conclusion section, para. 1).

Mirano develops the paper's thesis.

Brackets indicate Mirano's change in the quoted material.

The solutions proposed by a number of advocacy groups underscore this interest in political and cultural change. A report by the Henry J. Kaiser Family Foundation (2004) outlined trends that may have contributed to the childhood obesity crisis, including food advertising for children as well as

A quotation longer than forty words is indented without quotation marks.

> a reduction in physical education classes and after-school athletic programs, an increase in the availability of sodas and snacks in public schools, the growth in the number of fast-food outlets . . . , and the increasing number of highly processed high-calorie and high-fat grocery products. (p. 1)

Mirano interprets the evidence; she doesn't just report it.

Addressing each of these areas requires more than a doctor armed with a prescription pad; it requires a broad mobilization not just of doctors and concerned parents but of educators, food industry executives, advertisers, and media representatives.

The tone of the conclusion is objective.

The barrage of possible approaches to combating childhood obesity—from scientific research to political lobbying—indicates both the severity and the complexity of the problem. While none of the medications currently available is a miracle drug for curing the nation's nine million obese children, research has illuminated some of the underlying factors that affect obesity and has shown the need for a comprehensive approach to the problem that includes behavioral, medical, social, and political change.

CAN MEDICATION CURE OBESITY IN CHILDREN? 10

References

List of references begins on a new page. Heading is centered and not boldface.

List is alphabetized by authors' last names. All authors' names are inverted.

The first line of an entry is at the left margin; subsequent lines indent ½″.

Double-spacing is used throughout.

Berkowitz, R. I., Wadden, T. A., Tershakovec, A. M., & Cronquist, J. L. (2003). Behavior therapy and sibutramine for the treatment of adolescent obesity. *Journal of the American Medical Association, 289*, 1805-1812.

Carmona, R. H. (2004, March 2). *The growing epidemic of childhood obesity*. Testimony before the Subcommittee on Competition, Foreign Commerce, and Infrastructure of the U.S. Senate Committee on Commerce, Science, and Transportation. Retrieved from http://www.hhs.gov/asl/testify/t040302.html

Critser, G. (2003). *Fat land*. Boston, MA: Houghton Mifflin.

Duenwald, M. (2004, January 6). Slim pickings: Looking beyond ephedra. *The New York Times*, p. F1. Retrieved from http://nytimes.com/

Henry J. Kaiser Family Foundation. (2004, February). *The role of media in childhood obesity*. Retrieved from http://www.kff.org/entmedia/7030.cfm

Hilts, P. J. (2002, March 20). Petition asks for removal of diet drug from market. *The New York Times*, p. A26. Retrieved from http://nytimes.com/

Hoppin, A. G., & Taveras, E. M. (2004, June 25). Assessment and management of childhood and adolescent obesity. Clinical Update. Retrieved from http://www.medscape.com/viewarticle/481633

McDuffie, J. R., Calis, K. A., Uwaifo, G. I., Sebring, N. G., Fallon, E. M., Hubbard, V. S., & Yanovski, J. A. (2002). Three-month tolerability of orlistat in adolescents with obesity-related comorbid conditions. *Obesity Research, 10*, 642-650.

Roche Laboratories. (2003, December). *Xenical (orlistat) capsules: Complete product information.* Retrieved from http://www.rocheusa.com/products/xenical/pi.pdf

Yanovski, S. Z., & Yanovski, J. A. (2002). Drug therapy: Obesity. *The New England Journal of Medicine, 346,* 591-602.

Appendixes

Index

Appendixes 597

Index 636

APPENDIX

A document design gallery

Good document design promotes readability and increases the chances that you will achieve your purpose for writing and reach your readers. How you design a document — how you format it for the printed page or for a computer screen, for example — affects your readers' response to it. Most readers have expectations about document design and format, usually depending on the context and the purpose of the piece of writing.

This gallery features pages from both academic and business documents. The annotations on the sides of the pages point out design choices as well as important features of the writing.

Standard academic formatting

Use the manuscript format that is recommended for your academic discipline. In most English and some other humanities classes, you will be asked to use MLA (Modern Language Association) format (see 57). In most social science, business, education, and health-related classes, you'll be asked to use APA (American Psychological Association) format (see 62).

Pages 598–602 show basic formatting in MLA and APA styles. For complete student papers in MLA and APA formats, see 57b and 62b.

Standard professional formatting

It helps to look at examples when you are preparing to write a professional document such as a letter, a memo, or a résumé. (See pp. 604–6 for examples.) In general, business and professional writing is direct, clear, and courteous, and documents are designed to be read easily and quickly. When writing less formal documents such as e-mail messages in academic contexts, it's just as important to craft the document for easy readability. (See p. 607 for a sample e-mail message.)

MLA ESSAY FORMAT

1″

½″

Larson 1

Writer's name, instructor's name, course title, date flush left on first page; title centered.

Dan Larson

Professor Duncan

English 102

19 April 2013

Writer's last name and page number in upper right corner of each page.

The Transformation of Mrs. Peters:

An Analysis of "A Jury of Her Peers"

½″

In Susan Glaspell's 1917 short story "A Jury of Her Peers," two women accompany their husbands and a county attorney to an isolated house where a farmer named John Wright has been choked to death in his bed with a rope. The chief suspect is Wright's wife, Minnie, who is in jail awaiting trial. The sheriff's wife, Mrs. Peters, has come along to gather some personal items for Minnie, and Mrs. Hale has joined her. Early in the story, Mrs. Hale sympathizes with Minnie and objects to the way the male investigators are "snoopin' round and criticizin'" her kitchen (249). In contrast, Mrs. Peters shows respect for the law, saying that the men are doing "no more than their duty" (249). By the end of the story, however, Mrs. Peters has joined Mrs. Hale in a conspiracy of silence, lied to the men, and committed a crime—hiding key evidence. What causes this dramatic change?

Double-spacing throughout.

1″

Quotations from source cited with page numbers in parentheses.

One critic, Leonard Mustazza, argues that Mrs. Hale recruits Mrs. Peters "as a fellow 'juror' in the case, moving the sheriff's wife away from her sympathy for her husband's position and towards identification with the accused wom[a]n" (494). While this is true, Mrs. Peters also reaches insights on her own. Her observations in the kitchen lead her to understand Minnie's grim and lonely plight as the wife of an abusive farmer, and her identification with both Minnie and Mrs. Hale is strengthened as the men conducting the investigation trivialize the lives of women.

1″

The first evidence that Mrs. Peters reaches understanding on her own surfaces in the following passage:

> The sheriff's wife had looked from the stove to the sink—to the pail of water which had been carried in from outside. . . . That look of seeing into things, of seeing through a thing to something else, was in the eyes of the sheriff's wife now. (251-52)

A long quotation is set off by indenting; no quotation marks are needed; ellipsis dots indicate a sentence omitted from the source.

Something about the stove, the sink, and the pail of water connects

1″

MLA WORKS CITED PAGE

Larson 7

Works Cited

Ben-Zvi, Linda. "'Murder, She Wrote': The Genesis of Susan Glaspell's Trifles." *Theatre Journal* 44.2 (1992): 141-62. Rpt. in *Susan Glaspell: Essays on Her Theater and Fiction*. Ed. Ben-Zvi. Ann Arbor: U of Michigan P, 1995. 19-48. Print.

Glaspell, Susan. "A Jury of Her Peers." *Literature and Its Writers: A Compact Introduction to Fiction, Poetry, and Drama*. Ed. Ann Charters and Samuel Charters. 6th ed. Boston: Bedford, 2013. 243-58. Print.

Hedges, Elaine. "Small Things Reconsidered: 'A Jury of Her Peers.'" *Women's Studies* 12.1 (1986): 89-110. Rpt. in *Susan Glaspell: Essays on Her Theater and Fiction*. Ed. Linda Ben-Zvi. Ann Arbor: U of Michigan P, 1995. 49-69. Print.

Mustazza, Leonard. "Generic Translation and Thematic Shift in Susan Glaspell's *Trifles* and 'A Jury of Her Peers.'" *Studies in Short Fiction* 26.4 (1989): 489-96. Print.

Heading centered.

List alphabetized by authors' last names (or by title for works with no author).

First line of each entry at left margin; extra lines indented ½".

Double-spacing throughout; no extra space between entries.

APA TITLE PAGE

Header consists of shortened title (no more than 50 characters) in all capital letters at left margin and page number at right margin; on title page only, words "Running head" and colon precede shortened title.

Running head: REACTION TIMES IN VISUAL SEARCH TASKS 1

Full title, writer's name, and school centered halfway down page.

Reaction Times for Detection of Objects

in Two Visual Search Tasks

Allison Leigh Johnson

Carthage College

Author's note (optional) gives writer's affiliation, information about course, and possibly acknowledgments and contact information.

Author Note

Allison Leigh Johnson, Department of Psychology, Carthage College. This research was conducted for Psychology 2300, Cognition: Theories and Application, taught by Professor Leslie Cameron.

APA ABSTRACT

REACTION TIMES IN VISUAL SEARCH TASKS 2

Shortened title and page number on every page.

Abstract

Visual detection of an object can be automatic or can require attention. The reaction time varies depending on the type of search task being performed. In this visual search experiment, 3 independent variables were tested: type of search, number of distracters, and presence or absence of a target. A feature search contains distracters notably different from the target, while a conjunctive search contains distracters with features similar to the target. For this experiment, 14 Carthage College students participated in a setting of their choice. A green circle was the target. During the feature search, reaction times were similar regardless of the number of distracters and the presence or absence of the target. In the conjunctive search, the number of distracters and the presence or absence of the target affected reaction times. This visual search experiment supports the idea that feature searches are automatic and conjunctive searches require attention from the viewer.

Abstract, a 150-to-250-word overview of paper, appears on separate page. Heading centered, not boldface.

Numerals for all numbers in abstract, including numbers under 10.

Keywords: visual search, cognition, feature search, conjunctive search

Keywords (optional) help readers search for paper on the Web or in a database.

APA ESSAY FORMAT

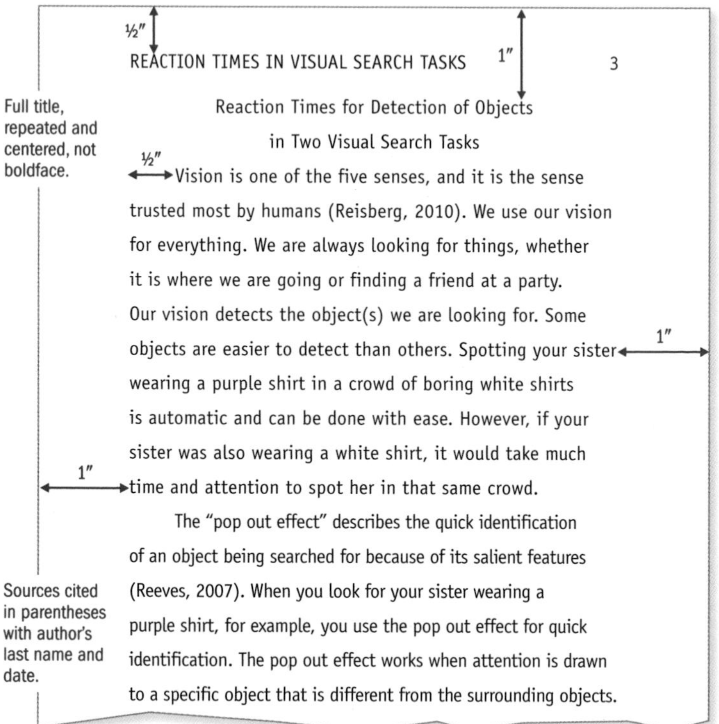

REACTION TIMES IN VISUAL SEARCH TASKS 3

Reaction Times for Detection of Objects
in Two Visual Search Tasks

Vision is one of the five senses, and it is the sense trusted most by humans (Reisberg, 2010). We use our vision for everything. We are always looking for things, whether it is where we are going or finding a friend at a party. Our vision detects the object(s) we are looking for. Some objects are easier to detect than others. Spotting your sister wearing a purple shirt in a crowd of boring white shirts is automatic and can be done with ease. However, if your sister was also wearing a white shirt, it would take much time and attention to spot her in that same crowd.

The "pop out effect" describes the quick identification of an object being searched for because of its salient features (Reeves, 2007). When you look for your sister wearing a purple shirt, for example, you use the pop out effect for quick identification. The pop out effect works when attention is drawn to a specific object that is different from the surrounding objects.

APA LIST OF REFERENCES

REACTION TIMES IN VISUAL SEARCH TASKS 8

List of references begins on new page; heading centered, not boldface.

List alphabetized by authors' last names.

First line of each entry flush left; additional lines indented ½″. Double-spacing throughout.

References

Reeves, R. (2007). *The Norton psychology labs workbook*. New York, NY: Norton.

Reisberg, D. (2010). *Cognition: Exploring the science of the mind*. New York, NY: Norton.

Treisman, A. (1986). Features and objects in visual processing. *Scientific American*, *255*, 114-125.

Wolfe, J. M. (1998). What do 1,000,000 trials tell us about visual search? *Psychological Science*, *9*, 33-39.

ZAPS: *The Norton psychology labs*. (2004). Retrieved from http://wwnorton.com/ZAPS/

BUSINESS REPORT WITH A VISUAL

Employee Motivation 5

Doug Ames, manager of operations for OAISYS, noted that some of these issues keep the company from outperforming expectations: "Communication is not timely or uniform, expectations are not clear and consistent, and some employees do not contribute significantly yet nothing is done" (personal communication, February 28, 2006).

Report formatted in typical business style, with citations in APA style.

Recommendations

It appears that a combination of steps can be used to unlock greater performance for OAISYS. Most important, steps can be taken to strengthen the corporate culture in key areas such as communication, accountability, and appreciation. Employee feedback indicates that these are areas of weakness or motivators that can be improved. This feedback is summarized in Figure 1.

Visual referred to in body of report.

A plan to use communication effectively to set expectations, share results in a timely fashion, and publicly offer appreciation to specific contributors will likely go a long way toward aligning individual motivation with corporate goals. Additionally, holding individuals accountable for results will bring parity to the workplace.

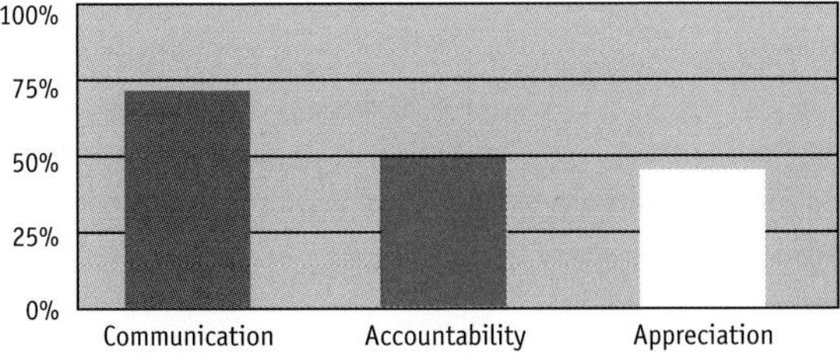

Figure 1. Areas of greatest need for improvements in motivation.

Figure, a bar graph, appears at bottom of page on which it is mentioned. Figure number and caption placed below figure.

BUSINESS LETTER IN FULL BLOCK STYLE

LatinoVoice

Date — March 16, 2013

Jonathan Ross
Managing Editor
Latino World Today
2971 East Oak Avenue
Baltimore, MD 21201

— Inside address

Salutation — Dear Mr. Ross:

Paragraphs single-spaced, not indented; double-spacing between paragraphs.

Thank you very much for taking the time yesterday to speak to the University of Maryland's Latino Club. A number of students have told me that they enjoyed your presentation and found your job search suggestions to be extremely helpful.

As I mentioned to you, the club publishes a monthly newsletter, *Latino Voice*. Our purpose is to share up-to-date information and expert advice with members of the university's Latino population. Considering how much students benefited from your talk, I would like to publish excerpts from it in our newsletter.

I have transcribed parts of your presentation and organized them into a question-and-answer format for our readers. Would you mind looking through the enclosed article and letting me know if I may have your permission to print it? I'm hoping to include this article in our next newsletter, so I would need your response by April 4.

Once again, Mr. Ross, thank you for sharing your experiences with us. I would love to be able to share your thoughts with students who couldn't hear you in person.

— Body

Sincerely, — Close

Jeffrey Richardson

Jeffrey Richardson
Associate Editor

— Signature

Indicates something enclosed with letter. — Enc.

210 Student Center University of Maryland College Park MD 20742

RÉSUMÉ

Alexis A. Smith

404 Ponce de Leon NE, #B7 — 404-231-1234
Atlanta, GA 30308 — asmith@smith.localhost

SKILLS SUMMARY

- Writing: competent communicating to different audiences, using a range of written forms (articles, reports, flyers, pamphlets, memos, letters)
- Design: capable of creating visually appealing, audience appropriate documents; skilled at taking and editing photographs
- Technical: proficient in Microsoft Office; comfortable with Dreamweaver, Photoshop, InDesign
- Language: fluent in spoken and written Spanish

EDUCATION

Bachelor of Arts, English — expected May 2014
Georgia State University, Atlanta, GA

- Emphasis areas: journalism and communication
- Study Abroad, Ecuador (Fall 2012)
- Dean's List (Fall 2012, Fall 2013, Spring 2014)

EXPERIENCE

Copyeditor — Sept. 2013-present
The Signal, Atlanta, GA

- copyedit articles for spelling, grammar, and style
- fact-check articles
- prepare copy for Web publication in Dreamweaver

Writing Tutor — Oct. 2011-present
Georgia State University Writing Studio, Atlanta, GA

- work with undergraduate and graduate students on writing projects in all subject areas
- provide technical support for multimedia projects

OUTREACH AND ACTIVITIES

- Publicity Director, English Department Student Organization — Aug. 2013-present
- Coordinator, Georgia State University Relay for Life Student Team — April 2013, 2014

Limit résumé to one page, if possible, two pages at most.

Information organized into clear categories—Skills Summary, Education, Experience, etc.—and formatted for easy scanning.

Information presented in reverse chronological order.

Bulleted lists organize information.

Present-tense verbs (*provide*) used for current activities.

PROFESSIONAL MEMO

Date, name of recipient, name of sender on separate lines.

Subject line describes topic clearly and concisely.

Introduction states point of memo.

Headings guide readers and promote quick scanning of document.

List calls attention to important information.

COMMONWEALTH PRESS

MEMORANDUM

February 26, 2013

To: Editorial assistants, Advertising Department

cc: Stephen Chapman

From: Helen Brown

Subject: Training for new database software

The new database software will be installed on your computers next week. I have scheduled a training program to help you become familiar with the software and with our new procedures for data entry and retrieval.

Training program

A member of our IT staff will teach in-house workshops on how to use the new software. If you try the software before the workshop, please be prepared to discuss any problems you encounter.

We will keep the training groups small to encourage hands-on participation and to provide individual attention. The workshops will take place in the training room on the third floor from 10:00 a.m. to 2:00 p.m.

Lunch will be provided in the cafeteria.

Sign-up

Please sign up by March 1 for one of the following dates by adding your name in the department's online calendar:

- Monday, March 4
- Wednesday, March 6
- Friday, March 8

If you will not be in the office on any of those dates, please let me know by March 1.

E-MAIL MESSAGE

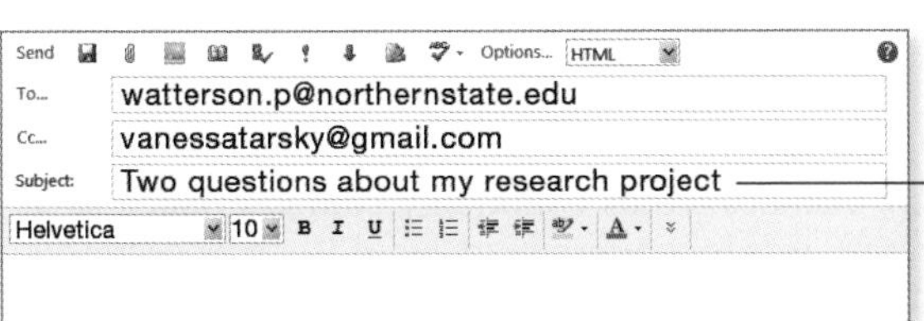

Clear, specific subject line gives purpose of message.

Hello, Professor Watterson.

Thank you for taking the time to meet with me yesterday to talk about my research project. I am excited to start the project this week. As we discussed, I am planning to meet with a reference librarian to learn more about NSU's online resources. And I will also develop an online survey to gather my fellow nursing students' perspectives on the topic. In the meantime, I have two questions:

- Do I need approval from the college's institutional review board before I conduct my survey?
- Do I need students' approval to quote their responses in my paper?

I know this is a busy time of year, but if possible, please let me know the answers to these questions before the end of the week.

Thanks for all your help with my project.

Sincerely,

Vanessa Tarsky

Introduction explains reason for writing.

Formal tone and language appropriate for communicating with professor.

Message formatted to be read quickly. Bullets draw reader's eye to important details.

Desired outcome of message: request stated briefly.

Message ends with brief, friendly closing.

APPENDIX

Glossary of usage

This glossary includes words commonly confused (such as *accept* and *except*), words commonly misused (such as *aggravate*), and words that are nonstandard (such as *hisself*). It also lists colloquialisms and jargon. Colloquialisms are casual expressions that may be appropriate in informal speech but are inappropriate in formal writing. Jargon is needlessly technical or pretentious language that is inappropriate in most contexts. If an item is not listed here, consult the index. For irregular verbs (such as *sing, sang, sung*), see 27a. For idiomatic use of prepositions, see 18d.

a, an Use *an* before a vowel sound, *a* before a consonant sound: *an apple, a peach.* Problems sometimes arise with words beginning with *h* or *u*. If the *h* is silent, the word begins with a vowel sound, so use *an*: *an hour, an honorable deed.* If the *h* is pronounced, the word begins with a consonant sound, so use *a*: *a hospital, a historian, a hotel.* Words such as *university* and *union* begin with a consonant sound (a *y* sound), so use *a*: *a union.* Words such as *uncle* and *umbrella* begin with a vowel sound, so use *an*: *an underground well.* When an abbreviation or an acronym begins with a vowel sound, use *an*: *an EKG, an MRI, an AIDS prevention program.*

accept, except *Accept* is a verb meaning "to receive." *Except* is usually a preposition meaning "excluding." *I will accept all the packages except that one. Except* is also a verb meaning "to exclude." *Please except that item from the list.*

adapt, adopt *Adapt* means "to adjust or become accustomed"; it is usually followed by *to. Adopt* means "to take as one's own." *Our family adopted a Vietnamese child, who quickly adapted to his new life.*

adverse, averse *Adverse* means "unfavorable." *Averse* means "opposed" or "reluctant"; it is usually followed by *to. I am averse to your proposal because it could have an adverse impact on the economy.*

advice, advise *Advice* is a noun, *advise* a verb. *We advise you to follow John's advice.*

affect, effect *Affect* is usually a verb meaning "to influence." *Effect* is usually a noun meaning "result." *The drug did not affect the disease, and it had adverse side effects. Effect* can also be a verb meaning "to bring about." *Only the president can effect such a dramatic change.*

aggravate *Aggravate* means "to make worse or more troublesome." *Overgrazing aggravated the soil erosion.* In formal writing, avoid the use of *aggravate* meaning "to annoy or irritate." *Her babbling annoyed* (not *aggravated*) *me.*

agree to, agree with *Agree to* means "to give consent to." *Agree with* means "to be in accord with" or "to come to an understanding with." *He agrees with me about the need for change, but he won't agree to my plan.*

ain't *Ain't* is nonstandard. Use *am not, are not* (*aren't*), or *is not* (*isn't*). *I am not* (not *ain't*) *going home for spring break.*

all ready, already *All ready* means "completely prepared." *Already* means "previously." *Susan was all ready for the concert, but her friends had already left.*

all right *All right*, written as two words, is correct. *Alright* is nonstandard.

all together, altogether *All together* means "everyone or everything in one place." *Altogether* means "entirely." *We were not altogether certain that we could bring the family all together for the reunion.*

allude To *allude* to something is to make an indirect reference to it. Do not use *allude* to mean "to refer directly." *In his lecture, the professor referred* (not *alluded*) *to several pre-Socratic philosophers.*

allusion, illusion An *allusion* is an indirect reference. An *illusion* is a misconception or false impression. *Did you catch my allusion to Shakespeare? Mirrors give the room an illusion of depth.*

a lot *A lot* is two words. Do not write *alot*. *Sam lost a lot of weight.* See also *lots, lots of.*

among, between See *between, among.*

amongst In American English, *among* is preferred.

amoral, immoral *Amoral* means "neither moral nor immoral"; it also means "not caring about moral judgments." *Immoral* means "morally wrong." *Until recently, most business courses were taught from an amoral perspective. Murder is immoral.*

amount, number Use *amount* with quantities that cannot be counted; use *number* with those that can. *This recipe calls for a large amount of sugar. We have a large number of toads in our garden.*

an See *a, an.*

and etc. *Et cetera* (*etc.*) means "and so forth"; *and etc.* is redundant. See also *etc.*

and/or Avoid the awkward construction *and/or* except in technical or legal documents.

angry at, angry with Use *angry with*, not *angry at*, when referring to a person. *The coach was angry with the referee.*

ante-, anti- The prefix *ante-* means "earlier" or "in front of"; the prefix *anti-* means "against" or "opposed to." *William Lloyd Garrison was a leader of the antislavery movement during the antebellum period. Anti-* should be used with a hyphen when it is followed by a capital letter (*anti-Semitic*) or a word beginning with *i* (*anti-intellectual*).

anxious *Anxious* means "worried" or "apprehensive." In formal writing, avoid using *anxious* to mean "eager." *We are eager* (not *anxious*) *to see your new house.*

anybody, anyone *Anybody* and *anyone* are singular. (See 21e and 22a.)

anymore Use the adverb *anymore* in a negative context to mean "any longer" or "now." *The factory isn't producing shoes anymore.* Using *anymore* in a positive context is colloquial; in formal writing, use *now* instead. *We order all our food online now* (not *anymore*).

anyone See *anybody, anyone.*

anyone, any one *Anyone,* an indefinite pronoun, means "any person at all." *Any one,* the pronoun *one* preceded by the adjective *any,* refers to a particular person or thing in a group. *Anyone from the winning team may choose any one of the games on display.*

anyplace *Anyplace* is colloquial. In formal writing, use *anywhere.*

anyways, anywheres *Anyways* and *anywheres* are nonstandard. Use *anyway* and *anywhere.*

as Do not use *as* to mean "because" if there is any chance of ambiguity. *We canceled the picnic because* (not *as*) *it began raining. As* here could mean either "because" or "when."

as, like See *like, as.*

as to *As to* is jargon for *about. He inquired about* (not *as to*) *the job.*

averse See *adverse, averse.*

awful The adjective *awful* and the adverb *awfully* are not appropriate in formal writing.

awhile, a while *Awhile* is an adverb; it can modify a verb, but it cannot be the object of a preposition such as *for*. The two-word form *a while* is a noun preceded by an article and therefore can be the object of a preposition. *Stay awhile. Stay for a while.*

back up, backup *Back up* is a verb phrase. *Back up the car carefully. Be sure to back up your hard drive. Backup* is a noun meaning "a copy of electronically stored data." *Keep your backup in a safe place. Backup* can also be used as an adjective. *I regularly create backup disks.*

bad, badly *Bad* is an adjective, *badly* an adverb. *They felt bad about ruining the surprise. Her arm hurt badly after she slid into second base.* (See 26a, 26b, and 26c.)

being as, being that *Being as* and *being that* are nonstandard expressions. Write *because* instead. *Because* (not *Being as*) *I slept late, I had to skip breakfast.*

beside, besides *Beside* is a preposition meaning "at the side of" or "next to." *Annie sleeps with a flashlight beside her bed. Besides* is a preposition meaning "except" or "in addition to." *No one besides Terrie can have that ice cream. Besides* is also an adverb meaning "in addition." *I'm not hungry; besides, I don't like ice cream.*

between, among Ordinarily, use *among* with three or more entities, *between* with two. *The prize was divided among several contestants. You have a choice between carrots and beans.*

bring, take Use *bring* when an object is being transported toward you, *take* when it is being moved away. *Please bring me a glass of water. Please take these forms to Mr. Scott.*

burst, bursted; bust, busted *Burst* is an irregular verb meaning "to come open or fly apart suddenly or violently." Its past tense is *burst*. The past-tense form *bursted* is nonstandard. *Bust* and *busted* are slang for *burst* and, along with *bursted*, should not be used in formal writing.

can, may The distinction between *can* and *may* is fading, but some writers still observe it in formal writing. *Can* is traditionally reserved for ability, *may* for permission. *Can you speak French? May I help you?*

capital, capitol *Capital* refers to a city, *capitol* to a building where lawmakers meet. *Capital* also refers to wealth or resources. *The residents of the state capital protested plans to close the streets surrounding the capitol.*

censor, censure *Censor* means "to remove or suppress material considered objectionable." *Censure* means "to criticize severely." *The administration's policy of censoring books has been censured by the media.*

cite, site *Cite* means "to quote as an authority or example." *Site* is usually a noun meaning "a particular place." *He cited the zoning law in his argument against the proposed site of the gas station.* Locations on the Internet are usually referred to as *sites*. *The library's Web site improves every week.*

climactic, climatic *Climactic* is derived from *climax*, the point of greatest intensity in a series or progression of events. *Climatic* is derived from *climate* and refers to meteorological conditions. *The climactic period in the dinosaurs' reign was reached just before severe climatic conditions brought on an ice age.*

coarse, course *Coarse* means "crude" or "rough in texture." *The coarse weave of the wall hanging gave it a three-dimensional quality. Course* usually refers to a path, a playing field, or a unit of study; the expression *of course* means "certainly." *I plan to take a course in car repair this summer. Of course, you are welcome to join me.*

compare to, compare with *Compare to* means "to represent as similar." *She compared him to a wild stallion. Compare with* means "to examine similarities and differences." *The study compared the language ability of apes with that of dolphins.*

complement, compliment *Complement* is a verb meaning "to go with or complete" or a noun meaning "something that completes." As a verb, *compliment* means "to flatter"; as a noun, it means "flattering remark." *Her skill at rushing the net complements his skill at volleying. Martha's flower arrangements receive many compliments.*

conscience, conscious *Conscience* is a noun meaning "moral principles." *Conscious* is an adjective meaning "aware or alert." *Let your conscience be your guide. Were you conscious of his love for you?*

continual, continuous *Continual* means "repeated regularly and frequently." *She grew weary of the continual telephone calls. Continuous* means "extended or prolonged without interruption." *The broken siren made a continuous wail.*

could care less *Could care less* is nonstandard. Write *couldn't care less* instead. *He couldn't* (not *could*) *care less about his psychology final.*

could of *Could of* is nonstandard for *could have. We could have* (not *could of*) *taken the train.*

council, counsel A *council* is a deliberative body, and a *councilor* is a member of such a body. *Counsel* usually means "advice" and can also mean "lawyer"; a *counselor* is one who gives advice or guidance. *The councilors met to draft the council's position paper. The pastor offered wise counsel to the troubled teenager.*

criteria *Criteria* is the plural of *criterion*, which means "a standard or rule or test on which a judgment or decision can be based." *The only criterion for the scholarship is ability.*

data *Data* is a plural noun technically meaning "facts or propositions." But *data* is increasingly being accepted as a singular noun. *The new data suggest* (or *suggests*) *that our theory is correct.* (The singular *datum* is rarely used.)

different from, different than Ordinarily, write *different from. Your sense of style is different from Jim's.* However, *different than* is acceptable to avoid an awkward construction. *Please let me know if your plans are different than* (to avoid *from what*) *they were six weeks ago.*

differ from, differ with *Differ from* means "to be unlike"; *differ with* means "to disagree with." *My approach to the problem differed from hers. She differed with me about the wording of the agreement.*

disinterested, uninterested *Disinterested* means "impartial, objective"; *uninterested* means "not interested." *We sought the advice of a disinterested counselor to help us solve our problem. Mark was uninterested in anyone's opinion but his own.*

don't *Don't* is the contraction for *do not. I don't want any. Don't* should not be used as the contraction for *does not*, which is *doesn't. He doesn't* (not *don't*) *want any.*

due to *Due to* is an adjective phrase and should not be used as a preposition meaning "because of." *The trip was canceled because of* (not *due to*) *lack of interest. Due to* is acceptable as a subject complement and usually follows a form of the verb *be. His success was due to hard work.*

each *Each* is singular. (See 21e and 22a.)

effect See *affect, effect.*

e.g. In formal writing, replace the Latin abbreviation *e.g.* with its English equivalent: *for example* or *for instance*.

either *Either* is singular. (See 21e and 22a.) For *either . . . or* constructions, see 21d and 22a.

elicit, illicit *Elicit* is a verb meaning "to bring out" or "to evoke." *Illicit* is an adjective meaning "unlawful." *The reporter was unable to elicit any information from the police about illicit drug traffic.*

emigrate from, immigrate to *Emigrate* means "to leave one country or region to settle in another." *In 1903, my great-grandfather emigrated from Russia to escape the religious pogroms. Immigrate* means "to enter another country and reside there." *More than fifty thousand Bosnians immigrated to the United States in the 1990s.*

eminent, imminent *Eminent* means "outstanding" or "distinguished." *We met an eminent professor of Greek history. Imminent* means "about to happen." *The snowstorm is imminent.*

enthused Avoid using *enthused* as an adjective. Use *enthusiastic* instead. *The children were enthusiastic* (not *enthused*) *about baking.*

etc. Avoid ending a list with *etc.* It is more emphatic to end with an example, and in most contexts readers will understand that the list is not exhaustive. When you don't wish to end with an example, *and so on* is more graceful than *etc.* (See also *and etc.*)

eventually, ultimately Often used interchangeably, *eventually* is the better choice to mean "at an unspecified time in the future," and *ultimately* is better to mean "the furthest possible extent or greatest extreme." *He knew that eventually he would complete his degree. The existentialists considered suicide the ultimately rational act.*

everybody, everyone *Everybody* and *everyone* are singular. (See 21e and 22a.)

everyone, every one *Everyone* is an indefinite pronoun. *Every one*, the pronoun *one* preceded by the adjective *every*, means "each individual or thing in a particular group." *Every one* is usually followed by *of. Everyone wanted to go. Every one of the missing books was found.*

except See *accept, except.*

expect Avoid the informal use of *expect* meaning "to believe, think, or suppose." *I think* (not *expect*) *it will rain tonight.*

explicit, implicit *Explicit* means "expressed directly" or "clearly defined"; *implicit* means "implied, unstated." *I gave him explicit instructions not to go swimming. My mother's silence indicated her implicit approval.*

farther, further *Farther* usually describes distances. *Further* usually suggests quantity or degree. *Chicago is farther from Miami than I thought. I would be grateful for further suggestions.*

fewer, less Use *fewer* for items that can be counted; use *less* for items that cannot be counted. *Fewer people are living in the city. Please put less sugar in my tea.*

finalize *Finalize* is jargon meaning "to make final or complete." Use ordinary English instead. *The architect prepared final drawings* (not *finalized the drawings*).

firstly *Firstly* sounds pretentious, and it leads to the ungainly series *firstly, secondly, thirdly,* and so on. Write *first, second, third* instead.

further See *farther, further.*

get *Get* has many colloquial uses. In writing, avoid using *get* to mean the following: "to evoke an emotional response" (*That music always gets to me*); "to annoy" (*After a while, his sulking got to me*); "to take revenge on" (*I got back at her by leaving the room*); "to become" (*He got sick*); "to start or begin" (*Let's get going*). Avoid using *have got to* in place of *must. I must* (not *have got to*) *finish this paper tonight.*

good, well *Good* is an adjective, *well* an adverb. (See 26a, 26b, and 26c.) *He hasn't felt good about his game since he sprained his wrist last season. She performed well on the uneven parallel bars.*

graduate Both of the following uses of *graduate* are standard: *My sister was graduated from UCLA last year. My sister graduated from UCLA last year.* It is nonstandard, however, to drop the word *from*: *My sister graduated UCLA last year.* Though this usage is common in informal English, many readers object to it.

grow Phrases such as *to grow the economy* and *to grow a business* are jargon. Usually the verb *grow* is intransitive (it does not take a direct object). *Our business has grown very quickly.* Use *grow* in a transitive sense, with a direct object, to mean "to cultivate" or "to allow to grow." *We plan to grow tomatoes this year. John is growing a beard.*

hanged, hung *Hanged* is the past-tense and past-participle form of the verb *hang* meaning "to execute." *The prisoner was hanged at dawn. Hung* is the past-tense and past-participle form of the verb *hang* meaning "to fasten or suspend." *The stockings were hung by the chimney with care.*

hardly Avoid expressions such as *can't hardly* and *not hardly,* which are considered double negatives. *I can* (not *can't*) *hardly describe my surprise at getting the job.* (See 26e.)

has got, have got *Got* is unnecessary and awkward in such constructions. It should be dropped. *We have* (not *have got*) *three days to prepare for the opening.*

he At one time *he* was commonly used to mean "he or she." Today such usage is inappropriate. (See 17e and 22a.)

he/she, his/her In formal writing, use *he or she* or *his or her.* For alternatives to these wordy constructions, see 17e and 22a.

hisself *Hisself* is nonstandard. Use *himself.*

hopefully *Hopefully* means "in a hopeful manner." *We looked hopefully to the future.* Some usage experts object to the use of *hopefully* as a sentence adverb, apparently on grounds of clarity. To be safe, avoid using *hopefully* in sentences such as the following: *Hopefully, your son will recover soon.* Instead, indicate who is doing the hoping: *I hope that your son will recover soon.*

however In the past, some writers objected to the conjunctive adverb *however* at the beginning of a sentence, but current experts allow placing the word according to the intended meaning and emphasis. All of the following sentences are correct. *Pam decided, however, to attend the lecture. However, Pam decided to attend the lecture.* (She had been considering other activities.) *Pam, however, decided to attend the lecture.* (Unlike someone else, Pam chose to attend the lecture.) (See 32f.)

hung See *hanged, hung.*

i.e. In formal writing, use "in other words" or "that is" rather than the Latin abbreviation *i.e.* to introduce a clarifying statement. *Exposure to borax usually causes only mild skin irritation; in other words* (not *i.e.*), *it's not especially toxic.*

if, whether Use *if* to express a condition and *whether* to express alternatives. *If you go on a trip, whether to Nebraska or Italy, remember to bring traveler's checks.*

illusion See *allusion, illusion.*

immigrate See *emigrate from, immigrate to.*

imminent See *eminent, imminent.*

immoral See *amoral, immoral.*

implement *Implement* is a pretentious way of saying "do," "carry out," or "accomplish." Use ordinary language instead. *We carried out* (not *implemented*) *the director's orders.*

implicit See *explicit, implicit.*

imply, infer *Imply* means "to suggest or state indirectly"; *infer* means "to draw a conclusion." *John implied that he knew all about computers, but the interviewer inferred that John was inexperienced.*

in, into *In* indicates location or condition; *into* indicates movement or a change in condition. *They found the lost letters in a box after moving into the house.*

in regards to *In regards to* confuses two different phrases: *in regard to* and *as regards.* Use one or the other. *In regard to* (or *As regards*) *the contract, ignore the first clause.*

irregardless *Irregardless* is nonstandard. Use *regardless.*

is when, is where These mixed constructions are often incorrectly used in definitions. *A runoff election is a second election held to break a tie* (not *is when a second election is held to break a tie*). (See 11c.)

its, it's *Its* is a possessive pronoun; *it's* is a contraction of *it is.* (See 36c and 36e.) *It's always fun to watch a dog chase its tail.*

kind(s) *Kind* is singular and should be treated as such. Don't write *These kind of chairs are rare.* Write instead *This kind of chair is rare. Kinds* is plural and should be used only when you mean more than one kind. *These kinds of chairs are rare.*

kind of, sort of Avoid using *kind of* or *sort of* to mean "somewhat." *The movie was somewhat* (not *sort of*) *boring.* Do not put *a* after either phrase. *That kind of* (not *kind of a*) *salesclerk annoys me.*

lay, lie See *lie, lay.*

lead, led *Lead* is a metallic element; it is a noun. *Led* is the past tense of the verb *lead. He led me to the treasure.*

learn, teach *Learn* means "to gain knowledge"; *teach* means "to impart knowledge." *I must teach* (not *learn*) *my sister to read.*

leave, let *Leave* means "to exit." Avoid using it with the nonstandard meaning "to permit." *Let* (not *Leave*) *me help you with the dishes.*

led See *lead, led.*

less See *fewer, less.*

let, leave See *leave, let.*

liable *Liable* means "obligated" or "responsible." Do not use it to mean "likely." *You're likely* (not *liable*) *to trip if you don't tie your shoelaces.*

lie, lay *Lie* is an intransitive verb meaning "to recline or rest on a surface." Its forms are *lie, lay, lain. Lay* is a transitive verb meaning "to put or place." Its forms are *lay, laid, laid.* (See 27b.)

like, as *Like* is a preposition, not a subordinating conjunction. It can be followed only by a noun or a noun phrase. *As* is a subordinating conjunction that introduces a subordinate clause. In casual speech, you may say *She looks like she hasn't slept* or *You don't know her like I do.* But in formal writing, use *as. She looks as if she hasn't slept. You don't know her as I do.* (See also 46f and 46g.)

loose, lose *Loose* is an adjective meaning "not securely fastened." *Lose* is a verb meaning "to misplace" or "to not win." *Did you lose your only loose pair of work pants?*

lots, lots of *Lots* and *lots of* are informal substitutes for *many, much,* or *a lot.* Avoid using them in formal writing.

mankind Avoid *mankind* whenever possible. It offends many readers because it excludes women. Use *humanity, humans, the human race,* or *humankind* instead. (See 17e.)

may See *can, may.*

maybe, may be *Maybe* is an adverb meaning "possibly." *Maybe the sun will shine tomorrow. May be* is a verb phrase. *Tomorrow may be brighter.*

may of, might of *May of* and *might of* are nonstandard for *may have* and *might have. We might have* (not *might of*) *had too many cookies.*

media, medium *Media* is the plural of *medium. Of all the media that cover the Olympics, television is the medium that best captures the spectacle of the events.*

might of See *may of, might of.*

most *Most* is informal when used to mean "almost" and should be avoided. *Almost* (not *Most*) *everyone went to the parade.*

must of See *may of, might of. Must of* is nonstandard for *must have.*

myself *Myself* is a reflexive or intensive pronoun. Reflexive: *I cut myself.* Intensive: *I will drive you myself.* Do not use *myself* in place of *I* or *me. He gave the pie to Ed and me* (not *myself*). (See also 24a and 24b.)

neither *Neither* is singular. For *neither . . . nor* constructions, see 21d, 22a, and 22d.

none *None* may be singular or plural. (See 21e.)

nowheres *Nowheres* is nonstandard. Use *nowhere* instead.

number See *amount, number.*

of Use the verb *have*, not the preposition *of*, after the verbs *could, should, would, may, might*, and *must. They must have* (not *must of*) *left early.*

off of *Off* is sufficient. Omit *of. The ball rolled off* (not *off of*) *the table.*

OK, O.K., okay All three spellings are acceptable, but avoid these expressions in formal speech and writing.

parameters *Parameter* is a mathematical term that has become jargon for "boundary" or "guideline." Use ordinary English instead. *The task force worked within certain guidelines* (not *parameters*).

passed, past *Passed* is the past tense of the verb *pass. Ann passed me another slice of cake. Past* usually means "belonging to a former time" or "beyond a time or place." *Our past president spoke until past midnight. The hotel is just past the next intersection.*

percent, per cent, percentage *Percent* (also spelled *per cent*) is always used with a specific number. *Percentage* is used with a descriptive term such as *large* or *small*, not with a specific number. *The candidate won 80 percent of the primary vote. A large percentage of registered voters turned out for the election.*

phenomena *Phenomena* is the plural of *phenomenon*, which means "an observable occurrence or fact." *Strange phenomena occur at all hours of the night in that house, but last night's phenomenon was the strangest of all.*

plus *Plus* should not be used to join independent clauses. *This raincoat is dirty; moreover* (not *plus*), *it has a hole in it.*

precede, proceed *Precede* means "to come before." *Proceed* means "to go forward." *As we proceeded up the mountain path, we noticed fresh tracks in the mud, evidence that a group of hikers had preceded us.*

principal, principle *Principal* is a noun meaning "the head of a school or an organization" or "a sum of money." It is also an adjective meaning "most important." *Principle* is a noun meaning "a basic truth or law." *The* *principal expelled her for three principal reasons. We believe in the principle of equal justice for all.*

proceed, precede See *precede, proceed.*

quote, quotation *Quote* is a verb; *quotation* is a noun. Avoid using *quote* as a shortened form of *quotation. Her quotations* (not *quotes*) *from current movies intrigued us.*

raise, rise *Raise* is a transitive verb meaning "to move or cause to move upward." It takes a direct object. *I raised the shades. Rise* is an intransitive verb meaning "to go up." *Heat rises.*

real, really *Real* is an adjective; *really* is an adverb. *Real* is sometimes used informally as an adverb, but avoid this use in formal writing. *She was really* (not *real*) *angry.* (See 26a and 26b.)

reason . . . is because Use *that* instead of *because. The reason she's cranky is that* (not *because*) *she didn't sleep last night.* (See 11c.)

reason why The expression *reason why* is redundant. *The reason* (not *The reason why*) *Jones lost the election is clear.*

relation, relationship *Relation* describes a connection between things. *Relationship* describes a connection between people. *There is a relation between poverty and infant mortality. Our business relationship has cooled over the years.*

respectfully, respectively *Respectfully* means "showing or marked by respect." *Respectively* means "each in the order given." *He respectfully submitted his opinion to the judge. John, Tom, and Larry were a butcher, a baker, and a lawyer, respectively.*

rise See *raise, rise.*

sensual, sensuous *Sensual* means "gratifying the physical senses," especially those associated with sexual pleasure. *Sensuous* means "pleasing to the senses," especially those involved in the experience of art, music, and nature. *The sensuous music and balmy air led the dancers to more sensual movements.*

set, sit *Set* is a transitive verb meaning "to put" or "to place." Its past tense is *set. She set the dough in a warm corner of the kitchen. Sit* is an intransitive verb meaning "to be seated." Its past tense is *sat. The cat sat in the doorway.*

shall, will *Shall* was once used in place of the helping verb *will* with *I* or *we*: *I shall, we shall.* Today, however, *will* is generally accepted even when the subject is *I* or *we*. The word *shall* occurs primarily in polite questions (*Shall I find you a pillow?*) and in legalistic sentences suggesting duty or obligation (*The applicant shall file form A by December 31*).

should of *Should of* is nonstandard for *should have. They should have* (not *should of*) *been home an hour ago.*

since Do not use *since* to mean "because" if there is any chance of ambiguity. *Because* (not *Since*) *we won the game, we have been celebrating* *with a pitcher of root beer. Since* here could mean "because" or "from the time that."

sit See *set, sit.*

site See *cite, site.*

somebody, someone *Somebody* and *someone* are singular. (See 21e and 22a.)

something *Something* is singular. (See 21e.)

sometime, some time, sometimes *Sometime* is an adverb meaning "at an indefinite time." *Some time* is the adjective *some* modifying the noun *time* and means "a period of time." *Sometimes* is an adverb meaning "at times, now and then." *I'll see you sometime soon. I haven't lived there for some time. Sometimes I see him at work.*

suppose to *Suppose to* is nonstandard for *supposed to. I was supposed to* (not *suppose to*) *be there by noon.*

sure and Write *sure to. We were all taught to be sure to* (not *sure and*) *look both ways before crossing a street.*

take See *bring, take.*

than, then *Than* is a conjunction used in comparisons; *then* is an adverb denoting time. *That pizza is more than I can eat. Tom laughed, and then we recognized him.*

that See *who, which, that.*

that, which Many writers reserve *that* for restrictive clauses, *which* for nonrestrictive clauses. (See 32e.)

theirselves *Theirselves* is nonstandard for *themselves. The crash victims pushed the car out of the way themselves* (not *theirselves*).

them The use of *them* in place of *those* is nonstandard. *Please take those* (not *them*) *flowers to the patient in room 220.*

then, than See *than, then.*

there, their, they're *There* is an adverb specifying place; it is also an expletive (placeholder). Adverb: *Sylvia is sitting there patiently.* Expletive: *There are two plums left. Their* is a possessive pronoun: *Fred and Jane finally washed their car. They're* is a contraction of *they are*: *They're later than usual today.*

they The use of *they* to indicate possession is nonstandard. Use *their* instead. *Cindy and Sam decided to sell their* (not *they*) *1975 Corvette.*

they, their The use of the plural pronouns *they* and *their* to refer to singular nouns or pronouns is nonstandard. *No one handed in his or her* (not *their*) *draft on time.* (See 22a.)

this kind See *kind(s).*

to, too, two *To* is a preposition; *too* is an adverb; *two* is a number. *Too many of your shots slice to the left, but the last two were just right.*

toward, towards *Toward* and *towards* are generally interchangeable, although *toward* is preferred in American English.

try and *Try and* is nonstandard for *try to. The teacher asked us all to try to* (not *try and*) *write an original haiku.*

ultimately, eventually See *eventually, ultimately.*

unique Avoid expressions such as *most unique, more straight, less perfect, very round.* Either something is unique or it isn't. It is illogical to suggest degrees of uniqueness. (See 26d.)

usage The noun *usage* should not be substituted for *use* when the meaning is "employment of." *The use* (not *usage*) *of insulated shades has cut fuel costs dramatically.*

use to *Use to* is nonstandard for *used to. I used to* (not *use to*) *take the bus to work.*

utilize *Utilize* means "to make use of." It often sounds pretentious; in most cases, *use* is sufficient. *I used* (not *utilized*) *the laser printer.*

wait for, wait on *Wait for* means "to be in readiness for" or "to await." *Wait on* means "to serve." *We're waiting for* (not *waiting on*) *Ruth to take us to the museum.*

ways *Ways* is nonstandard when used to mean "distance." *The city is a long way* (not *ways*) *from here.*

weather, whether The noun *weather* refers to the state of the atmosphere. *Whether* is a conjunction referring to a choice between alternatives. *We wondered whether the weather would clear.*

well, good See *good, well.*

where Do not use *where* in place of *that. I heard that* (not *where*) *the crime rate is increasing.*

whether See *if, whether.*

which See *that, which* and *who, which, that.*

while Avoid using *while* to mean "although" or "whereas" if there is any chance of ambiguity. *Although* (not *While*) *Gloria lost money in the slot machine, Tom won it at roulette.* Here *While* could mean either "although" or "at the same time that."

who, which, that Do not use *which* to refer to persons. Use *who* instead. *That*, though generally used to refer to things, may be used to refer to a group or class of people. *The player who* (not *that* or *which*) *made the basket at the buzzer was named MVP. The team that scores the most points in this game will win the tournament.*

who, whom *Who* is used for subjects and subject complements; *whom* is used for objects. (See 25.)

who's, whose *Who's* is a contraction of *who is*; *whose* is a possessive pronoun. *Who's ready for more popcorn? Whose coat is this?* (See 36c and 36e.)

will See *shall, will.*

would of *Would of* is nonstandard for *would have. She would have* (not *would of*) *had a chance to play if she had arrived on time.*

you In formal writing, avoid *you* in an indefinite sense meaning "anyone." (See 23d.) *Any spectator* (not *You*) *could tell by the way John caught the ball that his throw would be too late.*

your, you're *Your* is a possessive pronoun; *you're* is a contraction of *you are. Is that your new bike? You're in the finals.* (See 36c and 46b.)

Answers to Lettered Exercises

EXERCISE 6–1, page 102

a. hasty generalization; b. false analogy; c. *either . . . or* fallacy; d. biased language; e. faulty cause-and-effect reasoning

EXERCISE 8–1, page 129 *Possible revisions:*

a. The Prussians defeated the Saxons in 1745.
b. Ahmed, the producer, manages the entire operation.
c. The tour guides expertly paddled the sea kayaks.
d. Emphatic and active; no change
e. Protesters were shouting on the courthouse steps.

EXERCISE 9–1, page 132 *Possible revisions:*

a. Police dogs are used for finding lost children, tracking criminals, and detecting bombs and illegal drugs.
b. Hannah told her rock-climbing partner that she bought a new harness and that she wanted to climb Otter Cliffs.
c. It is more difficult to sustain an exercise program than to start one.
d. During basic training, I was told not only what to do but also what to think.
e. Jan wanted to drive to the wine country or at least to Sausalito.

EXERCISE 10–1, page 136 *Possible revisions:*

a. A grapefruit or an orange is a good source of vitamin C.
b. The women entering the military academy can expect haircuts as short as those of the male cadets.
c. Looking out the family room window, Sarah saw that her favorite tree, which she had climbed as a child, was gone.
d. The graphic designers are interested in and knowledgeable about producing posters for the balloon race.
e. The Great Barrier Reef is larger than any other coral reef in the world.

EXERCISE 11–1, page 140 *Possible revisions:*

a. Using surgical gloves is a precaution now taken by dentists to prevent contact with patients' blood and saliva.
b. A career in medicine, which my brother is pursuing, requires at least ten years of challenging work.
c. The pharaohs had bad teeth because tiny particles of sand found their way into Egyptian bread.
d. Recurring bouts of flu caused the team to forfeit a record number of games.
e. This box contains the key to your future.

EXERCISE 12–1, page 143 *Possible revisions:*

a. More research is needed to evaluate effectively the risks posed by volcanoes in the Pacific Northwest.
b. Many students graduate from college with debt totaling more than fifty thousand dollars.

c. It is a myth that humans use only 10 percent of their brains.
d. A coolhunter is a person who can find the next wave of fashion in the unnoticed corners of modern society.
e. Not all geese fly beyond Narragansett for the winter.

EXERCISE 12–6, page 146 *Possible revisions:*

a. To complete an online purchase with a credit card, you must enter the expiration date and the security code.
b. Though Martha was only sixteen, UCLA accepted her application.
c. As I settled in the cockpit, the pounding of the engine was muffled only slightly by my helmet.
d. After studying polymer chemistry, Phuong found computer games less complex.
e. When I was a young man, my mother enrolled me in tap dance classes.

EXERCISE 13–5, page 151 *Possible revisions:*

a. An incredibly talented musician, Ray Charles mastered R&B, soul, and gospel styles. He even performed country music well.
b. Environmentalists point out that shrimp farming in Southeast Asia is polluting water and making farmlands useless. They warn that governments must act before it is too late.
c. We observed the samples for five days before we detected any growth. *Or* The samples were observed for five days before any growth was detected.
d. In his famous soliloquy, Hamlet contemplates whether death would be preferable to his difficult life and, if so, whether he is capable of committing suicide.
e. The lawyer told the judge that Miranda Hale was innocent and asked that she be allowed to prove the allegations false. *Or* The lawyer told the judge, "Miranda Hale is innocent. Please allow her to prove the allegations false."

EXERCISE 13–6, page 152 *Possible revisions:*

a. Courtroom lawyers need to have more than a touch of theater in their blood.
b. The interviewer asked if we had brought our proof of citizenship and our passports.
c. Experienced reconnaissance scouts know how to make fast decisions and use sophisticated equipment to keep their teams from being detected.
d. After the animators finish their scenes, the production designer arranges the clips according to the storyboard and makes synchronization notes for the sound editor and the composer.
e. Madame Defarge is a sinister figure in Dickens's *A Tale of Two Cities*. On a symbolic level, she represents fate; like the Greek Fates, she knits the fabric of individual destiny.

EXERCISE 14–1, page 155 *Possible revisions:*

a. Williams played for the Boston Red Sox from 1939 to 1960, and he managed the Washington Senators and Texas Rangers for several years after retiring as a player.
b. In 1941, Williams finished the season with a batting average of .406; no player has hit over .400 for a season since then.
c. Although he acknowledged that Joe DiMaggio was a better all-around player, Williams felt that he was a better hitter than DiMaggio.

d. Williams was a stubborn man; for example, he always refused to tip his cap to the crowd after a home run because he claimed that fans were fickle.
e. Williams's relationship with the media was unfriendly at best; he sarcastically called baseball writers the "knights of the keyboard" in his memoir.

EXERCISE 14–2, page 158 *Possible revisions:*

a. The X-Men comic books and Japanese woodcuts of kabuki dancers, all part of Marlena's research project on popular culture, covered the tabletop and the chairs.
b. Our waitress, costumed in a kimono, had painted her face white and arranged her hair in a lacquered beehive.
c. Students can apply for a spot in the leadership program, which teaches thinking and communication skills.
d. Shore houses were flooded up to the first floor, beaches were washed away, and Brant's Lighthouse was swallowed by the sea.
e. Laura Thackray, an engineer at Volvo Car Corporation, addressed women's safety needs by designing a pregnant crash-test dummy.

EXERCISE 14–8, page 159 *Possible revisions:*

a. These particles, known as "stealth liposomes," can hide in the body for a long time without detection.
b. Irena, a competitive gymnast majoring in biochemistry, intends to apply her athletic experience and her science degree to a career in sports medicine.
c. Because students, textile workers, and labor unions have loudly protested sweatshop abuses, apparel makers have been forced to examine their labor practices.
d. Developed in a European university, IRC (Internet relay chat) was created as a way for a group of graduate students to talk from their dorm rooms about projects.
e. The cafeteria's new menu, which has an international flavor, includes everything from enchiladas and pizza to pad thai and sauerbraten.

EXERCISE 14–10, page 161 *Possible revisions:*

a. To help the relief effort, Gina distributed food and medical supplies.
b. Janbir, who spent every Saturday learning tabla drumming, noticed with each hour of practice that his memory for complex patterns was growing stronger.
c. When the rotor hit, it gouged a hole about an eighth of an inch deep in my helmet.
d. My grandfather, who was born eighty years ago in Puerto Rico, raised his daughters the old-fashioned way.
e. By reversing the depressive effect of the drug, the Narcan saved the patient's life.

EXERCISE 15–1, page 165 *Possible revisions:*

a. Across the hall from the fossils exhibit are the exhibits for insects and spiders.
b. After growing up desperately poor, Sayuri becomes a successful geisha.
c. Researchers who have been studying Mount St. Helens for years believe that earthquakes may have caused the 1980 eruption.

d. Ice cream typically contains 10 percent milk fat, but premium ice cream may contain up to 16 percent milk fat and has considerably less air in it.
e. If home values climb, the economy may recover quickly.

EXERCISE 16–1, page 169 *Possible revisions:*

a. Martin Luther King Jr. set a high standard for future leaders.
b. Alice has loved cooking since she could first peek over a kitchen tabletop.
c. Bloom's race for the governorship is futile.
d. A successful graphic designer must have technical knowledge and an eye for color and balance.
e. You will deliver mail to all employees.

EXERCISE 17–1, page 173 *Possible revisions:*

a. When I was young, my family was poor.
b. This conference will help me serve my clients better.
c. The meteorologist warned the public about the possible dangers of the coming storm.
d. Government studies show a need for after-school programs.
e. Passengers should try to complete the customs declaration form before leaving the plane.

EXERCISE 17–6, page 178 *Possible revisions:*

a. Dr. Geralyn Farmer is the chief surgeon at University Hospital. Dr. Paul Green is her assistant.
b. All applicants want to know how much they will earn.
c. Elementary school teachers should understand the concept of nurturing if they intend to be effective.
d. Obstetricians need to be available to their patients at all hours.
e. If we do not stop polluting our environment, we will perish.

EXERCISE 18–2, page 182 *Possible revisions:*

a. We regret this delay; thank you for your patience.
b. Ada's plan is to acquire education and experience to prepare herself for a position as property manager.
c. Serena Williams, the ultimate competitor, has earned millions of dollars just in endorsements.
d. Many people take for granted that public libraries have up-to-date computer systems.
e. The effect of Gao Xingjian's novels on other Chinese exiles is hard to gauge.

EXERCISE 18–5, page 183 *Possible revisions:*

a. Queen Anne was so angry with Sarah Churchill that she refused to see her again.
b. Correct
c. The parade moved off the street and onto the beach.
d. The frightened refugees intend to make the dangerous trek across the mountains.
e. What type of wedding are you planning?

EXERCISE 18–8, page 186 *Possible revisions:*

a. John stormed into the room like a hurricane.
b. Some people insist that they'll always be available to help, even when they haven't been before.
c. The Cubs easily beat the Mets, who were in trouble early in the game today at Wrigley Field.
d. We worked out the problems in our relationship.
e. My mother accused me of evading her questions when in fact I was just saying the first thing that came to mind.

EXERCISE 19–1, page 194 *Possible revisions:*

a. Listening to the CD her sister had sent, Mia was overcome with a mix of emotions: happiness, homesickness, and nostalgia.
b. Cortés and his soldiers were astonished when they looked down from the mountains and saw Tenochtitlán, the magnificent capital of the Aztecs.
c. Although my spoken Spanish is not very good, I can read the language with ease.
d. There are several reasons for not eating meat. One reason is that dangerous chemicals are used throughout the various stages of meat production.
e. To learn how to sculpt beauty from everyday life is my intention in studying art and archaeology.

EXERCISE 20–1, page 200 *Possible revisions:*

a. The city had one public swimming pool that stayed packed with children all summer long.
b. The building is being renovated, so at times we have no heat, water, or electricity.
c. The view was not what the travel agent had described. Where were the rolling hills and the shimmering rivers?
d. Walker's coming-of-age novel is set against a gloomy scientific backdrop; the earth's rotation has begun to slow down.
e. City officials had good reason to fear a major earthquake: Most [*or* most] of the business district was built on landfill.

EXERCISE 20–2, page 201 *Possible revisions:*

a. Wind power for the home is a supplementary source of energy that can be combined with electricity, gas, or solar energy.
b. Correct
c. In the Middle Ages, when the streets of London were dangerous places, it was safer to travel by boat along the Thames.
d. "He's not drunk," I said. "He's in a state of diabetic shock."
e. Are you able to endure extreme angle turns, high speeds, frequent jumps, and occasional crashes? Then supermoto racing may be a sport for you.

EXERCISE 21–1, page 211

a. One of the main reasons for elephant poaching is the profits received from selling the ivory tusks.
b. Correct
c. A number of students in the seminar were aware of the importance of joining the discussion.

d. Batik cloth from Bali, blue and white ceramics from Delft, and a bocce ball from Turin have made Angelie's room the talk of the dorm.
e. Correct

EXERCISE 22–1, page 217 *Possible revisions:*

a. Every presidential candidate must appeal to a wide variety of ethnic and social groups to win the election.
b. David lent his motorcycle to someone who allowed a friend to use it.
c. The aerobics teacher motioned for all the students to move their arms in wide, slow circles.
d. Correct
e. Applicants should be bilingual if they want to qualify for this position.

EXERCISE 23–1, page 221 *Possible revisions:*

a. Some professors say that engineering students should have hands-on experience with dismantling and reassembling machines.
b. Because she had decorated her living room with posters from chamber music festivals, her date thought that she was interested in classical music. Actually, she preferred rock.
c. In my high school, students didn't need to get all A's to be considered a success; they just needed to work to their ability.
d. Marianne told Jenny, "I am worried about your mother's illness." [*or* ". . . about my mother's illness."]
e. Though Lewis cried for several minutes after scraping his knee, eventually his crying subsided.

EXERCISE 24–1, page 226

a. Correct [But the writer could change the end of the sentence: . . . *than he was*.]
b. Correct [But the writer could change the end of the sentence: . . . *that she was the coach*.]
c. She appreciated his telling the truth in such a difficult situation.
d. The director has asked you and me to draft a proposal for a new recycling plan.
e. Five close friends and I rented a station wagon, packed it with food, and drove two hundred miles to Mardi Gras.

EXERCISE 25–1, page 230

a. Correct
b. The environmental policy conference featured scholars whom I had never heard of. [*or* . . . scholars I had never heard of.]
c. Correct
d. Daniel always gives a holiday donation to whoever needs it.
e. So many singers came to the audition that Natalia had trouble deciding whom to select for the choir.

EXERCISE 26–1, page 236

a. Do you expect to perform well on the exam next week?
b. With the budget deadline approaching, our office has hardly had time to handle routine correspondence.

c. Correct
d. The customer complained that he hadn't been treated nicely by the agent on the phone.
e. Of all the smart people in my family, Aunt Ida is the cleverest. [*or* . . . most clever.]

EXERCISE 27–1, page 242

a. When I get the urge to exercise, I lie down until it passes.
b. Grandmother had driven our new hybrid to the sunrise church service, so we were left with the station wagon.
c. A pile of dirty rags was lying at the bottom of the stairs.
d. How did the game know that the player had gone from the room with the blue ogre to the hall where the gold was heaped?
e. Abraham Lincoln took good care of his legal clients; the contracts he drew for the Illinois Central Railroad could never be broken.

EXERCISE 27–5, page 247

a. The glass sculptures of the Swan Boats were prominent in the brightly lit lobby.
b. Visitors to the glass museum were not supposed to touch the exhibits.
c. Our church has all the latest technology, even a closed-circuit television.
d. Christos didn't know about Marlo's promotion because he never listens. He is [*or* He's] always talking.
e. Correct

EXERCISE 27–9, page 254 *Possible revisions:*

a. Correct
b. Watson and Crick discovered the mechanism that controls inheritance in all life: the workings of the DNA molecule.
c. When city planners proposed rezoning the waterfront, did they know that the mayor had promised to curb development in that neighborhood?
d. Tonight's concert begins at 9:30. If it were earlier, I'd consider going.
e. Correct

EXERCISE 28–1, page 261

a. In the past, tobacco companies denied any connection between smoking and health problems.
b. The volunteer's compassion has touched many lives.
c. I want to register for a summer tutoring session.
d. By the end of the year, the state will have tested 139 birds for avian flu.
e. The golfers were prepared for all weather conditions.

EXERCISE 28–4, page 263

a. A major league pitcher can throw a baseball more than ninety-five miles per hour.
b. The writing center tutor will help you revise your essay.
c. A reptile must adjust its body temperature to its environment.
d. Correct
e. My uncle, a cartoonist, could sketch a face in less than two minutes.

EXERCISE 28–7, page 267 *Possible revisions:*

a. The electrician might have discovered the broken circuit if she had gone through the modules one at a time.
b. If Verena wins a scholarship, she will go to graduate school.
c. Whenever a rainbow appears after a storm, everybody comes out to see it.
d. Sarah did not understand the terms of her internship.
e. If I lived in Budapest with my cousin Szusza, she would teach me Hungarian cooking.

EXERCISE 28–10, page 270 *Possible answers:*

a. I enjoy riding my motorcycle.
b. The tutor told Samantha to come to the writing center.
c. The team hopes to work hard and win the championship.
d. Ricardo and his brothers miss surfing during the winter.
e. Jon remembered to lock the door. *Or* Jon remembered seeing that movie years ago.

EXERCISE 29–1, page 278

a. Doing volunteer work often brings satisfaction.
b. As I looked out the window of the plane, I could see Cape Cod.
c. Melina likes to drink her coffee with lots of cream.
d. Correct
e. I completed my homework assignment quickly. *Or* I completed the homework assignment quickly.

EXERCISE 30–1, page 283

a. There are some cartons of ice cream in the freezer.
b. I don't use the subway because I am afraid.
c. The prime minister is the most popular leader in my country.
d. We tried to get in touch with the same manager whom we spoke to earlier.
e. Recently there have been a number of earthquakes in Turkey.

EXERCISE 30–4, page 285 *Possible revisions:*

a. Although freshwater freezes at 32 degrees Fahrenheit, ocean water freezes at 28 degrees Fahrenheit.
b. Because we switched cable packages, our channel lineup has changed.
c. The competitor confidently mounted his skateboard.
d. My sister performs the *legong,* a Balinese dance, well.
e. Correct

EXERCISE 30–7, page 286

a. Listening to everyone's complaints all day was irritating.
b. The long flight to Singapore was exhausting.
c. Correct
d. After a great deal of research, the scientist made a fascinating discovery.
e. Surviving that tornado was one of the most frightening experiences I've ever had.

EXERCISE 30–10, page 288

a. an intelligent young Vietnamese sculptor
b. a dedicated Catholic priest

c. her old blue wool sweater
d. Joe's delicious Scandinavian bread
e. many beautiful antique jewelry boxes

EXERCISE 31–1, page 289

a. Whenever we eat at the Centerville Café, we sit at a small table in the corner of the room.
b. Correct
c. On Thursday, Nancy will attend her first home repair class at the community center.
d. Correct
e. We decided to go to a restaurant because there was no fresh food in the refrigerator.

EXERCISE 32–1, page 296

a. Alisa brought the injured bird home and fashioned a splint out of Popsicle sticks for its wing.
b. Considered a classic of early animation, *The Adventures of Prince Achmed* used hand-cut silhouettes against colored backgrounds.
c. If you complete the evaluation form and return it within two weeks, you will receive a free breakfast during your next stay.
d. Correct
e. Roger had always wanted a handmade violin, but he couldn't afford one.

EXERCISE 32–2, page 296

a. J. R. R. Tolkien finished writing his draft of *The Lord of the Rings* trilogy in 1949, but the first book in the series wasn't published until 1954.
b. In the first two minutes of its ascent, the space shuttle had broken the sound barrier and reached a height of over twenty-five miles.
c. German shepherds can be gentle guide dogs, or they can be fierce attack dogs.
d. Some former professional cyclists admit that the use of performance-enhancing drugs is widespread in cycling, but they argue that no rider can be competitive without doping.
e. As an intern, I learned most aspects of the broadcasting industry, but I never learned about fundraising.

EXERCISE 32–5, page 298

a. The cold, impersonal atmosphere of the university was unbearable.
b. An ambulance threaded its way through police cars, fire trucks, and irate citizens.
c. Correct
d. After two broken arms, three cracked ribs, and one concussion, Ken quit the varsity football team.
e. Correct

EXERCISE 32–6, page 299

a. NASA's rovers on Mars are equipped with special cameras that can take close-up, high-resolution pictures of the terrain.
b. Correct
c. Correct

d. Love, vengeance, greed, and betrayal are common themes in Western literature.
e. Many experts believe that shark attacks on surfers are a result of the sharks' mistaking surfboards for small injured seals.

EXERCISE 32–9, page 302

a. Choreographer Alvin Ailey's best-known work, *Revelations*, is more than just a crowd-pleaser.
b. Correct
c. Correct
d. A member of an organization that provides job training for teens was also appointed to the education commission.
e. Brian Eno, who began his career as a rock musician, turned to meditative compositions in the late 1970s.

EXERCISE 32–11, page 307

a. Cricket, which originated in England, is also popular in Australia, South Africa, and India.
b. At the sound of the starting pistol, the horses surged forward toward the first obstacle, a sharp incline three feet high.
c. After seeing an exhibition of Western art, Gerhard Richter escaped from East Berlin and smuggled out many of his notebooks.
d. Corrie's new wet suit has an intricate blue pattern.
e. We replaced the rickety old spiral staircase with a sturdy new ladder.

EXERCISE 32–12, page 308

a. On January 15, 2012, our office moved to 29 Commonwealth Avenue, Mechanicsville, VA 23111.
b. Correct
c. Ms. Carlson, you are a valued customer whose satisfaction is very important to us.
d. Mr. Mundy was born on July 22, 1939, in Arkansas, where his family had lived for four generations.
e. Correct

EXERCISE 33–1, page 312

a. Correct
b. Tricia's first artwork was a bright blue clay dolphin.
c. Some modern musicians (trumpeter John Hassell is an example) blend several cultural traditions into a unique sound.
d. Myra liked hot, spicy foods such as chili, kung pao chicken, and buffalo wings.
e. On the display screen was a soothing pattern of light and shadow.

EXERCISE 34–1, page 316

a. Do not ask me to be kind; just ask me to act as though I were.
b. When men talk about defense, they always claim to be protecting women and children, but they never ask the women and children what they think.
c. When I get a little money, I buy books; if any is left, I buy food and clothes.
d. Correct
e. Wit has truth in it; wisecracking is simply calisthenics with words.

EXERCISE 34–2, page 317

a. Strong black coffee will not sober you up; the truth is that time is the only way to get alcohol out of your system.
b. Margaret was not surprised to see hail and vivid lightning; conditions had been right for violent weather all day.
c. There is often a fine line between right and wrong, good and bad, truth and deception.
d. Correct
e. Severe, unremitting pain is a ravaging force, especially when the patient tries to hide it from others.

EXERCISE 35–1, page 319

a. Correct [Either *It* or *it* is correct.]
b. If we have come to fight, we are far too few; if we have come to die, we are far too many.
c. The travel package includes a round-trip ticket to Athens, a cruise through the Cyclades, and all hotel accommodations.
d. The news article portrays the land use proposal as reckless, although 62 percent of the town's residents support it.
e. Psychologists Kindlon and Thompson (2000) offer parents a simple starting point for raising male children: "Teach boys that there are many ways to be a man" (p. 256).

EXERCISE 36–1, page 322

a. Correct
b. The innovative shoe fastener was inspired by the designer's young son.
c. Each day's menu features a different European country's dish.
d. Sue worked overtime to increase her family's earnings.
e. Ms. Jacobs is unwilling to listen to students' complaints about computer failures.

EXERCISE 37–1, page 328

a. As for the advertisement "Sailors have more fun," if you consider chipping paint and swabbing decks fun, then you will have plenty of it.
b. Correct
c. After winning the lottery, Juanita said that she would give half the money to charity.
d. After the movie, Vicki said, "The reviewer called this flick 'trash of the first order.' I guess you can't believe everything you read."
e. Correct

EXERCISE 39–1, page 335

a. A client left his or her [*or* a] cell phone in our conference room after the meeting.
b. The films we made of Kilauea on our trip to Hawaii Volcanoes National Park illustrate a typical spatter cone eruption.
c. Correct
d. Of three engineering fields — chemical, mechanical, and materials — Keegan chose materials engineering for its application to toy manufacturing.
e. Correct

EXERCISE 40–1, page 341

a. Correct
b. Some combat soldiers are trained by government diplomats to be sensitive to issues of culture, history, and religion.
c. Correct
d. How many pounds have you lost since you began running four miles a day?
e. Denzil spent all night studying for his psychology exam.

EXERCISE 41–1, page 342

a. *MLA style:* The carpenters located three maple timbers, twenty-one sheets of cherry, and ten oblongs of polished ebony for the theater set. *APA style:* The carpenters located three maple timbers, 21 sheets of cherry, and 10 oblongs of polished ebony for the theater set.
b. Correct
c. Correct
d. Eight students in the class had been labeled "learning disabled."
e. The Vietnam Veterans Memorial in Washington, DC, had 58,132 names inscribed on it when it was dedicated in 1982.

EXERCISE 42–1, page 345

a. Howard Hughes commissioned the *Spruce Goose*, a beautifully built but thoroughly impractical wooden aircraft.
b. The old man screamed his anger, shouting to all of us, "I will not leave my money to you worthless layabouts!"
c. I learned the Latin term *ad infinitum* from an old nursery rhyme about fleas: "Great fleas have little fleas upon their back to bite 'em, / Little fleas have lesser fleas and so on *ad infinitum.*"
d. Correct
e. Neve Campbell's lifelong interest in ballet inspired her involvement in the film *The Company*, which portrays a season with the Joffrey Ballet.

EXERCISE 44–1, page 356

a. Correct
b. The swiftly moving tugboat pulled alongside the barge and directed it away from the oil spill in the harbor.
c. Correct
d. Your dog is well known in our neighborhood.
e. Roadblocks were set up along all the major highways leading out of the city.

EXERCISE 45–1, page 360

a. Assistant Dean Shirin Ahmadi recommended offering more world language courses.
b. Correct
c. Kalindi has an ambitious semester, studying differential calculus, classical Hebrew, brochure design, and Greek literature.
d. Lydia's aunt and uncle make modular houses as beautiful as modernist works of art.
e. We amused ourselves on the long flight by discussing how spring in Kyoto stacks up against summer in London.

EXERCISE 46–1, page 362

a. stage, confrontation, proportions; b. courage, mountain (noun/adjective), climber, inspiration, rescuers; c. need, guest, honor, fog; d. defense (noun/adjective), attorney, appeal, jury; e. museum, women (noun/adjective), artists, 1987

EXERCISE 46–5, page 365

a. his; b. that, our (pronoun/adjective); c. he, himself, some, his (pronoun/adjective); d. I, my (pronoun/adjective), you, one; e. no one, her

EXERCISE 46–9, page 367

a. told; b. were, killed; c. brought down; d. Stay, 'll [will] arrive; e. struggled, was trapped

EXERCISE 46–13, page 369

a. Adjectives: weak, unfocused; b. Adjectives: The (article), Spanish, flexible; adverb: wonderfully; c. Adjectives: The (article), fragrant, the (article), steady; adverb: especially; d. Adjectives: hot, cold; adverbs: rather, slightly, bitterly; e. Adjectives: The (article), its (pronoun/adjective), wicker (noun/adjective); adverb: soundly

EXERCISE 47–1, page 377

a. Complete subjects: The hills and mountains, the snow atop them; simple subjects: hills, mountains, snow; b. Complete subject: points; simple subject: points; c. Complete subject: (You); d. Complete subject: hundreds of fireflies; simple subject: hundreds; e. Complete subject: The evidence against the defendant; simple subject: evidence

EXERCISE 47–5, page 381

a. Subject complement: expensive; b. Direct object: death; c. Direct object: their players' efforts; d. Subject complement: the capital of the Russian Empire; e. Subject complement: bitter

EXERCISE 47–6, page 381

a. Direct objects: adults and children; object complement: weary; b. Indirect object: students; direct object: healthy meal choices; c. Direct object: the work; object complement: finished; d. Indirect objects: the agent, us; direct objects: our tickets, boarding passes; e. Direct object: community service; object complement: her priority

EXERCISE 48–1, page 385

a. In northern Italy (adverb phrase modifying *met*); as their first language (adverb phrase modifying *speak*); b. through the thick forest (adjective phrase modifying *hike*); with ease (adverb phrase modifying *completed*); c. To my boss's dismay (adverb phrase modifying *was*); for work (adverb phrase modifying *late*); d. of Mayan artifacts (adjective phrase modifying *exhibit*); into pre-Columbian culture (adjective phrase modifying *insight*); e. In 2002, in twelve European countries (adverb phrases modifying *became*)

EXERCISE 48–6, page 388

a. Updating your software (gerund phrase used as subject); b. decreasing the town budget (gerund phrase used as object of the preposition *in*); identifying nonessential services (gerund phrase used as subject complement); c. to help her mother by raking the lawn (infinitive phrase used as direct object); raking the lawn (gerund phrase used as object of the preposition *by*); d. Understanding little (participial phrase modifying *I*); passing my biology final (gerund phrase used as object of the preposition *of*); e. Working with animals (gerund phrase used as subject)

EXERCISE 48–10, page 391

a. so that every vote would count (adverb clause modifying *adjusted*); b. that targets baby boomers (adjective clause modifying *campaign*); c. After the Tambora volcano erupted in the southern Pacific in 1815 (adverb clause modifying *realized*); that it would contribute to the "year without a summer" in Europe and North America (noun clause used as direct object of *realized*); d. that at a certain point there will be no more oil to extract from the earth (noun clause used as direct object of *implies*); e. when you are rushing (adverb clause modifying *are overlooked*)

EXERCISE 49–1, page 394

a. Complex; that are ignited in dry areas (adjective clause); b. Compound; c. Simple; d. Complex; Before we leave for the station (adverb clause); e. Compound-complex; when you want to leave (noun clause)

Index

A

C

E

F

G

O

S

T

Multilingual Menu

A complete section for multilingual writers:

Multilingual and Academic English notes in other sections:

Writing about Literature

Writing about Literature L-1

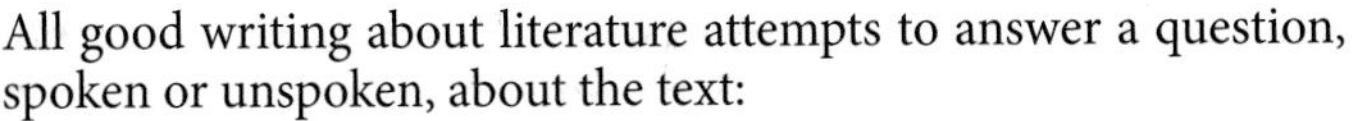

All good writing about literature attempts to answer a question, spoken or unspoken, about the text:

- Why does Hamlet hesitate for so long before killing his uncle, King Claudius?
- How does street language function in Gwendolyn Brooks's "We Real Cool"?
- What does George Orwell's "Shooting an Elephant" imply about the role the British played in colonial India?
- What does the relationship between Hana and Kip in Michael Ondaatje's novel *The English Patient* suggest about love and nationality?
- How does Suzanne Collins critique modern society in her depiction of a post-apocalyptic world in *The Hunger Games*?
- Why does Margaret Atwood make so many biblical allusions in *The Handmaid's Tale*?
- In what ways does Louise Erdrich's *Love Medicine* draw on oral narrative traditions?
- Why does it matter that Robert Hayden's poem "Those Winter Sundays" is about winter Sundays (as opposed to, say, winter Tuesdays)?

The goal of a literature analysis should be to answer such questions with a meaningful and persuasive interpretation.

L1 Reading to form an interpretation

L1-a Get involved in the work; be an active reader.

Responding to literature starts with becoming an engaged and active reader. Read the work through once, closely and carefully. Think of it as speaking to you: What is it telling you? Asking you? Trying to make you feel? Then go back and read it a second time. If the work provides an introduction and footnotes, read them as well. They may provide key information. Use the dictionary to look up unfamiliar words or words with connotations that may influence the work's meaning.

Rereading is a central part of the process of developing an analysis. You should read short works several times, first to get an overall impression and then again to focus on meaningful details. With longer works, such as novels or plays, read the most important chapters or scenes more than once while keeping in mind the work as a whole.

As you read and reread, interact with the work by posing questions and looking for possible answers. The chart that begins on page L-6 suggests some questions about literature that may help you become a more engaged, active reader.

Annotating the work

Annotating the work — in other words, interacting with the text by taking notes — is a way to focus your reading, capture your responses, and prepare for a class discussion. The first time you read the work through, you may want to indicate passages you find especially significant or puzzling. On a more careful rereading, pay particular attention to those passages, and jot down your ideas and reactions in a notebook or (if you own the text) on the pages. As you annotate, you can try out ideas and develop your questions and perspectives about the work.

Here is one student's annotation of a poem by Shakespeare.

Shall I compare thee to a summer's day?
Thou art more lovely and more temperate:
Rough winds do shake the darling buds of May,
And summer's lease hath all too short a date.
Sometime too hot the eye of heaven shines,
And often is his gold complexion dimmed;
And every fair from fair sometimes declines,
By chance, or nature's changing course, untrimmed.

Who? (Must be a loved one.)
Rhyming pattern of sonnet
Pleasant-natured (like pleasant weather)?
Fair = beauty, or more than beauty?
Summer is fleeting and not always perfect. (But lover is perfect?)

But thy eternal summer shall not fade,
Nor lose possession of that fair thou ow'st
Nor shall death brag thou wand'rest in his shade,
When in eternal lines to time thou grow'st.
So long as men can breathe or eyes can see,
So long lives this, and this gives life to thee.

What are "eternal lines to time"? Ask in class?

Death would be proud to claim the lover but can't?

Final couplet seems to signal a shift in thought.

This = the poem? (Art, like the writer's love, is eternal.)

NOTE TAKING ON A LITERARY WORK

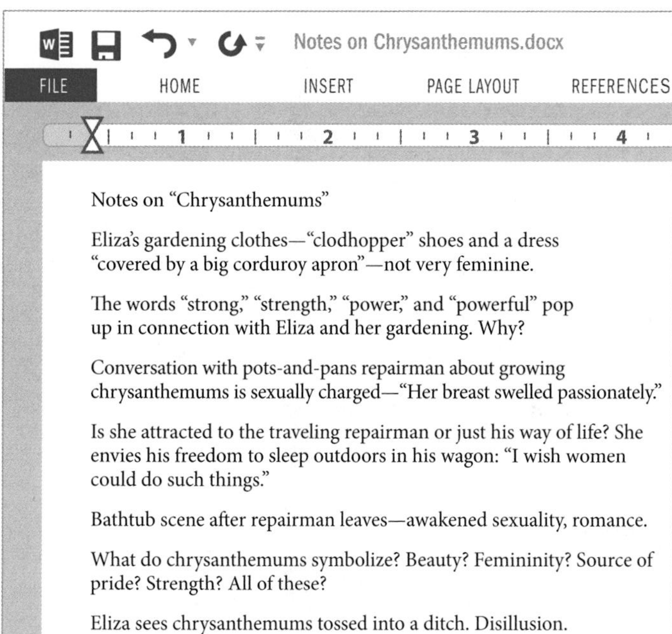

Notes on Chrysanthemums.docx
FILE
HOME
INSERT
PAGE LAYOUT
REFERENCES
Notes on "Chrysanthemums"
Eliza's gardening clothes—"clodhopper" shoes and a dress "covered by a big corduroy apron"—not very feminine.
The words "strong," "strength," "power," and "powerful" pop up in connection with Eliza and her gardening. Why?
Conversation with pots-and-pans repairman about growing chrysanthemums is sexually charged—"Her breast swelled passionately."
Is she attracted to the traveling repairman or just his way of life? She envies his freedom to sleep outdoors in his wagon: "I wish women could do such things."
Bathtub scene after repairman leaves—awakened sexuality, romance.
What do chrysanthemums symbolize? Beauty? Femininity? Source of pride? Strength? All of these?
Eliza sees chrysanthemums tossed into a ditch. Disillusion.

Taking notes

Note taking is also an important part of rereading a work of literature. In your notes you can try out ideas and develop your perspective on the work. Here are some notes one student took on a short story, "Chrysanthemums," by John Steinbeck. Notice that some of these notes pose questions for further thought.

CONVERSATION ABOUT A SUBJECT

Dr. Connolly's Blog | ENG 101, Section 4

1 **Who is Arnold Friend?**
Posted by **Professor Barbara Connolly**, Fri Mar 6, 2015 4:36 PM

At one point during the story, Arnold Friend demands, "Don't you know who I am?" Who do you think he is? Does the reader or Connie ever really know?

View comments | Add a comment

4 comments on
"Who is Arnold Friend?" **Original post**

2 Posted by **Zoe Marshall**, Fri Mar 6, 2015 7:23 PM
I think we're not supposed to know who Arnold Friend is. When he first arrives at Connie's house, she asks him, "Who the hell do you think you are?" but Arnold ignores her question by changing the subject. He never tells her who he really is, only that he's her friend and her lover.

Posted by **Mirabel Chavez**, Fri Mar 6, 2015 7:47 PM
Connie is always pretending to be something else to her friends, her boyfriends, and her family. Oates describes her as having two sides: one for home and one for when she's away from home. Pretending is something Connie and Arnold have in common.

Posted by **Jon Fietze**, Fri Mar 6, 2015 8:04 PM
I found a lot of parallels between Arnold and the wolf in "Little Red Riding Hood." For example, Connie notices Arnold's hair, his teeth, and his grin. It reminded me of that part in "Little Red Riding Hood" when Little Red says, "Oh, Grandmother, what big teeth you have!"

Posted by **Yuko Yoshikawa**, Fri Mar 6, 2015 11:11 PM
I was thinking the same thing. Plus, Arnold seems like he's dressing up to hide who he is. Connie thinks that his hair is like a wig, and later that his face is a mask. It reminded me of when the wolf puts on the grandmother's clothing to trick Little Red Riding Hood, just like Arnold is trying to trick Connie.

1 Instructor's prompt.

2 A series of student responses to the prompt.

Discussing the work

Class discussions can be a social experience and can often lead to interesting insights about a literary work, perhaps by calling attention to details that you failed to notice on a first reading. Discussions don't always need to occur face-to-face. In many classes, they happen online in discussion forums, chat rooms, blogs, or wikis. On page L-4, for example, is a set of blog postings about a character in Joyce Carol Oates's short story "Where Are You Going, Where Have You Been?"

L1-b Form an interpretation.

After rereading, taking notes, and perhaps discussing the work, you are ready to start forming an interpretation—your understanding of the meaning of details in the work. At this stage, try to focus on one aspect of the work. Look through your notes and annotations for recurring questions and insights.

Focusing on a central issue

In writing an analysis of literature, you will focus on a central issue. Your job is not to say everything about the work that can possibly be said. It is to develop a sustained, in-depth interpretation that illuminates the work in some specific way. For example, you may think that *Huckleberry Finn* is an interesting book because it not only contains humor and brilliant descriptions of scenery but also tells a serious story of one boy's coming of age. But to develop this general response into an interpretation, you will have to find a focus. For example, you might address the ways in which the runaway slave Jim uses humor to preserve his dignity. Or you might examine the ironic contradictions between what Huck says and what his heart tells him.

Asking questions that lead to an interpretation

Good interpretations generally arise from good questions. What is it about the work that puzzles or intrigues you? What do you want to know more about? By asking yourself such questions, you will push yourself to move beyond your first impressions to deeper insights.

In writing an analysis, you might answer questions about literary techniques, such as the author's handling of plot, setting, or character. Or you could respond to questions about social context as well — what a work reveals about the time and culture in which it was written. Both kinds of questions are included in the chart that begins at the bottom of the page.

Often you will find yourself writing about both technique and social context. For example, Margaret Peel, a student who wrote about Langston Hughes's poem "Ballad of the Landlord" (see p. L-27), addressed the following question, which touches on both language and race:

> How does the poem's language—through its four voices—dramatize the experience of a black man in a society dominated by whites?

Questions to ask about literature

Questions about technique

Plot: What central conflicts drive the plot? Are they internal (within a character) or external (between characters or between a character and a force)? How are conflicts resolved? Why are events revealed in a particular order?

Setting: Does the setting (time and place) create an atmosphere, give an insight into a character, suggest symbolic meanings, or hint at the theme of the work?

Character: What seems to motivate the central characters? Do any characters change significantly? If so, what have they learned from their experiences? Do contrasts between characters highlight important themes?

Point of view: Does the point of view — the perspective from which the story is narrated or the poem is spoken — influence our understanding of events? Does the narration reveal the character traits of the speaker, or does the speaker merely observe others? Is the narrator perhaps innocent, naive, or deceitful?

Theme: Does the work have an overall theme (a central insight about people or a truth about life, for example)? If so, how do details in the work serve to illuminate this theme?

Language: Does language — such as formal or informal, standard or dialect, ordinary or poetic, cool or passionate — reveal the character of speakers? How do metaphors, similes, and sensory images contribute to the work? How do recurring images enrich the work and hint at its meaning?

Questions about social context

Historical context: What does the work reveal about — or how was it shaped by — the time and place in which it was written? Does the work appear to promote or undermine a philosophy that was popular in its time, such as social Darwinism in the late nineteenth century or feminism in the mid-twentieth century?

Class: How does social class shape or influence characters' choices and actions? How does class affect the way characters view — or are viewed by — others? What economic struggles or power relationships does the work reflect or depict?

Race and culture: Are any characters portrayed as being caught between cultures: between a traditional and an emerging culture, for example? Are any characters engaged in a conflict with society because of their race or ethnic background? Does the work celebrate a specific culture and its traditions?

Gender: Are any characters' choices restricted because of gender? What are the power relationships between the sexes, and do these change during the course of the work? Do any characters resist the gender roles society has assigned to them? Do other characters choose to conform to those roles?

Archetypes (or universal types): Does a character, an image, or a plot fit a pattern — a type — that has been repeated in stories throughout history and across cultures? (For example, nearly every culture has stories about heroes, quests, redemption, and revenge.) How is an archetypal character, image, or plot line similar to or different from others like it?

In the introduction of your paper, you will usually announce your interpretation in a one- or two-sentence thesis. The thesis answers the central question that you posed. Here, for example, is Margaret Peel's two-sentence thesis:

> Langston Hughes's "Ballad of the Landlord" is narrated through four voices, each with its own perspective on the poem's action. These opposing voices—of a tenant, a landlord, the police, and the press—dramatize a black man's experience in a society dominated by whites.

L2 Planning the paper

L2-a Draft a thesis.

A thesis, which often appears in the introduction, announces an essay's main point. When planning your paper, it is good to have a working or preliminary thesis in mind. This preliminary thesis will reflect the current state of your thinking about the work and will likely change and evolve as you plan and draft. (See 1c for more on thesis statements.)

In a literature analysis, your thesis will answer the central question that you have asked about the work. When drafting your thesis, aim for a strong, assertive summary of your interpretation. For example, here are two successful thesis statements taken from student essays, together with the central question each student had posed.

> **QUESTION**
>
> What does Emily Dickinson's poem "I dwell in Possibility—" tell us about the writing of poetry?
>
> **THESIS**
>
> Emily Dickinson's poem "I dwell in Possibility—" implies that poetry itself is limitless and that the role of the poet is not to create poetry but to inhabit and shape it.
>
> **QUESTION**
>
> What is the significance of the explorer Robert Walton in Mary Shelley's novel *Frankenstein*?
>
> **THESIS**
>
> Through the character of Walton, Shelley suggests that the most profound and useful sort of knowledge is not a knowledge of nature's secrets but a knowledge of the limits of knowledge itself.

As in other college writing, the thesis of a literature paper should be open to interpretation; it should not be a statement of fact that all readers would agree is true. A thesis should also be focused — not too broad or too vague (see also 1c).

For an essay on Mark Twain's *Huckleberry Finn*, the first three examples would all make weak thesis statements.

TOO FACTUAL

As a runaway slave, Jim is in danger from the law.

TOO BROAD

In *Huckleberry Finn*, Twain criticizes mid-nineteenth-century American society.

TOO VAGUE

Huckleberry Finn is Twain's most exciting work.

The following thesis statement is sharply focused and presents a central idea that requires discussion and support. It connects a general point (that Twain objects to empty piety) to those specific aspects of the novel the paper will address (Huck's status as narrator, Huck's comments on religion).

EFFECTIVE THESIS

Because Huckleberry Finn is a naive narrator, his comments on conventional religion function ironically at every turn, allowing Twain to poke fun at empty piety.

L2-b Sketch an outline.

Your thesis may strongly suggest a method of organization, in which case you will have little difficulty jotting down your essay's key points. Consider, for example, the following informal outline, based on a thesis that leads naturally to a three-part organization (see p. L-10).

Thesis: In Zora Neale Hurston's novel *Their Eyes Were Watching God*, Janie grows into independence through a series of marriages: first to Logan Killicks, who treats her as a source of farm labor; next to Jody Starks, who sees her as a symbol of his own power; and then to Tea Cake, with whom she shares a passionate and satisfying love that leads her to self-discovery.

—Marriage to Logan Killicks: arranged by grandmother, Janie as labor, runs away

—Marriage to Jody Starks: Eatonville, Jody as mayor, violence, Jody's death

—Marriage to Tea Cake: younger man, love, shooting, return to Eatonville

If your thesis does not by itself suggest a method of organization, turn to your notes and begin putting them into categories that relate to the thesis. For example, one student who was writing about Euripides's play *Medea* constructed the following formal outline from her notes.

Thesis: Although Medea professes great love for her children, Euripides gives us reason to doubt her sincerity: Medea does not hesitate to use the children as weapons in her bloody battle with Jason, and from the outset she displays little real concern for their fate.

I. From the beginning of the play, Medea is a less than ideal mother.
   A. Her first words about the children are hostile.
   B. Her first actions suggest indifference.

II. In three scenes Medea appears to be a loving mother, but in each of these scenes we have reason to doubt her sincerity.

III. Throughout the play, as Medea plots her revenge, her overriding concern is not her children but her reputation.
   A. Fearing ridicule, she is proud of her reputation as one who can "help her friends and hurt her enemies."
   B. Her obsession with reputation may stem from the Greek view of reputation as a means of immortality.

IV. After she kills her children, Medea reveals her real concern.
   A. She shows no remorse.
   B. She revels in Jason's agony over their death.

Whether to use a formal or an informal outline is to some extent a matter of personal preference. For most purposes, you will probably find that an informal outline is sufficient, perhaps even preferable. (See 1d and 5b.)

L3 Writing the paper

L3-a Draft an introduction that announces your interpretation.

The introduction to a literature analysis is usually one paragraph long. In most cases, you will want to begin the paragraph with a few sentences that provide context for your main idea and to end it with a thesis statement that sums up your interpretation. You may also want to note the question or issue that motivated your interpretation. In this way, you will help your reader understand not only what your idea or thesis *is* but also why it *matters*.

The following is an introductory paragraph announcing a student's interpretation of one aspect of the novel *Frankenstein*; the thesis is highlighted.

> In Mary Shelley's novel *Frankenstein*, Walton's ambition as an explorer, to find a passage to the North Pole, mirrors Frankenstein's ambition as a scientist, to discover and master the secret of life. But where Frankenstein is ultimately destroyed by his quest for knowledge, Walton turns back from his quest when he learns of Frankenstein's fate. Walton's story might seem unimportant, but paired with Frankenstein's, it keeps us from missing one of the novel's most important themes. Through the character of Walton, Shelley suggests that the most profound and useful sort of knowledge is not a knowledge of nature's secrets but a knowledge of the limits of knowledge itself.

L3-b Support your interpretation with evidence from the work; avoid simple plot summary.

Your thesis and preliminary outline will point you toward details in the work relevant to your interpretation. As you begin drafting the body of your paper, make good use of those details.

Supporting your interpretation

As a rule, each paragraph in the body of your paper should focus on some aspect of your overall interpretation and should include a topic sentence that states the main idea of the paragraph. (See also "topic sentence" in your handbook.) The rest of the paragraph should present details and perhaps quotations from the work that back up your interpretation. In the following paragraph, which develops part of the outline sketched on pages L-9 to L-10, the topic sentence (highlighted) comes first. It sums up the significance of Janie's marriage to Logan Killicks in Zora Neale Hurston's novel *Their Eyes Were Watching God.*

> Janie finds her marriage to Logan Killicks unsatisfying because she did not choose him and cannot love him. The marriage is arranged by Janie's grandmother and caretaker, Nanny, so that Janie will have a secure home after Nanny dies. When Janie objects to the marriage, Nanny tells her, "'Tain't Logan Killicks Ah wants you to have, baby, it's protection" (15). Janie marries Logan even though she does not love him. She "wait[s] for love to begin" (22), but love never comes. At first, Logan dotes on Janie, but as time passes, he demands more and more work from her. Although she works hard in the kitchen, he wants her to perform traditionally masculine tasks such as chopping wood, plowing fields, and shoveling manure. When Janie suggests that they each have their roles—"Youse in yo' place and Ah'm in mine"—Logan asserts his authority over her and doesn't seem to relate to her as family: "You ain't got no particular place. It's wherever Ah need yuh" (31). As husband and wife, Janie and Logan are estranged from each other. Janie tells him, "You ain't done me no favor by marryin' me" (31). To escape this loveless and demeaning marriage, Janie runs away with Joe Starks.

Notice that the writer has quoted dialogue from the novel to lend both flavor and substance to her interpretation (quotations are cited with page numbers). Notice too that the writer is *interpreting* the work: She is not merely summarizing the plot.

Avoiding simple plot summary

In a literature paper, it is tempting to rely heavily on plot summary and avoid interpretation. You can resist this temptation by paying special attention to your topic sentences. The following rough-draft topic sentence, for instance, led to a plot summary rather than an interpretation.

DRAFT: A TOPIC SENTENCE THAT LEADS TO PLOT SUMMARY

As they drift down the river on a raft, Huck and the runaway slave Jim have many philosophical discussions.

REVISED: A TOPIC SENTENCE THAT ANNOUNCES AN INTERPRETATION

The theme of dawning moral awareness is reinforced by the many philosophical discussions between Huck and Jim, the runaway slave, as they drift down the river on a raft.

Remember that readers are interested in your ideas about a work — the questions you are asking and the details you find significant. To avoid simple plot summary, keep the following strategies in mind as you write.

- When you write for an academic audience, you can assume that readers have read the work. You need to include some summary as background, but the emphasis should be on your ideas about and your interpretation of the work.
- Pose questions that lead to an interpretation or a judgment of the work rather than to a summary. The questions in the chart that begins on page L-6 can help steer you away from summary and toward interpretation.
- Read your essay out loud. If you hear yourself listing events from the work, stop and revise.
- Rather than organizing your paper according to the work's sequence of events, organize it in a way that brings out the relationship among your ideas.

L4 Observing the conventions of literature papers

The academic discipline of English literature has certain conventions, or standard practices, that scholars in the field use when writing about literature. These conventions help scholars communicate their ideas clearly and efficiently. If you follow these conventions, you will enhance your credibility and enable your readers to focus more easily on your ideas.

L4-a Refer to authors, titles, and characters according to convention.

The first time you refer to an author of a literary work or a secondary source, such as a critical essay, use the author's full name: *Virginia Woolf is known for her experimental novels.* In subsequent references, you may use the last name only: *Woolf's early work was largely overlooked.* As a rule, do not use personal titles such as *Mr.* or *Ms.* or *Dr.* when referring to authors.

When you mention the title of a short story, an essay, or a short or medium-length poem, put the title in quotation marks.

"The Progress of Love," by Alice Munro

"Coming Home Again," by Chang-Rae Lee

"Promises like Pie-Crust," by Christina Rossetti

Italicize the titles of novels, nonfiction books, plays, and long poems.

The Poisonwood Bible, by Barbara Kingsolver

I Know Why the Caged Bird Sings, by Maya Angelou

M. Butterfly, by David Henry Hwang

Howl, by Allen Ginsberg

Refer to each character by the name most often used for him or her in the work. If, for instance, a character's name is Lambert Strether and he is always referred to as "Strether," do not call him "Lambert" or "Mr. Strether." Similarly, write "Lady Macbeth," not "Mrs. Macbeth."

L4-b Use the present tense to describe fictional events.

Perhaps because fictional events have not actually occurred in the past, the literary convention is to describe them in the present tense. Until you become used to this convention, you may find yourself shifting between present and past tense. As you revise your draft, make sure that you have used the present tense consistently.

INCONSISTENT USE OF TENSES

Octavia demands blind obedience from James and from all of her children. When James and Ty caught two redbirds in their trap, they wanted to play with them; Octavia, however, had other plans for the birds (89-90).

CONSISTENT USE OF THE PRESENT TENSE

Octavia demands blind obedience from James and from all of her children. When James and Ty catch two redbirds in their trap, they want to play with them; Octavia, however, has other plans for the birds (89-90).

NOTE: When integrating quotations from the work into your own text, you will need to be alert to the problem of shifting tenses. See L5-c.

L4-c Use MLA style to format passages quoted from the work.

Unless your instructor suggests otherwise, use MLA (Modern Language Association) style for formatting passages quoted from literary works.

MLA style usually requires that you name the author of the work quoted and give a page number for the exact location of the passage in the work. When writing about nonfiction articles and books, introduce a quotation with a signal phrase naming the author (*John Smith points out that* ". . .") or place the author's name and page number in parentheses at the end of the quoted passage: ". . ." *for all time (Smith 22).*

When writing about a single work of fiction, however, you do not need to include the author's name each time you quote from the work. You will mention the author's name in the introduction to your paper. Then, when you are quoting from the work, you may include just the page number in parentheses following the quotation (see p. L-20). You can still use the author's name in a signal phrase to highlight the author's role or technique (see p. L-18), but you are not required to do so. (See also L5-a.)

Additional MLA guidelines for handling citations in the text of your paper appear in L5.

L5 Integrating quotations from the text

Integrating quotations from a literary text can lend vivid support to your argument, but keep most quotations fairly short. You can use long quotations to present extended passages you will discuss at length, but use them sparingly. Excessive use of long quotations may interrupt the flow of your interpretation, making your paper more difficult to read and understand.

Integrating quotations smoothly into your own text can present a challenge. Because of the complexities of literature, do not be surprised to find yourself puzzling over the most graceful way to tuck in a short phrase or the clearest way to introduce a more extended passage from the work.

L5-a Do not confuse the work's author with a narrator, speaker, or character.

When introducing quotations from a literary work, make sure that you don't confuse the author with the narrator of a story, the speaker of a poem, or a character in a story or play. Instead of naming the author, you can refer to the narrator or speaker — or to the work itself.

INAPPROPRIATE

Poet Andrew Marvell describes his fear of death like this: "But at my back I always hear / Time's wingèd chariot hurrying near" (21-22).

APPROPRIATE

Addressing his beloved in an attempt to win her sexual favors, the speaker of the poem argues that death gives them no time to waste: "But at my back I always hear / Time's wingèd chariot hurrying near" (21-22).

APPROPRIATE

The poem "To His Coy Mistress" says as much about fleeting time and death as it does about sexual passion. Its most powerful lines are "But at my back I always hear / Time's wingèd chariot hurrying near" (21-22).

In the last example, you could mention the author as well: *Marvell's poem "To His Coy Mistress" says as much. . . .* Although the author is mentioned, readers will not confuse him with the speaker of the poem.

L5-b Provide context for quotations.

When you quote the words of a narrator, speaker, or character in a literary work, you should name who is speaking and provide a context for the quoted words. In the following examples, the quoted language is from Tennessee Williams's play *The Glass Menagerie* and Shirley Jackson's short story "The Lottery."

> Laura is so completely under Amanda's spell that when urged to make a wish on the moon, she asks, "What shall I wish for, Mother?" (1.5.140).

> When a neighbor suggests that the lottery should be abandoned, Old Man Warner responds, "There's *always* been a lottery" (284).

L5-c As you integrate quotations, avoid shifts in tense.

Because it is conventional to write about literature in the present tense (see L4-b) and because literary works often use other tenses, you will need to exercise some care when weaving quotations into your own writing. One student's first draft of a paper on Nadine Gordimer's short story "Friday's Footprint" included the following awkward sentence, in which the present-tense main verb *sees* is followed by the past-tense verb *blushed* in the quotation.

> TENSE SHIFT
>
> When Rita sees Johnny's relaxed attitude, "she blushed, like a wave of illness" (159).

When revising, the writer considered two ways to avoid the distracting shift from present to past tense: to paraphrase the reference to Rita's blushing and reduce the length of the quotation or to change the verb in the quotation to the present tense, using brackets to indicate the change (see p. L-18).

REVISION 1

When Rita sees Johnny's relaxed attitude, she is overcome with embarrassment, "like a wave of illness" (159).

REVISION 2

When Rita sees Johnny's relaxed attitude, "she blushe[s], like a wave of illness" (159).

Using brackets around just one letter of a word can seem fussy, so the writer chose the first revision. (See also L5-d.)

L5-d To indicate changes in a quotation, use brackets and the ellipsis mark.

Two marks of punctuation, square brackets and the ellipsis mark (three spaced periods), show readers that you have modified a quoted passage in some way.

Brackets are used for additions, as in the following example from a paper on Khaled Hosseini's novel *A Thousand Splendid Suns.*

> Laila, fearful, confides in Tariq: "It's the whistling, the damn whistling [of the rockets], I hate more than anything" (156).

Because some readers might not understand the meaning of *whistling* out of context, the writer has supplied a clarification in brackets. Brackets are also used to change words or letters to keep a quoted sentence grammatical in your context, as in the last example in L5-c, or to change a capital letter to lowercase or vice versa, as on page L-23.

The ellipsis mark is used to indicate omissions. In the following example from a paper on Tim O'Brien's "How to Tell a True War Story," the writer has omitted some words from the original in order to keep the quoted passage brief.

> O'Brien warns his readers bluntly that they should not seek noble themes in war stories: "If at the end of a war story you feel uplifted, . . . then you have been made the victim of a very old and terrible lie" (347).

If you want to omit one or more full sentences from a quotation, use a period before the three ellipsis dots.

O'Brien regards war as fundamentally immoral: "A true war story is never moral. . . . If a story seems moral, do not believe it" (347).

Usually you do not need an ellipsis mark at the beginning or at the end of a quotation. But if you have dropped words at the end of the final quoted sentence, put three ellipsis dots before the closing quotation mark and parenthetical reference, as in the example on page L-23.

Remember to use brackets and ellipsis marks sparingly. The purpose of quoting is to show your readers the actual language of the work. Excessive alterations can undermine a quotation's effectiveness as evidence.

L5-e Enclose embedded quotations in single quotation marks.

In writing about literature, you may sometimes want to use a quotation with another quotation embedded in it—when you are quoting dialogue in a novel, for example. In such cases, set off the main quotation with double quotation marks, as you usually would, and set off the embedded quotation with single quotation marks. The following example from a student paper quotes lines from Amy Tan's novel *The Hundred Secret Senses.*

Early in the novel the narrator's half-sister Kwan sees—or thinks she sees—ghosts: "'Libby-ah,' she'll say to me. 'Guess who I see yesterday, you guess.' And I don't have to guess that she's talking about someone dead" (3).

L5-f Use MLA style to cite passages from the work.

MLA guidelines for citing quotations differ somewhat for short stories or novels, poems, and plays.

Short stories or novels

To cite a passage from a short story or a novel, use a page number in parentheses after the quoted words (see the example on p. L-20).

> The narrator of Madeleine Thien's "Simple Recipes" remembers a conversation with her mother in which the mother described guilt as something one could "shrink" and "compress." After a time, according to the mother, "you can blow it off your body like a speck of dirt" (12).

If a novel has numbered divisions, give the page number and a semicolon; then indicate the book, part, or chapter in which the passage is found. Use abbreviations such as "bk." and "ch."

> White relies on past authors to help retell the legend of King Arthur. The narrator does not provide specifics about Lancelot's tournament at Corbin, instead telling readers, "If you want to read about the Corbin tournament, Malory has it" (489; bk. 3, ch. 39).

When a quotation from a work of fiction takes up four or fewer typed lines, put it in quotation marks and run it into the text of your essay, as in the two previous examples. When a quotation is five lines or longer, set it off from the text by indenting one inch from the left margin; when you set a quotation off from the text, do not use quotation marks. Put the parenthetical citation after the final mark of punctuation.

> Sister's tale begins with "I," and she makes every event revolve around herself, even her sister's marriage:
>
> > I was getting along fine with Mama, Papa-Daddy and Uncle Rondo until my sister Stella-Rondo just separated from her husband and came back home again. Mr. Whitaker! Of course I went with Mr. Whitaker first, when he first appeared here in China Grove, taking "Pose Yourself" photos, and Stella-Rondo broke us up. (88)

Poems

To cite lines from a poem, use line numbers in parentheses at the end of the quotation. For the first reference, use the word "lines": (lines 1-2). Thereafter use just the numbers: (12-13).

> The opening lines of Frost's "Fire and Ice" strike a conversational tone: "Some say the world will end in fire, / Some say in ice" (1-2).

Enclose quotations of three or fewer lines of poetry in quotation marks within your text, and indicate line breaks with a slash, as in the example just given.

When you quote four or more lines of poetry, set the quotation off from the text by indenting one inch, and omit the quotation marks. Put the line numbers in parentheses after the final mark of punctuation.

> In the second stanza of "A Noiseless Patient Spider," Whitman turns the spider's weaving into a metaphor for the activity of the human soul:
>
> > And you O my soul where you stand,
> > Surrounded, detached, in measureless oceans of
> > space,
> > Ceaselessly musing, venturing, throwing, seeking
> > the spheres to connect them,
> > Till the bridge you will need be form'd, till the
> > ductile anchor hold,
> > Till the gossamer thread you fling catch
> > somewhere, O my soul. (6-10)

NOTE: If any line of the poem takes up more than one line of your paper, carry the extra words to the next line of the paper and indent them an additional one-quarter inch, as in the previous example. Alternatively, you may indent the entire poem a little less than one inch to fit the long line.

Plays

To cite lines from a play, include the act number, scene number, and line numbers (as many of these as are available) in parentheses at the end of the quotation. Separate the numbers with periods, and use arabic numerals (1, 2, 3) unless your instructor prefers roman numerals.

> Two attendants silently watch as the sleepwalking Lady Macbeth struggles with her conscience: "Here's the smell of the blood still. All the perfumes of Arabia will not sweeten this little hand" (5.1.50-51).

If no act, scene, or line numbers are available, use a page number.

When a quotation from a play takes up four or fewer typed lines in your paper and is spoken by only one character, put quotation marks around it and run it into the text of your essay, as in the previous example. If the quotation consists of two or three lines from a verse play, use a slash for line breaks, as for poetry (see p. L-20). When a quotation by a single character in a play is five typed lines or longer (or more than three lines in a verse play), treat it like a passage from a short story or a novel (see p. L-20): Indent it one inch from the left margin and omit quotation marks. Include the citation in parentheses after the final mark of punctuation.

> Speaking to Electra, Clytemnestra complains about the sexual double standard that has allowed her husband to justify sacrificing her other daughter, Iphigenia, to the gods. She asks what would have happened if Menelaus, and not his wife Helen, had been seized by the Trojans:
>
> > If Menelaus had been raped from home on the sly,
> > should I have had to kill Orestes so my sister's
> > husband could be rescued? You think your father
> > would have borne it? He would have killed me.
> > Then why was it fair for him to kill what belonged
> > to me and not be killed? (1041-45)

When quoting dialogue between two or more characters in a play, set the quotation off from the text. Type each character's name in all capital letters at a one-inch indent from the left margin. Indent subsequent lines under the character's name an additional one-quarter inch.

> In the opening act of *Translations*, Friel pointedly contrasts the monolingual Captain Lancey with the multilingual Irish:
>
> > HUGH. . . . [Lancey] then explained that he does
> > not speak Irish. Latin? I asked. None. Greek?
> > Not a syllable. He speaks—on his own
> > admission—only English; and to his credit he
> > seemed suitably verecund—James?
> >
> > JIMMY. *Verecundus*—humble.
> >
> > HUGH. Indeed—he voiced some surprise that we
> > did not speak his language. (act 1)

L6 Using secondary sources

Many literature papers rely wholly on primary sources—the literary work or works under discussion. You document such papers with MLA in-text citations as explained in L5-f. If a list of works cited is required, it will consist of the literary work or works (see L6-a).

In addition to relying on primary sources, some literature papers draw on secondary sources: essays of literary criticism, a biography or autobiography of the author, or histories of the era in which the work was written. When you use secondary sources, you must document them with MLA in-text citations and a list of works cited as explained in L6-a. (For an example of a paper that uses secondary sources, see pp. L-32 to L-38.)

Keep in mind that even when you use secondary sources, your main goal should be to develop and communicate your own understanding and interpretation of the literary work.

L6-a Use MLA style to document secondary sources.

Most literature papers use the documentation system recommended by the Modern Language Association (MLA), as set forth in the *MLA Handbook for Writers of Research Papers*, 7th ed. (New York: MLA, 2009). (See 56.)

MLA recommends in-text citations that refer readers to a list of works cited. An in-text citation names the author of the source, often in a signal phrase, and gives the page number in parentheses. At the end of the paper, a list of works cited provides publication information about the sources used in the paper.

MLA IN-TEXT CITATION

Finding Butler's science fiction novel *Xenogenesis* more hopeful than *Frankenstein*, Theodora Goss and John Paul Riquelme note that "[h]uman and creature never bridge their differences in Shelley's narrative, but in Butler's they do . . ." (437).

The signal phrase names the authors of the secondary source; the number in parentheses is the page on which the quoted words appear.

The in-text citation is used in combination with a list of works cited at the end of the paper. Anyone interested in knowing additional information about the secondary source can consult the list of works cited. Here, for example, is the works cited entry for the work referred to in the sample in-text citation.

ENTRY IN THE LIST OF WORKS CITED

Goss, Theodora, and John Paul Riquelme. "From Superhuman to Posthuman: The Gothic Technological Imaginary in Mary Shelley's *Frankenstein* and Octavia Butler's *Xenogenesis*." *Modern Fiction Studies* 53.3 (2007): 434-59. Print.

As you document secondary sources with in-text citations and a list of works cited, you will need to consult section 56.

L6-b Avoid plagiarism.

The rules about plagiarism are the same for literature papers as for other academic and research writing. To be fair and ethical, you must acknowledge your responsibility to the writers of any sources you use. If you don't, you commit plagiarism, a serious academic offense.

In general, three different acts are considered plagiarism: (1) failing to cite quotations and borrowed ideas, (2) failing to enclose borrowed language in quotation marks, and (3) failing to put summaries and paraphrases in your own words. You may want to learn about your school's plagiarism policy if you are unfamiliar with it.

If another critic's work suggested an interpretation to you or if someone else's research clarified an obscure point, it is your responsibility to cite the source (as explained in L6-a). In addition to citing the source, you must place any borrowed language in quotation marks. In the example on page L-25, the plagiarized words are highlighted.

ORIGINAL SOURCE

Here again Glaspell's story reflects a larger truth about the lives of rural women. Their isolation induced madness in many. The rate of insanity in rural areas, especially for women, was a much-discussed subject in the second half of the nineteenth century.

— Elaine Hedges, "Small Things Reconsidered: 'A Jury of Her Peers,' " p. 59

PLAGIARISM

Glaspell may or may not want us to believe that Minnie Wright's murder of her husband is an insane act, but Minnie's isolation certainly could have driven her mad. As Elaine Hedges notes, the rate of insanity in rural areas, especially for women, was a much-discussed subject in the second half of the nineteenth century (59).

BORROWED LANGUAGE IN QUOTATION MARKS

Glaspell may or may not want us to believe that Minnie Wright's murder of her husband is an insane act, but Minnie's isolation certainly could have driven her mad. As Elaine Hedges notes, "The rate of insanity in rural areas, especially for women, was a much-discussed subject in the second half of the nineteenth century" (59).

Sometimes writers plagiarize unintentionally because they have difficulty paraphrasing a source's ideas. In the first paraphrase (p. L-26) of the following source, the writer has copied the highlighted words (without quotation marks) and followed the sentence structure of the source, merely plugging in synonyms (*prowess* for *skill*, *respect* for *esteem*, and so on).

ORIGINAL SOURCE

Mothers [in the late nineteenth century] were advised to teach their daughters to make small, exact stitches, not only for durability but as a way of instilling habits of patience, neatness, and diligence. But such stitches also became a badge of one's needlework skill, a source of self-esteem and of status, through the recognition and admiration of other women.

— Elaine Hedges, "Small Things Reconsidered: 'A Jury of Her Peers,' " p. 62

PLAGIARISM: UNACCEPTABLE BORROWING

One of the final clues in the story, the irregular stitching in Minnie's quilt patches, connects immediately with Mrs. Hale and Mrs. Peters. In the late nineteenth century, explains Elaine Hedges, small, exact stitches were valued not only for their durability. They became a badge of one's prowess with the needle, a source of self-respect and of prestige, through the recognition and approval of other women (62).

ACCEPTABLE PARAPHRASE

One of the final clues in the story, the irregular stitching in Minnie's quilt patches, connects immediately with Mrs. Hale and Mrs. Peters. In the late nineteenth century, explains Elaine Hedges, precise needlework was valued for more than its strength. It was a source of pride to women, a way of gaining status in the community of other women (62).

Although the acceptable version uses a few words found in the original source, it does not borrow entire phrases without quotation marks or closely mimic the structure of the original. To write an acceptable paraphrase, it may help to write from memory; resist the temptation to look at the source while you write. Ask yourself, "What is the author's meaning?" and then in your own words, state your understanding of the author's basic point.

L7 Sample papers

Following are two sample essays that analyze literary works. The first, by Margaret Peel, has no secondary sources. (Langston Hughes's "Ballad of the Landlord," the poem discussed in the essay, appears on p. L-31.) The second essay, by Dan Larson, uses secondary sources. (The short story discussed in the essay begins on p. L-39.)

Peel 1

Margaret Peel

Professor Lin

English 102

20 April 2010

Opposing Voices in "Ballad of the Landlord"

Langston Hughes's "Ballad of the Landlord" is narrated through four voices, each with its own perspective on the poem's action. These opposing voices—of a tenant, a landlord, the police, and the press—dramatize a black man's experience in a society dominated by whites.

Thesis states Peel's main idea.

The main voice in the poem is that of the tenant, who, as the last line tells us, is black. The tenant is characterized by his informal, nonstandard speech. He uses slang ("Ten Bucks"), contracted words (*'member, more'n*), and nonstandard grammar ("These steps is broken down"). This colloquial English suggests the tenant's separation from the world of convention, represented by the formal voices of the police and the press, which appear later in the poem.

Details from the poem illustrate Peel's point.

Although the tenant uses nonstandard English, his argument is organized and logical. He begins with a reasonable complaint and a gentle reminder that the complaint is already a week old: "My roof has sprung a leak. / Don't you 'member I told you about it / Way last week?" (lines 2-4). In the second stanza, he appeals diplomatically to the landlord's self-interest: "These steps is broken down. / When you come up yourself / It's a wonder you don't fall down" (6-8). In the third stanza, when the landlord has responded to his complaints with a demand for rent money, the tenant becomes more forceful, but his voice is still reasonable: "Ten Bucks you say is due? / Well, that's Ten Bucks more'n I'll pay you / Till you fix this house up new" (10-12).

The first citation for lines of the poem includes the word "lines." Subsequent citations from the poem are cited with line numbers alone.

Marginal annotations indicate MLA-style formatting and **effective writing**.

Peel 2

Topic sentence focuses on an interpretation.

The fourth stanza marks a shift in the tone of the argument. At this point the tenant responds more emotionally, in reaction to the landlord's threats to evict him. By the fifth stanza, the tenant has unleashed his anger: "Um-huh! You talking high and mighty" (17). Hughes uses an exclamation point for the first time; the tenant is raising his voice at last. As the argument gets more heated, the tenant finally resorts to the language of violence: "You ain't gonna be able to say a word / If I land my fist on you" (19-20).

Transition prepares readers for the next topic.

These are the last words the tenant speaks in the poem. Perhaps Hughes wants to show how black people who threaten violence are silenced. When a new voice is introduced—the landlord's—the poem shifts to a frantic tone:

> *Police! Police!*
> *Come and get this man!*
> *He's trying to ruin the government*
> *And overturn the land!* (21-24)

This response is clearly an overreaction to a small threat. Instead of dealing with the tenant directly, the landlord shouts for the police. His hysterical voice—marked by repetitions and punctuated with exclamation points—reveals his disproportionate fear and outrage. And his conclusions are equally excessive: this black man, he claims, is out to "ruin the government" and "overturn the land." Although the landlord's overreaction is humorous, it is sinister as well, because the landlord knows that, no matter how excessive his claims are, he has the police and the law on his side.

Peel interprets the landlord's response.

Peel shows how meter and rhyme support the poem's meaning.

In line 25, the regular meter and rhyme of the poem break down, perhaps showing how an arrest disrupts

Peel 3

everyday life. The “voice” in lines 25-29 has two parts: the clanging sound of the police (“Copper’s whistle! / Patrol bell!”) and, in sharp contrast, the unemotional, factual tone of a police report (“Arrest. / Precinct Station. / Iron cell.”).

The last voice in the poem is the voice of the press, represented in newspaper headlines: “MAN THREATENS LANDLORD / TENANT HELD NO BAIL / JUDGE GIVES NEGRO 90 DAYS IN COUNTY JAIL” (31-33). Meter and rhyme return here, as if to show that once the tenant is arrested, life can go on as usual. The language of the press, like that of the police, is cold and distant, and it gives the tenant less and less status. In line 31, he is a “man”; in line 32, he has been demoted to a “tenant”; and in line 33, he has become a “Negro,” or just another statistic.

Peel sums up her interpretation.

By using four opposing voices in “Ballad of the Landlord,” Hughes effectively dramatizes different views of minority assertiveness. To the tenant, assertiveness is informal and natural, as his language shows; to the landlord, it is a dangerous threat, as his hysterical response suggests. The police response is, like the language that describes it, short and sharp. Finally, the press’s view of events, represented by the headlines, is distant and unsympathetic.

By the end of the poem, we understand the predicament of the black man. Exploited by the landlord, politically oppressed by those who think he’s out “to ruin the government,” physically restrained by the police and the judicial system, and denied his individuality by the press, he is saved only by his own sense of humor. The very title of the poem suggests his—and Hughes’s—sense of humor.

Peel concludes with an analysis of the poem’s political significance.

Peel 4

The tenant is singing a *ballad* to his oppressors, but this ballad is no love song. It portrays the oppressors, through their own voices, in an unflattering light: the landlord as cowardly and ridiculous, the police and press as dull and soulless. The tenant may lack political power, but he speaks with vitality, and no one can say he lacks dignity or the spirit to survive.

Ballad of the Landlord

LANGSTON HUGHES

Landlord, landlord,
My roof has sprung a leak.
Don't you 'member I told you about it
Way last week?

Landlord, landlord,
These steps is broken down.
When you come up yourself
It's a wonder you don't fall down.

Ten Bucks you say I owe you?
Ten Bucks you say is due?
Well, that's Ten Bucks more'n I'll pay you
Till you fix this house up new.

What? You gonna get eviction orders?
You gonna cut off my heat?
You gonna take my furniture and
Throw it in the street?

Um-huh! You talking high and mighty.
Talk on — till you get through.
You ain't gonna be able to say a word
If I land my fist on you.

Police! Police!
Come and get this man!
He's trying to ruin the government
And overturn the land!

Copper's whistle!
Patrol bell!
Arrest.

Precinct Station.
Iron cell.
Headlines in press:

MAN THREATENS LANDLORD
TENANT HELD NO BAIL
JUDGE GIVES NEGRO 90 DAYS IN COUNTY JAIL

Larson 1

Dan Larson

Professor Duncan

English 102

17 April 2013

The Transformation of Mrs. Peters:
An Analysis of "A Jury of Her Peers"

The opening lines name the story and establish context.

Present tense is used to describe details from the story.

Quotations from the story are cited with page numbers in parentheses.

The opening paragraph ends with Larson's research question.

The thesis asserts Larson's main point.

In Susan Glaspell's 1917 short story "A Jury of Her Peers," two women accompany their husbands and a county attorney to an isolated house where a farmer named John Wright has been choked to death in his bed with a rope. The chief suspect is Wright's wife, Minnie, who is in jail awaiting trial. The sheriff's wife, Mrs. Peters, has come along to gather some personal items for Minnie, and Mrs. Hale has joined her. Early in the story, Mrs. Hale sympathizes with Minnie and objects to the way the male investigators are "snoopin' round and criticizin'" her kitchen (249). In contrast, Mrs. Peters shows respect for the law, saying that the men are doing "no more than their duty" (249). By the end of the story, however, Mrs. Peters has joined Mrs. Hale in a conspiracy of silence, lied to the men, and committed a crime—hiding key evidence. What causes this dramatic change?

One critic, Leonard Mustazza, argues that Mrs. Hale recruits Mrs. Peters "as a fellow 'juror' in the case, moving the sheriff's wife away from her sympathy for her husband's position and towards identification with the accused wom[a]n" (494). While this is true, Mrs. Peters also reaches insights on her own. Her observations in the kitchen lead her to understand Minnie's grim and lonely plight as the wife of an abusive farmer, and her identification with both Minnie and Mrs. Hale is strengthened as the men conducting the investigation trivialize the lives of women.

Marginal annotations indicate MLA-style formatting and **effective writing**.

Larson 2

The first evidence that Mrs. Peters reaches understanding on her own surfaces in the following passage:

> The sheriff's wife had looked from the stove to the sink—to the pail of water which had been carried in from outside. . . . That look of seeing into things, of seeing through a thing to something else, was in the eyes of the sheriff's wife now. (251-52)

Something about the stove, the sink, and the pail of water connects with her own experience, giving Mrs. Peters a glimpse into the life of Minnie Wright. The details resonate with meaning.

A long quotation is set off by indenting; no quotation marks are needed; ellipsis dots indicate a sentence omitted from the source.

Social historian Elaine Hedges argues that such details, which evoke the drudgery of a farm woman's work, would not have been lost on Glaspell's readers in 1917. Hedges tells us what the pail and the stove, along with another detail from the story—a dirty towel on a roller—would have meant to women of the time. Laundry was a dreaded all-day affair. Water had to be pumped, hauled, and boiled; then the wash was rubbed, rinsed, wrung through a wringer, carried outside, and hung on a line to dry. "What the women see, beyond the pail and the stove," writes Hedges, "are the hours of work it took Minnie to produce that one clean towel" (56).

Larson summarizes ideas from a secondary source and then quotes from that source; he names the author in a signal phrase and gives a page number in parentheses.

On her own, Mrs. Peters discovers clues about the motive for the murder. Her curiosity leads her to pick up a sewing basket filled with quilt pieces and then to notice something strange: a sudden row of badly sewn stitches. "What do you suppose she was so—nervous about?" asks Mrs. Peters (252). A short time later, Mrs. Peters spots another clue, an empty birdcage. Again she observes

Topic sentences present Larson's interpretation.

Larson 3

details on her own, in this case a broken door and hinge, suggesting that the cage has been roughly handled.

In addition to noticing details, both women draw conclusions from them and speculate on their significance. When Mrs. Hale finds the dead canary beneath a quilt patch, for example, the women conclude that its neck has been wrung and understand who must have wrung it.

Details from the story provide evidence for the interpretation.

As the women speculate on the significance of the dead canary, each connects the bird with her own experience. Mrs. Hale knows that Minnie once sang in the church choir, an activity that Mr. Wright put a stop to, just as he put a stop to the bird's singing. Also, as a farmer's wife, Mrs. Hale understands the desolation and loneliness of life on the prairie. She sees that the bird was both a thing of beauty and a companion. "If there had been years and years of—nothing, then a bird to sing to you," says Mrs. Hale, "it would be awful—still—after the bird was still" (256). To Mrs. Peters, the stillness of the canary evokes memories of the time when she and her husband homesteaded in the northern plains. "I know what stillness is," she says, as she recalls the death of her first child, with no one around to console her (256).

Elaine Hedges has written movingly of the isolation that women experienced on late-nineteenth- and early-twentieth-century farms of the West and Midwest:

Ellipsis dots indicate omitted words within the sentence and at the end of the sentence.

> Women themselves reported that it was not unusual to spend five months in a log cabin without seeing another woman . . . or to spend one and a half years after arriving before being able to take a trip to town. . . . (54)

Larson 4

To combat loneliness and monotony, says Hedges, many women bought canaries and hung the cages outside their sod huts. The canaries provided music and color, a "spot of beauty" that "might spell the difference between sanity and madness" (60).

Mrs. Peters and Mrs. Hale understand—and Glaspell's readers in 1917 would have understood—what the killing of the bird means to Minnie. For Mrs. Peters, in fact, the act has a special significance. When she was a child, a boy axed her kitten to death and, as she says, "If they hadn't held me back I would have . . . hurt him" (256). She has little difficulty comprehending Minnie's murderous rage, for she has felt it herself.

Although Mrs. Peters's growing empathy for Minnie stems largely from her observations, it is also prompted by her negative reaction to the patronizing comments of the male investigators. At several points in the story, her body language reveals her feelings. For example, when Mr. Hale remarks that "women are used to worrying over trifles," both women move closer together and remain silent. When the county attorney asks, "for all their worries, what would we do without the ladies?" the women do not speak, nor do they "unbend" (248). The fact that the women respond in exactly the same way reveals the extent to which they are bonding.

Transition serves as a bridge from one section of the paper to the next.

Both women are annoyed at the way in which the men criticize and trivialize the world of women. The men question the difficulty of women's work. For example, when the county attorney points to the dirty towel on the rack as evidence that Minnie wasn't much of a housekeeper, Mrs. Hale replies, "There's a great deal of work to be done on a farm" (248). Even the importance of women's work is questioned. The men kid the women for trying to decide if Minnie was going to quilt or knot patches together for a quilt and laugh about such trivial concerns. Those very quilts, of course, kept the men warm at night and cost them nothing beyond the price of thread.

The men also question the women's wisdom and intelligence. For example, when the county attorney tells the women to keep their eyes out for clues, Mr. Hale replies, "But would the women know a clue if they did come upon it?" (249). The women's response is to stand motionless and silent. The irony is that the men don't see the household clues that are right in front of them.

Larson gives evidence that Mrs. Peters has been transformed.

By the end of the story, Mrs. Peters has been so transformed that she risks lying to the men. When the county attorney walks into the kitchen and notices the birdcage the women have found, he asks about the whereabouts of the bird. Mrs. Hale replies, "We think the cat got it" (255), even though she knows from Mrs. Peters that Minnie was afraid of cats and would not have owned one. Instead of correcting the lie, Mrs. Peters elaborates on it, saying of cats, "They're superstitious, you know; they leave" (255). Clearly Mrs. Hale is willing to risk lying because she is confident that Mrs. Peters won't contradict her.

Larson draws on a secondary source that gives background on Glaspell's life.

The Mrs. Peters character may have been based on a real sheriff's wife. Seventeen years before writing "A Jury of Her Peers," Susan Glaspell covered a murder case for the *Des Moines Daily News*. A farmer's wife, Margaret Hossack, was accused of murdering her sleeping husband with two axe blows to the head. In one of her newspaper reports, Glaspell wrote that the sheriff's wife sat next to Mrs. Hossack and

Larson 6

"frequently applied her handkerchief to her eyes" (qtd. in Ben-Zvi 30).

We do not know from the short story the ultimate fate of Minnie Wright, but Margaret Hossack, whose case inspired the story, was found guilty, though the case was later thrown out by the Iowa Supreme Court. However, as Linda Ben-Zvi points out, the women's guilt or innocence is not the issue:

> Whether Margaret Hossack or Minnie Wright committed murder is moot; what is incontrovertible is the brutality of their lives, the lack of options they had to redress grievances or to escape abusive husbands, and the complete disregard of their plight by the courts and by society. (38)

These are the issues that Susan Glaspell wished to stress in "A Jury of Her Peers."

These are also the issues that Mrs. Peters comes to understand as the story unfolds, with her understanding deepening as she identifies with Minnie and Mrs. Hale and is repulsed by male attitudes. Her transformation becomes complete when the men joke that she is "married to the law" and she responds by violating the law: hiding key evidence, the dead canary.

Larson's conclusion echoes his main point without dully repeating it.

Larson 7

Works Cited

The works cited page lists the primary source (Glaspell's story) and secondary sources.

Ben-Zvi, Linda. "'Murder, She Wrote': The Genesis of Susan Glaspell's *Trifles*." *Theatre Journal* 44.2 (1992): 141-62. Rpt. in *Susan Glaspell: Essays on Her Theater and Fiction*. Ed. Linda Ben-Zvi. Ann Arbor: U of Michigan P, 1995. 19-48. Print.

Glaspell, Susan. "A Jury of Her Peers." *Literature and Its Writers: An Introduction to Fiction, Poetry, and Drama*. Ed. Ann Charters and Samuel Charters. 6th ed. Boston: Bedford, 2013. 243-58. Print.

Hedges, Elaine. "Small Things Reconsidered: 'A Jury of Her Peers.'" *Women's Studies* 12.1 (1986): 89-110. Rpt. in *Susan Glaspell: Essays on Her Theater and Fiction*. Ed. Linda Ben-Zvi. Ann Arbor: U of Michigan P, 1995. 49-69. Print.

Mustazza, Leonard. "Generic Translation and Thematic Shift in Susan Glaspell's *Trifles* and 'A Jury of Her Peers.'" *Studies in Short Fiction* 26.4 (1989): 489-96. Print.

A Jury of Her Peers

SUSAN GLASPELL

When Martha Hale opened the storm-door and got a cut of the north wind, she ran back for her big woolen scarf. As she hurriedly wound that round her head her eye made a scandalized sweep of her kitchen. It was no ordinary thing that called her away — it was probably further from ordinary than anything that had ever happened in Dickson County. But what her eye took in was that her kitchen was in no shape for leaving: her bread all ready for mixing, half the flour sifted and half unsifted.

She hated to see things half done; but she had been at that when the team from town stopped to get Mr. Hale, and then the sheriff came running in to say his wife wished Mrs. Hale would come too — adding, with a grin, that he guessed she was getting scary and wanted another woman along. So she had dropped everything right where it was.

"Martha!" now came her husband's impatient voice. "Don't keep folks waiting out here in the cold."

She again opened the storm-door, and this time joined the three men and the one woman waiting for her in the big two-seated buggy.

After she had the robes tucked around her she took another look at the woman who sat beside her on the back seat. She had met Mrs. Peters the year before at the county fair, and the thing she remembered about her was that she didn't seem like a sheriff's wife. She was small and thin and didn't have a strong voice. Mrs. Gorman, sheriff's wife before Gorman went out and Peters came in, had a voice that somehow seemed to be backing up the law with every word. But if Mrs. Peters didn't look like a sheriff's wife, Peters made it up in looking like a sheriff. He was to a dot the kind of man who could get himself elected sheriff — a heavy man with a big voice, who was particularly genial with the law-abiding, as if to make it plain that he knew the difference between criminals and non-criminals. And right there it came into Mrs. Hale's mind, with a stab, that this man who was so pleasant and lively with all of them was going to the Wrights' now as a sheriff.

"The country's not very pleasant this time of year," Mrs. Peters at last ventured, as if she felt they ought to be talking as well as the men.

Mrs. Hale scarcely finished her reply, for they had gone up a little hill and could see the Wright place now, and seeing it did not make her feel like talking. It looked very lonesome this cold March morning. It had always been a lonesome-looking place. It was down in a hollow, and the poplar trees around it were lonesome-looking trees. The men were looking at it and talking about what had happened. The county attorney was bending to one side of the buggy, and kept looking steadily at the place as they drew up to it.

"I'm glad you came with me," Mrs. Peters said nervously, as the two women were about to follow the men in through the kitchen door.

Even after she had her foot on the door-step, her hand on the knob, Martha Hale had a moment of feeling she could not cross that threshold. And the reason it seemed she couldn't cross it now was simply because she hadn't crossed it before. Time and time again it had been in her mind, "I ought to go over and see Minnie Foster" — she still thought of her as Minnie Foster, though for twenty years she had been Mrs. Wright. And then there was always something to do and Minnie Foster would go from her mind. But *now* she could come.

The men went over to the stove. The women stood close together by the door. Young Henderson, the county attorney, turned around and said, "Come up to the fire, ladies."

Mrs. Peters took a step forward, then stopped. "I'm not — cold," she said.

And so the two women stood by the door, at first not even so much as looking around the kitchen.

The men talked for a minute about what a good thing it was the sheriff had sent his deputy out that morning to make a fire for them, and then Sheriff Peters stepped back from the stove, unbuttoned his outer coat, and leaned his hands on the kitchen table in a way that seemed to mark the beginning of official business. "Now, Mr. Hale," he said in a sort of semi-official voice, "before we move things about, you tell Mr. Henderson just what it was you saw when you came here yesterday morning."

The county attorney was looking around the kitchen.

"By the way," he said, "has anything been moved?" He turned to the sheriff. "Are things just as you left them yesterday?"

Peters looked from cupboard to sink; from that to a small worn rocker a little to one side of the kitchen table.

"It's just the same."

"Somebody should have been left here yesterday," said the county attorney.

"Oh — yesterday," returned the sheriff, with a little gesture as of yesterday having been more than he could bear to think of. "When I had to send Frank to Morris Center for that man who went crazy — let me tell you. I had my hands full *yesterday.* I knew you could get back from Omaha by today, George, and as long as I went over everything here myself —"

"Well, Mr. Hale," said the county attorney, in a way of letting what was past and gone go, "tell just what happened when you came here yesterday morning."

Mrs. Hale, still leaning against the door, had that sinking feeling of the mother whose child is about to speak a piece. Lewis often wandered along and got things mixed up in a story. She hoped he would tell this straight and plain, and not say unnecessary things that would just make things harder for Minnie Foster. He didn't begin at once, and she noticed that he looked queer — as if standing in that kitchen and having to tell what he had seen there yesterday morning made him almost sick.

"Yes, Mr. Hale?" the county attorney reminded.

"Harry and I had started to town with a load of potatoes," Mrs. Hale's husband began.

Harry was Mrs. Hale's oldest boy. He wasn't with them now, for the very good reason that those potatoes never got to town yesterday and he was taking them this morning, so he hadn't been home when the sheriff stopped to say he wanted Mr. Hale to come over to the Wright place and tell the county attorney his story there, where he could point it all out. With all Mrs. Hale's other emotions came the fear now that maybe Harry wasn't dressed warm enough — they hadn't any of them realized how that north wind did bite.

"We come along this road," Hale was going on, with a motion of his hand to the road over which they had just come, "and as we got in sight of the house I says to Harry, 'I'm goin' to see if I can't get John Wright to take a telephone.' You see," he explained to Henderson, "unless I can get somebody to go in with me they won't come out this branch road except for a price *I* can't pay. I'd spoke to Wright about it once before; but he put me off, saying folks talked too much anyway, and all he asked was peace and quiet — guess you know about how much he talked himself. But I thought maybe if I went to the house and talked about it before his wife, and said all the women-folks liked the telephones, and that in this lonesome stretch of road it would be a good thing — well, I said to Harry that that was what I was going to say — though I said at the same time that I didn't know as what his wife wanted made much difference to John —"

Now there he was! — saying things he didn't need to say. Mrs. Hale tried to catch her husband's eye, but fortunately the county attorney interrupted with:

"Let's talk about that a little later, Mr. Hale. I do want to talk about that, but I'm anxious now to get along to just what happened when you got here."

When he began this time, it was very deliberately and carefully:

"I didn't see or hear anything. I knocked at the door. And still it was all quiet inside. I knew they must be up — it was past eight o'clock. So I knocked again, louder, and I thought I heard somebody say, 'Come in.' I wasn't sure — I'm not sure yet. But I opened the door — this door," jerking a hand toward the door by which the two women stood, "and there, in that rocker" — pointing to it — "sat Mrs. Wright."

Everyone in the kitchen looked at the rocker. It came into Mrs. Hale's mind that that rocker didn't look in the least like Minnie Foster — the Minnie Foster of twenty years before. It was a dingy red, with wooden rungs up the back, and the middle rung was gone, and the chair sagged to one side.

"How did she—look?" the county attorney was inquiring.

"Well," said Hale, "she looked—queer."

"How do you mean—queer?"

As he asked it he took out a note-book and pencil. Mrs. Hale did not like the sight of that pencil. She kept her eye fixed on her husband, as if to keep him from saying unnecessary things that would go into that note-book and make trouble.

Hale did speak guardedly, as if the pencil had affected him too.

"Well, as if she didn't know what she was going to do next. And kind of—done up."

"How did she seem to feel about your coming?"

"Why, I don't think she minded—one way or other. She didn't pay much attention. I said, 'Ho' do, Mrs. Wright? It's cold, ain't it?' And she said, 'Is it?'—and went on pleatin' at her apron.

"Well, I was surprised. She didn't ask me to come up to the stove, or to sit down, but just set there, not even lookin' at me. And so I said: 'I want to see John.'

"And then she—laughed. I guess you would call it a laugh.

"I thought of Harry and the team outside, so I said, a little sharp, 'Can I see John?' 'No,' says she—kind of dull like. 'Ain't he home?' says I. Then she looked at me. 'Yes,' says she, 'he's home.' 'Then why can't I see him?' I asked her, out of patience with her now. 'Cause he's dead,' says she, just as quiet and dull—and fell to pleatin' her apron. 'Dead?' says I, like you do when you can't take in what you've heard.

"She just nodded her head, not getting a bit excited, but rockin' back and forth.

"'Why—where is he?' says I, not knowing what to say.

"She just pointed upstairs—like this"—pointing to the room above.

"I got up, with the idea of going up there myself. By this time I—didn't know what to do. I walked from there to here; then I says: 'Why, what did he die of?'

"'He died of a rope around his neck,' says she; and just went on pleatin' at her apron."

Hale stopped speaking, and stood staring at the rocker, as if he were still seeing the woman who had sat there the morning before. Nobody spoke; it was as if every one were seeing the woman who had sat there the morning before.

"And what did you do then?" the county attorney at last broke the silence.

"I went out and called Harry. I thought I might—need help. I got Harry in, and we went upstairs." His voice fell almost to a whisper. "There he was—lying over the—"

"I think I'd rather have you go into that upstairs," the county attorney interrupted, "where you can point it all out. Just go on now with the rest of the story."

"Well, my first thought was to get that rope off. It looked—"

He stopped, his face twitching.

"But Harry, he went up to him, and he said, 'No, he's dead all right, and we'd better not touch anything.' So we went downstairs.

"She was still sitting that same way. 'Has anybody been notified?' I asked. 'No,' says she, unconcerned.

"'Who did this, Mrs. Wright?' said Harry. He said it businesslike, and she stopped pleatin' at her apron. 'I don't know,' she says. 'You don't *know*?' says Harry. 'Weren't you sleepin' in the bed with him?' 'Yes,' says she, 'but I was on the inside.' 'Somebody slipped a rope round his neck and strangled him, and you didn't wake up?' says Harry. 'I didn't wake up,' she said after him.

"We may have looked as if we didn't see how that could be, for after a minute she said, 'I sleep sound.'

"Harry was going to ask her more questions, but I said maybe that weren't our business; maybe we ought to let her tell her story first to the coroner or the sheriff. So Harry went fast as he could over to High Road—the Rivers' place, where there's a telephone."

"And what did she do when she knew you had gone for the coroner?" The attorney got his pencil in his hand all ready for writing.

"She moved from that chair to this one over here"—Hale pointed to a small chair in the corner—"and just sat there with her hands held together and looking down. I got a feeling that I ought to make some conversation, so I said I had come in to see if John wanted to put in a telephone; and at that she started to laugh, and then she stopped and looked at me—scared."

At the sound of a moving pencil the man who was telling the story looked up.

"I dunno—maybe it wasn't scared," he hastened: "I wouldn't like to say it was. Soon Harry got back, and then Dr. Lloyd came, and you, Mr. Peters, and so I guess that's all I know that you don't."

He said that last with relief, and moved a little, as if relaxing. Everyone moved a little. The county attorney walked toward the stair door.

"I guess we'll go upstairs first—then out to the barn and around there."

He paused and looked around the kitchen.

"You're convinced there was nothing important here?" he asked the sheriff. "Nothing that would—point to any motive?"

The sheriff too looked all around, as if to re-convince himself.

"Nothing here but kitchen things," he said, with a little laugh for the insignificance of kitchen things.

The county attorney was looking at the cupboard—a peculiar, ungainly structure, half closet and half cupboard, the upper part of it being built in the wall, and the lower part just the old-fashioned kitchen cupboard. As if its queerness attracted him, he got a chair and opened the upper part and looked in. After a moment he drew his hand away sticky.

"Here's a nice mess," he said resentfully.

The two women had drawn nearer, and now the sheriff's wife spoke.

"Oh — her fruit," she said, looking to Mrs. Hale for sympathetic understanding. She turned back to the county attorney and explained: "She worried about that when it turned so cold last night. She said the fire would go out and her jars might burst."

Mrs. Peters' husband broke into a laugh.

"Well, can you beat the woman! Held for murder, and worrying about her preserves!"

The young attorney set his lips.

"I guess before we're through with her she may have something more serious than preserves to worry about."

"Oh, well," said Mrs. Hale's husband, with good-natured superiority, "women are used to worrying over trifles."

The two women moved a little closer together. Neither of them spoke. The county attorney seemed suddenly to remember his manners — and think of his future.

"And yet," said he, with the gallantry of a young politician, "for all their worries, what would we do without the ladies?"

The women did not speak, did not unbend. He went to the sink and began washing his hands. He turned to wipe them on the roller towel — whirled it for a cleaner place.

"Dirty towels! Not much of a housekeeper, would you say, ladies?"

He kicked his foot against some dirty pans under the sink.

"There's a great deal of work to be done on a farm," said Mrs. Hale stiffly.

"To be sure. And yet" — with a little bow to her — "I know there are some Dickson County farm-houses that do not have such roller towels." He gave it a pull to expose its full length again.

"Those towels get dirty awful quick. Men's hands aren't always as clean as they might be."

"Ah, loyal to your sex, I see," he laughed. He stopped and gave her a keen look. "But you and Mrs. Wright were neighbors. I suppose you were friends, too."

Martha Hale shook her head.

"I've seen little enough of her of late years. I've not been in this house — it's more than a year."

"And why was that? You didn't like her?"

"I liked her well enough," she replied with spirit. "Farmers' wives have their hands full, Mr. Henderson. And then —" She looked around the kitchen.

"Yes?" he encouraged.

"It never seemed a very cheerful place," said she, more to herself than to him.

"No," he agreed; "I don't think anyone would call it cheerful. I shouldn't say she had the home-making instinct."

"Well, I don't know as Wright had, either," she muttered.

"You mean they didn't get on very well?" he was quick to ask.

"No; I don't mean anything," she answered, with decision. As she turned a little away from him, she added: "But I don't think a place would be any the cheerfuller for John Wright's bein' in it."

"I'd like to talk to you about that a little later, Mrs. Hale," he said. "I'm anxious to get the lay of things upstairs now."

He moved toward the stair door, followed by the two men.

"I suppose anything Mrs. Peters does'll be all right?" the sheriff inquired. "She was to take in some clothes for her, you know — and a few little things. We left in such a hurry yesterday."

The county attorney looked at the two women whom they were leaving alone there among the kitchen things.

"Yes — Mrs. Peters," he said, his glance resting on the woman who was not Mrs. Peters, the big farmer woman who stood behind the sheriff's wife. "Of course Mrs. Peters is one of us," he said, in a manner of entrusting responsibility. "And keep your eye out, Mrs. Peters, for anything that might be of use. No telling; you women might come upon a clue to the motive — and that's the thing we need."

Mr. Hale rubbed his face after the fashion of a showman getting ready for a pleasantry.

"But would the women know a clue if they did come upon it?" he said; and, having delivered himself of this, he followed the others through the stair door.

The women stood motionless and silent, listening to the footsteps, first upon the stairs, then in the room above them.

Then, as if releasing herself from something strange, Mrs. Hale began to arrange the dirty pans under the sink, which the county attorney's disdainful push of the foot had deranged.

"I'd hate to have men comin' into my kitchen," she said testily — "snoopin' round and criticizin.'"

"Of course it's no more than their duty," said the sheriff's wife, in her manner of timid acquiescence.

"Duty's all right," replied Mrs. Hale bluffly; "but I guess that deputy sheriff that come out to make the fire might have got a little of this on." She gave the roller towel a pull. "Wish I'd thought of that sooner! Seems mean to talk about her for not having things slicked up, when she had to come away in such a hurry."

She looked around the kitchen. Certainly it was not "slicked up." Her eye was held by a bucket of sugar on a low shelf. The cover was off the wooden bucket, and beside it was a paper bag — half full.

Mrs. Hale moved toward it.

"She was putting this in there," she said to herself — slowly.

She thought of the flour in her kitchen at home — half sifted, half not sifted. She had been interrupted, and had left things half done. What had interrupted Minnie Foster? Why had that work been left half done? She made a move as if to finish it, — unfinished things always bothered her, — and then she glanced around and saw that Mrs. Peters was watching her — and she didn't want Mrs. Peters to get that feeling she had got of work begun and then — for some reason — not finished.

"It's a shame about her fruit," she said, and walked toward the cupboard that the county attorney had opened, and got on the chair, murmuring: "I wonder if it's all gone."

It was a sorry enough looking sight, but "Here's one that's all right," she said at last. She held it toward the light. "This is cherries, too." She looked again. "I declare I believe that's the only one."

With a sigh, she got down from the chair, went to the sink, and wiped off the bottle.

"She'll feel awful bad, after all her hard work in the hot weather. I remember the afternoon I put up my cherries last summer."

She set the bottle on the table, and, with another sigh, started to sit down in the rocker. But she did not sit down. Something kept her from sitting down in that chair. She straightened — stepped back, and, half turned away, stood looking at it, seeing the woman who had sat there "pleatin' at her apron."

The thin voice of the sheriff's wife broke in upon her: "I must be getting those things from the front-room closet." She opened the door into the other room, started in, stepped back. "You coming with me, Mrs. Hale?" she asked nervously. "You — you could help me get them."

They were soon back — the stark coldness of that shut-up room was not a thing to linger in.

"My!" said Mrs. Peters, dropping the things on the table and hurrying to the stove.

Mrs. Hale stood examining the clothes the woman who was being detained in town had said she wanted.

"Wright was close!" she exclaimed, holding up a shabby black skirt that bore the marks of much making over. "I think maybe that's why she kept so much to herself. I s'pose she felt she couldn't do her part; and then, you don't enjoy things when you feel shabby. She used to wear pretty clothes and be lively — when she was Minnie Foster, one of the town girls, singing in the choir. But that — oh, that was twenty years ago."

With a carefulness in which there was something tender, she folded the shabby clothes and piled them at one corner of the table. She looked up at Mrs. Peters, and there was something in the other woman's look that irritated her.

"She don't care," she said to herself. "Much difference it makes to her whether Minnie Foster had pretty clothes when she was a girl."

Then she looked again, and she wasn't so sure; in fact, she hadn't at any time been perfectly sure about Mrs. Peters. She had that shrinking manner, and yet her eyes looked as if they could see a long way into things.

"This all you was to take in?" asked Mrs. Hale.

"No," said the sheriff's wife; "she said she wanted an apron. Funny thing to want," she ventured in her nervous little way, "for there's not much to get you dirty in jail, goodness knows. But I suppose just to make her feel more natural. If you're used to wearing an apron—. She said they were in the bottom drawer of this cupboard. Yes—here they are. And then her little shawl that always hung on the stair door."

She took the small gray shawl from behind the door leading upstairs, and stood a minute looking at it.

Suddenly Mrs. Hale took a quick step toward the other woman.

"Mrs. Peters!"

"Yes, Mrs. Hale?"

"Do you think she—did it?"

A frightened look blurred the other thing in Mrs. Peters' eyes.

"Oh, I don't know," she said, in a voice that seemed to shrink away from the subject.

"Well, I don't think she did," affirmed Mrs. Hale stoutly. "Asking for an apron, and her little shawl. Worryin' about her fruit."

"Mr. Peters says—." Footsteps were heard in the room above; she stopped, looked up, then went on in a lowered voice: "Mr. Peters says—it looks bad for her. Mr. Henderson is awful sarcastic in a speech, and he's going to make fun of her saying she didn't—wake up."

For a moment Mrs. Hale had no answer. Then, "Well, I guess John Wright didn't wake up—when they was slippin' that rope under his neck," she muttered.

"No, it's *strange*," breathed Mrs. Peters. "They think it was such a—funny way to kill a man."

She began to laugh; at the sound of the laugh, abruptly stopped.

"That's just what Mr. Hale said," said Mrs. Hale, in a resolutely natural voice. "There was a gun in the house. He says that's what he can't understand."

"Mr. Henderson said, coming out, that what was needed for the case was a motive. Something to show anger—or sudden feeling."

"Well, I don't see any signs of anger around here," said Mrs. Hale, "I don't—" She stopped. It was as if her mind tripped on something. Her eye was caught by a dishtowel in the middle of the kitchen table. Slowly she moved toward the table. One half of it was wiped clean, the other half messy. Her eyes made a slow, almost unwilling turn to the bucket of sugar and the half empty bag beside it. Things begun — and not finished.

After a moment she stepped back, and said, in that manner of releasing herself:

"Wonder how they're finding things upstairs? I hope she had it a little more redd up up there. You know," — she paused, and feeling gathered, — "it seems kind of *sneaking*: locking her up in town and coming out here to get her own house to turn against her!"

"But, Mrs. Hale," said the sheriff's wife, "the law is the law."

"I s'pose 'tis," answered Mrs. Hale shortly.

She turned to the stove, saying something about that fire not being much to brag of. She worked with it a minute, and when she straightened up she said aggressively:

"The law is the law — and a bad stove is a bad stove. How'd you like to cook on this?" — pointing with the poker to the broken lining. She opened the oven door and started to express her opinion of the oven; but she was swept into her own thoughts, thinking of what it would mean, year after year, to have that stove to wrestle with. The thought of Minnie Foster trying to bake in that oven — and the thought of her never going over to see Minnie Foster — .

She was startled by hearing Mrs. Peters say: "A person gets discouraged — and loses heart."

The sheriff's wife had looked from the stove to the sink — to the pail of water which had been carried in from outside. The two women stood there silent, above them the footsteps of the men who were looking for evidence against the woman who had worked in that kitchen. That look of seeing into things, of seeing through a thing to something else, was in the eyes of the sheriff's wife now. When Mrs. Hale next spoke to her, it was gently:

"Better loosen up your things, Mrs. Peters. We'll not feel them when we go out."

Mrs. Peters went to the back of the room to hang up the fur tippet she was wearing. A moment later she exclaimed, "Why, she was piecing a quilt," and held up a large sewing basket piled high with quilt pieces.

Mrs. Hale spread some of the blocks on the table.

"It's log-cabin pattern," she said, putting several of them together. "Pretty, isn't it?"

They were so engaged with the quilt that they did not hear the footsteps on the stairs. Just as the stair door opened Mrs. Hale was saying:

"Do you suppose she was going to quilt it or just knot it?"

The sheriff threw up his hands.

"They wonder whether she was going to quilt it or just knot it!"

There was a laugh for the ways of women, a warming of hands over the stove, and then the county attorney said briskly:

"Well, let's go right out to the barn and get that cleared up."

"I don't see as there's anything so strange," Mrs. Hale said resentfully, after the outside door had closed on the three men — "our taking up our time with little things while we're waiting for them to get the evidence. I don't see as it's anything to laugh about."

"Of course they've got awful important things on their minds," said the sheriff's wife apologetically.

They returned to an inspection of the block for the quilt. Mrs. Hale was looking at the fine, even sewing, and preoccupied with thoughts of the woman who had done that sewing, when she heard the sheriff's wife say, in a queer tone:

"Why, look at this one."

She turned to take the block held out to her.

"The sewing," said Mrs. Peters, in a troubled way. "All the rest of them have been so nice and even — but — this one. Why, it looks as if she didn't know what she was about!"

Their eyes met — something flashed to life, passed between them; then, as if with an effort, they seemed to pull away from each other. A moment Mrs. Hale sat there, her hands folded over that sewing which was so unlike all the rest of the sewing. Then she had pulled a knot and drawn the threads.

"Oh, what are you doing, Mrs. Hale?" asked the sheriff's wife, startled.

"Just pulling out a stitch or two that's not sewed very good," said Mrs. Hale mildly.

"I don't think we ought to touch things," Mrs. Peters said, a little helplessly.

"I'll just finish up this end," answered Mrs. Hale, still in that mild, matter-of-fact fashion.

She threaded a needle and started to replace bad sewing with good. For a little while she sewed in silence. Then, in that thin, timid voice, she heard:

"Mrs. Hale!"

"Yes, Mrs. Peters?"

"What do you suppose she was so — nervous about?"

"Oh, *I* don't know," said Mrs. Hale, as if dismissing a thing not important enough to spend much time on. "I don't know as she was — nervous. I sew awful queer sometimes when I'm just tired."

She cut a thread, and out of the corner of her eye looked up at Mrs. Peters. The small, lean face of the sheriff's wife seemed to have tightened up. Her eyes had that look of peering into something. But next moment she moved, and said in her thin, indecisive way:

"Well, I must get those clothes wrapped. They may be through sooner than we think. I wonder where I could find a piece of paper — and string."

"In that cupboard, maybe," suggested Mrs. Hale, after a glance around.

• • •

One piece of the crazy sewing remained unripped. Mrs. Peters' back turned, Martha Hale now scrutinized that piece, compared it with the dainty, accurate sewing of the other blocks. The difference was startling. Holding this block made her feel queer, as if the distracted thoughts of the woman who had perhaps turned to it to try and quiet herself were communicating themselves to her.

Mrs. Peters' voice roused her.

"Here's a bird-cage," she said. "Did she have a bird, Mrs. Hale?"

"Why, I don't know whether she did or not." She turned to look at the cage Mrs. Peters was holding up. "I've not been here in so long." She sighed. "There was a man round last year selling canaries cheap — but I don't know as she took one. Maybe she did. She used to sing real pretty herself."

Mrs. Peters looked around the kitchen.

"Seems kind of funny to think of a bird here." She half laughed — an attempt to put up a barrier. "But she must have had one — or why would she have a cage? I wonder what happened to it."

"I suppose maybe the cat got it," suggested Mrs. Hale, resuming her sewing.

"No; she didn't have a cat. She's got that feeling some people have about cats — being afraid of them. When they brought her to our house yesterday, my cat got in the room, and she was real upset and asked me to take it out."

"My sister Bessie was like that," laughed Mrs. Hale.

The sheriff's wife did not reply. The silence made Mrs. Hale turn round. Mrs. Peters was examining the bird-cage.

"Look at this door," she said slowly. "It's broke. One hinge has been pulled apart."

Mrs. Hale came nearer.

"Looks as if someone must have been — rough with it."

Again their eyes met — startled, questioning, apprehensive. For a moment neither spoke nor stirred. Then Mrs. Hale, turning away, said brusquely:

"If they're going to find any evidence, I wish they'd be about it. I don't like this place."

"But I'm awful glad you came with me, Mrs. Hale." Mrs. Peters put the bird-cage on the table and sat down. "It would be lonesome for me — sitting here alone."

"Yes, it would, wouldn't it?" agreed Mrs. Hale, a certain determined naturalness in her voice. She had picked up the sewing, but now it dropped in her lap, and she murmured in a different voice: "But I tell you what I *do* wish, Mrs. Peters. I wish I had come over sometimes when she was here. I wish — I had."

"But of course you were awful busy, Mrs. Hale. Your house — and your children."

"I could've come," retorted Mrs. Hale shortly. "I stayed away because it weren't cheerful — and that's why I ought to have come. I" — she looked around — "I've never liked this place. Maybe because it's down in a hollow and you don't see the road. I don't know what it is, but it's a lonesome place, and always was. I wish I had come over to see Minnie Foster sometimes. I can see now —" She did not put it into words.

"Well, you mustn't reproach yourself," counseled Mrs. Peters. "Somehow, we just don't see how it is with other folks till — something comes up."

"Not having children makes less work," mused Mrs. Hale, after a silence, "but it makes a quiet house — and Wright out to work all day — and no company when he did come in. Did you know John Wright, Mrs. Peters?"

"Not to know him. I've seen him in town. They say he was a good man."

"Yes — good," conceded John Wright's neighbor grimly. "He didn't drink, and kept his word as well as most, I guess, and paid his debts. But he was a hard man, Mrs. Peters. Just to pass the time of day with him — ." She stopped, shivered a little. "Like a raw wind that gets to the bone." Her eye fell upon the cage on the table before her, and she added, almost bitterly: "I should think she would've wanted a bird!"

Suddenly she leaned forward, looking intently at the cage. "But what do you s'pose went wrong with it?"

"I don't know," returned Mrs. Peters; "unless it got sick and died."

But after she said it she reached over and swung the broken door. Both women watched it as if somehow held by it.

"You didn't know — her?" Mrs. Hale asked, a gentler note in her voice.

"Not till they brought her yesterday," said the sheriff's wife.

"She — come to think of it, she was kind of like a bird herself. Real sweet and pretty, but kind of timid and — fluttery. How — she — did — change."

That held her for a long time. Finally, as if struck with a happy thought and relieved to get back to everyday things, she exclaimed:

"Tell you what, Mrs. Peters, why don't you take the quilt in with you? It might take up her mind."

"Why, I think that's a real nice idea, Mrs. Hale," agreed the sheriff's wife, as if she too were glad to come into the atmosphere of a simple kindness. "There couldn't possibly be any objection to that, could there? Now, just what will I take? I wonder if her patches are in here — and her things?"

They turned to the sewing basket.

"Here's some red," said Mrs. Hale, bringing out a roll of cloth. Underneath that was a box. "Here, maybe her scissors are in here — and her things." She held it up. "What a pretty box! I'll warrant that was something she had a long time ago — when she was a girl."

She held it in her hand a moment; then, with a little sigh, opened it. Instantly her hand went to her nose.

"Why—!"

Mrs. Peters drew nearer—then turned away.

"There's something wrapped up in this piece of silk," faltered Mrs. Hale.

"This isn't her scissors," said Mrs. Peters, in a shrinking voice.

Her hand not steady, Mrs. Hale raised the piece of silk. "Oh, Mrs. Peters!" she cried. "It's—"

Mrs. Peters bent closer.

"It's the bird," she whispered.

"But, Mrs. Peters!" cried Mrs. Hale. "*Look* at it! Its *neck*—look at its neck! It's all—other side *to*."

She held the box away from her.

The sheriff's wife again bent closer.

"Somebody wrung its neck," said she, in a voice that was slow and deep.

And then again the eyes of the two women met—this time clung together in a look of dawning comprehension, of growing horror. Mrs. Peters looked from the dead bird to the broken door of the cage. Again their eyes met. And just then there was a sound at the outside door.

Mrs. Hale slipped the box under the quilt pieces in the basket, and sank into the chair before it. Mrs. Peters stood holding to the table. The county attorney and the sheriff came in from outside.

"Well, ladies," said the county attorney, as one turning from serious things to little pleasantries, "have you decided whether she was going to quilt it or knot it?"

"We think," began the sheriff's wife in a flurried voice, "that she was going to—knot it."

He was too preoccupied to notice the change that came in her voice on that last.

"Well, that's very interesting, I'm sure," he said tolerantly. He caught sight of the bird-cage. "Has the bird flown?"

"We think the cat got it," said Mrs. Hale in a voice curiously even.

He was walking up and down, as if thinking something out.

"Is there a cat?" he asked absently.

Mrs. Hale shot a look up at the sheriff's wife.

"Well, not *now*," said Mrs. Peters. "They're superstitious, you know; they leave."

She sank into her chair.

The county attorney did not heed her. "No sign at all of anyone having come in from the outside," he said to Peters, in the manner of continuing an interrupted conversation. "Their own rope. Now let's go upstairs again and go over it, piece by piece. It would have to have been someone who knew just the—"

The stair door closed behind them and their voices were lost.

The two women sat motionless, not looking at each other, but as if peering into something and at the same time holding back. When they spoke now it was as if they were afraid of what they were saying, but as if they could not help saying it.

"She liked the bird," said Martha Hale, low and slowly. "She was going to bury it."

"When I was a girl," said Mrs. Peters, under her breath, "my kitten — there was a boy took a hatchet, and before my eyes — before I could get there —" She covered her face an instant. "If they hadn't held me back I would have" — she caught herself, looked upstairs where footsteps were heard, and finished weakly — "hurt him."

Then they sat without speaking or moving.

"I wonder how it would seem," Mrs. Hale at last began, as if feeling her way over strange ground — "never to have had any children around?" Her eyes made a slow sweep of the kitchen, as if seeing what that kitchen had meant through all the years. "No, Wright wouldn't like the bird," she said after that — "a thing that sang. She used to sing. He killed that too." Her voice tightened.

Mrs. Peters moved uneasily.

"Of course we don't know who killed the bird."

"I knew John Wright," was Mrs. Hale's answer.

"It was an awful thing was done in this house that night, Mrs. Hale," said the sheriff's wife. "Killing a man while he slept — slipping a thing round his neck that choked the life out of him."

Mrs. Hale's hand went out to the bird-cage.

"His neck. Choked the life out of him."

"We don't *know* who killed him," whispered Mrs. Peters wildly. "We don't *know*."

Mrs. Hale had not moved. "If there had been years and years of — nothing, then a bird to sing to you, it would be awful — still — after the bird was still."

It was as if something within her not herself had spoken, and it found in Mrs. Peters something she did not know as herself.

"I know what stillness is," she said, in a queer, monotonous voice. "When we homesteaded in Dakota, and my first baby died — after he was two years old — and me with no other then —"

Mrs. Hale stirred.

"How soon do you suppose they'll be through looking for the evidence?"

"I know what stillness is," repeated Mrs. Peters, in just the same way. Then she too pulled back. "The law has got to punish crime, Mrs. Hale," she said in her tight little way.

"I wish you'd seen Minnie Foster," was the answer, "when she wore a white dress with blue ribbons, and stood up there in the choir and sang."

The picture of that girl, the fact that she had lived neighbor to that girl for twenty years, and had let her die for lack of life, was suddenly more than she could bear.

"Oh, I *wish* I'd come over here once in a while!" she cried. "That was a crime! Who's going to punish that?"

"We mustn't take on," said Mrs. Peters, with a frightened look toward the stairs.

"I might 'a' known she needed help! I tell you, it's *queer*, Mrs. Peters. We live close together, and we live far apart. We all go through the same things — it's all just a different kind of the same thing! If it weren't — why do you and I *understand*? Why do we *know* — what we know this minute?"

She dashed her hand across her eyes. Then, seeing the jar of fruit on the table, she reached for it and choked out:

"If I was you I wouldn't *tell* her her fruit was gone! Tell her it *ain't*. Tell her it's all right — all of it. Here — take this in to prove it to her! She — she may never know whether it was broke or not."

She turned away.

Mrs. Peters reached out for the bottle of fruit as if she were glad to take it — as if touching a familiar thing, having something to do, could keep her from something else. She got up, looked about for something to wrap the fruit in, took a petticoat from the pile of clothes she had brought from the front room, and nervously started winding that round the bottle.

"My!" she began, in a high, false voice, "it's a good thing the men couldn't hear us! Getting all stirred up over a little thing like a — dead canary." She hurried over that. "As if that could have anything to do with — with — My, wouldn't they *laugh*?"

Footsteps were heard on the stairs.

"Maybe they would," muttered Mrs. Hale — "maybe they wouldn't."

"No, Peters," said the county attorney incisively; "it's all perfectly clear, except the reason for doing it. But you know juries when it comes to women. If there was some definite thing — something to show. Something to make a story about. A thing that would connect up with this clumsy way of doing it."

In a covert way Mrs. Hale looked at Mrs. Peters. Mrs. Peters was looking at her. Quickly they looked away from each other. The outer door opened and Mr. Hale came in.

"I've got the team round now," he said. "Pretty cold out there."

"I'm going to stay here awhile by myself," the county attorney suddenly announced. "You can send Frank out for me, can't you?" he asked the sheriff. "I want to go over everything. I'm not satisfied we can't do better."

Again, for one brief moment, the two women's eyes found one another.

The sheriff came up to the table.

"Did you want to see what Mrs. Peters was going to take in?"

The county attorney picked up the apron. He laughed.

"Oh, I guess they're not very dangerous things the ladies have picked out."

Mrs. Hale's hand was on the sewing basket in which the box was concealed. She felt that she ought to take her hand off the basket. She did not seem able to. He picked up one of the quilt blocks which she had piled on to cover the box. Her eyes felt like fire. She had a feeling that if he took up the basket she would snatch it from him.

But he did not take it up. With another little laugh, he turned away, saying:

"No; Mrs. Peters doesn't need supervising. For that matter, a sheriff's wife is married to the law. Ever think of it that way, Mrs. Peters?"

Mrs. Peters was standing beside the table. Mrs. Hale shot a look up at her; but she could not see her face. Mrs. Peters had turned away. When she spoke, her voice was muffled.

"Not — just that way," she said.

"Married to the law!" chuckled Mrs. Peters' husband. He moved toward the door into the front room, and said to the county attorney:

"I just want you to come in here a minute, George. We ought to take a look at these windows."

"Oh — windows," said the county attorney scoffingly.

"We'll be right out, Mr. Hale," said the sheriff to the farmer, who was still waiting by the door.

Hale went to look after the horses. The sheriff followed the county attorney into the other room. Again — for one final moment — the two women were alone in that kitchen.

Martha Hale sprang up, her hands tight together, looking at that other woman, with whom it rested. At first she could not see her eyes, for the sheriff's wife had not turned back since she turned away at that suggestion of being married to the law. But now Mrs. Hale made her turn back. Her eyes made her turn back. Slowly, unwillingly, Mrs. Peters turned her head until her eyes met the eyes of the other woman. There was a moment when they held each other in a steady, burning look in which there was no evasion nor flinching. Then Martha Hale's eyes pointed the way to the basket in which was hidden the thing that would make certain the conviction of the other woman — that woman who was not there and yet who had been there with them all through that hour.

For a moment Mrs. Peters did not move. And then she did it. With a rush forward, she threw back the quilt pieces, got the box, tried to put it in her handbag. It was too big. Desperately she opened it, started to take the bird out. But there she broke — she could not touch the bird. She stood there helpless, foolish.

There was the sound of a knob turning in the inner door. Martha Hale snatched the box from the sheriff's wife, and got it in the pocket of her big coat just as the sheriff and the county attorney came back into the kitchen.

"Well, Henry," said the county attorney facetiously, "at least we found out that she was not going to quilt it. She was going to — what is it you call it, ladies?"

Mrs. Hale's hand was against the pocket of her coat.

"We call it — knot it, Mr. Henderson."

This is the index for Writing about Literature only. For the handbook's main index, see pages 636–72.

Index for Writing about Literature

This is the index for Writing about Literature only. For the handbook's main index, see pages 636–72.

P

Q

R

S

T

U

W

Revision Symbols

Boldface numbers refer to sections of the handbook.

abbr	faulty abbreviation **40**
adj/adv	misuse of adjective or adverb **26**
add	add needed word **10**
agr	faulty agreement **21, 22**
appr	inappropriate language **17**
art	article (*a, an, the*) **29**
awk	awkward
cap	capital letter **45**
case	error in case **24, 25**
cliché	cliché **18e**
coh	coherence **3d**
coord	faulty coordination **14a**
cs	comma splice **20**
dev	inadequate development **3b, 6h**
dm	dangling modifier **12e**
-ed	*-ed* ending **27d**
emph	emphasis **14**
ESL	English as a second language, multilingual **28–31**
exact	inexact language **18**
frag	sentence fragment **19**
fs	fused sentence **20**
gl/us	see glossary of usage
hyph	hyphen **44**
idiom	idioms **18d**
inc	incomplete construction **10**
irreg	irregular verb **27a**
ital	italics **42**
jarg	jargon **17a**
lc	lowercase letter **45**
mix	mixed construction **11**
mm	misplaced modifier **12a–d**
mood	mood **27g**
nonst	nonstandard usage **17c, 27**
num	use of numbers **41**
om	omitted word **10, 30b**
p	punctuation
^,	comma **32**
no ,	no comma **33**
;	semicolon **34**
:	colon **35**
’	apostrophe **36**
“ ”	quotation marks **37**
. ?	period, question mark **38a–b**
!	exclamation point **38c**
— ( )	dash, parentheses **39a–b**
[ ] . . .	brackets, ellipsis mark **39c–d**
/	slash **39e**
¶	new paragraph **3e**
pass	ineffective passive **8**
pn agr	pronoun agreement **22**
proof	proofreading problem **2g**
ref	pronoun reference **23**
run-on	run-on sentence **20**
-*s*	-*s* ending **21, 27c**
sexist	sexist language **17e, 22a**
shift	distracting shift **13**
sl	slang **17c**
sp	misspelled word **43**
sub	subordination **14**
sv agr	subject-verb agreement **21, 27c**
t	verb tense **27f**
trans	transition needed **3d**
usage	see glossary of usage
v	voice **8a**
var	lack of variety in sentence structure **14, 15**
vb	verb problem **27, 28**
w	wordy **16**
//	parallelism **9**
^	insert
#	insert space
⁀‿	close up space

Detailed Menu

P9-DNT-582

A Canadian Writer's Reference

FOURTH EDITION

A Canadian Writer's Reference

Diana Hacker

Contributing Authors

Nancy Sommers
Tom Jehn
Jane Rosenzweig
Harvard University

Contributing ESL Specialist

Marcy Carbajal Van Horn
Santa Fe Community College

BEDFORD / ST. MARTIN'S Boston ◆ New York

For Bedford/St. Martin's

Executive Editor: Michelle M. Clark
Senior Development Editor: Barbara G. Flanagan
Senior Production Editor: Anne Noonan
Senior Production Supervisor: Joe Ford
Senior Marketing Manager: John Swanson
Associate Editors: Amy Hurd Gershman and Mara Weible
Editorial Assistants: Jennifer Lyford and Alicia Young
Assistant Production Editor: Amy Derjue
Copy Editor: Dawn Hunter
Text Design: Claire Seng-Niemoeller
Cover Design: Donna Lee Dennison
Composition: Monotype, LLC
Printing and Binding: R.R. Donnelley & Sons Company

President: Joan E. Feinberg
Editorial Director: Denise B. Wydra
Editor in Chief: Karen S. Henry
Director of Marketing: Karen Melton Soeltz
Director of Editing, Design, and Production: Marcia Cohen
Managing Editor: Elizabeth M. Schaaf

Library of Congress Control Number: 2007934303

Manufactured in the United States of America.

2 1 0 9 8 7
f e d c b a

For information, write: Bedford/St. Martin's, 75 Arlington Street, Boston, MA 02116 (617-399-4000)

ISBN-10: 0-312-47283-8
ISBN-13: 978-0-312-47823-2

ACKNOWLEDGMENTS

Scott Adams, "Dilbert and the Way of the Weasel." Copyright © 2000 by United Features Syndicate. Reprinted with permission of United Media.

American Heritage Dictionary, definition for "regard" from *The American Heritage Dictionary of the English Language, Fourth Edition*. Copyright © 2000 by Houghton Mifflin Company. Reprinted with permission.

How to use this book

A Canadian Writer's Reference is designed to save you time. As you can see, the book lies flat, making it easy to consult while you are revising and editing a draft. And the book's twelve section dividers will lead you quickly to the information you need.

Here are brief descriptions of the book's major reference aids, followed by a chart summarizing the content of the book's companion Web site.

THE MENU SYSTEM. The main menu inside the front cover displays the book's contents as briefly and simply as possible. Each of the twelve sections in the main menu leads you to a colour-coded tabbed divider, on the back of which you will find a more detailed menu. Let's say you have a question about the proper use of commas between items in a series. Your first step is to scan the main menu, where you will find the comma listed as the first item in section P (Punctuation). Next flip the book open to the blue tabbed divider marked P. Now consult the detailed menu for the precise subsection (P1-c) and the exact page number.

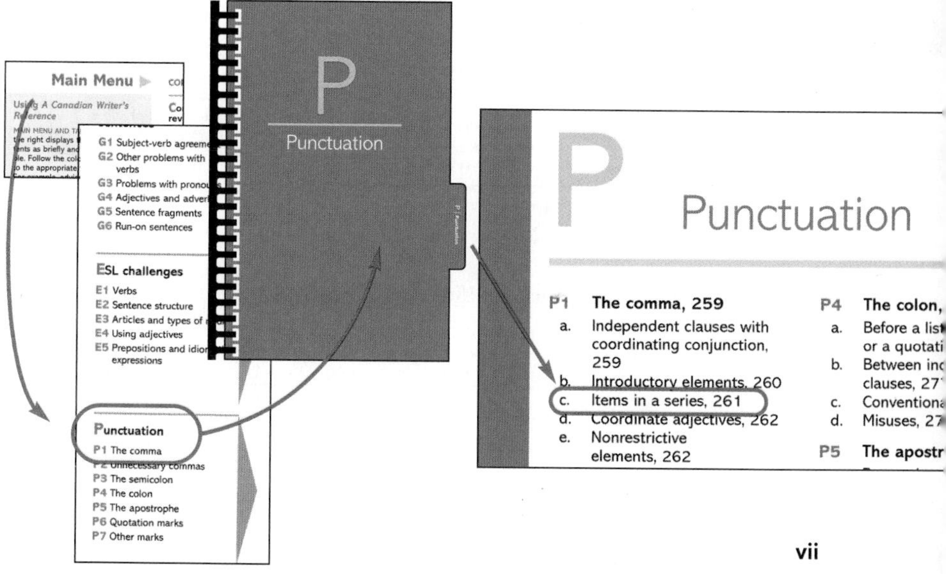

DETAILED MENU (inside the back cover). A menu more detailed than the main menu appears inside the back cover.

CODES AND REVISION SYMBOLS. Some instructors mark student papers with the codes given on the main menu and detailed menus — section numbers such as S1 or G3-d. When you are revising an essay marked with codes, tracking down information is simple. When you see G3-d, for example, flip to the G tab — and then let the blue tabs at the tops of the pages lead you to G3-d, clear advice about when to use *who* and *whom*. If your instructor uses an abbreviation such as *dm* or *cs* instead of a number, consult the list of revision symbols on the next to last page of the book. There you will find the name of the problem (*dangling modifier*; *comma splice*) and the section number that will help you solve the problem.

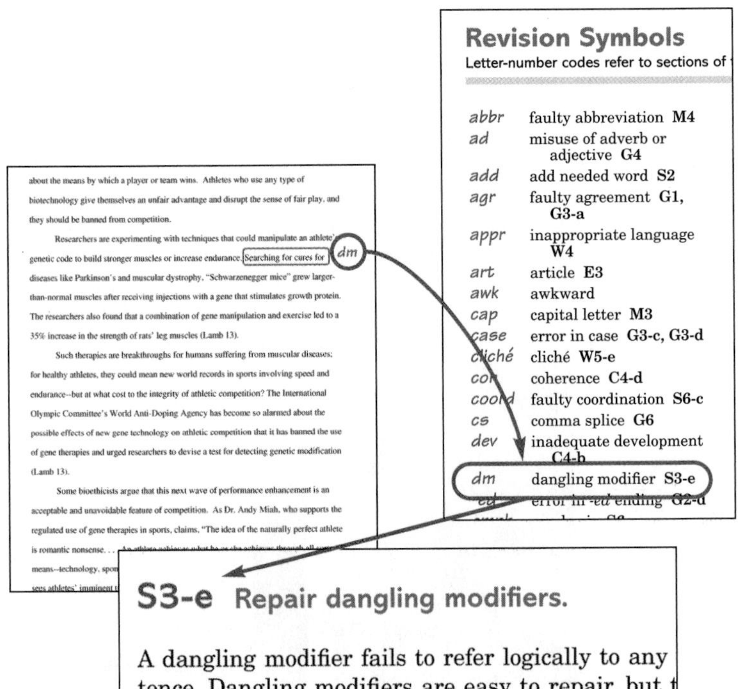

about the means by which a player or team wins. Athletes who use any type of
biotechnology give themselves an unfair advantage and disrupt the sense of fair play, and
they should be banned from competition.
Researchers are experimenting with techniques that could manipulate an athlete's
genetic code to build stronger muscles or increase endurance. Searching for cures for
dm
diseases like Parkinson's and muscular dystrophy, "Schwarzenegger mice" grew larger-
than-normal muscles after receiving injections with a gene that stimulates growth protein.
The researchers also found that a combination of gene manipulation and exercise led to a
35% increase in the strength of rats' leg muscles (Lamb 13).
Such therapies are breakthroughs for humans suffering from muscular diseases;
for healthy athletes, they could mean new world records in sports involving speed and
endurance--but at what cost to the integrity of athletic competition? The International
Olympic Committee's World Anti-Doping Agency has become so alarmed about the
possible effects of new gene technology on athletic competition that it has banned the use
of gene therapies and urged researchers to devise a test for detecting genetic modification
(Lamb 13).
Some bioethicists argue that this next wave of performance enhancement is an
acceptable and unavoidable feature of competition. As Dr. Andy Miah, who supports the
regulated use of gene therapies in sports, claims, "The idea of the naturally perfect athlete
is romantic nonsense. . .
means--technology, spo
Revision Symbols
Letter-number codes refer to sections of
abbr faulty abbreviation M4
ad misuse of adverb or adjective G4
add add needed word S2
agr faulty agreement G1, G3-a
appr inappropriate language W4
art article E3
awk awkward
cap capital letter M3
case error in case G3-c, G3-d
cliché cliché W5-e
coh coherence C4-d
coord faulty coordination S6-c
cs comma splice G6
dev inadequate development C4-b
dm dangling modifier S3-e
S3-e Repair dangling modifiers.
A dangling modifier fails to refer logically to any
tence. Dangling modifiers are easy to repair, but
to recognize, especially in your own writing.

RULES, EXPLANATIONS, AND EXAMPLES. Once you use a code to find a section, such as G1-b, the text presents three main types of help to solve your writing problem. The section number is accompanied by a rule, which is often a revision strategy. The rule is followed by a clear, brief explanation and, in some sections, by one or more hand-edited examples.

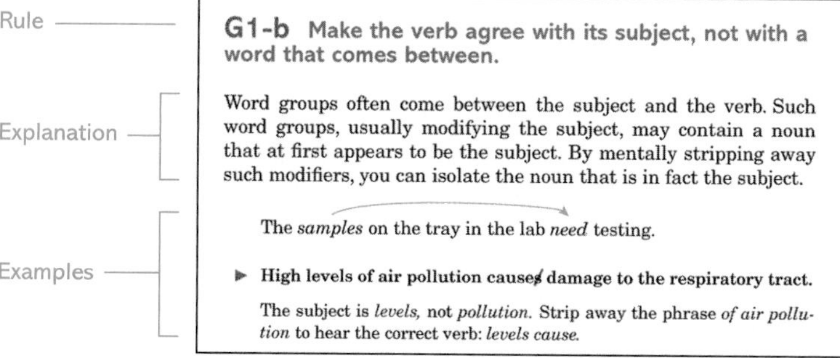

Rule
Explanation
Examples
G1-b Make the verb agree with its subject, not with a word that comes between.
Word groups often come between the subject and the verb. Such word groups, usually modifying the subject, may contain a noun that at first appears to be the subject. By mentally stripping away such modifiers, you can isolate the noun that is in fact the subject.
The samples on the tray in the lab need testing.
▶ High levels of air pollution causes damage to the respiratory tract.
The subject is levels, not pollution. Strip away the phrase of air pollution to hear the correct verb: levels cause.

THE INDEX. If you aren't sure what topic to choose from the main menu, consult the index at the back of the book. For example, you may not realize that the issue of whether to use *has* or *have* is a matter of subject-verb agreement (G1 on the main menu). In that case, simply look up "*has* vs. *have*" in the index. The boldface letter in the index entry leads you to the tabbed section G, and the page numbers pinpoint the specific page numbers in G. In addition, a cross-reference suggests another helpful index entry, "Subject-verb agreement."

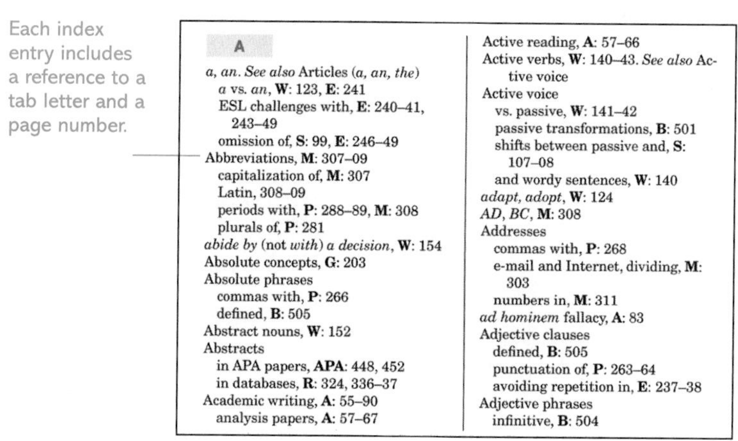

THE GLOSSARY OF USAGE. When in doubt about the correct use of a particular word (such as *affect* and *effect* or *among* and *between*), flip to section W1 and consult the alphabetically arranged glossary for the word in question. If the word you are looking for isn't in the glossary of usage, it may be in the index.

The glossary of usage begins on page 123.

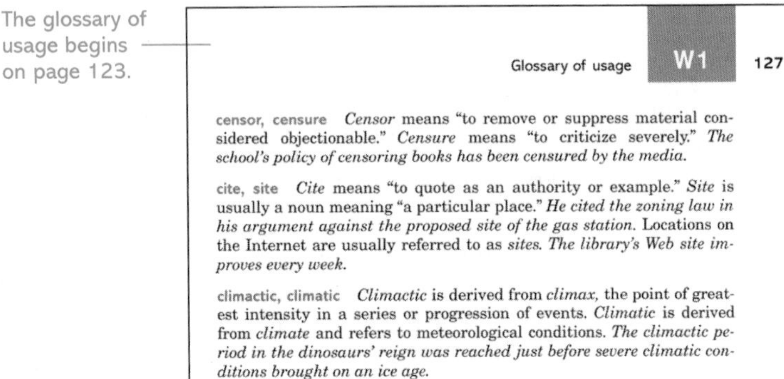
Glossary of usage W1 127

censor, censure *Censor* means "to remove or suppress material considered objectionable." *Censure* means "to criticize severely." *The school's policy of censoring books has been censured by the media.*

cite, site *Cite* means "to quote as an authority or example." *Site* is usually a noun meaning "a particular place." *He cited the zoning law in his argument against the proposed site of the gas station.* Locations on the Internet are usually referred to as *sites*. *The library's Web site improves every week.*

climactic, climatic *Climactic* is derived from *climax*, the point of greatest intensity in a series or progression of events. *Climatic* is derived from *climate* and refers to meteorological conditions. *The climactic period in the dinosaurs' reign was reached just before severe climatic conditions brought on an ice age.*

THE DIRECTORIES TO DOCUMENTATION MODELS. When you are writing a research paper, you don't need to memorize technical details about handling citations or constructing a list of works you have cited. Instead, you can rely on one of the book's directories to documentation models to help you find examples of the types of citations you will need to provide in your paper. If you are using the Modern Language Association (MLA) system of documentation, flip the book open to the tabbed section marked MLA and then scan the tab menu to find the appropriate directory. If you are using the American Psychological Association (APA) or the *Chicago Manual of Style* (CMS) system, scan the menu on the tab marked APA/CMS.

The directory to MLA works cited models begins on page 379.

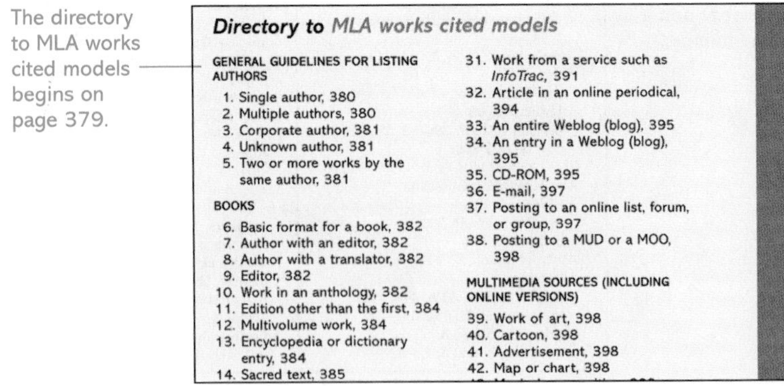
Directory to MLA works cited models

GENERAL GUIDELINES FOR LISTING AUTHORS

1. Single author, 380
2. Multiple authors, 380
3. Corporate author, 381
4. Unknown author, 381
5. Two or more works by the same author, 381

BOOKS

6. Basic format for a book, 382
7. Author with an editor, 382
8. Author with a translator, 382
9. Editor, 382
10. Work in an anthology, 382
11. Edition other than the first, 384
12. Multivolume work, 384
13. Encyclopedia or dictionary entry, 384
14. Sacred text, 385

31. Work from a service such as *InfoTrac*, 391
32. Article in an online periodical, 394
33. An entire Weblog (blog), 395
34. An entry in a Weblog (blog), 395
35. CD-ROM, 395
36. E-mail, 397
37. Posting to an online list, forum, or group, 397
38. Posting to a MUD or a MOO, 398

MULTIMEDIA SOURCES (INCLUDING ONLINE VERSIONS)

39. Work of art, 398
40. Cartoon, 398
41. Advertisement, 398
42. Map or chart, 398

COMPANION WEB SITE. The following chart describes student resources available on the book's companion Web site.

ON THE WEB > **dianahacker.com/writersref**

- Writing exercises

  Interactive exercises on topics such as choosing a thesis statement and conducting a peer review — with feedback for every correct and incorrect answer
- Grammar exercises

  Interactive exercises on grammar, style, and punctuation — with feedback for every correct and incorrect answer
- Research exercises

  Interactive exercises on topics such as integrating quotations, formatting in-text citations and bibliographic entries, and identifying elements needed for citing sources in MLA, APA, and CMS (*Chicago*) styles — with feedback for every correct and incorrect answer
- Language Debates

  Brief essays by Diana Hacker that explore controversial issues of grammar and usage, such as split infinitives
- ESL help

  Resources and strategies to help English language learners improve their academic writing skills
- Model papers

  Annotated sample papers in MLA, APA, CMS (*Chicago*), and CSE styles
- Research and Documentation Online

  Advice on finding sources and up-to-date guidelines for documenting print and online sources in MLA, APA, CMS (*Chicago*), and CSE styles
- Tutorials

  Interactive resources that teach essential skills such as navigating *A Canadian Writer's Reference*, integrating sources, and making the most of the writing centre
- Resources for writers and tutors

  Handouts, revision checklists, and tips for visiting the writing centre
- Additional resources

  Print-format exercises for practice and links to additional online resources

Tutorials

The following tutorials will give you practice using the book's menus, index, glossary of usage, and MLA directory. Answers to the tutorials begin on page xv.

TUTORIAL 1
Using the menus

Each of the following "rules" violates the principle it expresses. Using the brief menu inside the front cover or the detailed menu inside the back cover, find the section in *A Canadian Writer's Reference* that explains the principle. Then fix the problem. Examples:

▶ **~~In~~ [Tutors in] the writing centre/ ~~they~~ say that vague pronoun reference is unacceptable.** *G3-b*

▶ **Be alert for irregular verbs that have ~~came~~ [come] to you in the wrong form.** *G2-a*

1. A verb have to agree with its subject.
2. Each pronoun should agree with their antecedent.
3. About sentence fragments. You should avoid them.
4. Its important to use apostrophe's correctly.
5. Check for *-ed* verb endings that have been drop.
6. Discriminate careful between adjectives and adverbs.
7. If your sentence begins with a long introductory word group use a comma to separate the word group from the rest of the sentence.
8. Don't write a run-on sentence, you must connect independent clauses with a comma and a coordinating conjunction or with a semicolon.
9. A writer must be careful not to shift your point of view.
10. When dangling, watch your modifiers.

TUTORIAL 2

Using the index

Assume that you have written the following sentences and want to know the answers to the questions in brackets. Use the index at the back of the book to locate the information you need, and edit the sentences if necessary.

1. Each of the candidates have decided to participate in tonight's debate. [Should the verb be *has* or *have* to agree with *Each*?]
2. We had intended to go surfing but spent most of our vacation lying on the beach. [Should I use *lying* or *laying*?]
3. We only looked at two houses before buying the house of our dreams. [Is *only* in the right place?]
4. In Saudi Arabia it is considered ill mannered for you to accept a gift. [Is it okay to use *you* to mean "anyone in general"?]
5. Joanne picked up several bottles of maple syrup for her sister and me. [Should I write *for her sister and I*?]

TUTORIAL 3

Using the menu system or the index

Imagine that you are in the following situations. Using either the menus or the index, find the information you need.

1. You are Ray Farley, a community college student who has been out of high school for ten years. You recall learning to put a comma between all items in a series except the last two. But you have noticed that most writers use a comma between all items. You're curious about the current rule. Which section of *A Canadian Writer's Reference* will you consult?

2. You are Marie Bouchard, a peer tutor in your university's writing centre. Mike Lee, an English language learner, has come to you for help. He is working on a rough draft that contains a number of problems with articles (*a, an,* and *the*). You know how to use articles, but you aren't able to explain the complicated rules on their correct use. Which section of *A Canadian Writer's Reference* will you and Mike Lee consult?

3. You are John Pell, engaged to marry Sophia Ju. In a note to Sophia's parents, you have written, "Thank you for giving Sophia and myself such a generous contribution toward our honeymoon." You wonder if you should write "Sophia and I" or "Sophia and me." What does *A Canadian Writer's Reference* say?

4. You are Selena Young, an intern supervisor at a housing agency. Two of your interns, Jake Gilliam and Aisha Greene, have writing problems involving *-s* endings on verbs. Jake tends to drop *-s* endings; Aisha tends to add them where they don't belong. You suspect that both problems stem from nonstandard dialects spoken at home.

   Aisha and Jake are in danger of losing their jobs because your boss thinks that anyone who writes "the tenant refuse" or "the landlords agrees" is beyond hope. You disagree. Aisha and Jake have asked for your help. Where in *A Canadian Writer's Reference* can they find the rules they need?

5. You are Owen Thompson, a first-year university student. Your friend Samantha, who has completed two years of university, enjoys correcting your English. Yesterday she corrected your sentence "I felt badly about her death" to "I felt bad about her death." You're sure you've heard many educated people, including professors, say "I felt badly." Upon consulting *A Canadian Writer's Reference*, what do you discover?

TUTORIAL 4

Using the glossary of usage

Consult the glossary of usage (section W1) to see if the italicized words are used correctly. Then edit any sentences containing incorrect usage. If a sentence is correct, write "correct" after it. Example:

▶ **The pediatrician gave my daughter ~~a~~ an injection for her allergy.**

1. Changing attitudes *toward* alcohol have *effected* the beer industry.
2. It is *mankind's* nature to think wisely and act foolishly.
3. This afternoon I plan to *lie* in my hammock and read.
4. Our goal this year is to *grow* our profits by 9 percent.
5. Most sleds are pulled by no *less* than two dogs and no more than ten.

TUTORIAL 5
Using the directory to MLA works cited models

Assume that you have written a short research essay on the origins of hip-hop music. You have cited the following sources in your essay, using MLA documentation, and you are ready to type your list of works cited. Turn to page 379 and use the MLA directory to locate the appropriate models. Then write a correct entry for each source and arrange the entries in a properly formatted list of works cited.

A book by Jeff Chang titled *Can't Stop, Won't Stop: A History of the Hip-Hop Generation.* The book was published in New York by St. Martin's Press in 2005.

A podcast of a Kardinal Offishall concert and interview called "Kardinal Offishall in Session at CBC Studio 2," on May 2, 2001. The site is hosted by CBC/SRC. The podcast was produced by James Booth and is available on the CBC Radio 3 Web site, which you accessed on April 14, 2006. The URL is <http://radio3.cbc.ca/concerts/Kardinal-Offishall-2001-05-02>.

A journal article by H. Samy Alim titled "360 Degreez of Black Art Comin at You: Sista Sonia Sanchez and the Dimensions of a Black Arts Continuum." The article appears in the journal *BMa: The Sonia Sanchez Literary Review*, which is paginated by issue. The article appears on pages 15–33. The volume number is 6, the issue number is 1, and the year is 2000.

A sound recording entitled "Rapper's Delight" performed by the Sugarhill Gang on the LP *The Sugarhill Gang.* The album was released in 1979 by Sugarhill Records.

A magazine article accessed through the *InfoTrac* database *Expanded Academic ASAP*. The article, "The Roots Redefine Hip-Hop's Past," was written by Kimberly Davis and published in *Ebony* magazine in June 2003. The article appears on pages 162–64. You found this article at the Ray Cosgrove Library at Truman College in Chicago on April 13, 2006, using the URL <http://infotrac.galegroup.com>.

Answers to Tutorial 1

1. A verb has to agree with its subject. (G1-a)
2. Each pronoun should agree with its antecedent. (G3-a)
3. Avoid sentence fragments. (G5)
4. It's important to use apostrophes correctly. (P5-c and P5-e)
5. Check for *-ed* verb endings that have been dropped. (G2-d)
6. Discriminate carefully between adjectives and adverbs. (G4)
7. If your sentence begins with a long introductory word group, use a comma to separate the word group from the rest of the sentence. (P1-b)

8. Don't write a run-on sentence; you must connect independent clauses with a comma and a coordinating conjunction or with a semicolon. (G6)
9. A writer must be careful not to shift his or her [*not* their] point of view. *Or* Writers must be careful not to shift their point of view. (S4-a)
10. Watch out for dangling modifiers. (S3-e)

Answers to Tutorial 2

1. The index entry "*each*" mentions that the word is singular, so you might not need to look further to realize that the verb should be *has,* not *have.* The first page reference takes you to the entry for *each* in the glossary of usage, which directs you to G1-e and G3-a for details about why *has* is correct. The index entry "*has* vs. *have*" leads you to the chart in G1-a.
2. The index entry "*lying* vs. *laying*" takes you to section G2-b, where you will learn that *lying* (meaning "reclining or resting on a surface") is correct.
3. Look up "*only,* placement of" and you will be directed to section S3-a, which explains that limiting modifiers such as *only* should be placed before the words they modify. The sentence should read *We looked at only two houses before buying the house of our dreams.*
4. Looking up "*you,* inappropriate use of" leads you to the glossary of usage (W1) and section G3-b, which explain that *you* should not be used to mean "anyone in general." You can revise the sentence by using *a person* or *one* instead of *you,* or you can restructure the sentence completely: *In Saudi Arabia, accepting a gift is considered ill mannered.*
5. The index entries "*I* vs. *me*" and "*me* vs. *I*" take you to section G3-c, which explains why *me* is correct.

Answers to Tutorial 3

1. Section P1-c states that, although usage varies, most experts advise using a comma between all items in a series — to prevent possible misreadings or ambiguities. To find this section, Ray Farley would probably use the menu system.
2. Marie Bouchard and Mike Lee would consult section E3, on articles. This section is easy to locate in the menu system.
3. Section G3-c explains why *Sophia and me* is correct. To find section G3-c, John Pell could use the menu system if he knew to look under "Problems with pronouns." Otherwise, he could look up "*I* vs. *me*" in the index. Pell could also look up "*myself*" in the index or he could consult the glossary of usage (W1), where a cross-reference would direct him to section G3-c.
4. Selena Young's interns could turn to sections G1 and G2-c for help. Young could use the menu system to find these sections if she knew to look under "Subject-verb agreement" or "Standard English verb forms." If she wasn't sure about the grammatical terminology, she could look up "*-s,* as verb ending" or "Verbs, *-s* form of" in the index.
5. Section G4-b explains why *I felt bad about her death* is correct. To find section G4-b, Owen Thompson could use the menu system if he knew that *bad* versus *badly* is a choice between an adjective and an adverb. Otherwise he could look up "*bad, badly*" in the index or the glossary of usage (W1).

Answers to Tutorial 4

1. Changing attitudes toward alcohol have *affected* the beer industry.
2. It is *human* nature to think wisely and act foolishly.
3. Correct
4. Our goal this year is to *increase* our profits by 9 percent.
5. Most sleds are pulled by no *fewer* than two dogs and no more than ten.

Answers to Tutorial 5

Alim, H. Samy. "360 Degreez of Black Art Comin at You: Sista Sonia Sanchez and the Dimensions of a Black Arts Continuum." BMa: The Sonia Sanchez Literary Review 6.1 (2000): 15-33.

Chang, Jeff. Can't Stop, Won't Stop: A History of the Hip-Hop Generation. New York: St. Martin's, 2005.

Davis, Kimberly. "The Roots Redefine Hip-Hop's Past." Ebony June 2003: 162-64. Expanded Academic ASAP. InfoTrac. Ray Cosgrove Lib., Truman Coll., Chicago. 13 Apr. 2006 <http://infotrac.galegroup.com>.

Offishall, Kardinal. "Kardinal Offishall in Session at CBC Studio 2." Podcast. Prod. James Booth. CBC Radio 3. 2 May 2001. CBC/SRC. 14 Apr. 2006 <http://radio3.cbc.ca/concerts/Kardinal-Offishall-2001-05-02>.

Sugarhill Gang. "Rapper's Delight." The Sugarhill Gang. LP. Sugarhill, 1979.

Preface for instructors

Publisher's note

> When Bedford and I invented the quick-reference format — with its main menu, tabbed dividers, and lie-flat binding — . . . we had no idea that *A Writer's Reference* would become so popular (or so widely imitated). My goals were more modest. I hoped that the format and the title would send a clear message: *A Writer's Reference* is meant to be consulted as needed; it is not a set of grammar lessons to be studied in a vacuum. . . . Instructors across the country tell me that their students can and do use the book on their own, keeping it flipped open next to their computers.
>
> Diana Hacker (1942–2004),
> from the Preface for Instructors,
> *A Writer's Reference,* Fifth Edition

In her trademark lucid style, Diana Hacker describes making publishing history. *A Writer's Reference* is not only the most widely adopted English handbook on the market but also the best-selling college textbook of any kind in any discipline. It literally revolutionized the handbook genre. Users of the book routinely tell us that *A Writer's Reference,* from which *A Canadian Writer's Reference* is adapted, is the easiest handbook to use — a book that helps students find what they need and understand what they find.

Like all of the innovations that Diana Hacker brought to the genre of handbooks, the innovations of *A Writer's Reference* came from her teaching. She was able to take everything she knew from her thirty-five years of teaching and put it to work on every page of her books. Diana carefully observed how students actually used handbooks — mainly as references — and designed a book that would work better for them. The tabbed dividers and comb binding, which allow *A Writer's Reference* to lie open on any page, make it easier for students to find the information they need as quickly as possible. Once they get to the right page, the information is easy for them to understand on their own. The book's patient, respectful tone; its clear, concise explanations; and its hand-edited examples give students the help they need. Even though many other handbooks have imitated the format, no one understands as Diana did how format and content have to work together to make a truly useful handbook.

Although the first edition grew primarily out of Diana Hacker's own teaching experiences, subsequent editions reflect the experiences of the thousands of instructors using the books in their classrooms and of the millions of students who have found it helpful. For this new edition, we relied on advice from an extraordinary group of reviewers who kept reminding us what their students need. More than five hundred dedicated and experienced composition instructors reviewed the new edition. More than thirty of them served as an editorial advisory board; they read and commented on every word of this edition, making sure that it will work as well for their students as it always has and that the new material meets the high standards of a Hacker handbook.

With her team of Bedford editors, Diana had mapped out a plan for this edition. Based on this plan, a talented group of contributing authors revised this edition, putting themselves at the service of the book while bringing their own classroom experience to everything they did. Nancy Sommers, Tom Jehn, and Jane Rosenzweig — all of whom teach in the Harvard Expository Writing Program — helped revise the coverage of the writing process and research. Marcy Carbajal Van Horn, teacher of composition and ESL at Santa Fe Community College (FL), revised the ESL coverage. Diana was a huge fan of Nancy Sommers's work because it focused on student writing, drawing on Nancy's teaching at the University of Oklahoma and Rutgers as well as at Harvard. Diana was eager to have insights from Nancy's recent longitudinal study of student writing in the book. Tom Jehn is the clear and patient writing teacher that Diana always was, especially in helping students work with sources. Jane Rosenzweig is the skilled writer Diana always hoped for in a coauthor. Marcy Carbajal Van Horn creates practical and accessible content for a broad range of students — starting with her own — as Diana always did.

A Writer's Reference has always been a team effort between Diana and her editors at Bedford/St. Martin's, and that team is still in place. I was Diana's editor on the first edition of every one of her handbooks, including *A Writer's Reference*, and have been a part of every book since. Special thanks go to Chuck Christensen for understanding what makes a great handbook author and for knowing he had found one in Diana Hacker. At the heart of the Hacker team is Diana's longtime editor, executive editor Michelle Clark, the most skilled, creative editor we could wish for. Development editors Ellen Kuhl and Michelle McSweeney, veterans of many Hacker handbooks, made sure that every word in this book sounds like Diana's voice. Claire Seng-Niemoeller has designed every Hacker handbook since the first and has again retained the clean, uncluttered look of the book while making more use of colour. Having copy edited every Hacker handbook, Barbara Flanagan has been hearing Diana's voice for more than twenty years. Diana credited her with the clarity and consistency that is a Hacker hallmark. Copy editor Dawn Hunter has helped bring Canadian content and conventions to the new edition. Senior production editor Anne Noonan kept us all on track with her persistence, sharp eye, and concern for every detail. Assistant production editor Amy Derjue provided detailed assistance throughout the page proof review. Editor in chief Karen Henry and managing editor Elizabeth Schaaf have worked on these books from the beginning and remain committed to Diana's vision. New media editors Mara Weible and Amy Hurd Gershman expanded the new media offerings, making them as easy to use as the book itself. Stellar editorial assistants Jennifer Lyford and Alicia Young managed various projects and made sure that we heard from as many users as possible. We all remain committed to maintaining the high level of quality of Hacker handbooks.

Joan Feinberg
President, Bedford/St. Martin's

Features of the fourth Canadian edition

What's new

NEW VISUALS THAT TEACH CITATION AT A GLANCE. New full-colour, annotated facsimiles of original sources show students where to look for publication information in a book, a periodical, a Web site, and a source accessed in a database. These visuals help students find the information they need to cite print and online materials accurately and responsibly.

ADVICE THAT HELPS STUDENTS MAINTAIN THEIR VOICE WHILE WRITING FROM SOURCES. Thoroughly revised coverage of integrating sources teaches students how to go beyond patchwork research writing.

Section MLA-3 shows students how to lead into — and get out of — sources while keeping the source material in context and maintaining their own line of argument.

GUIDELINES THAT HELP STUDENTS UNDERSTAND HOW SOURCES CAN FUNCTION IN THEIR WRITING. A new section (MLA-1c) teaches students to consider the varying roles that sources can play in research writing.

NEW CHARTS THAT OFFER PRACTICAL ADVICE FOR USING SOURCES. New quick-reference charts on determining whether a source is "scholarly," on selecting appropriate versions of electronic sources, and on avoiding Internet plagiarism help students meet the challenges of research writing in the digital age.

A NEW EMPHASIS ON ACADEMIC WRITING. A new tabbed section (A) provides strategies for writing well in any postsecondary course; it brings new chapters on writing about texts and writing in the disciplines together with a revised chapter on argument.

GUIDELINES FOR WRITING ABOUT VERBAL AND VISUAL TEXTS. A new section (A1) provides advice and models for annotating, outlining, summarizing, and analyzing both verbal texts (such as essays and articles) and visual texts (such as advertisements and photographs).

A NEW CHAPTER ON WRITING IN THE DISCIPLINES. *A Canadian Writer's Reference* offers more help for students as they write in courses outside of the humanities. It explains the common features of all good postsecondary writing and provides practical advice for approaching writing assignments in all disciplines.

MORE HELP WITH WRITING ARGUMENTS. Revised coverage of counterargument teaches students how to strengthen their writing by anticipating and responding to objections.

NEW QUICK-ACCESS CHARTS. This edition features new charts that help writers navigate common writing challenges: understanding a writing assignment, making use of advice from peer reviewers, writing a conclusion, reading actively, and analyzing visuals.

MEETS THE NEEDS OF A BROADER RANGE OF ENGLISH LANGUAGE LEARNERS. Thoroughly revised ESL coverage considers the experiences of students who may be proficient English speakers but who struggle with writing well in English.

MORE HELP FOR THE MOST TROUBLESOME SENTENCE-LEVEL PROBLEMS. Developed with the help of ESL specialists, the fourth Canadian edition offers stronger support for using verbs, articles, and prepositions correctly. New charts offer at-a-glance help for English language learners.

CRUCIAL ADVICE ON ACADEMIC CONVENTIONS — FOR ENGLISH SPEAKERS AS WELL AS ENGLISH LANGUAGE LEARNERS. New boxed tips teach *academic English* — or how to go about writing well at college or university. Throughout the book, these nuggets of advice — on topics such as plagiarism, writing arguments, and understanding writing assignments — help students meet academic expectations.

AN UNCLUTTERED PAGE DESIGN. The book's new, more colourful design presents complex material and new visual elements as simply as possible. Because grammar rules and hand-edited examples are highlighted in colour, students can easily skim the book's central sections for quick answers to questions. Charts and boxes are easy to find and, just as important, easy to skip.

NEW SAMPLE PAPERS. Four new major papers show good writing and proper formatting: an argument essay; an analysis of an article; an MLA-style research essay; and an APA-style review of the literature.

UPDATED GRAMMAR CHECKER BOXES. A Diana Hacker innovation, the fifty grammar checker boxes have been updated to reflect the way current grammar and spell checker programs work. Students will read helpful advice about the capabilities and limitations of these programs.

FLEXIBLE CONTENT THAT HELPS YOU MEET THE NEEDS OF YOUR STUDENTS. Supplemental content for English language learners, writing in the disciplines, visual rhetoric, and writing about literature is available for packaging or for custom publishing to create a handbook that supports your course.

What's the same

We have kept the features that have made *A Canadian Writer's Reference* work so well for students and instructors. These features, detailed here, will be familiar to users of the previous edition.

COLOUR-CODED MAIN MENU AND TABBED DIVIDERS. The main menu directs students to orange, blue, green, and white tabbed dividers; the colour coding makes it easy for students to identify and flip to the section they need. The documentation sections are further colour-coded: blue for MLA, green for APA, and brown for CMS.

USER-FRIENDLY INDEX. This index, which Diana Hacker wrote herself and which was carefully updated for this edition, helps students find what they are looking for even if they don't know grammatical terminology. When facing a choice between *I* and *me*, for example, students may not know to look up "Case" or even "Pronoun, case of." They are more likely to look up "*I*" or "*me*," so the index includes entries for "*I* vs. *me*" and "*me* vs. *I*." Similar user-friendly entries appear throughout the index.

Index entries include the letter of the tabbed section before the page number of the indexed term (**G**: 192). Users can flip directly to the correct tabbed divider, such as G (for Grammatical sentences) before tracking down the page number.

QUICK-REFERENCE CHARTS. Many of the handbook's charts help students review for common problems in their own writing, such as fragments and subject-verb agreement. Other charts summarize important material: a checklist for global revision, strategies for avoiding sexist language, guidelines for evaluating Web sites, and so on.

DISCIPLINE-SPECIFIC RHETORICAL ADVICE FOR MLA, APA, AND CMS (*CHICAGO*) STYLES. Advice on drafting a thesis, avoiding plagiarism, and integrating sources is illustrated for all three major documentation styles — MLA, APA, and CMS (*Chicago*) — in three colour-coded sections. Examples are related to topics appropriate to the disciplines that typically use each style: English and other humanities (MLA), social sciences (APA), and history (CMS).

What's on the companion Web site <http://dianahacker.com/writersref>

RESOURCES FOR WRITERS AND TUTORS. New writing centre resources on the companion Web site offer help for both tutors and writers: checklists for responding to a wide array of assignments, tips for preparing for a visit to the writing centre, hints for making the best use of advice from tutors, and helpsheets for common writing problems — the same kinds of handouts students see in the writing centre — all available in printable format.

ELECTRONIC GRAMMAR EXERCISES. For online practice, students can access more than one thousand exercise items — on every topic in the handbook — with feedback written by Diana Hacker. Most of the exercises are scorable. Exercises that call for editing are labelled "edit and compare." They ask students to edit sentences and compare their versions with possible revisions.

ELECTRONIC RESEARCH AND WRITING EXERCISES. Scorable electronic exercises on matters such as avoiding plagiarism, integrating sources, documenting sources, and identifying citation elements give students ample practice with these critical topics. Scorable exercises on thesis statements, peer review, point of view, transitions, and other writing topics support students throughout the composing process.

LANGUAGE DEBATES. To encourage students to think about the rationales for a rule and then make their own rhetorical decisions, Diana Hacker wrote twenty brief essays that explore controversial issues of grammar and usage. The Web site features two additional debates written by style expert Barbara Wallraff.

MODEL PAPERS. Model papers for MLA, APA, CMS (*Chicago*), and CSE styles illustrate both the design and the content of researched writing. Annotations highlight key points about each paper's style, content, and documentation.

RESEARCH AND DOCUMENTATION ONLINE. This online resource helps students conduct research and document their sources. Reference librarian Barbara Fister has updated her advice on finding sources and has provided new links to resources in a variety of disciplines; she continues to maintain the research portion of the site. Guidelines for documenting print and online sources in MLA, APA, CMS (*Chicago*), and CSE styles are also kept up-to-date.

EXTRA HELP FOR ESL WRITERS. For English speakers and English language learners alike, this area of the site offers advice and strategies for understanding academic expectations and for writing well on assignments. Authored by Marcy Carbajal Van Horn (assistant professor of English and ESL at Santa Fe Community College, FL), it includes many helpful charts, exercises and activities, advice for working with sources, and an annotated student essay.

ACCESS TO AN ONLINE E-HANDBOOK. With the purchase of a print version of the handbook, students also have premium access to an electronic version of *A Writer's Reference*, conveniently located at the companion site.

THE INSTRUCTOR SITE. Accessible from the student site, this password-protected Web site offers additional resources such as diagnostic tests and tutorials and serves as a portal for retrieving student exercise results.

Ancillaries for students

PRINT RESOURCES

Exercises to Accompany A Canadian Writer's Reference (with answer key)

Developmental Exercises to Accompany A Writer's Reference (with answer key)

Working with Sources: Exercises to Accompany A Writer's Reference (with answer key)

Research and Documentation in the Electronic Age, Fourth Edition

Language Debates, Second Edition

Writing about Literature

Extra Help for ESL Writers

Writing in the Disciplines: Advice and Models

ONLINE RESOURCES

A Writer's Reference companion Web site (See the On the Web box on p. xi.)

Comment with *A Writer's Reference*

Ancillaries for instructors

PROFESSIONAL RESOURCES FOR INSTRUCTORS

Teaching Composition: Background Readings

The Bedford Guide for Writing Tutors, Fourth Edition

The Bedford Bibliography for Teachers of Writing, Sixth Edition

ONLINE RESOURCES FOR INSTRUCTORS

A Writer's Reference instructor site at <http://dianahacker.com/writersref>

Exercise Masters, print-format versions of all the exercises in the book

Quiz Masters, print-format quizzes on key topics in the book

Electronic Diagnostic Tests, a test bank for instructors' use

Transparency Masters, useful charts, examples, and visuals from the book

In addition, all of the resources within *Re:Writing* <http://bedfordstmartins.com/rewriting> are available for free to users of *A Canadian Writer's Reference*. Resources include tutorials, exercises, diagnostics, technology help, and model documents — all written by our most widely adopted authors.

Other composition resources by Bedford/St. Martin's

The following resources are available for packaging with *A Canadian Writer's Reference*:

ix visual exercises (CD-ROM), Cheryl E. Ball and Kristin L. Arola. Introduces the fundamentals of visual composition in an interactive medium

i·cite visualizing sources (CD-ROM), Doug Downs. Helps students work with all kinds of texts and provides opportunities for interactive practice

i·claim visualizing argument (CD-ROM), Patrick Clauss. Introduces argument concepts with a range of multimedia examples; includes assignments

Oral Presentations in the Composition Course: A Brief Guide, Matthew Duncan and Gustav W. Friedrich

For a complete list, contact your sales representative or visit <http://bedfordstmartins.com/composition>.

Course management content

A variety of student and instructor resources developed for *A Writer's Reference* are ready for use in course management systems.

Acknowledgments

Diana Hacker worked with us to map out her goals for this edition of *A Writer's Reference*. We called on a number of experienced, creative individuals to develop this edition with Diana's plan as the foundation.

Contributing authors

The contributors brought both expertise and enthusiasm to the project. They drafted new content and rethought existing content to make certain that *A Writer's Reference* reaches a broader range of students and meets their varied needs.

Nancy Sommers, Sosland Director of Expository Writing at Harvard University, has also taught composition at Rutgers University and at Monmouth College and has directed the writing program at the University of Oklahoma. A two-time Braddock Award winner, Sommers is well known for her research and publications on student writing. Her articles "Revision Strategies of Student and Experienced Writers" and "Responding to Student Writing" are two of the most widely read in the field. Her recent work involves a longitudinal study of undergraduate writing.

Tom Jehn teaches composition and directs the writing across the disciplines program at Harvard University. A recipient of numerous teaching awards both at Harvard and at the University of Virginia, he also leads professional development seminars on writing instruction for public high school teachers through the Calderwood Writing Fellows Project.

Jane Rosenzweig, a published author of fiction and nonfiction, teaches composition and directs the writing centre at Harvard University. She has also taught writing at Yale University and the University of Iowa.

Marcy Carbajal Van Horn, assistant professor of English and ESL at Santa Fe Community College (FL), teaches composition to English speakers and English language learners and teaches the advanced ESL writing course. She has also taught university-level academic writing and critical thinking at Instituto Tecnológico y de Estudios Superiores in Mexico.

Editorial Advisory Board

We asked a number of longtime users of the book and several nonusers to serve as editorial advisers. They looked carefully at all new and substantially revised sections of the new edition to make certain that the book is still as effective as it has always been in their classrooms. We thank them for their thoughtful and candid reviews.

Joanne Addison, University of Colorado, Denver

Derick Burleson, University of Alaska, Fairbanks

Paige Byam, Northern Kentucky University

Elizabeth Canfield, Virginia Commonwealth University
Richard Carr, University of Alaska, Fairbanks
Michele Cheung, University of Southern Maine, Portland
Jon Cullick, Northern Kentucky University
David Endicott, Tacoma Community College (WA)
Lin Fraser, Sacramento City College (CA)
Hank Galmish, Green River Community College (WA)
Nancy Gish, University of Southern Maine, Portland
Jacqueline Gray, St. Charles Community College (MO)
Barclay Green, Northern Kentucky University
Karen Grossweiner, University of Alaska, Fairbanks
D. J. Henry, Daytona Beach Community College
Kandace Knudson, Sacramento City College (CA)
Tonya Krouse, Northern Kentucky University
Tamara Kuzmenkov, Tacoma Community College (WA)
Cheryl Laz, University of Southern Maine, Portland
Lydia Lynn Lewellen, Tacoma Community College (WA)
Jeanette Lonia, Delaware Technical and Community College
Walter Lowe, Green River Community College (WA)
Michael Mackey, Community College of Denver (CO)
Tammy Mata, Tarrant County College (TX)
Holly McSpadden, Missouri Southern State University
Liora Moriel, University of Maryland, College Park
Patricia Murphy, Missouri Southern State University
Melissa Nicolas, University of Louisiana, Lafayette
Diane Allen O'Heron, Broome Community College (NY)
Sarah Quirk, Waubonsee Community College (IL)
Ann Smith, Modesto Junior College (CA)
Steve Thomas, Community College of Denver (CO)
Nick Tingle, University of California, Santa Barbara
Terry Myers Zawacki, George Mason University (VA)

Reviewers

For their many helpful suggestions, we would like to thank a perceptive group of reviewers. Some answered a detailed questionnaire about the previous edition; others reviewed manuscript for the new edition.

Barry Abrams, Sierra College (CA); Melanie Abrams, California State University, San Bernardino; Susan Achziger, Community College of Aurora (CO); Jo Acres-Devine, University of Alaska, Southeast; D. Michelle Adkerson, Nashville State Technical Community College (TN); Judy Andree, University of Alaska, Southeast; Rebecca Argall, University of Memphis (TN); Marianne Arieux, Empire State College (NY); Diann Arinder, Jackson Preparatory School (MS); Janice Aslanian, Hope College (MI); Greg Barnhisel, Duquesne University (PA); Dana Basinger, Samford University (AL); Dennis Beach, Saint John's University (MN); Diana Bell, University of Alabama, Huntsville; Sally Bell, University of Montevallo (AL); Barbara Bengels, Hofstra University (NY); Rick Beno, Padua Academy (DE); Cameron Bentley, Augusta Technical Institute (GA); Mary Bettley, Lesley University (MA); Nilanjana Bhattacharjya, Cornell University (NY); Desha Bierbaum, Lesley University (MA); Cynthia Bily, Adrian College (MI); Delmar Bishop, Pomona High School (CO); Shalom Black, Catholic University of America (DC); Keva Boone, Barry University (FL); Robin Bott, Adrian College (MI); Kimberly Bovee, Tidewater Community College (VA); Martha Bowden, Kennesaw State (GA); Brad Bowers, Barry University (FL); Mary Boyes, Tusculum College (TN); Molly Boyle, Massachusetts Bay Community College; Karla Braig, Loras College (IA); Angela Branch, John Tyler Community College (VA); Jennifer Brezina, College of the Canyons (CA); Kristi Brock, Northern Kentucky University; Angier Brock Caudle, Virginia Commonwealth University; Elaine Brooks, CUNY Brooklyn College (NY); Barry Brown, Missouri Southern State University; Cheryl Brown, Towson University (MD); Laura Brown, Central Alabama Community College; Shanti Bruce, Indiana University of Pennsylvania; Richard Bullock, Wright State University (OH); William Burgos, Long Island University, Brooklyn (NY); Richard Burke, Lynchburg College (VA); Charles Burm, Monroe Community College (NY); Ellen Butki, University of Texas at Austin; Barb Butler, Bellevue Community College (WA); Candace Byrne, Shasta College (CA); Stephen Calatrello, Calhoun State Community College (AL); Linda Caldwell, Towson University (MD); Catherine Calloway, Arkansas State University, Main Campus; Jorinde Canden Berg, Montgomery College, Germantown (MD); Phyllis Carey, Mount Mary College (WI); Cheryl Carpinello, Alameda Senior High School (CO); Pat Cearley, South Plains College (TX); Sherry Chapman, Modesto Junior College (CA); Nishi Chawla, University of Maryland University College; Marjorie Childers, Elms College (MA); Angela Christman, Loyola College (MD); Greg Clark, Brigham Young University (UT); Anne Clark, St. Cloud State University (MN); Gladys Cleland, SUNY Morrisville (NY); Joanne Clements, University of Rochester Medical School (NY); Cheryl Cobb, Tidewater Community College (VA); Jill Coe, Southwest Texas Junior College; Tammy Conard-Salvo, Purdue University (IA); Magana Conception, Garden City Community College (KS); Linda Conra, Curry College (MA); Trish Conrad, Hutchinson Community College (KS); Linda Conway, Howard College (TX); Cheryl Corbiell, Maui Community College (HI); Jennifer Courtney-Pooler, University of North Carolina, Charlotte; Julie Cox, University of California, Santa Cruz; Michelle Cox, University of New Hampshire; Donna Craine, Front Range Community College/Westminster (CO); Delmas Crisp, Wesleyan College (GA); Beth Crookston, Stark State College of Technology (OH); Pam Cross, Stockton State College (NJ); Eileen Crowe, University of North Carolina, Asheville; Debbie Cunningham, Adams State College (CO); Stephen Curley, Texas A&M, Galveston; Billye Currie, Samford University (AL); Sarah Curtis, Consumnes River College (CA); Christopher Dainele, Massachusetts Bay Community College; Helen Dale, University of Wisconsin, Eau Claire; Sarah Dangelantonio, Franklin Pierce College (NH); Cynthia Davidson, SUNY Stony Brook (NY); Matthew Davis, University of Puget Sound (WA); Sister Mary Davlin, Dominican University (IL); Mary De Nys, George Mason University (VA); Ann Dean, University of Southern Maine, Portland; Deborah Dean, Brigham Young University (UT); Renee Dechert, Northwest College (WY); Jeffrey Decker, University of California, Los Angeles; Margie Dernaika, Southwest Tennessee Community College; Kathryn De Zur, SUNY Delhi (NY); Kristen di Gennaro, Pace University (NY); Theresa Dolan, Los Angeles Trade Technical College (CA); Lynn Domina, SUNY Delhi (NY); Patricia Don, San Jose State University (CA); Cecilia Donohue, Madonna University (MI); Tony D'Souza, Shasta College (CA); Deb Dusek, North Dakota State College of Science; Chitralekha Duttagupta, Arizona State University; Scott Earle, Tacoma Community College (WA); Marie Eckstrom, Rio Hondo College (CA); Martha Edmonds, University of Richmond (VA); Richard Eichman, Sauk Valley Community College (IL); Mary Ellen, University of North Carolina, Charlotte; Lynette Emanuel, Wisconsin Indianhead Technical Institute; Charlene Engleking, Lindenwood University (MO); Bill Eppright, Northwestern College (MN); Douglas Eyman, Michigan State University; Deanna Fassett, San Jose State University (CA); Deborah Fleming, Ashland University (OH); John Fleming, De Anza College (CA); Maryann Fleming-McCall, Atlantic Cape Community College (NJ); Jessica Fordham Kidd, University of Alabama; P. Forson-Williams, McDaniel College (MD); Deanna Foster, Lassen College (CA); Bonnie Fox, D'Youville College (NY); Catherine Fraga, California State University, Sacramento; Martha Francescato, George Mason University (VA); Michael Frank, Bentley College (MA); Traci Freeman, University of Colorado, Colorado Springs; Christina French, Diablo Valley College (CA); Steve Frogge, Missouri Western State University; Jacqueline Fulmer, University of California, Berkeley; Karen Gardiner, University of Alabama; Wayne Garrett, Lipscomb University (TN); Susan Garrett, McDaniel College (MD); Steven

Gehring, SUNY Stony Brook (NY); Dennis Geisler, Columbia College (MO); Gina Genova, University of California, Santa Barbara; James Gifford, Mohawk Valley Community College (NY); Jane Gilligan, Assumption College (MA); Susan Gimprich, Fairleigh Dickinson University (NJ); Tracey Glaessgen, Southwest Missouri State University; Norman Golar, University of Alabama; Bertrand Goldgar, Lawrence University (WI); Amy Goodwin, Randolph-Macon College (VA); Ricia Gordon, Landmark College (VT); Rebecca Gorman, Metropolitan State College of Denver (CO); William Gorski, West Los Angeles College (CA); Susan Gorsky, University of California, Santa Cruz; Gwen Gray Schwartz, University of Arizona; Robert Greenwald, Dominican University (IL); Katie Guest, University of North Carolina, Greensboro; Max Guggenhiemer, Lynchburg College (VA); Diana Gyler, Azusa Pacific University (CA); Joan Haahr, Yeshiva University (NY); Thomas Hackett, CUNY Brooklyn College (NY); Michelle Halbach, Widener University (DE); Susan Halio, Long Island University, Brooklyn (NY); Peggy Hamilton, San Joaquin Delta College (CA); Robin Hammerman, Stevens Institute of Technology (NJ); Kathleen Hammond, Brookdale Community College (NJ); Jefferson Hancock, Cabrillo College (CA); Heidi Hanrahan, University of North Carolina, Greensboro; Katie Hanson, Augustana College (IL); John Hanvey, Barry University (FL); Lisa Harbo, University of Alaska, Fairbanks; Gloria Hardy, Saint John's University (MN); Eunice Hargett, Broward Community College, Central (FL); Mitchell Harris, University of Texas; Terese Hartman, Lynchburg College (VA); Kip Hartvigsen, Brigham Young University, Idaho; Lisa Hastings, Delaware Technical and Community College; Gary Hatch, Brigham Young University (UT); Nancy Hayward, Indiana University of Pennsylvania; Shelly Hedstrom, Palm Beach Community College (FL); Ruth Heller, Eastern Connecticut State University; Diane Henningfeld, Adrian College (MI); Bridgette Henry, University of Missouri, Kansas City; Patricia Henshaw, Sacramento City College (CA); Leah Herman, Pitzer College (CA); Kathleen Hickey, Dominican University (NY); Sharon Hileman, Sul Ross State University (TX); Cheryl Hill, Nova Southeastern University (FL); Vicki Hill, Brewton-Parker College (GA); Lisa Hodgens, Piedmont College (GA); Kathleen Hoffman, Cambridge Community College (MN); John Hogwood, Wayland Baptist University (TX); Deborah Holler, Empire State College (NY); Camille Lee Hornbeck, Tarrant County Community College (TX); Alice Horning, Oakland University (CA); Tai Houser, Broward Community College, North (FL); James Hunter, Gonzaga University (WA); Michael Hustedde, St. Ambrose University (IA); Marie Iglesias-Cardinale, Genessee Community College (NY); Robin Inboden, Wittenberg University (OH); Alyson Indrunas, Everett Community College (WA); James Inman, University of Tennessee, Chattanooga; Sherri Inness, Miami University, Hamilton (OH); Ginger Irwin, Colgate University (NY); James

Isbell, Santiago Canyon College (CA); Kathy Ivey, Lenoir-Rhyne College (NC); Lisa Jackson, University of North Texas; Ian Jacobs, New School University (NY); Dawnelle Jager, Syracuse University (NY); Glenda James, Calhoun State Community College (AL); Susan James, Curry College (MA); Mary Jo Stirling, Santa Monica College (CA); Carol Johnson, Virginia Wesleyan College; Sue Johnson, Sierra College (CA); Nancy Johnson Squaire, Sheridan College (WY); Jennifer Jones, University of Colorado, Boulder; Jay Jordan, Pennsylvania State University; Paul Juhasz, Tarrant County Community College (TX); Demetrios Kapetanakos, Queensborough Community College (NY); Elizabeth Katz, University of New Mexico; Janet Kay, Leeward Community College (HI); Laura Kay, John F. Kennedy University (CA); Joshua Keels, Community College of Vermont, Burlington; Elizabeth Keifer, Tunxis Community College (CT); Sue Keith, Guilford College (NC); Roberta Kelly, Washington State University; Gilda Kelsey, University of Delaware; Jan Kinch, Edinboro University of Pennsylvania; Lola King, Trinity Valley Community College (TX); Liz Kleinfeld, Red Rocks Community College (CO); Matt Kozusko, Ursinus College (PA); Carrie Krantz-Fischer, Washtenaw Community College (MI); Michelle Ladd, California State University, Los Angeles; Gina Ladinsky, Santa Monica College (CA); Lauren LaFauci, University of Michigan, Ann Arbor; John Lang, Emory and Henry College (VA); Margaret Lattimore, Gardner-Webb University (NC); Sally Lavender, Lipscomb University (TN); Joe Law, Wright State University (OH); Amy Lawlor, Pasadena City College (CA); Robert Lawrence, Jefferson Community College (KY); Kathleen Lazarus, Daytona Beach Community College (FL); Andria Leduc, Open Learning Agency (BC); Catharine Lee, Wesleyan College (GA); Michelle Lee, Minnesota State University; Kathy LeGrand, Olympic Heights High School (FL); Lindsay Lewan, Arapahoe Community College (CO); James Livingston, Northern Michigan University; Alice Longaker, University of Northern Colorado; Sonia Maasik, University of California, Los Angeles; Joan Maiers, Marylhurst University (OR); Ceil Malek, University of Colorado, Colorado Springs; Lisa Mallory, Atlanta Metropolitan College (GA); Ajuan Mance, Mills College (CA); Kate Mangelsdorf, University of Texas, El Paso; Travis Mann, Tarrant County Community College (TX); Nicole Marafioti, Cornell University (NY); Annette March, California State University, Monterey Bay; Pete Marcoux, El Camino Community College (CA); Barbara Martin, University of Cincinnati (OH); Joann Martin, Wisconsin Indianhead Technical Institute; Elizabeth Martinez, University of Connecticut; David Maruyama, Long Beach City College (CA); Pat Mathias, Itasca Community College (MN); Leanne Maunu, Palomar Community College (CA); Jennifer McCann, Bay de Noc Community College (MI); Barbara McClain, Contra Costa College (CA); Julia McGregor, Inver Hills Community College (MN); Andrea McKenzie, New York University; James McLaughlin, Master's College and Seminary (CA); Sara McLaughlin, Texas Technical University; Vicky Melograno, Atlantic Cape Community College (NJ); Agnetta Mendoza, Nashville State Technical Community College (TN); Gayle Mercer, Southwest Missouri State; Carol Messing, Northwood University (MI); Allan Metcalf, MacMurray College (IL); Donna Metcalf, Springfield College (IL); Steve Michael, Wayland Baptist University (TX); Marlene Michels, Mid Michigan Community College; Ilene Miele, University of California, Santa Barbara; David Miller, Victor Valley College (CA); Jack Miller, Normandale Community College (MN); Ruth Miller, University of Louisville (KY); Wendy Moffat, Dickinson College (PA); Scott Moncrieff, Andrews University (MI); Jayne Moneysmith, Kent State University (OH); Bryan Moore, Arkansas State University, Main Campus; Matthew Moore, Roberts Wesleyan College (NY); Robert Morace, Daemen College (NY); Dan Morgan, Scott Community College, Bettendorf (IA); Jennifer Morrison, Niagara University (NY); Gala Muench, North Idaho College (ID); Terry Muller, Cambridge College (MA); Deborah Mutnick, Long Island University, Brooklyn (NY); Linda Myers, California State University, Sacramento; Lyndall Nairn, Lynchburg College (VA); James Nash, Montclair State University (NJ); Michelle Nash, Union College (NE); Claire Nava, California State University, Fullerton; Jeffrey Nelson, University of Alabama; Stephen Newmann, Montgomery College, Germantown (MD); Corrine Nicolas, Tusculum College (TN); Jennifer Niester, Central Michigan University; Sylvia Nosworthy, Walla Walla College (WA); Catherine O'Callaghan, Community College of Vermont, Brattleboro; David Okamura-Wilson, East Carolina University (NC); Ben Opipari, Colgate College (NY); Scott Orme, Spokane Community College (WA); Christina Ortmeier-Hooper, University of New Hampshire; Mary O'Sullivan, Western Wisco Technical College (WI); Liz Parker, Nashville State Technical Community College (TN); Allison Parker, Southeastern Community College (NC); M. Elizabeth Parker, Nashville State Technical Community College (TN); Joanne Parsons, Eastern Oregon University (OR); Karen Pass, Empire State College (NY); Mary Pat, Dominican University (IL); David Paul, SUNY Morrisville (NY); Craig Payne, Indian Hills Community College (IA); Tammy Peery, Montgomery College, Germantown (MD); Myra Perry, University of North Carolina, Charlotte; Todd Petersen, Southern Utah University; Stephen Petrina, University of British Columbia; Diane Philen, Sinte Gleska University (SD); Christine Pipitone-Herron, Raritan Valley Community College (NJ); Susan Piqueira, Tunxis Community College (CT); Neil Placky, Broward Community College-South (FL); Faith Plvan, Syracuse University (NY); Robert Prescott, Bradley University (IL); Mary Lou Price, University of Texas, Austin; Ben Rafoth, Indiana University of Pennsylvania; Anniqua Rana, Canada College (CA); Vanessa Rasmussen, Rider University (NJ); Kokila Ravi, Atlanta Metropolitan College (GA);

Susan Regan, Cloud County Community College (KS); Paul Reid, Chippewa Valley Technical College (WI); Steven Reynolds, College of the Siskiyous (CA); Angela Ricciardi, Plymouth State College (NH); Clai Rice, University of Louisiana, Lafayette; Jeff Rice, Wayne State University (MI); Aaron Ritzenberg, Brandeis University (MA); Marilyn Roberts, Waynesburg College (PA); Lourdes Rodriguez-Florido, Broward Community College South (FL); Timothy Rogers, Furman University (SC); Teri Rosen, CUNY Hunter College (NY); Michelle Ross, Indiana University (IN); Deborah Rossen-Knill, University of Rochester (NY); Jennifer Rosti, Roanoke College (VA); Henry Ruminski, Wright State University (OH); Carol Russo, SUNY Stony Brook (NY); Leigh Ryan, University of Maryland; Kristen Salsbury, University of California, Irvine; Art Saltzmann, Missouri Southern State University; Mark Sanders, Three Rivers Community College (MO); Mark Sanford, Suffolk University (MA); Lilia Savova, Indiana University of Pennsylvania; Elizabeth Sawin, Missouri Western State University; Suzy Sayre, Towson University (MD); Bret Scaliter, Crafton Hills College (CA); Sandra Scheller, Wayland Baptist University (TX); Sandra Schroeder, Yakima Valley College (WA); Holly Schullo, University of Louisiana, Lafayette; Gloria Scott, Towson University (MD); Laine Scott, La Grange College (GA); Aparna Screenivasan, California State University, Monterey Bay; Michael Sewell, Wayland Baptist University (TX); Jolly Sharp, Cumberland College (KY); Meighan Sharp, Emory and Henry College (VA); Amy Sheldon, SUNY Geneseo (NY); Brandi Shelton, Nashville State Technical Community College (TN); Suzanne Shepard, Broome Community College (NY); Jean Sheridan, University of Southern Maine, Portland; John Silva, LaGuardia Community College (NY); Mary Beth Simmons, Villanova University (PA); Michele Singletary, Nashville State Technical Community College (TN); Beverly Six, Sul Ross State University (TX); Greta Skogseth, Montcalm Community College (MI); Bonnie Smith, Belmont University (TN); Mary Lou Smith, Alexandria Technical University (MN); Sally Smith, Alexandria Technical University (MN); Sean Smith, Ivy Technical Sate College (IN); James Southerland, Brenau College (GA); Sis Spencer, Trinidad State Junior College (CO); Barbara Steele, Towson University (MD); Sharon Steinberg, Tunxis Community College (CT); Lisa Steinman, Reed College (OR); Shari Stenberg, Creighton University (NE); Rebecca Suarez, University of Texas, El Paso; Jo Suzuki, Master's College and Seminary (CA); Kristine Swenson, University of Missouri, Rolla; Peggy Szczesniak, Genessee Community College (NY); Cynthia Taber, Schenectady County Community College (NY); Dean Taciuch, George Mason University (VA); Marguerite Tassi, University of Nebraska, Kearney; Lisa Terasa, Mount Mary College (WI); Matt Theado, Gardner-Webb University (NC); Catherine Thomas, College of Charleston (SC); Cliff Toliver, Missouri Southern State University; Jill Tucker,

San Diego Miramar College (CA); Anita Turpin, Roanoke College (VA); Pat Tyrer, West Texas A&M University; Wanda Umber, Wayland Baptist University (TX); Kim Van Alkamade, Shippensburg University (PA); Thomas Varner, J. Sargeant Reynolds Community College (VA); Angela Vogel, John Tyler Community College (VA); Michelle Von Euw, University of Maryland; Peter Vose, Falmouth High School (ME); Elizabeth Wagoner, Kent State University (OH); Ralph Wahlstrom, SUNY Buffalo (NY); Shelton Waldrep, University of Southern Maine; Teri Waters, Waubonsee Community College (IL); Pamela Watkins, Los Angeles Harbor Community College (CA); Cindy Welch, Carthage College (WI); Vicky Westacott, Alfred University (NY); Jennifer Whetham, Greenriver Community College (WA); Anne Whitney, University of California, Santa Barbara; John Wiltbank, Tidewater Community College (VA); Barbara Winborn, Asbury College (KY); Rosemary Winslow, Catholic University of America (DC); Kelli Wood-Mancha, El Paso Community College (TX); Michael Woodruff, Hargrave Military Academy (VA); Donna Y. Smith, Wayland Baptist University (OK); Ann Yearick, Radford University (VA); Julie Yen, California State University, Sacramento; Jonathan Ying, Cornell University (NY); Joann Yost, Bethel University (MN); Ben Young, Oregon State University; Michael Young, La Roche College (PA); Laura Zam, George Mason University (VA); Robbin Zeff, George Washington University (DC); Trudy Zimmerman, Hutchinson Community College (KS)

Student contributors

We are indebted to the students whose essays appear in this edition — Ned Bishop, Anna Orlov, Emilia Sanchez, Jamal Hammond, and Luisa Mirano — not only for permission to use their work but also for allowing us to adapt it for pedagogical purposes. Our thanks also go to the students who granted permission to use their paragraphs: Rosa Broderick, Connie Hailey, Craig Lee Hetherington, Kathleen Lewis, Laurie McDonough, Kevin Smith, Margaret Smith, Margaret Stack, and David Warren.

C

Composing and Revising

C Composing and Revising

Writing is not a matter of recording already developed thoughts but a process of figuring out what you think. Since it's not possible to think about everything all at once, most experienced writers handle a piece of writing in stages. You will generally move from planning to drafting to revising, but be prepared to return to earlier stages as your ideas develop.

C1

Planning

C1-a Assess the writing situation.

Begin by taking a look at the writing situation in which you find yourself. Consider your subject, the sources of information available to you, your purpose, your audience, and constraints such as length, document design, review sessions, and deadlines or other assignment requirements. It is likely that you will make final decisions about all of these matters later in the writing process — after a first draft, for example. Nevertheless, you can save yourself time by thinking about as many of them as possible in advance. For a quick checklist, see page 5.

> **ACADEMIC ENGLISH** What counts as good writing varies from culture to culture and even among groups within cultures. In some situations, you will need to become familiar with the writing styles—such as direct or indirect, personal or impersonal, plain or embellished—that are valued by the culture or discourse community for which you are writing.

C1-b Experiment with ways to explore your subject.

Instead of just plunging into a first draft, experiment with one or more techniques for exploring your subject — perhaps talking and listening, annotating texts and taking notes, listing, clustering, freewriting, or asking the journalist's questions. Whatever technique you turn to, the goal is the same: to generate a wealth of ideas that will lead you to a question, a problem, or an issue that you want to explore further. At this early stage of the writing process, don't censor yourself. Sometimes an idea that initially seems trivial or far-fetched will turn out to be worthwhile.

Understanding an assignment

Determining the purpose of the assignment

Usually the wording of an assignment will suggest its purpose. You might be expected to do one of the following:

- summarize information from textbooks, lectures, or research
- analyze ideas and concepts
- take a position on a topic and defend it with evidence
- create an original argument by combining ideas from different sources

Understanding how to answer an assignment's questions

Many assignments will ask a *how* or *why* question. Such a question cannot be answered using only facts; you will need to take a position. For example, the question "*What* are the survival rates for leukemia patients?" can be answered by reporting facts. The question "*Why* are the survival rates for leukemia patients in one province lower than in a neighbouring province?" must be answered with both facts and interpretation.

If a list of prompts appears in the assignment, you do not need to answer all of the questions in order. Look instead for topics, themes, or ideas that will help you ask your own questions.

Recognizing implied questions

An assignment to *discuss, analyze, agree or disagree,* or *consider* a topic will often expect you to answer a *how* or *why* question. For example, "*Discuss* the effects of the Employment Equity Act on equality in the workplace" is another way of saying "*How* has the Employment Equity Act affected equality in the workplace?" Similarly, "*Consider* the recent rise of attention deficit hyperactivity disorder diagnoses" is asking "*Why* are diagnoses of attention deficit hyperactivity disorder rising?"

ON THE WEB > **dianahacker.com/writersref**
Writing exercises > E-ex C1–1

ON THE WEB > **dianahacker.com/writersref**
Additional resources > Links Library > The writing process

Checklist for assessing the writing situation

Subject

- Has a subject (or a range of possible subjects) been given to you, or are you free to choose your own?
- What interests you about your subject? What questions would you like to explore?
- How broadly can you cover the subject? Do you need to narrow it to a more specific topic (because of length restrictions, for instance)?

Sources of information

- Where will your information come from: Reading? Personal experience? Direct observation? Interviews? Questionnaires?
- What sort of documentation is required?

Purpose and audience

- Why are you writing: To inform readers? To persuade them? To entertain them? To call them to action? Some combination of these?
- Who are your readers? How well informed are they about your subject? How will they benefit from reading your work?
- How interested and attentive are your readers? Will they care about your purpose? Will they resist any of your ideas?
- What is your relationship to them: Student to instructor? Employee to supervisor? Citizen to citizen? Expert to novice? Scholar to scholar?

Length and document design

- Do you have any length specifications? If not, what length seems appropriate, given your subject, purpose, and audience?
- Must you use a particular format for your document? If so, do you have guidelines to follow or examples to consult?

Reviewers and deadlines

- Who will be reviewing your draft in progress: Your instructor? A writing centre tutor? Your classmates? A friend? Someone in your family?
- What are your deadlines? How much time will you need to allow for the various stages of writing, including proofreading and printing the final draft?

Talking and listening

Since writing is a process of figuring out what you think about a subject, it can be useful to try out your ideas on other people. Conversation can deepen and refine your ideas before you even begin to set them down on paper. By talking and listening to others, you can also discover what they find interesting, what they are curious about, and where they disagree with you. If you are planning to advance an argument, you can try it out on listeners who have other points of view.

Many writers begin by brainstorming ideas in a group, debating a point with friends, or chatting with an instructor. Others turn to themselves for company — by talking into a tape recorder. Some writers exchange ideas by sending e-mails or instant messages, by joining an Internet chat group, or by following a mailing list discussion. If you are part of a networked classroom, you may be encouraged to share ideas with others in an electronic workshop. For example, a student who participated in the following chat was able to refine her argument before she started drafting her essay on federal campaign funding.

CONVERSATION ABOUT A SUBJECT

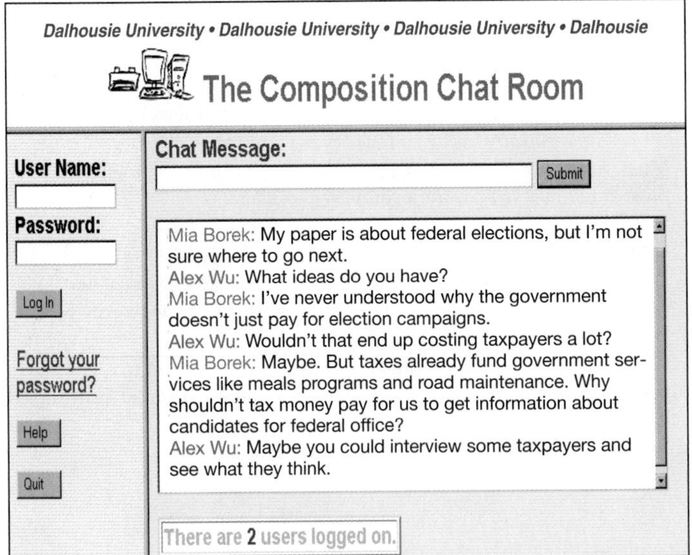

Annotating texts

When you write about reading, one of the best ways to explore ideas is to mark up the work — on the pages themselves if you own the work, on photocopies or sticky notes if you don't. Annotating a text encourages you to look at it more carefully — to underline key concepts, to note possible contradictions in an argument, to raise questions for further investigation. Here, for example, is a paragraph from an essay on medical ethics as one student annotated it:

What breakthroughs? Do all breakthroughs have the same consequences?

Is everyone really uneasy? Is something a breakthrough if it creates a predicament?

> Breakthroughs in genetics present us with a promise and a predicament. The promise is that we may soon be able to treat and prevent a host of debilitating diseases. The predicament is that our newfound genetic knowledge may also enable us to manipulate our own nature — to enhance our muscles, memories, and moods; to choose the sex, height, and other genetic traits of our children; to make ourselves "better than well." When science moves faster than moral understanding, as it does today, men and women struggle to articulate their unease. In liberal societies they reach first for the language of autonomy, fairness, and individual rights. But this part of our moral vocabulary is ill equipped to address the hardest questions posed by genetic engineering. The genomic revolution has induced a kind of moral vertigo.
>
> — Michael Sandel, "The Case against Perfection"

Stem cell research?

What does he mean by "moral understanding"?

Which questions? He doesn't seem to be taking sides.

Listing

Listing ideas is a good way to figure out what you know and what questions you have. You might simply write ideas in the order in which they occur to you — a technique sometimes known as *brainstorming*. Here is a list one student writer jotted down for an essay about funding for university athletics:

Football receives the most funding of any sport.

Funding comes from ticket sales, fundraisers, alumni contributions.

Biggest women's sport is soccer.

Women's soccer team is only ten years old; football team is fifty years old.

Football graduates have had time to earn more money than soccer graduates.

Soccer games don't draw as many fans.

Should funding be equal for all teams?

Do alumni have the right to fund whatever they want?

Feel free to rearrange ideas, to group them under general categories, to delete some, and to add others. In other words, treat the initial list as a source of ideas and a springboard to new ideas, not as an outline.

Clustering

Unlike listing, the technique of clustering highlights relationships among ideas. To cluster ideas, write your topic in the centre of a sheet of paper, draw a circle around it, and surround that circle with related ideas connected to it with lines. If some of the satellite ideas lead to more specific clusters, write them down as well. The writer of the following cluster diagram was exploring ideas for an essay on obesity in children.

CLUSTER DIAGRAM

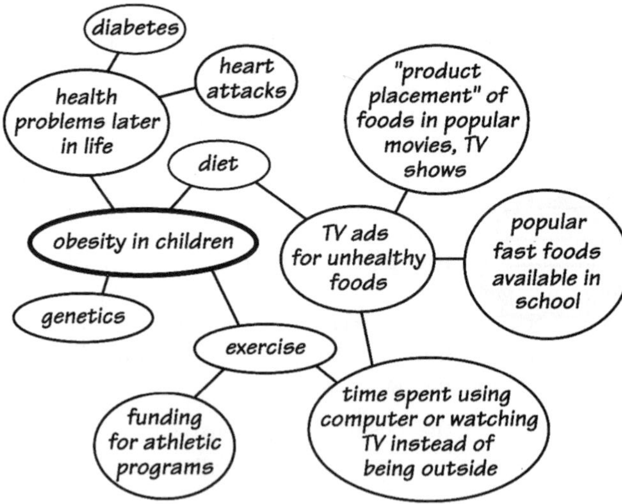

ON THE WEB > dianahacker.com/writersref
Resources for writers and tutors > Tips from writing tutors: Invention strategies

Freewriting

In its purest form, freewriting is simply nonstop writing. You set aside ten minutes or so and write whatever comes to you, without pausing to think about word choice, spelling, or even meaning. If you get stuck, you can write about being stuck, but you should keep your fingers moving. If nothing much happens, you have lost only ten minutes. It's more likely, though, that something interesting will emerge — an eloquent sentence, an honest expression of feeling, or an idea worth further investigation. To explore ideas on a particular topic, consider using a technique called *focused freewriting.* Again, you write quickly and freely, but this time you focus on a subject and pay attention to the connections among your ideas.

Asking the journalist's questions

By asking relevant questions, you can generate many ideas — and you can make sure that you have adequately surveyed your subject. When gathering material for a story, journalists routinely ask themselves Who? What? When? Where? Why? and How? In addition to helping journalists get started, these questions ensure that they will not overlook an important fact: the date of a prospective summit meeting, for example, or the exact location of a burglary.

Whenever you are writing about events, whether current or historical, asking the journalist's questions is one way to get started. One student, whose subject was the negative reaction in 1915 to D. W. Griffith's silent film *The Birth of a Nation*, began exploring her topic with this set of questions:

Who objected to the film?

What were the objections?

When were the protests first voiced?

Where were protests most strongly expressed?

Why did protesters object to the film?

How did protesters make their views known?

In the academic world, scholars often generate ideas with questions related to a specific discipline: one set of questions for analyzing short stories, another for evaluating experiments in social psychology, still another for reporting field experiences in anthropology. If you are writing in a particular discipline, try to discover the questions that its scholars typically explore (see A4).

C1-c Formulate a tentative thesis.

As you explore your subject and identify questions you would like to investigate, you will begin to see possible ways to focus your material. At this point, try to settle on a tentative central idea. The more complex your topic, the more your focus will change as your drafts evolve.

For many types of writing, you will be able to assert your central idea in a sentence or two. Such a statement, which ordinarily appears in the opening paragraph of your finished essay, is called a *thesis* (see also C2-a). A thesis is often the answer to a question, the resolution of a problem, or a statement that takes a position on a debatable topic. A successful thesis — like the following, all taken from articles in *Smithsonian* magazine — points both the writer and the reader in a definite direction.

> Much maligned and the subject of unwarranted fears, most bats are harmless and highly beneficial.
>
> There are some earth phenomena you can count on, but the magnetic field, some say, is not one of them.
>
> Raging in mines from Pennsylvania to China, coal fires threaten towns, poison air and water, and add to global warming.

The thesis sentence usually contains a key word or controlling idea that limits its focus. The first two example sentences, for instance, use key words to prepare for essays that focus on the *beneficial* aspects of bats and the unreliable aspects of Earth's *magnetic field*. The third example uses a controlling idea: the *effects* of coal fires.

It's a good idea to formulate a tentative thesis early in the writing process, perhaps by jotting it on scratch paper, by putting it at the head of a rough outline, or by drafting an introductory paragraph that includes it. This tentative thesis will help you shape your thoughts. Don't worry about the exact wording because your main point may change as you refine your ideas. Here, for example, is one student's early effort:

> In *Rebel without a Cause*, the protagonist, Jim Stark, is often seen literally on the edge of physical danger — walking too close to the swimming pool, leaning over an observation deck, and driving his car toward a cliff.

The thesis that appeared in the student's final draft not only was more polished but also reflected the evolution and refinement of the student's ideas.

Testing a tentative thesis

- Is the thesis too obvious? If you cannot come up with interpretations that oppose your own, consider revising your thesis.
- Can you support your thesis with the evidence available?
- Does the thesis require an essay's worth of development? Or will you run out of points too quickly?
- Can you explain why readers will want to read an essay with this thesis?

> The scenes in which Jim Stark is seen on the edge of physical danger — walking too close to the swimming pool, leaning over an observation deck, driving his car toward a cliff — suggest that he is becoming more agitated by the constraints of family and society.

For a more detailed discussion of thesis, see C2-a.

C1-d Sketch a plan.

Once you have generated some ideas and formulated a tentative thesis, you might want to sketch an informal outline to see how you will support your thesis and to begin to structure your ideas. Informal outlines can take many forms. Perhaps the most common is simply the thesis followed by a list of major ideas.

> Thesis: Television advertising should be regulated to help prevent childhood obesity.
>
> - Children watch more television than ever.
> - Snacks marketed to children are often unhealthy and fattening.
> - Childhood obesity can cause diabetes and other health problems.
> - Solving these health problems costs taxpayers billions of dollars.
> - Therefore, these ads are actually costing the public money.
> - But if advertising is free speech, do we have the right to regulate it?
> - We regulate liquor ads and have banned tobacco ads on television. Quebec prohibits advertising aimed at children, and so should the rest of Canada.

If you began by jotting down a list of ideas or drawing a clustering diagram, you may be able to turn that list or diagram into a rough outline by crossing out some ideas, adding others, and putting the ideas in a logical order.

When to use a formal outline

Early in the writing process, rough outlines have certain advantages over their more formal counterparts: They can be produced more quickly, they are more obviously tentative, and they can be revised more easily should the need arise. However, a formal outline may be useful later in the writing process, after you have written a rough draft, especially if your subject matter is complex.

The following formal outline brought order to the research paper that appears in MLA-5b, on Internet surveillance in the workplace. Notice that the student's thesis is an important part of the outline. Everything else in the outline supports it, directly or indirectly.

Thesis: Although companies often have legitimate concerns that lead them to monitor employees' Internet usage — from expensive security breaches to reduced productivity — the benefits of electronic surveillance are outweighed by its costs to employees' privacy and autonomy.

I. Although employers have always monitored employees, electronic surveillance is more efficient.
   - A. Employers can gather data in large quantities.
   - B. Electronic surveillance can be continuous.
   - C. Electronic surveillance can be conducted secretly, with keystroke logging programs.

II. Some experts argue that employers have legitimate reasons to monitor employees' Internet usage.
   - A. Unmonitored employees could accidentally breach security.
   - B. Companies are legally accountable for online actions of employees.

III. Despite valid concerns, employers should value employee morale and autonomy and avoid creating an atmosphere of distrust.
   - A. Setting the boundaries for employee autonomy is difficult in the wired workplace.
     1. Using the Internet is the most popular way of wasting time at work.
     2. Employers can't tell easily if employees are working or surfing the Web.
   - B. Surveillance can create resentment among employees.
     1. Web surfing can relieve stress, and restricting it can generate tension between managers and workers.
     2. Enforcing Internet usage can seem arbitrary.

IV. Surveillance may not increase employee productivity, and trust may benefit it.
   A. It shouldn't matter to the company how many hours salaried employees work as long as they get the job done.
   B. Casual Internet use can actually benefit companies.
      1. The Internet may spark business ideas.
      2. The Internet may suggest ideas about how to operate more efficiently.

V. Employees' rights to privacy are not well defined by the law.
   A. Few federal guidelines exist on electronic surveillance.
   B. Employers and employees are negotiating the boundaries without legal guidance.
   C. As technological capabilities increase, there will be an increased need to define boundaries.

Guidelines for constructing an outline

1. Put the thesis at the top.
2. Make items at the same level of generality as parallel as possible (see S1).
3. Use sentences unless phrases are clear.
4. Use the conventional system of numbers and letters for the levels of generality.

   I.
      A.
      B.
         1.
         2.
            a.
            b.
   II.
5. Always use at least two subdivisions for a category, since nothing can be divided into fewer than two parts.
6. Limit the number of major sections in the outline; if the list of roman numerals begins to look like a laundry list, find some way of clustering the items into a few major categories with more subcategories.
7. Be flexible; in other words, be prepared to change your outline as your drafts evolve.

C2

Drafting

As you rough out an initial draft, focus your attention on ideas and organization. You can think about sentence structure and word choice later. Writing tends to flow better when it is drafted relatively quickly, without many stops and starts. Keep your prewriting materials — lists, outlines, freewriting, and so on — close at hand. In addition to helping you get started, such notes and blueprints will encourage you to keep moving.

For most kinds of writing, an introduction announces the main point, the body paragraphs develop it, and the conclusion drives it home. You can begin drafting, however, at any point. If you find it difficult to introduce a paper that you have not yet written, try drafting the body first and saving the introduction for later.

ON THE WEB > **dianahacker.com/writersref**
Resources for writers and tutors > Tips from writing tutors: Writing introductions and conclusions

C2-a For most types of writing, draft an introduction that includes a thesis.

Your introduction will usually be a paragraph of 50 to 150 words (in a longer paper, it may be more than one paragraph). Perhaps the most common strategy is to open the paragraph with a few sentences that engage the reader, establish your purpose for writing, and conclude with your main point. The sentence stating the main point is called a *thesis*. (See also C1-c.) In the following examples, the thesis has been italicized.

> Credit card companies love to extend credit to college students, especially those just out of high school. Ads for credit cards line campus bulletin boards, flash across commercial Web sites for students, and get stuffed into shopping bags at college bookstores. Why do the companies market their product so vigorously to a population that lacks a substantial credit history and often has no steady source of income? The answer is that significant profits can be earned through high interest rates and assorted penalties and fees. *By granting college students liberal lending arrangements, credit card companies often hook them on a cycle of spending that can ultimately lead to financial ruin.* — Matt Watson, student

> As the United States industrialized in the nineteenth century, using desperate immigrant labor, social concerns took a backseat to the task of building a prosperous nation. The government did not regulate industries and did not provide an effective safety net for the poor or for those who became sick or injured on the job. Luckily, immigrants and the poor did have a few advocates. Settlement houses such as Hull-House in Chicago provided information, services, and a place for reform-minded individuals to gather and work to improve the conditions of the urban poor. Alice Hamilton was one of these reformers. *Hamilton's efforts helped to improve the lives of immigrants and drew attention and respect to the problems and people that until then had been virtually ignored.*
>
> — Laurie McDonough, student

Ideally, the sentences leading to the thesis should hook the reader, perhaps with one of the following:

a startling statistic, an unusual fact, or a vivid example

a paradoxical statement

a quotation or a bit of dialogue

a question

an analogy

an anecdote

Whether you are writing for a scholarly audience, a professional audience, or a general audience, you cannot assume your readers' interest in the topic. The hook should spark curiosity and offer readers a reason to continue reading.

Although the thesis frequently appears at the end of the introduction, it can also appear at the beginning. Much work-related writing, in which a straightforward approach is most effective, commonly begins with the thesis.

> *Flextime scheduling, which has proved its effectiveness at the Library of Congress, should be introduced on a trial basis at the main branch of the Montgomery County Public Library.* By offering flexible work hours, the library can boost employee morale, cut down on absenteeism, and expand its hours of operation.
>
> — David Warren, student

For some types of writing, it may be difficult or impossible to express the central idea in a thesis sentence; or it may be unwise or unnecessary to put a thesis sentence in the essay itself. A personal narrative, for example, may have a focus too subtle to be distilled in a single sentence, and such a sentence might ruin the story. Strictly informative writing, like that found in many business memos, may be difficult to summarize in a thesis. In such instances, do not try to force the central idea into a thesis sentence. Instead, think in terms of an overriding purpose, which may or may not be stated directly.

> ACADEMIC ENGLISH If you come from a culture that prefers an indirect approach in writing, you may feel that asserting a thesis early in an essay sounds unrefined or even rude. In Canada, however, readers appreciate a direct approach; when you state your point as directly as possible, you show that you value your readers' time.

Characteristics of an effective thesis

An effective thesis sentence is a central idea that requires supporting evidence; it is of adequate scope for an essay of the assigned length; and it is sharply focused.

A thesis must require proof or further development through facts and details; it cannot itself be a fact or a description.

TOO FACTUAL The polygraph was developed by Dr. John A. Larson in 1921.

REVISED Because the polygraph has not been proved reliable, even under controlled conditions, its use by employers should be banned.

A thesis should be of sufficient scope for your assignment, not too broad and not too narrow. Unless you are writing a book or a very long research paper, the following thesis is too broad.

TOO BROAD Mapping the human genome has many implications for health and science.

REVISED Although scientists can now detect genetic predisposition to specific diseases, not everyone should be tested for these diseases.

A thesis should be sharply focused, not too vague. Avoid fuzzy, hard-to-define words such as *interesting, good,* or *disgusting.*

TOO VAGUE The way the TV show *ER* portrays doctors and nurses is interesting.

REVISED In dramatizing the experiences of doctors and nurses as they treat patients, navigate medical bureaucracy, and negotiate bioethical dilemmas, the TV show *ER* portrays health care professionals as unfailingly caring and noble.

In the process of making a too-vague thesis more precise, you may find yourself outlining the major sections of your paper, as in the preceding example. This technique, known as *blueprinting*, helps readers know exactly what to expect as they read on. It also helps you, the writer, control the shape of your essay.

ON THE WEB > **dianahacker.com/writersref**
Writing exercises > E-ex C2–1 and C2–2

C2-b Draft the body.

The body of an essay develops support for a thesis, so it's important to have at least a tentative thesis before you start writing. What does your thesis promise readers? Try to keep your response to that question in mind as you draft the body.

If you have sketched a preliminary plan, try to block out your paragraphs accordingly. If you do not have a plan, you would be wise to pause a moment and sketch one (see C1-d). Keep in mind that often you might not know what you want to say until you have written a draft. It is possible to begin without a plan — assuming you are prepared to treat your first attempt as a "discovery draft" that will almost certainly be tossed or rewritten once you discover what you really want to say.

For more advice about paragraphs and paragraphing, see C4.

C2-c Draft a conclusion.

A conclusion should remind readers of the essay's main idea without dully repeating it. Often the concluding paragraph can be relatively short. By the end of the essay, readers should already understand your main point; your conclusion simply drives it home and, perhaps, leaves readers with something larger to consider.

In addition to echoing your main idea, a conclusion might briefly summarize the essay's key points, propose a course of action, discuss the topic's wider significance, offer advice, or pose a question for future study. To conclude an essay analyzing the shifting roles of women in the military services, one student discusses her topic's implications for society as a whole:

> As the military continues to train women in jobs formerly reserved for men, our understanding of women's roles in society will no doubt continue to change. When news reports of women

> training for and taking part in combat operations become commonplace, reports of women becoming CEOs, police chiefs, and even president of the United States will cease to surprise us. Or perhaps we have already reached this point. — Rosa Broderick, student

To make the conclusion memorable, you might include a detail, an example, or an image from the introduction to bring readers full circle; a quotation or a bit of dialogue; an anecdote; or a humorous or ironic comment.

Whatever concluding strategy you choose, keep in mind that an effective conclusion is decisive and unapologetic. Avoid introducing wholly new ideas at the end of an essay. Finally, because the conclusion is so closely tied to the rest of the essay in both content and tone, be prepared to rework it (or even replace it) when you revise.

C3

Revising

Revising is rarely a one-step process. Global matters — focus, purpose, organization, content, and overall strategy — generally receive attention first. Improvements in sentence structure, word choice, grammar, punctuation, and mechanics come later.

C3-a Make global revisions.

By the time you've written a draft, your ideas will probably have gone in directions you couldn't have predicted ahead of time. As a result, global revisions can be quite dramatic. It's possible, for example, that your thesis will evolve as you figure out how your ideas fit together. You might drop whole paragraphs and add others or condense material once stretched over two or three paragraphs. You might rearrange entire sections. You will save time if you handle global revisions before turning to sentence-level issues: There is little sense in revising sentences that may not appear in your final draft.

Many of us resist global revisions because we find it difficult to view our work from our audience's perspective. To distance yourself from a draft, put it aside for a while, preferably overnight or longer. When you return to it, try to play the role of your audience as you

EXAMPLE OF GLOBAL REVISIONS

Big Box Stores Aren't So Bad

In her essay Big Box Stores Are Bad for Main Street, Betsy Taylor shifts the focus away from the economic effects of these stores to the effects these stores have on the "soul" of America. She claims that stores like Home Depot and Target are bad for America, they draw people out of downtown shopping districts and cause them to focus exclusively on consumption. She believes that small businesses are good for America because they provide personal attention, foster community interaction, and make each city different from the other ones. But Taylor's argument is not strong because it is based on nostalgic images rather than true assumptions about the roles that businesses play in consumers lives and communities. Taylor reveals that she has a nostalgic view of American society and does not understand economic realities. ~~She focuses~~ on idealized shoppers and shopkeepers interacting on the quaint Main Streets of America ~~rather than the economic realities of the situation.~~ As a result, she incorrectly assumes that simply getting rid of big box stores would have a positive effect on us.

For example, in her first paragraph she refers to a big box store as a "25-acre slab of concrete with a 100,000 square foot box of stuff" that lands on a town, evoking images of something strong and powerful conquering something small and weak. But she oversimplifies a complex issue.

She ignores the more complex and economically driven relationship between large chain stores and the communities in which they exist.

read. If possible, enlist the help of reviewers — persons willing to read your draft, focusing on the larger issues, not on the fine points. The checklist for global revision on page 21 may help them get started.

EXAMPLE OF SENTENCE-LEVEL REVISIONS

Rethinking Big-Box Stores
~~Big Box Stores Aren't So Bad~~

" "
In her essay Big Box Stores Are Bad for Main Street, Betsy Taylor ~~shifts~~
focuses not on *large chain* *but on*
~~the focus away from~~ the economic effects of ~~these~~ stores ~~to~~ the effects these
argues
stores have on the "soul" of America. She ~~claims~~ that stores like Home Depot,
and Wal-Mart *because*
~~and~~ Target, are bad for America/ they draw people out of downtown shopping
In contrast, she
districts and cause them to focus exclusively on consumption. ~~She~~ believes
that small businesses are good for America because they provide personal
unique.
attention, foster community interaction, and make each city ~~different from~~
ultimately unconvincing
~~the other ones.~~ But Taylor's argument is ~~not strong~~ because it is based on
nostalgia *images of a*
~~nostalgic images~~--on idealized ~~shoppers and shopkeepers interacting on the~~
on
quaint Main Streets/ ~~of America~~--rather than ~~true assumptions about~~ the roles
' *By ignoring*
that businesses play in consumers lives and communities. ~~She ignores~~ the
more complex, ~~and~~ economically driven relationship between large chain stores
their *Taylor*
and ~~the~~ communities, ~~in which they exist. As a result, she~~ incorrectly assumes
- *America's communities.*
that simply getting rid of big box stores would have a positive effect on ~~us.~~

Taylor's colorful use of language
~~Taylor~~ reveals that she has a nostalgic view of American society and does
In *Taylor*
not understand economic realities. ~~For example, in~~ her first paragraph, ~~she~~
-
refers to a big box store as a "25-acre slab of concrete with a 100,000 square
" " *a monolithic*
foot box of stuff" that lands on a town, evoking images of ~~something strong~~
monster crushing the American way of life (1011).
~~and powerful conquering something small and weak.~~ But she oversimplifies
a complex issue.

TIP: When working on a computer, you might want to print out a hard copy and read the draft as a whole rather than screen by screen. Once you have decided what global revisions may be needed, the computer is an excellent tool for combining or rearranging paragraphs. With little risk, you can explore the possibilities. When a revision misfires, it is easy to return to your original draft.

ON THE WEB > **dianahacker.com/writersref**
Writing exercises > E-ex C3–1

Checklist for global revision

Purpose and audience

- Does the draft accomplish its purpose — to inform readers, to persuade them, to entertain them, to call them to action?
- Is the draft appropriate for its audience? Does it account for the audience's knowledge of the subject, level of interest in the subject, and possible attitudes toward the subject?

Focus

- Is the thesis clear? Is it placed prominently? If there is no thesis, is there a good reason for omitting one?
- Do the introduction and conclusion focus clearly on the central idea?
- Are any ideas obviously off the point?

Organization and paragraphing

- Are there enough organizational cues for readers (such as topic sentences or headings)?
- Are ideas presented in a logical order?
- Are any paragraphs too long or too short for easy reading?

Content

- Is the supporting material relevant and persuasive?
- Which ideas need further development?
- Are the parts proportioned sensibly? Do major ideas receive enough attention?
- Where might material be deleted?

Point of view

- Is the draft free of distracting shifts in point of view (from *I* to *you*, for example, or from *it* to *they*)?
- Is the dominant point of view — first person (*I* or *we*), second person (*you*), or third person (*he, she, it, one,* or *they*) — appropriate for your purpose and audience? (See S4-a.)

ON THE WEB > **diananhacker.com/writersref**

Writing exercises > E-ex C3–2

ON THE WEB > **dianahacker.com/writersref**

Resources for writers and tutors > Tips from writing tutors: Revising and editing

C3-b Revise and edit sentences.

Much of the rest of this book offers advice on revising sentences for style and clarity and on editing them for grammar, punctuation, and mechanics. Some writers handle sentence-level revisions directly at the computer, experimenting on-screen with a variety of improvements. Other writers prefer to print out a hard copy of the draft, mark it up, and then return to the computer. Here, for example, is a draft paragraph edited for a variety of sentence-level problems.

Although some cities have found creative ways to improve access to public transportation for people with disabilities, ~~and to fund other programs, there have been problems in~~ our city has struggled with ~~due to the need to address~~ budget constraints and competing ~~needs~~ priorities. ~~This~~ The budget crunch has led citizens to question how funds are distributed. ~~?~~ For example, last year ~~when~~ city officials voted to use available funds to support ~~had to choose between allocating funds for accessible transportation or allocating funds to~~ after-school programs rather than transportation upgrades. ~~, they voted for the after school programs.~~ It is not clear to some citizens why ~~these~~ after-school programs are more important.

The original paragraph was flawed by wordiness, a problem that can be addressed through any number of revisions. This revision would also be acceptable:

> Some cities have funded improved access to public transportation for people with disabilities. Because of budget constraints, our city chose to fund after-school programs rather than transportation programs. As a result, citizens have begun to question how funds are distributed and why certain programs are more important than others.

Some of the paragraph's improvements are not open to debate and must be fixed in any revision. The hyphen in *after-school programs* is necessary; a noun must be substituted for the pronoun *these* in the last sentence; and the question mark in the second sentence must be changed to a period.

GRAMMAR CHECKERS can help with some but by no means all of the sentence-level problems in a typical draft. Many problems — such as faulty parallelism and misplaced modifiers — require an understanding of grammatical structure that computer programs lack. Such problems often slip right past the grammar checker. Even when the grammar checker makes a suggestion for revision, it is your responsibility as the writer to decide whether the suggestion is more effective than your original.

C3-c Proofread the final manuscript.

After revising and editing, you are ready to prepare the final manuscript. (See C5.) Make sure to allow yourself enough time for proofreading — the final and most important step in manuscript preparation.

Proofreading is a special kind of reading: a slow and methodical search for misspellings, typographical mistakes, and omitted words or word endings. Such errors can be difficult to spot in your own work because you may read what you intended to write, not what is actually on the page. To fight this tendency, try proofreading out loud, articulating each word as it is actually written. You might also try proofreading your sentences in reverse order, a strategy that takes your attention away from the meanings you intended and forces you to focus on one word at a time.

Although proofreading may be dull, it is crucial. Errors strewn throughout an essay are distracting and annoying. A reader may think, If the writer doesn't care about this piece of writing, why should I? A carefully proofread essay, however, sends the message that you value your writing and respect your readers.

SPELL CHECKERS are more reliable than grammar checkers, but they too must be used with caution. Many typographical errors (such as *quiet* for *quite*) and misused words (such as *effect* for *affect*) slip past the spell checker because the checker flags only words not found in its dictionary.

ON THE WEB > **dianahacker.com/writersref**
Model papers > MLA paper-in-progress: Watson

C4

Writing paragraphs

Except for special-purpose paragraphs, such as introductions and conclusions (see C2-a and C2-c), paragraphs are clusters of information supporting an essay's main point (or advancing a story's action). Aim for paragraphs that are clearly focused, well developed, organized, coherent, and neither too long nor too short for easy reading.

C4-a Focus on a main point.

A paragraph should be unified around a main point. The point should be clear to readers, and all sentences in the paragraph should relate to it.

Stating the main point in a topic sentence

As a rule, you should state the main point of a paragraph in a topic sentence — a one-sentence summary that tells readers what to expect as they read on. Usually the topic sentence comes first in the paragraph.

> *All living creatures manage some form of communication.* The dance patterns of bees in their hive help to point the way to distant flower fields or announce successful foraging. Male stickleback fish regularly swim upside-down to indicate outrage in a courtship contest. Male deer and lemurs mark territorial ownership by rubbing their own body secretions on boundary stones or trees. Everyone has seen a frightened dog put his tail between his legs and run in panic. We, too, use gestures, expressions, postures, and movement to give our words point. [Italics added.]
>
> — Olivia Vlahos, *Human Beginnings*

Sometimes the topic sentence is introduced by a transitional sentence linking the paragraph to earlier material, and occasionally it is withheld until the end of the paragraph. And at times a topic sentence is not needed: if a paragraph continues developing an idea clearly introduced in an earlier paragraph, if the details of the paragraph unmistakably suggest its main point, or if the paragraph appears in a narrative of events where generalizations might interrupt the flow of the story.

Sticking to the point

Sentences that do not support the topic sentence destroy the unity of a paragraph. If the paragraph is otherwise well focused, such offending sentences can simply be deleted or perhaps moved elsewhere. In the following paragraph describing the inadequate facilities in a high school, the information about the chemistry instructor (in italics) is clearly off the point.

> As the result of budget cuts, the educational facilities of Macdonald High School have reached an all-time low. Some of the books date back to 1990 and have long since shed their covers. The few computers in working order must share one printer. The lack of lab equipment makes it necessary for four or five students to work at one table, with most watching rather than performing experiments. *Also, the chemistry instructor left to have a baby at the beginning of the semester, and most of the students don't like the substitute.* As for the furniture, many of the upright chairs have become recliners, and the desk legs are so unbalanced that they play seesaw on the floor. [Italics added.]

Sometimes the solution for a disunified paragraph is not as simple as deleting or moving material. Writers often wander into uncharted territory because they cannot think of enough evidence to support a topic sentence. Feeling that it is too soon to break into a new paragraph, they move on to new ideas for which they have not prepared the reader. When this happens, the writer is faced with a choice: Either find more evidence to support the topic sentence or adjust the topic sentence to mesh with the evidence that is available.

ON THE WEB > **dianahacker.com/writersref**
Writing exercises > E-ex C4–1

C4-b Develop the main point.

Though an occasional short paragraph is fine, particularly if it functions as a transition or emphasizes a point, a series of brief paragraphs suggests inadequate development. How much development is enough? That varies, depending on the writer's purpose and audience.

For example, when she wrote a paragraph attempting to convince readers that it is impossible to lose fat quickly, health columnist Jane Brody knew that she would have to present a great deal of evidence because many dieters want to believe the opposite. She did *not* write:

> When you think about it, it's impossible to lose — as many diets suggest — 10 pounds of *fat* in ten days, even on a total fast. Even a moderately active person cannot lose so much weight so fast. A less active person hasn't a prayer.

This three-sentence paragraph is too skimpy to be convincing. But the paragraph that Brody in fact wrote contains enough evidence to convince even skeptical readers.

> When you think about it, it's impossible to lose — as many . . . diets suggest — 10 pounds of *fat* in ten days, even on a total fast. A pound of body fat represents 3,500 calories. To lose 1 pound of fat, you must expend 3,500 more calories than you consume. Let's say you weigh 170 pounds and, as a moderately active person, you burn 2,500 calories a day. If your diet contains only 1,500 calories, you'd have an energy deficit of 1,000 calories a day. In a week's time that would add up to a 7,000-calorie deficit, or 2 pounds of real fat. In ten days, the accumulated deficit would represent nearly 3 pounds of lost body fat. Even if you ate nothing at all for ten days and maintained your usual level of activity, your caloric deficit would add up to 25,000 calories. . . . At 3,500 calories per pound of fat, that's still only 7 pounds of lost fat.
>
> — Jane Brody, *Jane Brody's Nutrition Book*

C4-c Choose a suitable pattern of organization.

Although paragraphs may be patterned in any number of ways, certain patterns of organization occur frequently, either alone or in combination: examples and illustrations, narration, description, process, comparison and contrast, analogy, cause and effect, classification and division, and definition. There is nothing particularly magical about these patterns (sometimes called *methods of development*). They simply reflect some of the ways in which we think.

Examples and illustrations

Examples, perhaps the most common pattern of organization, are appropriate whenever the reader might be tempted to ask, "For example?"

Normally my parents abided scrupulously by "The Budget," but several times a year Dad would dip into his battered black strongbox and splurge on some irrational, totally satisfying luxury. Once he bought over a hundred comic books at a flea market, doled out to us thereafter at the tantalizing rate of two a week. He always got a whole flat of pansies, Mom's favourite flower, for us to give her on Mother's Day. One day a boy stopped at our house selling fifty-cent raffle tickets on a sailboat and Dad bought every ticket the boy had left — three books' worth.

— Connie Hailey, student

Illustrations are extended examples, frequently presented in story form.

Part of [Harriet Tubman's] strategy of conducting was, as in all battle-field operations, the knowledge of how and when to retreat. Numerous allusions have been made to her moves when she suspected that she was in danger. When she feared the party was closely pursued, she would take it for a time on a train southward bound. No one seeing Negroes going in this direction would for an instant suppose them to be fugitives. Once on her return she was at a railroad station. She saw some men reading a poster and she heard one of them reading it aloud. It was a description of her, offering a reward for her capture. She took a southbound train to avert suspicion. At another time when Harriet heard men talking about her, she pretended to read a book which she carried. One man remarked, "This can't be the woman. The one we want can't read or write." Harriet devoutly hoped the book was right side up.

— Earl Conrad, *Harriet Tubman*

Narration

A paragraph of narration tells a story or part of a story. The following paragraph recounts one of the author's experiences in the African wild.

One evening when I was wading in the shallows of the lake to pass a rocky outcrop, I suddenly stopped dead as I saw the sinuous black body of a snake in the water. It was all of six feet long, and from the slight hood and the dark stripes at the back of the neck I knew it to be a Storm's water cobra — a deadly reptile for the bite of which there was, at that time, no serum. As I stared at it an incoming wave gently deposited part of its body on one of my feet. I remained motionless, not even breathing, until the wave rolled back into the lake, drawing the snake with it. Then I leaped out of the water as fast as I could, my heart hammering.

— Jane Goodall, *In the Shadow of Man*

Description

A descriptive paragraph sketches a portrait of a person, place, or thing by using concrete and specific details that appeal to one or more senses — sight, sound, smell, taste, and touch. Consider, for example, the following description of the grasshopper invasions that devastated the midwestern United States in the late 1860s.

> They came like dive bombers out of the west. They came by the millions with the rustle of their wings roaring overhead. They came in waves, like the rolls of the sea, descending with a terrifying speed, breaking now and again like a mighty surf. They came with the force of a williwaw and they formed a huge, ominous, dark brown cloud that eclipsed the sun. They dipped and touched earth, hitting objects and people like hailstones. But they were not hail. These were *live* demons. They popped, snapped, crackled, and roared. They were dark brown, an inch or longer in length, plump in the middle and tapered at the ends. They had transparent wings, slender legs, and two black eyes that flashed with a fierce intelligence. — Eugene Boe, "Pioneers to Eternity"

Process

A process paragraph is structured in chronological order. A writer may choose this pattern either to describe how something is made or done or to explain to readers, step by step, how to do something. The following paragraph explains how to perform a "roll cast," a popular fly-fishing technique.

> Begin by taking up a suitable stance, with one foot slightly in front of the other and the rod pointing down the line. Then begin a smooth, steady draw, raising your rod hand to just above shoulder height and lifting the rod to the 10:30 or 11:00 position. This steady draw allows a loop of line to form between the rod top and the water. While the line is still moving, raise the rod slightly, then punch it rapidly forward and down. The rod is now flexed and under maximum compression, and the line follows its path, bellying out slightly behind you and coming off the water close to your feet. As you power the rod down through the 3:00 position, the belly of line will roll forward. Follow through smoothly so that the line unfolds and straightens above the water.
> — *The Dorling Kindersley Encyclopedia of Fishing*

Comparison and contrast

To compare subjects is to draw attention to their similarities, although the word *compare* also has a broader meaning that includes a consideration of differences. To contrast is to focus only on differences.

Whether a paragraph stresses similarities or differences, it may be patterned in one of two ways. The two subjects may be presented one at a time, as in the following paragraph of contrast.

> So Grant and Lee were in complete contrast, representing two diametrically opposed elements in American life. Grant was the modern man emerging; beyond him, ready to come on the stage, was the great age of steel and machinery, of crowded cities and a restless, burgeoning vitality. Lee might have ridden down from the old age of chivalry, lance in hand, silken banner fluttering over his head. Each man was the perfect champion of his cause, drawing both his strengths and his weaknesses from the people he led.
>
> — Bruce Catton, "Grant and Lee: A Study in Contrasts"

Or a paragraph may proceed point by point, treating two subjects together, one aspect at a time. The following paragraph uses the point-by-point method to contrast the writer's experiences in a North American high school and an Irish convent.

> Strangely enough, instead of being academically inferior to my North American high school, the Irish convent was superior. In my class at home, *Love Story* was considered pretty heavy reading, so imagine my surprise at finding Irish students who could recite passages from *War and Peace*. In high school we complained about having to study *Romeo and Juliet* in one semester, whereas in Ireland we simultaneously studied *Macbeth* and Dickens's *Hard Times*, in addition to writing a composition a day in English class. In high school, I didn't even begin algebra until the ninth grade, while at the convent seventh graders (or their Irish equivalent) were doing calculus and trigonometry.
>
> — Margaret Stack, student

Analogy

Analogies draw comparisons between items that appear to have little in common. In the following paragraph, physician Lewis Thomas draws an analogy between the behaviour of ants and that of humans.

> Ants are so much like human beings as to be an embarrassment. They farm fungi, raise aphids as livestock, launch armies into wars, use chemical sprays to alarm and confuse enemies, capture slaves. The families of weaver ants engage in child labor, holding their larvae like shuttles to spin out the thread that sews the leaves together for their fungus gardens. They exchange information ceaselessly. They do everything but watch television.
>
> — Lewis Thomas, "On Societies as Organisms"

Cause and effect

A paragraph may move from cause to effects or from an effect to its causes. The topic sentence in the following paragraph mentions an effect; the rest of the paragraph lists several causes.

> The fantastic water clarity of the Mount Gambier sinkholes results from several factors. The holes are fed from aquifers holding rainwater that fell decades — even centuries — ago, and that has been filtered through miles of limestone. The high level of calcium that limestone adds causes the silty detritus from dead plants and animals to cling together and settle quickly to the bottom. Abundant bottom vegetation in the shallow sinkholes also helps bind the silt. And the rapid turnover of water prohibits stagnation.
>
> — Hillary Hauser, "Exploring a Sunken Realm in Australia"

Classification and division

Classification is the grouping of items into categories according to some consistent principle. The following paragraph classifies species of electric fish.

> Scientists sort electric fishes into three categories. The first comprises the strongly electric species like the marine electric rays or the freshwater African electric catfish and South American electric eel. Known since the dawn of history, these deliver a punch strong enough to stun a human. In recent years, biologists have focused on a second category: weakly electric fish in the South American and African rivers that use tiny voltages for communication and navigation. The third group contains sharks, nonelectric rays and catfish, which do not emit a field but possess sensors that enable them to detect the minute amounts of electricity that leak out of other organisms.
>
> — Anne and Jack Rudloe, "Electric Warfare: The Fish That Kill with Thunderbolts"

Division takes one item and divides it into parts. As with classification, division should be made according to some consistent principle. The following paragraph describes the components that make up a baseball.

> Like the game itself, a baseball is composed of many layers. One of the delicious joys of childhood is to take apart a baseball and examine the wonders within. You begin by removing the red cotton thread and peeling off the leather cover — which comes from the hide of a Holstein cow and has been tanned, cut, printed,

and punched with holes. Beneath the cover is a thin layer of cotton string, followed by several hundred yards of woolen yarn, which makes up the bulk of the ball. Finally, in the middle is a rubber ball, or "pill," which is a little smaller than a golf ball. Slice into the rubber and you'll find the ball's heart — a cork core. The cork is from Portugal, the rubber from southeast Asia, the covers are American, and the balls are assembled in Costa Rica.

— Dan Gutman, *The Way Baseball Works*

Definition

A definition puts a word or concept into a general class and then provides enough details to distinguish it from other members in the same class. In the following paragraph, the writer defines *envy* as a special kind of desire.

> Envy is so integral and so painful a part of what animates behavior in market societies that many people have forgotten the full meaning of the word, simplifying it into one of the synonyms of desire. It is that, which may be why it flourishes in market societies: democracies of desire, they might be called, with money for ballots, stuffing permitted. But envy is more or less than desire. It begins with an almost frantic sense of emptiness inside oneself, as if the pump of one's heart were sucking on air. One has to be blind to perceive the emptiness, of course, but that's just what envy is, a selective blindness. *Invidia*, Latin for envy, translates as "non-sight," and Dante has the envious plodding along under cloaks of lead, their eyes sewn shut with leaden wire. What they are blind to is what they have, God-given and humanly nurtured, in themselves.
>
> — Nelson W. Aldrich Jr., *Old Money*

C4-d Make paragraphs coherent.

When sentences and paragraphs flow from one to another without discernible bumps, gaps, or shifts, they are said to be coherent. Coherence can be improved by strengthening the various ties between old information and new. A number of techniques for strengthening those ties are detailed in this section.

Linking ideas clearly

Readers expect to learn a paragraph's main point in a topic sentence early in the paragraph. Then, as they move into the body of the paragraph, they expect to encounter specific facts, details, or examples that support the topic sentence — either directly or indirectly. Consider the following paragraph, in which all of the sentences following the topic sentence directly support it.

> A passenger list of the early years [of the Orient Express] would read like a *Who's Who of the World*, from art to politics. Sarah Bernhardt and her Italian counterpart Eleonora Duse used the train to thrill the stages of Europe. For musicians there were Toscanini and Mahler. Dancers Nijinsky and Pavlova were there, while lesser performers like Harry Houdini and the girls of the Ziegfeld Follies also rode the rails. Violinists were allowed to practice on the train, and occasionally one might see trapeze artists hanging like bats from the baggage racks.
>
> — Barnaby Conrad III, "Train of Kings"

If a sentence does not support the topic sentence directly, readers expect it to support another sentence in the paragraph. The following paragraph begins with a topic sentence. The italicized sentences are direct supports, and the rest of the sentences are indirect supports.

> Though the open-space classroom works for many children, it is not practical for my son, David. *First, David is hyperactive.* When he was placed in an open-space classroom, he became distracted and confused. He was tempted to watch the movement going on around him instead of concentrating on his own work. *Second, David has a tendency to transpose letters and numbers, a tendency that can be overcome only by individual attention from the instructor.* In the open classroom he was moved from teacher to teacher, with each one responsible for a different subject. No single teacher worked with David long enough to diagnose the problem, let alone help him with it. *Finally, David is not a highly motivated learner.* In the open classroom, he was graded "at his own level," not by criteria for a certain grade. He could receive a B in reading and still be a grade level behind, because he was doing satisfactory work "at his own level." [Italics added.]
>
> — Margaret Smith, student

Repeating key words

Repetition of key words is an important technique for gaining coherence. To prevent repetitions from becoming dull, you can use variations of the key word (*hike*, *hiker*, *hiking*), pronouns referring to the word (*gamblers . . . they*), and synonyms (*run*, *spring*, *race*, *dash*). In the following paragraph describing plots among indentured servants in the seventeenth century, historian Richard Hofstadter binds sentences together by repeating the key word *plots* and echoing it with variations (italicized).

> *Plots* hatched by several servants to run away together occurred mostly in the plantation colonies, and the few recorded servant *uprisings* were entirely limited to those colonies. Virginia had been forced from its very earliest years to take stringent steps against *mutinous plots*, and severe punishments for *such behavior* were recorded. Most servant *plots* occurred in the seventeenth century: a contemplated *uprising* was nipped in the bud in York County in 1661; apparently led by some left-wing offshoots of the *Great Rebellion*, servants *plotted* an *insurrection* in Gloucester County in 1663, and four leaders were condemned and executed; some discontented servants apparently joined *Bacon's Rebellion* in the 1670's. In the 1680's the planters became newly apprehensive of discontent among the servants "owing to their great necessities and want of clothes," and it was feared they would *rise up* and *plunder* the storehouses and ships; in 1682 there were plant-cutting *riots* in which servants and laborers, as well as some planters, took part. [Italics added.]
>
> — Richard Hofstadter, *America at 1750*

Using parallel structures

Parallel structures are frequently used within sentences to underscore the similarity of ideas (see S1). They may also be used to bind together a series of sentences expressing similar information. In the following passage describing folk beliefs, anthropologist Margaret Mead presents similar information in parallel grammatical form.

> Actually, almost every day, even in the most sophisticated home, something is likely to happen that evokes the memory of some old folk belief. The salt spills. A knife falls to the floor. Your nose tickles. Then perhaps, with a slightly embarrassed smile, the person who spilled the salt tosses a pinch over his left shoulder. Or someone recites the old rhyme, "Knife falls, gentleman calls." Or as you rub your nose you think, That means a letter. I wonder who's writing?
>
> — Margaret Mead, "New Superstitions for Old"

Maintaining consistency

Coherence suffers whenever a draft shifts confusingly from one point of view to another (for example, from *I* to *you* or from *anyone* to *they*). Coherence also suffers when a draft shifts without reason from one verb tense to another (for example, from *swam* to *swims*). For advice on avoiding shifts, see S4.

Providing transitions

Transitions are bridges between what has been read and what is about to be read. Transitions help readers move from sentence to sentence; they also alert readers to more global connections of ideas — those between paragraphs or even larger blocks of text.

> ACADEMIC ENGLISH Choose transitions carefully and vary them appropriately. For instance, avoid using a transition that signals a logical relationship (such as *therefore*) if no clear logical relationship exists. Each transition has a different meaning; if you do not use an appropriate signal, you might confuse your reader.
>
> ▶ **Although taking eight o'clock classes may seem unappealing, coming to school early has its advantages. ~~Moreover,~~ For example, students who arrive early typically avoid the worst traffic and find the best parking spaces.**

SENTENCE-LEVEL TRANSITIONS Certain words and phrases signal connections between (or within) sentences. Frequently used transitions are included in the chart on page 36.

Skilled writers use transitional expressions with care, making sure, for example, not to use *consequently* when *also* would be more precise. They are also careful to select transitions with an appropriate tone, perhaps preferring *so* to *thus* in an informal piece, *in summary* to *in short* for a scholarly essay.

In the following paragraph, taken from an argument that dinosaurs had the "'right-sized' brains for reptiles of their body size," biologist Stephen Jay Gould uses transitions (italicized) with skill.

> I don't wish to deny that the flattened, minuscule head of largebodied *Stegosaurus* houses little brain from our subjective, top-heavy perspective, *but* I do wish to assert that we should not expect more of the beast. *First of all*, large animals have relatively smaller brains than related, small animals. The correlation of brain size with body size among kindred animals (all reptiles, all mammals, *for example*) is remarkably regular. *As* we move from small to large animals, from mice to elephants or small lizards to Komodo dragons, brain size increases, *but* not so fast as body size. *In other words*, bodies grow faster than brains, *and* large animals have low ratios of brain weight to body weight. *In fact*, brains grow

only about two-thirds as fast as bodies. *Since* we have no reason to believe that large animals are consistently stupider than their smaller relatives, we must conclude that large animals require relatively less brain to do as well as smaller animals. *If* we do not recognize this relationship, we are likely to underestimate the mental power of very large animals, dinosaurs *in particular.*

— Stephen Jay Gould, "Were Dinosaurs Dumb?"

ON THE WEB > **dianahacker.com/writersref**
Writing exercises > E-ex C4–2

PARAGRAPH-LEVEL TRANSITIONS Transitions between paragraphs usually link the *first* sentence of a new paragraph with the *first* sentence of the previous paragraph. In other words, the topic sentences signal global connections.

Look for opportunities to allude to the subject of a previous paragraph (as summed up in its topic sentence) in the topic sentence of the next paragraph. In his essay "Little Green Lies," Jonathan H. Alder uses this strategy in the following topic sentences, which appear in a passage describing the benefits of plastic packaging.

> Consider aseptic packaging, the synthetic packaging for the "juice boxes" so many children bring to school with their lunch. One criticism of aseptic packaging is that it is nearly impossible to recycle, yet on almost every other count, aseptic packaging is environmentally preferable to the packaging alternatives. Not only do aseptic containers not require refrigeration to keep their contents from spoiling, but their manufacture requires less than one-10th the energy of making glass bottles.
>
> What is true for juice boxes is also true for other forms of synthetic packaging. The use of polystyrene, which is commonly (and mistakenly) referred to as "Styrofoam," can reduce food waste dramatically due to its insulating properties. (Thanks to these properties, polystyrene cups are much preferred over paper for that morning cup of coffee.) Polystyrene also requires significantly fewer resources to produce than its paper counterpart.

TRANSITIONS BETWEEN BLOCKS OF TEXT In long essays, you may need to alert readers to connections between large blocks of text. You can do this by inserting transitional paragraphs at key points in the essay. On the next page, for example, is a transitional paragraph from a student research paper. It announces that the first part of the paper has come to a close and the second part is about to begin.

Common transitions

TO SHOW ADDITION and, also, besides, further, furthermore, in addition, moreover, next, too, first, second

TO GIVE EXAMPLES for example, for instance, to illustrate, in fact, specifically

TO COMPARE also, in the same manner, similarly, likewise

TO CONTRAST but, however, on the other hand, in contrast, nevertheless, still, even though, on the contrary, yet, although

TO SUMMARIZE OR CONCLUDE in other words, in short, in summary, in conclusion, to sum up, that is, therefore

TO SHOW TIME after, as, before, next, during, later, finally, meanwhile, since, then, when, while, immediately

TO SHOW PLACE OR DIRECTION above, below, beyond, farther on, nearby, opposite, close, to the left

TO INDICATE LOGICAL RELATIONSHIP if, so, therefore, consequently, thus, as a result, for this reason, because, since

> Although the great apes have demonstrated significant language skills, one central question remains: Can they be taught to use that uniquely human language tool we call grammar, to learn the difference, for instance, between "ape bite human" and "human bite ape"? In other words, can an ape create a sentence?

C4-e If necessary, adjust paragraph length.

Most readers feel comfortable reading paragraphs that range between one hundred and two hundred words. Shorter paragraphs force too much starting and stopping, and longer ones strain the reader's attention span. There are exceptions to this guideline, however. Paragraphs longer than two hundred words frequently appear in scholarly writing, where they suggest seriousness and depth. Paragraphs shorter than one hundred words occur in newspapers because of narrow columns; in informal essays to quicken the pace; in business letters, where readers routinely skim for main ideas; and in e-mail and on Web sites for ease of reading on the computer screen.

In an essay, the first and last paragraphs will ordinarily be the introduction and conclusion. These special-purpose paragraphs are likely to be shorter than the paragraphs in the body of the essay.

Typically, the body paragraphs will follow the essay's outline: one paragraph per point in short essays, a group of paragraphs per point in longer ones. Some ideas require more development than others, however, so it is best to be flexible. If an idea stretches to a length unreasonable for a paragraph, you should divide the paragraph, even if you have presented comparable points in the essay in single paragraphs.

Paragraph breaks are not always made for strictly logical reasons. Writers use them for all of the following reasons.

REASONS FOR BEGINNING A NEW PARAGRAPH

- to mark off the introduction and the conclusion
- to signal a shift to a new idea
- to indicate an important shift in time or place
- to emphasize a point (by placing it at the beginning or the end, not in the middle, of a paragraph)
- to highlight a contrast
- to signal a change of speakers (in dialogue)
- to provide readers with a needed pause
- to break up text that looks too dense

Beware of using too many short, choppy paragraphs, however. Readers want to see how your ideas connect, and they become irritated when you break their momentum by forcing them to pause every few sentences. Here are some reasons you might have for combining some of the paragraphs in a rough draft.

REASONS FOR COMBINING PARAGRAPHS

- to clarify the essay's organization
- to connect closely related ideas
- to bind together text that looks too choppy

C5

Designing documents

The term *document* is broad enough to describe anything you might write in a college or university class, in business, and in everyday life. How you design a document (format it for the printed page or for a computer screen) will affect how readers respond to it.

Good document design promotes readability, but what *readability* means depends on your purpose and audience and perhaps on other elements of your writing situation, such as your subject and any length restrictions. All of your design choices — layout, word processing options such as margins and fonts, headings, and lists — should be made in light of your writing situation. Likewise, different types of visuals — tables, charts, and images — can support your writing if they are used appropriately.

C5-a Determine layout and format to suit your purpose and audience.

Word processing programs offer abundant options for layout, margins and line spacing, alignment, and fonts. As you use these options to design documents, always keep the purpose of the document and the needs of your readers in mind.

Layout

Most readers have set ideas about how different kinds of documents should look. Advertisements, for example, have a distinctive appearance, as do newsletters, flyers, brochures, and menus. Instructors have expectations about how a college or university paper should look (see C5-e). Employers expect documents such as letters, résumés, and memos to be presented in standard ways (see C5-f). And anyone who reads your writing online will appreciate a recognizable layout.

Unless you have a compelling reason to stray from convention, it's best to choose a document layout that conforms to your readers' expectations. If you're not sure what readers expect, look at examples of the kind of document you are producing.

Planning a document: Purpose and audience checklist

- What is the purpose of your document? How can your document design help you achieve this purpose?
- Who are your readers? What are their expectations?
- What format is required? What format options — layout, margins, line spacing, alignment, and fonts — will readers expect?
- How can you use visuals — charts, graphs, tables, images — to help you convey information?

Margins and line spacing

Margins help control the look of a page. For most academic and business documents, leave a margin of 1–1.5 inches (2.5–3.5 cm) on all sides. These margins create a visual frame for the text and provide room for annotations, such as an instructor's comments or a co-worker's suggestions. Narrower margins generally make a page crowded and difficult to read.

SINGLE-SPACED, UNFORMATTED

Obesity in Children 1

Can Medication Cure Obesity in Children?
A Review of the Literature

In March 2004, U.S. Surgeon General Richard Carmona called attention to a health problem in the United States that, until recently, has been overlooked: childhood obesity. Carmona said that the "astounding" 15% child obesity rate constitutes an "epidemic." Since the early 1980s, that rate has "doubled in children and tripled in adolescents." Now more than 9 million children are classified as obese (paras. 3, 6). While the traditional response to a medical epidemic is to hunt for a vaccine or a cure-all pill, childhood obesity has proven more elusive. The lack of success of recent initiatives suggests that medication might not be the answer for the escalating problem. This literature review considers whether the use of medication is a promising approach for solving the childhood obesity problem by responding to the following questions: What are the implications of childhood obesity? Is medication effective at treating childhood obesity? Is medication safe for children? Is medication the best solution? Understanding the limitations of medical treatments for children highlights the complexity of the childhood obesity problem in the United States and underscores the need for physicians, advocacy groups, and policymakers to search for other solutions.

Obesity can be a devastating problem from both an individual and a societal perspective. Obesity puts children at risk for a number of medical complications, including type 2 diabetes, hypertension, sleep apnea, and orthopedic problems (Henry J. Kaiser Family Foundation, 2004, p. 1). Researchers Hoppin and Taveras (2004) have noted that obesity is often associated with psychological issues such as depression, anxiety, and binge eating (Table 4).

Obesity also poses serious problems for a society struggling to cope with rising health care costs. The cost of treating obesity currently totals $117 billion per year--a price, according to the surgeon general, "second only to the cost of [treating] tobacco use" (Carmona, 2004, para. 9). And as the number of children who suffer from obesity grows, long-term costs will only increase.

The widening scope of the obesity problem has prompted medical professionals to rethink old conceptions of the disorder and its causes. As researchers Yanovski and Yanovski (2002) have explained, obesity

DOUBLE-SPACED, FORMATTED

Obesity in Children 1

Can Medication Cure Obesity in Children?

A Review of the Literature

In March 2004, U.S. Surgeon General Richard Carmona called attention to a health problem in the United States that, until recently, has been overlooked: childhood obesity. Carmona said that the "astounding" 15% child obesity rate constitutes an "epidemic." Since the early 1980s, that rate has "doubled in children and tripled in adolescents." Now more than 9 million children are classified as obese (paras. 3, 6).[1] While the traditional response to a medical epidemic is to hunt for a vaccine or a cure-all pill, childhood obesity has proven more elusive. The lack of success of recent initiatives suggests that medication might not be the answer for the escalating problem. This literature review considers whether the use of medication is a promising approach for solving the childhood obesity problem by responding to the following questions:

1. What are the implications of childhood obesity?
2. Is medication effective at treating childhood obesity?
3. Is medication safe for children?
4. Is medication the best solution?

Understanding the limitations of medical treatments for children highlights the complexity of the childhood obesity

[1]Obesity is measured in terms of body-mass index (BMI): weight in kilograms divided by square of height in meters. An adult with a BMI 30 or higher is considered obese. In children and adolescents, obesity is defined in relation to others of the same age and gender. An adolescent with a BMI in the 95th percentile for his or her age and gender is considered obese.

ACADEMIC ENGLISH If your word processing program was not purchased in North America, you may need to change the default settings. From your page setup menu (usually under the file menu) change the paper size to 8.5 × 11 inches (letter size). In most cases, change your margins to 1 inch (2.5 cm).

Most manuscripts in progress are double-spaced to allow room for editing. Final copy is often double-spaced as well, since single-spacing is less inviting to read. If you are unsure about margin and spacing requirements, check with your instructor or look at documents similar to the one you are writing. At times, the advantages of double-spacing are offset by other considerations. For example, most business and technical documents are single-spaced, with double-spacing between paragraphs, to save paper and to promote quick scanning. Your document's purpose and context should determine appropriate margins and line spacing.

Alignment

Word processing programs allow you to align text and visuals on a page in four ways: left, right, centred, and justified. Most academic and business documents are left-aligned for easy reading. Although justified margins may seem more professional, they tend to create awkward word spacing and should be avoided.

Fonts

If you have a choice, select a font that fits your writing situation in an easy-to-read size (usually 10–12 points). Although offbeat or decorative fonts, such as those that look handwritten, may seem attractive, they slow readers down and can distract them from your ideas. For example, using comic sans, a font with a handwritten, childish feel, can make an essay seem too informal or unpolished, regardless of how well it is written. Fonts that are easy to read and appropriate for college or university and workplace documents include the following:

Arial	Tahoma
Courier	Times New Roman
Garamond	Verdana
Georgia	

Font styles — such as **boldface**, *italics*, and underlining — can be useful for calling attention to parts of a document. On the whole, it is best to use restraint when selecting font styles. Applying too many different styles within a document results in busy-looking pages and confuses readers.

TIP: Never write a document in all capital or all lowercase letters. Doing so can frustrate or annoy readers. Although some readers have become accustomed to e-mails that omit capital letters entirely, their absence makes a message difficult to read.

ON THE WEB > **dianahacker.com/writersref**
Links Library > Document design

C5-b Use headings when appropriate.

You will have little need for headings in short essays, especially if you use paragraphing and clear topic sentences to guide readers. In more complex documents, however, such as research papers, grant proposals, business reports, and Web sites, headings can be a useful visual cue for readers.

Headings help readers see at a glance the organization of a document. If more than one level of heading is used, the headings also indicate the hierarchy of ideas — as they do throughout this book.

Headings can serve a number of functions for your readers. When readers are simply looking up information, headings will help them find it quickly. When readers are scanning, hoping to pick up the gist of things, headings will guide them. Even when readers are committed enough to read every word, headings can help. Efficient readers preview a document before they begin reading; when previewing and while reading, they are guided by any visual cues the writer provides.

TIP: Although headings can be useful, they cannot substitute for transitions between paragraphs. Keep this in mind as you write essays in college and university.

Phrasing headings

Headings should be as brief and as informative as possible. Certain styles of headings — the most common being *-ing* phrases, noun phrases, questions, and imperative sentences — work better for some purposes, audiences, and subjects than others.

Whatever style you choose, use it consistently. Headings on the same level of organization should be written in parallel structure (see S1), as in the following examples from a report, a history textbook, a financial brochure, and a nursing manual, respectively.

***-ING* HEADINGS**

Safeguarding the earth's atmosphere

Charting the path to sustainable energy

Conserving global forests

NOUN PHRASE HEADINGS

The economics of slavery

The sociology of slavery

The psychological effects of slavery

QUESTIONS AS HEADINGS

How do I buy shares?

How do I redeem shares?

What is the history of the fund's performance?

IMPERATIVE SENTENCES AS HEADINGS

Ask the patient to describe current symptoms.

Take a detailed medical history.

Record the patient's vital signs.

Placing and formatting headings

Headings on the same level of organization should be placed and formatted in a consistent way. If you have more than one level of heading, you might centre your first-level headings and make them boldface; then you might make the second-level headings left-aligned and italicized, like this:

First-level heading

Second-level heading

A college or university paper with headings typically has only one level, and the headings are often centred, as in the sample paper on pages 484–88. Business memos often include headings. Important headings can be highlighted by using white space around them. Less important headings can be downplayed by using less white space or by running them into the text.

C5-c Use lists to guide readers.

Lists are easy to read or scan when they are displayed rather than run into your text. You might choose to display the following kinds of lists:

- steps in a process
- materials needed for a project
- parts of an object
- advice or recommendations
- items to be discussed
- criteria for evaluation (as in checklists)

Lists should usually be introduced with an independent clause followed by a colon (*All mammals share the following five characteristics:*). Periods are not used after items in a list unless the items are complete sentences.

If the order of items is not important, use bullets (circles or squares) or dashes to draw readers' eyes to a list. If you are describing a sequence or a set of steps, number the list with arabic numerals (1, 2, 3) followed by periods.

TIP: Although lists can be useful visual cues, don't overdo them. Too many will clutter a document.

C5-d Add visuals to supplement your text.

Visuals can convey information concisely and powerfully. Charts, graphs, and tables, for example, can simplify complex numerical data. Images — including photographs and diagrams — often express an idea more vividly than words can. With access to the Internet, digital photography, and word processing or desktop publishing software, you can download or create your own visuals to enhance your document. If you download a visual, you must credit your source (see R3).

Choosing appropriate visuals

Use visuals to supplement your writing, not to substitute for it. Always consider how a visual supports your purpose and how your audience might respond to it. A student writing about electronic surveillance in the workplace, for example, used a cartoon to illustrate her point about employees' personal use of the Internet at work (see MLA-5b). Another student, writing about treatments for childhood obesity, created a table to display data she had found in two different sources and discussed in her paper (see APA-5b).

As you draft and revise a document, choose carefully the visuals that support your main point, and avoid overloading your text with too many images. The chart on pages 44–45 describes eight types of visuals and their purposes.

Placing and labeling visuals

A visual may be placed in the text of a document, near a discussion to which it relates, or it can be put in an appendix, labelled, and referred to in the text.

Choosing visuals to suit your purpose

Pie chart

Pie charts compare a part or parts with the whole. The parts are displayed as segments of the pie, represented as percentages of the whole (which is always 100 percent).

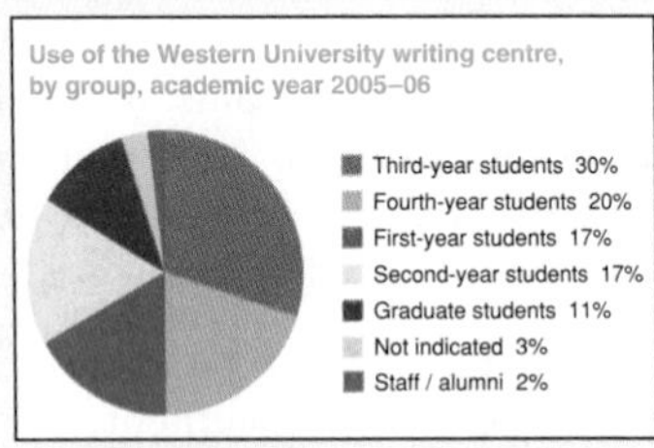

Line graph

Line graphs highlight trends over time or compare numerical data.

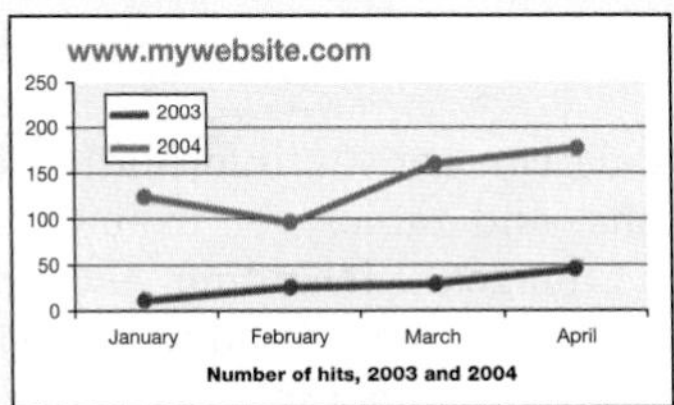

Bar graph

Bar graphs can be used for the same purpose as line graphs. This bar graph displays the same data as in the line graph above.

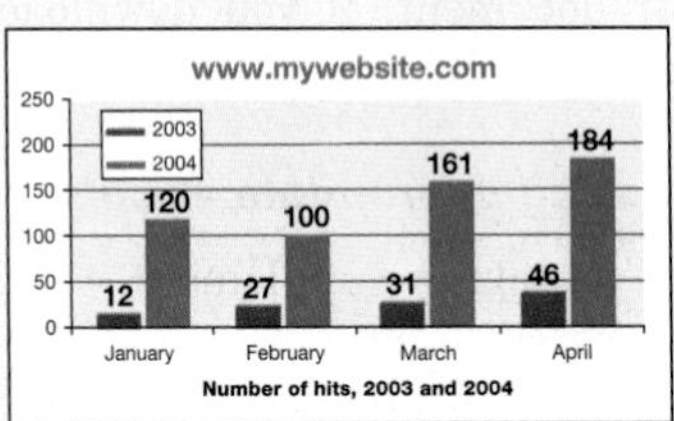

Table

Tables organize complicated numerical information into an accessible format.

Prices of daily doses of AIDS drugs
($US)

Drug	*Brazil*	*Uganda*	*Côte d'Ivoire*	*US*
3TC (Lamuvidine)	1.66	3.28	2.95	8.70
ddC (Zalcitabine)	0.24	4.17	3.75	8.80
Didanosine	2.04	5.26	3.48	7.25
Efavirenz	6.96	n/a	6.41	13.13
Indinavir	10.32	12.79	9.07	14.93
Nelfinavir	4.14	4.45	4.39	6.47
Nevirapine	5.04	n/a	n/a	8.48
Saquinavir	6.24	7.37	5.52	6.50
Stavudine	0.56	6.19	4.10	9.07
ZDV/3TC	1.44	7.34	n/a	18.78
Zidovudine	1.08	4.34	2.43	10.12

Source: UNAIDS, 2000

Photograph

Photographs vividly depict people, scenes, or objects discussed in a text.

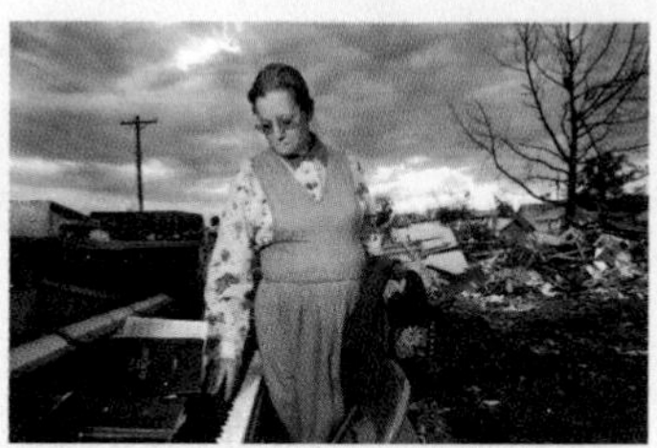

Diagram

Diagrams, useful in scientific and technical writing, concisely illustrate processes, structures, or interactions.

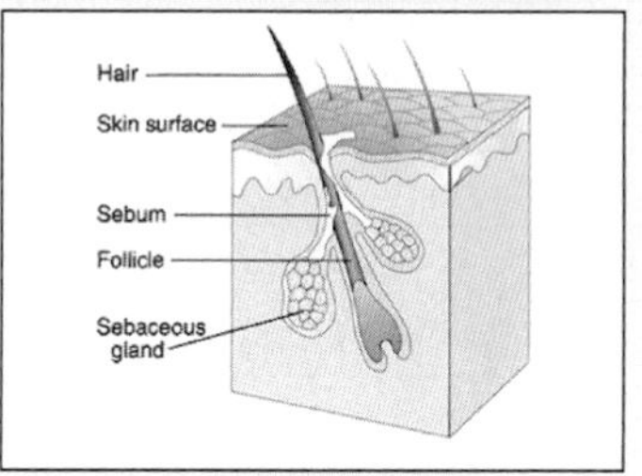

Map

Maps indicate locations, distances, and demographic information.

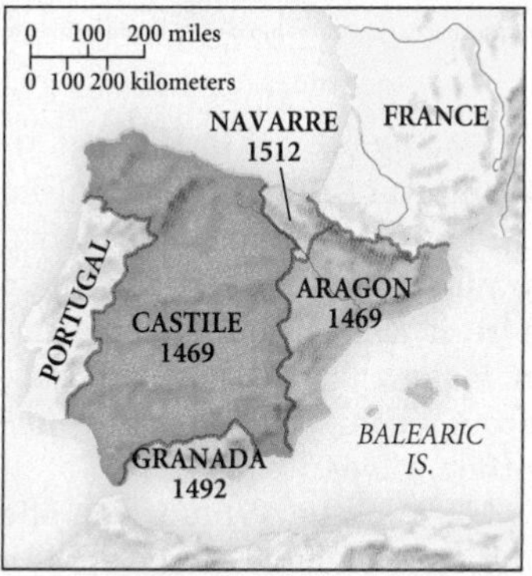

Flowchart

Flowcharts show structures or steps in a process. (For another example, see p. 104.)

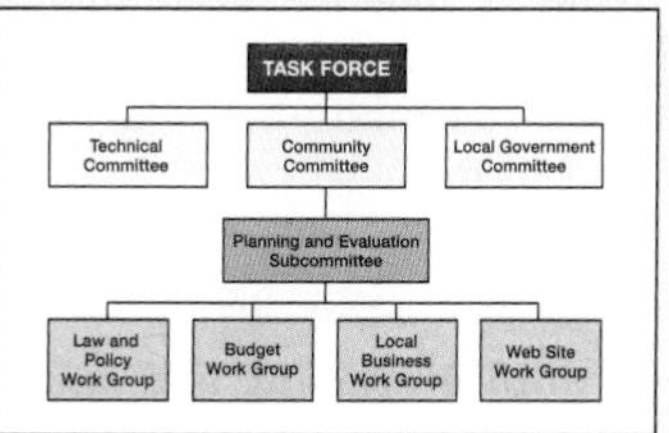

VISUAL WITH A SOURCE CREDITED

Fig. 6.

Top Companies in Alberta, by Number of Employees			
Rank	**Company**	**No. of Employees**	**Headquarters**
1	Government of Alberta (includes Agencies, Boards, & Commissions)	35 000	Edmonton
2	Canada Safeway Limited	30 000	Calgary
3	Westfair Foods Ltd.	29 000	Calgary
4	Calgary Health Region	18 000	Calgary
5	Canadian Pacific Railway Co.	16 106	Calgary
6	The Forzani Group Ltd.	10 733	Calgary
7	City of Calgary	10 000	Calgary
8	Sport-Check Intl 2000 Ltd.	9 700	Calgary
9	Calgary Board of Education	8 296	Calgary
10	Capital Health Authority	8 199	Edmonton

Source: Adapted from "Alberta's Top Companies Ranked by Employees," *Government of Alberta*, http://www.alberta-canada.com/statpub/albertaTopCompanies/byEmployees.cfm.

Placing visuals in the text of a document can be tricky. Usually you will want the visual to appear close to the sentences that relate to it, but page breaks won't always allow this placement. At times you may need to insert the visual at a later point and tell readers where it can be found; sometimes, with the help of software, you can make the text flow around the visual. No matter where you place a visual, refer to it in your text. Don't expect visuals to speak for themselves.

Most of the visuals you include in a document will require some sort of label. Labels, which are typically placed above or under the visuals, should be brief but descriptive. Most commonly, a visual is labelled with the word "Figure" or the abbreviation "Fig.," followed by a number: *Fig. 4.* Sometimes a title might be included to explain how the visual relates to the text: *Fig. 4. Voter turnout by age.*

Using visuals responsibly

Most word processing and spreadsheet software will allow you to produce your own visuals. If you create a chart, a table, or a graph using information from your research, you must cite the source of the information even though the visual is your own. The table on page 46 credits the source of its data.

If you download a photograph from the Web or scan an image from a magazine or book, you must credit the person or organization that created it, just as you would cite any other source you use in an academic paper (see R3). If your document is written for publication outside the classroom, you will need to request permission to use any visual you borrow.

Guidelines for using visuals vary by academic discipline. See MLA-5a, APA-5a, and CMS-5a for guidelines in English and humanities, social sciences, and history, respectively.

C5-e Use standard academic formatting.

Instructors have certain expectations about how a college or university paper should look. If your instructor provides guidelines for formatting an essay, report, or research paper, you should follow them. Otherwise, use the manuscript format that is recommended for your academic discipline.

In most English and humanities classes, you will be asked to use the MLA (Modern Language Association) format. The sample on pages 48–49 illustrates this format. For more detailed MLA manuscript guidelines and a sample research paper, see MLA-5. If you have been asked to use APA (American Psychological Association) or CMS (*Chicago Manual of Style*) manuscript guidelines, see APA-5 or CMS-5.

MLA ESSAY FORMAT

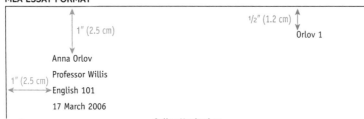

Orlov 1

Anna Orlov

Professor Willis

English 101

17 March 2006

Title is centered.

Online Monitoring:

A Threat to Employee Privacy in the Wired Workplace

1/2" (1.2 cm)

As the Internet has become an integral tool of businesses, company policies on Internet usage have become as common as policies regarding vacation days or sexual harassment. A 2005 study by the American Management Association and ePolicy Institute found that 76% of companies monitor employees' use of the Web, and the number of companies that block employees' access to certain Web sites has increased 27% since 2001 (1). Unlike other company rules, however, Internet usage policies often include language authorizing companies to secretly monitor their employees, a practice that raises questions about rights in the workplace. Although companies often have legitimate concerns that lead them to monitor employees' Internet usage--from expensive security breaches to reduced productivity--the benefits of electronic surveillance are outweighed by its costs to employees' privacy and autonomy.

Double-spacing is used throughout.

1" (2.5 cm)

While surveillance of employees is not a new phenomenon, electronic surveillance allows employers to monitor workers with unprecedented efficiency. In his book The Naked Employee, Frederick Lane describes offline ways in which employers have been permitted to intrude on employees' privacy for decades, such as drug testing, background checks, psychological exams, lie detector tests, and in-store video surveillance. The difference, Lane argues, between these old methods of data gathering and electronic surveillance involves quantity:

1" (2.5 cm)

> Technology makes it possible for employers to gather enormous amounts of data about employees, often far beyond what is necessary to satisfy safety or productivity concerns. And the trends that drive technology--faster, smaller, cheaper--make it possible for larger and larger numbers of employers to gather ever-greater amounts of personal data. (3-4)

1" (2.5 cm)

Marginal annotations indicate MLA-style formatting.

MLA ESSAY FORMAT (*continued*)

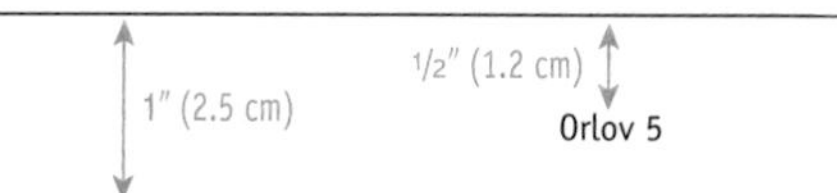

Works Cited

Heading is centered.

Adams, Scott. Dilbert and the Way of the Weasel. New York: Harper, 2002.

American Management Association and ePolicy Institute. "2005 Electronic Monitoring and Surveillance Survey." American Management Association. 2005. 15 Feb. 2006 <http://www.amanet.org/research/pdfs/EMS_summary05.pdf>.

"Automatically Record Everything They Do Online! Spector Pro 5.0 FAQ's." Netbus.org. SpectorSoft. 17 Feb. 2006 <http://www.netbus.org/sProFAQ.html>.

Flynn, Nancy. "Internet Policies." ePolicy Institute. 2001. 15 Feb. 2006 <http://www.epolicyinstitute.com/i_policies/index.html>.

Frauenheim, Ed. "Stop Reading This Headline and Get Back to Work." CNET News.com. 11 July 2005. 17 Feb. 2006 <http://news.com.com/Stop+reading+this+headline+and+get+back+to+work/2100-1022_3-5783552.html>.

Gonsalves, Chris. "Wasting Away on the Web." eWeek.com 8 Aug. 2005. 16 Feb. 2006 <http://www.eweek.com/article2/0,1895,1843242,00.asp>.

Kesan, Jay P. "Cyber-Working or Cyber-Shirking? A First Principles Examination of Electronic Privacy in the Workplace." Florida Law Review 54 (2002): 289-332.

Lane, Frederick S., III. The Naked Employee: How Technology Is Compromising Workplace Privacy. New York: Amer. Management Assn., 2003.

Tam, Pui-Wing, et al. "Snooping E-Mail by Software Is Now a Workplace Norm." Wall Street Journal 9 Mar. 2005: B1+.

Tynan, Daniel. "Your Boss Is Watching." PC World 6 Oct. 2004. 17 Feb. 2006 <http://www.pcworld.com/news/article/0,aid,118072,00.asp>.

Verespej, Michael A. "Inappropriate Internet Surfing." Industry Week 7 Feb. 2000. 16 Feb. 2006 <http://www.industryweek.com/ReadArticle.aspx?ArticleID=568>.

1" (2.5 cm)

1" (2.5 cm)

1/2" (1.2 cm)

Double-spacing is used throughout; no extra space between entries.

C5-f Use standard business formatting.

This section provides advice on preparing business letters, résumés, and memos. For a more detailed discussion of these and other business documents — proposals, reports, executive summaries, and so on — consult a business writing textbook or look at current examples at the organization for which you are writing.

ON THE WEB > **dianahacker.com/writersref**
Links Library > Document design

BUSINESS LETTER IN FULL BLOCK STYLE

FrancophoneVoice

March 16, 2006 — Date

Jonathan Ross
Managing Editor
Francophone World Today
2023 Meadow Place
Victoria BC V8R 1R2
— Inside address

Dear Mr. Ross: — Salutation

Body —

Thank you very much for taking the time yesterday to speak to the University of Victoria's Francophone Club. A number of students have told me that they enjoyed your presentation and found your job search suggestions to be extremely helpful.

As I mentioned to you when we first scheduled your appearance, the club publishes a monthly newsletter, *Francophone Voice*. Our purpose is to share up-to-date information and expert advice with members of the university's Francophone population. Considering how much students benefited from your talk, I would like to publish excerpts from it in our newsletter.

I have taken the liberty of transcribing parts of your presentation and organizing them into a question-and-answer format for our readers. When you have a moment, would you mind looking through the enclosed article and letting me know if I may have your permission to print it? I would be happy, of course, to make any changes or corrections that you request. I'm hoping to include this article in our next newsletter, so I would need your response by April 4.

Once again, Mr. Ross, thank you for sharing your experiences with us. You gave an informative and entertaining speech, and I would love to be able to share it with the students who couldn't hear it in person.

Sincerely, — Close

Jeffrey Richardson

Jeffrey Richardson
Associate Editor
— Signature

Enc.

210 Student Centre University of Victoria Victoria BC V8W 2Y2

Business letters

In writing a business letter, be direct, clear, and courteous. State your purpose or request at the beginning of the letter and include only relevant information in the body. Being as direct and concise as possible shows that you value your reader's time.

For the format of the letter, stick to established business conventions. A sample business letter in *full block* style appears on page 50.

Résumés and cover letters

An effective résumé gives relevant information in a clear, concise form. You may be asked to produce a traditional résumé, a scannable résumé, or a Web résumé. A cover letter gives a prospective employer a reason to look at your résumé. The goal is to present yourself in a favourable light without including unnecessary details and wasting your reader's time.

COVER LETTERS When you send out your résumé, always include a cover letter that introduces yourself, states the position you seek, and tells where you learned about it. The letter should also highlight past experiences that qualify you for the position and emphasize what you can do for the employer (not what the job will do for you). End the letter with a suggestion for a meeting, and tell your prospective employer when you will be available.

TRADITIONAL RÉSUMÉS Traditional paper résumés are screened by people, not by computers. Because screeners may face stacks of applications, they often spend very little time looking at each résumé. Therefore, you will need to make your résumé as reader-friendly as possible. Here are a few guidelines. See page 52 for an example.

- Limit your résumé to one page if possible, two pages at the most.
- Organize your information into clear categories — Education, Experience, and so on.
- Present the information in each category in reverse chronological order to highlight your most recent accomplishments.
- Use bulleted lists or some other simple, clear visual device to organize information.
- Use strong, active verbs to emphasize your accomplishments. (Use present-tense verbs, such as *manage,* for current activities and past-tense verbs, such as *managed,* for past activities.)

TRADITIONAL RÉSUMÉ

Jeffrey Richardson
608 Harbinger Avenue
Victoria BC V8V 4J1
205–555–2651
jrichardson@jrichardson.localhost

OBJECTIVE	To obtain an editorial internship with a magazine
EDUCATION	
Fall 2003 – present	University of Victoria • BA expected in June 2007 • Double major: English and journalism • GPA: 3.7 (on a 4-point scale)
EXPERIENCE	
Fall 2005 – present	Associate editor, *Francophone Voice*, newsletter of Francophone Club • Assign and edit feature articles • Coordinate community outreach
Fall 2004 – present	Photo editor, *The Martlet*, student paper • Shoot and print photographs • Select and lay out photographs and other visuals
Summer 2005	Intern, *The Globe,* Nanaimo, British Columbia • Wrote stories about local issues and personalities • Interviewed political candidates • Edited and proofread copy • Coedited "The Landscapes of Northern Canada: A Photoessay"
Summers 2004, 2005	Tutor, Nanaimo ESL Program • Tutored English language learners • Trained new tutors
ACTIVITIES	Photographers' Workshop, Francophone Club
PORTFOLIO	Available at http://jrichardson.localhost/jrportfolio.htm
REFERENCES	Available upon request

SCANNABLE RÉSUMÉS Scannable résumés might be submitted on paper, by e-mail, or through an online employment service. The prospective employer scans and searches the résumé electronically; a database matches keywords in the employer's job description with keywords in the résumé. A human screener then looks through the résumés filtered out by the database matching.

A scannable résumé must be very simply formatted so that the scanner can accurately pick up its content. In general, follow these guidelines when preparing a scannable résumé:

- Include a Keywords section that lists words likely to be searched by a scanner. (Use nouns such as *manager*, not verbs such as *manage*.)
- Use standard résumé headings (Education, Experience, and so on).
- Avoid special characters, graphics, or font styles such as boldface or italics.

WEB RÉSUMÉS Posting your résumé on a Web site is an easy way to provide prospective employers with up-to-date information about your experience and employment goals. Web résumés allow you to present details about yourself without overwhelming your readers. Most guidelines for traditional résumés apply to Web résumés. Always list the date that you last updated the résumé.

ON THE WEB > **dianahacker.com/writersref**
Model papers > Résumés

Memos

Usually brief and to the point, a memo reports information, makes a request, or recommends an action. The format of a memo, which varies from company to company, is designed for easy distribution, quick reading, and efficient filing.

Most memos display the date, the name of the recipient, the name of the sender, and the subject on separate lines at the top of the page. Many companies have preprinted forms for memos, and some word processing programs allow you to call up a memo template.

The subject line of a memo, on paper or in e-mail, should describe the topic as clearly and concisely as possible, and the introductory paragraph should get right to the point. In addition, the body of the memo should be well organized and easy to skim. To promote skimming, use headings where possible and display any items that deserve special attention by setting them off from the text — in a list, for example, or in boldface.

E-mail

E-mail is fast replacing regular mail in the business world and in most people's personal lives. Especially in business and academic contexts, you will want to show readers that you value their time. Your message may be just one of many that your readers have to wade through. Here are some strategies for writing effective e-mails:

- Fill in the subject line with a meaningful, concise subject to help readers sort through messages and set priorities.
- Put the most important part of your message at the beginning so it will be seen on the first screen.
- For long, detailed messages, consider providing a summary at the beginning.
- Write concisely, and keep paragraphs fairly short, especially if your audience is likely to read your message on the screen.
- Avoid writing in all capital letters or all lowercase letters, a practice that is easy on the writer but hard on the reader.
- Use formatting such as boldface and italics and special characters sparingly; not all e-mail systems handle such elements consistently.
- Proofread for typos and obvious errors that are likely to slow down or annoy readers.

A

Academic Writing

A Academic Writing

Writing is a fact of life in postsecondary education. No matter what you study, you will be expected to participate in ongoing conversations conducted by other students and scholars. To join in those conversations, you will analyze and respond to texts, evaluate other people's arguments, and put forth your own ideas. Whatever the discipline, the goal of academic writing is to argue a thesis and support it with appropriate evidence.

A1

Writing about texts

The word *texts* can refer to a variety of works: essays, periodical articles, government reports, books, and even visuals such as advertisements and photographs. Most assignments that ask you to respond to a text call for a summary or an analysis or both.

A summary is neutral in tone and demonstrates that you have understood the author's key ideas. Assignments calling for an analysis of a text vary widely, but they will usually ask you to look at how the text's parts contribute to its central argument or purpose, often with the aim of judging its evidence or overall effect.

When you write about a written text, you will need to read it several times to digest its full meaning. Two techniques will help you move beyond a superficial first reading: (1) annotating the text with your observations and questions and (2) outlining the text's key points. The same techniques will help you analyze visual texts.

A1-a Read actively: Annotate the text.

Read actively by jotting down your questions, thoughts, and reactions in the margins of the text or in a notebook. Use a pencil instead of a highlighter; with a pencil you can underline key concepts, mark points, or circle elements that intrigue you. If you change your mind, you can erase your early annotations and replace them with new ones.

ON THE WEB > **dianahacker.com/writersref**
Resources for writers and tutors > Tips from writing tutors: Benefits of reading

Guidelines for active reading

Familiarize yourself with the basic features and structure of a text.

- What kind of text are you reading? An essay? An editorial? A scholarly article? An advertisement? A photograph?
- What is the author's purpose? To inform? To persuade? To call to action?
- Who is the audience? How does the author attempt to appeal to the audience?
- What is the author's thesis? What question does the text attempt to answer?
- What evidence does the author provide to support the thesis?

Note details that surprise, puzzle, or intrigue you.

- Has the author revealed a fact or made a point that runs counter to what you had assumed was true? What exactly is surprising?
- Has the author made a generalization you disagree with? Can you think of evidence that would challenge the generalization?
- Are there any contradictions or inconsistencies in the text?
- Are there any words, statements, or phrases in the text that you don't understand? If so, what reference materials do you need to consult?

Read and reread to discover meaning.

- What do you notice on a second or third reading that you didn't notice earlier?
- Does the text raise questions that it does not resolve?
- If you could address the author directly, what questions would you pose? Where do you agree and disagree with the author? Why?

Apply critical thinking strategies to visual texts.

- What first strikes you about the image? What elements do you notice immediately?
- Who or what is the main subject of the image?
- What colours and textures dominate?
- What is in the background? In the foreground?
- What role, if any, do words play in the visual text?

Following are an article from a consumer-oriented newsletter and a magazine advertisement, annotated by students. The students, Emilia Sanchez and Albert Lee, were assigned to write a summary and an analysis. Each began by annotating the text.

ANNOTATED ARTICLE

Big Box Stores Are Bad for Main Street

BETSY TAYLOR

There is plenty of reason to be concerned about the proliferation of Wal-Marts and other so-called "big box" stores. The question, however, is not whether or not these types of stores create jobs (although several studies claim they produce a net job loss in local communities) or whether they ultimately save consumers money. The real concern about having a 25-acre slab of concrete with a 100,000 square foot box of stuff land on a town is whether it's good for a community's soul.

Opening strategy — the problem is not x, it's y.

Sentimental — what is a community's soul?

The worst thing about "big boxes" is that they have a tendency to produce Ross Perot's famous "big sucking sound" — sucking the life out of cities and small towns across the country. On the other hand, small businesses are great for a community. They offer more personal service; they won't threaten to pack up and leave town if they don't get tax breaks, free roads and other blandishments; and small-business owners are much more responsive to a customer's needs. (Ever try to complain about bad service or poor quality products to the president of Home Depot?)

Lumps all big boxes together.

Assumes all small businesses are attentive.

Logic problem? Why couldn't customer complain to store manager?

Yet, if big boxes are so bad, why are they so successful? One glaring reason is that we've become a nation of hyper-consumers, and the big-box boys know this. Downtown shopping districts comprised of small businesses take some of the efficiency out of overconsumption. There's all that hassle of having to travel from store to store, and having to pull out your credit card so many times. Occasionally, we even find ourselves chatting with the shopkeeper, wandering into a coffee shop to visit with a friend or otherwise wasting precious time that could be spent on acquiring more stuff.

True?

Nostalgia for a time that is long gone or never was.

But let's face it — bustling, thriving city centers are fun. They breathe life into a community. They allow cities and towns to stand out from each other. They provide an atmosphere for people to interact with each other that just cannot be found at Target, or Wal-Mart or Home Depot.

Community vs. economy. What about prices?

Is it anti-American to be against having a retail giant set up shop in one's community? Some people would say so. On the other hand, if you board up Main Street, what's left of America?

Ends with emotional appeal.

ANNOTATED ADVERTISEMENT

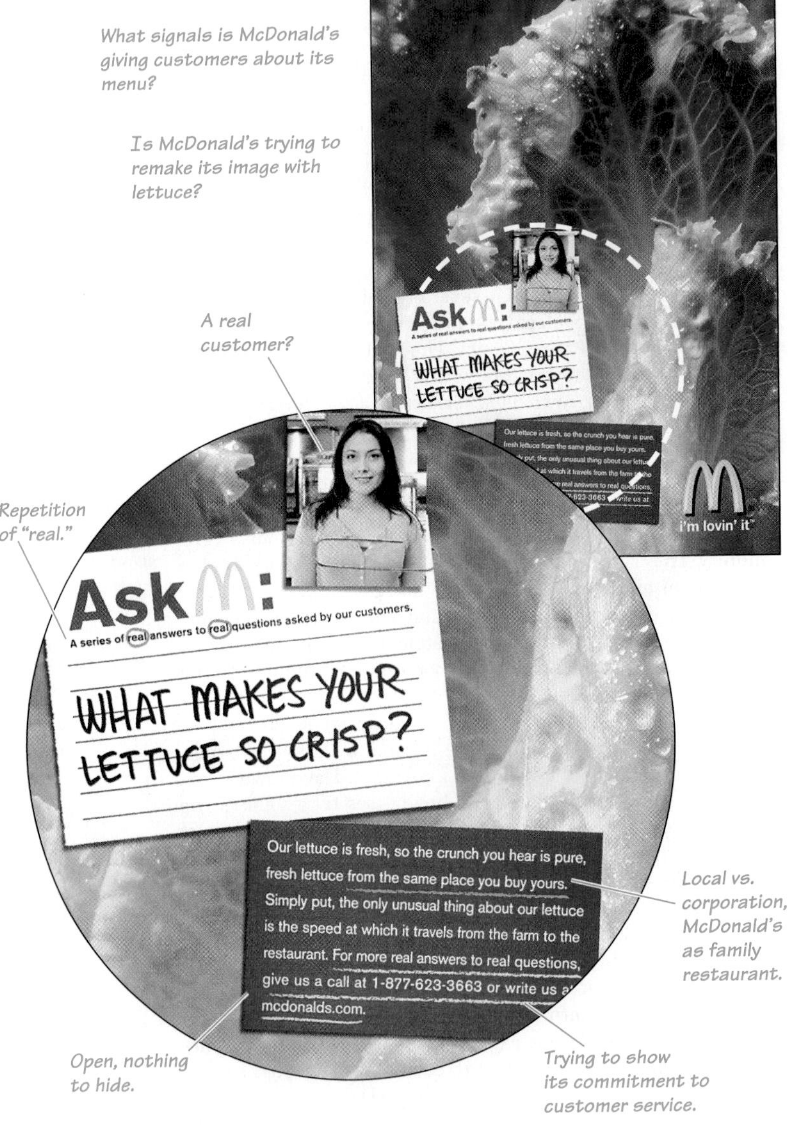

A1-b Try sketching a brief outline of the text.

After reading, rereading, and annotating a text, attempt to outline it. Seeing how the author has constructed a text can help you understand it. As you sketch an outline, pay special attention to the text's thesis (central idea) and its topic sentences. The thesis of a written text usually appears in the introduction, often in the first or second paragraph. Topic sentences can be found at the beginnings of most body paragraphs, where they announce a shift to a new topic. (See C2-a and C4-a.)

In your outline, put the author's thesis and key points in your own words. Here, for example, is the outline that Emilia Sanchez developed as she prepared to write her summary and analysis of the text printed on page 59. Notice that the outline does not simply trace the author's ideas paragraph by paragraph; instead, it sums up the article's central points.

OUTLINE OF "BIG BOX STORES ARE BAD FOR MAIN STREET"

Thesis: Whether or not they take jobs away from a community or offer low prices to consumers, we should be worried about "big-box" stores like Wal-Mart, Target, and Home Depot because they harm communities by taking the life out of downtown shopping districts.

I. Small businesses are better for cities and towns than big-box stores are.
   A. Small businesses offer personal service and big-box stores do not.
   B. Small businesses don't make demands on community resources as big-box stores do.
   C. Small businesses respond to customer concerns and big-box stores do not.

II. Big-box stores are successful because they cater to consumption at the expense of benefits to the community.
   A. Buying everything in one place is convenient.
   B. Shopping at small businesses may be inefficient, but it provides opportunities for socializing.
   C. Downtown shopping districts give each city or town a special identity.

Conclusion: While some people say that it's anti-American to oppose big-box stores, actually these stores threaten the communities that make up America by encouraging buying at the expense of the traditional interactions of Main Street.

A visual, of course, doesn't state an explicit thesis or an explicit line of reasoning. Instead, you must infer the meaning beneath the image's surface and interpret its central point and supporting ideas from the elements of its design. One way to outline a visual text is to try to define its purpose and sketch a list of its key elements. Here, for example, are the key features that Albert Lee identified for the advertisement printed on page 60.

> Purpose: To persuade readers that McDonald's is concerned about its customers' health.
>
> Key features:
>
> - A close-up of a fresh, green lettuce leaf makes up the entire background.
> - Near the centre there's a comment card with a handwritten question from a "real" McDonald's customer: "What makes your lettuce so crisp?"
> - A photograph of a smiling woman is clipped to the card.
> - Beneath the comment card is the company's response, which emphasizes the farm-fresh quality and purity of its vegetables and urges customers to ask other candid questions.
> - At the bottom of the ad is the McDonald's slogan "I'm lovin' it."

ON THE WEB > **dianahacker.com/writersref**
Model papers > MLA analysis papers > Albert Lee

A1-c Summarize to demonstrate your understanding.

Your goal in summarizing a text is to state the work's main ideas and key points simply, briefly, and accurately. If you have sketched a brief outline of the text (see A1-b), refer to it as you draft your summary.

To summarize a written text, first find the author's central idea — the thesis. Then divide the whole piece into a few major and perhaps minor ideas. Since a summary must be fairly short, you must make judgments about what is most important. To summarize a visual text, begin with information about who created the visual, who the intended audience is, and when and where the visual appeared. Briefly explain the visual's main point or purpose and point to its key features.

Following is Emilia Sanchez's summary of the article that is printed on page 59.

> In her essay "Big Box Stores Are Bad for Main Street," Betsy Taylor argues that chain stores harm communities by taking the life out of downtown shopping districts. Explaining that a commu-

Guidelines for writing a summary

- In the first sentence, mention the title of the text, the name of the author, and the author's thesis or the visual's central point.
- Maintain a neutral tone; be objective.
- Use the third-person point of view and the present tense.
- Keep your focus on the text. Don't state the author's ideas as if they were your own.
- Put all or most of your summary in your own words; if you borrow a phrase or a sentence from the text, put it in quotation marks and give the page number in parentheses.
- Limit yourself to presenting the text's key points.
- Be concise; make every word count.

nity's "soul" is more important than low prices or consumer convenience, she argues that small businesses are better than stores like Wal-Mart, Target, and Home Depot because they emphasize personal interactions and don't place demands on a community's resources. Taylor asserts that big-box stores are successful because "we've become a nation of hyper-consumers," although the convenience of shopping in these stores comes at the expense of benefits to the community. She concludes by suggesting that it's not "anti-American" to oppose big-box stores because the damage they inflict on downtown shopping districts extends to America itself.

— Emilia Sanchez, student

A1-d Analyze to demonstrate your critical thinking.

Whereas a summary most often answers the question of *what* a text says, an analysis looks at *how* a text makes its point.

Typically, an analysis takes the form of an essay that makes its own argument about a text. Include an introduction that briefly summarizes the text, a thesis that states your own judgment about the text, and body paragraphs that support your thesis with evidence. If you are analyzing an image, examine it as a whole and then reflect on how the individual elements contribute to its overall meaning. If you have written a summary of the text, you may find it useful to refer to the main points of the summary as you write your analysis.

Beginning on the next page is Emilia Sanchez's analysis of the article by Betsy Taylor (see p. 59).

Sanchez 1

Emilia Sanchez

Professor Goodwin

English 10

22 October 2005

Rethinking Big-Box Stores

Opening summarizes the article's purpose and thesis.

In her essay "Big Box Stores Are Bad for Main Street," Betsy Taylor focuses not on the economic effects of large chain stores but on the effects these stores have on the "soul" of America. She argues that stores like Home Depot, Target, and Wal-Mart are bad for America because they draw people out of downtown shopping districts and cause them to focus exclusively on consumption. In contrast, she believes that small businesses are good for America because they provide personal attention, foster community interaction, and make each city unique. But Taylor's argument is ultimately unconvincing because it is based on nostalgia--on idealized images of a quaint Main Street--rather than on the roles that businesses play in consumers' lives and communities. By ignoring the more complex, economically driven relationships between large chain stores and their communities, Taylor incorrectly assumes that simply getting rid of big-box stores would have a positive effect on America's communities.

Thesis expresses Sanchez's judgment of Taylor's article.

Signal phrase introduces quotations from the source; Sanchez uses an MLA in-text citation.

Sanchez begins to identify and challenge Taylor's assumptions.

Taylor's use of colorful language reveals that she has a nostalgic view of American society and does not understand economic realities. In her first paragraph, Taylor refers to a big-box store as a "25-acre slab of concrete with a 100,000 square foot box of stuff" that "lands on a town," evoking images of a monolithic monster crushing the American way of life (1011). But her assessment oversimplifies a complex issue. Taylor does not consider that many downtown business districts failed long before chain stores moved in, when factories and mills closed and workers lost their jobs. In cities with struggling economies, big-box stores can actually provide much-needed jobs. Similarly, while Taylor blames big-box stores for harming local economies by asking for tax breaks, free roads, and other perks, she doesn't acknowledge that these stores also enter into economic partnerships with the surrounding communities by offering financial benefits to schools and hospitals.

Marginal annotations indicate MLA-style formatting and effective writing.

Sanchez 2

Taylor's assumption that shopping in small businesses is always better for the customer also seems driven by nostalgia for an old-fashioned Main Street rather than by the facts. While she may be right that many small businesses offer personal service and are responsive to customer complaints, she does not consider that many customers appreciate the service at big-box stores. Just as customer service is better at some small businesses than at others, it is impossible to generalize about service at all big-box stores. For example, customers depend on the lenient return policies and the wide variety of products at stores like Target and Home Depot.

Clear topic sentence announces a shift to a new topic.

Sanchez refutes Taylor's claim.

Taylor blames big-box stores for encouraging American "hyper-consumerism," but she oversimplifies by equating big-box stores with bad values and small businesses with good values. Like her other points, this claim ignores the economic and social realities of American society today. Big-box stores do not force Americans to buy more. By offering lower prices in a convenient setting, however, they allow consumers to save time and purchase goods they might not be able to afford from small businesses. The existence of more small businesses would not change what most Americans can afford, nor would it reduce their desire to buy affordable merchandise.

Taylor may be right that some big-box stores have a negative impact on communities and that small businesses offer certain advantages. But she ignores the economic conditions that support big-box stores as well as the fact that Main Street was in decline before the big-box store arrived. Getting rid of big-box stores will not bring back a simpler America populated by thriving, unique Main Streets; in reality, Main Street will not survive if consumers cannot afford to shop there.

Sanchez treats the author fairly.

Conclusion returns to the thesis and shows the wider significance of Sanchez's analysis.

Work cited page is in MLA style.

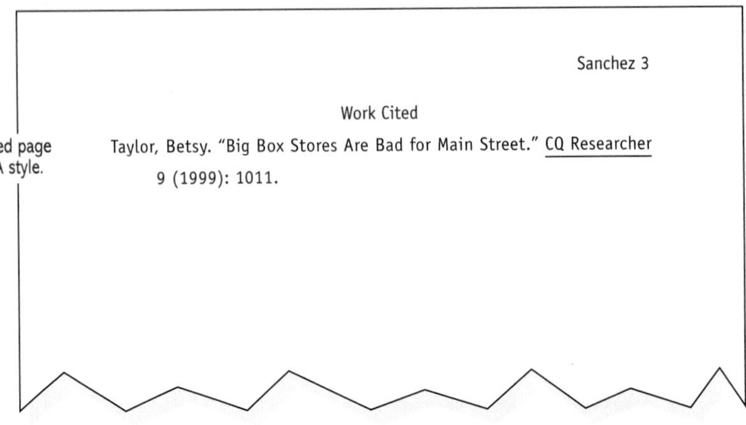

Sanchez 3

Work Cited

Taylor, Betsy. "Big Box Stores Are Bad for Main Street." CQ Researcher 9 (1999): 1011.

Guidelines for analyzing a text

Written texts. Instructors who ask you to analyze a written nonfiction text often expect you to address some of the following questions.

- What is the author's thesis or central idea? Who is the audience?
- What questions does the author address (implicitly or explicitly)?
- How does the author structure the text? What are the key parts and how do they relate to one another and to the thesis?
- What strategies has the author used to generate interest in the argument and to persuade readers of its merit?
- What evidence does the author use to support the thesis? How persuasive is the evidence?
- Does the author anticipate objections and counter opposing views?
- Does the author fall prey to any faulty reasoning?

Visual texts. If you are analyzing a visual text, the following additional questions will help you evaluate an image's purpose and meaning.

- What surprises, perplexes, or intrigues you about the image?
- What clues suggest the visual text's intended audience? How does the image appeal to its audience?
- If the text is an advertisement, what product is it selling? Does it attempt to sell an idea or a message as well?
- If the visual text includes words, how do the words contribute to the meaning of the image?
- How do design elements — colours, shapes, perspective, background, foreground — shape the visual text's meaning or serve its purpose?

A2

Constructing reasonable arguments

In writing an argument, you take a stand on a debatable issue. The question being debated might be a matter of public policy:

> Should religious groups be allowed to meet on public school property?
>
> What is the least dangerous way to dispose of nuclear waste?
>
> Should a province enact laws rationing medical care?

On such questions, reasonable people may disagree.

Reasonable people also disagree about scholarly issues. Psychologists debate the role of genes in behaviour; historians interpret causes of the War of 1812 differently; biologists challenge one another's predictions about the effects of global warming.

When you construct a *reasonable* argument, your goal is not simply to win or to have the last word. Your aim is to explain your understanding of the truth about a subject or to propose the best solution available for solving a problem — without being needlessly combative. In constructing your argument, you join a conversation with other writers and readers. Your aim is to convince readers to reconsider their opinions by offering new reasons to question an old viewpoint.

ACADEMIC ENGLISH Some cultures value writers who argue with force and express their superiority. Other cultures value writers who argue subtly or indirectly, often with an apology. Academic audiences in Canada will expect your writing to be assertive and confident — neither aggressive nor passive. Create an assertive tone by acknowledging different opinions and supporting your view with specific evidence.

TOO AGGRESSIVE	Of course prayer should be discouraged in public schools. Only foolish people think that organized prayer is good for everyone.
TOO PASSIVE	I might be wrong, but I think that organized prayer should be discouraged in public schools.
ASSERTIVE TONE	Organized prayer should be discouraged in public schools because it violates the religious freedom guaranteed by the Charter of Rights and Freedoms.

If you are uncertain about the tone of your work, ask for help at your school's writing centre.

A2-a Examine your issue's social and intellectual contexts.

Arguments appear in social and intellectual contexts. Public policy debates obviously arise in social contexts. Grounded in specific times and places, such debates are conducted among groups with competing values and interests. For example, the debate over nuclear power plants has been renewed in Canada in light of skyrocketing energy costs and terrorism concerns — with environmentalists, nuclear industry officials, and consumers all weighing in on the argument. Most public policy debates also have intellectual dimensions that address scientific or theoretical questions. In the case of the nuclear power issue, physicists, biologists, and economists all contribute their expertise.

Scholarly debates play out in intellectual contexts, but they have a social dimension too. Scholars and researchers rarely work in a vacuum: They respond to the contributions of other specialists in the field, often building on others' views and refining them, but at times challenging them.

Because many of your readers will be aware of the social and intellectual contexts in which your issue is grounded, you need to conduct some research before preparing your argument; consulting even a few sources can help. For example, the student whose paper appears on pages 74–76 became more knowledgeable about his issue — the ethics of performance-enhancing procedures in sports — after consulting a few brief sources.

A2-b View your audience as a panel of jurors.

Do not assume that your audience already agrees with you; instead, envision skeptical readers who, like a panel of jurors, will make up their minds after listening to all sides of the argument. If you are arguing a public policy issue, aim your paper at readers who represent a variety of opinions. In the case of the debate over nuclear power, for example, imagine a jury representative of those who have a stake in the matter: environmentalists, nuclear industry officials, and consumers.

At times, you can deliberately narrow your audience. If you are working within a word limit, for example, you might not have the space in which to address the concerns of all parties to the nuclear energy debate. Or you might be primarily interested in reaching one segment of a general audience, such as consumers. In such instances, you can still view your audience as a panel of jurors; the jury will simply be a less diverse group.

In the case of scholarly debates, you will be addressing readers who share your interest in a discipline such as literature or psychology. Such readers belong to a group with an agreed-upon way of investigating and talking about issues. Though they generally agree about procedures, scholars in an academic discipline often disagree about particular issues. Once you see how they disagree about your issue, you should be able to imagine a jury that reflects the variety of opinions they hold.

A2-c In your introduction, establish credibility and state your position.

When you construct an argument, make sure your introduction contains a thesis sentence that states your position on the issue you have chosen to debate (see also C2-a). In the sentences leading up to the thesis, establish your credibility with readers by showing that you are knowledgeable and fair-minded. If possible, build common ground with readers who may not be in initial agreement with your views and show them why they need to consider your thesis.

In the following introduction, student Kevin Smith presents himself as someone worth listening to. His opening sentence shows that he is familiar with the legal issues surrounding school prayer. His next sentence reveals him to be fair-minded, as he presents the views of both sides. Even Smith's thesis builds common ground: "Prayer is too important to be trusted to our public schools." Because Smith introduces both sides of the debate, readers are likely to approach his essay with an open mind.

> Although the US Supreme Court has ruled against prayer in public schools on First Amendment grounds, many people still feel that prayer should be allowed. Such people value prayer as a practice central to their faith and believe that prayer is a way for schools to reinforce moral principles. They also compellingly point out a paradox in the First Amendment itself: at what point does the separation of church and state restrict the freedom of those who wish to practise their religion? What proponents of school prayer fail to realize, however, is that the Supreme Court's decision, although it was made on legal grounds, makes sense on religious grounds as well. Prayer is too important to be trusted to the public schools.
>
> — Kevin Smith, student

A good way to test a thesis while drafting and revising is to imagine a counterargument to your argument (see A2-f). If you can't think of an opposing point of view, rethink your thesis or ask friends or classmates to respond to your argument.

A2-d Back up your thesis with persuasive lines of argument.

Arguments of any complexity contain lines of argument that, when taken together, might reasonably persuade readers that the thesis has merit. Here, for example, are the main lines of argument used by a student whose thesis was that athletes' use of biotechnology could constitute an unfair advantage in sports.

> Thesis: Athletes who use any type of biotechnology give themselves an unfair advantage and disrupt the sense of fair play, and they should be banned from competition.
>
> - Athletic achievement nowadays increasingly results from biological and high-tech intervention rather than strictly from hard work.
> - There is a difference between the use of state-of-the-art equipment and drugs and the modification of the body itself.
> - If the rules that guarantee an even playing field are violated, competitors and spectators alike are deprived of a sound basis of comparison on which to judge athletic effort and accomplishment.
> - If we let athletes alter their bodies through biotechnology, we might as well dispense with the human element altogether.

If you sum up your main lines of argument, you will have a rough outline of your essay. The outline will consist of your central claim — the thesis — and any supporting claims that back it up. In your paper, you will provide evidence for each of these claims.

ON THE WEB > **dianahacker.com/writersref**
Resources for writers and tutors > Tips from writing tutors: Writing arguments; Writing essays in English

A2-e Support your claims with specific evidence.

You will need to support your central claim and any subordinate claims with evidence: facts, statistics, examples and illustrations, expert opinion, and so on. Most debatable topics require that you consult some written sources to gather evidence. Always cite your sources. Documentation gives credit to the authors and shows readers how to locate a source in case they want to assess its credibility or explore the issue further (see R4).

Using facts and statistics

A fact is something that is known with certainty because it has been objectively verified: The capital of Nunavut is Iqaluit. Carbon has an atomic weight of 12. John F. Kennedy was assassinated on November 22, 1963. Statistics are collections of numerical facts: Alcohol abuse is a factor in nearly 40 percent of traffic deaths. Almost seven out of ten Canadian households own a DVD player. As of 2005, about 12 percent of board seats in the top five hundred Canadian companies were held by women.

Most arguments are supported at least to some extent by facts and statistics. For example, in the following passage the writer uses statistics to show that college students are granted unreasonably high credit limits.

> A 2001 study by Nellie Mae revealed that while the average credit card debt per college undergraduate is $2,327, more than 20% of undergraduates who have at least one credit card maintain a much higher debt level, from $3,000 to $7,000 (Barrett).

Writers and politicians often use statistics in selective ways to bolster their views. If you suspect that a writer's handling of statistics is not quite fair, read authors with opposing views, who may give you a fuller understanding of the numbers.

Using examples and illustrations

Examples and illustrations (extended examples, often in story form) rarely prove a point by themselves, but when used in combination with other forms of evidence they flesh out an argument and bring it to life. Because examples often are vivid, they can reach readers in ways that statistics cannot.

In a paper arguing that any athletes who use gene therapy should be banned from competition, Jamal Hammond gives a thought-provoking example of how running with genetically modified limbs is no different from riding a motorcycle in a footrace.

Citing expert opinion

Although they are no substitute for careful reasoning of your own, the views of an expert can contribute to the force of your argument. For example, to help him make the case that biotechnology could degrade the meaning of sports, Jamal Hammond quotes the remarks of an expert:

> Thomas Murray, chair of the ethics advisory panel for the World Anti-Doping Agency, says he hopes, not too optimistically, for an "alternative future . . . where we still find meaning in great performances as an alchemy of two factors, natural talents . . . and virtues" (qtd. in Jenkins D11).

When you rely on expert opinion, make sure that your source is an authority in the field you are writing about. In some cases you may need to provide credentials showing why your source is worth listening to. When including expert testimony in your paper, you can summarize or paraphrase the expert's opinion or you can quote the expert's exact words. You will of course need to document the source, as in the example just given (see R4).

A2-f Anticipate objections; counter opposing arguments.

Readers who already agree with you need no convincing, although most welcome a well-argued case for their position on an issue. Indifferent or skeptical readers, however, may resist an argument that conflicts with their point of view. In addition to presenting your own case, therefore, you should acknowledge opposing arguments and any contradictory evidence and explain why your position is stronger.

Countering opposing arguments

To anticipate a possible objection, consider the following questions:

- Could a reasonable person draw a different conclusion from your facts or examples?
- Might a reader question any of your assumptions?
- Could a reader offer an alternative explanation of this issue?

To respond to a potential objection, consider these questions:

- Can you concede the point to the opposition but challenge the point's importance or usefulness?
- Can you explain why readers should consider a new perspective or question a piece of evidence?
- Should you qualify your position in light of contradictory evidence?
- Can you suggest a different interpretation of the evidence?

When you write, use phrasing to signal to readers that you're about to present an objection. Often the signal phrase can go in the lead sentence of a paragraph:

- Critics of this view argue that. . . .
- Some readers might point out that. . . .
- Gray presents compelling challenges to. . . .
- But isn't it possible that . . . ?

There is no best place in an essay to deal with opposing views. Often it is useful to summarize the opposing position early in your essay. After stating your thesis but before developing your own arguments, you might have a paragraph that takes up the most important counterargument. Or you can anticipate objections paragraph by paragraph as you develop your case. Wherever you decide to address opposing points of view, explain the arguments of others accurately and fairly.

A2-g Build common ground.

As you counter opposing arguments, try to build common ground with readers who do not initially agree with your views. If you can show that you share your readers' values, they may be able to switch to your position without giving up what they feel is important. For example, to persuade people opposed to shooting deer, a provincial wildlife commission would have to show that it too cares about preserving deer and does not want them to die needlessly. Having established these values in common, the commission might be able to persuade critics that a carefully controlled hunting season is good for the deer population because it prevents starvation caused by overpopulation.

People believe that intelligence and decency support their side of an argument. To change sides, they must continue to feel intelligent and decent. Otherwise they will persist in their opposition.

A2-h Sample argument paper

In the following paper, student Jamal Hammond argues that we should ban the use of biotechnology by athletes because the practice degrades the values of hard work and natural ability. Notice that he is careful to present opposing views fairly before providing his counterarguments.

In writing the paper, Hammond consulted three newspaper articles, two in print and one online. When he quotes or uses information from a source, he cites the source with an MLA (Modern Language Association) in-text citation. Citations in the paper refer readers to the list of works cited at the end of the paper. (See MLA-4.)

ON THE WEB > **dianahacker.com/writersref**
Model papers > MLA papers: Orlov; Daly; Levi

Hammond 1

Jamal Hammond

Professor Paschal

English 102

17 March 2006

Performance Enhancement through Biotechnology
Has No Place in Sports

Opening sentences provide background for Hammond's thesis.

The debate over athletes' use of performance-enhancing substances is getting more complicated as biotechnologies such as gene therapy become a reality. The availability of these new methods of boosting performance will force us to decide what we value most in sports--displays of physical excellence developed through hard work or victory at all costs. For centuries, spectators and athletes have cherished the tradition of fairness in sports. While sports competition is, of course, largely about winning, it is also about the means by which a player or team wins. Athletes who use any type of biotechnology give themselves an unfair advantage and disrupt the sense of fair play, and they should be banned from competition.

Thesis states the main point.

Researchers are experimenting with techniques that could manipulate an athlete's genetic code to build stronger muscles or increase endurance. Searching for cures for diseases like Parkinson's and muscular dystrophy, scientists at the University of Pennsylvania have created "Schwarzenegger mice," rodents that grew larger-than-normal muscles after receiving injections with a gene that stimulates growth protein. The researchers also found that a combination of gene manipulation and exercise led to a 35% increase in the strength of rats' leg muscles (Lamb 13).

Hammond establishes his credibility by summarizing medical research.

Source is cited in MLA style.

Such therapies are breakthroughs for humans suffering from muscular diseases; for healthy athletes, they could mean new world records in sports involving speed and endurance--but at what cost to the integrity of athletic competition? The International Olympic Committee's World Anti-Doping Agency has become so alarmed about the possible effects of new gene technology on athletic competition that it has banned the use of gene therapies and urged researchers to devise a test for detecting genetic modification (Lamb 13).

Hammond uses specific evidence to support his thesis.

Marginal annotations indicate MLA-style formatting and effective writing.

Hammond 2

Some bioethicists argue that this next wave of performance enhancement is an acceptable and unavoidable feature of competition. As Dr. Andy Miah, who supports the regulated use of gene therapies in sports, claims, "The idea of the naturally perfect athlete is romantic nonsense. . . . An athlete achieves what he or she achieves through all sorts of means--technology, sponsorship, support and so on" (qtd. in Rudebeck). Miah, in fact, sees athletes' imminent turn to genetic modification as "merely a continuation of the way sport works; it allows us to create more extraordinary performances" (Rudebeck). Miah's approval of "extraordinary performances" as the goal of competition reflects our culture's tendency to demand and reward new heights of athletic achievement. The problem is that achievement nowadays increasingly results from biological and high-tech intervention rather than strictly from hard work.

Opposing views are presented fairly.

"Qtd. in" is used for an indirect source: words quoted in another source.

Hammond counters opposing arguments.

Better equipment, such as aerodynamic bicycles and fiberglass poles for pole vaulting, have made it possible for athletes to record achievements unthinkable a generation ago. But athletes themselves must put forth the physical effort of training and practice--they must still build their skills--even in the murky area of legal and illegal drug use (Jenkins D11). There is a difference between the use of state-of-the-art equipment and drugs and the modification of the body itself. Athletes who use medical technology to alter their bodies can bypass the hard work of training by taking on the powers of a machine. If they set new records this way, we lose the opportunity to witness sports as a spectacle of human effort and are left marveling at scientific advances, which have little relation to the athletic tradition of fair play.

Hammond develops the thesis.

Such a tradition has long defined athletic competition. Sports rely on equal conditions to ensure fair play, from regulations that demand similar equipment to referees who evenhandedly apply the rules to all participants. If the rules that guarantee an even playing field are violated, competitors and spectators alike are deprived of a sound basis of comparison on which to judge athletic effort and accomplishment. When major league baseball rules call for solid-wood bats, the player who uses a corked bat enhances his hitting statistics at the expense of players who use regulation equipment. When Ben Johnson tested

Transition moves from the writer's main argument to specific examples.

Hammond 3

positive for steroids after setting a world record in the 100-meter dash in the 1988 Olympics, his "achievement" devalued the intense training that his competitors had undergone to prepare for the event--and the International Olympic Committee responded by stripping Johnson of his medal and his world record. Likewise, athletes who use gene therapy to alter their bodies and enhance their performance will create an uneven playing field.

A vivid example helps the writer make his point.

If we let athletes alter their bodies through biotechnology, we might as well dispense with the human element altogether. Instead of watching the 100-meter dash to see who the fastest runner in the world is, we might just as well watch the sprinters mount motorcycles and race across the finish line. The absurdity of such an example, however, points to the damage that we will do to sports if we allow these therapies. Thomas Murray, chair of the ethics advisory panel for the World Anti-Doping Agency, says he hopes, not too optimistically, for an "alternative future . . . where we still find meaning in great performances as an alchemy of two factors, natural talents . . . and virtues" (qtd. in Jenkins D11).

Conclusion echoes the thesis without dully repeating it.

Unless we are willing to organize separate sporting events and leagues--an Olympics, say, for athletes who have opted for a boost from the test tube and another for athletes who have chosen to keep their bodies natural--we should ask from our athletes that they dazzle us less with extraordinary performance and more with the fruits of their hard work.

Hammond 4

Works cited page uses MLA style.

Works Cited

Jenkins, Sally. "The First Item in a Pandora's Box of Moral Ambiguities." Washington Post 4 Dec. 2004: D11.

Lamb, Gregory M. "Will Gene-Altered Athletes Kill Sports?" Christian Science Monitor 23 Aug. 2004: 12-13.

Rudebeck, Clare. "The Eyes Have It." Independent [London] 27 Apr. 2005. 28 Feb. 2006 <http://news.independent.co.uk/world/science_technology/article3597.ece>.

A3

Evaluating arguments

In your reading and in your own writing, evaluate all arguments for logic and fairness. Many arguments can stand up to critical scrutiny. Often, however, a line of argument that at first seems reasonable turns out to be fallacious, unfair, or both.

ON THE WEB > **dianahacker.com/writersref**
Additional resources > Links Library > Critical thinking

A3-a Distinguish between reasonable and fallacious argumentative tactics.

A number of unreasonable argumentative tactics are known as *logical fallacies*. Most of the fallacies — such as hasty generalizations and false analogies — are misguided or dishonest uses of legitimate argumentative strategies. The examples in this section suggest when such strategies are reasonable and when they are not.

Generalizing (inductive reasoning)

Writers and thinkers generalize all the time. We look at a sample of data and conclude that data we have not observed will most likely conform to what we have seen before. From a spoonful of soup, we conclude just how salty the whole bowl will be. After numerous bad experiences with an airline, we decide to book future flights with one of its competitors instead.

When we draw a conclusion from an array of facts, we are engaged in inductive reasoning. Such reasoning deals in probability, not certainty. For a conclusion to be highly probable, it must be based on evidence that is sufficient, representative, and relevant. (See the chart on p. 79.)

The fallacy known as *hasty generalization* is a conclusion based on insufficient or unrepresentative evidence.

HASTY GENERALIZATION

Deaths from drug overdoses in Vancouver have doubled in the past three years. Therefore, more Canadians than ever are dying from drug abuse.

Data from one city do not justify a conclusion about the whole of Canada.

A *stereotype* is a hasty generalization about a group. Here are a few examples.

STEREOTYPES

Women are bad bosses.

Politicians are corrupt.

Asian students are exceptionally intelligent.

Stereotyping is common because of our human tendency to perceive selectively. We tend to see what we want to see; that is, we notice evidence confirming our already formed opinions and fail to notice evidence to the contrary. For example, if you have concluded that politicians are corrupt, your stereotype will be confirmed by news reports of legislators being indicted — even though every day the media describe conscientious officials serving the public honestly and well.

NOTE: Many hasty generalizations contain words like *all*, *ever*, *always*, and *never*, when qualifiers such as *most*, *many*, *usually*, and *seldom* would be more accurate.

Drawing analogies

An analogy points out a similarity between two things that are otherwise different. Analogies can be an effective means of arguing a point. In fact, our system of case law, which relies heavily on precedents, makes extensive use of reasoning by analogy. A prosecutor may argue, for example, that Z is guilty because his actions resemble those of X and Y, who were judged guilty in previous rulings. In response, the defence may maintain that the actions of Z bear only a superficial resemblance to those of X and Y and that in legally relevant respects they are in fact quite different.

It is not always easy to draw the line between a reasonable and an unreasonable analogy. At times, however, an analogy is clearly off-base, in which case it is called a *false analogy*.

FALSE ANALOGY

If we can put humans on the moon, we should be able to find a cure for the common cold.

The writer has falsely assumed that because two things are alike in one respect, they must be alike in others. Putting human beings on the moon and finding a cure for the common cold are both scientific

Testing inductive reasoning

Though inductive reasoning leads to probable and not absolute truth, you can assess a conclusion's likely probability by asking three questions. This chart shows how to apply those questions to a sample conclusion based on a survey.

CONCLUSION The majority of students on our campus would subscribe to wireless Internet access if it were available.

EVIDENCE In a recent survey, 923 of 1515 students questioned say they would subscribe to wireless Internet access.

1. Is the evidence sufficient?
   That depends. On a small campus (say, 3000 students), the pool of students surveyed would be sufficient for market research, but on a large campus (say, 30 000), 1515 students are only 5 percent of the population. If that 5 percent were known to be truly representative of the other 95 percent, however, even such a small sample would be sufficient (see question 2).
2. Is the evidence representative?
   The evidence is representative if those responding to the survey reflect the characteristics of the entire student population: age, sex, level of technical expertise, amount of disposable income, and so on. If most of those surveyed are majoring in technical fields, for example, the researchers would be wise to question the survey's conclusion.
3. Is the evidence relevant?
   The answer is yes. The results of the survey are directly linked to the conclusion. A question about the number of hours spent on the Internet, by contrast, would not be relevant, because it would not be about *subscribing to wireless Internet access*.

challenges, but the technical problems confronting medical researchers are quite different from those solved by space scientists.

Tracing causes and effects

Demonstrating a connection between causes and effects is rarely a simple matter. For example, to explain why a chemistry course has a high failure rate, you would begin by listing possible causes: inadequate preparation of students, poor teaching, large class size, lack of qualified tutors, and so on. Next you would investigate each possible cause. To see whether inadequate preparation contributes to the high failure rate, for instance, you might compare the math and science backgrounds of successful and failing students. To see whether large class size is a contributing factor, you might run a pilot program of small classes and compare grades in the small classes with those in the larger ones. Only after investigating the possible causes would you be able to weigh the relative impact of each cause and suggest appropriate remedies.

Because cause-and-effect reasoning is so complex, it is not surprising that writers frequently oversimplify it. In particular, writers sometimes assume that because one event follows another, the first is the cause of the second. This common fallacy is known as *post hoc*, from the Latin *post hoc, ergo propter hoc*, meaning "after this, therefore because of this."

***POST HOC* FALLACY**

Since Mayor Cho took office, unemployment of minorities in the city has decreased by 7 percent. Mayor Cho should be applauded for reducing unemployment among minorities.

The writer must show that Mayor Cho's policies are responsible for the decrease in unemployment; it is not enough to show that the decrease followed the mayor's taking office.

Weighing options

Especially when reasoning about problems and solutions, writers must weigh options. To be fair, a writer should mention the full range of options, showing why one is superior to the others or might work well in combination with others.

It is unfair to suggest that there are only two alternatives when in fact there are more. Writers who set up a false choice between their preferred option and one that is clearly unsatisfactory are guilty of the *either . . . or* fallacy.

***EITHER . . . OR* FALLACY**

Our current war against drugs has not worked. Either we should legalize drugs or we should turn the drug war over to our armed forces and let them fight it.

Clearly there are other options, such as increased funding for drug prevention and treatment.

Making assumptions

An assumption is a claim that is taken to be true — without the need of proof. Most arguments are based to some extent on assumptions, since writers rarely have the time and space to prove all of the conceivable claims on which an argument is based. For example, someone arguing about the best means of limiting population growth in developing countries might well assume that the goal of limiting population growth is worthwhile. For most audiences, there would be no need to articulate this assumption or to defend it.

There is a danger, however, in failing to spell out and prove a claim that is clearly controversial. Consider the following short argument, in which a key claim is missing.

ARGUMENT WITH MISSING CLAIM

Violent crime is increasing.

Therefore, we should reintroduce the death penalty.

The writer seems to be assuming that the death penalty deters violent criminals — and that most audiences will agree. Obviously, neither is a safe assumption.

When a missing claim is an assertion that few would agree with, we say that a writer is guilty of a *non sequitur* (Latin for "does not follow").

NON SEQUITUR

Mariko loves good food; therefore, she will be an excellent chef.

Few people would agree with the missing claim — that lovers of good food always make excellent chefs.

Deducing conclusions (deductive reasoning)

When we deduce a conclusion, we — like Sherlock Holmes — put things together. We establish that a general principle is true, that a specific case is an example of that principle, and that therefore a particular conclusion is a certainty. In real life, such absolute reasoning rarely happens. Approximations of it, however, sometimes occur.

Deductive reasoning can often be structured in a three-step argument called a *syllogism*. The three steps are the major premise, the minor premise, and the conclusion.

1. Anything that increases radiation in the environment is dangerous to public health. (Major premise)
2. Nuclear reactors increase radiation in the environment. (Minor premise)
3. Therefore, nuclear reactors are dangerous to public health. (Conclusion)

The major premise is a generalization. The minor premise is a specific case. The conclusion follows from applying the generalization to the specific case.

Deductive arguments break down if one of the premises is not true or if the conclusion does not logically follow from the premises. In the following short argument, the major premise is very likely untrue.

ARGUMENT WITH A QUESTIONABLE PREMISE

The police do not give speeding tickets to people driving less than eight kilometres per hour over the limit. Sam is driving ninety-five kilometres per hour in a ninety kilometre-per-hour zone. Therefore, the police will not give Sam a speeding ticket.

The conclusion is true only if the premises are true. If the police sometimes give tickets for less than eight-kilometre-per-hour violations, Sam cannot safely conclude that he will avoid a ticket.

In the following argument, both premises might be true, but the conclusion does not follow logically from them.

CONCLUSION DOES NOT FOLLOW

All members of our club ran in this year's Royal Victoria Marathon. Jay ran in this year's Royal Victoria Marathon. Therefore, Jay is a member of our club.

The fact that Jay ran the marathon is no guarantee that he is a member of the club. Presumably, many runners are nonmembers.

Assuming that both premises are true, the following argument holds up.

CONCLUSION FOLLOWS

All members of our club ran in this year's Royal Victoria Marathon. Jay is a member of our club. Therefore, Jay ran in this year's Royal Victoria Marathon.

A3-b Distinguish between legitimate and unfair emotional appeals.

There is nothing wrong with appealing to readers' emotions. After all, many issues worth arguing about have an emotional as well as a logical dimension. Even the Greek logician Aristotle lists *pathos* (emotion) as a legitimate argumentative tactic. For example, in an essay criticizing big-box stores, writer Betsy Taylor has a good reason for tugging at readers' emotions: Her subject is the decline of city and town life. In her conclusion, Taylor appeals to readers' emotions by invoking their national pride.

LEGITIMATE EMOTIONAL APPEAL

Is it anti-American to be against having a retail giant set up shop in one's community? Some people would say so. On the other hand, if you board up Main Street, what's left of America?

As we all know, however, emotional appeals are frequently misused. Many of the arguments we see in the media, for instance, strive to win our sympathy rather than our intelligent agreement. A TV commercial suggesting that you will be thin and sexy if you drink a certain diet beverage is making a pitch to emotions. So is a political speech that recommends electing a candidate because he is a devoted husband and father who serves as a volunteer firefighter.

The following passage illustrates several types of unfair emotional appeals.

UNFAIR EMOTIONAL APPEALS

> This progressive proposal to build a ski resort has been carefully researched by RBC, the largest bank in the province; furthermore, it is favoured by a majority of the local merchants. The only opposition comes from narrow-minded, do-gooder environmentalists who care more about trees than they do about people; one of their leaders was actually arrested for disturbing the peace several years ago.

Words with strong positive or negative connotations, such as *progressive* and *do-gooder*, are examples of *biased language*. Attacking the persons who hold a belief (environmentalists) rather than refuting their argument is called *ad hominem*, a Latin term meaning "to the man." Associating a prestigious name (RBC) with the writer's side is called *transfer*. Claiming that an idea should be accepted because a large number of people are in favour (the majority of merchants) is called the *bandwagon appeal*. Bringing in irrelevant issues (the arrest) is a *red herring*, named after a trick used in fox hunts to mislead the dogs by dragging a smelly fish across the trail.

A3-c Judge how fairly a writer handles opposing views.

The way in which a writer deals with opposing views is telling. Some writers address the arguments of the opposition fairly, conceding points when necessary and countering others, all in a civil spirit. Other writers will do almost anything to win an argument: either ignoring opposing views altogether or misrepresenting such views and attacking their proponents.

In your own writing, you build credibility by addressing opposing arguments fairly. (See also A2-f.) In your reading, you can assess the credibility of your sources by looking at how they deal with views not in agreement with their own.

Describing the views of others

Writers and politicians often deliberately misrepresent the views of others. One way they do this is by setting up a "straw man," a character so weak that he is easily knocked down. The *straw man* fallacy consists of an oversimplification or outright distortion of opposing views. For example, in a debate over attempts to control the cougar population in British Columbia, pro-cougar groups characterized their opponents as trophy hunters bent on shooting harmless cougars and sticking them on the walls of their dens. In truth, such hunters were only one faction of those who saw a need to control the cougar population.

In response to the District of Columbia's request for voting representation, some politicians have set up a straw man, as shown in the following example.

> **STRAW MAN FALLACY**
>
> Washington, DC, residents are lobbying for statehood. Giving a city such as the District of Columbia the status of a state would be unfair.

The straw man wants statehood. In fact, most District citizens are lobbying for voting representation in any form, not necessarily through statehood.

Quoting opposing views

Writers often quote the words of writers who hold opposing views. In general, this is a good idea, for it assures some level of fairness and accuracy. At times, though, both the fairness and accuracy are an illusion.

A source may be misrepresented when it is quoted out of context. All quotations are to some extent taken out of context, but a fair writer will explain the context to readers. To select a provocative sentence from a source and to ignore the more moderate sentences surrounding it is both unfair and misleading. Sometimes a writer deliberately distorts a source through the device of ellipsis dots. Ellipsis dots tell readers that words have been omitted from the original source (see P7-g). When those words are crucial to an author's meaning, omitting them is obviously unfair.

> **ORIGINAL SOURCE**
>
> Johnson's *History of the American West* is riddled with inaccuracies and astonishing in its blatantly racist description of the Indian wars.
>
> — B. Smith, reviewer

MISLEADING QUOTATION

According to B. Smith, Johnson's *History of the American West* is "astonishing in its . . . description of the Indian wars."

A4

Writing in the disciplines

College and university courses expose you to the thinking of scholars in many disciplines, such as the humanities (literature, music, art), the social sciences (psychology, anthropology, sociology), and the sciences (biology, physics, chemistry). Writing in any discipline provides the opportunity to practise the methods used by scholars in these fields and to enter into their debates. Each field has its own questions, evidence, language, and conventions, but all disciplines share certain expectations for good writing.

A4-a Find commonalities across disciplines.

A good paper in any field needs to communicate a writer's purpose to an audience and to explore an engaging question about a subject (see C1-a). All effective writers make an argument and support their claims with evidence (see A2-e). Writers in any field need to show readers the thesis they're developing (or, in the sciences, the hypothesis they're testing) and how they counter opposing explanations or objections of other writers (see A2-f). All disciplines require writers to document where they found their evidence and from whom they borrowed ideas (see A4-e).

A4-b Recognize the questions writers in a discipline ask.

Disciplines are characterized by the kinds of questions their scholars attempt to answer. One way to understand how disciplines ask different questions is to look at assignments on the same topic in various fields. Many disciplines, for example, might be interested in cults. The questions on the next page show how writers in different fields approach the topic of cults.

SOCIOLOGY	What role does gender play in cult leadership?
HISTORY	Why did the cult of Caesar take hold in ancient Rome?
FILM	How does the movie *Fight Club* portray contemporary cults?
BIOLOGY	Do individuals susceptible to cult influence share genetic characteristics?
BUSINESS	How do multilevel marketing (MLM) practices depend on cult techniques for their success?

The questions you will ask in any discipline will form the basis of the thesis for your paper. Questions themselves don't communicate a central idea, but they may lead you to one. For example, the historian who asks "Why did the cult of Caesar take hold in ancient Rome?" might work out a thesis like this: *By raising Caesar to the status of a deity, imperial Rome attempted to unify the various peoples in its far-flung realm into one cult of worship centred on the emperor.*

A4-c Understand the kinds of evidence writers in a discipline use.

Regardless of the discipline in which you're writing, you must support any claims you make with evidence — facts, statistics, examples and illustrations, expert opinion, and so on.

The kinds of evidence used in different disciplines commonly overlap. Students of geography, media studies, and political science, for example, all might use census data to explore different topics. The evidence that one discipline values, however, might not be sufficient to support an interpretation or a conclusion in another field. For example, psychologists, who look for evidence in case studies and in the results of experiments, seldom use expert opinion as evidence. The chart at the top of the next page lists the kinds of evidence typically used in various disciplines.

A4-d Become familiar with a discipline's language conventions.

Every discipline has a specialized vocabulary. As you read the articles and books in a field, you'll notice certain words and phrases that come up repeatedly. Sociologists, for example, use terms like

Evidence typically used in various disciplines

Humanities: Literature, art, film, music, philosophy

- Passages of text or lines of a poem
- Details from an image or a work of art
- Passages of a musical composition
- Essays that analyze original works or put forth theories

Humanities: History

- Firsthand sources such as photographs, letters, maps, and government documents
- Scholarly books and articles that interpret evidence

Social sciences: Psychology, sociology, political science, anthropology

- Data from original experiments
- Results of field research such as interviews, observations, or surveys
- Statistics from government agencies
- Scholarly books and articles that interpret data from original experiments and from other researchers' studies

Sciences: Biology, chemistry, physics

- Data from original experiments
- Scholarly articles that report findings from experiments

independent variables, *political opportunity resources*, and *dyads* to describe social phenomena; computer scientists might refer to *algorithm design* and *loop invariants* to describe programming methods. Practitioners in health fields such as nursing use terms like *treatment plan* and *systemic assessment* to describe patient care. Use discipline-specific terms only when you are certain that you and your readers fully understand their meaning.

In addition to vocabulary, many fields of study have developed specialized conventions for point of view and verb tense. See the chart on the next page.

A4-e Use a discipline's preferred citation style.

In any discipline, you must give credit to those whose ideas or words you have borrowed. Avoid plagiarism by citing sources honestly and accurately (see R4).

Point of view and verb tense in academic writing

Point of view

- Writers of analytical or research essays in the humanities usually use the third-person point of view: *Austen presents* . . . or *Castel describes the battle as*. . . .
- Scientists and most social scientists, who depend on quantitative research to present findings, tend to use the third-person point of view: *The results indicated*. . . .
- Writers in the humanities and in some social sciences occasionally use the first person in discussing their personal experience or in writing a personal narrative: *After spending two years interviewing families affected by the war, I began to understand that* . . . or *Every July as we approached the Bay of Fundy, we could sense*. . . .

Present or past tense

- Literature scholars use the present tense to discuss a text: *Hughes effectively dramatizes different views of minority assertiveness.* (See MLA-3.)
- Science and social science writers use the past tense to describe experiments and the present tense to discuss the findings: *In 2003, Berkowitz released the first double-blind placebo study. . . . These results paint a murky picture.* (See APA-3.)
- Writers in history use the present tense or the present perfect tense to discuss a text: *Shelby Foote describes the scene like this* . . . or *Shelby Foote has described the scene like this*. . . . (See CMS-3.)

While all disciplines emphasize careful documentation, each follows a particular system of citation that its members have agreed on. Writers in the humanities usually use the system established by the Modern Language Association (MLA). Scholars in some social sciences, such as psychology and anthropology, follow the style guidelines of the American Psychological Association (APA); scholars in history and some humanities typically follow *The Chicago Manual of Style*. For guidance on using the MLA, APA, or *Chicago* (CMS) format, see MLA-4, APA-4, or CMS-4, respectively.

Approaching assignments in the disciplines

When you receive a writing assignment, look for key terms that alert you to the purpose of the assignment and to the specialized language of the field. Also determine the kinds of evidence that would be appropriate to support your argument. At first glance, the following four assignments might seem to have nothing in common. A closer look will show that they all use key terms specific to the field, they all use the vocabulary of the field to describe the purpose of the assignment, and they all explain or suggest the kinds of evidence the writers should use.

Environmental science

The El Niño Southern Oscillation (ENSO) is a worldwide climatic oscillation. Evaluate the scientific issues involved in enhancing our ability to predict ENSO events and current limitations to our forecasting ability. Use scientific papers, abstracts, review articles, and course readings to support your conclusions.

1. Key terms
2. Purpose: to summarize and analyze research findings
3. Appropriate evidence: articles, visuals, especially conflicting data

Business

Develop a position in response to the following question: Do corporate takeovers create or destroy value? To determine how these value changes come about, analyze case studies and Ontario Securities Commission documents.

1. Key terms
2. Purpose: to analyze certain evidence and to argue a position based on that analysis
3. Appropriate evidence: examples of corporate takeovers

→

Approaching assignments in the disciplines (continued)

Anthropology

Compare and contrast the male rites of passage among the Sambia of New Guinea and the Maasai of southern Kenya. Consult ethnographic descriptions of Sambian and Maasai rituals in course readings.

1. Key terms
2. Purpose: to analyze similarities and differences
3. Appropriate evidence: anthropologists' field research

Nursing

Compile a detailed, objective health history for a member of your family. Use interview notes and any available health records to build the patient history.

1. Key term
2. Purpose: to record information
3. Appropriate evidence: interviews, relevant health records

Once you have determined the expectations of a writing assignment, you must be sure to do the following, regardless of the discipline you are writing in.

- Determine your audience and purpose (see C1-a).
- Ask questions appropriate to the field (see A4-b).
- Formulate a thesis (see C2-a).
- Gather evidence. Conduct research if necessary (see R1).
- Identify the required citation style (see R4).

S

Sentence Style

S Sentence Style

S1

Parallelism

If two or more ideas are parallel, they are easier to grasp when expressed in parallel grammatical form. Single words should be balanced with single words, phrases with phrases, clauses with clauses.

> A kiss can be a comma, a question mark, or an exclamation point.
>
> —Mistinguett

> This novel is not to be tossed lightly aside, but to be hurled with great force.
>
> —Dorothy Parker

> In matters of principle, stand like a rock; in matters of taste, swim with the current.
>
> —Thomas Jefferson

GRAMMAR CHECKERS only occasionally flag faulty parallelism. Because the programs cannot assess whether ideas are parallel in grammatical form, they fail to catch the faulty parallelism in sentences such as this: *In my high school, boys were either jocks, preppies, or studied constantly.*

S1-a Balance parallel ideas in a series.

Readers expect items in a series to appear in parallel grammatical form. When one or more of the items violate readers' expectations, a sentence will be needlessly awkward.

► **Abused children commonly exhibit one or more of the following symptoms: withdrawal, rebelliousness, restlessness, and** *depression.* ~~**they are depressed.**~~

The revision presents all of the items as nouns.

▶ **Hooked on romance novels, I learned that nothing is more important than being rich, looking good, and ~~to have~~ *having* a good time.**

The revision uses *-ing* forms for all items in the series.

▶ **After assuring us that he was sober, Sam drove down the middle of the road, ran one red light, and *went through* two stop signs.**

The revision adds a verb to make the three items parallel: *drove . . . , ran . . . , went through. . . .*

NOTE: For parallelism in headings and lists, see C5-b and C5-c.

S1-b Balance parallel ideas presented as pairs.

When pairing ideas, underscore their connection by expressing them in similar grammatical form. Paired ideas are usually connected in one of these ways:

- with a coordinating conjunction such as *and, but,* or *or*
- with a pair of correlative conjunctions such as *either . . . or* or *not only . . . but also*
- with a word introducing a comparison, usually *than* or *as*

Parallel ideas linked with coordinating conjunctions

Coordinating conjunctions (*and, but, or, nor, for, so,* and *yet*) link ideas of equal importance. When those ideas are closely parallel in content, they should be expressed in parallel grammatical form.

▶ **At Cedarbrae Collegiate, vandalism can result in suspension or even ~~being expelled~~ *expulsion* from school.**

The revision balances the nouns *suspension* and *expulsion.*

▶ **Many cities are reducing property taxes for home owners and ~~extend~~ *extending* financial aid in the form of tax credits to renters.**

The revision balances the *-ing* verb forms *reducing* and *extending.*

Parallel ideas linked with correlative conjunctions

Correlative conjunctions come in pairs: *either . . . or, neither . . . nor, not only . . . but also, both . . . and, whether . . . or.* Make sure that the grammatical structure following the second half of the pair is the same as that following the first half.

▶ **Alexander Graham Bell was not only a prolific inventor but also ~~was~~ a devoted educator.**

A prolific inventor follows *not only,* so *a devoted educator* should follow *but also.* Repeating *was* creates an unbalanced effect.

▶ **The clerk told me either to change my flight or** *to* **take the train.**

To change my flight, which follows *either,* should be balanced with *to take the train,* which follows *or.*

Comparisons linked with than *or* as

In comparisons linked with *than* or *as,* the elements being compared should be expressed in parallel grammatical structure.

▶ **It is easier to speak in abstractions than ~~grounding~~** *to ground* **one's thoughts in reality.**

▶ **Mother could not persuade me that giving is as much a joy as ~~to receive.~~** *receiving.*

To speak in abstractions is balanced with *to ground one's thoughts in reality. Giving* is balanced with *receiving.*

NOTE: Comparisons should also be logical and complete. See S2-c.

S1-c Repeat function words to clarify parallels.

Function words such as prepositions (*by, to*) and subordinating conjunctions (*that, because*) signal the grammatical nature of the word groups to follow. Although they can sometimes be omitted, include them whenever they signal parallel structures that might otherwise be missed by readers.

▶ **Many hooked smokers try switching to a brand they find distasteful or** *to* **a low tar and nicotine cigarette.**

In the original sentence, the prepositional phrase was too complex for easy reading. The repetition of the preposition *to* prevents readers from losing their way.

ON THE WEB > **dianahacker.com/writersref**
Grammar exercises > Sentence style > E-ex S1–1 through S1–3

S2

Needed words

Do not omit words necessary for grammatical or logical completeness. Readers need to see at a glance how the parts of a sentence are connected.

Languages sometimes differ in the need for certain words. In particular, be alert for missing articles, verbs, subjects, or expletives. See E3, E2-a, and E2-b.

GRAMMAR CHECKERS do not flag the vast majority of missing words. They can, however, catch some missing verbs (see G2-e). Although they can flag some missing articles (*a, an,* and *the*), they often suggest that an article is missing when in fact it is not. (See also E3.)

S2-a Add words needed to complete compound structures.

In compound structures, words are often omitted for economy: *Anwar is a man who means what he says and* [*who*] *says what he means.* Such omissions are perfectly acceptable as long as the omitted word is common to both parts of the compound structure.

If the shorter version defies grammar or idiom because an omitted word is not common to both parts of the compound structure, the word must be put back in.

▶ **Some of the regulars are acquaintances whom we see at work or** *who* **live in our community.**

The word *who* must be included because *whom . . . live in our community* is not grammatically correct.

▶ **Mayor Davis never has** *accepted* **and never will accept a bribe from anyone.**

Has . . . accept is not grammatically correct.

▶ **Many South Pacific tribes still believe** *in* **and live by ancient laws.**

Believe . . . by is not idiomatic English.

S2-b Add the word *that* if there is any danger of misreading without it.

If there is no danger of misreading, the word *that* may sometimes be omitted when it introduces a subordinate clause: *The value of a principle is the number of things* [*that*] *it will explain.* Occasionally, however, a sentence might be misread without *that.*

▶ **Looking out the family room window, Sarah saw** *that* **her favourite tree, which she had climbed so often as a child, was gone.**

Sarah didn't see the tree; she saw that the tree was gone. The word *that* tells readers to expect a clause, not just *tree,* as the direct object of *saw.*

S2-c Add words needed to make comparisons logical and complete.

Comparisons should be made between items that are alike. To compare unlike items is illogical and distracting.

▶ **The forests of North America are much more extensive than** *those of* **Europe.**

Forests must be compared with forests.

▶ ~~The graduation rate of our~~ [Our] student athletes ~~is higher~~ [graduate at a higher rate] than the rest of the student population.

A rate cannot be logically compared with a population. The writer could revise the sentence by inserting *that of* after *than,* but the preceding revision is more concise.

▶ Some say that Ella Fitzgerald's renditions of Cole Porter's songs are better than any other ~~singer.~~ [singer's.]

Ella Fitzgerald's renditions cannot be logically compared with a singer. The revision uses the possessive form *singer's,* with the word *renditions* being implied.

Sometimes the word *other* must be inserted to make a comparison logical.

▶ Jupiter is larger than any [other] planet in our solar system.

Jupiter cannot be larger than itself.

Sometimes the word *as* must be inserted to make a comparison grammatically correct.

▶ The city of Lowell is as old, [as] if not older than, the city of Lawrence.

The construction *as old* is not complete without a second *as: as old as . . . the city of Lawrence.*

Comparisons should be complete enough so that readers will understand what is being compared.

INCOMPLETE Brand X is less salty.

COMPLETE Brand X is less salty than Brand Y.

Also, comparisons should leave no ambiguity for readers. If more than one interpretation is possible, revise the sentence to state clearly which interpretation you intend. In the following sentence, two interpretations are possible.

AMBIGUOUS Ken helped me more than my roommate.

CLEAR Ken helped me more than *he helped* my roommate.

CLEAR Ken helped me more than my roommate *did.*

S2-d Add the articles *a, an,* and *the* where necessary for grammatical completeness.

Articles are sometimes omitted in recipes and other instructions that are meant to be followed while they are being read. Such omissions are inappropriate, however, in nearly all other forms of writing, whether formal or informal.

▶ **Blood can be drawn only by ^a doctor or by ^an authorized person who has been trained in ^the procedure.**

It is not always necessary to repeat articles with paired items: *We bought a computer and printer.* However, if one of the items requires *a* and the other requires *an,* both articles must be included.

▶ **We bought a computer and ^an antivirus program at a discount.**

ON THE WEB > **dianahacker.com/writersref**
Grammar exercises > Sentence style > E-ex S2–1 and S2–2

S3

Problems with modifiers

Modifiers, whether they are single words, phrases, or clauses, should point clearly to the words they modify. As a rule, related words should be kept together.

GRAMMAR CHECKERS can flag split infinitives, such as *to carefully and thoroughly sift* (S3-d). However, they don't alert you to other misplaced modifiers (*I only ate three radishes*) or dangling modifiers, including danglers like this one: *When a young man, my mother enrolled me in tap dance classes, hoping I would become the next Savion Glover.*

S3-a Put limiting modifiers in front of the words they modify.

Limiting modifiers such as *only, even, almost, nearly,* and *just* should appear in front of a verb only if they modify the verb: *At first I couldn't even touch my toes, much less grasp them.* If they limit the meaning of some other word in the sentence, they should be placed in front of that word.

▶ **Lasers ~~only~~ destroy ^only the target, leaving the surrounding healthy tissue intact.**

Only limits the meaning of *the target,* not *destroy.*

▶ **The turtle ~~only~~ makes progress ^only when it sticks its neck out.**

Only limits the meaning of the *when* clause.

When the limiting modifier *not* is misplaced, the sentence usually suggests a meaning the writer did not intend.

▶ **In the United States in 1860, ^not all black southerners were ~~not~~ slaves.**

The original sentence says that no black southerners were slaves. The revision makes the writer's real meaning clear: Some (but not all) black southerners were slaves.

S3-b Place phrases and clauses so that readers can see at a glance what they modify.

Although phrases and clauses can appear at some distance from the words they modify, make sure that your meaning is clear. When phrases or clauses are oddly placed, absurd misreadings can result.

MISPLACED The soccer player returned to the clinic where he had undergone emergency surgery in 2004 in a limousine sent by Adidas.

REVISED Travelling in a limousine sent by Adidas, the soccer player returned to the clinic where he had undergone emergency surgery in 2004.

The revision corrects the false impression that the soccer player underwent emergency surgery in a limousine.

▶ ~~**There**~~ *On the walls* **are many pictures of comedians who have performed at Gavin's.** ~~**on the walls.**~~

The comedians weren't performing on the walls; the pictures were on the walls.

▶ **The robber was described as a** *150-pound,* **six-foot-tall man with a mustache.** ~~**weighing 150 pounds.**~~

The robber, not the mustache, weighed 150 pounds.

Occasionally the placement of a modifier leads to an ambiguity, in which case two revisions will be possible, depending on the writer's intended meaning.

AMBIGUOUS	The exchange students we met for coffee occasionally questioned us about our latest slang.
CLEAR	The exchange students we occasionally met for coffee questioned us about our latest slang.
CLEAR	The exchange students we met for coffee questioned us occasionally about our latest slang.

In the original version, it was not clear whether the meeting or the questioning happened occasionally. The revisions eliminate the ambiguity.

S3-c Move awkwardly placed modifiers.

As a rule, a sentence should flow from subject to verb to object, without lengthy detours along the way. When a long adverbial element separates a subject from its verb, a verb from its object, or a helping verb from its main verb, the result is often awkward.

▶ ~~**Hong Kong,**~~ *A* **after more than 150 years of British rule,** *Hong Kong* **was transferred back to Chinese control in 1997.**

There is no reason to separate the subject, *Hong Kong,* from the verb, *was transferred,* with a long adverb phrase.

EXCEPTION: Occasionally a writer may choose to delay a verb or an object to create suspense. In the following passage, for example, Robert Mueller inserts the *after* phrase between the subject *women* and the verb *walk* to heighten the dramatic effect.

> I asked a Burmese why women, after centuries of following their men, now walk ahead. He said there were many unexploded land mines since the war.
> —Robert Mueller

ESL English does not allow an adverb to appear between a verb and its object. See E2-f.

easily
▶ **Yolanda lifted ~~easily~~ the twenty-five-kilogram weight.**

S3-d Avoid split infinitives when they are awkward.

An infinitive consists of *to* plus a verb: *to think, to breathe, to dance.* When a modifier appears between its two parts, an infinitive is said to be "split": *to carefully balance, to completely understand.*

When a long word or a phrase appears between the parts of the infinitive, the result is usually awkward.

If possible, patients
▶ **~~Patients~~ should try to ~~if possible~~ avoid going up and down stairs by themselves.**

Attempts to avoid split infinitives can result in equally awkward sentences. When alternative phrasing sounds unnatural, most experts allow—and even encourage—splitting the infinitive.

AWKWARD We decided actually to enforce the law.

BETTER We decided to actually enforce the law.

At times, neither the split infinitive nor its alternative sounds particularly awkward. In such situations, you may want to unsplit the infinitive, especially in formal writing.

formally.
▶ **The candidate decided to ~~formally~~ launch her campaign.**

ON THE WEB > dianahacker.com/writersref
Language Debates > Split infinitives

S3-e Repair dangling modifiers.

A dangling modifier fails to refer logically to any word in the sentence. Dangling modifiers are easy to repair, but they can be hard to recognize, especially in your own writing.

Recognizing dangling modifiers

Dangling modifiers are usually word groups (such as verbal phrases) that suggest but do not name an actor. When a sentence opens with such a modifier, readers expect the subject of the next clause to name the actor. If it doesn't, the modifier dangles.

When the driver opened
▶ **~~Opening~~ the window to let out a huge bumblebee, the car accidentally swerved into an oncoming car.**

The car didn't open the window; the driver did.

women have often been denied
▶ **After completing seminary training, ~~women's~~ access to the pulpit. ~~has often been denied.~~**

The women (not their access to the pulpit) complete the training.

The following sentences illustrate four common kinds of dangling modifiers.

DANGLING *Deciding to join the navy,* the recruiter enthusiastically pumped Joe's hand. [Participial phrase]

DANGLING *Upon entering the doctor's office,* a skeleton caught my attention. [Preposition followed by a gerund phrase]

DANGLING *To please the children,* some fireworks were set off a day early. [Infinitive phrase]

DANGLING *Though only sixteen,* the University of Calgary accepted Martha's application. [Elliptical clause with an understood subject and verb]

These dangling modifiers falsely suggest that the recruiter decided to join the navy, that the skeleton entered the doctor's office, that the fireworks intended to please the children, and that the University of Calgary is sixteen years old.

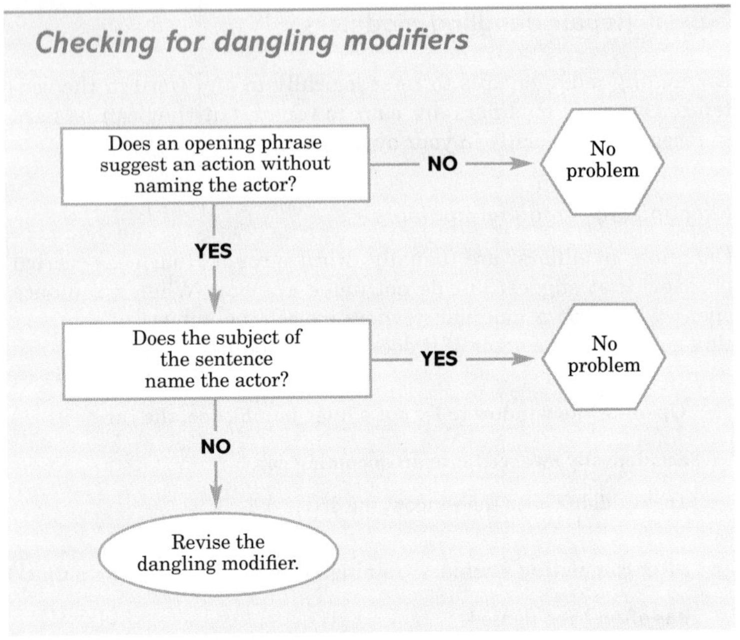
Checking for dangling modifiers
Does an opening phrase suggest an action without naming the actor?
NO
No problem
YES
Does the subject of the sentence name the actor?
YES
No problem
NO
Revise the dangling modifier.

Although most readers will understand the writer's intended meaning in such sentences, the inadvertent humour can be distracting, and it can make the writer appear somewhat foolish.

ON THE WEB > **dianahacker.com/writersref**
Language Debates > Dangling modifiers

Repairing dangling modifiers

To repair a dangling modifier, you can revise the sentence in one of two ways:

1. Name the actor in the subject of the sentence, or
2. name the actor in the modifier.

Depending on your sentence, one of these revision strategies may be more appropriate than the other.

ACTOR NAMED IN SUBJECT

▶ **Upon entering the doctor's office, ^*I noticed* a skeleton^. ~~caught my attention.~~**

▶ To please the children, ~~some fireworks were set off~~ we set off some fireworks a day early.

ACTOR NAMED IN MODIFIER

▶ ~~Deciding~~ When Joe decided to join the navy, the recruiter enthusiastically pumped ~~Joe's~~ his hand.

▶ Though Martha was only sixteen years old, the University of Calgary accepted ~~Martha's~~ her application.

NOTE: You cannot repair a dangling modifier just by moving it. Consider, for example, the sentence about the skeleton. If you put the modifier at the end of the sentence (*A skeleton caught my attention upon entering the doctor's office*), you are still suggesting—absurdly, of course—that the skeleton entered the office. The only way to avoid the problem is to put the word *I* in the sentence, either as the subject or in the modifier.

▶ Upon entering the doctor's office, I noticed a skeleton. ~~caught my attention.~~

▶ ~~Upon entering~~ As I entered the doctor's office, a skeleton caught my attention.

ON THE WEB > dianahacker.com/writersref
Grammar exercises > Sentence style > E-ex S3–1 through S3–4

S4

Shifts

GRAMMAR CHECKERS usually do not flag shifts in point of view or in verb tense, mood, or voice. Even obvious errors, like the following shift in tense, slip right past the grammar checker: *My three-year-old fell into the pool and to my surprise she swims to the shallow end.*

Sometimes grammar checkers mark a shift from direct to indirect question or quotation but do not make any suggestions for revision. You must decide where the structure is faulty and determine how to fix it.

S4-a Make the point of view consistent.

The point of view of a piece of writing is the perspective from which it is written: first person (*I* or *we*), second person (*you*), or third person (*he*/*she*/*it*/*one* or *they*).

The *I* (or *we*) point of view, which emphasizes the writer, is a good choice for informal letters and writing based primarily on personal experience. The *you* point of view, which emphasizes the reader, works well for giving advice or explaining how to do something. The third-person point of view, which emphasizes the subject, is appropriate in formal academic and professional writing.

Writers who are having difficulty settling on an appropriate point of view sometimes shift confusingly from one to another. The solution is to choose a suitable perspective and then stay with it.

▶ **One week our class met in a junkyard to practise rescuing a victim trapped in a wrecked car. We learned to dismantle the car with the essential tools.** *We* **~~You~~ were graded on** *our* **~~your~~ speed and** *our* **~~your~~ skill in extricating the victim.**

The writer should have stayed with the *we* point of view. *You* is inappropriate because the writer is not addressing readers directly. *You* should not be used in a vague sense meaning "anyone." (See also G3-b.)

▶ *You need* **~~One needs~~ a password and a credit card number to access this database. You will be billed at an hourly rate.**

You is an appropriate choice because the writer is giving advice directly to readers.

Shifts from the third-person singular to the third-person plural are especially common.

▶ *Police officers are* **~~A police officer is~~ often criticized for always being there when they aren't needed and never being there when they are.**

Although the writer might have changed *they* to *he or she* (to match the singular *officer*), the revision in the plural is more concise. (See also G3-a.)

S4-b Maintain consistent verb tenses.

Consistent verb tenses clearly establish the time of the actions being described. When a passage begins in one tense and then shifts without warning and for no reason to another, readers are distracted and confused.

► **There was no way I could fight the current. Just as I was losing hope, a stranger ~~jumps~~ *jumped* off a passing boat and ~~swims~~ *swam* toward me.**

Writers often encounter difficulty with verb tenses when writing about literature. Because fictional events occur outside the time frames of real life, the past and the present tenses may seem equally appropriate. The literary convention, however, is to describe fictional events consistently in the present tense. (See also G2-f.)

► **The scarlet letter is a punishment sternly placed on Hester's breast by the community, and yet it ~~was~~ *is* an extremely fanciful and imaginative product of Hester's own needlework.**

S4-c Make verbs consistent in mood and voice.

Unnecessary shifts in the mood of a verb can be as distracting as needless shifts in tense. There are three moods in English: the indicative, used for facts, opinions, and questions; the imperative, used for orders or advice; and the subjunctive, used for wishes or conditions contrary to fact. (See G2-g.)

The following passage shifts confusingly from the indicative to the imperative mood.

► **The officers advised us not to allow anyone into our homes without proper identification. ~~Also,~~ *They also suggested that we* alert neighbours to our vacation schedules.**

Since the writer's purpose was to report the officers' advice, the revision puts both sentences in the indicative.

A verb may be in either the active voice (with the subject doing the action) or the passive voice (with the subject receiving the action). (See W3-a.) If a writer shifts without warning from one to the other, readers may be left wondering why.

▶ **When the tickets are ready, the travel agent notifies the client, lists each ~~Each~~ ticket ~~is then listed~~ on a daily register form, and files a copy of the itinerary. ~~is filed.~~**

The passage began in the active voice (*agent notifies*) and then switched to the passive (*ticket is listed . . . copy is filed*). Because the active voice is clearer and more direct, the writer changed all the verbs to the active voice.

S4-d Avoid sudden shifts from indirect to direct questions or quotations.

An indirect question reports a question without asking it: *We asked whether we could visit Mimo.* A direct question asks directly: *Can we visit Mimo?* Sudden shifts from indirect to direct questions are awkward. In addition, sentences containing such shifts are impossible to punctuate because indirect questions must end with a period and direct questions must end with a question mark. (See P7-b.)

▶ **I wonder whether Karla knew of the theft and, if so, ~~did~~ whether she reported ~~she report~~ it to the police~~?~~.**

The revision poses both questions indirectly. The writer could also ask both questions directly: *Did Karla know of the theft and, if so, did she report it to the police?*

An indirect quotation reports someone's words without quoting word for word: *Annabelle said that she is a Virgo.* A direct quotation presents the exact words of a speaker or writer, set off with quotation marks: *Annabelle said, "I am a Virgo."* Unannounced shifts from indirect to direct quotations are distracting and confusing, especially when the writer fails to insert the necessary quotation marks, as in the following example.

▶ **Mother said that she would be late for dinner and asked me not to ~~please do not~~ leave for choir practice until Dad came ~~comes~~ home.**

The revision reports all of the mother's words. The writer could also quote directly: *Mother said, "I will be late for dinner. Please do not leave for choir practice until Dad comes home."*

ON THE WEB > **dianahacker.com/writersref**
Grammar exercises > Sentence style > E-ex S4–1 through S4–4

S5

Mixed constructions

A mixed construction contains elements that do not sensibly fit together. The mismatch may be a matter of grammar or of logic.

GRAMMAR CHECKERS can flag *is when, is where,* and *reason . . . is because* constructions (S5-c), but they fail to identify nearly all other mixed constructions, including sentences as tangled as this one: *Depending on our method of travel and our destination determines how many suitcases we are allowed to pack.*

S5-a Untangle the grammatical structure.

Once you head into a sentence, your choices are limited by the range of grammatical patterns in English. (See B2 and B3.) You cannot begin with one grammatical plan and switch without warning to another.

MIXED For most drivers who have a blood alcohol level of 0.05 percent double their risk of causing an accident.

REVISED For most drivers who have a blood alcohol level of 0.05 percent, the risk of causing an accident is doubled.

REVISED Most drivers who have a blood alcohol level of 0.05 percent double their risk of causing an accident.

The writer began with a long prepositional phrase that was destined to be a modifier but then tried to press it into service as the subject of the sentence. A prepositional phrase cannot serve as the subject of a sentence. If the sentence is to begin with the prepositional phrase, the writer must finish the sentence with a subject and verb (*risk . . . is doubled*). The writer who wishes to stay with the original verb (*double*) must head into the sentence another way (*Most drivers . . .*).

▶ ~~When an employee is~~ *Being* promoted without warning can be exciting or alarming.

The adverb clause *When an employee is promoted without warning* cannot serve as the subject of the sentence. The revision replaces the adverb clause with a gerund phrase, a word group that can function as the subject. (See B3-b and B3-e.)

▶ **Although Canada is one of the wealthiest nations in the world, ~~but~~ 5.6 percent of our children live in poverty.**

The *Although* clause is subordinate, so it cannot be linked to an independent clause with the coordinating conjunction *but*. (If you speak English as a second language, see also E2-e.)

Occasionally a mixed construction is so tangled that it defies grammatical analysis. When this happens, back away from the sentence, rethink what you want to say, and then say it again as clearly as you can.

MIXED In the whole-word method children learn to recognize entire words rather than by the phonics method in which they learn to sound out letters and groups of letters.

REVISED The whole-word method teaches children to recognize entire words; the phonics method teaches them to sound out letters and groups of letters.

ESL English does not allow double subjects, nor does it allow an object or an adverb to be repeated in an adjective clause. See E2-c and E2-d. Unlike some languages, English does not allow a noun and a pronoun to be repeated in a sentence if they serve the same grammatical purpose. See E2-c.

▶ **My father ~~he~~ moved to Saskatchewan before he met my mother.**

▶ **~~The final exam~~ I should really study for ~~it~~ *the final exam* to pass the course.**

S5-b Straighten out the logical connections.

The subject and the predicate should make sense together. When they don't, the error is known as *faulty predication.*

▶ **Reluctantly we decided that ~~Tiffany's welfare~~** *Tiffany* **would not be safe living with her mother.**

Tiffany, not her welfare, may not be safe.

▶ **Under the revised plan, seniors/ ~~who now receive a double personal exemption,~~** *the double personal exemption for* **seniors will be abolished.**

The exemption, not seniors, will be abolished.

An appositive and the noun to which it refers should be logically equivalent. When they are not, the error is known as *faulty apposition.*

▶ **~~The tax accountant,~~** *Tax accounting,* **a very lucrative field, requires intelligence, patience, and attention to detail.**

The tax accountant is a person, not a field.

S5-c Avoid *is when, is where,* and *reason . . . is because* constructions.

In formal English, many readers object to *is when, is where,* and *reason . . . is because* constructions on either logical or grammatical grounds.

▶ **Anorexia nervosa is ~~where people,~~** *a disorder suffered by people who,* **believing they are too fat, diet to the point of starvation.**

Anorexia nervosa is a disorder, not a place.

▶ **~~The reason~~ I was late ~~is~~ because my motorcycle broke down.**

The writer might have replaced the word *because* with *that,* but the preceding revision is more concise.

ON THE WEB > dianahacker.com/writersref
Grammar exercises > Sentence style > E-ex S5–1 and S5–2

S6

Sentence emphasis

Within each sentence, emphasize your point by expressing it in the subject and verb of an independent clause, the words that receive the most attention from readers (see S6-a to S6-e).

Within longer stretches of prose, you can draw attention to ideas deserving special emphasis by using a variety of techniques, often involving an unusual twist or some element of surprise (see S6-f).

S6-a Coordinate equal ideas; subordinate minor ideas.

When combining two or more ideas in one sentence, you have two choices: coordination or subordination. Choose coordination to indicate that the ideas are equal or nearly equal in importance. Choose subordination to indicate that one idea is less important than another.

GRAMMAR CHECKERS do not catch the problems with coordination and subordination discussed in this section. Not surprisingly, computer programs have no way of sensing the relative importance of ideas.

Coordination

Coordination draws attention equally to two or more ideas. To coordinate single words or phrases, join them with a coordinating conjunction or with a pair of correlative conjunctions (see S1-b). To coordinate independent clauses—word groups that could each stand alone as a sentence—join them with a comma and a coordinating conjunction or with a semicolon. The semicolon is often accompanied by a conjunctive adverb such as *moreover, therefore,* or *however* or by a transitional phrase such as *for example* or *in other words.* (For a longer list, see P3-b.)

Grandmother lost her sight, but her hearing sharpened.

Grandmother lost her sight; however, her hearing sharpened.

Subordination

To give unequal emphasis to two or more ideas, express the major idea in an independent clause and place any minor ideas in subordinate clauses or phrases. (See B3.) Subordinate clauses, which cannot stand alone, typically begin with one of the following subordinating conjunctions or relative pronouns.

after	before	unless	which
although	if	until	while
as	since	when	who
as if	that	where	whom
because	though	whether	whose

Deciding which idea to emphasize is not a matter of right and wrong but is determined by the meaning you intend. Consider the two ideas about Grandmother's sight and hearing.

Grandmother lost her sight. Her hearing sharpened.

If your purpose is to stress your grandmother's acute hearing rather than her blindness, subordinate the idea concerning her blindness.

As Grandmother lost her sight, her hearing sharpened.

To focus on your grandmother's blindness, subordinate the idea about her hearing.

Though her hearing sharpened, Grandmother lost her sight.

S6-b Combine choppy sentences.

Short sentences demand attention, so you should use them primarily for emphasis. Too many short sentences, one after the other, make for a choppy style.

If an idea is not important enough to deserve its own sentence, try combining it with a sentence close by. Put any minor ideas in subordinate structures such as phrases or subordinate clauses. (See B3.)

▶ **We keep our use of insecticides to a minimum~~.~~ ~~We~~** *because we* **are concerned about their effect on the environment.**

A minor idea is now expressed in a subordinate clause beginning with *because.*

▶ ~~Sister Consilio was~~ Enveloped in a black robe with only her face and hands visible, Sister Consilio ~~She~~ was an imposing figure.

A minor idea is now expressed in a participial phrase beginning with *Enveloped.* (See B3-b.)

▶ **My sister owes much of her recovery to a bodybuilding program that she ~~She~~ began ~~the program~~ three years ago.**

A minor idea is now expressed in an adjective clause beginning with *that.* (See B3-e.)

ESL

Unlike Arabic, Farsi, and other languages, English does not repeat objects or adverbs in adjective clauses. The relative pronoun (*that, which, whom*) or relative adverb (*where*) in the adjective clause represents the object or adverb. See E2-d.

▶ **The apartment that we rented ~~it~~ needed repairs.**

The pronoun *it* cannot repeat the relative pronoun *that.*

▶ **The small town where my grandfather was born ~~there~~ is now a big city.**

The adverb *there* cannot repeat the relative adverb *where.*

Although subordination is ordinarily the most effective technique for combining short, choppy sentences, coordination is appropriate when the ideas are equal in importance.

▶ **The hospital decides when patients will sleep and wake, ~~It~~ dictates what and when they will eat, and ~~It~~ tells them when they may be with family and friends.**

Equivalent ideas are expressed as parallel elements of a compound predicate: *decides . . . dictates . . . tells.*

ON THE WEB > **dianahacker.com/writersref**
Grammar exercises > Sentence style > E-ex S6–1 and S6–2

S6-c Avoid ineffective coordination.

Coordinate structures are appropriate only when you intend to draw the reader's attention equally to two or more ideas: *Professor Sakellarios praises loudly, and she criticizes softly.* If one idea is more important than another—or if a coordinating conjunction does not clearly signal the relation between the ideas—you should subordinate the lesser idea.

After four hours,
▶ ~~Four hours went by, and~~ a rescue truck finally arrived, but by that time the injured swimmer had been evacuated in a helicopter.

Three independent clauses were excessive. The least important idea has become a prepositional phrase. (See B3-a.)

S6-d Do not subordinate major ideas.

If a sentence buries its major idea in a subordinate construction, readers may not give the idea enough attention. Express the major idea in an independent clause and subordinate any minor ideas.

had polio as a child,
▶ Lanie, who now walks with the help of braces/. ~~had polio as a child.~~

The writer wanted to focus on Lanie's ability to walk, but the original sentence buried this idea in an adjective clause. The revision puts the major idea in an independent clause and tucks the less important idea into an adjective clause (*who had polio as a child*). (See B3-e.)

noticing
▶ My uncle, ~~noticed~~ my frightened look, ~~and~~ told me that the dentures in the glass were not real teeth.

The less important idea has become a participial phrase modifying the noun *uncle*.

ON THE WEB > dianahacker.com/writersref
Grammar exercises > Sentence style > E-ex S6–3

S6-e Do not subordinate excessively.

In attempting to avoid short, choppy sentences, writers sometimes move to the opposite extreme, putting more subordinate ideas into a sentence than its structure can bear. If a sentence collapses under its own weight, occasionally it can be restructured. More often, however, such sentences must be divided.

▶ **Our job is to stay between the stacker and the tie machine to see if the newspapers jam~~,~~. If they do, ~~in which case~~ we pull the bundles off and stack them on a skid, because otherwise they would back up in the stacker.**

S6-f Experiment with techniques for gaining special emphasis.

By experimenting with certain techniques, usually involving some element of surprise, you can draw attention to ideas that deserve special emphasis. Use such techniques sparingly, however, or they will lose their punch. The writer who tries to emphasize everything ends up emphasizing nothing.

Using sentence endings for emphasis

You can highlight an idea simply by withholding it until the end of a sentence. The technique works something like a punch line. In the following example, the sentence's meaning is not revealed until its very last word.

> The only completely consistent people are the dead.
> —Aldous Huxley

Using parallel structure for emphasis

Parallel grammatical structure draws special attention to paired ideas or to items in a series. (See S1.) When parallel ideas are paired, the emphasis falls on words that underscore comparisons or contrasts, especially when they occur at the end of a phrase or clause.

> We must *stop talking* about the *American dream* and *start listening* to the *dreams of Americans*.
> —Reubin Askew

In a parallel series, the emphasis falls at the end, so it is generally best to end with the most dramatic or climactic item in the series.

> Sister Charity enjoyed passing out writing punishments: translate the Ten Commandments into Latin, type a thousand-word essay on good manners, copy the New Testament with a quill pen.
>
> —Marie Visosky, student

Using an occasional short sentence for emphasis

Too many short sentences in a row will fast become monotonous (see S6-b), but an occasional short sentence, when played off against longer sentences in the same passage, will draw attention to an idea.

> The great secret, known to internists and learned early in marriage by internists' wives [or husbands], but still hidden from the general public, is that most things get better by themselves. Most things, in fact, are better by morning. —Lewis Thomas

S7

Sentence variety

When a rough draft is filled with too many same-sounding sentences, try to inject some variety—as long as you can do so without sacrificing clarity or ease of reading.

GRAMMAR CHECKERS are of little help with sentence variety. It takes a human ear to know when and why sentence variety is needed.

Some programs tell you when you have used the same word to open several sentences, but sometimes it is a good idea to do so—if you are trying to highlight parallel ideas, for example (see p. 33).

S7-a Use a variety of sentence structures.

A writer should not rely too heavily on simple sentences and compound sentences, for the effect tends to be both monotonous and choppy. (See S6-a and S6-b.) Too many complex sentences, however, can be equally monotonous. If your style tends to one or the other extreme, try to achieve a better mix of sentence types.

For a discussion of sentence types, see B4-a.

S7-b Use a variety of sentence openings.

Most sentences in English begin with the subject, move to the verb, and continue to an object, with modifiers tucked in along the way or put at the end. For the most part, such sentences are fine. Put too many of them in a row, however, and they become monotonous.

Adverbial modifiers, being easily movable, can often be inserted at the beginning of the sentence, ahead of the subject. Such modifiers might be single words, phrases, or clauses.

Eventually a
▶ ~~A~~ few drops of sap ~~eventually~~ began to trickle from the tree into the pail.

Just as the sun was coming up, a
▶ ~~A~~ pair of black ducks flew over the lake. ~~just as the sun was coming up.~~

For variety, adjectives and participial phrases can frequently be moved to the beginning of a sentence without loss of clarity. (See B3-b.)

Dejected and withdrawn,
▶ Edward/ ~~dejected and withdrawn,~~ nearly gave up his search for a job.

A *Roberto and I*
▶ ~~Roberto and I,~~ anticipating a peaceful evening, sat cross-legged at the campfire to brew a cup of coffee and plan the rest of our hike.

TIP: When beginning a sentence with a participial phrase, make sure that the subject of the sentence names the person or thing described in the introductory phrase. If it doesn't, the phrase will dangle. (See S3-e.)

S7-c Try inverting sentences occasionally.

A sentence is inverted if it does not follow the normal subject-verb-object pattern. Many inversions sound artificial and should be avoided except in the most formal contexts. But if an inversion sounds natural, it can provide a welcome touch of variety.

Opposite the produce section is a
▶ ~~A~~ refrigerated case of mouth-watering cheeses. ~~is opposite the produce section.~~

Set at the top two corners of the stage were huge
▶ ~~Huge~~ lavender hearts outlined in bright white lights. ~~were set at the top two corners of the stage.~~

W

Word Choice

W Word Choice

W1

Glossary of usage

This glossary includes words commonly confused (such as *accept* and *except*), words commonly misused (such as *aggravate*), and words that are nonstandard (such as *hisself*). It also lists colloquialisms and jargon. Colloquialisms are expressions that may be appropriate in informal speech but are inappropriate in formal writing. Jargon is needlessly technical or pretentious language that is inappropriate in most contexts. If an item is not listed here, consult the index. For irregular verbs (such as *sing, sang, sung*), see G2-a. For idiomatic use of prepositions, see W5-d.

GRAMMAR CHECKERS can point out commonly confused words and suggest that you check your usage. It is up to you, however, to determine the correct word for your intended meaning.

ON THE WEB > **dianahacker.com/writersref**

Language Debates > Absolute concepts such as *unique*
bad versus *badly*
however at the beginning of a sentence
lie versus *lay*
myself
that versus *which*
who versus *which* or *that*
who versus *whom*
you

a, an Use *an* before a vowel sound, *a* before a consonant sound: *an apple, a peach.* Problems sometimes arise with words beginning with *h* or *u*. If the *h* is silent, the word begins with a vowel sound, so use *an*: *an hour, an honourable deed.* If the *h* is pronounced, the word begins with a consonant sound, so use *a*: *a hospital, a historian, a hotel.* Words such as *university* and *union* begin with a consonant sound (a *y* sound), so use *a*: *a union.* Words such as *uncle* and *umbrella* begin with a vowel sound, so use *an*: *an underground well.* When an abbreviation or an acronym begins with a vowel sound, use *an*: *an EKG, an MRI, an AIDS fundraiser.*

accept, except *Accept* is a verb meaning "to receive." *Except* is usually a preposition meaning "excluding." *I will accept all the packages except* *that one. Except* is also a verb meaning "to exclude." *Please except that item from the list.*

adapt, adopt *Adapt* means "to adjust or become accustomed"; it is usually followed by *to. Adopt* means "to take as one's own." *Our family adopted a Vietnamese orphan, who quickly adapted to his new life.*

adverse, averse *Adverse* means "unfavourable." *Averse* means "opposed" or "reluctant"; it is usually followed by *to. I am averse to your proposal because it could have an adverse impact on the economy.*

advice, advise *Advice* is a noun, *advise* a verb. *We advise you to follow John's advice.*

affect, effect *Affect* is usually a verb meaning "to influence." *Effect* is usually a noun meaning "result." *The drug did not affect the disease, and it had adverse side effects. Effect* can also be a verb meaning "to bring about." *Only the president can effect such a dramatic change.*

aggravate *Aggravate* means "to make worse or more troublesome." *Overgrazing aggravated the soil erosion.* In formal writing, avoid the colloquial use of *aggravate* meaning "to annoy or irritate." *Her babbling annoyed* (not *aggravated*) *me.*

agree to, agree with *Agree to* means "to give consent." *Agree with* means "to be in accord" or "to come to an understanding." *He agrees with me about the need for change, but he won't agree to my plan.*

ain't *Ain't* is nonstandard. Use *am not, are not* (*aren't*), or *is not* (*isn't*). *I am not* (not *ain't*) *going home for spring break.*

all ready, already *All ready* means "completely prepared." *Already* means "previously." *Susan was all ready for the concert, but her friends had already left.*

all right *All right* is written as two words. *Alright* is nonstandard.

all together, altogether *All together* means "everyone gathered." *Altogether* means "entirely." *We were not altogether certain that we could bring the family all together for the reunion.*

allude To *allude* to something is to make an indirect reference to it. Do not use *allude* to mean "to refer directly." *In his lecture the professor referred* (not *alluded*) *to several pre-Socratic philosophers.*

allusion, illusion An *allusion* is an indirect reference. An *illusion* is a misconception or false impression. *Did you catch my allusion to Shakespeare? Mirrors give the room an illusion of depth.*

a lot *A lot* is two words. Do not write *alot. Sam lost a lot of weight.*

among, between See *between, among.*

amongst In North American English, *among* is preferred.

amoral, immoral *Amoral* means "neither moral nor immoral"; it also means "not caring about moral judgments." *Immoral* means "morally wrong." *Until recently, most business courses were taught from an amoral perspective. Murder is immoral.*

amount, number Use *amount* with quantities that cannot be counted; use *number* with those that can. *This recipe calls for a large amount of sugar. We have a large number of toads in our garden.*

an See *a, an.*

and etc. *Et cetera* (*etc.*) means "and so forth," so *and etc.* is redundant. See also *etc.*

and/or Avoid the awkward construction *and/or* except in technical or legal documents.

angry at, angry with To write that one is *angry at* another person is nonstandard. Use *angry with* instead.

ante-, anti- The prefix *ante-* means "earlier" or "in front of"; the prefix *anti-* means "against" or "opposed to." *William Lloyd Garrison was a leader of the antislavery movement during the antebellum period. Anti-* should be used with a hyphen when it is followed by a capital letter or a word beginning with *i.*

anxious *Anxious* means "worried" or "apprehensive." In formal writing, avoid using *anxious* to mean "eager." *We are eager* (not *anxious*) *to see your new house.*

anybody, anyone *Anybody* and *anyone* are singular. (See G1-e and G3-a.)

anymore Reserve the adverb *anymore* for negative contexts, where it means "any longer." *Moviegoers are rarely shocked anymore by profanity.* Do not use *anymore* in positive contexts. Use *now* or *nowadays* instead. *Interest rates are so low nowadays* (not *anymore*) *that more people can afford to buy homes.*

anyone See *anybody, anyone.*

anyone, any one *Anyone,* an indefinite pronoun, means "any person at all." *Any one,* the pronoun *one* preceded by the adjective *any,* refers to a particular person or thing in a group. *Anyone from Halifax may choose any one of the games on display.*

anyplace In formal writing, use *anywhere.*

anyways, anywheres *Anyways* and *anywheres* are nonstandard. Use *anyway* and *anywhere.*

as *As* is sometimes used to mean "because." But do not use it if there is any chance of ambiguity. *We cancelled the picnic because* (not *as*) *it began raining. As* here could mean "because" or "when."

as, like See *like, as.*

as to *As to* is jargon for *about. He inquired about* (not *as to*) *the job.*

averse See *adverse, averse.*

awful The adjective *awful* and the adverb *awfully* are too colloquial for formal writing.

awhile, a while *Awhile* is an adverb; it can modify a verb, but it cannot be the object of a preposition such as *for.* The two-word form *a while* is a noun preceded by an article and therefore can be the object of a preposition. *Stay awhile. Stay for a while.*

back up, backup *Back up* is a verb phrase. *Back up the car carefully. Be sure to back up your hard drive. Backup* is a noun meaning "a duplicate of electronically stored data." *Keep your backup in a safe place. Backup* can also be used as an adjective. *I regularly create backup disks.*

bad, badly *Bad* is an adjective, *badly* an adverb. (See G4-a and G4-b.) *They felt bad about being early and ruining the surprise. Her arm hurt badly after she slid headfirst into second base.*

being as, being that *Being as* and *being that* are nonstandard expressions. Write *because* instead. *Because* (not *Being as*) *I slept late, I had to skip breakfast.*

beside, besides *Beside* is a preposition meaning "at the side of" or "next to." *Annie Oakley slept with her gun beside her bed. Besides* is a preposition meaning "except" or "in addition to." *No one besides Terrie can have that ice cream. Besides* is also an adverb meaning "in addition." *I'm not hungry; besides, I don't like ice cream.*

between, among Ordinarily, use *among* with three or more entities, *between* with two. *The prize was divided among several contestants. You have a choice between carrots and beans.*

bring, take Use *bring* when an object is being transported toward you, *take* when it is being moved away. *Please bring me a glass of water. Please take these flowers to Mr. Leung.*

burst, bursted; bust, busted *Burst* is an irregular verb meaning "to come open or fly apart suddenly or violently." Its principal parts are *burst, burst, burst.* The past-tense form *bursted* is nonstandard. *Bust* and *busted* are slang for *burst* and, along with *bursted,* should not be used in formal writing.

can, may The distinction between *can* and *may* is fading, but some writers still observe it in formal writing. *Can* is traditionally reserved for ability, *may* for permission. *Can you speak French? May I help you?*

capital, capitol *Capital* refers to a city, *capitol* to a building where lawmakers meet. *Capital* also refers to wealth or resources. *The capitol has undergone extensive renovations. The residents of the provincial capital protested the development plans.*

censor, censure *Censor* means "to remove or suppress material considered objectionable." *Censure* means "to criticize severely." *The school's policy of censoring books has been censured by the media.*

cite, site *Cite* means "to quote as an authority or example." *Site* is usually a noun meaning "a particular place." *He cited the zoning law in his argument against the proposed site of the gas station.* Locations on the Internet are usually referred to as *sites. The library's Web site improves every week.*

climactic, climatic *Climactic* is derived from *climax,* the point of greatest intensity in a series or progression of events. *Climatic* is derived from *climate* and refers to meteorological conditions. *The climactic period in the dinosaurs' reign was reached just before severe climatic conditions brought on an ice age.*

coarse, course *Coarse* means "crude" or "rough in texture." *The coarse weave of the wall hanging gave it a three-dimensional quality. Course* usually refers to a path, a playing field, or a unit of study; the expression *of course* means "certainly." *I plan to take a course in car repair this summer. Of course, you are welcome to join me.*

compare to, compare with *Compare to* means "to represent as similar." *She compared him to a wild stallion. Compare with* means "to examine similarities and differences." *The study compared the language ability of apes with that of dolphins.*

complement, compliment *Complement* is a verb meaning "to go with or complete" or a noun meaning "something that completes." *Compliment* as a verb means "to flatter"; as a noun it means "flattering remark." *Her skill at rushing the net complements his skill at volleying. Mother's flower arrangements receive many compliments.*

conscience, conscious *Conscience* is a noun meaning "moral principles." *Conscious* is an adjective meaning "aware or alert." *Let your conscience be your guide. Were you conscious of his love for you?*

continual, continuous *Continual* means "repeated regularly and frequently." *She grew weary of the continual telephone calls. Continuous* means "extended or prolonged without interruption." *The broken siren made a continuous wail.*

could care less *Could care less* is a nonstandard expression. Write *couldn't care less* instead. *He couldn't* (not *could*) *care less about his psychology final.*

could of *Could of* is nonstandard for *could have. We could have* (not *could of*) *taken the train.*

council, counsel A *council* is a deliberative body, and a *councillor* is a member of such a body. *Counsel* usually means "advice" and can also mean "lawyer"; *counsellor* is one who gives advice or guidance. *The* *councillors met to draft the council's position paper. The pastor offered wise counsel to the troubled teenager.*

criteria *Criteria* is the plural of *criterion,* which means "a standard or rule or test on which a judgment or decision can be based." *The only criterion for the scholarship is ability.*

data *Data* is a plural noun technically meaning "facts or propositions." But *data* is increasingly being accepted as a singular noun. *The new data suggest* (or *suggests*) *that our theory is correct.* (The singular *datum* is rarely used.)

different from, different than Ordinarily, write *different from. Your sense of style is different from Jim's.* However, *different than* is acceptable to avoid an awkward construction. *Please let me know if your plans are different than* (to avoid *from what*) *they were six weeks ago.*

differ from, differ with *Differ from* means "to be unlike"; *differ with* means "to disagree." *She differed with me about the wording of the agreement. My approach to the problem differed from hers.*

disinterested, uninterested *Disinterested* means "impartial, objective"; *uninterested* means "not interested." *We sought the advice of a disinterested counsellor to help us solve our problem. He was uninterested in anyone's opinion but his own.*

don't *Don't* is the contraction for *do not. I don't want any. Don't* should not be used as the contraction for *does not,* which is *doesn't.* He *doesn't* (not *don't*) *want any.*

due to *Due to* is an adjective phrase and should not be used as a preposition meaning "because of." *The trip was cancelled because of* (not *due to*) *lack of interest. Due to* is acceptable as a subject complement and usually follows a form of the verb *be. His success was due to hard work.*

each *Each* is singular. (See G1-e and G3-a.)

effect See *affect, effect.*

e.g. In formal writing, replace the Latin abbreviation *e.g.* with its English equivalent: *for example* or *for instance.*

either *Either* is singular. (See G1-e and G3-a.) For *either . . . or* constructions, see G1-d and G3-a.

elicit, illicit *Elicit* is a verb meaning "to bring out" or "to evoke." *Illicit* is an adjective meaning "unlawful." *The reporter was unable to elicit any information from the police about illicit drug traffic.*

emigrate from, immigrate to *Emigrate* means "to leave one country or region to settle in another." *In 1900, my grandfather emigrated from Russia to escape the religious pogroms. Immigrate* means "to enter another country and reside there." *Many Filipinos immigrate to Canada to find work.*

eminent, imminent *Eminent* means "outstanding" or "distinguished." *We met an eminent professor of Greek history. Imminent* means "about to happen." *The announcement is imminent.*

enthused Many people object to the use of *enthused* as an adjective. Use *enthusiastic* instead. *The children were enthusiastic* (not *enthused*) *about going to the circus.*

etc. Avoid ending a list with *etc.* It is more emphatic to end with an example, and in most contexts readers will understand that the list is not exhaustive. When you don't wish to end with an example, *and so on* is more graceful than *etc.*

eventually, ultimately Often used interchangeably, *eventually* is the better choice to mean "at an unspecified time in the future" and *ultimately* is better to mean "the furthest possible extent or greatest extreme." *He knew that eventually he would complete his degree. The existentialist considered suicide the ultimately rational act.*

everybody, everyone *Everybody* and *everyone* are singular. (See G1-e and G3-a.)

everyone, every one *Everyone* is an indefinite pronoun. *Every one,* the pronoun *one* preceded by the adjective *every,* means "each individual or thing in a particular group." *Every one* is usually followed by *of. Everyone wanted to go. Every one of the missing books was found.*

except See *accept, except.*

expect Avoid the colloquial use of *expect* meaning "to believe, think, or suppose." *I think* (not *expect*) *it will rain tonight.*

explicit, implicit *Explicit* means "expressed directly" or "clearly defined"; *implicit* means "implied, unstated." *I gave him explicit instructions not to go swimming. My mother's silence indicated her implicit approval.*

farther, further *Farther* usually describes distances. *Further* usually suggests quantity or degree. *Altona is farther from Kenora than I thought. You extended the curfew further than you should have.*

fewer, less *Fewer* refers to items that can be counted; *less* refers to items that cannot be counted. *Fewer people are living in the city. Please put less sugar in my tea.*

finalize *Finalize* is jargon meaning "to make final or complete." Use ordinary English instead. *The architect prepared final drawings* (not *finalized the drawings*).

firstly *Firstly* sounds pretentious, and it leads to the ungainly series *firstly, secondly, thirdly,* and so on. Write *first, second, third* instead.

further See *farther, further.*

get *Get* has many colloquial uses. In writing, avoid using *get* to mean the following: "to evoke an emotional response" (*That music always gets to me*); "to annoy" (*After a while his sulking got to me*); "to take revenge on" (*I got back at him by leaving the room*); "to become" (*He got sick*); "to start or begin" (*Let's get going*). Avoid using *have got to* in place of *must. I must* (not *have got to*) *finish this paper tonight.*

good, well *Good* is an adjective, *well* an adverb. (See G4.) *He hasn't felt good about his game since he sprained his wrist last season. She performed well on the uneven parallel bars.*

graduate Both of the following uses of *graduate* are standard: *My sister was graduated from U of T last year. My sister graduated from U of T last year.* It is nonstandard, however, to drop the word *from*: *My sister graduated U of T last year.* Though this usage is common in informal English, many readers object to it.

grow Phrases such as *to grow the economy* and *to grow a business* are jargon. Usually the verb *grow* is intransitive (it does not take a direct object). *Our business has grown very quickly.* When *grow* is used in a transitive sense, with a direct object, it means "to cultivate" or "to allow to grow." *We plan to grow tomatoes this year. John is growing a beard.*

hanged, hung *Hanged* is the past-tense and past-participle form of the verb *hang* meaning "to execute." *The prisoner was hanged at dawn. Hung* is the past-tense and past-participle form of the verb *hang* meaning "to fasten or suspend." *The stockings were hung by the chimney with care.*

hardly Avoid expressions such as *can't hardly* and *not hardly,* which are considerable double negatives. *I can* (not *can't*) *hardly describe my elation at getting the job.* (See G4-d.)

has got, have got *Got* is unnecessary and awkward in such constructions. It should be dropped. *We have* (not *have got*) *three days to prepare for the opening.*

he At one time *he* was commonly used to mean "he or she." Today such usage is inappropriate. (See W4-e and G3-a.)

he/she, his/her In formal writing, use *he or she* or *his or her.* For alternatives to these wordy constructions, see W4-e and G3-a.

hisself *Hisself* is nonstandard. Use *himself.*

hopefully *Hopefully* means "in a hopeful manner." *We looked hopefully to the future.* Some usage experts object to the use of *hopefully* as a sentence adverb, apparently on grounds of clarity. To be safe, avoid using *hopefully* in sentences such as the following: *Hopefully, your son will recover soon.* At least some educated readers will want you to indicate who is doing the hoping: *I hope that your son will recover soon.*

however In the past, some writers objected to *however* at the beginning of a sentence, but current experts advise you to place the word according to your meaning and desired emphasis. Any of the following sentences is correct, depending on the intended contrast. *Pam decided, however, to attend Harvard. However, Pam decided to attend Harvard.* (She had been considering other schools.) *Pam, however, decided to attend Harvard.* (Unlike someone else, Pam opted for Harvard.)

hung See *hanged, hung.*

i.e. In formal writing, replace the Latin abbreviation *i.e.* with its English equivalent: *that is.*

if, whether Use *if* to express a condition and *whether* to express alternatives. *If you go on a trip, whether to Nebraska or New Jersey, remember to bring traveller's cheques.*

illusion See *allusion, illusion.*

immigrate See *emigrate from, immigrate to.*

imminent See *eminent, imminent.*

immoral See *amoral, immoral.*

implement *Implement* is a pretentious way of saying "do," "carry out," or "accomplish." Use ordinary language instead. *We carried out* (not *implemented*) *the director's orders with some reluctance.*

imply, infer *Imply* means "to suggest or state indirectly"; *infer* means "to draw a conclusion." *John implied that he knew all about computers, but the interviewer inferred that John was inexperienced.*

in, into *In* indicates location or condition; *into* indicates movement or a change in condition. *They found the lost letters in a box after moving into the house.*

in regards to *In regards to* confuses two different phrases: *in regard to* and *as regards.* Use one or the other. *In regard to* (or *As regards*) *the contract, ignore the first clause.*

irregardless *Irregardless* is nonstandard. Use *regardless.*

is when, is where These mixed constructions are often incorrectly used in definitions. *A run-off election is a second election held to break a tie* (not *is when a second election breaks a tie*). (See S5-c.)

its, it's *Its* is a possessive pronoun; *it's* is a contraction for *it is.* (See P5-c and P5-e.) *The dog licked its wound whenever its owner walked into the room. It's a perfect day to walk the thirty-kilometre trail.*

kind(s) *Kind* is singular and should be treated as such. Don't write *These kind of chairs are rare.* Write instead *This kind of chair is rare. Kinds* is plural and should be used only when you mean more than one kind. *These kinds of chairs are rare.*

kind of, sort of Avoid using *kind of* or *sort of* to mean "somewhat." *The movie was somewhat* (not *kind of*) *boring.* Do not put *a* after either phrase. *That kind of* (not *kind of a*) *salesclerk annoys me.*

lay, lie See *lie, lay.*

lead, led *Lead* is a metallic element; it is a noun. *Led* is the past tense of the verb *lead. He led me to the treasure.*

learn, teach *Learn* means "to gain knowledge"; *teach* means "to impart knowledge." *I must teach* (not *learn*) *my sister to read.*

leave, let *Leave* means "to exit." Avoid using it with the nonstandard meaning "to permit." *Let* (not *Leave*) *me help you with the dishes.*

less See *fewer, less.*

let, leave See *leave, let.*

liable *Liable* means "obligated" or "responsible." Do not use it to mean "likely." *You're likely* (not *liable*) *to trip if you don't tie your shoelaces.*

lie, lay *Lie* is an intransitive verb meaning "to recline or rest on a surface." Its principal parts are *lie, lay, lain. Lay* is a transitive verb meaning "to put or place." Its principal parts are *lay, laid, laid.* (See G2-b.)

like, as *Like* is a preposition, not a subordinating conjunction. It can be followed only by a noun or a noun phrase. *As* is a subordinating conjunction that introduces a subordinate clause. In casual speech you may say *She looks like she hasn't slept* or *You don't know her like I do.* But in formal writing, use *as. She looks as if she hasn't slept. You don't know her as I do.* (See also B1-f and B1-g.)

loose, lose *Loose* is an adjective meaning "not securely fastened." *Lose* is a verb meaning "to misplace" or "to not win." *Did you lose your only loose pair of work pants?*

lots, lots of *Lots* and *lots of* are colloquial substitutes for *many, much,* or *a lot.* Avoid using them in formal writing.

mankind Avoid *mankind* whenever possible. It offends many readers because it excludes women. Use *humanity, humans, the human race,* or *humankind* instead. (See W4-e.)

may See *can, may.*

maybe, may be *Maybe* is an adverb meaning "possibly." *May be* is a verb phrase. *Maybe the sun will shine tomorrow. Tomorrow may be a brighter day.*

may of, might of *May of* and *might of* are nonstandard for *may have* and *might have. We may have* (not *may of*) *had too many cookies.*

media, medium *Media* is the plural of *medium. Of all the media that cover the Olympics, television is the medium that best captures the spectacle of the events.*

most *Most* is colloquial when used to mean "almost" and should be avoided. *Almost* (not *Most*) *everyone went to the parade.*

must of See *may of.*

myself *Myself* is a reflexive or intensive pronoun. Reflexive: *I cut myself.* Intensive: *I will drive you myself.* Do not use *myself* in place of *I* or *me. He gave the flowers to Melinda and me* (not *myself*). (See also G3-c.)

neither *Neither* is singular. (See G1-e and G3-a.) For *neither . . . nor* constructions, see G1-d and G3-a.

none *None* may be singular or plural. (See G1-e.)

nowheres *Nowheres* is nonstandard for *nowhere.*

number See *amount, number.*

of Use the verb *have,* not the preposition *of,* after the verbs *could, should, would, may, might,* and *must. They must have* (not *must of*) *left early.*

off of *Off* is sufficient. Omit *of. The ball rolled off* (not *off of*) *the table.*

OK, O.K., okay All three spellings are acceptable, but in formal speech and writing avoid these colloquial expressions.

parameters *Parameter* is a mathematical term that has become jargon for "fixed limit," "boundary," or "guideline." Use ordinary English instead. *The task force was asked to work within certain guidelines* (not *parameters*).

passed, past *Passed* is the past tense of the verb *pass. Mother passed me another slice of cake. Past* usually means "belonging to a former time" or "beyond a time or place." *Our past president spoke until past midnight. The hotel is just past the next intersection.*

percent, per cent, percentage *Percent* (also spelled *per cent*) is always used with a specific number. *Percentage* is used with a descriptive term such as *large* or *small,* not with a specific number. *The candidate won 80 percent of the primary vote. Only a small percentage of registered voters turned out for the election.*

phenomena *Phenomena* is the plural of *phenomenon,* which means "an observable occurrence or fact." *Strange phenomena occur at all hours of the night in that house, but last night's phenomenon was the strangest of all.*

plus *Plus* should not be used to join independent clauses. *This raincoat is dirty; moreover* (not *plus*), *it has a hole in it.*

precede, proceed *Precede* means "to come before." *Proceed* means "to go forward." *As we proceeded up the mountain path, we noticed fresh tracks in the mud, evidence that a group of hikers had preceded us.*

principal, principle *Principal* is a noun meaning "the head of a school or an organization" or "a sum of money." It is also an adjective meaning "most important." *Principle* is a noun meaning "a basic truth or law." *The principal expelled her for three principal reasons. We believe in the principle of equal justice for all.*

proceed, precede See *precede, proceed.*

quote, quotation *Quote* is a verb; *quotation* is a noun. Avoid using *quote* as a shortened form of *quotation. Her quotations* (not *quotes*) *from Shakespeare intrigued us.*

raise, rise *Raise* is a transitive verb meaning "to move or cause to move upward." It takes a direct object. *I raised the shades. Rise* is an intransitive verb meaning "to go up." *Heat rises.*

real, really *Real* is an adjective; *really* is an adverb. *Real* is sometimes used informally as an adverb, but avoid this use in formal writing. *She was really* (not *real*) *angry.* (See G4-a.)

reason . . . is because Use *that* instead of *because. The reason she's cranky is that* (not *because*) *she didn't sleep last night.* (See S5-c.)

reason why The expression *reason why* is redundant. *The reason* (not *The reason why*) *Jones lost the election is clear.*

relation, relationship *Relation* describes a connection between things. *Relationship* describes a connection between people. *There is a relation between poverty and infant mortality. Our business relationship has cooled over the years.*

respectfully, respectively *Respectfully* means "showing or marked by respect." *Respectively* means "each in the order given." *He respectfully submitted his opinion to the judge. John, Tom, and Larry were a butcher, a baker, and a lawyer, respectively.*

sensual, sensuous *Sensual* means "gratifying the physical senses," especially those associated with sexual pleasure. *Sensuous* means "pleasing to the senses," especially those involved in the experience of art, music, and nature. *The sensuous music and balmy air led the dancers to more sensual movements.*

set, sit *Set* is a transitive verb meaning "to put" or "to place." Its principal parts are *set, set, set. Sit* is an intransitive verb meaning "to be seated." Its principal parts are *sit, sat, sat. She set the dough in a warm corner of the kitchen. The cat sat in the warmest part of the room.*

shall, will *Shall* was once used as the helping verb with *I* or *we*: *I shall, we shall, you will, he/she/it will, they will.* Today, however, *will* is generally accepted even when the subject is *I* or *we.* The word *shall* occurs primarily in polite questions (*Shall I find you a pillow?*) and in legalistic sentences suggesting duty or obligation (*The applicant shall file form 1080 by December 31*).

should of *Should of* is nonstandard for *should have. They should have* (not *should of*) *been home an hour ago.*

since Do not use *since* to mean "because" if there is any chance of ambiguity. *Because* (not *Since*) *we won the game, we have been celebrating with a pitcher of root beer. Since* here could mean "because" or "from the time that."

sit See *set, sit.*

site See *cite, site.*

somebody, someone *Somebody* and *someone* are singular. (See G1-e and G3-a.)

something *Something* is singular. (See G1-e.)

sometime, some time, sometimes *Sometime* is an adverb meaning "at an indefinite or unstated time." *Some time* is the adjective *some* modifying the noun *time* and is spelled as two words to mean "a period of time." *Sometimes* is an adverb meaning "at times, now and then." *I'll see you sometime soon. I haven't lived there for some time. Sometimes I run into him at the library.*

suppose to Write *supposed to.*

sure and Write *sure to. We were all taught to be sure to* (not *and*) *look both ways before crossing a street.*

take See *bring, take.*

than, then *Than* is a conjunction used in comparisons; *then* is an adverb denoting time. *That pizza is more than I can eat. Tom laughed, and then we recognized him.*

that See *who, which, that.*

that, which Many writers reserve *that* for restrictive clauses, *which* for nonrestrictive clauses. (See P1-e.)

theirselves *Theirselves* is nonstandard for *themselves. The crash victims pushed the car out of the way themselves* (not *theirselves*).

them The use of *them* in place of *those* is nonstandard. *Please send those* (not *them*) *flowers to the patient in room 220.*

there, their, they're *There* is an adverb specifying place; it is also an expletive. Adverb: *Sylvia is lying there unconscious.* Expletive: *There are two plums left. Their* is a possessive pronoun. *Fred and Jane finally washed their car. They're* is a contraction of *they are. They're later than usual today.*

they The use of *they* to indicate possession is nonstandard. Use *their* instead. *Cindy and Syed decided to sell their* (not *they*) *1975 Corvette.*

this kind See *kind(s).*

to, too, two *To* is a preposition; *too* is an adverb; *two* is a number. *Too many of your shots slice to the left, but the last two were just right.*

toward, towards *Toward* and *towards* are generally interchangeable, although *toward* is preferred in North American English.

try and *Try and* is nonstandard for *try to. The teacher asked us all to try to* (not *try and*) *write an original haiku.*

ultimately, eventually See *eventually, ultimately.*

unique Avoid expressions such as *most unique, more straight, less perfect, very round.* Either something is unique or it isn't. It is illogical to suggest degrees of uniqueness. (See G4-c.)

usage The noun *usage* should not be substituted for *use* when the meaning is "employment of." *The use* (not *usage*) *of computers dramatically increased the company's profits.*

use to Write *used to.*

utilize *Utilize* means "to make use of." It often sounds pretentious; in most cases, *use* is sufficient. *I used* (not *utilized*) *the laser printer.*

wait for, wait on *Wait for* means "to be in readiness for" or "await." *Wait on* means "to serve." *We're only waiting for* (not *waiting on*) *Ruth to take us to the game.*

ways *Ways* is colloquial when used to mean "distance." *The city is a long way* (not *ways*) *from here.*

weather, whether The noun *weather* refers to the state of the atmosphere. *Whether* is a conjunction referring to a choice between alternatives. *We wondered whether the weather would clear.*

well, good See *good, well.*

where Do not use *where* in place of *that. I heard that* (not *where*) *the crime rate is increasing.*

which See *that, which* and *who, which, that.*

while Avoid using *while* to mean "although" or "whereas" if there is any chance of ambiguity. *Although* (not *While*) *Gloria lost money in the slot machine, Angelo won it at roulette.* Here *While* could mean either "although" or "at the same time that."

who, which, that Do not use *which* to refer to persons. Use *who* instead. *That,* though generally used to refer to things, may be used to refer to a group or class of people. *The player who* (not *that* or *which*) *made the basket at the buzzer was named MVP. The team that scores the most points in this game will win the tournament.*

who, whom *Who* is used for subjects and subject complements; *whom* is used for objects. (See G3-d.)

who's, whose *Who's* is a contraction of *who is*; *whose* is a possessive pronoun. *Who's ready for more popcorn? Whose coat is this?* (See P5-c and P5-e.)

will See *shall, will.*

would of *Would of* is nonstandard for *would have. She would have* (not *would of*) *had a chance to play if she had arrived on time.*

you In formal writing, avoid *you* in an indefinite sense meaning "anyone." (See G3-b.) *Any spectator* (not *You*) *could tell by the way Jin caught the ball that his throw would be too late.*

your, you're *Your* is a possessive pronoun; *you're* is a contraction of *you are. Is that your new motorcycle? You're on the list of finalists.* (See P5-c and P5-e.)

W2

Wordy sentences

Long sentences are not necessarily wordy, nor are short sentences always concise. A sentence is wordy if it can be tightened without loss of meaning.

GRAMMAR CHECKERS flag wordy constructions only occasionally. They sometimes alert you to common redundancies, such as *true fact,* but they overlook more redundancies than they catch. They may miss empty or inflated phrases, such as *in my opinion* and *in order that,* and they rarely identify sentences with needlessly complex structures. Grammar checkers are very good, however, at flagging and suggesting revisions for wordy constructions beginning with *there is* and *there are.*

W2-a Eliminate redundancies.

Redundancies such as *cooperate together, close proximity, basic essentials,* and *true fact* are a common source of wordiness. There is no need to say the same thing twice.

► **Daniel ~~is now employed~~ [works] at a private rehabilitation centre ~~working~~ as a registered physical therapist.**

Though modifiers ordinarily add meaning to the words they modify, occasionally they are redundant.

▶ Sylvia ~~very hurriedly~~ scribbled her name, address, and phone number on the back of a greasy napkin.

▶ Joel was determined ~~in his mind~~ to lose weight.

The words *scribbled* and *determined* already contain the notions suggested by the modifiers *very hurriedly* and *in his mind.*

W2-b Avoid unnecessary repetition of words.

Though words may be repeated deliberately, for effect, repetitions will seem awkward if they are clearly unnecessary. When a more concise version is possible, choose it.

▶ **Our fifth patient, in room six, ~~is a patient with~~ has a mental illness.**

▶ **The best teachers help each student to ~~become a better student~~ grow both academically and emotionally.**

W2-c Cut empty or inflated phrases.

An empty phrase can be cut with little or no loss of meaning. Common examples are introductory word groups that apologize or hedge: *in my opinion, I think that, it seems that, one must admit that,* and so on.

▶ **~~In my opinion, o~~Our current immigration policy is misguided.**

Inflated phrases can be reduced to a word or two without loss of meaning.

INFLATED	CONCISE
along the lines of	like
as a matter of fact	in fact
at all times	always
at the present time	now, currently
at this point in time	now, currently

INFLATED	CONCISE
because of the fact that	because
by means of	by
due to the fact that	because
for the purpose of	for
for the reason that	because
have the ability to	can, be able to
in order to	to
in spite of the fact that	although, though
in the event that	if
in the final analysis	finally
in the nature of	like
in the neighbourhood of	about
until such time as	until

▶ **We will file the appropriate papers ~~in the event that~~ *if* we are unable to meet the deadline.**

W2-d Simplify the structure.

If the structure of a sentence is needlessly indirect, try simplifying it. Look for opportunities to strengthen the verb.

▶ **The CEO claimed that because of volatile market conditions she could not ~~make an~~ estimate ~~of~~ the company's future profits.**

The verb *estimate* is more vigorous and more concise than *make an estimate of.*

The colourless verbs *is, are, was,* and *were* frequently generate excess words. (See also W3-b.)

▶ **Eduartina ~~is responsible for monitoring and balancing~~ *monitors and balances* the budgets for travel and personnel.**

The revision is more direct and concise. Actions orginally appearing in subordinate structures have become verbs replacing *is.*

The expletive constructions *there is* and *there are* (or *there was* and *there were*) can also generate excess words. The same is true of expletive constructions beginning with *it.*

▶ ~~There is~~ ~~a~~A nother module ~~that~~ tells the story of Charles Darwin and introduces the theory of evolution.

▶ ~~It is imperative that~~ ~~a~~A ll police officers *must* follow strict procedures when apprehending a suspect.

Finally, verbs in the passive voice may be needlessly indirect. When the active voice expresses your meaning as well, use it. (See also W3-a.)

▶ All too often, *our coaches have recruited* athletes with marginal academic skills. ~~have been recruited by our coaches.~~

W2-e Reduce clauses to phrases, phrases to single words.

Word groups functioning as modifiers can often be made more compact. Look for any opportunities to reduce clauses to phrases or phrases to single words.

▶ We visited Monticello, ~~which was~~ the home of Thomas Jefferson.

▶ For her birthday we gave Jess a stylish *silk* vest. ~~made of silk.~~

ON THE WEB > dianahacker.com/writersref
Grammar exercises > Word choice > E-ex W2–1 through W2–3

W3

Active verbs

As a rule, choose an active verb and pair it with a subject that names the person or thing doing the action. Active verbs express meaning more emphatically and vigorously than their weaker counterparts—forms of the verb *be* or verbs in the passive voice.

Verbs in the passive voice lack strength because their subjects receive the action instead of doing it (see also B2-b). Forms of the verb *be* (*be, am, is, are, was, were, being, been*) lack vigour because they convey no action.

Although passive verbs and the forms of *be* have legitimate uses, if an active verb can carry your meaning, use it.

PASSIVE	The coolant pumps *were destroyed* by a surge of power.
BE VERB	A surge of power *was* responsible for the destruction of the coolant pumps.
ACTIVE	A surge of power *destroyed* the coolant pumps.

Even among active verbs, some are more active — and therefore more vigorous and colourful — than others. Carefully selected verbs can energize a piece of writing.

▶ **The goalie crouched low, ~~reached~~ swept out his stick, and ~~sent~~ hooked the rebound away from the mouth of the net.**

ACADEMIC ENGLISH Although you may be tempted to avoid the passive voice completely, keep in mind that it is preferred in some writing situations, especially in scientific writing. For appropriate uses of the passive voice, see W3-a; for advice about forming the passive, see E1-c.

GRAMMAR CHECKERS are fairly good at flagging passive verbs, such as *is used.* However, because passive verbs are sometimes appropriate, you — not the computer program — must decide whether to change a verb from passive to active. Grammar checkers tend to suggest revisions only when the passive sentence contains a *by* phrase (*Carbon dating is used by scientists to determine an object's approximate age*). Occasionally they make inappropriate suggestions for revision (*Scientists to determine an object's approximate age use carbon dating*). Only you can determine the most sensible word order for your sentence.

W3-a Use the active voice unless you have a good reason for choosing the passive.

In the active voice, the subject of the sentence does the action; in the passive voice, the subject receives the action. (See also B2-b.)

ACTIVE Hernando *caught* the fly ball.

PASSIVE The fly ball *was caught* by Hernando.

In passive sentences, the actor (in this case *Hernando*) frequently disappears from the sentence: *The fly ball was caught.*

In most cases, you will want to emphasize the actor, so you should use the active voice. To replace a passive verb with an active alternative, make the actor the subject of the sentence.

> A bolt of lightning struck the transformer.
> ▶ ~~The transformer was struck by a bolt of lightning.~~
>
> The active verb (*struck*) makes the point more forcefully than the passive verb (*was struck*).

The passive voice is appropriate if you wish to emphasize the receiver of the action or to minimize the importance of the actor.

APPROPRIATE PASSIVE Many native Hawaiians *are forced* to leave their beautiful beaches to make room for hotels and condominiums.

APPROPRIATE PASSIVE As the time for harvest approaches, the tobacco plants *are sprayed* with a chemical to retard the growth of suckers.

The writer of the first sentence wished to emphasize the receivers of the action, Hawaiians. The writer of the second sentence wished to focus on the tobacco plants, not on the people spraying them.

In much scientific writing, the passive voice properly emphasizes the experiment or process being described, not the researcher.

APPROPRIATE PASSIVE The solution *was heated* to the boiling point, and then it was reduced in volume by 50 percent.

ON THE WEB > **dianahacker.com/writersref**
Language Debates > Passive voice

W3-b Replace *be* verbs that result in dull or wordy sentences.

Not every *be* verb needs replacing. The forms of *be* (*be, am, is, are, was, were, being, been*) work well when you want to link a subject to a noun that clearly renames it or to an adjective that describes it: *History is a bucket of ashes. Scoundrels are always sociable.* (See B2-b.) And when used as helping verbs before present participles (*is flying, are disappearing*) to express ongoing action, *be* verbs are fine: *Derrick was plowing the field when his wife went into labour.* (See G2-f.)

If using a *be* verb makes a sentence needlessly dull or wordy, however, consider replacing it. Often a phrase following the verb will contain a word (such as *violation*) that suggests a more vigorous, active alternative (*violate*).

▶ **Burying nuclear waste in Antarctica would ~~be in violation of~~ [violate] an international treaty.**

Violate is less wordy and more vigorous than *be in violation of.*

▶ **When Rosa Parks ~~was resistant to~~ [resisted] giving up her seat on the bus, she became a civil rights hero.**

Resisted is stronger than *was resistant to.*

GRAMMAR CHECKERS usually do not flag wordiness caused by *be* verbs: *is in violation of.* Only you can find ways to strengthen your sentences by using vigorous, active verbs in place of *be.*

ON THE WEB > **dianahacker.com/writersref**
Grammar exercises > Word choice > E-ex W3–1 through W3–3

W4

Appropriate language

Language is appropriate when it suits your subject, engages your audience, and blends naturally with your own voice.

W4-a Stay away from jargon.

Jargon is specialized language used among members of a trade, profession, or group. Use jargon only when readers will be familiar with it; even then, use it only when plain English will not do as well.

JARGON For years the indigenous body politic of South Africa attempted to negotiate legal enfranchisement without result.

REVISED For years the indigenous people of South Africa negotiated in vain for the right to vote.

Broadly defined, jargon includes puffed-up language designed more to impress readers than to inform them. The following are common examples from business, government, higher education, and the military, with plain English translations in parentheses.

ameliorate (improve)
commence (begin)
components (parts)
endeavour (try)
exit (leave)
facilitate (help)
factor (consideration, cause)
impact (v.) (affect)
indicator (sign)
optimal (best, most favourable)
parameters (boundaries, limits)
peruse (read, look over)
prior to (before)
utilize (use)
viable (workable)

Sentences filled with jargon are hard to read, and they are often wordy as well.

▶ All ~~employees functioning in the capacity of~~ work-study students *must prove that they are currently enrolled.* ~~are required to give evidence of current enrollment.~~

▶ Mayor Summers will *begin* ~~commence~~ his term of office by *improving* ~~ameliorating~~ living conditions in *poor neighbourhoods.* ~~economically deprived zones.~~

W4-b Avoid pretentious language, most euphemisms, and "doublespeak."

Hoping to sound profound or poetic, some writers embroider their thoughts with large words and flowery phrases, language that in fact sounds pretentious. Pretentious language is so ornate and often so wordy that it obscures the thought that lies beneath.

▶ We ~~mere mortals~~ often find ~~that~~ it *difficult* ~~requires cerebral exertion~~ to *face* ~~confront~~ the *harsh* ~~virtually unendurable~~ reality that we all *die.* ~~ultimately perish from this life.~~

Euphemisms, nice-sounding words or phrases substituted for words thought to sound harsh or ugly, are sometimes appropriate. It is customary, for example, to say that a couple is "sleeping together" or that someone has "passed away." Most euphemisms, however, are needlessly evasive or even deceitful. Like pretentious language, they obscure the intended meaning.

EUPHEMISM	PLAIN ENGLISH
adult entertainment	pornography
preowned automobile	used car
economically deprived	poor
selected out	fired
negative savings	debts
strategic withdrawal	retreat or defeat
revenue enhancers	taxes
chemical dependency	drug addiction
downsize	lay off
correctional facility	prison

The term *doublespeak* applies to any deliberately evasive or deceptive language, including euphemisms. Doublespeak is especially common in politics, where missiles are named "Peacekeepers," airplane crashes are termed "uncontrolled contact with the ground," and a military retreat is described as "tactical redeployment." Business also gives us its share of doublespeak. When the manufacturer of a pacemaker writes that its product "may result in adverse health consequences in pacemaker-dependent patients as a result of sudden 'no output' failure," it takes an alert reader to grasp the message: The pacemaker might suddenly stop functioning and cause a heart attack or even death.

GRAMMAR CHECKERS rarely identify jargon and only occasionally flag pretentious language. Sometimes they flag language that is acceptable in academic writing. You should be alert to your own use of jargon and pretentious language and simplify it whenever possible. If your grammar checker continually questions language that is appropriate in an academic setting, check to see whether you can set the program to a formal style level.

ON THE WEB > **dianahacker.com/writersref**
Grammar exercises > Word choice > E-ex W4–1

W4-c In most contexts, avoid slang, regional expressions, and nonstandard English.

Slang is an informal and sometimes private vocabulary that expresses the solidarity of a group such as teenagers, rock musicians, or football fans; it is subject to more rapid change than standard English. For example, the slang teenagers use to express approval changes every few years; *cool, groovy, neat, awesome, phat,* and *sweet* have replaced one another within the last three decades. Sometimes slang becomes so widespread that it is accepted as standard vocabulary. *Jazz,* for example, started as slang but is now generally accepted to describe a style of music.

Although slang has a certain vitality, it is a code that not everyone understands, and it is very informal. Therefore, it is inappropriate in most written work.

▶ **If we don't begin studying for the final, a whole semester's work ~~is~~ *will be wasted.* ~~going down the tubes.~~**

▶ **The government's "filth" guidelines for food will *disgust you.* ~~gross you out.~~**

Regional expressions are common to a group in a geographical area. *He's from away* (for *He wasn't born here*) is an expression in Prince Edward Island, for example. Regional expressions have the same limitations as slang and are therefore inappropriate in most writing.

▶ **John was four blocks from the house before he remembered to *turn on* ~~cut~~ the headlights. ~~on.~~**

▶ **I'm not ~~for~~ sure, but I think the dance has been postponed.**

Standard English is the language used in all academic, business, and professional fields. Nonstandard English is spoken by people with a common regional or social heritage. Although nonstandard English may be appropriate when spoken within a close group, it is out of place in most formal and informal writing.

▶ **The counsellor *has* ~~have~~ so many problems in her own life that she *doesn't* ~~don't~~ know how to advise anyone else.**

If you speak a nonstandard dialect, try to identify the ways in which your dialect differs from standard English. Look especially for the following features of nonstandard English, which commonly cause problems in writing:

Misuse of verb forms such as *began* and *begun* (See G2-a.)

Omission of *-s* endings on verbs (See G2-c.)

Omission of *-ed* endings on verbs (See G2-d.)

Omission of necessary verbs (See G2-e.)

Double negatives (See G4-d.)

You might also scan the glossary of usage (W1), which alerts you to nonstandard words and expressions such as *ain't, could of, hisself, theirselves, them* (meaning "those"), *they* (meaning "their"), and so on.

W4-d Choose an appropriate level of formality.

In deciding on a level of formality, consider both your subject and your audience. Does the subject demand a dignified treatment, or is a relaxed tone more suitable? Will the audience be put off if you assume too close a relationship with them, or might you alienate them by seeming too distant?

For most postsecondary and professional writing, some degree of formality is appropriate. In a letter applying for a job, for example, it is a mistake to sound too breezy and informal.

TOO INFORMAL	I'd like to get that technician job you've got in the paper.
MORE FORMAL	I would like to apply for the technician position listed in the *Brandon Sun*.

Informal writing is appropriate for private letters, business correspondence between close associates, articles in popular magazines, and personal narratives. In such writing, formal language can seem out of place.

▶ **Bob's pitching lesson ~~commenced~~** *began* **with his famous sucker pitch, ~~implemented~~** *which he threw* **as a slow ball coming behind a fast windup.**

Formal words such as *commenced* and *implemented* clash with appropriate informal terms such as *sucker pitch* and *fast windup.*

GRAMMAR CHECKERS rarely flag slang and informal language. They do, however, flag contractions. If your ear tells you that a contraction such as *isn't* or *doesn't* strikes the right tone, stay with it.

W4-e Avoid sexist language.

Sexist language is language that stereotypes or demeans men or women, usually women. Using nonsexist language is a matter of courtesy—of respect for and sensitivity to the feelings of others.

GRAMMAR CHECKERS are good at flagging obviously sexist terms, such as *mankind* and *fireman,* but they do not flag language that might be demeaning to women (*woman doctor*) or stereotypical (referring to assistants as women and lawyers as men, for instance). They also have no way of identifying the generic use of *he* or *his* (*An obstetrician needs to be available to his patients at all hours*). You must use your common sense to tell when a word or a construction is offensive.

ON THE WEB > **dianahacker.com/writersref**
Language Debates > Sexist language

Recognizing sexist language

Some sexist language is easy to recognize because it reflects genuine contempt for women: referring to a woman as a "chick," for example, or calling a lawyer a "lady lawyer," or saying in an advertisement, "If our new sports car were a lady, it would get its bottom pinched."

Other forms of sexist language are less blatant. The following practices, while they may not result from conscious sexism, reflect stereotypical thinking: referring to nurses as women and doctors as men, using different conventions when naming or identifying women and men, or assuming that all of one's readers are men.

STEREOTYPICAL LANGUAGE

After the nursing student graduates, *she* must face a difficult licensing board examination. [Not all nursing students are women.]

Running for city council are Jake Stein, an attorney, and *Mrs.* Cynthia Jones, a professor of English *and mother of three.* [The title *Mrs.* and the phrase *and mother of three* are irrelevant.]

Wives of senior government officials are required to report any gifts they receive that are valued at more than $100. [Not all senior government officials are men.]

Still other forms of sexist language result from outmoded traditions. The pronouns *he, him,* and *his,* for instance, were traditionally used to refer generically to persons of either sex.

GENERIC *HE* OR *HIS*

When a senior physician is harassed by managed care professionals, *he* may be tempted to leave the profession.

A journalist is stimulated by *his* deadline.

Today, however, such usage is widely viewed as sexist because it excludes women and encourages sex-role stereotyping—the view that men are somehow more suited than women to be doctors, journalists, and so on.

Like the pronouns *he, him,* and *his,* the nouns *man* and *men* were once used indefinitely to refer to persons of either sex. Current usage demands gender-neutral terms instead.

INAPPROPRIATE	APPROPRIATE
anchorman	anchor
chairman	chairperson, moderator, chair, head
clergyman	member of the clergy, minister, pastor
congressman	member of Congress, representative, legislator
fireman	firefighter
foreman	supervisor
mailman	mail carrier, postal worker, letter carrier
(to) man	to operate, to staff
mankind	people, humans
manpower	personnel
policeman	police officer
salesman	sales associate, sales representative
weatherman	weather forecaster, meteorologist
workman	worker, labourer

Revising sexist language

When revising sexist language, be sparing in your use of the wordy constructions *he or she* and *his or her.* Although these constructions are fine in small doses, they become awkward when repeated throughout an essay. A better revision strategy, many writers have discovered, is to write in the plural; yet another strategy is to recast the sentence so that the problem does not arise.

SEXIST

When a senior physician is harassed by managed care professionals, *he* may be tempted to leave the profession.

A journalist is stimulated by *his* deadline.

ACCEPTABLE BUT WORDY

When a senior physician is harassed by managed care professionals, *he or she* may be tempted to leave the profession.

A journalist is stimulated by *his or her* deadline.

BETTER: USING THE PLURAL

When senior *physicians* are harassed by managed care professionals, *they* may be tempted to leave the profession.

Journalists are stimulated by *their* deadlines.

BETTER: RECASTING THE SENTENCE

When harassed by managed care professionals, *a senior physician* may be tempted to leave the profession.

A journalist is stimulated by *a* deadline.

For more examples of these revision strategies, see G3-a.

ON THE WEB > **dianahacker.com/writersref**
Grammar exercises > Word choice > E-ex W4–2

W4-f Revise language that may offend groups of people.

Obviously it is impolite to use offensive terms such as *Polack* or *redneck*. But biased language can take more subtle forms. Because language evolves over time, names once thought acceptable may become offensive. When describing groups of people, choose names that the groups currently use to describe themselves.

▶ Nunavut takes its name from the ~~Eskimo~~ Inuit word meaning "friend" or "ally."

▶ Many ~~Oriental~~ Asian immigrants have recently settled in our small town in British Columbia.

Negative stereotypes (such as "drives like a teenager" or "haggard as an old crone") are of course offensive. But you should avoid stereotyping a person or a group even if you believe your generalization to be positive.

▶ It was no surprise that Greer, ~~a Chinese Canadian,~~ an excellent math and science student, was selected for the honours chemistry program.

W5

Exact language

Two reference works (or their online equivalents) will help you find words to express your meaning exactly: a good dictionary, such as the *Canadian Oxford Dictionary* or the *Nelson Canadian Dictionary of the English Language,* and a book of synonyms and antonyms, such as *Roget's International Thesaurus.* (See W6.)

GRAMMAR CHECKERS flag some nonstandard idioms, such as *comply to,* but few clichés. They do not identify commonly confused words, such as *principal* and *principle*, or misused word forms, such as *significance* and *significant.* You must be alert for such words and use your dictionary if you are unsure of the correct form. Grammar checkers are of little help with the other problems discussed in W5: choosing words with appropriate connotations, using concrete language, and using figures of speech appropriately.

W5-a Select words with appropriate connotations.

In addition to their strict dictionary meanings (or *denotations*), words have *connotations,* emotional colorings that affect how readers respond to them. The word *steel* denotes "made of or resembling commercial iron that contains carbon," but it also calls up a cluster of images associated with steel, such as the sensation of touching it. These associations give the word its connotations—cold, smooth, unbending.

If the connotation of a word does not seem appropriate for your purpose, your audience, or your subject matter, you should change the word. When a more appropriate synonym does not come quickly to mind, consult a dictionary or a thesaurus. (See W6.)

▶ **The model was ~~skinny~~ *slender* and fashionable.**

The connotation of the word *skinny* is too negative.

▶ **As I covered the boats with marsh grass, the ~~perspiration~~ *sweat* I had worked up evaporated in the wind, and the cold morning air seemed even colder.**

The term *perspiration* is too dainty for the context, which suggests vigorous exercise.

W5-b Prefer specific, concrete nouns.

Unlike general nouns, which refer to broad classes of things, specific nouns point to definite and particular items. *Film,* for example, names a general class, *fantasy film* names a narrower class, and *Lord of the Rings: Return of the King* is more specific still.

Unlike abstract nouns, which refer to qualities and ideas (*justice, beauty, realism, dignity*), concrete nouns point to immediate, often sensory experience and to physical objects (*steeple, asphalt, lilac, stone, garlic*).

Specific, concrete nouns express meaning more vividly than general or abstract ones. Although general and abstract language is sometimes necessary to convey your meaning, ordinarily prefer specific, concrete alternatives.

▶ **The senator spoke about the challenges of the future: ~~the environment and world peace.~~** *famine, pollution, dwindling resources, and terrorism.*

Nouns such as *thing, area, factor,* and *individual* are especially dull and imprecise.

▶ **A career in city planning offers many ~~things.~~** *rewards.*

▶ **Try pairing a trainee with an ~~individual with technical experience.~~** *experienced technician.*

W5-c Do not misuse words.

If a word is not in your active vocabulary, you may find yourself misusing it, sometimes with embarrassing consequences. When in doubt, check the dictionary.

▶ **The fans were ~~migrating~~** *climbing* **up the bleachers in search of good seats.**

▶ **The Internet has so ~~diffused~~** *permeated* **our culture that it touches all segments of society.**

Be especially alert for misused word forms—using a noun such as *absence, significance,* or *persistence,* for example, when your meaning requires the adjective *absent, significant,* or *persistent.*

▶ **Most dieters are not ~~persistence~~** *persistent* **enough to make a permanent change in their eating habits.**

ON THE WEB > **dianahacker.com/writersref**
Grammar exercises > Word choice > E-ex W5–1

W5-d Use standard idioms.

Idioms are speech forms that follow no easily specified rules. The English say "Maria went *to hospital,*" an idiom strange to American ears, which are accustomed to hearing *the* in front of *hospital.* Native speakers of a language seldom have problems with idioms, but prepositions sometimes cause trouble, especially when they follow certain verbs and adjectives. When in doubt, consult a good desk dictionary: Look up the word preceding the troublesome preposition.

UNIDIOMATIC	IDIOMATIC
abide with (a decision)	abide by (a decision)
according with	according to
agree to (an idea)	agree with (an idea)
angry at (a person)	angry with (a person)
capable to	capable of
comply to	comply with
desirous to	desirous of
different than (a person or thing)	different from (a person or thing)
intend on doing	intend to do
off of	off
plan on doing	plan to do
preferable than	preferable to
prior than	prior to
superior than	superior to
sure and	sure to
try and	try to
type of a	type of

Because idioms follow no particular rules, you must learn them individually. You may find it helpful to keep a list of idioms that you frequently encounter in your reading. For idiomatic combinations of adjectives and prepositions (such as *afraid of*), see E5-c. For idiomatic combinations of verbs and prepositions (such as *search for*), see E5-d.

ON THE WEB > **dianahacker.com/writersref**
Grammar exercises > Word choice > E-ex W5–2

W5-e Do not rely heavily on clichés.

The pioneer who first announced that he had "slept like a log" no doubt amused his companions with a fresh and unlikely comparison. Today, however, that comparison is a cliché, a saying that has lost its dazzle from overuse. No longer can it surprise.

To see just how predictable clichés are, put your hand over the right-hand column on the next page and then finish the phrases given on the left.

cool as a	cucumber
beat around	the bush
blind as a	bat
busy as a	bee, beaver
crystal	clear
dead as a	doornail
out of the frying pan and	into the fire
light as a	feather
like a bull	in a china shop
playing with	fire
nutty as a	fruitcake
selling like	hotcakes
starting out at the bottom	of the ladder
water under the	bridge
white as a	sheet, ghost
avoid clichés like the	plague

The cure for clichés is frequently simple: Just delete them. When this won't work, try adding some element of surprise. One student, for example, who had written that she had butterflies in her stomach, revised her cliché like this:

> If all of the action in my stomach is caused by butterflies, there must be a horde of them, with horseshoes on.

The image of butterflies wearing horseshoes is fresh and unlikely, not dully predictable like the original cliché.

ON THE WEB > **dianahacker.com/writersref**
Language Debates > Clichés

W5-f Use figures of speech with care.

A figure of speech is an expression that uses words imaginatively (rather than literally) to make abstract ideas concrete. Most often, figures of speech compare two seemingly unlike things to reveal surprising similarities.

In a *simile,* the writer makes the comparison explicitly, usually by introducing it with *like* or *as*: "By the time cotton had to be picked, grandfather's neck was as red as the clay he plowed." In a *metaphor,* the *like* or *as* is omitted, and the comparison is implied.

For example, in the Old Testament Song of Solomon, a young woman compares the man she loves to a fruit tree: "With great delight I sat in his shadow, and his fruit was sweet to my taste."

Although figures of speech are useful devices, writers sometimes use them without thinking through the images they evoke. The result is sometimes a *mixed metaphor,* the combination of two or more images that don't make sense together.

▶ **Crossing Utah's salt flats in his new convertible, my father flew** *at jet speed.* **~~under a full head of steam.~~**

Flew suggests an airplane, while *under a full head of steam* suggests a steamboat or a train. To clarify the image, the writer should stick with one comparison or the other.

▶ **Our office had decided to put all controversial issues on a back burner. ~~in a holding pattern.~~**

Here the writer is mixing stoves and airplanes. Simply deleting one of the images corrects the problem.

ON THE WEB > **dianahacker.com/writersref**
Grammar exercises > Word choice > E-ex W5–3

W6

The dictionary and thesaurus

W6-a The dictionary

A good dictionary, whether print or online—such as the *Gage Canadian Dictionary,* the *Canadian Oxford Dictionary,* the *Nelson Canadian Dictionary of the English Language,* or *The American Heritage Dictionary of the English Language*—is an indispensable writer's aid.

The entry on page 157 is taken from *The American Heritage Dictionary*. Labels show where various kinds of information about a word can be found in that dictionary. A sample entry from an online dictionary, *Merriam-Webster Online,* appears on page 158.

PRINT DICTIONARY ENTRY

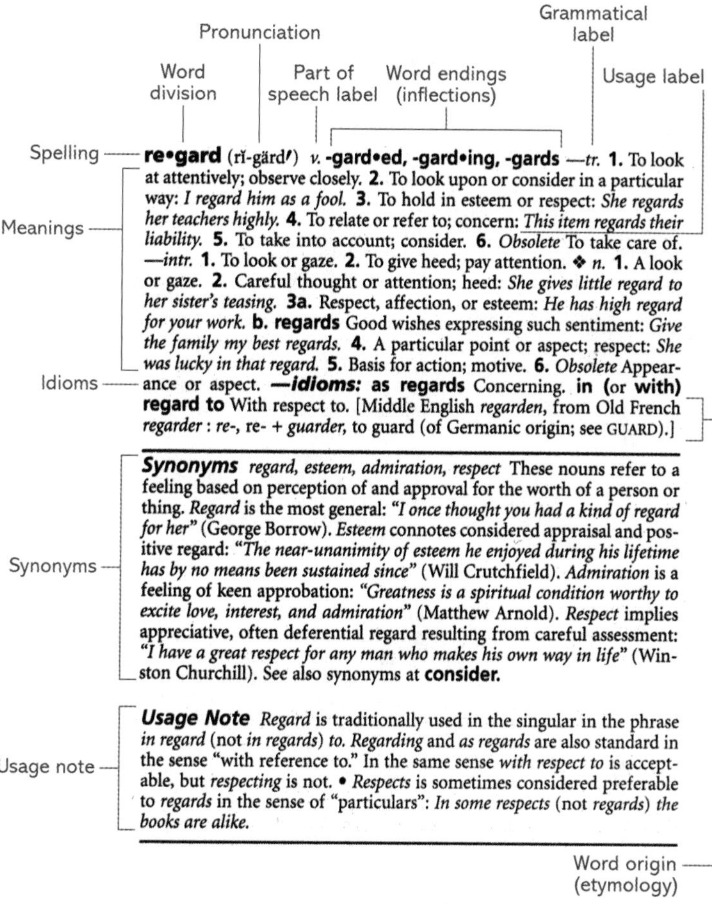

re•gard (rĭ-gärd′) *v.* **-gard•ed, -gard•ing, -gards** —*tr.* **1.** To look at attentively; observe closely. **2.** To look upon or consider in a particular way: *I regard him as a fool.* **3.** To hold in esteem or respect: *She regards her teachers highly.* **4.** To relate or refer to; concern: *This item regards their liability.* **5.** To take into account; consider. **6.** *Obsolete* To take care of. —*intr.* **1.** To look or gaze. **2.** To give heed; pay attention. ❖ *n.* **1.** A look or gaze. **2.** Careful thought or attention; heed: *She gives little regard to her sister's teasing.* **3a.** Respect, affection, or esteem: *He has high regard for your work.* **b. regards** Good wishes expressing such sentiment: *Give the family my best regards.* **4.** A particular point or aspect; respect: *She was lucky in that regard.* **5.** Basis for action; motive. **6.** *Obsolete* Appearance or aspect. ***—idioms:*** **as regards** Concerning. **in** (or **with**) **regard to** With respect to. [Middle English *regarden,* from Old French *regarder* : *re-,* re- + *guarder,* to guard (of Germanic origin; see GUARD).]

Synonyms *regard, esteem, admiration, respect* These nouns refer to a feeling based on perception of and approval for the worth of a person or thing. *Regard* is the most general: *"I once thought you had a kind of regard for her"* (George Borrow). *Esteem* connotes considered appraisal and positive regard: *"The near-unanimity of esteem he enjoyed during his lifetime has by no means been sustained since"* (Will Crutchfield). *Admiration* is a feeling of keen approbation: *"Greatness is a spiritual condition worthy to excite love, interest, and admiration"* (Matthew Arnold). *Respect* implies appreciative, often deferential regard resulting from careful assessment: *"I have a great respect for any man who makes his own way in life"* (Winston Churchill). See also synonyms at **consider.**

Usage Note *Regard* is traditionally used in the singular in the phrase *in regard* (not *in regards*) *to. Regarding* and *as regards* are also standard in the sense "with reference to." In the same sense *with respect to* is acceptable, but *respecting* is not. • *Respects* is sometimes considered preferable to *regards* in the sense of "particulars": *In some respects* (not *regards*) *the books are alike.*

Spelling, word division, and pronunciation

The main entry (*re•gard* in the sample entries) shows the correct spelling of the word. When there are two correct spellings of a word (as in *collectible, collectable,* for example), both are given, with the preferred spelling usually appearing first.

The main entry also shows how the word is divided into syllables. The dot between *re* and *gard* separates the word's two syllables. When a word is compound, the main entry shows how to write it: as one word (*crossroad*), as a hyphenated word (*cross-stitch*), or as two words (*cross section*).

ONLINE DICTIONARY ENTRY

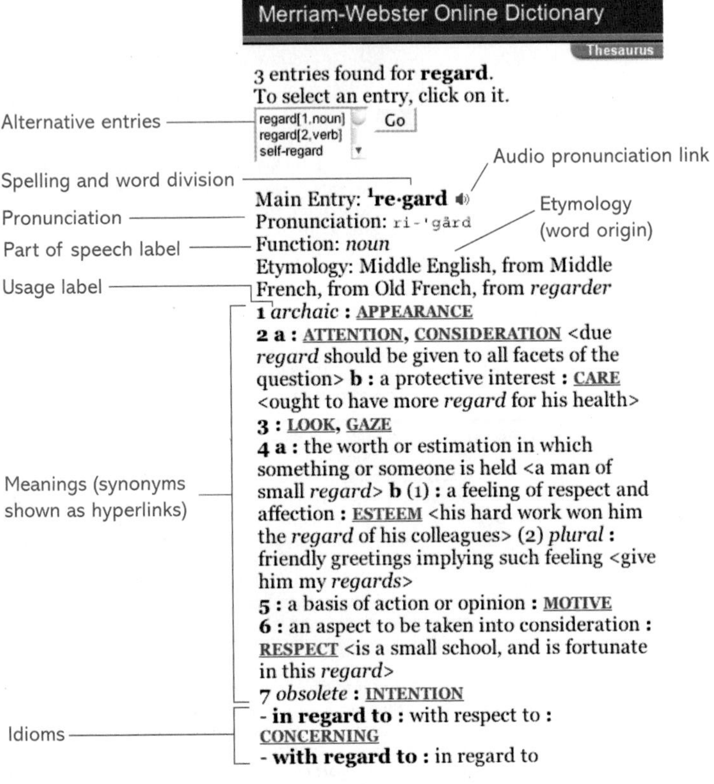

The word's pronunciation is given just after the main entry. The accents indicate which syllables are stressed; the other marks are explained in the dictionary's pronunciation key. In print dictionaries this key usually appears at the bottom of every page or every other page. Many online entries include an audio link to a person's voice pronouncing the word. And most online dictionaries have an audio pronunciation guide.

Word endings and grammatical labels

When a word takes endings to indicate grammatical functions (called *inflections*), the endings are listed in boldface, as with *-garded, -garding,* and *-gards* in the sample print entry.

Labels for the parts of speech and for other grammatical terms are sometimes abbreviated, as they are in the print entry. The most commonly used abbreviations are these:

n.	noun	adj.	adjective
pl.	plural	adv.	adverb
sing.	singular	pron.	pronoun
v.	verb	prep.	preposition
tr.	transitive verb	conj.	conjunction
int.	intransitive verb	interj.	interjection

Meanings, word origin, synonyms, and antonyms

Each meaning for the word is given a number. Occasionally a word's use is illustrated in a quoted sentence.

Sometimes a word can be used as more than one part of speech (*regard,* for instance, can be used as either a verb or a noun). In such a case, all the meanings for one part of speech are given before all the meanings for another, as in the sample entries. The entries also give idiomatic uses of the word.

The origin of the word, called its *etymology,* appears in brackets after all the meanings in the print version; in the online version, it appears before the meanings.

Synonyms, words similar in meaning to the main entry, are frequently listed. In the sample print entry, the dictionary draws distinctions in meaning among the various synonyms. In the online entry, synonyms appear as hyperlinks. Antonyms, which do not appear in the sample entries, are words having a meaning opposite from that of the main entry.

Usage

Usage labels indicate when, where, or under what conditions a particular meaning for a word is appropriately used. Common labels are *informal* (or *colloquial*), *slang, nonstandard, dialect, obsolete, archaic, poetic,* and *British.* In the sample print entry, two meanings of *regard* are labelled *obsolete* because they are no longer in use. The online entry has meanings labelled both *archaic* and *obsolete.*

Dictionaries sometimes include usage notes as well. In the sample print entry, the dictionary offers advice on several uses of *regard* not specifically covered by the meanings. Such advice is based on the opinions of many experts and on actual usage in current magazines, newspapers, and books.

W6-b The thesaurus

When you are looking for just the right word, you may want to consult a book of synonyms and antonyms such as *Roget's International Thesaurus* (or its online equivalent). Look up (or click on) the adjective *still,* for example, and you will find synonyms such as *tranquil, quiet, quiescent, reposeful, calm, pacific, halcyon, placid,* and *unruffled.* Unless your vocabulary is better than average, the list will contain words you've never heard of or with which you are only vaguely familiar. Whenever you are tempted to use one of these words, look it up in the dictionary first to avoid misusing it.

On discovering the thesaurus, many writers use it for the wrong reasons, so a word of caution is in order. Do not turn to a thesaurus in search of exotic, fancy words—such as *halcyon*—with which to embellish your essays. Look instead for words that express your meaning exactly. Most of the time these words will be familiar to both you and your readers. The first synonym on the list—*tranquil*—was probably the word you were looking for all along.

G

Grammatical Sentences

G Grammatical Sentences

G1

Subject-verb agreement

Native speakers of standard English know by ear that *he teaches, she has,* and *it doesn't* (not *he teach, she have,* and *it don't*) are standard subject-verb combinations. For such speakers, problems with subject-verb agreement arise only in certain tricky situations, which are detailed in G1-b to G1-k.

If you don't trust your ear—perhaps because you speak English as a second language or because you speak or hear nonstandard English in your community—you will need to learn the standard forms explained in G1-a. Even if you do trust your ear, take a quick look at G1-a to see what "subject-verb agreement" means.

GRAMMAR CHECKERS are fairly good at flagging subject-verb agreement problems. They occasionally flag a correct sentence, usually because they misidentify the subject, the verb, or both. Sometimes they miss an agreement problem because they don't recognize a pronoun's antecedent. In the following sentence, for example, the grammar checker did not detect that *eggs* is the antecedent of *which*: *Some animal rights groups oppose eating eggs, which comes from animals.* Because *eggs* is plural, the correct verb is *come.*

G1-a Consult this section for standard subject-verb combinations.

In the present tense, verbs agree with their subjects in number (singular or plural) and in person (first, second, or third). The present-tense ending *-s* (or *-es*) is used on a verb if its subject is third-person singular; otherwise the verb takes no ending. Consider, for example, the present-tense forms of the verb *love,* given at the beginning of the chart on page 164.

The verb *be* varies from this pattern; unlike any other verb, it has special forms in *both* the present and the past tense. These forms appear at the end of the chart on page 164.

If you aren't confident that you know the standard forms, use the charts on pages 164 and 165 as you proofread for subject-verb agreement. You may also want to look at G2-c, on *-s* endings.

Subject-verb agreement at a glance

Present-tense forms of *love* and *try* (typical verbs)

	SINGULAR		PLURAL	
FIRST PERSON	I	love	we	love
SECOND PERSON	you	love	you	love
THIRD PERSON	he/she/it	loves	they	love

	SINGULAR		PLURAL	
FIRST PERSON	I	try	we	try
SECOND PERSON	you	try	you	try
THIRD PERSON	he/she/it	tries	they	try

Present-tense forms of *have*

	SINGULAR		PLURAL	
FIRST PERSON	I	have	we	have
SECOND PERSON	you	have	you	have
THIRD PERSON	he/she/it	has	they	have

Present-tense forms of *do*

	SINGULAR		PLURAL	
FIRST PERSON	I	do/don't	we	do/don't
SECOND PERSON	you	do/don't	you	do/don't
THIRD PERSON	he/she/it	does/doesn't	they	do/don't

Present-tense and past-tense forms of *be*

	SINGULAR		PLURAL	
FIRST PERSON	I	am/was	we	are/were
SECOND PERSON	you	are/were	you	are/were
THIRD PERSON	he/she/it	is/was	they	are/were

When to use the -s (or -es) form of a present-tense verb

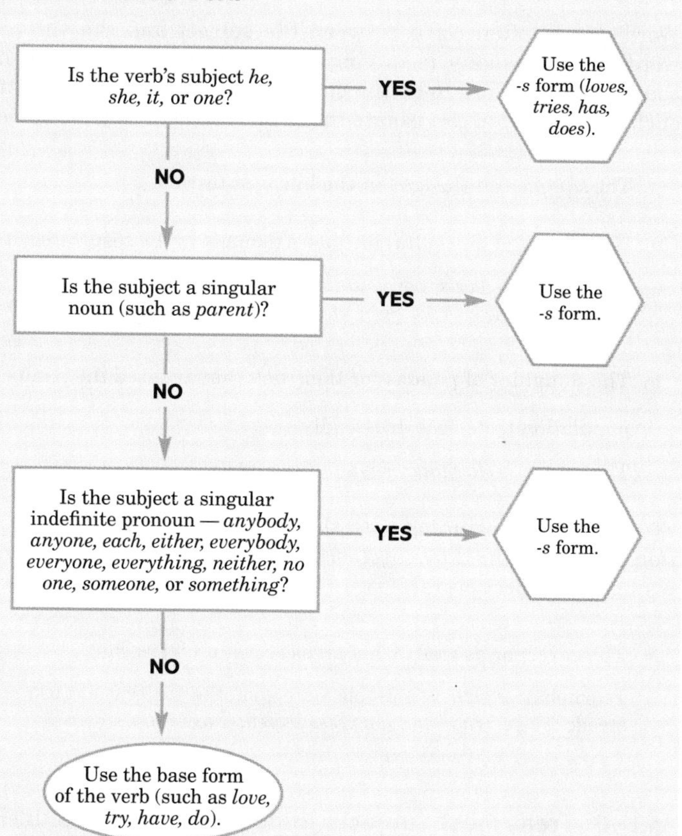
Is the verb's subject *he, she, it,* or *one*?
YES
Use the -*s* form (*loves, tries, has, does*).
NO
Is the subject a singular noun (such as *parent*)?
YES
Use the -*s* form.
NO
Is the subject a singular indefinite pronoun — *anybody, anyone, each, either, everybody, everyone, everything, neither, no one, someone,* or *something*?
YES
Use the -*s* form.
NO
Use the base form of the verb (such as *love, try, have, do*).

EXCEPTION: Choosing the correct present-tense form of *be* (*am, is,* or *are*) is not quite so simple. See the chart on the previous page for both present- and past-tense forms of *be.*

ESL TIP: Do not use the -*s* form of a verb that follows a modal or another helping verb such as *can, must,* or *do.* (See E1-b.)

G1-b Make the verb agree with its subject, not with a word that comes between.

Word groups often come between the subject and the verb. Such word groups, usually modifying the subject, may contain a noun that at first appears to be the subject. By mentally stripping away such modifiers, you can isolate the noun that is in fact the subject.

The *samples* on the tray in the lab *need* testing.

▶ **High levels of air pollution causes damage to the respiratory tract.**

The subject is *levels,* not *pollution.* Strip away the phrase *of air pollution* to hear the correct verb: *levels cause.*

▶ **The slaughter of pandas for their pelts ~~have~~ has caused the panda population to decline drastically.**

The subject is *slaughter,* not *pandas* or *pelts.*

NOTE: Phrases beginning with the prepositions *as well as, in addition to, accompanied by, together with,* and *along with* do not make a singular subject plural.

▶ **The governor as well as his press secretary ~~were~~ was shot.**

To emphasize that two people were shot, the writer could use *and* instead: *The governor and his press secretary were shot.*

G1-c Treat most subjects joined with *and* as plural.

A subject with two or more parts is said to be compound. If the parts are connected by *and,* the subject is nearly always plural.

Leon and Jan often *jog* together.

▶ **Jill's natural ability and her desire to help others ~~has~~ have led to a career in the ministry.**

Ability and desire is a plural subject, so its verb should be *have.*

EXCEPTIONS: When the parts of the subject form a single unit or refer to the same person or thing, treat the subject as singular.

Strawberries and cream was a last-minute addition to the menu.

Sue's friend and adviser was surprised by her decision.

When a compound subject is preceded by *each* or *every,* treat the subject as singular.

Each tree, shrub, and vine needs to be sprayed.

This exception does not apply when a compound subject is followed by *each*: *Alain and Marcia each have different ideas.*

G1-d With subjects joined with *or* or *nor* (or with *either . . . or* or *neither . . . nor*), make the verb agree with the part of the subject nearer to the verb.

A driver's *licence* or credit *card is* required.

A driver's *licence* or two credit *cards are* required.

▶ **If an infant or a child ~~are~~ [is] having difficulty breathing, seek medical attention immediately.**

▶ **Neither the teacher nor the students ~~was~~ [were] in the lab.**

The verb must be matched with the part of the subject closer to it: *child is* in the first sentence, *students were* in the second.

NOTE: If one part of the subject is singular and the other is plural, put the plural one last to avoid awkwardness.

G1-e Treat most indefinite pronouns as singular.

Indefinite pronouns are pronouns that do not refer to specific persons or things. The following commonly used indefinite pronouns are singular: *anybody, anyone, anything, each, either, everybody, everyone, everything, neither, nobody, no one, somebody, someone, something.*

Everyone on the team *supports* the coach.

▶ **Each of the furrows ~~have~~ [has] been seeded.**

▶ **Everybody who signed up for the ski trip ~~were~~ [was] taking lessons.**

The subjects of these sentences are *Each* and *Everybody*. These indefinite pronouns are third-person singular, so the verbs must be *has* and *was.*

A few indefinite pronouns (*all, any, none, some*) may be singular or plural depending on the noun or pronoun they refer to.

Some of our *luggage was* lost. *None* of his *advice makes* sense.

Some of the *rocks are* slippery. *None* of the *eggs were* broken.

NOTE: When the meaning of *none* is emphatically "not one," *none* may be treated as singular: *None* [meaning "Not one"] *of the eggs was broken.* However, some experts advise using *not one* instead: *Not one of the eggs was broken.*

ON THE WEB > **diahacker.com/writersref**
Language Debates > *none*

G1-f Treat collective nouns as singular unless the meaning is clearly plural.

Collective nouns, such as *jury, committee, audience, crowd, class, troop, family,* and *couple,* name a class or a group. In North American English, collective nouns are usually treated as singular: They emphasize the group as a unit. Occasionally, when there is some reason to draw attention to the individual members of the group, a collective noun may be treated as plural. (See also G3-a.)

SINGULAR The *class respects* the teacher.

PLURAL The *class are* debating among themselves.

To underscore the notion of individuality in the second sentence, many writers would add a clearly plural noun such as *members*: *The members of the class are debating among themselves.*

▶ **The board of trustees ~~meet~~** *meets* **in Toronto twice a year.**

The board as a whole meets; there is no reason to draw attention to its individual members.

▶ **A young couple ~~was~~** *were* **arguing about politics while holding hands.**

The meaning is clearly plural. Only individuals can argue and hold hands.

NOTE: Treat *the number* as singular, *a number* as plural.

SINGULAR *The number* of school-age children *is* declining.

PLURAL *A number* of children *are* attending the wedding.

NOTE: In general, when units of measurement are used with a singular noun, treat them as singular; when they are used with a plural noun, treat them as plural.

SINGULAR *Three-fourths* of the pie *has* been eaten.

PLURAL *One-fourth* of the truck drivers *were* women.

G1-g Make the verb agree with its subject even when the subject follows the verb.

Verbs ordinarily follow subjects. When this normal order is reversed, it is easy to become confused. Sentences beginning with *there is* or *there are* (or *there was* or *there were*) are inverted; the subject follows the verb.

There *are* surprisingly few *children* in our neighbourhood.

Occasionally you may decide to invert a sentence for variety or effect. When you do so, check to make sure that your subject and verb agree.

▶ **At the back of the room ~~is~~ *are* a small aquarium and an enormous terrarium.**

The subject, *aquarium and terrarium,* is plural, so the verb must be *are.* If the correct sentence seems awkward, begin with the subject: *A small aquarium and an enormous terrarium are at the back of the room.*

G1-h Make the verb agree with its subject, not with a subject complement.

One sentence pattern in English consists of a subject, a linking verb, and a subject complement: *Jack is a securities lawyer.* (See B2-b.) Because the subject complement names or describes the subject, it is sometimes mistaken for the subject.

► **A tent and a sleeping bag ~~is~~ *are* the required equipment.**

Tent and bag is the subject, not *equipment.*

► **A major force in today's economy ~~are~~ *is* women — as earners, consumers, and investors.**

Force is the subject, not *women.* If the corrected version seems awkward, make *women* the subject: *Women are a major force in today's economy — as earners, consumers, and investors.*

G1-i *Who, which,* and *that* take verbs that agree with their antecedents.

Like most pronouns, the relative pronouns *who, which,* and *that* have antecedents, nouns or pronouns to which they refer. Relative pronouns used as subjects of subordinate clauses take verbs that agree with their antecedents. (See B3-e.)

Take a *suit that travels* well.

Constructions such as *one of the students who* [or *one of the things that*] cause problems for writers. Do not assume that the antecedent must be *one.* Instead, consider the logic of the sentence.

► **Our ability to use language is one of the things that set~~s~~ us apart from animals.**

The antecedent of *that* is *things,* not *one.* Several things set us apart from animals.

When the word *only* comes before *one,* you are safe in assuming that *one* is the antecedent of the relative pronoun.

► **Veronica was the only one of the first-year French students who ~~were~~ *was* fluent enough to apply for the exchange program.**

The antecedent of *who* is *one,* not *students.* Only one student was fluent enough.

ON THE WEB > **dianahacker.com/writersref**
Language Debates > *one of those who* (or *that*)

G1-j Words such as *athletics, economics, mathematics, physics, statistics, measles,* and *news* are usually singular, despite their plural form.

▶ Statistics ~~are~~ ^is^ among the most difficult courses in our program.

EXCEPTION: When they describe separate items rather than a collective body of knowledge, words such as *athletics, mathematics, physics,* and *statistics* are plural: *The statistics on steroid use are alarming.*

G1-k Titles of works, company names, words mentioned as words, and gerund phrases are singular.

▶ *Lost Cities* ~~describe~~ ^describes^ the discoveries of many ancient civilizations.

▶ Delmonico Brothers ~~specialize~~ ^specializes^ in organic produce and additive-free meats.

▶ *Controlled substances* ~~are~~ ^is^ a euphemism for illegal drugs.

A gerund phrase consists of an *-ing* verb form followed by any objects, complements, or modifiers. (See B3-b.) Treat gerund phrases as singular.

▶ Encountering busy signals ~~are~~ ^is^ troublesome to our clients, so we have hired two new switchboard operators.

ON THE WEB > **dianahacker.com/writersref**
Grammar exercises > Grammatical sentences > E-ex G1–1 through G1–3

G2

Other problems with verbs

The verb is the heart of the sentence, so it is important to get it right. Section G1 deals with the problem of subject-verb agreement, and section W3 offers advice on active and passive verbs. This section describes other potential problems with verbs:

a. irregular verb forms (such as *drive, drove, driven*)
b. *lie* and *lay*
c. *-s* (or *-es*) endings on verbs
d. *-ed* endings on verbs
e. omitted verbs
f. tense
g. subjunctive mood

If English is not your first language, see also E1 for more help with verbs.

G2-a Choose standard English forms of irregular verbs.

Except for the verb *be,* all main verbs in English have five forms. The following list shows the five forms and provides a sample sentence in which each might appear.

BASE FORM	Usually I (*walk, ride*).
PAST TENSE	Yesterday I (*walked, rode*).
PAST PARTICIPLE	I have (*walked, ridden*) many times before.
PRESENT PARTICIPLE	I am (*walking, riding*) right now.
-S FORM	He/she/it (*walks, rides*) regularly.

For regular verbs, the past-tense and past-participle forms end in *-ed* or *-d*: *walked, walked*. For irregular verbs, the past tense and past participle are formed differently: *rode, ridden*; *began, begun.*

The past-tense form always occurs alone, without a helping verb. It expresses action that occurred entirely in the past: *I rode to work yesterday. I walked to work last Tuesday.* The past participle is used with a helping verb. It forms the perfect tenses with *has, have,* or *had*; it forms the passive voice with *be, am, is are, was, were, being,* or *been.* (See B1-c for a complete list of helping verbs and G2-f for a survey of tenses.)

PAST TENSE	Last July, we *went* to Paris.
HELPING VERB + PAST PARTICIPLE	We *have gone* to Paris twice.

The list of common irregular verbs beginning at the bottom of this page will help you distinguish between past tense and past participle. Choose the past-participle form if the verb in your sentence requires a helping verb; choose the past-tense form if the verb does not require a helping verb.

▶ **Yesterday we ~~seen~~ saw an unidentified flying object.**

▶ **The reality of the situation ~~sunk~~ sank in.**

The past-tense forms *saw* and *sank* are required.

▶ **The truck was apparently ~~stole~~ stolen while the driver ate lunch.**

▶ **By Friday, the stock market had ~~fell~~ fallen two hundred points.**

Because of the helping verbs, the past-participle forms are required: *was stolen, had fallen.*

GRAMMAR CHECKERS sometimes flag misused irregular verbs in sentences, such as *I had drove the car to school* and *Lucia seen the movie already.* But you cannot rely on grammar checkers to identify problems with irregular verbs — they miss about twice as many errors as they find.

Common irregular verbs

When in doubt about the standard English forms of irregular verbs, consult the following list or look up the base form of the verb in the dictionary, which also lists any irregular forms. (If no additional forms are listed in the dictionary, the verb is regular, not irregular.)

BASE FORM	PAST TENSE	PAST PARTICIPLE
arise	arose	arisen
awake	awoke, awaked	awaked, awoke
be	was, were	been
beat	beat	beaten, beat
become	became	become
begin	began	begun
bend	bent	bent
bite	bit	bitten, bit

BASE FORM	PAST TENSE	PAST PARTICIPLE
blow	blew	blown
break	broke	broken
bring	brought	brought
build	built	built
burst	burst	burst
buy	bought	bought
catch	caught	caught
choose	chose	chosen
cling	clung	clung
come	came	come
cost	cost	cost
deal	dealt	dealt
dig	dug	dug
dive	dived, dove	dived
do	did	done
drag	dragged	dragged
draw	drew	drawn
dream	dreamed, dreamt	dreamed, dreamt
drink	drank	drunk
drive	drove	driven
eat	ate	eaten
fall	fell	fallen
fight	fought	fought
find	found	found
fly	flew	flown
forget	forgot	forgotten, forgot
freeze	froze	frozen
get	got	gotten, got
give	gave	given
go	went	gone
grow	grew	grown
hang (suspend)	hung	hung
hang (execute)	hanged	hanged
have	had	had
hear	heard	heard
hide	hid	hidden
hurt	hurt	hurt
keep	kept	kept

BASE FORM	PAST TENSE	PAST PARTICIPLE
know	knew	known
lay (put)	laid	laid
lead	led	led
lend	lent	lent
let (allow)	let	let
lie (recline)	lay	lain
lose	lost	lost
make	made	made
prove	proved	proved, proven
read	read	read
ride	rode	ridden
ring	rang	rung
rise (get up)	rose	risen
run	ran	run
say	said	said
see	saw	seen
send	sent	sent
set (place)	set	set
shake	shook	shaken
shoot	shot	shot
shrink	shrank	shrunk, shrunken
sing	sang	sung
sink	sank	sunk
sit (be seated)	sat	sat
slay	slew	slain
sleep	slept	slept
speak	spoke	spoken
spin	spun	spun
spring	sprang	sprung
stand	stood	stood
steal	stole	stolen
sting	stung	stung
strike	struck	struck, stricken
swear	swore	sworn
swim	swam	swum
swing	swung	swung
take	took	taken
teach	taught	taught
throw	threw	thrown

BASE FORM	PAST TENSE	PAST PARTICIPLE
wake	woke, waked	waked, woken
wear	wore	worn
wring	wrung	wrung
write	wrote	written

ON THE WEB > **dianahacker.com/writersref**
Grammar exercises > Grammatical sentences > E-ex G2–1

G2-b Distinguish among the forms of *lie* and *lay.*

Writers and speakers frequently confuse the various forms of *lie* (meaning "to recline or rest on a surface") and *lay* (meaning "to put or place something"). *Lie* is an intransitive verb; it does not take a direct object: *The tax forms lie on the table.* The verb *lay* is transitive; it takes a direct object: *Please lay the tax forms on the table.* (See B2-b.)

In addition to confusing the meaning of *lie* and *lay,* writers and speakers are often unfamiliar with the standard English forms of these verbs.

BASE FORM	PAST TENSE	PAST PARTICIPLE	PRESENT PARTICIPLE
lie	lay	lain	lying
lay	laid	laid	laying

▶ **Su Mei was so exhausted that she ~~laid~~ *lay* down for a nap.**

The past-tense form of *lie* ("to recline") is *lay.*

▶ **The patient had ~~laid~~ *lain* in an uncomfortable position all night.**

The past-participle form of *lie* ("to recline") is *lain.* If the correct English seems too stilted, recast the sentence: *The patient had been lying in an uncomfortable position all night.*

▶ **The prosecutor ~~lay~~ *laid* the pistol on a table close to the jurors.**

The past-tense form of *lay* ("to place") is *laid.*

▶ **Letters dating from the Boer War were ~~laying~~ *lying* in the corner of the chest.**

The present participle of *lie* ("to rest on a surface") is *lying.*

ON THE WEB > **dianahacker.com/writersref**
Language Debates > *lie* versus *lay*

G2-c Use *-s* (or *-es*) endings on present-tense verbs that have third-person singular subjects.

When the subject of a sentence is third-person singular, its verb takes an *-s* or *-es* ending in the present tense. (See also G1-a and the charts on pp. 164–65.)

	SINGULAR		PLURAL	
FIRST PERSON	I	know	we	know
SECOND PERSON	you	know	you	know
THIRD PERSON	he/she/it	knows	they	know
	child	knows	parents	know
	everyone	knows		

All singular nouns (such as *child*) and the pronouns *he, she,* and *it* are third-person singular; indefinite pronouns (such as *everyone*) are also third-person singular.

In nonstandard speech, the *-s* ending required by standard English is sometimes omitted.

▶ **Sulphur dioxide ~~turn~~ *turns* leaves yellow, ~~dissolve~~ *dissolves* marble, and ~~eat~~ *eats* away iron and steel.**

The subject, *sulphur dioxide*, is third-person singular, so the verbs must end in *-s*.

TIP: Do not add the *-s* ending to the verb if the subject is not third-person singular.

▶ **I prepare~~s~~ program specifications and logic diagrams.**

The writer mistakenly concluded that the *-s* ending belongs on present-tense verbs used with *all* singular subjects, not just *third-person* singular subjects. The pronoun *I* is first-person singular, so its verb does not require the *-s*.

▶ **The dirt floors require~~s~~ continual sweeping.**

The writer mistakenly thought that the *-s* ending on the verb indicated plurality. The *-s* goes on present-tense verbs used with third-person *singular* subjects.

In nonstandard speech, the *-s* verb form *has, does,* or *doesn't* is sometimes replaced with *have, do,* or *don't.* In standard English, use *has, does,* or *doesn't* with a third-person singular subject. (See also G1-a.)

▶ **This respected musician always ~~have~~ *has* a message in his work.**

▶ **~~Do~~ *Does* she know the correct procedure for the experiment?**

▶ **My uncle ~~don't~~ *doesn't* want to change jobs right now.**

GRAMMAR CHECKERS are fairly good at catching missing *-s* endings on verbs and some misused *-s* forms of the verb, consistently flagging errors such as *The training session take place later today* and *The careful camper learn to feel the signs of a coming storm.* (See the grammar checker advice on p. 163 for more information about subject-verb agreement.)

G2-d Do not omit *-ed* endings on verbs.

Speakers who do not fully pronounce *-ed* endings sometimes omit them unintentionally in writing. Failure to pronounce *-ed* endings is common in many dialects and in informal speech. In the following frequently used words and phrases, for example, the *-ed* ending is not always fully pronounced.

advised	developed	prejudiced	supposed to
asked	fixed	pronounced	used to
concerned	frightened	stereotyped	

When a verb is regular, both the past tense and the past participle are formed by adding *-ed* to the base form of the verb.

Past tense

Use an *-ed* or *-d* ending to express the past tense of regular verbs. The past tense is used when the action occurred entirely in the past.

▶ **Over the weekend, Ed ~~fix~~ *fixed* his brother's skateboard and tuned up his mother's 1977 Cougar.**

▶ **Last summer my counsellor ~~advise~~ *advised* me to ask my family for help.**

Past participles

Past participles are used in three ways: (1) following *have, has,* or *had* to form one of the perfect tenses; (2) following *be, am, is, are, was, were, being,* or *been* to form the passive voice; and (3) as adjectives modifying nouns or pronouns. The perfect tenses are listed on page 181, and the passive voice is discussed in W3-a. For a discussion of participles functioning as adjectives, see B3-b.

▶ **Robin has ~~ask~~ *asked* me to go to California with her.**

Has asked is present perfect tense (*have* or *has* followed by a past participle).

▶ **Though it is not a new phenomenon, domestic violence is ~~publicize~~ *publicized* more frequently than before.**

Is publicized is in the passive voice (a form of *be* followed by a past participle).

▶ **All aerobics classes end in a cool-down period to stretch ~~tighten~~ *tightened* muscles.**

Tightened is a participle used as an adjective to modify the noun *muscles.*

GRAMMAR CHECKERS flag missing *-ed* endings on verbs more often than not. Unfortunately, they often suggest an *-ing* ending (*passing*) rather than the missing *-ed* ending (*passed*), as in the following sentence: *The law was pass last week.*

G2-e Do not omit needed verbs.

Although standard English allows some linking verbs and helping verbs to be contracted, at least in informal contexts, it does not allow them to be omitted.

Linking verbs, used to link subjects to subject complements, are frequently a form of *be*: *be, am, is, are, was, were, being, been.*

(See B2-b.) Some of these forms may be contracted (*I'm, she's, we're*), but they should not be omitted altogether.

▶ **Alvin** *is* **a man who can defend himself.**

Helping verbs, used with main verbs, include forms of *be, do,* and *have* and the modal verbs *can, will, shall, could, would, should, may, might,* and *must.* (See B1-c.) Some helping verbs may be contracted (*he's leaving, we'll celebrate, they've been told*), but they should not be omitted altogether.

▶ **Do you know someone who** *would* **be good for the job?**

Several languages, including Russian and Turkish, do not require a linking verb between a subject and its complement. English, however, requires a verb in every sentence. See E2-a.

▶ **Every night, I read a short book to my daughter. When I** *am* **too busy, my husband reads to her.**

GRAMMAR CHECKERS flag omitted verbs about half the time — but they often miss needed helping verbs. For example, a grammar checker caught the missing verb in this sentence: *We seen the* Shrek *sequel three times already.* However, this sentence went unflagged: *The plot built around a family reunion.*

ON THE WEB > **dianahacker.com/writersref**
Grammar exercises > Grammatical sentences > E-ex G2–2

G2-f Choose the appropriate verb tense.

Tenses indicate the time of an action in relation to the time of the speaking or writing about that action.

The most common problem with tenses — shifting from one tense to another — is discussed in S4-b. Other problems with tenses are detailed in this section, after the following survey of tenses.

For additional help with verb tense, see E1-a.

Survey of tenses

Tenses are classified as present, past, and future, with simple, perfect, and progressive forms for each.

The simple tenses indicate relatively simple time relations. The simple present tense is used primarily for actions occurring at the time of the speaking or for actions occurring regularly. The simple past tense is used for actions completed in the past. The simple future tense is used for actions that will occur in the future. In the following table, the simple tenses are given for the regular verb *walk,* the irregular verb *ride,* and the highly irregular verb *be.*

SIMPLE PRESENT

SINGULAR		PLURAL	
I	walk, ride, am	we	walk, ride, are
you	walk, ride, are	you	walk, ride, are
he/she/it	walks, rides, is	they	walk, ride, are

SIMPLE PAST

SINGULAR		PLURAL	
I	walked, rode, was	we	walked, rode, were
you	walked, rode, were	you	walked, rode, were
he/she/it	walked, rode, was	they	walked, rode, were

SIMPLE FUTURE

I, you, he/she/it, we, they — will walk, ride, be

More complex time relations are indicated by the perfect tenses. A verb in one of the perfect tenses (a form of *have* plus the past participle) expresses an action that was or will be completed at the time of another action.

PRESENT PERFECT

I, you, we, they	have walked, ridden, been
he/she/it	has walked, ridden, been

PAST PERFECT

I, you, he/she/it, we, they — had walked, ridden, been

FUTURE PERFECT

I, you, he/she/it, we, they — will have walked, ridden, been

The simple and perfect tenses just discussed have progressive forms that describe actions in progress. A progressive verb consists of a form of *be* followed by a present participle. The progressive forms are not normally used with mental activity verbs such as *believe, know,* and *think.*

PRESENT PROGRESSIVE

I	am walking, riding, being
he/she/it	is walking, riding, being
you, we, they	are walking, riding, being

PAST PROGRESSIVE

I, he/she/it	was walking, riding, being
you, we, they	were walking, riding, being

FUTURE PROGRESSIVE

I, you, he/she/it, we, they	will be walking, riding, being

PRESENT PERFECT PROGRESSIVE

I, you, we, they	have been walking, riding, being
he/she/it	has been walking, riding, being

PAST PERFECT PROGRESSIVE

I, you, he/she/it, we, they	had been walking, riding, being

FUTURE PERFECT PROGRESSIVE

I, you, he/she/it, we, they	will have been walking, riding, being

Special uses of the present tense

Use the present tense when expressing general truths, when writing about literature, and when quoting, summarizing, or paraphrasing an author's views.

General truths or scientific principles should appear in the present tense, unless such principles have been disproved.

▶ **Galileo taught that Earth ~~revolved~~ revolves around the sun.**

Since Galileo's teaching has not been discredited, the verb should be in the present tense. The following sentence, however, is acceptable: *Ptolemy taught that the sun revolved around Earth.*

When writing about a work of literature, you may be tempted to use the past tense. The convention, however, is to describe fictional events in the present tense.

▶ **In Masuji Ibuse's *Black Rain,* a child ~~reached~~ reaches for a pomegranate in his mother's garden, and a moment later he ~~was~~ is dead, killed by the blast of the atomic bomb.**

When you are quoting, summarizing, or paraphrasing the author of a nonliterary work, use present-tense verbs such as *writes, reports, asserts,* and so on. This convention is usually followed even when the author is dead (unless a date or the context specifies the time of writing).

▶ **Baron Bowan of Colwood ~~wrote~~ writes that "a metaphysician is one who goes into a dark cellar at midnight without a light, looking for a black cat that is not there."**

EXCEPTION: When you are documenting a paper with the APA (American Psychological Association) style of in-text citations, use past-tense verbs such as *reported* or *demonstrated* or present perfect verbs such as *has reported* or *has demonstrated.*

E. Wilson (1994) reported that positive reinforcement alone was a less effective teaching technique than a mixture of positive reinforcement and constructive criticism.

The past perfect tense

The past perfect tense consists of a past participle preceded by *had* (*had worked, had gone*). This tense is used for an action already completed by the time of another past action or for an action already completed at some specific past time.

Everyone *had spoken* by the time I arrived.

Everyone *had spoken* by 10:00 a.m.

Writers sometimes use the simple past tense when they should use the past perfect.

▶ **We built our cabin high on a pine knoll, fifteen metres above an abandoned quarry that ~~was~~ had been flooded in 1920 to create a lake.**

The building of the cabin and the flooding of the quarry both occurred in the past, but the flooding was completed before the time of building.

had
▶ **By the time dinner was served, the guest of honour left.**

The past perfect tense is needed because the action of leaving was completed at a specific past time (by the time dinner was served).

Some writers tend to overuse the past perfect tense. Do not use the past perfect if two past actions occurred at the same time.

▶ **When we arrived in Paris, Pauline ~~had~~ met us at the train station.**

Sequence of tenses with infinitives and participles

An infinitive is the base form of a verb preceded by *to*. (See B3-b.) Use the present infinitive to show action at the same time as or later than the action of the verb in the sentence.

raise
▶ **The club had hoped to ~~have raised~~ a thousand dollars by April 1.**

The action expressed in the infinitive (*to raise*) occurred later than the action of the sentence's verb (*had hoped*).

Use the perfect form of an infinitive (*to have* followed by the past participle) for an action occurring earlier than that of the verb in the sentence.

have joined
▶ **Dan would like to ~~join~~ the navy, but he did not pass the physical.**

The liking occurs in the present; the joining would have occurred in the past.

Like the tense of an infinitive, the tense of a participle is governed by the tense of the sentence's verb. Use the present participle (ending in *-ing*) for an action occurring at the same time as that of the sentence's verb.

Hiking the Appalachian Trail in early spring, we spotted many wildflowers.

Use the past participle (such as *given* or *helped*) or the present perfect participle (*having* plus the past participle) for an action occurring before that of the verb.

Discovered off the coast of Florida, the *Atocha* yielded many treasures.

Having worked her way through university, Lee graduated debt-free.

G2-g Use the subjunctive mood in the few contexts that require it.

There are three moods in English: the *indicative,* used for facts, opinions, and questions; the *imperative,* used for orders or advice; and the *subjunctive,* used in certain contexts to express wishes, requests, or conditions contrary to fact. Of these moods, the subjunctive is most likely to cause problems for writers.

Forms of the subjunctive

In the subjunctive mood, present-tense verbs do not change form to indicate the number and person of the subject (see G1-a). Instead, the subjunctive uses the base form of the verb (*be, drive, employ*) with all subjects.

It is important that you *be* [not *are*] prepared for the interview.

We asked that she *drive* [not *drives*] more slowly.

Also, in the subjunctive mood, there is only one past-tense form of *be: were* (never *was*).

If I *were* [not *was*] you, I'd proceed more cautiously.

Uses of the subjunctive

The subjunctive mood appears in only a few contexts: in contrary-to-fact clauses beginning with *if* or expressing a wish; in *that* clauses following verbs such as *ask, insist, recommend, request,* and *suggest*; and in certain set expressions.

IN CONTRARY-TO-FACT CLAUSES BEGINNING WITH *IF* When a subordinate clause beginning with *if* expresses a condition contrary to fact, use the subjunctive mood.

▶ **If I ~~was~~ *were* a member of the Senate, I would vote for that bill.**

▶ **We could be less cautious if Jake ~~was~~ *were* more trustworthy.**

The verbs in these sentences express conditions that do not exist: The writer is not a member of the Senate, and Jake is not trustworthy.

Do not use the subjunctive mood in *if* clauses expressing conditions that exist or may exist.

If Dana *wins* the contest, she will leave for Spain in June.

IN CONTRARY-TO-FACT CLAUSES EXPRESSING A WISH In formal English, the subjunctive is used in clauses expressing a wish or desire; in informal speech, however, the indicative is more commonly used.

FORMAL I wish that Dr. Vaughn *were* my professor.

INFORMAL I wish that Dr. Vaughn *was* my professor.

IN *THAT* CLAUSES FOLLOWING VERBS SUCH AS *ASK, INSIST, RECOMMEND, REQUEST,* AND *SUGGEST* Because requests have not yet become reality, they are expressed in the subjunctive mood.

▶ **Professor Moore insists that her students ~~are~~ *be* on time.**

▶ **We recommend that Lambert ~~files~~ *file* form 1050 soon.**

IN CERTAIN SET EXPRESSIONS The subjunctive mood, once more widely used, remains in certain set expressions: *be that as it may, as it were, far be it from me,* and so on.

ON THE WEB > **dianahacker.com/writersref**
Grammar exercises > Grammatical sentences > E-ex G2–3

GRAMMAR CHECKERS only sometimes flag problems with the subjunctive mood. What they catch is very spotty, so you must be alert to the correct uses of the subjunctive in your own writing.

G3

Problems with pronouns

Pronouns are words that substitute for nouns (see B1-b). Four frequently encountered problems with pronouns are discussed in this section:

a. pronoun-antecedent agreement (singular vs. plural)
b. pronoun reference (clarity)
c. pronoun case (personal pronouns such as *I* vs. *me, she* vs. *her*)
d. pronoun case (*who* vs. *whom*)

For other problems with pronouns, consult the glossary of usage (W1).

G3-a Make pronouns and antecedents agree.

Many pronouns have antecedents, nouns or pronouns to which they refer. A pronoun and its antecedent agree when they are both singular or both plural.

SINGULAR *Dr. Ava Berto* finished *her* rounds.

PLURAL The *hospital interns* finished *their* rounds.

The pronouns *he, his, she, her, it,* and *its* must agree in gender (masculine, feminine, or neuter) with their antecedents (the words they refer to), not with the words that follow them.

▶ **Elvis Presley had an unusually close bond with ~~her~~ his mother.**

Because the pronoun refers to the masculine noun *Elvis Presley,* the pronoun must also be masculine.

GRAMMAR CHECKERS do not flag problems with pronoun-antecedent agreement. It takes a human eye to see that a plural pronoun, such as *their,* does not agree with a singular antecedent, such as *logger,* in a sentence like this: *The logger in the Northwest relies on the old forest growth for their living.*

When grammar checkers do flag agreement problems, they often suggest (correctly) substituting the singular phrase *his or her* for the plural pronoun *their.* For alternatives to the wordy *his or her* construction, see "Revising sexist language" on page 150.

Indefinite pronouns

Indefinite pronouns refer to nonspecific persons or things. Even though some of the following indefinite pronouns may seem to have plural meanings, treat them as singular in formal English: *anybody, anyone, anything, each, either, everybody, everyone, everything, neither, nobody, no one, nothing, somebody, someone, something.*

In this class *everyone* performs at *his or her* [not *their*] fitness level.

When a plural pronoun refers mistakenly to a singular indefinite pronoun, you can usually choose one of three options for revision.

1. Replace the plural pronoun with *he or she* (or *his or her*).
2. Make the antecedent plural.
3. Rewrite the sentence so that no problem of agreement exists.

he or she is
▶ **When someone has been drinking, ~~they are~~ likely to speed.**

drivers have
▶ **When ~~someone~~ has been drinking, they are likely to speed.**

A driver who / is
▶ **~~When someone~~ has been drinking, ~~they are~~ likely to speed.**

Because the *he or she* construction is wordy, often the second or third revision strategy is more effective.

NOTE: The traditional use of *he* (or *his*) to refer to persons of either sex is now widely considered sexist (see W4-e).

Generic nouns

A generic noun represents a typical member of a group, such as a typical student, or any member of a group, such as any lawyer. Although generic nouns may seem to have plural meanings, they are singular.

Every *runner* must train vigorously if *he or she* wants [not *they want*] to excel.

When a plural pronoun refers mistakenly to a generic noun, you will usually have the same three revision options as mentioned at the top of this page for indefinite pronouns.

he or she wants
▶ **A medical student must study hard if ~~they want~~ to succeed.**

Medical students
▶ **~~A medical student~~ must study hard if they want to succeed.**

▶ **A medical student must study hard ~~if they want~~ to succeed.**

Collective nouns

Collective nouns, such as *jury, committee, audience, crowd, class, troop, family, team,* and *couple,* name a class or group. Ordinarily the group functions as a unit, so the noun should be treated as singular; if the members of the group function as individuals, however, the noun should be treated as plural.

AS A UNIT The planning *committee* granted *its* permission to build.

AS INDIVIDUALS The *committee* put *their* signatures on the document.

When treating a collective noun as plural, many writers prefer to add a clearly plural antecedent such as *members* to the sentence: *The members of the committee put their signatures on the document.*

To some extent, you can choose whether to treat a collective noun as singular or plural depending on your meaning. Make sure, however, that you are consistent.

▶ **The jury has reached ~~their~~ ^its decision.**

There is no reason to draw attention to the individual members of the jury, so *jury* should be treated as singular. Notice also that the writer treated the noun as singular when choosing the verb *has,* so for consistency the pronoun must be *its.*

Compound antecedents

Treat compound antecedents joined by *and* as plural.

Joanne and John moved to Luray, where *they* built a log cabin.

With compound antecedents joined by *or* or *nor,* make the pronoun agree with the nearer antecedent.

Either *Bruce* or *Khalil* should receive first prize for *his* poem.

Neither the *mouse* nor the *rats* could find *their* way through the maze.

NOTE: If one of the antecedents is singular and the other plural, as in the second example, put the plural one last to avoid awkwardness.

EXCEPTION: If one antecedent is male and the other female, do not follow the traditional rule. The sentence *Either Bruce or Anita should receive first prize for her story* makes no sense. The best solution is to recast the sentence: *The prize for best story should go to Bruce or Anita.*

ON THE WEB > **dianahacker.com/writersref**
Language Debates > Pronoun-antecedent agreement

ON THE WEB > **dianahacker.com/writersref**
Grammar exercises > Grammatical sentences > E-ex G3–1 through G3–3

G3-b Make pronoun references clear.

Pronouns substitute for nouns; they are a kind of shorthand. In a sentence like *After Andrew intercepted the ball, he kicked it as hard as he could,* the pronouns *he* and *it* substitute for the nouns *Andrew* and *ball.* The word a pronoun refers to is called its *antecedent.*

GRAMMAR CHECKERS do not flag problems with faulty pronoun reference. Although a computer program can identify pronouns, it has no way of knowing which words, if any, they refer to. For example, grammar checkers miss the fact that the pronoun *it* has an ambiguous reference in the following sentence: *The thief stole the woman's purse and her car and then destroyed it.* Did the thief destroy the purse or the car? It takes human judgment to realize that readers might be confused.

Ambiguous reference

Ambiguous pronoun reference occurs when a pronoun could refer to two possible antecedents.

▶ *The pitcher broke when Gloria set it* ~~**When Gloria set the pitcher**~~ **on the glass-topped table**. ~~**, it broke.**~~

▶ **Tom told James,** *"You have* ~~**that he had**~~ **won the lottery."**

What broke — the table or the pitcher? Who won the lottery — Tom or James? The revisions eliminate the ambiguity.

Implied reference

A pronoun must refer to a specific antecedent, not to a word that is implied but not present in the sentence.

> ▶ **After braiding Ann's hair, Sue decorated ~~them~~ ^the braids^ with brightly coloured ribbons.**

The pronoun *them* referred to Ann's braids (implied by the term *braiding*), but the word *braids* did not appear in the sentence.

Modifiers, such as possessives, cannot serve as antecedents. A modifier may strongly imply the noun that the pronoun might logically refer to, but it is not itself that noun.

> ▶ **In ~~Mary Gordon's~~ *The Shadow Man,* ~~she~~ ^Mary Gordon^ writes about her father's mysterious and startling past.**

The pronoun *she* cannot refer logically to the possessive modifier *Mary Gordon's.* The revision substitutes the noun *Mary Gordon* for the pronoun *she,* thereby eliminating the problem.

ON THE WEB > **dianahacker.com/writersref**
Language Debates > Possessives as antecedents

Broad reference of this, that, which, *and* it

For clarity, the pronouns *this, that, which,* and *it* should ordinarily refer to specific antecedents rather than to whole ideas or sentences. When a pronoun's reference is needlessly broad, either replace the pronoun with a noun or supply an antecedent to which the pronoun clearly refers.

> ▶ **More and more often, we are finding ourselves victims of serious crimes. We learn to accept ~~this~~ ^our fate^ with minor complaints.**

For clarity, the writer substituted a noun (*fate*) for the pronoun *this,* which referred broadly to the idea expressed in the preceding sentence.

> ▶ **Romeo and Juliet were both too young to have acquired much wisdom, ^a fact^ which accounts for their rash actions.**

Indefinite reference of they, it, *or* you

Do not use *they* to refer indefinitely to persons who have not been specifically mentioned. The pronoun *they* should refer to a specific antecedent.

> ▶ **In 2007, ~~they~~ *Parliament* voted not to extend two controversial provisions in Canada's antiterrorism legislation.**

The word *it* should not be used indefinitely in constructions such as "In the article it says that. . . ."

> ▶ **~~In the~~ *The* encyclopedia ~~it~~ states that male moths can smell female moths from several kilometres away.**

The pronoun *you* is appropriate when the writer is addressing the reader directly: *Once you have kneaded the dough, let it rise in a warm place.* Except in very informal contexts, however, the indefinite *you* (meaning "anyone in general") is inappropriate.

> ▶ **Ms. Pickersgill's *Guide to Etiquette* stipulates that ~~you~~ *a guest* should not arrive at a party too early or leave too late.**
>
> The writer could have replaced *you* with *one,* but in North American English the pronoun *one* can seem stilted.

ON THE WEB > **diianahacker.com/writersref**
Language Debates > *you*

ON THE WEB > **dianahacker.com/writersref**
Grammar exercises > Grammatical sentences > E-ex G3–4 through G3–6

G3-c Distinguish between pronouns such as *I* and *me.*

The personal pronouns in the following chart change what is known as case form according to their grammatical function in a sentence. Pronouns functioning as subjects (or subject complements) appear in the *subjective* case; those functioning as objects appear in the *objective* case; and those functioning as possessives appear in the *possessive* case.

	SUBJECTIVE CASE	OBJECTIVE CASE	POSSESSIVE CASE
SINGULAR	I	me	my
	you	you	your
	he/she/it	him/her/it	his/her/its
PLURAL	we	us	our
	you	you	your
	they	them	their

This section explains the difference between the subjective and objective cases; then it alerts you to certain structures that may tempt you to choose the wrong pronoun. Finally, it describes a special use of possessive-case pronouns.

GRAMMAR CHECKERS sometimes flag incorrect pronouns and suggest using the correct form: *I* or *me, he* or *him, she* or *her, we* or *us, they* or *them.* A grammar checker flagged *we* in the following sentence and correctly advised using *us* instead: *I say it is about time for we parents to revolt.* Grammar checkers miss more incorrect pronouns than they catch, however, and their suggestions for revision are sometimes off the mark. A grammar checker caught the error in the following sentence: *I am a little jealous that my dog likes my neighbour more than I.* But instead of suggesting changing the final *I* to *me* (*. . . more than me*), it suggested adding *do* (*. . . more than I do*), which does not fit the meaning of the sentence.

Subjective case

When a pronoun functions as a subject or a subject complement, it must be in the subjective case (*I, we, you, he, she, it, they*).

SUBJECT	Sylvia and *he* shared the award.
SUBJECT COMPLEMENT	Greg announced that the winners were Sylvia and *he.*

Subject complements — words following linking verbs that complete the meaning of the subject — frequently cause problems for writers, since we rarely hear the correct form in casual speech. (See B2-b.)

▶ **During the Lindbergh trial, Bruno Hauptmann repeatedly denied that the kidnapper was ~~him.~~** *he.*

If *kidnapper was he* seems too stilted, rewrite the sentence: *During the Lindbergh trial, Bruno Hauptmann repeatedly denied that he was the kidnapper.*

Objective case

When a personal pronoun is used as a direct object, an indirect object, or the object of a preposition, it must be in the objective case (*me, us, you, him, her, it, them*).

DIRECT OBJECT	Bruce found Tony and brought *him* home.
INDIRECT OBJECT	Mina gave *me* a surprise party.
OBJECT OF A PREPOSITION	Jessica wondered if the call was for *her.*

Compound word groups

When a subject or an object appears as part of a compound structure, you may occasionally become confused. To test for the correct pronoun, mentally strip away all of the compound word group except the pronoun in question.

▶ **Joel ran away from home because his stepfather and ~~him~~** *he* **had quarrelled.**

His stepfather and he is the subject of the verb *had quarrelled.* If we strip away the words *his stepfather and,* the correct pronoun becomes clear: *he had quarrelled* (not *him had quarrelled*).

▶ **The most traumatic experience for her father and ~~I~~** *me* **occurred long after her operation.**

Her father and me is the object of the preposition *for.* Strip away the words *her father and* to test for the correct pronoun: *for me* (not *for I*).

When in doubt about the correct pronoun, some writers try to avoid making the choice by using a reflexive pronoun such as *myself.* Such evasions are nonstandard, even though they are used by some educated persons.

▶ **The Indian cab driver gave my husband and ~~myself~~ *me* some good tips on travelling in New Delhi.**

My husband and me is the indirect object of the verb *gave.* For correct uses of *myself,* see the glossary of usage (W1).

ON THE WEB > **dianahacker.com/writersref**
Language Debates > *myself*

Appositives

Appositives are noun phrases that rename nouns or pronouns. A pronoun used as an appositive has the same function (usually subject or object) as the word(s) it renames.

▶ **The chief strategists, Dr. Bell and ~~me,~~ *I,* could not agree on a plan.**

The appositive *Dr. Bell and I* renames the subject, *strategists.* Test: *I could not agree* (not *me could not agree*).

▶ **The reporter interviewed only two witnesses, the bicyclist and ~~I.~~ *me.***

The appositive *the bicyclist and me* renames the direct object *witnesses.* Test: *interviewed me* (not *interviewed I*).

We *or* us *before a noun*

When deciding whether *we* or *us* should precede a noun, choose the pronoun that would be appropriate if the noun were omitted.

▶ **~~Us~~ *We* tenants would rather fight than move.**

▶ **Management is shortchanging ~~we~~ *us* tenants.**

No one would say *Us would rather fight than move* or *Management is shortchanging we.*

Comparisons with than *or* as

Sentence parts, usually verbs, are often omitted in comparisons beginning with *than* or *as.* To test for the correct pronoun, mentally complete the sentence.

▶ **Even though he is sometimes ridiculed by the other boys, Norman is much better off than ~~them.~~** *they.*

They is the subject of the verb *are,* which is understood: *Norman is much better off than they* [*are*]. If the correct English seems too formal, you can always add the verb.

▶ **We respected no other candidate for the city council as much as ~~she.~~** *her.*

This sentence means that we respected no other candidate as much as *we respected her. Her* is the direct object of the understood verb *respected.*

Subjects and objects of infinitives

An infinitive is the word *to* followed by the base form of a verb. (See B3-b.) Subjects of infinitives are an exception to the rule that subjects must be in the subjective case. Whenever an infinitive has a subject, it must be in the objective case. Objects of infinitives also are in the objective case.

▶ **Ms. Wong asked John and ~~I~~** *me* **to drive the senator and ~~she~~** *her* **to the airport.**

John and me is the subject of the infinitive *to drive; senator and her* is the direct object of the infinitive.

Possessive case to modify a gerund

A pronoun that modifies a gerund or a gerund phrase should appear in the possessive case (*my, our, your, his, her, its, their*). A gerund is a verb form ending in *-ing* that functions as a noun. Gerunds frequently appear in phrases, in which case the whole gerund phrase functions as a noun. (See B3-b.)

▶ **The chances against ~~you~~** *your* **being hit by lightning are about two million to one.**

Your modifies the gerund phrase *being hit by lightning.*

Nouns as well as pronouns may modify gerunds. To form the possessive case of a noun, use an apostrophe and an *-s* (*victim's*) or just an apostrophe (*victims'*). See P5-a.

▶ **The old order in France paid a high price for the ~~aristocracy~~ aristocracy's exploiting the lower classes.**

The possessive noun *aristocracy's* modifies the gerund phrase *exploiting the lower classes.*

ON THE WEB > **dianahacker.com/writersref**
Language Debates > Possessive before a gerund

ON THE WEB > **dianahacker.com/writersref**
Grammar exercises > Grammatical sentences > E-ex G3–7 and G3–8

G3-d Distinguish between *who* and *whom.*

The choice between *who* and *whom* (or *whoever* and *whomever*) occurs primarily in subordinate clauses and in questions. *Who* and *whoever,* subjective-case pronouns, are used for subjects and subject complements. *Whom* and *whomever,* objective-case pronouns, are used for objects.

An exception to this general rule occurs when the pronoun functions as the subject of an infinitive. See page 199.

GRAMMAR CHECKERS catch misuses of *who* and *whom* (*whoever* and *whomever*) only about half the time. A grammar checker flagged the incorrect use of *whomever* in the sentence *Daniel always volunteers this information to whomever will listen,* recognizing that *whoever* is required as the subject of the verb *will listen.* But it did not flag the incorrect use of *who* in this sentence: *My cousin Sylvie, who I am teaching to fly a kite, watches us every time we compete.*

In subordinate clauses

The case of a relative pronoun in a subordinate clause is determined by its function *within the subordinate clause it introduces.*

▶ **The prize goes to the runner ~~whom~~ who collects the most points.**

The subordinate clause is *who collects the most points.* The verb of the clause is *collects,* and its subject is *who.*

When it functions as an object in a subordinate clause, *whom* appears out of order, before both the subject and the verb. To choose the correct pronoun, you can mentally restructure the clause.

▶ **You will work with our senior engineers, ~~who~~ whom you will meet later.**

The subordinate clause is *whom you will meet later.* The subject of the clause is *you* and the verb is *will meet. Whom* is the direct object of the verb. The correct choice becomes clear if you mentally restructure the clause: *you will meet whom.*

When functioning as the object of a preposition in a subordinate clause, *whom* is often separated from its preposition.

▶ **The tutor ~~who~~ whom I was assigned to was very supportive.**

Whom is the object of the preposition *to.* If the correct English seems too formal, drop *whom*: *The tutor I was assigned to. . . .*

NOTE: Inserted expressions such as *they know, I think,* and *she says* should be ignored in determining whether to use *who* or *whom*.

▶ **All of the school bullies want to take on a big guy ~~whom~~ who they know will not hurt them.**

Who is the subject of *will hurt,* not the object of *know.*

In questions

The case of an interrogative pronoun is determined by its function within the question.

▶ **~~Whom~~ Who was responsible for creating that computer virus?**

Who is the subject of the verb *was.*

When *whom* functions as an object in a question, it appears out of normal order, before both the subject and the verb. To choose the correct pronoun, you must mentally restructure the question.

▶ **~~Who~~ Whom did the New Democratic Party elect in 1992?**

Whom is the direct object of the verb *did nominate.* This becomes clear if you restructure the question: *The New Democratic Party did elect whom in 1992?*

For subjects or objects of infinitives

An infinitive is the word *to* followed by the base form of a verb. (See B3-b.) Subjects of infinitives are an exception to the rule that subjects must be in the subjective case. Whenever an infinitive has a subject, it must be in the objective case. Objects of infinitives also are in the objective case.

▶ **On the subject of health care, I don't know ~~who~~ *whom* to believe.**

ON THE WEB > **dianahacker.com/writersref**
Language Debates > *who* versus *whom*

ON THE WEB > **dianahacker.com/writersref**
Grammar exercises > Grammatical sentences > E-ex G3–9 and G3–10

G4

Adjectives and adverbs

Adjectives ordinarily modify nouns or pronouns; occasionally they function as subject complements following linking verbs. Adverbs modify verbs, adjectives, or other adverbs.

Many adverbs are formed by adding *-ly* to adjectives (*normal, normally*). But don't assume that all words ending in *-ly* are adverbs or that all adverbs end in *-ly*. Some adjectives end in *-ly* (*lovely, friendly*) and some adverbs don't (*always, here, there*). When in doubt, consult a dictionary.

In English, adjectives are not pluralized to agree with the words they modify: *The red* [not *reds*] *roses were a wonderful surprise.*

GRAMMAR CHECKERS can flag a number of problems with adjectives and adverbs: some misuses of *bad* or *badly* and *good* or *well*; some double comparisons, such as *more meaner*; some absolute comparisons, such as *most unique*; and some double negatives, such as *can't hardly*. However, the programs miss more problems than they find. Programs ignored errors like these: *could have been handled more professional* and *hadn't been bathed regular.*

G4-a Use adverbs, not adjectives, to modify verbs, adjectives, and adverbs.

When adverbs modify verbs (or verbals), they nearly always answer the question When? Where? How? Why? Under what conditions? How often? or To what degree? When adverbs modify adjectives or other adverbs, they usually qualify or intensify the meaning of the word they modify.

Adjectives are often used incorrectly in place of adverbs in casual or nonstandard speech.

> ▶ **The manager must see that the office runs ~~smooth~~ *smoothly* and ~~efficient.~~ *efficiently.***
>
> The adverbs *smoothly* and *efficiently* modify the verb *runs.*

> ▶ **In the early 1970s, chances for survival of the bald eagle looked ~~real~~ *really* slim.**
>
> Only adverbs can be used to modify adjectives or other adverbs. *Really* intensifies the meaning of the adjective *slim.*

NOTE: The incorrect use of the adjective *good* in place of the adverb *well* to modify a verb is especially common in casual and nonstandard speech. Use *well,* not *good,* to modify a verb in your writing.

> ▶ **We were glad that Sanya had done ~~good~~ *well* on the CPA exam.**
>
> The adverb *well* should be used to modify the verb *had done.*

The word *well* is an adjective, however, when it means "healthy," "satisfactory," or "fortunate": *I feel very well today. All is well. It is just as well.*

ESL The placement of adverbs varies from language to language. Unlike some languages, such as French and Spanish, English does not allow an adverb between a verb (*poured*) and its direct object (*the liquid*). See E2-f.

> ▶ **In the last stage of our experiment, we *slowly* poured ~~slowly~~ the liquid into the container.**

G4-b Use adjectives, not adverbs, as subject complements.

Adjectives ordinarily precede nouns, but they can also function as subject complements following linking verbs (see B2-b). When an adjective functions as a subject complement, it describes the subject.

Justice is *blind.*

Problems can arise with verbs such as *smell, taste, look,* and *feel,* which sometimes, but not always, function as linking verbs. If the word following one of these verbs describes the subject, use an adjective; if it modifies the verb, use an adverb.

ADJECTIVE The detective looked *cautious.*

ADVERB The detective looked *cautiously* for fingerprints.

The adjective *cautious* describes the detective; the adverb *cautiously* modifies the verb *looked.*

Linking verbs suggest states of being, not actions. Notice, for example, the different meanings of *looked* in the preceding examples. To look cautious suggests the state of being cautious; to look cautiously is to perform an action in a cautious way.

► **The lilacs in our backyard smell especially ~~sweetly~~ sweet this year.**

► **Lori looked ~~well~~ good in her new go-go boots.**

► **We felt ~~badly~~ bad upon hearing of your grandmother's death.**

The verbs *smell, looked,* and *felt* suggest states of being, not actions. Therefore, they should be followed by adjectives, not adverbs.

ON THE WEB > **dianahacker.com/writersref**
Language Debates > *bad* versus *badly*

G4-c Use comparatives and superlatives with care.

Most adjectives and adverbs have three forms: the positive, the comparative, and the superlative.

POSITIVE	COMPARATIVE	SUPERLATIVE
soft	softer	softest
fast	faster	fastest
careful	more careful	most careful
bad	worse	worst
good	better	best

Comparative versus superlative

Use the comparative to compare two things, the superlative to compare three or more.

> ▶ **Which of these two low-carb drinks is ~~best?~~** *better?*

> ▶ **Though Shaw and Jackson are impressive, Hobbs is the ~~more~~** *most* **qualified of the three candidates running for mayor.**

Form of comparatives and superlatives

To form comparatives and superlatives of most one- and two-syllable adjectives, use the endings *-er* and *-est*: *smooth, smoother, smoothest; easy, easier, easiest.* With longer adjectives, use *more* and *most* (or *less* and *least* for downward comparisons): *exciting, more exciting, most exciting; less helpful, least helpful.*

Some one-syllable adverbs take the endings *-er* and *-est* (*fast, faster, fastest*), but longer adverbs and all of those ending in *-ly* form the comparative and superlative with *more* and *most* (or *less* and *least*).

The comparative and superlative forms of the following adjectives and adverbs are irregular: *good, better, best; well, better, best; bad, worse, worst; badly, worse, worst.*

> ▶ **The Kirov was the ~~talentedest~~** *most talented* **ballet company we had ever seen.**

> ▶ **Lloyd's luck couldn't have been ~~worser~~** *worse* **than David's.**

Double comparatives or superlatives

Do not use double comparatives or superlatives. When you have added *-er* or *-est* to an adjective or adverb, do not also use *more* or *most* (or *less* or *least*).

> ▶ **The polls indicated that Harper was more ~~likelier~~** *likely* **to win than Mann.**

▶ **Of all her family, Julia is the ~~most~~ happiest about the move.**

Absolute concepts

Avoid expressions such as *more straight, less perfect, very round,* and *most unique.* Either something is unique or it isn't. It is illogical to suggest that absolute concepts come in degrees.

▶ **That is the most ~~unique~~** unusual **wedding gown I have ever seen.**

▶ **The painting would have been even more ~~priceless~~** valuable **had it been signed.**

ON THE WEB > **dianahacker.com/writersref**
Language Debates > Absolute concepts such as *unique*

G4-d Avoid double negatives.

Standard English allows two negatives only if a positive meaning is intended: *The orchestra was not unhappy with its performance.* Double negatives used to emphasize negation are nonstandard.

Negative modifiers such as *never, no,* and *not* should not be paired with other negative modifiers or with negative words such as *neither, none, no one, nobody,* and *nothing.*

▶ **Management is not doing ~~nothing~~** anything **to see that the trash is picked up.**

The double negative *not . . . nothing* is nonstandard.

The modifiers *hardly, barely,* and *scarcely* are considered negatives in standard English, so they should not be used with other negatives such as *not, no one,* and *never.*

▶ **Maxine is so weak from her surgery she ~~can't~~** can **hardly climb stairs.**

ON THE WEB > **dianahacker.com/writersref**
Grammar exercises > Grammatical sentences > E-ex G4–1 and G4–2

G5

Sentence fragments

A sentence fragment is a word group that pretends to be a sentence. Sentence fragments are easy to recognize when they appear out of context, like these:

> On the old wooden stool in the corner of my grandmother's kitchen.
>
> And immediately popped their flares and life vests.

When fragments appear next to related sentences, however, they are harder to spot.

> On that morning I sat in my usual spot. On the old wooden stool in the corner of my grandmother's kitchen.
>
> The pilots ejected from the burning plane, landing in the water not far from the ship. And immediately popped their flares and life vests.

GRAMMAR CHECKERS can flag as many as half of the sentence fragments in a sample; but that means, of course, that they miss half or more of them. If fragments are a serious problem for you, you will still need to proofread for them.

Sometimes the grammar checker will identify "false positives," sentences that have been flagged but are not fragments. For example, a grammar checker flagged this complete sentence as a possible fragment: *I bent down to crawl into the bunker.* When a program spots a possible fragment, you should check to see if it is really a fragment by using the flowchart on page 206.

Unlike some languages, English requires a subject and a verb in every sentence (except in commands, where the subject *you* is understood but not present: *Sit down*). See E2-a and E2-b.

▶ ~~**Is**~~ *It is* **often hot and humid during the summer.**

▶ **Students** *are* **usually very busy at the end of the semester.**

Recognizing sentence fragments

To be a sentence, a word group must consist of at least one full independent clause. An independent clause has a subject and a verb, and it either stands alone or could stand alone.

To test a word group for sentence completeness, use the flowchart on page 206. For example, by using the flowchart, you can see exactly why *On the old wooden stool in the corner of my grandmother's kitchen* is a fragment: It lacks both a subject and a verb. *And immediately popped their flares and life vests* is a fragment because it lacks a subject.

Repairing sentence fragments

You can repair most fragments in one of two ways: Either pull the fragment into a nearby sentence or turn the fragment into a sentence.

▶ **On that morning I sat in my usual spot~~.~~ ~~On~~ *on* the old wooden stool in the corner of my grandmother's kitchen.**

▶ **The pilots ejected from the burning plane, landing in the water not far from the ship. ~~And~~ *They* immediately popped their flares and life vests.**

G5-a Attach fragmented subordinate clauses or turn them into sentences.

A subordinate clause is patterned like a sentence, with both a subject and a verb, but it begins with a word that marks it as subordinate. The following words commonly introduce subordinate clauses: *after, although, because, before, if, though, unless, until, when, where, who, which,* and *that.* (See B3-e.)

Most fragmented subordinate clauses beg to be pulled into a sentence nearby.

▶ **North Americans have come to fear the West Nile virus~~.~~ ~~Because~~ *because* it is transmitted by the common mosquito.**

Because introduces a subordinate clause. (For punctuation of a subordinate clause appearing at the end of a sentence, see P2-f.)

Test for sentence completeness

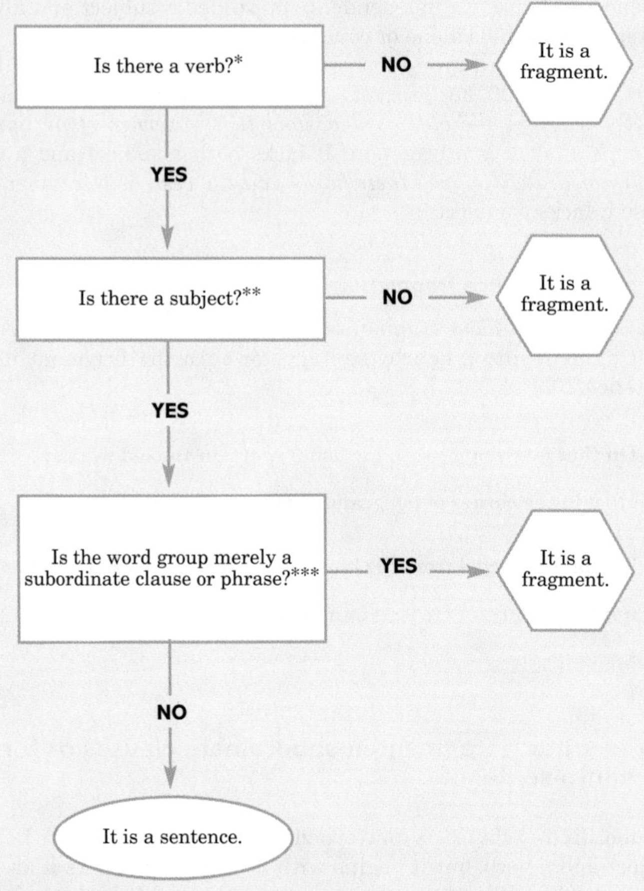
Is there a verb?*
NO
It is a fragment.
YES
Is there a subject?**
NO
It is a fragment.
YES
Is the word group merely a subordinate clause or phrase?***
YES
It is a fragment.
NO
It is a sentence.

*Do not mistake verbals for verbs. (See B3-b.)
**The subject of a sentence may be *you,* understood. (See B2-a.)
***A sentence may open with a subordinate clause or phrase, but the sentence must also include an independent clause. (See B3.)

If you find any fragments, try one of these methods of revision:

1. Attach the fragment to a nearby sentence.
2. Turn the fragment into a sentence.

If a fragmented clause cannot be attached to a nearby sentence or if you feel that attaching it would be awkward, try turning it into a sentence. The simplest way to do this is to delete the opening word or words that mark it as subordinate.

▶ **Population increases and uncontrolled development are taking a deadly toll on the environment. ~~So that in~~ In many parts of the world, fragile ecosystems are collapsing.**

G5-b Attach fragmented phrases or turn them into sentences.

Like subordinate clauses, phrases function within sentences as adjectives, as adverbs, or as nouns. They cannot stand alone. Fragmented phrases are often prepositional or verbal phrases; sometimes they are appositives, words or word groups that rename nouns or pronouns. (See B3-a, B3-b, and B3-c.)

Often a fragmented phrase may simply be pulled into a nearby sentence.

▶ **The archaeologists worked slowly~~.~~, ~~Examining~~ examining and labelling every pottery shard they uncovered.**

The word group beginning with *Examining* is a verbal phrase.

▶ **Mary is suffering from agoraphobia~~.~~, ~~A~~ a fear of the outside world.**

A fear of the outside world is an appositive renaming the noun *agoraphobia.*

If a fragmented phrase cannot be pulled into a nearby sentence effectively, turn the phrase into a sentence. You may need to add a subject, a verb, or both.

▶ **In the training session, Jamie explained how to access our new database. ~~Also~~ She also taught us how to submit expense reports and request vendor payments.**

The revision turns the fragmented phrase into a sentence by adding a subject and a verb.

G5-c Attach other fragmented word groups or turn them into sentences.

Other word groups that are commonly fragmented include parts of compound predicates, lists, and examples introduced by *such as, for example,* or similar expressions.

Parts of compound predicates

A predicate consists of a verb and its objects, complements, and modifiers. A compound predicate includes two or more predicates joined by a coordinating conjunction such as *and, but,* or *or.* Because the parts of a compound predicate have the same subject, they should appear in the same sentence.

▶ **The woodpecker finch of the Galápagos Islands carefully selects a twig of a certain size and shape. ~~And~~ and then uses this tool to pry out grubs from trees.**

Notice that no comma appears between the parts of a compound predicate. (See P2-a.)

Lists

When a list is mistakenly fragmented, it can often be attached to a nearby sentence with a colon or a dash. (See P4-a and P7-d.)

▶ **It has been said that there are only three indigenous American art forms. : Jazz j, musical comedy, and soap opera.**

Examples introduced by such as, for example, *or similar expressions*

Expressions that introduce examples (or explanations) can lead to unintentional fragments. Although you may begin a sentence with some of the following words or phrases, make sure that what you have written is a sentence, not a fragment.

also	especially	in addition	namely	that is
and	for example	like	or	
but	for instance	mainly	such as	

Sometimes fragmented examples can be attached to the preceding sentence.

▶ **In the twentieth century, Canada produced some great writers~~.~~, ~~Such~~ such as Margaret Atwood, June Callwood, Michael Ondaatje, Alice Munro, and Robertson Davies.**

At times, however, it may be necessary to turn the fragment into a sentence.

▶ **If Eric doesn't get his way, he goes into a fit of rage. For example, ~~lying~~ he lies on the floor screaming or ~~opening~~ opens the cabinet doors and then ~~slamming~~ slams them shut.**

The writer corrected this fragment by adding a subject — *he* — and substituting verbs — *lies, opens,* and *slams* — for the verbals *lying, opening,* and *slamming.*

G5-d Exception: Fragments may be used for special purposes.

Skilled writers occasionally use sentence fragments for the following special purposes.

FOR EMPHASIS	Madison Avenue is a very powerful aggression against private consciousness. *A demand that you yield your private consciousness to public manipulation.* — Marshall McLuhan
TO ANSWER A QUESTION	Are these new drug tests 100 percent reliable? *Not in the opinion of most experts.*
AS A TRANSITION	*And now the opposing arguments.*
EXCLAMATIONS	*Not again!*
IN ADVERTISING	*Fewer carbs. Improved taste.*

Although fragments are sometimes appropriate, writers and readers do not always agree on when they are appropriate. Therefore, you will find it safer to write in complete sentences.

ON THE WEB > **dianahacker.com/writersref**
Grammar exercises > Grammatical sentences > E-ex G5–1 through G5–3

G6

Run-on sentences

Run-on sentences are independent clauses that have not been joined correctly. An independent clause is a word group that can stand alone as a sentence. (See B4.) When two independent clauses appear in one sentence, they must be joined in one of these ways:

- with a comma and a coordinating conjunction (*and, but, or, nor, for, so, yet*)
- with a semicolon (or occasionally with a colon or a dash)

Recognizing run-on sentences

There are two types of run-on sentences. When a writer puts no mark of punctuation and no coordinating conjunction between independent clauses, the result is called a *fused sentence.*

INDEPENDENT CLAUSE

FUSED Air pollution poses risks to all humans it can be

INDEPENDENT CLAUSE

deadly for asthma sufferers.

A far more common type of run-on sentence is the *comma splice* — two or more independent clauses joined by a comma without a coordinating conjunction. In some comma splices, the comma appears alone.

COMMA SPLICE Air pollution poses risks to all humans, it can be deadly for asthma sufferers.

In other comma splices, the comma is accompanied by a joining word that is *not* a coordinating conjunction. There are only seven coordinating conjunctions in English: *and, but, or, nor, for, so,* and *yet.* Notice that all of these words are short — only two or three letters long. (See also G6-a.)

COMMA SPLICE Air pollution poses risks to all humans, however, it can be deadly for asthma sufferers.

However is a transitional expression, not a coordinating conjunction.

To review your writing for possible run-on sentences, use the flowchart on page 213.

ON THE WEB > **diandahacker.com/writersref**
Language Debates > Comma splices

GRAMMAR CHECKERS flag fewer than half the run-on sentences in a sample. They usually suggest a semicolon as a method of revision, but you can consult G6-a through G6-d for other revision strategies that might be more suitable in a particular situation. If you have repeated problems with run-ons, the flowchart on page 213 will help you identify them.

Revising run-on sentences

To revise a run-on sentence, you have four choices:

1. Use a comma and a coordinating conjunction (*and, but, or, nor, for, so, yet*).

but
▶ **Air pollution poses risks to all humans, ^ it can be deadly for asthma sufferers.**

2. Use a semicolon (or, if appropriate, a colon or a dash). A semicolon may be used alone; it can also be accompanied by a transitional expression (see also G6-b and P3-b).

▶ **Air pollution poses risks to all humans,; it can be deadly for asthma sufferers.**

; however,
▶ **Air pollution poses risks to all humans, ^ it can be deadly for asthma sufferers.**

3. Make the clauses into separate sentences.

It
▶ **Air pollution poses risks to all humans,. ~~it~~ can be deadly for asthma sufferers.**

4. Restructure the sentence, perhaps by subordinating one of the clauses.

   ▶ *Although air* **~~Air~~ pollution poses risks to all humans, it can be deadly for asthma sufferers.**

One of these revision techniques will often work better than the others for a particular sentence. The fourth technique, the one requiring the most extensive revision, is frequently the most effective.

G6-a Consider separating the clauses with a comma and a coordinating conjunction.

There are seven coordinating conjunctions in English: *and, but, or, nor, for, so,* and *yet.* When a coordinating conjunction joins independent clauses, it is usually preceded by a comma. (See P1-a.)

▶ **The paramedic asked where I was hurt,** *and* **as soon as I motioned toward my pain, he cut up the leg of my favourite pair of jeans.**

▶ **Many government officials privately admit that the polygraph is unreliable,** *yet* **~~however,~~ they continue to use it as a security measure.**

However is a transitional expression, not a coordinating conjunction, so it cannot be used with only a comma to join independent clauses.

G6-b Consider separating the clauses with a semicolon (or, if appropriate, with a colon or a dash).

When the independent clauses are closely related and their relation is clear without a coordinating conjunction, a semicolon is an acceptable method of revision. (See P3-a.)

▶ **Tragedy depicts the individual confronted with the fact of death~~,~~; comedy depicts the adaptability of human society.**

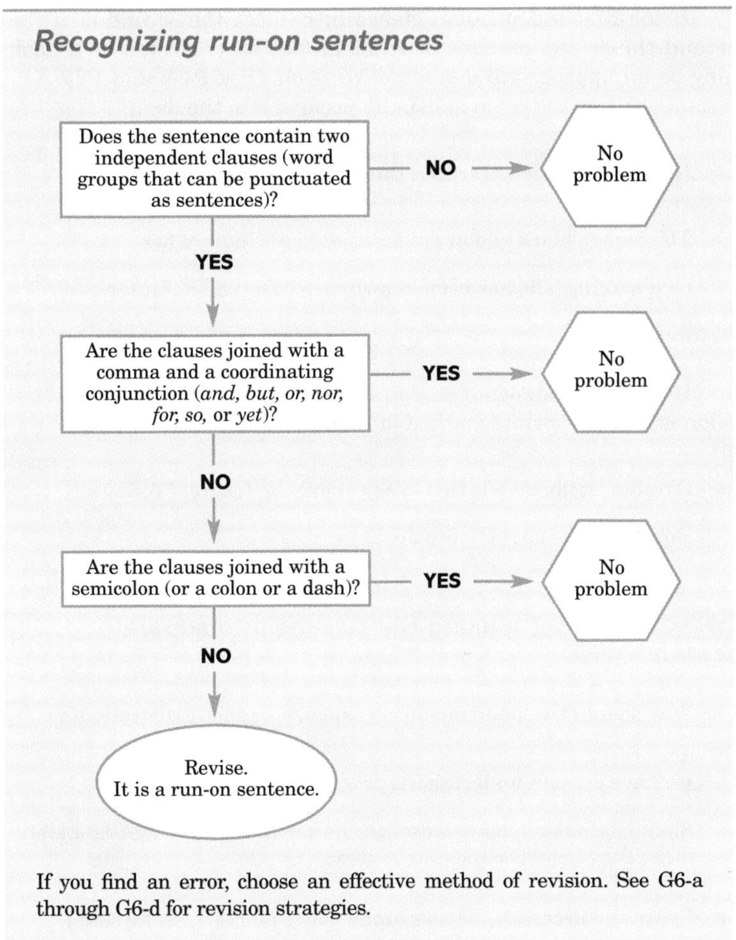
Recognizing run-on sentences
Does the sentence contain two independent clauses (word groups that can be punctuated as sentences)?
NO
No problem
YES
Are the clauses joined with a comma and a coordinating conjunction (and, but, or, nor, for, so, or yet)?
YES
No problem
NO
Are the clauses joined with a semicolon (or a colon or a dash)?
YES
No problem
NO
Revise.
It is a run-on sentence.

If you find an error, choose an effective method of revision. See G6-a through G6-d for revision strategies.

A semicolon is required beween independent clauses that have been linked with a transitional expression (such as *however, therefore, moreover, in fact,* or *for example*). For a longer list, see P3-b.

▶ **Handheld PDAs are gaining in popularity,; however, they are not nearly as popular as cell phones.**

If the first independent clause introduces the second or if the second clause summarizes or explains the first, a colon or a dash may be an appropriate method of revision. (See P4-b and P7-d.) In formal writing, the colon is usually preferred to the dash.

▶ **Nuclear waste is hazardous: ~~this~~ This is an indisputable fact.**

▶ **The female black widow spider is often a widow of her own making— she has been known to eat her partner after mating.**

If the first independent clause introduces a quoted sentence, a colon is an appropriate method of revision.

▶ **Carolyn Heilbrun has this to say about the future: "Today's shocks are tomorrow's conventions."**

G6-c Consider making the clauses into separate sentences.

▶ **Why should we spend money on expensive space exploration? ~~we~~ We have enough underfunded programs here on Earth.**

Since one independent clause is a question and the other is a statement, they should be separate sentences.

▶ **I gave the necessary papers to the police officer. ~~then~~ Then he said I would have to accompany him to the police station, where a counsellor would talk with me and call my parents.**

Because the second independent clause is quite long, a sensible revision is to use separate sentences.

NOTE: When two quoted independent clauses are divided by explanatory words, make each clause its own sentence.

▶ **"It's always smart to learn from your mistakes," quipped my supervisor. ~~"it's~~ "It's even smarter to learn from the mistakes of others."**

G6-d Consider restructuring the sentence, perhaps by subordinating one of the clauses.

If one of the independent clauses is less important than the other, turn it into a subordinate clause or phrase. (See S6-a.)

▶ *Although many* ~~Many~~ scholars dismiss the abominable snowman of the Himalayas as a myth, others claim it may be a kind of ape.

▶ Of the many geysers in Yellowstone National Park, the most famous is Old Faithful, *which* ~~it~~ sometimes reaches forty-five metres in height.

▶ Mary McLeod Bethune, ~~was~~ the seventeenth child of former slaves, ~~she~~ founded the National Council of Negro Women in 1935.

Minor ideas in these sentences are now expressed in subordinate clauses or phrases.

ON THE WEB > **dianahacker.com/writersref**
Grammar exercises > Grammatical sentences > E-ex G6–1 through G6–3

E

ESL Challenges

E ESL Challenges

This section of *A Canadian Writer's Reference* is primarily for multilingual writers. You may find this section helpful if you learned English as a second language (ESL) or if you speak a language other than English with your friends and family.

ON THE WEB > **dianahacker.com/writersref**
ESL help

E1

Verbs

Both English speakers and English language learners encounter the following challenges with verbs, which are treated elsewhere in this book:

making subjects and verbs agree (G1)

using irregular verb forms (G2-a)

leaving off verb endings (G2-c, G2-d)

choosing the correct verb tense (G2-f)

avoiding inappropriate uses of the passive voice (W3-a)

This section focuses on the major challenges that verbs can cause for multilingual writers.

ON THE WEB > **dianahacker.com/writersref**
Grammar exercises > ESL challenges > E-ex E1–1 through E1–4

E1-a Use the appropriate verb form and tense.

This section offers a brief review of the various English verb forms and tenses. See the chart on pages 226–28 for an overview of verb usage. For additional help with verb form and tense, see G2-f and B1-c.

Basic verb forms

VERB FORM	REGULAR VERB *HELP*	IRREGULAR VERB *GIVE*	IRREGULAR VERB *BE*
BASE FORM	help	give	be
PAST TENSE	helped	gave	was, were
PAST PARTICIPLE	helped	given	been
PRESENT PARTICIPLE	helping	giving	being
-S FORM	helps	gives	is

Basic verb forms

Every main verb in English has five forms, which are used to create all of the verb tenses in standard English. The chart at the top of this page shows these forms for the regular verb *help* and the irregular verbs *give* and *be.* (*Be* has the six forms listed in the chart as well as *am* and *are,* used in the present tense. See G2-a for a list of common irregular verbs.)

Simple tenses for general facts, states of being, habitual actions

SIMPLE PRESENT (BASE FORM OR *-S* FORM) Simple present tense shows general facts, constant states, or habitual or repetitive actions. It is also used for scheduled future events. (For uses of the present tense in writing about literature, see G2-f.)

We *donate* to a different charity each year.

The sun *rises* in the east and *sets* in the west.

The plane *leaves* tomorrow at 6:30 p.m.

SIMPLE PAST (BASE FORM + *-ED* OR *-D* OR IRREGULAR FORM) Simple past tense expresses actions that happened at a specific time or during a specific period in the past. It can also show states of being and repetitive actions that have ended. It is often accompanied by a word (such as *ago* or *yesterday*) or a phrase (*in 1902*, *last year*) that indicates a specific past time. (See G2-a for irregular past-tense forms.)

She *drove* to Montreal three years ago.

When I *was* young, I usually *walked* to school with my sister.

SIMPLE FUTURE (*WILL* + BASE FORM) Simple future tense expresses actions that will happen at some time in the future as well as promises or predictions of future events.

I *will call* you next week.

Simple progressive forms for continuing actions

PRESENT PROGRESSIVE (*AM, IS, ARE* + PRESENT PARTICIPLE) Present progressive verbs show actions that are in progress at the present time but are not expected to remain constant or to continue indefinitely. Present progressive forms of verbs such as *leave*, *go*, *come*, and *move* are also used to express future actions.

Carlos *is building* his house on a cliff overlooking the ocean.

We *are going* to the circus tomorrow.

PAST PROGRESSIVE (*WAS, WERE* + PRESENT PARTICIPLE) Past progressive verbs express actions that were in progress at a specific past time. They often indicate a continuing action that was interrupted by another action. The past progressive form *was going to* or *were going to* is used for past plans that did not happen.

Roy *was driving* a brand-new red Corvette yesterday.

When my roommate walked in, we *were planning* her party.

We *were going to* spend spring break in Florida, but we went to New York instead.

FUTURE PROGRESSIVE (*WILL* + *BE* + PRESENT PARTICIPLE) Future progressive verbs show actions that will be in progress at a certain time in the future.

Naomi *will be flying* home tomorrow.

TIP: Certain verbs are not usually used in the progressive sense in English. In general, these verbs express a state of being or mental activity, not a dynamic action. Common examples are *appear, believe, belong, contain, have, hear, know, like, need, see, seem, taste, think, understand,* and *want.*

▶ **I ~~am wanting~~ [want] to see August Wilson's *Gem of the Ocean.***

Some of these verbs, however, have special uses in which progressive forms are normal (*We are thinking about going to the Bahamas*). You should note exceptions as you encounter them.

Perfect tenses for actions that happened or will happen before another time

PRESENT PERFECT (*HAVE*, *HAS* + PAST PARTICIPLE) Present perfect tense expresses actions that began in the past and continue to the present or actions that happened at an unspecific time in the past.

> An-Mei *has* not *spoken* Chinese since she was a child.
>
> My parents *have travelled* to South Africa twice.

PAST PERFECT (*HAD* + PAST PARTICIPLE) The past perfect tense conveys actions that began in the past and continued to a more recent past time. It is also used for an action that happened at an unspecific time before another past event. (For uses of the past perfect in conditional sentences, see E1-e.)

> By the time Hakan was fifteen, he *had* already *learned* to drive.
>
> I *had* just *finished* the test when the professor announced that time was up.

FUTURE PERFECT (*WILL* + *HAVE* + PAST PARTICIPLE) The future perfect tense expresses actions that will be completed before or at a specified future time.

> By the time I graduate, I *will have taken* five composition classes.

Perfect progressive forms for continuous past actions before another time

PRESENT PERFECT PROGRESSIVE (*HAVE*, *HAS* + *BEEN* + PRESENT PARTICIPLE) Present perfect progressive verbs express continuous actions that began in the past and continue to the present.

> My sister *has been living* in Winnipeg since 2001.

PAST PERFECT PROGRESSIVE (*HAD* + *BEEN* + PRESENT PARTICIPLE) Past perfect progressive verbs convey actions that began and continued in the past until some other past action.

> By the time I moved to Regina, I *had been supporting* myself for five years.

FUTURE PERFECT PROGRESSIVE (*WILL* + *HAVE* + *BEEN* + PRESENT PARTICIPLE) Future perfect progressive verbs indicate actions that are or will be in progress before a specified time in the future.

> By the time we reach the register, we *will have been waiting* in line for two full hours.

E1-b Use the base form of the verb after a modal.

A modal verb—*can, could, may, might, must, shall, should, will,* or *would*—is used with the base form of a verb to show certainty, necessity, or possibility. Modals do not change form to indicate tense. For a summary of modals and their meanings, see the chart beginning on this page. (Along with forms of *have*, *do*, and *be*, modals are also called *helping verbs*. See B1-c.)

▶ **My cousin will ~~sends~~ send us photographs from her wedding when she returns from Portugal.**

▶ **We could ~~spoke~~ speak Portuguese when we were young.**

TIP: Do not use *to* in front of a main verb that follows a modal.

▶ **Gina can ~~to~~ drive us home from the party if we miss the last subway train.**

For the use of modals in conditional sentences, see E1-e.

Modals and their meanings

Can

- General ability (present)

  Valerie *can sing*.

  Jorge *can run* the marathon faster than his brother.

- Informal requests or permission

  Can you *tell* me where the bookstore is?

  You *can borrow* my calculator until Wednesday.

Could

- General ability (past)

  Hilit *could speak* three languages when she was only five years old.

- Polite, informal requests or suggestions

  Could you *give* me that pen?

→

May

- Formal requests or permission

  May I *use* your pen?

  Students *may park* only in the yellow zone.

- Possibility

  I *may try* to finish my homework tonight, or I *may wake up* early and finish it tomorrow.

Might

- Possibility

  The population of New Delhi *might reach* thirteen million by 2010.

Must

- Necessity (present or future)

  To be effective, welfare-to-work programs *must provide* access to job training.

- Strong possibility or near certainty (present or past)

  Amy doesn't look well this morning. She *must be* sick. [She is probably sick.]

  I *must have left* my wallet at home. [I probably left my wallet at home.]

Should

- Suggestions or advice

  Frank *should join* student government.

  You *should drink* plenty of water every day.

- Obligations or duties

  The government *should protect* the rights of citizens.

- Expectations

  The books *should arrive* soon. [We expect the books to arrive soon.]

Will

- Certainty

  If you don't leave now, you *will be* late.

- Requests

  Will you *help* me study for my history test?

- Promises and offers

  I *will arrange* the carpool.

NOTE: *Shall* traditionally was the modal used with *I* or *we* in place of *will*. It is now used mainly for polite requests or in very formal contexts (*Shall I call you soon?*).

Would

- Polite requests

  Would you *help* me carry these books?

  I *would like* some coffee. [Polite for *want*.]

- Habitual or repeated actions (past)

  Whenever I needed help with sewing, I *would call* my aunt.

E1-c Use a form of *be* with the past participle to write a verb in the passive voice.

When a sentence is written in the passive voice, the subject receives the action instead of doing it. (See B2-b.)

S: The control group; V: was given

The control group was given a placebo.

Melissa *was taken* to the hospital.

To form the passive voice, use a form of *be*—*am*, *is*, *are*, *was*, *were*, *being*, *be*, or *been*—followed by the past participle of the main verb.

▶ ***Dreaming in Cuban* was ~~writing~~ written by Cristina García.**

The past participle *written*, not the present participle *writing*, must be used following *was* (the past tense of *be*) in the passive voice.

▶ **Councillor Dixon will ^be defeated.**

The passive voice requires a form of *be* before the past participle.

▶ **The child was being ~~tease.~~ ^teased.**

The past participle *teased*, not the base form *tease*, must be used with *was being* to form the passive voice.

For details on forming the passive in various tenses, consult the chart at the bottom of this page. (For appropriate uses of the passive voice, see W3-a.)

TIP: Only transitive verbs, those that take direct objects, may be used in the passive voice. Intransitive verbs such as *occur, happen, sleep, die,* and *fall* are not used in the passive. (See B2-b.)

▶ **The accident ~~was~~ happened suddenly.**

Verbs at a glance

Simple tenses

	ACTIVE VOICE	PASSIVE VOICE
Simple present • general facts • states of being • habitual, repetitive actions	**Base form or *-s* form** University students often *study* late at night.	***am, is, are* + past participle** Breakfast *is served* daily at 8:00.
Simple past • completed past actions • facts or states of being in the past	**Base form + *-ed* or *-d* or irregular form** The storm *destroyed* their property.	***was, were* + past participle** He *was punished* for being late.
Simple future • future actions, promises, or predictions	***will* + base form** I *will exercise* tomorrow.	***will be* + past participle** The mayor *will be elected* next week.

→

Simple progressive forms

	ACTIVE VOICE	PASSIVE VOICE
Present progressive	***am, is, are* + present participle**	***am, is, are* + *being* + past participle**
• actions in progress at the present time	The students *are taking* an exam in Room 105.	Dinner *is being served* now.
• future actions (with *leave*, *go*, *come*, *move*, etc.)	I *am leaving* tomorrow morning.	Jo *is being moved* to a new class next month.
Past progressive	***was, were* + present participle**	***was, were* + *being* + past participle**
• actions in progress at a specific time in the past	They *were swimming* when the storm struck.	We thought we *were being followed.*
Future progressive	***will* + *be* + present participle**	
• actions in progress at a specific time in the future	Brad *will be cooking* when his parents arrive.	[Future progressive is usually not used in the passive voice.]

Perfect tenses

	ACTIVE VOICE	PASSIVE VOICE
Present perfect	***has, have* + past participle**	***has, have* + *been* + past participle**
• repetitive or constant actions that began in the past and continue to the present	I *have loved* cats since I was a child.	Wars *have been fought* throughout history.
• actions that happened at an unknown or unspecific time in the past	Steph *has visited* Wales three times.	
Past perfect	***had* + past participle**	***had* + *been* + past participle**
• actions that began or occurred before another time in the past	She *had* just *crossed* the street when the runaway car plowed into the building.	He *had been given* all the hints he needed to complete the puzzle.

→

	ACTIVE VOICE	PASSIVE VOICE
Future perfect • actions that will be completed before or at a specific future time	***will*** **+** ***have*** **+ past participle** By the end of this year, I *will have seen* three concerts.	[Future perfect is usually not used in the passive voice.]

Perfect progressive forms

	ACTIVE VOICE
Present perfect progressive • continuous actions that began in the past and continue to the present	***has, have*** **+** ***been*** **+ present participle** My sister *has been trying* to get a job in Vancouver for five years.
Past perfect progressive • actions that began and continued in the past until some other past action	***had*** **+** ***been*** **+ present participle** By the time I entered high school, I *had been taking* piano lessons for eight years.
Future perfect progressive • actions that are or will be in progress before a specified future time	***will*** **+** ***have*** **+** ***been*** **+ present participle** When Carol is eighty years old, she *will have been living* in North Bay for sixty-two years.

E1-d To make negative verb forms, add *not* in the appropriate place.

If the verb is the simple present or past tense of *be* (*am*, *is*, *are*, *was*, *were*), add *not* after the verb.

Mario *is not* a member of the club.

For simple present-tense verbs other than *be*, use *do* or *does* plus *not* before the base form of the verb. (For the correct use of *do* and *does*, see the chart in G1-a.)

▶ **Mariko** *does not* **~~no~~ want more dessert.**

▶ **Mariko does not want~~s~~ more dessert.**

For simple past-tense verbs other than *be*, use *did* plus *not* before the base form of the verb.

▶ **They did not** *plant* **~~planted~~ corn this year.**

In a verb phrase consisting of one or more helping verbs and a present or past participle (*is watching*, *were living*, *has played*, *could have been driven*), use the word *not* after the first helping verb.

▶ **Inna should** *not* **have ~~not~~ gone dancing last night.**

▶ **Bonnie is** *not* **~~no~~ singing this weekend.**

NOTE: The word *not* can be contracted to *n't* when used with some forms of *be* (*is*, *are*, *was*, *were*) and with other helping verbs and modals. Use *isn't* for *is not*, *don't* for *do not*, *doesn't* for *does not*, *shouldn't* for *should not*, and so on. *Won't* is the contracted form of *will not*. The contracted form of *am not*, used only in questions, is *aren't*.

English allows only one negative in an independent clause to express a negative idea; using more than one is an error known as a *double negative* (see also G4-d). Double negatives can be corrected by eliminating one of the two negative words or by replacing one of them with an article or another noun marker such as *any*.

▶ **I don't have ~~no~~ homework this weekend.**

▶ **We could not find** *any* **~~no~~ books about the history of our school.**

▶ **The smoke detector doesn't have** *a* **~~no~~ battery in it.**

E1-e In a conditional sentence, choose verb tenses according to the type of condition expressed in the sentence.

Conditional sentences contain two clauses: a subordinate clause (usually starting with *if, when,* or *unless*) and an independent clause. The subordinate clause (sometimes called the *if* or *unless* clause) states the condition or cause; the independent clause states the result or effect.

Verb tenses in conditional sentences usually express the nature of the condition rather than the time of an action or event. Present tenses typically express factual or true conditions, and past tenses typically express speculative or imaginary conditions.

Three kinds of conditional sentences are discussed in this section: factual, predictive, and speculative. In each example, the subordinate clause is marked SUB, and the independent clause is marked IND.

Factual

Factual conditional sentences express factual relationships. If the relationship is a scientific truth, use the present tense in both clauses.

SUB — IND

If water *cools* to 0° C, it *freezes.*

If the sentence describes a condition that is (or was) habitually true, use the same tense in both clauses.

SUB — IND

When Sue *jogs* along the canal, her dog *runs* ahead of her.

SUB — IND

Whenever the coach *asked* for help, I *volunteered.*

Predictive

Predictive conditional sentences are used to predict the future or to express future plans or possibilities. To form a predictive sentence, use a present-tense verb in the subordinate clause; in the independent clause, use the modal *will*, *can*, *may*, *should*, or *might* plus the base form of the verb.

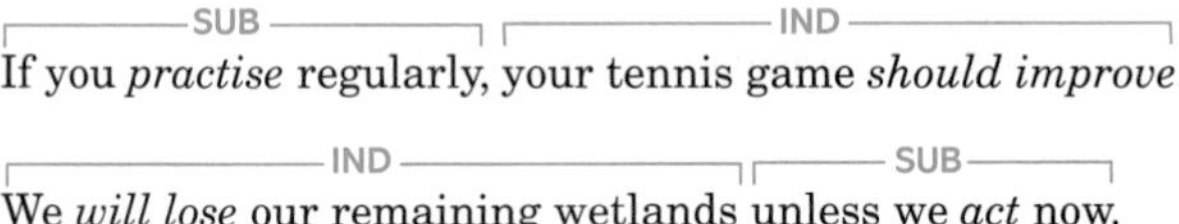
SUB — IND

If you *practise* regularly, your tennis game *should improve.*

IND — SUB

We *will lose* our remaining wetlands unless we *act* now.

TIP: In all types of conditional sentences (factual, predictive, and speculative), *if* or *unless* clauses do not use the modal verb *will.*

▶ **If Jenna ~~will pass~~ *passes* her history test, she will graduate this year.**

Speculative

Speculative conditional sentences, sometimes called *unreal conditionals*, show unlikely, contrary-to-fact, or impossible conditions. To show distance from truth or reality, English uses past or past perfect tense in the *if* clause, even for conditions in the present and future.

UNLIKELY POSSIBILITIES If the condition is possible but unlikely in the present or future, use the past tense in the subordinate clause; in the independent clause, use *would*, *could*, or *might* plus the base form of the verb.

SUB IND

If I *won* the lottery, I *would travel* to Egypt.

The writer does not expect to win the lottery. Because this is a possible but unlikely present or future situation, the subordinate clause uses the past tense.

CONDITIONS CONTRARY TO FACT In conditions that are currently unreal or contrary to fact, use the past-tense verb *were* (not *was*) in the *if* clause for all subjects. (See G2-g for more details.)

were

▶ **If I ~~was~~ prime minister, I would make children's issues a priority.**

The writer is not prime minister, so *were* is correct in the *if* clause.

EVENTS THAT DID NOT HAPPEN In a conditional sentence that speculates about an event that did not happen or was impossible in the past, use the past perfect tense in the *if* clause; in the independent clause, use *would have*, *could have*, or *might have* with the past participle. (See also past perfect tense, p. 222.)

SUB IND

If I *had saved* enough money, I *would have visited* Senegal last year.

The writer did not save enough money and did not travel to Senegal. This sentence shows a possibility that did not happen.

SUB IND

If Aunt Grace *had been* alive for your graduation, she *would have been* very proud.

Aunt Grace was not alive at the time of the graduation. This sentence shows an impossible situation in the past.

E1-f Become familiar with verbs that may be followed by gerunds or infinitives.

A gerund is a verb form that ends in *-ing* and is used as a noun: *sleeping, dreaming.* (See B3-b.) An infinitive is the word *to* plus the base form of the verb: *to sleep, to dream.* The word *to* is not a preposition in this use but an infinitive marker.

A few verbs may be followed by either a gerund or an infinitive; others may be followed by a gerund but not by an infinitive; still others may be followed by an infinitive but not by a gerund.

Verb + gerund or infinitive (no change in meaning)

The following commonly used verbs may be followed by a gerund or an infinitive, with little or no difference in meaning:

begin	hate	love
continue	like	start

I love *skiing.* I love *to ski.*

Verb + gerund or infinitive (change in meaning)

With a few verbs, the choice of a gerund or an infinitive changes the meaning dramatically:

forget remember stop try

She stopped *speaking* to Lucia. [She no longer spoke to Lucia.]

She stopped *to speak* to Lucia. [She paused so that she could speak to Lucia.]

Verb + gerund

These verbs may be followed by a gerund but not by an infinitive:

admit	enjoy	postpone	resist
appreciate	escape	practise	risk
avoid	finish	put off	suggest
deny	imagine	quit	tolerate
discuss	miss	recall	

Bill enjoys *playing* [not *to play*] the piano.

Jamie quit *smoking.*

Verb + infinitive

These verbs may be followed by an infinitive but not by a gerund:

agree	expect	need	refuse
ask	help	offer	wait
beg	hope	plan	want
claim	manage	pretend	wish
decide	mean	promise	would like

Jill has offered *to water* [not *watering*] the plants while we are away.

Joe finally managed *to find* a parking space.

The man refused *to join* the rebellion.

A few of these verbs may be followed either by an infinitive directly or by a noun or pronoun plus an infinitive:

ask	help	promise	would like
expect	need	want	

We asked *to speak* to the congregation.

We asked *Rabbi Abrams to speak* to our congregation.

Alex expected *to get* the lead in the play.

Ira expected *Alex to get* the lead in the play.

Verb + noun or pronoun + infinitive

With certain verbs in the active voice, a noun or pronoun must come between the verb and the infinitive that follows it. The noun or pronoun usually names a person who is affected by the action.

advise	convince	order	tell
allow	encourage	persuade	urge
cause	have ("own")	remind	warn
command	instruct	require	

V N INF
The class encouraged Luis to tell the story of his escape.

The counsellor *advised Haley to take* four courses instead of five.

Professor Howlett *instructed us to write* our names on the left side of the paper.

Verb + noun or pronoun + unmarked infinitive

An unmarked infinitive is an infinitive without *to.* A few verbs (often called *causative verbs*) may be followed by a noun or pronoun and an unmarked infinitive.

have ("cause") help let ("allow") make ("force")

Hon *had the valet park* his car.

▶ **Please let me ~~to~~ pay for the tickets.**

▶ **Frank made me ~~to~~ carry his book for him.**

NOTE: *Help* can be followed by a noun or pronoun and either an unmarked or a marked infinitive: *Emma helped Brian wash the dishes. Emma helped Brian to wash the dishes.*

E2

Sentence structure

Although their structure can vary widely, sentences in English generally flow from subject to verb to object or complement: *Bears eat fish*. This section focuses on the major challenges that English language learners face when writing sentences in English. For more details on the parts of speech and how they work together to form sentences, consult B, Basic Grammar.

ON THE WEB > **dianahacker.com/writersref**
Grammar exercises > ESL challenges > E-ex E2–1 and E2–2

E2-a Use a linking verb between a subject and its complement.

Some languages, such as Russian and Turkish, do not use linking verbs (*is, are, was, were*) between subjects and complements (nouns or adjectives that rename or describe the subject). Every English sentence, however, must include a verb. For more on linking verbs, see G2-e.

▶ Jim ^is intelligent.

▶ Many streets in Halifax ^are very steep.

E2-b Include a subject in every sentence.

Some languages, such as Spanish and Japanese, do not require a subject in every sentence. Every English sentence, however, needs a subject. An exception is commands, in which the subject *you* is understood but not present (*Give to the poor*).

▶ **Your aunt is very energetic. ^She seems ~~Seems~~ young for her age.**

The word *it* is used as the subject of a sentence describing the weather or temperature, stating the time, indicating distance, or suggesting an environmental fact.

▶ **^It is ~~Is~~ raining in the valley and snowing in the mountains.**

▶ **In July, ^it is very hot in Toronto.**

▶ **^It is ~~Is~~ 9:15 a.m.**

▶ **^It is ~~Is~~ three hundred kilometres to Ottawa.**

▶ **^It gets ~~Gets~~ noisy in our dorm on weekends.**

In most English sentences, the subject appears before the verb. Some sentences, however, are inverted: The subject comes after the verb. In these sentences, a placeholder called an *expletive* (*there* or *it*) often comes before the verb.

EXP V S S V
There are many people here today. (Many people are here today.)

▶ **^There is ~~Is~~ an apple in the refrigerator.**

▶ **As you know, ^there are many religious sects in India.**

Notice that the verb agrees with the subject that follows it: *apple is, sects are.* (See G1-g.)

In inverted sentences that have an infinitive (*to work*) or a noun clause (*that she is intelligent*) as the subject, the placeholder *it* is needed to open the sentence. *It* is followed by a linking verb (*is*, *was*, *seems*, and so on), an adjective, and then the subject. (See B3-b and B3-e.)

EXP V S S V
It is important to study daily. (To study daily is important.)

It is
▶ ~~Is~~ healthy to eat fruit and grains.

It is
▶ ~~Is~~ clear that we must change our approach.

TIP: The words *here* and *there* are not used as subjects. When they mean "in this place" (*here*) or "in that place" (*there*), they are adverbs—not nouns.

It there.
▶ **I just returned from a vacation in Japan. ~~There~~ is very beautiful~~.~~**

This school that school
▶ **~~Here~~ offers a master's degree in physical therapy; ~~there~~ has only a bachelor's program.**

GRAMMAR CHECKERS can flag some sentences with a missing expletive, or placeholder (*there* or *it*), but they often misdiagnose the problem, suggesting that if a sentence opens with a word such as *Is* or *Are,* it may need a question mark at the end. Consider this sentence, which a grammar checker flagged as requiring a question mark: *Are two grocery stores on Elm Street.* The sentence is missing the placeholder *there*, whether it is phrased as a question or as a statement: *There are two grocery stores on Elm Street. Are there two grocery stores on Elm Street?*

E2-c Do not use both a noun and a pronoun to perform the same grammatical function in a sentence.

English does not allow a subject to be repeated in its own clause.

▶ **The doctor ~~she~~ advised me to cut down on salt.**

▶ **Andrea ~~she~~ is late all the time.**

The pronoun *she* cannot repeat the subject, *doctor*, in the first sentence or the subject, *Andrea*, in the second.

Do not add a pronoun even when a word group comes between the subject and the verb.

▶ **The watch that had been lost on vacation ~~it~~ was in my backpack.**

The pronoun *it* cannot repeat the subject, *watch*.

Some languages allow "topic fronting," or placing a word or phrase (a "topic") at the beginning of a sentence and following it with an independent clause that explains something about the topic. This form is not allowed in English.

TOPIC | IND CLAUSE

INCORRECT The seeds I planted them last fall.

The pronoun *them* repeats the "topic," *the seeds*. The sentence can be revised by replacing *them* with *the seeds*.

▶ **~~The seeds~~ I planted ~~them~~ last fall.** [inserted: *the seeds*]

E2-d Do not repeat an object or an adverb in an adjective clause.

Adjective clauses begin with relative pronouns (*who, whom, whose, which, that*) or relative adverbs (*when, where*). Relative pronouns usually serve as subjects or objects in the clauses they introduce; another word in the clause cannot serve the same function. Relative adverbs should not be repeated by other adverbs later in the clause.

ADJ CLAUSE

The cat ran under the car that was parked on the street.

▶ **The cat ran under the car that ~~it~~ was parked on the street.**

The relative pronoun *that* is the subject of the adjective clause, so the pronoun *it* cannot be added as the subject.

▶ **Myrna enjoyed the investment seminars that she attended ~~them~~ last week.**

The relative pronoun *that* is the object of the verb *attended*. The pronoun *them* cannot also serve as object.

Even when the relative pronoun has been omitted, do not add another word with its same function.

▶ **Myrna enjoyed the investment seminars she attended ~~them~~ last week.**

The relative pronoun *that* is understood even though it is not present in the sentence.

If the clause begins with a relative adverb, do not use another adverb with the same meaning later in the clause.

▶ **The office where I work ~~there~~ is one hour from the city.**

The adverb *there* cannot repeat the relative adverb *where*.

GRAMMAR CHECKERS usually fail to mark sentences with repeated subjects or objects. One program flagged some sentences with repeated subjects, such as this one: *The yarn that she ordered it will arrive next Monday.* But the program misdiagnosed the problem and did not recognize that *it* repeats the subject, *yarn*.

E2-e Do not mix *although* or *because* with other linking words that serve the same purpose in a sentence.

A word group that begins with *although* cannot be linked to a word group that begins with *but* or *however* (both words have the same meaning as *although*). Similarly, a word group that begins with *because* cannot be linked to a word group that begins with *so* or *therefore*.

If you want to keep *although* or *because,* drop the other linking word.

▶ **Although the sales figures look impressive, ~~but~~ the company is losing money.**

▶ **Because finance laws are not always enforced, ~~therefore~~ investing in the Commonwealth of Independent States can be very risky.**

If you want to keep the other linking word, omit *although* or *because.*

> ▶ ~~Because finance~~ Finance laws are not always enforced; therefore, investing in the Commonwealth of Independent States can be very risky.

> ▶ ~~Although the~~ The sales figures look impressive, but the company is losing money.

For advice about using commas and semicolons with linking words, see P1-a and P3-b.

E2-f Do not place an adverb between a verb and its direct object.

Adverbs modifying verbs can appear in various positions:

- at the beginning or end of the sentence

  Slowly, we drove along the rain-slick road.

  Mother wrapped the gift *carefully.*

- before or after the verb

  Martin *always* wins our tennis matches.

  Christina is *rarely* late for our lunch dates.

- between a helping verb and a main verb

  My daughter has *often* spoken of you.

  The election results were being *closely* followed by analysts.

However, an adverb cannot appear between a verb and its direct object.

> ▶ Mother carefully wrapped ~~carefully~~ the gift.

The adverb *carefully* may be placed at the beginning or at the end of this sentence or before the verb, *wrapped*. It cannot appear after the verb because the verb is followed by a direct object, *the gift*.

E3

Articles and types of nouns

Articles (*a, an, the*) are part of a category of words known as *noun markers* or *determiners*. Standard English uses noun markers to help identify the nouns that follow. In addition to articles, noun markers include

- possessive nouns, such as *Elena's* (See P5-a.)
- possessive pronoun/adjectives: *my, your, his, her, its, our, their* (See B1-b.)
- demonstrative pronoun/adjectives: *this, that, these, those* (See B1-b.)
- quantifiers: *all, any, each, either, every, few, many, more, most, much, neither, several, some,* and so on (See E3-e.)
- numbers: *one, two,* and so on

ON THE WEB > **dianahacker.com/writersref**
Grammar exercises > ESL challenges > E-ex E3–1 and E3–2

E3-a Be familiar with articles and other noun markers.

Articles and other noun markers always appear before nouns. If you use an adjective with a noun, put the article before the adjective.

ART N
Felix is reading a book about mythology.

ART ADJ N
We took an exciting trip to Yukon last summer.

In most cases, do not use an article with another noun marker, such as *Natalie's* or *this*.

▶ **When did you buy ~~the~~ this round pine table?**

▶ **~~The~~ Natalie's older brother lives in Joliette.**

Types of articles

Indefinite articles

Indefinite articles (*a, an*) are used with nouns that are not specific. See E3-d.

a — *A* means "one" or "one among many." Use *a* before a consonant sound: *a banana, a tree, a picture, a hand, a happy child.*

an — *An* also means "one" or "one among many." Use *an* before a vowel sound: *an eggplant, an occasion, an uncle, an hour, an honourable person.*

NOTE: Words beginning with *h* and *u* can have either a consonant sound (*a hand, a happy baby, a university, a union*) or a vowel sound (*an hour, an honourable person, an umbrella, an uncle*). (See also W1.)

Definite article

The definite article (*the*) is used with specific nouns. See E3-c.

the — *The* makes nouns specific; it does not refer to a number or amount. Use *the* with one or more than one specific thing: *the newspaper, the soldiers.*

EXCEPTION: Expressions like *a few, the most,* and *all the* are exceptions. See E3-e.

Did you bring *all the books* with you?

We got *the most snow* ever in January.

E3-b Understand the different types of nouns.

To choose an appropriate article for a noun, you must first determine whether the noun is common or proper, specific or general, count or noncount, and singular or plural.

Common or proper

Common nouns name general persons, places, things, or ideas. Proper nouns, which are marked in English with capital letters, name specific persons, places, things, or ideas. (See also M3.)

- common: religion, student, country
- proper: Hinduism, Philip, Vietnam

Specific (definite) or general (indefinite)

Specific or definite nouns represent persons, places, things, or ideas that can be identified within a group of nouns of the same type. General or indefinite nouns represent whole categories in general; they can also name nonspecific persons, places, things, or ideas that represent a group.

SPECIFIC The *students* in Professor Martin's class should study harder. [The specific students in the class]

GENERAL *Students* should study. [All students, students in general]

SPECIFIC The *airplane* carrying Premier Chen took off at 1:30. [The specific airplane carrying the premier]

GENERAL The *airplane* has made commuting between major cities easy. [All airplanes as a category of transportation]

Count or noncount

Count nouns refer to persons, places, things, or ideas that can be counted. Only count nouns have plural forms. Noncount nouns refer to things or abstract ideas that cannot be counted or made plural.

- count: *one girl*, *two girls*; *one city*, *three cities*; *one goose*, *four geese*; *one philosophy*, *five philosophies*
- noncount: *water*, *silver*, *air*, *furniture*, *patience*, *knowledge*

Some nouns can be used in both a count and a noncount sense.

COUNT	NONCOUNT
I'll have *a coffee*.	I'll have *coffee*.
There are many *democracies* in the world.	We learned that *democracy* originated in ancient Greece.

Some nouns (such as *advice* and *information*) may be countable in some languages but not in English. If you do not know whether a noun is count or noncount, refer to the chart on page 243 or consult an ESL dictionary.

Singular or plural

Singular nouns represent one person, place, thing, or idea; plural nouns represent more than one. Only count nouns can be made plural. (For more information on forming plural nouns, see M1-a.)

- singular: *backpack*, *country*, *woman*, *achievement*
- plural: *backpacks*, *countries*, *women*, *achievements*

GRAMMAR CHECKERS rarely flag missing or misused articles. They cannot distinguish when *a* or *an* is appropriate and when *the* is correct, nor can they tell when an article is missing.

E3-c Use *the* with most specific common nouns.

The definite article *the* is used with most nouns—both count and noncount—that the reader can identify specifically. Usually the identity will be clear to the reader for one of the following reasons.

1. The noun has been previously mentioned.

▶ **A truck cut in front of our van. When ^the truck skidded a few seconds later, we almost crashed into it.**

The article *A* is used before *truck* when the noun is first mentioned. When the noun is mentioned again, it needs the article *the* because readers can now identify which truck skidded.

Commonly used noncount nouns

Food and drink

beef, bread, butter, candy, cereal, cheese, cream, meat, milk, pasta, rice, salt, sugar, water, wine

Nonfood substances

air, cement, coal, dirt, gasoline, gold, paper, petroleum, plastic, rain, silver, snow, soap, steel, wood, wool

Abstract nouns

advice, anger, beauty, confidence, courage, employment, fun, happiness, health, honesty, information, intelligence, knowledge, love, poverty, satisfaction, wealth

Other

biology (and other areas of study), clothing, equipment, furniture, homework, jewellery, luggage, machinery, mail, money, news, poetry, pollution, research, scenery, traffic, transportation, violence, weather, work

NOTE: A few noncount nouns can also be used as count nouns: *You can't buy love. He had two loves: music and archery.*

Choosing articles for common nouns

This chart summarizes the most frequent uses of articles with common nouns. For help choosing articles with proper nouns, see E3-g.

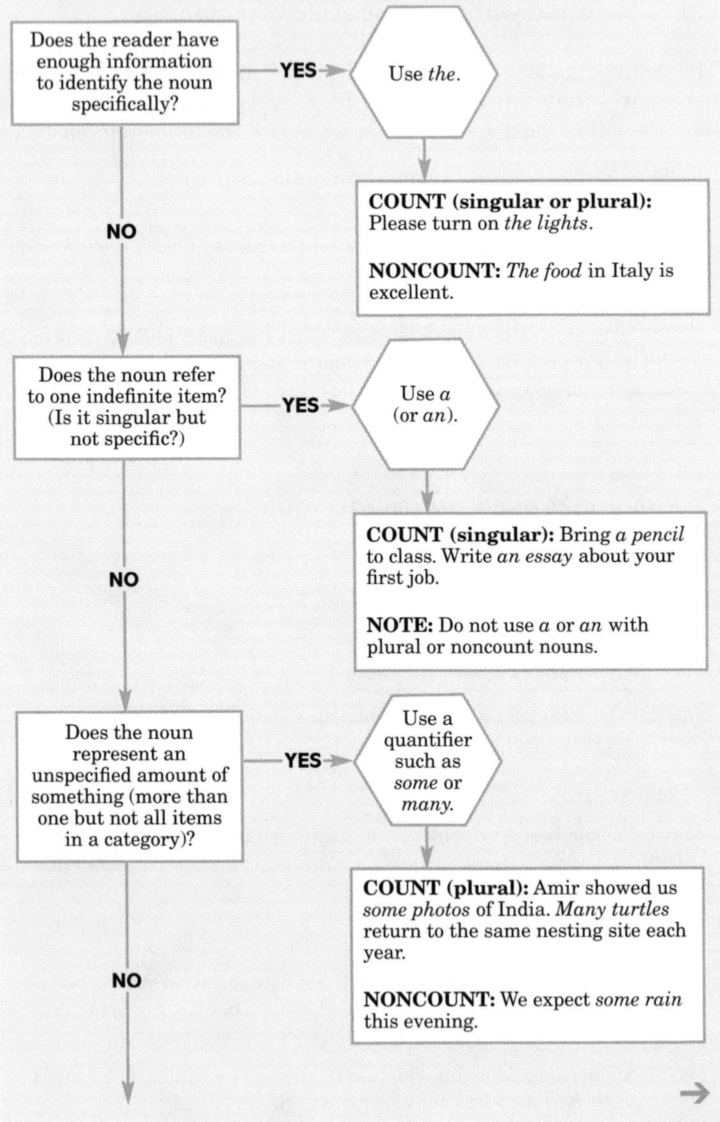
Does the reader have enough information to identify the noun specifically?
YES
Use *the*.
COUNT (singular or plural): Please turn on *the lights*.
NONCOUNT: *The food* in Italy is excellent.
NO
Does the noun refer to one indefinite item? (Is it singular but not specific?)
YES
Use *a* (or *an*).
COUNT (singular): Bring *a pencil* to class. Write *an essay* about your first job.
NOTE: Do not use *a* or *an* with plural or noncount nouns.
NO
Does the noun represent an unspecified amount of something (more than one but not all items in a category)?
YES
Use a quantifier such as *some* or *many*.
COUNT (plural): Amir showed us *some photos* of India. *Many turtles* return to the same nesting site each year.
NONCOUNT: We expect *some rain* this evening.
NO

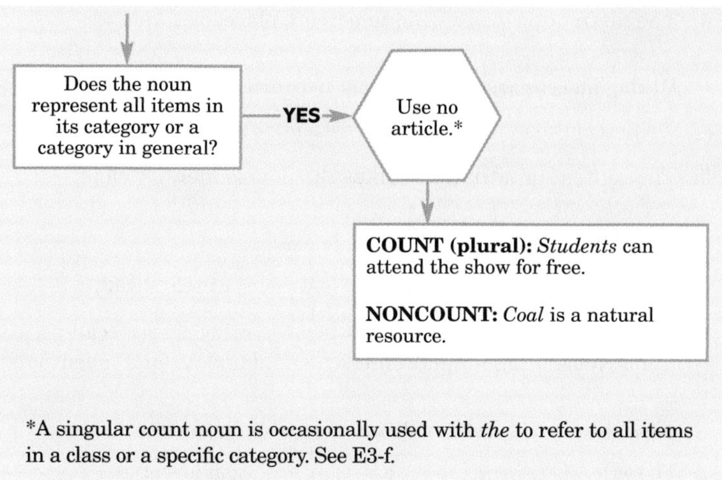

*A singular count noun is occasionally used with *the* to refer to all items in a class or a specific category. See E3-f.

2. A phrase or clause following the noun restricts its identity.

► **Bryce warned me that** ^the **computer on his desk had just crashed.**

The phrase *on his desk* identifies the specific computer.

NOTE: Descriptive adjectives do not necessarily make a noun specific. A specific noun is one that readers can identify within a group of nouns of the same type.

► **If I win the lottery, I will buy** ^a ~~**the**~~ **brand-new bright red sports car.**

The reader cannot identify which specific brand-new bright red sports car the writer will buy. Even though *car* has many adjectives in front of it, it is a general noun in this sentence.

3. A superlative adjective such as *best* or *most intelligent* makes the noun's identity specific. (See also G4-c on comparatives and superlatives.)

► **Our petite daughter dated** ^the **tallest boy in her class.**

The superlative *tallest* makes the noun *boy* specific. Although there might be several tall boys, only one boy can be the tallest.

4. The noun describes a unique person, place, or thing.

▶ **During an eclipse, one should not look directly at ^the sun.**

There is only one sun in our solar system, so its identity is clear.

5. The context or situation makes the noun's identity clear.

▶ **Please don't slam ^the door when you leave.**

Both the speaker and the listener know which door is meant.

6. The noun is singular and refers to a scientific class or category of items (most often animals, musical instruments, and inventions).

▶ ^The assembly **~~Assembly~~ line transformed manufacturing in North America.**

The writer is referring to the assembly line as an invention.

E3-d Use *a* (or *an*) with common singular count nouns that refer to "one" or "any."

If a count noun refers to one unspecific item (not a whole category), use the indefinite article *a* (or *an*). *A* and *an* usually mean "one among many" but can also mean "any one."

▶ **My English professor asked me to bring ^a dictionary to class.**

The noun *dictionary* refers to "one unspecific dictionary" or "any dictionary."

▶ **We want to rent ^an apartment close to the lake.**

The noun *apartment* refers to "any apartment close to the lake," not a specific apartment.

E3-e Use a quantifier such as *some* or *more*, not *a* (or *an*), with a noncount noun to express an approximate amount.

Do not use *a* (or *an*) with noncount nouns. Also do not use numbers or words such as *several* or *many* because they must be used with plural nouns, and noncount nouns do not have plural forms.

▶ **Dr. Snyder gave us ~~an~~ information about the Peace Corps.**

▶ **Do you have ~~many~~ money with you?**

You can use quantifiers such as the following to suggest approximate amounts or nonspecific quantities of noncount nouns.

QUANTIFIER	NONCOUNT NOUN
a little	salt, rain, knowledge, time
any	sugar, homework
enough	bread, wood, money
less	meat, violence
more	coffee, information
much (*or* a lot of)	snow, pollution
plenty of	paper, lumber
some	tea, news, work

some
▶ **Claudia's mother told her that she had ~~a~~ news that would surprise her.**

E3-f Do not use articles with nouns that refer to all of something or something in general.

When a noncount noun refers to all of its type or to a concept in general, it is not marked with an article.

Kindness
▶ **~~The kindness~~ is a virtue.**

The noun represents kindness in general; it does not represent a specific type of kindness.

▶ **In some parts of the world, ~~the~~ rice is preferred to all other grains.**

The noun *rice* represents rice in general, not a specific type or serving of rice.

In most cases, when you use a count noun to represent a general category, make the noun plural. Do not use unmarked singular count nouns to represent whole categories.

Fountains are
▶ **~~Fountain is~~ an expensive element of landscape design.**

Fountains is a count noun that represents fountains in general.

EXCEPTION: In some cases, *the* can be used with singular count nouns to represent a class or specific category: *The American alligator is no longer listed as an endangered species.* Also see number 6 in E3-c.

E3-g Do not use articles with most singular proper nouns. Use *the* with most plural proper nouns.

Since singular proper nouns are already specific, they typically do not need an article: *Prime Minister Blair, Jamaica, Lake Huron, Mount Etna.*

There are, however, many exceptions. In most cases, if the proper noun consists of a common noun with modifiers (adjectives or an *of* phrase), use *the* with the proper noun.

Using the *with geographical nouns*

When to omit *the*

streets, squares, parks	Ivy Street, Union Square, Denali National Park
cities, provinces or territories, counties	Miami, Northwest Territories, Bee County
most countries, continents	Italy, Nigeria, China, South America, Africa
bays, single lakes	Hudson Bay, Lake Geneva
single mountains, islands	Mount Everest, Crete

When to use *the*

country names with *of* phrase	the United States (of America), the People's Republic of China
large regions, deserts	the East Coast, the Sahara
peninsulas	the Iberian Peninsula
oceans, seas, gulfs	the Pacific Ocean, the Dead Sea, the Persian Gulf
canals and rivers	the Panama Canal, the Amazon
mountain ranges	the Rocky Mountains, the Alps
groups of islands	the Solomon Islands

▶ We visited ^the Great Wall of China last year.

▶ Rob wants to be a translator for ^the Central Intelligence Agency.

The is used with most plural proper nouns: *the McGregors, the Bahamas, the Finger Lakes, the United States.*

Geographical names create problems because there are so many exceptions to the rules. When in doubt, consult the chart on page 248, check a dictionary, or ask an English speaker.

E4

Using adjectives

ON THE WEB > **dianahacker.com/writersref**
Grammar exercises > ESL challenges > E-ex E4–1 and E4–2

E4-a Distinguish between present participles and past participles used as adjectives.

Both present and past participles may be used as adjectives. The present participle always ends in *-ing.* Past participles usually end in *-ed, -d, -en, -n,* or *-t.* (See G2-a.)

PRESENT PARTICIPLES	confusing, speaking, boring
PAST PARTICIPLES	confused, spoken, bored

Like all other adjectives, participles can come before nouns; they also can follow linking verbs, in which case they describe the subject of the sentence. (See B2-b.)

It was a depressing (ADJ) movie (N).

The movie was (V) depressing (ADJ).

The *confused tourists* stared at the map.

The *tourists* were *confused* by the map.

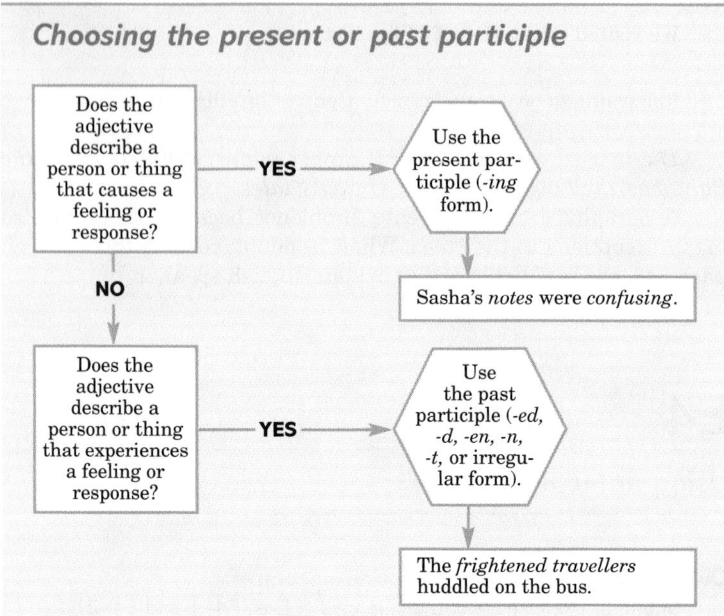

Use a present participle to describe a person or thing *causing or stimulating an experience*.

The *boring lecture* put us to sleep. [The lecture caused boredom; it didn't experience it.]

Use a past participle to describe a person or thing *undergoing an experience*.

The *audience* was *bored* by the lecture. [The audience experienced boredom; it didn't cause boredom.]

Participles that describe emotions or mental states often cause the most confusion.

▶ **Our hike was ~~exhausted.~~** exhausting.

Exhausting describes how the hike made us feel.

▶ **The ~~exhausting~~** exhausted **hikers reached camp at sunset.**

Exhausted describes how the hikers felt.

The chart on page 250 can help you use these participles correctly.

annoying/annoyed	exhausting/exhausted
boring/bored	fascinating/fascinated
confusing/confused	frightening/frightened
depressing/depressed	satisfying/satisfied
exciting/excited	surprising/surprised

GRAMMAR CHECKERS do not flag problems with present and past participles used as adjectives. Not surprisingly, the programs have no way of knowing the meaning a writer intends.

E4-b Place cumulative adjectives in an appropriate order.

Adjectives usually come before the nouns that they modify and may also come after linking verbs. (See B1-d, B1-e, and B2-b.)

Janine wore a new[ADJ] necklace[N]. Janine's necklace was[V] new[ADJ].

Order of cumulative adjectives

FIRST **ARTICLE OR OTHER NOUN MARKER** a, an, the, her, Joe's, two, many, some

EVALUATIVE WORD attractive, dedicated, delicious, ugly

SIZE large, enormous, small, little

LENGTH OR SHAPE long, short, round, square

AGE new, old, young, antique

COLOUR yellow, blue, crimson

NATIONALITY French, Peruvian, Vietnamese

RELIGION Catholic, Protestant, Jewish, Muslim

MATERIAL silver, walnut, wool, marble

LAST **NOUN/ADJECTIVE** tree (as in *tree* house)

THE NOUN MODIFIED house, sweater, bicycle, bread, woman, priest

my long green wool coat

Cumulative adjectives, which cannot be joined by the word *and* or separated by commas, must come in a particular order. If you use cumulative adjectives before a noun, see the chart on page 251. The chart is only a guide; don't be surprised if you encounter exceptions. (See also P2-d.)

▶ **My dorm room has only a small desk and a ~~plastic red smelly~~** *smelly red plastic* **chair.**

▶ **Nice weather, ~~blue clear~~** *clear blue* **water, and ancient monuments attract many people to Italy.**

E5

Prepositions and idiomatic expressions

E5-a Become familiar with prepositions that show time and place.

The most frequently used prepositions in English are *at, by, for, from, in, of, on, to,* and *with.* Prepositions can be difficult to master because the differences among them are subtle and idiomatic. The chart on page 253 is limited to three troublesome prepositions that show time and place: *at, on,* and *in.*

Not every possible use is listed in the chart, so don't be surprised when you encounter exceptions and idiomatic uses that you must learn one at a time. For example, in English we ride *in* a car but *on* a bus, plane, train, or subway.

▶ **My first class starts ~~on~~** *at* **8:00 a.m.**

▶ **The farmers go to market ~~in~~** *on* **Wednesday.**

▶ **I want to work at one of the biggest companies ~~on~~** *in* **the world.**

ON THE WEB > **dianahacker.com/writersref**
Grammar exercises > ESL challenges > E-ex E5–1

At, on, *and* in *to show time and place*

Showing time

AT *at* a specific time: *at* 7:20, *at* dawn, *at* dinner

ON *on* a specific day or date: *on* Tuesday, *on* June 4

IN *in* a part of a 24-hour period: *in* the afternoon, *in* the daytime [but *at* night]

in a year or month: *in* 1999, *in* July

in a period of time: finished *in* three hours

Showing place

AT *at* a meeting place or location: *at* home, *at* the club

at the edge of something: sitting *at* the desk

at the corner of something: turning *at* the intersection

at a target: throwing the snowball *at* Lucy

ON *on* a surface: placed *on* the table, hanging *on* the wall

on a street: the house *on* Spring Street

on an electronic medium: *on* television, *on* the Internet

IN *in* an enclosed space: *in* the garage, *in* an envelope

in a geographic location: *in* Nelson, *in* Alberta

in a print medium: *in* a book, *in* a magazine

E5-b Use nouns (including *-ing* forms) after prepositions.

In a prepositional phrase, use a noun (not a verb) after the preposition. Sometimes the noun will be a gerund, the *-ing* verb form that functions as a noun (see B3-b).

▶ **Our student government is good at ~~save~~ *saving* money.**

Distinguish between the preposition *to* and the infinitive marker *to*. If *to* is a preposition, it should be followed by a noun or a gerund.

▶ **We are dedicated to ~~help~~ *helping* the poor.**

If *to* is an infinitive marker, it should be followed by the base form of the verb.

▶ **We want to ~~helping~~ help the poor.**

TIP: To test whether *to* is a preposition or an infinitive marker, insert a word that you know is a noun after the word *to*. If the noun sounds right in that position, *to* is a preposition.

Zoe is addicted to ____________.

In this case, a noun (such as *magazines*) makes sense after *to*, so *to* is a preposition and should be followed by a noun or a gerund: *Zoe is addicted to magazines. Zoe is addicted to reading.*

They are planning to _________.

In this case, a noun (such as *house*) does not make sense after *to*, so *to* is an infinitive marker and must be followed by the base form of the verb: *They are planning to build a new house.*

E5-c Become familiar with common adjective + preposition combinations.

Some adjectives appear only with certain prepositions. These expressions are idiomatic and may be different from the combinations used in your native language.

Adjective + preposition combinations

accustomed to	connected to	interested in	proud of
addicted to	covered with	involved in	responsible for
afraid of	dedicated to	involved with	satisfied with
angry with	devoted to	known as	scared of
ashamed of	different from	known for	similar to
aware of	engaged to	made of (*or* made from)	tired of
committed to	excited about	married to	worried about
concerned about	familiar with	opposed to	
concerned with	full of	preferable to	
	guilty of		

▶ **Paula is married ~~with~~ Jon.** *(to)*

Check an ESL dictionary for combinations that are not listed in the chart on page 254.

E5-d Become familiar with common verb + preposition combinations.

Many verbs and prepositions appear together in idiomatic phrases. Pay special attention to the combinations that are different from the combinations used in your native language.

▶ **Your success depends ~~of~~ your effort.** *(on)*

Check an ESL dictionary for combinations that are not listed in the following chart.

Verb + preposition combinations

agree with	compare with	forget about	speak to (*or* speak with)
apply to	concentrate on	happen to	stare at
approve of	consist of	hope for	succeed at
arrive in	count on	insist on	succeed in
arrive at	decide on	listen to	take advantage of
ask for	depend on	participate in	take care of
believe in	differ from	rely on	think about
belong to	disagree with	reply to	think of
care about	dream about	respond to	wait for
care for	dream of	result in	wait on
compare to	feel like	search for	

P

Punctuation

P Punctuation

P1

The comma

The comma was invented to help readers. Without it, sentence parts can collide into one another unexpectedly, causing misreadings.

CONFUSING If you cook Eri will do the dishes.

CONFUSING While we were eating a rattlesnake approached our campsite.

Add commas in the logical places (after *cook* and *eating*), and suddenly all is clear. No longer is Eri being cooked, the rattlesnake being eaten.

Various rules have evolved to prevent such misreadings and to speed readers along through complex grammatical structures. Those rules are detailed in this section.

GRAMMAR CHECKERS rarely flag missing or misused commas. They sometimes recognize that a comma belongs before a *which* clause but not before a *that* clause (see P1-e). For all other uses of the comma — after introductory word groups, between items in a series, between coordinate adjectives, around appositives, and so on — they are unreliable. When a grammar checker does note a missing comma, its suggested revision is often incorrect and sometimes even amusing. One program, for example, suggested a comma after the word *delivery* in the following sentence: *While I was driving a huge delivery truck ran through a red light.*

P1-a Use a comma before a coordinating conjunction joining independent clauses.

When a coordinating conjunction connects two or more independent clauses — word groups that could stand alone as separate sentences — a comma must precede it. There are seven coordinating conjunctions in English: *and, but, or, nor, for, so,* and *yet.*

A comma tells readers that one independent clause has come to a close and that another is about to begin.

▶ **Nearly everyone has heard of love at first sight, but I fell in love at first dance.**

EXCEPTION: If the two independent clauses are short and there is no danger of misreading, the comma may be omitted.

The plane took off and we were on our way.

TIP: As a rule, do *not* use a comma to separate coordinate word groups that are not independent clauses. (See P2-a.)

▶ **A good money manager controls expenses/and invests surplus dollars to meet future needs.**

The word group following *and* is not an independent clause; it is the second half of a compound predicate.

P1-b Use a comma after an introductory word group.

The most common introductory word groups are clauses and phrases functioning as adverbs. Such word groups usually tell when, where, how, why, or under what conditions the main action of the sentence occurred. (See B3-a, B3-b, and B3-e.)

A comma tells readers that the introductory clause or phrase has come to a close and that the main part of the sentence is about to begin.

▶ **When Irwin was ready to iron, his cat tripped on the cord.**

Without the comma, readers may have Irwin ironing his cat. The comma signals that *his cat* is the subject of a new clause, not part of the introductory one.

▶ **Near a small stream at the bottom of the canyon, the park rangers discovered an abandoned mine.**

The comma tells readers that the introductory prepositional phrase has come to a close.

EXCEPTION: The comma may be omitted after a short adverb clause or phrase if there is no danger of misreading.

In no time we were at eight hundred metres.

Sentences also frequently begin with participial phrases describing the noun or pronoun immediately following them. The comma tells readers that they are about to learn the identity of the person or thing described; therefore, the comma is usually required even when the phrase is short. (See also B3-b.)

▶ **Thinking his entrance into St. Peter's Square was routine, Pope John Paul II smiled and waved at the crowds.**

▶ **Buried under layers of younger rocks, Earth's oldest rocks contain no fossils.**

NOTE: Other introductory word groups include transitional expressions and absolute phrases. (See P1-f.)

P1-c Use a comma between all items in a series.

When three or more items are presented in a series, those items should be separated from one another with commas. Items in a series may be single words, phrases, or clauses.

▶ **Bubbles of air, leaves, ferns, bits of wood, and insects are often found trapped in amber.**

Although some publications omit the comma between the last two items, be aware that its omission can result in ambiguity or misreading.

▶ **My uncle willed me all of his property, houses, and warehouses.**

Did the uncle will his property *and* houses *and* warehouses — or simply his property, consisting of houses and warehouses? If the first meaning is intended, a comma is necessary to prevent ambiguity.

▶ **The activities include a search for lost treasure, dubious financial dealings, much discussion of ancient heresies, and midnight orgies.**

Without the comma, the people seem to be discussing orgies, not participating in them. The comma makes it clear that *midnight orgies* is a separate item in the series.

ON THE WEB > **dianahacker.com/writersref**
Language Debates > Commas with items in a series

P1-d Use a comma between coordinate adjectives not joined by *and*. Do not use a comma between cumulative adjectives.

When two or more adjectives each modify a noun separately, they are *coordinate.*

Roberto is a *warm, gentle, affectionate* father.

Adjectives are coordinate if they can be joined with *and* (warm *and* gentle *and* affectionate).

Two or more adjectives that do not modify the noun separately are cumulative.

Three large grey shapes moved slowly toward us.

Beginning with the adjective closest to the noun *shapes,* these modifiers lean on one another, piggyback style, with each modifying a larger word group. *Grey* modifies *shapes, large* modifies *grey shapes,* and *three* modifies *large grey shapes.* Cumulative adjectives cannot be joined with *and* (three *and* large *and* grey shapes).

COORDINATE ADJECTIVES

▶ **Patients with severe, irreversible brain damage should not be put on life support systems.**

CUMULATIVE ADJECTIVES

▶ **Ira ordered a rich/chocolate/layer cake.**

P1-e Use commas to set off nonrestrictive elements. Do not use commas to set off restrictive elements.

Word groups describing nouns or pronouns (adjective clauses, adjective phrases, and appositives) are restrictive or nonrestrictive. A *restrictive* element defines or limits the meaning of the word it modifies and is therefore essential to the meaning of the sentence. Because it contains essential information, a restrictive element is not set off with commas.

RESTRICTIVE For camp the children need clothes *that are washable.*

If you remove a restrictive element from a sentence, the meaning changes significantly, becoming more general than you intended. The writer of the example sentence does not mean that the children need clothes in general. The intended meaning is more limited: The children need *washable* clothes.

A *nonrestrictive* element describes a noun or pronoun whose meaning has already been clearly defined or limited. Because it contains nonessential or parenthetical information, a nonrestrictive element is set off with commas.

NONRESTRICTIVE For camp the children need sturdy shoes, *which are expensive.*

If you remove a nonrestrictive element from a sentence, the meaning does not change dramatically. Some meaning is lost, to be sure, but the defining characteristics of the person or thing described remain the same as before. The children need *sturdy shoes,* and these happen to be expensive.

NOTE: Often it is difficult to tell whether a word group is restrictive or nonrestrictive without seeing it in context and considering the writer's meaning. Both of the following sentences are grammatically correct, but their meaning is slightly different.

The dessert made with fresh raspberries was delicious.

The dessert, made with fresh raspberries, was delicious.

In the example without commas, the phrase *made with fresh raspberries* tells readers which of two or more desserts the writer is referring to. In the example with commas, the phrase merely adds information about the particular dessert.

Adjective clauses

Adjective clauses are patterned like sentences, containing subjects and verbs, but they function within sentences as modifiers of nouns or pronouns. They always follow the word they modify, usually immediately. Adjective clauses begin with a relative pronoun (*who, whom, whose, which, that*) or with a relative adverb (*where, when*).

Nonrestrictive adjective clauses are set off with commas; restrictive adjective clauses are not.

NONRESTRICTIVE CLAUSE

▶ **Ed's house, which is located on five hectares, was furnished with bats in the rafters and mice in the kitchen.**

The clause *which is located on five hectares* does not restrict the meaning of *Ed's house,* so the information is nonessential.

RESTRICTIVE CLAUSE

▶ **Ramona's cat/ that just had kittens/ became defensive around the other cats in the house.**

Because the adjective clause *that just had kittens* identifies the particular cat, the information is essential.

NOTE: Use *that* only with restrictive clauses. Many writers prefer to use *which* only with nonrestrictive clauses, but usage varies.

ON THE WEB > dianahacker.com/writersref
Language Debates > *that* versus *which*

Phrases functioning as adjectives

Prepositional or verbal phrases functioning as adjectives may be restrictive or nonrestrictive. Nonrestrictive phrases are set off with commas; restrictive phrases are not.

NONRESTRICTIVE PHRASE

▶ **The helicopter, with its million-candlepower spotlight illuminating the area, circled above.**

The *with* phrase is nonessential because its purpose is not to specify which of two or more helicopters is being discussed.

RESTRICTIVE PHRASE

▶ **One corner of the attic was filled with newspapers/ dating from the turn of the twentieth century.**

Dating from the turn of the twentieth century restricts the meaning of *newspapers,* so the comma should be omitted.

Appositives

An appositive is a noun or noun phrase that renames a nearby noun. Nonrestrictive appositives are set off with commas; restrictive appositives are not.

NONRESTRICTIVE APPOSITIVE

▶ **Darwin's most important book, *On the Origin of Species,* was the result of many years of research.**

Most important restricts the meaning to one book, so the appositive *On the Origin of Species* is nonrestrictive and should be set off with commas.

RESTRICTIVE APPOSITIVE

▶ **The song, "Vertigo," was blasted out of huge amplifiers.**

Once they've read *song,* readers still don't know precisely which song the writer means. The appositive following *song* restricts its meaning.

P1-f Use commas to set off transitional and parenthetical expressions, absolute phrases, and contrasted elements.

Transitional expressions

Transitional expressions serve as bridges between sentences or parts of sentences. They include conjunctive adverbs such as *however, therefore,* and *moreover* and transitional phrases such as *for example, as a matter of fact,* and *in other words.* (For more complete lists, see P3-b.)

When a transitional expression appears between independent clauses in a compound sentence, it is preceded by a semicolon and is usually followed by a comma.

▶ **Minh did not understand our language; moreover, he was unfamiliar with our customs.**

When a transitional expression appears at the beginning of a sentence or in the middle of an independent clause, it is usually set off with commas.

▶ **As a matter of fact, American football was established by fans who wanted to play a more organized game of rugby.**

▶ **Natural foods are not always salt free; celery, for example, contains more sodium than most people would imagine.**

EXCEPTION: If a transitional expression blends smoothly with the rest of the sentence, calling for little or no pause in reading, it does not need to be set off with commas. Expressions such as *also, at least, certainly, consequently, indeed, of course, no doubt, perhaps, then,* and *therefore* do not always call for a pause.

Alice's bicycle is broken; *therefore* you will need to borrow Sue's.

Alice's bicycle is broken; you will *therefore* need to borrow Sue's.

Parenthetical expressions

Expressions that are distinctly parenthetical should be set off with commas. Providing supplemental information, they interrupt the flow of a sentence or appear at the end as afterthoughts.

▶ **Evolution, so far as we know, doesn't work this way.**

▶ **The bass weighed five kilograms, give or take a few grams.**

Absolute phrases

An absolute phrase, which modifies the whole sentence, usually consists of a noun followed by a participle or participial phrase. (See B3-d.) Absolute phrases may appear at the beginning or at the end of a sentence. Wherever they appear, they should be set off with commas.

▶ **The sun appearing for the first time in a week, we were at last able to begin the archaeological dig.**

▶ **Elvis Presley made music industry history in the 1950s, his records having sold more than ten million copies.**

TIP: Do not insert a comma between the noun and the participle in an absolute construction.

▶ **The next contestant, being five years old, the emcee adjusted the height of the microphone.**

Contrasted elements

Sharp contrasts beginning with words such as *not, never,* and *unlike* are set off with commas.

▶ The Epicurean philosophers sought mental, not bodily, pleasures.

▶ Unlike Robert, Celia loved dance contests.

P1-g Use commas to set off nouns of direct address, the words *yes* and *no,* interrogative tags, and mild interjections.

▶ Forgive us, Dr. Atkins, for having rolls with dinner.

▶ Yes, the loan will probably be approved.

▶ The film was faithful to the book, wasn't it?

▶ Well, cases like these are difficult to decide.

P1-h Use commas with expressions such as *he said* to set off direct quotations. (See also P6-f.)

▶ Naturalist Arthur Cleveland Bent once remarked, "In part the peregrine declined unnoticed because it is not adorable."

▶ "Convictions are more dangerous foes of truth than lies," wrote philosopher Friedrich Nietzsche.

P1-i Use commas with dates, addresses, titles, and numbers.

Dates

In dates, the year is set off from the rest of the sentence with a pair of commas.

▶ On December 12, 1890, orders were sent out for the arrest of Sitting Bull.

EXCEPTIONS: Commas are not needed if the date is inverted or if only the month and year are given.

The recycling plan went into effect on 15 April 2002.

January 2004 was an extremely cold month.

Addresses

The elements of an address or a place name are separated by commas. A postal code, however, is not preceded by a comma.

▶ **John Lennon was born in Liverpool, England, in 1940.**

▶ **Please send the package to Greg Tarvin at 708 Spring Street, Washington, Illinois 61571.**

Titles

If a title follows a name, separate it from the rest of the sentence with a pair of commas.

▶ **Sandra Belinsky, MD, has been appointed to the board of trustees.**

Numbers

In numbers more than four digits long, use spaces to separate the numbers into groups of three, starting from the right. In numbers four digits long, a space is optional.

3 500 [*or* 3500]
100 000
5 000 000

EXCEPTIONS: Do not use spaces in street numbers, US zip codes, telephone numbers, or years.

P1-j Use a comma to prevent confusion.

In certain contexts, a comma is necessary to prevent confusion. If the writer has omitted a word or phrase, for example, a comma may be needed to signal the omission.

▶ **To err is human; to forgive, divine.**

If two words in a row echo each other, a comma may be needed for ease of reading.

▶ **All of the catastrophes that we had feared might happen, happened.**

Sometimes a comma is needed to prevent readers from grouping words in ways that do not match the writer's intention.

▶ **Patients who can, walk up and down the halls several times a day.**

ON THE WEB > **dianahacker.com/writersref**
Grammar exercises > Punctuation > E-ex P1–1 through P1–3

P2

Unnecessary commas

P2-a Do not use a comma between compound elements that are not independent clauses.

Though a comma should be used before a coordinating conjunction joining independent clauses (see P1-a), this rule should not be extended to other compound word groups.

▶ **Marie Curie discovered radium, and later applied her work on radioactivity to medicine.**

And links two verbs in a compound predicate: *discovered* and *applied.*

▶ **Jake still does not realize that his illness is serious, and that he will have to alter his diet to improve.**

And links two subordinate clauses, each beginning with *that.*

P2-b Do not use a comma to separate a verb from its subject or object.

A sentence should flow from subject to verb to object without unnecessary pauses. Commas may appear between these major sentence elements only when a specific rule calls for them.

▶ **Zoos large enough to give the animals freedom to roam/ are becoming more popular.**

The comma should not separate the subject, *zoos,* from the verb, *are becoming.*

▶ **Francesca explained to him/ that she was busy and would see him later.**

The comma should not separate the verb, *explained,* from its object, the subordinate clause *that she was busy and would see him later.*

P2-c Do not use a comma before the first or after the last item in a series.

Though commas are required between items in a series (see P1-c), do not place them either before or after the whole series.

▶ **Other causes of asthmatic attacks are/ stress, change in temperature, and cold air.**

▶ **Ironically, this job that appears so glamorous, carefree, and easy/ carries a high degree of responsibility.**

P2-d Do not use a comma between cumulative adjectives, between an adjective and a noun, or between an adverb and an adjective.

Though commas are required between coordinate adjectives (those that can be joined with *and*), they do not belong between cumulative adjectives (those that cannot be joined with *and*). (For a full discussion, see P1-d.)

▶ **In the corner of the closet we found an old/ maroon hatbox from Sears.**

A comma should never be used to separate an adjective from the noun that follows it.

▶ **It was a senseless, dangerous/ mission.**

Nor should a comma be used between an adverb and an adjective that follows it.

▶ **The Hurst Home is unsuitable as a rehab facility for severely/ injured soldiers.**

P2-e Do not use commas to set off restrictive or mildly parenthetical elements.

Restrictive elements are modifiers or appositives that restrict the meaning of the nouns they follow. Because they are essential to the meaning of the sentence, they are not set off with commas. (For a full discussion, see P1-e.)

▶ **Drivers/ who think they own the road/ make cycling a dangerous sport.**

The modifier *who think they own the road* restricts the meaning of *Drivers* and is therefore essential to the meaning of the sentence. Putting commas around the *who* clause falsely suggests that all drivers think they own the road.

▶ **Margaret Mead's book/ *Coming of Age in Samoa*/ stirred up considerable controversy when it was published in 1928.**

Since Mead wrote more than one book, the appositive contains information essential to the meaning of the sentence.

Although commas should be used with distinctly parenthetical expressions (see P1-f), do not use them to set off elements that are only mildly parenthetical.

▶ **Charisse believes that the Internet is/ essentially/ one giant billboard.**

P2-f Do not use a comma to set off a concluding adverb clause that is essential to the meaning of the sentence.

When adverb clauses introduce a sentence, they are nearly always followed by a comma (see P1-b). When they conclude a sentence, however, they are not set off by commas if their content is essential to the meaning of the earlier part of the sentence. Adverb clauses beginning with *after, as soon as, before, because, if, since, unless, until,* and *when* are usually essential.

▶ **Don't visit Paris at the height of the tourist season/ unless you have booked hotel reservations.**

Without the concluding *unless* clause, the meaning of the sentence would be broader than the writer intended.

When a concluding adverb clause is nonessential, it should be preceded by a comma. Clauses beginning with *although, even though, though,* and *whereas* are usually nonessential.

▶ **The lecture seemed to last only a short time, although the clock said it had gone on for more than an hour.**

P2-g Avoid other common misuses of the comma.

Do not use a comma in the following situations.

AFTER A COORDINATING CONJUNCTION (*AND, BUT, OR, NOR, FOR, SO, YET*)

▶ **I have an iPod, but/ I don't have a sound dock.**

AFTER *SUCH AS* OR *LIKE*

▶ **Many shade-loving plants, such as/ begonias, impatiens, and coleus, can add colour to a shady garden.**

BEFORE *THAN*

▶ **Touring Crete was more thrilling for us/ than visiting the Greek islands frequented by rich Europeans.**

AFTER *ALTHOUGH*

▶ **Although, the air was balmy, the water was too cold for swimming.**

BEFORE A PARENTHESIS

▶ **At Telus Sylvia began at the bottom, (with only three and a half walls and a swivel chair), but within five years she had been promoted to supervisor.**

TO SET OFF AN INDIRECT (REPORTED) QUOTATION

▶ **Samuel Goldwyn once said, that a verbal contract isn't worth the paper it's written on.**

WITH A QUESTION MARK OR AN EXCLAMATION POINT

▶ **"Why don't you try it?," she coaxed.**

ON THE WEB > **dianahacker.com/writersref**
Grammar exercises > Punctuation > E-ex P2–1

P3

The semicolon

The semicolon is used to connect major sentence elements of equal grammatical rank.

GRAMMAR CHECKERS flag some, but not all, misused semicolons (P3-d). In addition, they can alert you to some run-on sentences (G6). However, they miss more run-on sentences than they identify, and they sometimes flag correct sentences as possible run-ons. (See also the grammar checker advice in G6.)

P3-a Use a semicolon between closely related independent clauses not joined with a coordinating conjunction.

When related independent clauses appear in one sentence, they are ordinarily linked with a comma and a coordinating conjunction (*and, but, or, nor, for, so, yet*). The coordinating conjunction signals the relation between the clauses. If the clauses are closely related and the relation is clear without the conjunction, they may be linked with a semicolon instead.

> Popular art is the dream of society; it does not examine itself.
> — Margaret Atwood

A semicolon must be used whenever a coordinating conjunction has been omitted between independent clauses. To use merely a comma creates a kind of run-on sentence known as a comma splice. (See G6.)

▶ **In 1800, a traveller needed six weeks to get from New York City to Chicago~~,~~; in 1860, the trip by railroad took two days.**

TIP: Do not overuse the semicolon as a means of revising run-on sentences. For other revision strategies, see G6.

P3-b Use a semicolon between independent clauses linked with a transitional expression.

Transitional expressions include conjunctive adverbs and transitional phrases.

CONJUNCTIVE ADVERBS

accordingly	finally	meanwhile	similarly
also	furthermore	moreover	specifically
anyway	hence	nevertheless	still
besides	however	next	subsequently
certainly	indeed	nonetheless	then
consequently	instead	now	therefore
conversely	likewise	otherwise	thus

TRANSITIONAL PHRASES

after all	even so	in fact
as a matter of fact	for example	in other words
as a result	for instance	in the first place
at any rate	in addition	on the contrary
at the same time	in conclusion	on the other hand

When a transitional expression appears between independent clauses, it is preceded by a semicolon and usually followed by a comma.

▶ **Many corals grow very gradually~~,~~; in fact, the creation of a coral reef can take centuries.**

When a transitional expression appears in the middle or at the end of the second independent clause, the semicolon goes *between the clauses.*

Most singers gain fame through hard work and dedication; Evita, however, found other means.

Transitional expressions should not be confused with the coordinating conjunctions *and, but, or, nor, for, so,* and *yet,* which are preceded by a comma when they link independent clauses. (See P1-a and G6-a.)

P3-c Use a semicolon between items in a series containing internal punctuation.

▶ **Classic science fiction sagas are *Star Trek,* with Mr. Spock and his large pointed ears~~,~~; *Battlestar Galactica,* with its Cylon Raiders~~,~~; and *Star Wars,* with Han Solo, Luke Skywalker, and Darth Vader.**

Without the semicolons, the reader must sort out the major groupings, distinguishing between important and less important pauses according to the logic of the sentence. By inserting semicolons at the major breaks, the writer does this work for the reader.

P3-d Avoid common misuses of the semicolon.

Do not use a semicolon in the following situations.

BETWEEN A SUBORDINATE CLAUSE AND THE REST OF THE SENTENCE

▶ **Unless you brush your teeth within ten or fifteen minutes after eating; brushing does almost no good.**

BETWEEN AN APPOSITIVE AND THE WORD IT REFERS TO

▶ **The scientists were fascinated by the species *Argyroneta acquatica*; a spider that lives underwater.**

TO INTRODUCE A LIST

▶ **Some of my favourite film stars have home pages on the Web;: Uma Thurman, Billy Bob Thornton, and Halle Berry.**

BETWEEN INDEPENDENT CLAUSES JOINED BY *AND, BUT, OR, NOR, FOR, SO,* OR *YET*

▶ **Five of the applicants had worked with spreadsheets;, but only one was familiar with database management.**

EXCEPTIONS: If at least one of the independent clauses contains internal punctuation, you may use a semicolon even though the clauses are joined with a coordinating conjunction.

> As a vehicle [the model T] was hard-working, commonplace, and heroic; and it often seemed to transmit those qualities to the person who rode in it. — E. B. White

Although a comma would also be correct in this sentence, the semicolon effectively indicates the relative weights of the pauses.

Occasionally, a semicolon may be used to emphasize a sharp contrast or a firm distinction between clauses joined with a coordinating conjunction.

> It no longer bothers me that I may be constantly searching for father figures; by this time, I have found several and dearly enjoyed knowing them all. — Alice Walker

ON THE WEB > **dianahacker.com/writersref**
Grammar exercises > Punctuation > E-ex P3–1 and P3–2

P4

The colon

The colon is used primarily to call attention to the words that follow it. In addition, the colon has some conventional uses.

GRAMMAR CHECKERS are fairly good at flagging colons that incorrectly follow a verb (*The office work includes: typing, filing, and answering the phone*). They also point out semicolons used where colons are needed, although they don't suggest revisions.

P4-a Use a colon after an independent clause to direct attention to a list, an appositive, or a quotation.

A LIST

The daily routine should include at least the following: twenty knee bends, fifty sit-ups, fifteen leg lifts, and five minutes of running in place.

AN APPOSITIVE

My roommate is guilty of two of the seven deadly sins: gluttony and sloth.

A QUOTATION

Consider the words of Pierre Trudeau: "I will not leave Ottawa until the country and the government are irreversibly bilingual."

For other ways of introducing quotations, see P6-f.

P4-b Use a colon between independent clauses if the second summarizes or explains the first.

Faith is like love: It cannot be forced.

NOTE: When an independent clause follows a colon, it may begin with a capital or a lowercase letter. (See M3-f.)

P4-c Use a colon after the salutation in a formal letter, to indicate hours and minutes, to show proportions, between a title and subtitle, and between city and publisher in bibliographic entries.

Dear Sir or Madam:

5:30 p.m.

The ratio of women to men was 2:1.

The Glory of Hera: Greek Mythology and the Greek Family

Boston: Bedford, 2005

NOTE: In biblical references, a colon is ordinarily used between chapter and verse (Luke 2:14). The Modern Language Association recommends a period instead (Luke 2.14).

P4-d Avoid common misuses of the colon.

A colon must be preceded by a full independent clause. Therefore, avoid using it in the following situations.

BETWEEN A VERB AND ITS OBJECT OR COMPLEMENT

▶ **Some important vitamins and minerals in vegetables are: vitamin A, thiamine, niacin, and vitamin C.**

BETWEEN A PREPOSITION AND ITS OBJECT

▶ **The heart's two pumps each consist of: an upper chamber, or atrium, and a lower chamber, or ventricle.**

AFTER *SUCH AS, INCLUDING,* OR *FOR EXAMPLE*

▶ **The trees on our campus include many fine Japanese specimens such as: black pines, ginkgos, and weeping cherries.**

ON THE WEB > dianahacker.com/writersref
Grammar exercises > Punctuation > E-ex P4–1

P5

The apostrophe

GRAMMAR CHECKERS flag only some missing or misused apostrophes. They catch missing apostrophes in contractions, such as *don't*. They also flag problems with possessives (*sled dogs feet, a babys eyes*), although they miss as many problems as they identify. Only you can decide when to add an apostrophe and whether to put it before or after the *-s* in possessives.

P5-a Use an apostrophe to indicate that a noun is possessive.

Possessive nouns usually indicate ownership, as in *Tim's hat* or *the lawyer's desk*. Frequently, however, ownership is only loosely implied: *the tree's roots, a day's work*. If you are not sure whether a noun is possessive, try turning it into an *of* phrase: *the roots of the tree, the work of a day*.

When to add -'s

If the noun does not end in *-s,* add *-'s.*

> Rikke managed to climb out on the driver's side.
>
> Thank you for refunding the children's money.

If the noun is singular and ends in *-s* or an *s* sound, add *-'s.*

> Lois's sister spent last year in India.
>
> Her article presents an overview of Marx's teachings.

EXCEPTION: To avoid potentially awkward pronunciation, some writers use only the apostrophe with a singular noun ending in *-s*: *Sophocles'*.

ON THE WEB > **dianahacker.com/writersref**
Language Debates > *-'s* for singular nouns ending in *-s* or an *s* sound

When to add only an apostrophe

If the noun is plural and ends in *-s,* add only an apostrophe.

> Both diplomats' briefcases were searched by guards.

Joint possession

To show joint possession, use *-'s* (or *-s'*) with the last noun only; to show individual possession, make all nouns possessive.

> Have you seen Joyce and Greg's new camper?
>
> Hernando's and Maria's expectations of marriage couldn't have been more different.

Joyce and Greg jointly own one camper. Hernando and Maria individually have different expectations.

Compound nouns

If a noun is compound, use *-'s* (or *-s'*) with the last element.

> Her father-in-law's sculpture won first place.

P5-b Use an apostrophe and *-s* to indicate that an indefinite pronoun is possessive.

Indefinite pronouns refer to no specific person or thing: *everyone, someone, no one, something.* (See B1-b.)

> Someone's raincoat has been left behind.

P5-c Use an apostrophe to mark contractions.

In contractions, the apostrophe takes the place of missing letters.

> It's a shame that Frank can't go on the tour.

It's stands for *It is* and *can't* for *cannot.*

The apostrophe is also used to mark the omission of the first two digits of a year (*the class of '99*) or years (*the '60s generation*).

P5-d An apostrophe is often optional in plural numbers, letters, abbreviations, and words mentioned as words.

An apostrophe typically is not used to pluralize numbers, letters, abbreviations, and words mentioned as words. Note the few exceptions and be consistent throughout your paper.

PLURAL NUMBERS Omit the apostrophe in the plural of all numbers, including decades.

> Oksana skated nearly perfect figure 8s.
>
> The 1920s are known as the Jazz Age.

PLURAL LETTERS Italicize the letter and use roman (regular) font style for the *-s* ending. Do not italicize academic grades. Use of an apostrophe is usually optional; the Modern Language Association recommends the apostrophe for the plural of both capital and lowercase letters.

> Two large *J*s (*or* *J*'s) were painted on the door.

PLURAL ABBREVIATIONS Do not use an apostrophe to pluralize an abbreviation.

> We collected only four IOUs out of forty.
>
> Marco earned two PhDs before his thirtieth birthday.

PLURAL OF WORDS MENTIONED AS WORDS Generally, omit the apostrophe to form the plural of words mentioned as words. If the word is italicized, the *-s* ending appears in roman type.

> We've heard enough *maybe*s.

Words mentioned as words may also appear in quotation marks. When you choose this option, use the apostrophe: *We've heard enough "maybe's."*

P5-e Avoid common misuses of the apostrophe.

Do not use an apostrophe in the following situations.

WITH NOUNS THAT ARE NOT POSSESSIVE

▶ Some ~~outpatient's~~ outpatients are given special parking permits.

IN THE POSSESSIVE PRONOUNS *ITS, WHOSE, HIS, HERS, OURS, YOURS,* AND *THEIRS*

▶ **Each area has ~~it's~~ its own conference room.**

It's means "it is." The possessive pronoun *its* contains no apostrophe despite the fact that it is possessive.

ON THE WEB > **dianahacker.com/writersref**
Grammar exercises > Punctuation > E-ex P5–1

P6

Quotation marks

GRAMMAR CHECKERS are no help with quotation marks. They do not recognize direct and indirect quotations, they fail to identify quotation marks used incorrectly inside periods and commas, and they do not point out a missing quotation mark in a pair.

P6-a Use quotation marks to enclose direct quotations.

Direct quotations of a person's words, whether spoken or written, must be in quotation marks.

> "A foolish consistency is the hobgoblin of little minds," wrote Ralph Waldo Emerson.

CAUTION: Do not use quotation marks around indirect quotations. An indirect quotation reports someone's ideas without using that person's exact words.

> Ralph Waldo Emerson believed that consistency for its own sake is the mark of a small mind.

NOTE: In dialogue, begin a new paragraph to mark a change in speaker.

> "Mom, his name is Willie, not William. A thousand times I've told you, it's *Willie.*"
>
> "Willie is a derivative of William, Lester. Surely his birth certificate doesn't have Willie on it, and I like calling people by their proper names."
>
> "Yes, it does, ma'am. My mother named me Willie K. Mason."
>
> — Gloria Naylor

If a single speaker utters more than one paragraph, introduce each paragraph with quotation marks, but do not use closing quotation marks until the end of the speech.

P6-b Set off long quotations of prose or poetry by indenting.

The guidelines in this section are those of the Modern Language Association (MLA). The American Psychological Association (APA) and *The Chicago Manual of Style* (CMS) have slightly different guidelines (see APA-2a and CMS-2a).

When a quotation of prose runs to more than four typed lines in your paper, set it off by indenting one inch (or ten spaces) from the left margin. Quotation marks are not required because the indented format tells readers that the quotation is taken word-for-word from a source. Long quotations are ordinarily introduced by a sentence ending with a colon.

> After studying the historical record, James Horan evaluates Billy the Kid like this:
>
>> The portrait that emerges of [the Kid] from the thousands of pages of affidavits, reports, trial transcripts, his letters, and his testimony is neither the mythical Robin Hood nor the stereotyped adenoidal moron and pathological killer. Rather Billy appears as a disturbed, lonely young man, honest, loyal to his friends, dedicated to his beliefs, and betrayed by our institutions and the corrupt, ambitious, and compromising politicians of his time. (158)

The number in parentheses is a citation handled according to the Modern Language Association style. (See MLA-4a.)

NOTE: When you quote two or more paragraphs from the source, indent the first line of each paragraph an additional 0.5 inch (1.2 cm or five spaces).

When you quote more than three lines of a poem, set the quoted lines off from the text by indenting 1 inch (2.5 cm or ten spaces) from the left margin. Use no quotation marks unless they appear in the poem. (To quote two or three lines of poetry, see P7-h.)

> Although many anthologizers "modernize" her punctuation, Emily Dickinson relied heavily on dashes, using them, perhaps, as a musical device. Here, for example, is the original version of the opening stanza from "The Snake":
>
> A narrow Fellow in the Grass
> Occasionally rides--
> You may have met Him--did you not
> His notice sudden is--

P6-c Use single quotation marks to enclose a quotation within a quotation.

> According to Paul Eliott, Inuit hunters "chant an ancient magic song to the seal they are after: 'Beast of the sea! Come and place yourself before me in the early morning!' "

P6-d Use quotation marks around the titles of short works: newspaper and magazine articles, poems, short stories, songs, episodes of television and radio programs, and chapters or subdivisions of books.

> Mavis Gallant's "The Doctor" provoked a lively discussion in our short-story class last night.

NOTE: Titles of books, plays, Web sites, television and radio programs, films, magazines, and newspapers are put in italics or underlined. (See M6-a.)

P6-e Quotation marks may be used to set off words used as words.

Although words used as words are ordinarily italicized (see M6-d), quotation marks are also acceptable. Just be sure to follow consistent practice throughout a paper.

> The words "accept" and "except" are frequently confused.
>
> The words *accept* and *except* are frequently confused.

P6-f Use punctuation with quotation marks according to convention.

This section describes the conventions used by Canadian and American publishers in placing various marks of punctuation inside or outside quotation marks. It also explains how to punctuate when introducing quoted material.

Periods and commas

Place periods and commas inside quotation marks.

> "This is a stick-up," said the well-dressed young couple. "We want all your money."

This rule applies to single quotation marks as well as double quotation marks. (See P6-c.) It also applies to all uses of quotation marks: for quoted material, for titles of works, and for words used as words.

EXCEPTION: In the Modern Language Association's style of parenthetical in-text citations (see MLA-4a), the period follows the citation in parentheses.

> In his discussion of the fate of linguistic minorities if Canada and Quebec become separate national entities, Kenneth McRoberts stresses that minority linguistic rights should be "one of the elements of partnership" (27).

Colons and semicolons

Put colons and semicolons outside quotation marks.

> Harold wrote, "I regret that I am unable to attend the fundraiser for AIDS research"; his letter, however, contained a substantial contribution.

Question marks and exclamation points

Put question marks and exclamation points inside quotation marks unless they apply to the sentence as a whole.

> Contrary to tradition, bedtime at my house is marked by "Mommy, can I tell you a story now?"

> Have you heard the old proverb "Do not climb the hill until you reach it"?

In the first sentence, the question mark applies only to the quoted question. In the second sentence, the question mark applies to the whole sentence.

NOTE: In MLA style for a quotation that ends with a question mark or an exclamation point, the parenthetical citation and a period should follow the entire quotation: *Rosie Thomas asks, "Is nothing in life ever straight and clear, the way children see it?" (77).*

Introducing quoted material

After a word group introducing a quotation, choose a colon, a comma, or no punctuation at all, whichever is appropriate in context.

FORMAL INTRODUCTION If a quotation has been formally introduced, a colon is appropriate. A formal introduction is a full independent clause, not just an expression such as *he said* or *she remarked.*

> Morrow views personal ads in the classifieds as an art form: "The personal ad is like a haiku of self-celebration, a brief solo played on one's own horn."

EXPRESSION SUCH AS *HE SAID* If a quotation is introduced with an expression such as *he said* or *she remarked* — or if it is followed by such an expression — a comma is needed.

> Stephen Leacock once said, "I am a great believer in luck, and I find the harder I work the more I have of it."

> "You can be a little ungrammatical if you come from the right part of the country," writes Robert Frost.

BLENDED QUOTATION When a quotation is blended into the writer's own sentence, either a comma or no punctuation is appropriate, depending on the way in which the quotation fits into the sentence structure.

> The future champion could, as he put it, "float like a butterfly and sting like a bee."

> Charles Hudson noted that the prisoners escaped "by squeezing through a tiny window eighteen feet above the floor of their cell."

BEGINNING OF SENTENCE If a quotation appears at the beginning of a sentence, set it off with a comma unless the quotation ends with a question mark or an exclamation point.

> "We shot them like dogs," boasted Davy Crockett, who was among Jackson's troops.
>
> "What is it?" I asked, bracing myself.

INTERRUPTED QUOTATION If a quoted sentence is interrupted by explanatory words, use commas to set off the explanatory words.

> "A great many people think they are thinking," wrote William James, "when they are merely rearranging their prejudices."

If two successive quoted sentences from the same source are interrupted by explanatory words, use a comma before the explanatory words and a period after them.

> "I was a flop as a daily reporter," admitted E. B. White. "Every piece had to be a masterpiece — and before you knew it, Tuesday was Wednesday."

P6-g Avoid common misuses of quotation marks.

Do not use quotation marks to draw attention to familiar slang, to disown trite expressions, or to justify an attempt at humor.

► **Between Thanksgiving and Super Bowl Sunday, many American wives become "football widows."**

Do not use quotation marks around indirect quotations. (See also P6-a.)

► **After leaving the scene of the domestic quarrel, the officer said that "he was due for a coffee break."**

Do not use quotation marks around the title of your own essay.

ON THE WEB > dianahacker.com/writersref
Grammar exercises > Punctuation > E-ex P6–1

P7

Other marks

GRAMMAR CHECKERS occasionally flag sentences beginning with words like *Why* or *Are* and suggest that a question mark may be needed. On the whole, however, grammar checkers are of little help with end punctuation. Most notably, they neglect to tell you when your sentence is missing end punctuation.

P7-a The period

Use a period to end all sentences except direct questions or genuine exclamations. Also use periods in abbreviations according to convention.

To end sentences

Everyone knows that a period should be used to end most sentences. The only problems that arise concern the choice between a period and a question mark or between a period and an exclamation point.

If a sentence reports a question instead of asking it directly, it should end with a period, not a question mark.

▶ **Joelle asked whether the picnic would be cancelled?.**

If a sentence is not a genuine exclamation, it should end with a period, not an exclamation point.

▶ **After years of working her way through school, Geeta finally graduated with high honours!.**

In abbreviations

A period is conventionally used in abbreviations such as these:

Mr.	i.e.	a.m. (or AM)
Ms.	e.g.	p.m. (or PM)
Dr.	etc.	

NOTE: If a sentence ends with a period marking an abbreviation, do not add a second period.

A period is not used in Canada Post abbreviations for provinces and territories: YK, NB, NL.

Current usage is to omit the period in abbreviations of organization names, academic degrees, and designations for eras.

NATO	UNESCO	TSSA	BSC	BC (or BCE)
CSA	CUPE	NHL	PhD	AD (or CE)
USA	CAW	RCMP	RN	NDP

P7-b The question mark

Obviously a direct question should be followed by a question mark.

> What is the horsepower of a 777 engine?

If a polite request is written in the form of a question, it may be followed by a period.

> Would you please send me your catalogue of lilies.

CAUTION: Do not use a question mark after an indirect question, one that is reported rather than asked directly. Use a period instead.

> ▶ **He asked me who was teaching the mythology course~~?~~.**

NOTE: Questions in a series may be followed by question marks even when they are not complete sentences.

> We wondered where Calamity had hidden this time. Under the sink? Behind the furnace? On top of the bookcase?

P7-c The exclamation point

Use an exclamation point after a word group or sentence to express exceptional feeling or to provide special emphasis.

> When Gloria entered the room, I switched on the lights and we all yelled "Surprise!"

TIP: Do not overuse the exclamation point.

▶ **In the fisherman's memory the fish lives on, increasing in length and weight with each passing year, until at last it is big enough to shade a fishing boat!.**

This sentence doesn't need to be pumped up with an exclamation point. It is emphatic enough without it.

▶ **Whenever I see Venus lunging forward to put away an overhead smash, it might as well be me!. She does it just the way I would!**

The first exclamation point should be deleted so that the second one will have more force.

P7-d The dash

When typing, use two hyphens to form a dash (--). Do not put spaces before or after the dash. (If your word processing program has what is known as an "em-dash," you may use it instead, with no space before or after it.) Dashes are used for the following purposes.

To set off parenthetical material that deserves emphasis

Everything that went wrong — from the peeping Tom at her window last night to my head-on collision today — we blamed on our move.

To set off appositives that contain commas

An appositive is a noun or noun phrase that renames a nearby noun. Ordinarily most appositives are set off with commas (see P1-e), but when the appositive itself contains commas, a pair of dashes helps readers see the relative importance of all the pauses.

In my hometown the basic needs of people — food, clothing, and shelter — are less costly than in a big city like Toronto.

To prepare for a list, a restatement, an amplification, or a dramatic shift in tone or thought

Along the wall are the bulk liquids — sesame seed oil, honey, safflower oil, maple syrup, and peanut butter.

> Consider the amount of sugar in the average person's diet — forty-seven kilograms per year, 90 percent more than that consumed by our ancestors.
>
> Everywhere we looked there were little kids — a box of Cracker Jacks in one hand and mommy's or daddy's sleeve in the other.
>
> Kiere took a few steps back, came running full speed, kicked a mighty kick — and missed the ball.

In the first two examples, the writer could also use a colon. (See P4-a.) The colon is more formal than the dash and not quite as dramatic.

CAUTION: Unless there is a specific reason for using the dash, avoid it. Unnecessary dashes create a choppy effect.

► **Insisting that our young people learn to use computers as instructional tools ~~—~~ for information retrieval ~~—~~ makes good sense. Herding them ~~—~~ sheeplike ~~—~~ into computer technology does not.**

P7-e Parentheses

Use parentheses to enclose supplemental material, minor digressions, and afterthoughts.

> After taking her vital signs (temperature, pulse, and blood pressure), the nurse made Becky as comfortable as possible.
>
> The weights Javid was first able to move (not lift, mind you) were measured in fractions of kilograms.

Use parentheses to enclose letters or numbers labeling items in a series.

> Regulations stipulated that only the following equipment could be used on the survival mission: (1) a knife, (2) ten metres of parachute line, (3) a book of matches, (4) two ponchos, (5) an *E* tool, and (6) a signal flare.

TIP: Do not overuse parentheses. Rough drafts are likely to contain more afterthoughts than necessary. As writers head into a sentence, they often think of additional details, occasionally working them in as best they can with parentheses. Such sentences should be revised so that the additional details no longer seem to be afterthoughts.

between two and three million

▶ **Researchers have said that ~~two million (some say three million)~~ Canadians have diabetes.**

P7-f Brackets

Use brackets to enclose any words or phrases that you have inserted into an otherwise word-for-word quotation.

> *Audubon* reports that "if there are not enough young to balance deaths, the end of the species [California condor] is inevitable."

The sentence quoted from the *Audubon* article did not contain the words *California condor* (since the context made clear what species was meant), so the writer needed to add the name in brackets.

The Latin word "sic" in brackets indicates that an error in a quoted sentence appears in the original source.

> According to the review, Nelly Furtado's performance was brilliant, "exceding [sic] the expectations of even her most loyal fans."

Do not overuse "sic," however, since calling attention to others' mistakes can appear snobbish. The preceding quotation, for example, might have been paraphrased instead: *According to the review, even Nelly Furtado's most loyal fans were surprised by the brilliance of her performance.*

P7-g The ellipsis mark

The ellipsis mark consists of three spaced periods. Use an ellipsis mark to indicate that you have deleted material from an otherwise word-for-word quotation.

> Reuben reports that "when the amount of cholesterol circulating in the blood rises over . . . 300 milligrams per 100, the chances of a heart attack increase dramatically."

If you delete a full sentence or more in the middle of a quoted passage, use a period before the three ellipsis dots.

> "Most of our efforts," writes Dave Erikson, "are directed toward saving the bald eagle's wintering habitat along the Mississippi River. . . . It's important that the wintering birds have a place to roost, where they can get out of the cold wind."

TIP: Ordinarily, do not use the ellipsis mark at the beginning or at the end of a quotation. Readers will understand that the quoted material is taken from a longer passage. If you have cut some words from the end of the final sentence quoted, however, MLA requires an ellipsis mark, as in the second example on page 363.

In quoted poetry, use a full line of dots to indicate that you have dropped a line or more from the poem:

> Had we but world enough, and time,
> This coyness, lady, were no crime.
> . . . .
> But at my back I always hear
> Time's wingèd chariot hurrying near;
>
> —Andrew Marvell

The ellipsis mark may also be used to mark a hesitation or an interruption in speech or to suggest unfinished thoughts.

> "The apartment building next door . . . it's going up in flames!" yelled Marcia.

> Before falling into a coma, the victim whispered, "It was a man with a tattoo on his . . ."

P7-h The slash

Use the slash to separate two or three lines of poetry that have been run into your text. Add a space both before and after the slash.

> In the opening lines of "Jordan," George Herbert pokes gentle fun at popular poems of his time: "Who says that fictions only and false hair / Become a verse? Is there in truth no beauty?"

More than three lines of poetry should be handled as an indented quotation. (See P6-b.)

The slash may occasionally be used to separate paired terms such as *pass/fail* and *producer/director*. Do not use a space before or after the slash.

> Roger, the producer/director, announced a casting change.

Be sparing, however, in this use of the slash. In particular, avoid the use of *and/or, he/she,* and *his/her*.

ON THE WEB > dianahacker.com/writersref
Grammar exercises > Punctuation > E-ex P7–1

M

Mechanics

M Mechanics

M1

Spelling

You learned to spell from repeated experience with words in both reading and writing, but especially writing. Words have a look, a sound, and even a feel to them as the hand moves across the page. As you proofread, you can probably tell if a word doesn't look quite right. In such cases, the solution is obvious: Look up the word in the dictionary. (See W6-a.)

SPELL CHECKERS are useful alternatives to a dictionary, but only to a point. A spell checker will not tell you how to spell words not listed in its dictionary; nor will it help you catch words commonly confused, such as *accept* and *except,* or some typographical errors, such as *own* for *won.* You will still need to proofread, and for some words you may need to turn to the dictionary.

M1-a Become familiar with the major spelling rules.

i *before* e *except after* c

Use *i* before *e* except after *c* or when sounded like *ay,* as in *neighbour* and *weigh.*

I* BEFORE *E	relieve, believe, sieve, niece, fierce, frieze
E* BEFORE *I	receive, deceive, sleigh, freight, eight
EXCEPTIONS	seize, either, weird, height, foreign, leisure

Suffixes

FINAL SILENT *-E* Generally, drop a final silent *-e* when adding a suffix that begins with a vowel. Keep the final *-e* if the suffix begins with a consonant.

combine, combination	achieve, achievement
desire, desiring	care, careful
prude, prudish	entire, entirety
remove, removable	gentle, gentleness

Words such as *changeable, judgment, argument,* and *truly* are exceptions.

FINAL *-Y* When adding *-s* or *-d* to words ending in *-y,* ordinarily change *-y* to *-ie* when the *-y* is preceded by a consonant but not when it is preceded by a vowel.

comedy, comedies	monkey, monkeys
dry, dried	play, played

With proper names ending in *-y,* however, do not change the *-y* to *-ie* even if it is preceded by a consonant: *the Dougherty family, the Doughertys.*

FINAL CONSONANTS If a final consonant is preceded by a single vowel *and* the consonant ends a one-syllable word or a stressed syllable, double the consonant when adding a suffix beginning with a vowel.

bet, betting	occur, occurrence
commit, committed	

Plurals

-S OR *-ES* Add *-s* to form the plural of most nouns; add *-es* to singular nouns ending in *-s, -sh, -ch,* and *-x.*

table, tables	church, churches
paper, papers	dish, dishes

Ordinarily add *-s* to nouns ending in *-o* when the *-o* is preceded by a vowel. Add *-es* when it is preceded by a consonant.

radio, radios	hero, heroes
video, videos	tomato, tomatoes

OTHER PLURALS To form the plural of a hyphenated compound word, add *-s* to the chief word even if it does not appear at the end.

mother-in-law, mothers-in-law

English words derived from other languages such as Latin or French sometimes form the plural as they would in their original language.

medium, media	chateau, chateaux
criterion, criteria	

Spelling may vary slightly among English-speaking countries. If you studied British or American English before you began studying Canadian English, be aware of the different forms listed here. Consult a dictionary for others.

CANADIAN	AMERICAN	BRITISH
cancelled	canceled	cancelled
colour	color	colour
judgment	judgment	judgement
cheque	check	cheque
realize	realize	realise
defence	defense	defence
anemia	anemia	anaemia
theatre	theater	theatre
fetus	fetus	foetus
mould	mold	mould
civilization	civilization	civilisation
connection	connection	connexion
licorice	licorice	liquorice

NOTE: For rules on pluralizing numbers, letters, abbreviations, and words mentioned as words, see P5-d.

M1-b Discriminate between words that sound alike but have different meanings.

Words that sound alike or nearly alike but have different meanings and spellings are called *homophones*. The following sets of words are so commonly confused that a good proofreader will double-check their every use.

affect (verb: to exert an influence)
effect (verb: to accomplish; noun: result)

its (possessive pronoun: of or belonging to it)
it's (contraction for *it is*)

loose (adjective: free, not securely attached)
lose (verb: to fail to keep, to be deprived of)

principal (adjective: most important; noun: head of a school)
principle (noun: a general or fundamental truth)

their (possessive pronoun: belonging to them)
they're (contraction for *they are*)
there (adverb: that place or position)

who's (contraction for *who is*)
whose (possessive form of *who*)

your (possessive form of *you*)
you're (contraction of *you are*)

To check for correct use of these and other commonly confused words, consult the Glossary of Usage in this book (W1).

ON THE WEB > **dianahacker.com/writersref**
Links Library > Grammar, style, punctuation, and usage

M2

The hyphen

GRAMMAR CHECKERS can flag some, but not all, missing or misused hyphens. For example, the programs can often tell you that a hyphen is needed in compound numbers, such as *sixty-four.* They can also tell you how to spell certain compound words, such as *breakup* (not *break-up*).

M2-a Consult the dictionary to determine how to treat a compound word.

The dictionary will tell you whether to treat a compound word as a hyphenated compound (*water-repellent*), one word (*waterproof*), or two words (*water table*). If the compound word is not in the dictionary, treat it as two words.

- ▶ **The Crown attorney chose not to cross-examine any witnesses.**
- ▶ **Imogene kept her sketches in a small note book.**

▶ Alice walked through the looking/glass into a backward world.

M2-b Use a hyphen to connect two or more words functioning together as an adjective before a noun.

▶ Mrs. Douglas gave Toshiko a seashell and some newspaper-wrapped fish to take home to her mother.

▶ Richa Gupta is not yet a well-known candidate.

Newspaper-wrapped and *well-known* are adjectives used before the nouns *fish* and *candidate.*

Generally, do not use a hyphen when such compounds follow the noun.

▶ After our television campaign, Richa Gupta will be well/known.

Do not use a hyphen to connect *-ly* adverbs to the words they modify.

▶ A slowly/moving truck tied up traffic.

NOTE: In a series, hyphens are suspended.

Do you prefer first-, second-, or third-class tickets?

M2-c Hyphenate the written form of fractions and of compound numbers from twenty-one to ninety-nine.

▶ One-fourth of my salary goes to pay my child care expenses.

M2-d Use a hyphen with the prefixes *all-*, *ex-*, and *self-* and with the suffix *-elect.*

▶ The charity is funnelling more money into self-help projects.

▶ Anne King is our club's president-elect.

M2-e A hyphen is used in some words to avoid ambiguity or to separate awkward double or triple letters.

Without the hyphen there would be no way to distinguish between words such as *re-creation* and *recreation.*

> Bicycling in the city is my favourite form of recreation.
>
> The film was praised for its astonishing re-creation of nineteenth-century London.

Hyphens are sometimes used to separate awkward double or triple letters in compound words (*anti-intellectual, cross-stitch*). Always check a dictionary for the standard form of the word.

M2-f If a word must be divided at the end of a line, divide it correctly.

Divide words between syllables; never divide a one-syllable word.

▶ **When I returned from my semester overseas, I didn't ~~reco-~~** *recog-*
nize
~~gnize~~ one face on the magazine covers.

▶ **He didn't have the courage or the ~~stren-~~**
strength
~~gth~~ to open the door.

Never divide a word so that a single letter stands alone at the end of a line or fewer than three letters begin a line.

▶ **She'll bring her brother with her when she comes ~~a-~~**
again.
~~gain.~~

▶ **As audience to the play *The Mousetrap,* Hamlet is a ~~watch-~~**
watcher
~~er~~ watching watchers.

When dividing a compound word at the end of a line, either make the break between the words that form the compound or put the whole word on the next line.

▶ **My niece Marielena is determined to become a long-~~dis-~~**
distance
~~tance~~ runner when she grows up.

To divide long e-mail and Internet addresses (URLs), do not use a hyphen. Break an e-mail address after the @ symbol or before a period. Break a URL after a colon, a slash, or a double slash or before a period or other punctuation mark.

> I repeatedly e-mailed Janine at janine.r.rose@dunbaracademy .org before I gave up and called her cell phone.

> To find a postal code quickly, I always use the Canada Post Web site at http://www.canadapost.ca/personal/tools/pcl/ bin/advanced-e.asp.

NOTE: For breaks in URLs in MLA and APA documentation styles, see MLA-5 and APA-5.

ON THE WEB > **dianahacker.com/writersref**
Grammar exercises > Mechanics > E-ex M2–1

M3

Capitalization

In addition to the rules in this section, a good dictionary can tell you when to use capital letters.

GRAMMAR CHECKERS remind you that sentences should begin with capital letters and that some words, such as *Métis,* are proper nouns. Many words, however, should be capitalized only in certain contexts, and you must determine when to do so.

M3-a Capitalize proper nouns and words derived from them; do not capitalize common nouns.

Proper nouns are the names of specific persons, places, and things. All other nouns are common nouns. The following types of words are usually capitalized: names for the deity, religions, religious followers, sacred books; words of family relationship used as names; particular places; nationalities and their languages, races, tribes, or bands; educational institutions, departments, degrees, particular courses; government departments, organizations, political parties;

historical movements, periods, events, documents; specific electronic sources; and trade names.

PROPER NOUNS	COMMON NOUNS
God (used as a name)	a god
Book of Common Prayer	a book
Uncle Pedro	my uncle
Father (used as a name)	my father
Lake Ontario	a picturesque lake
the Capital Centre	a centre for advanced studies
the Prairies	a Canadian province
the Rogers Centre	a baseball stadium
University of Windsor	a good university
Geology 101	geology
Environment Canada	a federal agency
Phi Kappa Psi	a fraternity
a Liberal	an independent
the Enlightenment	the eighteenth century
the Charter of Rights and Freedoms	a treaty
the World Wide Web, the Web	a home page
the Internet, the Net	a computer network
Advil	a painkiller

Months, holidays, and days of the week are treated as proper nouns; the seasons and numbers of the days of the month are not.

> Our academic year begins on a Tuesday in early September, right after Labour Day.
>
> My mother's birthday is in early summer, on the second of June.

EXCEPTION: Capitalize Fourth of July (or July Fourth) when referring to the holiday.

Names of school subjects are capitalized only if they are names of languages. Names of particular courses are capitalized.

> This semester Austin is taking math, geography, geology, French, and English.
>
> Professor Obembe offers Modern American Fiction 501 to graduate students.

TIP: Do not capitalize common nouns to make them seem important. *Our company is currently hiring computer programmers* [not *Company, Computer Programmers*].

M3-b Capitalize titles of persons when used as part of a proper name but usually not when used alone.

> Prof. Margaret Barnes; Dr. Sinyee Sein; John Scott Williams Jr.; Anne Tilton, LLD
>
> Crown Attorney Marshall was reprimanded for badgering the witness.
>
> The attorney general was appointed last year.

Usage varies when the title of an important public figure is used alone. *The prime minister* [or *Prime Minister*] *signed the bill.*

M3-c Capitalize the first, last, and all major words in titles and subtitles of works such as books, articles, songs, and online documents.

In both titles and subtitles, major words such as nouns, pronouns, verbs, adjectives, and adverbs should be capitalized. Minor words such as articles, prepositions, and coordinating conjunctions are not capitalized unless they are the first or last word of a title or subtitle. Capitalize the second part of a hyphenated term in a title if it is a major word but not if it is a minor word.

> *Seizing the Enigma: The Race to Break the German U-Boat Codes*
> "Fire and Ice"
> "I Want to Hold Your Hand"
> *The Canadian Green Page*

Capitalize chapter titles and the titles of other major divisions of a work following the same guidelines used for titles of complete works.

> "Work and Play" in Santayana's *The Nature of Beauty*
>
> "Size Matters" on the Web site *Discovery Channel Online*

M3-d Capitalize the first word of a sentence.

Obviously the first word of a sentence should be capitalized.

When lightning struck the house, the chimney collapsed.

When a sentence appears within parentheses, capitalize its first word unless the parentheses appear within another sentence.

Early detection of breast cancer significantly increases survival rates. (See table 2.)

Early detection of breast cancer significantly increases survival rates (see table 2).

M3-e Capitalize the first word of a quoted sentence but not a quoted phrase.

In *Time* magazine Robert Hughes writes, "There are only about sixty Watteau paintings on whose authenticity all experts agree."

Russell Baker has written that sports are "the opiate of the masses."

If a quoted sentence is interrupted by explanatory words, do not capitalize the first word after the interruption. (See also P6-f.)

"If you want to go out," he said, "tell me now."

When quoting poetry, copy the poet's capitalization exactly. Many poets capitalize the first word of every line of poetry; a few contemporary poets dismiss capitalization altogether.

When I consider everything that grows
Holds in perfection but a little moment —Shakespeare

it was the week that
i felt the city's narrow breezes rush about
me —Don L. Lee

M3-f Capitalize the first word after a colon if it begins an independent clause.

I came to a startling conclusion: The house must be haunted.

NOTE: MLA and CMS styles use a lowercase letter to begin an independent clause following a colon; APA style uses a capital letter.

Use lowercase after a colon to introduce a list or an appositive.

The students were divided into two groups: residents and commuters.

M3-g Capitalize abbreviations for departments and agencies of government, other organizations, and corporations; capitalize the call letters of radio and television stations.

CSA, CSIS, OPEC, IBM, WCTV, YTV

ON THE WEB > **dianahacker.com/writersref**
Grammar exercises > Mechanics > E-ex M3–1

M4

Abbreviations

GRAMMAR CHECKERS can flag a few inappropriate abbreviations, such as *Xmas* and *e.g.,* but do not assume that a program will catch all problems with abbreviations.

M4-a Use standard abbreviations for titles immediately before and after proper names.

TITLES BEFORE PROPER NAMES	TITLES AFTER PROPER NAMES
Mr. Rafael Zabala	William Albert Sr.
Ms. Nancy Linehan	Thomas Hines Jr.
Mrs. Edward Horn	Anita Lor, PhD
Dr. Margaret Simmons	Robert Simkowski, MD
the Rev. John Stone	Margaret Chin, LLD
Prof. James Russo	Polly Stein, DDS

Do not abbreviate a title if it is not used with a proper name.

▶ **My history ~~prof.~~ *professor* is an expert on race relations in South Africa.**

Avoid redundant titles such as *Dr. Amy Day, MD.* Choose one title or the other: *Dr. Amy Day* or *Amy Day, MD.*

M4-b Use abbreviations only when you are sure your readers will understand them.

Familiar abbreviations, written without periods, are acceptable.

> USB, RCMP, CUPE, RSVP, HTML, IBM, CBS, USA, IOU, CD-ROM, ESL
>
> The YMCA has opened a new gym close to my office.

NOTE: When using an unfamiliar abbreviation (such as CASW for Canadian Association of Social Workers) throughout a paper, write the full name followed by the abbreviation in parentheses at the first mention of the name. Then use the abbreviation throughout the rest of the paper.

M4-c Use BC, AD, a.m., p.m., No., and $ only with specific dates, times, numbers, and amounts.

The abbreviation BC ("before Christ") follows a date, and AD ("*anno Domini*") precedes a date. Acceptable alternatives are BCE ("before the common era") and CE ("common era"), both of which follow a date.

40 BC (or 40 BCE)	4:00 a.m. (or AM)	No. 12 (or no. 12)
AD 44 (or 44 CE)	6:00 p.m. (or PM)	$150

Avoid using a.m., p.m., No., or $ when not accompanied by a specific figure.

▶ **We set off for the lake early in the ~~a.m.~~** *morning.*

M4-d Be sparing in your use of Latin abbreviations.

Latin abbreviations are acceptable in footnotes and bibliographies and in informal writing for comments in parentheses.

> cf. (Latin *confer,* "compare")
> e.g. (Latin *exempli gratia,* "for example")
> et al. (Latin *et alii,* "and others")
> etc. (Latin *et cetera,* "and so forth")

i.e. (Latin *id est,* "that is")
N.B. (Latin *nota bene,* "note well")

Harold Simms et al., *The Race for Space*

Alfred Hitchcock directed many classic thrillers (e.g., *Psycho, Rear Window,* and *Vertigo*).

In formal writing, use the appropriate English phrases.

▶ **Many obsolete laws remain on the books; ~~e.g.,~~** *for example,* **a law in Fort Qu'Appelle, Saskatchewan, forbids teenagers to walk down Main Street with their shoes untied.**

M4-e Avoid inappropriate abbreviations.

In formal writing, abbreviations for the following are not commonly accepted: personal names, units of measurement, days of the week, holidays, months, courses of study, divisions of written works, states, provinces, territories, and countries (except in addresses and except Washington, DC). Do not abbreviate *Company* and *Incorporated* unless their abbreviated forms are part of an official name.

PERSONAL NAME Charles (*not* Chas.)

UNITS OF MEASUREMENT kilogram (*not* kg)

DAYS OF THE WEEK Monday (*not* Mon.)

HOLIDAYS Christmas (*not* Xmas)

MONTHS January, February, March (*not* Jan., Feb., Mar.)

COURSES OF STUDY political science (*not* poli. sci.)

DIVISIONS OF WRITTEN WORKS chapter, page (*not* ch., p.)

STATES, PROVINCES, TERRITORIES, COUNTRIES Alberta (*not* AB or Alta.)

PARTS OF A BUSINESS NAME Adams Lighting Company (*not* Adams Lighting Co.); Kim and Brothers, Inc. (*not* Kim and Bros., Inc.)

▶ **Blood donors must be at least seventeen ~~yrs~~** *years* **old and weigh 110 ~~lb.~~** *pounds.*

ON THE WEB > dianahacker.com/writersref
Grammar exercises > Mechanics > E-ex M4–1

M5

Numbers

GRAMMAR CHECKERS can tell you to spell out certain numbers, such as *thirty-three* and numbers that begin a sentence, but they won't help you understand when it is acceptable to use figures.

M5-a Spell out numbers of one or two words or those that begin a sentence. Use figures for numbers that require more than two words to spell out.

▶ **It's been ~~8~~ *eight* years since I visited Peru.**

▶ **I counted ~~one hundred seventy six~~ *176* DVDs on the shelf.**

If a sentence begins with a number, spell out the number or rewrite the sentence.

▶ **~~150~~ *One hundred fifty* children in our program need expensive dental treatment.**

Rewriting the sentence will also correct the error and may be less awkward if the number is long: *In our program 150 children need expensive dental treatment.*

EXCEPTIONS: In technical and some business writing, figures are preferred even when spellings would be brief, but usage varies. When in doubt, consult the style guide of the organization for which you are writing.

When several numbers appear in the same passage, many writers choose consistency rather than strict adherence to the rule.

When one number immediately follows another, spell out one and use figures for the other: *three 100-meter events, 25 four-poster beds.*

M5-b Generally, figures are acceptable for dates, addresses, percentages, fractions, decimals, scores, statistics and other numerical results, exact amounts of money, divisions of books and plays, pages, identification numbers, and the time.

DATES July 4, 1776, 56 BC, AD 30

ADDRESSES 77 Latches Lane, 519 West 42nd Street

PERCENTAGES 55 percent (or 55%)

FRACTIONS, DECIMALS ½, 0.047

SCORES 7 to 3, 21–18

STATISTICS average age 37, average weight 180

SURVEYS 4 out of 5

EXACT AMOUNTS OF MONEY $105.37, $106 000

DIVISIONS OF BOOKS volume 3, chapter 4, page 189

DIVISIONS OF PLAYS act 3; scene 3 (*or* act III, scene iii)

IDENTIFICATION NUMBERS serial number 10988675

TIME OF DAY 4:00 p.m., 1:30 a.m.

▶ **Several doctors put up ~~two hundred fifty-five thousand dollars~~ $255 000 for the construction of a golf course.**

NOTE: When not using a.m. or p.m., write out the time in words (*four o'clock in the afternoon, twelve noon, seven in the morning*).

ON THE WEB > **dianahacker.com/writersref**
Grammar exercises > Mechanics > E-ex M5–1

M6

Italics (underlining)

Italics, a slanting font style used in printed material, can be produced by word processing programs. In handwritten or typed papers, underlining is used instead. Some instructors prefer underlining even though their students can produce italics.

NOTE: Some e-mail systems do not allow for italics or underlining. Many people indicate words that should be italicized by preceding and ending them with underscore marks or asterisks. Punctuation should follow the coding.

> I am planning to write my senior thesis on _Memoirs of a Geisha_.

In less formal e-mail messages, normally italicized words aren't marked at all.

> I finally finished reading Memoirs of a Geisha--what a story!

TIP: In World Wide Web documents, underlining indicates a hot link. When creating a Web document, use italics, not underlining, for the conventions described in this section.

GRAMMAR CHECKERS do not flag problems with italics or underlining.

M6-a Underline or italicize the titles of works according to convention.

Titles of the following works, including electronic works, should be underlined or italicized.

TITLES OF BOOKS *The Color Purple, Middlesex, Encarta*

MAGAZINES *Time, Canadian Geographic, Salon.com*

NEWSPAPERS the *Toronto Sun*, the *Globe and Mail*

PAMPHLETS *Common Sense, Facts about Marijuana*

LONG POEMS *The Waste Land, Paradise Lost*

PLAYS *King Lear, Rent*

FILMS *Casablanca, Million Dollar Baby*

TELEVISION PROGRAMS *Survivor, 60 Minutes*

RADIO PROGRAMS *All Things Considered*

MUSICAL COMPOSITIONS *Porgy and Bess*

CHOREOGRAPHIC WORKS *Brief Fling*

WORKS OF VISUAL ART Rodin's *The Thinker*

COMIC STRIPS *Dilbert*

ELECTRONIC DATABASES *InfoTrac*

WEB SITES *ZDNet, Google*

ELECTRONIC GAMES *Free Cell, Zuma*

The titles of other works, such as short stories, essays, episodes of radio or television programs, songs, and short poems, are enclosed in quotation marks. (See P6-d.)

NOTE: Do not use underlining or italics when referring to the Bible, titles of books in the Bible (Genesis, not *Genesis*), or titles of legal documents (the Charter of Rights and Freedoms, not the *Charter of Rights and Freedoms*). Do not underline the titles of computer software (WordPerfect, Photoshop). Do not underline the title of your own paper.

M6-b Underline or italicize the names of spacecraft, aircraft, ships, and trains.

Challenger, Spirit of St. Louis, Queen Mary 2, Silver Streak

► **The success of the Soviets' Sputnik galvanized the US space program.**

M6-c Underline or italicize foreign words in an English sentence.

► **Caroline's joie de vivre should be a model for all of us.**

EXCEPTION: Do not underline or italicize foreign words that have become part of the English language—"laissez-faire," "fait accompli," "modus operandi," and "per diem," for example.

M6-d Underline or italicize words, letters, and numbers mentioned as themselves.

► **Tim assured us that the howling probably came from his bloodhound, Hill Billy, but his probably stuck in our minds.**

▶ **Sarah called her father by his given name, Johnny, but she was unable to pronounce the J.**

▶ **A big 3 was painted on the door.**

NOTE: Quotation marks may be used instead of underlining or italics to set off words mentioned as words. (See P6-e.)

M6-e Avoid excessive underlining or italics for emphasis.

Frequent underlining or italicizing to emphasize words or ideas is distracting and should be used sparingly.

▶ **In-line skating is a popular sport that has become almost an addiction.**

ON THE WEB > **dianahacker.com/writersref**
Grammar exercises > Mechanics > E-ex M6–1

R

Researching

R Researching

College and university research assignments ask you to pose a question worth exploring, to read widely in search of possible answers, to interpret what you read, to draw reasoned conclusions, and to support those conclusions with valid and well-documented evidence. The process takes time: time for researching and time for drafting, revising, and documenting the paper in the style recommended by your instructor (see the tabbed dividers marked MLA and APA/CMS). Before beginning a research project, set a realistic schedule of deadlines. One student created a calendar to map out her tasks for a paper assigned on October 3 and due October 31.

SAMPLE CALENDAR FOR A RESEARCH ASSIGNMENT

2	3 **Receive assignment.**	4 Pose questions worth exploring. →	5 Talk with a librarian; plan a search strategy. →	6	7 Settle on a topic. Locate sources. →	8
9 →	10	11 Read and take notes.	12	13 Draft a tentaive thesis and an outline.	14 Draft the paper. →	15
16 → Draft the paper. →	17	18	19 Visit the writing centre to get help with ideas for revision.	20 Do further research if necessary.	21	22
23 Revise the paper. →	24	25	26	27	28 Prepare a list of works cited.	29
30 Proofread the final draft.	31 **Final draft due.**					

R1 Conducting research

Throughout this tabbed section, you will encounter examples related to three sample research papers:

- A paper on the dangers of Internet surveillance in the workplace, written by a student in an English composition class (see p. 408). The student, Anna Orlov, uses the MLA (Modern Language Association) style of documentation.
- A paper on the limitations of medications to treat childhood obesity, written by a student in a psychology class (see p. 451). The student, Luisa Mirano, uses the APA (American Psychological Association) style of documentation.
- A paper on the extent to which Civil War general Nathan Bedford Forrest can be held responsible for the Fort Pillow massacre, written by a student in a history class (see p. 484). The student, Ned Bishop, uses the CMS (*Chicago Manual of Style*) documentation system.

R1-a Pose possible questions worth exploring.

Working within the guidelines of your assignment, pose a few questions that seem worth researching. Here, for example, are some preliminary questions jotted down by students enrolled in a variety of classes in different disciplines.

- Should the CRTC broaden its definition of indecent programming to include violence?
- Which geological formations are the safest repositories for nuclear waste?
- What was Marcus Garvey's contribution to the fight for racial equality?
- How can governments and zoos help preserve Asia's endangered snow leopard?
- Why was amateur archaeologist Heinrich Schliemann such a controversial figure in his own time?

As you formulate possible questions, make sure that they are appropriate lines of inquiry for a research paper. Choose questions that are narrow (not too broad), challenging (not too bland), and grounded (not too speculative).

Choosing a narrow question

If your initial question is too broad, given the length of the paper you plan to write, look for ways to restrict your focus. Here, for example, is how two students narrowed their initial questions.

TOO BROAD

What are the hazards of fad diets?

Is the Canadian government seriously addressing the problem of prisoner abuse?

NARROWER

What are the hazards of low-carbohydrate diets?

To what extent have the Canadian Forces addressed the problem of prisoner abuse since the Somalia Affair?

Choosing a challenging question

Your research paper will be more interesting to both you and your audience if you base it on an intellectually challenging line of inquiry. Avoid bland questions that fail to provoke thought or engage readers in a debate.

TOO BLAND

What is obsessive-compulsive disorder?

How does DNA testing work?

CHALLENGING

What treatments for obsessive-compulsive disorder show the most promise?

How reliable is DNA testing?

You may need to address a bland question in the course of answering a more challenging one. For example, if you were writing about promising treatments for obsessive-compulsive disorder, you would no doubt answer the question "What is obsessive-compulsive disorder?" at some point in your paper. It would be a mistake, however, to use the bland question as the focus for the whole paper.

Choosing a grounded question

Finally, you will want to make sure that your research question is grounded, not too speculative. Although speculative questions — such as those that address philosophical, ethical, or religious issues — are worth asking and may receive some attention in a research paper, they are inappropriate central questions. The central argument of a research paper should be grounded in facts; it should not be based entirely on beliefs.

TOO SPECULATIVE

Is it wrong to share music files on the Internet?

Do medical scientists have the right to experiment on animals?

GROUNDED

How has Internet file sharing affected the earning potential of musicians?

How have technology breakthroughs made medical experiments on animals increasingly unnecessary?

ON THE WEB > **dianahacker.com/writersref**
Research exercises > E-ex R1–1

R1-b Map out a search strategy.

A search strategy is a systematic plan for tracking down sources. To create a search strategy appropriate for your research question, consult a reference librarian and take a look at your library's Web site, which will give you an overview of available resources.

> ACADEMIC ENGLISH Whether it is your first or fiftieth time writing a research paper, you may initially feel overwhelmed by the number of resources available to you both in print and online. Instead of turning immediately to a popular search engine like *Google*, step back and think about the best way to find the right information for your purpose. You can start by consulting the advice in this section.

Getting started

Reference librarians are information specialists who can save you time by steering you toward relevant and reliable sources. With the help of an expert, you can make the best use of electronic databases, Web search engines, and other reference tools.

When you ask a reference librarian for help, be prepared to answer a number of questions:

- What is your assignment?
- In which academic discipline are you writing?
- What is your tentative research question?
- How long will the paper be?
- How much time can you spend on the project?

It's a good idea to bring a copy of the assignment with you.

In addition to speaking with a reference librarian, take some time to explore your library's Web site. You will typically find links to the library's catalogue and to a variety of databases and electronic sources that you can access from any networked computer. In addition, you may find resources listed by subject, research guides, information about interlibrary loans, and links to Web sites selected by librarians for their quality. Many libraries also offer online reference assistance.

LIBRARY HOME PAGE

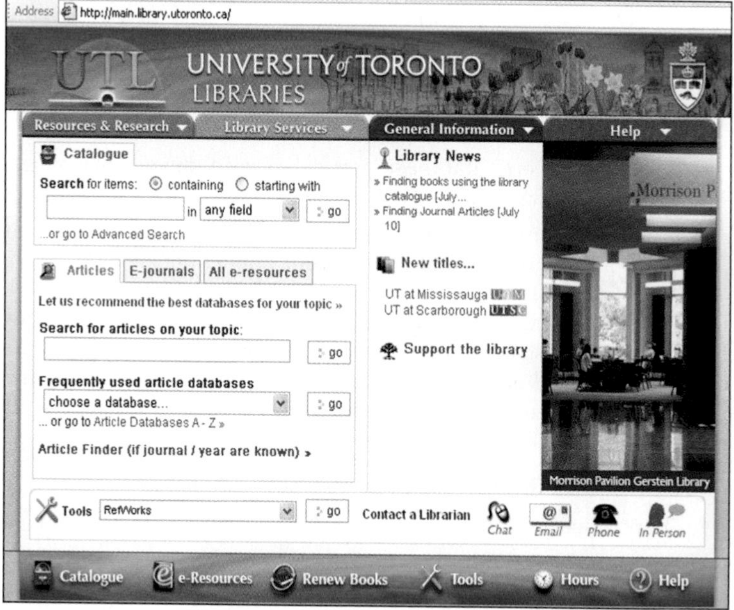

Including the library in your plan

Resist the temptation to do all of your work on the Internet. Most assignments will require using at least some formally published sources, and libraries offer a wider range of quality materials than the Web does. Although you can locate some newspaper, magazine, and journal articles online, you may have to pay a fee to access them. Most libraries subscribe to databases that will give you unlimited access to these materials as well as scholarly resources that won't turn up in a Web search. Keep in mind that databases don't always include full-text articles of everything they cite. Often you'll need to track down print copies in your library's stacks or request them through interlibrary loan.

Choosing an appropriate search strategy

No single search strategy works for every topic. For some topics, it may be appropriate to search for information in newspapers, magazines, and Web sites. For others, the best sources might be found in scholarly journals and books and specialized reference works. Still other topics might be enhanced by field research — interviews, surveys, or direct observation. With the help of a reference librarian, each of the students mentioned on page 318 constructed a search strategy appropriate for his or her research question.

ANNA ORLOV Anna Orlov's topic, the dangers of Internet surveillance in the workplace, was so current that books were an unlikely source. To find up-to-date information on her topic, Orlov decided to

- search a general database for articles in magazines, newspapers, and journals
- use Web search engines, such as *Google*, to locate relevant sites, online articles, and government publications

LUISA MIRANO Luisa Mirano's topic, the limitations of medications for childhood obesity, has recently become the subject of psychological studies as well as articles in the popular press (newspapers and magazines aimed at the general public). Thinking that both popular and scholarly works would be appropriate, Mirano decided to

- locate books through the library's online catalogue
- check a specialized encyclopedia, *Encyclopedia of Psychology*
- search a general database for popular articles
- search a specialized database, *PsycINFO*, for scholarly articles

NED BISHOP Ned Bishop's topic, the role played by Nathan Bedford Forrest in the Fort Pillow massacre, is an issue that has been investigated and debated by professional historians. Given the nature of his historical topic, Ned Bishop decided to

- locate books through the library's online catalogue
- locate scholarly articles by searching a specialized database, *America: History and Life*
- locate newspaper articles from 1864 by using a print index
- search the Web for other historical primary sources

R1-c To locate articles, search a database or consult a print index.

Libraries subscribe to a variety of electronic databases (sometimes called *periodical databases*) that give students access to articles and other materials without charge. Because many databases are limited to relatively recent works, you may need to consult a print index as well.

What databases offer

Your library has access to databases that can lead you to articles in newspapers, magazines, and scholarly or technical journals. Some databases cover several subjects; others cover one subject in depth. Your library might subscribe to some of the following resources.

GENERAL DATABASES

EBSCOhost. A portal to more than one hundred databases that include periodical articles, government documents, pamphlets, and other types of documents.

InfoTrac. A collection of databases, some of which index periodical articles.

LexisNexis. A set of databases that are particularly strong in coverage of news, business, legal, and political topics.

ProQuest. A database of periodical articles.

SUBJECT-SPECIFIC DATABASES

ERIC. An education database.

PubMed. A database offering abstracts of medical research studies.

MLA Bibliography. A database of literary criticism.

PsycINFO. A database of psychology research.

Refining keyword searches in databases and search engines

Although command terms and characters vary among electronic databases and Web search engines, some of the most commonly used functions are listed here.

- Use quotation marks around words that are part of a phrase: "Broadway musicals".
- Use AND to connect words that must appear in a document: Ireland AND peace. Some search engines require a plus sign instead: Ireland +peace.
- Use NOT in front of words that must not appear in a document: Titanic NOT movie. Some search engines require a minus sign (hyphen) instead: Titanic -movie.
- Use OR if only one of the terms must appear in a document: "mountain lion" OR cougar.
- Use an asterisk as a substitute for letters that might vary: "marine biolog*" (to find *marine biology* or *marine biologist,* for example).
- Use parentheses to group a search expression and combine it with another: (cigarettes OR tobacco OR smok*) AND lawsuits.

NOTE: Many search engines and databases offer an advanced search option that makes it easy to refine your search.

Many databases include the full text of at least some articles; others list only citations or citations with short summaries called *abstracts*. When full text is not available, the citation will give you enough information to track down an article.

How to search a database

To find articles on your topic in a database, start with a keyword search. If the first keyword you try results in no matches, experiment with synonyms or ask a librarian for suggestions. For example, if you're searching for sources on a topic related to education, you might also want to try the terms *teaching*, *learning*, *pedagogy*, and *curriculum*. If your keyword search results in too many matches, narrow it by using one of the strategies in the chart at the top of this page.

For her paper on Internet surveillance in the workplace, Anna Orlov conducted a keyword search in a general periodical database.

DATABASE SCREEN: RESULTS OF A KEYWORD SEARCH

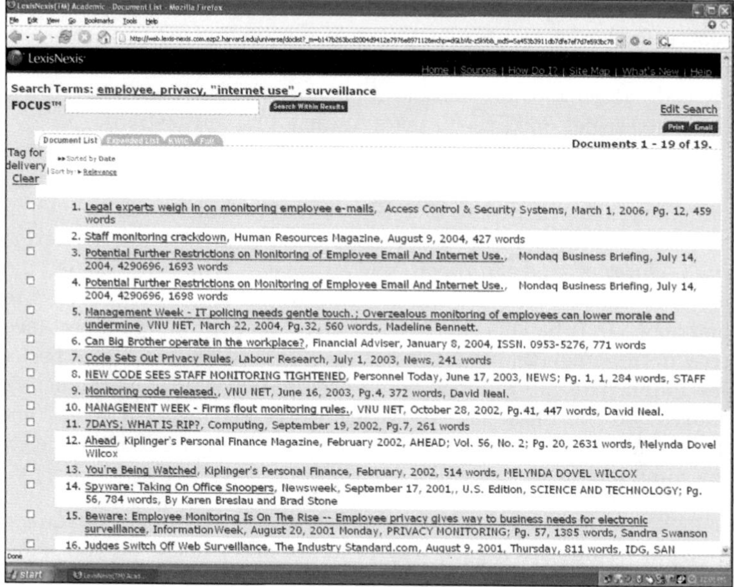

She typed in *employee* and *privacy* and *"internet use"* and *surveillance*; her search brought up nineteen possible articles, some of which looked promising (see the screen above).

When to use a print index

If you want to search for articles published before the 1980s, you may need to turn to a print index. For example, Ned Bishop consulted the *New York Times Index* to locate newspaper articles written in April 1864, just after the battle at Fort Pillow. To find older magazine articles, consult the *Readers' Guide to Periodical Literature* or *Poole's Index to Periodical Literature* or ask a librarian for help.

R1-d To locate books, consult the library's catalogue.

The books your library owns are listed in its computer catalogue, along with other resources such as videos. You can search the catalogue by author, title, or topic keywords.

Don't be surprised if your first search calls up too few or too many results. If you have too few results, try different keywords or search for books on broader topics. If a search gives you too many results, use the strategies in the chart on page 324 or try an advanced search tool to combine concepts and limit your results. If those strategies don't work, ask a librarian for suggestions.

When Luisa Mirano, whose topic was childhood obesity, entered the term *obesity* into the computer catalogue, she was faced with an unmanageable number of hits. She narrowed her search by adding two more specific terms to *obesity*: *child** (to include the terms *child*, *children*, and *childhood*) and *treatment*. When she still got too many results, she limited the first two terms to subject searches to find books that had obesity in children as their primary subject (see screen 1). Screen 2 shows the complete record for one of the books she found. The call number, listed beside *Availability*, is the book's address on the library shelf. (When you're retrieving a book from the shelf, scan other books in the area since they are likely to be on the same topic.)

LIBRARIAN'S TIP: The record for a book lists related subject headings. These headings are a good way to locate other books on your subject. For example, the record in screen 2 lists the terms *obesity in children* and *obesity in adolescence* as related subject headings. By clicking on these new terms, Mirano found a few more books on her subject.

LIBRARY CATALOGUE SCREEN 1: ADVANCED SEARCH

LIBRARY CATALOGUE SCREEN 2: COMPLETE RECORD FOR A BOOK

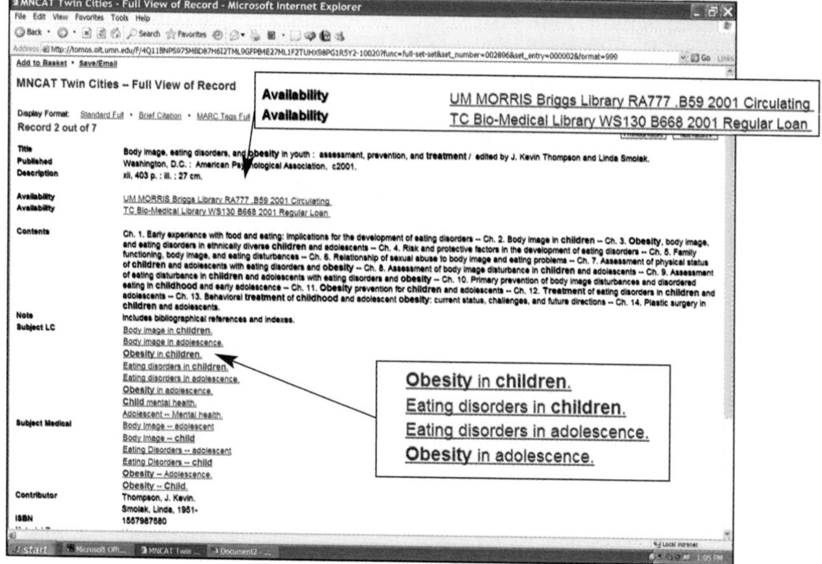

R1-e To locate a wide variety of sources, turn to the Web.

For some (but not all) topics, the Web is an excellent resource. For example, government agencies post information on the Web, and the sites of many organizations are filled with information about the issues they cover. Museums and libraries often post digital versions of primary sources, such as photographs, political speeches, and classic literary texts.

Although the Web can be a rich source of information, some of which can't be found anywhere else, it lacks quality control. Anyone can publish on the Web, so you'll need to evaluate online sources with special care (see R2).

This section describes the following Web resources: search engines, directories, digital archives, government and news sites, and discussion forums.

ON THE WEB > dianahacker.com/writersref
Additional resources > Links Library > Conducting research

Search engines

Search engines take your search terms and seek matches among millions of Web pages. Some search engines go into more depth than others, but none can search the entire Web. Often it is a good idea to try more than one search engine, since each locates sources in its own way. For current information about search engines, visit *Search Engine Showdown* at <http://www.searchengineshowdown.com>. This site classifies search engines, evaluates them, and provides updates on new search features. Following are some popular search engines:

Google <http://www.google.com>

MSN Search <http://search.msn.com>

Teoma <http://www.teoma.com>

Yahoo! <http://www.yahoo.com>

In using a search engine, focus your search as narrowly as possible. You can sharpen your search by using many of the tips listed in the chart on page 324 or by using the search engine's advanced search form.

SEARCH ENGINE SCREEN: RESULTS OF AN ADVANCED SEARCH

Web Results **1** - **5** of about **9** over the **past 3 months** for "**Internet surveillance**" **employee** "**workplace privacy**" **site:.org** (**0.44** seconds)

Tip: Try removing quotes from your search to get more results.

EPIC/PI - Privacy & Human Rights 2000
Now the supervision of **employee**'s performance, behavior and... [89]Information and Privacy Commissioner/Ontario, **Workplace Privacy**: The Need for a..
www.privacyinternational.org/survey/phr2000/threats.html - 131k Cached - Similar pages

Privacy and Human Rights 2003: Threats to Privacy
Other issues that raise **workplace privacy** concerns are employer requirements that **employees** complete medical tests, questionnaires, and polygraph tests..
www.privacyinternational.org/survey/phr2003/threats.htm - 279k Cached - Similar pages
[More results from www.privacyinternational.org]

[PDF] Monitoring **Employee** E-Mail And Internet Usage: Avoiding The..
File Format: PDF/Adobe Acrobat - View as HTML
Internet surveillance by employers in the American workplace. At present, US **employees** in the private workplace have no constitutional, common law or statu
lsr.nellco.org/cgi/viewcontent.cgi?article=1006&context=suffolk/ip - Similar pages

Previous EPIC Top News
The agencies plan to use RFID to track **employees**' movements and in ID cards... For more information on **workplace privacy**, see the EPIC **Workplace Privacy**...
www.epic.org/news/2005.html - 163k Cached - Similar pages

For her paper on Internet surveillance in the workplace, Anna Orlov had difficulty restricting the number of hits. When she typed the words *internet, surveillance, workplace*, and *privacy* into a search engine, she got more than 80 000 matches. To narrow her search, Orlov tried typing in the phrases *"internet surveillance"*, *employee*, and *"workplace privacy"*. The result was 422 matches, still too many, so Orlov clicked on Advanced Search and restricted her search to sites with URLs ending in *.org* and to those updated only in the last three months. (See the screen on p. 328.)

Directories

Unlike search engines, which hunt for Web pages automatically, directories are put together by information specialists who choose reputable sites and arrange them by topic: education, health, politics, and so on.

Some directories are more selective and therefore more useful for scholarly research than the directories that typically accompany a search engine. For example, the directory for the *Internet Scout Project* was created for a research audience; it includes annotations that are both descriptive and evaluative. The following directories are especially useful for scholarly research:

Internet Scout Project <http://scout.wisc.edu/Archives>

Librarian's Internet Index <http://www.lii.org>

Open Directory Project <http://www.dmoz.org>

WWW Virtual Library <http://www.vlib.org>

Digital archives

Archives may contain the texts of poems, books, speeches, political cartoons, and historically significant documents such as the British North America Act and the Constitutional Act. The materials in these sites are usually limited to official documents and older works because of copyright laws. The following online archives are impressive collections:

Archives Canada <http://www.archivescanada.ca>

CBC Archives <http://archives.cbc.ca>

Collections Canada <http://www.collectionscanada.ca>

Electronic Text Center <http://etext.lib.virginia.edu>

Eurodocs <http://library.byu.edu/~rdh/eurodocs>

Internet History Sourcebooks <http://www.fordham.edu/halsall>

Online Books Page <http://digital.library.upenn.edu/books>

Government and news sites

For current topics, both government and news sites can prove useful. Many government agencies at every level provide online information. Government-maintained sites include resources such as legal texts, facts and statistics, government reports, and searchable reference databases. Here are just a few government sites:

Census of Canada <http://www12.statcan.ca/english/census/Index.cfm>

Justice Laws <http://laws.justice.gc.ca/en/index.html>

Statistics Canada <http://www.statcan.ca>

Strategis: Industry Canada <http://strategis.ic.gc.ca>

United Nations <http://www.un.org>

Many news organizations offer up-to-date information on the Web. These online services often allow nonsubscribers to read current stories for free. Some allow users to log on as guests and search archives without cost, but to read actual articles users typically must pay a fee. Check with your library to see if it subscribes to a news archive that you can access at no charge. The following are some free news sites:

Canoe <http://www.canoe.ca>

Google News Canada <http://news.google.ca>

NewsLink <http://newslink.org>

Discussion forums

The Web offers various ways of communicating with experts and others who have an interest in your topic. You might join an online mailing list, for example, to send and receive e-mail messages relevant to your topic. Or you may wish to search a newsgroup's postings. Newsgroups resemble bulletin boards on which messages are posted and connected through "threads" as others respond. In addition, you might log on to real-time discussion forums. To find mailing lists, newsgroups, and forums, try one of these sites:

CataList <http://www.lsoft.com/catalist.html>

Google Groups <http://groups.google.ca>

Tile.Net <http://tile.net/lists>

NOTE: Be aware that many of the people you contact in discussion forums will not be experts on your topic. Although you are more likely to find serious and worthwhile commentary in moderated mailing lists and scholarly discussion forums than in more free-wheeling newsgroups, it is difficult to guarantee the credibility of anyone you meet online.

R1-f Use other search tools.

In addition to articles, books, and Web sources, you may want to consult reference works such as encyclopedias and almanacs. Bibliographies (lists of works written on a topic) and citations in scholarly works can lead you to additional sources.

Reference works

The reference section of the library holds both general and specialized encyclopedias, dictionaries, almanacs, atlases, and biographical references, some available in electronic format. Such works often serve as a good overview of a subject and include references to the most significant works on a topic. Check with a reference librarian to see which works are most appropriate for your project.

GENERAL REFERENCE WORKS General reference works are good places to check facts and get basic information. Here are a few frequently used general references:

The Canadian Encyclopedia

Dictionary of Canadian Biography

National Geographic Atlas of the World

The New Encyclopaedia Britannica

The Oxford English Dictionary

Statistical Abstract of the United States

World Almanac and Book of Facts

Although general encyclopedias are often a good place to find background about your topic, you should rarely use them in your final paper. Most instructors expect you to rely on more specialized sources.

SPECIALIZED REFERENCE WORKS Specialized reference works often go into a topic in depth, sometimes in the form of articles written by leading authorities. Many specialized works are available, including these:

Contemporary Authors

Encyclopedia of Applied Ethics

Encyclopedia of Crime and Justice

Encyclopedia of Psychology

McGraw-Hill Encyclopedia of Science and Technology

ON THE WEB > **dianahacker.com/writersref**
Research and Documentation Online > Finding sources

Bibliographies and scholarly citations

Bibliographies are lists of works written on a particular topic. They include enough information about each work (author's name, title, publication data) so that you can locate the book or article. In some cases bibliographies are annotated: They contain abstracts giving a brief overview of each work's contents.

In addition to book-length bibliographies, scholarly books and articles list the works the author has cited, usually at the end. These lists are useful shortcuts. For example, most of the scholarly articles Luisa Mirano consulted contained citations to related research studies; through these citations, she quickly located additional relevant sources on her topic, treatments for childhood obesity.

R1-g Conduct field research, if appropriate.

Writing projects may be enhanced by, and sometimes focused on, your own field research. For a composition class, for example, you might want to interview a local politician about some aspect of a current issue, such as the use of cell phones while driving. For a sociology class, you might decide to conduct a survey regarding campus trends in community service. At work, you might need to learn how food industry executives have responded to reports that their products are contributing to health problems.

R2

Evaluating sources

With electronic search tools, you can often locate dozens or even hundreds of potential sources for your topic — far more than you will have time to read. Your challenge will be to determine what kinds of sources you need and to zero in on a reasonable number of quality sources, those truly worthy of your time and attention.

Later, once you have decided on some sources worth consulting, your challenge will be to read them with an open mind and a critical eye.

R2-a Determine how a source will contribute to your writing.

Before you even begin to research your topic, think about how the sources you encounter could help you make your argument. How you plan to use a source will affect how you will evaluate it. Not every source must directly support your thesis. Sources can have various functions in a paper. They can

- provide background information or context for your topic
- explain terms or concepts that your readers might not understand
- provide evidence for your argument
- lend authority to your argument
- offer counterevidence and alternative interpretations to your argument

For examples of how student writers use sources for a variety of purposes, see MLA-1c, APA-1c, and CMS-1c.

R2-b Select sources worth your time and attention.

The chart on page 324 shows how to refine your searches in the library's book catalogue, in databases, and in search engines. This section explains how to scan through the results for the most promising sources and how to preview them — without actually reading them — to see whether they are likely to live up to your expectations and meet your needs.

Scanning search results

You will need to use somewhat different strategies when scanning search results from a book catalogue, a database, and a Web search engine.

BOOK CATALOGUES The library's book catalogue usually gives you a fairly short list of hits. A book's title and date of publication will often be your first clues as to whether the book is worth consulting. If a title looks interesting, you can click on it for further information: the book's subject matter and its length, for example.

DATABASES Most databases, such as *ProQuest* and *LexisNexis*, list at least the following information, which can help you decide if a source is relevant, current, scholarly enough (see the chart on p. 336), and a suitable length for your purposes.

Title and brief description (How relevant?)

Date (How current?)

Name of periodical (How scholarly?)

Length (How extensive in coverage?)

At the bottom of this page are just a few of the hits Ned Bishop came up with when he consulted a general database for articles on the Fort Pillow massacre, using the search term *Fort Pillow*.

By scanning the titles, Bishop saw that only one contained the words *Fort Pillow*. This title and the name of the periodical, *Jour-*

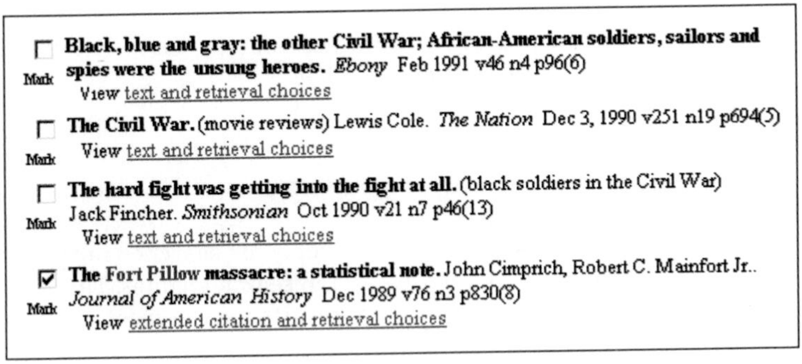

☐ Mark **Black, blue and gray: the other Civil War; African-American soldiers, sailors and spies were the unsung heroes.** *Ebony* Feb 1991 v46 n4 p96(6)
View text and retrieval choices

☐ Mark **The Civil War.** (movie reviews) Lewis Cole. *The Nation* Dec 3, 1990 v251 n19 p694(5)
View text and retrieval choices

☐ Mark **The hard fight was getting into the fight at all.** (black soldiers in the Civil War) Jack Fincher. *Smithsonian* Oct 1990 v21 n7 p46(13)
View text and retrieval choices

☑ Mark **The Fort Pillow massacre: a statistical note.** John Cimprich, Robert C. Mainfort Jr.. *Journal of American History* Dec 1989 v76 n3 p830(8)
View extended citation and retrieval choices

nal of American History, suggested that the source was scholarly. The 1989 publication date was not a problem, since currency is not necessarily a key issue for historical topics. The article's length (eight pages) is given in parentheses at the end of the citation. While the article may seem short, the topic — a statistical note — is narrow enough to ensure adequate depth of coverage. Bishop decided the article was worth consulting.

Bishop chose not to consult the other sources. The first is a brief article in a popular magazine, the second is a movie review, and the third surveys a topic that is far too broad, "black soldiers in the Civil War."

WEB SEARCH ENGINES Anyone can publish on the Web, and unreliable sites often masquerade as legitimate sources of information. As you scan through search results, look for the following clues about the probable relevance, currency, and reliability of a site — but be aware that the clues are by no means foolproof.

Title, keywords, and lead-in text (How relevant?)

A date (How current?)

An indication of the site's sponsor or purpose (How reliable?)

The URL, especially the domain name: .ca, .edu, .gov, or .org (How relevant? How reliable?)

The following are a few of the results that Luisa Mirano retrieved after typing the keywords *childhood obesity* into a search engine; she limited her search to works with those words in the title.

American **Obesity** Association - **Childhood Obesity**
Childhood Obesity. **Obesity** in **children** ... Note: The term "**childhood obesity**" may refer to both **children** and adolescents. In general, we ...
www.**obesity**.org/subs/**childhood**/ - 17k - Jan 8, 2005 - Cached - Similar pages

Childhood Obesity
KS Logo, **Childhood Obesity**. advertisement. Source. ERIC Clearinghouse on Teaching and Teacher Education. Contents. ... Back to the Top Causes of **Childhood Obesity**. ...
www.kidsource.com/kidsource/content2/**obesity**.html - 18k - Cached - Similar pages

Childhood Obesity, June 2002 Word on Health - National Institutes ...
Childhood Obesity on the Rise, an article in the June 2002 edition of The NIH Word on Health - Consumer Information Based on Research from the National ...
www.nih.gov/news/WordonHealth/ jun2002/**childhoodobesity**.htm - 22k - Cached - Similar pages

MayoClinic.com - **Childhood obesity**: Parenting advice
... **Childhood obesity**: Parenting advice By Mayo Clinic staff. ... Here are some other tips to help your **obese child** — and yourself: Be a positive role model. ...
www.mayoclinic.com/invoke.cfm?id=FL00058 - 42k - Jan 8, 2005 - Cached - Similar pages

Determining if a source is scholarly

For many college or university assignments, you will be asked to use scholarly sources. These are written by experts for a knowledgeable audience and usually go into more depth than books and articles written for a general audience. (Scholarly sources are sometimes called *refereed* or *peer-reviewed* because the work is evaluated by experts in the field before publication.) To determine if a source is scholarly, look for the following:

- Formal language and presentation
- Authors who are academics or scientists, not journalists
- Footnotes or a bibliography documenting the works cited by the author in the source
- Original research and interpretation (rather than a summary of other people's work)
- Quotations from and analysis of primary sources (in humanities disciplines such as literature, history, and philosophy)
- A description of research methods or a review of related research (in the sciences and social sciences)

NOTE: In some databases, searches can be limited to refereed or peer-reviewed journals.

Mirano found the first site, which was sponsored by a research-based organization, promising enough to explore for her paper. The second and fourth sites held less promise, because they seemed to offer popular rather than scholarly information. In addition, the *KidSource* site was populated by advertisements. Mirano rejected the third source not because of its reliability — in fact, research from the National Institutes of Health was what she was looking for — but because a quick skim of its contents revealed that the information was too general for her purposes.

Selecting appropriate versions of electronic sources

An electronic source may appear as an abstract, an excerpt, or a full-text article or book. It is important to distinguish among these versions and to use a complete source, preferably one with page numbers, for your research.

Abstracts and excerpts are shortened versions of complete works. An abstract — a summary of a work's contents — might ap-

DATABASE RECORD WITH AN ABSTRACT

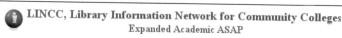

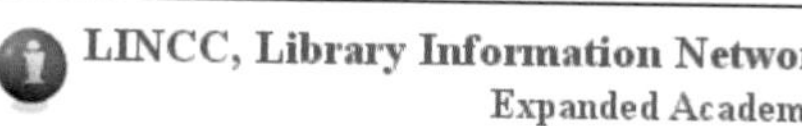
LINCC, Library Information Network for Community Colleges
Expanded Academic ASAP

— Article 1 of 2 —

☐ *Civil War History*, June 1996 v42 n2 p116(17)
Mark

"These devils are not fit to live on God's earth": war crimes and the Committee on the Conduct of the War, 1864-1865. *Bruce Tap.*

Abstract: The Committee on the Conduct of the War's report on the April 1864 Fort Pillow massacre of black Union soldiers by Confederate forces influenced public opinion against the atrocities of the Confederate troops and accelerated the reconstruction program. Hostility against blacks and abolition in the South prompted the Confederates to target black troops and deny them prisoner of war status. Investigation exposed the barbaric act and the Northern prisoners' suffering in Southern prisons. The report helped the inclusion of black troops in the prisoner exchange program.

Article A18749078

pear in a database record for a periodical article (see above) or in a catalogue listing for a book. An excerpt is the first few sentences or paragraphs (the *lead*) of a newspaper or magazine article and usually appears in a list of hits in an online search (see the example on p. 338). Abstracts or excerpts can give you clues about the usefulness of an article for your paper, but by themselves they do not contain enough information to cite. To understand an author's argument and use it in your own paper, you must track down and read the complete article. (See R1-c and R1-d.)

A full-text work may appear online as a PDF (for *portable document format*) file or as an HTML file (sometimes called a *text file*). A PDF file is usually an exact copy of the pages of a periodical article as they appeared in print, including the page numbers. Some corporate and government reports are presented online as PDF files, and these too are usually paginated. A full-text document that appears as an HTML or a text file is not paginated. If your source is available in both formats, choose the PDF file for your research because you will be able to cite specific page numbers.

SEARCH RESULT WITH AN EXCERPT

▾ **BOSTON GLOBE ARCHIVES**

Your search for **((fort AND pillow AND massacre))** returned **1** article(s) matching your terms. To purchase the full-text of an article, follow the link that says "Click for complete article."

| **Perform a new search** |

Your search results:

TALES OF BLACKS IN THE CIVIL WAR, FOR ALL AGES
Published on March 23, 1998
Author(s): Scott Alarik, Globe Correspondent

For African Americans, the Civil War was always two wars. It was, of course, the war to save the union and destroy slavery, but for the nearly 180,000 black soldiers who served in the Union Army, it was also a war to establish their rights as citizens and human beings in the United States. Their role in defeating the Confederacy is grandly chronicled in two new books, the massively complete "Like Men of War" and the superbly readable children's book "Black, Blue and
Click for complete article *(782 words)*

R2-c Read with an open mind and a critical eye.

As you begin reading the sources you have chosen, keep an open mind. Do not let your personal beliefs prevent you from listening to new ideas and opposing viewpoints. Your research question — not a snap judgment about the question — should guide your reading.

When you read critically, you are not necessarily judging an author's work harshly; you are simply examining its assumptions, assessing its evidence, and weighing its conclusions.

ACADEMIC ENGLISH When you research on the Web, it is easy to ignore views different from your own. Web pages that appeal to you will often link to other pages that support the same viewpoint. If your sources all seem to agree with you — and with one another — seek out opposing views and evaluate them with an open mind.

Distinguishing between primary and secondary sources

As you begin assessing evidence in a source, determine whether you are reading a primary or a secondary source. Primary sources are original documents such as letters, diaries, legislative bills, laboratory studies, field research reports, and eyewitness accounts. Secondary sources are commentaries on primary sources — another source's opinions about or interpretation of a primary source. A primary source for Ned Bishop was Nathan Bedford Forrest's official report on the battle at Fort Pillow. Bishop also consulted a number of secondary sources, some of which relied heavily on primary sources such as letters.

Although a primary source is not necessarily more reliable than a secondary source, it has the advantage of being a firsthand account. Naturally, you can better evaluate what a secondary source says if you have first read any primary sources it discusses.

Being alert for signs of bias

Both in print and online, some sources are more objective than others. If you were exploring the conspiracy theories surrounding John F. Kennedy's assassination, for example, you wouldn't look to a supermarket tabloid, such as the *National Enquirer*, for answers. Even publications that are considered reputable can be editorially biased. For example, *Canadian Business Magazine,* the *National Post,* and *Maclean's* are all credible sources, but they are also likely

Evaluating all sources

CHECKING FOR SIGNS OF BIAS

- Does the author or publisher have political leanings or religious views that could affect objectivity?
- Is the author or publisher associated with a special-interest group, such as Greenpeace or the National Firearms Association of Canada, that might see only one side of an issue?
- Are alternative views presented and addressed? How fairly does the author treat opposing views?
- Does the author's language show signs of bias?

ASSESSING AN ARGUMENT

- What is the author's central claim or thesis?
- How does the author support this claim — with relevant and sufficient evidence or with just a few anecdotes or emotional examples?
- Are statistics consistent with those you encounter in other sources? Have they been used fairly? Does the author explain where the statistics come from? (It is possible to "lie" with statistics by using them selectively or by omitting mathematical details.)
- Are any of the author's assumptions questionable?
- Does the author consider opposing arguments and refute them persuasively? (See A3-c.)
- Does the author fall prey to any logical fallacies? (See A3-a.)

Evaluating Web sources

AUTHORSHIP

- Does the Web site or document have an author? You may need to do some clicking and scrolling to find the author's name. If you have landed directly on an internal page of a site, for example, you may need to navigate to the home page or find an "about this site" link.
- If there is an author, can you tell whether he or she is knowledgeable and credible? When the author's qualifications aren't listed on the site itself, look for links to the author's home page, which may provide evidence of his or her interests and expertise.

SPONSORSHIP

- Who, if anyone, sponsors the site? The sponsor of a site is often named and described on the home page.
- What does the URL tell you? The URL ending often specifies the type of group hosting the site: commercial (.com), educational (.edu), nonprofit (.org), governmental (.gc), military (.mil), or network (.net). URLs may also indicate a country of origin: .uk (United Kingdom) or .ca (Canada), for instance.

PURPOSE AND AUDIENCE

- Why was the site created: To argue a position? To sell a product? To inform readers?
- Who is the site's intended audience? If you do not fit the audience profile, is information on the site still relevant to your topic?

CURRENCY

- How current is the site? Check for the date of publication or the latest update, often located at the bottom of the home page or at the beginning or end of an internal page.
- How current are the site's links? If many of the links no longer work, the site may be too dated for your purposes.

TIP: If the authorship and the sponsorship of a site are both unclear, think twice about using the site for your research.

TIP: To discover a site's sponsor, you may have to truncate, or shorten, the URL. For example, to find the sponsor of a Web site featuring an article on environmentally friendly neighbourhood development, you might need to shorten the full URL <http://www.eng.mcmaster.ca/civil/sustain/designparam/dparameters10.htm> to its base URL <http://www.eng.mcmaster.ca> to find that the sponsor is McMaster University Faculty of Engineering.

to interpret events quite differently from one another. If you are uncertain about a periodical's special interests, consult *Magazines for Libraries*. To check for bias in a book, see *Book Review Digest*. A reference librarian can help you locate these resources.

Like publishers, some authors are more objective than others. If you have reason to believe that a writer is particularly biased, you will want to assess his or her arguments with special care. For a list of questions worth asking, see the chart on page 339.

Assessing the author's argument

In nearly all subjects worth writing about, there is some element of argument, so don't be surprised to encounter experts who disagree. When you find areas of disagreement, you will want to read each source's arguments with special care, testing them with your own critical intelligence. For a list of questions worth asking, see the chart on page 339.

R2-d Assess Web sources with special care.

Web sources can be deceptive. Sophisticated-looking sites can be full of dubious information, and the identities of those who created a site are often hidden, along with their motives for having created it. Even hate sites may be cleverly disguised to look legitimate. In contrast, sites with reliable information can stand up to careful scrutiny. For a checklist on evaluating Web sources, see page 340.

In researching her topic on Internet surveillance and workplace privacy, Anna Orlov encountered sites that raised her suspicions. In particular, some sites were authored by surveillance software companies, which have an obvious interest in focusing on the benefits of such software to company management.

R3

Managing information; avoiding plagiarism

An effective researcher is a good record keeper. Whether you decide to keep records on paper or on your computer — or both — your challenge as a researcher will be to find systematic ways of managing information. More specifically, you will need methods for maintaining a working bibliography (see R3-a), keeping track of source materials (see R3-b), and taking notes without plagiarizing (stealing from) your sources (see R3-c).

R3-a Maintain a working bibliography.

Keep a record of any sources you decide to consult. You will need this record, called a *working bibliography*, when you compile the list of sources that will appear at the end of your paper. (The format of this list depends on the documentation style you are using. For MLA style, see MLA-4b; for APA style, see APA-4b; for *Chicago* style, see CMS-4c.) Your working bibliography will probably contain more sources than you will actually include in your list of works cited.

Most researchers print or save bibliographic information from the library's computer catalogue, its periodical databases, and the Web. The information you need to collect is given in the chart on page 343. If you download a visual, you must gather the same information as for a print source.

For Web sources, some bibliographic information may not be available, but spend time looking for it before assuming that it doesn't exist. When information isn't available on the home page, you may have to drill into the site, following links to interior pages. Look especially for the author's name, the date of publication (or latest update), and the name of any sponsoring organization. Do not omit such information unless it is genuinely unavailable.

Once you have created a working bibliography, you can annotate it. Writing several brief sentences summarizing key points of a source will help you to identify the source's role in your paper. Also, clarifying the source's ideas at this stage will help you avoid plagiarizing them later.

ON THE WEB > **dianahacker.com/writersref**
Model papers > Annotated bibliography (MLA)

R3-b Keep track of source materials.

The best way to keep track of source materials is to photocopy them or print them out. Many database subscription services will allow you to e-mail citations or full copies of articles to yourself. Some researchers choose to save these and online sources on a computer or disk.

Information for a working bibliography

FOR A BOOK

- All authors; any editors or translators
- Title and subtitle
- Edition (if not the first)
- Publication information: city, publisher, and date

FOR A PERIODICAL ARTICLE

- All authors of the article
- Title and subtitle of the article
- Title of the magazine, journal, or newspaper
- Date; volume, issue, and page numbers, if available

FOR A PERIODICAL ARTICLE RETRIEVED FROM A DATABASE (IN ADDITION TO PRECEDING INFORMATION)

- Name of the database and an item number, if available
- Name of the subscription service
- URL of the subscription service (for an online database)
- Library where you retrieved the source
- Date you retrieved the source

NOTE: Use particular care when printing or saving articles in PDF files. These may not include some of the elements you need to cite the electronic source properly.

FOR A WEB SOURCE (INCLUDING VISUALS)

- All authors, editors, or creators of the source
- Editor or compiler of the Web site, if there is one
- Title and subtitle of the source and title of the longer work, if applicable
- Title of the site, if available
- Publication information for the source, if available
- Page or paragraph numbers, if any
- Date of online publication (or latest update), if available
- Sponsor of the site
- Date you accessed the source
- The site's URL

NOTE: For the exact bibliographic format to use in the final paper, see MLA-4b, APA-4b, or CMS-4c.

Working with photocopies, printouts, and electronic files — as opposed to relying on memory or hastily written notes — has several benefits. You save time spent in the library. You can highlight key passages, perhaps even colour-coding them to reflect topics in your outline. You can annotate the source in the margins and get a head start on note taking. Finally, you reduce the chances of unintentional plagiarism, since you will be able to compare your use of a source in your paper with the actual source, not just with your notes (see R3-c).

NOTE: It's especially important to keep print or electronic copies of Web sources, which may change or even become inaccessible. Make sure that your copy includes the site's URL and your date of access, information needed for your list of works cited.

R3-c As you take notes, avoid unintentional plagiarism.

When you take notes and jot down ideas, be very careful not to borrow language from your sources. Even if you half-copy the author's sentences — either by mixing the author's phrases with your own without using quotation marks or by plugging your synonyms into the author's sentence structure — you are committing plagiarism, a serious academic offence. (For examples of this kind of plagiarism, see MLA-2, APA-2, and CMS-2.)

To prevent unintentional borrowing, resist the temptation to look at the source as you take notes — except when you are quoting. Keep the source close by so you can check for accuracy, but don't try to put ideas in your own words with the source's sentences in front of you. When you need to quote the exact words of a source, make sure you copy the words precisely and put quotation marks around them.

ACADEMIC ENGLISH Even when you are in the early stages of note taking, it is important to keep in mind that, in Canada, written texts are considered to be an author's property. (This "property" isn't a physical object, so it is often referred to as *intellectual property*.) The author (or publisher) owns the language as well as any original ideas contained in the writing, whether the source is published in print or electronic form. When you use another author's property in your own writing, you are required to follow certain conventions or risk committing the ethical and legal offence known as *plagiarism*.

There are three kinds of note taking: summarizing, paraphrasing, and quoting. Be sure to include exact page references for all three types of notes, since you will need the page numbers later if you use the information in your paper.

Summarizing without plagiarizing

A summary condenses information, perhaps reducing a chapter to a short paragraph or a paragraph to a single sentence. A summary should be written in your own words; if you use phrases from the source, put them in quotation marks.

Here is a passage from an original source read by student John Garcia in researching a paper on mountain lions. Following the passage is Garcia's summary of the source.

ORIGINAL SOURCE

> In some respects, the increasing frequency of mountain lion encounters in California has as much to do with a growing *human* population as it does with rising mountain lion numbers. The scenic solitude of the western ranges is prime cougar habitat, and it is falling swiftly to the developer's spade. Meanwhile, with their ideal habitat already at its carrying capacity, mountain lions are forcing younger cats into less suitable terrain, including residential areas. Add that cougars have generally grown bolder under a lengthy ban on their being hunted, and an unsettling scenario begins to emerge.
>
> — Ray Rychnovsky, "Clawing into Controversy," p. 40

SUMMARY

> Source: Rychnovsky, "Clawing into Controversy" (40)
>
> Encounters between mountain lions and humans are on the rise in California because increasing numbers of lions are competing for a shrinking habitat. As the lions' wild habitat shrinks, older lions force younger lions into residential areas. These lions have lost some of their fear of humans because of a ban on hunting.

Paraphrasing without plagiarizing

Like a summary, a paraphrase is written in your own words; but whereas a summary reports significant information in fewer words than the source, a paraphrase retells the information in roughly the same number of words. If you retain occasional choice phrases from the source, use quotation marks so you will know later which phrases are not your own.

As you read the following paraphrase of the original source (see p. 345), notice that the language is significantly different from that in the original.

PARAPHRASE

> Source: Rychnovsky, "Clawing into Controversy" (40)
>
> Californians are encountering mountain lions more frequently because increasing numbers of humans and a rising population of lions are competing for the same territory. Humans have moved into mountainous regions once dominated by the lions, and the wild habitat that is left cannot sustain the current lion population. Therefore, the older lions are forcing younger lions into residential areas. And because of a ban on hunting, these younger lions have become bolder — less fearful of encounters with humans.

Using quotation marks to avoid plagiarizing

A quotation consists of the exact words from a source. In your notes, put all quoted material in quotation marks; do not assume that you will remember later which words, phrases, and passages you have quoted and which are your own. When you quote, be sure to copy the words of your source exactly, including punctuation and capitalization. In the following example, John Garcia quotes from the original source on page 345.

QUOTATION

> Source: Rychnovsky, "Clawing into Controversy" (40)
>
> Rychnovsky explains that as humans expand residential areas into mountain ranges, the cougar's natural habitat "is falling swiftly to the developer's spade."

Avoiding Internet plagiarism

Understand what plagiarism is. When you use another author's intellectual property — language, visuals, or ideas — in your own writing without giving proper credit, you commit a kind of academic theft called *plagiarism.*

Treat Web sources in the same way you treat print sources. Any language that you find on the Internet must be carefully cited, even if the material is in the public domain or is publicly accessible on free sites. When you use material from Web sites authored by federal, provincial or territorial, or municipal governments and by nonprofit organizations, you must acknowledge that material, too, as intellectual property owned by those agencies.

Keep track of which words come from sources and which are your own. To prevent unintentional plagiarism when you copy passages from Web sources to an electronic file, put quotation marks around any text that you have inserted into your own work. In addition, during note taking and drafting, you might use a different colour font or your word processor's highlighting feature to indicate text taken from sources — so that source material stands out unmistakably as someone else's writing.

Avoid Web sites that bill themselves as "research services" and sell essays. When you use Web search engines to research a topic, you will often see links to sites that appear to offer legitimate writing support but that actually sell term papers. Of course, submitting a paper that you have purchased is cheating, but even using material from one counts as plagiarizing.

R4

Choosing a documentation style

The various academic disciplines use their own editorial style for citing sources and for listing the works that are cited in a paper. *A Canadian Writer's Reference* describes three commonly used styles: MLA (Modern Language Association), APA (American Psychological Association), and CMS (*Chicago Manual of Style*). See the appropriate tabbed section for each style. For a list of style manuals in a variety of disciplines, see R4-b.

R4-a Select a style appropriate for your discipline.

In researched writing, sources are cited for several reasons. First, it is important to acknowledge the contributions of others. If you fail to credit sources properly, you commit plagiarism, a serious academic offence. Second, choosing good sources will add credibility to your work; in a sense, you are calling on authorities to serve as expert witnesses. The more care you have taken in choosing reliable sources, the stronger your argument will be. Finally — and most importantly — you are helping to build knowledge by showing readers where they can pursue your topic in greater depth.

All of the academic disciplines cite sources for these same reasons. However, the different styles for citing sources are based on the values and intellectual goals of scholars in different disciplines.

MLA and APA in-text citations

The Modern Language Association (MLA) style and the American Psychological Association (APA) style both use citations in the text of a paper that refer to a list of works at the end of the paper. The systems work somewhat differently, however, because MLA style was created for scholars in English composition and literature, and APA style was created for researchers in the social sciences.

MLA IN-TEXT CITATION

Brandon Conran argues that the story is written from "a bifocal point of view" (111).

APA IN-TEXT CITATION

As researchers Yanovski and Yanovski (2002) have explained, obesity was once considered "either a moral failing or evidence of underlying psychopathology" (p. 592).

While MLA and APA styles work in a similar way, some basic disciplinary differences show up in these key elements:

- author's name
- date of publication
- page numbers
- verb tense in signal phrases

MLA style, which gives the author's full name on first mention, reflects the respect that English scholars have for authors of written words. APA style usually uses last names only, not out of disrespect but to emphasize the objectivity of scientific inquiry. APA style, which gives a date after the author's name, reflects the social scientist's concern with the currency of experimental results. MLA style omits the date in the text citation because English scholars are less concerned with currency; what someone had to say a century ago may be as significant as the latest contribution to the field.

Both styles include page numbers for quotations. MLA style requires page numbers for summaries and paraphrases as well; with a page number, readers can easily find the exact passage that has been summarized or paraphrased. While APA does not require page numbers for summaries and paraphrases, it recommends that writers use a page number if doing so would help readers find the passage in a longer work.

Finally, MLA style uses the present tense (such as *argues*) to introduce cited material, whereas APA style uses the past or present perfect tense (such as *argued* or *have argued*). The present tense evokes the timelessness of a literary text; the past or present perfect tense emphasizes that an experiment was conducted in the past.

CMS footnotes or endnotes

Most historians and many scholars in the humanities use the style of footnotes or endnotes recommended by *The Chicago Manual of Style* (CMS). Historians base their work on a wide variety of primary and secondary sources, all of which must be cited. The CMS note system has the virtue of being relatively unobtrusive; even when a paper or an article is thick with citations, readers will not be overwhelmed. In the text of the paper, only a raised number appears. Readers who are interested can consult the accompanying numbered note, which is given either at the foot of the page or at the end of the paper.

TEXT

Historian Albert Castel quotes several eyewitnesses on both the Union and the Confederate sides as saying that Forrest ordered his men to stop firing.[7]

NOTE

7. Albert Castel, "The Fort Pillow Massacre: A Fresh Examination of the Evidence," *Civil War History* 4, no. 1 (1958): 44–45.

The CMS system gives as much information as the MLA or APA system, but less of that information appears in the text of the paper.

R4-b If necessary, consult a style manual.

Following is a list of style manuals used in a variety of disciplines.

BIOLOGY (See <http://dianahacker.com/resdoc> for more information.)

Council of Science Editors. *Scientific Style and Format: The CSE Manual for Authors, Editors, and Publishers.* 7th ed. Reston: Council of Science Eds., 2006.

BUSINESS

Translation Bureau of Public Works and Government Services Canada. *The Canadian Style: A Guide to Writing and Editing.* 2nd ed. Toronto: Dundurn, 1997.

CHEMISTRY

Dodd, Janet S., ed. *The ACS Style Guide: A Manual for Authors and Editors.* 2nd ed. Washington: Amer. Chemical Soc., 1997.

ENGINEERING

Institute of Electrical and Electronics Engineers. *IEEE Standards Style Manual*. Rev. ed. New York: IEEE, 2005 <http://standards.ieee.org/guides/style/2005Style.pdf>.

ENGLISH AND THE HUMANITIES (See MLA-1 to MLA-5.)

Gibaldi, Joseph. *MLA Handbook for Writers of Research Papers.* 6th ed. New York: MLA, 2003.

GEOLOGY

Bates, Robert L., Rex Buchanan, and Marla Adkins-Heljeson, eds. *Geowriting: A Guide to Writing, Editing, and Printing in Earth Science.* 5th ed. Alexandria: Amer. Geological Inst., 1995.

GOVERNMENT DOCUMENTS

Statistics Canada. *How to Cite Statistics Canada Products.* Updated ed. Ottawa: Statistics Canada, 2006 <http://www.statcan.ca/english/freepub/12-591-XIE/12-591-XIE2006001.htm>.

United States Government Printing Office. *Style Manual.* Washington: GPO, 2000.

HISTORY (See CMS-1 to CMS-5.)

The Chicago Manual of Style. 15th ed. Chicago: U of Chicago P, 2003.

JOURNALISM

Tasko, Patti, ed. *The Canadian Press Stylebook.* 14th ed. Toronto: Canadian Press, 1989.

LAW

McGill Law Journal. *Canadian Guide to Uniform Legal Citation.* 6th ed. Toronto: Carswell, 2006.

LINGUISTICS

Linguistic Society of America. "LSA Style Sheet." Published annually in the December issue of the *LSA Bulletin.*

MATHEMATICS

American Mathematical Society. *Author Resource Center* <http://www.ams.org/authors>.

MEDICINE

Iverson, Cheryl, et al. *American Medical Association Manual of Style: A Guide for Authors and Editors.* 9th ed. Baltimore: Williams, 1998.

MUSIC

Holoman, D. Kern, ed. *Writing about Music: A Style Sheet from the Editors of* 19th-Century Music. Berkeley: U of California P, 1988.

PHYSICS

American Institute of Physics. *Style Manual: Instructions to Authors and Volume Editors for the Preparation of AIP Book Manuscripts.* 5th ed. New York: AIP, 1995.

POLITICAL SCIENCE

American Political Science Association. *Style Manual for Political Science.* Rev. ed. Washington: APSA, 2001.

PSYCHOLOGY AND OTHER SOCIAL SCIENCES (See APA-1 to APA-5.)

American Psychological Association. *Publication Manual of the American Psychological Association.* 5th ed. Washington: APA, 2001.

SCIENCE AND TECHNICAL WRITING

American National Standards Institute. *American National Standard for the Preparation of Scientific Papers for Written or Oral Presentation.* New York: ANSI, 1979.

Microsoft Corporation. *Microsoft Manual of Style for Technical Publications.* 3rd ed. Redmond: Microsoft, 2004.

Rubens, Philip, ed. *Science and Technical Writing: A Manual of Style.* 2nd ed. New York: Routledge, 2001.

SOCIAL WORK

National Association of Social Workers. *Writing for the NASW Press: Information for Authors* <http://naswpress.org/resources/tools/01-write/guidelines_toc.htm>.

MLA

MLA Papers

MLA
MLA Papers

MLA Papers

Most English instructors and some humanities instructors will ask you to document your sources with the Modern Language Association (MLA) system of citations described in MLA-4. When writing an MLA paper that is based on sources, you face three main challenges: (1) supporting a thesis, (2) citing your sources and avoiding plagiarism, and (3) integrating quotations and other source material.

Examples in this tabbed section are drawn from research a student conducted on online monitoring of employees' computer use. Anna Orlov's research paper, which argues that electronic surveillance in the workplace threatens employees' privacy and autonomy, appears on pages 408–12.

MLA-1

Supporting a thesis

Most research assignments ask you to form a thesis, or main idea, and to support that thesis with well-organized evidence.

MLA-1a Form a tentative thesis.

Once you have read a variety of sources and considered all sides of your issue, you are ready to form a tentative thesis: a one-sentence (or occasionally a two-sentence) statement of your central idea (see C2-a). In a research paper, your thesis will answer the central research question you posed earlier (see R1-a). Here, for example, are Anna Orlov's research question and her tentative thesis statement.

ORLOV'S RESEARCH QUESTION

Should employers monitor their employees' online activities in the workplace?

ORLOV'S TENTATIVE THESIS

Employers should not monitor their employees' online activities because electronic surveillance can compromise workers' privacy.

After you have written a rough draft and perhaps done more reading, you may decide to revise your tentative thesis, as did Orlov.

ORLOV'S REVISED THESIS

Although companies often have legitimate concerns that lead them to monitor employees' Internet usage--from expensive security breaches to reduced productivity--the benefits of electronic surveillance are outweighed by its costs to employees' privacy and autonomy.

The thesis usually appears at the end of the introductory paragraph. To read Anna Orlov's thesis in the context of her introduction, see page 408.

ON THE WEB > **dianahacker.com/writersref**
Research exercises > E-ex MLA 1–1

MLA-1b Organize your evidence.

The body of your paper will consist of evidence in support of your thesis. Instead of getting tangled up in a complex, formal outline, sketch an informal plan that organizes your ideas in bold strokes. Anna Orlov, for example, used this simple plan to outline the structure of her argument:

- Electronic surveillance allows employers to monitor workers more efficiently than older types of surveillance.
- Some experts have argued that companies have important financial and legal reasons to monitor employees' Internet usage.
- But monitoring employees' Internet usage may lower worker productivity when the threat to privacy creates distrust.
- Current laws do little to protect employees' privacy rights, so employees and employers have to negotiate the potential risks and benefits of electronic surveillance.

After you have written a rough draft, a more formal outline can be a useful way to shape the complexities of your argument. See C1-d for an example.

MLA-1c Use sources to inform and support your argument.

Used thoughtfully, the source materials you have gathered will make your argument more complex and convincing for readers.

Sources can play several different roles as you develop your points.

Providing background information or context

You can use facts and statistics to support generalizations or to establish the importance of your topic, as student writer Anna Orlov does in her introduction.

> As the Internet has become an integral tool of businesses, company policies on Internet usage have become as common as policies regarding vacation days or sexual harassment. A 2005 study by the American Management Association and ePolicy Institute found that 76% of companies monitor employees' use of the Web, and the number of companies that block employees' access to certain Web sites has increased 27% since 2001 (1).

Explaining terms or concepts

If readers are unlikely to be familiar with a word, a phrase, or an idea important to your topic, you must explain it for them. Quoting or paraphrasing a source can help you define terms and concepts in neutral, accessible language.

> One popular monitoring method is keystroke logging, which is done by means of an undetectable program on employees' computers. . . . As Lane explains, these programs record every key entered into the computer in hidden directories that can later be accessed or uploaded by supervisors; at their most sophisticated, the programs can even scan for keywords tailored to individual companies (128-29).

Supporting your claims

As you draft your argument, make sure to back up your assertions with facts, examples, and other evidence from your research (see also A2-e). Orlov, for example, uses an anecdote from one of her sources to support her claim that limiting computer access causes resentment among a company's staff.

> Monitoring online activities can have the unintended effect of making employees resentful. . . . Kesan warns that "prohibiting personal use can seem extremely arbitrary and can seriously harm morale. . . . Imagine a concerned parent who is prohibited from checking on a sick child by a draconian company policy" (315-16). As this analysis indicates, employees can become disgruntled when Internet usage policies are enforced to their full extent.

Lending authority to your argument

Expert opinion can give weight to your argument (see also A2-e). But don't rely on experts to make your argument for you. Construct your argument in your own words and, when appropriate, cite the judgment of an authority in the field to support your position.

> Additionally, many experts disagree with employers' assumption that online monitoring can increase productivity. Employment law attorney Joseph G. Schmitt argues that, particularly for employees who are paid a salary rather than by the hour, "a company shouldn't care whether employees spend one or 10 hours on the Internet as long as they are getting their jobs done--and provided that they are not accessing inappropriate sites" (qtd. in Verespej).

Anticipating and countering objections

Do not ignore sources that seem contrary to your position or that offer arguments different from your own. Instead, use them to give voice to opposing points of view and to state potential objections to your argument before you counter them (see A-2f). Anna Orlov, for example, cites conflicting evidence to acknowledge that readers may disagree with her position that online monitoring is bad for businesses.

> On the one hand, computers and Internet access give employees powerful tools to carry out their jobs; on the other hand, the same technology offers constant temptations to avoid work. As a 2005 study by Salary.com and America Online indicates, the Internet ranked as the top choice among employees for ways of wasting time on the job; it beat talking with co-workers--the second most popular method--by a margin of nearly two to one (Frauenheim).

MLA-2

Citing sources; avoiding plagiarism

Your research paper is a collaboration between you and your sources. To be fair and ethical, you must acknowledge your debt to the writers of those sources. If you don't, you commit plagiarism, a serious academic offence.

Three different acts are considered plagiarism: (1) failing to cite quotations and borrowed ideas, (2) failing to enclose borrowed language in quotation marks, and (3) failing to put summaries and paraphrases in your own words.

MLA-2a Cite quotations and borrowed ideas.

You must of course cite all direct quotations. You must also cite any ideas borrowed from a source: summaries and paraphrases; statistics and other specific facts; and visuals such as cartoons, graphs, and diagrams.

The only exception is common knowledge — information your readers could easily find in any number of general sources. For example, it is well known that Vincent Lam won the Giller Prize in 2006 and that Emily Dickinson published only a handful of her many poems during her lifetime.

As a rule, when you have seen information repeatedly in your reading, you don't need to cite it. However, when information has appeared in only one or two sources or when it is controversial, you should cite the source. If a topic is new to you and you are not sure what is considered common knowledge or what is controversial, ask someone with expertise. When in doubt, cite the source.

The Modern Language Association recommends a system of in-text citations. Here, briefly, is how the MLA citation system usually works:

1. The source is introduced by a signal phrase that names its author.
2. The material being cited is followed by a page number in parentheses.
3. At the end of the paper, a list of works cited (arranged alphabetically according to authors' last names) gives complete publication information about the source.

IN-TEXT CITATION

Legal scholar Jay Kesan points out that the law holds employers liable for employees' actions such as violations of copyright laws, the distribution of offensive or graphic sexual material, and illegal disclosure of confidential information (312).

ENTRY IN THE LIST OF WORKS CITED

Kesan, Jay P. "Cyber-Working or Cyber-Shirking? A First Principles Examination of Electronic Privacy in the Workplace." Florida Law Review 54 (2002): 289-332.

Handling an MLA citation is not always this simple. For a detailed discussion of possible variations, see MLA-4.

MLA-2b Enclose borrowed language in quotation marks.

To indicate that you are using a source's exact phrases or sentences, you must enclose them in quotation marks unless they have been set off from the text by indenting (see p. 364). To omit the quotation marks is to claim — falsely — that the language is your own. Such an omission is plagiarism even if you have cited the source.

ORIGINAL SOURCE

> Without adequate discipline, the World Wide Web can be a tremendous time sink; no other medium comes close to matching the Internet's depth of materials, interactivity, and sheer distractive potential.
>
> — Frederick Lane, *The Naked Employee*, p. 142

PLAGIARISM

Frederick Lane points out that if people do not have adequate discipline, the World Wide Web can be a tremendous time sink; no other medium comes close to matching the Internet's depth of materials, interactivity, and sheer distractive potential (142).

BORROWED LANGUAGE IN QUOTATION MARKS

Frederick Lane points out that for those not exercising self-control, "the World Wide Web can be a tremendous time sink; no other medium comes close to matching the Internet's depth of materials, interactivity, and sheer distractive potential" (142).

MLA-2c Put summaries and paraphrases in your own words.

A summary condenses information from a source; a paraphrase repeats the information in about the same number of words. When you summarize or paraphrase, it is not enough to name the source; you must restate the source's meaning using your own language. (See also R3-c.) You commit plagiarism if you half-copy the author's sentences — either by mixing the author's phrases with your own without using quotation marks or by plugging your synonyms into the author's sentence structure.

The first paraphrase of the following source is plagiarized—even though the source is cited—because too much of its language is borrowed from the original. The underlined strings of words have been copied word-for-word (without quotation marks). In addition, the writer has closely echoed the sentence structure of the source, merely substituting some synonyms (*restricted* for *limited, modern era* for *computer age, monitoring* for *surveillance,* and *inexpensive* for *cheap*).

ORIGINAL SOURCE

In earlier times, surveillance was limited to the information that a supervisor could observe and record firsthand and to primitive counting devices. In the computer age surveillance can be instantaneous, unblinking, cheap, and, maybe most importantly, easy.

—Carl Botan and Mihaela Vorvoreanu, "What Do Employees Think about Electronic Surveillance at Work?" p. 126

PLAGIARISM: UNACCEPTABLE BORROWING

Scholars Carl Botan and Mihaela Vorvoreanu argue that in earlier times monitoring of employees was restricted to the information that a supervisor could observe and record firsthand. In the modern era, monitoring can be instantaneous, inexpensive, and, most importantly, easy (126).

To avoid plagiarizing an author's language, resist the temptation to look at the source while you are summarizing or paraphrasing. Close the book, write from memory, and then open the book to check for accuracy. This technique prevents you from being captivated by the words on the page.

ACCEPTABLE PARAPHRASE

Scholars Carl Botan and Mihaela Vorvoreanu claim that the nature of workplace surveillance has changed over time. Before the arrival of computers, managers could collect only small amounts of information about their employees based on what they saw or heard. However, because computers are now standard workplace technology, employers can monitor employees efficiently (126).

ON THE WEB > **dianahacker.com/writersref**
Research exercises > E-ex MLA 2–1 through MLA 2–6

MLA-3

Integrating sources

Quotations, summaries, paraphrases, and facts will help you make your argument, but they cannot speak for you. You can use several strategies to integrate information from research sources into your paper while maintaining your own voice.

MLA-3a Limit your use of quotations.

Using quotations appropriately

Although it is tempting to insert many quotations in your paper and to use your own words only for connecting passages, do not quote excessively. It is almost impossible to integrate numerous long quotations smoothly into your own text.

Except for the following legitimate uses of quotations, use your own words to summarize and paraphrase your sources and to explain your own ideas.

WHEN TO USE QUOTATIONS

- When language is especially vivid or expressive
- When exact wording is needed for technical accuracy
- When it is important to let the debaters of an issue explain their positions in their own words
- When the words of an important authority lend weight to an argument
- When language of a source is the topic of your discussion (as in an analysis or interpretation)

It is not always necessary to quote full sentences from a source. To reduce your reliance on the words of others, you can often integrate language from a source into your own sentence structure. (For the use of signal phrases in integrating quotations, see MLA-3b.)

> Kizza and Ssanyu observe that technology in the workplace has been accompanied by "an array of problems that needed quick answers" such as electronic monitoring to prevent security breaches (4).

Using the ellipsis mark and brackets

Two useful marks of punctuation, the ellipsis mark and brackets, allow you to keep quoted material to a minimum and to integrate it smoothly into your text.

THE ELLIPSIS MARK To condense a quoted passage, you can use the ellipsis mark (three periods, with spaces between) to indicate that you have omitted words. What remains must be grammatically complete.

> Lane acknowledges the legitimate reasons that many companies have for monitoring their employees' online activities, particularly management's concern about preventing "the theft of information that can be downloaded to a . . . disk, e-mailed to oneself . . . , or even posted to a Web page for the entire world to see" (12).

The writer has omitted from the source the words *floppy or Zip* before *disk* and *or a confederate* after *oneself*.

On the rare occasions when you want to omit one or more full sentences, use a period before the three ellipsis dots.

> Charles Lewis, director of the Center for Public Integrity, points out that "by 1987, employers were administering nearly 2,000,000 polygraph tests a year to job applicants and employees. . . . Millions of workers were required to produce urine samples under observation for drug testing . . ." (22).

Ordinarily, do not use an ellipsis mark at the beginning or at the end of a quotation. Your readers will understand that the quoted material is taken from a longer passage, so such marks are not necessary. The only exception occurs when words have been dropped at the end of the final quoted sentence. In such cases, put three ellipsis dots before the closing quotation mark and parenthetical reference, as in the previous example.

Do not use an ellipsis mark to distort the meaning of your source.

BRACKETS Brackets allow you to insert your own words into quoted material. You can insert words in brackets to explain a confusing reference or to keep a sentence grammatical in your context.

> Legal scholar Jay Kesan notes that "a decade ago, losses [from employees' computer crimes] were already mounting to five billion dollars annually" (311).

To indicate an error such as a misspelling in a quotation, insert [sic] after the error.

> Johnson argues that "while online monitoring is often imagined as harmles [sic], the practice may well threaten employees' rights to privacy" (14).

Setting off long quotations

When you quote more than four typed lines of prose or more than three lines of poetry, set off the quotation by indenting it 1 inch (2.5 cm or ten spaces) from the left margin.

Long quotations should be introduced by an informative sentence, usually followed by a colon. Quotation marks are unnecessary because the indented format tells readers that the words are taken word-for-word from the source.

> Botan and Vorvoreanu examine the role of gender in company practices of electronic surveillance:
>
> > There has never been accurate documentation of the extent of gender differences in surveillance, but by the middle 1990s, estimates of the proportion of surveilled employees that were women ranged from 75% to 85%. . . . Ironically, this gender imbalance in workplace surveillance may be evening out today because advances in surveillance technology are making surveillance of traditionally male dominated fields, such as long-distance truck driving, cheap, easy, and frequently unobtrusive. (127)

Notice that at the end of an indented quotation the parenthetical citation goes outside the final mark of punctuation. (When a quotation is run into your text, the opposite is true. See the sample citations on p. 363.)

MLA-3b Use signal phrases to integrate sources.

Whenever you include a paraphrase, summary, or direct quotation of another writer in your paper, prepare your readers for it with an introduction called a *signal phrase.* A signal phrase names the author of the source and often provides some context for the source material.

Using signal phrases in MLA papers

To avoid monotony, try to vary both the language and the placement of your signal phrases.

Model signal phrases

In the words of researchers Greenfield and Davis, ". . ."

As legal scholar Jay Kesan has noted, ". . ."

The ePolicy Institute, an organization that advises companies about reducing risks from technology, reported that ". . ."

". . . ," writes Daniel Tynan, ". . ."

". . . ," claims attorney Schmitt.

Kizza and Ssanyu offer a persuasive counterargument: ". . ."

Verbs in signal phrases

acknowledges	comments	endorses	reasons
adds	compares	grants	refutes
admits	confirms	illustrates	rejects
agrees	contends	implies	reports
argues	declares	insists	responds
asserts	denies	notes	suggests
believes	disputes	observes	thinks
claims	emphasizes	points out	writes

When you write a signal phrase, choose a verb that is appropriate for the way you are using the source (see MLA-1c). Are you providing background, explaining a concept, supporting a claim, lending authority, or refuting a belief? See the chart at the top of this page for a list of verbs commonly used in signal phrases. Note that MLA style calls for present-tense verbs (*argues*) to introduce source material unless a date specifies the time of writing.

Marking boundaries

Readers need to move from your words to the words of a source without feeling a jolt. Avoid dropping quotations into the text without warning. Instead, provide clear signal phrases, including at least the author's name, to indicate the boundary between your words and the source's words.

DROPPED QUOTATION

Some experts have argued that a range of legitimate concerns justifies employer monitoring of employee Internet usage. "Employees could accidentally (or deliberately) spill confidential corporate information . . . or allow worms to spread throughout a corporate network" (Tynan).

QUOTATION WITH SIGNAL PHRASE

Some experts have argued that a range of legitimate concerns justifies employer monitoring of employee Internet usage. As PC World columnist Daniel Tynan explains, companies that don't monitor network traffic can be penalized for their ignorance: "Employees could accidentally (or deliberately) spill confidential information . . . or allow worms to spread throughout a corporate network."

Establishing authority

Good research writing uses evidence from reliable sources. The first time you mention a source, briefly include the author's title, credentials, or experience — anything that would help your readers recognize the source's authority.

SOURCE WITH NO CREDENTIALS

Jay Kesan points out that the law holds employers liable for employees' actions such as violations of copyright laws, the distribution of offensive or graphic sexual material, and illegal disclosure of confidential information (312).

SOURCE WITH CREDENTIALS

Legal scholar Jay Kesan points out that the law holds employers liable for employees' actions such as violations of copyright laws, the distribution of offensive or graphic sexual material, and illegal disclosure of confidential information (312).

When you establish your source's authority, as with the phrase *Legal scholar* in the previous example, you also signal to readers your own credibility as a responsible researcher, one who has located trustworthy sources.

Introducing summaries and paraphrases

Introduce most summaries and paraphrases with a signal phrase that names the author and places the material in the context of your argument. Readers will then understand that everything between the signal phrase and the parenthetical citation summarizes or paraphrases the cited source.

Without the signal phrase (underlined) in the following example, readers might think that only the quotation at the end is being cited, when in fact the whole paragraph is based on the source.

> <u>Frederick Lane believes that</u> the personal computer has posed new challenges for employers worried about workplace productivity. Whereas early desktop computers were primitive enough to prevent employees from using them to waste time, the machines have become so sophisticated that they now make non-work-related computer activities easy and inviting. Many employees enjoy adjusting and readjusting features of their computers, from the desktop wallpaper to software they can quickly download. Many workers spend considerable company time playing games on their computers. But perhaps most problematic from the employer's point of view, Lane asserts, is giving employees access to the Internet, "roughly the equivalent of installing a gazillion-channel television set for each employee" (15-16).

There are times when a summary or paraphrase does not require a signal phrase. Readers will understand, for example, that the citation at the end of the following passage applies to the entire paragraph, not just part of it.

> In 2005, the American Management Association and the ePolicy Institute cosponsored a survey on electronic surveillance in the workplace, including the monitoring of employees' use of e-mail, instant messaging, the Web, and voice mail. The organizations received responses to a detailed questionnaire from 526 companies, with nearly half of the respondents representing companies employing up to five hundred workers (12).

Putting direct quotations in context

Because a source cannot reveal its meaning or function by itself, you must make the connection between a source and your own ideas. A signal phrase can show readers how a quotation supports or challenges a point you are making.

Efforts by the music industry to stop Internet file sharing have been unsuccessful and, worse, divisive. Industry analysts share this view. Salon's Scott Rosenberg, for example, writes that the only thing the music industry's "legal strategy has accomplished is to radicalize the community of online music fans and accelerate the process of technological change" (2).

Readers should not have to guess why a quotation appears in your paper. If you use another writer's words, you must explain how they contribute to your point. It's a good idea to embed a quotation — especially a long one — between sentences of your own. In addition to introducing it with a signal phrase, follow it with interpretive comments that link the quotation to your paper's argument.

QUOTATION WITH INSUFFICIENT CONTEXT

The difference, Lane argues, between these old methods of data gathering and electronic surveillance involves quantity:

> Technology makes it possible for employers to gather enormous amounts of data about employees, often far beyond what is necessary to satisfy safety or productivity concerns. And the trends that drive technology--faster, smaller, cheaper--make it possible for larger and larger numbers of employers to gather ever-greater amounts of personal data. (3-4)

QUOTATION WITH EFFECTIVE CONTEXT

The difference, Lane argues, between these old methods of data gathering and electronic surveillance involves quantity:

> Technology makes it possible for employers to gather enormous amounts of data about employees, often far beyond what is necessary to satisfy safety or productivity concerns. And the trends that drive technology--faster, smaller, cheaper--make it possible for larger and larger numbers of employers to gather ever-greater amounts of personal data. (3-4)

Lane points out that employers can collect data whenever employees use their computers--for example, when they send e-mail, surf the Web, or even arrive at or depart from their workstations.

Integrating statistics and other facts

When you are citing a statistic or other specific fact, a signal phrase is often not necessary. In most cases, readers will understand that the citation refers to the statistic or fact (not the whole paragraph).

> According to a 2002 survey, 60% of responding companies reported disciplining employees who had used the Internet in ways the companies deemed inappropriate; 30% had fired their employees for those transgressions (Greenfield and Davis 347).

There is nothing wrong, however, with using a signal phrase to introduce a statistic or other fact.

ON THE WEB > **dianahacker.com/writersref**
Research exercises > E-ex MLA 3–1 through MLA 3–4

Reviewing an MLA paper: Use of sources

Use of quotations

- Is quoted material enclosed within quotation marks (unless it has been set off from the text)? (See MLA-2b.)
- Is quoted language word-for-word accurate? If not, do brackets or ellipsis marks indicate the changes or omissions? (See pp. 363–64.)
- Does a clear signal phrase (usually naming the author) prepare readers for each quotation and for the purpose the quotation serves? (See MLA-3b.)
- Does a parenthetical citation follow each quotation? (See MLA-4a.)
- Is each quotation put in context? (See pp. 367–68.)

Use of summaries and paraphrases

- Are summaries and paraphrases free of plagiarized wording—not copied or half-copied from the source? (See MLA-2c.)
- Are summaries and paraphrases documented with parenthetical citations? (See MLA-4a.)
- Do readers know where the cited material begins? In other words, does a signal phrase mark the boundary between your words and the summary or paraphrase, unless the context makes clear exactly what you are citing? (See pp. 367–68.)
- Does a clear signal phrase prepare readers for the purpose the summary or paraphrase has in your argument?

Use of statistics and other facts

- Are statistics and facts (other than common knowledge) documented with parenthetical citations? (See MLA-2a.)
- If there is no signal phrase, will readers understand exactly which facts are being cited? (See MLA-3b.)

MLA-4

Documenting sources

In English and in some humanities classes, you will be asked to use the MLA (Modern Language Association) system for documenting sources, which is set forth in the *MLA Handbook for Writers of Research Papers,* 6th ed. (New York: MLA, 2003). MLA recommends in-text citations that refer readers to a list of works cited.

An in-text citation names the author of the source, often in a signal phrase, and gives the page number in parentheses. At the end of the paper, a list of works cited provides publication information about the source; the list is alphabetized by authors' last names (or by titles for works without authors). There is a direct connection between the in-text citation and the alphabetical listing. In the following example, that link is highlighted in orange.

IN-TEXT CITATION

Jay Kesan notes that even though many companies now routinely monitor employees through electronic means, "there may exist less intrusive safeguards for employers" (293).

ENTRY IN THE LIST OF WORKS CITED

Kesan, Jay P. "Cyber-Working or Cyber-Shirking? A First Principles Examination of Electronic Privacy in the Workplace." Florida Law Review 54 (2002): 289–332.

For a list of works cited that includes this entry, see page 412.

NOTE: If your instructor allows italics for the titles of long works and for the names of publications, substitute italics for underlining in all the models in this section.

MLA-4a MLA in-text citations

MLA in-text citations are made with a combination of signal phrases and parenthetical references. A signal phrase indicates that something taken from a source (a quotation, summary, paraphrase, or fact) is about to be used; usually the signal phrase includes the author's name. The parenthetical reference, which comes

Directory to MLA in-text citation models

after the cited material, normally includes at least a page number. In the models in this section, the elements of the in-text citation are shown in orange.

IN-TEXT CITATION

Kwon points out that the Fourth Amendment does not give employees any protections from employers' "unreasonable searches and seizures" (6).

Readers can look up the author's last name in the alphabetized list of works cited, where they will learn the work's title and other publication information. If readers decide to consult the source, the page number will take them straight to the passage that has been cited.

Basic rules for print and electronic sources

The MLA system of in-text citations, which depends heavily on authors' names and page numbers, was created in the early 1980s with print sources in mind. Because some of today's electronic sources have unclear authorship and lack page numbers, they present a special challenge. Nevertheless, the basic rules are the same for both print and electronic sources.

The models in this section (items 1–5) show how the MLA system usually works and explain what to do if your source has no author or page numbers.

■ **1. AUTHOR NAMED IN A SIGNAL PHRASE** Ordinarily, introduce the material being cited with a signal phrase that includes the author's name. In addition to preparing readers for the source, the signal phrase allows you to keep the parenthetical citation brief.

> Frederick Lane reports that employers do not necessarily have to use software to monitor how their employees use the Web: employers can "use a hidden video camera pointed at an employee's monitor" and even position a camera "so that a number of monitors [can] be viewed at the same time" (147).

The signal phrase — *Frederick Lane reports that* — names the author; the parenthetical citation gives the page number of the book in which the quoted words may be found.

Notice that the period follows the parenthetical citation. When a quotation ends with a question mark or an exclamation point, leave the end punctuation inside the quotation mark and add a period after the parentheses: ". . . ?" (8). (See also the note on p. 286.)

■ **2. AUTHOR NAMED IN PARENTHESES** If a signal phrase does not name the author, put the author's last name in parentheses along with the page number.

> Companies can monitor employees' every keystroke without legal penalty, but they may have to combat low morale as a result (Lane 129).

Use no punctuation between the name and the page number.

■ **3. AUTHOR UNKNOWN** Either use the complete title in a signal phrase or use a short form of the title in parentheses. Titles of books are underlined; titles of articles are put in quotation marks.

> A popular keystroke logging program operates invisibly on workers' computers yet provides supervisors with details of the workers' online activities ("Automatically").

TIP: Before assuming that a Web source has no author, do some detective work. Often the author's name is available but is not easy to find. For example, it may appear at the end of the source, in tiny print. Or it may appear on another page of the site, such as the home page.

NOTE: If a source has no author and is sponsored by a corporate entity, such as an organization or a government agency, name the corporate entity as the author (see item 9 on p. 375).

■ **4. PAGE NUMBER UNKNOWN** You may omit the page number if a work lacks page numbers, as is the case with many Web sources. Although printouts from Web sites usually show page numbers, printers don't always provide the same page breaks; for this reason, MLA recommends treating such sources as unpaginated.

> As a 2005 study by Salary.com and America Online indicates, the Internet ranked as the top choice among employees for ways of wasting time on the job; it beat talking with co-workers--the second most popular method--by a margin of nearly two to one (Frauenheim).

When the pages of a Web source are stable (as in PDF files), however, supply a page number in your in-text citation. (For example, the source cited in the first paragraph of the student paper is a PDF file with stable pages, so a page number is included in the citation. See p. 408.)

NOTE: If a Web source numbers its paragraphs or screens, give the abbreviation "par." or "pars." or the word "screen" or "screens" in the parentheses: (Smith, par. 4).

5. ONE-PAGE SOURCE If the source is one page long, MLA allows (but does not require) you to omit the page number. Many instructors will want you to supply the page number because without it readers may not know where your citation ends or, worse, may not realize that you have provided a citation at all.

No page number given

> Anush Yegyazarian reports that in 2000 the National Labor Relations Board's Office of the General Counsel helped win restitution for two workers who had been dismissed because their employers were displeased by the employees' e-mails about work-related issues. The case points to the ongoing struggle to define what constitutes protected speech in the workplace.

Page number given

> Anush Yegyazarian reports that in 2000 the National Labor Relations Board's Office of the General Counsel helped win restitution for two workers who had been dismissed because their employers were displeased by the employees' e-mails about work-related issues (62). This case points to the ongoing struggle to define what constitutes protected speech in the workplace.

Variations on the basic rules

This section describes the MLA guidelines for handling a variety of situations not covered by the basic rules just given. These rules on in-text citations are the same for both traditional print sources and electronic sources.

6. TWO OR MORE TITLES BY THE SAME AUTHOR If your list of works cited includes two or more titles by the same author, mention the title of the work in the signal phrase or include a short version of the title in the parentheses.

> The American Management Association and ePolicy Institute have tracked employers' practices in monitoring employees' e-mail use. The groups' 2003 survey found that one-third of companies had a policy of keeping and reviewing employees' e-mail messages ("2003 E-mail" 2); in 2005, more than 55% of companies engaged in e-mail monitoring ("2005 Electronic" 1).

Titles of articles and other short works are placed in quotation marks, as in the example just given. Titles of books are underlined.

In the rare case when both the author's name and a short title must be given in parentheses, separate them with a comma.

> A 2004 survey found that 20% of employers responding had employees' e-mail "subpoenaed in the course of a lawsuit or regulatory investigation," up 7% from the previous year (Amer. Management Assn. and ePolicy Inst., "2004 Workplace" 1).

7. TWO OR THREE AUTHORS Name the authors in a signal phrase, as in the following example, or include their last names in the parenthetical reference: (Kizza and Ssanyu 2).

> Kizza and Ssanyu note that "employee monitoring is a dependable, capable, and very affordable process of electronically or otherwise recording all employee activities at work and also increasingly outside the workplace" (2).

When three authors are named in the parentheses, separate the names with commas: (Alton, Davies, and Rice 56).

8. FOUR OR MORE AUTHORS Name all of the authors or include only the first author's name followed by "et al." (Latin for "and others"). Make sure that your citation matches the entry in the list of works cited (see item 2 on p. 380).

> The study was extended for two years, and only after results were reviewed by an independent panel did the researchers publish their findings (Blaine et al. 35).

9. CORPORATE AUTHOR When the author is a corporation, an organization, or a government agency, name the corporate author either in the signal phrase or in the parentheses.

> According to a 2001 survey of human resources managers by the American Management Association, more than three-quarters of the responding companies reported disciplining employees for "misuse or personal use of office telecommunications equipment" (2).

In the list of works cited, the American Management Association is treated as the author and alphabetized under *A*.

When a government agency is treated as the author, it will be alphabetized in the list of works cited under the name of the government, such as "Canada" (see item 3 on p. 381). For this reason, you must name the government in your in-text citation.

> Transport Canada administers regulations and provides services for all of Canada's transportation systems.

10. AUTHORS WITH THE SAME LAST NAME If your list of works cited includes works by two or more authors with the same last name, include the author's first name in the signal phrase or first initial in the parentheses.

> Estimates of the frequency with which employers monitor employees' use of the Internet each day vary widely (A. Jones 15).

11. INDIRECT SOURCE (SOURCE QUOTED IN ANOTHER SOURCE) When a writer's or a speaker's quoted words appear in a source written by someone else, begin the parenthetical citation with the abbreviation "qtd. in."

> Researchers Botan and McCreadie point out that "workers are objects of information collection without participating in the process of exchanging the information . . ." (qtd. in Kizza and Ssanyu 14).

12. ENCYCLOPEDIA OR DICTIONARY Unless an encyclopedia or a dictionary has an author, it will be alphabetized in the list of works cited under the word or entry that you consulted — not under the title of the reference work itself (see item 13 on p. 384). Either in your text or in your parenthetical reference, mention the word or the entry. No page number is required, since readers can easily look up the word or entry.

> The word crocodile has a surprisingly complex etymology ("Crocodile").

■ **13. MULTIVOLUME WORK** If your paper cites more than one volume of a multivolume work, indicate in the parentheses the volume you are referring to, followed by a colon and the page number.

> In his studies of gifted children, Terman describes a pattern of accelerated language acquisition (2: 279).

If your paper cites only one volume of a multivolume work, you will include the volume number in the list of works cited and will not need to include it in the parentheses.

■ **14. TWO OR MORE WORKS** To cite more than one source in the parentheses, give the citations in alphabetical order and separate them with a semicolon.

> The effects of sleep deprivation have been well documented (Cahill 42; Leduc 114; Vasquez 73).

Multiple citations can be distracting, however, so you should not overuse the technique. If you want to alert readers to several sources that discuss a particular topic, consider using an information note instead (see MLA-4c).

■ **15. AN ENTIRE WORK** Use the author's name in a signal phrase or a parenthetical reference. There is of course no need to use a page number.

> Lane explores the evolution of surveillance in the workplace.

■ **16. WORK IN AN ANTHOLOGY** Put the name of the author of the work (not the editor of the anthology) in the signal phrase or the parentheses.

> In "A Jury of Her Peers," Mrs. Hale describes both a style of quilting and a murder weapon when she utters the last words of the story: "We call it--knot it, Mr. Henderson" (Glaspell 210).

In the list of works cited, the work is alphabetized under Glaspell, not under the name of the editor of the anthology.

> Glaspell, Susan. "A Jury of Her Peers." Literature and Its Writers: A Compact Introduction to Fiction, Poetry, and Drama. Ed. Ann Charters and Samuel Charters. 3rd ed. Boston: Bedford, 2004. 194-210.

17. LEGAL SOURCE For well-known historical documents, such as articles of the Canadian Constitution, and for laws in the Criminal Code of Canada, provide a parenthetical citation in the text: (Can. Const., pt. 3, sec. 36) or (CCC pt. 3, sec. 99). There is no need to provide a works cited entry.

Legislative acts and court cases are included in the works cited list (see item 53 on p. 402). Your in-text citation should name the act or case either in a signal phrase or in parentheses. In the text of a paper, names of acts are not underlined, but names of cases are.

> The Young Criminal Justice Act replaced the Young Offenders Act in 2003.

> In 1992, Justice Dufour of the Quebec Superior Court ruled in the case of Nancy B. v. Hôtel-Dieu de Québec that Nancy B. was competent to make decisions for herself and had a right to refuse treatment.

Literary works and sacred texts

Literary works and sacred texts are usually available in a variety of editions. Your list of works cited will specify which edition you are using, and your in-text citation will usually consist of a page number from the edition you consulted (see item 18).

However, MLA suggests that when possible you should give enough information — such as book parts, play divisions, or line numbers — so that readers can locate the cited passage in any edition of the work (see items 19–21).

18. LITERARY WORKS WITHOUT PARTS OR LINE NUMBERS Many literary works, such as most short stories and many novels and plays, do not have parts or line numbers that you can refer to. In such cases, simply cite the page number.

> At the end of Kate Chopin's "The Story of an Hour," Mrs. Mallard drops dead upon learning that her husband is alive. In the final irony of the story, doctors report that she has died of a "joy that kills" (25).

19. VERSE PLAYS AND POEMS For verse plays, MLA recommends giving act, scene, and line numbers that can be located in any edition of the work. Use arabic numerals, and separate the numbers with periods.

> In Shakespeare's King Lear, Gloucester, blinded for suspected treason, learns a profound lesson from his tragic experience: "A man may see how this world goes / with no eyes" (4.2.148-49).

For a poem, cite the part (if there are a number of parts) and the line numbers, separated by a period.

> When Homer's Odysseus comes to the hall of Circe, he finds his men "mild / in her soft spell, fed on her drug of evil" (10.209-10).

For poems that are not divided into parts, use line numbers. For a first reference, use the word "lines": (lines 5-8). Thereafter use just the numbers: (12-13).

20. NOVELS WITH NUMBERED DIVISIONS When a novel has numbered divisions, put the page number first, followed by a semicolon, and then indicate the book, part, or chapter in which the passage may be found. Use abbreviations such as "bk." and "ch."

> One of Kingsolver's narrators, teenager Rachel, pushes her vocabulary beyond its limits. For example, Rachel complains that being forced to live in the Congo with her missionary family is "a sheer tapestry of justice" because her chances of finding a boyfriend are "dull and void" (117; bk. 2, ch. 10).

21. SACRED TEXTS When citing a sacred text such as the Bible or the Qur'an, name the edition you are using in your works cited entry (see item 14 on p. 385). In your parenthetical citation, give the book, chapter, and verse (or their equivalent), separated by periods. Common abbreviations for books of the Bible are acceptable.

> Consider the words of Solomon: "If your enemies are hungry, give them food to eat. If they are thirsty, give them water to drink" (Holy Bible, Prov. 25.21).

ON THE WEB > **dianahacker.com/writersref**
Research exercises > E-ex MLA 4–1 and MLA 4–2

MLA-4b MLA list of works cited

An alphabetized list of works cited, which appears at the end of your research paper, gives publication information for each of the sources you have cited in the paper. (For information about preparing the list, see p. 406; for a sample list of works cited, see p. 412.)

NOTE: Unless your instructor asks for them, omit sources not actually cited in the paper, even if you read them.

Directory to MLA works cited models

ON THE WEB > **dianahacker.com/writersref**
Research exercises > E-ex MLA 4–3

ON THE WEB > **dianahacker.com/writersref**
Research and Documentation Online > Humanities: Documenting sources (MLA)

General guidelines for listing authors

Alphabetize entries in the list of works cited by authors' last names (if a work has no author, alphabetize it by its title). The author's name is important because citations in the text of the paper refer to it and readers will be looking for it at the beginning of an entry in the alphabetized list.

NAME CITED IN TEXT

According to Nancy Flynn, . . .

BEGINNING OF WORKS CITED ENTRY

Flynn, Nancy.

Items 1–5 show how to begin an entry for a work with a single author, multiple authors, a corporate author, an unknown author, and multiple works by the same author. What comes after this first element of your citation will depend on the kind of source you are citing. (See items 6–60.)

NOTE: For a book, an entry in the works cited list will sometimes begin with an editor (see item 9 on p. 382).

■ **1. SINGLE AUTHOR** For a work with one author, begin with the author's last name, followed by a comma; then give the author's first name, followed by a period.

Tannen, Deborah.

■ **2. MULTIPLE AUTHORS** For works with two or three authors, name the authors in the order in which they are listed in the source. Reverse the name of only the first author.

Walker, Janice R., and Todd Taylor.

Wilmut, Ian, Keith Campbell, and Colin Tudge.

For a work with four or more authors, either name all of the authors or name the first author, followed by "et al." (Latin for "and others").

Sloan, Frank A., Emily M. Stout, Kathryn Whetten-Goldstein, and Lan Liang.

Sloan, Frank A., et al.

3. CORPORATE AUTHOR When the author of a print document or Web site is a corporation, a government agency, or some other organization, begin your entry with the name of the group.

Farm Credit Canada.

Canada. Dept. of Justice.

Canadian Association of Management Consultants.

NOTE: Make sure that your in-text citation also treats the organization as the author (see item 9 on p. 375).

4. UNKNOWN AUTHOR When the author of a work is unknown, begin with the work's title. Titles of articles and other short works, such as brief documents from Web sites, are put in quotation marks. Titles of books and other long works, such as entire Web sites, are underlined.

Article or other short work

"Media Giants."

Book or other long work

Atlas of the World.

Before concluding that the author of a Web source is unknown, check carefully (see the tip on p. 372). Also remember that an organization may be the author (see item 3 at the top of this page).

5. TWO OR MORE WORKS BY THE SAME AUTHOR If your list of works cited includes two or more works by the same author, use the author's name only for the first entry. For other entries, use three hyphens followed by a period. The three hyphens must stand for exactly the same name or names as in the first entry. List the titles in alphabetical order (ignoring the article *A, An,* or *The* at the beginning of a title).

Callwood, June. The Man Who Lost Himself. Toronto: McClellan, 2000.

---. The Sleepwalker. Toronto: Lester, 1990.

Books

Items 6–19 apply to print books. For online books, see item 29.

6. BASIC FORMAT FOR A BOOK For most books, arrange the information into three units, each followed by a period and one space: the author's name; the title and subtitle, underlined; and the place of publication, the publisher, and the date.

Tan, Amy. The Bonesetter's Daughter. New York: Putnam, 2001.

Take the information about the book from its title page and copyright page. Use a short form of the publisher's name; omit terms such as *Press, Inc.,* and *Co.* except when naming university presses (Oxford UP, for example). If the copyright page lists more than one date, use the most recent one.

7. AUTHOR WITH AN EDITOR Begin with the author and title, followed by the name of the editor. In this case the abbreviation "Ed." means "Edited by," so it is the same for one or multiple editors.

Plath, Sylvia. The Unabridged Journals of Sylvia Plath. Ed. Karen V. Kukil. New York: Anchor-Doubleday, 2000.

8. AUTHOR WITH A TRANSLATOR Begin with the name of the author. After the title, write "Trans." (for "Translated by") and the name of the translator.

Allende, Isabel. Zorro. Trans. Margaret Sayers Peden. London: Fourth Estate, 2005.

9. EDITOR An entry for a work with an editor is similar to that for a work with an author except that the name is followed by a comma and the abbreviation "ed." for "editor" (or "eds." for "editors").

Craig, Patricia, ed. The Oxford Book of Travel Stories. Oxford: Oxford UP, 1996.

10. WORK IN AN ANTHOLOGY Begin with (1) the name of the author of the selection, not with the name of the editor of the anthology. Then give (2) the title of the selection; (3) the title of the anthology; (4) the name of the editor (preceded by "Ed." for "Edited by"); (5) publication information; and (6) the pages on which the selection appears.

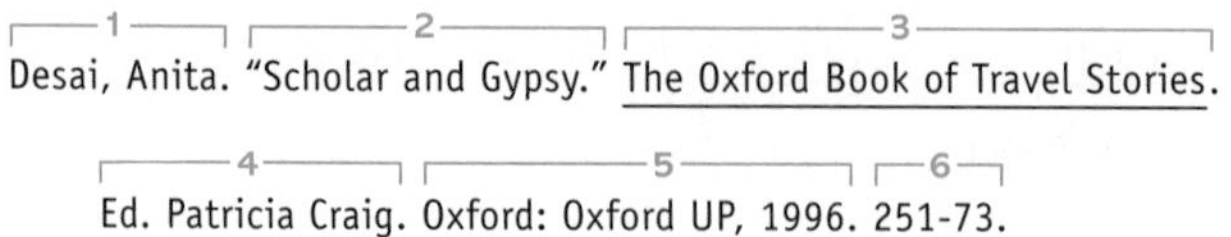

Citation at a glance: Book (MLA)

To cite a book in MLA style, include the following elements:

1 Author
2 Title and subtitle
3 City of publication
4 Publisher
5 Date of publication

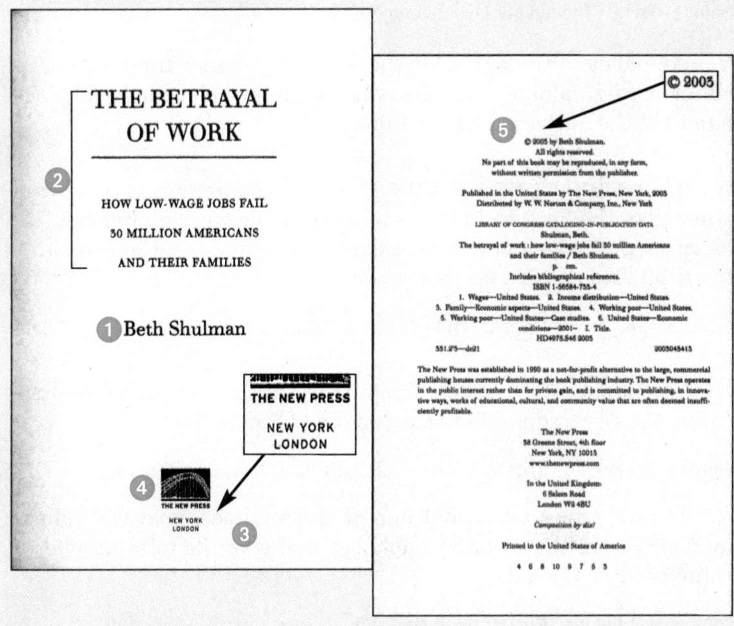

WORKS CITED ENTRY FOR A BOOK

1 — 2 — 3 — 4 — 5

Shulman, Beth. The Betrayal of Work: How Low-Wage Jobs Fail 30 Million Americans and Their Families. New York: New, 2003.

For more on citing books in MLA style, see pages 382–86.

If you wish, you may cross-reference two or more works from the same anthology. Provide an entry for the anthology (see item 9 on p. 382). Then in separate entries list the author and title of each selection, followed by the last name of the editor of the anthology and the page numbers on which the selection appears.

Desai, Anita. "Scholar and Gypsy." Craig 251-73.

Malouf, David. "The Kyogle Line." Craig 390-96.

Alphabetize the entry for the anthology under the name of its editor (Craig); alphabetize the entries for the selections under the names of the authors (Desai, Malouf).

■ **11. EDITION OTHER THAN THE FIRST** If you are citing an edition other than the first, include the number of the edition after the title (or after the names of any translators or editors that appear after the title): 2nd ed., 3rd ed., and so on.

Auletta, Ken. The Underclass. 2nd ed. Woodstock: Overlook, 2000.

■ **12. MULTIVOLUME WORK** Include the total number of volumes before the city and publisher, using the abbreviation "vols."

Conway, Jill Ker, ed. Written by Herself. 2 vols. New York: Random, 1996.

If your paper cites only one of the volumes, give the volume number before the city and publisher and give the total number of volumes after the date.

Conway, Jill Ker, ed. Written by Herself. Vol. 2. New York: Random, 1996. 2 vols.

■ **13. ENCYCLOPEDIA OR DICTIONARY ENTRY** When an encyclopedia or a dictionary is well known, simply list the author of the entry (if there is one), the title of the entry, the title of the reference work, the edition number (if any), and the date of the edition.

Posner, Rebecca. "Romance Languages." The Encyclopaedia Britannica: Macropaedia. 15th ed. 1987.

"Sonata." Canadian Oxford Dictionary. 2nd ed. 2004.

Volume and page numbers are not necessary because the entries in the source are arranged alphabetically and therefore are easy to locate.

If a reference work is not well known, provide full publication information as well.

14. SACRED TEXT Give the title of the edition of the sacred text (taken from the title page), underlined; the editor's or translator's name (if any); and publication information.

Holy Bible. Wheaton: Tyndale, 2005.

The Qur'an: Translation. Trans. Abdullah Yusuf Ali. Elmhurst: Tahrike, 2000.

15. FOREWORD, INTRODUCTION, PREFACE, OR AFTERWORD Begin with the author of the foreword or other book part, followed by the name of that part. Then give the title of the book; the author of the book, preceded by the word "By"; and the editor of the book (if any). After the publication information, give the page numbers for the part of the book being cited.

Morris, Jan. Introduction. Letters from the Field, 1925-1975. By Margaret Mead. New York: Perennial-Harper, 2001. xix-xxiii.

If the book part being cited has a title, include it in quotation marks immediately after the author's name.

Ozick, Cynthia. "Portrait of the Essay as a Warm Body." Introduction. The Best American Essays 1998. Ed. Ozick. Boston: Houghton, 1998. xv-xxi.

16. BOOK WITH A TITLE IN ITS TITLE If the book title contains a title normally underlined, neither underline the internal title nor place it in quotation marks.

King, John N. Milton and Religious Controversy: Satire and Polemic in Paradise Lost. Cambridge: Cambridge UP, 2000.

If the title within the title is normally put in quotation marks, retain the quotation marks and underline the entire title.

Knight, Denise D., and Cynthia J. Davis. Approaches to Teaching Gilman's "The Yellow Wall-Paper" and Herland. New York: Mod. Lang. Assn., 2003.

17. BOOK IN A SERIES Before the publication information, cite the series name as it appears on the title page, followed by the series number, if any.

Malena, Anne. The Dynamics of Identity in Francophone Caribbean Narrative. Francophone Cultures and Lits. Ser. 24. New York: Lang, 1998.

18. REPUBLISHED BOOK After the title of the book, cite the original publication date, followed by the current publication information. If the republished book contains new material, such as an introduction or afterword, include information about the new material after the original date.

Hughes, Langston. Black Misery. 1969. Afterword Robert O'Meally. New York: Oxford UP, 2000.

19. PUBLISHER'S IMPRINT If a book was published by an imprint (a division) of a publishing company, link the name of the imprint and the name of the publisher with a hyphen, putting the imprint first.

Truan, Barry. Acoustic Communication. Westport: Ablex-Greenwood, 2000.

Articles in periodicals

This section shows how to prepare works cited entries for articles in magazines, scholarly journals, and newspapers. In addition to consulting the models in this section, you will at times need to turn to other models as well:

- More than one author: see item 2
- Corporate author: see item 3
- Unknown author: see item 4
- Online article: see item 32
- Article from a subscription service: see item 31

NOTE: For articles appearing on consecutive pages, provide the range of pages (see items 21 and 22). When an article does not appear on consecutive pages, give the number of the first page followed by a plus sign: 32+.

20. ARTICLE IN A MAGAZINE List, in order, separated by periods, the author's name; the title of the article, in quotation marks; and the title of the magazine, underlined. Then give the date and the page numbers, separated by a colon. If the magazine is issued monthly, give just the month and year. Abbreviate the names of the months except May, June, and July.

Silverman, Craig. "Nice Rack." Report on Business Magazine July-Aug. 2006: 133.

If the magazine is issued weekly, give the exact date.

Lord, Lewis. "There's Something about Mary Todd." US News and World Report 19 Feb. 2001: 53.

21. ARTICLE IN A JOURNAL PAGINATED BY VOLUME Many scholarly journals continue page numbers throughout the year instead of beginning each issue with page 1; at the end of the year, the issues are collected in a volume. To find an article, readers need only the volume number, the year, and the page numbers.

Aboud, Frances, and Anna-Beth Doyle. "Does Talk of Race Foster Prejudice or Tolerance in Children?" Canadian Journal of Behavioural Science 28 (1996): 161-70.

22. ARTICLE IN A JOURNAL PAGINATED BY ISSUE If each issue of the journal begins with page 1, you need to indicate the number of the issue. After the volume number, put a period and the issue number.

Wood, Michael. "Broken Dates: Fiction and the Century." Kenyon Review 22.3 (2000): 50-64.

23. ARTICLE IN A DAILY NEWSPAPER Begin with the name of the author, if known, followed by the title of the article. Next give the name of the newspaper, the date, and the page numbers (including the section letter). Use a plus sign (+) after the page number if the article does not appear on consecutive pages.

Walton, Dawn. "Police in Calgary Make Big Ecstasy Bust." Globe and Mail 30 Oct. 2002: A10.

If the section is marked with a number rather than a letter, handle the entry as follows:

Wilford, John Noble. "In a Golden Age of Discovery, Faraway Worlds Beckon." New York Times 9 Feb. 1997, late ed., sec. 1: 1+.

When an edition of the newspaper is specified on the masthead, name the edition after the date and before the page reference (eastern ed., late ed., natl. ed., and so on), as in the example just given.

If the city of publication is not obvious, include it in brackets after the name of the newspaper: Citizen [Blyth, ON].

Citation at a glance: Article in a periodical (MLA)

To cite an article in a periodical in MLA style, include the following elements:

1 Author
2 Title of article
3 Name of periodical
4 Date of publication
5 Page numbers

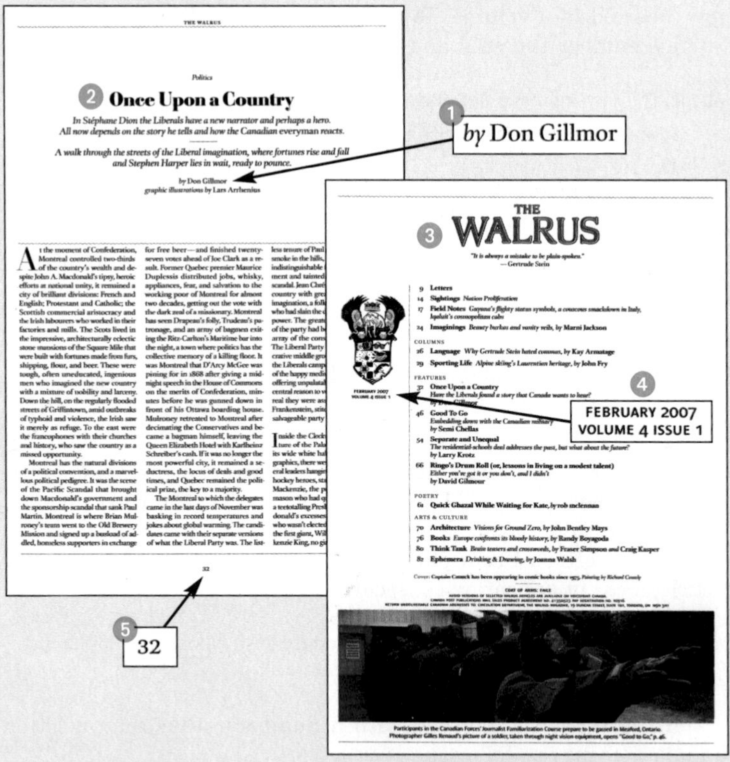

WORKS CITED ENTRY FOR AN ARTICLE IN A PERIODICAL

Gillmor, Don. "Once upon a Country." Walrus Feb. 2007: 32-45.

For more on citing periodical articles in MLA style, see pages 386–89.

■ **24. EDITORIAL IN A NEWSPAPER** Cite an editorial as you would an article with an unknown author, adding the word "Editorial" after the title.

"All Wet." Editorial. Boston Globe 12 Feb. 2001: A14.

■ **25. LETTER TO THE EDITOR** Name the writer, followed by the word "Letter" and the publication information for the periodical in which the letter appears.

Shrewsbury, Toni. Letter. Atlanta Journal-Constitution 17 Feb. 2001: A13.

■ **26. BOOK OR FILM REVIEW** Name the reviewer and the title of the review, if any, followed by the words "Rev. of" and the title and author or director of the work reviewed. Add the publication information for the periodical in which the review appears.

Gleick, Elizabeth. "The Burdens of Genius." Rev. of The Last Samurai, by Helen DeWitt. Time 4 Dec. 2000: 171.

Farquharson, Vanessa. "In Praise of Scrunchy-Faced Women." Rev. of Miss Potter, dir. Chris Noonan. National Post 12 Jan. 2007: E4.

Electronic sources

This section shows how to prepare works cited entries for a variety of electronic sources, including Web sites, online books, articles in online periodicals and databases, blogs, e-mail, and Web postings.

NOTE: When a Web address in a works cited entry must be divided at the end of a line, MLA recommends that you break it after a slash. Do not insert a hyphen.

■ **27. AN ENTIRE WEB SITE** Begin with the name of the author or corporate author (if known) and the title of the site, underlined. Then give the names of any editors, the date of publication or last update, the name of any sponsoring organization, the date you accessed the source, and the URL in angle brackets. Provide as much of this information as is available.

With author

Peterson, Susan Lynn. The Life of Martin Luther. 2002. 24 Jan. 2006 <http://www.susanlynnpeterson.com/luther/home.html>.

With corporate (group) author

Canada. Health Canada. Drinking Water. 26 July 2006. 12 Jan. 2007 <http://www.hc-sc.gc.ca/ewh-semt/water-eau/drink-potab/index_e.html>.

Author unknown

Margaret Sanger Papers Project. 18 Oct. 2000. History Dept., New York U. 6 Feb. 2006 <http://www.nyu.edu/projects/sanger>.

With editor

Internet Modern History Sourcebook. Ed. Paul Halsall. 22 Sept. 2001. Fordham U. 22 Feb. 2006 <http://www.fordham.edu/HALSALL/mod/modsbook.html>.

NOTE: If the site has no title, substitute a description, such as "Home page," for the title. Do not underline the words or put them in quotation marks.

Yoon, Mina. Home page. 29 Sept. 2004. 12 Jan. 2005 <http://www.pa.msu.edu/~mnyoon>.

■ **28. SHORT WORK FROM A WEB SITE** Short works are those that appear in quotation marks in MLA style: articles, poems, and other documents that are not book length. For a short work from a Web site, include as many of the following elements as apply and as are available: author's name; title of the short work, in quotation marks; title of the site, underlined; date of publication or last update; sponsor of the site (if not named as the author or given as the title of the site); date you accessed the source; and the URL in angle brackets.

Usually at least some of these elements will not apply or will be unavailable. In the following example, no sponsor or date of publication was available. (The date given is the date on which the researcher accessed the source.) For an annotated example, see pages 392–93.

With author

Shiva, Vandana. "Bioethics: A Third World Issue." NativeWeb. 22 Feb. 2006 <http://www.nativeweb.org/pages/legal/shiva.html>.

Author unknown

"Media Giants." Frontline: The Merchants of Cool. 2001. PBS Online. 7 Feb. 2006 <http://www.pbs.org/wgbh/pages/frontline/shows/cool/giants>.

NOTE: When the URL for a short work from a Web site is very long, you may give the URL for the home page and indicate the path by which readers can access the source.

"US Obesity Trends 1985-2004." Centers for Disease Control and Prevention. 3 Jan. 2003. 17 Feb. 2006 <http://www.cdc.gov>. Path: A-Z Index; Overweight and Obesity; Obesity Trends; US Obesity Trends 1985 to 2004.

■ **29. ONLINE BOOK** When a book or a book-length work such as a play or a long poem is posted on the Web as its own site, give as much publication information as is available, followed by your date of access and the URL. (See also the models for print books: items 6–19.)

Rawlins, Gregory J. E. Moths to the Flame. Cambridge: MIT P, 1996. 17 Jan. 2006 <http://mitpress.mit.edu/e-books/Moths/contents.html>.

If the book-length work is posted on a scholarly Web site, provide information about that site.

Jacobs, Harriet Ann. Incidents in the Life of a Slave Girl. Boston, 1861. Documenting the American South: The Southern Experience in Nineteenth-Century America. Ed. Ji-Hae Yoon and Natalia Smith. 1998. Academic Affairs Lib., U of North Carolina, Chapel Hill. 3 Mar. 2006 <http://docsouth.unc.edu/jacobs/jacobs.html>.

■ **30. PART OF AN ONLINE BOOK** Place the part title before the book's title. If the part is a short work such as a poem or an essay, put its title in quotation marks. If the part is an introduction or other division of the book, do not use quotation marks.

Adams, Henry. "Diplomacy." The Education of Henry Adams. Boston: Houghton, 1918. Bartleby.com: Great Books Online. 1999. 8 Jan. 2005 <http://bartleby.com/159/8.html>.

■ **31. WORK FROM A SERVICE SUCH AS *INFOTRAC*** For sources retrieved from a library's subscription database service, give as much of the following information as is available: publication information for the source (see items 20–26); the name of the database, underlined; the name of the service; the name and location of the library where you retrieved the source; your date of access; and the URL of the service.

The following models are for articles retrieved through three popular library subscription services. The *InfoTrac* source is a

Citation at a glance: Short work from a Web site (MLA)

To cite a short work from a Web site in MLA style, include the following elements:

1 Author
2 Title of short work
3 Title of Web site
4 Date of publication or latest update
5 Sponsor of site
6 Date of access
7 URL

ON-SCREEN VIEW OF SHORT WORK

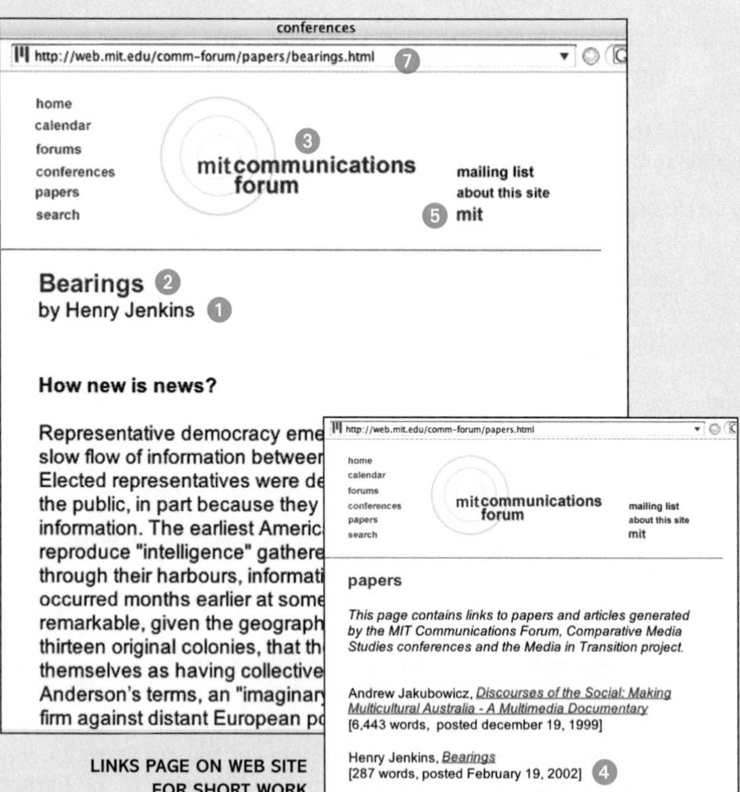

LINKS PAGE ON WEB SITE FOR SHORT WORK

BROWSER PRINTOUT OF SHORT WORK

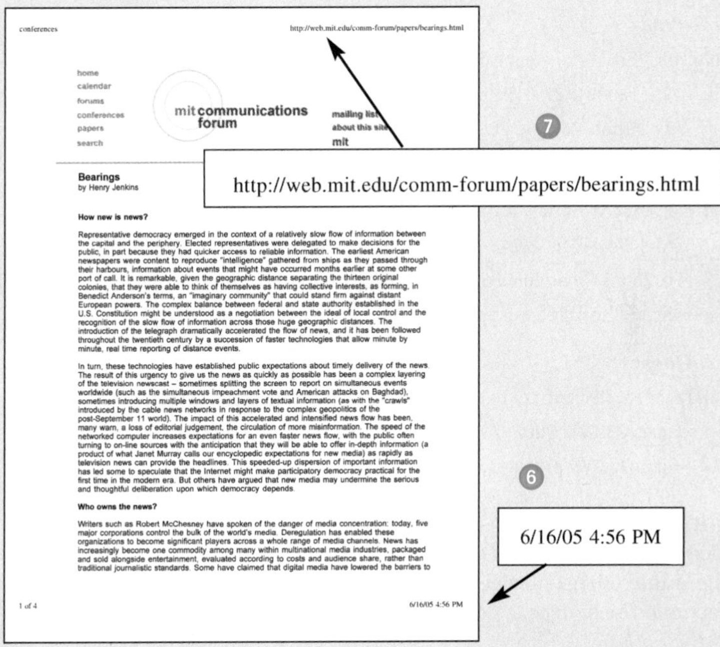

conferences http://web.mit.edu/comm-forum/papers/bearings.html

home
calendar
forums
conferences
papers
search

mit communications forum

mailing list
about this site
mit

Bearings
by Henry Jenkins

How new is news?

Representative democracy emerged in the context of a relatively slow flow of information between the capital and the periphery. Elected representatives were delegated to make decisions for the public, in part because they had quicker access to reliable information. The earliest American newspapers were content to reproduce "intelligence" gathered from ships as they passed through their harbours, information about events that might have occurred months earlier at some other port of call. It is remarkable, given the geographic distance separating the thirteen original colonies, that they were able to think of themselves as having collective interests, as forming, in Benedict Anderson's terms, an "imaginary community" that could stand firm against distant European powers. The complex balance between federal and state authority established in the U.S. Constitution might be understood as a negotiation between the ideal of local control and the recognition of the slow flow of information across those huge geographic distances. The introduction of the telegraph dramatically accelerated the flow of news, and it has been followed throughout the twentieth century by a succession of faster technologies that allow minute by minute, real time reporting of distance events.

In turn, these technologies have established public expectations about timely delivery of the news. The result of this urgency to give us the news as quickly as possible has been a complex layering of the television newscast – sometimes splitting the screen to report on simultaneous events worldwide (such as the simultaneous impeachment vote and American attacks on Baghdad), sometimes introducing multiple windows and layers of textual information (as with the "crawls" introduced by the cable news networks in response to the complex geopolitics of the post-September 11 world). The impact of this accelerated and intensified news flow has been, many warn, a loss of editorial judgement, the circulation of more misinformation. The speed of the networked computer increases expectations for an even faster news flow, with the public often turning to on-line sources with the anticipation that they will be able to offer in-depth information (a product of what Janet Murray calls our encyclopedic expectations for new media) as rapidly as television news can provide the headlines. This speeded-up dispersion of important information has led some to speculate that the Internet might make participatory democracy practical for the first time in the modern era. But others have argued that new media may undermine the serious and thoughtful deliberation upon which democracy depends.

Who owns the news?

Writers such as Robert McChesney have spoken of the danger of media concentration: today, five major corporations control the bulk of the world's media. Deregulation has enabled these organizations to become significant players across a whole range of media channels. News has increasingly become one commodity among many within multinational media industries, packaged and sold alongside entertainment, evaluated according to costs and audience share, rather than traditional journalistic standards. Some have claimed that digital media have lowered the barriers to

1 of 4 6/16/05 4:56 PM

WORKS CITED ENTRY FOR A SHORT WORK FROM A WEB SITE

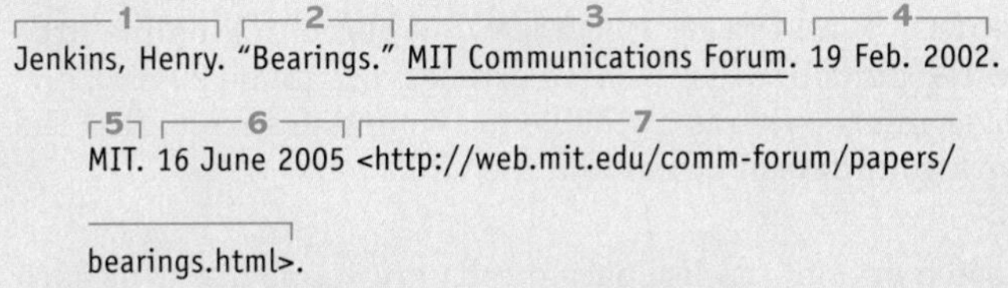

For more on citing sources from Web sites in MLA style, see pages 389–91.

scholarly article in a journal paginated by volume (see item 21); the *EBSCOhost* source is an article in a bimonthly magazine (see item 20); and the *ProQuest* source is an article in a daily newspaper (see item 23). An annotated example appears on pages 396–97.

InfoTrac

Johnson, Kirk. "The Mountain Lions of Michigan." Endangered Species Update 19.2 (2002): 27+. Expanded Academic Index. InfoTrac. U of Michigan Lib., Ann Arbor. 26 Nov. 2005 <http://infotrac.galegroup.com>.

EBSCOhost

Barrera, Rebeca María. "A Case for Bilingual Education." Scholastic Parent and Child Nov.-Dec. 2004: 72-73. Academic Search Premier. EBSCOhost. St. Johns River Community Coll. Lib., Palatka, FL. 1 Feb. 2006 <http://search.epnet.com>.

ProQuest

Kolata, Gina. "Scientists Debating Future of Hormone Replacement." New York Times 23 Oct. 2002: A20. ProQuest. Drew U Lib., Madison, NJ. 26 Nov. 2005 <http://www.proquest.com>.

NOTE: When you access a work through a personal subscription service such as *America Online,* give the information about the source, the name of the service, the date of access, and the keyword used to retrieve the source.

Conniff, Richard. "The House That John Built." Smithsonian Feb. 2001. America Online. 11 Mar. 2006. Keyword: Smithsonian Magazine.

■ **32. ARTICLE IN AN ONLINE PERIODICAL** When citing online articles, follow the guidelines for printed articles (see items 20–26), giving whatever information is available in the online source. End the citation with your date of access and the URL.

NOTE: In some online articles, paragraphs are numbered. For such articles, include the total number of paragraphs in your citation, as in the next example.

From an online scholarly journal

Belau, Linda. "Trauma and the Material Signifier." Postmodern Culture 11.2 (2001): 37 pars. 20 Feb. 2006 <http://muse.jhu.edu/journals/postmodern_culture/toc/pmc11.2.html#articles>.

From an online magazine

Morgan, Fiona. "Banning the Bullies." Salon.com 15 Mar. 2001. 21 Jan. 2006 <http://www.salon.com/news/feature/2001/03/15/bullying/index.html>.

From an online newspaper

Grant, Matthew. "Ex-Mayor Begins His Next Career." Whitehorse Daily Star 12 Jan. 2007. 15 Jan. 2007 <http://www.whitehorsestar.com/auth.php?r=45603>.

■ **33. AN ENTIRE WEBLOG (BLOG)** To cite an entire Weblog, give the author's name; the title of the Weblog, underlined; the word "Weblog"; the date of most recent update; the sponsor of the site, if any; the date of access; and the URL. MLA currently provides no guidelines for documenting a blog. Items 33 and 34 are based on MLA's guidelines for Web sites and short works from Web sites.

Mayer, Caroline. The Checkout. Weblog. 27 Apr. 2006. Washingtonpost.com. 29 Apr. 2006 <http://blog.washingtonpost.com/thecheckout>.

■ **34. AN ENTRY IN A WEBLOG (BLOG)** To cite an entry or a comment (a response to an entry) in a Weblog, give the author of the entry or comment; the title, if any, in quotation marks; the words "Weblog post" or "Weblog comment"; and the information about the entire blog as in item 33.

Mayer, Caroline. "Some Surprising Findings about Identity Theft." Weblog post. The Checkout. 28 Feb. 2006. Washingtonpost.com. 2 Mar. 2006 <http://blog.washingtonpost.com/thecheckout/02/some_surprising_findings_about.html>.

Burdick, Dennis. Weblog comment. The Checkout. 28 Feb. 2006. Washingtonpost.com. 2 Mar. 2006 <http://blog.washingtonpost.com/thecheckout/02/some_surprising_findings_about.html#comments>.

■ **35. CD-ROM** Treat a CD-ROM as you would any other source, but name the medium before the publication information.

"Pimpernel." Canadian Oxford Dictionary. 2nd ed. CD-ROM. Toronto: Oxford UP, 2004.

Wattenberg, Ruth. "Helping Students in the Middle." American Educator 19.4 (1996): 2-18. ERIC. CD-ROM. SilverPlatter. Sept. 1996.

Citation at a glance: Article from a database (MLA)

To cite an article from a database in MLA style, include the following elements:

1 Author
2 Title of article
3 Name of periodical, volume and issue numbers
4 Date of publication
5 Inclusive pages
6 Name of database
7 Name of subscription service
8 Library at which you retrieved the source
9 Date of access
10 URL of service

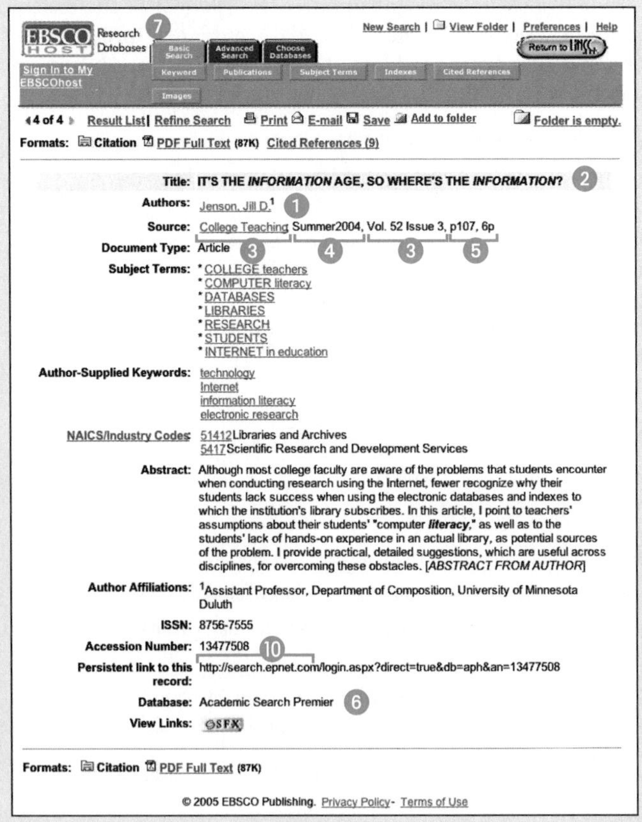
EBSCO HOST Research Databases (7)

New Search | View Folder | Preferences | Help

Return to LINK

Basic Search | Advanced Search | Choose Databases

Sign In to My EBSCOhost

Keyword | Publications | Subject Terms | Indexes | Cited References | Images

4 of 4 Result List | Refine Search Print E-mail Save Add to folder Folder is empty.

Formats: Citation PDF Full Text (87K) Cited References (9)

Title: IT'S THE *INFORMATION* AGE, SO WHERE'S THE *INFORMATION*? (2)

Authors: Jenson, Jill D.[1] (1)

Source: College Teaching (3) Summer2004, (4) Vol. 52 Issue 3, (3) p107, 6p (5)

Document Type: Article

Subject Terms:
* COLLEGE teachers
* COMPUTER literacy
* DATABASES
* LIBRARIES
* RESEARCH
* STUDENTS
* INTERNET in education

Author-Supplied Keywords: technology
Internet
information literacy
electronic research

NAICS/Industry Codes: 51412 Libraries and Archives
5417 Scientific Research and Development Services

Abstract: Although most college faculty are aware of the problems that students encounter when conducting research using the Internet, fewer recognize why their students lack success when using the electronic databases and indexes to which the institution's library subscribes. In this article, I point to teachers' assumptions about their students' "computer ***literacy***," as well as to the students' lack of hands-on experience in an actual library, as potential sources of the problem. I provide practical, detailed suggestions, which are useful across disciplines, for overcoming these obstacles. [*ABSTRACT FROM AUTHOR*]

Author Affiliations: [1]Assistant Professor, Department of Composition, University of Minnesota Duluth

ISSN: 8756-7555

Accession Number: 13477508

Persistent link to this record: (10) http://search.epnet.com/login.aspx?direct=true&db=aph&an=13477508

Database: Academic Search Premier (6)

View Links: SFX

Formats: Citation PDF Full Text (87K)

© 2005 EBSCO Publishing. Privacy Policy - Terms of Use

WORKS CITED ENTRY FOR AN ARTICLE FROM A DATABASE

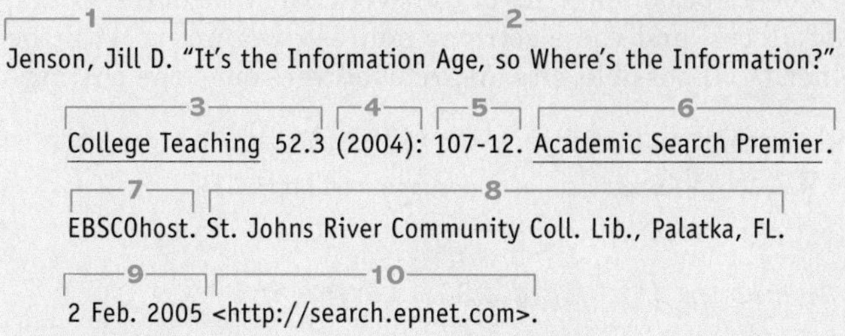

For more on citing articles from a database in MLA style, see pages 391 and 394.

■ **36. E-MAIL** To cite an e-mail, begin with the writer's name and the subject line. Then write "E-mail to" followed by the name of the recipient. End with the date of the message.

Lowe, Walter. "Review questions." E-mail to the author. 15 Mar. 2006.

■ **37. POSTING TO AN ONLINE LIST, FORUM, OR GROUP** When possible, cite archived versions of postings. If you cannot locate an archived version, keep a copy of the posting for your records. Begin with the author's name, followed by the title or subject line; the words "Online posting"; the date of the posting; the name of the list, forum, or newsgroup; and your date of access. For a discussion list, give the URL of the list if it is available; otherwise give the e-mail address of the list moderator. For a Web forum, give the network address. For a Usenet group, use the prefix "news:" followed by the name of the newsgroup.

Discussion list posting

Edwards, David. "Media Lens." Online posting. 20 Dec. 2001. Media Lens Archives. 10 Apr. 2002 <http://groups.yahoo.com/group/medialens/message/25>.

Web forum posting

Brown, Oliver. "Welcome." Online posting. 8 Oct. 2002. Chester Coll. Students Web Forum. 20 Feb. 2003 <http://www.voy.com/113243>.

Newsgroup posting

Reedy, Tom. "Re: Macbeth an Existential Nightmare?" Online posting. 9 Mar. 2002. 8 Apr. 2002 <news:humanities.lit.authors.shakespeare>.

■ **38. POSTING TO A MUD OR A MOO** Include the writer's name (if relevant), a description and date of the event, the title of the forum, the date of access, and the electronic address, beginning with the prefix "telnet://." If possible, cite an archived version of the posting.

Carbone, Nick. Planning for the future. 1 Mar. 2001. TechRhet's Thursday night MOO. 1 Mar. 2001 <telnet://connections.moo.mud.org:3333>.

Multimedia sources (including online versions)

Multimedia sources include visuals (such as works of art), audio works (such as sound recordings), audiovisuals (such as films), podcasts, and live events.

When citing multimedia sources that you retrieved online, consult the appropriate model in this section and give whatever information is available for the online source; then end the citation with your date of access and the URL. (See items 39, 42, 46, and 48 for examples.)

■ **39. WORK OF ART** Cite the artist's name, followed by the title of the artwork, usually underlined, and the institution and city in which the artwork can be found. If you want to indicate the work's date, include it after the title. For a work of art you viewed online, end your citation with your date of access and the URL.

Constable, John. Dedham Vale. Victoria and Albert Museum, London.

van Gogh, Vincent. The Starry Night. 1889. Museum of Mod. Art, New York. 3 Feb. 2006 <http://moma.org/collection/browse_results.php?object_id=79802>.

■ **40. CARTOON** Begin with the cartoonist's name, the title of the cartoon (if it has one) in quotation marks, the word "Cartoon," and the publication information for the publication in which the cartoon appears.

Sutton, Ward. "Why Wait 'til November?" Cartoon. Village Voice 7-13 July 2004: 6.

■ **41. ADVERTISEMENT** Name the product or company being advertised, followed by the word "Advertisement." Give publication information for the source in which the advertisement appears.

Truth by Calvin Klein. Advertisement. Vogue Dec. 2000: 95-98.

■ **42. MAP OR CHART** Cite a map or a chart as you would a book or a short work within a longer work. Add the word "Map" or "Chart" following the title.

Serbia. Map. 2 Feb. 2001. 17 Mar. 2006 <http://www.biega.com/serbia.html>.

Joseph, Lori, and Bob Laird. "Driving While Phoning Is Dangerous." Chart. USA Today 16 Feb. 2001: 1A.

■ **43. MUSICAL COMPOSITION** Cite the composer's name, followed by the title of the work. Underline the title of an opera, a ballet, or a composition identified by name, but do not underline or use quotation marks around a composition identified by number or form.

Ellington, Duke. Conga Brava.

Haydn, Franz Joseph. Symphony no. 88 in G.

■ **44. SOUND RECORDING** Begin with the name of the person you want to emphasize: the composer, conductor, or performer. For a long work, give the title, underlined, followed by names of pertinent artists (such as performers, readers, or musicians) and the orchestra and conductor (if relevant). End with the manufacturer and the date.

Bizet, Georges. Carmen. Perf. Jennifer Laramore, Thomas Moser, Angela Gheorghiu, and Samuel Ramey. Bavarian State Orch. and Chorus. Cond. Giuseppe Sinopoli. Warner, 1996.

For a song, put the title in quotation marks. If you include the name of the album or CD, underline it.

Blige, Mary J. "Be without You." The Breakthrough. Geffen, 2005.

■ **45. FILM OR VIDEO** Begin with the title, underlined. For a film, cite the director and the lead actors or narrator ("Perf." or "Narr."), followed by the name of the distributor and the year of the film's release. For a videotape or DVD, add "Videocassette" or "DVD" before the name of the distributor.

Finding Neverland. Dir. Marc Forster. Perf. Johnny Depp, Kate Winslet, Julie Christie, Radha Mitchell, and Dustin Hoffman. Miramax, 2004.

High Fidelity. Dir. Stephen Frears. Perf. John Cusack, Iben Hjejle, Jack Black, and Todd Louiso. 2000. Videocassette. Walt Disney Video, 2001.

■ **46. RADIO OR TELEVISION PROGRAM** Begin with the title of the radio segment or television episode (if there is one) in quotation marks, followed by the title of the program, underlined. Next give relevant information about the program's writer ("By"), director ("Dir."), performers ("Perf."), or host ("Host"). Then name the network, the local station (if any), and the date the program was broadcast.

"Monkey Trial." American Experience. PBS. WGBH, Boston. 18 Mar. 2003.

"Live at NPR: The Music and Life of Richard Thompson." Fresh Air. Natl. Public Radio. 17 Feb. 2006. 22 Feb. 2006 <http://www.npr.org/templates/story/story.php?storyId=5221211>.

If there is a series title, include it after the title of the program, neither underlined nor in quotation marks.

Mysteries of the Pyramids. On the Inside. Discovery Channel. 7 Feb. 2001.

■ **47. RADIO OR TELEVISION INTERVIEW** Begin with the name of the person who was interviewed, followed by the word "Interview." End with the information about the program as in item 46.

McGovern, George. Interview. Charlie Rose. PBS. WNET, New York. 1 Feb. 2001.

■ **48. PODCAST** A podcast can refer to digital audio content—downloadable lectures, interviews, or essays—or to the method of delivery. In an entry for a podcast, include as many of the following elements as apply and as are available: the author's (or speaker's) name; the title of the podcast, in quotation marks; the word "Podcast"; the names of the performers or the host; the title of the site on which it appears, underlined; the date of posting; the sponsor of the site; the date you accessed the source; and the URL.

Patterson, Chris. "Will School Consolidation Improve Education?" Podcast. Host Michael Quinn Sullivan. Texas PolicyCast. 13 Apr. 2006. Texas Public Policy Foundation. 27 Apr. 2006 <http://www.texaspolicy.com/texaspolicycast.php>.

NOTE: The Modern Language Association currently provides no guidelines for documenting a podcast. The model shown here is based on MLA's guidelines for a short work from a Web site.

■ **49. LIVE PERFORMANCE** For a live performance of a play, a ballet, an opera, or a concert, begin with the title of the work performed. Then name the author or composer of the work (preceded by the word "By"), followed by as much information about the performance as is available: the director ("Dir."), choreographer ("Chor."), or conductor ("Cond."); the major performers ("Perf."); the theatre, ballet, or opera company; the theatre and its city; and the date of the performance.

Art. By Yasmina Reza. Dir. Matthew Warchus. Perf. Philip Franks, Leigh Lawson, and Simon Shephard. Whitehall Theatre, London. 3 Dec. 2001.

Cello Concerto no. 2. By Eric Tanguy. Cond. Seiji Ozawa. Perf. Mstislav Rostropovich. Boston Symphony Orch. Symphony Hall, Boston. 5 Apr. 2002.

■ **50. LECTURE OR PUBLIC ADDRESS** Cite the speaker's name, followed by the title of the lecture (if any), the organization sponsoring the lecture, the location, and the date.

Wellbery, David E. "On a Sentence of Franz Kafka." Franke Inst. for the Humanities. Gleacher Center, Chicago. 1 Feb. 2006.

■ **51. PERSONAL INTERVIEW** To cite an interview that you conducted, begin with the name of the person interviewed. Then write "Personal interview," followed by the date of the interview.

Akufo, Dautey. Personal interview. 11 Aug. 2006.

Other sources (including online versions)

This section includes a variety of traditional print sources not covered elsewhere. For sources obtained on the Web, consult the appropriate model in this section and give whatever information is available for the online source; then end the citation with the date on which you accessed the source and the URL. (See the second example under item 52.)

■ **52. GOVERNMENT PUBLICATION** Treat the government agency as the author, giving the name of the government followed by the name of the agency.

Canada. Minister of Indian Affairs and Northern Dev. Gathering Strength: Canada's Aboriginal Action Plan. Ottawa: Minister of Public Works and Govt. Services Canada, 2000.

For government documents published online, give as much publication information as is available and end your citation with the date of access and the URL.

Canada. Agriculture and Agri-Food Canada. "How to Get the Most Bang for Your Buck." Agri-Science E-zine. 11 Nov. 2006. 12 Jan. 2007 <http://www.agr.gc.ca/index_e.php?s1=re&s2=zine&page=buc-arg>.

■ **53. LEGAL SOURCE** For articles of the Canadian Constitution and laws in the Criminal Code of Canada, no works cited entry is required; instead, simply give an in-text citation (see item 17 on p. 377).

For a legislative act, begin with the name of the act. Then provide the act's number and date of enactment.

Personal Information Protection and Electronic Documents Act. SC 2000, chap. 5.

For a court case, name the first plaintiff and first defendant. Then give the court name and the date of the decision, followed by the law report volume, series, and page. In a works cited entry, the name of the case is not underlined.

Nancy B. v. Hôtel-Dieu de Québec. Quebec Superior Ct. 1992. 86 DLR (4th) 385.

■ **54. PAMPHLET** Cite a pamphlet as you would a book.

Zimmer, Henry B. Canplan: Your Canadian Financial Planning Software. Calgary: Springbank, 1994.

■ **55. DISSERTATION** Begin with the author's name, followed by the dissertation title in quotation marks, the abbreviation "Diss.," the name of the institution, and the year the dissertation was accepted.

Gregory, T. R. "The C-Value Enigma." Diss. U of Guelph, ON, 2002.

For dissertations that have been published in book form, underline the title. After the title and before the book's publication information, add the abbreviation "Diss.," the name of the institution, and the year the dissertation was accepted.

Damberg, Cheryl L. Healthcare Reform: Distributional Consequences of an Employer Mandate for Workers in Small Firms. Diss. Rand Graduate School, 1995. Santa Monica: Rand, 1996.

■ **56. ABSTRACT OF A DISSERTATION** Cite an abstract as you would an unpublished dissertation. After the dissertation date, give the abbreviation *DA* or *DAI* (for *Dissertation Abstracts* or *Dissertation Abstracts International*), followed by the volume number, the date of publication, and the page number.

Chen, Shu-Ling. "Mothers and Daughters in Morrison, Tan, Marshall, and Kincaid." Diss. U of Washington, 2000. DAI 61 (2000): 2289.

57. PUBLISHED PROCEEDINGS OF A CONFERENCE Cite published conference proceedings as you would a book, adding information about the conference after the title.

Kartiganer, Donald M., and Ann J. Abadie. Faulkner at 100: Retrospect and Prospect. Proc. of Faulkner and Yoknapatawpha Conf., 27 July-1 Aug. 1997, U of Mississippi. Jackson: UP of Mississippi, 2000.

58. PUBLISHED INTERVIEW Name the person interviewed, followed by the title of the interview (if there is one). If the interview does not have a title, include the word "Interview" followed by a period after the interviewee's name. Give publication information for the work in which the interview was published.

Armstrong, Lance. "Lance in France." Sports Illustrated 28 June 2004: 46+.

If the name of the interviewer is relevant, include it after the name of the interviewee.

Prince. Interview with Bilge Ebiri. Yahoo! Internet Life 7.6 (2001): 82-85.

59. PERSONAL LETTER To cite a letter that you have received, begin with the writer's name and add the phrase "Letter to the author," followed by the date.

Primak, Shoshana. Letter to the author. 6 May 2006.

60. ENTRY IN A WIKI A wiki is an online reference that is openly edited by its users. Treat it as you would a short work from a Web site (see item 28 on p. 390). Because wiki content is, by definition, collectively edited and continually updated, do not include an author. Include the title of the entry; the name of the wiki; the date of last update; the sponsor of the wiki, if any; your date of access; and the URL.

"Hip Hop Music." Wikipedia. 2 Mar. 2006. Wikimedia Foundation. 18 Mar. 2006 <http://en.wikipedia.org/wiki/Hip_hop_music>.

"Negation in Languages." UniLang.org. 22 Apr. 2006. UniLang. 9 June 2006 <http://home.unilang.org/wiki3/index.php/Negation_in_languages>.

ON THE WEB > **dianahacker.com/writersref**
Research exercises > E-ex MLA 4–4 through MLA 4–6

MLA-4c MLA information notes (optional)

Researchers who use the MLA system of parenthetical documentation (see MLA-4a) may also use information notes for one of two purposes:

1. to provide additional material that might interrupt the flow of the paper yet is important enough to include
2. to refer readers to any sources not discussed in the paper

Information notes may be either footnotes or endnotes. Footnotes appear at the foot of the page; endnotes appear on a separate page at the end of the paper, just before the list of works cited. For either style, the notes are numbered consecutively throughout the paper. The text of the paper contains a raised arabic numeral that corresponds to the number of the note.

TEXT

In the past several years, employees have filed a number of lawsuits against employers because of online monitoring practices.[1]

NOTE

[1] For a discussion of federal law applicable to electronic surveillance in the workplace, see Kesan 293.

MLA-5

Manuscript format; sample paper

MLA-5a Manuscript format

The following guidelines are consistent with advice given in the *MLA Handbook for Writers of Research Papers,* 6th ed. (New York: MLA, 2003). For a sample MLA paper, see MLA-5b.

Formatting the paper

Papers written in MLA style should be formatted as follows.

MATERIALS Use good-quality 8½″ × 11″ (letter-size) white paper. Secure the pages with a paper clip. Unless your instructor suggests otherwise, do not staple or bind the pages.

TITLE AND IDENTIFICATION MLA does not require a title page. On the first page of your paper, place your name, your instructor's name, the course title, and the date on separate lines against the left margin. Then centre your title. (See p. 408 for a sample first page.)

If your instructor requires a title page, ask for guidelines on formatting it. A format similar to the one on page 451 may be acceptable.

PAGINATION Put the page number preceded by your last name in the upper right corner of each page, 0.5 inch (1.2 cm) below the top edge. Use arabic numerals (1, 2, 3, and so on).

MARGINS, LINE SPACING, AND PARAGRAPH INDENTS Leave margins of 1 inch (2.5 cm) on all sides of the page. Left-align the text.

Double-space throughout the paper. Do not add extra line spaces above or below the title of the paper or between paragraphs.

Indent the first line of each paragraph 0.5 inch (1.2 cm or five spaces) from the left margin.

LONG QUOTATIONS When a quotation is longer than four typed lines of prose or three lines of verse, set it off from the text by indenting the entire quotation 1 inch (2.5 cm or ten spaces) from the left margin. Double-space the indented quotation, and don't add extra space above or below it.

Quotation marks are not needed when a quotation has been set off from the text by indenting. See page 408 for an example.

WEB ADDRESSES When a Web address (URL) mentioned in the text of your paper must be divided at the end of a line, do not insert a hyphen (a hyphen could appear to be part of the address). For MLA rules on dividing Web addresses in your list of works cited, see page 406.

HEADINGS MLA neither encourages nor discourages the use of headings and currently provides no guidelines for their use. If you would like to insert headings in a long essay or research paper, check first with your instructor.

VISUALS MLA classifies visuals as tables and figures (figures include graphs, charts, maps, photographs, and drawings). Label each table with an arabic numeral (Table 1, Table 2, and so on) and provide a clear caption that identifies the subject. The label and caption should appear on separate lines above the table, flush left. Below the table, give its source in a note like this one:

> Source: David N. Greenfield and Richard A. Davis, "Lost in Cyberspace: The Web @ Work," Cyberpsychology and Behavior 5 (2002): 349.

For each figure, place a label and a caption below the figure, flush left. They need not appear on separate lines. The word "Figure" may be abbreviated to "Fig." Include source information following the caption.

Visuals should be placed in the text, as close as possible to the sentences that relate to them unless your instructor prefers them in an appendix. See page 410 for an example of a visual in the text of a paper.

Preparing the list of works cited

Begin the list of works cited on a new page at the end of the paper. Centre the title Works Cited about 1 inch (2.5 cm) from the top of the page. Double-space throughout. See page 412 for a sample list of works cited.

ALPHABETIZING THE LIST Alphabetize the list by the last names of the authors (or editors); if a work has no author or editor, alphabetize by the first word of the title other than *A, An,* or *The.*

If your list includes two or more works by the same author, use the author's name only for the first entry. For subsequent entries use three hyphens followed by a period. List the titles in alphabetical order. See item 5 on page 381.

INDENTING Do not indent the first line of each works cited entry, but indent any additional lines 0.5 inch (1.2 cm or five spaces). This technique highlights the names of the authors, making it easy for readers to scan the alphabetized list.

WEB ADDRESSES Do not insert a hyphen when dividing a Web address (URL) at the end of a line. Break the line after a slash. Also insert angle brackets around the URL.

For advice about how to cite sources with long URLs, see the note at the top of page 391.

If your word processing program automatically turns Web addresses into hot links (by underlining them and highlighting them in colour), turn off this feature.

ON THE WEB > **dianahacker.com/writersref**
Additional resources > Formatting help

MLA-5b Sample MLA research paper

On the following pages is a research paper on the topic of electronic surveillance in the workplace, written by Anna Orlov, a student in a composition class. Orlov's paper is documented with MLA-style in-text citations and list of works cited. Annotations in the margins of the paper draw your attention to Orlov's use of MLA style and her effective writing.

ON THE WEB > **dianahacker.com/writersref**
Model papers > MLA papers: Orlov; Daly; Levi
> MLA annotated bibliography: Orlov

Orlov 1

Anna Orlov

Professor Willis

English 101

17 March 2006

Title is centred.

Online Monitoring:

A Threat to Employee Privacy in the Wired Workplace

Opening sentences provide background for thesis.

As the Internet has become an integral tool of businesses, company policies on Internet usage have become as common as policies regarding vacation days or sexual harassment. A 2005 study by the American Management Association and ePolicy Institute found that 76% of companies monitor employees' use of the Web, and the number of companies that block employees' access to certain Web sites has increased 27% since 2001 (1). Unlike other company rules, however, Internet usage policies often include language authorizing companies to secretly monitor their employees, a practice that raises questions about rights in the workplace. Although companies often have legitimate concerns that lead them to monitor employees' Internet usage--from expensive security breaches to reduced productivity--the benefits of electronic surveillance are outweighed by its costs to employees' privacy and autonomy.

Thesis asserts Orlov's main point.

While surveillance of employees is not a new phenomenon, electronic surveillance allows employers to monitor workers with unprecedented efficiency. In his book The Naked Employee, Frederick Lane describes offline ways in which employers have been permitted to intrude on employees' privacy for decades, such as drug testing, background checks, psychological exams, lie detector tests, and in-store video surveillance. The difference, Lane argues, between these old methods of data gathering and electronic surveillance involves quantity:

Summary and long quotation are introduced with a signal phrase naming the author.

> Technology makes it possible for employers to gather enormous amounts of data about employees, often far beyond what is necessary to satisfy safety or productivity concerns. And the trends that drive technology--faster, smaller, cheaper--make it possible for larger and larger numbers of employers to gather ever-greater amounts of personal data. (3-4)

Long quotation is set off from the text; quotation marks are omitted.

Page number is given in parentheses after the final period.

Marginal annotations indicate MLA-style formatting and effective writing.

Orlov 2

Lane points out that employers can collect data whenever employees use their computers--for example, when they send e-mail, surf the Web, or even arrive at or depart from their workstations.

Another key difference between traditional surveillance and electronic surveillance is that employers can monitor workers' computer use secretly. One popular monitoring method is keystroke logging, which is done by means of an undetectable program on employees' computers. The Web site of a vendor for Spector Pro, a popular keystroke logging program, explains that the software can be installed to operate in "Stealth" mode so that it "does not show up as an icon, does not appear in the Windows system tray, . . . [and] cannot be uninstalled without the Spector Pro password which YOU specify" ("Automatically"). As Lane explains, these programs record every key entered into the computer in hidden directories that can later be accessed or uploaded by supervisors; at their most sophisticated, the programs can even scan for keywords tailored to individual companies (128-29).

Clear topic sentences, like this one, are used throughout the paper.

Source with an unknown author is cited by a shortened title.

Some experts have argued that a range of legitimate concerns justifies employer monitoring of employee Internet usage. As PC World columnist Daniel Tynan explains, companies that don't monitor network traffic can be penalized for their ignorance: "Employees could accidentally (or deliberately) spill confidential information . . . or allow worms to spread throughout a corporate network." The ePolicy Institute, an organization that advises companies about reducing risks from technology, reported that breaches in computer security cost institutions $100 million in 1999 alone (Flynn). Companies also are held legally accountable for many of the transactions conducted on their networks and with their technology. Legal scholar Jay Kesan points out that the law holds employers liable for employees' actions such as violations of copyright laws, the distribution of offensive or graphic sexual material, and illegal disclosure of confidential information (312).

Orlov anticipates objections and provides sources for opposing views.

These kinds of concerns should give employers, in certain instances, the right to monitor employee behavior. But employers rushing to adopt surveillance programs might not be adequately weighing the effect such programs can have on employee morale.

Transition helps readers move from one paragraph to the next.

Orlov 3

Fig. 1. Scott Adams, Dilbert and the Way of the Weasel (New York: Harper, 2002) 106.

Illustration has figure number and source information.

Employers must consider the possibility that employees will perceive surveillance as a breach of trust that can make them feel like disobedient children, not responsible adults who wish to perform their jobs professionally and autonomously.

Orlov treats both sides fairly; she provides a transition to her own argument.

Yet determining how much autonomy workers should be given is complicated by the ambiguous nature of productivity in the wired workplace. On the one hand, computers and Internet access give employees powerful tools to carry out their jobs; on the other hand, the same technology offers constant temptations to avoid work. As a 2005 study by Salary.com and America Online indicates, the Internet ranked as the top choice among employees for ways of wasting time on the job; it beat talking with co-workers--the second most popular method--by a margin of nearly two to one (Frauenheim). Chris Gonsalves, an editor for eWeek.com, argues that the technology has changed the terms between employers and employees: "While bosses can easily detect and interrupt water-cooler chatter," he writes, "the employee who is shopping at Lands' End or IMing with fellow fantasy baseball managers may actually appear to be working." The gap between behaviors that are observable to managers and the employee's actual activities when sitting behind a computer has created additional motivations for employers to invest in surveillance programs. "Dilbert," a popular cartoon that spoofs office culture, aptly captures how rampant recreational Internet use has become in the workplace (see Fig. 1).

No page number is available for this Web source.

Orlov counters opposing views and provides support for her argument.

But monitoring online activities can have the unintended effect of making employees resentful. As many workers would be quick to point out, Web surfing and other personal uses of the Internet can provide needed outlets in the stressful work environment; many scholars have

Orlov 4

argued that limiting and policing these outlets can exacerbate tensions between employees and managers. Kesan warns that "prohibiting personal use can seem extremely arbitrary and can seriously harm morale. . . . Imagine a concerned parent who is prohibited from checking on a sick child by a draconian company policy" (315-16). As this analysis indicates, employees can become disgruntled when Internet usage policies are enforced to their full extent.

Orlov uses a brief signal phrase to move from her argument to the words of a source.

Additionally, many experts disagree with employers' assumption that online monitoring can increase productivity. Employment law attorney Joseph Schmitt argues that, particularly for employees who are paid a salary rather than by the hour, "a company shouldn't care whether employees spend one or 10 hours on the Internet as long as they are getting their jobs done--and provided that they are not accessing inappropriate sites" (qtd. in Verespej). Other experts even argue that time spent on personal Internet browsing can actually be productive for companies. According to Bill Coleman, an executive at Salary.com, "Personal Internet use and casual office conversations often turn into new business ideas or suggestions for gaining operating efficiencies" (qtd. in Frauenheim). Employers, in other words, may benefit from showing more faith in their employees' ability to exercise their autonomy.

Orlov cites an indirect source: words quoted in another source.

Employees' right to privacy and autonomy in the workplace, however, remains a murky area of the law. Although evaluating where to draw the line between employee rights and employer powers is often a duty that falls to the judicial system, the courts have shown little willingness to intrude on employers' exercise of control over their computer networks. Federal law provides few guidelines related to online monitoring of employees, and only Connecticut and Delaware require companies to disclose this type of surveillance to employees (Tam et al.). "It is unlikely that we will see a legally guaranteed zone of privacy in the American workplace," predicts Kesan (293). This reality leaves employees and employers to sort the potential risks and benefits of technology in contract agreements and terms of employment. With continuing advances in technology, protecting both employers and employees will require greater awareness of these programs, better disclosure to employees, and a more public discussion about what types of protections are necessary to guard individual freedoms in the wired workplace.

Orlov sums up her argument and suggests a course of action.

Heading is centred.

List is alphabetized by authors' last names (or by title when a work has no author).

The URL is broken after a slash. No hyphen is inserted.

First line of each entry is at the left margin; extra lines are indented 1/2" (1.2 cm or five spaces).

Double-spacing is used throughout.

A work with four authors is listed by the first author's name and the abbreviation "et al." (for "and others").

Orlov 5

Works Cited

Adams, Scott. Dilbert and the Way of the Weasel. New York: Harper, 2002.

American Management Association and ePolicy Institute. "2005 Electronic Monitoring and Surveillance Survey." American Management Association. 2005. 15 Feb. 2006 <http://www.amanet.org/research/pdfs/EMS_summary05.pdf>.

"Automatically Record Everything They Do Online! Spector Pro 5.0 FAQ's." Netbus.org. SpectorSoft. 17 Feb. 2006 <http://www.netbus.org/sProFAQ.html>.

Flynn, Nancy. "Internet Policies." ePolicy Institute. 2001. 15 Feb. 2006 <http://www.epolicyinstitute.com/i_policies/index.html>.

Frauenheim, Ed. "Stop Reading This Headline and Get Back to Work." CNET News.com. 11 July 2005. 17 Feb. 2006 <http://news.com.com/Stop+reading+this+headline+and+get+back+to+work/2100-1022_3-5783552.html>.

Gonsalves, Chris. "Wasting Away on the Web." eWeek.com 8 Aug. 2005. 16 Feb. 2006 <http://www.eweek.com/article2/0,1895,1843242,00.asp>.

Kesan, Jay P. "Cyber-Working or Cyber-Shirking? A First Principles Examination of Electronic Privacy in the Workplace." Florida Law Review 54 (2002): 289-332.

Lane, Frederick S., III. The Naked Employee: How Technology Is Compromising Workplace Privacy. New York: Amer. Management Assn., 2003.

Tam, Pui-Wing, et al. "Snooping E-Mail by Software Is Now a Workplace Norm." Wall Street Journal 9 Mar. 2005: B1+.

Tynan, Daniel. "Your Boss Is Watching." PC World 6 Oct. 2004. 17 Feb. 2006 <http://www.pcworld.com/news/article/0,aid,118072,00.asp>.

Verespej, Michael A. "Inappropriate Internet Surfing." Industry Week 7 Feb. 2000. 16 Feb. 2006 <http://www.industryweek.com/ReadArticle.aspx?ArticleID=568>.

APA
CMS

APA and CMS Papers

APA • CMS
APA/CMS Papers

This tabbed section shows how to document sources in psychology and other social science classes (APA style) and in history and some humanities classes (CMS style). It also includes discipline-specific advice on three important topics: supporting a thesis, citing sources and avoiding plagiarism, and integrating sources. Examples are documented with the appropriate style.

NOTE: For cross-disciplinary advice on finding and evaluating sources and on managing information, see the tabbed section R, Researching.

APA Papers

Most writing assignments in the social sciences are either reports of original research or reviews of the literature written about a research topic. Often an original research report contains a "review of the literature" section that places the writer's project in the context of previous research.

Most social science instructors will ask you to document your sources with the American Psychological Association (APA) system of in-text citations and references described in APA-4. You face three main challenges when writing a social science paper that draws on written sources: (1) supporting a thesis, (2) citing your sources and avoiding plagiarism, and (3) integrating quotations and other source material.

APA-1

Supporting a thesis

Most assignments ask you to form a thesis, or main idea, and to support that thesis with well-organized evidence. In a paper reviewing the literature on a topic, this thesis analyzes the often competing conclusions drawn by a variety of researchers.

APA-1a Form a thesis.

A thesis, which usually appears at the end of the introduction, is a one-sentence (or occasionally a two-sentence) statement of your central idea. You will be reading articles and other sources that address a central research question. Your thesis will express a reasonable answer to that question, given the current state of research in the field. Here, for example, is a research question posed by Luisa Mirano, a student in a psychology class, followed by a thesis that answers the question.

RESEARCH QUESTION

Is medication the right treatment for the escalating problem of childhood obesity?

POSSIBLE THESIS

Understanding the limitations of medical treatments for children highlights the complexity of the childhood obesity problem in the United States and underscores the need for physicians, advocacy groups, and policymakers to search for other solutions.

ON THE WEB > **dianahacker.com/writersref**
Research exercises > E-ex APA 1–1

APA-1b Organize your evidence.

The American Psychological Association encourages the use of headings to help readers follow the organization of a paper. For an original research report, the major headings often follow a standard model: Method, Results, Discussion. The introduction is not given a heading; it consists of the material between the title of the paper and the first heading.

For a literature review, headings will vary. The student who wrote about treatments for childhood obesity used four questions to focus her research; the questions then became headings in her paper (see pp. 451–59).

APA-1c Use sources to inform and support your argument.

Used thoughtfully, the source materials you have gathered will make your argument more complex and convincing for readers. Sources can play several different roles as you develop your points.

Providing background information or context

You can use facts and statistics to support generalizations or to establish the importance of your topic, as student writer Luisa Mirano does in her introduction.

> In March 2004, U.S. Surgeon General Richard Carmona called attention to a health problem in the United States that, until recently, has been overlooked: childhood obesity. Carmona said that the "astounding" 15% child obesity rate constitutes an "epidemic." Since the early 1980s, that rate has "doubled in children and tripled in adolescents." Now more than 9 million children are classified as obese (paras. 3, 6).

Explaining terms or concepts

If readers are unlikely to be familiar with a word, a phrase, or an idea important to your topic, you must explain it for them. Quoting or paraphrasing a source can help you define terms and concepts in neutral, accessible language.

> Sibutramine suppresses appetite by blocking the reuptake of the neurotransmitters serotonin and norepinephrine in the brain (Yanovski & Yanovski, 2002, p. 594).

Supporting your claims

As you draft your argument, make sure to back up your assertions with facts, examples, and other evidence from your research (see also A2-e). Luisa Mirano, for example, uses one source's findings to support her central idea that the medical treatment of childhood obesity has limitations.

> As journalist Greg Critser (2003) noted in his book *Fat Land,* use of weight-loss drugs is unlikely to have an effect without the proper "support system"--one that includes doctors, facilities, time, and money (p. 3).

Lending authority to your argument

Expert opinion can give weight to your argument (see also A2-e). But don't rely on experts to make your argument for you. Construct your argument in your own words and, when appropriate, cite the judgment of an authority in the field to support your position.

> Both medical experts and policymakers recognize that solutions might come not only from a laboratory but also from policy, education, and advocacy. Indeed, a handbook designed to educate doctors on obesity recommended a notably nonmedical course of action, calling for "major changes in some aspects of western culture" (Hoppin & Taveras, 2004, Conclusion section, para. 1).

Anticipating and countering alternative interpretations

Do not ignore sources that seem contrary to your position or that offer interpretations different from your own. Instead, use them to give voice to opposing points of view and to state potential objections before you counter them (see A2-f). Mirano uses a source to show readers that there is substance to her opponents' position that medication is the preferable approach to treating childhood obesity.

> As researchers Yanovski and Yanovski (2002) have explained, obesity was once considered "either a moral failing or evidence of underlying psychopathology" (p. 592). But this view has shifted: Many medical professionals now consider obesity a biomedical rather than a moral condition, influenced by both genetic and environmental factors. Yanovski and Yanovski have further noted that the development of weight-loss medications in the early 1990s showed that "obesity should be treated in the same manner as any other chronic disease . . . through the long-term use of medication" (p. 592).

APA-2

Citing sources; avoiding plagiarism

Your research paper is a collaboration between you and your sources. To be fair and ethical, you must acknowledge your debt to the writers of those sources. If you don't, you commit plagiarism, a serious academic offence.

Three different acts are considered plagiarism: (1) failing to cite quotations and borrowed ideas, (2) failing to enclose borrowed language in quotation marks, and (3) failing to put summaries and paraphrases in your own words.

APA-2a Cite quotations and borrowed ideas.

You must of course cite all direct quotations. You must also cite any ideas borrowed from a source: summaries and paraphrases; statistics and other specific facts; and visuals such as cartoons, graphs, and diagrams.

The only exception is common knowledge—information that your readers may know or could easily locate in any number of reference sources. For example, the current population of Canada is common knowledge among sociologists and economists, and psychologists are familiar with Freud's theory of the unconscious. As a rule, when you have seen certain information repeatedly in your reading, you don't need to cite it. However, when information has appeared in only a few sources, when it is highly specific (as with statistics), or when it is controversial, you should cite the source.

The American Psychological Association recommends an author-date system of citations. Here, very briefly, is how the author-date system usually works. See APA-4 for a detailed discussion of variations.

1. The source is introduced by a signal phrase that includes the last names of the authors followed by the date of publication in parentheses.
2. The material being cited is followed by a page number in parentheses.
3. At the end of the paper, an alphabetized list of references gives complete publication information about the source.

IN-TEXT CITATION

As researchers Yanovski and Yanovski (2002) have explained, obesity was once considered "either a moral failing or evidence of underlying psychopathology" (p. 592).

ENTRY IN THE LIST OF REFERENCES

Yanovski, S. Z., & Yanovski, J. A. (2002). Drug therapy: Obesity [Electronic version]. *The New England Journal of Medicine, 346*, 591-602.

APA-2b Enclose borrowed language in quotation marks.

To indicate that you are using a source's exact phrases or sentences, you must enclose them in quotation marks. To omit the quotation marks is to claim—falsely—that the language is your own. Such an omission is plagiarism even if you have cited the source.

ORIGINAL SOURCE

In an effort to seek the causes of this disturbing trend, experts have pointed to a range of important potential contributors to the rise in childhood obesity that are unrelated to media: a reduction in physical education classes and after-school athletic programs, an increase in the availability of sodas and snacks in public schools, the growth in the number of fast-food outlets across the country, the trend toward "super-sizing" food portions in restaurants, and the increasing number of highly processed high-calorie and high-fat grocery products.

—Henry J. Kaiser Family Foundation,
"The Role of Media in Childhood Obesity" (2004), p. 1

PLAGIARISM

According to the Henry J. Kaiser Family Foundation (2004), experts have pointed to a range of important potential contributors to the rise in childhood obesity that are unrelated to media (p. 1).

BORROWED LANGUAGE IN QUOTATION MARKS

According to the Henry J. Kaiser Family Foundation (2004), "experts have pointed to a range of important potential contributors to the rise in childhood obesity that are unrelated to media" (p. 1).

NOTE: When quoted sentences are set off from the text by indenting, quotation marks are not needed (see p. 423).

APA-2c Put summaries and paraphrases in your own words.

Summaries and paraphrases are written in your own words. A summary condenses information; a paraphrase reports information in about the same number of words as in the source. When you summarize or paraphrase, you must restate the source's meaning using your own language. You commit plagiarism if you half-copy the author's sentences—either by mixing the author's well-chosen phrases with your own without using quotation marks or by plugging your own synonyms into the author's sentence structure. The following paraphrases are plagiarized—even though the source is cited—because their language is too close to that of the source.

ORIGINAL SOURCE

In an effort to seek the causes of this disturbing trend, experts have pointed to a range of important potential contributors to the rise in childhood obesity that are unrelated to media.

—Henry J. Kaiser Family Foundation,
"The Role of Media in Childhood Obesity" (2004), p. 1

UNACCEPTABLE BORROWING OF PHRASES

According to the Henry J. Kaiser Family Foundation (2004), experts have indicated a range of significant potential contributors to the rise in childhood obesity that are not linked to media (p. 1).

UNACCEPTABLE BORROWING OF STRUCTURE

According to the Henry J. Kaiser Family Foundation (2004), experts have identified a variety of significant factors causing a rise in childhood obesity, factors that are not linked to media (p. 1).

To avoid plagiarizing an author's language, set the source aside, write from memory, and consult the source later to check for accuracy. This strategy prevents you from being captivated by the words on the page.

ACCEPTABLE PARAPHRASE

A report by the Henry J. Kaiser Family Foundation (2004) described sources other than media for the childhood obesity crisis.

ON THE WEB > **dianahacker.com/writersref**
Research exercises > E-ex APA 2–1 through APA 2–5

APA-3

Integrating sources

Quotations, summaries, paraphrases, and facts will support your argument, but they cannot speak for you. You can use several strategies to integrate information from research sources into your paper while maintaining your own voice.

APA-3a Limit your use of quotations.

Using quotations appropriately

Although it is tempting to insert many quotations in your paper and to use your own words only for connecting passages, do not quote excessively. It is almost impossible to integrate numerous long quotations smoothly into your own text.

It is not always necessary to quote full sentences from a source. At times you may wish to borrow only a phrase or to weave part of a source's sentence into your own sentence structure.

> Carmona (2004) advised the subcommittee that the situation constitutes an "epidemic" and that the skyrocketing statistics are "astounding" (para. 3).

> As researchers continue to face a number of unknowns about obesity, it may be helpful to envision treating the disorder, as Yanovski and Yanovski (2002) suggested, "in the same manner as any other chronic disease" (p. 592).

USING THE ELLIPSIS MARK To condense a quoted passage, you can use the ellipsis mark (three periods, with spaces between) to indicate that you have omitted words. What remains must be grammatically complete.

> Roman (2003) reported that "social factors are nearly as significant as individual metabolism in the formation of . . . dietary habits of adolescents" (p. 345).

The writer has omitted the words *both healthy and unhealthy.*

When you want to omit a full sentence or more, use a period before the three ellipsis dots.

> According to Sothern and Gordon (2003), "Environmental factors may contribute as much as 80% to the causes of childhood obesity. . . . Research suggests that obese children demonstrate decreased levels of physical activity and increased psychosocial problems" (p. 104).

Ordinarily, do not use an ellipsis mark at the beginning or at the end of a quotation. Readers will understand that the quoted material is taken from a longer passage. The only exception occurs when you think that the author's meaning might be misinterpreted without ellipsis marks.

USING BRACKETS Brackets (square parentheses) allow you to insert your own words into quoted material to explain a confusing reference or to keep a sentence grammatical in your context.

> The cost of treating obesity currently totals $117 billion per year--a price, according to the surgeon general, "second only to the cost of [treating] tobacco use" (Carmona, 2004, para. 9).

To indicate an error in a quotation, insert [*sic*] right after the error. Notice that the term *sic* is italicized and appears in brackets.

SETTING OFF LONG QUOTATIONS When you quote forty or more words, set off the quotation by indenting it 0.5 inch (1.2 cm or five spaces) from the left margin. Use the normal right margin and do not single-space.

Long quotations should be introduced by an informative sentence, usually followed by a colon. Quotation marks are unnecessary because the indented format tells readers that the words are taken directly from the source.

> Yanovski and Yanovski (2002) have described earlier treatments of obesity that focused on behavior modification:
>
> > With the advent of behavioral treatments for obesity in the 1960s, hope arose that modification of maladaptive eating and exercise habits would lead to sustained weight loss, and that time-limited programs would produce permanent changes in weight. Medications for the treatment of obesity were proposed as short-term adjuncts for patients, who would presumably then acquire the skills necessary to continue to lose weight, reach "ideal body weight," and maintain a reduced weight indefinitely. (p. 592)

APA-3b Use signal phrases to integrate sources.

The information you gather from sources cannot speak for itself. Whenever you include a paraphrase, summary, or direct quotation of another writer in your paper, prepare your readers for it with an introduction called a *signal phrase.* A signal phrase usually names the author of the source and gives the publication date in parentheses.

When the signal phrase includes a verb, choose one that is appropriate for the way you are using the source (see APA-1c). Are you arguing a point, making an observation, reporting a fact, drawing a conclusion, or refuting an argument? By choosing an appropriate verb, you can make your source's role clear. See the chart on page 424 for a list of verbs commonly used in signal phrases.

The American Psychological Association requires using past tense or present perfect tense in phrases that introduce quotations and other source material: *Davis (2005) noted that* or *Davis (2005) has noted that*, not *Davis (2005) notes that.* Use the present tense only for discussing the results of an experiment (*the results show*) or knowledge that has clearly been established (*researchers agree*).

It is generally acceptable in the social sciences to call authors by their last name only, even on a first mention. If your paper refers to two authors with same last name, use initials as well.

Using signal phrases in APA papers

To avoid monotony, try to vary the language and placement of your signal phrases.

MODEL SIGNAL PHRASES

In the words of Carmona (2004), "..."

As Yanovski and Yanovski (2002) have noted, "..."

Hoppin and Taveras (2004), medical researchers, pointed out that "..."

"...," claimed Critser (2003).

"...," wrote Duenwald (2004), "..."

Researchers McDuffie et al. (2003) have offered an odd argument for this view: "..."

Hilts (2002) answered these objections with the following analysis: "..."

VERBS IN SIGNAL PHRASES

admitted	contended	reasoned
agreed	declared	refuted
argued	denied	rejected
asserted	emphasized	reported
believed	insisted	responded
claimed	noted	suggested
compared	observed	thought
confirmed	pointed out	wrote

Marking boundaries

Readers need to move from your words to the words of a source without feeling a jolt. Avoid dropping direct quotations into your text without warning. Instead, provide clear signal phrases, including at least the author's name and the date of publication. A signal phrase indicates the boundary between your words and the source's words and can also tell readers why a source is trustworthy.

DROPPED QUOTATION

Obesity was once considered in a very different light. "For many years, obesity was approached as it if were either a moral failing or evidence of underlying psychopathology" (Yanovski & Yanovski, 2002, p. 592).

QUOTATION WITH SIGNAL PHRASE

As researchers Yanovski and Yanovski (2002) have explained, obesity was once considered "either a moral failing or evidence of underlying psychopathology" (p. 592).

Introducing summaries and paraphrases

As with quotations, you should introduce most summaries and paraphrases with a signal phrase that mentions the author and the date of publication and places the material in context. Readers will then understand where the summary or paraphrase begins.

Without the signal phrase (underlined) in the following example, readers might think that only the last sentence is being cited, when in fact the whole paragraph is based on the source.

> Carmona (2004) advised a Senate subcommittee that the problem of childhood obesity is dire and that the skyrocketing statistics--which put the child obesity rate at 15%--are cause for alarm. More than 9 million children, double the number in the early 1980s, are classified as obese. Carmona warned that obesity can cause myriad physical problems that only worsen as children grow older (para. 6).

There are times, however, when a summary or a paraphrase does not require a signal phrase naming the author. When the context makes clear where the cited material begins, omit the signal phrase and include the author's name in the parentheses. Unless the work is short, also include the page number in the parentheses: (Saltzman, 2004, p. D8).

Putting source material in context

Readers need to understand how your source is relevant to your paper's thesis. It's a good idea, in other words, to embed your quotation—especially a long one—between sentences of your own, introducing it with a signal phrase and following it up with interpretive comments that link the source material to your paper's thesis.

QUOTATION WITH INSUFFICIENT CONTEXT

A report by the Henry J. Kaiser Family Foundation (2004) outlined trends that may have contributed to the childhood obesity crisis, including food advertising for children as well as

> a reduction in physical education classes . . . , an increase in the availability of sodas and snacks in public schools, the growth in the

> number of fast-food outlets . . . , and the increasing number of highly processed high-calorie and high-fat grocery products. (p. 1)

QUOTATION WITH EFFECTIVE CONTEXT

A report by the Henry J. Kaiser Family Foundation (2004) outlined trends that may have contributed to the childhood obesity crisis, including food advertising for children as well as

> a reduction in physical education classes . . . , an increase in the availability of sodas and snacks in public schools, the growth in the number of fast-food outlets . . . , and the increasing number of highly processed high-calorie and high-fat grocery products. (p. 1)

Addressing each of these areas requires more than a doctor armed with a prescription pad; it requires a broad mobilization not just of doctors and concerned parents but of educators, food industry executives, advertisers, and media representatives.

Integrating statistics and other facts

When you are citing a statistic or another specific fact, a signal phrase is often not necessary. In most cases, readers will understand that the citation refers to the statistic or fact (not the whole paragraph).

> In purely financial terms, the drugs cost more than $3 a day on average (Duenwald, 2004, paras. 33, 36).

There is nothing wrong, however, with using a signal phrase.

> Duenwald (2004) reported that the drugs cost more than $3 a day on average (paras. 33, 36).

ON THE WEB > **dianahacker.com/writersref**
Research exercises > E-ex APA 3–1 through APA 3–4

APA-4

Documenting sources

In most social science classes, you will be asked to use the APA system for documenting sources, which is set forth in the *Publication Manual of the American Psychological Association,* 5th ed. (Washington: APA, 2001). APA recommends in-text citations that refer readers to a list of references.

An in-text citation gives the author of the source (often in a signal phrase), the date of publication, and at times a page number in parentheses. At the end of the paper, a list of references provides publication information about the source (see p. 459). The direct link between the in-text citation and the entry in the reference list is highlighted in green in the following example.

IN-TEXT CITATION

Yanovski and Yanovski (2002) reported that "the current state of the treatment for obesity is similar to the state of the treatment of hypertension several decades ago" (p. 600).

ENTRY IN THE LIST OF REFERENCES

Yanovski, S. Z., & Yanovski, J. A. (2002). Drug therapy: Obesity [Electronic version]. *The New England Journal of Medicine, 346,* 591-602.

For a reference list that includes this entry, see page 459.

Directory to APA in-text citations

APA-4a APA in-text citations

The APA's in-text citations provide at least the author's last name and the date of publication. For direct quotations and some paraphrases, a page number is given as well.

NOTE: APA style requires the use of the past tense or the present perfect tense in signal phrases introducing cited material: *Smith (2005) reported, Smith (2005) has argued.*

1. BASIC FORMAT FOR A QUOTATION Ordinarily, introduce the quotation with a signal phrase that includes the author's last name followed by the year of publication in parentheses. Put the page number (preceded by "p.") in parentheses after the quotation.

> Critser (2003) noted that despite growing numbers of overweight Americans, many health care providers still "remain either in ignorance or outright denial about the health danger to the poor and the young" (p. 5).

If the author is not named in the signal phrase, place the author's name, the year, and the page number in parentheses after the quotation: (Critser, 2003, p. 5).

NOTE: APA style requires the year of publication in an in-text citation. Do not include a month, even if the source is listed by month and year.

2. BASIC FORMAT FOR A SUMMARY OR A PARAPHRASE Include the author's last name and the year either in a signal phrase introducing the material or in parentheses following it. A page number or another locator is not required for a summary or a paraphrase, but include one if it would help readers find the passage in a long work.

> According to Carmona (2004), the cost of treating obesity is exceeded only by the cost of treating illnesses from tobacco use (para. 9).

> The cost of treating obesity is exceeded only by the cost of treating illnesses from tobacco use (Carmona, 2004, para. 9).

3. A WORK WITH TWO AUTHORS Name both authors in the signal phrase or parentheses each time you cite the work. In the parentheses, use "&" between the authors' names; in the signal phrase, use "and."

> According to Sothern and Gordon (2003), "Environmental factors may contribute as much as 80% to the causes of childhood obesity" (p. 104).

> Obese children often engage in limited physical activity (Sothern & Gordon, 2003, p. 104).

4. A WORK WITH THREE TO FIVE AUTHORS Identify all authors in the signal phrase or parentheses the first time you cite the source.

> In 2003, Berkowitz, Wadden, Tershakovec, and Cronquist concluded, "Sibutramine . . . must be carefully monitored in adolescents, as in adults, to control increases in [blood pressure] and pulse rate" (p. 1811).

In subsequent citations, use the first author's name followed by "et al." in either the signal phrase or the parentheses.

> As Berkowitz et al. (2003) advised, "Until more extensive safety and efficacy data are available, . . . weight-loss medications should be used only on an experimental basis for adolescents" (p. 1811).

5. A WORK WITH SIX OR MORE AUTHORS Use the first author's name followed by "et al." in the signal phrase or the parentheses.

> McDuffie et al. (2002) tested 20 adolescents, aged 12-16, over a three-month period and found that orlistat, combined with behavioral therapy, produced an average weight loss of 4.4 kg, or 9.7 pounds (p. 646).

6. UNKNOWN AUTHOR If the author is unknown, mention the work's title in the signal phrase or give the first word or two of the title in the parenthetical citation. Titles of articles and chapters are put in quotation marks; titles of books and reports are italicized.

> Children struggling to control their weight must also struggle with the pressures of television advertising that, on the one hand, encourages the consumption of junk food and, on the other, celebrates thin celebrities ("Television," 2002).

NOTE: In the rare case when "Anonymous" is specified as the author, treat it as if it were a real name: (Anonymous, 2001). In the list of references, also use the name Anonymous as author.

7. ORGANIZATION AS AUTHOR If the author is a government agency or other organization, name the organization in the signal phrase or in the parenthetical citation the first time you cite the source.

> Obesity puts children at risk for a number of medical complications, including type 2 diabetes, hypertension, sleep apnea, and orthopedic problems (Henry J. Kaiser Family Foundation, 2004, p. 1).

If the organization has a familiar abbreviation, you may include it in brackets the first time you cite the source and use the abbreviation alone in later citations.

FIRST CITATION (National Institute of Mental Health [NIMH], 2001)

LATER CITATIONS (NIMH, 2001)

8. TWO OR MORE WORKS IN THE SAME PARENTHESES When your parenthetical citation names two or more works, put them in the same order that they appear in the reference list, separated by semicolons.

> Researchers have indicated that studies of pharmacological treatments for childhood obesity are inconclusive (Berkowitz et al., 2003; McDuffie et al., 2003).

9. AUTHORS WITH THE SAME LAST NAME To avoid confusion, use initials with the last names if your reference list includes two or more authors with the same last name.

> Research by E. Smith (1989) revealed that . . .

10. PERSONAL COMMUNICATION Interviews, memos, letters, e-mail, and similar unpublished person-to-person communications should be cited as follows:

> One of Atkinson's colleagues, who has studied the effect of the media on children's eating habits, has contended that advertisers for snack foods will need to design ads responsibly for their younger viewers (F. Johnson, personal communication, October 20, 2004).

Do not include personal communications in your reference list.

11. AN ELECTRONIC DOCUMENT When possible, cite an electronic document as you would any other document (using the author-date style).

> Atkinson (2001) found that children who spent at least four hours a day watching TV were less likely to engage in adequate physical activity during the week.

Electronic sources may lack authors' names or dates. In addition, they may lack page numbers (required in some citations). Here are APA's guidelines for handling sources without authors' names, dates, or page numbers.

Unknown author

If no author is named, mention the title of the document in a signal phrase or give the first word or two of the title in parentheses (see also item 6). (If an organization serves as the author, see item 7.)

> The body's basal metabolic rate, or BMR, is a measure of its at-rest energy requirement ("Exercise," 2003).

Unknown date
When the date is unknown, APA recommends using the abbreviation "n.d." (for "no date").

> Attempts to establish a definitive link between television programming and children's eating habits have been problematic (Magnus, n.d.).

No page numbers
APA ordinarily requires page numbers for quotations, and it recommends them for summaries or paraphrases from long sources. When an electronic source lacks stable numbered pages, your citation should include—if possible—information that will help readers locate the particular passage being cited.

When an electronic document has numbered paragraphs, use the paragraph number preceded by the symbol ¶ or by the abbreviation "para.": (Hall, 2001, ¶ 5) *or* (Hall, 2001, para. 5). If neither a page nor a paragraph number is given and the document contains headings, cite the appropriate heading and indicate which paragraph under that heading you are referring to.

> Hoppin and Taveras (2004) pointed out that several other medications were classified by the Drug Enforcement Administration as having the "potential for abuse" (Weight-Loss Drugs section, para. 6).

NOTE: Electronic files in portable document format (PDF) often have stable page numbers. For such sources, give the page number in the parenthetical citation.

12. INDIRECT SOURCE If you use a source that was cited in another source (a secondary source), name the original source in your signal phrase. List the secondary source in your reference list and include it in your parenthetical citation, preceded by the words "as cited in." In the following example, Critser is the secondary source.

> Former surgeon general Dr. David Satcher described "a nation of young people seriously at risk of starting out obese and dooming themselves to the difficult task of overcoming a tough illness" (as cited in Critser, 2003, p. 4).

13. TWO OR MORE WORKS BY THE SAME AUTHOR IN THE SAME YEAR When your list of references includes more than one work by the same author in the same year, use lowercase letters ("a," "b," and so on) with the year to order the entries in the reference list. (See item 6 on p. 434.) Use those same letters with the year in the in-text citation.

> Research by Durgin (2003b) has yielded new findings about the role of counseling in treating childhood obesity.

ON THE WEB > **dianahacker.com/writersref**
Research exercises > E-ex APA 4–1 through APA 4–3

APA-4b APA references

In APA style, the alphabetical list of works cited, which appears at the end of the paper, is titled "References." Following are models illustrating APA style for entries in the list of references. Observe all details: capitalization, punctuation, use of italics, and so on. For advice on preparing the reference list, see pages 449–50. For a sample reference list, see page 459.

ON THE WEB > **dianahacker.com/writersref**
Research exercises > E-ex APA 4–4

ON THE WEB > **dianahacker.com/writersref**
Research and Documentation Online > Social sciences: Documenting sources (APA)

General guidelines for listing authors

Alphabetize entries in the list of references by authors' last names; if a work has no author, alphabetize it by its title. The first element of each entry is important because citations in the text of the paper refer to it and readers will be looking for it in the alphabetized list. The date of publication appears immediately after the first element of the citation.

NAME AND DATE CITED IN TEXT

Duncan (2006) has reported that . . .

BEGINNING OF ENTRY IN THE LIST OF REFERENCES

Duncan, B. (2006).

Items 1–4 show how to begin an entry for a work with a single author, multiple authors, an organization as author, and an unknown author. Items 5 and 6 show how to begin an entry when your list includes two or more works by the same author or two or more works by the same author in the same year. What comes after the first element of your citation will depend on the kind of source you are citing (see items 7–32).

Directory to APA references (bibliographic entries)

1. SINGLE AUTHOR Begin the entry with the author's last name, followed by a comma and the author's initial(s). Then give the date in parentheses.

Perez, E. (2006).

2. MULTIPLE AUTHORS List up to six authors by last names followed by initials. Use an ampersand (&) between the names of two authors or, if there are more than two authors, before the name of the last author.

DuNann, D. W., & Koger, S. M. (2004).

Sloan, F. A., Stout, E. M., Whetten-Goldstein, K., & Liang, L. (2000).

If there are more than six authors, list the first six and "et al." (meaning "and others") to indicate that there are others.

3. ORGANIZATION AS AUTHOR When the author is an organization, begin with the name of the organization.

Canadian Psychological Association. (2005).

NOTE: If the organization is also the publisher, see item 29.

4. UNKNOWN AUTHOR Begin the entry with the work's title. Titles of books are italicized; titles of articles are neither italicized nor put in quotation marks. (For rules on capitalization of titles, see p. 449.)

Oxford essential world atlas. (2001).

Omega-3 fatty acids. (2004, November 23).

5. TWO OR MORE WORKS BY THE SAME AUTHOR Use the author's name for all entries. List the entries by year, the earliest first.

Schlechty, P. C. (1997).

Schlechty, P. C. (2001).

6. TWO OR MORE WORKS BY THE SAME AUTHOR IN THE SAME YEAR List the works alphabetically by title. In the parentheses, following the year, add "a," "b," and so on. Use these same letters when giving the year in the in-text citation. (See also p. 449.)

Durgin, P. A. (2003a). At-risk behaviors in children.

Durgin, P. A. (2003b). Treating obesity with psychotherapy.

Articles in periodicals

This section shows how to prepare an entry for an article in a periodical such as a scholarly journal, a magazine, or a newspaper. In addition to consulting the models in this section, you may need to refer to items 1–6 (general guidelines for listing authors).

NOTE: For articles on consecutive pages, provide the range of pages at the end of the citation (see item 7 for an example). When an article does not appear on consecutive pages, give all page numbers: A1, A17.

7. ARTICLE IN A JOURNAL PAGINATED BY VOLUME Many professional journals continue page numbers throughout the year instead of beginning each issue with page 1; at the end of the year,

Citation at a glance: Article in a periodical (APA)

To cite an article in a periodical in APA style, include the following elements:

1. Author
2. Date of publication
3. Title of article
4. Name of periodical
5. Volume and issue numbers
6. Page numbers

REFERENCE LIST ENTRY FOR AN ARTICLE IN A PERIODICAL

1 2 3 4 5 6

Hoxby, C. M. (2002). The power of peers. *Education Next, 2*(2), 57-63.

For more on citing periodicals in APA style, see pages 434–37.

the issues are collected in a volume. After the italicized title of the journal, give the volume number (also italicized), followed by the page numbers.

Hoff, T. (1992). Psychology in Canada one hundred years ago: James Mark Baldwin at the University of Toronto. *Canadian Psychology, 33,* 683-694.

8. ARTICLE IN A JOURNAL PAGINATED BY ISSUE When each issue of a journal begins with page 1, include the issue number in parentheses after the volume number. Italicize the volume number but not the issue number.

Wyrostok, N., & Paulson, B. (2000). Traditional healing practices among First Nations students. *Canadian Journal of Counselling, 34*(1), 14-24.

9. ARTICLE IN A MAGAZINE In addition to the year of publication, list the month and, for weekly magazines, the day. If there is a volume number, include it (italicized) after the title.

Raloff, J. (2001, May 12). Lead therapy won't help most kids. *Science News, 159,* 292.

10. ARTICLE IN A NEWSPAPER Begin with the name of the author followed by the exact date of publication. (If the author is unknown, see also item 4.) Page numbers are introduced with "p." (or "pp.").

Walton, D. (2002, October 30). Police in Calgary make big ecstasy bust. *The Globe and Mail,* p. A10.

11. LETTER TO THE EDITOR Letters to the editor appear in journals, magazines, and newspapers. Follow the appropriate model and insert the words "Letter to the editor" in brackets before the name of the periodical.

Carter, R. (2006, July). Lost in translation? [Letter to the editor]. *Scientific American, 295*(1), 12.

12. REVIEW Reviews of books and other media appear in a variety of periodicals. Follow the appropriate model for the periodical. For a review of a book, give the title of the review (if there is one), followed in brackets by the words "Review of the book" and the title of the book.

Gleick, E. (2000, December 14). The burdens of genius [Review of the book *The Last Samurai*]. *Time, 156,* 171.

For a film review, write "Review of the motion picture," and for a TV review, write "Review of the television program." Treat other media in a similar way.

Books

In addition to consulting the items in this section, you may need to refer to items 1–6 (general guidelines for listing authors).

13. BASIC FORMAT FOR A BOOK Begin with the author's name, followed by the date and the book's title. End with the place of publication and the name of the publisher. Take the information about the book from its title page and copyright page. If more than one place of publication is given, use only the first; if more than one date is given, use the most recent one.

Wilde, G. J. S. (1994). *Target risk: Dealing with the danger of death, disease, and damage in everyday decisions.* Toronto: PDE.

14. BOOK WITH AN EDITOR For a book with an editor but no author, begin with the name of the editor (or editors) followed by the abbreviation "Ed." (or "Eds.") in parentheses.

Schuller, R. A., & Ogloff, J. R. P. (Eds.). (2001). *Introduction to psychology and law: Canadian perspectives.* Toronto: University of Toronto Press.

For a book with an author and an editor, begin with the author's name. Give the editor's name in parentheses after the title of the book, followed by the abbreviation "Ed." (or "Eds.").

Plath, S. (2000). *The unabridged journals* (K. V. Kukil, Ed.). New York: Anchor.

15. TRANSLATION After the title, give the translator and the abbreviation "Trans.," in parentheses. Add the original date of the work's publication in parentheses at the end of the entry.

Steinberg, M. D. (2003). *Voices of revolution, 1917* (M. Schwartz, Trans.). New Haven, CT: Yale University Press. (Original work published 2001)

16. EDITION OTHER THAN THE FIRST Include the number of the edition in parentheses after the title.

Clark, S. D. (1968). *The developing Canadian community* (2nd ed.). Toronto: University of Toronto Press.

Citation at a glance: Book (APA)

To cite a book in APA style, include the following elements:

1 Author
2 Date of publication
3 Title and subtitle
4 City of publication
5 Publisher

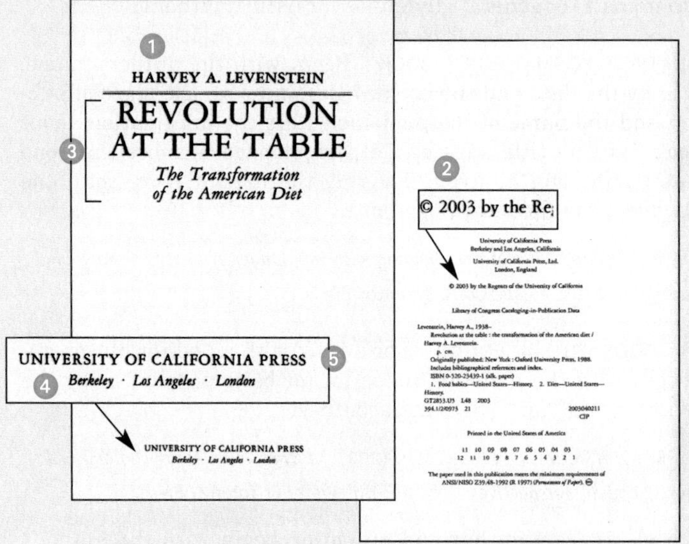

REFERENCE LIST ENTRY FOR A BOOK

1 2 3
Levenstein, H. A. (2003). *Revolution at the table: The transformation of*
4 5
the American diet. Berkeley: University of California Press.

For more on citing books in APA style, see pages 437–39.

17. ARTICLE OR CHAPTER IN AN EDITED BOOK Begin with the author, year of publication, and title of the article or chapter. Then write "In" and give the editor's name, followed by "Ed." in parentheses; the title of the book; and the page numbers of the article or chapter in parentheses. End with the book's publication information.

Aboud, F. E. (1993). A fifth grade program to reduce prejudice. In K. McLeod (Ed.), *Multicultural education: The state of the art* (pp. 20-27). Toronto: University of Toronto Press.

18. MULTIVOLUME WORK Give the number of volumes after the title.

Luo, J. (Ed.). (2005). *China today: An encyclopedia of life in the People's Republic* (Vols. 1-2). Westport, CT: Greenwood Press.

Electronic sources

This section shows how to prepare reference list entries for a variety of electronic sources, including articles in online periodicals and databases, Web documents, Weblogs, and e-mail.

19. ARTICLE FROM AN ONLINE PERIODICAL When citing online articles, follow the guidelines for printed articles (see items 7–12), giving whatever information is available in the online source. If the article also appears in a printed journal, a URL is not required; instead, include "Electronic version" in brackets after the title of the article.

Whitmeyer, J. M. (2000). Power through appointment [Electronic version]. *Social Science Research, 29*, 535-555.

If there is no print version, include the date you accessed the source and the article's URL.

Ashe, D. D., & McCutcheon, L. E. (2001). Shyness, loneliness, and attitude toward celebrities. *Current Research in Social Psychology, 6*(9). Retrieved March 2, 2006, from http://www.uiowa.edu/~grpproc/crisp/crisp.6.9.htm

NOTE: When you have retrieved an article from a newspaper's searchable Web site, give the URL for the site, not for the article.

Steffenhagen, J. (2006, February 10). B.C. First Nations to run own schools. *Edmonton Journal*. Retrieved January 17, 2007, from http://www.canada.com/edmontonjournal

20. ARTICLE FROM A DATABASE To cite an article from a library's subscription database, include the publication information from the source (see items 7–12). End the citation with your date of access, the name of the database, and the document number (if applicable).

Holliday, R. E., & Hayes, B. K. (2001). Dissociating automatic and intentional processes in children's eyewitness memory. *Journal of Experimental Child Psychology, 75*(1), 1-5. Retrieved February 21, 2001, from Expanded Academic ASAP database (A59317972).

21. NONPERIODICAL WEB DOCUMENT To cite a nonperiodical Web document, such as a report, list as many of the following elements as are available.

Author's name
Date of publication (if there is no date, use "n.d.")
Title of document (in italics)
Date you accessed the source
A URL that will take readers directly to the source

In the first model, the source has both an author and a date; in the second, the source lacks a date.

Cain, A., & Burris, M. (1999, April). *Investigation of the use of mobile phones while driving.* Retrieved January 15, 2000, from http://www.cutr.eng .usf.edu/its/mobile_phone_text.htm

Archer, D. (n.d.). *Exploring nonverbal communication.* Retrieved March 2, 2006, from http://nonverbal.ucsc.edu

If a source has no author, begin with the title and follow it with the date in parentheses.

NOTE: If you retrieved the source from a university program's Web site, name the program in your retrieval statement.

Cosmides, L., & Tooby, J. (1997). *Evolutionary psychology: A primer.* Retrieved March 1, 2006, from the University of California, Santa Barbara, Center for Evolutionary Psychology Web site: http://www.psych.ucsb.edu/research/cep/primer.html

22. CHAPTER OR SECTION IN A WEB DOCUMENT Begin with the author, the year of publication, and the title of the chapter or section. Then write "In" and give the title of the document, followed by any identifying information in parentheses. End with your date of access and the URL for the chapter or section.

Heuer, R. J., Jr. (1999). Keeping an open mind. In *Psychology of intelligence analysis* (chap. 6). Retrieved January 7, 2006, from http://www.cia.gov/csi/books/19104/art9.html

23. ENTRY IN A WEBLOG (BLOG) To cite an entry in a Weblog, give the author's name, the title of the entry, the name of the Weblog, the date on which you retrieved the source, and the URL.

Mayer, C. (2006, February 28). Some surprising findings about identity theft. *The Checkout.* Retrieved March 2, 2006, from http://blog.washingtonpost.com/thecheckout/2006/02/some_surprising_findings_about.html

24. E-MAIL E-mail messages and other personal communications are not included in the list of references.

25. ONLINE POSTING If an online posting is not maintained in an archive, cite it as a personal communication in the text of your paper and do not include it in the list of references. If the posting can be retrieved from an archive, give as much information as is available.

Eaton, S. (2001, June 12). Online transactions [Msg 2]. Message posted to news://sci.psychology.psychotherapy.moderated

26. COMPUTER PROGRAM Add the words "Computer software" in brackets after the title of the program.

Kaufmann, W. J., III, & Comins, N. F. (2003). Discovering the universe (Version 6.0) [Computer software]. New York: Freeman.

Other sources

27. DISSERTATION ABSTRACT

Yoshida, Y. (2001). Essays in urban transportation (Doctoral dissertation, Boston College, 2001). *Dissertation Abstracts International, 62,* 7741A.

28. GOVERNMENT DOCUMENT

Health reports: Regional differences in obesity. (2006, August 22). *The Daily.* Ottawa, ON: Statistics Canada. (Catalogue No. 11-001-XIE)

Citation at a glance: Article from a database (APA)

To cite an article from a database in APA style, include the following elements:

1 Author
2 Date of publication
3 Title of article
4 Name of periodical
5 Volume and issue numbers
6 Page numbers
7 Date of access
8 Name of database
9 Document number

ON-SCREEN VIEW OF DATABASE RECORD

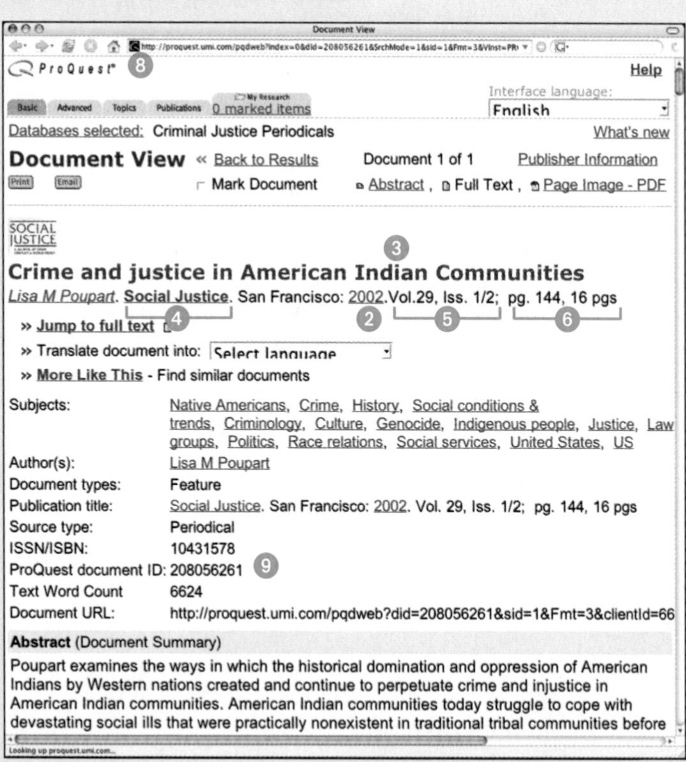

PRINTOUT OF RECORD AND BEGINNING OF ARTICLE

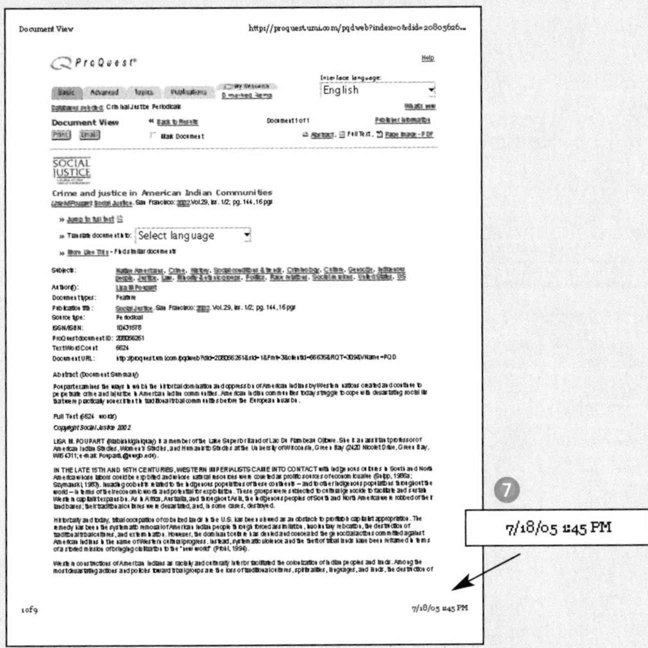
Document View https://proquest.umi.com/pqdweb?index=0&did=20805626...

ProQuest

Help

Interface language: English

Basic Advanced Topics Publications My Research 0 marked items

Databases selected: Criminal Justice Periodicals

What's new

Document View « Back to Results Document 1 of 1 Publisher information

Print Email Mark Document Abstract, Full Text, Page Image - PDF

SOCIAL JUSTICE

Crime and justice in American Indian Communities

Lisa M Poupart. Social Justice. San Francisco: 2002. Vol. 29, Iss. 1/2; pg. 144, 16 pgs

» Jump to full text

» Translate document into: Select language

» More Like This - Find similar documents

Subjects:	Native Americans, Crime, History, Social conditions & trends, Criminology, Culture, Genocide, Indigenous people, Justice, Law, Minority & ethnic groups, Politics, Race relations, Socialization, United States, US
Author(s):	Lisa M Poupart
Document types:	Feature
Publication title:	Social Justice. San Francisco: 2002. Vol. 29, Iss. 1/2; pg. 144, 16 pgs
Source type:	Periodical
ISSN/ISBN:	10431578
ProQuest document ID:	208056261
Text Word Count	6624
Document URL:	http://proquest.umi.com/pqdweb?did=208056261&sid=1&Fmt=3&clientId=65635&RQT=309&VName=PQD

Abstract (Document Summary)

Full Text (6624 words)

Copyright Social Justice 2002

1 of 9 7/18/05 11:45 PM

REFERENCE LIST ENTRY FOR AN ARTICLE FROM A DATABASE

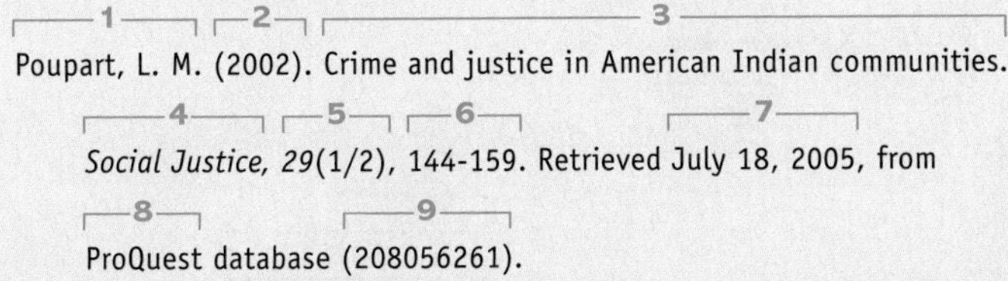

Poupart, L. M. (2002). Crime and justice in American Indian communities. *Social Justice, 29*(1/2), 144-159. Retrieved July 18, 2005, from ProQuest database (208056261).

For more on citing articles from a database in APA style, see page 440.

Citation at a glance: Document from a Web site (APA)

To cite a document from a Web site in APA style, include the following elements:

1 Author
2 Date of publication or most recent update
3 Title of document on Web site
4 Title of Web site or section of site
5 Date of access
6 URL of document

BROWSER PRINTOUT OF WEB SITE

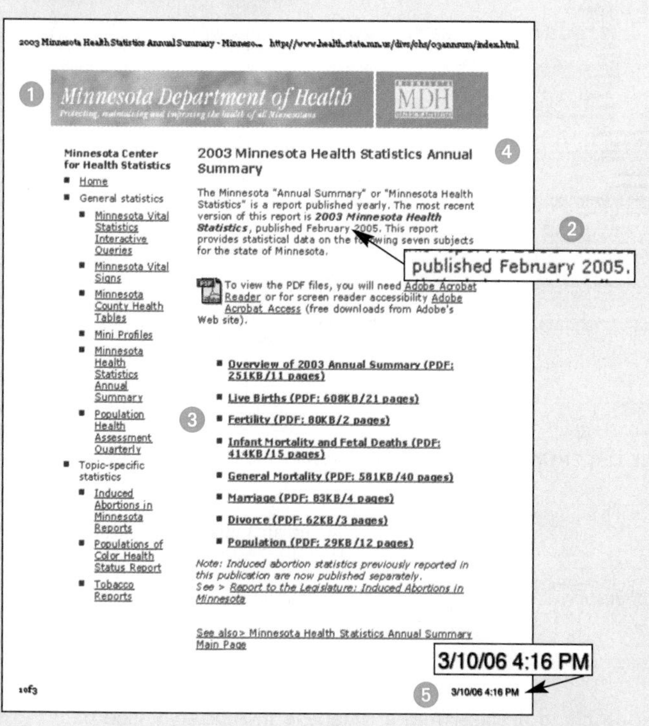
2003 Minnesota Health Statistics Annual Summary - Minneso... http://www.health.state.mn.us/divs/chs/03annsum/index.html

1 Minnesota Department of Health
Protecting, maintaining and improving the health of all Minnesotans
MDH

Minnesota Center for Health Statistics
- Home
- General statistics
  - Minnesota Vital Statistics Interactive Queries
  - Minnesota Vital Signs
  - Minnesota County Health Tables
  - Mini Profiles
  - Minnesota Health Statistics Annual Summary
  - Population Health Assessment Quarterly
- Topic-specific statistics
  - Induced Abortions in Minnesota Reports
  - Populations of Color Health Status Report
  - Tobacco Reports

4 2003 Minnesota Health Statistics Annual Summary

The Minnesota "Annual Summary" or "Minnesota Health Statistics" is a report published yearly. The most recent version of this report is ***2003 Minnesota Health Statistics***, published February 2005. This report provides statistical data on the following seven subjects for the state of Minnesota.

2 published February 2005.

To view the PDF files, you will need Adobe Acrobat Reader or for screen reader accessibility Adobe Acrobat Access (free downloads from Adobe's Web site).

3
- Overview of 2003 Annual Summary (PDF: 251KB/11 pages)
- Live Births (PDF: 608KB/21 pages)
- Fertility (PDF: 80KB/2 pages)
- Infant Mortality and Fetal Deaths (PDF: 414KB/15 pages)
- General Mortality (PDF: 581KB/40 pages)
- Marriage (PDF: 83KB/4 pages)
- Divorce (PDF: 62KB/3 pages)
- Population (PDF: 29KB/12 pages)

Note: Induced abortion statistics previously reported in this publication are now published separately.
See > Report to the Legislature: Induced Abortions in Minnesota

See also> Minnesota Health Statistics Annual Summary Main Page

1of3

5 3/10/06 4:16 PM

3/10/06 4:16 PM

ON-SCREEN VIEW OF DOCUMENT

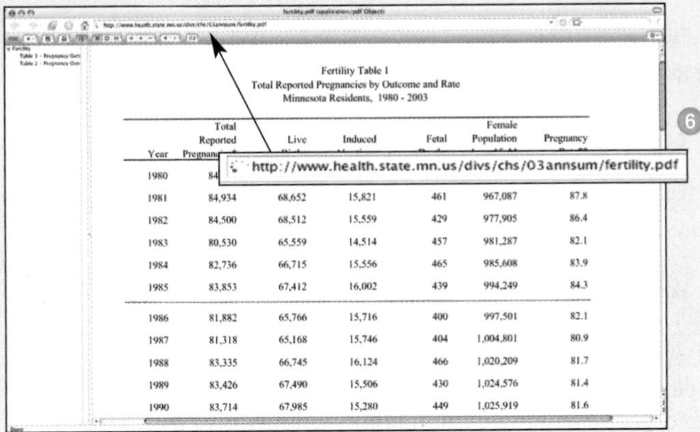

Fertility Table 1
Total Reported Pregnancies by Outcome and Rate
Minnesota Residents, 1980 - 2003

Year	Total Reported Pregnan[illegible]	Live [illegible]	Induced [illegible]	Fetal [illegible]	Female Population [illegible]	Pregnancy [illegible]
1980	84[illegible]	[illegible]	[illegible]	[illegible]	[illegible]	[illegible]
1981	84,934	68,652	15,821	461	967,087	87.8
1982	84,500	68,512	15,559	429	977,905	86.4
1983	80,530	65,559	14,514	457	981,287	82.1
1984	82,736	66,715	15,556	465	985,608	83.9
1985	83,853	67,412	16,002	439	994,249	84.3
1986	81,882	65,766	15,716	400	997,501	82.1
1987	81,318	65,168	15,746	404	1,004,801	80.9
1988	83,335	66,745	16,124	466	1,020,209	81.7
1989	83,426	67,490	15,506	430	1,024,576	81.4
1990	83,714	67,985	15,280	449	1,025,919	81.6

REFERENCE LIST ENTRY FOR A DOCUMENT FROM A WEB SITE

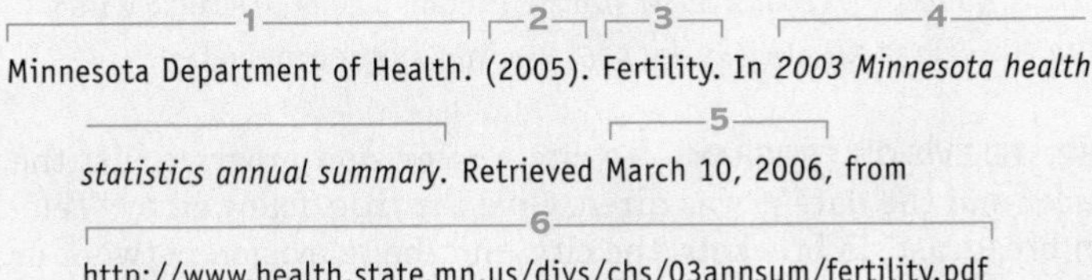

Minnesota Department of Health. (2005). Fertility. In *2003 Minnesota health statistics annual summary*. Retrieved March 10, 2006, from http://www.health.state.mn.us/divs/chs/03annsum/fertility.pdf

For more on citing documents from Web sites in APA style, see pages 439–41.

29. REPORT FROM A PRIVATE ORGANIZATION If the publisher and the author are the same, use the word "Author" as the publisher. If a person is named as the author, begin with that person and give the organization as publisher at the end.

Canadian Psychological Association. (1991). *Canadian code of ethics for psychologists.* Ottawa, ON: Author.

30. CONFERENCE PROCEEDINGS

Stahl, G. (Ed.). (2002). *Proceedings of CSCL '02: Computer support for collaborative learning.* Hillsdale, NJ: Erlbaum.

31. MOTION PICTURE To cite a motion picture (film, video, or DVD), list the director and the year of the picture's release. Give the title, followed by "Motion picture" in brackets, the country where it was made, and the name of the studio. If the motion picture is difficult to find, include instead the name and address of its distributor.

Gaghan, S. (Director). (2005). *Syriana* [Motion picture]. United States: Warner Brothers Pictures.

Spurlock, M. (Director). (2004). *Super size me* [Motion picture]. (Available from IDP Films, 1133 Broadway, Suite 926, New York, NY 10010)

32. TELEVISION PROGRAM To cite a television program, list the producer and the date it was aired. Give the title, followed by "Television broadcast" in brackets, the city, and the television network or service.

Pratt, C. (Executive Producer). (2006, February 19). *Face the nation* [Television broadcast]. Washington, DC: CBS News.

For a television series, use the year in which the series was produced, and follow the title with "Television series" in brackets. For an episode in a series, list the writer and director and the year. After the episode title, put "Television series episode" in brackets. Follow with information about the series.

Janows, J. (Executive Producer). (2000). *Culture shock* [Television series]. Boston: WGBH.

Loeterman, B. (Writer), & Gale, B. (Director). (2000). Real justice [Television series episode]. In M. Sullivan (Executive Producer), *Frontline.* Boston: WGBH.

ON THE WEB > dianahacker.com/writersref
Electronic research exercises > E-ex APA 4–5 and APA 4–6

APA-5

Manuscript format; sample paper

APA-5a Manuscript format

The American Psychological Association makes a number of recommendations for formatting a paper and preparing a list of references. The following guidelines are consistent with advice given in the *Publication Manual of the American Psychological Association,* 5th ed. (Washington: APA, 2001).

Formatting the paper

APA guidelines for formatting a paper are endorsed by many instructors in the social sciences.

MATERIALS AND TYPEFACE Use good-quality 8½″ × 11″ (letter-size) white paper. Avoid a typeface that is unusual or hard to read.

TITLE PAGE The APA manual does not provide guidelines for preparing the title page of a college or university paper, but most instructors will want you to include one. See page 451 for an example.

PAGE NUMBERS AND RUNNING HEAD The title page is numbered as page i; the abstract page, if there is one, is numbered as page ii. Use arabic numerals, beginning with 1, for the rest of the paper. In the upper right-hand corner of each page, type a short version of your title, followed by five spaces and the page number. Number all pages, including the title page.

MARGINS, LINE SPACING, AND PARAGRAPH INDENTS Use margins of 1 inch (2.5 cm) on all sides of the page. Left-align the text.

Double-space throughout, but single-space footnotes. Indent the first line of each paragraph 0.5 inch (1.2 cm or five spaces).

LONG QUOTATIONS AND FOOTNOTES When a quotation is longer than forty words, set it off from the text by indenting it 0.5 inch

(1.2 cm or five spaces) from the left margin. Double-space the quotation. Quotation marks are not needed when a quotation has been set off from the text. See page 458 for an example.

Place each footnote, if any, at the bottom of the page on which the text reference occurs. Double-space between the last line of text on the page and the footnote. Indent the first line of the footnote 0.5 inch (1.2 cm or five spaces). Begin the note with the superscript arabic numeral that corresponds to the number in the text. See page 453 for an example.

ABSTRACT If your instructor requires one, include an abstract immediately after the title page. Centre the word Abstract 1 inch (2.5 cm) from the top of the page; double-space the abstract as you do the body of your paper.

An abstract is a 100-to-120-word paragraph that provides readers with a quick overview of your essay. It should express your main idea and your key points; it might also briefly suggest any implications or applications of the research you discuss in the paper. See page 452 for an example.

HEADINGS Although headings are not always necessary, their use is encouraged in the social sciences. For most undergraduate papers, one level of heading will usually be sufficient.

In APA style, major headings are centred. Capitalize the first word of the heading, along with all words except articles, short prepositions, and coordinating conjunctions.

VISUALS The APA classifies visuals as tables and figures (figures include graphs, charts, drawings, and photographs). Keep visuals as simple as possible. Label each table with an arabic numeral (Table 1, Table 2, and so on) and provide a clear title. The label and title should appear on separate lines above the table, flush left and single-spaced. Below the table, give its source in a note. If any data in the table require an explanatory footnote, use a superscript lowercase letter in the body of the table and in a footnote following the source note. Single-space source notes and footnotes and do not indent the first line of each note. See page 455 for an example.

For each figure, place a label and a caption below the figure, flush left and single-spaced. They need not appear on separate lines.

In the text of your paper, discuss the most significant features of each visual. Place the visual as close as possible to the sentences that relate to it unless your instructor prefers it in an appendix.

Preparing the list of references

Begin your list of references on a new page at the end of the paper. Center the title References 1 inch (2.5 cm) from the top of the page. Double-space throughout. For a sample reference list, see page 459.

INDENTING ENTRIES APA recommends using a hanging indent: Type the first line of an entry flush left and indent any additional lines 0.5 inch (1.2 cm or five spaces), as shown on page 459.

ALPHABETIZING THE LIST Alphabetize the reference list by the last names of the authors (or editors); when a work has no author or editor, alphabetize by the first word of the title other than *A, An,* or *The.*

If your list includes two or more works by the same author, arrange the entries by year, the earliest first. If your list includes two or more works by the same author in the same year, arrange them alphabetically by title. Add the letters "a," "b," and so on within the parentheses after the year. Use only the year for articles in journals: (2002a). Use the full date for articles in magazines and newspapers in the reference list: (2005a, July 7). Use only the year in the in-text citation.

AUTHORS' NAMES Invert all authors' names and use initials instead of first names. With two or more authors, use an ampersand (&) before the last author's name. Separate the names with commas. Include names for the first six authors; if there are additional authors, end the list with "et al." (Latin for "and others").

TITLES OF BOOKS AND ARTICLES Italicize the titles and subtitles of books. Do not use quotation marks around the titles of articles. Capitalize only the first word of the title and subtitle (and all proper nouns) of books and articles. Capitalize names of periodicals as you would capitalize them normally (see M3-c).

ABBREVIATIONS FOR PAGE NUMBERS Abbreviations for "page" and "pages" ("p." and "pp.") are used before page numbers of newspaper articles and articles in edited books (see item 10 on p. 436 and item 17 on p. 439) but not before page numbers of articles appearing in magazines and scholarly journals (see items 7–9 on pp. 434–36).

BREAKING A URL When a URL must be divided, break it after a slash or before a period. Do not insert a hyphen.

See page 459 for an example of how to type your list of references. For information about the exact format of each entry in your list, consult the models on pages 433–46.

APA-5b Sample research paper: APA style

On the following pages is a research paper written by Luisa Mirano, a student in a psychology class. Mirano's assignment was to write a review of the literature paper documented with APA-style citations and references.

ON THE WEB > **dianahacker.com/writersref**
Model papers > APA papers: Mirano; Shaw
> APA annotated bibliography: Haddad

Obesity in Children i

Short title and page number for student papers. Lowercase roman numerals are used on title page and abstract page, arabic numerals on all text pages.

Can Medication Cure Obesity in Children?

A Review of the Literature

Full title, writer's name, and section number of course, instructor's name, and date (all centred).

Luisa Mirano

Psychology 107, Section B

Professor Kang

October 31, 2004

Marginal annotations indicate APA-style formatting and effective writing.

Abstract appears on a separate page.

Abstract

In recent years, policymakers and medical experts have expressed alarm about the growing problem of childhood obesity in the United States. While most agree that the issue deserves attention, consensus dissolves around how to respond to the problem. This literature review examines one approach to treating childhood obesity: medication. The paper compares the effectiveness for adolescents of the only two drugs approved by the Food and Drug Administration (FDA) for long-term treatment of obesity, sibutramine and orlistat. This examination of pharmacological treatments for obesity points out the limitations of medication and suggests the need for a comprehensive solution that combines medical, social, behavioral, and political approaches to this complex problem.

Can Medication Cure Obesity in Children?
A Review of the Literature

Full title, centred.

In March 2004, U.S. Surgeon General Richard Carmona called attention to a health problem in the United States that, until recently, has been overlooked: childhood obesity. Carmona said that the "astounding" 15% child obesity rate constitutes an "epidemic." Since the early 1980s, that rate has "doubled in children and tripled in adolescents." Now more than 9 million children are classified as obese (paras. 3, 6).[1] While the traditional response to a medical epidemic is to hunt for a vaccine or a cure-all pill, childhood obesity has proven more elusive. The lack of success of recent initiatives suggests that medication might not be the answer for the escalating problem. This literature review considers whether the use of medication is a promising approach for solving the childhood obesity problem by responding to the following questions:

1. What are the implications of childhood obesity?
2. Is medication effective at treating childhood obesity?
3. Is medication safe for children?
4. Is medication the best solution?

The writer sets up her organization by posing four questions.

Understanding the limitations of medical treatments for children highlights the complexity of the childhood obesity problem in the United States and underscores the need for physicians, advocacy groups, and policymakers to search for other solutions.

The writer states her thesis.

What Are the Implications of Childhood Obesity?

Headings, centred, help readers follow the organization.

Obesity can be a devastating problem from both an individual and a societal perspective. Obesity puts children at risk for a number of medical complications, including type 2 diabetes, hypertension, sleep apnea, and orthopedic problems (Henry J. Kaiser Family Foundation, 2004, p. 1). Researchers Hoppin and Taveras (2004) have noted that obesity is often associated with psychological issues such as depression, anxiety, and binge eating (Table 4).

In a signal phrase, the word "and" links the names of two authors; the date is given in parentheses.

[1]Obesity is measured in terms of body-mass index (BMI): weight in kilograms divided by square of height in meters. An adult with a BMI 30 or higher is considered obese. In children and adolescents, obesity is defined in relation to others of the same age and gender. An adolescent with a BMI in the 95th percentile for his or her age and gender is considered obese.

The writer uses a footnote to define an essential term that would be cumbersome to define within the text.

Obesity also poses serious problems for a society struggling to cope with rising health care costs. The cost of treating obesity currently totals $117 billion per year--a price, according to the surgeon general, "second only to the cost of [treating] tobacco use" (Carmona, 2004, para. 9). And as the number of children who suffer from obesity grows, long-term costs will only increase.

Because the author (Carmona) is not named in the signal phrase, his name and the date appear in parentheses, along with the paragraph number of the electronic source.

Is Medication Effective at Treating Childhood Obesity?

The widening scope of the obesity problem has prompted medical professionals to rethink old conceptions of the disorder and its causes. As researchers Yanovski and Yanovski (2002) have explained, obesity was once considered "either a moral failing or evidence of underlying psychopathology" (p. 592). But this view has shifted: Many medical professionals now consider obesity a biomedical rather than a moral condition, influenced by both genetic and environmental factors. Yanovski and Yanovski have further noted that the development of weight-loss medications in the early 1990s showed that "obesity should be treated in the same manner as any other chronic disease . . . through the long-term use of medication" (p. 592).

Ellipsis mark indicates omitted words.

The search for the right long-term medication has been complicated. Many of the drugs authorized by the Food and Drug Administration (FDA) in the early 1990s proved to be a disappointment. Two of the medications--fenfluramine and dexfenfluramine--were withdrawn from the market because of severe side effects (Yanovski & Yanovski, 2002, p. 592), and several others were classified by the Drug Enforcement Administration as having the "potential for abuse" (Hoppin & Taveras, 2004, Weight-Loss Drugs section, para. 6). Currently only two medications have been approved by the FDA for long-term treatment of obesity: sibutramine (marketed as Meridia) and orlistat (marketed as Xenical). This section compares studies on the effectiveness of each.

An ampersand links the names of two authors in parentheses.

Sibutramine suppresses appetite by blocking the reuptake of the neurotransmitters serotonin and norepinephrine in the brain (Yanovski & Yanovski, 2002, p. 594). Though the drug won FDA approval in 1998, experiments to test its effectiveness for younger patients came considerably later. In 2003, University of Pennsylvania researchers Berkowitz, Wadden, Tershakovec, and Cronquist released the first double-blind placebo study testing the effect of sibutramine on adolescents, aged 13-17, over a 12-month period. Their findings are summarized in Table 1.

The writer draws attention to an important article.

Table 1

Effectiveness of Sibutramine and Orlistat in Adolescents

Medication	Subjects	Treatment[a]	Side effects	Average weight loss/gain
Sibutramine	Control	0-6 mos.: placebo 6-12 mos.: sibutramine	Mos. 6-12: increased blood pressure; increased pulse rate	After 6 mos.: loss of 3.2 kg (7 lb) After 12 mos.: loss of 4.5 kg (9.9 lb)
	Medicated	0-12 mos.: sibutramine	Increased blood pressure; increased pulse rate	After 6 mos.: loss of 7.8 kg (17.2 lb) After 12 mos.: loss of 7.0 kg (15.4 lb)
Orlistat	Control	0-12 mos.: placebo	None	Gain of 0.67 kg (1.5 lb)
	Medicated	0-12 mos.: orlistat	Oily spotting; flatulence; abdominal discomfort	Loss of 1.3 kg (2.9 lb)

Note. The data on sibutramine are adapted from "Behavior Therapy and Sibutramine for the Treatment of Adolescent Obesity" [Electronic version], by R. I. Berkowitz, T. A. Wadden, A. M. Tershakovec, & J. L. Cronquist, 2003, *Journal of the American Medical Association, 289,* pp. 1807-1809. The data on orlistat are adapted from *Xenical (Orlistat) Capsules: Complete Product Information,* by Roche Laboratories, December 2003, retrieved October 11, 2004, from http://www.rocheusa.com/products/xenical/pi.pdf

[a]The medication and/or placebo were combined with behavioral therapy in all groups over all time periods.

The writer uses a table to summarize the findings presented in two sources.

A note gives the source of the data.

A content note explains data common to all subjects.

After 6 months, the group receiving medication had lost 4.6 kg (about 10 pounds) more than the control group. But during the second half of the study, when both groups received sibutramine, the results were more ambiguous. In months 6-12, the group that continued to take sibutramine gained an average of 0.8 kg, or roughly 2 pounds; the control group, which switched from placebo to sibutramine, lost 1.3 kg, or roughly 3 pounds (p. 1808). Both groups received behavioral therapy covering diet, exercise, and mental health.

These results paint a murky picture of the effectiveness of the medication: While initial data seemed promising, the results after one year raised questions about whether medication-induced weight loss could be sustained over time. As Berkowitz et al. (2003) advised, "Until more extensive safety and efficacy data are available, . . . weight-loss medications should be used only on an experimental basis for adolescents" (p. 1811).

When this article was first cited, all four authors were named. In subsequent citations of a work with three to five authors, "et al." is used after the first author's name.

A study testing the effectiveness of orlistat in adolescents showed similarly ambiguous results. The FDA approved orlistat in 1999 but did not authorize it for adolescents until December 2003. Roche Laboratories (2003), maker of orlistat, released results of a one-year study testing the drug on 539 obese adolescents, aged 12-16. The drug, which promotes weight loss by blocking fat absorption in the large intestine, showed some effectiveness in adolescents: an average loss of 1.3 kg, or roughly 3 pounds, for subjects taking orlistat for one year, as opposed to an average gain of 0.67 kg, or 1.5 pounds, for the control group (pp. 8-9). See Table 1.

Short-term studies of orlistat have shown slightly more dramatic results. Researchers at the National Institute of Child Health and Human Development tested 20 adolescents, aged 12-16, over a three-month period and found that orlistat, combined with behavioral therapy, produced an average weight loss of 4.4 kg, or 9.7 pounds (McDuffie et al., 2002, p. 646). The study was not controlled against a placebo group; therefore, the relative effectiveness of orlistat in this case remains unclear.

For a source with six or more authors, the first author's surname followed by "et al." is used for the first and subsequent references.

Is Medication Safe for Children?

While modest weight loss has been documented for both medications, each carries risks of certain side effects. Sibutramine has been observed to increase blood pressure and pulse rate. In 2002, a consumer group claimed that the medication was related to the deaths of 19 people and filed a petition with the Department of Health and Human Services to ban the medication (Hilts, 2002). The sibutramine study by Berkowitz et al. (2003) noted elevated blood pressure as a side effect, and dosages had to be reduced or the medication discontinued in 19 of the 43 subjects in the first six months (p. 1809).

The main side effects associated with orlistat were abdominal discomfort, oily spotting, fecal incontinence, and nausea (Roche Laboratories, 2003, p. 13). More serious for long-term health is the concern that orlistat, being a fat-blocker, would affect absorption of fat-soluble vitamins, such as vitamin D. However, the study found that this side effect can be minimized or eliminated if patients take vitamin supplements two hours before or after administration of orlistat (p. 10). With close monitoring of patients taking the medication, many of the risks can be reduced.

Is Medication the Best Solution?

The data on the safety and efficacy of pharmacological treatments of childhood obesity raise the question of whether medication is the best solution for the problem. The treatments have clear costs for individual patients, including unpleasant side effects, little information about long-term use, and uncertainty that they will yield significant weight loss.

In purely financial terms, the drugs cost more than $3 a day on average (Duenwald, 2004, paras. 33, 36). In each of the clinical trials, use of medication was accompanied by an expensive regime of behavioral therapies, including counseling, nutritional education, fitness advising, and monitoring. As journalist Greg Critser (2003) noted in his book *Fat Land,* use of weight-loss drugs is unlikely to have an effect without the proper "support system"--one that includes doctors, facilities, time, and money (p. 3). For some, this level of care is prohibitively expensive.

A third complication is that the studies focused on adolescents aged 12-16, but obesity can begin at a much younger age. Little data exist to establish the safety or efficacy of medication for treating very young children.

The writer develops the paper's thesis.

While the scientific data on the concrete effects of these medications in children remain somewhat unclear, medication is not the only avenue for addressing the crisis. Both medical experts and policymakers recognize that solutions might come not only from a laboratory but also from policy, education, and advocacy. Indeed, a handbook designed to educate doctors on obesity recommended a notably nonmedical course of action, calling for "major changes in some aspects of western culture" (Hoppin & Taveras, 2004, Conclusion section, para. 1). Cultural change may not be the typical realm of medical professionals, but the handbook urged doctors to be proactive and "focus [their] energy on public policies and interventions" (Conclusion section, para. 1).

Brackets indicate a word not in the original source.

The solutions proposed by a number of advocacy groups underscore this interest in political and cultural change. A report by the Henry J. Kaiser Family Foundation (2004) outlined trends that may have contributed to the childhood obesity crisis, including food advertising for children as well as

A quotation longer than 40 words is set off from the text without quotation marks.

> a reduction in physical education classes and after-school athletic programs, an increase in the availability of sodas and snacks in public schools, the growth in the number of fast-food outlets . . . , and the increasing number of highly processed high-calorie and high-fat grocery products. (p. 1)

The writer interprets the evidence; she doesn't just report it.

Addressing each of these areas requires more than a doctor armed with a prescription pad; it requires a broad mobilization not just of doctors and concerned parents but of educators, food industry executives, advertisers, and media representatives.

The tone of the conclusion is objective.

The barrage of possible approaches to combating childhood obesity--from scientific research to political lobbying--indicates both the severity and the complexity of the problem. While none of the medications currently available is a miracle drug for curing the nation's 9 million obese children, research has illuminated some of the underlying factors that affect obesity and has shown the need for a comprehensive approach to the problem that includes behavioral, medical, social, and political change.

References

List of references begins on a new page. Heading is centred.

Berkowitz, R. I., Wadden, T. A., Tershakovec, A. M., & Cronquist, J. L. (2003). Behavior therapy and sibutramine for the treatment of adolescent obesity [Electronic version]. *Journal of the American Medical Association, 289*, 1805-1812.

Carmona, R. H. (2004, March 2). *The growing epidemic of childhood obesity*. Testimony before the Subcommittee on Competition, Foreign Commerce, and Infrastructure of the U.S. Senate Committee on Commerce, Science, and Transportation. Retrieved October 10, 2004, from http://www.hhs.gov/asl/testify/t040302.html

Critser, G. (2003). *Fat land: How Americans became the fattest people in the world*. Boston: Houghton Mifflin.

Duenwald, M. (2004, January 6). Slim pickings: Looking beyond ephedra. *The New York Times,* p. F1. Retrieved October 12, 2004, from LexisNexis.

Henry J. Kaiser Family Foundation. (2004, February). *The role of media in childhood obesity*. Retrieved October 10, 2004, from http://www.kff.org/entmedia/7030.cfm

Hilts, P. J. (2002, March 20). Petition asks for removal of diet drug from market. *The New York Times,* p. A26. Retrieved October 12, 2004, from LexisNexis.

Hoppin, A. G., & Taveras, E. M. (2004, June 25). Assessment and management of childhood and adolescent obesity. *Clinical Update*. Retrieved October 12, 2004, from Medscape Web site: http://www.medscape.com/viewarticle/481633

McDuffie, J. R., Calis, K. A., Uwaifo, G. I., Sebring, N. G., Fallon, E. M., Hubbard, V. S., et al. (2003). Three-month tolerability of orlistat in adolescents with obesity-related comorbid conditions [Electronic version]. *Obesity Research, 10,* 642-650.

Roche Laboratories. (2003, December). *Xenical (orlistat) capsules: Complete product information*. Retrieved October 11, 2004, from http://www.rocheusa.com/products/xenical/pi.pdf

Yanovski, S. Z., & Yanovski, J. A. (2002). Drug therapy: Obesity [Electronic version]. *The New England Journal of Medicine, 346*, 591-602.

List is alphabetized by authors' last names. All authors' names are inverted.

The first line of an entry is at the left margin; subsequent lines indent ½" (1.2 cm or five spaces).

Double-spacing is used throughout.

CMS (*Chicago*) Papers

Most assignments in history and other humanities classes are based to some extent on reading. At times you will be asked to respond to one or two readings, such as essays or historical documents. At other times you may be asked to write a research paper that draws on a wide variety of sources.

Most history instructors and some humanities instructors require you to document sources with footnotes or endnotes based on *The Chicago Manual of Style,* 15th ed. (Chicago: U of Chicago P, 2003). (See CMS-4.)

When you write a paper using sources, you face three main challenges in addition to documenting your sources: (1) supporting a thesis, (2) citing your sources and avoiding plagiarism, and (3) integrating quotations and other source material.

CMS-1

Supporting a thesis

Most assignments ask you to form a thesis, or main idea, and to support that thesis with well-organized evidence.

CMS-1a Form a thesis.

A thesis is a one-sentence (or occasionally a two-sentence) statement of your central idea. Usually your thesis will appear at the end of the first paragraph (as on p. 485), but if you need to provide readers with considerable background information, you may place it in the second paragraph.

The thesis of your paper will be a reasoned answer to the central question you pose. Here is a research question posed by Ned Bishop, a student in a history course, followed by a thesis that answers the question.

RESEARCH QUESTION

To what extent was Confederate Major General Nathan Bedford Forrest responsible for the massacre of Union troops at Fort Pillow?

POSSIBLE THESIS

Although we will never know whether Nathan Bedford Forrest directly ordered the massacre of Union troops at Fort Pillow, evidence suggests that he was responsible for it.

Notice that the thesis expresses a view on a debatable issue—an issue about which intelligent, well-meaning people might disagree. The writer's job is to convince such readers that this view is worth taking seriously.

ON THE WEB > **dianahacker.com/writersref**
Research exercises > E-ex CMS 1–1

CMS-1b Organize your evidence.

The body of your paper will consist of evidence in support of your thesis. Instead of getting tangled up in a complex, formal outline, sketch an informal plan that organizes your evidence in bold strokes. Ned Bishop, the student who wrote about Fort Pillow, used a simple list of questions as the blueprint for his paper. In the paper itself, these became headings that help readers follow Bishop's line of argument.

What happened at Fort Pillow?

Did Forrest order the massacre?

Can Forrest be held responsible for the massacre?

CMS-1c Use sources to inform and support your argument.

Used thoughtfully, the source materials you have gathered will make your argument more complex and convincing for readers. Sources can play several different roles as you develop your points.

Providing background information or context

You can use facts and statistics to support generalizations or to establish the importance of your topic, as student writer Ned Bishop does early in his paper.

> Fort Pillow, Tennessee, which sat on a bluff overlooking the Mississippi River, had been held by the Union for two years. It was garrisoned by 580 men, 292 of them from United States Colored Heavy and Light Artillery regiments, 285 from the white Thirteenth Tennessee Cavalry. Nathan Bedford Forrest commanded about 1,500 troops.[1]

Explaining terms or concepts

If readers are unlikely to be familiar with a word, a phrase, or an idea important to your topic, you must explain it for them. Quoting or paraphrasing a source can help you define terms and concepts in neutral, accessible language.

> The Civil War practice of giving no quarter to an ememy--in other words "denying [an enemy] the right of survival"--defied Lincoln's mandate for humane and merciful treatment of prisoners.[9]

Supporting your claims

As you draft your argument, make sure to back up your assertions with facts, examples, and other evidence from your research (see also A2-e). Ned Bishop, for example, uses an eyewitness report of the racially motivated violence perpetrated by Nathan Bedford Forrest's troops.

> The slaughter at Fort Pillow was no doubt driven in large part by racial hatred. . . . A Southern reporter traveling with Forrest makes clear that the discrimination was deliberate: "Our troops maddened by the excitement, shot down the ret[r]eating Yankees, and not until they had attained t[h]e water's edge and turned to beg for mercy, did any prisoners fall in [t]o our hands--Thus the whites received quarter, but the negroes were shown no mercy."[19]

Lending authority to your argument

Expert opinion can give weight to your argument (see also A2-e). But don't rely on experts to make your argument for you. Construct your argument in your own words and, when appropriate, cite the judgment of an authority in the field to support your position.

> Fort Pillow is not the only instance of a massacre or threatened massacre of black soldiers by troops under Forrest's command. Biographer Brian Steel Wills points out that at Brice's Cross Roads in June 1864, "black soldiers suffered inordinately" as Forrest looked the other way and Confederate soldiers deliberately sought out those they termed "the damned negroes."[21]

Anticipating and countering objections

Do not ignore sources that seem contrary to your position or that offer arguments different from your own. Instead, use them to give voice to opposing points of view and to state potential objections to your arguments before you counter them (see A2-f). Ned Bishop, for example, presents evidence from a source that challenges his thesis.

> Hurst suggests that the temperamental Forrest "may have ragingly ordered a massacre and even intended to carry it out--until he rode inside the fort and viewed the horrifying result" and ordered it stopped.[15] While this is an intriguing interpretation of events, even Hurst would probably admit that it is merely speculation.

CMS-2

Citing sources; avoiding plagiarism

Your research paper is a collaboration between you and your sources. To be fair and ethical, you must acknowledge your debt to the writers of those sources. If you don't, you commit plagiarism, a serious academic offence.

Three different acts are considered plagiarism: (1) failing to cite quotations and borrowed ideas, (2) failing to enclose borrowed language in quotation marks, and (3) failing to put summaries and paraphrases in your own words.

CMS-2a Cite quotations and borrowed ideas.

You must of course cite all direct quotations. You must also cite any ideas borrowed from a source: summaries and paraphrases; statistics and other specific facts; and visuals such as cartoons, graphs, and diagrams.

The only exception is common knowledge—information your readers could easily locate in any number of reference sources. For example, the population of Canada is common knowledge among sociologists and economists, and historians are familiar with facts such as the date of the British North America Act. As a rule, when you have seen certain information repeatedly in your reading, you don't need to cite it. However, when information has appeared in only a few sources, when it is highly specific (as with statistics), or when it is controversial, you should cite the source.

CMS citations consist of superscript numbers in the text of the paper that refer readers to notes with corresponding numbers either at the foot of the page (footnotes) or at the end of the paper (endnotes).

TEXT

Governor John Andrew was not allowed to recruit black soldiers from out of state. "Ostensibly," writes Peter Burchard, "no recruiting was done outside Massachusetts but it was an open secret that Andrew's agents were working far and wide."[1]

NOTE

1. Peter Burchard, *One Gallant Rush: Robert Gould Shaw and His Brave Black Regiment* (New York: St. Martin's, 1965), 85.

For detailed advice on using CMS-style notes, see CMS-4. When you use footnotes or endnotes, you will usually need to provide a bibliography as well (see CMS-4b).

CMS-2b Enclose borrowed language in quotation marks.

To indicate that you are using a source's exact phrases or sentences, you must enclose them in quotation marks. To omit the quotation marks is to claim—falsely—that the language is your own. Such an omission is plagiarism even if you have cited the source.

ORIGINAL SOURCE

For many Southerners it was psychologically impossible to see a black man bearing arms as anything but an incipient slave uprising complete with arson, murder, pillage, and rapine.

—Dudley Taylor Cornish, *The Sable Arm,* p. 158

PLAGIARISM

According to Civil War historian Dudley Taylor Cornish, for many Southerners it was psychologically impossible to see a black man bearing arms as anything but an incipient slave uprising complete with arson, murder, pillage, and rapine.[2]

BORROWED LANGUAGE IN QUOTATION MARKS

According to Civil War historian Dudley Taylor Cornish, "For many Southerners it was psychologically impossible to see a black man bearing arms as anything but an incipient slave uprising complete with arson, murder, pillage, and rapine."[2]

NOTE: When quoted sentences are set off from the text by indenting, quotation marks are not needed (see pp. 467–68).

CMS-2c Put summaries and paraphrases in your own words.

Summaries and paraphrases are written in your own words. A summary condenses information; a paraphrase reports information in about the same number of words as in the source. When you summarize or paraphrase, you must restate the source's meaning using your own language. You commit plagiarism if you half-copy the author's sentences—either by mixing the author's well-chosen phrases with your own without using quotation marks or by plugging your own synonyms into the author's sentence structure. The following paraphrase is plagiarized—even though the source is cited—because too much of its language is borrowed from the source without quotation marks. The underlined phrases have been copied word-for-word. In addition, the writer has closely followed the sentence structure of the original source, merely plugging in some synonyms (such as *Fifty percent* for *half* and *savage hatred* for *fierce, bitter animosity*).

ORIGINAL SOURCE

> Half of the force holding Fort Pillow were Negroes, former slaves now enrolled in the Union Army. Toward them Forrest's troops had the fierce, bitter animosity of men who had been educated to regard the colored race as inferior and who for the first time had encountered that race armed and fighting against white men. The sight enraged and perhaps terrified many of the Confederates and aroused in them the ugly spirit of a lynching mob.
>
> —Albert Castel, "The Fort Pillow Massacre," pp. 46–47

PLAGIARISM: UNACCEPTABLE BORROWING

> Albert Castel suggests that much of the brutality at Fort Pillow can be traced to racial attitudes. Fifty percent of the troops <u>holding Fort Pillow were Negroes, former slaves</u> who had joined the Union Army. <u>Toward them Forrest's</u> soldiers displayed the savage hatred <u>of men who had been</u> taught the inferiority of blacks <u>and who for the first time had</u> confronted them <u>armed and fighting against white men</u>. The vision angered and perhaps frightened the Confederates and <u>aroused in them the ugly spirit of a lynching mob</u>.[3]

To avoid plagiarizing an author's language, set the source aside, write from memory, and consult the source later to check for accuracy. This strategy prevents you from being captivated by the words on the page.

ACCEPTABLE PARAPHRASE

Albert Castel suggests that much of the brutality at Fort Pillow can be traced to racial attitudes. Nearly half of the Union troops were blacks, men whom the Confederates had been raised to consider their inferiors. The shock and perhaps fear of facing armed ex-slaves in battle for the first time may well have unleashed the fury that led to the massacre.[3]

ON THE WEB > **dianahacker.com/writersref**
Research exercises > E-ex CMS 2–1 through CMS 2–5

CMS-3

Integrating sources

Quotations, summaries, paraphrases, and facts will support your argument, but they cannot speak for you. You can use several strategies to integrate information from research sources into your paper while maintaining your own voice.

CMS-3a Limit your use of quotations.

Using quotations appropriately

Although it is tempting to insert many quotations in your paper and to use your own words only for connecting passages, do not quote excessively. It is almost impossible to integrate numerous long quotations smoothly into your own text.

It is not always necessary to quote full sentences from a source. At times you may wish to borrow only a phrase or to weave part of a source's sentence into your own sentence structure.

As Hurst has pointed out, until "an outcry erupted in the Northern press," even the Confederates did not deny that there had been a massacre at Fort Pillow.[4]

Union surgeon Dr. Charles Fitch testified that after he was in custody he "saw" Confederate soldiers "kill every negro that made his appearance dressed in Federal uniform."[20]

USING THE ELLIPSIS MARK To condense a quoted passage, you can use the ellipsis mark (three periods, with spaces between) to indicate that you have omitted words. What remains must be grammatically complete.

> Union surgeon Fitch's testimony that all women and children had been evacuated from Fort Pillow before the attack conflicts with Forrest's report: "We captured . . . about 40 negro women and children."[6]

The writer has omitted several words not relevant to the issue at hand: *164 Federals, 75 negro troops, and.*

When you want to omit a full sentence or more, use a period before the three ellipsis dots. For an example, see the long quotation on page 468.

Ordinarily, do not use the ellipsis mark at the beginning or at the end of a quotation. Readers will understand that the quoted material is taken from a longer passage.

USING BRACKETS Brackets allow you to insert words of your own into quoted material, perhaps to explain a confusing reference or to keep a sentence grammatical in your context.

> According to Albert Castel, "It can be reasonably argued that he [Forrest] was justified in believing that the approaching steamships intended to aid the garrison [at Fort Pillow]."[7]

NOTE: Use [*sic*] to indicate that an error in a quoted sentence appears in the original source. (An example appears on p. 468.) However, if a source is filled with errors, as is the case with many historical documents, this use of [*sic*] can become distracting and is best avoided.

SETTING OFF LONG QUOTATIONS CMS style allows you some leeway in deciding whether to set off a long quotation or run it into your text. For emphasis you may want to set off a quotation of more than four or five lines of text; almost certainly you should set off quotations of ten lines or more. To set off a quotation, indent it 0.5 inch (1.2 cm or five spaces) from the left margin and use the normal right margin. Double-space the indented quotation.

Long quotations should be introduced by an informative sentence, usually followed by a colon. Quotation marks are unnecessary because the indented format tells readers that the words are taken directly from the source.

In a letter home, Confederate officer Achilles V. Clark recounted what happened at Fort Pillow:

> Words cannot describe the scene. The poor deluded negroes would run up to our men fall upon their knees and with uplifted hands scream for mercy but they were ordered to their feet and then shot down. The whitte [*sic*] men fared but little better. . . . I with several others tried to stop the butchery and at one time had partially succeeded[,] but Gen. Forrest ordered them shot down like dogs[,] and the carnage continued.[8]

CMS-3b Use signal phrases to integrate sources.

The information you gather from sources cannot speak for itself. Whenever you include a paraphrase, summary, or direct quotation of another writer in your paper, prepare your readers for it with an introduction called a *signal phrase.* A signal phrase names the author of the source and often provides some context for the source material.

When the signal phrase includes a verb, choose one that is appropriate for the way you are using the source (see CMS-1c). Are you arguing a point, making an observation, reporting a fact, drawing a conclusion, or refuting an argument? By choosing an appropriate verb, you can make your source's role clear. See the chart on page 469 for a list of verbs commonly used in signal phrases.

In a CMS-style paper, use the present tense or present perfect tense in phrases that introduce quotations or other source material from nonfiction sources: *Foote points out that* or *Foote has pointed out that* (not *Foote pointed out that*). If you have good reason to emphasize that the author's language or opinion was articulated in the past, however, the past tense is acceptable.

The first time you mention an author, use the full name: *Shelby Foote argues. . . .* When you refer to the author again, you may use the last name only: *Foote raises an important question.*

Marking boundaries

Readers should be able to move from your words to the words of a source without feeling a jolt. Avoid dropping direct quotations into your text without warning. Instead, provide clear signal phrases, including the author's name, to prepare readers for the quotation. A signal phrase indicates the boundary between your words and

Using signal phrases in CMS papers

To avoid monotony, try to vary the language and placement of your signal phrases.

MODEL SIGNAL PHRASES

In the words of historian James M. McPherson, ". . ."[1]

As Dudley Taylor Cornish has argued, ". . ."[2]

In a letter to his wife, a Confederate soldier who witnessed the massacre wrote that ". . ."[3]

". . . ," claims Benjamin Quarles.[4]

". . . ," writes Albert Castel, ". . ."[5]

Shelby Foote offers an intriguing interpretation: ". . ."[6]

VERBS IN SIGNAL PHRASES

admits	compares	insists	rejects
agrees	confirms	notes	reports
argues	contends	observes	responds
asserts	declares	points out	suggests
believes	denies	reasons	thinks
claims	emphasizes	refutes	writes

the source's words and can also tell readers why a source is trustworthy.

DROPPED QUOTATION

Not surprisingly, those testifying on the Union and Confederate sides recalled events at Fort Pillow quite differently. Unionists claimed that their troops had abandoned their arms and were in full retreat. "The Confederates, however, all agreed that the Union troops retreated to the river with arms in their hands."[9]

QUOTATION WITH SIGNAL PHRASE

Not surprisingly, those testifying on the Union and Confederate sides recalled events at Fort Pillow quite differently. Unionists claimed that their troops had abandoned their arms and were in full retreat. "The Confederates, however," writes historian Albert Castel, "all agreed that the Union troops retreated to the river with arms in their hands."[9]

Introducing summaries and paraphrases

As with quotations, you should introduce most summaries and paraphrases with a signal phrase that mentions the author and places the material in context. Readers will then understand where the summary or paraphrase begins.

Without the signal phrase (underlined) in the following example, readers might think that only the last sentence is being cited, when in fact the whole paragraph is based on the source.

> According to Jack Hurst, official Confederate policy was that black soldiers were to be treated as runaway slaves; in addition, the Confederate Congress decreed that white Union officers commanding black troops be killed. Confederate Lieutenant General Kirby Smith went one step further, declaring that he would kill all captured black troops. Smith's policy never met with strong opposition from the Richmond government.[10]

Putting source material in context

Readers need to understand how your source is relevant to your paper's argument. It's a good idea, in other words, to embed your quotation—especially a long one—between sentences of your own, introducing it with a signal phrase and following it up with interpretive comments that link the source material to your paper's argument.

QUOTATION WITH INSUFFICIENT CONTEXT

> In a respected biography of Nathan Bedford Forrest, Hurst suggests that the temperamental Forrest "may have ragingly ordered a massacre and even intended to carry it out--until he rode inside the fort and viewed the horrifying result" and ordered it stopped.[11]

QUOTATION WITH EFFECTIVE CONTEXT

> In a respected biography of Nathan Bedford Forrest, Hurst suggests that the temperamental Forrest "may have ragingly ordered a massacre and even intended to carry it out--until he rode inside the fort and viewed the horrifying result" and ordered it stopped.[11] While this is an intriguing interpretation of events, even Hurst would probably admit that it is merely speculation.

Integrating statistics and other facts

When you are citing a statistic or another specific fact, a signal phrase is often not necessary. In most cases, readers will understand that the citation refers to the statistic or fact (not the whole paragraph).

Of 295 white troops garrisoned at Fort Pillow, 168 were taken prisoner. Black troops fared worse, with only 58 of 262 captured and most of the rest presumably killed or wounded.[12]

There is nothing wrong, however, with using a signal phrase.

Shelby Foote notes that of 295 white troops garrisoned at Fort Pillow, 168 were taken prisoner but that black troops fared worse, with only 58 of 262 captured and most of the rest presumably killed or wounded.[12]

ON THE WEB > **dianahacker.com/writersref**
Research exercises > E-ex CMS 3–1 through CMS 3–4

CMS-4

Documenting sources

Professors in history and some humanities courses often require footnotes or endnotes based on *The Chicago Manual of Style.* When you use CMS-style notes, you will usually be asked to include a bibliography at the end of your paper (see CMS-4b).

TEXT

A Union soldier, Jacob Thompson, claimed to have seen Forrest order the killing, but when asked to describe the six-foot-two general, he called him "a little bit of a man."[13]

FOOTNOTE OR ENDNOTE

13. Brian Steel Wills, *A Battle from the Start: The Life of Nathan Bedford Forrest* (New York: HarperCollins, 1992), 187.

BIBLIOGRAPHY ENTRY

Wills, Brian Steel. *A Battle from the Start: The Life of Nathan Bedford Forrest.* New York: HarperCollins, 1992.

CMS-4a First and subsequent notes for a source

The first time you cite a source, the note should include publication information for that work as well as the page number on which the passage being cited may be found.

1. Peter Burchard, *One Gallant Rush: Robert Gould Shaw and His Brave Black Regiment* (New York: St. Martin's, 1965), 85.

For subsequent references to a source you have already cited, you may simply give the author's last name, a short form of the title, and the page or pages cited. A short form of the title of a book is italicized; a short form of the title of an article is put in quotation marks.

4. Burchard, *One Gallant Rush,* 31.

When you have two consecutive notes from the same source, you may use "Ibid." (meaning "in the same place") and the page number for the second note. Use "Ibid." alone if the page number is the same.

5. Jack Hurst, *Nathan Bedford Forrest: A Biography* (New York: Knopf, 1993), 8.

6. Ibid., 174.

CMS-4b CMS-style bibliography

A bibliography, which appears at the end of your paper, lists every work you have cited in your notes; in addition, it may include works that you consulted but did not cite. For advice on constructing the list, see page 483. A sample bibliography appears on page 488.

NOTE: If you include a bibliography, *The Chicago Manual of Style* suggests that you shorten all notes, including the first reference to a source, as described in CMS-4a. Check with your instructor, however, to see whether using an abbreviated note for a first reference to a source is acceptable.

CMS-4c Model notes and bibliography entries

The following models are consistent with guidelines set forth in *The Chicago Manual of Style,* 15th ed. For each type of source, a model note appears first, followed by a model bibliography entry. The model note shows the format you should use when citing a source for the first time. For subsequent citations of a source, use shortened notes (see CMS-4a).

ON THE WEB > **dianahacker.com/writersref**
Research exercises > E-ex CMS 4–1

Directory to CMS-style notes and bibliography entries

ON THE WEB > **dianahacker.com/writersref**
Research and Documentation Online > History: Documenting sources (*Chicago*)

Books (print and online)

1. BASIC FORMAT FOR A PRINT BOOK

1. Dale Thomson, *Jean Lesage and the Quiet Revolution* (Toronto: Macmillan, 1984), 10.

Thomson, Dale. *Jean Lesage and the Quiet Revolution*. Toronto: Macmillan, 1984.

1. Stephen Clarkson, *Uncle Sam and Us: Globalization, Neoconservatism, and the Canadian State* (Toronto: University of Toronto Press, 2002), 98.

Clarkson, Stephen. *Uncle Sam and Us: Globalization, Neoconservatism, and the Canadian State*. Toronto: University of Toronto Press, 2002.

2. BASIC FORMAT FOR AN ONLINE BOOK

2. Heinz Kramer, *A Changing Turkey: The Challenge to Europe and the United States* (Washington, DC: Brookings Press, 2000), 85, http://brookings.nap.edu/books/0815750234/html/R1.html.

Kramer, Heinz. *A Changing Turkey: The Challenge to Europe and the United States.* Washington, DC: Brookings Press, 2000. http://brookings.nap.edu/books/0815750234/html/R1.html.

3. TWO OR THREE AUTHORS

3. Stephen McBride and John Shields, *Dismantling a Nation: Canada and the New World Order* (Halifax: Fernwood Publishing, 1993), 20.

McBride, Stephen, and John Shields. *Dismantling a Nation: Canada and the New World Order.* Halifax: Fernwood Publishing, 1993.

4. FOUR OR MORE AUTHORS

4. Steven Langdon, Judy Rebick, Rosemary Warskett, and Ed Finn, *In the Public Interest: The Value of Public Services* (Prescott: Voyageur Publishing, 1995), 23.

Langdon, Steven, Judy Rebick, Rosemary Warskett, and Ed Finn. *In the Public Interest: The Value of Public Services.* Prescott: Voyageur Publishing, 1995.

5. UNKNOWN AUTHOR

5. *The Men's League Handbook on Women's Suffrage* (London, 1912), 23.

The Men's League Handbook on Women's Suffrage. London, 1912.

6. EDITED WORK WITHOUT AN AUTHOR

6. S. A. Yelaja, ed., *Canadian Social Policy* (Waterloo: Wilfrid Laurier University Press, 1978), 127.

Yelaja, S. A., ed. *Canadian Social Policy.* Waterloo: Wilfrid Laurier University Press, 1978.

7. EDITED WORK WITH AN AUTHOR

7. Ted Poston, *A First Draft of History,* ed. Kathleen A. Hauke (Athens: University of Georgia Press, 2000), 46.

Poston, Ted. *A First Draft of History.* Edited by Kathleen A. Hauke. Athens: University of Georgia Press, 2000.

8. TRANSLATED WORK

8. Tonino Guerra, *Abandoned Places,* trans. Adria Bernardi (Barcelona: Guernica, 1999), 71.

Guerra, Tonino. *Abandoned Places.* Translated by Adria Bernardi. Barcelona: Guernica, 1999.

9. EDITION OTHER THAN THE FIRST

9. Kenneth McRoberts, *Quebec: Social Change and Political Crisis,* 3rd ed. (Toronto: McClelland and Stewart, 1993), 198.

McRoberts, Kenneth. *Quebec: Social Change and Political Crisis.* 3rd ed. Toronto: McClelland and Stewart, 1993.

10. VOLUME IN A MULTIVOLUME WORK

10. Peter C. Newman, *The Canadian Establishment,* vol. 2, *The Acquisitors* (Toronto: McClelland and Stewart, 1990), 569.

Newman, Peter C. *The Canadian Establishment.* Vol. 2, *The Acquisitors.* Toronto: McClelland and Stewart, 1990.

11. WORK IN AN ANTHOLOGY

11. Michael Whittington, "Aboriginal Self-Government in Canada," in *Canadian Politics in the 21st Century,* 6th ed., ed. Michael Whittington and Glen Williams (Toronto: Nelson, 2004), 111.

Whittington, Michael. "Aboriginal Self-Government in Canada." In *Canadian Politics in the 21st Century,* 6th ed., edited by Michael Whittington and Glen Williams, 104-25. Toronto: Nelson, 2004.

12. LETTER IN A PUBLISHED COLLECTION

12. Thomas Gainsborough to Elizabeth Rasse, 1753, in *The Letters of Thomas Gainsborough,* ed. John Hayes (New Haven: Yale University Press, 2001), 5.

Gainsborough, Thomas. Letter to Elizabeth Rasse, 1753. In *The Letters of Thomas Gainsborough,* edited by John Hayes, 5. New Haven: Yale University Press, 2001.

13. WORK IN A SERIES

13. R. Keith Schoppa, *The Columbia Guide to Modern Chinese History,* Columbia Guides to Asian History (New York: Columbia University Press, 2000), 256-58.

Schoppa, R. Keith. *The Columbia Guide to Modern Chinese History.* Columbia Guides to Asian History. New York: Columbia University Press, 2000.

14. ENCYCLOPEDIA OR DICTIONARY

14. *Encyclopaedia Britannica,* 15th ed., s.v. "Monroe Doctrine."

14. Bryan A. Garner, *Garner's Modern American Usage* (Oxford: Oxford University Press, 2003), s.v. "brideprice."

Garner, Bryan A. *Garner's Modern American Usage.* Oxford: Oxford University Press, 2003.

The abbreviation "s.v." is for the Latin *sub verbo* ("under the word").

Well-known reference works such as encyclopedias do not require publication information and are usually not included in the bibliography.

15. SACRED TEXT

15. Matt. 20.4-9 (Revised Standard Version).

15. Qur'an 18:1-3.

Sacred texts are usually not included in the bibliography.

Articles in periodicals (print and online)

16. ARTICLE IN A JOURNAL For an article in a print journal, include the volume and issue numbers and the date; end the bibliography entry with the page range of the article.

16. Guy Vanderhaeghe, "History and Fiction," *Canadian Journal of History* 40, no. 3 (2005): 430.

Vanderhaeghe, Guy. "History and Fiction." *Canadian Journal of History* 40, no. 3 (2005): 429-30.

For an article accessed through a database service such as *EBSCOhost* or for an article published online, include a URL. If the article is paginated, give a page number in the note and a page range in the bibliography. For unpaginated articles, page references are not possible, but in your note you may include a "locator," such as a numbered paragraph or a heading from the article, as in the example for an article published online.

Journal article from a database service

16. Eugene F. Provenzo Jr., "Time Exposure," *Educational Studies* 34, no. 2 (2003): 266, http://search.epnet.com.

Provenzo, Eugene F., Jr. "Time Exposure." *Educational Studies* 34, no. 2 (2003): 266-67. http://search.epnet.com.

Journal article published online

16. Linda Belau, "Trauma and the Material Signifier," *Postmodern Culture* 11, no. 2 (2001): par. 6, http://www.iath.virginia.edu/pmc/text-only/issue.101/11.2belau.txt.

Belau, Linda. "Trauma and the Material Signifier." *Postmodern Culture* 11, no. 2 (2001). http://www.iath.virginia.edu/pmc/text-only/issue.101/11.2belau.txt.

17. ARTICLE IN A MAGAZINE For a print article, provide a page number in the note and a page range in the bibliography.

17. Bissell, Tom. "Improvised, Explosive, and Divisive." *Harper's,* January 2006, 42.

Bissell, Tom. "Improvised, Explosive, and Divisive." *Harper's,* January 2006, 41-54.

For an article accessed through a database service such as *FirstSearch* or for an article published online, include a URL. If the article is paginated, give a page number in the note and a page range in the bibliography. For unpaginated articles, page references are not possible.

Magazine article from a database service

17. David Pryce-Jones, "The Great Sorting Out: Postwar Iraq," *National Review,* May 5, 2003, 17, http://newfirstsearch.oclc.org.

Pryce-Jones, David. "The Great Sorting Out: Postwar Iraq." *National Review,* May 5, 2003, 17-18. http://newfirstsearch.oclc.org.

Magazine article published online

17. Fiona Morgan, "Banning the Bullies," *Salon,* March 15, 2001, http://www.salon.com/news/feature/2001/03/15/bullying/index.html.

Morgan, Fiona. "Banning the Bullies." *Salon,* March 15, 2001. http://www.salon.com/news/feature/2001/03/15/bullying/index.html.

18. ARTICLE IN A NEWSPAPER For newspaper articles—whether in print or online—page numbers are not necessary. A section letter or number, if available, is sufficient.

18. David Olive, "Corporate Welfare Never Ends," *Toronto Star,* September 8, 2003, sec. A.

Olive, David. "Corporate Welfare Never Ends." *Toronto Star,* September 8, 2003, sec. A.

For an article accessed through a database such as *ProQuest* or for an article published online, include a URL.

Newspaper article from a database service

18. Gina Kolata, "Scientists Debating Future of Hormone Replacement," *New York Times,* October 23, 2002, http://www.proquest.com.

Kolata, Gina. "Scientists Debating Future of Hormone Replacement." *New York Times,* October 23, 2002. http://www.proquest.com.

Newpaper article published online

18. David Arnot, "A Place beyond the Indian Act," *Globe and Mail,* March 22, 2007, http://www.theglobeandmail.com/.

Arnot, David. "A Place beyond the Indian Act." *Globe and Mail,* March 22, 2007. http://www.theglobeandmail.com/.

■ **19. UNSIGNED ARTICLE** When the author of a periodical article is unknown, treat the periodical itself as the author.

19. *Boston Globe,* "Renewable Energy Rules," August 11, 2003, sec. A.

Boston Globe. "Renewable Energy Rules." August 11, 2003, sec. A.

■ **20. BOOK REVIEW**

20. Nancy Gabin, review of *The Other Feminists: Activists in the Liberal Establishment,* by Susan M. Hartman, *Journal of Women's History* 12, no. 3 (2000): 230.

Gabin, Nancy. Review of *The Other Feminists: Activists in the Liberal Establishment,* by Susan M. Hartman. *Journal of Women's History* 12, no. 3 (2000): 227-34.

Web sites and postings

■ **21. WEB SITE** Include as much of the following information as is available: author, title of the site, sponsor of the site, and the site's URL. When no author is named, treat the sponsor as the author.

21. *Canadian Wildlife Service,* Environment Canada, http://www.cws-scf.ec.gc.ca/index_e.cfm.

Canadian Wildlife Service. Environment Canada. http://www.cws-scf.ec.gc.ca/index_e.cfm.

NOTE: *The Chicago Manual of Style* does not advise including the date you accessed a Web source, but you may provide an access date after the URL if the cited material is time-sensitive: for example, http://www.historychannel.com/today (accessed May 1, 2006).

22. SHORT DOCUMENT FROM A WEB SITE Include as many of the following elements as are available: author's name, title of the short work, title of the site, sponsor of the site, and the URL. When no author is named, treat the site's sponsor as the author.

22. Gérald-A. Beaufoin, "The 'Persons' Case," *Library and Archives of Canada,* http://www.collectionscanada.ca/04/0432_e.html.

Beaufoin, Gérald-A. "The 'Persons' Case." *Library and Archives of Canada.* http://www.collectionscanada.ca/04/0432_e.html.

22. PBS Online, "Media Giants," *Frontline: The Merchants of Cool,* http://www.pbs.org/wgbh/pages/frontline/shows/cool/giants.

PBS Online. "Media Giants." *Frontline: The Merchants of Cool.* http://www.pbs.org/wgbh/pages/frontline/shows/cool/giants.

23. AN ENTRY IN A WEBLOG (BLOG) Treat an entry for a Weblog as you would a short document from a Web site, including as many of the following elements as are available: the author's name; the title of the entry; the title of the blog; the sponsor, if any; and the URL.

23. Andrew Reeves, "Electoral Politics and FEMA's Poor Performance in the Aftermath of Hurricane Katrina," *Political Behavior Blog,* Institute for Quantitative Social Science at Harvard University, http://www.iq.harvard.edu/blog/pb/2005/09/electoral_politics_and_femas_p.html.

Reeves, Andrew. "Electoral Politics and FEMA's Poor Performance in the Aftermath of Hurricane Katrina." *Political Behavior Blog.* Institute for Quantitative Social Science at Harvard University. http://www.iq.harvard.edu/blog/pb/2005/09/electoral_politics_and_femas_p.html.

24. ONLINE POSTING OR E-MAIL If an online posting has been archived, include a URL, as in the following example. E-mails that are not part of an online discussion are treated as personal communications (see item 27). Online postings and e-mails are not included in the bibliography.

24. Janice Klein, posting to State Museum Association discussion list, June 19, 2003, http://listserv.nmmnh-abq.mus.nm.us/scripts/wa.exe?A2=ind0306c&L=sma-l&F=lf&S=&P=81.

Other sources (print, online, multimedia)

25. GOVERNMENT DOCUMENT

25. Statistics Canada, *Foreign and Domestic Investment in Canada* (Ottawa: Minister of Industry, 2005), 10.

Statistics Canada. *Foreign and Domestic Investment in Canada.* Ottawa: Minister of Industry, 2005.

26. UNPUBLISHED DISSERTATION

26. Thomas G. Arnold, "The Ice-Free Corridor: Biogeographical Highway or Environmental Cul-de-Sac" (PhD diss., Simon Fraser University, Burnaby, 2006), 164.

Arnold, Thomas G. "The Ice-Free Corridor: Biogeographical Highway or Environmental Cul-de-Sac." PhD diss., Simon Fraser University, Burnaby, 2006.

27. PERSONAL COMMUNICATION

27. Sara Lehman, e-mail message to author, August 13, 2003.

Personal communications are not included in the bibliography.

28. PUBLISHED OR BROADCAST INTERVIEW

28. Ron Haviv, interview by Charlie Rose, *The Charlie Rose Show,* PBS, February 12, 2001.

Haviv, Ron. Interview by Charlie Rose. *The Charlie Rose Show,* PBS, February 12, 2001.

29. PODCAST Treat an entry for a podcast as you would a short document from a Web site, including as many of the following elements as are available: the author's (or speaker's) name; the title of the podcast, in quotation marks; the title of the site on which it appears; the sponsor of the site; and the URL.

29. Chris Patterson, "Will School Consolidation Improve Education?" *Texas PolicyCast,* Texas Public Policy Foundation, http://www.texaspolicy.com/texaspolicycast.php.

Patterson, Chris. "Will School Consolidation Improve Education?" *Texas PolicyCast.* Texas Public Policy Foundation. http://www.texaspolicy.com/texaspolicycast.php.

30. VIDEO OR DVD

30. *The Secret of Roan Inish,* DVD, directed by John Sayles (1993; Culver City, CA: Columbia TriStar Home Video, 2000).

The Secret of Roan Inish. DVD. Directed by John Sayles. 1993; Culver City, CA: Columbia TriStar Home Video, 2000.

31. SOUND RECORDING

31. Gustav Holst, *The Planets,* Royal Philharmonic, André Previn, Telarc compact disc 80133.

Holst, Gustav. *The Planets.* Royal Philharmonic. André Previn. Telarc compact disc 80133.

32. SOURCE QUOTED IN ANOTHER SOURCE

32. Adam Smith, *The Wealth of Nations* (New York: Random House, 1965), 11, quoted in Mark Skousen, *The Making of Modern Economics: The Lives and the Ideas of the Great Thinkers* (Armonk, NY: M. E. Sharpe, 2001), 15.

Smith, Adam. *The Wealth of Nations,* 11. New York: Random House, 1965. Quoted in Mark Skousen, *The Making of Modern Economics: The Lives and the Ideas of the Great Thinkers* (Armonk, NY: M. E. Sharpe, 2001), 15.

ON THE WEB > **dianahacker.com/writersref**
Electronic research exercises > E-ex CMS 4–2 through CMS 4–6

CMS-5

Manuscript format; sample pages

CMS-5a Manuscript format

The following guidelines for formatting a CMS paper and preparing its endnotes and bibliography are based on *The Chicago Manual of Style,* 15th ed. For pages from a sample paper, see CMS-5b.

Formatting the paper

CMS manuscript guidelines are fairly generic, since they were not created with a specific type of writing in mind.

TITLE PAGE Include the full title of your paper, your name, the course title, the instructor's name, and the date. Do not number the title page but count it in the manuscript numbering; that is, the first page of the text will be numbered 2. See page 484 for a sample title page.

PAGINATION Using arabic numerals, number all pages except the title page in the upper right corner. Depending on your instructor's preference, you may also use a short title or your last name before the page numbers to help identify pages in case they come loose from your manuscript.

MARGINS AND LINE SPACING Leave margins of at least 1 inch (2.5 cm) at the top, bottom, and sides of the page. Double-space the entire manuscript, including long quotations that have been set off from the text. (For line spacing in notes and the bibliography, see the bottom of this page and p. 483.) Left-align the text.

LONG QUOTATIONS When a quotation is fairly long, set it off from the text by indenting (see also pp. 467–68). Indent the full quotation 0.5 inch (1.2 cm or five spaces) from the left margin. Quotation marks are not needed when a quotation has been set off from the text.

VISUALS *The Chicago Manual* classifies visuals as tables and illustrations (illustrations, or figures, include drawings, photographs, maps, and charts). Keep visuals as simple as possible. Label each table with an arabic numeral (Table 1, Table 2, and so on) and provide a clear title that identifies the subject. The label and title should appear on separate lines above the table, flush left. Below the table, give its source in a note like this one:

> *Source:* Jamie Brownlee, *Ruling Canada: Corporate Cohesion and Democracy* (Black Point, NS: Fernwood Publishing, 2005), 145.

For each figure, place a label and a caption below the figure, flush left. The label and caption need not appear on separate lines. The word "Figure" may be abbreviated to "Fig."

In the text of your paper, discuss the most significant features of each visual. Place visuals as close as possible to the sentences that relate to them unless your instructor prefers them in an appendix.

Preparing the endnotes

Begin the endnotes on a new page at the end of the paper. Centre the title Notes about 1 inch (2.5 cm) from the top of the page, and number the pages consecutively with the rest of the manuscript. See page 487 for an example.

INDENTING AND NUMBERING Indent the first line of each note 0.5 inch (1.2 cm or five spaces) from the left margin; do not indent additional lines in the note. Begin the note with the arabic numeral that corresponds to the number in the text. Put a period after the number.

LINE SPACING Single-space each note and double-space between notes (unless your instructor prefers double-spacing throughout).

Preparing the bibliography

Typically, the notes in CMS-style papers are followed by a bibliography, an alphabetically arranged list of all the works cited or consulted (see p. 488 for an example). Centre the title Bibliography about 1 inch (2.5 cm) from the top of the page. Number bibliography pages consecutively with the rest of the paper.

ALPHABETIZING THE LIST Alphabetize the bibliography by the last names of the authors (or editors); when a work has no author or editor, alphabetize it by the first word of the title other than *A, An,* or *The.*

If your list includes two or more works by the same author, use three hyphens instead of the author's name in all entries after the first. You may arrange the entries alphabetically by title or by date; be consistent throughout the bibliography.

INDENTING AND LINE SPACING Begin each entry at the left margin, and indent any additional lines 0.5 inch (1.2 cm or five spaces). Single-space each entry and double-space between entries (unless your instructor prefers double-spacing throughout).

CMS-5b Sample pages from a research paper: CMS style

Following are sample pages from a research paper by Ned Bishop, a student in a history class. (The complete paper is available on the *Writer's Reference* Web site.) Bishop was asked to document his paper using CMS-style endnotes and a bibliography. In preparing his manuscript, Bishop also followed CMS guidelines.

ON THE WEB > **dianahacker.com/writersref**
Model papers > *Chicago* (CMS) paper: Bishop

Title of paper.

The Massacre at Fort Pillow:

Holding Nathan Bedford Forrest Accountable

Writer's name.

Ned Bishop

Title of course, instructor's name, and date.

History 214

Professor Citro

March 22, 2001

Marginal annotations indicate CMS-style formatting and effective writing.

Bishop 2

Although Northern newspapers of the time no doubt exaggerated some of the Confederate atrocities at Fort Pillow, most modern sources agree that a massacre of Union troops took place there on April 12, 1864. It seems clear that Union soldiers, particularly black soldiers, were killed after they had stopped fighting or had surrendered or were being held prisoner. Less clear is the role played by Major General Nathan Bedford Forrest in leading his troops. Although we will never know whether Forrest directly ordered the massacre, evidence suggests that he was responsible for it.

Thesis asserts writer's main point.

What happened at Fort Pillow?

Headings help readers follow the organization.

Fort Pillow, Tennessee, which sat on a bluff overlooking the Mississippi River, had been held by the Union for two years. It was garrisoned by 580 men, 292 of them from United States Colored Heavy and Light Artillery regiments, 285 from the white Thirteenth Tennessee Cavalry. Nathan Bedford Forrest commanded about 1,500 troops.[1]

Statistics are cited with an endnote.

The Confederates attacked Fort Pillow on April 12, 1864, and had virtually surrounded the fort by the time Forrest arrived on the battlefield. At 3:30 p.m., Forrest demanded the surrender of the Union forces, sending in a message of the sort he had used before: "The conduct of the officers and men garrisoning Fort Pillow has been such as to entitle them to being treated as prisoners of war. . . . Should my demand be refused, I cannot be responsible for the fate of your command."[2] Union Major William Bradford, who had replaced Major Booth, killed earlier by sharpshooters, asked for an hour to consider the demand. Forrest, worried that vessels in the river were bringing in more troops, "shortened the time to twenty minutes."[3] Bradford refused to surrender, and Forrest quickly ordered the attack.

Quotation is cited with an endnote.

The Confederates charged to the fort, scaled the parapet, and fired on the forces within. Victory came quickly, with the Union forces running toward the river or surrendering. Shelby Foote describes the scene like this:

> Some kept going, right on into the river, where a number drowned and the swimmers became targets for marksmen on the bluff. Others, dropping their guns in terror, ran back toward the Confederates with their hands up, and of these some were spared as prisoners, while others were shot down in the act of surrender.[4]

Long quotation is set off from text by indenting. Quotation marks are omitted.

Bishop 3

Writer uses a primary source as well as secondary sources.

Quotation is introduced with a signal phrase.

In his own official report, Forrest makes no mention of the massacre. He does make much of the fact that the Union flag was not lowered by the Union forces, saying that if his own men had not taken down the flag, "few, if any, would have survived unhurt another volley."[5] However, as Jack Hurst points out and Forrest must have known, in this twenty-minute battle, "Federals running for their lives had little time to concern themselves with a flag."[6]

The writer draws attention to an important article containing primary sources.

The federal congressional report on Fort Pillow, which charged the Confederates with appalling atrocities, was strongly criticized by Southerners. Respected writer Shelby Foote, while agreeing that the report was "largely" fabrication, points out that the "casualty figures . . . indicated strongly that unnecessary killing had occurred."[7] In an important article, John Cimprich and Robert C. Mainfort Jr. argue that the most trustworthy evidence is that written within about ten days of the battle, before word of the congressional hearings circulated and Southerners realized the extent of Northern outrage. The article reprints a group of letters and newspaper sources written before April 22 and thus "untainted by the political overtones the controversy later assumed."[8] Cimprich and Mainfort conclude that these sources "support the case for the occurrence of a massacre" but that Forrest's role remains "clouded" because of inconsistencies in testimony.[9]

Did Forrest order the massacre?

Topic sentence states the main idea for this section.

Writer presents a balanced view of the evidence.

We will never really know whether Forrest directly ordered the massacre, but it seems unlikely. True, Confederate soldier Achilles Clark, who had no reason to lie, wrote to his sisters that "I with several others tried to stop the butchery . . . but Gen. Forrest ordered them [Negro and white Union troops] shot down like dogs[,] and the carnage continued."[10] But it is not clear whether Clark heard Forrest giving the orders or was just reporting hearsay. Many Confederates had been shouting "No quarter! No quarter!" and, as Shelby Foote points out, these shouts were "thought by some to be at Forrest's command."[11] A Union soldier, Jacob Thompson, claimed to have seen Forrest order the killing, but when asked to describe the six-foot-two general, he called him "a little bit of a man."[12]

Perhaps the most convincing evidence that Forrest did not order the massacre is that he tried to stop it once it had begun. Historian

Bishop 8

Notes

1. John Cimprich and Robert C. Mainfort Jr., eds., "Fort Pillow Revisited: New Evidence about an Old Controversy," *Civil War History* 28, no. 4 (1982): 293-94.

2. Quoted in Brian Steel Wills, *A Battle from the Start: The Life of Nathan Bedford Forrest* (New York: HarperCollins, 1992), 182.

3. Ibid., 183.

4. Shelby Foote, *The Civil War, a Narrative: Red River to Appomattox* (New York: Vintage, 1986), 110.

5. Nathan Bedford Forrest, "Report of Maj. Gen. Nathan B. Forrest, C. S. Army, Commanding Cavalry, of the Capture of Fort Pillow," *Shotgun's Home of the American Civil War,* http://www.civilwarhome.com/forrest.htm.

6. Jack Hurst, *Nathan Bedford Forrest: A Biography* (New York: Knopf, 1993), 174.

7. Foote, *Civil War,* 111.

8. Cimprich and Mainfort, "Fort Pillow," 305.

9. Ibid., 305.

10. Ibid., 299.

11. Foote, *Civil War,* 110.

12. Quoted in Wills, *Battle from the Start,* 187.

13. Albert Castel, "The Fort Pillow Massacre: A Fresh Examination of the Evidence," *Civil War History* 4, no. 1 (1958): 44-45.

14. Cimprich and Mainfort, "Fort Pillow," 300.

15. Hurst, *Nathan Bedford Forrest,* 177.

16. Ibid.

17. Dudley Taylor Cornish, *The Sable Arm: Black Troops in the Union Army, 1861-1865* (Lawrence, KS: University Press of Kansas, 1987), 175.

18. Foote, *Civil War,* 111.

19. Cimprich and Mainfort, "Fort Pillow," 304.

20. Quoted in Wills, *Battle from the Start,* 189.

21. Ibid., 215.

22. Quoted in Hurst, *Nathan Bedford Forrest,* 177.

First line of each note is indented ½" (1.2 cm or five spaces).

Note number is not raised and is followed by a period.

Authors' names are not inverted.

Last name and title refer to an earlier note by the same author.

Notes are single-spaced, with double-spacing between notes. (Some instructors may prefer double-spacing throughout.)

Entries are alphabetized by authors' last names.

First line of entry is at left margin; additional lines are indented ½" (1.2 cm or five spaces).

Entries are single-spaced, with double-spacing between entries. (Some instructors may prefer double-spacing throughout.)

Bishop 10

Bibliography

Castel, Albert. "The Fort Pillow Massacre: A Fresh Examination of the Evidence." *Civil War History* 4, no. 1 (1958): 37-50.

Cimprich, John, and Robert C. Mainfort Jr., eds. "Fort Pillow Revisited: New Evidence about an Old Controversy." *Civil War History* 28, no. 4 (1982): 293-306.

Cornish, Dudley Taylor. *The Sable Arm: Black Troops in the Union Army, 1861-1865*. Lawrence, KS: University Press of Kansas, 1987.

Foote, Shelby. *The Civil War, a Narrative: Red River to Appomattox*. New York: Vintage, 1986.

Forrest, Nathan Bedford. "Report of Maj. Gen. Nathan B. Forrest, C. S. Army, Commanding Cavalry, of the Capture of Fort Pillow." *Shotgun's Home of the American Civil War*. http://www.civilwarhome.com/forrest.htm.

Hurst, Jack. *Nathan Bedford Forrest: A Biography*. New York: Knopf, 1993.

McPherson, James M. *Battle Cry of Freedom: The Civil War Era*. New York: Oxford University Press, 1988.

Wills, Brian Steel. *A Battle from the Start: The Life of Nathan Bedford Forrest*. New York: HarperCollins, 1992.

B

Basic Grammar *Index*

B Basic Grammar

B1

Parts of speech

Traditional grammar recognizes eight parts of speech: noun, pronoun, verb, adjective, adverb, preposition, conjunction, and interjection. Many words can function as more than one part of speech. For example, depending on its use in a sentence, the word *paint* can be a noun (*The paint is wet*) or a verb (*Please paint the ceiling next*).

ON THE WEB > **dianahacker.com/writersref**
Grammar exercises > Basic grammar > E-ex B1–1 through B1–7

B1-a Nouns

A noun is the name of a person, place, thing, or an idea. Nouns are often but not always signalled by an article (*a, an, the*).

N N N
The *cat* in *gloves* catches no *mice.*

N N N
Repetition does not transform a *lie* into *truth*.

Nouns sometimes function as adjectives modifying other nouns. Because of their dual roles, nouns used in this manner may be called *noun/adjectives.*

N/ADJ N/ADJ
You can't make a *silk* purse out of a *sow's* ear.

Nouns are classified for a variety of purposes. When capitalization is the issue, we speak of *proper* versus *common* nouns (see M3-a). If the problem is one of word choice, we may speak of *concrete* versus *abstract* nouns (see W5-b). The distinction between *count nouns* and *noncount nouns* is useful for English language learners (see E3-b). Most nouns come in *singular* and *plural* forms; *collective* nouns may be either singular or plural (see G1-f and G3-a). *Possessive* nouns require an apostrophe (see P5-a).

B1-b Pronouns

A pronoun is a word used in place of a noun. Usually the pronoun substitutes for a specific noun, known as its *antecedent.*

When the *wheel* squeaks, *it* is greased.

Although most pronouns function as substitutes for nouns, some can function as adjectives modifying nouns.

PN/ADJ
This bird always catches the worm.

Most of the pronouns in English are listed in this section.

PERSONAL PRONOUNS Personal pronouns refer to specific persons or things. They always function as noun equivalents.

Singular: I, me, you, she, her, he, him, it

Plural: we, us, you, they, them

POSSESSIVE PRONOUNS Possessive pronouns indicate ownership.

Singular: my, mine, your, yours, her, hers, his, its

Plural: our, ours, your, yours, their, theirs

Some of these possessive pronouns function as adjectives modifying nouns: *my, your, his, her, its, our, their.*

INTENSIVE AND REFLEXIVE PRONOUNS Intensive pronouns emphasize a noun or another pronoun (The senator *herself* met us at the door). Reflexive pronouns name a receiver of an action identical with the doer of the action (Paula cut *herself*).

Singular: myself, yourself, himself, herself, itself

Plural: ourselves, yourselves, themselves

RELATIVE PRONOUNS Relative pronouns introduce subordinate clauses functioning as adjectives (The man *who helped us* was never identified). In addition to introducing the clause, the relative pronoun, in this case *who,* points back to a noun or pronoun that the clause modifies (*man*). (See B3-e.)

who, whom, whose, which, that

INTERROGATIVE PRONOUNS Interrogative pronouns introduce questions (*Who* is expected to win the election?).

who, whom, whose, which, what

DEMONSTRATIVE PRONOUNS Demonstrative pronouns identify or point to nouns. Frequently they function as adjectives (*This* chair is my favourite), but they may also function as noun equivalents (*This* is my favourite chair).

this, that, these, those

INDEFINITE PRONOUNS Indefinite pronouns refer to nonspecific persons or things. Most are singular (*everyone, each*); some are plural (*both, many*); a few may be singular or plural (see G1-e). Most indefinite pronouns function as noun equivalents (*Something* is burning), but some can also function as adjectives (*All* campers must check in at the lodge).

all, another, any, anybody, anyone, anything, both, each, either, everybody, everyone, everything, few, many, neither, nobody, none, no one, nothing, one, several, some, somebody, someone, something

RECIPROCAL PRONOUNS Reciprocal pronouns refer to individual parts of a plural antecedent (By turns, we helped *each other* through university).

each other, one another

NOTE: Pronouns cause a variety of problems for writers. See pronoun-antecedent agreement (G3-a), pronoun reference (G3-b), distinguishing between pronouns such as *I* and *me* (G3-c), and distinguishing between *who* and *whom* (G3-d).

B1-c Verbs

The verb of a sentence usually expresses action (*jump, think*) or being (*is, become*). It is composed of a main verb possibly preceded by one or more helping verbs.

MV
The best fish *swim* near the bottom.

HV MV
A marriage *is* not *built* in a day.

Notice that words can intervene between the helping and the main verb (*is* not *built*).

Helping verbs

There are twenty-three helping verbs in English: forms of *have, do,* and *be,* which may also function as main verbs; and nine modals, which function only as helping verbs. The forms of *have, do,* and *be* change form to indicate tense; the nine modals do not.

FORMS OF *HAVE, DO,* AND *BE*

have, has, had

do, does, did

be, am, is, are, was, were, being, been

MODALS

can, could, may, might, must, shall, should, will, would

The verb phrase *ought to* is often classified as a modal as well.

Main verbs

The main verb of a sentence is always the kind of word that would change form if put into these test sentences:

BASE FORM	Usually I (*walk, ride*).
PAST TENSE	Yesterday I (*walked, rode*).
PAST PARTICIPLE	I have (*walked, ridden*) many times before.
PRESENT PARTICIPLE	I am (*walking, riding*) right now.
-*S* FORM	Usually he/she/it (*walks, rides*).

If a word doesn't change form when slipped into these test sentences, you can be certain that it is not a main verb. For example, the noun *revolution,* though it may seem to suggest an action, can never function as a main verb. Just try to make it behave like one (*Today I revolution . . . Yesterday I revolutioned . . .*) and you'll see why.

When both the past-tense and the past-participle forms of a verb end in *-ed,* the verb is regular (*walked, walked*). Otherwise, the verb is irregular (*rode, ridden*). (See G2-a.)

The verb *be* is highly irregular, having eight forms instead of the usual five: the base form *be*; the present-tense forms *am, is,* and *are;* the past-tense forms *was* and *were*; the present participle *being;* and the past participle *been.*

NOTE: Some verbs are followed by words that look like prepositions but are so closely associated with the verb that they are a part of its meaning. These words are known as *particles.* Common verb-particle combinations include *bring up, call off, drop off, give in, look up, run into,* and *take off.*

> A lot of parents *pack up* their troubles and *send* them *off* to camp.
> —Raymond Duncan

NOTE: Verbs cause many problems for writers. See active verbs (W3), subject-verb agreement (G1), standard English verb forms (G2-a through G2-e), verb tense and mood (G2-f and G2-g), and ESL problems with verbs (E1).

B1-d Adjectives and articles

An adjective is a word used to modify, or describe, a noun or pronoun. An adjective usually answers one of these questions: Which one? What kind of? How many?

ADJ
the *lame* elephant [Which elephant?]

ADJ ADJ
valuable old stamps [What kind of stamps?]

ADJ
sixteen candles [How many candles?]

Adjectives usually precede the words they modify. However, they may also follow linking verbs, in which case they describe the subject. (See B2-b.)

ADJ
Good medicine always tastes *bitter.*

Articles, sometimes classified as adjectives, are used to mark nouns. There are only three: the definite article *the* and the indefinite articles *a* and *an.*

ART ART
A country can be judged by *the* quality of its proverbs.

Some possessive, demonstrative, and indefinite pronouns can function as adjectives: *their, its, this* (see B1-b).

NOTE: Writers sometimes misuse adjectives (see G4). Multilingual speakers often encounter problems with the articles *a, an,* and *the* and occasionally have trouble placing adjectives correctly (see E3 and E4-b).

B1-e Adverbs

An adverb is a word used to modify, or qualify, a verb (or verbal), an adjective, or another adverb. It usually answers one of these questions: When? Where? How? Why? Under what conditions? To what degree?

> ADV
> Pull *gently* at a weak rope. [Pull how?]

> ADV
> Read the best books *first*. [Read when?]

Adverbs modifying adjectives or other adverbs usually intensify or limit the intensity of the word they modify.

> ADV ADV
> Be *extremely* good, and you will be *very* lonesome.

The negators *not* and *never* are classified as adverbs.

B1-f Prepositions

A preposition is a word placed before a noun or pronoun to form a phrase modifying another word in the sentence. The prepositional phrase nearly always functions as an adjective or as an adverb. (See B3-a.)

> P P
> The road *to* hell is paved *with* good intentions.

To hell functions as an adjective modifying the noun *road*; *with good intentions* functions as an adverb modifying the verb *is paved.*

There are a limited number of prepositions in English. The most common are included in the following list.

about
above
across
after
against
along
among
around
as
at
before
behind
below
beneath
beside
besides
between
beyond
but
by
concerning
considering
despite
down
during
except
for
from
in
inside
into
like
near
next
of
off
on
onto
opposite
out
outside
over
past
plus
regarding
respecting
round
since
than
through

throughout	under	unto	within
till	underneath	up	without
to	unlike	upon	
toward	until	with	

Some prepositions are more than one word long. *Along with, as well as, in addition to,* and *next to* are common examples.

NOTE: Except for certain idiomatic uses (see W5-d), prepositions cause few problems for native speakers of English. For multilingual speakers, however, prepositions can cause considerable difficulty (see E5).

B1-g Conjunctions

Conjunctions join words, phrases, or clauses, and they indicate the relation between the elements joined.

COORDINATING CONJUNCTIONS A coordinating conjunction is used to connect grammatically equal elements. (See S1-b and S6.)

and but or nor for so yet

CORRELATIVE CONJUNCTIONS Correlative conjunctions are pairs of conjunctions that connect grammatically equal elements. (See S1-b.)

either . . . or	neither . . . nor	not only . . . but also
whether . . . or	both . . . and	

SUBORDINATING CONJUNCTIONS A subordinating conjunction introduces a subordinate clause and indicates its relation to the rest of the sentence.

after, although, as, as if, because, before, even though, if, in order that, once, rather than, since, so that, than, that, though, unless, until, when, where, whether, while

CONJUNCTIVE ADVERBS A conjunctive adverb is used to indicate the relation between independent clauses. (See P3-b.)

accordingly, also, anyway, besides, certainly, consequently, conversely, finally, furthermore, hence, however, incidentally, indeed, instead, likewise, meanwhile, moreover, nevertheless, next, nonetheless, once, otherwise, similarly, specifically, still, subsequently, then, therefore, thus

NOTE: The ability to distinguish between conjunctive adverbs and coordinating conjunctions will help you avoid run-on sentences and make punctuation decisions (see G6, P1-a, and P3-b). The ability to recognize subordinating conjunctions will help you avoid sentence fragments (see G5).

B1-h Interjections

Interjections are words used to express surprise or emotion (*Oh! Hey! Wow!*).

B2

Parts of sentences

Most English sentences flow from subject to verb to any objects or complements. *Predicate* is the grammatical term given to the verb plus its objects, complements, and modifiers.

ON THE WEB > **dianahacker.com/writersref**
Grammar exercises > Basic grammar > E-ex B2–1 through B2–5

B2-a Subjects

The subject of a sentence names who or what the sentence is about. The simple subject is always a noun or a pronoun; the complete subject consists of the simple subject and any words or word groups modifying the simple subject.

To find the complete subject, ask Who? or What?, insert the verb, and finish the question. The answer is the complete subject.

COMPLETE SUBJECT
The purity of a revolution usually lasts about two weeks.

Who or what lasts about two weeks? *The purity of a revolution.*

COMPLETE SUBJECT
Historical books that contain no lies are extremely tedious.

Who or what are extremely tedious? *Historical books that contain no lies.*

COMPLETE SUBJECT

In every country the sun rises in the morning.

Who or what rises in the morning? *The sun.* Notice that *In every country the sun* is not a sensible answer to the question.

The simple subject

To find the simple subject (SS), strip away all modifiers in the complete subject. This includes single-word modifiers such as *the* and *historical,* phrases such as *of a revolution,* and subordinate clauses such as *that contain no lies.*

A sentence may have a compound subject containing two or more simple subjects joined with a coordinating conjunction such as *and* or *or.*

SS SS

Much industry and little conscience make us rich.

In imperative sentences, which give advice or issue commands, the subject is an understood *you.*

[*You*] Hitch your wagon to a star.

Although the subject ordinarily comes before the verb, occasionally it does not. When a sentence begins with *There is* or *There are* (or *There was* or *There were*), the subject follows the verb. The word *There* is an expletive in such constructions, an empty word serving merely to get the sentence started.

SS

There is *no substitute* for victory.

Sometimes a writer will invert a sentence for effect.

SS

Happy is *the nation that has no history.*

In questions, the subject may appear before the verb, after the verb, or between the helping verb (HV) and main verb (MV).

S V

Who will take the first step?

V S

Why is the first step so difficult?

HV S MV

Will you take the first step?

NOTE: The ability to recognize the subject of a sentence will help you edit for a variety of problems such as sentence fragments (G5), subject-verb agreement (G1), and choice of pronouns such as *I* and *me* (G3-c). If English is not your native language, see also E2-b and E2-c.

B2-b Verbs, objects, and complements

Section B1-c explains how to find the verb of a sentence, which consists of a main verb possibly preceded by one or more helping verbs. A sentence's verb is classified as linking, transitive, or intransitive, depending on the kinds of objects or complements the verb can (or cannot) take.

Linking verbs and subject complements

Linking verbs (V) link the subject to a subject complement (SC), a word or word group that completes the meaning of the subject (S) by renaming or describing it.

S — V — SC
The handwriting on the wall may be a forgery.

S V SC
Love is blind.

When the simple subject complement renames the subject, it is a noun or noun equivalent (sometimes called a *predicate noun*), such as *forgery*. When it describes the subject, it is an adjective or adjective equivalent (sometimes called a *predicate adjective*), such as *blind*.

Linking verbs are usually a form of *be*: *be, am, is, are, was, were, being, been*. Verbs such as *appear, become, feel, grow, look, make, prove, remain, seem, smell, sound,* and *taste* are linking when they are followed by a word group that names or describes the subject.

Transitive verbs and direct objects

A transitive verb takes a direct object (DO), a word or word group that names a receiver of the action.

S — V — DO
The little snake studies the ways of the big serpent.

The simple direct object is always a noun, such as *ways,* or a pronoun. To find it, simply strip away all modifiers.

Transitive verbs usually appear in the active voice, with the subject doing the action and a direct object receiving the action. Active-voice sentences can be transformed into the passive voice, with the subject receiving the action instead.

ACTIVE VOICE	The early bird sometimes catches the early worm.
PASSIVE VOICE	The early worm is sometimes caught by the early bird.

What was once the direct object (*the early worm*) has become the subject in the passive-voice transformation, and the original subject appears in a prepositional phrase beginning with *by*. The *by* phrase is frequently omitted in passive-voice constructions: *The early worm is sometimes caught.* (See also W3-a.)

Transitive verbs, indirect objects, and direct objects

The direct object of a transitive verb is sometimes preceded by an indirect object (IO), a noun or pronoun telling to whom or for whom the action of the sentence is done.

S V IO DO S V IO DO
You show [to] me a hero, and I will write [for] you a tragedy.

Transitive verbs, direct objects, and object complements

The direct object of a transitive verb is sometimes followed by an object complement (OC), a word or word group that completes the direct object's meaning by renaming or describing it.

S V DO OC
Some people call a spade an agricultural implement.

S V DO OC
Love makes all hard hearts gentle.

When the object complement renames the direct object, it is a noun or pronoun (such as *implement*). When it describes the direct object, it is an adjective (such as *gentle*).

Intransitive verbs

Intransitive verbs take no objects or complements.

S V
Money talks.

S V
Revolutions never go backward.

Nothing receives the actions of talking and going in these sentences, so the verbs are intransitive. Such verbs may have adverbial modifiers. In the preceding sentence, *never* and *backward* are adverbs modifying *go*.

NOTE: The dictionary will tell you whether a verb is transitive or intransitive. Some verbs have both transitive and intransitive functions.

TRANSITIVE Sandra flew her Cessna over the canyon.

INTRANSITIVE A bald eagle flew overhead.

In the first example, *flew* has a direct object that receives the action: *her Cessna*. In the second example, the verb is followed by an adverb (*overhead*), not by a direct object.

B3

Subordinate word groups

Subordinate word groups cannot stand alone. They function only within sentences, usually as adjectives, adverbs, or nouns.

ON THE WEB > **dianahacker.com/writersref**
Grammar exercises > Basic grammar > E-ex B3–1 through B3–9

B3-a Prepositional phrases

A prepositional phrase begins with a preposition such as *at, by, for, from, in, of, on, to,* or *with* (see B1-f) and usually ends with a noun or a noun equivalent called the *object of the preposition*.

Prepositional phrases function as adjectives or adverbs. When functioning as an adjective, a prepositional phrase nearly always appears immediately following the noun or pronoun it modifies.

Variety is the spice *of life.*

Adjective phrases answer one or both of the questions Which one? and What kind of? If we ask Which spice? or What kind of spice? we get a sensible answer: *the spice of life.*

Adverbial prepositional phrases that modify the verb can appear nearly anywhere in a sentence.

Do not *judge* a tree *by its bark.*

Tyranny will *in time lead* to revolution.

To the ant, a few drops of rain *are* a flood.

Adverbial word groups usually answer one of these questions: When? Where? How? Why? Under what conditions? To what degree?

Do not judge a tree *how*? *By its bark.*

Tyranny will lead to revolution *when*? *In time.*

A few drops of rain are a flood *under what conditions*? *To the ant.*

B3-b Verbal phrases

A verbal is a verb form that does not function as the verb of a clause. Verbals include infinitives (the word *to* plus the base form of the verb), present participles (the *-ing* form of the verb), and past participles (the verb form usually ending in *-d, -ed, -n, -en,* or *-t*). (See G2-a.)

Verbals can take objects, complements, and modifiers to form verbal phrases. These phrases are classified as participial, gerund, and infinitive.

Participial phrases

Participial phrases always function as adjectives. Their verbals are either present participles, always ending in *-ing,* or past participles, frequently ending in *-d, -ed, -n, -en,* or *-t* (see G2-a).

Participial phrases frequently appear immediately following the noun or pronoun they modify.

Truth kept in the dark will never save the world.

Unlike other adjectival word groups, however, which must always follow the noun or pronoun they modify, participial phrases are often movable. They can precede the word they modify.

Being weak, foxes are distinguished by superior tact.

They may also appear at some distance from the word they modify.

History is *something* that never happened, *written by someone who wasn't there.*

Gerund phrases

Gerund phrases are built around present participles (verb forms ending in *-ing*), and they always function as nouns: usually as subjects, subject complements, direct objects, or objects of the preposition.

S
Justifying a fault doubles it.

DO
Kleptomaniacs can't help helping themselves.

Infinitive phrases

Infinitive phrases, usually constructed around *to* plus the base form of the verb (*to call, to drink*), can function as adjectives, adverbs, or nouns. When functioning as a noun, an infinitive phrase may appear in almost any slot in a sentence, usually as a subject, subject complement, or direct object.

We do not have the *right to abandon the poor.* [Adjective]

He *cut off* his nose *to spite his face.* [Adverb]

S
To side with truth is noble. [Noun]

NOTE: In some constructions, the infinitive is unmarked; in other words, the *to* does not appear: *No one can make you* [*to*] *feel inferior without your consent.*

B3-c Appositive phrases

Appositive phrases describe nouns or pronouns. In form they are nouns or noun equivalents.

> Politicians, *acrobats at heart,* can sit on a fence and yet keep both ears to the ground.

B3-d Absolute phrases

An absolute phrase modifies a whole clause or sentence, not just one word. It consists of a noun or noun equivalent usually followed by a participial phrase.

> *His words dipped in honey*, the senator mesmerized the crowd.

B3-e Subordinate clauses

Subordinate clauses are patterned like sentences, having subjects and verbs and sometimes objects or complements, but they function within sentences as adjectives, adverbs, or nouns. They cannot stand alone as complete sentences.

Adjective clauses

Adjective clauses modify nouns or pronouns, usually answering the question Which one? or What kind of? They begin with a relative pronoun (*who, whom, whose, which,* or *that*) or a relative adverb (*when, where,* or *why*).

> The *arrow that has left the bow* never returns.

In addition to introducing the clause, the relative pronoun points back to the noun that the clause modifies.

> The *fur that warms a monarch* once warmed a bear.

Relative pronouns are sometimes "understood."

> The things [*that*] *we know best* are the things [*that*] *we haven't been taught.*

The parts of an adjective clause are often arranged as in sentences (subject/verb/object or complement).

S V DO
We often forgive the people who bore us.

Frequently, however, the object or complement appears first, violating the normal order of subject/verb/object.

DO S V
We rarely forgive those whom we bore.

NOTE: For punctuation of adjective clauses, see P1-e and P2-e. If English is not your native language, see E2-d for a common problem with adjective clauses.

Adverb clauses

Adverb clauses modify verbs, adjectives, or other adverbs, usually answering one of these questions: When? Where? Why? How? Under what conditions? To what degree? They always begin with a subordinating conjunction (*after, although, as, as if, because, before, even though, if, in order that, once, rather than, since, so that, than, that, though, unless, until, when, where, whether, while*).

When the well is dry, we *know* the worth of water.

Venice *would be* a fine city *if it were only drained.*

Noun clauses

A noun clause functions just like a single-word noun, usually as a subject, subject complement, direct object, or object of a preposition. It usually begins with one of the following words: *how, that, which, who, whoever, whom, whomever, what, whatever, when, where, whether, whose, why.*

S
Whoever gossips to you will gossip of you.

DO
We will never forget that we buried the hatchet.

The word introducing the clause may or may not play a significant role in the clause. In the preceding example sentences, *Whoever* is the subject of its clause, but *that* does not perform a function in its clause.

As with adjective clauses, the parts of a noun clause may appear out of their normal order (subject/verb/object).

DO S V
Talent is what you possess.

The parts of a noun clause may also appear in their normal order.

S V DO
Genius is what possesses you.

B4

Sentence types

Sentences are classified in two ways: according to their structure (simple, compound, complex, and compound-complex) and according to their purpose (declarative, imperative, interrogative, and exclamatory).

ON THE WEB > **dianahacker.com/writersref**
Grammar exercises > Basic grammar > E-ex B4–1

B4-a Sentence structures

Depending on the number and types of clauses they contain, sentences are classified as simple, compound, complex, or compound-complex.

Clauses come in two varieties: independent and subordinate. An independent clause contains a subject and a predicate, and it either stands alone or could stand alone. A subordinate clause also contains a subject and a predicate, but it functions within a sentence as an adjective, an adverb, or a noun; it cannot stand alone.

SIMPLE SENTENCE A simple sentence is one independent clause with no subordinate clauses.

INDEPENDENT CLAUSE
Without music, life would be a mistake.

COMPOUND SENTENCE A compound sentence is composed of two or more independent clauses with no subordinate clauses. The independent clauses are usually joined with a comma and a coordinating conjunction (*and, but, or, nor, for, so, yet*) or with a semicolon.

INDEPENDENT CLAUSE — INDEPENDENT CLAUSE

One arrow is easily broken, but you can't break a bundle of ten.

COMPLEX SENTENCE A complex sentence is composed of one independent clause with one or more subordinate clauses.

SUBORDINATE CLAUSE

If you scatter thorns, don't go barefoot.

COMPOUND-COMPLEX SENTENCE A compound-complex sentence contains at least two independent clauses and at least one subordinate clause. The following sentence contains two independent clauses, each of which contains a subordinate clause.

IND CLAUSE — IND CLAUSE

SUB CLAUSE — SUB CLAUSE

Tell me what you eat, and I will tell you what you are.

B4-b Sentence purposes

Writers use declarative sentences to make statements, imperative sentences to issue requests or commands, interrogative sentences to ask questions, and exclamatory sentences to make exclamations.

DECLARATIVE	The echo always has the last word.
IMPERATIVE	Love your neighbour.
INTERROGATIVE	Are second thoughts always wisest?
EXCLAMATORY	I want to wash the flag, not burn it!

(Continued from page vi)

Screen shot of database search results Blackwell Synergy Web site, www.blackwell-synergy.com. Reprinted with the permission of Blackwell Publishers, Ltd.

Eugene Boe, excerpt from "Pioneers to Eternity" from *The Immigrant Experience*, edited by Thomas C. Wheeler. Copyright © 1971 by Thomas C. Wheeler. Reprinted with the permission of Doubleday, a division of Random House, Inc.

Albert Castel, excerpts from "The Fort Pillow Massacre: A Fresh Examination of the Evidence" from *Civil War History* 4, no. 1 (1958). Reprinted with the permission of The Kent State University Press.

EBSCO Information Services. Various screen shots. Reprinted with the permission of EBSCO Information Services.

Don Gillmor, "Once upon a Country," *The Walrus,* February 2007. Reprinted with permission.

Google screen shots. Reprinted with the permission of Google, Inc.

Government of Alberta, "Alberta's Top Companies Ranked by Employees." Used with permission.

Caroline M. Hoxby. "The Power of Peers." Front page of article and the TOC. From *Education Next*, Summer 2002. www.educationnext.org. Reprinted with the permission of *Education Next*.

Lynn Hunt et al., *The Making of the West,* Volume II. Copyright © 2005 by Bedford/St. Martin's. Reprinted by permission of Bedford/St. Martin's.

Henry Jenkins. Excerpted data from "Bearings." Copyright © 2006. The Massachusetts Institute of Technology. Posted online within the *MIT Communications Forum*. Reprinted with permission.

Jill D. Jenson, excerpt from "It's the Information Age, so Where's the Information?" from *College Teaching* (Summer 2004). Copyright © 2004. Reprinted with the permission of the Helen Dwight Reed Educational Foundation. Published by Heldref Publications, 1319 18th Street NW, Washington, DC 20036.

Harvey A. Levenstein. Reprint of the title and copyright pages from *Revolution at the Table: The Transformation of the American Diet* by Harvey A. Levenstein. Copyright © 2003 by the Regents of the University of California. Reprinted with the permission of the University of California Press.

LexisNexis. Screen shots. Copyright © 2006 LexisNexis, a division of Reed Elsevier Inc.

McDonald's Corporation, "What makes your lettuce so crisp?" advertisement. Copyright © 2004 by McDonald's Corporation. Reprinted with permission.

Anne McGrath, "A loss of foreign talent" from *U.S. News & World Report* (November 27, 2004). Copyright © 2004 by U.S. News & World Report, LP. Reprinted with permission. This figure includes a photo by Kenneth Dickerman which is reprinted by permission.

Merriam-Webster Online, screen shot of thesaurus entry for "regard" from www.MerriamWebster.com. Copyright © 2005 by Merriam-Webster Incorporated. Reprinted with permission.

"The Minnesota Annual Summary" or "Minnesota Health Statistics" report. Copyright © 2005 by the Minnesota Department of Health. www.health.state.mn.us.

L. M. Poupart. Page from "Crime and Justice in American Indian Communities." Copyright © 2002. Reprinted with the permission of *Social Justice*. Screenshot copyright © 2006 by ProQuest Information and Learning. Reprinted by permission.

Beth Shulman. Reprint of title and copyright pages from *Betrayal of Work* by Beth Shulman. Copyright © 2005 by Beth Shulman. Reprinted with the permission of The New Press.

Betsy Taylor, "Big Box Stores Are Bad for Main Street" from *CQ Researcher* (November 1999). Copyright © 1999 by Congressional Quarterly, Inc. Reprinted with permission.

United Nations Department of Public Information, *Africa Recovery* (June 2004), www.un.org/ecosocdev/geninfo/afrec/vol15no1/drugpr1.htm. Reprinted with the permission of UN Africa Renewal.

University of Toronto Libraries, screen shot. Reprinted with permission.

Fred Zwicky, "Tornado Touch." Copyright © 2004. This photograph originally appeared in the *Peoria Journal Star*. Used with permission.

Index

In addition to giving you page numbers, this index shows you which tabbed section to flip to. For example, the entry "*a* vs. *an*" directs you to section **W** (Word Choice), page 123, and to section **E** (ESL Challenges), page 241. Just flip to the appropriate tabbed section and then track down the exact pages you need.

A

C

E

G

H

I

J

K

M

O

R

S

T

U

V

W

Y

Using A Canadian Writer's Reference *in all of your college or university courses*

Good writing in any discipline communicates a writer's purpose to an audience and explores an engaging question about a subject. Effective postsecondary writers respond appropriately to an assignment or problem with a thesis, support their claims with evidence, document their research sources, and format documents in the style appropriate for their discipline.

A Canadian Writer's Reference provides help for writing well in all postsecondary courses. Consult the sections noted here for advice about writing in any discipline.

- Understand the writing assignment: C1-b, A4-e
- Determine your purpose: C1-a, C1-b
- Determine your audience: C1-a, C1-b
- Ask questions appropriate to the field: A4-b
- Formulate a thesis or main idea: C2-a, MLA-1a, APA-1a, CMS-1a
- Determine what types of evidence to gather: A4
- Conduct research if necessary: R1
- Support your claim: A2-d, A2-e, MLA-1c, APA-1c, CMS-1c
- Counter opposing arguments or objections: A2-f
- Identify the required documentation style: R4
- Integrate sources: MLA-3, APA-3, CMS-3
- Document your sources: MLA-4, APA-4, CMS-4
- Design your document: C5, MLA-5a, APA-5a, CMS-5a

NOTE: Modern Language Association (MLA) style is used in English and in other humanities courses such as art and music. American Psychological Association (APA) style is often used in nursing courses and in social science courses such as psychology, sociology, and anthropology. *The Chicago Manual of Style* (CMS) is often used for history courses and some other humanities.

ESL Menu

A complete section on major ESL problems:

ESL and Academic English notes in other sections:

Revision Symbols

Letter-number codes refer to sections of this book.

abbr	faulty abbreviation **M4**
ad	misuse of adverb or adjective **G4**
add	add needed word **S2**
agr	faulty agreement **G1, G3-a**
appr	inappropriate language **W4**
art	article **E3**
awk	awkward
cap	capital letter **M3**
case	error in case **G3-c, G3-d**
cliché	cliché **W5-e**
coh	coherence **C4-d**
coord	faulty coordination **S6-c**
cs	comma splice **G6**
dev	inadequate development **C4-b**
dm	dangling modifier **S3-e**
-ed	error in *-ed* ending **G2-d**
emph	emphasis **S6**
ESL	ESL grammar **E1, E2, E3, E4, E5**
exact	inexact language **W5**
frag	sentence fragment **G5**
fs	fused sentence **G6**
gl/us	see glossary of usage **W1**
hyph	error in use of hyphen **M2**
idiom	idiom **W5-d**
inc	incomplete construction **S2**
irreg	error in irregular verb **G2-a**
ital	italics (underlining) **M6**
jarg	jargon **W4-a**
lc	lowercase letter **M3**
mix	mixed construction **S5**
mm	misplaced modifier **S3-b**
mood	error in mood **G2-g**
nonst	nonstandard usage **W4-c**
num	error in use of number **M5**
om	omitted word **S2**
¶	new paragraph **C4**
p	error in punctuation
^ ,	comma **P1**
no ,	no comma **P2**
;	semicolon **P3**
:	colon **P4**
’	apostrophe **P5**
“ ”	quotation marks **P6**
. ? ! — ( ) [ ] . . . /	period, question mark, exclamation point, dash, parentheses, brackets, ellipsis mark, slash **P7**
pass	ineffective passive **W3**
pn agr	pronoun agreement **G3-a**
proof	proofreading problem **C3-c**
ref	error in pronoun reference **G3-b**
run-on	run-on sentence **G6**
-s	error in *-s* ending **G2-c**
sexist	sexist language **W4-e**
shift	distracting shift **S4**
sl	slang **W4-c**
sp	misspelled word **M1**
sub	faulty subordination **S6-d**
sv agr	subject-verb agreement **G1, G2-c**
t	error in verb tense **G2-f**
trans	transition needed **C4-d**
usage	see glossary of usage **W1**
v	voice **W3**
var	sentence variety **S6-b, S6-c, S7**
vb	verb error **G2**
w	wordy **W2**
//	faulty parallelism **S1**
^	insert
x	obvious error
#	insert space
⁀	close up space

Detailed Menu